DAY BY DAY: THE SEVENTIES

Volume II
1976–Index

DAY BY DAY: THE SEVENTIES

Volume II
1976–Index

by **Thomas Leonard, Cynthia Crippen**
and
Marc Aronson

Facts On File Publications
460 Park Avenue South
New York, N.Y. 10016

DAY BY DAY: THE SEVENTIES

Library of Congress Cataloging-in-Publication Data

Leonard, Thomas, 1955-
  Day by day, the seventies.

  Includes index.
  1. History, Modern—1945-   —Chronology.
I. Cryptin, Cynthia. II. Aronson, Marc. III. Title.
D848.L4   1987   909.82'02'02   83-11520
ISBN 0-8160-1020-X

Photographs courtesy of Wide World Photos

British CIP data available on request

Printed in the United States of America

10 9 8 7 6 5 4 3 2

CONTENTS

DAY BY DAY: THE SEVENTIES

Volume II
1976–Index

1976

The United States celebrates the bicentennial of its independence with festivities across the nation.

	World Affairs	Europe	Africa & the Middle East	The Americas	Asia & the Pacific
Jan.	Ford administration speaks out against Soviet involvement in Angolan civil war,. . . .U.N. censures South Africa.	The 13-month-old government of Italian Premier Aldo Moro collapses when the Socialist Party withdraws its support.	PLO forces clash with Lebanese Christian Phalangist Party militiamen. . . .Fighting intensifies in Angolan civil war.	Political violence continues unabated in Argentina. . . .Venezuelan oil industry is formally nationalized.	Chou En-lai, premier of the People's Republic of China, dies at age 78.
Feb.	U.S. State Secy. Henry Kissinger says that Cuba has resumed "exporting revolution" on its own initiative, now to Angola, the Sahara and possibly other places outside the Western Hemisphere.	Street demonstrations and protests occur in Barcelona, Spain.	Rhodesia's P.M. Ian Smith says in a nationwide broadcast that guerrilla warfare along Rhodesia's border with Mozambique has recently intensified.	Labor and student unrest spreads through Colombia.	The Communist Chinese govt. invites former Pres. Richard Nixon to visit China.
March	The U.S. vetoes a U.N. Security Council resolution assailing Israel's occupation policies in the Old City of Jerusalem and the West Bank.	A treaty providing for the return to West Germany of up to 125,000 ethnic Germans living in Poland is unanimously ratified by the upper house of the West German parliament.	Talks between the white minority government of P.M. Ian Smith and the African National Council faction headed by Joshua Nkomo break down.	Argentine Pres. Isabel Martinez de Peron is overthrown in a bloodless coup lead by commanders of the three armed forces.	South Korean government arrests 11 of 12 signers of an anti-government statement calling for the resignation of Pres. Chung Hee Park.
April	U.N. Economic and Social Council resumes debate on racism.	James Callaghan is elected leader of the Labor Party and British P.M..	The Arab League's Boycott Office blacklists 16 firms doing business with Israel.	Brig. Gen. Omar Torrijos, Panama's military strongman, accuses Pres. Ford and Ronald Reagan of "irresponsibility" in dealing with the Panama Canal treaty issue.	Chinese Deputy Premier Teng Hsiao-ping is deposed and Acting Premier Hua Kuo-feng is promoted to the second-ranked position after Communist Party Chairman Mao Tse-tung.
May	U.S.-Soviet Treaty on Underground Nuclear Tests for Peaceful Purposes is signed.	The Presidium of Supreme Soviet promotes Communist Party General Secretary Leonid Brezhnev to field marshall of the army, the Soviet Union's highest military rank.	U.S. State Secy. Henry Kissinger completes an African tour.	A federal judge in Buenos Aires, Argentina, announces that preliminary criminal charges have been filed against ex-President Peron for alleged misuse of government funds.	India and Pakistan agree to resume diplomatic relations that had been broken off since 1971.
June	The International Monetary Fund, in its first of 16 planned auctions, sells 780,000 ounces of gold at $126 an ounce. The auction was the first in the IMF's 32-year history.	NATO defense ministers meet in Brussels and reach agreement in principle to increase defense spending by up to 5% in real terms between 1977 and 1982.	Riots take place in the all-back township of Soweto outside of Johannesburg.	The Bolivian government imposes a nationwide state of seige following widespread protests of the assassination in Argentina of Bolivian ex-president Juan Jose Torres.	A boatload of 91 South Vietnamese arrives in Thailand and is granted political asylum while about a dozen other boatloads are said to be moored off the Thai coast.
July	Diplomatic sources are quoted as saying that Libya's leader, Col. Muammar el-Qaddafi, is financing, training and arming a wide-spread network of terrorist gangs.	Spanish King Juan Carlos I dismisses Premier Carlos Arrias Navarro and replaces him with Adolfo Suarez Gonzalez.	Israeli commandos land at Entebbe Airport and rescue 91 passengers and 12 crew members of a hijacked Air France plane.	Jose Lopez Portillo, candidate of the ruling Institutional Revolutionary Party (PRI), wins a landslide victory in Mexican presidential election.	The U.S. completes its military withdrawal from Thailand. . . .North and South Vietnam are officially reunited after 22 years of separation.
Aug.	Argentine Finance Minister Jose Martinez de Hoz announces, on returning from trip to the U.S. and Canada, that he has renegotiated payment of Argentina's $9-billion foreign debt.	Rival claims by Greece and Turkey to the continental shelf in the Aegean precipitates crisis in relations between the two countries.	Egyptian Pres. Anwar Sadat blames Libyan leader Muammar el-Qaddafi for the bombing of a train in Alexandria.	At least five Peruvian army officers described as left-wing reformists are arrested for attempting to organize a coup to reinstate ousted left-wing reformist Premier Gen. Jorge Fernandez Maldonado.	Former Philippine Sen. Benigno Aquino, a political rival of Pres. Ferdinand Marcos, is arraigned before a military tribunal in Manila on charges of murder and subversion.
Sept.	The Geneva disarmament conference agrees on a joint U.S.-Soviet pact to ban major forms of environmental warfare.	Portugal and Angola agree to reestablish diplomatic relations at the ambassadorial level, broken off because of Portugal's alleged hostility to its pro-Communist government.	Blacks stage a second three-day strike in the all-black township of Soweto in South Africa. Violent unrest continues in nonwhite townships of Cape Town.	A report on bilingualism in the Canadian civil service calls for evaluation of 65,000 bilingual positions in the government to determine what language competence they actually require.	Communist Chinese leader Mao-Tse-tung dies.
Oct.	Robert S. McNamara, World Bank president, calls for increase in direct and indirect aid to the 900 million persons, more than 20% of the earth's population, who live in poverty.	Italian Treasury Minister Gaetano Stammati announces anti-inflation measures to replace the 10% surcharge on foreign currency purchases that had been instituted Oct. 1.	A Syrian-Lebanese-Christian offensive launched in mountains east of Beirut routs Palestinians and their Lebanese-Moslem allies from most of their strategic positions north of the Beirut-Damascus highway.	James A. Richardson, Canada's defense minister, resigns to protest P.M. Pierre Elliott Trudeau's plan to give French official status with English in Canada's proposed constitution.	Hua Kuo-feng is officially reported to have succeeded Mao Tse-tung as Chinese Communist Party chairman.
Nov.	The U.N. General Assembly approves a resolution calling on Israel to halt transfer of Palestinian refugees in the Gaza Strip from their camps to new homes.	Greece and Turkey announce that they have agreed on procedures for future talks on continental-shelf rights in the Aegean Sea.	Egyptian Pres. Anwar Sadat asks a U.S. congressional group visiting Cairo to tell Israeli Premier Yitzhak Rabin that he and other Arab leaders are ready to negotiate a peace settlement.	Parti Quebecois (PQ) scores a major upset in provincial elections, moving from a minority of six seats to a majority of 69 in the 110-seat Quebec provincial parliament.	The 50th anniversary of the reign of Emperor Hirohito is celebrated in Japan. . . .The Philippine government deports two U.S. missionaries in a crack-down on activist church groups.
Dec.	Western European NATO defense ministers express concern over "the growing military capability of the Warsaw Pact."	Libya agrees to buy a 9.6% stake in Fiat S.p.A., Italy's largest private employer.	Rival black groups fight in Cape Town black townships over the celebration of Christmas.	Jose Lopez Portillo assumes the presidency of Mexico with a call for national unity and strict austerity to overcome the country's acute economic crisis.	Japanese Deputy Premier Takeo Fukuda is elected premier by the Japanese Diet.

A	B	C	D	E
Includes developments that affect more than one world region, international organizations and important meetings of major world leaders.	Includes all domestic and regional developments in Europe, including the Soviet Union, Turkey, Cyprus and Malta.	Includes all domestic and regional developments in Africa and the Middle East, including Iraq and Iran and excluding Cyprus, Turkey and Afghanistan.	Includes all domestic and regional developments in Latin America, the Caribbean and Canada.	Includes all domestic and regional developments in Asia and Pacific nations, extending from Afghanistan through all the Pacific Islands, except Hawaii.

U.S. Politics & Social Issues	U.S. Foreign Policy & Defense	U.S. Economy & Environment	Science, Technology & Nature	Culture, Leisure & Life Style	
Former California Gov. Ronald Reagan launches his 1976 presidential campaign with a tour of northern New Hampshire.	U.S. State Secy. Henry Kissinger says that "significant progress" has been achieved on elements of a new SALT II agreement.	Pres. Ford vetoes a construction site picketing bill on the grounds that it could lead to "greater, not lesser conflict in the construction industry."	HEW makes public its first report assessing the state of health of the U.S. population. The report says that Americans are generally healthy.	The Pittsburgh Steelers win the Super Bowl with a 21-17 victory over the Dallas Cowboys.	Jan.
The trial of Party Hearst begins.	Daniel Patrick Moynihan resigns as U.S. ambassador to the U.N.	Elliott Richardson is sworn in as Commerce Secy.	An earthquake shakes Guatemala and Honduras.	The 12th Winter Olympics are held in Innsbruck, Austria.	Feb.
Patricia Hearst is found guilty of robbing a bank and using a firearm in the commission of a felony.	William Scranton is confirmed as U.S. representative to the U.N.	Twenty-two major U.S. companies give written assurances that they would refuse to participate in the Arab boycott against Israel.	Pres. Ford calls for a government-supported campaign to vaccinate the entire population against a virus strain closely related to swine influenza.	*One Flew Over the Cuckoo's Nest* wins the Academy Award for Best Picture. The film's stars, Jack Nicholson and Louise Fletcher, win for Best Actor and Best Actress.	March
Democratic presidential candidate Jimmy Carter apologizes for remarks he had made upholding the "ethnic purity" of urban neighborhoods.	The U.S. Supreme Ct. declines to review the conviction of former Lt. William L. Calley Jr. for the murder of Vietnamese civilians at My Lai.	American billionaire Howard Hughes dies.	Full-scale testing of the vaccine to be used in the U.S. national flu immunization program begins.	Ray Floyd wins the Masters Golf Tournament in Augusta, Georgia.	April
The 1974 conviction of John D. Ehrlichman for his role in the 1971 break-in at the office of Daniel Ellsberg's former psychiatrist is unanimously upheld by the U.S. Court of Appeals in the District of Columbia.	Pres. Gerald R. Ford vetoes a $4.4 billion foreign-aid authorization bill on the ground that it represents "congressional encroachment" on presidential authority on foreign policy.	The British-French Concorde inaugurates SST service to the U.S.	A severe earthquake, measuring 7.3 on the open-ended Richter scale, strikes Soviet Union's Uzbek Republic in Central Asia.	*Bold Forbes* wins the 102nd running of the Kentucky Derby at Churchill Downs.	May
Jimmy Carter wins the Ohio Democratic primary and places second in California and N.J....Pres. Ford and Ronald Reagan remain locked in the Republican race.	Spanish King Juan Carlos I and Queen Sophia visit the U.S. and confer with government and business leaders. The king also addresses Congress.	Billionaire oilman J. Paul Getty dies at the age of 83....California voters reject Proposition 15, which called for the curbing of nuclear-power development.	The collapse of Idaho's Teton River Dam results in the death of at least nine people and leaves at least 30 others missing.	Jerry Pate, a rookie on the Professional Golf Association tour, wins the U.S. Open.	June
Jimmy Carter wins the Democratic Party's nomination for President.	West Germany and the U.S. agree to discontinue West Germany's contribution to the stationing of U.S. troops in that nation.	Pres. Ford vetoes legislation that would have revised regulations covering the leasing of federally-owned coal lands and increased states' shares of the royalties derived from the leases.	The U.S. Viking I spacecraft lands on Mars and successfully scoops up some Martian dirt.	The United States celebrates its 200th birthday with parades and festivities. Six million gather in the New York City area to watch a flotilla of sailing ships ply New York Harbor and the Hudson River.	July
Pres. Gerald Ford wins the Republican nomination in a close contest with Ronald Reagan and selects Kansas Sen. Robert Dole as his running mate.	Jimmy Carter says that he opposes a "blanket amnesty" for those who violated the Selective Service Law during the Vietnam War, but he says he supports a "blanket pardon."	General Motors raises prices on 1977 cars....A uniform air pollution index is proposed by a U.S. federal task force.	Reported cases of a mysterious ailment, the so-called legion fever, reached 179 in the U.S. as federal officials continued their investigation into the origin of the disease.	Noted film director Fritz Lang dies.	Aug.
Democratic presidential nominee Jimmy Carter stirs controversy with an interview granted to *Playboy* in which he gives his views on lust and adultery.	Over strong White House opposition, the House approves a bill that bars U.S. companies from complying with the Arab League's trade boycott against Israel.	United Auto Workers go on strike against Ford Motor Co....More than 165,000 workers stay off the job, shutting off production at 102 Ford plants in 22 states.	U.S. spacecraft Viking I continues soil tests on Mars.	The Episcopal Church formally approves the ordination of women to the priesthood and an extensive revision of the *Book of Common Prayer*.	Sept.
Pres. Gerald Ford and Democratic presidential candidate Jimmy Carter continue their televised debates....Carter continues to hold an edge in public opinion polls.	A GAO study questions whether the Ford Administration had exhausted all diplomatic possibilities of resolving *Mayaguez* crisis before it ordered a rescue strike.	Pres. Gerald Ford signs a toxic substance bill requiring pre-release testing of potentially dangerous chemicals.	The U.S. confirms that it has approved the sale to China of two computers that will be used in exploring for oil and predicting earthquakes.	Saul Bellow wins the Nobel Prize for Literature.	Oct.
Jimmy Carter is elected President of the United States by a narrow margin over Pres. Gerald Ford.	The U.S. Justice Dept. engages in a major investigation of a South Korean scheme to bribe U.S. legislators and top executive officials.	Arthur F. Burns, warns that inflation might worsen if "traditional policies" were used to stimulate the current sluggish pace of economic recovery.	An earthquake measuring 7.6 on Richter scale kills more than 4,000 people in Turkey.	The artist Alexander Calder dies.	Nov.
President-elect Jimmy Carter names Cyrus Vance as State Secy. and Bert Lance as the head of the Office of Management and Budget....Chicago Mayor Richard Daley dies.	Carter says he has heard from Soviet leader Brezhnev that the USSR "would bend over backwards not to create any sort of test in the early days" of the new Administration.	Pres. Carter names W. Michael Blumenthal Treasury Secy.	The U.S. government halts its swine-flu inoculations program.	An unprecedented Roman Catholic rite of general absolution in Memphis, Tenn. allows divorced, remarried Catholics and other estranged members of the church to receive Holy Communion.	Dec.

F	G	H	I	J
Includes elections, federal-state relations, civil rights and liberties, crime, the judiciary, education, health care, poverty, urban affairs and population.	Includes formation and debate of U.S. foreign and defense policies, veterans' affairs and defense spending. (Relations with specific foreign countries are usually found under the region concerned.)	Includes business, labor, agriculture, taxation, transportation, consumer affairs, monetary and fiscal policy, natural resources, and pollution.	Includes worldwide scientific, medical and technological developments, natural phenomena, U.S. weather, natural disasters, and accidents.	Includes the arts, religion, scholarship, communications media, sports, entertainments, fashions, fads and social life.

	World Affairs	Europe	Africa & the Middle East	The Americas	Asia & the Pacific
Jan. 1		A woman's rights bill goes into effect in Austria that gives married women the right to maintain their maiden name, choose where they live, have careers or be subsidized for being housewives — all areas previously controlled by their husbands. . . . Three persons are killed and 15 wounded during a demonstration near the gates of Oporto Prison, Portugal as paramilitary guards open fire on the crowd.	Somalia's ruling Supreme Revolutionary Council is dissolved and its powers transferred to the Somali Socialist Revolutionary Party, organized the same day to be the country's sole party.	The Venezuelan oil industry is nationalized. . . . The 1944–45 diaries of William Mackenzie King, Canadian prime minister from 1921 to 1948, are made public after a 30-year prohibition on their publication as secret government documents.	Two poems written by Chmn. Mao in 1965, just before the Cultural Revolution, are published, along with an editorial warning the Chinese against ideological laxity.
Jan. 2			White House denies a *Christian Science Monitor* report of mercenaries being trained by the U.S. Army to join other U.S.-trained forces helping pro-Western fighters in Angola.		
Jan. 3			Jeremy Thorpe, head of the British Liberal Party, charges that the Soviet govt. paid $50 million to an unnamed African leader to get him to recognize the Soviet-supported govt. in Angola.	AP reports that the 1975 death toll from continuing political violence in Argentina was 898.	A Saigon broadcast reports that since Aug. 12, 1975 a total of 4,600 foreigners have been evacuated from Saigon in 85 special flights arranged by France.
Jan. 4			Lebanese Christian Phalangists and the PLO clash after Christians blockade PLO refugee camps in Beirut, preventing arrival of fresh food.		
Jan. 5		John Costello, 84, twice the prime minister of Ireland and leader of Ireland's first coalition government, dies in Dublin.	South Africa begins its first full nationwide TV broadcasting after more than 10 years of controversy over TV's possible corrupting influence.	The National Statistics Institute reports that the 1975 inflation rate in Argentina was 334.8 percent, compared to a 40 percent increase in 1974. . . . Chilean govt. denies torturing Sheila Cassidy, a British doctor imprisoned in Chile for two months in 1975. . . . Canadian P.M. Pierre Trudeau calls for more government intervention in the economy, drawing criticism from his own Liberal Party and from business and labor.	Cambodia's new Constitution, approved by a national congress, goes into effect. It provides for a 250-member legislative assembly, freedom of religion, state control of production, full employment guarantees, and a ban on foreign bases. . . . A new no-fault divorce law takes effect in Australia.
Jan. 6		Ten Protestants are killed and one wounded in Northern Ireland in an apparent reprisal for the Jan. 4 murder of five Roman Catholics.		Bolivian Pres. Hugo Banzer Suarez dismisses his three military commanders after indications of armed forces' discontent about Bolivia's plan to cede national territory to Chile in exchange for a corridor to the Pacific Ocean. . . . The National Statistics Institute reports that the 1975 inflation rate in Chile was 340 percent, down from a 375 percent rate in 1974.	A Communist Chinese publication, *Peking Review*, reports that 12 million school graduates have relocated to rural areas since 1966, calling their resettlement voluntary and an indication of "a profound socialist revolution."

A	B	C	D	E
Includes developments that affect more than one world region, international organizations and important meetings of major world leaders.	Includes all domestic and regional developments in Europe, including the Soviet Union, Turkey, Cyprus and Malta.	Includes all domestic and regional developments in Africa and the Middle East, including Iraq and Iran and excluding Cyprus, Turkey and Afghanistan.	Includes all domestic and regional developments in Latin America, the Caribbean and Canada.	Includes all domestic and regional developments in Asia and Pacific nations, extending from Afghanistan through all the Pacific Islands, except Hawaii.

U.S. Politics & Social Issues	U.S. Foreign Policy & Defense	U.S. Economy & Environment	Science, Technology & Nature	Culture, Leisure & Life Style	
Explosives are found outside a Bureau of Indian Affairs office in Ariz. Supporters of the American Indian Movement (AIM) are believed to be involved. . . . House Select Committee on Intelligence accuses the FBI of trying to squelch a witness on possible FBI purchasing improprieties and asks Atty. Gen. Edward Levi to investigate.			National Transportation Safety Bd. attributes the 1975 Eastern Airlines 747 jet crash at Kennedy Airport, N.Y.C., to an underestimation of severe weather conditions.	Paul Brown, 67, resigns as head coach of the Cincinnati Bengals after an illustrious football career. . . . In major football bowl games, Oklahoma beats Michigan in the Orange Bowl, 14–6; Arkansas beats Georgia in the Cotton Bowl, 31–10; and U.C.L.A. beats Ohio in the Rose Bowl, 23–10. . . . Fred Millet, 85, who in 1954, as president of the American Assn. of University Professors, attacked censorship in what was seen as an indirect attack against Sen. Joseph McCarthy, dies.	Jan. 1
Treasury Dept. begins distributing $1.88 million to presidential contenders who qualify for subsidies under the 1974 Federal Election Campaign Act, which provides matching funds to candidates who were able to raise at least $5,000 in private donations of $250 or less in each of 20 states. . . . Sen. Lloyd Bentsen (D, Tex.) receives $492,030 in matching federal funds for his presidential campaign, the largest amount distributed to a candidate.		Pres. Ford vetoes a construction site picketing bill, citing possible loss of jobs for construction trades and higher costs for the public.		Previously unknown Renaissance frescos, attributed to Michelangelo by some art experts, are uncovered by workmen restoring the basilica of San Lorenzo in Florence, Italy.	Jan. 2
Chief Justice Warren Burger criticizes Congress for its failure to create more federal judgeships.				Freda Kirchwey, 82, editor and publisher of The Nation magazine from 1937–55, dies in St. Petersburg, Fla. . . . The annual Gallup Poll on church-going shows that 40 percent of U.S. adults attended church or synagogue in a typical week in 1975.	Jan. 3
		Flight attendants at National Airlines end their 127-day strike, the longest ever at National and the third longest in U.S. airline history.		Pope Paul VI urges the defense of the unborn in a speech in St. Peter's Square in Rome.	Jan. 4
	Former Gov. Ronald Reagan (R, Calif.) criticizes the U.S. policy of detente as he begins his 1976 presidential campaign.	EPA uges Transportation Secy. William Coleman Jr. to deny U.S. landing rights to the Concorde, the British–French supersonic transport. . . . Calif. Air Resources Bd. fines American Motors Corp. $4.2 million for violation of the state air-pollution law and bans the sale of the three AMC car models involved.			Jan. 5
	ACLU contests the presidential Clemency Bd.'s claim of success, saying that it underrated the number of Vietnam-era draft evaders and deserters eligible for clemency and thus its figure for the percentage who applied is too high.	The eighth U.S. Circuit Ct. of Appeals, St. Louis removes Judge Miles Lord from the Reserve Mining Co. antipollution case because of "gross bias" against the company, which is accused of polluting Lake Superior with daily waste discharges.		The N.Y. Rangers hockey team dismiss Emile Francis as manager, replacing him with Ron Stewart.	Jan. 6

F	G	H	I	J
Includes elections, federal-state relations, civil rights and liberties, crime, the judiciary, education, health care, poverty, urban affairs and population.	Includes formation and debate of U.S. foreign and defense policies, veterans' affairs and defense spending. (Relations with specific foreign countries are usually found under the region concerned.)	Includes business, labor, agriculture, taxation, transportation, consumer affairs, monetary and fiscal policy, natural resources, and pollution.	Includes worldwide scientific, medical and technological developments, natural phenomena, U.S. weather, natural disasters, and accidents.	Includes the arts, religion, scholarship, communications media, sports, entertainments, fashions, fads and social life.

	World Affairs	Europe	Africa & the Middle East	The Americas	Asia & the Pacific
Jan. 7	Ford administration declares that intelligence reports of Soviet warships heading for the Angolan coast constitute further evidence of continuing Soviet involvement in an area where they have no legitimate interest.	The 13-month-old government of Premier Aldo Moro, Italy's thirty-second govt. since the end of WWII, collapses when the Socialist Party withdraws its support.	Iran recalls its ambassadors from the seven Persian Gulf countries after reports that they were forming the Arabian Gulf News Agency, indicating their intention to rename the Gulf. . . . Syrian For. Min. Abdel Halim Khaddam warns that if Lebanon were partitioned between Moslems and Christians, Syria would intervene militarily.	The "National Project," the political testament of the late Argentinean Pres. Juan Peron, is published by a Buenos Aires newspaper.	
Jan. 8	Finance ministers attending the IMF Jamaica conference agree to reform the world currency system to legitimize current floating exchange rates and to give developing nations more aid.		The OAU meets briefly in Ethiopia but engages in no preparatory negotiations for its Jan. 10 emergency summit meeting on Angola. . . . Lebanese fighting between Moslem and Christian forces continues and intensifies, causing several hundred deaths.	The bodies of eight metalworkers are found outside Rosario, Argentina, a day after they were kidnapped by presumed right-wing terrorists.	Chou En-lai, 78, premier of the People's Republic of China since its founding in 1949, dies in Peking. . . . Without giving a reason, the Indian govt. suspends freedom of speech and assembly, the right to own property, and four other rights guaranteed by the Constitution. It is the fourth curb since emergency rule was imposed in 1975.
Jan. 9					Scholars identify several Chinese leaders as possible successors to the late Premier Chou En-lai and the ailing Chmn. Mao Tse-tung. They include Teng Hsiao-Ping, Chang Chun-chiao, Wang Hung-wen, and Hua Kuo-feng.
Jan. 10					
Jan. 11				Ecuador Pres. Guillermo Rodriguez Lara is deposed in a bloodless coup led by the three armed forces commanders who formed a military junta. . . . Cuban Deputy Premier Carlos Rodriguez says Cuba will continue to provide troops to the MPLA and will ignore any resolution the OAU may adopt about foreign intervention in Angola.	
Jan. 12	The U.N. Security Council begins its debate on the Middle East by voting to permit the PLO to participate in the debate with the rights of a member nation.	Merlyn Rees, British State Secy. for Northern Ireland, announces he is reconvening the constitutional convention to try to reach a solution to Ulster's sectarian violence.	Arab students at Bir Zeit College in the West Bank boycott classes in support of the PLO and its participation in the U.N. Security Council debate on the Middle East. . . . Egypt warns Israel that it will take military action if Israel intervenes in Lebanon. . . . Lebanese Phalangist militiamen lay siege to a refugee camp near Dbaiye in wake of intensified clashes between Moslem and Christian forces.		Thai Premier Kukrit Pramoj resigns, King Phumiphol Aduldet dissolves Parliament, and new elections are called for April 4.

A	B	C	D	E
Includes developments that affect more than one world region, international organizations and important meetings of major world leaders.	Includes all domestic and regional developments in Europe, including the Soviet Union, Turkey, Cyprus and Malta.	Includes all domestic and regional developments in Africa and the Middle East, including Iraq and Iran and excluding Cyprus, Turkey and Afghanistan.	Includes all domestic and regional developments in Latin America, the Caribbean and Canada.	Includes all domestic and regional developments in Asia and Pacific nations, extending from Afghanistan through all the Pacific Islands, except Hawaii.

U.S. Politics & Social Issues	U.S. Foreign Policy & Defense	U.S. Economy & Environment	Science, Technology & Nature	Culture, Leisure & Life Style	
The FBI arrests David Fine, one of four men indicted for the bombing of a University of Wisconsin building in 1970, which killed one person and injured four.... A special three-judge panel upholds a 1974 law giving control over former Pres. Richard Nixon's presidential papers and tape recordings to the government.... *The New York Times* reports a GAO audit of HEW records revealed that HEW failed to require states to file plans for enforcing HEW regulations on the length of Medicaid hospital stays.		Democratic presidential candidate Sargent Shriver releases an economic plan that he says would reduce both unemployment and inflation.			Jan. 7
				The first National Book Critics Circle Awards are presented. E.L. Doctorow receives the fiction prize for *Ragtime* and R.W.B. Lewis receives the nonfiction prize for *Edith Wharton* .	Jan. 8
Gov. George Wallace of Ala. opens his Mass. presidential primary campaign.... Sen. Robert Byrd (D, W. Va.) announces that he is a candidate for the Democratic presidential nomination.	State Secy. Henry Kissinger sets a policy of linking the amount of U.S. foreign aid to a country's support on important U.N. votes.	Forty-three black employes of Birmingham Southern Railroad win a $120,000 ct. award in a racial discrimination suit.... The FDA proposes a ban against the use of diethylstilbestrol (DES) in animal feed. ... Labor Dept. announces the December 1975 unemployment rate is unchanged at 8.3 percent of the work force.		The American Ballet Theater, N.Y.C., premieres Twyla Tharp's classical ballet-jazz dance production *Push Comes to Shove* .	Jan. 9
The IRS and Justice Dept. release guidelines covering the participation of IRS employes in Justice Dept. investigations.	Alice Olson, whose husband, Frank Olson, committed suicide in 1953 after he was given LSD without his knowledge in a CIA experiment, makes public CIA documents on the case.		Harvard professor Dr. Robert Kistner says his previous endorsement of the safety of birth control pills and the use of estrogen for menopause cannot be substantiated.	Chester (Howlin' Wolf) Burnett, 65, a blues singer and musician, dies in Chicago.	Jan. 10
FBI Dir. Clarence Kelley acknowledges that the FBI maintained an informant within a Calif. right-wing terrorist group, but denies a *San Diego Union* report that the FBI helped form the group and gave it weapons and explosives.... The Treasury Dept. completes its distribution of $1.88 million to presidential contenders who qualified for federal campaign subsidies.		Datsun, made by the Japanese Nissan Motor Co. is reported leading the 1975 foreign car sales, thereby ousting the 20-year sales leader Volkswagen .... The nation's second and third largest banks, First National City Bank of N.Y. and Chase Manhattan (N.Y.) are placed on the Comptroller of the Currency's "problem" list as needing scrutiny.		Frank Schoonmaker, 70, wine expert, dies in N.Y.C.... *Pacific Overtures* , a musical by Stephen Sondheim based on the 1853 Perry expedition to Japan, opens at the Winter Garden Theater, N.Y.C.... Chris Evert wins the $50,000 top prize in the L'eggs world series of women's tennis, beating Evonne Goolagong.	Jan. 11
Roy Wilkins, 74, executive director of the NAACP, announces his resignation effective Jan. 1, 1977. ... Former Calif. Gov. Ronald Reagan, campaigning in Ill. for the Republican presidential nomination, accuses the press of distorting his proposal to shift federal programs to state and local govts.... The Supreme Ct. unanimously rules that provisions of N.Y.S.'s fair campaign practices plan that bar candidates from making racial attacks or misrepresenting their opponents' qualifications are unconstitutional under the First Amendment.			The HEW Dept. releases its first report assessing the U.S. population's state of heath, finding Americans to be generally healthy with lowered infant mortality and heart disease rates.	Agatha Christie, 85, popular and prolific mystery writer, dies in Wallingford, England.... The National Endowment for the Arts awards 100 orchestras grants totaling $8.02 million.	Jan. 12

F	G	H	I	J
Includes elections, federal-state relations, civil rights and liberties, crime, the judiciary, education, health care, poverty, urban affairs and population.	*Includes formation and debate of U.S. foreign and defense policies, veterans' affairs and defense spending. (Relations with specific foreign countries are usually found under the region concerned.)*	*Includes business, labor, agriculture, taxation, transportation, consumer affairs, monetary and fiscal policy, natural resources, and pollution.*	*Includes worldwide scientific, medical and technological developments, natural phenomena, U.S. weather, natural disasters, and accidents.*	*Includes the arts, religion, scholarship, communications media, sports, entertainments, fashions, fads and social life.*

	World Affairs	Europe	Africa & the Middle East	The Americas	Asia & the Pacific
Jan. 13		The radical Paris newspaper *Liberation* publishes a list of 32 people it says are amoung the top 50 U.S. CIA agents in Paris.	An extraordinary session of the OAU, convened to discuss the Angolan crisis, ends its meetings in a deadlock over recognizing the Soviet-backed Popular Movement for the Liberation of Angola (MPLA) and condemning all foreign intervention.	Great Britain's Amb. to Argentina is ousted after Britain refuses to discuss Argentina's claim of sovereignty over the Falkland Islands.	
Jan. 14		Pres. Valery Giscard d'Estaing outlines his government's objectives for the next six months, emphasizing the economy, "structural reforms," and the improvement of the quality of French life.	Portugal suspends the regular daily flights of its airline, TAP, to Mozambique. . . . John Wrathall is sworn in as Rhodesia's second president. . . . Lebanese Christian Phalangists capture a Palestinian refugee camp at Dbaiye, leaving a casualty toll of 100 killed and 250 wounded, mainly Palestinians.	An Ecuadoran Cabinet of three civilians and 11 military officers is sworn in three days after Pres. Guillermo Rodriguez Lara was replaced by a military junta.	P.M. Indira Gandhi says India will continue to conduct nuclear explosions for peaceful purposes despite international protests.
Jan. 15			The *Financial Times* of London reports that Morocco has ordered 25 French Mirage F1 fighter jets, and placed options on buying 50 more. . . . Forces of the pro-Western National Front for the Liberation of Angola (FNLA) are reported collapsing in fighting against Soviet-backed Popular Movement for the Liberation of Angola (MPLA).	Argentinean Pres. Maria Estela Martinez de Peron dismisses four Cabinet ministers in a move seen as an attempt to strengthen right-wing forces in her government.	The six days of public mourning for the late Chinese Premier Chou En-lai end with a memorial ceremony attended by 5,000 Chinese Communist leaders and officials. . . . South Korea's Pres. Chung Hee Park confirms the discovery of oil about 200 miles southeast of Seoul.
Jan. 16		The West German Parliament votes stricter curbs against public advocacy of terrorist violence, drawing criticism from civil libertarians.	The Lebanese air force goes into action for the first time since the current fighting began in April 1975. . . . Holden Roberto, a leader of the National Front for the Liberation of Angola (FNLA), denies a U.S. assessment that his forces have almost collapsed in fighting in the north.	The Ontario, Canada, legislature enacts legislation ordering teachers back to work so that 135 Toronto high schools, closed since Nov. 12, 1975 by a teachers' strike, can reopen.	
Jan. 17	The second Bertrand Russell Tribunal issues a verdict condemning U.S. actions in Latin America and 11 Latin American governments for violations of human rights.		Algerian officials announce signing an agreement under which Algeria will supply 300,000 tons of oil products to North Vietnam in 1976.		
Jan. 18	U.N. Secy. Gen. Kurt Waldheim calls for a halt to the violence in Lebanon.	Leaders of the 19 Western European Socialist and Social Democratic parties begin two days of talks in Elsinore, Denmark on common problems, focusing on the economy and the divisive issue of cooperating with the Communist parties.			Australian P.M. Malcolm Fraser ends a three-day tour of Southeast Asia during which he held talks with the heads of Singapore, Thailand, Malaysia, and the Philippines.
Jan. 19	According to a Freedom House survey, only 19.8 percent of the world's population has full political and civil rights and 35.5 percent is "partially free."	Former Portuguese Gen. Otelo Saralva de Carvalho is arrested on charges of promoting the abortive November 1975 revolt by leftist military officers. . . . The British govt. announces it is withdrawing the small fleet of warships it had sent into Icelandic waters in November 1975 to protect British fishing vessels.		A U.N. Human Rights Commission panel receives testimony on torture in Chilean prisons from Dr. Sheila Cassidy, a British surgeon jailed in Chile for two months in 1975.	*The New York Times* reports that Cambodian authorities are again forcibly transferring hundreds of thousands of people from the cities to rural areas.

A	B	C	D	E
Includes developments that affect more than one world region, international organizations and important meetings of major world leaders.	Includes all domestic and regional developments in Europe, including the Soviet Union, Turkey, Cyprus and Malta.	Includes all domestic and regional developments in Africa and the Middle East, including Iraq and Iran and excluding Cyprus, Turkey and Afghanistan.	Includes all domestic and regional developments in Latin America, the Caribbean and Canada.	Includes all domestic and regional developments in Asia and Pacific nations, extending from Afghanistan through all the Pacific Islands, except Hawaii.

U.S. Politics & Social Issues	U.S. Foreign Policy & Defense	U.S. Economy & Environment	Science, Technology & Nature	Culture, Leisure & Life Style	
Pres. Ford appoints outgoing Commerce Secy. Rogers Morton as a Cabinet-rank counselor to the President on economic and domestic policy.... Federal Ct. rules that Ala. must reform its prison system to guarantee prisoners minimum standards of treatment.... Fed. Judge June Green seeks to inspect all documents withheld when the U.S. released in December 1975 30,000 pages in connection with Julius and Ethel Rosenberg, executed for espionage in 1949.		Supreme Ct., 5–3, rules that the IRS cannot arbitrarily set a date as the end of a taxpayer's taxable year and demand taxes at that time because it fears tax evasion.		AP poll names Fred Lynn, Boston Red Sox outfielder, 1975 Male Athlete of the Year.... Margaret Leighton, 53, Tony Award-winning British stage and screen actress, dies in Chichester, England.... AP follows the UPI and names Minnesota Vikings quarterback Fran Tarkenton the NFL's mvp.... Sarah Caldwell, Boston Opera Co. founder, is the first woman to conduct at the Metropolitan Opera House, N.Y.C., with a performance of Verdi's *La Traviata*.	Jan. 13
A U.S. Appeals Ct. upholds a lower court ruling ordering extensive busing of Boston, Mass. school children.	State Secy. Henry Kissinger announces plans to go to Moscow Jan. 20–23 to seek a breakthrough in SALT talks, despite Soviet involvement in Angola.	Labor Secy. John Dunlop announces his resignation, but says that he is not resigning to protest Pres. Ford's veto of the construction-site picketing bill.	The American Hospital Assn. reports a 0.4 percent decline in the number of people admitted to U.S. hospitals in the first nine months of 1975.... I.M. Laddon, 81, aircraft pioneer who designed the first all-metal plane, dies in San Diego, Calif.		Jan. 14
Sara Jane Moore is sentenced to life in prison for her attempted assassination of Pres. Ford on Sept. 22, 1975.	Charles Goodell, former chairman of the Presidential Clemency Bd., urges that the board be revived so more Vietnam War-era draft evaders and deserters can seek clemency.	Gulf Oil Corp.'s board of directors, embarrassed by reports that the company maintained a $12-million political slush fund, fires the board chairman, Bob Dorsey, and three other top officials.		Chris Evert, record tennis money-winner for 1975, is named female athlete of the year by the AP.... The Vatican issues a declaration on sexual ethics, assailing the "unbridled exaltation of sex" and reaffirming the doctrine that sex has its true meaning in marriage.	Jan. 15
		The Justice Dept sues the Bechtel Corp. for allegedly boycotting individuals and firms blacklisted by Arab League countries.... FRB announces that production in the nation's factories, mines, and utilities increased 1 percent during December 1975.			Jan. 16
				The NCAA, ending its annual convention, turns down economy moves intended to save money for member schools.	Jan. 17
		The National Wildlife Federation's annual environmental report finds ratings declined in five of seven categories assessed in 1974 and rose in only one category, the reduction of air pollution.		The Pittsburgh Steelers beat the Dallas Cowboys in the tenth annual Super Bowl, 21–17.	Jan. 18
The second session of the ninety-fourth Congress convenes.... Former Ga. Gov. Jimmy Carter (D) makes an impressive showing in the Iowa precinct caucuses, the first formal action toward selection of presidential nominees.... Former anti-Vietnam War activists Daniel and Philip Berrigan begin serving jail terms for digging holes in the White House lawn on Nov. 26, 1975 as a protest against the proliferation of nuclear weapons.		A GAO report criticizes the FDA for failing to enforce conflict-of-interest rules, saying more than 150 FDA officials have investments that violate the rules.... In his State of the Union address, Pres. Ford focuses largely on the economy, saying his first objective is sound economic growth without inflation.	The FDA bans Red No. 2 dye, the most widely used dye in foods, drugs, and cosmetics, because of cancer-linked safety concerns.	The official Chinese news agency announces that a new edition of 39 poems by Mao Tse-tung has been published.	Jan. 19

F	G	H	I	J
Includes elections, federal-state relations, civil rights and liberties, crime, the judiciary, education, health care, poverty, urban affairs and population.	Includes formation and debate of U.S. foreign and defense policies, veterans' affairs and defense spending. (Relations with specific foreign countries are usually found under the region concerned.)	Includes business, labor, agriculture, taxation, transportation, consumer affairs, monetary and fiscal policy, natural resources, and pollution.	Includes worldwide scientific, medical and technological developments, natural phenomena, U.S. weather, natural disasters, and accidents.	Includes the arts, religion, scholarship, communications media, sports, entertainments, fashions, fads and social life.

	World Affairs	Europe	Africa & the Middle East	The Americas	Asia & the Pacific
Jan. 20		The British Dept. of Employment releases unemployment figures showing a seasonally adjusted jobless total of 1.16 million persons, or 5.1 percent.... Spanish police break up a demonstration called by the Socialist Workers Party in Madrid with what is reported as one of the largest shows of force in years.	Troops of the PLO are reported to have entered Lebanon from Syria.	The Panamanian govt. exiles 11 critics of its policies, causing business executives to begin an indefinite protest strike.	The *Journal of Commerce* reports that the Japanese Economic Planning Agency has released figures indicating 1.3 million unemployed and 2.5 million underemployed.
Jan. 21	The IMF approves a standby loan to South Africa of 80 million special drawing rights (SDRs), equivalent to $93.6 million.		The Popular Movement for the Liberation of Angola (MPLA) claims to have captured the strategic town of Cela, a major supply camp.		Philippines President Ferdinand Marcos says there will be no national elections in the immediate future and announces formation of a national people's council to advise him.... P.M. Malcolm Fraser reinstates the British national anthem, "God Save the Queen," as the Australian national anthem.... A civilian administration replaces the military government of South Vietnam. Called the People's Revolutionary Committee of Saigon City, it consists of 15 members headed by Vo Van Kiet, formerly deputy chairman of the Military Management Committee.
Jan. 22		Moscow announces that 11,700 Soviet citizens left the country in 1975 to emigrate to Israel, about half the 1974 figure and one-third the 1973 figure.	Syrian Pres. Suleiman Franjieh, following a week of violence in Lebanon, announces a Syrian-negotiated truce aimed at ending the warfare.		
Jan. 23	U.S. State Secy. Kissinger says significant progress was made on the SALT agreement during the three days of Moscow meetings just ending.		The Moroccan Embassy in Madrid denies Spanish press reports that Moroccan troops dropped napalm bombs on refugee camps in the Spanish Sahara.	The Chilean govt. authorizes publication of a book by ex-Pres. Eduardo Frei Montalva, which criticizes the military govt.'s policies and calls for a return to democracy.	The official Chinese news agency reports the debate on post-Cultural Revolution educational policies is continuing under CP control.
Jan. 24		U.S. and Spain sign in Madrid a five-year Treaty of Friendship and Cooperation, which joins their defense policies more tightly then did their recently expired agreement.... In Italy a bid by caretaker Premier Aldo Moro to form a new governing coalition to replace the two-party government that fell on January 7 ends in failure.	Pinhas Lavon, 71, Israeli defense minister in 1954 who was a key figure in an espionage case that clouded Israel's political scene for a decade, dies in Tel Aviv.... Lebanese Premier Rashid Karami withdraws his resignation as the Syrian-negotiated truce begins to take hold in Lebanon.		
Jan. 25		*The New York Times* reports that the Swiss Union for the Decriminalization of Abortion has gathered 70,000 signatures on a petition to submit the abortion question to a national referendum.	Israel announces army commanders will permit free entry into Israel of Lebanese Christians fleeing the Lebanese civil war.		
Jan. 26	The U.N. Security Council's debate on the Middle East ends with the defeat of a pro-Palestinian resolution by a U.S. veto on a 9–1 vote.	EEC member countries, which normally produce 40 million tons of potatoes annually, are reported suffering from an acute potato shortage.... Rainer Schubert, a West Berliner, is sentenced in East Berlin to 15 years in prison for helping 86 East Germans and a Czech flee to the West.	Nigeria reports that it repatriated more than 20,000 contract laborers from Equatorial Guinea since mid-1975 because the workers were being treated brutally.	Rep. Michael Harrington (D, Mass.) reports the U.S. gave Chile $276 million in economic and military aid in 1975, despite a law banning military aid and placing a $25-million ceiling on economic aid.	

A	B	C	D	E
Includes developments that affect more than one world region, international organizations and important meetings of major world leaders.	Includes all domestic and regional developments in Europe, including the Soviet Union, Turkey, Cyprus and Malta.	Includes all domestic and regional developments in Africa and the Middle East, including Iraq and Iran and excluding Cyprus, Turkey and Afghanistan.	Includes all domestic and regional developments in Latin America, the Caribbean and Canada.	Includes all domestic and regional developments in Asia and Pacific nations, extending from Afghanistan through all the Pacific Islands, except Hawaii.

U.S. Politics & Social Issues	U.S. Foreign Policy & Defense	U.S. Economy & Environment	Science, Technology & Nature	Culture, Leisure & Life Style	
About 300 persons at East Boston High School demonstrate against court-ordered busing.	*The New York Times* and *Washington Post* begin publishing accounts of the still-unreleased House Intelligence Committee report on CIA questionable activities, which include involvement with the news media, secret aid to foreign leaders, and misrepresented aid to specific foreign political factions.	Gov. Milton Shapp of Pa., a Democratic presidential aspirant, attacks Pres. Ford's State of the Union address, saying his economic plan would lead to one million more jobless.... The Commerce Dept. announces that real GNP expanded at a rate of 5.4 percent annually during the fourth quarter of 1975, compared with 12 percent in the third quarter.			Jan. 20
Sen. Edmund Muskie (Me.) delivers the congressional Democrats' rebuttal to Pres. Ford's State of the Union Message, deploring Ford's "jobless policies" and questionable entanglements abroad.... Pres. Ford's 1977 budget proposes major revision of the Medicare program of health insurance for the elderly, with new "catastrophe" coverage.	Pres. Ford's 1977 budget includes $100.1 billion for defense, which represents 5.4 percent of the GNP and $8.9 billion more than the fiscal 1976 estimate.	Pres. Ford submits a $394.2 billion budget for fiscal 1977 to the Congress, with a projected deficit of $43 billion.	The Anglo-French Concorde, a supersonic passenger plane, begins service: London to Bahrain and Paris to Brazil.		Jan. 21
Pres. Ford names eight Republicans as among those he is considering as a running mate on the 1976 presidential ticket.		Pres. Ford nominates W.J. Usery Jr., director of the Federal Mediation and Conciliation Service, to be Labor Secy.		The New York City Ballet premieres George Balanchine's *Chaconne* to music by Christoph Willibald von Gluck.	Jan. 22
The U.S. Appeals Ct. extends the powers of the EEOC to investigate charges of discrimination, even if the discrimination does not affect the original complainant.... Former N.C. Gov. Terry Sanford withdraws from the race for the Democratic presidential nomination.	U.N. Amb. Daniel Moynihan accuses the State Dept. of not supporting his successful policy of breaking up the anti-U.S. voting bloc at the U.N.		China conducts its eighteenth nuclear weapons test.... Milton Reynolds, creator of the world's first mass-produced ball-point pen and an around-the-world flight record-setter, dies at the age of 83 in Mexico City.	Paul Robeson, 77, singer, actor, and black activist, dies in Philadelphia.... Actor Sidney Poitier marries actress Joanna Shimkus in Los Angeles.	Jan. 23
Ala. Gov. George Wallace wins in the Miss. Democratic precinct caucuses, beating former Ga. Gov. Jimmy Carter by a 3–1 margin.					Jan. 24
				Chinese CP official newspaper declares that Mao's two recently published poems inspired China's Jan. 23 nuclear weapons tests.... Top best-selling books, according to *The New York Times*, are (fiction) *Curtain* by Agatha Christie and *Ragtime* by E.L. Doctorow and (nonfiction) *Bring on the Empty Horses* by David Niven and *Sylvia Porter's Money Book* .	Jan. 25
Court-ordered busing to desegregate Detroit, Mich. schools goes into effect with virtually no disturbances.... The Supreme Ct. rules that police can make arrests in public places without a warrant, even if there is prior opportunity to get a warrant.	According to *The New York Times* account of the House Intelligence Committee report, the CIA secretly gave funds to many foreign political parties and individuals, mostly in developing countries.	Pres. Ford and his economic advisers urge a moderate and steady pace of recovery and caution against inflation.... J. William Fulbright, former chairman of the Senate Foreign Relations Committee, registers with the Justice Dept. as a United Arab Emirates agent.	*Journal of the American Medical Assn.* article links increased admissions to mental health facilities to the poor economy.	A rare seventeenth-century oil sketch on oak by Peter Paul Rubens, *The Visitation* is stolen from a museum in France.	Jan. 26

F	G	H	I	J
Includes elections, federal-state relations, civil rights and liberties, crime, the judiciary, education, health care, poverty, urban affairs and population.	*Includes formation and debate of U.S. foreign and defense policies, veterans' affairs and defense spending. (Relations with specific foreign countries are usually found under the region concerned.)*	*Includes business, labor, agriculture, taxation, transportation, consumer affairs, monetary and fiscal policy, natural resources, and pollution.*	*Includes worldwide scientific, medical and technological developments, natural phenomena, U.S. weather, natural disasters, and accidents.*	*Includes the arts, religion, scholarship, communications media, sports, entertainments, fashions, fads and social life.*

	World Affairs	Europe	Africa & the Middle East	The Americas	Asia & the Pacific
Jan. 27	The PLO is accepted as a new member of the Group of 77 developing nations of UNCTAD.... China will reportedly send a delegation to Brussels in the next few months to begin negotiations with the EEC a commercial trade pact.	King Juan Carlos of Spain issues a decree to postpone holding elections to the Cortes (Parliament) for at least one year to allow time for electoral law changes guaranteeing universal suffrage.	Pres. Ford greets visiting Israeli P.M. Yitzhak Rabin at a White House reception, pledging continued U.S. aid to Israel and urging that steps be taken to further peace negotiations.... Western-backed National Union for the Total Independence of Angola (UNITA) abandons Huambo, capital of the coalition govt. it had proclaimed with FNLA in November 1975, as the pro-Communist MPLA forces advance to within 50 miles of the city.		Former Australian P.M. Gough Whitlam wins reelection as parliamentary leader of his party.
Jan. 28	OPEC establishes an $800-million fund to provide developing nations with interest-free, long-term loans.	To the disappointment of a broad range of Spanish political groups, Premier Carlos Arias Navarro outlines a series of political reforms, but says little about political parties, ignores demands for free trade unions, and rules out a general political amnesty program.... Spanish CP calls the proposed political reforms "a pure and simple" continuation of the Franco regime.	Pres. Kenneth Kaunda of Zambia assumes emergency powers, which he justifies by the deteriorating conditions in Angola, Rhodesia, and South-West Africa.... More than 100 British mercenaries fly to Zaire to serve as "military advisers" to the National Front for the Liberation of Angola (FNLA).	Chilean Pres. Augusto Pinochet Ugarte signs a decree establishing certain rights for prisoners and setting measures to prevent the torture of those in custody.	
Jan. 29		British Liberal Party head Jeremy Thorpe denies potentially damaging charges about his financial and private life.... The EEC Commission replies affirmatively to the Greek govt.'s request for full admission, and recommends a delay so that Greece can make necessary structural reforms.	Angolan UNITA leader Jonas Savimbi appeals to all Western embassies in Kinshasa, Zaire for immediate military aid to stave off the MPLA onslaught.	In Canada a new government plan is announced to reorganize the nation's ailing rail passenger system by 1980.	In Australia a large number of people begin divorce actions under the new liberalized divorce law that went into effect January 5.
Jan. 30		EEC officials and those of its member states provisionally agree on an EEC fishing-rights policy based on a 200-mile national fishing limit.	Two top officials of the Popular Movement for the Liberation of Angola (MPLA) indicate their willingness to establish better relations with the West.		The Indian Parliament adopts a law guaranteeing equal pay for women doing similar work as men.
Jan. 31	The governing bd. of the 18-nation International Energy Agency (IEA) agrees to a long-term program of energy development to make its members less dependent on OPEC.... The U.N. Security Council unanimously approves a resolution calling for U.N.-supervised elections in South-West Africa (Namibia) and condemning South Africa's use of that territory as a base for attacks on neighboring countries.		Offices of two pro-Iraqi newspapers in a Beirut, Lebanon suburb are attacked by a pro-Syrian guerrilla group, killing seven newsmen, wounding another seven, and kidnapping five.... French Pres. Valery Giscard d'Estaing contends that since Algeria says it has no territorial claim to the Spanish Sahara, the Sahara's future should be decided by Morocco, Mauritania, and Spain.		The Indian central govt. takes over the administration of Tamil Nadu after accusing the state govt. of misrule and failure to obey the laws of the national emergency.
Feb. 1		As street demonstrations and labor protests continue in Spain, the police use tear gas and rubber bullets to counter Barcelona demonstrations by over 10,000 persons.... Portuguese farmers continue their month-long protests against the agrarian reform law, demanding it be suspended and illegal land ocupations be stopped.			

A	B	C	D	E
Includes developments that affect more than one world region, international organizations and important meetings of major world leaders.	Includes all domestic and regional developments in Europe, including the Soviet Union, Turkey, Cyprus and Malta.	Includes all domestic and regional developments in Africa and the Middle East, including Iraq and Iran and excluding Cyprus, Turkey and Afghanistan.	Includes all domestic and regional developments in Latin America, the Caribbean and Canada.	Includes all domestic and regional developments in Asia and Pacific nations, extending from Afghanistan through all the Pacific Islands, except Hawaii.

U.S. Politics & Social Issues	U.S. Foreign Policy & Defense	U.S. Economy & Environment	Science, Technology & Nature	Culture, Leisure & Life Style	
Jury selection begins in the trial of Patricia Hearst, kidnapped by the SLA in 1974, who is accused of bank robbery.	Anne Armstrong, counselor to Presidents Richard Nixon and Gerald Ford, is named Ambassador to Great Britain.... George Bush is confirmed as CIA director.... Marion Javits, wife of Jacob Javits (R, N.Y.), who is a member of the Sen. For. Rel. Committee, resigns as a $67,500-a-year consultant to Iran Air, in wake of conflict-of-interest charges.... Defense Secy. Donald Rumsfeld tells the House Armed Services Committee that Soviet military strength has increased steadily in recent years while U.S. investment in the military has declined.	The Commerce Dept announces that the U.S. posted a record $11.05-billion trade surplus during 1975, compared to $2.34 billion in 1974. The previous record was $7.08 billion.		Libby Howie, 24, is appointed the first woman auctioneer in the 232-year history of Sotheby Parke Bernet Inc., the world's largest fine art auction firm.... The largest lottery prize in U.S. history to date — $1,776 a week for life with a $1.8 million minimum guarantee — is won in N.J. by Eric Leek, a 26-year-old hairdresser.	Jan. 27
	The New York Times reports charges that Sen. Henry Jackson (D, Wash.) and Sen. Stuart Symington (D, Mo.) had, in 1974, given former CIA Dir. Richard Helms advice on dealing with congressional probes of Helms's and the CIA's Watergate involvement.	The Commerce Dept. announces that the government's composite index of leading economic indicators rose 0.4 percent in December 1975.... The Treasury Dept. announces the budget deficit for December 1975 was $5.8 billion, smaller than November but far larger than the $2.5 billion deficit in December 1974.	A National Cancer Institute spokesman attributes the seeming 1975 rise in cancer deaths to an irregularity in data compilation.	Variety lists Dog Day Afternoon as the top-grossing film during the previous week and "Convoy" as the best-selling single record.... Victor Goldbloom, the Quebec govt. minister in charge of the Olympics, says the Montreal Summer Games will start on time even though the facilities will not be completed.	Jan. 28
Dr. Gail Thain Parker, who at 32 is the nation's youngest woman college president, resigns from her post at Bennington College, Vt., citing intense faculty pressure and waning trustee support.... In a London Times article, Dr. William Sargent, a British psychiatrist who visited Patricia Hearst in jail, says there is no double she was brainwashed.		The House passes, 321–80 a public works–urban aid bill hours after Pres. Ford says he will veto it if it comes to him.		A painting by Henri de Toulouse-Lautrec, Marcelle , stolen from a Kyoto, Japan museum in 1968, is returned undamaged.	Jan. 29
The Supreme Ct. rules on the 1974 Federal Election Campaign Act, upholding the financing provisions and striking down limits on political expenditures.... Eighteen elderly residents of the Wincrest Manor Nursing and Rest Home, Chicago, Ill., die in wake of a fire.	David K. Bruce resigns as U.S. Amb. to NATO after 50 years of diplomatic service.	Pres. Ford vetoes a bill to increase federal price supports for milk, saying it would produce unnecessarily high prices and huge surpluses.		Public Broadcasting System initiates its nationwide TV series of telecasts of live performances from Lincoln Center, N.Y.C., with a program featuring the New York Philharmonic, Andre Previn conducting and Van Cliburn as piano soloist.	Jan. 30
Pres. Ford takes his campaign against federal encroachment on private and local initiatives into the South and Midwest.			An announcement is made that British archaeologists excavated eight tombs of the tenth century B.C. near the palace of Knossos on Crete, finding precious Minoan artifacts.	Pope Paul VI warns that feminism runs the risk "of either virilizing women or of depersonalizing them" and affirms woman's primary importance as custodian of the family.... Three gunmen steal 119 paintings by Pablo Picasso, worth $4.5 million, from the papal palace in Avignon, France.	Jan. 31
	Rep. Paul McCloskey Jr. (R, Calif.) says that North Vietnamese officials claimed, during a 1975 visit to Hanoi by members of a House Select Committee on Missing in Action, that then-Pres. Richard Nixon pledged $3.25 billion in postwar economic aid after the Paris accords to end the Vietnam War were signed.		The London Times reports that the prison where Socrates drank hemlock in 399 B.C. has been identified by an American archaelogist.	Jimmy Connors wins the U.S. professional indoor tennis tournament, defeating Bjorn Borg, 7–6, 6–4, 6–0.... Hilmar Baukhage, 87, radio commentator and columnist, dies in Wash., D.C.	Feb. 1

F	G	H	I	J
Includes elections, federal-state relations, civil rights and liberties, crime, the judiciary, education, health care, poverty, urban affairs and population.	Includes formation and debate of U.S. foreign and defense policies, veterans' affairs and defense spending. (Relations with specific foreign countries are usually found under the region concerned.)	Includes business, labor, agriculture, taxation, transportation, consumer affairs, monetary and fiscal policy, natural resources, and pollution.	Includes worldwide scientific, medical and technological developments, natural phenomena, U.S. weather, natural disasters, and accidents.	Includes the arts, religion, scholarship, communications media, sports, entertainments, fashions, fads and social life.

	World Affairs	Europe	Africa & the Middle East	The Americas	Asia & the Pacific
Feb. 2			The U.S. denies any involvement in financing the recruitment of mercenaries to fight in Angola alongside Western-backed forces.	P.M. Pierre Trudeau ends his Latin American tour during which he visited Mexico, Cuba, and Venezuela in an effort to stimulate Canadian trade and promote Canada's separate economic and political identity from the U.S.	
Feb. 3	The World Bank approves a $33-million loan to help Chile build a plant to process copper ore and by-products.	*London Financial Times* reports that in 1975 the number of foreign residents in Switzerland dropped 4.9 percent from the previous year to a total of 1,012,710.... Leonid Plyushch, dissident Soviet mathematician who was allowed to leave the country in January, holds his first press conference and details his experiences.	Zaire Pres. Mobutu Sese Seko, a major supporter of the Western-backed forces fighting in Angola, bars foreign mercenaries from passing through Zaire en route to battle.... The Iranian govt. reports that a sharp reduction in oil revenue has slowed the country's growth rate by 60 percent since spring, 1975.... Gen. Murtala Mohammed, the Nigerian head of state, announces a new national capital will be established at an undisclosed site in the center of the country.		
Feb. 4	UNESCO calls its 10-year program to eradicate world illiteracy a failure, saying that there are now 800 million illiterates in the world compared to 735 million in 1965.		A military parade in Luanda, Angola commemorates the fifteenth anniversary of the beginning of the MPLA's war of independence from Portugal.... French troops in Djibouti storm a school bus near the Somali border and kill six guerrillas who had threatened to murder the 30 French children aboard.	An Argentine ship fires two warning shots at a British ship near the Falkland Islands, which are ruled by Britain despite Argentine claims of sovereignty.	The Cambodian govt. announces that nationwide elections will he held March 20 for the newly established People's Representative Assembly.... Documents released by a Senate subcommittee show Lockheed Aircraft Corp. secretly paid $7.1 million to a right-wing Japanese militarist to promote the sale of the L-1011.
Feb. 5	*The New York Times* reports that State Secy. Kissinger has concluded that Cuba has resumed "exporting revolution," to Angola, the Sahara, and possibly other places.	The W. Ger. Federal Labor Office reports that January unemployment rose to 1.341 million, or 5.9 percent of the work force, the highest level in 20 years.... French wine growers, supported by leftist unions, stage a 24-hour work stoppage to dramatize their grievances against Italian wine imports.	The AP cites U.S. intelligence sources as saying the Cuban airlift to Angola was halted on January 21.	The Colombian govt. announces that a state of siege will remain in effect indefinitely following a resurgence of civil unrest.	
Feb. 6		Spanish govt. bans further concerts by the Catalonian protest singer Raimon Pelejero, after he appears the previous day before a 6,000-member audience, displaying Spanish Republican flags and cheering exiled Communist leaders.... W. Ger. Lower Saxony gubernatorial candidate Ernst Albrecht forms a minority Christian Democratic government after his party wins, for the second time in a month, a majority in secret balloting for the state governorship.	Rhodesian P.M. Ian Smith, saying guerrilla warfare along the border with Mozambique has recently intensified, announces an increased military call-up.	Margaret Trudeau, who committed protocol gaffes while accompanying her husband, Canadian P.M. Pierre Trudeau, on his Latin American tour, defends her actions in phone calls to an Ottawa radio program.	Japanese Premier Takeo Miki tells the Diet that he will investigate reports of official involvement in $12.6 million of Lockheed payoffs made since 1958.... Former Pres. Richard Nixon reportedly will visit China as a private citizen, beginning Feb. 21.... The Chinese foreign ministry says that a document, which was represented as the last political will of Chou En-lai, is "groundless fabrication."
Feb. 7		The French C.P. holds its twenty-second party congress, attended by 80 delegations of foreign Communist parties and a delegation from the French Socialist Party.			The official Chinese news agency discloses that sixth-ranked Deputy Premier Hua Kuo-feng, who is also public security minister, has been named acting premier.
Feb. 8		The Dutch Cabinet confirms that Prince Bernhard is thought to be the "high government official" named in U.S. Senate testimony as receiving $1.1 million to promote Lockheed aircraft sales.... The Israeli office for economic affairs in West Berlin is heavily damaged by a bomb. The Arm of the Arab Revolution claims responsibility.	Mayotte residents vote overwhelmingly to remain French, thus severing Mayotte's ties to the other three Comoro Islands.... Huambo, the capital of the Angolan govt. as proclaimed by UNITA, and the movement's military headquarters are captured by forces of the MPLA.	The Colombian govt. begins an investigation into reports that two air force generals received illegal payments from Lockheed as the bribery scandal spreads.	

A	B	C	D	E
Includes developments that affect more than one world region, international organizations and important meetings of major world leaders.	Includes all domestic and regional developments in Europe, including the Soviet Union, Turkey, Cyprus and Malta.	Includes all domestic and regional developments in Africa and the Middle East, including Iraq and Iran and excluding Cyprus, Turkey and Afghanistan.	Includes all domestic and regional developments in Latin America, the Caribbean and Canada.	Includes all domestic and regional developments in Asia and Pacific nations, extending from Afghanistan through all the Pacific Islands, except Hawaii.

U.S. Politics & Social Issues	U.S. Foreign Policy & Defense	U.S. Economy & Environment	Science, Technology & Nature	Culture, Leisure & Life Style	
The New York Times reports that Social Security officials confirm reports that millions of dollars are wasted by renting rather than buying medical equipment for Medicare patients.	Daniel Moynihan resigns as U.S. representative to the U.N.	Elliot Richardson is sworn in as Commerce Secy.			Feb. 2
Pres. Ford says that he doesn't believe in abortion on demand, doesn't agree with the Supreme Ct.'s 1973 decision, and doesn't think a constitutional amendment is the remedy.... Denise Watson, 21, a nurse's aide at the Chicago Wincrest Manor Nursing and Rest Home, is charged with arson and 54 counts of murder.	State Secy. Kissinger explains his view of detente and appeals for public and congressional support of his policy.	Three high-level GE nuclear engineers resign to join a campaign for a Calif. initiative against nuclear power.	The National Center for Health Statistics reports that the U.S. death rate for 1974 was 9.2 per 1,000 population, the lowest since statistics began to be kept in 1900.	Swedish film director Ingmar Bergman is hospitalized for what is described as a nervous breakdown following his arrest in Sweden on income-tax evasion charges.	Feb. 3
The trial of Patricia Hearst, charged with bank robbery, begins.		Transportation Secy. William Coleman Jr. decides to allow a 16-month trial of the British–French supersonic transport plane, the Concorde, to both Wash. D.C. and N.Y.... The Environmental Defense Fund sues to contest Coleman's decision to permit Concorde flights to the U.S.... Pres. Ford's milk-price-support veto is sustained by the Senate.	A major earthquake hits Guatemala and Honduras, causing massive destruction.... The U.S. detonates two medium-size underground nuclear devices, bringing to 285 the number of announced tests since the ban on atmospheric testing took effect.	The twelfth Winter Olympics open at Innsbruck, Austria, with 1,054 athletes representing 37 nations in skiing, skating, and ice hockey competitions.	Feb. 4
Southern Calif. doctors end a 35-day work slowdown protesting an escalation in the cost of malpractice insurance.... Eugene McCarthy names William Clay Ford, vice president of the Ford Motor Co., as his running mate on an independent third-party presidential ticket.		Pres. Ford signs the railroad aid bill, which provides financial aid and regulation reforms that he says will make reorganization of bankrupt lines a success.... House defeats a bill to deregulate natural gas prices set by major producers. ... Ben Kahn, 89, leading furrier, dies in N.Y.C.			Feb. 5
		Comptroller of the Currency James Smith says that 28 national banks, with assets totaling $11.53 billion, are on the agency's problem list.		U.S. medalist Sheila Young breaks an Olympic record in the 500-meter speed skating event with a time of 42.76.	Feb. 6
				Philadelphia's Schubert Theater, refurbished as an adjunct to the Academy of Music, opens with a revival of *My Fair Lady* .	Feb. 7
Pres. Ford campaigns in N.H., stressing his "common sense" policies of "economic discipline."	Brookings Institution releases a study opposing production of the B-1 bomber as unnecessary and more expensive than alternate ways of modernizing the strategic bomber force.	Newark, N.J. teachers ratify a new contract with an average salary increase of 8.5 percent over a two-and-a-half-year period, thereby ending a strike that began on Feb. 3.	*Washington Post* tells of a National Cancer Inst. study that found that the area with the greatest concentration of chemical plants along the New Jersey Turnpike had the highest U.S. cancer death rate.... The Fermi National Accelerator Laboratory in Ill. report that a new atomic particle has been detected and named upsilon.		Feb. 8

F	G	H	I	J
Includes elections, federal-state relations, civil rights and liberties, crime, the judiciary, education, health care, poverty, urban affairs and population.	*Includes formation and debate of U.S. foreign and defense policies, veterans' affairs and defense spending. (Relations with specific foreign countries are usually found under the region concerned.)*	*Includes business, labor, agriculture, taxation, transportation, consumer affairs, monetary and fiscal policy, natural resources, and pollution.*	*Includes worldwide scientific, medical and technological developments, natural phenomena, U.S. weather, natural disasters, and accidents.*	*Includes the arts, religion, scholarship, communications media, sports, entertainments, fashions, fads and social life.*

	World Affairs	Europe	Africa & the Middle East	The Americas	Asia & the Pacific
Feb. 9		Serge Klarsfeld, a French lawyer charged in a 1971 abortive attempt to kidnap a former head of the Paris Gestapo, is given a two-month suspended sentence by a Cologne court.	UNITA For. Affairs Secy. Jorge Sangumba calls the fall of Huambo his movement's most serious defeat, charges that the MPLA drive had been led by 6,000 Cuban troops and few Angolans, and foresees a return to guerrilla tactics. . . . The Israeli Knesset defeats 63–35, an opposition Likud Party vote of no confidence in Premier Yitzhak Rabin.		
Feb. 10	*Christian Science Monitor*, citing Soviet sources, says Moscow does not feel the appointment of Hua Kuo-feng as acting premier will help improve its ties with China. . . . The meeting of the Group of 77 of the U.N. Conference on Trade and Development calls for the restructuring of international trade in commodities.	U.S. officials confirm that the U.S. Embassy in Moscow has warned its employes of a potential health hazard arising from microwave radiation present in the embassy.	British P.M. Harold Wilson says 13 or 14 British mercenaries in Angola were executed by a firing squad of fellow countrymen who were forced to do so by a "Col. Callan."	Anguilla's new Constitution becomes effective, establishing the Caribbean island as a self-governing British territory.	ASEAN foreign Ministers at a meeting in Thailand agree on a treaty of friendship, but are still at odds over trade, tariffs, and arbitration of political disputes.
Feb. 11		Italian Premier Aldo Moro announces the formation oa minority Christian Democratic govt. to replace the coalition, which fell January 7. . . . Italian Interior Min. Luigi Gui calls for a court inquiry into allegations that he received more than $50,000 from Lockheed in connection with Italy's 1970–71 purchase of planes, but he also resigns his post. . . . In the one-year period since the Feb. 10, 1975 cease-fire between the Provisional wing of the Irish Republican Army (IRA) and the British army, 289 people are reported to have died.	OAU recognizes the government proclaimed by the Communist-backed MPLA and admits the People's Republic of Angola to membership.		Indonesian Defense Min. Maraden Panggabean says the left-wing Fretelin movement no longer administers any territory in East Timor, now controlled by the pro-Jakarta forces.
Feb. 12		Francis Stagg, 34, a former Provisional IRA staff officer, dies in an English prison after a 61-day hunger strike. . . . In the Netherlands the public prosecutor asks for an acquittal in the Dassault Breguet Aviation bribery case, citing insubstantial evidence.	UNITA, driven from all of the major sites it had held in southern Angola, says it will abandon conventional warfare against the MPLA, turning to intensive guerrilla tactics.		The Japanese Nissan Motor Co. announces it has purchased a large assembly plant located near Melbourne, Australia from Volkswagenwerk, A.G. of West Germany.
Feb. 13	The U.S. Commission of Human Rights accuses Israel of having committed war crimes by continued violations of international law in the occupied Arab territories.	Former W. Ger. Defense Min. Franz Josef Strauss, denies reports that he or his party, the Christian Social Union, received Lockheed money to promote the sale of its aircraft.	One thousand Arabs stage a violent demonstration in the Old City of Jerusalem to protest a recent Israeli court decision permitting Jews to pray on the Temple Mount. . . . Gen. Murtala Mohammed, the Nigerian head of state, is assassinated by a small group of self-described young revolutionaries.		In South Vietnam security forces storm a Roman Catholic church to stop a rebellion by armed dissidents.
Feb. 14			Nigeria's 20-member ruling Supreme Military Council announces that Lt. Gen. Olusegun Obasanjo, armed forces chief of staff, is the new head of state, after Gen. Murtala Mohammed's assassins fail in their coup attempt. . . . The Lebanese Cabinet approves a series of political reforms aimed at giving Lebanese Moslems a greater share in government and ending the civil strife.	The Venezuelan govt. names seven persons who allegedly received illegal payments from Occidental Petroleum Corp., including Alberto Flores Ortega, minister to OPEC.	The Indian govt. withdraws the accreditation of more than 40 Indian newspaper correspondents, depriving them of admission to news conference and Parliament sessions.

A	B	C	D	E
Includes developments that affect more than one world region, international organizations and important meetings of major world leaders.	*Includes all domestic and regional developments in Europe, including the Soviet Union, Turkey, Cyprus and Malta.*	*Includes all domestic and regional developments in Africa and the Middle East, including Iraq and Iran and excluding Cyprus, Turkey and Afghanistan.*	*Includes all domestic and regional developments in Latin America, the Caribbean and Canada.*	*Includes all domestic and regional developments in Asia and Pacific nations, extending from Afghanistan through all the Pacific Islands, except Hawaii.*

U.S. Politics & Social Issues	U.S. Foreign Policy & Defense	U.S. Economy & Environment	Science, Technology & Nature	Culture, Leisure & Life Style	
Patricia Hearst testifies at her trial, admitting participation in the bank robbery but claiming she was coerced by threats of death from her SLA captors.			The Guatemalan National Emergency Committee reports that 17,032 people died, 54,285 were injured, and more than a million were left homeles by the February 4 earthquake.	Percy Faith, 67, music arranger, composer, and conductor, dies in Los Angeles, Calif.... The first Avery Fisher Prizes for promising young instrumentalists are awarded to pianists Ursula Oppens and Paul Shenly, violonist Ani Kavafian, and harpist Heidi Lehwalder.	Feb. 9
Sen. Lloyd Bentsen (Tex.) withdraws from the Democratic presidential nomination race.... Republican presidential aspirant Ronald Reagan, campaigning in N.H., attacks the Ford administration foreign policy as bereft of a "coherent global view."	Pres. Ford assures reporters that former Pres. Nixon was invited to China as a private citizen, and that he has not asked for any "special report" from Nixon.... The House Select Intelligence Committee, before disbanding, votes, 9–4, to submit 20 proposals, including the creation of a permanent House Intelligence Committee.	W.J. Usery Jr., is sworn in as Labor Secy.... Pres. Ford orders a high-level investigation of the overseas practices of U.S. corporations.			Feb. 10
At the Privacy Protection Study Commission hearings, credit and other companies say that clients' records are often given to government agencies without notification. ... The Agriculture Dept. releases a report on misallocation of food stamps received by households in which at least one member is not receiving public assistance.... Forty-four federal judges sue in the U.S. Ct. of Claims for compensation for the reduction in the value of their salaries caused by inflation since 1969.	Village Voice , a N.Y.C. weekly, begins publishing leaked portions of the secret House Intelligence Committee report.... CIA Director George Bush says the CIA will no longer enter into any paid or contractual relationships with employes of U.S. news organizations.			Lee J. Cobb, 64, leading U.S. stage and screen actor known for his portrayal of Willy Loman in Death of a Salesman, dies in Los Angeles, Calif.	Feb. 11
The FBI says 69 persons were killed in 1975 in 2,053 reported bombing incidents.... Pres. Ford releases a personal financial statement showing a net worth of $323,489.	CBS News correspondent Daniel Schorr says he gave the Village Voice a copy of the secret House Intelligence Committee report so that it could be published.... Army Secy. Martin Hoffman says that if the tank developed by the West Germans, called the Leopart II, proves superior in performance and cost to tanks currently being developed by Chrysler Corp. and GM, the Army will purchase it as its official new main battle tank at a projected cost of $4.4 billion.		A FDA ban against manufacture of Red No. 2 dye, the most widely used food coloring in the U.S., goes into effect while a court challenge against the ban continues.	Sal Mineo, 37, screen, stage, and TV actor, is stabbed to death in Hollywood, Calif.	Feb. 12
Patricia Hearst testifies at her trial, describing her kidnapping and early treatment by the SLA and telling of death threats she had received from her captors.... Phyllis Schlafly, chairman of the Stop ERA organization, charges that supporters of the ERA want to turn child care over to the government.		Pres. Ford vetoes a $6.1 million public works employment bill.... Lockheed's two top executives, Daniel Haughton and A. Carl Kotchian, resign after disclosures of payments to foreign government officials to promote arms sales.		U.S. ice skater Dorothy Hamil wins a gold medal in the Winter Olympics.... State Secy. Kissinger protests the International Olympic Committee's decision to exclude Radio Free Europe from official coverage of the 1976 games.... Lily Pons, 71, leading coloratura soprano of the Metropolitain Opera from 1931 to 1960, dies in Dallas, Tex.	Feb. 13
					Feb. 14

F	G	H	I	J
Includes elections, federal-state relations, civil rights and liberties, crime, the judiciary, education, health care, poverty, urban affairs and population.	Includes formation and debate of U.S. foreign and defense policies, veterans' affairs and defense spending. (Relations with specific foreign countries are usually found under the region concerned.)	Includes business, labor, agriculture, taxation, transportation, consumer affairs, monetary and fiscal policy, natural resources, and pollution.	Includes worldwide scientific, medical and technological developments, natural phenomena, U.S. weather, natural disasters, and accidents.	Includes the arts, religion, scholarship, communications media, sports, entertainments, fashions, fads and social life.

	World Affairs	Europe	Africa & the Middle East	The Americas	Asia & the Pacific
Feb. 15			The Israeli Cabinet approves the appointment of Prof. Shlomo Avineri, a critic of Premier Yitzhak Rabin's Palestinian policies, as director general of the foreign ministry.	A new Cuban Constitution declaring the country is a socialist state, recognizing the leading role of the CP, and institutionalizing Pres. Castro's social and economic changes since 1959 is approved by a 97.7 percent vote in a national referendum.	
Feb. 16	Delegates of 12 countries sign a convention to control pollution in the Mediterranean and protect the marine environment in that area.	Soviet officials deny allegations of anti-Semitism and defend their policies regarding religion and emigration.		Transport workers and shopowners in San Felipe, Venezuela strike to protest the deaths of two students killed during a demonstration demanding improved school facilities. . . . U.S. State Secy. Henri Kissinger beings a Latin American tour to promote good will and smooth over bilateral trade problems. . . . Argentinian Pres. Maria de Peron closes the special session of Congress as political, labor, and management leaders urge her to resign to avoid a military coup.	A Shanghai radio broadcast identifies a Chinese wall poster campaign attacking Deputy Premier Teng Hsiao-ping as having been personally initiated by Chairman Mao.
Feb. 17		Yugoslavia's foreign trade deficit for 1975 is reported to be $3.624 billion, $266.68 million less than the 1974 figure.	The British high commissions in Lagos is sacked by Nigerian students following released reports that Lt. Col. B.S. Dimka, leader of the abortive Feb. 13 coup, sought the help of British Comr. Sir Martin Le Quesne for the return of exiled Nigerian leader Yakubu Gowon.	Venezuelan Mines Min. Valentin Hernandez-Acosta says that Alberto Flores Ortega must resign from his OPEC post so that he can defend himself against charges that he accepted bribes from the Occidental Petroleum Corp., whose assets were nationalized on Jan. 1.	The Japanese Diet holds two days of hearings on the Lockheed scandal, during which Kenji Osano, a confidant and financial supporter of Kakuei Tanaka, and representatives of All-American Airways and the Marubeni Corp. deny all charges of influence-peddling and corruptions. . . . Australian P.M. Malcolm Fraser announces that he will approve a U.S. request to build a $12 million navigation station near the Tasman Sea, thereby reversing a foreign policy principle of the former Labor govt. . . . The State Dept. reports the U.S. has broken off discussions with India on a $65 million economic development package because of the Indian govt.'s hostility to the U.S.
Feb. 18		EEC proposes extending exclusive national coastal fishing zones within the EEC from six to 12 miles and creating a 200-mile EEC-controlled zone in which fishing quotas would be negotiated among the nine member-countries. . . . Thousands of striking Barcelona municipal workers are drafted into the Spanish army to force them back to work. . . . London Times reports over 6,000 Finnish police have gone on strike demanding a 50 percent pay increase and rejecting a 3.5 percent increase granted in January.	Addis Ababa radio says Abuna (Archbishop) Tewoflos of the Ethiopian Orthodox Church was removed from office by the military government and accused of serious crimes.	In an apparent effort to avert a coup without resigning, Pres. Maria de Peron says she won't run for a full term later in 1976, but will complete her current term, which ends May 1977.	
Feb. 19	Former Israeli P.M. Golda Meir, speaking at the second World Conference on Soviet Jewry, calls on the U.S.S.R. to remove all obstacles in the way of those who wish to leave.	Iceland severs diplomatic relations with Great Britain in its continuing dispute over the amount of cod British fishermen can take from Icelandic territorial waters. . . . The British govt. sets out a series of economic programs designed to curb inflation, reduce government spending, and alleviate unemployment while boosting industrial investment.		Amnesty International, in a world-wide campaign to publicize alleged human-rights abuses in Uruguay, charges that 22 political prisoners have been tortured to death between May 1972 and November 1975 and two more had been killed since then. . . . Venezuelan OPEC minister Alberto Flores Ortega, accused of accepting Occidental Petroleum Corp. bribes, is reported to have offered to resign from his post in a letter to Mines Min. Valentin Hernandez Acosta.	Japanese Premier Takeo Miki appoints a Cabinet-level committee and says democracy would be fatally wounded if the Lockheed bribery allegations were not thoroughly investigated.

A	B	C	D	E
Includes developments that affect more than one world region, international organizations and important meetings of major world leaders.	*Includes all domestic and regional developments in Europe, including the Soviet Union, Turkey, Cyprus and Malta.*	*Includes all domestic and regional developments in Africa and the Middle East, including Iraq and Iran and excluding Cyprus, Turkey and Afghanistan.*	*Includes all domestic and regional developments in Latin America, the Caribbean and Canada.*	*Includes all domestic and regional developments in Asia and Pacific nations, extending from Afghanistan through all the Pacific Islands, except Hawaii.*

U.S. Politics & Social Issues	U.S. Foreign Policy & Defense	U.S. Economy & Environment	Science, Technology & Nature	Culture, Leisure & Life Style	
A violent confrontation takes place between police and antibusing demonstrators in front of South Boston High School.				The twelfth Winter Olympics end in Innsbruck, Austria. . . . Rosi Mittermaier of W. Germany emerges from the Winter Olympics competitions with the greatest overall Alpine performance for a woman in Olympic history.	Feb. 15
The announced results of the Okla. Democratic precinct caucuses show Jimmy Carter leading with 18.5 percent of the vote and former Okla. Sen. Fred Harris with 17 percent.		Firestone Tire & Rubber Co. agrees to pay $50,000 in penalties and to spend $750,000 on tire-safety ads to settle federal charges brought on behalf of the FTC. . . . AFL–CIO Pres. Georges Meany accuses Pres. Ford of lacking compassion for the working person and of being concerned, instead, with big corporations.			Feb. 16
Pres. Ford says that Ronald Reagan is too conservative to be elected president, citing pragmatic over philosophic differences. . . . The House of Delegates of the American Bar Assn. (ABA) votes to allow limited advertising by lawyers.	CBS Radio affiliates' executive committee urges CBS News to consider dismissing Daniel Schorr for leaking the House Intelligence Committee's report on the CIA to the *Village Voice* . . . . Pres. Ford announces his plans for revision of the command structure of U.S. foreign intelligence operations and establishment of guidelines for such operations.	The House gives final approval to a bill placing all areas within the National Wildlife Refuge System under the administration of the Interior Dept.'s Fish and Wildlife Service.	An article in the *Journal of the American Medical Association*, reports a new drug, metaproterenol sulfate, which has been proven safe and effective in the treatment of childhood asthma.	*Wolf* , a work for solo cello by Michael Colgrass, is performed for the first time by Ronald Thomas at the Hunter College Playhouse, N.Y.C.	Feb. 17
The New York Times reports that Ala. Atty. Gen. Bill Baxley has begin an investigation into the 1963 bombing of a Birmingham, Ala. church that killed four black girls. . . . The Ky. state house of representatives votes, 57–40, to rescind its 1972 approval of the ERA. . . . Pres. Ford issues an executive order curtailing domestic surveillance of U.S. citizens and proscribing burglaries and illegal use of tax returns. . . . Reagan's N.H. campaign chmn. Hugh Gregg charges that Pres. Ford distorted Reagan's positions on Social Security and says Reagan supports the mandatory system.	The Senate approves legislation authorizing $3 billion in foreign military aid and giving Congress new authority over military exports.	The House votes to appropriate $2.031 billion for fiscal years 1976–79 for Conrail (Consolidated Rail Corp.) a federally funded corporation that operates Penn Central and six other railroads. . . . The Commerce Dept. announces that January construction of new housing was at the lowest monthly rate since July 1975 and 5 percent below the revised rate for December 1975.	The EPA orders an immediate ban on production of most pesticides containing mercury, which has been linked to nervous-system disorders. . . . *The New York Times* reports that a new method of testing intelligence, free from cultural bias, has been developed by Jane Mercer, a University of California sociologist. . . . Guatemalan National Emergency Committee says that the death toll from the Feb. 4 earthquake has reached 22, 419, with 74,105 injured, and 5,000 more lost in the rubble.	Eddie Dowling, 81, Broadway playwright, song writer, actor, and director, dies in Smithfield, R.I.	Feb. 18
James Farmer, one of the founders of the Congress of Racial Equality (CORE), resigns to protest actions taken by CORE director Roy Innis regarding support of anti-Communist forces in Angola.	The House votes, 269–115, to have its Ethics Committee investigate the circumstances surrounding the *Village Voice* publication of the secret Intelligence Committee report.			Frank Sullivan, 83, humorist and writer, dies in Saratoga Springs, N.Y.	Feb. 19

F	G	H	I	J
Includes elections, federal-state relations, civil rights and liberties, crime, the judiciary, education, health care, poverty, urban affairs and population.	*Includes formation and debate of U.S. foreign and defense policies, veterans' affairs and defense spending. (Relations with specific foreign countries are usually found under the region concerned.)*	*Includes business, labor, agriculture, taxation, transportation, consumer affairs, monetary and fiscal policy, natural resources, and pollution.*	*Includes worldwide scientific, medical and technological developments, natural phenomena, U.S. weather, natural disasters, and accidents.*	*Includes the arts, religion, scholarship, communications media, sports, entertainments, fashions, fads and social life.*

	World Affairs	Europe	Africa & the Middle East	The Americas	Asia & the Pacific
Feb. 20	Rene Cassin, 88, principal author of the U.N. Declaration on Human Rights and Nobel Peace Prize winner, dies in Paris.			A Quebec superior ct. judge alleges that three Cabinet ministers made 'unwarranted attempts to interfere with the judicial process' by talking to judges about cases before them.	SEATO formally disbands in Manila ceremonies.
Feb. 21		Greek and Turkish Cypriot leaders end their talks, held under the auspice of U.N. Secy. Gen. Kurt Waldheim, but do not disclose the outcome.	The Arab League has reportedly blacklisted six ships that have passed through the Suez Canal since the Israeli–Egyptian Sinai disengagement agreement was signed in September 1975.... A U.N. commissioner says that the Lebanese govt's toll of casualties in the past 10 months of civil strife is 10–12,000 killed, 30–40,000 wounded, and 180,000 displaced.	U.S. State Secy. Kissinger meets with Brazilian Pres. Ernesto Geisel and signs a consultative agreement by which the U.S. recognizes Brazil as the major power in Latin America.	A Jakarta newspaper reports that the bodies of 500 members of pro-Indonesian factions in Timor were discovered in four mass graves, presumably slain by retreating Fretelin forces.... At a banquet in China, former Pres. Richard Nixon's toast includes remarks interpreted as critical of the U.S. policy of detente and the 1975 Helsinki Conference.
Feb. 22			Portugal recognizes the Angolan govt. established in its former colony by the Communist-supported MPLA.... The Israeli Cabinet employers the U.S. to consult with Egypt, Jordan, and Syria about the possibility of negotiating an 'end to the state of war' instead of formal peace accords.... The final phase of the Israeli–Egyptian troop disengagement agreement is implemented as U.S. emergency Force gives Egypt 89 square miles of the Sinai territory.		South Vietnamese authorities release the bodies of the last two U.S. servicemen to die in the Vietnam War.
Feb. 23		Germain Baudrin, former head of the Belgium state-run telephone company, is sentenced to nine months in prison for accepting bribes from ITT's Bell Telephone of Belgium.	The Northrop Corp. says it paid Iran $2.1 million as an apparent repayment for the use of a third party as an agent in Northrop's sales of military aircraft to Iran.... The European Community extends diplomatic recognition to the Angolan Luanda govt. proclaimed by the MPLA and offers a program of economic aid and political cooperation. ... Seven armed men led by Mohammed Haymour, a Canadian of Lebanese extraction with a grievance against the Canadian govt., storm the Canadian Embassy in Beirut and hold 27 hostages for almost eight hours.	Mexican, Colombian, and Venezuelan press reports denounce U.S. State Secy. Kissinger's pact with Brazil.... The Canadian Progressive Conservative Party, the official opposition, elects Joseph Clark as its leader after a party convention.	Former Pres. Nixon talks for nearly two hours with CP Chairman Mao, and also meets three times with recently appointed Acting Premier Hua Kuo-feng.
Feb. 24		Gen. Secy. Leonid Brezhnev delivers a five-and-a-half hour speech before the Soviet CP Congress, dispelling earlier rumors of failing health.	British envoy Lord Greenhill meets with Rhodesian P.M. Ian Smith and Joshua Nkomo, head of the moderate faction of the African National Congress (ANC), to access the progress of constitutional talks and Britain's rule in the process.	State Secy. Kissinger ends a nine-day, six-nation Latin American tour during which he conferred on trade and other bilateral and international issues.	Leaders of the Association of Southeast Asian Nations (ASEAN) conclude their first summit meeting in Bali, Indonesia, and sign accord to provide organizational procedures and cooperative economic ventures.... In the Tokyo area, officials raid more than 25 homes and offices of executives of Lockheed and its national trading agent and impound more than 600 boxes of documents.

A	B	C	D	E
Includes developments that affect more than one world region, international organizations and important meetings of major world leaders.	Includes all domestic and regional developments in Europe, including the Soviet Union, Turkey, Cyprus and Malta.	Includes all domestic and regional developments in Africa and the Middle East, including Iraq and Iran and excluding Cyprus, Turkey and Afghanistan.	Includes all domestic and regional developments in Latin America, the Caribbean and Canada.	Includes all domestic and regional developments in Asia and Pacific nations, extending from Afghanistan through all the Pacific Islands, except Hawaii.

U.S. Politics & Social Issues	U.S. Foreign Policy & Defense	U.S. Economy & Environment	Science, Technology & Nature	Culture, Leisure & Life Style	
In his final campaign swing before the N.H. primary, Republican presidential aspirant Ronald Reagan expresses surplise about Pres. Ford's charges that he is too conservative, revealing that Ford had offered him several Cabinet posts.	Several Vietnamese refugee groups in the U.S. are at odds on adopting a common policy approach toward the Communist government in Vietnam.	Hamilton Bancshares Inc., a major regional bank-holding company with banking interests in Tenn. and Ga., files for voluntary bankruptcy. ... The Labor Dept. announces the consumer price index increased at an adjusted annual rate of 4.8 percent during January, slower than the rate of the last three months.... The U.S. govt. sues N.Y. and N.Y.C. for failing to carry out a program to reduce polluting emissions from city taxis.			**Feb. 20**
					Feb. 21
In a *New Times* magazine article by SLA members William and Emily Harris, Patricia Hearst's testimony of coercion and involuntary partipation in the bank robbery is contradicted.			Energy Research and Development Administration (ERDA) confirms that the U.S. govt. had injected plutonium into human subjects from 1945–47 to determine the effect of radioactive substances on workers making the atomic bomb.... Michael Polanyi, 84, Hungarian-born physical chemist and philosopher who developed the use of rotating crystals in x-ray analysis and later attacked the 'reductionism' concept that science is the only source of knowledge, dies of a stroke in England.	Angela Baddeley, 71, the British actress known for the role of Mrs. Bridges in the popular British TV series *Upstairs, Downstairs*, dies in Essex, England.	**Feb. 22**
Pres. Ford asks the nation's governors to back him in pushing Congress for extension of revenue sharing.... Joseph Sisco resigns as undersecretary of state to become pres. of American University, Wash., D.C.	CBS News suspends its correspondent Daniel Schorr for an indefinite period after he leaked the secret House Intelligence Committee report to the *Village Voice* .	Consumer advocate Ralph Nader cites some progress as well as shortcomings in the effort for car safety.		H. Allen Smith, 69, best-selling humorous author, dies in San Francisco, Calif.	**Feb. 23**
Judge W. Arthur Garrity imposes a 20 percent quota for black administrators in Boston's public schools. ... Rep. Andrew Hinshaw (R, Calif.), convicted Jan. 26 on two counts of bribery, is sentenced to serve one to 14 years in prison.... Pres. Ford wins the Republican primary in N.H. by a 51–49 percent margin over Ronald Reagan. Jimmy Carter wins the Democratic primary with 29 percent of the vote. ... In the Hearst trial, Dr. Louis West, a psychiatrist, testifies that Heart's experiences were a 'classic case of coercive percuasion'.	The Senate votes commonwealth status to the northern Mariana Islands in the Pacific.		Researchers from the Univ. of Michigan and Wayne State Univ. reports an advance in the treatment of sickle-cell anemia by the use of zinc.	The House approves a fiscal 1976 appropriation of $33 million for completion of the James A. Madison Memorial Building in the Library of Congress.	**Feb. 24**

F	G	H	I	J
Includes elections, federal-state relations, civil rights and liberties, crime, the judiciary, education, health care, poverty, urban affairs and population.	Includes formation and debate of U.S. foreign and defense policies, veterans' affairs and defense spending. (Relations with specific foreign countries are usually found under the region concerned.)	Includes business, labor, agriculture, taxation, transportation, consumer affairs, monetary and fiscal policy, natural resources, and pollution.	Includes worldwide scientific, medical and technological developments, natural phenomena, U.S. weather, natural disasters, and accidents.	Includes the arts, religion, scholarship, communications media, sports, entertainments, fashions, fads and social life.

	World Affairs	Europe	Africa & the Middle East	The Americas	Asia & the Pacific
Feb. 25			Two employees of the U.S. Information Agency Beirut office, kidnapped on Oct. 25, are released. . . . *London Times* reports that the Kurdistan Democratic Party is organizing in Iraq and abroad to renew the rebellion against the Iraqi govt.		Former Australian Labor P.M. Gough Whitlam denies newspaper charges that he received a gift of $630,000 from Iraqi govt. representatives to help pay political expenses.
Feb. 26	The newly formed U.N. Committee on the Exercise of the Inalienable Rights of the Palestinian People opens a three-month session considering Palestinian claims against Israel.	*The New York Times* cites Washington sources who report that Moscow for the first time has conceded that microwaves were beamed at the U.S. Embassy in Moscow to disable U.S. rooftop minotoring equipment. . . . At the Soviet CP Congress, Rumanian leader Nicolae Ceausescu says his party seeks a new unity based on the right of each party to develop freely its own political strategy. . . . An agreement is reached between the British govt. and the U.S. Gulf Oil Corp. and Continental Oil Co. on the distribution of ownership rights to North Sea oil concessions.	Spain withdraws all of its officials from its former Spanish Saharan colony two days before the scheduled departure date. . . . Syria's mediation team returns home after failing to get rival Christian and Moslem factions in Lebanon to agree on the formation of a Cabinet of national unity.		Increasing evidence is seem indicating that Chmn. Mao's wife, Chiang Ching is playing a key role in an anti-rightist campaign against Deputy Premier Teng Hsiao-ping. . . . Radio Australia reports an agreement has been reached between representatives of domestic sugar suppliers and the Japanese Sugar Refiners' Assn.
Feb. 27		Thirty-one ethnic Albanians, accused of fomenting 'irredentist' activities in Yugoslavia, are sentenced to prison terms. . . . Italian Communist Party leader Enrico Berlinguer, at the Soviet Party Congress, says the Italian working class's mission will only be fulfilled within a democratic society.	The Popular Front for the Liberation of Sakiet el Hamra and Rio de Ora (Polisario), fighting for an independent Western Sahara, declare it the Saharan Arab Democratic Republic.	William Niehous, vice president Owens-Illinois Inc., a U.S.-based company, is kidnapped from his home in Caracas, Venezuela, apparently by left-wing guerrillas.	
Feb. 28			Israel assures Jerusalem's Moslem Arabs that the government would respect their exclusive prayer rights on the Temple Mount in the Old City. . . . Zaire Pres. Mobutu Sese Seko announces Zaire's recognition of the MPLA-proclaimed People's Republic of Angola, in a distinct policy reversal. . . . *The New York Times* reports that in Ethiopia from 150 to 2,000 persons have been arrested as 'reactionary elements opposed to the Ethiopian socialist revolution.'		The Secy. Gen of Thailand's Socialist Party, Boonsanong Punyodyana, is killed by an unknown assailant, the eighth political figure assassinated since Jan. 12. . . . An article in *Jenmin Jih Pao*, the official Chinese CP newspaper, indicates that Deputy Premier Teng Hsias-ping is clinging to his position of power despite a wall poster campaign against his more moderate policies.
Feb. 29	A study sponsored by the Arms Control Organization, the Institute for World Order, and Members of Congress for Peace Through Law finds a global increase in arms spending.		Egyptian Pres. Anwar Sadat, ending a visit to the Arab oil states that resulted in pledges of aid, says he made a three-point 'secret agreement' on the Mideast U.S. as part of the 1975 Sinai accords. . . . An Israeli Cabinet plan to expropriate 2,500 acres of privately owned land in the upper Galilee for housing development draws sharp protest from area Arabs.		

A	B	C	D	E
Includes developments that affect more than one world region, international organizations and important meetings of major world leaders.	Includes all domestic and regional developments in Europe, including the Soviet Union, Turkey, Cyprus and Malta.	Includes all domestic and regional developments in Africa and the Middle East, including Iraq and Iran and excluding Cyprus, Turkey and Afghanistan.	Includes all domestic and regional developments in Latin America, the Caribbean and Canada.	Includes all domestic and regional developments in Asia and Pacific nations, extending from Afghanistan through all the Pacific Islands, except Hawaii.

U.S. Politics & Social Issues	U.S. Foreign Policy & Defense	U.S. Economy & Environment	Science, Technology & Nature	Culture, Leisure & Life Style	
ERAmerica, an organization recently created specifically to win ratification of the ERA, opens its offices in Wash., D.C. It is headed by Democrat Liz Carpenter and Republican Elly Peterson.... Republican presidential aspirant Ronald Reagan issues a personal financial statement putting his net worth at $1.45 million.... A group of parents, Christian clergy, and religious libertarians seek a court order barring the teaching of transcendental meditation (TM) in N.J. public schools.	Three U.S. Senators propose a joint U.S.–U.S.S.R. moratorium on flight testing of the cruise missile, pending a SALT accord on the new weapon.... William Scranton, a former governor of Pa., is nominated by Pres. Ford as the U.S. representative to the U.N.	Time Inc. announces it will stop publication of its Canadian edition of *Time* as a result of a change in Canadian tax law.	At the request of the FDA, three major drug compagies are stopping the marketing and distribution of sequential oral contraceptives.	*One Flew Over the Cuckoo's Nest* is the top-grossing film in the week just ended.	Feb. 25
The Agriculture Dept. proposes to cut back the food-stamp program, eliminating five million of the current 19 million beneficiaries to save $1.2 billion a year.	Sen. Edward Kennedy (D, Mass.) chides State Secy. Kissinger for favoring Brazil's repressive military govt. over more democratic Latin American govts.	Pres. Ford sends Congress a special message on energy, emphasizing the need to 'regain our energy independence.'	The Senate approved a bill intented to modernize U.S. patent law.		Feb. 26
		The White House Council on Environmental Quality reports that air and water pollution is down in the U.S., but the estimated cost of pollution abatement has increased.			Feb. 27
	Pres. Ford, campaigning in Florida for the support of Cuban-Americans, calls Cuban P.M. Fidel Castro an 'international outlaw.'	A Nuclear Regulatory Commission investigation of the 1975 fire at an Ala. nuclear power plant finds deficient federal attention to fire prevention and control.	Rosalie Joseph Leventritt, 84, patron of music and founder of the Leventritt International Competition, dies in N.Y.... The British medical journal *The Lancet* reports that the brains of patients with multiple sclerosis contain a virus that might be the cause of the disease.	The National Theatre Company of Great Britain honors Old Vic Theater founder Lilian Bayliss with the play, *Tribute to a Lady*, before moving to its new home on the South Bank of the Thames.... Grammy Awards are presented to Paul Simon, as best male pop vocalist, and to Janis Ian, as best female pop vocalist.	Feb. 28
				Ned Rorem's *Book of Hours* for flute and harp is premiered at Alice Tully Hall, N.Y.C.... *Helter Skelter* by Vincent Bugliosi and *The Moneychangers* by Arthur Hailey head the best-seller list of mass-market paperback books.	Feb. 29

F	G	H	I	J
Includes elections, federal-state relations, civil rights and liberties, crime, the judiciary, education, health care, poverty, urban affairs and population.	Includes formation and debate of U.S. foreign and defense policies, veterans' affairs and defense spending. (Relations with specific foreign countries are usually found under the region concerned.)	Includes business, labor, agriculture, taxation, transportation, consumer affairs, monetary and fiscal policy, natural resources, and pollution.	Includes worldwide scientific, medical and technological developments, natural phenomena, U.S. weather, natural disasters, and accidents.	Includes the arts, religion, scholarship, communications media, sports, entertainments, fashions, fads and social life.

	World Affairs	Europe	Africa & the Middle East	The Americas	Asia & the Pacific
March 1		Italian central bank reopens its foreign exchange market, which closed on Jan. 21 after a run on the lira consumed nearly half of its reserves.		*Washington Post* reports that Chile turned over all its top cocaine-trafficking suspects to U.S. authorities in an effort to maintain good relations with the U.S.	
March 2				The Colombian army occupies the National University after police clash with thousands of student rioters.	
March 3			Mozambique Pres. Samora Machel declares that Mozambique is at war with Rhodesia and will apply full economic sanctions, a move lauded by the British govt.		Indian govt. files suit in the U.S. Dist. Ct., N.Y., charging five U.S. grain companies with fraudulent shipments over the past 15 years and seeking a total of $215 million in damages.
March 4	Antiwar activist Jane Kennedy, serving a three-year prison sentence for destroying U.S. draft records, is nominated for the 1976 Nobel Peace Prize.	Netherlands Prince Bernhard cancels a planned trip to Latin America to expedite the investigation into his alleged dealings with Lockheed.	British govt. recalls its high commissioner in Lagos, Sir Martin Le Quesne, at the Nigerian govt.'s request. . . . Ivory Coast Pres. Felix Houphouet-Boigny names a former opponent Jean-Baptiste Mockey, minister of health, in his new Cabinet.		Seventeen people are reported detained in S. Korea in connection with an antigovernment statement signed by some of them on March 1, calling for restoration of full civil rights and the resignation of Pres. Chung Hee Park.
March 5		The twenty-fifth Congress of the Soviet Communist Party ends after hearing Premier Alexei Kosygin's report on economic performance and unanimously approving a new five-year plan. . . . The commander of the Turkish air force, Gen. Emin Alpkaya, resigns after investigators probing alleged Lockheed payoffs find $30,000 in a safe at air force headquarters. . . . British State Secy. Merlyn Rees announces that London is abandoning its latest attempt to achieve a constitutional settlement of Northern Ireland's sectarian divisions, and declares that British direct rule of Ulster will continue indefinitely.	Nigerian police arrest Lt. Col. B.S. Dimka, leader of the attempted coup of Feb. 13, after a three-week nationwide manhunt. . . . Former Israeli Premier Golda Meir comes out of retirement to join the new "leadership forum" created by Premier Yitzhak Rabin and the 40-member Labor Party's governing bureau.	An Argentinian emergency plan announced by Economy Min. Emilio Mondelli, and approved by the IMF, sets off a wave of strikes and protests against the Peronist govt.'s faltering economic policies. . . . Canadian P.M. Pierre Trudeau says that if the provinces can't agree on a formula to repatriate the Canadian Constitution, the federal government will consider taking action itself.	
March 6		Cuban Premier Fidel Castro arrives in Yogoslavia for two days of talks with Pres. Josip Tito.		Guyanan Premier Forbes Burnham denies rumors that Georgetown had allowed Cuban aircraft to refuel in Guyana en route to Angola's civil war, but says that he would allow Cuban planes to refuel if they were carrying soldiers to aid Mozambique in its conflict with Rhodesia.	

A	B	C	D	E
Includes developments that affect more than one world region, international organizations and important meetings of major world leaders.	Includes all domestic and regional developments in Europe, including the Soviet Union, Turkey, Cyprus and Malta.	Includes all domestic and regional developments in Africa and the Middle East, including Iraq and Iran and excluding Cyprus, Turkey and Afghanistan.	Includes all domestic and regional developments in Latin America, the Caribbean and Canada.	Includes all domestic and regional developments in Asia and Pacific nations, extending from Afghanistan through all the Pacific Islands, except Hawaii.

U.S. Politics & Social Issues	U.S. Foreign Policy & Defense	U.S. Economy & Environment	Science, Technology & Nature	Culture, Leisure & Life Style	
Ariz. State Senate fails to approve the Equal Rights Amendment for women after the House had killed the ERA in committee, setting back the national drive to gain ratification. . . . Breaking an earlier tie vote, the U.S. Parole Bd. decides against freeing Dr. Timothy Leary from a 10-year prison term he is serving for a narcotics conviction.	Campaigning in Florida, Pres. Ford expresses dislike for the term detente.	Wis. Sen William Proxmire (D), chairman of the Senate Banking Committee, says the office of the Comptroller of the Currency, now held by James Smith, should be abolished, and criticizes Smith's spending habits, noting that Smith has earned the title of, "King Farouk of the Potomac." . . . Anheuser–Busch Inc. Teamsters union locals strike at bottling plants in Calif., N.H., Va., Ohio, Fla., and Tex.		Jean Martinon, 66, French composer-conductor, dies in Paris.	March 1
Sen. Henry Jackson (D, Wash.) wins the Mass. Democratic presidential primary, and Pres. Ford wins the Republican primary with 62 percent of the vote compared to 35 percent for Ronald Reagan. . . . Stanley Lundine wins a special election in New York State's thirty-ninth congressional district to become the first Democrat to represent the district in 106 years. . . . In a libel ruling, the Supreme Ct. holds that Fla. socialite Mary Alice Firestone, one of "the 400 of Palm Beach," is not a public figure although she has held news conferences.	State Dept. spokesman stresses that Ford was speaking of discarding the term detente, not the policy.	The House passes a bill designed to liberalize black-lung disease benefits and ensure that the cost of the benefits will be bourne by the private sector.		*Bubblin' Brown Sugar* , a musical revue featuring music of Eubie Blake, Cab Calloway, and Duke Ellington, opens on Broadway.	March 2
The House Ethics Committee investigating the publication leaks of the classified Intelligence Committee report, receives the authority to subpoena individuals and documents.	Consultations between the White House and Congress begin on the proposed sale of military transport jets to Egypt, the first step toward ending the arms embargo. . . . William Scranton, former Pa. governor is confirmed as chief delegate to the U.N.				March 3
Sen. Birch Bayh (Ind.) withdraws as a candidate for the Democratic presidential nomination. . . . Sen. Majority Leader Mike Mansfield (D, Mont.), party leader since 1961, announces he will not seek reelection.	Ronald Reagan charges the U.S. has fallen behind the Soviets in military might during Pres. Ford's administration.	The continuing investigation into corruption in the grain industry results in three companies receiving maximum fines of $10,000 each on charges of conspiracy to defraud.			March 4
The National Center for Health Statistics reports that the national birth rate declined in 1975 for the fifth time in five years.	Pres. Ford talks about nuclear weapons and defends his world leadership, saying, "America has seen too much of war in the twentieth century." . . . Wis. Sen. William Proxmire (D) challenges the Pentagon's estimate of Soviet military spending.	The Labor Dept. announces that the nation's unemployment rate improved in February for the fourth straight month and is at its lowest level since December 1974.		Frances Lewine, White House correspondent for the AP, becomes the second elected woman member (after Helen Thomas of UPI) of the Gridiron Club, formerly all-male.	March 5
				Dorothy Hamil wins the women's singles figure skating world title in Goteborg, Sweden.	March 6

F	G	H	I	J
Includes elections, federal-state relations, civil rights and liberties, crime, the judiciary, education, health care, poverty, urban affairs and population.	*Includes formation and debate of U.S. foreign and defense policies, veterans' affairs and defense spending. (Relations with specific foreign countries are usually found under the region concerned.)*	*Includes business, labor, agriculture, taxation, transportation, consumer affairs, monetary and fiscal policy, natural resources, and pollution.*	*Includes worldwide scientific, medical and technological developments, natural phenomena, U.S. weather, natural disasters, and accidents.*	*Includes the arts, religion, scholarship, communications media, sports, entertainments, fashions, fads and social life.*

	World Affairs	Europe	Africa & the Middle East	The Americas	Asia & the Pacific
March 7		The Common Market increases community farm commodity prices 7.5 percent in 1976–77, with retail price increases of 1.5 percent expected.	Morocco and Mauritania sever diplomatic relations with Algeria after Algiers recognizes the Saharan state proclaimed by the Polisario Front, an independence movement.		Former Australian P.M. Gough Whitlam is censured by his Labor Party in wake of allegations that he received $630,000 in campaign contributions from Iraq's governing Baath Party.
March 8		Political violence sweeping college and university campuses throughout Turkey causes a thirty-first death when a student is shot during a confrontation between left and right-wing students.		Chilean Pres. Augusto Pinochet Ugarte replaces his labor, health, and transportation ministers after the entire Cabinet resigned March 5 to give him a "free hand" in developing new policies.	Nearly 4,000 Japanese workers demonstrate in Tokyo to protest the Lockheed scandal.
March 9					Chinese Deputy Premier Teng Hsiao-ping is attacked by the Peking Women's Assn. as being insensitive to women's causes.
March 10		A Czech intelligence agent charges that former CP leader Alexander Dubcek and his supporters maintained links with the CIA dating back to the liberal government of 1968.			The South Korean govt. announces the arrest of 11 of 12 signers of an antigovernment statement calling for the resignation of Pres. Chung Hee Park, including the opposition party leader Kim Dae Jung.
March 11			A new leader in the Lebanese civil war emerges when the commander of the Beirut garrison, Gen. Abdel Aziz al- Ahdab proclaims himself military governor of Lebanon and demands that Premier Rashid Karami and Pres. Suleiman Franjieh resign immediately.... Washington Post says that CIA officials told members of the American Institute of Aeronautics and Astronautics that it estimates Israel has 10 to 20 nuclear weapons available for use.	Former Pres. Richard Nixon's sworn congressional testimony is released disclosing that he authorized secret CIA efforts in 1970 to undermine the late Salvador Allende's presidency in Chile.... Amnesty International releases photographs, said to have been sent from Uruguay by an unidentified army officer, showing torture of political prisoners.	
March 12		*Financial Times* of London reports that the U.S.S.R. has made its first purchases of sugar on the world market since the Soviet sugar shortage of 1974.... A Polish–West German pact providing for the return to West Germany within four years of up to 125,000 ethnic Germans now living in Poland is ratified by the Bonn Bundesrat.	Lebanese Parliament Speaker Kamal al- Assad hands Pres. Suleiman Franjieh a petition signed by 60 of the legislature's 99 members seeking Franjieh's resignation, which Franjieh immediately rejects.	Three U.S. Democratic congressmen — Toby Moffett (Conn.), Thomas Harkin (Iowa), and George Miller (Calif.) — find in a visit to Chile "a silent and pervasive fear" in all segments of society.	The Japanese govt. accepts Pres. Ford's March 11 offer of all available information on Lockheed's alleged payoffs in Japan, on condition that the data remain secret during the SEC investigation.... In another crackdown against political dissidents, the South Korean govt. is reported as having forced the dismissal or resignation of more than 400 university professors.... The Indian central govt. imposes direct presidential rule over Gujarat, thereby putting all 22 states under control of the governing Congress Party.

A	B	C	D	E
Includes developments that affect more than one world region, international organizations and important meetings of major world leaders.	Includes all domestic and regional developments in Europe, including the Soviet Union, Turkey, Cyprus and Malta.	Includes all domestic and regional developments in Africa and the Middle East, including Iraq and Iran and excluding Cyprus, Turkey and Afghanistan.	Includes all domestic and regional developments in Latin America, the Caribbean and Canada.	Includes all domestic and regional developments in Asia and Pacific nations, extending from Afghanistan through all the Pacific Islands, except Hawaii.

U.S. Politics & Social Issues	U.S. Foreign Policy & Defense	U.S. Economy & Environment	Science, Technology & Nature	Culture, Leisure & Life Style	
Rep. Wright Patman (D, Tex.), 82, former chairman of the House Banking Committee, dies in Bethesda, Md. after the fourth longest congressional career in U.S. history.	Rep. Les Aspin, in a published article echoing Sen. Proxmire's assertion, says that Pentagon estimates of Soviet arms spending were based on the 1972–74 period when Soviet production was expanding, but current figures show U.S. arms production increasing and the Soviet production decreasing.	Comptroller James Smith announces that he will reimburse his office for nearly $3,000 in personal limousine service used while attending three bankers' conventions.			March 7
					March 8
Ronald Reagan, campaigning in Ill., says Ford's nomination would keep the Watergate issue alive. . . . Pres. Ford finishes well ahead of Reagan in the Fla. presidential primary, and Carter upsets Ala. Gov. George Wallace, winning first place in a field of 12.	Rep. Otis Pike (D, N.Y.), chairman of the expired House Intelligence Committee, accuses the CIA of running a media event aimed at discrediting him and the committee, in wake of CIA statements that the committee had failed to return 232 classified documents.	Six former executives of the Franklin National Bank, N.Y. are sentenced on charges stemming from the bank's loss of more than $30 million in unauthorized foreign currency speculation. . . . Three drug companies, American Home Products Corp., Johnson & Johnson, and Sterling Drug Inc. report to the SEC that they made improper foreign payments from 1970 or 1971 to 1975.	Fifteen people are killed in a methane gas explosion that occurs in a southeastern Ky. coal mine just after the mine section had been inspected and cited for safety violations.		March 9
According to a court deposition, former Pres. Richard Nixon has testified that he ordered telephone wiretaps of 17 government officials and newsmen selected by State Secy. Kissinger. . . . The Justice Dept. issues provisional guidelines for the conduct of intelligence activities by the FBI, prohibiting incitement to riot, illegal entry, and other activities. . . . Barbara White, fifth-ranking member of the U.S. delegation to the U.N., resigns to become president of Mills College, Calif.		A N.Y. state judge dismisses a 1974 indictment against three of the nation's largest oil companies — Gulf Oil, Exxon, and Mobil Oil Corp. — charged with violating state antitrust laws during the 1973 energy crisis.		Ernst Neizvestny, a Soviet sculptor who had a public dispute over modern art in 1962 with then Premier Nikita Khrushchev, arrives in Vienna after getting permission to emigrate.	March 10
Senate Select Committee on Intelligence chmn. Sen. Frank Church (D, Ida.) denounces Nixon's advocacy of the sovereign presidency doctrine as dangerous.	Former Pres. Nixon is disclosed as having defended clandestine U.S. efforts to overthrow the Allende govt. in Chile by invoking a sovereign's actions as being above the laws applied to private citizens. . . . State Secy. Kissinger assails his foreign policy critics, saying that "our greatest foreign policy problem is our division at home" and calling for "national cohesion."	The Dow Jones industrial average closes above the psychologically important 1,000 mark.		Greek Ministry of Culture and Science reports that ancient sculptures in the Athens Acropolis are in dire need of protection against decay and pollution.	March 11
Pa. Gov. Milton Shapp withdraws from the Democratic presidential race.					March 12

F	G	H	I	J
Includes elections, federal-state relations, civil rights and liberties, crime, the judiciary, education, health care, poverty, urban affairs and population.	Includes formation and debate of U.S. foreign and defense policies, veterans' affairs and defense spending. (Relations with specific foreign countries are usually found under the region concerned.)	Includes business, labor, agriculture, taxation, transportation, consumer affairs, monetary and fiscal policy, natural resources, and pollution.	Includes worldwide scientific, medical and technological developments, natural phenomena, U.S. weather, natural disasters, and accidents.	Includes the arts, religion, scholarship, communications media, sports, entertainments, fashions, fads and social life.

	World Affairs	Europe	Africa & the Middle East	The Americas	Asia & the Pacific
March 13	The Chinese official CP newspaper charges that the U.S.S.R. is attempting to establish its domination over the Indian Ocean.... According to *The New York Times*, the seven nuclear-exporting nations, which agreed in January on secret safeguard guidelines, will be joined by as many as seven other countries.	The leaders of nine European Socialist and Social Democratic parties meet in Oporto, Portugal and endorse a statement that the primary threat to democracy in Portugal is no longer communism, but a weakened economy.			
March 14		The Soviet journal *Pravda* charges that Pres. Ford's recent comments about the word detente reflect a move by the administration to revise U.S. policy toward the Soviet Union.	Israeli govt. increases basic commodity prices and announces a 2 percent devaluation of the Israeli pound, setting it at 7.52 to the U.S. dollar.... Pres. Anwar Sadat reorganizes Egypt's nationalized newspapers, appointing editors with "no hatred against the Socialist Revolution."	Guatemala's ruling National Conciliation Party (PCN) sweeps the congressional and municipal elections, winning all 54 deputies' seats and 261 mayoralties at stake.	
March 15		The French govt. withdraws the franc from the joint Eurocurrency float, called the "snake," for the second time since 1974.	The U.S. suspends diplomatic relations with Equatorial Guinea after two U.S. diplomats there had been declared personae non gratae.... Legislation to end the Soviet-Egyptian Treaty of Friendship and Cooperation, signed in 1971, is approved by the Egyptian People's Assembly, 307–2.... Niger Pres. Seyni Kountche announces that loyal troops have foiled an attempted coup d'etat.... West Bank Arabs riot in Ramallah, prompting Israeli authorities to impose an indefinite 24-hour curfew there and in nearby El Bireh.	In wake of a wave of violence in Argentina, a bomb explodes in a Buenos Aires parking lot, killing one person and seriously wounding 29.... Seven hundred U.S. employes of the Panama Canal Co. call in sick in a wildcat strike against austerity measures recently proposed by the U.S. Army, which owns the company.	
March 16	The U.S. State Dept. announces the U.S. has decided to defer further Cabinet-level meetings of joint U.S.–Soviet commissions, because of the Soviet actions in Angola.	British P.M. Harold Wilson, in office for eight years, announces he will resign as soon as his Labor Party names a successor.... Danish Premier Anker Jorgensen announces that 200 Vietnamese orphans who arrived in Denmark in April 1975 will be permitted to stay.... Former Greek military dictator Gen. Demetrios Ioannides is sentenced to 14 years' imprisonment for conspiracy in connection with his role in the abortive revolt of February 1975.	Syria renews its mediation efforts in the Lebanese civil war.		
March 17		Liberal Party members of the British House of Commons unanimously vote to retain the leadership of Jeremy Thorpe despite recent allegations about him.			The Indian Congress Party widens its majority in the upper house of Parliament in nationwide elections, regaining its two-thirds majority.... Australian Labor Party leader Gough Whitlam survives two attempts to oust him from his position amid charges of a scheme to obtain Arab money for his 1975 campaign.
March 18				Colombian Pres. Alfonso Lopez Michelsen and his Cabinet issue a set of strict new security measures under the existing state of siege.	

A	B	C	D	E
Includes developments that affect more than one world region, international organizations and important meetings of major world leaders.	Includes all domestic and regional developments in Europe, including the Soviet Union, Turkey, Cyprus and Malta.	Includes all domestic and regional developments in Africa and the Middle East, including Iraq and Iran and excluding Cyprus, Turkey and Afghanistan.	Includes all domestic and regional developments in Latin America, the Caribbean and Canada.	Includes all domestic and regional developments in Asia and Pacific nations, extending from Afghanistan through all the Pacific Islands, except Hawaii.

U.S. Politics & Social Issues	U.S. Foreign Policy & Defense	U.S. Economy & Environment	Science, Technology & Nature	Culture, Leisure & Life Style	
The Citizens for Reagan Committee protests to the Fed. Election Commission that State Secy. Kissinger is serving as a surrogate speaker for the President's campaign. . . . A jury in San Francisco, Calif. finds four black men guilty of murder and conspiracy to commit murder in the so-called Zebra killings of whites in late 1973 and early 1974.	A Marine Corps recruit, Lynn McClure, dies after a severe beating during combat training at the Marine camp in San Diego, Calif.				March 13
				Busby Berkeley, 80, choreographer known for lavish movie musical productions, dies in Palm Desert, Calif.	March 14
Democratic presidential aspirant Rep. Morris Udall (Ariz.) says he stopped calling himself a liberal because of the word's controversial connotations, preferring progressive.	Jimmy Carter criticizes State Secy. Kissinger, saying Kissinger has identified foreign policy in general and detente in particular with his own reputation.			Jo Mielziner, 74, Tony Award-winning designer who created sets and lighting for over 300 productions, including dramas, musicals, operas, and ballets, dies in N.Y.C.	March 15
Pres. Ford and Jimmy Carter win by wide margins in the Ill. presidential primary.	CIA Director George Bush denies that the CIA used reports of missing documents as a media weapon against Rep. Otis Pike (D, N.Y.) or the House Intelligence Committee, which Pike headed. . . . *The New York Times* reports that CIA Dir. George Bush is displeased that the *Washington Post* reported the CIA disclosure about the Israeli stock of nuclear weapons.	Pres. Ford says he will impose three-year quotas on imports of specialty steel unless trade negotiators work out voluntary reductions of steel exports to the U.S.			March 16
The N.J. Supreme Ct. orders a new trial for Rubin (Hurricane) Carter and John Artis, who were convicted nine years ago of three murders.	Former CIA Director William Colby asserts that disclosure of the CIA's annual budget, sought in a suit filed by the ACLU and Morton Halperin, would injure U.S. security.		Two underground nuclear devices are tested as the U.S. intensifies its testing in anticipation of the proposed test-limitation treaty to go into effect March 31.		March 17
The defense and prosecution give their closing statements in the trial of Patricia Hearst. . . . Sen. Frank Church (Ida.) announces his candidacy for the Democratic presidential nomination.	In an upcoming article in the *New York Review of Books* Smith College historian Allen Weinstein charges that Alger Hiss had been lying about his relations with Whittaker Chambers for 30 years. . . . Alger Hiss, convicted of perjury about his alleged espionage link with Whittaker Chambers, assails Weinstein's statements and reasserts his innocence.	Rabbi Arthur Hertzberg, president of the American Jewish Congress, says that 22 major U.S. firms have pledged in writing that they will not comply with the Arab League's economic boycott of Israel.			March 18

F	G	H	I	J
Includes elections, federal-state relations, civil rights and liberties, crime, the judiciary, education, health care, poverty, urban affairs and population.	Includes formation and debate of U.S. foreign and defense policies, veterans' affairs and defense spending. (Relations with specific foreign countries are usually found under the region concerned.)	Includes business, labor, agriculture, taxation, transportation, consumer affairs, monetary and fiscal policy, natural resources, and pollution.	Includes worldwide scientific, medical and technological developments, natural phenomena, U.S. weather, natural disasters, and accidents.	Includes the arts, religion, scholarship, communications media, sports, entertainments, fashions, fads and social life.

	World Affairs	Europe	Africa & the Middle East	The Americas	Asia & the Pacific
March 19		An announcement is made that British Princess Margaret and Lord Snowdon (Antony Armstrong-Jones) have agreed to a separation after 16 years of marriage, but that there are no plans for a divorce.	The talks between Rhodesia's white minority government and the African Nat. Council faction, headed by Joshua Nkomo, break down after three months, raising the possibility of warfare.		
March 20				Guerrillas of the Colombian Revolutionary Armed Forces (FARC) kidnap the wealthy industrialist Octavio Echevarria. . . . Argentina suffers from a wave of political violence directed against both policemen and civilians and presumed to come from both rightist and leftist groups. . . . Striking U.S. employes of the Panama Canal Co., return to work after the Canal Zone's governor, Maj. Gen. Harold Parfitt, agrees to oppose U.S. Army austerity measures and to institute collective bargaining.	With about 98 percent of eligible voters participating, Cambodians elect 250 members to a newly formed People's Representative Assembly.
March 21		Polish voters elect a new Sejm. The Polish United Workers' Party — the nation's CP — holds 255 seats, the United Peasants 117, Democratic Party 39, and independents 49.	Israeli Maj. Gen. Ariel Sharon announces his resignation as military adviser to P.M. Yitzhak Rabin and warns of grave deterioration in Israel's political and military stance.		The U.S. ends all operations at its military bases in Thailand in response to a Thai govt. order to leave.
March 22			British For. Secy. James Callaghan outlines a two-stage plan for Rhodesian independence, in wake of the collapse of constitutional talks in Salisbury, and pledges that Britain will provide financial and diplomatic aid in the transfer of power to the black majority. . . . Lebanese Cabinet approves a constitutional amendment that would allow Parliament to elect a new president immediately instead of two months before the expiration of Pres. Suleiman Franjieh's term on Sept. 23.	The U.S. and Canada exchange instruments of ratification for a new treaty that formally extends joint extradition procedures to curb airplane hijacking and terrorism. . . . State Secy. Kissinger again stresses his warning to Cuba that the U.S. "will not accept further Cuban military interventions abroad."	
March 23	The IMF agrees to Zaire's purchase of the equivalent of 56.5 million special drawing rights (SDRs). . . . U.S. Rep. Henry Reuss (D, Wis.) charges that documents of the World Bank show that the bank has recently loaned Chile $33 million for political reasons. . . . U.S. Amb. to the U.N. William Scranton, in U.N. debate, criticizes Israeli settlements in occupied areas and questions Israel's rule over all of Jerusalem.		Rhodesian P.M. Ian Smith rejects the two-stage British plan to resolve Rhodesia's internal crisis after the collapse of constitutional talks. . . . West Bank Arabs stage violent demonstrations and strikes, sparked by the Moslem-Jewish religious controversy over the Temple Mount in Jerusalem.		
March 24		Field Marshal Viscount Montgomery, 88, British WWII hero, dies in Isington, England.	Lebanese fighting mounts in intensity as Moslems accelerate their advances against Christian positions in Beirut and elsewhere.	Argentinean Pres. Maria de Peron is overthrown in an apparently bloodless coup led by the commanders of the three armed forces. . . . Kennecott Copper Corp. of the U.S. says it has signed an agreement with Haiti for continued exploration, development, and mining on Haiti's northern coast. . . . The International Fund for Animal Welfare and the Greenpeace Foundation end their campaigns to protest and disrupt the annual hunting of baby seals off Newfoundland.	

A	B	C	D	E
Includes developments that affect more than one world region, international organizations and important meetings of major world leaders.	Includes all domestic and regional developments in Europe, including the Soviet Union, Turkey, Cyprus and Malta.	Includes all domestic and regional developments in Africa and the Middle East, including Iraq and Iran and excluding Cyprus, Turkey and Afghanistan.	Includes all domestic and regional developments in Latin America, the Caribbean and Canada.	Includes all domestic and regional developments in Asia and Pacific nations, extending from Afghanistan through all the Pacific Islands, except Hawaii.

U.S. Politics & Social Issues	U.S. Foreign Policy & Defense	U.S. Economy & Environment	Science, Technology & Nature	Culture, Leisure & Life Style	
Pres. Ford signs a bill that establishes, for a three-year period, a White House office for the coordination of federal efforts against drug abuse.... George Wallace says one of the issues of the Democratic presidential campaign is still-existing school segregation, and explains that he defended segregation 10 years ago because, "that's the way I was raised."		The Labor Dept. announces that the CPI rose a seasonally adjusted 0.1 percent in February to 167.1 percent of the 1967 average, the smallest monthly increase since September 1971.... Federal Appeals Ct. upholds the authority of the EPA to regulate the amount of lead in gasoline.			March 19
Patricia Hearst is found guilty of robbing a bank and using a firearm in the commission of a felony.... The National Black Political Convention affirms its intention to run a black candidate for U.S. President in 1976 under the banner of the Independent Freedom Party.				Council for Financial Aid to Education reports that gifts to colleges during the 1974–75 academic year declined $80 million from the previous year (3.6 percent), citing the recession as the reason.	March 20
AP report discloses recently released CIA documents on the 1963 assassination of John Kennedy that raise questions about a link between Lee Harvey Oswald and Cuban intelligence officers.					March 21
Sargent Shriver formally ends his bid for the Democratic presidential nomination.	By a 54–31 vote, the Senate returns a bipartisan resolution endorsing detente to the Foreign Relations Committee for further study.... Thomas Gates Jr., U.S. liaison office chief in Peking, is named ambassador to China, succeeding George Bush.	The NLRB rules that hospital interns and resident physicians are not covered by federal labor laws because they are students, not employes.			March 22
The Supreme Ct. declares the original Federal Election Commission had been illegally appointed and cuts off federal funds to candidates.... A proposed constitutional amendment to give District of Columbia residents voting representation in Congress is voted down by the House, 229–181.... Ronald Reagan wins an upset victory over Pres. Ford in the N.C. presidential primary. Carter leads the Democrats with a majority vote.		Pres. Ford signs a bill prohibiting credit discrimination on the basis of age, race, color, religion, or national origin.		According to a survey by the National Opinion Research Center, Pope Paul VI's ban on artificial birth control has led to a decline in Roman Catholic religious devotion.	March 23
Congress clears a $125 million day-care funds bill, which was reportedly opposed by Pres. Gerald Ford.		The Supreme Ct. rules that if someone is denied a job because of race, and is later hired, he should have the seniority and benefits he would have accrued if hired in the first place.	Pres. Ford calls for a government-supported campaign to vaccinate the entire population against the swine-flu virus.	Swedish govt. drops income-tax evasion charges against film director Ingmar Bergman.	March 24

F	G	H	I	J
Includes elections, federal-state relations, civil rights and liberties, crime, the judiciary, education, health care, poverty, urban affairs and population.	Includes formation and debate of U.S. foreign and defense policies, veterans' affairs and defense spending. (Relations with specific foreign countries are usually found under the region concerned.)	Includes business, labor, agriculture, taxation, transportation, consumer affairs, monetary and fiscal policy, natural resources, and pollution.	Includes worldwide scientific, medical and technological developments, natural phenomena, U.S. weather, natural disasters, and accidents.	Includes the arts, religion, scholarship, communications media, sports, entertainments, fashions, fads and social life.

	World Affairs	Europe	Africa & the Middle East	The Americas	Asia & the Pacific
March 25	The U.S. vetoes a U.N. Security Council resolution assailing Israel's occupation policies in the Old City of Jerusalem and the West Bank.	In Finland 43,000 food industry workers strike, reducing food supplies throughout the country.	Lebanese Pres. Suleiman Franjieh is forced to flee the presidential palace after it comes under artillery attack, establishing new headquarters in Junieh.	Industrialist Octavio Echevarria, kidnapped by the FARC on March 20, is found dead of a bullet wound in Puerto Berrio, Colombia.	The U.S. proposes to North Vietnam that they open discussions on normalization of relations.
March 26	Israeli P.M. Yitzhak Rabin says that the U.S. rejection of the U.N. anti-Israel resolution doesn't reduce the seriousness of Amb. William Scranton's remarks in Security Council debate, criticizing Israeli settlements and rule over Jerusalem. . . . Egypt's chief U.N. delegate Ahmed Meguid says that despite the U.S. veto the "fact remains that the world community deplored Israeli practices in the occupied territories."	The U.S. and Turkey agree on a new four-year accord to reopen U.S. military installations in Turkey in return for $1 billion in military aid plus other military and economic aid.	Sierra Leone Pres. Siaka Stevens is unanimously reelected to a second five-year term by Parliament.	Argentina's military junta issues a new security law providing stiff prison sentences and even the death penalty for a wide variety of offenses.	In Papua New Guinea, Premier Michael Somare tells Parliament that Bougainville leaders have agreed to call off their drive to secede.
March 27		Gaston Thorn, premier of Luxembourg, is elected president of the newly formed European liberal federation, which represents eight European liberal party leaders.	South Africa withdraws the last contingent of its forces from the buffer zone it maintained in southern Angola, bringing to an end its involvement in the Angolan civil war.		Philippines Pres. Ferdinand Marcos shakes up the armed forces for the first time in three years, retiring the commanders of all three armed services and five other generals.
March 28			Moslems score another victory in Beirut, capturing the unfinished Hilton Hotel, which was a vital defense position for the Christian Phalangist militia guarding the port. . . . Egypt's National Security Council urges Arab nations to intervene in Lebanon by sending joint Arab symbolic peace-keeping forces.		
March 29		In Finland over 17,000 merchant seamen strike in a dispute over demands to be paid for Sunday and night work. . . . The eleventh Congress of the Bulgarian CP begins. Todor Zhivkov is unanimously reelected as party first secretary and president.	The worst internal strife in Israel's 28-year history erupts in wake of a strike by Rakah, the Arab-dominated Israeli CP to protest a govt. plan to expropriate Arab, as well as Jewish-owned, land in the Galilee for a predominantly Jewish housing project.	New Argentine Pres. Lt. Gen. Jorge Videla, formally assumes power five days after the armed forces overthrew the government of Pres. Maria de Peron. . . . Brazilian Pres. Ernesto Geisel dismisses three federal deputies and suspends their political rights for 10 years after they publicly criticized the government.	Hanoi responds to the U.S. proposal to normalize relations by reiterating its demand that the U.S. fulfill its pledge of postwar aid as a condition for any talks.
March 30	U.N. Secy. Gen. Kurt Waldheim warns the Security Council that the fighting in Lebanon has implications extending far beyond the country's boundaries.	Egyptian Pres. Sadat visits West Germany and signs an agreement under which West Germany will provide Egypt with $90 million in capital material aid. . . . West Germany and the Soviet Union drop plans to construct the world's largest nuclear power station, which was to have supplied electricity to West Germany and West Berlin. . . . British For. Secy. James Callaghan is the front-runner in the second round of voting for prime minister, although he does not get a majority.	Six are killed and over 70 people wounded in the Israeli Galilee disturbances.	A Brink's Inc. armored truck is hijacked outside a Montreal bank and thieves escape with an estimated $2.8 million in cash and silver coins, the largest such incident in Brink's history.	
March 31	The U.N. Security Council censures South Africa's aggression against Angola and calls on the South African govt. to pay compensation to the People's Republic of Angola.		Jordan King Hussein tells a U.S. congressional committee that only direct Syrian military intervention could stop the fighting in Lebanon, but this would risk an Israeli response. . . . U.S. special envoy L. Dean Brown arrives in Beirut on a fact-finding mission, reflecting U.S. concern with events in Lebanon.	Keith Spicer, the Canadian commissioner of official languages, criticizes the government's program of bilingualism in the public service as costly and ineffective.	U.S. V.P. Nelson Rockefeller completes a two-day visit to Australia and pledges the U.S. will match any Soviet naval build-up in the Indian Ocean. . . . Japanese exports for fiscal year 1975 ending today are down 2 percent from 1975, but imports declined 6 percent, for a $5.88 billion net trade surplus.

A	B	C	D	E
Includes developments that affect more than one world region, international organizations and important meetings of major world leaders.	*Includes all domestic and regional developments in Europe, including the Soviet Union, Turkey, Cyprus and Malta.*	*Includes all domestic and regional developments in Africa and the Middle East, including Iraq and Iran and excluding Cyprus, Turkey and Afghanistan.*	*Includes all domestic and regional developments in Latin America, the Caribbean and Canada.*	*Includes all domestic and regional developments in Asia and Pacific nations, extending from Afghanistan through all the Pacific Islands, except Hawaii.*

U.S. Politics & Social Issues	U.S. Foreign Policy & Defense	U.S. Economy & Environment	Science, Technology & Nature	Culture, Leisure & Life Style	
The FBI announces a 9 percent rise in reported crime in the U.S. in 1975, which is increasing at a faster rate in small towns, suburbs, and rural areas than in big cities.		Environmental Action Inc. issues its fourth "dirty dozen" listing of congressmen it will seek to defeat in the fall and claims credit for defeating 22 of 31 previously listed.		Benjamin Franklin Miessner, 85, inventor of electronic musical devices and perfecter of the Wurlitzer organ, dies in Miami, Fla.	March 25
HEW Secy. F. David Mathews initiates a campaign against Medicaid fraud and abuse that costs the govt. at present an estimated $750 million a year.		The FTC rules unanimously that Encyclopaedia Britannica Inc. has used deceptive acts in recruiting sales people, in gaining entry to consumers' homes, and in selling practices.		Lin Yutang, 80, classical Chinese philospher-scholar who produced best-selling novels as well as academic works, dies in Hong Kong.	March 26
					March 27
According to just-released official FBI papers, the FBI burglarized the N.Y.C. offices of the Socialist Workers Party at least 92 times between 1960 and 1966.			About 1,000 bamboo slips, inscribed with laws and documents of the Chin Dynasty over 2,200 years old, are found in a tomb being excavated in China.	Richard Arlen, 75, film actor who starred in the first movie to win an Academy Award, dies in North Hollywood. . . . John Cogley, 60, leader of reform in the Roman Catholic Church, *Commonweal* writer-editor, and a founder of the Center for the Study of Democratic Institutions, dies of a heart attack in Santa Barbara, Calif.	March 28
				At the forty-eighth annual Academy Awards, *One Flew Over the Cuckoo's Nest* wins the best picture, best director, best actor, and best actress award.	March 29
		Pres. Ford signs legislation appropriating $2.143 million for Conrail (Consolidated Rail Corp.) funding.		Luchino Visconti, 69, Italian film director, dies in Rome, Italy. . . . Supreme Ct. affirms a lower ct. ruling to uphold a Va. ban on homosexual acts, even when committed in private between consenting adults.	March 30
Ronald Reagan makes a TV speech challenging Pres. Ford's bid for the Republican presidential nomination in which he portrays himself primarily as a non-politican, unclear of why he emerged on the political scene except that he is concerned about society's problems. . . . Despite warnings of a presidential veto, Congress clears a bill repealing the Hatch Act, which banned political activity by federal employes.	Protesting Chilean human-rights abuses, a House–Senate conference votes to maintain the U.S. ban on military aid but to allow arms sales for cash. . . . In his TV speech challenging Pres. Ford's renomination bid, Ronald Reagan deplores Ford's foreign policies, attacks State Secy. Kissinger, and charges that the U.S. has become militarily second to the Soviet Union in a world where it is dangerous to be second-best.	The Senate rejects, 49–45, a bill that would have required states to set up no-fault auto insurance plans within three years in accord with federal guidelines. . . . Pres. Ford names a Cabinet-level task force to conduct a sweeping policy review of foreign payoffs by U.S. corporations.	The N.J. Supreme Ct. rules unanimously that the mechanical respirator that is keeping Karen Anne Quinlan alive can be disconnected.	Paul Strand, 85, internationally known photographer and filmmaker who was an exponent of social and documentary realism, dies in Oregeval, France. . . . The U.S. premiere of Roger Sessions' opera *Montezuma* is presented by Sarah Caldwell's Opera Company of Boston.	March 31

F	G	H	I	J
Includes elections, federal-state relations, civil rights and liberties, crime, the judiciary, education, health care, poverty, urban affairs and population.	*Includes formation and debate of U.S. foreign and defense policies, veterans' affairs and defense spending. (Relations with specific foreign countries are usually found under the region concerned.)*	*Includes business, labor, agriculture, taxation, transportation, consumer affairs, monetary and fiscal policy, natural resources, and pollution.*	*Includes worldwide scientific, medical and technological developments, natural phenomena, U.S. weather, natural disasters, and accidents.*	*Includes the arts, religion, scholarship, communications media, sports, entertainments, fashions, fads and social life.*

	World Affairs	Europe	Africa & the Middle East	The Americas	Asia & the Pacific
April 1	The IMF concludes the final round of borrowing operations for its oil facility for 1975.	The Italian minority Christian Democrats, with help from the neofascist Italian Socialists, narrowly pass a restrictive amendment to the abortion bill.	Moslem and Christian factions in Lebanon agree to a 10-day truce so that Parliament can elect a new president to replace Suleiman Franjieh, who has refused demands to resign.	Juan Antonio Tack resigns as Panama's foreign minister and chief negotiator in talks with the U.S. over the Panama Canal and Zone and is replaced by Aquilino Boyd. . . . Haitian Pres. Jean-Claude Duvalier replaces six of his 11 Cabinet ministers, including Interior and Defense Min. Paul Blanchet, who had been considered the most powerful official in Haiti after Duvalier. . . . A new Argentinian Supreme Ct., comprised of five conservative civilian lawyers, is sworn in to reorganize the civil justice system.	Former Philippines Pres. Diosdado Macapagal (1961–65) assails Pres. Ferdinand Marcos for his martial-law rule, and then seeks and is denied political asylum in the U.S. Embassy.
April 2	Two shots are fired into the Soviet mission to the U.N. in N.Y.C. as a series of hostile anti-soviet activities intensifies. Jewish Armed Resistance claims responsibility and threatens other violance until Moscow changes its policies towards Jews.	The Portuguese Constituent Assembly approves a radical new Constitution, Portugal's first since the right-wing civilian dictatorship was overthrown in 1974.			Former Japanese Premier Kakuei Tanaka says he deplores the irresponsible remarks that sought to link him to the Lockheed bribes scandals.
April 3			The Arab League's Boycott Office ends its semi-annual conference in Alexandria, Egypt by blacklisting 16 firms doing business with Israel and removing 43 others from its roster.		Huge crowds seek to place wreaths honoring the late Chinese Premier Chou En-lai in Peking's Tien An Men Square prior to the Ching Ming festival honoring the Chinese dead.
April 4			Egyptian Pres. Anwar Sadat says the Soviet navy can no longer use the Egyptian ports of Alexandria, Port Said, and Matruh in wake of Egypt's abrogation of its 15-year friendship treaty with Moscow. . . . Jordanian King Hussein ends his U.S. visit, saying that his country's negotiations for the purchase of 14 Hawk missile batteries had bogged down.		The 17-party governing coalition of Thai Premier Kukrit Pramoj is defeated in elections for the National Assembly.
April 5	A second Soviet protest is lodged at the U.S. mission to the U.N. and at the U.N. itself, calling for a halt to the 'escalation of the heated anti-Soviet hysteria,' a reference to militant Jewish Armed Resistance harassment.	James Callaghan, British foreign secretary, is elected the new leader of the Labor Party, succeeding retiring P.M. Harold Wilson.	Israel denies a *Time* magazine report that it had assembled 13 atomic bombs at the start of the 1973 Yom Kippur war and then stored them when the war turned in Israel's favor.		Japanese steel industry sources say that China has cancelled emergency imports of nearly 2 million tons of Japanese steel and steel products negotiated in 1975. . . . An apparently spontaneous day-long riot takes place in Peking's Tien An Men Square by demonstrators expressing support for the late Premier Chou En-lai and his associates.
April 6		British Chancellor of the Exchequer Denis Healey presents Parliament the new Labor govt.'s 1976–77 budget. . . . Two thousand Greek Cypriots attack the U.S. Embassy in Nicosia to protest the pending resumption of U.S. military aid to Turkey.			

A	B	C	D	E
Includes developments that affect more than one world region, international organizations and important meetings of major world leaders.	Includes all domestic and regional developments in Europe, including the Soviet Union, Turkey, Cyprus and Malta.	Includes all domestic and regional developments in Africa and the Middle East, including Iraq and Iran and excluding Cyprus, Turkey and Afghanistan.	Includes all domestic and regional developments in Latin America, the Caribbean and Canada.	Includes all domestic and regional developments in Asia and Pacific nations, extending from Afghanistan through all the Pacific Islands, except Hawaii.

U.S. Politics & Social Issues	U.S. Foreign Policy & Defense	U.S. Economy & Environment	Science, Technology & Nature	Culture, Leisure & Life Style	
		Conrail (Consolidated Rail Corp.) operation of six bankrupt railroads in the Northeast begins. ... A N.Y.C. transit strike, which would have halted the city's subway and bus service, is averted by a last-minute settlement on a two-year contract without a direct wage increase.		Max Ernst, 84, painter and sculptor prominent in the Surrealist and Dada art movements, dies in Paris. ... Edward Albee's play *Who's Afraid of Virginia Wolf*, starring Colleen Dewhurst and Ben Gazarra, returns to Broadway.... Polish-born pianist Arthur Rubinstein is awarded the U.S. Medal of Freedom by Pres. Gerald Ford.	April 1
Rogers Morton, a presidential counsel and political aide, takes over as Pres. Ford's campaign chairman after the resignation of Howard Callaway.... HEW announces that the full $187.5 million appropriated by Congress for meals for the elderly will be released.			France conducts its third underground nuclear test in the Pacific atoll of Muroroa.	FCC eases some requirements for cable-TV operations.... In a literary-rights suit, Pulitzer Prize-winning playwright Frank Gilroy wins a settlement of over $1 million for the illegal use of his fictional character Amos Burke in a television series *Burke's Law*.	April 2
				Italian soprano Magda Olivero makes her Metropolitan Opera debut in *Tosca* at the age of 63.	April 3
The New York Times reports that a Library of Congress study of Senate committee activity found that 28 subcommittees, with budgets totaling $750,000, had never met in 1975.... Jimmy Carter, when asked about scattered site subsidized housing in a *New York Daily News* interview, says he sees "nothing wrong with ethnic purity being maintained."		The Interior Dept.'s Bureau of Mines reports petroleum remains the nation's largest single energy source, providing 46 percent of the energy used in the U.S. in 1975.			April 4
The FBI releases documents, in response to a freedom of information suit, that set forth its aims in initiating a counterintelligence program against black groups.	The Supreme Ct. declines to review the conviction of former Lt. William Calley Jr. for the murder of 22 Vietnamese civilians at My Law in 1968.	The NLRB holds that newspaper journalists are not professional employes in terms of the federal labor law.... Reclusive billionaire industrialist, aviator, and filmmaker Howard Hughes, 70, dies of kidney failure en route from Mexico to Houston, Tex. for medical treatment.	Wilder Penfield, pioneering neurosurgeon who perfected a surgical cure for epilepsy, dies at age 85 of abdominal cancer in Montreal, Canada.	Congress gives final approval to a resolution authorizing 25 of its members to go to England to accept to loan of an original copy of the Magna Carta for U.S. Bicentennial celebrations.... Meyer Davis, 81, reknowned society bandleader, dies in New York City.	April 5
Sen Henry Jackson (Wash.) wins a plurality of the delegate seats in the N.Y.S. Democratic presidential primary after a campaign stressing labor and economic issues.		According to the *Wall Street Journal* new-car sales totaled 946,600 in March, up 36 percent from March 1975, but 16 percent below 1973's record pace.	FDA proposes banning the use of chloroform in drugs and cosmetics because of a potential health risk.	The Australian Lawn Tennis Assn. reportedly will be sending a team of players to the People's Republic of China in May, as part of a cultural exchange program.	April 6

F	G	H	I	J
Includes elections, federal-state relations, civil rights and liberties, crime, the judiciary, education, health care, poverty, urban affairs and population.	*Includes formation and debate of U.S. foreign and defense policies, veterans' affairs and defense spending. (Relations with specific foreign countries are usually found under the region concerned.)*	*Includes business, labor, agriculture, taxation, transportation, consumer affairs, monetary and fiscal policy, natural resources, and pollution.*	*Includes worldwide scientific, medical and technological developments, natural phenomena, U.S. weather, natural disasters, and accidents.*	*Includes the arts, religion, scholarship, communications media, sports, entertainments, fashions, fads and social life.*

	World Affairs	Europe	Africa & the Middle East	The Americas	Asia & the Pacific
April 7		The Italian Socialist Party calls for the formation of a government of national emergency that would include members of the Communist Party. . . . Four Turkish officers on trial for falsifying records to conceal the diversion of funds received from an affiliate of Lockheed plead innocent.	In Beirut a curfew is imposed so that Parliament deputies can meet to amend the Lebanese Constitution to permit the selection of a new president.	Political violence continues in Argentina with the death toll since the March 24 military coup placed at more than 100 people.	Three Moslem rebel gunmen hijack a Philippine Air Lines passenger plane shortly after takeoff. . . . The Chinese govt. announces that Deputy Premier Teng has been deposed and Acting Premier Hua Kuo-feng is now premier and first deputy chairman of the Communist Party. . . . Cambodian Chief of State Prince Norodom Sihanouk and his Cabinet resign, causing a major shake-up in the government. Deputy Premier Khieu Samphan replaces Sihanouk.
April 8	The U.S.S.R. warns against any American intervention in Lebanon after reported movement of ships of the U.S. Sixth Fleet to Lebanese waters.	A new West German law grants women equal rights in marriage and provides more equitable divorces. It allows women to hold jobs without their husbands' prior approval. . . . The Finnish food workers' strike ends with the workers winning a 15 percent pay increase, almost 12 percent greater than the official limit established in January. . . . Newly elected British P.M. James Callaghan announces his Cabinet, naming Anthony Crosland, former state secy. for the environment, as foreign secy. and Michael Foot as lord president of the privy council.			
April 9		David O'Connell, reportedly the leader of the Provisional IRA in Northern Ireland prior to his arrest in 1975, is released from prison. . . . EEC agricultural commissioner Pierre Lardinois resigns, implying that he is in part protesting the planned budgetary ceiling on EEC farm expenditures.	Syrian troops begin to move into Lebanon in small force in an apparent attempt to apply pressure to hasten a political resolution of the Lebanese civil war. . . . Israeli officials criticize U.S. Amb. Malcolm Toon for anonymously accusing Israel of pressuring the U.S. Congress for more aid.	Canadian P.M. Pierre Trudeau outlines his proposals to make the Constitution a domestic document instead of a statute of the British Parliament, now called the British North America Act of 1867.	
April 10		Egyptian Pres. Sadat ends a European tour in Vienna, where he conferred with Austrian Chancellor Bruno Kreisky.	South African and Israel agree to a sweeping economic-cooperation pact following P.M. John Vorster's visit to Israel.		In Burma government troops and Communist guerrillas clash in fighting near the Chinese border.
April 11			Lebanese leftists agree to extend the 10-day truce to the end of April to provide more time for the election of a new president. They also demand the withdrawal of Syrian troops.		The Loatian govt. reports it has launched a 'cultural revolution' aimed at rooting out reactionaries and 'the depraved' Western way of life.
April 12	World Bank Pres. Robert McNamara defends its Chilean loan, saying the same criteria were used for Chile's present government as for its predecessor.	Soviet historian and author Andrei Amalrik and his wife are reported to have applied for visas to emigrate to Israel, prompted by KGB harassment although neither are Jewish nor had they originally sought permission to emigrate. . . . Hundreds of Turkish police repulse 2,000 to 3,000 Greek Cypriot demonstrators trying to storm the U.S. Embassy in Nicosia, protesting the recently concluded U.S.–Turkish defense pact.	Palestinian militant nationalists and Arab radicals score a major victory in elections held for mayors and municipal councils in the Israeli-occupied West Bank.		

A	B	C	D	E
Includes developments that affect more than one world region, international organizations and important meetings of major world leaders.	Includes all domestic and regional developments in Europe, including the Soviet Union, Turkey, Cyprus and Malta.	Includes all domestic and regional developments in Africa and the Middle East, including Iraq and Iran and excluding Cyprus, Turkey and Afghanistan.	Includes all domestic and regional developments in Latin America, the Caribbean and Canada.	Includes all domestic and regional developments in Asia and Pacific nations, extending from Afghanistan through all the Pacific Islands, except Hawaii.

U.S. Politics & Social Issues	U.S. Foreign Policy & Defense	U.S. Economy & Environment	Science, Technology & Nature	Culture, Leisure & Life Style	
				Mary Margaret McBride, 76, outspoken daily radio talk show host for more than 20 years, dies in West Shokun, N.Y.	April 7
Jimmy Carter, campaigning for the Democratic presidential nomination, apologizes for remarks he made about upholding the 'ethnic purity' of urban neighborhoods. . . . Jimmy Carter's remarks about 'ethnic purity' draw immediate criticism from Democratic presidential candidates Morris Undall and Henry Jackson and from black leaders and organizations. . . . Rep. Andrew Young (D, Ga.), Carter's leading advocate in the black community, defends Carter's position, but the congressional Black Caucus that National Urban League demand an explanation. . . . The Senate approves a compromise bill revising the food stamp program, setting new elegibility requirements that would reduce recipients from 19 to 17.5 million persons.		The NLRB says a newspaper's management can set up a code of ethics for editorial employes without consulting the union, but penalty provisions must be negotiated.		The Cincinnati Reds beat the Houston Astros, 11–5, as the National League opens its centennial season. Hank Aaron drives in three runs as the Milwaukee Brewers beat the N.Y. Yankees, in the American League opener.	April 8
Pres. Ford pledges to 'spare no effort to crush the menace of drug abuse.'	The U.S. completes a draft treaty with the U.S.S.R. limiting the size of underground nuclear tests for peaceful purposes and setting out procedures for on-side inspections.			Phil Ochs, 35, Vietnam War-era protest singer, commits suicide in Far Rockaway, N.Y.	April 9
	Pres. Ford says the U.S. will never give up its defense rights to the Panama Canal and never give up its operational rights as far as Panama is concerned. . . . Ronald Reagan charges that the administration is dealing from weakness not strength in its foreign policy, and the Soviet defense investment is 50 percent over the U.S.				April 10
	The New York Times reports that the family of Pvt. Lynn McClure, the recruit who died during combat training, has filed a $3.5 million damage suit against the Marine Corps.			Raymond Floyd wins the fortieth Masters Golf Tournament by eight strokes, with a total score of 271, equaling the event record set by Jack Nicklaus in 1965.	April 11
U.S. Circuit Judge William Miller, 68, whose decision on reapportionment led to the Supreme Ct.'s 'one man, one vote' rule, dies in Cincinnati, Ohio. . . . Patricia Hearst is ordered to concurrently serve the maximum prison term of 25 years for her bank robery conviction and 10 years for using a weapon during a felony.		Myra Wolfgang, 61, pioneer in the battle for working women's rights, dies in Detroit, Mich.	Congress clears legislation authorizing funding for a number of health programs and providing for the establishment of health research centers.		April 12

F	G	H	I	J
Includes elections, federal-state relations, civil rights and liberties, crime, the judiciary, education, health care, poverty, urban affairs and population.	Includes formation and debate of U.S. foreign and defense policies, veterans' affairs and defense spending. (Relations with specific foreign countries are usually found under the region concerned.)	Includes business, labor, agriculture, taxation, transportation, consumer affairs, monetary and fiscal policy, natural resources, and pollution.	Includes worldwide scientific, medical and technological developments, natural phenomena, U.S. weather, natural disasters, and accidents.	Includes the arts, religion, scholarship, communications media, sports, entertainments, fashions, fads and social life.

	World Affairs	Europe	Africa & the Middle East	The Americas	Asia & the Pacific
April 13	The U.N. Economic and Social Council resumes debate on the Decade for Action to Combat Racism and Racial Distrimination, 1973–83.	U.S. State Secy. Kissinger cautions that the advent of communist governments in Western Europe would result in an historic change in the relationship between the U.S. and Europe. . . . The London *Financial Times* reports that the Dutch commission investigating the Lockheed scandal has widened the scope of its inquiry.	In Chad four are killed and 72 wounded in a grenade attack on Pres. Felix Malloum, who is uninjured in the attack.	More than 90,000 Quebec teachers stage a one-day strike in defiance of a special law that suspends for 80 days their right to strike or conduct other disruptive actions.	North Vietnam replies to the U.S. suggestion of talks on possible normalization of relations in a message discribed by the State Dept. as 'very hardline' or 'negative.'
April 14		Human-rights activist Andrei Skaharov and his wife are detained for several hours in the Siberian city of Omsk after they scuffled with police at a dissident's slander trial.	Morocco and Mauritania conclude an accord in which they are dividing the disputed Western Sahara between themselves, despite challenges by third parties. . . . U.S. State Secy. Kissinger warns that Syria's military moves into Lebanon are getting close to the point of provoking Israeli retaliation. . . . Israeli Premier Yitzhak Rabin says that if Syria oversteps a 'definite red line' in Lebanon, it 'would prompt an Israeli action.'	Mariano Ospina Perez, 84, leader of Colombia's Conservative party for nearly three decades and president of the country from 1946–50, dies in Bogota. . . . An Ecuadoran magazine quotes Gen. Luis Reque Teran, who had commanded the Bolivan army division that tracked down Cuban revolutionary Ernesto (Che) Guevara in 1967, as saying that Guevara was executed on the orders of Bolivian leftist leaders Juan Jose Torres and Gen. Alfredo Ovando Candia.	The hijacking of a Phillipine plane ends after 8,000 miles, the longest hijacking ever, with the release of 12 Filipino hostages and a surrender to Libyan authorities. . . . The Cambodian People's Representative Assembly approves the selection of a new government at its first session. Khieu Samphan is made chief of state replacing Sihanouk. . . . Australian For. Min. Andrew Peacock announces, during a visit to Jakarta, that Australia will provide Indonesia with a three-year $108 million aid program.
April 15		Culminating in a national day of action, 250,000 French university students boycott classes to protest proposed governmental changes in the educational system. . . . The U.S. and Greece reach an agreement-in-principle that would permit continued operation of four U.S. military bases in Greece in return for $700 million in military aid.	The last five Soviet warships leave Alexandria, one hour before the deadline for ending Egyptian service to the Soviet fleet in the Mediterranean. . . . Lt. Gen. David Elazar, 50, commander of Israeli troops during the 1973 October War, dies in Tel Aviv.		
April 16			A plan aimed at ending the Lebanese civil war is announced following a meeting between PLO leader Yasir Arafat and Syrian Pres. Hafez al-Assad.	Panama's For. Min. Aquilino Boyd says that Ronald Reagan is 'willfully deceiving the people' of the U.S. and that 'Panama has never given up sovereignty over the Canal and Zone.'	Twelve hijacked hostages flown to Libya return to Manila, and Philippine Air Lines says that the $300,000 ransom paid to the Filipino Moslem gunmen for their release has been returned by the Libyan govt. . . . The Indian govt. announces a new birth-control policy to curb its population growth, including a higher minimum marriage age and cash incentives for sterilization.
April 17		Greek Premier Constantine Caramanlis proposes a non-aggression pact with Turkey and a peaceful settlement of the disputes between the two countries.	Rioting breaks out again in the Israeli-occupied West Bank as two Arabs are killed and many are injured in clashes with Israeli security forces.		
April 18		*Pravda* charges that Washington is interfering in the internal affairs of Western European governments by warning them against allowing communist participation. . . . The sixtieth anniversary of the 1916 Easter rebellion, which marked the beginning of the struggle that led to the establishment of an independent Irish republic, is commemorated in Northern Ireland, the Irish Republic, and in London.		The Colombian ruling Liberal and Conservative parties win more than 90 percent of the vote in elections for departmental (state) assemblies and municipal councils.	
April 19	The White House denies that State Secy. Kissinger's statement about Communist Party participation in Western European governments was a warning.			Colombian labor leader Raquel Mercado is killed by guerrillas of the leftist M-19 movement who had kidnapped him two months ago.	Indian P.M. Indira Gandhi, in a letter to Pakistan P.M. Zulfikar Ali Bhutto, offers to discuss resumption of diplomatic relations with Pakistan.

A	B	C	D	E
Includes developments that affect more than one world region, international organizations and important meetings of major world leaders.	Includes all domestic and regional developments in Europe, including the Soviet Union, Turkey, Cyprus and Malta.	Includes all domestic and regional developments in Africa and the Middle East, including Iraq and Iran and excluding Cyprus, Turkey and Afghanistan.	Includes all domestic and regional developments in Latin America, the Caribbean and Canada.	Includes all domestic and regional developments in Asia and Pacific nations, extending from Afghanistan through all the Pacific Islands, except Hawaii.

U.S. Politics & Social Issues	U.S. Foreign Policy & Defense	U.S. Economy & Environment	Science, Technology & Nature	Culture, Leisure & Life Style	
Pres. Ford says he would never use the phrase 'ethnic purity' but that 'ethnic heritage is a great treasure of this country.' . . . N.Y.S. Supreme Ct. Justice Aloysius Melia dismisses all charges in a perjury and bribery indictment against Albert Blumenthal, state Assembly majority leader.		Lockheed settles SEC charges that it violated fed. securities law by making secret payoffs to foreign government officials, totaling $25 million from 1968 to 1975.			April 13
		The Commerce Dept announces business inventories and sales rose strongly during February, which government analysts say are signs of continuing economic recovery.			April 14
The U.S. Ct. of Appeals rules that the Biscayne Bay Yacht Club in Miami, Fla. is not legally obliged to admit blacks or Jews.	White House press secy. Ron Nessen says the administration seeks a treaty protecting U.S. interests in the Canal Zone for the 'useful life of the canal,' 30 to 50 years.	The Commerce Dept. announces that Americans' personal income increased at an annual rate of $7.6 billion during March.	Pres. Ford signs a bill appropriating $135 million for a national swine flu immunization program.	Gerald L.K. Smith, 78, extreme right-wing preacher, Huey Long supporter, and vocal opponent of Franklin D. Roosevelt, dies in Glendale, Calif.	April 15
Jimmy Carter proposes a nationwide mandatory health insurance program as the key point in a revised federal health-care system.					April 16
			Henrik Dam, 81, Danish biochemist who discovered Vitamin K and won the Nobel Prize, dies in Copenhagen, Denmark.	Allardyce Nicoll, theater historian specializing in British drama, dies at the age of 81.	April 17
Samuel Belkin, 64, chancellor of Yeshiva University, N.Y.C., and instrumental in its growth from a small Jewish seminary to a distinguished institution, dies in N.Y.C.	The Defense Manpower Commission, a civilian group created by Congress, issues a report assessing the new U.S. volunteer army and future defense personnel needs. It finds the quality of volunteer recruits improved and urges against cutting manpower or funds for a standby draft.			Tony awards are presented for the following: best play, *Travesties* by Tom Stoppard; best musical, *A Chorus Line*; best actor in a drama, John Wood; best actress in a drama, Irene Worth.	April 18
	Campaigning in Texas, Pres. Ford says that Ronald Reagan's statements about the Panama Canal indicate that Reagan would end the canal negotiations, which Ford states is a 'position of irresponsibility.'	The Commerce Dept. says that the nation's real GNP increased at a seasonally adjusted annual rate of 7.5 percent during the first quarter, the fourth increase in a row.		The announced winners of the twenty-seventh annual National Book Awards are William Gaddis, Paul Fussell, John Ashbery, Walter Edmonds, Michael Arlen, and David Davis. . . . Jack Fultz, 27, wins the eightieth Boston Marathon in a time of two hours, 20 minutes, and 19 seconds; Kim Merritt leads the women.	April 19
F	G	H	I	J	
Includes elections, federal-state relations, civil rights and liberties, crime, the judiciary, education, health care, poverty, urban affairs and population.	Includes formation and debate of U.S. foreign and defense policies, veterans' affairs and defense spending. (Relations with specific foreign countries are usually found under the region concerned.)	Includes business, labor, agriculture, taxation, transportation, consumer affairs, monetary and fiscal policy, natural resources, and pollution.	Includes worldwide scientific, medical and technological developments, natural phenomena, U.S. weather, natural disasters, and accidents.	Includes the arts, religion, scholarship, communications media, sports, entertainments, fashions, fads and social life.	

	World Affairs	Europe	Africa & the Middle East	The Americas	Asia & the Pacific
April 20			A new Lebanese cease-fire goes into effect but it is ignored by Christian and Moslem forces with resultant high fatalities on both sides. . . . Israeli Premier Yitzhak Rabin tours the Jordan Valley in the West Bank and assures Jewish settlers that they would not be removed despite Arab protests and opposition within Israel.	Panama Canal Co. strikers return to work after the Canal Zone governor, Maj. Gen. Harold Parfitt, agrees to oppose austerity measures and to institute collective bargaining.	
April 21		Col. Valerie Andre becomes the first woman general in the French armed forces. . . . Political violence erupts in Rome as Giovanni Theodoli, managing director of the Italian subsidiary of Chevron Oil Co., is seriously wounded by urban guerrillas.	One account says 110 persons died in the previous 24 hours in Lebanon during the so-called cease-fire. . . . Egypt and China agree that China will provide Egypt with spare parts for its Soviet-supplied MiG-17 jets in wake of Soviet refusal to ship the parts or other military equipment to Egypt. . . . The Ethiopian provisional military govt. issues a major policy statement calling for all working-class parties to ultimately establish a peoples' democratic republic.	Rep. Edward Koch (D, N.Y.) charges that Uruguay has become the torture chamber of Latin America in view of recent reports of abuse of political prisoners.	Thai King Phumiphol Aduldet signs a proclamation appointing a new four-party coalition government headed by Seni Pramoj as premier.
April 22		Italian newspapers report that an unnamed premier during the 1960s accepted payments from Lockheed.		A federal senator, the president of the NHL, and three businessmen are charged with conspiring to influence the Canadian govt. to extend the lease on a duty-free airport concession.	
April 23		Soviet Gen. Sergei Shtemenko, 69, on the Warsaw Pact chiefs of staff since 1968 and a prominent member of the Stalin govt., dies of cancer in Moscow.		The Venezuelan Senate denounces the 'fascist distatorship that shames the people of Chile' and expresses 'solidarity with exiled, persecuted, jailed, and tortured' Chileans.	A militant Roman Catholic group circulates a document accusing the Philippine govt. of torturing prisoners.
April 24			State Secy, Kissinger, starting a two-week visit to Africa, says that the U.S. identifies with Africa's aspirations to human dignity, racial equality, and to economic progress.		An international conference of 300 overseas Indians is held in London to plan a drive against P.M. Indira Gandhi's restrictive rule in India. . . . North Vietnamese officials say they were surprised by last year's sudden collapse of Pres. Nguyen Van Thieu's govt., which led to the Communist victory in South Vietnam.
April 25	The Middle East Economic Survey reports that world oil production dropped 11.5 percent in 1975 from the 1974 figure. Middle East oil output fell 10.5 percent.	The Portuguese Socialist Party wins a plurality of the vote in elections for the Nat. Assembly (Parliament), the first free parliamentary elections in 50 years.	Kissinger says the U.S. welcomes Tanzania's efforts as mediator and conciliator in southern Africa, although Tanzania had supported the Soviet-backed Angolan nationalist movement.		
	A	**B**	**C**	**D**	**E**
	Includes developments that affect more than one world region, international organizations and important meetings of major world leaders.	*Includes all domestic and regional developments in Europe, including the Soviet Union, Turkey, Cyprus and Malta.*	*Includes all domestic and regional developments in Africa and the Middle East, including Iraq and Iran and excluding Cyprus, Turkey and Afghanistan.*	*Includes all domestic and regional developments in Latin America, the Caribbean and Canada.*	*Includes all domestic and regional developments in Asia and Pacific nations, extending from Afghanistan through all the Pacific Islands, except Hawaii.*

U.S. Politics & Social Issues	U.S. Foreign Policy & Defense	U.S. Economy & Environment	Science, Technology & Nature	Culture, Leisure & Life Style	
William Rentschler, manager of former Pres. Nixon's 1968 presidential campaign in Ill., pleads guilty to one count of defrauding First National City Bank of N.Y. (Citibank).... The Supreme Ct. rules, 8–0, that federal courts can order that law-income public housing be located in white suburbs.			The FAA is petitioned by two Ralph Nader organizations and an airline pilots', group to ban smoking in airline cockpits and smoking by pilots for eight hours before their flights.	*The Heiress*, a dramatization of Henry James's novel *Washington Square* , opens on Broadway with Jane Alexander and Richard Kiley.	April 20
The Supreme Ct. rules, 7–2, that individuals cannot challenge on Fourth Amendment grounds government subpoenas of their bank records because the records are the bank's property not the individual's.... Justice Dept. rules that 513 political entities in 30 states must hold elections in more than one language, in face of a provision to protect the voting rights of minorities as stipulated in the 1965 Voting Rights Act.	Republican presidential aspirant Ronald Reagan continues to call Panama's Gen Omar Torrijos a 'tinhorn dictator' and demands continued U.S. sovereignty over the Canal Zone.... Pres. Ford, intensifying his rebuttal of Reagan's charges, says allegations that the U.S. is in a position of military inferiority are 'complete and utter nonsense.'	The AFL–CIO United Rubber Workers strikes in a contract dispute with the four largest tire and rubber companies in the U.S.... U.S. auto industry's production of convertibles ends as GM makes the last Cadillac Eldorado .... The Natural Resources Defense Council challenges the FDA's interim approval of plastic soft-drink and beer bottles.	Full-scale testing of the swine flu vaccine to be used in the national flu immunization program begins in Washington, D.C.		April 21
	Army officials say that cadet honor boards at West Point found 50 third-year cadets guilty of cheating on an engineering take-home exam.			Swedish film director Ingmar Bergman and Swedish actress Bibi Anderson, who has worked closely with Bergman, announce they are leaving Sweden because of harassment by Swedish tax officials.... Barbara Walters becomes the first anchorwoman of a network television news program and the highest-paid journalist in history by accepting ABC's offer of a five-year contract at $1 million annually.	April 22
Rose Mary Woods, former Pres. Richard Nixon's personal secretary, wins the return of personal items that had been impounded in a legal battle over Nixon's papers and tapes.	*The New York Times* says that it has learned that the many more West Point cadets cheated than had been reported, but a limited number were being prosecuted to minimize the scandal.	Toni Schmuecker, board chairman of West German auto-maker Volkswagenwerk, A.G., announces that, in response to a drop in U.S. sales, the company will set up its first assembly plant in the U.S.... Jimmy Carter, campaigning for the Democratic presidential nomination, issues an economic-policy position paper in which he gives short-term priority to the generation of jobs in the private sector by the federal government.			April 23
				Mark Tobey, 85, American abstract painter who was influenced by Oriental art and philosophy, dies in Basel, Switzerland.... Pope Paul VI, in a departure from papal practice, directly criticizes an individual cleric, French Bishop Marcel Lefebvre, for founding a Swiss seminary to train priests in the pre-Second Vatican Council tradition.	April 24
Washington Post and *The New York Times* report that a new book by Herbert Alexander sets 1972 election campaign costs at a record $425 million and that, contrary to popular belief, the Democrats spent almost the same amount on their presidential campaign as did the Republicans.... *Rolling Stone* magazine publishes an account of Patricia Hearst's life with the SLA prior to her arrest, recounting how she gradually turned against the SLA doctrine of violence.				Renowned Russian pianist Alexander Brailowsky, best known for his Chopin interpretations, dies at the age of 80 in N.Y.... Sir Carol Reed, 69, British film director who won an Academy Award for *Oliver*, dies in London.	April 25

F	G	H	I	J
Includes elections, federal-state relations, civil rights and liberties, crime, the judiciary, education, health care, poverty, urban affairs and population.	Includes formation and debate of U.S. foreign and defense policies, veterans' affairs and defense spending. (Relations with specific foreign countries are usually found under the region concerned.)	Includes business, labor, agriculture, taxation, transportation, consumer affairs, monetary and fiscal policy, natural resources, and pollution.	Includes worldwide scientific, medical and technological developments, natural phenomena, U.S. weather, natural disasters, and accidents.	Includes the arts, religion, scholarship, communications media, sports, entertainments, fashions, fads and social life.

	World Affairs	Europe	Africa & the Middle East	The Americas	Asia & the Pacific
April 26					Philippine military sources report that at least 40 Philippine soldiers were killed in clashes with Moslem rebels in March. . . . More than 500 Laotian political and other prisoners escape from jail in Vientiane. . . . North and South Vietnam elect a joint National Assembly for the nation's first unified government in 30 years. All candidates were reportedly hand-picked by the Communist Party.
April 27	Zionism comes under attack by some of the Arab delegates during the UNESCO debate on the Decade for Action to Combat Racism and Racial Discrimination.	Marshal Andrei Grechko, 72, Soviet defense minister whose military career spanned over 50 years of Russian history, dies in Moscow. . . . The trial of British M.P. John Stonehouse begins. He is charged with 21 counts of forgery, theft, conspiracy, and fraud.	Rhodesian P.M. Ian Smith announces a new political initiative to include blacks in his white minority government, an action deplored by black leaders as 'irrelevant.' . . . State Secy. Kissinger, speaking in Zambia, declares U.S. support for majority rule in Rhodesia, an independent Namibia, and the end of apartheid in South Africa.		
April 28		In West Germany a nationwide strike of union printers is followed immediately by a lockout that shuts down about 450 daily newspapers and 6,000 printing plants.	U.S. State Secy. Kissinger, speaking in Zaire, offers the help of the U.S. in constitutional negotiations on swift progress toward black majority role in Rhodesia.		
April 29	A bomb explodes outside the gates of the Soviet Embassy in Peking, killing two Chinese guards, leaving extensive damage, but no Soviet casualties.				Gough Whitlam charges that between 1958 and 1960 a former civil aviation minister in Australia's Liberal-Country Party coalition government received Lockheed bribes.
April 30		Italian Premier Aldo Moro's minority Christian Democratic govt. resigns after the breakdown of a fragile parliamentary arrangement with the Socialists and two other parties. . . . Official sources in Tbilisi, the capital of the Georgian Soviet Socialist Republic, confirm that a wave of bombings and arson has erupted. . . . Thirteen center-right parties from seven of the nine EEC member-nations organize the European People's Party for the 1978 campaign for direct elections to the European Parliament.	State Secy. Kissinger says the U.S. would be willing to consider the normalization of relations with Angola if Cuban troops there were withdrawn. . . . Violence begins again in Lebanon following a parliamentary decision to postpone from May 1 to May 8 the election of a successor to Pres. Suleiman Franjieh.	The Canadian govt. and Lockheed sign a contract valued at more than $1 billion for the purchase of 18 specially modified P-3 Orio long-range patrol planes.	A South Korean court sentences 11 persons on charges of spying for North Korea, two receiving the death penalty and the others getting prison terms ranging up to 10 years.
May 1		Alexandros Panagoulis, Greek opposition party M.P. who had recently begun releasing documents from official military police archives, dies at the age of 37 in an automobile accident outside of Athens. . . . In the aftermath of the resignation of Italy's minority Christian Democratic govt., Pres. Giovanni Leone dissolves Parliament in preparation for national elections. . . . Hundreds of persons are arrested in Spain after heated clashes between authorities and demonstrators asking for greater political freedom.			Bangladesh Air Vice Marshal Mohammed Gholam Tawab resigns as air force chief and one of the country's three martial law administrators and is replaced by Air Commodore Mohammed Khademul Bashar.

A	B	C	D	E
Includes developments that affect more than one world region, international organizations and important meetings of major world leaders.	Includes all domestic and regional developments in Europe, including the Soviet Union, Turkey, Cyprus and Malta.	Includes all domestic and regional developments in Africa and the Middle East, including Iraq and Iran and excluding Cyprus, Turkey and Afghanistan.	Includes all domestic and regional developments in Latin America, the Caribbean and Canada.	Includes all domestic and regional developments in Asia and Pacific nations, extending from Afghanistan through all the Pacific Islands, except Hawaii.

U.S. Politics & Social Issues	U.S. Foreign Policy & Defense	U.S. Economy & Environment	Science, Technology & Nature	Culture, Leisure & Life Style	
	The Senate Select Committee on Intelligence issues a heavily censored report describing the U.S. intelligence community as routinely engaged in covert operations.	The Labor Dept. announces labor productivity increased at a seasonally adjusted annual rate of 4.6 percent in the first quarter.... U.S. Appeals Ct. upholds a 1973 plan to reduce air pollution and traffic congestion in N.Y.C.	The Senate Intelligence Committee report charges that the CIA has shown a disregard for human life in tests of biological and chemical agents.	The Senate Intelligence Committee report says that, despite new guidelines, the CIA continues to employ more than 26 newsmen and subsidized well over 200 books in 1967.... Sidney Franklin, 72, Brooklyn-born, world-renowned bullfighter and reputedly the first Jewish matador, dies in N.Y.C.	April 26
Jimmy Carter wins the Pa. Democratic presidential primary, his first victory in a northern industrial state and a counterindication to Henry Jackson's big-state strategy to win the nomination.... Pres. Ford calls for an aggressive program against drug abuse, including mandatory minimum prison sentences and preventive detention for high-level traffickers.... The Supreme Ct. rules, 5–3, that persons can be convicted of selling contraband such as drugs, even though government undercover agents supplied the contraband and bought it.		James Needham, chairman and chief executive officer of the NYSE, announces he is resigning as of May 19. William Batten is named to succeed him.	An American Airlines jet with 99 persons aboard crashes during an attempted landing in the U.S. Virgin Islands, leaving 37 persons dead and many seriously burned survivors.... A Census report on women says black women have a shorter life expectancy, with more TB and diabetes deaths and homicides but fewer suicides.	The Vatican announces the appointment of 21 new cardinals, including the Most Rev. William Wakefield Baum, archbishop of Washington, D.C.... The Census Bureau issues a report that assembled data gathered by various government agencies to provide a composite picture of women in America and their progress in various aspects of life, including employment, education, and overall status.	April 27
Calif. Gov. Jerry Brown opens his campaign for the Democratic presidential nomination in Md, greeted at the Baltimore airport by Md. Gov. Marvin Mandel and other the state democratic leaders.... The Senate Select Committee on Intelligence charges that the FBI and other U.S. agencies had conducted investigations, often using illegal methods, of many Americans.	The Marine Corps announces that three drill instructors and a captain will be court-martialed on charges stemming from the death of a recruit, Pvt. Lynn McClure.	Labor Dept. announces that the number of days lost to strikes in the first quarter of 1976 totaled 3.2 million, down from 5.1 million in the first quarter of 1975, and the fewest for any first quarter since 1964.... The Commerce Dept. reports the composite index of leading economic indicators for March declined .4 percent from February, the first decline since October.		*The Bell of Amherst*, a one-character play starring Julie Harris as the nineteenth century New England poet Emily Dickinson, opens at the Longacre Theater, N.Y.C.	April 28
Sen. Hubert Humphrey (D, Minn.) reaffirms his decision not to run for the Democratic presidential nomination.					April 29
			The EPA reports that asbestos fibers have been detected in water supplies for Boston, Philadelphia, Atlanta, San Francisco, and Seattle, but the samplings were inconclusive.	In an obscenity case, pornographic film star Harry Reems is among those convicted in a Memphis, Tenn. federal court for distributing the film *Deep Throat* across state lines.	April 30
Ronald Reagan wins all 96 Republican delegates in the Texas presidential primary to shut out Pres. Ford, the worst defeat to date by an incumbent in a presidential primary.... Sen. Henry Jackson (Wash.) announces he is ending active pursuit of the Democratic presidential nomination.				*Bold Forbes* wins the 102nd running of the Kentucky Derby at Churchill Downs. *Honest Pleasure*, the 2–5 favorite, is second, and *Elocutionist* is third.	May 1

F	G	H	I	J
Includes elections, federal-state relations, civil rights and liberties, crime, the judiciary, education, health care, poverty, urban affairs and population.	*Includes formation and debate of U.S. foreign and defense policies, veterans' affairs and defense spending. (Relations with specific foreign countries are usually found under the region concerned.)*	*Includes business, labor, agriculture, taxation, transportation, consumer affairs, monetary and fiscal policy, natural resources, and pollution.*	*Includes worldwide scientific, medical and technological developments, natural phenomena, U.S. weather, natural disasters, and accidents.*	*Includes the arts, religion, scholarship, communications media, sports, entertainments, fashions, fads and social life.*

	World Affairs	Europe	Africa & the Middle East	The Americas	Asia & the Pacific
May 2			A leftist radio station in Beirut assails U.S. special envoy to Lebanon L. Dean Brown, accusing him of bringing "conspiratorial instructions" for the Christian rightists to implement.		Leading world newspapers report an unusual display of Chinese CP unity during May Day celebrations in Peking.
May 3			Kamal Jumblat, head of Lebanon's Moslem Nat. Movement of Parties, says that if there's a conspiracy in Lebanon, Syria is mounting it.... Portuguese Pres. Agostinho Neto announces that Angola has adopted a law allowing the confiscation of economic assets abandoned by Portuguese settlers when they fled.		
May 4	The U.N. Security Council reopens deliberations on alleged Israeli atrocities against Palestinians in the West Bank and Gaza Strip.		Iranian police shoot and kill two alleged terrorists in Teheran, bringing to 31 the number of guerrillas executed or killed by police in shootouts since January.... *The New York Times* reports widespread opposition to Rhodesian P.M. Ian Smith's appointment of black tribal chiefs to the Cabinet. ... U.S. envoy L. Dean Brown resumes his mediation in Lebanon, conferring with Premier Rashid Karami.		
May 5	The fourth U.N. Conference on Trade and Development (UNCTAD) opens in Nairobi, Kenya, boycotted by Kenyan Pres. Jomo Kenyatta who objects to Philippine Pres. Marcos's presence.	The U.S.S.R. reports a trade deficit of nearly $3.6 billion in 1975, reversing a trend of increasing trade surpluses from sales of raw materials and rising oil prices.	South Africa's antiapartheid opposition scores an upset victory in an important by-election in Durban, the first legislative seat it has won in a traditionally moderate province.... Christian-Moslem fighting in Lebanon tapers off as the ceasefire appears to be taking hold. PLO troops separate forces on both sides, forming a buffer zone.... *The New York Times* reports that Egypt and the PLO have reached an understanding for cooperation in Lebanon and elsewhere, which was mediated by Saudi Arabia.	In the wake of numerous Argentinian bombings and kidnappings, presumed rightists abduct writer Haroldo Conti and leftist ERP members kidnap Vice Commodore Roberto Echegoyen, while unidentified guerrillas seize army Col. Juan Pita.	New Zealand P.M. Robert Muldoon, who met with Chinese Chmn. Mao April 30, says he had been told that Mao suffered a stroke and was not healthy, but that Mao appeared to be frail but not senile.
May 6	State Secy. Kissinger outlines a U.S. proposal for an international resources bank to serve as a mediator between a country and private foreign investors.	West German Bundesrat passes a limited abortion bill.	*The New York Times* reports the Israeli Parliament Finance Committee has approved an agreement for the development of a new oil field in the Israeli-occupied Sinai.... State Secy. Kissinger completes his two-weeks trip to six Central and West African nations, where he discussed economic problems and emphasized the necessity of freeing Africa from foreign intervention.	An Argentinean judge says preliminary criminal charges have been filed against ex-Pres. Maria de Peron and some former aides for alleged misuse of government funds.	

A	B	C	D	E
Includes developments that affect more than one world region, international organizations and important meetings of major world leaders.	*Includes all domestic and regional developments in Europe, including the Soviet Union, Turkey, Cyprus and Malta.*	*Includes all domestic and regional developments in Africa and the Middle East, including Iraq and Iran and excluding Cyprus, Turkey and Afghanistan.*	*Includes all domestic and regional developments in Latin America, the Caribbean and Canada.*	*Includes all domestic and regional developments in Asia and Pacific nations, extending from Afghanistan through all the Pacific Islands, except Hawaii.*

U.S. Politics & Social Issues	U.S. Foreign Policy & Defense	U.S. Economy & Environment	Science, Technology & Nature	Culture, Leisure & Life Style	
Republican presidential aspirant Ronald Reagan admits that he is "a little stunned" by his strong showings in the Tex. and Ind. primaries.	Defense Secy. Donald Rumsfeld announces that he has ordered a review of training practices in all branches of the service. . . . Sen. Barry Goldwater (R, Ariz.) defends Pres. Ford and scores Ronald Reagan's Panama Canal stance, asking if Reagan were willing to "go to war" over the Canal.		A Pan American Airways airliner completes the world's longest non-stop commercial flight, covering 8,088 miles in 13 hours and 31 minutes.	Distinguished Harvard University Shakespearean scholar Alfred Harbage dies at the age of 74.	May 2
Democratic presidential aspirant Jimmy Carter is endorsed by Sen. Birch Bayh (D, Ind.), the first former primary opponent to endorse him.	V.P. Rockefeller calls Ronald Reagan's position on the Panama Canal, "one of the worst forms of destructive demagoguery."	Chmn. Arthur Burns announces "small but prudent steps" that the FRB is taking to limit the projected growth rate in the money supply and thereby counter inflation.	A surgical team at Johns Hopkins University, Md., replaces the cancerous portion of a boy's thigh bone with part of his lower leg bone and rebuilds the diseased blood vessels.	Pulitzer Prizes are awarded to novelist Saul Bellow, biographer R.W.B. Lewis, historian Paul Horgan, nonfiction author Robert N. Butler, and poet John Ashbery. . . . Sydney Schanberg is among the recipients of Pulitzer Prizes for journalism for his coverage of the Communist takeover of Cambodia. . . . U.S. composer Ned Rorem is awarded a Pulitzer Prize for music for *Air Music, 10 etudes for orchestra* , and Scott Joplin is awarded a posthumous prize for his contribution to American music.	May 3
Jimmy Carter advocates a "compensatory opportunity" program for blacks to make up for the wrongs of the past. . . . In the Democratic presidential primaries, Carter's delegate count mounts by 104, reaching a total of 553, more than one-third of the 1,505 necessary for nomination. . . . The Agriculture Dept. announces new food-stamp regulations that would reduce the scope of the $5.8-billion program by $1.2 billion and eliminate benefits for an estimated five million.	Republican presidential aspirant Ronald Reagan avows that, hypothetically, he would risk a guerrilla war with Panama to keep U.S. control of the Canal.	The U.S. Treasury Dept. announces it will end its investigation of the U.S. marketing practices of 28 foreign-car manufacturers and notes evidence of dumping. . . . U.S. District Judge Edward J. Devitt orders that Reserve Mining Co. pay fines totaling more than $1 million for polluting Lake Superior.		Alexander Solzhenitsyn, the dissident Soviet author expelled from the U.S.S.R. in February 1974, is reported to be working at Stanford University's Hoover Institution, Calif. . . . Australian P.M. Malcolm Fraser announces that "Waltzing Matilda" will be the national anthem played at the summer Olympic games, reserving "God Save the Queen" for royal occasions.	May 4
The Senate Select Intelligence Committee staff study charges that the FBI's campaign against the late civil rights leader Dr. Martin Luther King was "marked by extreme personal vindictiveness."		IRS reports that 255 people with adjusted gross incomes of over $200,000 in 1974 filed no federal income tax returns.		The disposition of Howard Hughes's personal and corporate holdings, valued at between $1.5 and $2 billion, is still being argued a month after he died. . . . United Methodist Church's convention delegates condemn sanctioning homosexuality. . . . The British D'Oyle Carte Opera Co. returns to N.Y.C., opening at the Uris Theater with Gilbert and Sullivan's *The Mikado*.	May 5
The Senate Select Intelligence Committee's staff study details reports that the FBI tried to destroy the Black Panther Party by bringing it into conflict with other violence-prone groups.		The FRB announces consumer installment credit in March rose a seasonally adjusted $1.51 billion, the tenth increase in a row and a sign of continuing economic recession. . . . The Labor Dept. announces the government's wholesale price index rose a seasonally adjusted .8 percent in April.	A massive earthquake hits northeastern Italy's Friuli region, killing hundreds of people and injuring thousands. . . . The Niels Bohr Gold Medal, awarded every three years for outstanding contributions to the peaceful use of atomic energy, is awarded to Hans Bethe, Nobel Prize-winning nuclear physicist.		May 6

F	G	H	I	J
Includes elections, federal-state relations, civil rights and liberties, crime, the judiciary, education, health care, poverty, urban affairs and population.	*Includes formation and debate of U.S. foreign and defense policies, veterans' affairs and defense spending. (Relations with specific foreign countries are usually found under the region concerned.)*	*Includes business, labor, agriculture, taxation, transportation, consumer affairs, monetary and fiscal policy, natural resources, and pollution.*	*Includes worldwide scientific, medical and technological developments, natural phenomena, U.S. weather, natural disasters, and accidents.*	*Includes the arts, religion, scholarship, communications media, sports, entertainments, fashions, fads and social life.*

	World Affairs	Europe	Africa & the Middle East	The Americas	Asia & the Pacific
May 7		U.S. State Secy. Kissinger meets with French Pres. Valery Giscard d'Estaing and reportedly they agree that Africa must be free of all foreign intervention.			Two former Cambodian officers who escaped to Thailand report that 300 officers and soldiers, captured in the 1975 Communist takeover, were executed on Jan. 6 and on Jan. 15 by the Khmer Rouge.
May 8		The Presidium of the Supreme Soviet promotes CP Gen. Secy. Leonid Brezhnev, 69, to field marshal of the army, highest Soviet military rank.	The Lebanese Parliament elects Elias Sarkis to replace Pres. Suleiman Franjieh, but because of strong Moslem leftist opposition, it is uncertain when Franjieh will resign.	AP sources report that more than 1,000 people were arrested in Paraguay after an April 3 shootout between police and leftist guerrillas.	The Saigon govt. has ordered foreign consulates and news bureaus to shift from South Vietnam to Hanoi, making Hanoi the only point of origin for foreign news reports.
May 9		Ulrike Meinhof, 41, the co-founder of the W. Ger. left-wing terrorist Red Army Faction, also known as the Baader-Meinhof Gang, commits suicide in her West German jail cell. . . . Jean Royer, the conservative mayor of Tours and a former national commerce minister, is reelected to the French National Assembly.	The Israeli Cabinet orders the removal of about 130 ultranationalist Jewish settlers from the Camp Kadum army base in the West Bank.	Former Bolivian Pres. Alfredo Ovando Candia, implicated in the 1967 execution of Cuban revolutionary Ernesto (Che) Guevara, is quoted attributing Chevara's execution order to then-Bolivian Pres. Gen. Rene Barrientos Ortuno.	
May 10	The U.N. World Heath Organization survey on medical care in the West Bank and Gaza Strip says there has been "slow but steady" improvement since Israel's takeover in 1967.	Jeremy Thorpe resigns as head of the British Liberal Party after nine years, his political position damaged since January by charges of homosexuality and financial improprieties.	The third summit meeting of French and African officials convenes in Paris with 19 African nations participating, including Seychelles and Mauritius. . . . Pierre Gemayel, Phalangist Party leader in Lebanon, charges that Palestinian intervention in the Lebanese civil war breaches the agreement regulating Palestinian presence in the country.	AP reports that Argentina's ex-Pres. Hector Campora escaped arrest following the March coup and is taking political asylum in the Mexican Embassy in Buenos Aires.	
May 11	The World Bank suspends loans valued at several million dollars to the East African Community (grouping Kenya, Tanzania, and Uganda).	Joaquin Zenteno Anaya, 53, the Bolivian amb. to France, is shot and killed on a Paris street. Terrorists known as the International Che Guevara Brigade claim responsibility, accusing Zenteno of having masterminded Ernesto (Che) Guevara's assassination in 1967.	Lebanese Phalangist Party leader Pierre Gemayel, who strongly supports Pres. Elias Sarkis, calls for Syrian troops to protect Lebanese security for a limited period. . . . U.S. envoy to Beirut L. Dean Brown concludes his mission with praise for Pres. Sarkis and Syria's role in Lebanon, commenting that it is up to Sarkis to decide if Syrian troops should keep peace in the country.		
May 12	The Conference of Islamic States' seventh annual meeting begins, with foreign ministers and other representatives of 42 nations attending.	Peter Bessell, a former British Liberal Party member of Parliament, tells of his role in an asserted 10-year cover-up conspiracy to protect Jeremy Thorpe's reputation.	According to official Rhodesian govt. announcements, 69 black nationalist guerrillas and six Rhodesian soldiers have been killed in clashes since April 26. . . . Kamal Jumblat, Moslem leftist leader in Lebanon, offers to cooperate with newly elected Pres. Elias Sarkis on the condition that Sarkis keeps Syria out of Lebanon's internal affairs and protects the Palestinian presence in the country.		

A	B	C	D	E
Includes developments that affect more than one world region, international organizations and important meetings of major world leaders.	Includes all domestic and regional developments in Europe, including the Soviet Union, Turkey, Cyprus and Malta.	Includes all domestic and regional developments in Africa and the Middle East, including Iraq and Iran and excluding Cyprus, Turkey and Afghanistan.	Includes all domestic and regional developments in Latin America, the Caribbean and Canada.	Includes all domestic and regional developments in Asia and Pacific nations, extending from Afghanistan through all the Pacific Islands, except Hawaii.

U.S. Politics & Social Issues	U.S. Foreign Policy & Defense	U.S. Economy & Environment	Science, Technology & Nature	Culture, Leisure & Life Style	
Characterizing Calif. Gov. Jerry Brown as "a nice young man" whose administration in Calif. is based on "positive non-action," Jimmy Carter charges that Brown is not really running for the Democratic presidential nomination, but is being used by the Md. Democratic machine in a "stop-Carter" move.... Pres. Ford seeks a "fresh mandate" as he campaigns in Neb. in a last-minute effort to stop his recent string of primary defeats.	Pres. Ford vetoes a $4.4-billion foreign-aid authorization bill on the ground that it is congressional encroachment on presidential authority over foreign policy.	A federal grand jury indicts the Allied Chemical Corp. on 1,094 criminal charges involving discharge of industrial wastes containing Kepone into the James River.			May 7
FBI Dir. Clarence Kelley apologizes to the American public for FBI activities that were "clearly wrong and quite indefensible."		The 39-day San Francisco, Calif. strike of municipal, transportation, and other workers ends with an agreement to form a fact-finding commission on wage scales and working conditions.			May 8
Dem. presidential aspirant Jerry Brown asks on CBS, "Where's the real Jimmy Carter? What's behind the smile?" . . . The Senate Select Intelligence Committee's staff report on FBI wiretapping says that congressmen's phone conversations were recorded on wiretaps for Presidents Johnson and Nixon, but they weren't the targets of the taps.				Rev. Alison Cheek and three other irregularly ordained women Episcopal priests announce formation of an "Episcopal Church in Exodus" in Wash., D.C.... Bjorn Borg wins the World Championship Tennis singles title in Dallas, Tex., defeating Guillermo Vilas.	May 9
Hedrick Smith, of *The New York Times*, sues former Pres. Nixon, State Secy. Kissinger, and others allegedly responsible for wiretapping his home phone in 1969 when he was diplomatic correspondent.		The SEC files a suit accusing General Tire and Rubber Co. of making a wide array of foreign and domestic payoffs, the broadest charges yet in their investigation of management fraud.... The House passes and sends to the Senate a weakened version of a bill designed to restructure the FRB and reduce its autonomous status in the federal government.		Christopher Durang, a young playwright-parodist from the Yale School of Drama, has his spoof *Titanic* and his mock-Brecht cabaret, *Das Lusitania Songspiel* presented at the Van Dam Theatre in N.Y.C.	May 10
Ronald Reagan wins over Pres. Ford in the Neb. Republican presidential primary, Ford's fifth primary loss to Reagan in 10 days. Frank Church leads front-runner Jimmy Carter by 1,800 votes in the Democratic primary.		U.S. District Judge Charles Richey orders an end to commercial tuna fishing practices that cause the incidental destruction of porpoises.... The Interior Dept. issues rules requiring reclamation of federal lands strip-mined for coal to their approximate original contour and vegetation levels.	Alvar Aalto, 78, Finnish master of modern architecture and designer of curvilinear, laminated wood furniture, dies in Helsinki.	Rudolf Kempe, 65, German conductor connected with the London and Munich Philharmonic orchestras, dies in Zurich.... New York Drama Critics Award goes to the following: best play, *Travesties* ; best American play, *Streamers* ; best musical, *Pacific Overtures* . . . . *Pas de Duke* , choreographed by Alvin Ailey in honor of jazz musician Duke Ellington, is premiered in N.Y.C. and danced by Mikhail Baryshnikov and Judith Jamison.	May 11
		The Federal Home Loan Bank Board announces the median sale price for a new house in February was $43,000, compared with $38,000 in February 1975.... Sen. Frank Moss (D, Utah) says the differences between the congressional budget and the President's budget may mean a "long summer of futile confrontation." . . . SEC lists 79 U.S. corporations charged with making foreign payments of dubious legality.	Pittsburgh medical authorities are reported looking for 10,000 people who underwent radiation treatment for cancer 20 years ago, suspecting that about 7 percent probably have thyroid cancer.	*Union Jack* , a ballet choreographed by George Balanchine to music by Hershey Kay, is premiered by the New York City Ballet at Lincoln Center, N.Y.C.	May 12

F	G	H	I	J
Includes elections, federal-state relations, civil rights and liberties, crime, the judiciary, education, health care, poverty, urban affairs and population.	*Includes formation and debate of U.S. foreign and defense policies, veterans' affairs and defense spending. (Relations with specific foreign countries are usually found under the region concerned.)*	*Includes business, labor, agriculture, taxation, transportation, consumer affairs, monetary and fiscal policy, natural resources, and pollution.*	*Includes worldwide scientific, medical and technological developments, natural phenomena, U.S. weather, natural disasters, and accidents.*	*Includes the arts, religion, scholarship, communications media, sports, entertainments, fashions, fads and social life.*

	World Affairs	Europe	Africa & the Middle East	The Americas	Asia & the Pacific
May 13		Finland's five-party coalition government, in office since November 1975, resigns. It was the only Western European government with Communists in its Cabinet.	As the Lebanese civil war flares up, Beirut radio report says about 300 persons were killed or wounded in the last 24 hours and that the fighting, fiercest of the 13-month conflict, has spread to the edges of a nearby Palestinian refugee camp.... South African Information Secy. Eschel Rhoodie says South Africa will not intervene militarily to preserve Rhodesia's white minority government.		
May 14	Japanese police announce the arrest in Tokyo of Soviet press correspondent Alexander Machkhin, charged with attempting to buy U.S. military secrets.		The PLO calls on Syria for the first time to end its military intervention in Lebanon and to stop using Palestine Liberation Army troops for its own political purposes.... The Ethiopian provisional military govt. is reported preparing a major offensive against Eritrean rebels, deploying more than half the army and many thousands of peasant volunteers.		India and Pakistan agree to resume diplomatic relations that were broken off in 1971 and restore air and land transportation between the two countries.
May 15		The French Socialist Party special congress in Dijon unanimously approves a resolution to cooperate with the French CP and Left Radical Party in the upcoming spring 1977 elections.... *Washington Post* reports that meatless days in public eating places have been instituted in Soviet cities in a campaign to save meat.		Bolivian army commander Gen. Raul Alvarez Penaranda denounces Gen. Luis Reque Teran for revealing military secrets in describing the 1967 capture of revolutionary Ernesto (Che) Guevara.	
May 16		Italian Communist Party leader Enrico Berlinguer formally opens his party's election campaign, calling for an end to the 30 years of Christian Democratic hegemony.	Lebanese fighting leaves an estimated 150 dead and 600 wounded, many of them civilians including 34 dead and 110 wounded when a shell hit a Beirut movie house.... Ethiopian Head of State Brig. Gen. Teferi Bante offers the rebels conciliation and appeals to progressive forces in Eritrea.... Nigerian Lt. Col. B.S. Dimka and six accomplices are executed by firing squad for their roles in the Feb. 13 coup attempt in which the head of state was assassinated.		Thousands of Bangladeshi stage a 45-mile march near the Indian border to protest India's diversion of water from the Ganges River. It is led by Abdu Hamid Kha Bhashani, the 95-year-old nationalist leader.
May 17	IDB annual report cites record loans to Latin American in 1975. ... The U.N. WHO rejects a survey by its three-nation committee of experts reporting improved health services in the Israeli-occupied West Bank and Gaza Strip.	French Pres. Valery Giscard d'Estaing pays an official state visit to the U.S., arriving on the first official Concorde flight.... The British pound slips below $1.80 in trading on the London exchange, a new low.... British Leyland Ltd., Britain's largest car maker, announces a net pre-tax profit of $25.6 million for the six months ending March 27, compared with a $35.6 million loss last year.	Arabs in the West Bank and Jerusalem stage violent anti-Israeli demonstrations and riots.	Bolivian army commander Gen. Luis Reque Teran charges that Amb. Joaquin Zenteno Anaya's murder in Paris was ordered by Bolivian Pres. Hugo Banzer Suarez and accuses Banzer of genocide in the slaying of hundreds of peasants and political prisoners.	Indian Home Affairs State Min. Om Mehta says more than 7,000 people were arrested in a campaign to halt publication of "objectionable literature" criticizing the government.

A	B	C	D	E
Includes developments that affect more than one world region, international organizations and important meetings of major world leaders.	Includes all domestic and regional developments in Europe, including the Soviet Union, Turkey, Cyprus and Malta.	Includes all domestic and regional developments in Africa and the Middle East, including Iraq and Iran and excluding Cyprus, Turkey and Afghanistan.	Includes all domestic and regional developments in Latin America, the Caribbean and Canada.	Includes all domestic and regional developments in Asia and Pacific nations, extending from Afghanistan through all the Pacific Islands, except Hawaii.

U.S. Politics & Social Issues	U.S. Foreign Policy & Defense	U.S. Economy & Environment	Science, Technology & Nature	Culture, Leisure & Life Style	
		Commerce Dept. announces that business inventories increased .6 percent and combined business sales increased 1.6 percent in March.	Congress votes to expand the FDA's regulatory powers over medical devices, ranging from crutches to pacemakers, but it can require pre-market testing for certain devices.... U.S. and Thai scholars in Philadelphia, Pa. display bronze implements and jewelry from Thailand, which date further back than the oldest-known Bronze Age artifacts.	The New York Nets defeat the Denver Nuggets, 112–104, to win the ABA championship for the second time in three years.	May 13
The Justice Dept. tentatively decides to file a brief in support of a suit opposing court-ordered busing in Boston.... R.I. Gov. Philip Noel resigns as temporary chairman of the Democratic platform committee because of controversy over remarks he made about black parents while defending his antibusing stance.					May 14
Boston Mayor Kevin White says the proposed Justice Dept. antibusing action is welcome news to the city.... Samuel Eliot Morison, 88, twice-winning Pulitzer Prize historian and a professor at Harvard Univ. for 40 years, dies from the effects of a stroke, in Boston, Mass.				Campaigning for Jimmy Carter, Detroit's black mayor, Coleman Young, tells a group of black ministers that they have a "choice between a man from Ga. who fights to let you into his church and a man from Ariz. (Morris Udall) whose church won't let you in the front door."... Responding to Mayor Young's remarks, Rep. Morris Udall says that he had left the Mormon church some 30 years ago because of its barrier to blacks.... *Elocutionist*, a 20 to 1 shot, wins the 101st Preakness at Pimlico, Md.	May 15
				Hockey's Montreal Canadiens win their nineteenth Stanley Cup by defeating the Philadelphia Flyers, 5–3, in a four-game sweep.	May 16
U.S. Appeals Ct., Wash., D.C. unanimously upholds the 1974 conviction of John Ehrlichman for his role in the 1971 break-in at the office of Dr. Daniel Ellsberg's former psychiatrist, Lewis Fielding.	State Secy. Kissinger, in an NBC interview, says he would prefer to leave office even if Pres. Ford wins the election in November.		A severe earthquake measuring 7.3 on the Richter scale strikes the USSR's Uzbek Republic in central Asia.	Emmy Awards for the best television dramatic performances go to Anthony Hopkins, Susan Clark, Ed Asner, and Kathryn Walker. *The Mary Tyler Moore Show* sweeps the comedy awards.	May 17

F	G	H	I	J
Includes elections, federal-state relations, civil rights and liberties, crime, the judiciary, education, health care, poverty, urban affairs and population.	Includes formation and debate of U.S. foreign and defense policies, veterans' affairs and defense spending. (Relations with specific foreign countries are usually found under the region concerned.)	Includes business, labor, agriculture, taxation, transportation, consumer affairs, monetary and fiscal policy, natural resources, and pollution.	Includes worldwide scientific, medical and technological developments, natural phenomena, U.S. weather, natural disasters, and accidents.	Includes the arts, religion, scholarship, communications media, sports, entertainments, fashions, fads and social life.

	World Affairs	Europe	Africa & the Middle East	The Americas	Asia & the Pacific
May 18		In his speech opening East Germany's ruling CP congress, Erich Honecker, first secy., reaffirms East Germany's policy of detente with West Germany.	Libyan Premier Abdel Salam Jalloud unsuccessfully tries to mediate Syria's dispute with the PLO and Lebanon's leftist Moslem factions.	Canada's $1-billion contract with Lockheed collapses after Lockheed fails to secure $375 million in financing.... Two prominent Uruguayan political exiles, Zelmar Michelini and Hector Gutierrez Ruiz, are kidnapped from their homes in Buenos Aires. Argentina.	
May 19	U.N. WHO assembly votes, 57–16, to condemn Israeli practices in its occupied territories.	Former British P.M. Harold Wilson is knighted by Queen Elizabeth II. ... EEC announces a 1975 reduction in its member countries' external trade deficit to about $2.61 billion.	The Angolan govt. severs diplomatic relations with Portugal and orders Lisbon's representative to leave immediately.... Reconciliation talks between Syria and Egypt are postponed indefinitely, without explanation, just as they were about to start.... South Africa plans to establish a 1,000-mile buffer zone along the Namibian–Angolan border, aimed at stemming recurrent forays by black nationalist guerrillas into Namibia.		
May 20	The 18-nation International Energy Agency (IEA) agrees on cooperation in the fields of nuclear energy and petroleum.			The bodies of kidnapped Uruguayans Zelmar Michelini and Hector Gutierrez Ruiz are found, along with the bodies of two other Uruguayans kidnapped a week earlier.... Bolivian Pres. Hugo Banzer Suarez threatens to curb the country's press in wake of published charges implicating him in the murder of Amb. Joaquin Zenteno Anaya in Paris.... The Mexican foreign minister announces that his country will boycott the upcoming OAS gen. assembly meeting in Santiago, Chile because of Chile's repeated human-rights violations.	
May 21		NATO expresses increasing concern over the U.S.S.R.'s international motives and military build-up, and their effect on detente.... France offers to send troops, ready for combat if necessary, to Lebanon on 48 hours' notice to help end the civil war there.		Cuban Premier Fidel Castro, in a letter to Swedish Premier Olof Palme, says Cuban troops will be withdrawn from Angola at a rate of 200 per week.	A Philippine Air Lines passenger plane is hijacked by six rebel Moslem gunman who demand $375,000 ransom and a jet to fly them to Libya.
May 22			The newspaper of Iran's ruling Rastakhiz Party says that Libya supplied arms and money to Iranian terrorists.		

A	B	C	D	E
Includes developments that affect more than one world region, international organizations and important meetings of major world leaders.	Includes all domestic and regional developments in Europe, including the Soviet Union, Turkey, Cyprus and Malta.	Includes all domestic and regional developments in Africa and the Middle East, including Iraq and Iran and excluding Cyprus, Turkey and Afghanistan.	Includes all domestic and regional developments in Latin America, the Caribbean and Canada.	Includes all domestic and regional developments in Asia and Pacific nations, extending from Afghanistan through all the Pacific Islands, except Hawaii.

U.S. Politics & Social Issues	U.S. Foreign Policy & Defense	U.S. Economy & Environment	Science, Technology & Nature	Culture, Leisure & Life Style	
The Bureau of Statistics discloses that the nation's population through Dec. 31, 1975 is 13,600,800, an increase of 115,800 over 1974 and the smallest yearly rise since 1946. . . . Pres. Ford reportedly has instructed Atty. Gen. Edward Levi to look for an appropriate case for the Supreme Ct. to reconsider the use of court-ordered busing to desegregate schools. . . . Pres. Ford revives his campaign for the Republican nomination, winning the primary in his home state of Mich. by a 2–1 margin and leading Reagan by 16 percent in Md., where neither had campaigned. . . . Jimmy Carter barely defeats Rep. Morris Udall (Ariz.) in the Mich. Democratic presidential primary and loses to newcomer aspirant Calif. Gov. Jerry Brown in the Md. primary.		The Labor Dept. clears UMW top officials of charges of mismanaging union funds.	The French and West German govts. agree to exchange information and technology on the development of fast-breeder nuclear reactors.	An all-star concert, highlight of a 6.5 million fund drive to refurbish Carnegie Hall in N.Y.C., features musicians including Leonard Bernstein, Yehudi Menuhin, Vladimir Horowitz, and Isaac Stern.	May 18
The Senate votes to create a permanent Select Committee on Intelligence, an action recommended by an earlier Senate unit that investigated U.S. intelligence agencies. . . . Dr. Mario Jascalevich is indicted on five counts of murdering patients at a N.J. hospital while he was head surgeon there almost 10 years ago.	At Democratic platform hearings, Adm. Elmo R. Zumwalt Jr. (ret.) says that critical analysis of a government's foreign policy is not an irresponsible act.		Professional golfer Arnold Palmer completes a record-setting around-the-world jet flight in 57 hours, 25 minutes with two co-pilots and a timer-observer.		May 19
Sen. Edward Kennedy (D, Mass.) denies a report that he is easing his total renunciation of the 1976 Democratic presidential nomination. . . . Rev. Jesse Jackson, speaking of black needs at Democratic platform hearings, says, "We don't want more affirmative action. We want more economic action."	State Secy. Kissinger says U.S. foreign policy will continue to support a firm defense against Soviet military and ideological agression, regardless of who wins the election in November.	Congress gives final approval to a bill authorizing funds for the EPA to administer noise pollution control programs in fiscal 1976–77. . . . Sen. Edmund Muskie (D, Me.), speaking at the Democratic platform hearings, says "What's so damn liberal about wasting money?"	Typhoon Olga strikes the Philippines, with 16.1 inches of rain falling in 24 hours.		May 20
Morris Ernst, 87, noted lawyer who won the case that cleared James Joyce's book *Ulysses* of obscenity charges, dies in N.Y.C. . . . The Federal Election Commission is revived and dispatches $3.2 million in matching funds to nine presidential candidates. Pres. Ford gets $1.3 million, and Ronald Reagan $509,000. . . . Rep. Torbert Macdonald (D, Mass.), 58, influential in legislation dealing with broadcasting and television, dies in Bethesda, Md.	Ronald Reagan says that he opposes limited war, commenting, "If those who first put the troops in [Vietnam] had intended to get the war over with, it could have been done in a very short time."		Twenty-eight members of the Yuba City, Calif. high school choir are killed when the bus taking them to a performance crashes.		May 21
			Karen Anne Quinlan is removed from a mechanical respirator that had been credited with keeping her alive.		May 22

F	G	H	I	J
Includes elections, federal-state relations, civil rights and liberties, crime, the judiciary, education, health care, poverty, urban affairs and population.	*Includes formation and debate of U.S. foreign and defense policies, veterans' affairs and defense spending. (Relations with specific foreign countries are usually found under the region concerned.)*	*Includes business, labor, agriculture, taxation, transportation, consumer affairs, monetary and fiscal policy, natural resources, and pollution.*	*Includes worldwide scientific, medical and technological developments, natural phenomena, U.S. weather, natural disasters, and accidents.*	*Includes the arts, religion, scholarship, communications media, sports, entertainments, fashions, fads and social life.*

	World Affairs	Europe	Africa & the Middle East	The Americas	Asia & the Pacific
May 23			The Israeli Cabinet approves the formation of committees to study the grievances of Arabs living in Israel and to help reconcile differences between Jewish and Arab communities. . . . Lebanon Premier Rashid Karami rejects France's offer of troops, saying, "We will never go back to the days of the [French] mandate."	Bolivian Pres. Hugo Banzer Suarez withdraws his warning to the nation's press after nationwide strikes on the previous day by newspapers and radio stations.	
May 24	State Dept. officials say that the U.S.S.R. acknowledged that it committed a technical violation of the 1972 SALT accord and it is taking measures to rectify the infraction. . . . Japan becomes the 100th country to ratify the nuclear Non-Proliferation Treaty.	British M.P. Enoch Powell, known for his antiimmigration stance, says that the influx of Asians and blacks into Great Britian threatens the country with racial strife.			
May 25		The Soviet weekly newspaper *Literaturnaya Gazeta* reports allegations that three U.S. news correspondents in Moscow are associated with the CIA. . . . The annual meeting of Italian Catholic bishops endorses a statement calling for the excommunication of Catholics running on the Italian CP ticket.			Australian Defense Minister James Killen says the government will spend $15 billion on defense in the next five years. . . . Hanoi and Saigon radios announce that past and present enemies of the South Vietnamese govt. will be brought to trial, including persons who served with pro-U.S. governments.
May 26	The U.N. Security Council ends its debate on Israel's policy in the occupied Arab territories by adopting a statement deploring the establishment of Israeli settlements.	The U.S. State Dept. releases figures showing that the U.S.S.R. issued 5,000 exit visas for Israel during the first four months of 1976, a slight increase over 1975. . . . France denies that it had offered to intervene militarily in the Lebanese civil war.			
May 27	U.N. Secy. Gen. Kurt Waldheim, completes a three-day visit to Syria that had been opposed by both the U.S. and Israel.		Syria's Pres. Hafez al-Assad says he doesn't want the U.N. observer force on the Golan Heights to become a permanent institution.		
May 28	The U.N. Security Council votes to renew for another six months the mandate of the U.N. Disengagement Observer Force on the Golan Heights. . . . The oil ministers of OPEC end two days of talks with a decision to retain for now OPEC's nine-month freeze on crude oil prices. . . . Pres. Ford and Soviet CP Gen. Secy. Leonid Brezhnev sign a joint treaty placing limits on the size of underground nuclear explosions for peaceful purposes.	The British pound hits a new record low during trading on the London international exchange, dipping to $1.7535. . . . Yugoslavian Pres. Tito opens a new 296-mile rail link between Belgrade and the Adriatic port of Bar.	The International Commission of Jurists charges that Savak, Iran's secret police organization personally controlled by the Shah, tortures political prisoners. . . . Zambian Pres. Kenneth Kaunda says his government will permit Zimbabwe guerrillas (black Rhodesians) to use Zambia as a base for conducting raids into Rhodesia.		
May 29		East Germany's ruling CP announces a series of social reforms to be instituted during the 1976–80 five-year-plan period.			

A	B	C	D	E
Includes developments that affect more than one world region, international organizations and important meetings of major world leaders.	Includes all domestic and regional developments in Europe, including the Soviet Union, Turkey, Cyprus and Malta.	Includes all domestic and regional developments in Africa and the Middle East, including Iraq and Iran and excluding Cyprus, Turkey and Afghanistan.	Includes all domestic and regional developments in Latin America, the Caribbean and Canada.	Includes all domestic and regional developments in Asia and Pacific nations, extending from Afghanistan through all the Pacific Islands, except Hawaii.

U.S. Politics & Social Issues	U.S. Foreign Policy & Defense	U.S. Economy & Environment	Science, Technology & Nature	Culture, Leisure & Life Style	
				The NBA championship playoffs between the Boston Celtics and the Phoenix Suns begin.	May 23
Pres. Ford gets a big boost in delegate strength when 119 N.Y.S. previously uncommitted delegates vote to endorse him in a shift engineered by V.P. Nelson Rockefeller. . . . Presidential primaries held in Ida., Nev., Ore., Ky., Tenn., and Ark. yield three wins each for Pres. Ford and his challenger Ronald Reagan. . . . On the Democratic side, front-runner Jimmy Carter wins three primaries, Sen. Frank Church (Ida.) wins two, and late-starter Gov. Jerry Brown (Calif.) wins in Ore. with the most successful write-in vote in primary history.		The Supreme Ct. strikes down a Va. law that barred pharmacists from advertising drug prices. The FTC estimates that the move might save consumers millions of dollars annually.	Supersonic transport (SST) service to Washington, D.C. begins with flights by the British–French Concorde jet. The flights take under four hours. . . . Phillippine Pres. Ferdinand Marcos declares the island of Luzon a disaster area, in wake of four days of torrential rains causing floods in which 215 die and 630,000 are left homeless.	Hanoi's Roman Catholic Archbishop Joseph Trinh Nhu Khue is among 20 new cardinals installed by Pope Paul VI after his secret appointment in April.	May 24
Rep. Wayne Hays (D, Ohio) admits that he had a "personal relationship" with Elizabeth Ray, a member of the House Administrations Committee staff, but denies he gave her the $14,000 congressional job so that she could be his mistress.			National Science Foundation reports that two University of Arizona scientists have discovered large clouds of gas in what was previously thought to be empty spaces in the universe. . . . Iranian Premier Amir Abbas Hoveida announces signing a contract to buy two nuclear power plants from France.	Muhammad Ali knocks Richard Dunn down five times before the world heavyweight boxing title fight is stopped midway in the fifth round. . . . Metropolitan Museum of Art, N.Y.C., names Sir John Pope-Hennessey, former director of the British Museum, as consultative chairman of its European paintings department.	May 25
Democratic presidential aspirant Jimmy Carter gains the endorsement of N.Y.C. Mayor Abraham Beame.		The Commerce Dept. announces the U.S. posted its fourth consecutive monthly trade deficit in April, with imports exceeding exports by a seasonally adjusted $202.1 million.	U.S. Appeals Ct., N.Y., bars commercial use of plutonium as a nuclear fuel until the NRC completes a safety study, reversing a 1975 decision, which had been challenged by environmental groups.	Walter Wurzburger, 56, is installed as president of the Rabbinical Council of America, representing 1.5 million Orthodox Jews. . . . Martin Heidegger, 86, one of the most influential philosophers of the century, dies in Messkirch, West Germany. . . . English soprano Maggie Teyte, 88, who was chosen by Claude Debussy in 1908 to succeed Mary Garden as Melisande and who specialized in French music, dies in London.	May 26
The bipartisan National Women's Political Caucus charges that both major political parties failed to represent women and minorities adequately in convention delegate selection.		The Dow Jones average registers its lowest close in more than three months, at 965.57.		Abby Rockefeller Mauze, 72, eldest child and only daughter of John D. Rockefeller Jr. dies in N.Y.C.	May 27
At a Los Angeles meeting with reporters, Ronald Reagan says that he expects to win the Republican presidential nomination, but that if he does not, he would not throw his support automatically to Pres. Ford in the name of party unity.				Martin Scorsese's *Taxi Driver* wins the Golden Palm award at the 1976 Cannes Film Festival.	May 28
Atty. Gen. Edward Levi says that the Justice Dept. will wait until the Supreme Ct. agrees to hear an appeal on the Boston school integration busing case before filing a brief.			South Africa announces a $1 billion contract with a French consortium to buy a nuclear-power station, the first on the African continent.	Earl Bell of Arkansas State University sets a world pole-vault record of 18 feet 7 ¼ inches at the U.S. Track and Field Federation championships.	May 29
F	G	H	I	J	
Includes elections, federal-state relations, civil rights and liberties, crime, the judiciary, education, health care, poverty, urban affairs and population.	*Includes formation and debate of U.S. foreign and defense policies, veterans' affairs and defense spending. (Relations with specific foreign countries are usually found under the region concerned.)*	*Includes business, labor, agriculture, taxation, transportation, consumer affairs, monetary and fiscal policy, natural resources, and pollution.*	*Includes worldwide scientific, medical and technological developments, natural phenomena, U.S. weather, natural disasters, and accidents.*	*Includes the arts, religion, scholarship, communications media, sports, entertainments, fashions, fads and social life.*	

	World Affairs	Europe	Africa & the Middle East	The Americas	Asia & the Pacific
May 30	The U.N. Conference on Trade and Development (UNCTAD) adopts a compromise proposal to establish a fund to regulate world commodity prices.			The political death toll in Argentina mounts with more than 200 reported dead since the March military coup.	
May 31			An estimated 2,000 Syrian troops enter northern Lebanon.		
June 1	The International League for Human Rights calls on the U.N. to investigate charges that the Indian govt. is suppressing individual freedom and torturing political dissidents. . . . Australian P.M. Malcolm Fraser criticizes Soviet military expansion, saying the U.S.S.R. is still seeking to expand its influence throughout the world to achieve primacy.	British and Icelandic foreign ministers sign an interim pact to end their so-called cod war, which had resulted in the severing of diplomatic ties and threatened to disrupt NATO relations.			
June 2	A U.N. study recommends $432 million in foreign aid from the international community for postwar Vietnam, in addition to aid already being received. . . . The IMF, in its first of 16 planned gold auctions, sells 780,000 ounces at $126 an ounce.	King Juan Carlos I and Queen Sofia of Spain visit the U.S. and are officially greeted by Pres. Ford and his wife, Betty Ford. . . . Nicolae Ceausescu, Rumanian Pres. and CP first secy., calls for greater contributions from education and cultural activities to socialist goals. . . . Swedish Parliament passes a law giving employes a voice in company policy, thereby abolishing an employer's exclusive right to hire or fire.		The body of retired Bolivian Gen. Juan Jose Torres, who led a leftist government in 1970–71, is found a day after he is kidnapped in Argentina.	Philippines Pres. Ferdinand Marcos and U.S.S.R. Pres. Nikolai Podgorny establish diplomatic relations between the two countries.
June 3		Viggo Kampmann, 65, former Danish prime minister, dies in Copenhagen.		Bolivian mineworkers strike to protest the slaying of Gen. Juan Jose Torres in Argentina, blaming his death on "international fascists." . . . About 5,000 Quebec dairy farmers riot during a demonstration protesting reduced production quotas and the resulting loss in subsidies.	
June 4		An 18-year-old Sikh, Gurdip Singh Chaggar, dies of knife wounds in London after a racially motivated attack. -		Chilean Pres. Augusto Pinochet Ugarte, addressing the opening session of the OAS gen. assembly, denies human-rights abuses and says that Chile is establishing a democracy, having freed itself from Marxist-Leninist tyranny. . . . Argentina's ruling military junta bans political activities in the country, dissolving 48 organizations and declaring 22 of them illegal.	

A	B	C	D	E
Includes developments that affect more than one world region, international organizations and important meetings of major world leaders.	Includes all domestic and regional developments in Europe, including the Soviet Union, Turkey, Cyprus and Malta.	Includes all domestic and regional developments in Africa and the Middle East, including Iraq and Iran and excluding Cyprus, Turkey and Afghanistan.	Includes all domestic and regional developments in Latin America, the Caribbean and Canada.	Includes all domestic and regional developments in Asia and Pacific nations, extending from Afghanistan through all the Pacific Islands, except Hawaii.

U.S. Politics & Social Issues	U.S. Foreign Policy & Defense	U.S. Economy & Environment	Science, Technology & Nature	Culture, Leisure & Life Style	
			A group of seven doctors agree to look after Karen Anne Quinlan, removed from a life-support system by court order, as a chronic-care patient, and she is moved to a nursing home.	Johnny Rutherford wins the sixtieth running of the Indianapolis 500 in a rain-shortened 255-mile auto race. ... Betty Burfeindt defeats Judy Rankin by one stroke to win the LPGA championship.	May 30
The UPI says two Boston newspapers received phone calls saying that a window smashing and fire that occurred hours after Atty. Gen. Edward Levi's decision on the Boston school busing issue were the South Boston Defense League's protest against the decision.			Jacques Monod, 66, French molecular and cellular biologist who shared the 1965 Nobel Prize for medecine and physiology, dies in Cannes, France,	Martha Mitchell, 57, outspoken estranged wife of former Atty. Gen. John Mitchell, who denounced the Nixon administration for corrupting her husband, dies in N.Y.C. ... Leningrad police detain 10 Soviet artists for several hours after they try to stage an unauthorized exhibit of their paintings in defiance of a City Council ban. ... Rosi Mittermaier, 25, West Germany's Olympic champion alpine skier, announces she is retiring from competitive skiing.	May 31
In the next-to-the-last week of primary season, Pres. Ford wins a total of 28 delegates to 11 for Ronald Reagan, and Jimmy Carter loses two primaries in Mont. and R.I. and wins one in S.D., capturing the most delegates. ... The Supreme Ct. rules, 5–4, that the Civil Service Commission's regulations barring resident aliens from federal jobs violates the Fifth Amendment.		Seven independent oil companies are indicted on federal charges that they fixed the retail prices of gasoline they sold in the Middle Atlantic region.	The World Health Organization reports that Dr. William Trager has discovered a way of growing the most lethal form of the malaria parasite.		June 1
Ronald Reagan deplores the major adverse influence of the federal government in the nation's schools and suggests vouchers as an alternative to busing. ... Don Bolles, award-winning investigative reporter for the *Arizona Republic*, is fatally injured when a bomb explodes in his car. ... House Majority Leader Thomas (Tip) O'Neill asks Rep. Wayne Hays to temporarily resign his committee chairmanships until charges made against him by Elizabeth Ray are resolved.		Members of the N.Y. Newspaper Guild go on strike against Time Inc., the first strike against Time since it was founded in 1922.	Dr. Theodore Cooper, assistant secy. of HEW, says one of the four companies producing swine-flu vaccine made about two million doses using the wrong strain of the virus.		June 2
		The AFL-CIO Amalgamated Clothing and Textile Workers Union is established when the Amalgamated Clothing Workers of American merges with the Textile Workers Union.	Karen Anne Quinlan is described by her doctors as being in stable condition after the removal of the mechanical respirator on May 22. ... The International Agency for Research on Cancer reports that studies are underway to examine cancer-frequencies in different countries. ... *Washington Post* reports on studies that appear to confirm research linking the use of estrogen with uterine cancer.		June 3
		The Labor Dept. announces unemployment in May fell to a seasonally adjusted 7.3 percent of the work force, a record 17-month low. ... Merrill Lynch, Pierce, Fenner & Smith Inc. files consent decrees agreeing to pay about $1.9 million to victims of past discrimination and spend $1.3 million on recruiting ads.		Col. Jack Brennan, a Nixon aide, says letters in the possession of literary agent Scott Meredith, said to be love letters from Nixon to a married woman, are obvious forgeries.	June 4

F	G	H	I	J
Includes elections, federal-state relations, civil rights and liberties, crime, the judiciary, education, health care, poverty, urban affairs and population.	Includes formation and debate of U.S. foreign and defense policies, veterans' affairs and defense spending. (Relations with specific foreign countries are usually found under the region concerned.)	Includes business, labor, agriculture, taxation, transportation, consumer affairs, monetary and fiscal policy, natural resources, and pollution.	Includes worldwide scientific, medical and technological developments, natural phenomena, U.S. weather, natural disasters, and accidents.	Includes the arts, religion, scholarship, communications media, sports, entertainments, fashions, fads and social life.

	World Affairs	Europe	Africa & the Middle East	The Americas	Asia & the Pacific
June 5	The Soviet CP newspaper *Pravda* charges that the Ford administration is not doing enough to help bring the SALT II talks to a swift, successful conclusion.		Egypt assails Syria for invading Lebanon, recalling its entire diplomatic mission and ordering the Syrian Embassy in Cairo to close.		
June 6		Pres. Valery Giscard d'Estaing and Premier Jacques Chirac confer in an attempt to reconcile divisions within France's coalition government.			Mohammed Stephens, chief minister of the Malaysian state of Sabah, and three Cabinet ministers, are among 14 killed in a plane crash. Harris Saleh is sworn in to succeed Stephens.
June 7	Eight members of the Group of 10 industrialized democracies, Switzerland, and the Bank for International Settlements offer Great Britain a $5.3 billion credit line to prop the pound.		The South African Parliament debates a bill under which Xhosa tribe members would forfeit their citizenship and become citizens of the Transkei when it became independent.		
June 8		Francesco Coco, the Genoa state prosecutor, is shot dead by terrorists on a Genoa, Italy street, along with his bodyguard and driver.... Edward Gierek, first secy. of the Polish CP, visits West Germany and holds talks with Chancellor Helmut Schmidt.		Emmas Obleas de Torres, widow of the slain Bolivian president, charges that the Argentine and Bolivian govts. were responsible for her husband's death.... Mexico and the U.S. announce that most of the opium poppy fields in Mexico were destroyed in an intensified joint eradication campaign. ... State Secy. Kissinger, speaking before the OAS gen. assembly meeting, notes Chilean human-rights abuses, but refrains from condemning the Chilean government.	
June 9		The Spanish Parliament approves a bill allowing other political parties besides the right-wing National Movement to operate for the first time since 1939.	Israeli Amb. to the U.N. Chaim Herzog criticizes the U.N. for not dealing with the crisis in Lebanon, warning that it threatens to engulf Israel and the rest of the Middle East.	The Bolivian govt. imposes a nationwide state of siege following widespread student and mine-worker protests of the assassination in Argentina of ex-Pres. Juan Jose Torres.	
June 10		Defense ministers from 13 of the 15 NATO nations meet for a semiannual conference.	The Arab League agrees to send a symbolic peace-keeping force to Lebanon to oversee a truce arranged to halt the increased fighting.... Rhodesian planes destroy a Mozambique army post in retaliation for a three-hour mortar-and-rocket barrage against a tea plantation near the southeastern Rhodesia border.		Hanoi and Saigon radios announce that past and present enemies of the South Vietnamese govt. will be brought to trial.

A	B	C	D	E
Includes developments that affect more than one world region, international organizations and important meetings of major world leaders.	Includes all domestic and regional developments in Europe, including the Soviet Union, Turkey, Cyprus and Malta.	Includes all domestic and regional developments in Africa and the Middle East, including Iraq and Iran and excluding Cyprus, Turkey and Afghanistan.	Includes all domestic and regional developments in Latin America, the Caribbean and Canada.	Includes all domestic and regional developments in Asia and Pacific nations, extending from Afghanistan through all the Pacific Islands, except Hawaii.

U.S. Politics & Social Issues	U.S. Foreign Policy & Defense	U.S. Economy & Environment	Science, Technology & Nature	Culture, Leisure & Life Style	
Speaker of the House Carl Albert, 68, announces he has made an irreversible decision to retire from Congress at the end of the term.	A House subcommittee passes an amendment prohibiting U.S. military aid to Uruguay because of alleged governmental abuse of human rights.		The collapse of Teton River Dam (Idaho) results in nine persons dead, at least 30 missing, and 4,000 homes and businesses destroyed.	East German swimmers set 14 world records at their national championships in East Berlin.... Dwight Stones raises his world high-jump record to seven ft., seven inches in the NCAA track-and-field championship finals in Philadelphia.... Favored *Bold Forbes*, the Kentucky Derby winner, wins the 108th running of the Belmont Stakes, N.Y. in 2:29 minutes.	June 5
		A 14-week strike by Teamsters Union locals against Anheuser–Busch Inc. ends. The strike, which began March 1, was the longest in the brewery firm's history.... J. Paul Getty, 83, American oil billionaire considered the world's wealthiest man, dies in Surrey, England.		The Boston Celtics win their thirteenth NBA title by defeating the Phoenix Suns, 87–80.... Elisabeth Rethberg, 81, a leading Metropolitan Opera soprano for 20 years, dies in Yorktown Heights, N.Y.	June 6
Dr. Timothy Leary is released from jail for a 1970 narcotics conviction after the Parole Bd. reverses an earlier decision denying him parole. ... The Supreme Ct. upholds a test given to Washington D.C. police force applicants after a lower ct. had thrown out the test because of a racially disproportionate impact.... Pres. Ford says the nomination of Reagan would be a debacle for the Republican Party, similar to that of 1964 when Barry Goldwater was the nominee.		Pres. Ford approves import quotas on specially-steel products, effective June 14.	Congress passes a bill authorizing $234 million in fiscal 1976–78 for a variety of programs aimed at curbing diseases and improving public knowledge in health matters.	Organist E. Power Biggs criticizes the management of Carnegie Hall (N.Y.C.) for installing an electronic organ, which he argues cheapens the hall and ruins its image as a place of excellence.	June 7
In the Calif. Democratic senatorial primary, Sen. John Tunney wins over Tom Hayden, a campus radical leader in the Vietnam era. Dr. S.I. Hayakawa wins the Republican nomination.... Jimmy Carter gains 126 delegates in the Ohio primary, which, with 67 delegates garnered in his second-place Calif. primary finish and 25 from a second-place win in N.J., takes his total delegate count to within 388 of the 1,505 needed to win the Democratic presidential nomination.			Calif. voters defeat a proposition to curb the operation of existing nuclear power plants and ban additional construction.		June 8
James Farley, 88, the master-mind of former Pres. Franklin Roosevelt's campaign strategy during the 1930s, dies in N.Y.C.... Chicago Mayor Richard Daley endorses Carter and suggests Sen. Adlai Stevenson (D, Ill.) as his running mate.	The military manpower subcommittee of the House Armed Services Committee continues hearing testimony in a probe of Marine Corps recruitment and training practices. ... State Secy. Kissinger pledges that the U.S. will improve trade relations with Latin America and urges that Latin nations reciprocate.			Dame Sybil Thorndike, 93, acclaimed British actress renowned for her role in George Bernard Shaw's *Saint Joan*, dies in London.	June 9
Pa. Gov. Milton Shapp, Tex Sen. Lloyd Bentsen, Phila. Mayor Frank Rizzo, and Mayor Walter Washington of the District of Columbia endorse Carter. W.Va. Sen. Robert Byrd releases his delegates.... Rep. Wayne Hays (D, Ohio) is rushed to a hospital in a coma, which his doctor says was caused by an overreaction to a commonly prescribed sleeping pill.		Delaware and the FDIC announce the completion of their joint rescue effort to save the Farmers Bank of the State of Delaware, the state's second largest bank.	The National Council on Alcoholism calls "dangerous and misleading" a Rand Corp. study that said some alcoholics could safely go back to drinking normal amounts of liquor.	Neil Simon's *California Suite*, starring Tammy Grimes and Jack Weston, opens on Broadway.... Adolph Zukor, 103, movie pioneer and builder of the Paramount Pictures empire, dies in Los Angeles, Calif.	June 10

F	G	H	I	J
Includes elections, federal-state relations, civil rights and liberties, crime, the judiciary, education, health care, poverty, urban affairs and population.	Includes formation and debate of U.S. foreign and defense policies, veterans' affairs and defense spending. (Relations with specific foreign countries are usually found under the region concerned.)	Includes business, labor, agriculture, taxation, transportation, consumer affairs, monetary and fiscal policy, natural resources, and pollution.	Includes worldwide scientific, medical and technological developments, natural phenomena, U.S. weather, natural disasters, and accidents.	Includes the arts, religion, scholarship, communications media, sports, entertainments, fashions, fads and social life.

	World Affairs	Europe	Africa & the Middle East	The Americas	Asia & the Pacific
June 11		Italian Christian Democratic Pres. Amintore Fanfani declares that a CP victory would mean the progressive isolation of Italy.... Indian P.M. Indira Gandhi visits Moscow where she and Soviet CP Chmn. Leonid Brezhnev pledge continued friendship and cooperation between their two countries.		Bolivian Pres. Hugo Banzer Suarez visits mines occupied by striking workers and vows to raise miners' wages, while students at the metropolitan university in La Paz strike in solidarity with the miners.	South Korean opposition leader Kim Young Sam resigns following a ruling by the party's election committee that he was illegally reelected at a conference of a party faction.
June 12			All Iraqi reservists are ordered to report to their units as Iraqi troops mass near Syria.		
June 13		A senior Italian CP official, Giorgio Napolitano, says the CP has abandoned its proposal for a coalition with the Christian Democrats.		Ousted Bolivian Pres. Juan Bordaberry resumes management of his large cattle ranch outside of Montevideo, Chile.	
June 14		French legislators, responding to recent political violence, amend the Constitution so that a presidential election can be postponed if a candidate should die or withdraw during the campaign.	Syrian troops capture the Lebanese Arab Army garrison at Rasheiya after a week's siege.	Bolivian mineworkers begin an indefinite general strike in response to the arrest of mineworkers' leaders under the govt.'s state of siege.	Six members of Japan's ruling Liberal Democratic Party announce plans to form a new conservative political force to oppose Premier Takeo Miki and revitalize Japanese politics.
June 15		Rumanian Pres. Nicolae Ceausescu dismisses his defense minister and three other high officials in a major Cabinet shuffle.... Italian CP leader Enrico Berlinguer says his party intends to keep Italy in NATO and dismisses the risk of a Soviet-led invasion of Italy similar to the 1968 attack on Czechoslovakia.... P.M. James Callaghan assures Asian immigrants that the British govt. will protect them against the racial violence that has become increasingly widespread throughout the country.	Libyan Premier Abdel Salam Jalloud conducts separate mediation talks with all sides in Lebanon and he is reported saying that Syria is willing to make a phased withdrawal.	The first continuous flow of crude oil from western Canada arrives in Montreal through the new 520–mile pipeline extension from Ontario.	The Chinese Foreign Ministry announces that CP Chmn. Mao Tse-tung, 82, will no longer receive visits from foreign distinguished guests.
June 16	The U.N. Security Council approves a resolution renewing for another six months the mandate of the 2,900-man U.N. Force in Cyprus.	The Bank of England releases its quarterly bulletin giving the first authoritative explanation for the pound's decline. It cites pressures from OPEC members.... Leaders of Britain's Trades Union Congress, representing more than 10 million workers, vote to support the Labor govt.'s new pay restraint formula.	Francis Meloy Jr. the U.S. ambassador to Lebanon, and Robert Waring, his economic counselor, are kidnapped and shot to death.... The worst racial violence in South Africa's history breaks out in Soweto, a black township near Johannesburg.		A new presidential order permits the Indian govt. to detain political prisoners without trial or formal charges for up to two years.
June 17			Three Lebanese, arrested by Al Fatah security agents, confess to killing U.S. Amb. Francis Meloy Jr. and Robert Waring and will be turned over to an Arab League peacekeeping force.... The U.S. considers evacuating the remaining 1,400 Americans in Lebanon as State Secy. Kissinger says the U.S. "will not be driven off its course by violence."	The Canadian armed forces show photographs which spokesmen say demonstrate that the U.S.S.R. is occupying ice islands in the Arctic territory claimed by Canada.	

A	B	C	D	E
Includes developments that affect more than one world region, international organizations and important meetings of major world leaders.	Includes all domestic and regional developments in Europe, including the Soviet Union, Turkey, Cyprus and Malta.	Includes all domestic and regional developments in Africa and the Middle East, including Iraq and Iran and excluding Cyprus, Turkey and Afghanistan.	Includes all domestic and regional developments in Latin America, the Caribbean and Canada.	Includes all domestic and regional developments in Asia and Pacific nations, extending from Afghanistan through all the Pacific Islands, except Hawaii.

U.S. Politics & Social Issues	U.S. Foreign Policy & Defense	U.S. Economy & Environment	Science, Technology & Nature	Culture, Leisure & Life Style	
The New York Times reports charges by Colleen Gardner that Rep. John Young (D, Tex.) paid her a high salary as a secretary primarily to have sex with him.		Commerce Dept. sets a porpoise-kill limit for U.S. tuna fishermen of 78,000 for 1976.			June 11
The New York Times reports that authorities are probing Elizabeth Ray's charges that Rep. Kenneth Gray (D, Ill.) ordered her to have sex with Sen. Mike Gravel (D, Alaska) to get his backing on a bill.				Henry McDonald, first black pro football player, dies at the age of 85 in Geneva, N.Y.	June 12
Salt Lake City, Utah, police release transcripts of a conversation between Rep. Allan Turner Howe (D, Utah) and a policewoman posing as a decoy prostitute after Howe is arrested on the previous day on sex solicitation charges.				Hungarian pianist Geza Anda, famous for his performances of Bela Bartok's music, dies at the age of 54 in Zurich, Switzerland.	June 13
The Supreme Ct. declines to review, and so leaves effective, the lower ct. rulings that ordered extensive busing of students to achieve desegregation of Boston's schools. . . . Sen. Frank Church (D, Ida.) and Rep. Morris Udall (D, Utah) withdraw their candidacy for the Democratic presidential primary. Sen. Church endorses Carter. . . . Calif. Gov. Jerry Brown, resisting the Carter bandwagon, takes his case to N.Y. delegates and receives an enthusiastic response, if no delegates.	The court martial begins of S. Sgt. Harold Bronson, charged with manslaughter in the death of Pvt. Lynn McClure during Marine Corps combat training.			Jack Davis, a Bermuda businessman, is unanimously elected as 1977–78 president of Rotary International, after Wolfgang Wick, an ex-Nazi SS trooper withdraws his candidacy.	June 14
The Democratic platform committee adopts a platform with widespread support from all party factions that is said to reflect Carter's views. . . . The Agriculture Dept. proposed regulations to reduce food-stamp eligibility are held up by a temporary restraining order.			Center for Disease Control survey reveals a decrease in all adult American cigarette smoking from 1970–75 and an increasingly negative attitude toward smoking. . . . Parke-Davis & Co., one of the drug companies producing swine flu vaccine for the upcoming inoculation campaign, is reported to be on the verge of losing its liability insurance covering the project.	Oakland A's owner, Charles Finley, sells three star players — Vida Blue, Joe Rudi, and Rollie Fingers — for $3.5 million, just hours before baseball major league's midnight trading deadline.	June 15
Two Filipino nurses are charged with murdering five patients and poisoning 10 others at a VA hospital in Ann Arbor, Mich.		Frank Fitzsimmons is reelected to a five-year term as president of the Teamsters Union.		Benjamin Britten's *Phaedra* receives its premiere performance by the English Chamber Orchestra and soprano Janet Baker in Aldeburgh, England.	June 16
				Eighteen teams of the NBA merge with four of the six remaining ABA teams.	June 17

F	G	H	I	J
Includes elections, federal-state relations, civil rights and liberties, crime, the judiciary, education, health care, poverty, urban affairs and population.	Includes formation and debate of U.S. foreign and defense policies, veterans' affairs and defense spending. (Relations with specific foreign countries are usually found under the region concerned.)	Includes business, labor, agriculture, taxation, transportation, consumer affairs, monetary and fiscal policy, natural resources, and pollution.	Includes worldwide scientific, medical and technological developments, natural phenomena, U.S. weather, natural disasters, and accidents.	Includes the arts, religion, scholarship, communications media, sports, entertainments, fashions, fads and social life.

	World Affairs	Europe	Africa & the Middle East	The Americas	Asia & the Pacific
June 18	The U.N. ILO unanimously adopts a program aimed at creating tens of thousands of new jobs, largely in the developing countries, by the year 2000.		South Africa P.M. John Vorster, making his first public statement on the racial violence in Soweto, says, "there is definitely no reason for any panic." However, he places the army on alert.	OAS Gen. Assembly, meeting in Chile, passes a compromise resolution urging Chile to continue adopting measures to guarantee human rights. . . . Jamaican delegate Patricia Durrant denounces the OAS resolution as too mild, in wake of reports of widespread torture and other human-rights abuses in Chile.	
June 19	The U.N. Committee on the Exercise of the Inalienable Rights of the Palestinian People adopts a series of recommendations supporting the Palestinians' "right to return". . . . The U.N. Security Council adopts a resolution strongly condemning the South African govt. for its use of massive violence against black Africans.	Syrian Pres. Hafez al-Assad and French Pres. Valery Giscard d'Estaing meet and confirm the French offer to facilitate a round table among the diverse Lebanese components.	The Ethiopian govt. officially halts the advance by tens of thousands of Christian peasants toward the Moslem province of Eritrea.	Jamaican govt. declares a state of emergency after six months of political violence resulting in over 100 deaths.	
June 20		Turkish Cypriots elect Rauf Denktash as president of the Turkish Federated State of Cyprus, but the Greek Cypriot majority does not recognize the elections as valid. . . . Italian Christian Democrats' power is seen threatened by the country's Communist Party as general elections begin.	The Iranian govt. plans to buy $125 million worth of shares in Occidental Petroleum Corp. in a series of joint ventures with the company. . . . The U.S. Navy evacuates 110 Americans and 166 persons from 25 other countries from Beirut, and the U.S. Embassy has strongly urged all remaining U.S. citizens to leave.	Canadian airline pilots strike in support of air-traffic controllers, who have threatened to strike over the issue of bilingualism in air-traffic control.	
June 21	State Secy. Kissinger addresses the annual ministerial meeting of the OECD and endorses its code on multinational corporations.	Enrico Berlinguer, Italian CP leader, says the "era when governments could govern with an anti-Communist bias is over."	The Saharan independence movement, the Polisario Front, confirms the death of Sayed el- Wali, the front's secretary general but does not explain the circumstances of his death. . . . The vanguard of an Arab League peacekeeping force arrives in Lebanon from Damascus to implement the League's plan to help end the fighting in Lebanon. . . . The U.S., through a third party, thanks Al Fatah, the Palestinian guerrilla group, for providing escorts for the civilians assembling on the Beirut beach preparatory to evacuation. . . . Rioting leaves at least 10 people dead in Mabopane, Pretoria's largest black township, 20 miles north of the South African capital, and in two other townships. . . . South African commissioner of police, Gen. Gert Prinsloo, discloses that 128 persons were killed and 1,112 injured in the rioting last week in Johannesburg's black townships.		
June 22		The Italian CP makes major gains in parliamentary and municipal govt. elections, placing in doubt the ability of the Christian Democrats to continue governing alone.	With the Christians on the offensive, Lebanese fighting resumes around Beirut, Palestinian refugee camps, and the Moslem quarter.		Tokyo police arrest four persons in connection with the Lockheed scandal in Japan.

A	B	C	D	E
Includes developments that affect more than one world region, international organizations and important meetings of major world leaders.	Includes all domestic and regional developments in Europe, including the Soviet Union, Turkey, Cyprus and Malta.	Includes all domestic and regional developments in Africa and the Middle East, including Iraq and Iran and excluding Cyprus, Turkey and Afghanistan.	Includes all domestic and regional developments in Latin America, the Caribbean and Canada.	Includes all domestic and regional developments in Asia and Pacific nations, extending from Afghanistan through all the Pacific Islands, except Hawaii.

U.S. Politics & Social Issues	U.S. Foreign Policy & Defense	U.S. Economy & Environment	Science, Technology & Nature	Culture, Leisure & Life Style	
Pres. Ford cancels an election campaign trip to Iowa to oversee evacuation of U.S. citizens from Lebanon.				Baseball Comr. Bowie Kuhn nullifies the sales, largest in Baseball history, of three Oakland A's stars, saying they were not consistent with the best interests of baseball.	June 18
Senators Jacob Javits (R, N.Y.) and Edward Brooke (R, Mass.) release federal statistics showing a slight decline in the segregation of black schoolchildren in the 1970s balanced by a slight increase in the segregation of Spanish-surnamed children. . . . School integration efforts in the South and in border states during the 1970s are reported to far exceed those in the North and Middle West. . . . Ronald Reagan gains 16 delegates over Pres. Ford, the result of state and district conventions in five states.					June 19
				U.S. Open golf tournament is won in an upset by golf rookie Jerry Pate, who beat Tom Weiskopf and Al Geiberger by two strokes.	June 20
John Adamson, a racing-dog owner and two-truck operator, is charged with murdering *Arizona Dispatch* reporter Don Bolles.		Striking editorial employes vote to end their 20-day walkout against Time Inc. and to accept in essence the contract offered just before the strike began.			June 21
		The Labor Dept. announces the government's index of consumer prices rose a seasonally adjusted .6 percent in May, the largest increase in six months.			June 22

F	G	H	I	J
Includes elections, federal-state relations, civil rights and liberties, crime, the judiciary, education, health care, poverty, urban affairs and population.	*Includes formation and debate of U.S. foreign and defense policies, veterans' affairs and defense spending. (Relations with specific foreign countries are usually found under the region concerned.)*	*Includes business, labor, agriculture, taxation, transportation, consumer affairs, monetary and fiscal policy, natural resources, and pollution.*	*Includes worldwide scientific, medical and technological developments, natural phenomena, U.S. weather, natural disasters, and accidents.*	*Includes the arts, religion, scholarship, communications media, sports, entertainments, fashions, fads and social life.*

	World Affairs	Europe	Africa & the Middle East	The Americas	Asia & the Pacific
June 23	In a Security Council vote, the U.S. vetoes Angola's application for U.N. membership, saying that Angola fails to meet the membership requirements of being an independent state.	Members of West Germany's Maoist Communist Party and its neo-Nazi National Democratic Party demonstrate, protesting the talks between U.S. State Secy. Kissinger and South African P.M. John Vorster.	Syria and Egypt hold a long-delayed meeting to discuss the major issues dividing the two countries, in an effort to restore political and military cooperation.	Canadian P.M. Pierre Trudeau asks pilots and controllers to work with the government in devising bilingual procedures for air traffic.	
June 24		French Pres. Valery Giscard d'Estaing ends a three-day visit to Great Britain, after agreeing with British P.M. James Callaghan to meet annually.	South African P.M. John Voster and U.S. State Secy. Kissinger talk on the southern Africa situation, the first such high-level meeting since WWII.... Rhodesian Min. of Law and Order Hilary Squires announces a renewal of the state of emergency, citing increased guerrilla warfare, continuing U.N. sanctions, and other factors.		Manila officially replaces adjacent Quezon City as the capital of the Philippines.
June 25		Yugoslavia Pres. Tito plans to attend the June 29 meeting of East and West European Communist Party leaders in Berlin, thus ending a 19-year Yugoslav boycott of international communist conferences.... Michele Sindona, an Italian financier reportedly living in the U.S., is found guilty in Milan of bank fraud and conflict-of-interest involving the collapse of his bank and is sentenced in absentia.... Polish workers stage violent demonstrations and strikes in response to a government plan to drastically increase food prices.	South African Justice Min. James Kruger says the official casualty toll following five days of rioting about the use of the Afrikaans language in black township schools is 176 killed, 1,139 wounded. He charges that the riots were organized by the black movement.... Ugandan Pres. Idi Amin is proclaimed president for life by the Defense Council, the government ruling body since Amin's takeover in 1971.	Cesar Augusto Salinas, Sandinista chief in northern Nicaragua, is killed in a clash with National Guard troops.... Argentinean Finance Min. Jose de Martinez Hoz announces that he has renegotiated payment of Argentina's $9-billion foreign debt.	
June 26				The death penalty is restored to the Argentine penal code by government decree.	
June 27		Portuguese Gen. Antonio Ramalho Eanes, the army chief of staff, wins a landslide victory in Portugal's presidential election.	Intense fighting rages around Lebanese refugee camps and across the Christian–Moslem confrontation line in Beirut. More than 200 persons are killed and 300 wounded in 24 hours.... Seven pro-Palestinian guerrillas hijack an Air France plane carrying 270 on a flight from Tel Aviv to Paris. The pilot is forced to refuel in Libya and then fly to Uganda.		
June 28	In an economic summit meeting in Puerto Rico, the leaders of seven industrialized nations agree to adopt a go-slow policy of economic growth to solve their shared problems of inflation and unemployment.	Jordan's King Hussein visits Moscow to discuss the Middle East crisis, but there is no mention of possible purchases of Soviet arms in the joint communique at the end of the talks.	Negotiators in Uganda persuade the Palestinian hijackers to let the passengers and crew leave the Air France plane and rest in a transit lounge at Entebbe Airport where they remain under their captors' control, awaiting further developments.... The Seychelle Islands in the Indian Ocean off the African coast become an independant republic, ending more than 160 years of British colonial rule. ... An American and three Britons who fought as mercenaries for a defeated faction in the Angolan civil war are sentenced to death by firing squad.	A nine-day strike by Canadian airline pilots ends when the government says it will reexamine plans to increase the use of the French language at airports in Quebec.... Jean Marchand, Canadian environment minister and a close political associate of P.M. Pierre Trudeau, resigns in protest against the terms of the strike agreement with pilots and air controllers.	

A	B	C	D	E
Includes developments that affect more than one world region, international organizations and important meetings of major world leaders.	*Includes all domestic and regional developments in Europe, including the Soviet Union, Turkey, Cyprus and Malta.*	*Includes all domestic and regional developments in Africa and the Middle East, including Iraq and Iran and excluding Cyprus, Turkey and Afghanistan.*	*Includes all domestic and regional developments in Latin America, the Caribbean and Canada.*	*Includes all domestic and regional developments in Asia and Pacific nations, extending from Afghanistan through all the Pacific Islands, except Hawaii.*

U.S. Politics & Social Issues	U.S. Foreign Policy & Defense	U.S. Economy & Environment	Science, Technology & Nature	Culture, Leisure & Life Style	
N.J. Teamster Union official Anthony (Tony Pro) Provenzano, and three others, are indicted on charges involving the kidnap-slaying of a Teamster official in 1961.	Jimmy Carter criticizes the "secretive" and "amoral" foreign policies of the Ford administration and characterizes State Secy. Kissinger as a "Lone Ranger" pursuing a "one-man policy of international adventure."	A large barge running aground in the St. Lawrence Seaway spills more than 300,000 gallons of oil, which spread 30 miles downstream.	N.Y.S. Gov. Hugh Carey declares two of the state's counties, Nassau and Suffolk, disaster areas due to the raw sewage and other contaminants that washed up on a 70-mile stretch of beaches on the Long Island south shore.... The National Institutes of Health (NIH) issues guidelines banning certain forms of genetic experimentation and strongly regulating others in wake of years of debate about potential hazards.		June 23
The Justice Dept. begins an investigation of illegal burglaries alleged to have been carried out by the FBI. ... Pres. Ford submits to Congress his proposed curbs on court-ordered busing to desegregate schools. Roy Wilkins, executive director of the NAACP, denounces the proposals.		The Supreme Ct. holds, 5–4, that federal minimum-wage laws are not binding on state and local governments, reversing a 1968 decision.		Joseph Papp's New York Shakespeare Festival opens in Central Park, N.Y.C., with *Henry V*, featuring Paul Rudd and Meryl Streep. ... Imogen Cunningham, 93, a distinguished American photographer for 75 years, dies in San Francisco.	June 24
The New York Times reports an FBI source said that FBI agents had anonymously kidnapped a radical political activist within the past five years to disrupt his activities.... Maurice Nadjari is dismissed from his post as special N.Y.S. prosecutor investigating N.Y.C.'s criminal-justice system in wake of much criticism of his methods and a N.Y.S. Appeals Ct. ruling on June 3 limiting his jurisdiction to criminal, not civil, justice.... The Supreme Ct. rules, 7–2, against discrimination by private nonsectarian schools, holding that denial of entry to black children is not protected by the right of free association.	State Secy. Kissinger makes a major foreign-policy statement in London on Western European cooperation and East–West relations, emphasizing the importance of European unity.	The Supreme Ct. affirms, 7–1, the right of a state to set a mandatory retirement age for its employes, provided the age is related to the duties of the job.		Alfred Friendly Jr, a Moscow correspondent for *Newsweek*, sues the Soviet weekly *Literaturnaya Gazeta* over an article that accused him of being a CIA agent. ... Johnny Mercer, 66, singer and composer of 75 hit songs of which four won Academy Awards, dies in Calif.	June 25
Pres. Ford wins 17 of 18 delegates in Minn., leaving him 90 delegates short of the nomination. Reagan trails Ford by 50 delegates.			Two devastating earthquakes, measuring 7.1 and 5.6 on the Richter scale, strike two widely distant parts of Indonesia, killing 1,000 people.	Most of the 16 tall ships scheduled for the U.S. Bicentennial Operation Sail on Independence Day arrive in Newport, R.I.	June 26
				Prince Stanislas Radziwill, 62, former husband of Jacqueline Onassis' younger sister Lee Bouvier, dies of a heart attack in London.	June 27
The Supreme Ct. rules that public employes may not be fired because of political beliefs but restricts the ruling to employes not in policy-making jobs or confidential advisory positions.	S.Sgt. Harold Bronson, one of three soldiers charged in the training-camp death of Marine recruit Pvt. Lynn McClure, is acquitted after a court-martial.	The Supreme Ct. approves strip mining of coal in Wyoming, Montana, and North and South Dakota, rejecting a request by the Sierra Club for a delay until a regional environmental impact study is completed.... The Commerce Dept. announces that in May the U.S. posted its first trade surplus in five months, which showed that exports exceeded imports by a seasonally adjusted $395.6 million.			June 28

F	G	H	I	J
Includes elections, federal-state relations, civil rights and liberties, crime, the judiciary, education, health care, poverty, urban affairs and population.	*Includes formation and debate of U.S. foreign and defense policies, veterans' affairs and defense spending. (Relations with specific foreign countries are usually found under the region concerned.)*	*Includes business, labor, agriculture, taxation, transportation, consumer affairs, monetary and fiscal policy, natural resources, and pollution.*	*Includes worldwide scientific, medical and technological developments, natural phenomena, U.S. weather, natural disasters, and accidents.*	*Includes the arts, religion, scholarship, communications media, sports, entertainments, fashions, fads and social life.*

	World Affairs	Europe	Africa & the Middle East	The Americas	Asia & the Pacific
June 29	The U.S. vetoes a U.N. Security Council resolution calling on Israel to withdraw from occupied Arab lands. The vote is 10–1, with Britain, France, Italy, and Sweden abstaining.	Soviet leader Leonid Brezhnev delivers the keynote speech to the opening meeting of 29 East and West European CP leaders and sets a conciliatory tone toward European Communist parties seeking to stay clear of Soviet influence.	Hijackers of the Air France plane, now held at Entebbe Airport in Uganda, reveal their threat to kill its hostage passengers and blow up the plane if 53 Palestinian terrorists are not released from prisons in Israel and four other countries by July 1. . . . Libyan Premier Abdel Salam Jalloud, who had been trying to mediate the Lebanese conflict, announces he is going home to escalate Libyan support for the Palestinians and their Lebanese allies.	Jamaican P.M. Michael Manley charges that there is evidence of a terrorist plot against his government.	
June 30		Twenty-nine East and West CP leaders conclude their two-day meeting in Berlin by rebuffing the Soviet role as the center of communism and endorsing each party's right to seek its own means of socialism.	Ugandan Pres. Idi Amin appeals to Israel, France, West Germany, Kenya, and Switzerland to free their Palestinian prisoners as demanded by the hijackers of the Air France plane now held at Entebbe Airport. . . . Israel's District Ct. nullifies a magistrate ct's decision on prayer rights on the Temple Mount in the Old City, in wake of the controversy-sparked Arab riots in March.	The British Columbia Ct. of Appeals rules, 3–2, that the provincial govt. owns the land and mineral resources on the ocean floor between Vancouver Island and the mainland.	The U.S. closes its last two major military installations in Thailand.
July 1		British Petroleum Co. Ltd. and its largest shareholder, the British govt., agree that the state-owned British National Oil Corp. will obtain a 51 percent interest in BP's North Sea oil fields.	Reversing its policy of refusing to deal with Arab hijackers, Israel says it is prepared to negotiate the Entebbe operation and is ready to release an unspecified number of Arab detainees.	The Peru govt. declares a nationwide state of emergency after students and workers riot in Lima to protest a new set of economic austerity measures.	
July 2			Christian forces overrun the outer defenses of Tel Zaatar, a Palestinian refugee camp in Beirut. . . . The OAU thirteenth annual summit meeting opens in Port Louis, Mauritius, and its chairman, Ugandan Pres. Idi Amin, turns his duties over to his successor, Sir Seewoosagur Ramgoolam, Mauritius prime minister.		North and South Vietnam are officially reunited after 22 years of separation. Hanoi is declared the capital of the new country, now known as the Socialist Republic of Vietnam. . . . Japanese police arrest two more persons in connection with the Lockheed scandal.
July 3		In a suprise move, King Juan Carlos of Spain dismisses Premier Carlos Arias Navarro and replaces him with Adolfo Suarez Gonzalez, the Cabinet minister in charge of the National Movement, a close associate of the king's and considered more sympathetic to instigating the democratic reforms the king seeks.	Morocco and Mauritania threaten to withdraw from the OAU unless all discussions about the Western Saharan region, which is partitioned between them, are ended immediately. . . . Israeli commandos land at Uganda's Entebbe Airport and rescue 103 passengers and crew of the Air France hijacked plane. Thirty-one people die, including all seven hijackers, 20 Ugandan soldiers, and three Israeli hostages.		

A	B	C	D	E
Includes developments that affect more than one world region, international organizations and important meetings of major world leaders.	*Includes all domestic and regional developments in Europe, including the Soviet Union, Turkey, Cyprus and Malta.*	*Includes all domestic and regional developments in Africa and the Middle East, including Iraq and Iran and excluding Cyprus, Turkey and Afghanistan.*	*Includes all domestic and regional developments in Latin America, the Caribbean and Canada.*	*Includes all domestic and regional developments in Asia and Pacific nations, extending from Afghanistan through all the Pacific Islands, except Hawaii.*

U.S. Politics & Social Issues	U.S. Foreign Policy & Defense	U.S. Economy & Environment	Science, Technology & Nature	Culture, Leisure & Life Style	
The Supreme Ct. upholds, 6–3, provisions of the Social Security Act that make it more difficult for illegitimate children to obtain survivor's benefits on a parent's death.	Warrant Officer Jennie Vallance, the first woman graduate of the U.S. Army's Helicopter Flight School, says she is resigning from the Army, charging sex discrimination.			Jimmy Connors, the 1974 Wimbledon champion and the betting favorite, is defeated by Roscoe Tanner in the Wimbledon semifinals, 6–4, 6–2, 8–6.	June 29
The Supreme Ct. unanimously voids a Nebraska judge's order barring pre-trial news coverage of a mass-murder case.... Sen. Barry Goldwater (R, Ariz.), the unsuccessful GOP presidential nominee in 1964, endorses Pres. Ford for the Republican presidential nomination.... FBI Dir. Clarence Kelley admits that the FBI carried out a limited number of break-ins in 1972 and 1973, targeted against radical groups.	Pres. Ford signs a bill authorizing $6.9 billion in foreign military aid for fiscal 1976–77. The bill expands Congress's role in the oversight of foreign-arms aid and sales.	The Senate gives final congressional approval and Pres. Ford signs a bill raising the temporary ceiling on the federal debt to $700 billion through Sept. 30, 1977.		The first live television broadcast of a full-length ballet occurs when *Swan Lake* is performed by the American Ballet Theater at Lincoln Center (N.Y.C.).	June 30
The House sets up a commission to study congressional accounting and personnel practices and also strips the Administration Committee of its power to unilaterally alter members' benefits and allowances.... The Supreme Ct. rules that in abortion cases a woman cannot be required to obtain her husband's consent and under-18-year-olds cannot be absolutely required to have parental consent.... Mayor Kenneth Gibson of Newark, N.J. becomes the first black president of the U.S. Conference of Mayors, succeeding Mayor Moon Landrieu of New Orleans.		The Supreme Ct. upholds a federal law requiring coal-mine operators to pay benefits to miners suffering from black-lung disease.			July 1
The Supreme Ct. affirms, in a landmark 7–2 ruling, that the death penalty for murder convictions does not violate the Constitution's ban on 'cruel and unusual' punishment. ... The NAACP's bd. of directors votes to postpone until September its decision on whether its director Roy Wilkins, 74, will be forced to retire at the end of the year.	Pres. Ford vetoes a bill authorizing $3.324 billion for military construction in fiscal 1977.	The Labor Dept. announces unemployment increased to 7.5 percent during June, compared with 7.3 percent in May, but blames the increase on statistical quirks.		A 76-hour vigil begins at the National Archives, Wash., D.C. to honor the signing of the Declaration of Independence.	July 2
		Pres. Ford vetoes legislation that revised regulations covering the leasing of federally owned coal lands and increased states' shares of the royalties derived.		Bjorn Borg, a 20-year-old Swede, becomes the youngest Wimbledon champion in 45 years, when he wins the men's singles title by defeating favored Ilie Nastase.	July 3

F	G	H	I	J
Includes elections, federal-state relations, civil rights and liberties, crime, the judiciary, education, health care, poverty, urban affairs and population.	Includes formation and debate of U.S. foreign and defense policies, veterans' affairs and defense spending. (Relations with specific foreign countries are usually found under the region concerned.)	Includes business, labor, agriculture, taxation, transportation, consumer affairs, monetary and fiscal policy, natural resources, and pollution.	Includes worldwide scientific, medical and technological developments, natural phenomena, U.S. weather, natural disasters, and accidents.	Includes the arts, religion, scholarship, communications media, sports, entertainments, fashions, fads and social life.

	World Affairs	Europe	Africa & the Middle East	The Americas	Asia & the Pacific
July 4			French officials and previously released hostages of the hijacked Air France plane say they have substantial proof of Ugandan cooperation with the hijackers.... A Sudanese newspaper reports 300 persons were killed and 300 wounded when dissident Sudanese army elements were defeated during an attempt to overthrow the government.	Jose Lopez Portillo, candidate of Mexico's ruling Institutional Revolutionary Party, wins a landslide victory in the presidential election.	
July 5		The French Socialist Party praises the Israeli Entebbe operation, but the CP newspaper *L'Humanité* assails it as unjustifiable.... British P.M. James Callaghan tours Belfast in his first visit to the area since becoming prime minister and pledges that Northern Ireland will remain part of the U.K.... Employes of *France-Soir*, the largest-selling Parisian newspaper, are told it is being sold to a publishing firm headed by Paul Winkler.... Peitro Ingrao is elected speaker of the Italian Chamber of Deputies, giving the Communist Party its most important parliamentary role since the republic was created 30 years ago.	Israeli officials say the Popular Front for the Liberation of Palestine lost key operatives in the Israeli attack at Entebbe Airport. ... Ugandan Pres. Idi Amin threatens to retaliate for the Israeli raid on Entebbe Airport.		
July 6		French Pres. Valery Giscard d'Estaing meets in Hamburg with West German Chancellor Helmut Schmidt under terms of a treaty of friendship and cooperation.	The OAU summit conference ends after passing a resolution prohibiting all OAU member states from recognizing the independence of Transkei or any other South African Bantustans.... A Libyan Arab Airlines plane is hijacked and diverted to Majorca after being refused permission to land in Tunisia and Algeria. The hijacker surrenders without a struggle.... The South African govt. revokes a law requiring the use of the Afrikaans language as a teaching medium in black township schools after the issue caused five days of riots.	Venezuela suspends diplomatic relations with Uruguay a week after alleged Uruguayan officers invaded the grounds of the Venezuela Embassy and abducted a Uruguayan woman.... The *London Times* says at least 150 persons were killed from June 1 to July 5 in Argentina as political violence increased throughout the country, leaving the political death toll to date at over 600.	Chu Teh, 90, China's most famous military leader in modern times and the head of China's Parliament, dies. He led the Communist armies during the long March of 1934–35.
July 7		British M.P. David Steel is elected as leader of the Liberal Party, taking over from Jo Grimond, who served in an interim capacity for two months.... An agreement between Paris newspaper owners and printers' unions is announced, ending a situation that kept newsstands virtually empty seven times last year.... Austria's Parliament approves a bill allowing minority groups to use their own languages in government, schools and business, and on signposts.			
July 8		A new Spanish Cabinet takes office with a mandate from King Juan Carlos to continue his reform program and to organize parliamentary elections for the spring of 1977.		Julio Scherer Garcia, liberal head of Mexico's leading newspaper, *Excelsior*, is ousted by a minority of conservative employees.	Seoul Church sources say 18 Christian missionaries arrested in South Korea on suspicion of pro-Communist activities have been released after they promised not to work among slum dwellers.... John Hodges, the chairman of an Australian House subcommittee, reveals the existence of a multimillion-dollar smuggling ring in remote areas of the northern part of the country.

A	B	C	D	E
Includes developments that affect more than one world region, international organizations and important meetings of major world leaders.	Includes all domestic and regional developments in Europe, including the Soviet Union, Turkey, Cyprus and Malta.	Includes all domestic and regional developments in Africa and the Middle East, including Iraq and Iran and excluding Cyprus, Turkey and Afghanistan.	Includes all domestic and regional developments in Latin America, the Caribbean and Canada.	Includes all domestic and regional developments in Asia and Pacific nations, extending from Afghanistan through all the Pacific Islands, except Hawaii.

U.S. Politics & Social Issues	U.S. Foreign Policy & Defense	U.S. Economy & Environment	Science, Technology & Nature	Culture, Leisure & Life Style	
	A military helicopter patrol finds 26 wild horses dead or near death next to a waterhold on the Dugway Proving Ground (Utah). They showed no symptoms of any known disease, although the base is a testing ground for chemical weapons.			The U.S. celebrates its Bicentennial with parades and festivities as 6 million gather in N.Y.C. to watch a flotilla of sailing ships known as Operation Sail.... In Boston an estimated crowd of 400,000 gather on the Esplanade to hear Arthur Fiedler conduct the Boston Pops Orchestra and see a fireworks display.... The works of 10 U.S. sculptors are unveiled along a 455-mile stretch of Interstate 80 in Nebraska.	July 4
Supreme Ct. Justice Thurgood Marshall enters a hospital after experiencing a mild heart disturbance.		According to a report published by the Public Interest Research Group, a Ralph Nader organization, the U.S. banking industry has been weakened significantly by the expansion of banks into nonbanking fields.			July 5
The Supreme Ct. holds that federal cts. cannot set aside a state conviction because of illegally obtained evidence if the defendant could have appealed the issue in the state ct.... The National Governors Conference's major recommendation is a national welfare program with a minimum level of payment.... Ronald Reagan assails both Pres. Ford and Jimmy Carter in a 30-minute, paid television telecast and directs an appeal to the white ethnic voter, saying "you are a victim of reverse discrimination."			The federal ban on Red No. 2 Dye is upheld by the U.S. Ct. of Appeals in Washington, D.C.	Great Britain's Queen Elizabeth II arrives in Philadelphia to begin a six-day visit to the U.S. and presents a bell, cast in the same foundry as the Liberty Bell, as a Bicentennial gift.... At its summit conference, the OAU asks member nations to consider boycotting the Olympic games if New Zealand, which had played rugby with South Africa, is allowed to participate.	July 6
Pres. Ford suspends an HEW ruling banning father–son or mother–daughter school events, which was based on Title IX of the 1972 educational amendments against discrimination.	According to a New York Times interview, Jimmy Carter expects foreign policy to be a major issue in the presidential campaign.	A strike by the National Union of Hospital and Health Care Employees begins against 33 private non-profit hospitals in N.Y.C.	The Cambridge (Mass). City Council votes to establish a three-month moratorium on DNA research at Harvard University, where plans have been approved for a genetics research lab.		July 7
Former Pres. Nixon is ordered disbarred in N.Y.S., effective August 9, after charges are brought by the Association of the Bar of the City of New York.		N.J. becomes the forty-third state in the nation to enact a personal income tax bill, thus ending a legal dispute over the financing of the state's public schools.... Pres. Ford signs a bill authorizing $35 million in both fiscal 1977 and 1978 for federal railroad safety programs, although he has opposed the measure as not in the executive or congressional sphere.		Patricia Nixon, wife of former Pres. Nixon, enters a hospital after suffering a stroke.	July 8

F	G	H	I	J
Includes elections, federal-state relations, civil rights and liberties, crime, the judiciary, education, health care, poverty, urban affairs and population.	Includes formation and debate of U.S. foreign and defense policies, veterans' affairs and defense spending. (Relations with specific foreign countries are usually found under the region concerned.)	Includes business, labor, agriculture, taxation, transportation, consumer affairs, monetary and fiscal policy, natural resources, and pollution.	Includes worldwide scientific, medical and technological developments, natural phenomena, U.S. weather, natural disasters, and accidents.	Includes the arts, religion, scholarship, communications media, sports, entertainments, fashions, fads and social life.

	World Affairs	Europe	Africa & the Middle East	The Americas	Asia & the Pacific
July 9		Italian Premier Aldo Moro resigns in a move designed to enable Italy to form a new government following the June 20–21 national elections.... A new witness in the investigation of the death of Greek opposition party M.P. Alexandros Panagoulis tells the Athens magistrate that the legislator's fatal car crash was not an accident, but that he was killed by a right-wing group.		Canadian P.M. Pierre Trudeau, in a nationwide broadcast, urges Canadians to renew their commitment to bilingualism.	All Nippon Airways v.p. Naoje Watanabe is arrested on charges of having lied when he told an investigating committee that he never received $170,200 of Lockheed payoffs.
July 10		The Rome state prosecutor, Vittorio Occorsio, is shot dead by three men with submachine guns outside his home almost one month to the day that the Genoa state prosecutor was fatally shot.	Four mercenaries, condemned to death for their part in the Angolan civil war, are executed by firing squad in Luanda.... Damascus radio reports that 3,866 persons were killed in the previous three days of Lebanese fighting. The death toll in 16 months of civil war is estimated at 32,000.... At least 13 are killed and 50 injured in clashes between rival tribesmen in Djibouti, capital of the French Territory of the Afars & Issas.	Argentinian air force Vice Commodore Roberto Echegoyen is presumably killed by ERP guerrillas, who had kidnapped him in April, during an Argentinian army raid on a ERP hideout in suburban Buenos Aires.	
July 11		A Madrid newspaper columnist charges that three ministers of the new Spanish Cabinet telephoned newspapers to interfere in the publication of articles although censorship had been abolished in 1968.	Kamal Jumblat, head of the Moslem-Lebanese leftist alliance, asks Saudi Arabia, Algeria, Libya, Iraq, and Egypt for military and political intervention against the Syrian forces in Lebanon.		The ashes of Chu Teh are buried in Peking after laying in state at the Workers' Cultural Palace.
July 12	OECD statistics show that the per capita income of Americans for 1975 ranks third behind that of Switzerland and Sweden.	The European Council, composed of the heads of government of the European Community, agrees on the distribution of seats for the new 410-member European Parliament. ... The British Parliament is told that a hijacking hostage holding British and Israeli citizenship, who disappeared from a Ugandan hospital after the Entebbe Airport raid, is thought to have been killed.	Right-wing Christian forces are reported to be in the outskirts of leftist-held Tripoli in their advance against combined Palestinian and Lebanese forces.	The bishops' council of the Paraguayan Roman Catholic Church accuses the government of a wide range of abuses of priests and other Paraguayans.... The Canadian Supreme Ct. rules, 7–2, that the federal govt.'s antiinflation program is legal and was correctly imposed under the Constitution.	Vietnam agrees to establish diplomatic relations with the Philippines.
July 13	Representatives of 58 developing countries, meeting in New Delhi, India, vote to pool their news agencies to replace reports made by Western agencies.	The Austrian central bank allows the schilling to float freely against the U.S. dollar, and its value moves quickly upward against both the dollar and the mark.... Italian Pres. Giovanni Leone accepts Premier Aldo Moro's resignation and appoints Giulio Andreotti, the budget minister in the outgoing government, to succeed Moro.... The Polish govt. announces a 35 percent rise in meat prices two weeks after proposed food price increases incited workers' riots.			

A	B	C	D	E
Includes developments that affect more than one world region, international organizations and important meetings of major world leaders.	Includes all domestic and regional developments in Europe, including the Soviet Union, Turkey, Cyprus and Malta.	Includes all domestic and regional developments in Africa and the Middle East, including Iraq and Iran and excluding Cyprus, Turkey and Afghanistan.	Includes all domestic and regional developments in Latin America, the Caribbean and Canada.	Includes all domestic and regional developments in Asia and Pacific nations, extending from Afghanistan through all the Pacific Islands, except Hawaii.

U.S. Politics & Social Issues	U.S. Foreign Policy & Defense	U.S. Economy & Environment	Science, Technology & Nature	Culture, Leisure & Life Style	
Pres. Ford says he considers Ronald Reagan qualified to be President and tempers his previous harsh criticism of Reagan by saying that in a controversial campaign you make a point with "political license."		The FRB announces that consumer installment credit expanded a seasonally adjusted $1.48 billion in May, the largest increase since December 1975. . . . Aluminum Company of America (ALCOA) discloses that between 1970 and 1972 it had made $80,000 in illegal payments abroad and that its foreign subsidiaries had made nearly $270,000 in payments.	London *Financial Times* reports three new oil and gas finds in the North Sea, including one believed to contain major reserves. . . . The National Institute of Drug Abuse reports that alcohol and Valium were responsible for the greatest number of drug-related illnesses from April 1974 to April 1975.	Tanzania announces it won't attend the Olympics because New Zealand, a participant, sent its national rugby team on a tour of South Africa.	July 9
					July 10
Jimmy Carter says that he will select his running mate from a final list of seven men, six of whom are U.S. senators. The list includes Walter Mondale (Minn.), Frank Church (Ida.), Adlai Stevenson (Ill.), John Glenn (Ohio), Henry Jackson (Wash.), and Edmund Muskie (Me.).		The Commerce Dept. says per-capita disposable income in the U.S. rose 140 percent between 1960 and 1974. Adjusted for inflation, the real disposable income rose 45–50 percent.		Singer Frank Sinatra is married to Barbara Marx, a former showgirl and ex-wife of Zeppo Marx.	July 11
A 24-hour general strike is called by the Australian Council of Trade Unions to protest scheduled changes in the national health scheme. . . . Jimmy Carter meets with National Women's Political Caucus representatives, gives full support to the Equal Rights Amendment, and promises to appoint women to Cabinet, ambassadorial, and judicial posts. . . . Rep. Barbara Jordan (Tex.) becomes the first black and first woman to deliver a Democratic Nat. Convention keynote speech, with a stirring call for a national community where "all of us are equal."		The AFL–CIO International Brotherhood of Electrical Workers (IBEW) initiates a national strike against Westinghouse Electric Corp.		James Wong Howe, 76, Academy Award-winning cinemaphotographer, dies in Hollywood. . . . Pres. Ford telephones Philip Krumm, U.S. Olympic Committee head, to deplore the injection of politics into the Olympic competition and to denounce efforts to bar Taiwan.	July 12
				Baseball's National League team beats the American League team, 7–1, in the All-Star game, pushing its winning streak to five straight and 13 of the last 14.	July 13

F	G	H	I	J
Includes elections, federal-state relations, civil rights and liberties, crime, the judiciary, education, health care, poverty, urban affairs and population.	*Includes formation and debate of U.S. foreign and defense policies, veterans' affairs and defense spending. (Relations with specific foreign countries are usually found under the region concerned.)*	*Includes business, labor, agriculture, taxation, transportation, consumer affairs, monetary and fiscal policy, natural resources, and pollution.*	*Includes worldwide scientific, medical and technological developments, natural phenomena, U.S. weather, natural disasters, and accidents.*	*Includes the arts, religion, scholarship, communications media, sports, entertainments, fashions, fads and social life.*

	World Affairs	Europe	Africa & the Middle East	The Americas	Asia & the Pacific
July 14	The IMF sells 780,000 ounces of gold at $122.05 an ounce, a price decline from the first auction price of $126, bringing in $95.2 million. . . . The U.N. Security Council inconclusively ends its debate on the Israeli Entebbe Airport raid.	Gen. Antonio Ramalho Eanes assumes the presidency of Portugal and vows to eliminate a climate of coups and anarchy.		The Canadian House of Commons abolishes capital punishment for all but traitorous military offenses and awaits Senate approval. . . . The Argentinian Roman Catholic Episcopal Conference expresses concern over the political violence in the country. . . . The ruling Nat. Council choses Aparicio Mendez to be Uruguay's new president, succeeding Alberto Demicheli, who was interim president after the army overthrew Pres. Juan Bordaberry.	
July 15	*The New York Times* quotes diplomatic sources as saying that Libya's leader, Col. Muammer el-Qaddafi, is financing, training, and arming a network of terrorist gangs throughout the world.	Andrei Amalrik, the dissident Soviet author and historian, renounces his Soviet citizenship and flies to Amsterdam, accompanied by his wife. . . . French Finance Min. Jean-Pierre Fourcade denies rumors that the franc would be devalued in the face of international speculation.	A Soweto administrator is killed and another wounded as disturbances and violence in South African black townships continue.	At his first press conference, Uruguay's Pres. Aparicio Mendez says he plans a civic purge to root out any Marxists remaining in political institutions, public administration, and the universities.	
July 16		W. Ger. Chancellor Helmut Schmidt reveals that the U.S., W. Germany, France, and England have informally agreed not to grant further loans to Italy if it allows Communists to hold Cabinet positions. . . . A gang of thieves launches a complex underground looting operation and escapes with $10 to $15 million in money and valuables from a bank in Nice, France. . . . Francesco De Martino, secy. gen. of the Italian Socialist Party, resigns and is replaced by Bettino Craxi. . . . The U.S.S.R. and France agree on safeguards to prevent either country from launching accidental nuclear attacks on the other and establish a "hot line." . . . Portuguese Pres. Antonio Ramalho Eanes asks Socialist leader Mario Soares to be his premier.	Zambian Pres. Kenneth Kaunda charges that South African troops are operating an intensive antiguerrilla campaign in Namibia, near the Zambian border.	The International Commission of Jurists says that torture of men, women, and children by Uruguayan authorities is an everyday practice. . . . Peru Pres. Francisco Morales Bermudez revises his Cabinet, dismissing the last prominent left-wing reformists from the government. . . . The Paraguayan Nat. Assembly votes to amend the Constitution to allow the reelection of Pres. Alfredo Stroessner, who seized power in a military coup in 1954.	The Bangladesh govt. announces the release of 44 political prisoners in the previous eight days, bringing to 1,457 the number of such detainees thus far set free.
July 17		The Cabinet of Spanish Premier Adolfo Suarez Gonzalez announces it will request a royal amnesty for political prisoners and it will arrange legislative elections by June 30, 1977.	Ali Aref Bourhan resigns as president of the French Territory of the Afars & Issas upon his arrival in Paris from Djibouti, claiming that the French had forced his resignation.		Indonesian Pres. Suharto signs a bill establishing East Timor as Indonesia's twenty-seventh province, thus ending more than 400 years of Portuguese rule in the territory. . . . *London Times* reports that Australian P.M. Malcolm Fraser has asked police to investigate the leak of 15 secret government documents to the press since he took office.
July 18	The Israeli govt. removes the Israeli pound from its exclusive link with the U.S. dollar and will match it instead against a basket of currencies.	Extreme leftists set off bombs at public buildings and monuments in eight Spanish cities on the fortieth anniversary of the uprising that began the Spanish Civil War.		*Washington Post* reports a resurgence of political violence in Guatemala after a brief lull caused by the February earthquake.	

A	B	C	D	E
Includes developments that affect more than one world region, international organizations and important meetings of major world leaders.	Includes all domestic and regional developments in Europe, including the Soviet Union, Turkey, Cyprus and Malta.	Includes all domestic and regional developments in Africa and the Middle East, including Iraq and Iran and excluding Cyprus, Turkey and Afghanistan.	Includes all domestic and regional developments in Latin America, the Caribbean and Canada.	Includes all domestic and regional developments in Asia and Pacific nations, extending from Afghanistan through all the Pacific Islands, except Hawaii.

U.S. Politics & Social Issues	U.S. Foreign Policy & Defense	U.S. Economy & Environment	Science, Technology & Nature	Culture, Leisure & Life Style	
Jimmy Carter is declared the Democratic presidential nominee by acclamation after he led by an overwhelming margin on first-ballot voting. . . . Four men are indicted in Boston and Portland in connection with 11 terrorist bombings in Mass., N.H., and Maine between April 22 and July 2 this year.	The U.S. Navy says it won't use live ammunition in test bombings by its planes north of the Subic Bay base pending an investigation of the deaths of several Filipino fishermen in the area. . . . Pres. Ford signs legislation authorizing $32.5 billion in fiscal 1977 for arms procurement and research.			International Olympic Committee (IOC), backed by the U.S. Olympic Committee, proposes that the five coaches and athletes from Taiwan already in Canada for the Olympic Games be allowed to compete using the flag and anthem of the Republic of China.	July 14
Carter accepts the Democratic presidential nomination, proclaiming it's a "time for healing" and holding forth the prospect of an America on the move again. . . . Carter announces that Sen. Walter Mondale (Minn.) is his choice as the Democratic vice-presidential nominee. . . . Twenty-six schoolchildren and their bus driver are kidnapped on their way home from school in Chowchilla, Calif.				Writer Paul Gallico dies at age 78 of a heart attack in Monaco. . . . Canada proposes a compromise on Taiwan's Olympic participation, which would have all 42 participants use their anthem and flag but not be designated as representing the Republic of China.	July 15
Charles Tuller and his two sons are each sentenced to 100 years in prison for air piracy and kidnapping in connection with the 1972 hijacking of a plane to Cuba.		The Ford administration predicts 1976 will be a year of faster economic growth, lower unemployment, and less inflation than forecast in January.		Taiwan withdraws from the Olympic Games in wake of a dispute with the Canadian govt. which objected to Taiwan's competing using the name Republic of China.	July 16
The Republican Party's selection of 2,259 convention delegates is completed without resolution of the struggle between Ford and Reagan for the presidential nomination.	Chancellor Helmut Schmidt ends a three-day U.S. visit, during which he negotiates an agreement to end offset arrangements for the stationing of U.S. troops in W. Germany.	The longest and largest hospital strike in N.Y.C. history ends after ratification of an agreement to submit to binding arbitration.		Hollywood and Broadway producer Arthur Hornblow Jr., 83, dies in N.Y. . . . The Summer Olympic Games are opened in Montreal by Queen Elizabeth II. . . . *The New York Times* reports that much of the support for Tanzania's boycott of the Olympic Games was provided by two officials of an umbrella organization for sports in Africa.	July 17
			Venezuela's worst floods in 30 years leave at least 50,000 people homeless. . . . A new strain of infectious arthritis called Lyme disease, believed to be transmitted by an insect-borne virus, is reported to have afflicted 39 children and 12 adults in Conn.	U.N. Secy. Gen. Kurt Waldheim appeals to the African countries that have withdrawn from the Olympics or are intending to do so.	July 18

F	G	H	I	J
Includes elections, federal-state relations, civil rights and liberties, crime, the judiciary, education, health care, poverty, urban affairs and population.	Includes formation and debate of U.S. foreign and defense policies, veterans' affairs and defense spending. (Relations with specific foreign countries are usually found under the region concerned.)	Includes business, labor, agriculture, taxation, transportation, consumer affairs, monetary and fiscal policy, natural resources, and pollution.	Includes worldwide scientific, medical and technological developments, natural phenomena, U.S. weather, natural disasters, and accidents.	Includes the arts, religion, scholarship, communications media, sports, entertainments, fashions, fads and social life.

	World Affairs	Europe	Africa & the Middle East	The Americas	Asia & the Pacific
July 19		Credit for the Spanish bombings is claimed by an extreme leftist movement calling itself Groups of Anti-Fascist Resistance — October 1. ... The Paris newspaper *Le Monde* reports that Soviet leader Leonid Brezhnev has accused Syria of prolonging the Lebanese war and has urged that it pull its troops out. ... Christian Bonnet, French minister of agriculture, seeks additional drought relief from the EEC because the severe summer drought hit France more severely than other member countries.	A U.S. plan to carry out a second evacuation of U.S. citizens and other foreign nationals from war-torn Lebanon is postponed because of the deteriorating situation. ... Egypt, Saudi Arabia, and Sudan announce that they are establishing joint organizations and institutions for close political, military, and economic cooperation.	Mario Santucho, founder and leader of Argentina's leftist People's Revolutionary Army (ERP), is killed in a gun battle with police and soldiers. ... Jamaican P.M. Michael Manley acknowledges that his ruling party had received $20,000 from Alcoa, which has extensive bauxite holdings in the country, for its 1972 political campaign. ... The U.N. refugee office in Buenos Aires, Argentina reports that 30 Uruguayan refugees in the city were kidnapped in recent days.	
July 20		According to released figures, the British jobless rate has risen to 6.3 percent of the working population, the highest level since WWII.			The Tokyo High Ct. reverses a lower ct. acquittal of newsman Takichi Nishiyama and gives him a suspended four-month sentence on charges of illegally obtaining foreign ministry documents. ... The U.S. ends its military withdrawal from Thailand, meeting the deadline set by the Thai govt. in March. Simultaneously, the U.S. Military Assistance Command Thailand ends.
July 21		British Industry Secy. Eric Varley reveals the government will give British Leyland Ltd., Britain's largest auto company, a capital loan of $180 million. ... The British Ambassador to Ireland, Christopher Ewart-Biggs, is killed near his home in Dublin by a land mine exploding beneath the car he was in. ... Irish P.M. Liam Cosgrave and British P.M. James Callaghan condemn the terrorist attack. ... Mikhail Menshikov, former Soviet ambassador to the U.S. in the late 1950s who advocated detente, dies at the age of 73 in Moscow.			India and Pakistan formally reestablish diplomatic relations as both nations exchange ambassadors and resume passenger flights between the two countries.
July 22		In a further drastic move to bolster the economy, the British govt. announces it plans a reduction of $1.78 million in public spending for fiscal 1978. ... The French govt. raises the central bank's discount lending rate from 8 percent to 9.5 percent in an effort to halt the franc's continuing decline in international money markets.	Schools in South African black townships reopen, but few students attend. Most black areas appear calm, but tear gas is used to break up a group of 200 rock-throwing demonstrators. ... Libyan–Egyptian relations deteriorate as Egyptian Pres. Anwar Sadat charges Libya was involved in the attempted Sudanese coup. ... Lebanese Moslem-leftist alliance leader Kamal Jumblat says that his faction has formed a civil administration in Moslem-held areas, an action that virtually makes formal the partition of Lebanon between Christians and Moslems. ... According to a UPI report, Rwanda's economy appears to be on the brink of collapse because its supplies of oil from Kenya are not getting through neighboring Uganda.	A delegation of Argentinean Catholic church leaders meet with Pres. Jorge Rafael Videla, who admits that the government has arrested 10 priests in recent months.	N. Korean Pres. Kim Il Sung calls for a congress of North and South Koreans to drive the "U.S. imperialist" troops out of [South] Korea and to overthrow S. Korea's Chung Hee Park government.

A	B	C	D	E
Includes developments that affect more than one world region, international organizations and important meetings of major world leaders.	Includes all domestic and regional developments in Europe, including the Soviet Union, Turkey, Cyprus and Malta.	Includes all domestic and regional developments in Africa and the Middle East, including Iraq and Iran and excluding Cyprus, Turkey and Afghanistan.	Includes all domestic and regional developments in Latin America, the Caribbean and Canada.	Includes all domestic and regional developments in Asia and Pacific nations, extending from Afghanistan through all the Pacific Islands, except Hawaii.

U.S. Politics & Social Issues	U.S. Foreign Policy & Defense	U.S. Economy & Environment	Science, Technology & Nature	Culture, Leisure & Life Style	
Pres. Ford proposes a substitute Watergate reform bill and defends his pardon of Nixon, saying he did it because he felt it was in the national interest and that he would do it again.	A four-man court-martial bd. finds S.Sgt. Henry Wallraff guilty of dereliction of duty in connection with the death of Marine recruit Pvt. Lynn McClure and acquits him on two other charges.	UAW's negotiations for new national contracts with the major auto companies begin.... The AFL–CIO Executive Council endorses the Democratic ticket of Carter and Mondale.			July 19
The Fed. Election Commission certifies the payment of $21.8 million to the Carter–Mondale Democratic ticket, marking the first publicly financed general election in U.S. history.... Jimmy Carter calls Pres. Ford's pardon of Nixon "improper" and "ill-advised," but doesn't question or criticize Ford's motives.		The Commerce Dept. announces the real gross national product rose at a seasonally adjusted annual rate of 4.4 percent during the second quarter.... Westinghouse and three major unions sign new three-year contracts to end a brief national strike, the first against the company since 1956.	The unmanned U.S. spacecraft Viking I lands on Mars, the first man-made object to reach the Martian surface in working condition, after a journey that started on Aug. 20, 1975.		July 20
			Fourteen consecutive days of heavy rain cause flooding in 11 of Mexico's 31 states, killing at least 120 and leaving 200,000 homeless.... The first Martian weather report, prepared on the basis of data supplied by Viking I, is issued: Light winds, a low temperature of minus 122 F., and a high of minus 22 F.... Viking I transmits color photographs of its immediate surroundings, provoking a controversy about the color of the sky, which could reveal something about the Martian atmosphere.	Earle Combs, 77, member of baseball's Hall of Fame who played center field for the New York Yankees in 1924–34, dies in Richmond, Ky.... The musical *Guys and Dolls* is revived on Broadway with an entirely black cast.... Tunisia becomes the thirty-first nation to pull out of the Olympics in support of the Tanzanian boycott.	July 21
The Contra Costa County, Calif. district attorney says there is insufficient evidence to warrant criminal prosecution in the May 21 fatal crash of a Yuba City school bus.... Supreme Ct. Justice Lewis Powell orders a stay of execution in the cases of three men sentenced to die in Florida, Georgia, and Texas. ... Republican presidential aspirant Ronald Reagan calls Pres. Ford's courtship of delegates a "little heavy-handed," but the White House denies promising favors to line up delegates.	State Secy. Kissinger suggests that the U.S., China, N. Korea, and S. Korea meet to discuss ways of preserving the 1953 Korean armistice agreement and of reducing tensions.	Nathaniel Goldfinger, 59, top economist and director of research for the AFL–CIO, dies in Washington, D.C.	British archaeological pioneer Sir Mortimer Wheeler dies at age 85 in England.	The International Amateur Athletic Federation (IAAF), the governing body for amateur track and field, expels South Africa because of its racial policies.... The Olympic women's gymnastics competition is marked by the emergence of two new stars, Nadia Comaneci, 14, of Rumania and Nelli Kim, 18, of the U.S.S.R.	July 22

F	G	H	I	J
Includes elections, federal-state relations, civil rights and liberties, crime, the judiciary, education, health care, poverty, urban affairs and population.	*Includes formation and debate of U.S. foreign and defense policies, veterans' affairs and defense spending. (Relations with specific foreign countries are usually found under the region concerned.)*	*Includes business, labor, agriculture, taxation, transportation, consumer affairs, monetary and fiscal policy, natural resources, and pollution.*	*Includes worldwide scientific, medical and technological developments, natural phenomena, U.S. weather, natural disasters, and accidents.*	*Includes the arts, religion, scholarship, communications media, sports, entertainments, fashions, fads and social life.*

	World Affairs	Europe	Africa & the Middle East	The Americas	Asia & the Pacific
July 23		Laszlo Toth, a Yugoslav-born naturalized American sentenced on espionage charges by Yugoslavia, is released and immediately flies to the U.S. . . . Mario Soares takes office as Portuguese premier with a minority Cabinet of 13 Socialists, three independents, and two military officers.	Rhodesian P.M. Ian Smith dismisses as impractical the main proposals of the Commission on Racial Discrimination, including the provision that land set aside for whites should be opened up to all. . . . Three Red Cross representatives enter the Lebanese Tel Zaatar refugee camp to try to arrange the evacuation of more than 1,000 wounded after four previous efforts to enter had been stopped by shelling.	The Canadian govt. issues temporary regulations barring the use of the French language for air-traffic control anywhere except in six small airports in Quebec, which were already using it.	
July 24			The Arab League's Boycott Office warns that Arab states would boycott oil companies that help Israel in prospecting for oil in the Israeli-occupied Sinai desert. . . . *London Times* reports that a five-year banning order has been served on Fatima Meer, an Indian sociologist in Durban, South Africa, under the new Internal Security Act.		Peking Mayor Wu Teh is reported by Indian officials to have been selected as chairman of the Nat. People's Congress, described as China's nearest equivalent to a head of state.
July 25			A Lebanese cease-fire agreement signed on July 24 is immediately shattered as Sudanese and Saudi troops of the Arab League peace-keeping force come under fire. . . . In a speech, Libyan leader Col. Muammer el-Qaddafi charges that Egyptian Pres. Anwar Sadat moved Egyptian troops from the front lines with the "Zionist enemy" and massed them against Libya after Sadat had forged an alliance with Sudan and Saudi Arabia.		
July 26		Rory O'Brady, president of the Provisional Sinn Fein, the political wing of the Provisional IRA, is ordered deported from Northern Ireland by Merlyn Rees, reflecting a hardening of Britain's attitude toward Sinn Fein. . . . The franc continues to fall to a new low of 4.9443 francs to the dollar. Since leaving the European snake, or joint float, the franc has depreciated by 8 percent against the dollar. . . . The Italian CP wins the chairmanships of four major committees in the Chamber of Deputies, adding to the party's parliamentary power.	According to reports, Kurdish rebels are resuming their guerrilla attacks against Iraqi army forces, sparked by Iraq's policy of dispersing Kurds to other parts of the country.	A research study by the Canadian-American Committee finds relations between the two countries are undergoing a period of tension and are unlikely to improve soon.	
July 27		EEC foreign ministers agree to extend their collective fishing limits to 200 miles beyond the coasts of each of the nine member-countries.	The Transkei Legislative Assembly approves plans earlier ratified by the S. African govt. for it to become the first tribal homeland to be independent. . . . The U.S. Navy evacuates 160 Americans and 148 other foreigners from the Moslem section of Beirut, Lebanon. . . . Militiamen of the Christian Phalangists and Nat. Liberal Party clash, reflecting long-standing rivalry between the opposing Christian groups in Lebanon.	A French-speaking group of air-traffic controllers plans to take legal action against the Canadian govt.'s decision about the use of the French language for air-traffic control. . . . The body of Jorge Antonio Rodriguez, leader of the Venezuelan Socialist League who died after being interrogated by police intelligence squad agents, is reported to show signs of torture.	Former Japanese Premier Kakuei Tanaka is arrested for alleged involvement in the Lockheed bribery scandal. He is believed to have accepted almost $2 million in Lockheed funds.

A	B	C	D	E
Includes developments that affect more than one world region, international organizations and important meetings of major world leaders.	Includes all domestic and regional developments in Europe, including the Soviet Union, Turkey, Cyprus and Malta.	Includes all domestic and regional developments in Africa and the Middle East, including Iraq and Iran and excluding Cyprus, Turkey and Afghanistan.	Includes all domestic and regional developments in Latin America, the Caribbean and Canada.	Includes all domestic and regional developments in Asia and Pacific nations, extending from Afghanistan through all the Pacific Islands, except Hawaii.

U.S. Politics & Social Issues	U.S. Foreign Policy & Defense	U.S. Economy & Environment	Science, Technology & Nature	Culture, Leisure & Life Style	
		The Labor Dept. announces that the average first-year wage increase for the second quarter was 8.2 percent, compared with 8.8 percent for first quarter contracts.			July 23
In response to speculation on a Ford–Reagan ticket, Reagan emphatically denies the possibility that he would accept a vice-presidential nomination.	*Washington Post* reports that the toll of dead horses on the Dugway, Utah Army base has reached 53, but that scientists confirm that the deaths were not caused by lethal substances.	A wildcat strike begun by W. Va. coal miners spreads into four other states and idles 30,000 miners.		French Bishop Marcel Lefebvre is suspended for persistently rejecting Second Vatican Council reforms.	July 24
Chester Plummer Jr., a 30-year-old Wash., D.C. cab driver, is fatally shot by a White House guard after scaling the White House fence, armed with a three-foot section of metal pipe.			Henry K. Beecher, 72, anesthesiologist and medical ethics advocate, dies in Boston.		July 25
In a surprise move, Ronald Reagan announces that he has selected liberal Republican Sen. Richard Schweiker (Pa.) to be his running mate if he wins the Republican presidential nomination.	Australian P.M. Malcolm Fraser meets in the U.S. with Jimmy Carter's foreign policy adviser Zbigniew Brzezinski and says that he is reassured that there would be little change in foreign policy if Carter wins.	The Labor Dept. announces that productivity in the private sector increased at a more normal pace in the second quarter than in the first quarter of 1976.	Scientists say that measurements taken on the Mars surface confirm Viking I findings that nitrogen accounts for two to three percent of the Martian atmosphere.	*90 Minutes at Entebbe* , a book by William Stevenson purporting to shed more light on the Israeli raid freeing the hostages at Uganda's airport, is published by Bantam Books.	July 26
N.H. Gov. Meldrim Thomson Jr., Rep. John Ashbrook (Ohio), and other former Reagan supporters withdraw their endorsements after he chooses liberal Republican Richard Schweiker as his running mate, should he win the presidential nomination. . . . Claude Wild Jr., a former Gulf Oil lobbyist, is acquitted of making an illegal political contribution to Sen. Daniel Inouye (D, Hawaii) because the statute of limitations had expired. . . . Former Treasury Secy. and former Texas governor John Connally endorses Pres. Ford's candidacy for the Republican presidential nomination.		Commerce Dept. announces a U.S. balance of trade deficit in June as imports exceeded exports by $377.3 million after adjustment for seasonal variation. . . . The FPC revamps the national rate structure for gas sold in the interstate market and orders the largest rate increase in the agency's history for new gas.		Soviet citizen Viktor Korchnoi, the world's second-ranking chess player, asks for political asylum in Amsterdam. . . . John Lennon, a member of the defunct Beatles rock group, wins formal permission to remain in the U.S. as a permanent resident and will be eligible for citizenship in five years.	July 27

F	G	H	I	J
Includes elections, federal-state relations, civil rights and liberties, crime, the judiciary, education, health care, poverty, urban affairs and population.	*Includes formation and debate of U.S. foreign and defense policies, veterans' affairs and defense spending. (Relations with specific foreign countries are usually found under the region concerned.)*	*Includes business, labor, agriculture, taxation, transportation, consumer affairs, monetary and fiscal policy, natural resources, and pollution.*	*Includes worldwide scientific, medical and technological developments, natural phenomena, U.S. weather, natural disasters, and accidents.*	*Includes the arts, religion, scholarship, communications media, sports, entertainments, fashions, fads and social life.*

	World Affairs	Europe	Africa & the Middle East	The Americas	Asia & the Pacific
July 28		Lord Feather (Victor Feather), 69, prominent British trade unionist, dies of a stroke in London.... Christian Ranucci, 22 is guillotined in Marseilles for having murdered an 8-year-old girl, the first person executed in more than three years. ... Britain breaks diplomatic relations with Uganda, precipitated by Uganda's failure to explain the disappearance and presumed death of Dora Bloch, a hostage left behind after the Entebbe Airport raid.	The Israeli Foreign Ministry says its government expressed its displeasure to the U.S. State Dept. about the direct contact made by the U.S. with the PLO for the evacuation of foreign nationals from Lebanon.		
July 29		The W. Ger. Bundesrat approves a new antiterrorist law, which allows judges to read letters between jailed terrorists and their lawyers.	Abdallah Mohammed Kamil, a member of the Afars tribe, succeeds Ali Aref Bourhan as president of the French Territory of the Afars & Issas.... Syria and the PLO sign an agreement providing for a cease-fire in the Lebanese civil war and for measures to pave the way for a political solution to the crisis.	Angolan Pres. Agostinho Neto leaves Cuba after a seven-day official visit.	Former Australian P.M. Gough Whitlam, in China during the earthquakes, says his hotel had been "literally split down the middle," but despite the damage, the building remained standing.... New Zealand P.M. Robert Muldoon presents a new austere budget designed to stimulate economic recovery.
July 30		The French Foreign Ministry says it has asked Cambodia to suspend the activities of its diplomatic mission in France, the only Western European country where the Khmer Rouge is represented.... Italy's first woman Cabinet minister, Tina Anselmi, is given the labor portfolio. Her appointment is praised by the CP-dominated Italian Woman's Union.	*The New York Times* reports the Syrian-PLO Lebanese cease-fire agreement represents a major concession by the PLO, reaffirming the predominant role of Syria in Lebanon.... PLO leader Yasir Arafat is reported to have disavowed the Damascus peace accord, saying a clause within it was aimed at driving a wedge between the PLO and Egypt.	The French press reports that 186 were killed in political violence in Argentina during July, bringing the 1976 political death toll to near 700.	
July 31			The Lebanese Christians' extreme right-wing faction formally bars the Red Cross from going beyond the Christian lines to enter Tel Zaatar refugee camp in Beirut to rescue victims of fighting.... Ford administration officials disclose that the U.S. has decided to sell Saudi Arabia quantities of a new generation of missiles and laser-guided missiles.		
Aug. 1			Mahmoud al-Ayoubi resigns as Syrian premier and is immediately replaced by Maj. Gen. Abdel Rahman Khleifawi, who had held the post until his resignation for health reasons in 1972.		The New China News Agency says formal use of a new Romanized script is beginning in the first step toward converting all written Chinese to an alphabet.... A Gallup Poll gives Jimmy Carter margins of 62 to 29 percent over Pres. Ford and 64 to 27 percent over Ronald Reagan.

A	B	C	D	E
Includes developments that affect more than one world region, international organizations and important meetings of major world leaders.	*Includes all domestic and regional developments in Europe, including the Soviet Union, Turkey, Cyprus and Malta.*	*Includes all domestic and regional developments in Africa and the Middle East, including Iraq and Iran and excluding Cyprus, Turkey and Afghanistan.*	*Includes all domestic and regional developments in Latin America, the Caribbean and Canada.*	*Includes all domestic and regional developments in Asia and Pacific nations, extending from Afghanistan through all the Pacific Islands, except Hawaii.*

U.S. Politics & Social Issues	U.S. Foreign Policy & Defense	U.S. Economy & Environment	Science, Technology & Nature	Culture, Leisure & Life Style	
Journal of Commerce reports a National Assn. of Insurance Commissioners study showing that in a recent seven-month period doctors who were sued for malpractice won four out of five cases brought to trial.		The Commerce Dept. announces the index of leading economic indicators increased .3 percent in June. It rose 2 percent during the second quarter.	Two major earthquakes cause serious damage in heavily populated areas of northern China, leaving at least 100,000 dead. . . . The Viking I spacecraft's arm gathers up dirt and drops it into miniaturized labs programmed to carry out tests to detect evidence of life on the surface of Mars.		July 28
Police arrest the last of three suspects in the school bus kidnapping of a group of Chowchilla, Calif. schoolchildren, who were kept in a buried truck trailer. . . . The House votes, 381–3, to reprimand Rep. Robert Sikes (D, Fla.) on conflict-of-interest charges.		Josephine Roche, 89, who was the first woman Treasury Dept. assistant secretary and former UMW executive, dies in Bethesda, Md.	The White House reports that the U.S. liaison office in Peking has offered any assistance that might be wanted in the relief effort after the Chinese earthquakes.		July 29
	Washington Post reports that State Secy. Kissinger has tied U.S. support of Spanish King Juan Carlo's govt. with a continued ban of the Spanish CP.	Richard Schweiker, whose Senate voting record is strongly pro-labor, tells newsmen he would take the antilabor side, if necessary, to conform to the Republican Party platform.		The International Olympic Committee announces that three athletes were ejected from the 1976 games for using anabolic steroids, which are muscle-building drugs. . . . Finland's Lasse Viren, the 1972 gold medalist in the 10,000-and 5,000-meter runs, wins those races again in the 1976 games, but his wins are marred by AP reports of blood doping. . . . Rudolf Bultmann, 92, German theologian influential in New Testament studies, dies in Germany.	July 30
		Some 30,000 Calif. cannery workers end an 11-day strike during the harvest season for peaches, pears, tomatoes, and other crops.	U.S. 1975 death rate is reported at a record low, the first time it has dropped below nine per 1,000 people. . . . Torrential rains and a resultant flash flood in Colorado's Big Thompson River canyon kill 100, strand 2,000, and cause $29-million in damage.	Six Eastern European athletes, one from the U.S.S.R. and five from Rumania, defect during the Olympics. . . . Soviet officials withdraw their threat to pull out of the 1976 Olympics after conferring with IOC officials about the disappearance of a Soviet diver Sergei Nemtsanov, 17, who had applied for permanent residence status in Canada while participating in the Olympics. . . . The Martha Graham Dance Co., celebrating its fiftieth anniversary, concludes a 12-day engagement at the Royal Opera House, London, England, the first modern-dance troupe to perform there.	July 31
	Sen. Hubert Humphrey (D, Minn.) says U.S. arms sales to Iran, totaling $10 billion since 1972, have been out of control.		Many foreigners leave Peking after Chinese officials warn of continuing post-quake tremors and warn that the epicenter of the new disturbances seems to be moving toward Peking. . . . *Washington Post* reports that a high Chinese official said that 1 million persons may have been killed or injured in the Chinese earthquakes. . . . Vienna's Empire Bridge collapses into the Danube River.	The twenty-first Olympiad games end in Montreal. They were the most expensive and controversial in Olympics history, marked by the withdrawal of 32 nations, the defection to Canada of six E. European athletes, the dismissal of a Soviet athlete for cheating, the disqualification of three other participants for steroid use, and reports of a death threat to a Soviet sprinter.	Aug. 1

F	G	H	I	J
Includes elections, federal-state relations, civil rights and liberties, crime, the judiciary, education, health care, poverty, urban affairs and population.	Includes formation and debate of U.S. foreign and defense policies, veterans' affairs and defense spending. (Relations with specific foreign countries are usually found under the region concerned.)	Includes business, labor, agriculture, taxation, transportation, consumer affairs, monetary and fiscal policy, natural resources, and pollution.	Includes worldwide scientific, medical and technological developments, natural phenomena, U.S. weather, natural disasters, and accidents.	Includes the arts, religion, scholarship, communications media, sports, entertainments, fashions, fads and social life.

	World Affairs	Europe	Africa & the Middle East	The Americas	Asia & the Pacific
Aug. 2		A British House of Lords committee upholds the tradition of special schools for gifted children, determined by administering proficiency exams at age 11.			
Aug. 3			Right-wing Christian forces permit members of the Red Cross to enter the Tel Zaatar refugee camp in Beirut and remove a total of 334 victims of recent fighting.		Former Philippine Sen. Benigno Aquino, political rival of Pres. Ferdinand Marcos, is arraigned before a military tribunal on charges of murder and subversion. . . . Australian Defense Min. James Killen says an inquiry he ordered Aug. 2 failed to produce any evidence that Australian troops massacred 27 unarmed Vietnamese villagers in 1970.
Aug. 4		Italian Premier Giulio Andreotti presents an economic austerity program to Parliament for consideration with a vote of confidence. . . . The Spanish govt. decrees amnesty for all political prisoners and exiles not convicted of terrorism.	A Red Cross vehicle in Lebanon is pierced by bullets. Red Cross operations are suspended until the safety of those participating can be guaranteed. . . . In wake of new violence erupting in South Africa, the home of Winnie Mandela is fire-bombed. She is the wife of black activist leader Nelson Mandela, who is serving a two-year prison term. . . . Eighty-one persons, including Muhammed Nur Saeed, are executed in Khartoum following their trials and convictions on charges of an attempted coup against Sudanese Pres. Mohammed Gaafar el-Nimeiry in July.		
Aug. 5		Danish Finance Min. Knud Heinesen signs the largest foreign loan in Denmark's history, $292.5 million, to cover Denmark's record first-half trade deficit.	Mapetla Mohapi, a former official of the S. African Students Organization, dies in police custody. . . . Heavy fighting continues in Beirut and other parts of Lebanon despite a cease-fire, which was to go into effect today as part of an overall peace accord signed in Damascus. . . . Lebanese Interior Min. Camille Chamoun charges that Iraqi troops were sent to Beirut to fight on the Palestinians' side.		
Aug. 6	The IMF announces it has approved a stand-by arrangement authorizing the Argentine govt. to buy currencies up to the equivalent of $300 million.	The Italian Senate votes confidence in Premier Giulio Andreotti's minority Christian Democratic govt., a vote made possible by a CP abstention. . . . Former British Labor govt. min. and M.P. John Stonehouse is convicted of 18 charges connected with his life insurance fraud and faked disappearance in Miami, and he is sentenced to seven years in prison.	Officials of the S. African Electricity Supply Commission sign a contract for a German consortium to build two nuclear power plants in S. Africa. . . . The Israeli govt. announces a series of measures of humanitarian relief for the Lebanese and says that it is also prepared to send agricultural experts to assist farmers there.		Vietnam agrees to establish diplomatic relations with Thailand.

A	B	C	D	E
Includes developments that affect more than one world region, international organizations and important meetings of major world leaders.	Includes all domestic and regional developments in Europe, including the Soviet Union, Turkey, Cyprus and Malta.	Includes all domestic and regional developments in Africa and the Middle East, including Iraq and Iran and excluding Cyprus, Turkey and Afghanistan.	Includes all domestic and regional developments in Latin America, the Caribbean and Canada.	Includes all domestic and regional developments in Asia and Pacific nations, extending from Afghanistan through all the Pacific Islands, except Hawaii.

U.S. Politics & Social Issues	U.S. Foreign Policy & Defense	U.S. Economy & Environment	Science, Technology & Nature	Culture, Leisure & Life Style	
	State Secy. Kissinger is booed by a predominantly black audience at the Urban League's annual convention in Boston, when he says that there are few blacks in the State Dept. because it serves no purpose to appoint black personnel unless they meet all qualifications. . . . In a letter to Sen. Abraham Ribicoff (D, Conn.) State Secy. Kissinger acknowledges that there is a high probability that heavy water supplied by the U.S. was used by India in its 1974 nuclear explosion.	EPA regulations easing air-pollution standards in certain areas are upheld by the U.S. Ct. of Appeals for the District of Columbia.	Health officials recognize an outbreak of a mystery disease that killed 23 persons attending an American Legion convention in Philadelphia, July 21–24.	Fritz Lang, 85, film pioneer famous for his movie *M*, dies in Beverly Hills, Calif.	Aug. 2
The FBI is told to turn over to the Socialist Workers Party all of its files on six alleged informants in wake of a SWP $37-million suit against the FBI and other agencies. . . . *The New York Times* Republican delegate count is 1,108 for Ford, 1,030 for Reagan, and 121 uncommitted. . . . Rep. Jerry Litton (D, Mo.) and his family are killed in a plane crash hours after he won an upset victory in the Missouri Democratic senatorial primary.	State Dept. reveals figures showing that 1,585 of its 12,247 employes are black, 262 professionals are black, and five ambassadors (out of 140) are black.	Pres. Ford submits to Congress legislation requiring companies to disclose payments, "proper or improper", that they made to officials of foreign governments to foster sales.			Aug. 3
	U.S. Army Secy. Martin Hoffman says the U.S. and W. Germany have agreed on a plan to standardize components of a new battle tank.	About 18,000 nonprofessional employes at 16 municipal hospitals in N.Y.C. go on strike to protest a city plan to lay off 1,350 workers. . . . For the tenth time, Congress overrides a veto by Pres. Ford, thereby enacting a bill to establish new regulations on leasing federal lands with coal reserves. . . . William Lummis is named board chairman of the Summa Corp., the late Howard Hughes' multibillion-dollar conglomerate.	A severe drought in Ethiopia is reported, threatening 65,000 persons with starvation.	Commissioned for the Bicentennial, Gian-Carlo Menotti's Symphony No. 1 has its world premiere at the Saratoga Performing Arts Center, N.Y. by the Philadelphia Orchestra.	Aug. 4
			Scientists studying the mysterious epidemic that felled American Legion convention delegates in Phila. announce plans to take samples from the hotels' air-conditioning systems and kitchens, focusing on the Bellevue Stratford Hotel, where most convention activities took place.	A theological symposium reaches a consensus among Catholic, Protestant, and Orthodox Christian scholars on the nature of the Eucharist.	Aug. 5
Russell Means, the American Indian Movement (AIM) leader charged with murder in a barroom slaying is acquitted. A codefendant, Richard Marshall, had previously been convicted and sentenced to life.		The Senate votes to approve a massive bill revising income tax law, defeating efforts by liberals to make corporations and the wealthy bear a larger tax burden. . . . The Labor Dept. announces the unemployment rate rose sharply in July to 7.8 percent, its highest level since January.	New criteria for determining victims of the so-called "Legion fever" are initiated by Center for Disease Control's epidemiologists.	Acclaimed cellist Gregor Piatigorsky, 73, dies in Los Angeles.	Aug. 6

F	G	H	I	J
Includes elections, federal-state relations, civil rights and liberties, crime, the judiciary, education, health care, poverty, urban affairs and population.	*Includes formation and debate of U.S. foreign and defense policies, veterans' affairs and defense spending. (Relations with specific foreign countries are usually found under the region concerned.)*	*Includes business, labor, agriculture, taxation, transportation, consumer affairs, monetary and fiscal policy, natural resources, and pollution.*	*Includes worldwide scientific, medical and technological developments, natural phenomena, U.S. weather, natural disasters, and accidents.*	*Includes the arts, religion, scholarship, communications media, sports, entertainments, fashions, fads and social life.*

	World Affairs	Europe	Africa & the Middle East	The Americas	Asia & the Pacific
Aug. 7		Rival claims by Greece and Turkey to the continental shelf in the Aegean Sea create a crisis intensified by the dispatch of a Turkish oil research vessel to the Aegean. . . . A meeting organized by the neo-Nazi National Democrats in Hamburg, W. Germany, attended by 900 neofascists from several European countries, leads to a violent left-wing protest demonstration.	State Secy. Kissinger signs an agreement whereby Iran will buy $10 billion in arms from the U.S. as part of a 1975–80 trade arrangement that will total about $50 billion. He defends the size of the arms transaction as in the best interests of the U.S. . . . Kenyan Pres. Jomo Kenyatta and Ugandan Pres. Idi Amin sign an agreement ending the state of tension that existed between the two countries in recent weeks. . . . Saeb Salam, a former Lebanese Moslem premier, and Pierre Gemayel, the Phalangist Party leader, meet informally after which Salam tells newsmen he is concerned about the reunification of Lebanon. . . . *London Times* notes that in recent years 23 persons in South Africa have died while in police custody.		One of the last four Americans known to be in Vietnam leaves the country.
Aug. 8		A coalition of Communists, Socialists, and Social Democrats win control of the Roman Italy city govt. and Communist Giulio Argan is named mayor.	Rhodesian forces again cross into Mozambique in purported retaliation for attacks being launched against the Salisbury govt. from there by Rhodesian black nationalists. . . . Dozens are arrested as Israeli security forces clash with suspected agitators in an attempt to break an Arab West Bank merchants' strike.		
Aug. 9		Roman Catholic M.P. Gerry Fitt, leader of the Ulster Social and Democratic Labor Party, uses a gun to hold off a stone-throwing mob of 30, which entered his home in Belfast. . . . Britain reestablishes diplomatic relations with Cambodia that were broken in April 1975 when the Khmer Rouge ousted Pres. Lon Nol's govt. . . . In the first war crimes trial held in E. Germany for many years, former Nazi SS leader Herbert Drabant, 61, is sentenced to life imprisonment.	P.M. John Vorster indicates a willingness to improve the status of S. Africa's blacks, but he attributes the country's recent unrest to outside causes.		State Secy. Kissinger announces that the U.S. and Pakistan have agreed to settle their dispute over the projected sale of a French nuclear-processing plant to Pakistan.
Aug. 10		Antonio de Spinola, who fled Portugal 17 months ago when a right-wing coup attempt failed, is arrested upon his return to Lisbon airport amidst fears of a resurgence of right-wing activities in Portugal.	The Jerusalem press indicates that Israel is becoming increasingly involved in the Lebanese conflict, stepping up naval activity in Lebanese waters to block arms shipments.	Government-owned Air Canada applies for a fare increase as a result of losses incurred in the work stoppage by English-speaking pilots and controllers.	
Aug. 11		British Leyland Ltd., faced with shortages because of a 25-worker strike at a body-shop plant in Liverpool, lays off 1,400 assembly-line workers in Coventry. . . . Two Palestinian guerrillas shoot and kill four and wound 30 others in an El Al Air Line line in a Turkish airport. Turkish police capture the terrorists, thwarting a hijack attempt. . . . A Greek protest against a Turkish ship's alleged violation of Greek sovereignty in the Aegean Sea is rejected by Turkey, which charges that Greek warships and planes are harassing the ship.		David Jimenez Sarmiento, alleged leader of the September 23 Communist League, is killed in Mexico City during a guerrilla attack on President-elect Jose Lopez Portillo's sister.	

A	B	C	D	E
Includes developments that affect more than one world region, international organizations and important meetings of major world leaders.	Includes all domestic and regional developments in Europe, including the Soviet Union, Turkey, Cyprus and Malta.	Includes all domestic and regional developments in Africa and the Middle East, including Iraq and Iran and excluding Cyprus, Turkey and Afghanistan.	Includes all domestic and regional developments in Latin America, the Caribbean and Canada.	Includes all domestic and regional developments in Asia and Pacific nations, extending from Afghanistan through all the Pacific Islands, except Hawaii.

U.S. Politics & Social Issues	U.S. Foreign Policy & Defense	U.S. Economy & Environment	Science, Technology & Nature	Culture, Leisure & Life Style	
An AP poll comparing delegates to the Republican and Democratic National Conventions reveals that there are, statistically, more white Republican delegates and that they are older and more affluent than their Democratic counterparts. Ford delegates have more education and higher incomes than delegates pledged to Reagan.		A settlement is reached that ends the N.Y.C. hospital workers' strike and averts the planned layoffs. . . . Consumer advocate Ralph Nader praises Democratic presidential candidate Carter, saying his positions on consumer issues are a "breath of fresh air", but he declines to endorse Carter's candidacy.	Laboratory soil tests from the Viking I lander, on Mars since July 20, suggest the possibility of life on the planet.		Aug. 7
Herman Long, 64, race-relations expert, educator, and president of the United Negro College Fund, dies in Talladega, Ala.			Two new reports published by the Rutgers University Center of Alcohol Studies support the Rand Corp.'s contention that some recovered alcoholics can learn to drink in a controlled way.	At a service ending the forty-first International Euchariastic Congress, 100,000 people hear Pres. Ford express concern for the "increased irreverence for life," an apparent appeal to antiabortionists.	Aug. 8
White merchants in Port Gibson, Miss. win a $1.251 million judgment against the NAACP in a suit stemming from a 1966 black boycott of white businesses. . . . The New York Times reports that John Connally remains a Republican vice presidential possibility, but that he would more likely be offered the chairmanship of the Ford campaign committee. . . . A jury finds SLA members William and Emily Harris guilty of two counts of kidnapping, two of car theft, and one of armed robbery, but acquits them of other charges related to the 1974 kidnapping of Patricia Hearst.		A coalition of consumer-interest groups wins a temporary stay of the natural gas rate hike in a ruling by the U.S. Ct. of Appeals, Wash, D.C.	Hurricane Belle, the first full-fledged hurricane spawned in the Caribbean in 1976, sweeps up the East Coast.	John Candelaria pitches a no-hitter for the Pittsburgh Pirates for a 2–0 victory over the Los Angeles Dodgers. . . . Baseball Hall of Fame inducts players Bob Lemon, Robin Roberts, Fred Lindstrom, and umpire Cal Hubbard, as well as two nineteenth-century players, Oscar Charleston and Roger Connor.	Aug. 9
The New York Times reports that Pres. Ford has seven leading vice presidential prospects, including Sen. Howard Baker (Tenn.), Sen. Robert Dole (Kan.) and William Ruckelshaus, former deputy attorney general.			Chinese officials repeat their warning that another serious earthquake is imminent and say Peking residents should remain out of doors after six new aftershocks. . . . Congress clears a bill that provides manufacturers of swine-flu vaccine with a federal shield against damage suits.		Aug. 10
FBI Dir. Clarence Kelley says he has ordered extensive restructuring of the agency, including removing responsibility for investigating domestic radical groups from the agency's intelligence division. . . . Jimmy Carter, Democratic presidential candidate, says if elected he will take a "new broom to Washington to sweep the house of government clean," an allusion to his charge that Pres. Ford has failed to restore public confidence in wake of the Watergate scandal.					Aug. 11

F	G	H	I	J
Includes elections, federal-state relations, civil rights and liberties, crime, the judiciary, education, health care, poverty, urban affairs and population.	Includes formation and debate of U.S. foreign and defense policies, veterans' affairs and defense spending. (Relations with specific foreign countries are usually found under the region concerned.)	Includes business, labor, agriculture, taxation, transportation, consumer affairs, monetary and fiscal policy, natural resources, and pollution.	Includes worldwide scientific, medical and technological developments, natural phenomena, U.S. weather, natural disasters, and accidents.	Includes the arts, religion, scholarship, communications media, sports, entertainments, fashions, fads and social life.

	World Affairs	Europe	Africa & the Middle East	The Americas	Asia & the Pacific
Aug. 12	The U.N. Security Council debates the Aegean Sea dispute at the request of Greece.	Former Portuguese provisional pres. Antonio de Spinola is released unconditionally after his return from exile because officials say there is no evidence that he committed a crime.... British troops are ordered into London-derry to prevent violence during a parade by 10,000 marchers mark-ing the anniversary of the 1969 start of the current Northern Ireland violence.... Special W. German envoy Gunter Gaus meets with E. German CP chief Erich Honecker in an attempt to ease tensions resulting from recent E. German border shootings.... In a modification of its previous sup-port of the Lebanese–Palestinian leftist alliance, the Soviet Union assails what it calls ultra-leftist ele-ments for having rejected all Leba-nese peace efforts.	Christian right-wing forces capture the Palestinian refugee camp of Tel Zaatar in eastern Beirut. It is the last Moslem enclave in the Chris-tian area of Beirut to fall.... The Palestinians repeat their charge of Syrian collusion with the Lebanese Christians and assert that Syrian Col. Ali al-Madani was in the mili-tary operations room during the fighting.... An estimated 35–40 persons are killed and hundreds injured after more than a week of rioting that began in Soweto and spread to Cape Town where two days of riots kill 27 more.	Charging subversion, Ecuadoran police arrest over 50 foreign Roman Catholic priests and lay-men who are attending an interna-tional meeting in Riomba.	
Aug. 13			Kamal Jumblat, head of the 11-party Moslem–leftist alliance, announces plans to recruit a 4,000-man popular army to launch an all-out offensive to drive the Syrians out of Lebanon.... S. Afri-can For. Min. Hilgard Muller calls for unspecified reforms in the gov-ernment's racial policy, while affirming its commitment to apart-heid.... S. African security police round up 20–50 black leaders, including Winnie Mandela, through-out the country and hold them with-out charge.... Evacuees from Tel Zaatar say Lebanese rightist forces committed atrocities on entering the camp. PLO leader Yasir Arafat speaks of massacres and calls for an Arab meeting at the highest level.	Colombian Fin. Min. Rodrigo Botero minimizes the role of mounting inflation in sparking the wave of student riots, guerrilla attacks, and kidnappings through-out the country since the year began.... The London newsletter *Latin America* reports that at least five Peruvian army officers were arrested for trying to organize a coup to reinstate the ousted left-wing reformist premier, Gen. Jorge Fernandez Maldonado.	
Aug. 14					
Aug. 15			Egyptian Pres. Anwar Sadat blames Libyan leader Muammer el-Qaddafi for an Aug. 14th bomb blast in a train in Alexandria and for earlier bombings in Egypt, charges that Libya denies.	With the tacit support of Chilean govt. troops, a rock-throwing mob attacks three Catholic bishops at the Santiago airport.	Indian P.M. Indira Gandhi declares the emergency laws curbing civil liberties have been gradually relaxed for many months now, but their elimination depends on the opposition.... Praphas Charusa-thien, former deputy premier of Thai-land, returns secretly to Thai-land after nearly three years in exile on Taiwan, where he had fled in 1973 after student riots toppled Thanom Kittikachorn's regime.... The official Chinese *People's Daily* newspaper urges the U.S. to pull its troops out of S. Korea and sign a peace pact replacing the existing armistice agreement.

A	B	C	D	E
Includes developments that affect more than one world region, international orga-nizations and important meetings of major world leaders.	Includes all domestic and regional devel-opments in Europe, including the Soviet Union, Turkey, Cyprus and Malta.	Includes all domestic and regional devel-opments in Africa and the Middle East, including Iraq and Iran and excluding Cyprus, Turkey and Afghanistan.	Includes all domestic and regional devel-opments in Latin America, the Caribbean and Canada.	Includes all domestic and regional devel-opments in Asia and Pacific nations, extending from Afghanistan through all the Pacific Islands, except Hawaii.

U.S. Politics & Social Issues	U.S. Foreign Policy & Defense	U.S. Economy & Environment	Science, Technology & Nature	Culture, Leisure & Life Style	
A Gallup Poll reveals that Reagan's selection of liberal Republican Richard Schweiker as his potential running mate neither hurt nor helped him in winning Republican delegates' support, but a Harris survey shows a negative reaction to his choice.		United Rubber Workers and Firestone negotiators reach an understanding on economic issues after five days of nearly continuous talks. Firestone was the target company for negotiations.			Aug. 12
In the wake of a sex scandal, Rep. Wayne Hays (D, Ohio), in the House for 28 years, says he will not seek reelection, explaining that ill health, coupled with alleged harassment from the *Washington Post* led to the decision.... The GOP Platform Committee approves a document generally supporting Pres. Ford's foreign policies. It also contains conservative planks on domestic issues to satisfy Reagan.... Jimmy Carter disavows a staff memo charging that federal agencies are a "dumping ground" for defeated Republican candidates.	The GOP Platform Committee adopts a plank avowing that the 1903 treaty with Panama gives the U.S. rights in the Canal Zone as if it were the sovereign and that any new treaty should not cede those rights necessary for U.S. protection in the Western Hemisphere.... A Reagan-backed proposal that the U.S. affirm its sovereign rights over the Panama Canal is rejected by the Republican Platform Committee.	Pres. Ford vetoes a bill authorizing $19.7 million for pesticide programs run by the EPA, objecting to a clause granting Congress authority to veto any pesticide regulation.... NRC announces a moratorium on licensing new nuclear power plants until an environmental hazard study is completed.			Aug. 13
Manson cultist Susan Murphy, serving a five-year sentence for conspiring to send threatening letters, escapes from a Calif. prison with a fellow inmate, a convicted bank robber Diane Ellis.... Howard Swearer, 46, president of Carlton College in Minnesota, is named president of Brown University in Rhode Island.... Rep. Otto Passman, (La.), 76, loses a bid for renomination to a sixteenth term in the Democratic primary to Jerry Huckaby, 35, a dairy farmer and businessman.		Pres. Ford signs a bill raising the price of domestic oil and authorizing loans and other incentives to spur energy conservation investments.			Aug. 14
The New York Times reports that a government motion to dismiss the Socialist Workers Party 1973 damage claim against the FBI, which charges illegal surveillance, has been rejected by Judge Thomas Griesa.		A House Banking Committee staff study charges big business representatives and the banking industry dominate the Federal Reserve System's 12 district banks.		Black youth gangs in Detroit attack white teenagers during a rock concert at Cobb Hall.	Aug. 15

F	G	H	I	J
Includes elections, federal-state relations, civil rights and liberties, crime, the judiciary, education, health care, poverty, urban affairs and population.	*Includes formation and debate of U.S. foreign and defense policies, veterans' affairs and defense spending. (Relations with specific foreign countries are usually found under the region concerned.)*	*Includes business, labor, agriculture, taxation, transportation, consumer affairs, monetary and fiscal policy, natural resources, and pollution.*	*Includes worldwide scientific, medical and technological developments, natural phenomena, U.S. weather, natural disasters, and accidents.*	*Includes the arts, religion, scholarship, communications media, sports, entertainments, fashions, fads and social life.*

	World Affairs	Europe	Africa & the Middle East	The Americas	Asia & the Pacific
Aug. 16		Thieves escape with an estimated $5 million from a Paris bank after entering it through a sewer on Aug. 13.	Lebanese Pres. Suleiman Franjieh proposes a truce so that rival factions can reach a political settlement, conditioned on acceptance of the 1969 agreement restricting Palestinian activity.		Former Japanese Premier Kakuei Tanaka is indicted on charges of having accepted $1.6 million in bribes to arrange the purchase of Lockheed aircraft by All Nippon Airways.
Aug. 17	North Korean Premier Pak Sung Chul tells members of the nonaligned nations conference, meeting in Sri Lanka, that the U.S. should be urged to withdraw its troops and nuclear weapons from South Korea or face the prospect of a new war breaking out in that area.	British Agriculture Min. Frederick Peart reports on the unprecedented severe damage inflicted by a widespread drought after a two-day tour of Britain's southeast and southwest.	Israeli Defense Min. Shimon Peres denies reports that Israel has imposed a naval blockade around Lebanon to prevent arms shipments from reaching Palestinian guerrillas.		Vietnamese Premier Pham Van Dong expresses his nation's interest in developing economic ties with industrial nations and normal diplomatic relations with the U.S.
Aug. 18		British Parliament passes an emergency Drought Act allowing local authorities to curtail both domestic and industrial water usage. . . . U.S. firm PepsiCo Inc. signs an agreement with the Soviet foreign ministry to quadruple the amount of Pepsi-Cola produced in the Soviet Union.	The South-West African (Namibian) constitutional conference says it has set Dec. 31, 1978 as the date for full independence for Namibia.		Thirty N. Korean soldiers attack a U.S.-S. Korean work team pruning a tree at Panmunjom in the DMZ, killing two U.S. Army officers and wounding four Americans and five S. Koreans.
Aug. 19	The U.N. and many black African nations criticize the Namibian constitutional convention for excluding SWAPO because it is considered political and not tribally representative.	Thousands of Danish workers participate in wildcat strikes to protest the passage of a new austerity plan in the Parliament. . . . Brian Faulkner, a former Protestant prime minister, announces his retirement from the leadership of the Protestant Unionist Party of Northern Ireland.			U.S. State Secy. Kissinger discusses the Korean crisis with Huang Chen, head of the Chinese liason mission in Washington, D.C., where he repeats a U.S. proposal for four-way talks (China, U.S., North and South Korea) to resolve long-standing tensions resulting from the Korean War.
Aug. 20	Representatives of the 85-member Nonaligned Nations Movement, concluding their fifth conference in Sri Lanka, warn the world's rich countries of the need to yield more of their wealth in a rearranged economic order.		The Arab peacekeeping force unsuccessfully tries to pacify the situation east of Beirut, where Christians and Moslems are deployed for a possible confrontation.	Forty-seven Montoneros are slain before dawn by presumed Argentian rightists, who shoot and mutilate 30 of the victims.	

A	B	C	D	E
Includes developments that affect more than one world region, international organizations and important meetings of major world leaders.	Includes all domestic and regional developments in Europe, including the Soviet Union, Turkey, Cyprus and Malta.	Includes all domestic and regional developments in Africa and the Middle East, including Iraq and Iran and excluding Cyprus, Turkey and Afghanistan.	Includes all domestic and regional developments in Latin America, the Caribbean and Canada.	Includes all domestic and regional developments in Asia and Pacific nations, extending from Afghanistan through all the Pacific Islands, except Hawaii.

U.S. Politics & Social Issues	U.S. Foreign Policy & Defense	U.S. Economy & Environment	Science, Technology & Nature	Culture, Leisure & Life Style	
The Justice Dept. confirms that it has cleared Rep. John Young (D, Tex.) of charges that he paid a former aide a salary primarily to serve as his mistress.... *The New York Times* reports that the announced restructuring of the FBI will still allow the agency to continue its surveillance of the Socialist Workers Party because its activity is regarded as a counterintelligence — rather than domestic security — investigation.... Republican National Convention keynoter Sen. Howard Baker (Tenn.) calls Jimmy Carter the nominee of the party (Democratic) with the original credibility gap and says that the Carter-Mondale ticket promises more of the same old Democratic government programs, controls, and spending.			A strong new earthquake hits Szechuan, China, but only slight damage occurs, according to the official Chinese news agency.	Dave Stockton wins the fifty-eighth PGA championship when he sinks a 12-foot putt for a birdie, earning $45,000.	Aug. 16
Retired FBI associate director Mark Felt says the policy of allowing domestic break-ins was approved directly by L. Patrick Gray, acting FBI director from May 1972 to April 1973.	Pres. Ford's supporters decide to avoid confrontation with the Reagan camp over the Republican platform and offer no resistance to a "morality in foreign policy" plank proposed by Reagan.		Thousands are reported dead and missing and thousands are left homeless after an earthquake in the Philippine island of Mindanao and neighboring islands.		Aug. 17
Edward Miller, former FBI intelligence chief, supports Mark Felt's statement that domestic break-ins were approved by then Acting Dir. L. Patrick Gray, saying that Gray had told him privately that he would permit the break-ins.... Pres. Ford and Ronald Reagan continue their search for delegates to the day that the Republican National Convention begins balloting, leaving only eight delegates uncommitted.... Opponents of the Republican platform's antiabortion plank, led by Rep. Millicent Fenwick (N.J.), seek to eliminate all platform references to abortion, but decide not to force a roll-call vote.	Marine Corp Maj. Gen. Kenneth Houghton dismisses or reduces charges against the two remaining defendants in the beating death of Pvt. Lynn McClure.				Aug. 18
Ford wins the Republican presidential nomination on the first ballot in a close race: 1,187 for Ford and 1,070 for Reagan out of the 1,130 needed to win.... Pres. Ford surprises most delegates and political observes by choosing conservative Sen. Robert Dole (Kan.) as his running mate.... An unscheduled 45-minute floor demonstration by Reagan supporters prevents Ford's nomination victory from being seen by prime-time viewers in the East, South, and part of the Middle West.	The consensus on the results of a special National Security Council meeting on the crisis in N. Korea is that an outbreak of war is not likely there.		U.S. oil firm Mesa Petroleum reports an oil find 12 miles off Scotland's coast that is significant because it is in shallow waters.		Aug. 19
Jake Jacobsen, former dairy lobbyist and chief prosecution witness in the bribery trial of former Treasury Secy. John Connally, is sentenced to two years probation.... Pres. Ford accompanies his running mate, Sen. Robert Dole, to Dole's hometown of Russell, Kan. for a celebration of "Bob Dole Day."... Defeated Republican presidential aspirant Ronald Reagan says, "It wasn't so much that I wanted to be President. I never really hungered for the job. But there were important issues that face the nation."				Pope Paul VI contends that the growing Anglican acceptance of women priests could harm Roman Catholic-Anglican relations.... British actor Alastair Sim, 75, known for his performance of Scrooge in *A Christmas Carol*, dies of cancer in London.	Aug. 20

F	G	H	I	J
Includes elections, federal-state relations, civil rights and liberties, crime, the judiciary, education, health care, poverty, urban affairs and population.	Includes formation and debate of U.S. foreign and defense policies, veterans' affairs and defense spending. (Relations with specific foreign countries are usually found under the region concerned.)	Includes business, labor, agriculture, taxation, transportation, consumer affairs, monetary and fiscal policy, natural resources, and pollution.	Includes worldwide scientific, medical and technological developments, natural phenomena, U.S. weather, natural disasters, and accidents.	Includes the arts, religion, scholarship, communications media, sports, entertainments, fashions, fads and social life.

	World Affairs	Europe	Africa & the Middle East	The Americas	Asia & the Pacific
Aug. 21			Chiefs of seven of S. Africa's nine tribal homelands meet and condemn apartheid. Two homelands — Transkei, which will become independant in October, and Swaziland — do not participate.		The U.S. increases its air and naval activities in the Korean DMZ, and American and S. Korean personnel chop down the tree that was the center of controversy leading to the killing of two Americans by the N. Koreans. . . . Praphas Charusathien is deported from Thailand following riots and political unrest sparked by his return from exile on Aug. 15. . . . N. Korean Pres. Kim Il Sung expresses regret over the Aug. 18 DMZ incident in a message to the U.N. Military Command at Panmunjom.
Aug. 22		Protestant clergyman Rev. Oskar Bruesewitz immolates himself in Zeitz to protest E. German religious oppression.		Chilean Catholic Bishop Carlos Camus charges that underneath his country's seeming calm, the public is repressed and terrified.	U.S. State Dept. calls North Korean Pres. Kim Il Sung's apology over the DMZ tree incident not acceptable because it does not acknowledge what it terms the brutal and premeditated murder of two Americans.
Aug. 23			An Egyptian airliner is hijacked by three Arab guerrillas after takeoff from Cairo but is recaptured by Egyptian army commandos when it lands in Luxor with the hostages unharmed.		Australian P.M. Malcolm Fraser and Gov. Gen. Sir John Kerr flee two separate violent university student demonstrations protesting cuts in student allowances, in migrant education allocations, and in health insurance. . . . In an apparent softening of reaction, the U.S. State Dept. calls N. Korean Pres. Kim Il Sung's expression of regret a positive step, and calls for an early meeting of the Military Armistice Commission.
Aug. 24		British P.M. James Callaghan appoints Denis Howell to deal with Britain's dwindling water supplies in wake of the worst European drought in more than 200 years. . . . The British Dept. of Employment says July 18–Aug. 12 unemployment rose to 6.4 percent, up .1 percent.	A group of 1,500 Zulu vigilantes, whose formation was encouraged openly by S. African white officials, fight in Soweto with young black demonstrators who intimidated black workers into a strike-work boycott.		Gough Whitlam, former Australian Labor P.M., calls Liberal P.M. Malcolm Fraser's proposed 1976–1977 budget irrelevant to the nation's needs. . . . Members of Japan's ruling Liberal-Democratic Party urge Premier Takeo Miki to resign in wake of the Lockheed bribe scandal.
Aug. 25	The U.N. Security Council adopts a resolution calling on Greece and Turkey to resume discussions in their dispute over the search for oil in the Aegean Sea.	French Premier Jacques Chirac resigns, charging that Pres. Valery Giscard d'Estaing did not allow him sufficient authority to deal with France's economic problems. He is replaced by Raymond Barre.	Esso Standard Near East, an Exxon subsidiary, says it is ending its operations in Lebanon because of the civil war there and dismisses 200 employes. . . . The Arab League presses plans to hold another summit meeting on the Lebanese civil war, but must commit three more members to attend besides the eight already lined up.		Thai Defense Min. Tawit Seniwong is reported to have resigned in wake of critism of his involvement in the secret return to Thailand of exiled former deputy Premier Praphas Charusathien.
Aug. 26	A paid *New York Times* advertisement signed by Western European socialist and social-democratic leaders condemns the Argentian military junta for promoting violence.	Dutch Prince Bernhard resigns nearly all of his military and business posts after a government investigatory commission strongly criticizes his relationship with Lockheed officials.	The Polisario Front (Sarahan independence movement) holds its third congress and 40 foreign delegations attend.		A 140-man Philippine security force captures Bernabe Buscayano, head of the New People's Army, the military arm of the Philippine Communist Party.

A	B	C	D	E
Includes developments that affect more than one world region, international organizations and important meetings of major world leaders.	Includes all domestic and regional developments in Europe, including the Soviet Union, Turkey, Cyprus and Malta.	Includes all domestic and regional developments in Africa and the Middle East, including Iraq and Iran and excluding Cyprus, Turkey and Afghanistan.	Includes all domestic and regional developments in Latin America, the Caribbean and Canada.	Includes all domestic and regional developments in Asia and Pacific nations, extending from Afghanistan through all the Pacific Islands, except Hawaii.

U.S. Politics & Social Issues	U.S. Foreign Policy & Defense	U.S. Economy & Environment	Science, Technology & Nature	Culture, Leisure & Life Style	
Former Missouri Gov. Warren Hearnes is chosen by the Democratic State Committee as the party's U.S. senatorial nominee, replacing Rep. Jerry Litton, who died in a plane crash.			A second earthquake hits China's Szechuan Province.	Danish foreign ministry bars the Taiwan National Opera from performing in Denmark because the EEC, of which Denmark is a member, recognizes the Peoples Republic of China but not Nationalist China.	Aug. 21
			Philippine Pres. Ferdinand Marcos announces that 8,000 persons have died in the earthquake and tidal wave that struck the Philippines on Aug. 17, and that 35,138 families were left homeless.	The Edinburgh Festival, Scotland presents N.Y.C.'s La Mama troupe in Andrei Serban's production of *The Good Woman of Setzuan* by Bertolt Brecht, plus two parts of Serban's *Trilogy*, his version of *Electra* and *The Trojan Women*. . . . Pianist Gina Bachauer, 63, dies of a heart attack in Athens.	Aug. 22
John Connally denies a report in the *Dallas Times Herald* that he was offered the GOP National Committee chairmanship but turned it down because he doesn't think Ford can win the presidency. . . . A strike by inmates at the Attica State Correctional Facility, N.Y. begins when 95 percent of the inmates refuse to leave their cells.	Army Secy. Martin Hoffman says cadets expelled from West Point in connection with the cheating scandal will be given a chance to apply for readmission after a year's absence. . . . A group of black Americans led by Rev. Jesse Jackson urge State Secy. Kissinger to communicate to South Africa in the strongest terms U.S. opposition to South African racial policies.	A federal task force proposes a uniform air-pollution index, with ratings ranging from numerals zero to 500, the emergency point being set at 400.	*London Times* reports that the July 28 Chinese earthquake killed 100,000 people in the Tangstan area. . . . The National Cancer Institute's new guidelines on the use of X-ray techniques, known as mammography, to detect breast cancer recommend against routine mammograms for women ages 35–50.		Aug. 23
Clarence Mitchell, head of the NAACP's Washington office, criticizes both Democrats and Republicans for their platform planks on civil rights.	Carter draws boos from the American Legion convention by declaring that his intention, if he is elected President, is to grant a blanket pardon to Vietnam War draft resisters.				Aug. 24
Pres. Ford names James Baker III his national campaign chairman, replacing Rogers C.B. Morton. . . . Democratic vice presidential nominee Walter Mondale makes a coast-to-coast campaign trip and meets in Chicago with Mayor Richard Daley. . . . A Gallup Poll finds 49 percent of the electorate support Carter, 39 percent support Ford, and 12 percent are undecided, a 13-point gain for Ford.	Republican vice presidential nominee Robert Dole, speaking to the American Legion convention, takes issues with Carter's remarks on Vietnam War draft resister, saying there is no such distinction, as Carter made, between "amnesty" and "pardon". . . . The State Dept. criticizes those nations at the Nonaligned Nations Movement conference that supported a N. Korean resolution condemning the U.S. and S. Korea for plotting a war against N. Korea.	GM says it is raising prices on its 1977 auto models an average $344 a unit, or 5.9 percent. The base sticker price for the average standard-sized car will be more than $6,000.			Aug. 25
Ford and Carter campaign representatives meet, under the auspices of the League of Women Voters, to negotiate the ground rules for proposed TV debates.		The Commerce Dept. announces the U.S. posted an $827.1 million trade deficit in July, its largest since August 1974.	British Airways show a $4.14 million loss for the first 10 weeks of the Concorde's operation. . . . Contradictory results of experiments based on Viking samples neither prove nor disprove that there is life on Mars.	Lotte Lehman, German-born operatic soprano and lieder singer who sang in every major opera house in Europe and the U.S., dies at the age of 88 of a heart attack in Santa Barbara, Calif.	Aug. 26

F	G	H	I	J
Includes elections, federal-state relations, civil rights and liberties, crime, the judiciary, education, health care, poverty, urban affairs and population.	*Includes formation and debate of U.S. foreign and defense policies, veterans' affairs and defense spending. (Relations with specific foreign countries are usually found under the region concerned.)*	*Includes business, labor, agriculture, taxation, transportation, consumer affairs, monetary and fiscal policy, natural resources, and pollution.*	*Includes worldwide scientific, medical and technological developments, natural phenomena, U.S. weather, natural disasters, and accidents.*	*Includes the arts, religion, scholarship, communications media, sports, entertainments, fashions, fads and social life.*

	World Affairs	Europe	Africa & the Middle East	The Americas	Asia & the Pacific
Aug. 27		John Stonehouse, former British Labor govt. minister imprisoned on ethics charges, resigns from Parliament.... French Premier Raymond Barre names his Cabinet and increases the number of ministerial posts from 15 to 17, but decreases the total government members from 41 to 36.	Iran and the U.S.-based Occidental Petroleum Corp. cancel a $125-million transaction to develop Caspian Sea oil and to process and market other Iranian petroleum.... S. African P.M. John Vorster, in a speech marking his tenth anniversary as prime minister, says S. Africa faces domestic and international problems but denies that an internal crisis exists.		Philippine Pres. Ferdinand Marcos announces that martial law will continue to be imposed.
Aug. 28		Italian right-wing terrorists Giovanni Ventura and Franco Freda are released from prison seven years after their arrest for a Milan bombing incident.			U.S. and N. Korean representatives meet at Panmunjom to discuss easing tension around the truce village in the DMZ.... The Seoul District Criminal Ct. convicts and sentences 18 prominent S. Korean Chistians on charges of violating the 1975 emergency decree prohibiting all acts of dissent.
Aug. 29		The Soviet CP newspaper *Pravda* says that Syrian withdrawal from Lebanon, and Palestinian cooperation, would be significant steps toward a Lebanese crisis settlement.	Kuwaiti Premier Sheik Jaber al-Ahmed al-Sabah and his Cabinet resign, the Nat. Assembly dissolves, and constitutional provisions on press freedom and elections are suspended, following tensions arising from the large Palestinian population in the country and the government's pro-Syrian policy toward the Lebanese civil war.		
Aug. 30		The Dutch Parliament votes, 148–2, to reject a left-wing motion calling for criminal prosecution of Prince Bernhard for his involvement in the Lockheed bribery scandal.	Soviet CP newspaper *Pravda* charges that Egyptian imperialists and reactionaries are plotting against the Libyan govt.... Armed Lebanese Christians clash with Palestinian guerrillas near the Israeli frontier, according to Israeli sources.		Japanese Premier Takeo Miki offers to reshuffle his Cabinet in wake of the Lockheed bribery scandal.
Aug. 31	Gold prices, falling steadily since January, continue to decline to $104 an ounce, nearly a three-year low.		U.S. State Secy. Kissinger warns whites in Namibia and Rhodesia that black majority rule is inevitable and calls South Africa's internal structure incompatible with any concept of human dignity.	The Quebec Catholic teachers' union accepts the government's pay offer despite a union directive to reject the proposal.... The Mexican govt. allows the peso to float, ending its 22-year fixed parity with the U.S. dollar.	

A	B	C	D	E
Includes developments that affect more than one world region, international organizations and important meetings of major world leaders.	*Includes all domestic and regional developments in Europe, including the Soviet Union, Turkey, Cyprus and Malta.*	*Includes all domestic and regional developments in Africa and the Middle East, including Iraq and Iran and excluding Cyprus, Turkey and Afghanistan.*	*Includes all domestic and regional developments in Latin America, the Caribbean and Canada.*	*Includes all domestic and regional developments in Asia and Pacific nations, extending from Afghanistan through all the Pacific Islands, except Hawaii.*

U.S. Politics & Social Issues	U.S. Foreign Policy & Defense	U.S. Economy & Environment	Science, Technology & Nature	Culture, Leisure & Life Style	
The American Independent Party selects former Ga. Gov. Lester Maddox as its presidential nominee. . . . Pres. Ford says there is "fear and apprehension" among Americans about Carter, especially about the prospect of an inexperienced person conducting foreign policy.		The Commerce Dept. announces the government's index of leading economic indicators rose .5 percent in July, the seventeenth consecutive monthly advance.		Dr. Renee Richards, a transsexual who had a sex-change operation, is barred from the U.S. Open tennis competition after she refuses to take a just-instituted chromosome test.	Aug. 27
A six-day strike by inmates at the Attica N.Y. State Correctional Facility ends peacefully after convict leaders and corrections officers agree upon several reforms.	Sen. Edward Kennedy (D, Mass.) an advocate of normalized U.S.–Cuban relations, criticizes the Cuban govt. for barring representatives of international organizations from observing the condition of political prisoners.	United Rubber Workers end a 130-day strike against Goodyear Tire and Rubber Co. and gain an immediate wage increase of $.80 an hour, and cost-of-living increases.	Massachusetts Institute of Technology scientists say they have successfully constructed a bacterial gene, complete with regulatory mechanisms, and implanted it in a living cell where it functioned normally.	The North American Soccer League championship is won by the Toronto Metros, 3–0, over the Minnesota Kicks.	Aug. 28
		Pres. Ford proposes a 10-year, $1.5 billion program to increase national park and recreation land acreage, a plan the Environmental Policy Center calls "the height of hypocrisy." . . . Amtrak and the U.S. Transportation Dept. agree on a plan for Amtrak to buy from Conrail the Boston-Washington Northeast rail corridor.	*Washington Post* reports U.S. intelligence has found that Taiwan is secretly reprocessing used uranium fuel to obtain plutonium.	Defying a papal ban, suspended Bishop Marcel Lefebvre celebrates a Latin Mass in Lille, France, and in his sermon denounces ecumenism, communists, liberal Catholics, and the use of the vernacular instead of Latin in the liturgy.	Aug. 29
A Senate report says rampant fraud and abuse, combined with abysmal administration, is costing the government between 25–50 percent of Medicaid's budget. . . . Over 100 Haitian refugees, crowded in a 16-meter sailboat, reach Miami and seek political asylum in the U.S.		A chemical explosion in a container of radioactive wastes at the Hanford Nuclear Reservation in Washington State injures a workman and contaminates him and nine others with radioactivity. . . . Competitive pressures force major steel producers to withdraw a planned Oct. 1 price increase of 4.5 percent on flat-rolled products. . . . Alan Greenspan, chairman of the President's Council of Economic Advisers, says the economy is at a pause stage in its pause–spurt pattern of recovery.	La Soufriere volcano on the French Caribbean island of Guadeloupe erupts, injuring three scientists. The eruption was preceded by 294 earth tremors.	Helene Berg, 92, widow of composer Alban Berg who held up a performance of the final act of his opera *Lulu* because she said her husband's spirit asked her to, dies in Vienna, Austria.	Aug. 30
FBI Dir. Clarence Kelley admits, in response to press charges, that some of his home furnishings were provided without charge by the FBI and that he had received gifts from top aides. . . . SLA members William and Emily Harris, convicted on five charges including kidnapping and armed robbery, are sentenced to 11 years to life in prison. They were involved in the Patricia Hearst kidnapping.		The Agriculture Dept. says farm prices declined 4 percent in the 30-day period that ended Aug. 15.	Reports of cases of so-called legion fever reach 179 as federal officials continue their investigation into the disease's origin. Twenty-eight have died of the disease and 11 remain hospitalized.		Aug. 31

F	G	H	I	J
Includes elections, federal-state relations, civil rights and liberties, crime, the judiciary, education, health care, poverty, urban affairs and population.	*Includes formation and debate of U.S. foreign and defense policies, veterans' affairs and defense spending. (Relations with specific foreign countries are usually found under the region concerned.)*	*Includes business, labor, agriculture, taxation, transportation, consumer affairs, monetary and fiscal policy, natural resources, and pollution.*	*Includes worldwide scientific, medical and technological developments, natural phenomena, U.S. weather, natural disasters, and accidents.*	*Includes the arts, religion, scholarship, communications media, sports, entertainments, fashions, fads and social life.*

	World Affairs	Europe	Africa & the Middle East	The Americas	Asia & the Pacific
Sept. 1	U.S. State Secy. Kissinger tries to break the deadlocked U.N. Conference on the Law of the Sea by offering U.S. aid to permit Third World countries to establish an international deep-mining enterprise.	According to a report by Netherlands Premier Joop den Uyl, Lockheed officals approached three Parliament members to gain support for the sale of their *Orion* antisubmarine aircraft to the Dutch navy.... Italian leftist weekly *L'Espresso* publishes letters apparently showing that Premier Giulio Andreotti was the intended recipient of $43,000 in Lockheed bribes.... Both houses of the Irish Parliament approve P.M. Liam Cosgrave's request for a declared state of emergency, anticipating a crisis over legislation to curb activities of the IRA and other terrorist acts.	South African P.M. John Vorster, reacting to U.S. State Secy. Kissinger's condemnation of apartheid, holds that South Africa sets its own internal policy and does not follow outsiders' prescriptions.	Aparicio Mendez begins a five-year term as president of Uruguay and suspends for 15 years the political rights of the leaders of all existing parties.	The Burmese govt. announces the lifting of martial law imposed on Rangoon following student riots in December 1974, after ordering the phased release of 1,600 persons. ... Two U.S. officials say N. Korean guards warned a U.N. Command team against cutting down the tree in the DMZ 12 days before the incident that led to the slaying of two Americans.... China reports a record summer harvest.
Sept. 2		According to published letters, Netherlands Prince Bernhard asked W. German Chancellor Helmut Schmidt in 1971 to buy Northrop Corp. planes.... European Commission on Human Rights issues a report finding Great Britain guilty of torturing suspected terrorists in Northern Ireland from August to December 1971. The policy ended in December 1975.	Libyan leader Muammer el-Qaddafi denies responsibility for recent bombings in Cairo and Alexandria and for the Aug. 23 hijacking of an Egyptian airliner.... Violence in Cape Town is the first unrest to reach the white area of a S. African city. Justice Min. James Kruger extends the ban, which expired on Aug. 31, on outdoor meetings and demonstrations.		
Sept. 3		Railroad workers throughout France strike to protest the institution of a new hierachical grade for motormen.		The opposition Barbados Labor Party wins 17 of the 24 seats in the House of Assembly (Parliament) elections. J.M.G. (Tom) Adams, party leader, is sworn in as prime minister.	
Sept. 4		A KLM Royal Dutch Airlines plane, en route from Spain to Amsterdam, is hijacked by three pro-Palestinian gunmen shortly after takeoff from a stopover in Nice, France.	U.S. State Secy. Kissinger meets with S. African P.M. John Vorster in Zurich, Switzerland for a second round of talks on the southern African situation.	More than 100 persons are killed in political violence throughout Argentina, raising the 1976 political death toll to at least 875.	
Sept. 5		The KLM Royal Dutch Airlines hijacked plane flies to Cyprus, and then departs for Tel Aviv but is intercepted by Israeli jets and returns to Cyprus where the gunmen surrender and release the hostages.	S. African P.M. John Vorster for the first time publicly legitimizes the South-West Africa People's Organization (SWAPO) and says, "It is for the peoples of South-West Africa" to decide their future.		
Sept. 6		Lieut. Viktor Belenko, the pilot of a MiG-25 jet fighter, one of the newest and most secret Soviet planes, lands in Japan and asks for U.S. asylum.	The Arab League unanimously raises the status of the PLO from a non-voting member to the league's twenty-first full voting member, in a move sponsored by Egypt.... Kuwait Premier Crown Prince Jaber al-Ahmed al-Sahmed forms a new 18-member Cabinet, retaining all members of his previous Cabinet, which resigned August 29.	More than 7,000 Colombian doctors employed by the Colombian Social Security Institute strike to protest a Labor Ministry decree classifying them as public servants.	The Indian govt. orders a birth-control plan as an amendment to the civil service conduct rules for its three million employes, limiting children to three per family.... The U.S.-led U.N. Command and N. Korea agree to partition the Joint Security Area at the Panmunjom truce site in the DMZ to prevent further clashes, thereby amending the 1953 truce.

A	B	C	D	E
Includes developments that affect more than one world region, international organizations and important meetings of major world leaders.	*Includes all domestic and regional developments in Europe, including the Soviet Union, Turkey, Cyprus and Malta.*	*Includes all domestic and regional developments in Africa and the Middle East, including Iraq and Iran and excluding Cyprus, Turkey and Afghanistan.*	*Includes all domestic and regional developments in Latin America, the Caribbean and Canada.*	*Includes all domestic and regional developments in Asia and Pacific nations, extending from Afghanistan through all the Pacific Islands, except Hawaii.*

U.S. Politics & Social Issues	U.S. Foreign Policy & Defense	U.S. Economy & Environment	Science, Technology & Nature	Culture, Leisure & Life Style	
Washington Post quotes FBI sources who recall that when J. Edgar Hoover headed the FBI, it was common practice for the director and other top executives to receive special favors.... Ford and Carter representatives agree on the basic format for a series of nationally televised debates. It will be the first time an incumbent President debates an opponent. ... Rep. Wayne Hays, (D, Ohio), center of a Capitol Hill sex-payroll scandal and target of Justice Dept. and federal grand-jury probes, says he is resigning effective immediately.			Figures released by HEW indicate that Pres. Ford's nationwide immunization plan against swine flu is more than two months behind schedule.	The racetrack of the $340-million Hackensack Meadowlands Sports Complex (N.J.) opens to an overflow crowd of harness-racing enthusiasts.	Sept. 1
FBI Dir. Clarence Kelley gives the FBI a check for $335 to cover the cost of labor and window fixtures installed in his home by bureau employes at no cost to him.	The congressional Black Caucus criticizes State Secy. Kissinger and urges that he not meet with South African P.M. John Vorster unless the talks result in a trip to South Africa and an announcement that the U.S. will break all ties until apartheid ends.	Phillips Petroleum Co., its chairman, and two former CEOs are indicted on tax-fraud charges related to a previously disclosed corporate fund for secret illegal political contributions.	French volcanologist Haroun Tazieff charges that other scientists studying La Soufriere volcano emissions on Guadeloupe island were incompetent and calls the evacuation of 72,000 islanders in face of the Aug. 30 eruption a panic reaction.	Rev. Luther Weigle, 95, dean emeritus of the Yale Divinity School who directed the writing of the Revised Standard Version of the Bible, dies in New Haven, Conn.	Sept. 2
Paul Gilly and Claude Edward Vealey receive life sentences for the 1969 murders of UMW dissident Joseph Yablonski, his wife, and his daughter.		Jimmy Carter stresses the need to curb inflation and balance the federal budget, saying this effort has priority over new programs.... The Labor Dept. says that the August 7.9 percent unemployment rate is at its highest level for the year. CEA chmn. Alan Greenspan blames the rise on the extremely abnormal growth in the number of people seeking work.	The Viking 2 lander safely sets down on the Martian plain known as Utopia, about 4,600 miles northeast of the Viking 1 landing site, after an 11-month journey.		Sept. 3
Pres. Ford says that he will not dismiss FBI Dir. Clarence Kelley, after reading a report by Atty. Gen. Edward Levi that recommends that Kelley not be disciplined nor asked to resign for using FBI money and personnel for his personal projects.			A Venezuelan air force transport crashes while trying to land at the U.S. Air Force base in the Azores. All 68 aboard are killed.	*Steve Lobell* , driven by Billy Haughton, wins the fifty-first Hambletonian Stakes for three-year-old trotters, in the richest race in American harness-racing history. ... FBI Dir. Clarence Kelley, 64, says he will marry Shirley Dyckes, a former Roman Catholic nun. His first wife died of cancer on Nov. 9, 1975.... Archbishop Nikon (Nicolas P. Rklitsky), 84, leader of the Russian Orthodox Church Outside of Russia, dies in the Bronx, N.Y.	Sept. 4
		Washington Post and *The New York Times* report congressional investigators have serious doubts that the 800-mile Alaskan pipeline will be operational by mid-1977.			Sept. 5
Jimmy Carter formally kicks off his presidential election campaign with a call for a new generation of leadership and says that no one seems to be in charge of Pres. Ford's administration. ... John Shattuck is appointed director of the ACLU's Washington office, succeeding Charles Morgan Jr. who resigned in April when he was asked to keep his political views separate from the organization's.					Sept. 6
F Includes elections, federal-state relations, civil rights and liberties, crime, the judiciary, education, health care, poverty, urban affairs and population.	**G** Includes formation and debate of U.S. foreign and defense policies, veterans' affairs and defense spending. (Relations with specific foreign countries are usually found under the region concerned.)	**H** Includes business, labor, agriculture, taxation, transportation, consumer affairs, monetary and fiscal policy, natural resources, and pollution.	**I** Includes worldwide scientific, medical and technological developments, natural phenomena, U.S. weather, natural disasters, and accidents.	**J** Includes the arts, religion, scholarship, communications media, sports, entertainments, fashions, fads and social life.	

	World Affairs	Europe	Africa & the Middle East	The Americas	Asia & the Pacific
Sept. 7		Corsican separatists blow up an Air France jet at Ajaccio airport, after ordering all passengers out of the plane. No injuries are reported.	A conference of five African heads of state, seeking a common strategy for dealing with the Rhodesian and S. African govts., can't reconcile the opposing ANC factions.... A secret Israeli govt. report, leaked by an Israeli newspaper, warns that Israeli Arabs will outnumber Jews in the Galilee by 1978 and recommends increasing Jewish settlements there, decreasing state subsidies to Arabs with large families, and encouraging Arabs to go abroad to study.	A Quebec court rules that Air Canada pilots can speak French in the cockpit and in air-to-ground communications	The U.S. nuclear-powered cruiser *Truxton* arrives in Melbourne, where 10,000 Australian maritime workers strike for 24 hours to protest its presence in Australian waters and the dangers of radioactive leakages.
Sept. 8	The 18-member U.N. Special Committee against Apartheid approves a report citing the ever-closer collaboration between Israel and S. Africa.				Australian P.M. Malcolm Fraser announces new measures to aid victims of the prolonged droughts in southwestern Australia.... The United Buddhist Church of Vietnam reports 12 Buddhist nuns and monks burned themselves to death in November 1974 to protest Communist persecution.
Sept. 9		Danish Premier Anker Jorgensen changes two positions in his minority Social Democratic govt., following Labor Min. Erling Dinesen's resignation for personal reasons.... Portuguese Premier Mario Soares announces a broad economic austerity program that includes wage and price controls, rationing, import surcharge increases, public works projects, and new budget guidelines for nationalized firms.	After conferring in Zurich with U.S. State Secy. Kissinger, South African P.M. John Vorster agrees to a U.S. - British plan to recompensate Rhodesian whites who choose to emigrate and assure their rights in an independent Rhodesia under black majority rule.... New offical maps issued by Libya expand its southern border to include more than 52,000 square miles of territory from Algeria, Chad, and Niger, none of which protest publicly.... Rev. Ndabaningi Sithole, an African National Council leader in Rhodesia, withdraws from the organization, citing its failure to unify rival factions. He then claims sole leadership of the Zimbabwe African National Union (ZANU).... Palestinian-Lebanese leftist alliance members go to the Soviet Embassy in Beirut to see if Moscow's policy on Lebanon has changed. Christian right-wing leaders laud the Soviet statement condemning left-wing extremists.		Mao Tse-tung, the leader of the People's Republic of China since its creation in 1949 and a founder of the Chinese CP, dies in Peking at the age of 82.... The Laotian govt. bans birth control in an effort to build up the country's population, cut sharply by years of war and the flight of a large portion of its residents into exile.
Sept. 10	Five Croatian nationalists hijack a N.Y.-to-Chicago Trans-World Airlines (TWA) jet and commandeer it on a 30-hour international campaign against "genocidal Yugoslavism."	British P.M. James Callaghan reshuffles his Cabinet after Home Secy. Roy Jenkins resigns to become EEC president and replaces Jenkins with the former minister to Northern Ireland Merlyn Rees.... A series of strikes by British Leyland Ltd. workers at plants throughout the country ends.			
Sept. 11		The Yugoslavian govt. announces that Pres. Josip Tito has canceled a visit by French Pres. Valery Giscard d'Estaing scheduled for Sept. 15 because Tito is ill with severe liver trouble.... A group of Catholic and Protestant women in Northern Ireland stage six separate peace marches, the largest at Antrim, 18 miles from Belfast, where 8,000 Catholics and Protestants sing and pray.	Kissinger, before talking with African leaders, says his goal is not a permanent settlement of southern Africa's racial crises, but the creation of a basis for negotiations.	British P.M. James Callaghan begins a week-long visit to Canada. ... *Washington Post* reports that Argentine army officers have admitted that violence by police death squads has become as big a problem in the country as guerrilla terrorism.	

A	B	C	D	E
Includes developments that affect more than one world region, international organizations and important meetings of major world leaders.	Includes all domestic and regional developments in Europe, including the Soviet Union, Turkey, Cyprus and Malta.	Includes all domestic and regional developments in Africa and the Middle East, including Iraq and Iran and excluding Cyprus, Turkey and Afghanistan.	Includes all domestic and regional developments in Latin America, the Caribbean and Canada.	Includes all domestic and regional developments in Asia and Pacific nations, extending from Afghanistan through all the Pacific Islands, except Hawaii.

U.S. Politics & Social Issues	U.S. Foreign Policy & Defense	U.S. Economy & Environment	Science, Technology & Nature	Culture, Leisure & Life Style	
Pres. Ford signs legislation providing $240 million in aid to day-care centers for low-income families.		A nuclear energy expert's report sees an existing major radioactive waste problem in the U.S. and says that the system of storing wastes soon will be unworkable.		Milan, Italy's La Scala Opera Co. makes its U.S. debut at the Kennedy Center for the Performing Arts, Wash., D.C.	Sept. 7
	Former Army Lt. William Calley Jr., convicted in the slaying of 22 Vietnamese civilians at My Lai, says he favors unconditional amnesty for Vietnam draft evaders. . . . Jimmy Carter tells a convention of B'nai B'rith, a national Jewish organization, that morality belongs in foreign affairs and that the U.S. should not ignore another country's abuse of human rights when formulating policy.	N.Y.S. and the General Electric Co. agree on a cooperative $7-million program to end PCB pollution of the Hudson River. . . . URW ratifies a new three-year contract with B.F. Goodrich Co. after ratifying one with Uniroyal Inc., thus ending the longest strike against major U.S. tire producers.	The FDA approves 10 prescription cold, asthma, and allergy medicines for over-the-counter sales. An advisory panel says no treatment can prevent, cure, or shorten common colds.	The Paris Opera Co. makes its U.S. debut at the Metropolitan Opera House, N.Y.C., with Wolfgang Amadeus Mozart's *The Marriage of Figaro*. . . . U.S. District Ct. Judge William Bryant rules that the annual draft of college players by the National Football League violates antitrust laws.	Sept. 8
	Former U.S. Pres. Richard Nixon, who met Mao twice, calls him "a unique man in a generation of great revolutionary leaders" and praises his courage and ideological determination.			*The New York Times* reports that exiled Soviet writer Alexander Solzhenitsyn has moved from Zurich, Switzerland to Cavendish, Vt. because he believed he was being spied on in Zurich by Russians. . . . Roundabout Theater, N.Y.C., opens its new season with George Bernard Shaw's *The Philanderer* , staged by Stephen Hollis.	Sept. 9
Robert Dole, the GOP vice-presidential nominee, sharply attacks the Democratic presidential ticket during a campaign visit to Texas, charging that Carter has no record or issues and that Mondale totally follows the liberal line. . . . Mordecai Johnson, 86, first black president of Howard University, dies in Wash., D.C.		R.J. Reynolds Industries Inc. admits it made more than $25 million in questionable corporate payments in the U.S. and abroad since 1968 to promote its interests.	In history's worst to date mid-air disaster, a British Airways Trident and a Yugoslav DC-9 charter jet collide 33,000 feet over northern Yugoslavia, killing 176. . . . The 11-member Nat. Commission for the Protection of Human Subjects of Biomedical and Behavioral Research says controversial psychosurgery should not be categorically prohibited.	Dalton Trumbo, 70, novelist and Oscar-winning screenwriter who was blacklisted and jailed for refusing in 1947 to tell a congressional committee whether he was a Communist, dies in Los Angeles.	Sept. 10
High school seniors are reported scoring slightly lower in their 1976 verbal Scholastic Aptitude Tests (SAT) scores than in 1975, but maintaining their mathematical scores, with the average verbal score down three points to 431 and the math score at 472.				At the U.S. Open, Forest Hills, N.Y., Chris Evert beats Evonne Goolagong, 6–3, 6–0, in a tennis match that lasts only 52 minutes. . . . Dorothy Kathleen Benham, 20, of Minn., wins the Miss America title at Atlantic City, N.J.	Sept. 11

F	G	H	I	J
Includes elections, federal-state relations, civil rights and liberties, crime, the judiciary, education, health care, poverty, urban affairs and population.	Includes formation and debate of U.S. foreign and defense policies, veterans' affairs and defense spending. (Relations with specific foreign countries are usually found under the region concerned.)	Includes business, labor, agriculture, taxation, transportation, consumer affairs, monetary and fiscal policy, natural resources, and pollution.	Includes worldwide scientific, medical and technological developments, natural phenomena, U.S. weather, natural disasters, and accidents.	Includes the arts, religion, scholarship, communications media, sports, entertainments, fashions, fads and social life.

	World Affairs	Europe	Africa & the Middle East	The Americas	Asia & the Pacific
Sept. 12	The Croatian hijacking of a TWA jet, the first successful hijacking of a U.S. domestic airliner since 1972, ends with the arrest of four men and one woman and the passengers and crew unharmed.		*The New York Times* reports U.S. defense sources believe that the build-up of troops on the Egyptian–Libyan border has seriously affected military balance in the Middle East.	The Mexican govt. stabilizes the exchange rate at 19.9 pesos to the dollar, an effective devaluation of 37 percent from the previous fixed rate.	
Sept. 13	The Geneva disarmament conference (U.N. Conference of the Committee on Disarmament) agrees on a joint U.S.-Soviet pact to ban major forms of environmental warfare, such as triggering earthquakes or hurricanes.	Thousands are stranded at stations throughout Italy as 15,000 members of a small railway workers' union strike for better pay and a reorganization of the railway company.	Israeli Foreign Min. Yigal Allon denounces a leaked government report on the need to curb the growth and influence of Israeli Arabs in Galilee. . . . South African blacks stage a second three-day protest strike in the Johannesburg township of Soweto. There is more black participation and less violence than in the first protest.	Trinidad & Tobago's ruling People's Nat. Movement wins the general elections, giving P.M. Eric Williams a fifth consecutive five-year term of office.	
Sept. 14	The U.N. Security Council, faced with a threatened U.S. veto because of Hanoi's failure to account for all Vietnam War missing U.S. soldiers, delays action on Vietnam's application for membership.	Swedish Gen. Stig Synnergren confirms that $250,000 in secret payments were made to the U.S. to buy electronic devices to monitor Soviet-bloc military movements, but contends the payments were legitimate.	U.S. State Secy. Kissinger arrives in Tanzania where the Tanzanian govt. calls for the U.S. to declare its support for the liberation forces in Namibia and Rhodesia should negotiations with their governments fail. . . . Rhodesian P.M. Ian Smith and South African P.M. John Vorster meet in Pretoria for a five-hour discussion on the Rhodesian situation.	In a major reorganization of Canada's Cabinet, P.M. Pierre Trudeau names 15 new ministers. Allan MacEachen replaces Mitchell Sharp as president of the Privy Council. . . . Camilo Ponce, 64, last constitutionally elected president of Ecuador to complete his term in office (1956–1960), dies of a heart attack in Ecuador. . . . Cuban For. Min. Raul Roa Garcia contends that Cuba will never rejoin the OAS.	The Red Cross ends its evacuation from Vietnam of foreigners who had remained behind when Communist forces conquered the South in 1975, having removed more than 3,000 people. . . . The Indian govt. withdraws its case against *The Statesman*, ending its threats to close down the paper after it printed a magazine containing articles regarded politically critical.
Sept. 15	Vietnam wins a seat on the International Monetary Fund. . . . IMF holds its third gold auction, selling 780,000 ounces at an average price of $109.40 an ounce.		The South African strike spreads to Cape Town, the first time its 250,000 coloreds (mixed-race) have participated in an organized protest on such a large scale, and the first time they have joined with blacks. . . . After meeting with U.S. State Secy. Kissinger, Tanzanian Pres. Julius Nyerere says he feels more pessimistic than before on the prospects for African peace. He also warns the U.S. against S. African and Rhodesian claims that they are fighting communism. . . . Lebanese Pres. Suleiman Franjieh, due to be replaced Sept. 23, reshuffles his Cabinet, reducing the powers of Premier Rashid Karami, a Moslem, to the protest of Moslem leftists. . . . Under an agreement reached by Syria and Israel, Arab Druses in the Israeli-occupied Golan Heights are permitted to meet with relatives from Syria in the U.N. buffer zone.		Japanese Premier Takeo Miki reshuffles his Cabinet and top leadership of the ruling Liberal Democratic Party in an attempt to satisfy party rivals who oppose him because of the Lockheed scandal. . . . Amnesty International accuses the Philippine govt. of using frequent and extremely cruel torture on martial law detainees.

A	B	C	D	E
Includes developments that affect more than one world region, international organizations and important meetings of major world leaders.	Includes all domestic and regional developments in Europe, including the Soviet Union, Turkey, Cyprus and Malta.	Includes all domestic and regional developments in Africa and the Middle East, including Iraq and Iran and excluding Cyprus, Turkey and Afghanistan.	Includes all domestic and regional developments in Latin America, the Caribbean and Canada.	Includes all domestic and regional developments in Asia and Pacific nations, extending from Afghanistan through all the Pacific Islands, except Hawaii.

U.S. Politics & Social Issues	U.S. Foreign Policy & Defense	U.S. Economy & Environment	Science, Technology & Nature	Culture, Leisure & Life Style	
			The Viking 2 lander extends its arm and scoops up a sample of Martian soil, which it feeds to three miniature biological laboratories on the spacecraft.	Jimmy Connors beats Bjorn Borg in the men's tennis final of the U.S. Open at Forest Hills, N.Y.	Sept. 12
Pres. Ford signs a bill requiring nearly every executive-branch agency, except Cabinet offices, to open their meetings to the public except when confidential matters are discussed.... Carter appears in Birmingham, Ala. with Ala. Gov. George Wallace where Wallace remarks, "Oh, how I've longed to see a Deep Southerner, like you and me and Jimmy Carter, in the White House." ... A former Grumman Corp. official, Thomas Cheatham, tells a Sen. For. Relations subcommittee that Nixon White House aide Richard V. Allen had suggested that a $1 million contribution to Nixon's reelection campaign would gain administration assistance in winning an arms contract abroad.		A National Academy of Sciences committee says that fluorocarbon use, particularly in aerosol spray cans, will almost certainly have to be regulated to prevent weakening of the atmosphere's ozone layer.... The Senate approves legislation allowing the eventual tripling of federal funding for the national park and recreation system.	Typhoon Fran leaves 104 known dead, 57 missing, and nearly 325,000 homeless in Japan after five days of 100 mph winds and five feet of rain.		Sept. 13
Richard Lorber, a political unknown, defeats R.I. Gov. Philip Noel by 100 votes in the Democratic primary for the Senate seat of retiring John Pastore.... Daniel Patrick Moynihan, former U.S. Ambassador to the U.N., narrowly defeats Rep. Bella Abzug in N.Y.'s five-sided Democratic senatorial primary.... Pres. Ford signs legislation providing for regular congressional review of future states of national emergency declared by the President.		UAW goes on strike against the Ford Motor Co., with more than 165,000 workers staying off the job, thereby shutting off production at 102 plants and facilities in 22 states.	An American Cancer Society survey supports previous findings that pipe and cigar smokers' lung-cancer death rate is double that of nonsmokers and that their lip, tongue, mouth, and esophgeal cancer rate is high or higher than cigarette smokers.		Sept. 14
Pres. Ford opens his election campaign at the University of Michigan attacking Carter by saying, "It is not enough for anyone to say,'trust me.' Trust must be earned." ... Sen. Select Committee on Standards and Conduct votes, 5–1, to end without charges its investigation of Senate Minority Leader Hugh Scott (R, Pa.) and other senators who had allegedly received illegal contributions from the Gulf Oil Corp.... Parole is denied to Richard Speck, 34, serving a sentence of 400–1,200 years in prison for the 1966 murders of eight Chicago nurses.		The Senate approves, 86–0, a bill making it a criminal offense for U.S. corporations to bribe foreign officials. Sen. William Proxmire (D, Wis.) is the bill's chief sponsor.... Closing of the American Bank & Trust Co., (N.Y.C.) marks the fourth-largest bank failure in U.S. history.... AT&T announces a 25 percent profit rise in the quarter ending Aug. 31, thus becoming the first publicly owned U.S. corporation to earn $1 billion in any three-month period.	The U.S.S.R. launches Soyuz 22, with Col. Valery Bykovsky and Vladimir Aksenov aboard, to study the geological and geographical characteristics of the earth's surface.	The U.S. Protestant Episcopal Church votes formal approval of the ordination of women.	Sept. 15

F	G	H	I	J
Includes elections, federal-state relations, civil rights and liberties, crime, the judiciary, education, health care, poverty, urban affairs and population.	Includes formation and debate of U.S. foreign and defense policies, veterans' affairs and defense spending. (Relations with specific foreign countries are usually found under the region concerned.)	Includes business, labor, agriculture, taxation, transportation, consumer affairs, monetary and fiscal policy, natural resources, and pollution.	Includes worldwide scientific, medical and technological developments, natural phenomena, U.S. weather, natural disasters, and accidents.	Includes the arts, religion, scholarship, communications media, sports, entertainments, fashions, fads and social life.

	World Affairs	Europe	Africa & the Middle East	The Americas	Asia & the Pacific
Sept. 16		Prince Paul, 83, Yugoslavia's regent (1934–41) who signed a secret pact with Hitler, dies in Paris.	Egyptian Pres. Anwar Sadat is elected to a second six-year term in a national referendum, receiving 99.94 percent of the vote after running unopposed.... The ruling Rhodesian Front Party gives P.M. Ian Smith full power to decide Rhodesia's future in negotiations with U.S. State Secy. Kissinger.		The new military demarcation line separating U.S. and N. Korean forces at the Panmunjom truce village in the Korean DMZ goes into effect.
Sept. 17	The U.N. Conference on the Law of the Sea meets and is deadlocked in another fruitless attempt to draft a legal code regulating the mineral wealth of the deep seabed.	Finnish Premier Martti Miettunen and his coalition Cabinet resign. Pres. Urho Kaleva Kekkonen asks the Cabinet to remain until he can form a new government.... The Soviet press denounces U.S. State Secy. Kissinger's mission to Rhodesia, accusing him of trying to protect the white minority regimes of southern Africa.	S. African police fire on a group of Soweto schoolchildren protesting the arrival of U.S. State Secy. Kissinger. Police say one is killed, but a Soweto hospital reports three children died.... U.S. State Secy. Kissinger and South African P.M. John Vorster meet in Pretoria for five hours of talks, described as constructive.... An Israeli peace plan calling for Israeli withdrawal from most of the Arab territory occupied since the 1967 war is proposed by Foreign Min. Yigal Allon in a *Foreign Affairs* article.	Panamanian govt. charges that student riots in Panama City on Sept. 10 and 15 were part of a CIA destabilization campaign against the govt. of Brig. Gen. Omar Torrijos.	
Sept. 18			A Cairo military ct. convicts and sentences to life in prison two Palestinians and an Egyptian on charges of hijacking an Egyptian airliner on Aug. 23.		India announces the lifting of censorship regulations it imposed on the foreign press in 1975.... An eight-day mourning for Chinese Chmn. Mao ends with a brief rally of an estimated one million persons in Peking's Tien An Men Square.
Sept. 19		Anthimos, 72, former bishop of Kitium, Cyprus, who was defrocked for trying to oust Archbishop Makarios in 1973, dies of an apparent heart attack in Limassol, Cyprus.	U.S. State Secy. Kissinger meets with Rhodesian P.M. Ian Smith, and they discuss U.S.-British proposals for establishing black majority rule within two years, with compensation for whites who lose property or emigrate.... Palestinians and Egypt are blamed for the impasse in Lebanese truce efforts.		S. Korean Pres. Park Chung Hee imposes a series of "social purification" measures, which the opposition denounces as infringements on physical freedom and violations of human rights.
Sept. 20	Soviet Union statistics show a decreasing trade gap with the West in the first quarter of 1976.	Swedish Premier Olof Palme resigns after his Social Democratic Party suffers its first defeat in 44 years. Thorbjorn Falldin, Center Party leader, reportedly will take office.... Maltese P.M. Dominic Mintoff's Labor Party wins a three-seat majority in the 65-member House of Representatives, assuring Mintoff of another five-year term as prime minister. ... Representatives of the EEC's nine members agree to hold direct elections to the European Parliament in May or June 1978.... Two British Royal Navy warships collide 80 miles off the Netherlands coast, killing two people and leaving 10 listed as missing.	The Christian Institute of Southern Africa, an antiapartheid group, says 280 persons have been detained by South African authorities since the beginning of unrest in June.		

A	B	C	D	E
Includes developments that affect more than one world region, international organizations and important meetings of major world leaders.	Includes all domestic and regional developments in Europe, including the Soviet Union, Turkey, Cyprus and Malta.	Includes all domestic and regional developments in Africa and the Middle East, including Iraq and Iran and excluding Cyprus, Turkey and Afghanistan.	Includes all domestic and regional developments in Latin America, the Caribbean and Canada.	Includes all domestic and regional developments in Asia and Pacific nations, extending from Afghanistan through all the Pacific Islands, except Hawaii.

U.S. Politics & Social Issues	U.S. Foreign Policy & Defense	U.S. Economy & Environment	Science, Technology & Nature	Culture, Leisure & Life Style	
Archbishop Joseph Berardin of Cincinnati, Ohio, says the Catholic Church is absolutely neutral in the presidential contest but the bishops approve of Pres. Ford's antiabortion stand after meeting with him on Sept. 10.		Congress clears a major income-tax revision bill, which extends antirecession tax cuts enacted in 1975 and makes large changes in estate and gift taxes. . . . The House gives final congressional approval to a bill strengthening enforcement of antitrust laws, which would allow state attorney generals to bring triple-damage *parens patriae* suits. . . . RCA Corp. accepts the resignation of Anthony Conrad as chairman, president, and CEO after he tells the board of directors of his failure to file 1971–75 personal tax returns.	Six days of new tremors in earth-quake-shattered Italy leave at least four dead, 60 injured, and 20,000 homeless.		Sept. 16
The House creates a special select committee to investigate the assassinations of Pres. John Kennedy and Martin Luther King Jr., and other political assassinations if it so chooses. . . . Four Calif. newsmen with the *Fresno Bee* , jailed for refusing to identify the source of information for articles containing material from a grand-jury transcript, are released after 14 days. . . . U.S. Dist. Ct. Judge William O'Kelly sentences William A.H. Williams to 50 years in jail for the 1974 kidnapping of *Atlanta Constitution* newspaper executive J. Reginald Murphy.		Congress achieves its eleventh override of a Ford veto, enacting legislation to aid development of a practical electric automobile. . . . The Commerce Dept. says construction of new housing in August was at its highest level in six months and permits for future construction at the highest rate since March 1974.			Sept. 17
				Boston, Mass. philanthropist and financier George Peabody Gardner dies at the age of 88 in Dresden Hills, Maine. . . . Rev. Sun Myung Moon, controversial leader of the evangelical, anticommunist Unification Church, ends his personal four-year ministry in the U.S. with a "God Bless America" rally at the Washington Monument.	Sept. 18
			A Turkish Airlines Boeing 727 crashes into the Karakaya Mountain, killing all 155 aboard. The accident was attributed to the pilot's miscalculation of altitude.		Sept. 19
In a *Playboy* magazine interview, Jimmy Carter says he has "looked on a lot of women with lust" and had "committed adultery in my heart many times, but God forgives sinners."	W. Averell Harriman, former U.S. ambassador to the Soviet Union and current Carter adviser, meets with Soviet CP Gen. Secy. Leonid Brezhnev to discuss the upcoming U.S. presidential election.			Kermit Bloomgarden, 71, Broadway producer whose plays included *The Music Man* and *Death of a Salesman*, dies in N.Y. . . . The Episcopal Church's House of Bishops approves an extensively revised Book of Common Prayer, the first major revisions in 427 years.	Sept. 20

F	G	H	I	J
Includes elections, federal-state relations, civil rights and liberties, crime, the judiciary, education, health care, poverty, urban affairs and population.	*Includes formation and debate of U.S. foreign and defense policies, veterans' affairs and defense spending. (Relations with specific foreign countries are usually found under the region concerned.)*	*Includes business, labor, agriculture, taxation, transportation, consumer affairs, monetary and fiscal policy, natural resources, and pollution.*	*Includes worldwide scientific, medical and technological developments, natural phenomena, U.S. weather, natural disasters, and accidents.*	*Includes the arts, religion, scholarship, communications media, sports, entertainments, fashions, fads and social life.*

	World Affairs	Europe	Africa & the Middle East	The Americas	Asia & the Pacific
Sept. 21	The U.N. General Assembly's thirty-first session convenes with the crisis in southern Africa looming as a major issue of debate.... Vietnam wins a seat on the World Bank.... SALT talks resume in Geneva with both sides still deadlocked.	Netherlands Finance Min. Willem Duisenberg reports a deficit of $5.6 billion on a $33.2 billion budget. Queen Juliana says strict price and wage controls will continue.		Orlando Letelier, a former Chilean minister and ambassador to the U.S. who has criticized Chile's human-rights abuses, is killed by a bomb under his car in Wash., D.C. Associates charge he was murdered by agents of Chile's military govt.	
Sept. 22		French Premier Raymond Barre announces a price freeze and recommends a series of tax reforms and wage-and-price controls to curb inflation.... The Council of Europe formally admits Portugal as its nineteenth member. ... The U.S. Embassy in Bonn says that an alleged 1958 letter from former CIA head Allen Dulles to former W. Ger. Defense Min. Franz Josef Strauss regarding Lockheed purchase kickbacks is a forgery.		The Quebec Ct. of Appeals rejects an attempt by Air Canada to upset an injunction barring the airline from enforcing an English-only policy for pilots.	Indonesian State Secy. Sudharmono discloses that the government arrested four persons on charges of planning to overthrow Pres. Suharto and replace him with Mohamad Hatta.
Sept. 23		Three of the four most powerful French trade unions call for a 24-hour protest strike on Oct. 7 to show their disapproval of the government's antiinflation program. ... Four members of two popular Czech rock groups, Plastic People of the Universe and DG307, are sentenced in Prague to varying jail terms on charges that include antisocial behavior and anarchism. ... Exiled Czech Social Democratic Party leader Blazej Vilim, 67, dies in London.	Elias Sarkis, a moderate Christian, is inaugurated as Lebanon's sixth president, replacing hard-line Suleiman Franjieh, whose refusal to resign contributed to the intensification of the civil war.... A South African black student demonstration in downtown Johannesburg is the first incident of unrest in the white center of the city since riots began in June. Four hundred Africans are arrested.		Vietnam wins a seat on the Manila-based Asian Development Bank.
Sept. 24			Rhodesian P.M. Ian Smith accepts the proposal presented by U.S. State Secy. Kissinger for the transfer of power to Rhodesia's black majority within two years and an interim government until then. The proposal was first made by British P.M. James Callaghan on March 22, when he was foreign secretary, and endorsed by the U.S. on Aug. 2.		
Sept. 25		Pro-Makarios parties sweep the first Cypriot elections in the Greek-controlled area since the 1974 Turkish invasion.	A Kissinger aide says the Rhodesian agreement would not have been possible without the persuasion of S. African P.M. John Vorster.		the Indian National Development Council approves a revised fifth five-year economic plan, delayed since April 1974 because of inflation and internal political unrest.
Sept. 26	The U.S. State Dept. issues a statement that black African leaders have accepted basic proposals for majority rule in Rhodesia and that the U.S. and Great Britain will organize a meeting to form an interim government.	Netherlands police report the seizure of $5 million worth of hashish, one of the largest such drug interceptions ever made in Europe.	Four pro-Palestinian guerrillas seize a Damascus hotel and fight for seven hours with Syrian troops before being captured. The guerrilla leader and four of the 90 hostages are killed.... Leaders of African nations bordering Rhodesia and South Africa (so-called front-line states) meet in Lusaka and criticize the British Callaghan plan for Rhodesian majority rule, saying that it would legalize the white Rhodesian power structure. They do not mention U.S. State Secy. Kissinger's diplomatic role in the plan's acceptance.	Over 2,000 people, including Hortensia Bussi de Allende, widow of the late Chilean president, attend a memorial mass in St. Matthew's Cathedral, Wash., D.C., for Chilean ex-minister Orlando Letelier, who was killed when a bomb exploded under his car in Washington on Sept. 21.	

A	B	C	D	E
Includes developments that affect more than one world region, international organizations and important meetings of major world leaders.	*Includes all domestic and regional developments in Europe, including the Soviet Union, Turkey, Cyprus and Malta.*	*Includes all domestic and regional developments in Africa and the Middle East, including Iraq and Iran and excluding Cyprus, Turkey and Afghanistan.*	*Includes all domestic and regional developments in Latin America, the Caribbean and Canada.*	*Includes all domestic and regional developments in Asia and Pacific nations, extending from Afghanistan through all the Pacific Islands, except Hawaii.*

U.S. Politics & Social Issues	U.S. Foreign Policy & Defense	U.S. Economy & Environment	Science, Technology & Nature	Culture, Leisure & Life Style	
Wall Street Journal reports that Charles Ruff, Watergate special prosecutor, is investigating political contributions that may involve Pres. Ford's past congressional campaigns.... Former AEC head Dixy Lee Ray narrowly wins the Washington State Democratic gubernatorial primary.		Pres. Ford triples the duty on imported sugar to 1.875 cents a pound, the maximum allowed by law, from .625 a pound.... Carter calls for a new Cabinet-level dept. to reorganize federal energy and power agencies and charges that "our country still has no energy policy."			Sept. 21
The House drops its probe of CBS correspondent Daniel Schorr's sources of classified information about U.S. intelligence activities after Schorr refused nine times to testify.... Carter press secy. Jody Powell reports that Carter has called Lady Bird Johnson to apologize about his *Playboy* interview reference to her late husband, which linked him with former Pres. Nixon in distorting the truth.	Pres. Ford signs legislation appropriating $104.3 billion for defense in fiscal 1977, $3.6 billion less than the Pentagon requested, but almost $14 billion more than in 1976.... A bill, sponsored by Rep. Jonathan Bingham (D, N.Y.), barring U.S. companies from participating in the Arab League's economic boycott of Israel is approved by the House over strong White House opposition.	The Senate passes two key bills that will help achieve the Democrats' goal of creating more jobs. ... EPA reports that 1977-model cars had a 6 percent gain in fuel economy, averaging 18.6 m.p.g., and a substantial reduction in auto-exhaust emissions.	The FDA bans the use of Red No. 4 dye (used in maraschino cherries) in foods and ingested drugs and the use of carbon black (used in licorice) in foods, drugs, and cosmetics.		Sept. 22
Presidential contenders Ford and Carter meet in the first of three televised debates, marred by a technical mishap, which loses 27 minutes of sound. Ford accuses Carter of not being specific, and Carter charges bureaucracy and lack of leadership in Washington.... Former Postmaster Gen. Marvin Watson pleads guilty to helping Armand Hammer, chairman of Occidental Petroleum Corp., cover up illegal contributions to Nixon's presidential campaign.			Center for Disease Control (CDC) holds live-virus oral polio vaccine responsible for over half the U.S. cases of polio between 1973 and 1975. Dr. Jonas Salk, who discovered the killed-virus injectable vaccines, contends that the live-virus vaccine discovered by Dr. Albert Sabin was the main cause of 140 polio cases reported since 1960.	South African govt. announces that sports matches between black and white teams will be allowed and that integrated teams can now represent the country in international competitions.	Sept. 23
Patricia Hearst is sentenced to concurrent sentences of seven years for armed romed robbery and two years for using a firearm in the commission of a felony.... Paul H. Douglas, 84, economist and Democratic senator from Illinois (1948–1966), dies in Washington.		EPA announces a relaxed timetable for gasoline lead-content reduction, in face of possible gas shortages in the next two years.		Kenneth Tynan's sex-revue *Oh! Calcutta!* returns to Broadway after a successful 610-performance run in 1971.	Sept. 24
		Carter pledges to end sales of nuclear fuel and technology to countries engaging in nuclear weapons development or building a plant for reprocessing reactor fuel.... The collapse of Teton River Dam (Idaho) in June is called a man-made disaster by Rep. Leo Ryan (D, Calif.), chairman of the congressional subcommittee that investigated it.	Carter pledges to end sales of nuclear fuel and technology to countries engaging in nuclear weapons development or building a plant for reprocessing reactor fuel.... The collapse of Teton River Dam (Idaho) in June is called a man-made disaster by Rep. Leo Ryan (D, Calif.), chairman of the congressional subcommittee that investigated it.	A newly staged production of George Gershwin's opera *Porgy and Bess* opens on Broadway.	Sept. 25
			China is reported to have concluded its nineteenth nuclear weapons test, viewed as a morale booster in wake of Mao's death.	The Circle in the Square (N.Y.C.) opens its new season with Marguerite Duras's play *Days in the Trees* .	Sept. 26

F	G	H	I	J
Includes elections, federal-state relations, civil rights and liberties, crime, the judiciary, education, health care, poverty, urban affairs and population.	*Includes formation and debate of U.S. foreign and defense policies, veterans' affairs and defense spending. (Relations with specific foreign countries are usually found under the region concerned.)*	*Includes business, labor, agriculture, taxation, transportation, consumer affairs, monetary and fiscal policy, natural resources, and pollution.*	*Includes worldwide scientific, medical and technological developments, natural phenomena, U.S. weather, natural disasters, and accidents.*	*Includes the arts, religion, scholarship, communications media, sports, entertainments, fashions, fads and social life.*

	World Affairs	Europe	Africa & the Middle East	The Americas	Asia & the Pacific
Sept. 27	At the close of the U.N. International Atomic Energy Agency annual conference in Rio de Janeiro, Yugoslavia proposes an international nuclear fuel cycle pool to assist developing countries in building their nuclear energy potential and help developed countries in stabilizing uranium supply.	Portuguese govt. begins to return to their owners 101 small and medium-sized farms occupied by leftist and Communist farm workers in 1975.	The three captured Palestinian guerrillas who seized a Damascus hotel are hanged in public after confessing to be Al Fatah members, protesting Syria's involvement in Lebanon. . . . Al Fatah denies any involvement in the Damascus hotel raid, claims that the captured guerrillas sought to discredit PLO leader Yasir Arafat, and accuses a group headed by Abou Nidal, whom it had expelled from the organization in 1970.	Pope Paul VI demands that the Argentine govt. provide an adequate explanation for the killing of several priests earlier this year. . . . Premier Fidel Castro blames Cuba's economic problems on the sharp fall of world sugar prices and charges that U.S. policy contributed to the price decline. . . . Inmates of a British Columbia maximum-security prison seize hostages and demand a meeting to air their grievances.	
Sept. 28	Addressing the U.N. General Assembly, Soviet Foreign Min. Andrei Gromyko sharply attacks U.S. State Secy. Kissinger's diplomatic efforts in Africa, saying they were aimed at containing the "just struggle of the people" for their legitimate rights. . . . In his U.N. address, Soviet For. Min. Gromyko makes a conciliatory reference to China, the first Soviet reference to that country in an international forum since the death of Chmn. Mao Tse-tung.		Syrian and Lebanese Christian forces launch a long-expected major attack against Palestinian forces in the mountains east of Beirut. Syria demands that PLO leader Yasir Arafat accept Syrian intervention.		
Sept. 29	Following an unprecedented drop in the pound's value to $1.64, British Exchequer Chancellor Denis Healey announces the British Treasury will apply for a $3.9 billion loan from the IMF. . . . British For. Secy. Anthony Crosland announces that Britain will convene a conference to discuss the formation of a Rhodesian interim government.	Finland's Premier Martti Miettunen and his coalition Cabinet are sworn in. . . . British Labor Party conference rejects the EEC agreement for direct elections to the European Parliament. . . . Lagonegro, Italy court sentences Giuseppe Lamanna and Antonio Mancuso to eight years in prison for the 1973 kidnapping of J. Paul Getty III. . . . Gibraltar's pro-British Labor Party wins a majority of legislative seats.	Three British citizens are sentenced in Cape Town, South Africa on charges of printing and distributing illegal political literature. . . . Mozambique Pres. Samora Machel says that guerrilla war will not end until a concrete timetable for transfer of power is established in Rhodesia.	Orlando Letelier, killed in a Wash., D.C. bomb explosion, is buried in Caracas, Venezuela. Venezuelan Pres. Carlos Andres Perez offers condolences to Letelier's widow and expresses solidarity for Chileans who believe in freedom and democracy.	Phillipine Pres. Ferdinand Marcos orders punishment for six soldiers accused of torturing three detained women.
Sept. 30	In a speech before the U.N. General Assembly, U.S. State Secy. Kissinger responds to Soviet For. Min. Gromyko's Sept. 28 charges before the U.N., and declares that the U.S. is impartial in southern Africa and wants black leaders there to devise their own political future without outside interference.	Portugal and Angola agree to reestablish diplomatic relations, broken off by Angola in May.	Rhodesian P.M. Ian Smith accepts a British proposal to convene a black-white Rhodesian conference to lay plans for black majority rule.		

A	B	C	D	E
Includes developments that affect more than one world region, international organizations and important meetings of major world leaders.	Includes all domestic and regional developments in Europe, including the Soviet Union, Turkey, Cyprus and Malta.	Includes all domestic and regional developments in Africa and the Middle East, including Iraq and Iran and excluding Cyprus, Turkey and Afghanistan.	Includes all domestic and regional developments in Latin America, the Caribbean and Canada.	Includes all domestic and regional developments in Asia and Pacific nations, extending from Afghanistan through all the Pacific Islands, except Hawaii.

U.S. Politics & Social Issues	U.S. Foreign Policy & Defense	U.S. Economy & Environment	Science, Technology & Nature	Culture, Leisure & Life Style	
Jimmy Carter explains his controversial interview in *Playboy* by saying that he is trying to run an accessible campaign and that the magazine has a wide readership, but admits that his choice of adultery to illustrate his views on religious intolerance was unfortunate. . . . Ford, in a strong law-and-order stance, urges all citizens to join in a crusade against crime, ruling out vigilante action, but calling for swift and certain justice.		The Justice Dept. files suit against Chrysler Corp. for $91 million in penalties for alleged auto-emission violations. . . . Commerce Dept. announces a $757.7 million U.S. trade deficit for August, the third largest on record.	Dr. Morris Fishbein, 87, *Journal of the American Medical Association* editor from 1924 to 1949, whose controversial views forced his retirement from the AMA, dies after a long illness in Chicago.		Sept. 27
		Commerce Dept. announces a 1.5 percent decline of leading economic indicators in August, the first decline since February 1975 and the steepest slide since January 1975. . . . The Toxic Substances Control Act, prohibiting the marketing of new chemical compounds before testing their health and environmental impact, is passed by Congress.		World heavyweight boxing champion Muhammad Ali wins a unanimous 15-round decision over Ken Norton at Madison Square Garden, N.Y.C.	Sept. 28
A Calif. grand jury indicts William and Emily Harris on charges stemming from the February 1974 kidnapping of Patricia Hearst.		House Government Operations Committee reports that virtually all U.S. banks engaged in international business have "willingly" complied with the Arab economic boycott of Israel.		Former Pres. Richard Nixon is reported to have signed a $2 million contract for his memoirs and will receive an additional $300,000 for related expenses. . . . San Francisco Giant John Montefusco pitches a no-hitter against the Atlanta Braves to win, 9–0. . . . The Brooklyn Academy of Music (BAM) Theater Co. is incorporated with Frank Dunlop as artistic director. . . . Industrialist Armand Hammer buys the Rembrandt painting *Juno* for $3.25 million, setting a new record price for a Rembrandt art work. . . . John Cage's *Renga with Apartment House 1776* , receives its world premiere by the Boston Symphony Orchestra, conducted by Seiji Ozawa.	Sept. 29
A Gallup Poll on the results of the first presidential TV debate finds that of the 67 percent of the nation's adults viewing it, 32 percent favored Ford, 25 percent favored Carter, and 33 percent saw a tie. . . . Congress overrides Pres. Ford's veto of legislation appropriating $56.6 billion for the Labor Dept. and HEW in fiscal 1977, the twelfth veto override since Ford took office. . . . The Senate gives final approval, 77–4, to a $25.6 billion extension of the federal revenue sharing program from Jan. 1, 1977 to Sept. 30, 1980.	William H. (Hap) Arnold, 75, retired U.S. Army general who commanded the American Division in the South Pacific during WWII, dies in Lake Forest, Ill.	Commerce Dept. reports that the Arab economic boycott of Israel has been supported by 94 percent of the U.S. companies surveyed between September 1975 and March 1976. . . . William Zeckendorf, 71, U.S. and Canadian real-estate developer who assembled the site for U.N. headquarters, dies of a stroke in Wash., D.C.	Calif. Gov. Jerry Brown signs right-to-die legislation, the first enacted by any U.S. state, thus allowing adult patients to authorize termination of life-sustaining equipment if they are facing certain death.	The Senate, 75–0, and the House, by voice vote, clear the first major revision of U.S. copyright laws since 1909.	Sept. 30

F	G	H	I	J
Includes elections, federal-state relations, civil rights and liberties, crime, the judiciary, education, health care, poverty, urban affairs and population.	*Includes formation and debate of U.S. foreign and defense policies, veterans' affairs and defense spending. (Relations with specific foreign countries are usually found under the region concerned.)*	*Includes business, labor, agriculture, taxation, transportation, consumer affairs, monetary and fiscal policy, natural resources, and pollution.*	*Includes worldwide scientific, medical and technological developments, natural phenomena, U.S. weather, natural disasters, and accidents.*	*Includes the arts, religion, scholarship, communications media, sports, entertainments, fashions, fads and social life.*

	World Affairs	Europe	Africa & the Middle East	The Americas	Asia & the Pacific
Oct. 1	The Soviet Union calls for the resumption of the Geneva Middle East peace conference to consider terms of its proposal: the withdrawal of Israeli troops from 1967-occupied Arab lands, creation of a Palestinian state, international guarantees for the independence of Israel and its Arab neighboring states, and an end to the Israel-Arab war.... Pres. Ford meets with Soviet Foreign Min. Andrei Gromyko in Washington for talks on the stalemate in the SALT II talks, but no progress is reported. ... The Soviet CP newspaper *Pravda*, marking the twenty-seventh anniversary of the Communists' takeover of China, indicates official willingness to improve relations with Peking.	*Wall Street Journal* reports that stockholders of French auto makers Peugeot S.A. and Citroen S.A. have approved plans to merge and create a group to rival France's largest car producer, Renault Co.. ... Extensive changes in Portuguese labor laws are announced that directly challenge Communist power in the trade unions.... Italian Premier Giulio Andreotti announces on national TV a series of emergency measures designed to protect the lira and to increase industrial productivity.	The Syrians and Christians renew their offensive at Aleih after the Palestinian refusal Sept. 30 to accept Syrian cease-fire terms. The Christians suffer heavy losses.	A riot by inmates of a maximum-security penitentiary in British Columbia ends with two hostages released and most of the prisoners' demands reportedly met.... Guyanan Parliament reportedly approves a bill, which had been bitterly opposed by Catholic and Anglican churches, enabling the government to take over all schools.... About 6,700 Protestant teachers strike more than 320 Quebec elementary and secondary schools in a dispute over class sizes and workload.	Reuters says an Australian govt. report to Parliament shows the birth rate is at a long-term no-growth level and a net yearly immigration loss of 5,000.
Oct. 2			The Syrian–Lebanese Christian offensive, launched in the mountains east of Beirut Sept. 28, routs the Palestinians from most of their strategic positions.... The Syrian-Christian attacks are suspended, apparently to permit further political negotiations.	The embalmed remains of Eva Duarte de Peron, second wife of the late Argentinian Pres. Juan Peron, are removed from the crypt of the presidential residence and buried in her family's vault in another Buenos Aires cemetery.	
Oct. 3		British Undersecretary of State for Energy John Cunningham says oil production from the five operating North Sea fields totals more than one million tons per month.... W. Ger. Chancellor Helmut Schmidt's ruling coalition of the Social Democratic Party and the Free Democratic Party win a narrow majority in nationwide parliamentary elections against a strong challenge.	Syrians announce that Saudi Arabia's 4,000-man force, on the Golan Heights since October 1973, will be withdrawn.... Arabs and Jews clash in the Israeli-occupied West Bank town of Hebron in a religious dispute involving a Moslem shrine. Hundreds of Arab youths desecrate Jewish artifacts.		
Oct. 4	The IMF and the World Bank meet in Manila where World Bank head Robert McNamara calls for an increase in the Bank's capital resources and in direct and indirect aid to the world's 900 million poor.	Juan Maria de Araluce y Villar, an adviser to Spanish King Juan Carlos I, is killed by presumed members of ETA, the Basque separatist movement.... A Czech Presidium member says Soviet deliveries of crude oil to Czechoslovakia will be sharply reduced in 1976–80, but the extent of the cutbacks and their cause are not disclosed.	Syria levels sharp criticism at PLO leader Yasir Arafat, charging him with misusing power to the detriment of the Palestinian cause.	Former Canadian P.M. John Diefenbaker accuses the late U.S. Pres. John Kennedy of causing his ouster from office by arranging a foreign-exchange crisis that forced the devaluation of the Canadian dollar.	In India New Delhi police padlock the presses of the *Indian Express*, the English-language newspaper opposed to government policies. ... Thai students demonstrate against the return to Thailand on Sept. 19 of exiled former Premier Thanom Kittikachorn.
Oct. 5	Chinese Foreign Min. Chiao Kuanhua denounces the U.S.S.R. in an address to the thirty-first session of the U.N. General Assembly, rebuffing Soviet peace overtures and disarmament proposals.... U.S. Treasury Secy. William Simon restates his opposition to an enlargement of the World Bank's capital resources, a view shared by French, Japanese, and Australian meeting participants.	In an interview with a French TV reporter, Soviet leader Leonid Brezhnev blames the Soviet arms build-up on Western military pressure.... Protesting the assassination of royal adviser Juan Maria de Araluce y Villar, Spanish rightists go on a rampage in San Sebastian after Araluce's funeral, reportedly unhampered by riot police.			

A	B	C	D	E
Includes developments that affect more than one world region, international organizations and important meetings of major world leaders.	Includes all domestic and regional developments in Europe, including the Soviet Union, Turkey, Cyprus and Malta.	Includes all domestic and regional developments in Africa and the Middle East, including Iraq and Iran and excluding Cyprus, Turkey and Afghanistan.	Includes all domestic and regional developments in Latin America, the Caribbean and Canada.	Includes all domestic and regional developments in Asia and Pacific nations, extending from Afghanistan through all the Pacific Islands, except Hawaii.

U.S. Politics & Social Issues	U.S. Foreign Policy & Defense	U.S. Economy & Environment	Science, Technology & Nature	Culture, Leisure & Life Style	
A racial slur made by Agriculture Secy. Earl Butz in conversation with former White House counsel John Dean, and reported by Dean, creates a storm of controversy.	Pres. Ford signs the $5.1-billion Foreign Assistance Appropriations Act, which allocates 43 percent of the funds to the Middle East and contains an amendment cutting off military aid to Uruguay because of alleged torture and other human-rights violations.				Oct. 1
Criticism of Agr. Secy. Earl Butz widens as members of both parties call for his resignation or dismissal, using words such as "poisonous," "revolting" and "stupid" to describe his racial quip. . . . Republican vice presidential candidate Robert Dole criticizes Carter for his stand on taxation of church properties such as church-owned hospitals, schools, senior citizens homes, and orphanages.		Rep. Charles Vanik (D, Ohio) charges that eleven major corporations with combined earnings of more than $1 billion in 1975 paid no federal income taxes that year. . . . Arnold Miller's UMW presidency receives a setback during a turbulent union convention in which delegates withdraw UMW support of federal strip-mining controls and favor less-strict state controls.	The Center for Disease Control reports that 12 cases of a new strain of gonorrhea, resistent to penicillin, have been detected in seven states.		Oct. 2
No public officials defend Agriculture Secy. Earl Butz, but two Republican governors — James Edwards (S.C.) and Robert Bennett (Kan.) — say that Butz's remark was no more serious than Carter's comments on adultery in *Playboy*.				Walter Alston resigns from the Los Angeles Dodgers after 23 seasons as manager and is replaced by Tom LaSorda.	Oct. 3
The Supreme Ct. announces it will not reconsider its July 2 ruling that upheld the death penalty and lifts a stay on executions in three states signed by Justice Lewis Powell Jr. on July 22.		Agriculture Secy. Earl Butz resigns, acknowledging he was guilty of "gross indiscretion" in a remark he made about blacks. Undersecy. John Knebel becomes acting secretary. . . . The Supreme Ct. vacates a lower-court ruling that found it lawful for strikers to picket businesses retailing the struck company's products.		The baseball major leagues' first and only black manager, Frank Robinson, is signed to a third one-year contract with the Cleveland Indians. He announces his retirement as a player.	Oct. 4
The New York Times says a team of 18 reporters, motivated by the murder of newsman Don Bolles, are jointly preparing a series of articles on crime and corruption in Arizona. . . . Pres. Ford describes the ninety-fourth Congress as one marked by "weak compromises and evasions." . . . Osborne Elliott resigns as *Newsweek* magazine chairman and editor-in-chief to become N.Y.C.'s deputy mayor for economic development, a dollar-a-year post, the first in the city.	A GAO study questions whether the Ford administration exhausted all diplomatic possibilities with Cambodia before it ordered the *Mayaquez* rescue strike in May 1975, resulting in the death of 41 servicemen.	The Census Bureau announces the nation's farm population was an estimated 8.9 million in 1975, or 4.2 percent of the total population. It has been steadily declining since 1920. . . . Asst. Atty. Gen. Donald Baker, head of the Justice Dept.'s antitrust division, personally presents the government's sentencing recommendations to a Chicago court regarding 48 paperboard company officials who pleaded no-contest to price-fixing charges. . . . Allied Chemical Corp. is fined $13.3 million for polluting the James River with the toxic insecticide Kepone.	Nobel laureate and chemistry professor Lars Onsager, 72, dies in Coral Gables, Fla. . . . The FDA says it has approved a plan by Dr. John Merritt to use marijuana to treat severe cases of glaucoma. . . . The drought in western Australia, South Australia, Victoria, and New South Wales ends with heavy rain and hail storms, severely flooding Victoria and New South Wales.	Syndicated Broadway columnist Leonard Lyons dies at the age of 70 in N.Y. after a long illness.	Oct. 5

F	G	H	I	J
Includes elections, federal-state relations, civil rights and liberties, crime, the judiciary, education, health care, poverty, urban affairs and population.	Includes formation and debate of U.S. foreign and defense policies, veterans' affairs and defense spending. (Relations with specific foreign countries are usually found under the region concerned.)	Includes business, labor, agriculture, taxation, transportation, consumer affairs, monetary and fiscal policy, natural resources, and pollution.	Includes worldwide scientific, medical and technological developments, natural phenomena, U.S. weather, natural disasters, and accidents.	Includes the arts, religion, scholarship, communications media, sports, entertainments, fashions, fads and social life.

	World Affairs	Europe	Africa & the Middle East	The Americas	Asia & the Pacific
Oct. 6	Gold closes at $115.25.		A religious funeral service for the Jewish Torah scrolls and holy books desecrated by the Arabs during unrest in Hebron is attended by 3,000 religious Jews while Israeli soldiers stand by.	A Cuban passenger jet crashes after bombs explode following takeoff. The bombing, which kills all 73 on board, is attributed to Cuban exiles and Venezuelans opposing Premier Fidel Castro.... Honduras and El Salvador agree to arbitrate the border dispute stemming from their brief but intense war in July 1969.... Chile withdraws from the Andean Group after unsuccessful attempts to change the group's limits on foreign investment and its common external tariff.	The Thai govt. of Premier Seni Pramoj is ousted and replaced by the Thai military following bloody clashes in Bangkok between police and left-wing students, resulting in the arrests of 1,700 students.... In response to an appeal by the *Indian Express*, the Delhi High Ct. rules that the police padlocking of its presses was improper and orders the seals and locks removed.
Oct. 7	The U.S., Britain, and S. Africa discuss establishing a fund to aid the transition to majority rule in Rhodesia. It is to be used to provide economic security for all citizens.	Helmut Kohl announces he will give up his post as prime minister of the West German Rhineland–Palatinate state to lead the opposition coalition of Christian Democrats and Christian Social Unionists in the W. Ger. Bundestag.		At least 16 are arrested in Trinidad & Tabago and in Venezuela in connection with the Cuban plane bombing.... Colombian Pres. Alfonso Lopez Michelsen reimposes a state of siege to combat what he calls a wave of subversive civil unrest.	An Australian House of Representative's Committee warns that rampant alcoholism could destroy the Aborigines in the Northern Territory unless immediate action is taken.... Chiang Ching, Mao's widow, and four other key leaders of the CP's radical faction are purged after reportedly trying to forge Mao's will and oust Hua Kuofeng as party chairman.
Oct. 8		Soviet CP Secy. Gen. Leonid Brezhnev and Angolan Pres. Agostinho Neto conclude two days of talks in Moscow by signing a 20-year treaty of friendship and cooperation between the two countries and between the Soviet CP and Neto's MPLA.... Swedish Premier Thorbjorn Falldin names a 20-member Cabinet that includes five women, and delivers a policy speech in which he abandons his campaign pledge to end nuclear power plant construction and operation in the country.... The Portuguese govt. announces three austerity decrees to reduce Portugal's balance of payments deficit.	S. African P.M. John Vorster meets with the chiefs of eight of the nine tribal homelands (Bantustans), his first such conference since black unrest began in June.	In a newspaper interview, Uruguayan Pres. Aparicio Mendez blames the U.S. foreign aid ban on the U.S. Democratic Party and Sen. Edward Kennedy (D, Mass.).	Vietnam, Laos, and the U.S.S.R. accuse the U.S. of fomenting the coup in Thailand, saying the Thai junta officers are pro-U.S. militarists known to be working for the CIA.... An announcement is made that Mao's body will be embalmed and enshrined in a crystal sarcophagus and displayed in a mausoleum to be constructed in Peking.
Oct. 9		The Provisional Sinn Fein, political arm of the IRA, begins a propaganda campaign against the Northern Ireland women's peace movement, saying its rallies had duped thousands.	Leaders of two factions of the African Nat. Council, Joshua Nkomo and Robert Mugabe, demand immediate Rhodesian majority rule and release of all political prisoners.	The Venezuelan govt. admits there are no new leads in its investigation of the February kidnapping of William Niehous, a U.S. business executive.	
Oct. 10			Israeli P.M. Yitzhak Rabin declares that as a result of the Hebron unrest, he and his ministers will become more involved in occupied area policy, hitherto under the sole jurisdiction of the military and defense ministers.	Uruguayan Pres. Aparicio Mendez disavows his comments about the U.S. Democratic Party and Sen. Edward Kennedy, and his government confiscates the edition of *La Manana* that contained the interview.	Australian P.M. Malcolm Fraser and Indonesian Pres. Suharto agree that Australian representatives will confer with the five member countries of ASEAN on economic issues.
Oct. 11	The U.S. accuses U.N. Secy. Gen. Kurt Waldheim of yielding to pressure from governments seeking Secretariat jobs for unqualified candidates.	British Parliament approves Exchequer Chancellor Denis Healey's decision to raise the Bank of England's 13 percent minimum lending rate to a record 15 percent so that Britain can get a $3.9 billion IMF loan.... *Democratie Francaise*, French Pres. Valery Giscard d'Estaing's book on French liberalism and its future, is published, and the first printing of 200,000 copies sells out in a few hours.	Pres. Ford says the U.S. has agreed to lift the ban on sales to Israel of some sophisticated weapons and to hasten the delivery of already-approved equipment.	Patrick Rice, a Roman Catholic Irish priest working with the poor in Buenos Aires, Argentina, is reported arrested and subjected to electric-shock torture.... *Washington Post* reports four policemen are under arrest in Rio de Janeiro in connection with a Brazilian Death Squad execution in which one of the intended victims survived.	
	A Includes developments that affect more than one world region, international organizations and important meetings of major world leaders.	**B** Includes all domestic and regional developments in Europe, including the Soviet Union, Turkey, Cyprus and Malta.	**C** Includes all domestic and regional developments in Africa and the Middle East, including Iraq and Iran and excluding Cyprus, Turkey and Afghanistan.	**D** Includes all domestic and regional developments in Latin America, the Caribbean and Canada.	**E** Includes all domestic and regional developments in Asia and Pacific nations, extending from Afghanistan through all the Pacific Islands, except Hawaii.

U.S. Politics & Social Issues	U.S. Foreign Policy & Defense	U.S. Economy & Environment	Science, Technology & Nature	Culture, Leisure & Life Style	
The second nationally televised debate between Ford and Carter features sharp attacks by Carter on Ford's foreign policy and a strong defense by Ford of his record.	In the debate Ford asserts that there is no Soviet domination of Eastern Europe and there never will be under a Ford administration. ... In the debate Carter says the U.S. has lost world prestige through lack of leadership, morality, and openness in foreign dealings, and charges that State Secy. Kissinger "has been President" concerning foreign policy.... Ford announces during the second presidential debate that the Commerce Dept. will tomorrow release the names of companies that complied with Arab requests to boycott Israel.	House Government Operations Committee accuses the Comptroller of the Currency's office of failing to take aggressive corrective action against Franklin National Bank, N.Y., which, when it collapsed in October 1974, was the largest bank failure in U.S. history.		Jackson Pollock's last privately owned painting, *Lavender Mist*, is reported sold to the National Gallery of Art, Wash., D.C. for $2 million.	Oct. 6
Gary Gilmore, convicted Utah murderer, is sentenced to death and pleads for prompt execution by a firing squad.	Pres. Ford modifies his announced position on the Commerce Dept. disclosure of companies participating in the Arab boycott, saying that it should make available all "future" reports.... Carter says Ford's claim of Eastern European freedom "is a cruel hoax upon millions of Eastern Europeans who have lived under Soviet domination for their entire lives." ... Ethnic group leaders in the U.S. deplore Pres. Ford's statement that the Soviets do not dominate Eastern Europe.			David Del Tredici's *The Final Alice*, a tonal orchestral work in a series inspired by *Alice in Wonderland*, is premiered in Chicago.... The Cooper-Hewitt Museum of Design opens in the former Andrew Carnegie mansion, N.Y.C.	Oct. 7
	The Commerce Dept. issues new rules requiring that all demands made to U.S. companies to participate in the Arab boycott of Israel must be reported within 15 days of receipt.	The Labor Dept. announces that unemployment declined one-tenth of one point during September to 7.8 percent, the first labor-force shrinkage since February.			Oct. 8
		Pres. Ford signs a proclamation imposing a meat import quota of 1.233 billion pounds in 1976, the first time a quota is set since enactment of the 1964 Beef Import Law.		Czech dissident playwright Vaclav Havel is not allowed to attend the Austrian premieres of two of his plays in Vienna.	Oct. 9
					Oct. 10
			Three elderly persons die hours after they receive the swine flu vaccine. The Center for Disease Control finds no evidence that the flu vaccinations caused the deaths. ... The French govt. announces its willingness to discuss international limitations on the spread of nuclear technology.	Connee Boswell, 68, radio singing star of the 1930s who went on to film and television, dies in N.Y.	Oct. 11

F	G	H	I	J
Includes elections, federal-state relations, civil rights and liberties, crime, the judiciary, education, health care, poverty, urban affairs and population.	Includes formation and debate of U.S. foreign and defense policies, veterans' affairs and defense spending. (Relations with specific foreign countries are usually found under the region concerned.)	Includes business, labor, agriculture, taxation, transportation, consumer affairs, monetary and fiscal policy, natural resources, and pollution.	Includes worldwide scientific, medical and technological developments, natural phenomena, U.S. weather, natural disasters, and accidents.	Includes the arts, religion, scholarship, communications media, sports, entertainments, fashions, fads and social life.

	World Affairs	Europe	Africa & the Middle East	The Americas	Asia & the Pacific
Oct. 12		Six former officers of the Greek security police are found guilty of torturing political prisoners and are sentenced to terms ranging from 10 months to two years.... In a formal protest, the Austrian govt. says that the Czech govt. ban on playwright Vaclav Havel's travel to Vienna violates the spirit of the Helsinki agreement.		P.M. Pierre Trudeau pledges to combat Canadian inflation and unemployment and says more emphasis will be placed on teaching French in schools and less on teaching it to civil servants.... A Jesuit priest, Rev. Joao Bosco Penido Burnier, is killed by police in Brazil when he goes to a police station to ask clemency for two female prisoners who had been tortured.	Premier Hua Kuo-feng succeeds Mao as chairman of the Chinese Communist Party and the Military Affairs Commission, thereby holding the country's three highest government posts.
Oct. 13	A U.S. Dept. of Economic and Social Affairs report holds that the world's natural resources are sufficient to sustain a growing population and higher standard of living, thereby directly challenging a 1972 Club of Rome private study that warned that the planet could not provide for advancing growth.... Supreme Allied Commander Alexander Haig acknowledges NATO's shortcomings, but defends basic NATO strategic assumptions against too rapid changes in doctrine.	The Italian parliamentary commission probing Premier Giulio Andreotti's alleged involvement in the Lockheed payoff scandal votes, 19–1, to drop the investigation.	Syrian forces open a new drive against Palestinian positions near Beirut, forcing cancellation of truce talks scheduled to resume today. ... Five Palestinians, taken into custody after landing a speedboat in daylight on a beach in Tel Aviv, are identified as Al Fatah guerrillas who planned terrorist operations in Israel.	Canadian Nat. Defense Min. James Richardson resigns to protest P.M. Pierre Trudeau's plan to give French official status with English in Canada's proposed Constitution.	
Oct. 14	Edouard Ghorra, Lebanon's chief U.N. representative, denounces the Palestinian role in Lebanon, saying the Palestinian revolution is entirely to blame for the civil war.	Mikhail Soloviev, a member of the Soviet Embassy in France's trade department, is expelled for spying.		*London Financial Times* reports that unnamed persons sent a letter bomb in September to Brazilian Gen. Dilermando Gomes Monteiro, who was largely responsible for ending police brutality and torture in recent months, as part of a war of nerves against the Geisel govt. ... More than half of Canada's 2.2 million unionized workers walk off their jobs in a one-day strike to protest the government's antiinflation program.	
Oct. 15	For the nineteenth time since the Nobel Prize awards began in 1901, the Nobel Committee of the Norwegian Parliament decides to award no peace prize.	Italian Tres. Min. Gaetano Stammati announces antiinflation measures designed to replace the 10 percent surcharge on foreign currency purchases, which were instituted Oct. 1.... The Irish Supreme Ct. approves the Emergency Powers Bill after Pres. Cearbhall O Dalaigh asked that a section of it be judged to see if it were constitutional.		Cuban Premier Fidel Castro says he will cancel the 1973 Cuban–U.S. antihijacking agreement because the CIA participated directly in the Oct. 6 bombing of a Cuban airline jet.	Thailand's ruling military council announces it has launched a nationwide roundup of leftist writers, educators, and intellectuals suspected of being subversives. ... The Japanese govt. submits to the Diet (parliament) an interim report on its eight-month investigation of the Lockheed scandal that implicates 14 Diet members.
Oct. 16	Britain says the conference on Rhodesian majority rule will open formally in Geneva on Oct. 28, with preliminary sessions beginning on Oct. 21.		Egyptian Pres. Anwar Sadat is sworn in for a second six-year term of office.	Brazilian Jesuit priests issue a statement saying that Rev. Joao Bosco Penido Burnier's murder by the police was not an isolated incident as the government claims, but stems from a system that abuses human rights.	
Oct. 17		Comte Robert-Jean de Vogue, 80, WWII French Resistance hero who later was managing director of Moet & Chandon champagne concern, dies in Paris.... Finnish Socialists lose control of 19 municipal councils and gain control of four in elections.	Approximately 700 blacks damage official vehicles in the Johannesburg black township of Soweto, S. Africa after the funeral of a 16-year-old student, who died in jail.... Rabbi Meir Kahane, leader of the U.S. Jewish Defense League, announces in Jerusalem that 20 families of JDL members, including his own, will move into Qiryat Arba, the Jewish settlement adjacent to Hebron, to encourage opposition to Israeli moderates.		One of Indian P.M. Indira Gandhi's major political foes, Jayaprakash Narayan, heads the People's Union for Civil Liberties and Democratic Rights, a newly formed group opposed to Gandhi.... Vietnam criticizes Thai's military rulers, accusing the junta of rounding up several thousand Vietnamese and incarcerating them in disguised concentration camps.

A	B	C	D	E
Includes developments that affect more than one world region, international organizations and important meetings of major world leaders.	Includes all domestic and regional developments in Europe, including the Soviet Union, Turkey, Cyprus and Malta.	Includes all domestic and regional developments in Africa and the Middle East, including Iraq and Iran and excluding Cyprus, Turkey and Afghanistan.	Includes all domestic and regional developments in Latin America, the Caribbean and Canada.	Includes all domestic and regional developments in Asia and Pacific nations, extending from Afghanistan through all the Pacific Islands, except Hawaii.

U.S. Politics & Social Issues	U.S. Foreign Policy & Defense	U.S. Economy & Environment	Science, Technology & Nature	Culture, Leisure & Life Style	
The Supreme Ct. refuses to review, and thus leaves in effect, a 1975 FCC ruling interpreting equal political broadcast time. The FCC ruling provided the legal basis for the Ford–Carter debates.... The second murder trial of Rubin (Hurricane) Carter and John Artis begins in Jersey City, N.J.... A federal appeals ct. upholds, 5–1, the Watergate conspiracy convictions of John Mitchell, H.R. Haldeman, and John Ehrlichman, but reverses the conviction of Robert Mardian.	After trying on several occasions to clarify his remarks about Soviet influence on Eastern Europe, Pres. Ford meets with ethnic group leaders in the White House and afterwards acknowledges his mistake in expression. Clarifying, he says that he recognizes Soviet military domination in Eastern Europe, but does not "accept" or "acquiesce" to it.	Pres. Ford signs a bill, long sought by environmentalists, requiring prerelease testing of potentially dangerous chemicals.... UAW's 170,000 striking Ford workers ratify a three-year nationwide contract with annual 3 percent pay increases and cost-of-living adjustments, thereby ending a 28-day strike.		Baseball's Cincinnati Reds win their second National league pennant in succession and their fourth in seven years, beating the Philadelphia Phillies.	Oct. 12
A mistrial is declared in the Boston bank robbery–murder case of Susan Saxe, the antiwar activist who had been on the FBI's 10-most-wanted list for five years. ... Pres. Ford signs into law a medical education-aid bill aimed at increasing the proportion of doctors and other health professionals working in medically deprived areas.		Pres. Ford raises the price-support loan rates to farmers for wheat, corn and other feed grains, to give farmers an opportunity to hold their crops for higher prices.		CBS Inc. ousts Arthur Taylor as president to be replaced by John Backe, head of the CBS Publishing Group. The move is attributed to Taylor's conflict with William Paley, CBS chairman.	Oct. 13
Watergate special prosecutor Charles Ruff says a three-month investigation found no evidence substantiating an informant's allegation that Pres. Ford misused political contributions.		Milton Friedman wins the Nobel Prize in Economics. He heads the monetarist or "Chicago" school of economics, which emphasizes the importance of a nation's money supply and advocates a free policy toward business and trade.	The Nobel Prize in Medicine or Physiology is awarded jointly to Drs. Baruch Blumberg and Daniel Carleton Gajdusek for their discoveries concerning new mechanisms for the origin and spread of infectious diseases.... A mysterious disease that has killed more than 300 in northern Zaire and the Sudan since Oct. 7 is identified as a variant of the hemorrhagic viral fever, Green Monkey.	The New York Yankees win their first American League championship since 1964 by beating the Kansas City Royals in the fifth and final game of the league's playoffs. ... The Medal of Freedom, the nation's highest civilian award, is presented to modern dancer and choreographer Martha Graham, 82.... British actress Dame Edith Evans dies at the age of 88 in Kent, England.	Oct. 14
Vice presidential candidates Dole and Mondale engage in a lively, acerbic debate televised nationally from the Alley Theater in Houston, the first campaign debate ever between vice presidential nominees.... A Gallup Poll shows that Carter has widened his narrow lead over Ford after their second TV debate, by six percentage points, 48–45 percent.... Carlo Gambino, 74, Sicilian-born leader of N.Y.'s largest Mafia family, dies in N.Y.		The Commerce Dept. announces that Americans' personal income rose .5 percent in September to an adjusted annual rate of $1.392 trillion.	The American Cancer Society begins a five-year campaign against cigarette smoking aiming at persuading 12.5 million of the 50 million adult smokers in the U.S. to quit.		Oct. 15
			Authorities in Canberra, Australia evacuate 4,000 of the 22,000 persons living in the nearby town of Queanbeyan as the Googong dam threatens to burst because of floodwaters.		Oct. 16
			Washington Post reports that an important enzyme, neuraminidase, is missing from the swine flu vaccine, that its lack does not reduce the vaccine's effectiveness, but if a vaccinated person should contract the disease, he or she would become more sick than if the vaccine had contained the enzyme.		Oct. 17

F	G	H	I	J
Includes elections, federal-state relations, civil rights and liberties, crime, the judiciary, education, health care, poverty, urban affairs and population.	*Includes formation and debate of U.S. foreign and defense policies, veterans' affairs and defense spending. (Relations with specific foreign countries are usually found under the region concerned.)*	*Includes business, labor, agriculture, taxation, transportation, consumer affairs, monetary and fiscal policy, natural resources, and pollution.*	*Includes worldwide scientific, medical and technological developments, natural phenomena, U.S. weather, natural disasters, and accidents.*	*Includes the arts, religion, scholarship, communications media, sports, entertainments, fashions, fads and social life.*

	World Affairs	Europe	Africa & the Middle East	The Americas	Asia & the Pacific
Oct. 18	The U.N. General Assembly accords observer status to the 36-member Commonwealth of Nations.... According to the IMF analysis of the Oct. 4–8 Manila conference, developing countries' representatives tempered their demands and industrial countries acknowledged the urgency of helping the poorer countries toward economic health.	The West German mark is revalued within the seven-nation snake, or joint float, after a meeting in Frankfurt of finance ministers and bankers from the seven nations.... The lira falls from 845 to 870 to the dollar in wake of Italy's economic austerity program. Italian CP leader Enrico Berlinguer says that the party had no choice but to support the program by abstaining in the vote on wage freeze and tax reform measures.... The Hungarian news agency reports that the Hungarian army began joint maneuvers with Soviet troops stationed in Hungary as part of its annual training program.	S. African P.M. John Vorster rejects black participation in S. African politics, but says outdated apartheid regulations will be abolished.... A truce to end the Lebanese civil war is signed in Riyadh after a two-day meeting attended by the heads of Syria, Egypt, Lebanon, Saudi Arabia, and Kuwait, and by Yasir Arafat, PLO head.... The Riyadh accord provides for expansion of the Arab League peacekeeping force in Lebanon, withdrawal of all combatants to pre-April 1975 positions, and Palestinian adherence to the 1969 Cairo agreement that confined Palestinian guerrilla forces in Lebanon to refugee camps and to the Arkub section in the southeast.	The Canadian opposition Progressive Conservative Party wins both district by-elections in what is seen as an indication of voter dissatisfaction with Liberal Party rule.	In a referendum preceded by violence and calls for a boycott, a reported 91 percent of Philippine voters approve continuing martial law.
Oct. 19	U.S. Amb. to the U.N. William Scranton defends the U.S. veto of a Security Council resolution imposing an arms embargo on South Africa by saying that its approval would have undermined substantial progress made in negotiations on Namibia.	The EEC and Greek delegates agree on a sequence of meetings leading to Greek entry, and Greece is assured it will not be opposed by poorer member-nations.		The Caracas newspaper *El Nacional* says Venezuelan police discovered plans by right-wing Cuban exiles to carry out terrorist attacks and link them to the murder of Orlando Letelier in Wash., D.C. ... Chilean Pres. Augusto Pinochet Ugarte announces that his govt. has rejected a $27.5-million grant from the U.S. because the grant is conditional on an improvement in the human-rights situation.	
Oct. 20			Israel reopens the Tomb of the Patriarchs in Hebron to Jewish and Moslem prayer for the first time since militants from each faith desecrated religious objects in the shrines.		
Oct. 21			Fighting in Lebanon's civil war eases as a cease-fire, negotiated by six Arab leaders, takes effect. The Moslem leftist-controlled radio reports about 60 percent effectiveness.	Three U.S. journalists, who flew to Venezuela to report on the Cuban plane-sabotage case, are detained by police after their arrival and deported to the U.S. the next day.	Canadian P.M. Pierre Trudeau and Japanese P.M. Takeo Miki, meeting in Tokyo, sign a pact to expand trade and technical cooperation between their two countries.... A group of 65 Indian journalists, in a letter to P.M. Indira Gandhi, say they are gravely disturbed about the government's actions against the *Indian Express* and other newspapers.

A	B	C	D	E
Includes developments that affect more than one world region, international organizations and important meetings of major world leaders.	Includes all domestic and regional developments in Europe, including the Soviet Union, Turkey, Cyprus and Malta.	Includes all domestic and regional developments in Africa and the Middle East, including Iraq and Iran and excluding Cyprus, Turkey and Afghanistan.	Includes all domestic and regional developments in Latin America, the Caribbean and Canada.	Includes all domestic and regional developments in Asia and Pacific nations, extending from Afghanistan through all the Pacific Islands, except Hawaii.

U.S. Politics & Social Issues	U.S. Foreign Policy & Defense	U.S. Economy & Environment	Science, Technology & Nature	Culture, Leisure & Life Style	
	In a press conference, Gen. George Brown, chairman of the Joint Chiefs of Staff, tries to put in proper perspective an earlier statement he made that Israel is a military burden for the U.S.... The Commerce Dept. makes public 59 reports from 40 companies asked to participate in the Arab boycott of Israel. All did so, usually by affirming goods were not Israeli nor shipped on Israeli ships.		Pres. Ford presents the nation's highest award for scientific achievement, the Medal of Science, to 15 scientists, one of which is presented posthumously. ... The Nobel Prize in Chemistry is awarded to William Lipscomb Jr. for his studies of boranes. The Prize in Physics is awarded to Burton Richter and Samuel Ting for their discovery of the psi, or J particle.		Oct. 18
	Jimmy Carter, speaking to a predominantly Jewish audience, pledges to end the Arab boycott of American firms doing business with Israel, saying it is "a matter of morality."	The Commerce Dept. says the nation's real GNP increased at a 4 percent annual rate during the third quarter.... The Commerce Dept. announces the pace of new housing construction quickened in September with housing starts rising 18 percent, the highest monthly rate since February.		Avery Fisher Hall, part of the Lincoln Center complex in N.Y.C. reopens after a $6.4 million construction program to improve its acoustics.	Oct. 19
Pres. Ford denies a 1972 talk with then Pres. Nixon on an administration attempt to block a House inquiry into the Watergate burglary. Atty. Gen. Edward Levi rejects a request by Rep. Elizabeth Holtzman (D, N.Y.) for a new inquiry.... Pres. Ford signs a bill allowing federal courts to award attorneys' fees to private parties who successfully brought suit to enforce various civil-rights laws.	*Wall Street Journal* says some U.S. companies whose Arab boycott compliance was reported were unaware of their compliance, indicating that decisions were made by low-level management. ... Sen. James Buckley (R-Cons., N.Y.), Sen. Charles Percy (R, Ill.), and Zionist Organization of America pres. Joseph Sternstein issue statements calling for Gen. George Brown's dismissal.... Pres. Ford defends Joint Chiefs of Staff Chmn. George Brown, saying that his interview with Israeli journalist Ranan Lurie, in which he called Israel a military burden to the U.S., had been released before Brown had anticipated it would be and that it had been excerpted.	Pres. Ford signs a bill extending the coverage of the regular unemployment compensation system and revising the system's financing to cope with its deficits.... The 159-year-old *Hartford Times*, Conn., ceases publication, describing itself in its final issue as "a newspaper strangled by litigation." ... Commerce Clearing House (CCH) reports fiscal 1976 bankruptcy petitions are down 3.1 percent compared to fiscal 1975.	A Mississippi River ferryboat-tanker collision, 20 miles above New Orleans, La., kills 78 people.		Oct. 20
A mistrial is declared in the case of John Adamson, accused of killing Ariz. reporter Don Bolles, on the grounds that prejudicial pretrial publicity made it impossible to select a fair jury.... A 1968 federal firearms charge against black activist H. Rap Brown is dropped in New Orleans, and Brown is paroled from a 1971 assault and robbery conviction in N.Y.S.	According to a book by Thomas McCann, United Brands Co., then known as United Fruit Co., actively took part in the 1961 Bay of Pigs invasion of Cuba at the CIA's request, and had dealt directly with the then attorney general, the late Robert F. Kennedy.	Pres. Ford announces that he is directing the FAA to extend the noise standard for new wide-bodied jetliners to all older and noisier aircraft in airline fleets.... Pres. Ford signs legislation authorizing $366 million for solid-waste programs, including establishment of an Office of Solid Waste and a directive that the EPA characterize and specify hazardous wastes.	N.Y. Atty. Gen. Louis Lefkowitz holds a hearing to discuss whether legal restrictions should be placed on potentially dangerous genetic engineering experiments in the state in face of lenient federal restrictions.	All seven winners of the Nobel Prizes are Americans, the first year citizens of one nation win all the prizes.... The Nobel Prize in Literature is awarded to Saul Bellow, a professor of English at the University of Chicago and the first American to win the prize since John Steinbeck did in 1962.... The Cincinnati Reds win their second consecutive World Series and are the first National League team to defend their championship successfully since 1922.	Oct. 21

F	G	H	I	J
Includes elections, federal-state relations, civil rights and liberties, crime, the judiciary, education, health care, poverty, urban affairs and population.	Includes formation and debate of U.S. foreign and defense policies, veterans' affairs and defense spending. (Relations with specific foreign countries are usually found under the region concerned.)	Includes business, labor, agriculture, taxation, transportation, consumer affairs, monetary and fiscal policy, natural resources, and pollution.	Includes worldwide scientific, medical and technological developments, natural phenomena, U.S. weather, natural disasters, and accidents.	Includes the arts, religion, scholarship, communications media, sports, entertainments, fashions, fads and social life.

	World Affairs	Europe	Africa & the Middle East	The Americas	Asia & the Pacific
Oct. 22		Sweden announces that five N. Korean diplomats, including the ambassador, were recalled home to avoid expulsion for illegal sales of narcotics, cigarettes, and alcohol to the Swedish public. . . . President of the Republic of Ireland Cearbhall O Dalaigh resigns after he is publicly criticized for sending the antiterrorist Emergency Powers Act to the Supreme Court for evaluation.	S. African blacks vandalize liquor stores and illegal bars in Soweto, demanding that they close as a sign of respect for blacks who were killed or arrested in recent disturbances. . . . Israeli cooperation with Christian forces in Lebanon is seen further manifested in a border meeting of six Christian military officers in civilian clothing and a number of Israeli officers.		A new 17-member Thai Cabinet, dominated by the right-wing and the military, takes office after being approved by King Phumiphol Aduldet. . . . The official Chinese news agency Hsinhua, says a coup attempt by Mao's widow Chiang Ching and three others has been crushed by Hua Kuo-feng and the CP Central Committee, in the first official report to China that Hua is party chairman.
Oct. 23		Portuguese Maj. Otelo Saralva de Carvalho is arrested and sentenced to 20 days in jail for expressing political views at a public meeting. . . . A group of Soviet dissidents, who have been denied exit visas, conclude a five day sit-in in a reception room of the Supreme Soviet, attempting to get written statements on their status.	Christian forces in Lebanon expand their military security zone along the Israeli frontier by capturing the Moslem stronghold of Khiam, five miles north of the border.		
Oct. 24	Robert Mugabe, leader of the Zimbabwe African National Union (ZANU), arrives in Geneva and repeats his rejection of U.S. State Secy. Kissinger's proposals for the transition to Rhodesian majority rule, saying that armed struggle will continue until total power is transferred to the black majority.	University of Chicago economist Milton Friedman, speaking about British economic difficulties, says British govt. spending is 60 percent of its national income and that Britain is on the verge of collapse.			One million Chinese demonstrators in Peking rallies celebrate the appointment of Hua Kuo-feng as successor to Mao. The second rally marks Hua's first public appearance since his eulogy for Mao.
Oct. 25	Brezhnev affirms his government's support of detente, but criticizes both U.S. presidential contenders — Pres. Ford and Jimmy Carter — for making contradictory statements about the Soviet Union.	Soviet CP Secy. Gen. Leonid Brezhnev reports to the Central Committee that the grain harvest has exceeded expectations and might reach a record. . . . Soviet police arrest 30 more activists in an effort to prevent further demonstrations about exit visas.	P.M. Yitzhak Rabin cites Israeli policy of nonintervention in Lebanese affairs in denying a meeting sought by representatives of Christian villages in southern Lebanon to request Israeli protection following an alleged massacre of 400 Christians in Aichiye on Oct. 20. . . . Iran returns Soviet pilot Lt. Valentin Zasimov to the Soviet Union under a 1973 Soviet–Iranian hijacking extradition agreement, after Zasimov had sought political asylum in Iran on Sept. 23.	The Ecuadorean govt. begins negotiations to buy Ecuadorean Gulf Oil Co., the local subsidiary of Gulf Oil Corp. of the U.S. . . . The Indian Brotherhood of the Northwest Territories files a formal claim with the Canadian govt. to political jurisdiction over 450,000 square miles of the territory now under federal control. . . . Former Argentine Pres. Maria Estela Martinez de Peron is indicted and placed under preventive detention on charges of embezzling nine checks drawn on funds of a public charity that she had headed before the March coup.	
Oct. 26	The U.N. Gen. Assembly approves a resolution urging member states to withhold recognition of the newly independent country of Transkei, the former S. African black homeland. . . . *The New York Times* reports the IMF is running low on money because of exceptionally heavy borrowing by member nations in 1975 and 1976.		An Arab League summit conference approves the general peacemaking proposals for Lebanon agreed to at a meeting of six Arab leaders in Riyadh, Saudi Arabia, Oct. 17–18. . . . In an elaborate ceremony, Paramount Chief Kaiser Dallwonga Matanzima proclaims the Xhosa Republic of the Transkei independent from S. Africa. It is the first tribal homeland to gain independence.		

A	B	C	D	E
Includes developments that affect more than one world region, international organizations and important meetings of major world leaders.	*Includes all domestic and regional developments in Europe, including the Soviet Union, Turkey, Cyprus and Malta.*	*Includes all domestic and regional developments in Africa and the Middle East, including Iraq and Iran and excluding Cyprus, Turkey and Afghanistan.*	*Includes all domestic and regional developments in Latin America, the Caribbean and Canada.*	*Includes all domestic and regional developments in Asia and Pacific nations, extending from Afghanistan through all the Pacific Islands, except Hawaii.*

U.S. Politics & Social Issues	U.S. Foreign Policy & Defense	U.S. Economy & Environment	Science, Technology & Nature	Culture, Leisure & Life Style	
Pres. Ford and Jimmy Carter hold their third and last televised presidential debate, and each speaks of a ''new spirit'' in America. The questions are blunt and the overall tone is subdued.... In the debate Carter says he is strongly against abortion, but doesn't favor a constitutional amendment. Ford says he supports an abortion amendment, but favors one that would let each state decide individually by referendum.	In the debate Pres. Ford calls Gen. George Brown the outstanding U.S. military leader and strategist and says that Brown has indicated his apology for remarks about Israel considered embarrassing to the U.S.	The Labor Dept. says wage and benefit increases provided in major labor contracts during the third quarter were higher than in the second quarter, but lower than 1975 averages.... U.S. Dist. Ct. Judge Albert Bryan Jr. orders Western Electric Co. to pay damages to blacks and women who were victims of employment bias at the company's Arlington, Va. plant.			Oct. 22
				Call to Action, called the most representative assembly of U.S. Roman Catholics ever to meet, convenes in Detroit, Mich. and adopts resolutions supporting the ordination of women, priests' right to marry, and married couples' right to use artifical birth control.	Oct. 23
	Washington Post reports that the Justice Dept. is investigating the activities of a South Korean lobby, reportedly approved by Pres. Park Chung Hee and led by Korean businessman Park Tong Sun, to influence U.S. congressmen and other government officials by bribes and campaign contributions.			John Kani and Winston Ntshona, who shared the 1975 Tony award in N.Y.C. for best dramatic actor, are ordered to leave the Transkei after being detained since Oct. 8 for acting in an anti-apartheid play, Sizwe Banzi is Dead .... The seventh New York City Marathon is won by Bill Rodgers, with a time of 2 hours, 10 minutes, 10 seconds, and by Miki Gorman, in the women's division, with a time of 2 hours, 39 minutes, 11 seconds. It is the first city-wide marathon and is not run in the confines of Central Park.	Oct. 24
Ala. Gov. George Wallace pardons Clarence Norris, last known survivor of the Scottsboro Boys. He had been a fugitive since 1946 when he broke parole by fleeing Alabama.	Jimmy Carter sends a telegram to the wife of Soviet dissident Vladimir Slepak, expressing his personal interest in the outcome of Slepak's participation and arrest in a dissidents' demonstration over exit visas.			Queen Elizabeth II formally opens Britain's new National Theatre complex on the South Bank of the Thames in London.	Oct. 25
The U.S. Ct. of Appeals rules that White House tapes used in the Watergate trial are no longer confidential and can be cleared for reproduction, broadcast, and sale. ... U.S. Dist. Ct. Judge Thomas Flannery dismisses taxpayers' suits against former Rep. Wayne Hays (D, Ohio) that sought restitution of federal funds allegedly paid to Hays' mistress, Elizabeth Ray.	Rep. John Brademas (D, Ind.) says that since 1972 he has received $5,150 in campaign contributions from Korean businessman Park Tong Sun. A spokesman notes that Brademas's voting record has consistently opposed aid to S. Korea.		Ten Nobel laureate scientists charge Pres. Ford with using the U.S. sweep of the prizes to make inaccurate claims about the administration's role in promoting science.		Oct. 26

F	G	H	I	J
Includes elections, federal-state relations, civil rights and liberties, crime, the judiciary, education, health care, poverty, urban affairs and population.	Includes formation and debate of U.S. foreign and defense policies, veterans' affairs and defense spending. (Relations with specific foreign countries are usually found under the region concerned.)	Includes business, labor, agriculture, taxation, transportation, consumer affairs, monetary and fiscal policy, natural resources, and pollution.	Includes worldwide scientific, medical and technological developments, natural phenomena, U.S. weather, natural disasters, and accidents.	Includes the arts, religion, scholarship, communications media, sports, entertainments, fashions, fads and social life.

	World Affairs	Europe	Africa & the Middle East	The Americas	Asia & the Pacific
Oct. 27	Two African Nat. Council faction leaders, Robert Mugabe and Joshua Nkomo, accuse Britain of collaboration with Rhodesian P.M. Ian Smith to wreck the Geneva conference on Rhodesian majority rule.... The IMF auctions 779,200 ounces of gold at an average price of $117.71 an ounce, generating $60.2 million for low-interest loans to the poorest developing nations.				At least 50 are killed as police shoot Indian villagers demonstrating against the government's sterilization policy. Rumors fly that the government plans to force men to be sterilized.
Oct. 28	The Geneva conference on Rhodesian majority rule holds its opening session with Ivor Richard, Britain's chief U.N. delegate, serving as chairman.... The Worldwatch Institute says that for the first time in history the rate of global population growth is declining, attributable to more extensive birth control and more starvation deaths.	East Germany is the first country to achieve zero population growth, according to the Worldwatch Institute.... The British pound sterling falls to a record low of $1.5090.			The Worldwatch Institute finds that China has experienced the most precipitous decline in birth rate of any country in history.... An Australian govt.-sponsored inquiry, in its interim report, endorses the mining and selling of uranium under strict conditions.
Oct. 29	The first session of the Geneva conference is adjourned after Rhodesian P.M. Ian Smith denies accusations that Rhodesian security forces tortured civilians.	The Supreme Soviet, the U.S.S.R.'s Parliament, unanimously approves the nation's five-year plan for 1976–80. It projects a 36 percent increase in industrial production.... E. German CP Secy. Gen. Erich Honecker is unanimously elected chairman of the Council of State, the country's highest government body, thereby strengthening his authority.		The London newsletter *Latin America* says residents of Ribeirao Bonito, Brazil destroyed the local police station after attending a memorial mass for Jesuit priest Rev. Joao Bosco Penido Burnier, who was shot dead by policemen on Oct. 12.	Japanese Premier Takeo Miki cancels a convention of the ruling Liberal Democratic Party at which there were plans to replace him as party leader.
Oct. 30					Elections for the lower house of the Indian Parliament are again postponed until early 1978. The balloting had previously been scheduled for March 1976.... Pakistani Air Marshal Asghar Khan, leader of the right-wing opposition Teherik-i-Istiqal Party, says the government has jailed more than 50,000 people for political activities.... The Chinese govt. announces the appointment of Su Chen-hua and two others as the new CP leaders of Shanghai. Chiang Ching's three associates are dismissed from all posts.
Oct. 31			*Washington Post* reports that Israel has negotiated a deal to buy S. African coal to lessen Israeli dependence on Middle East oil.... Amnesty International reports a rise in Latin American human rights abuses in 1975–1976, particularly in Argentina, Chile, Uruguay, Brazil, Paraguay, and Bolivia.		Pakistani troops are reported to have crushed a revolt of Kohistani tribesmen, leaving 250–300 persons killed.
Nov. 1	U.N. High Commissioner for Refugess Prince Sadruddin Aga Khan sends a note to Iran protesting the return to the Soviet Union of defector Valentin Zasimov.... The U.N. Security Council gives the Palestinian Liberation Organization the right to participate as an observer in the debate concerning Israel's policies in occupied Arab lands.	The Albanian Communist Party holds its seventh congress. First secy. Enver Hoxha stresses Albanian self-reliance, indicating a move away from dependence upon China.... W. German defense Min. Georg Leber dismisses the air force commander and deputy commander for defending the appearance of a former Nazi pilot Hans-Ulrich Rudel at a WWII pilots' meeting.	Despite S. African black students' demands for a general strike, most black workers in the Johannesburg and Cape Town areas show up at work.		
	A	**B**	**C**	**D**	**E**
	Includes developments that affect more than one world region, international organizations and important meetings of major world leaders.	*Includes all domestic and regional developments in Europe, including the Soviet Union, Turkey, Cyprus and Malta.*	*Includes all domestic and regional developments in Africa and the Middle East, including Iraq and Iran and excluding Cyprus, Turkey and Afghanistan.*	*Includes all domestic and regional developments in Latin America, the Caribbean and Canada.*	*Includes all domestic and regional developments in Asia and Pacific nations, extending from Afghanistan through all the Pacific Islands, except Hawaii.*

U.S. Politics & Social Issues	U.S. Foreign Policy & Defense	U.S. Economy & Environment	Science, Technology & Nature	Culture, Leisure & Life Style	
Former Sen. Edward Gurney (R, Fla.) is acquitted of the last of seven felony charges brought against him by the Justice Dept. before he resigned his Senate seat in 1974.					Oct. 27
John Ehrlichman, a top White House aide of Nixon, enters a federal prison camp to serve his sentence, a minimum of 30 months, for his Watergate conviction.	Defense Dept. confirms Wis. Dem. Sen. William Proxmire's charges that collusive bidding by South Korean contractors is raising the cost of U.S. military contracts with South Korean firms by $15 to $25 million annually.... *The New York Times* reports that State Secy. Kissinger told CBS-TV interviewers that he is ordering an inquiry into charges that the Iranian intelligence service, Savak, is harassing Iranian dissidents in the U.S.	The Commerce Dept. announces the U.S. merchandise-trade deficit widened during September. The monthly deficit of $778.9 million is the second largest of the year.			Oct. 28
	The New York Times reports that the Justice Dept., FBI, and State Dept. are investigating a wide range of allegations that S. Korean intelligence agents (KCIA) have harassed, coerced, and violated the civil rights of Korean aliens and Korean-Americans living in the U.S. ... The U.S. State Dept. announces it has expelled a Malagasy diplomat in retaliation for a "series of unfriendly acts" by the Malagasy govt.	The Commerce Dept. announces the government's index of leading economic indicators declined .7 percent in September, the second monthly decline in a row.	The first mandatory examination to determine if U.S. doctors have kept pace with medical advances is administered throughout the U.S. to over 1,400 specialists in family practice.... An earthquake strikes West Irian Province, Indonesia, leaving 133 dead. The worst-hit settlement is Bime, which was a refugee center for victims of an earthquake last June.		Oct. 29
Editor and Publisher magazine reports that 411 of 661 daily newspapers responding to its poll endorsed the Ford–Dole ticket, 80 backed Carter–Mondale, and 168 endorsed neither.					Oct. 30
The Plains, Ga. Baptist Church, where Carter is a deacon, cancels services when a black minister and three other blacks, who seek membership in the church, show up for services.... Carter charges that the incident in the Plains Baptist Church was "politically inspired," as Ford's campaign committee sends telegrams to 400 black ministers about the incident.					Oct. 31
Coretta King, widow of Martin Luther King Jr., joins Democratic presidential candidate Carter and appears at a rally of tens of thousands in his support.				Cardinal Stefan Wyszynski announces that he will continue to lead Poland's 30 million Roman Catholics at the request of Pope Paul VI, although he offered to resign on Aug. 3 when he turned 75, the customary age for residential bishops to step down.	Nov. 1

F	G	H	I	J
Includes elections, federal-state relations, civil rights and liberties, crime, the judiciary, education, health care, poverty, urban affairs and population.	*Includes formation and debate of U.S. foreign and defense policies, veterans' affairs and defense spending. (Relations with specific foreign countries are usually found under the region concerned.)*	*Includes business, labor, agriculture, taxation, transportation, consumer affairs, monetary and fiscal policy, natural resources, and pollution.*	*Includes worldwide scientific, medical and technological developments, natural phenomena, U.S. weather, natural disasters, and accidents.*	*Includes the arts, religion, scholarship, communications media, sports, entertainments, fashions, fads and social life.*

	World Affairs	Europe	Africa & the Middle East	The Americas	Asia & the Pacific
Nov. 2	The Rhodesian govt. delegation at the majority-rule conference in Geneva refuses to agree to nationalist demands for an early Rhodesian independence date, and Rhodesian P.M. Ian Smith says he will return to Rhodesia.	Talks between Greece and Turkey on continental shelf rights in the Aegean Sea resume.... *Journal of Commerce* says shipping magnates Stratis Andreadis, Stavros Niarchos, and Ioannis Latsis face charges of moral complicity in breaches of duty committed by Greek govt. officials.... *Journal of Commerce* reports the Lockheed Aircraft Corp. is formally cleared of bribery in connection with aircraft sales to Greece under the ousted dictatorship.	A broadcast says Burundi Pres. Michel Micombero was ousted in a bloodless army coup led by Lt. Col. Jean-Baptist Bagaza and Uprona, Burundi's only political party, was dissolved.	Canada extends offshore fishing limits to 200 miles from 12 miles, effective on Jan. 1, 1977.... A Venezuelen district judge charges four Cuban exiles with the murder of 73 persons who died Oct. 6 when a Cuban passenger jet crashed in the Caribbean after two bombs exploded on board.... Costa Rica repeals a 1974 law, known as the "Vesco" Law because it reputedly was enacted to protect fugitive U.S. financier Robert Vesco who lived in Costa Rica, that gave the president final say on extraditions.	The Chinese CP newspaper *Jen-min Jih Pao* charges that Chiang Ching and her three associates criminally tried to disrupt China's industrial production and the management of the economy.... The lower house of the Indian Parliament approves a sweeping series of constitutional amendments that will expand the legislature's and prime minister's power.... Arnold Zeitlin, AP bureau chief in Manila, is denied reentry to the Philippines when he returns from a two-day visit to Hong Kong.
Nov. 3	Rhodesian P.M. Ian Smith leaves the Geneva conference on Rhodesian majority rule, expressing dissatisfaction with the lack of progress and charging that Britain is too ready to appease.... The basic continuity of U.S. foreign policy, no matter who is President, is reported to be the underrunning theme of foreign reaction to Carter's election.		Israeli P.M. Yitzhak Rabin voices confidence that U.S. Pres.-elect Carter will continue traditional bipartisan support for Israel, but remarks that "there will be days when we'll recall with nostalgia the era of Dr. Kissinger."	The Canadian Immigration Dept. says immigration fell 22.3 percent to 73,735 persons during the first six months of 1976, compared to the first six months of 1975.	
Nov. 4	Britain proposes March 1, 1978 as the date for Rhodesian independence and the establishment of majority rule.... ZANU leader Robert Mugabe rejects Western proposals for an international fund to aid Rhodesian development and to compensate whites who choose to leave the country.	Commenting on the U.S. presidential elections, Yves Guena, the secy. gen. of France's Gaullist party, says U.S. foreign policy doesn't change with a change in the presidency, and Italian C.P. leader Enrico Berlinguer sees an end to State Secy. Kissinger's pressure on Italian politics.... Soviet Foreign Min. Andrei Gromyko and Ismail Fahmy, his Egyptian counterpart, confer in Bulgaria in an effort to improve relations between the two countries.	Egypt expresses strong apprehension about U.S. Pres.-elect Carter's pro-Israel stance, while Palestinians in Lebanon rejoice over Pres. Ford's defeat.... The cost of basic commodities in Israel sharply rises after the withdrawal of government subsidies. Food prices increase 20 percent and fuel 11 percent.	An official of Venezuela's ruling Democratic Action Party, Carlos Canache Mata, reports elation over Jimmy Carter's U.S. presidential victory because, he charges, Pres. Ford had supported Latin American dictatorships.	
Nov. 5	GATT special panel, meeting in Geneva, rules that the U.S. export-tax incentive program, known as DISC, is illegal.	A U.S. congressional fact-finding commission, touring Europe to check compliance with the 1975 Helsinki pact is barred from all Communist countries except Yugoslavia. The U.S.S.R. charges it with trying to sow distrust against Warsaw Pact countries.		*Miami Herald* says Chilean govt. statistics report inflation in Chile for the first 10 months of 1976 is 151.3 percent, down from 280 percent in the same period last year.	Takeo Fukuda resigns from the Japanese Cabinet as deputy premier and director-general of the Economic Planning Agency. Uichi Noda replaces him as head of the economic body.

A	B	C	D	E
Includes developments that affect more than one world region, international organizations and important meetings of major world leaders.	*Includes all domestic and regional developments in Europe, including the Soviet Union, Turkey, Cyprus and Malta.*	*Includes all domestic and regional developments in Africa and the Middle East, including Iraq and Iran and excluding Cyprus, Turkey and Afghanistan.*	*Includes all domestic and regional developments in Latin America, the Caribbean and Canada.*	*Includes all domestic and regional developments in Asia and Pacific nations, extending from Afghanistan through all the Pacific Islands, except Hawaii.*

U.S. Politics & Social Issues	U.S. Foreign Policy & Defense	U.S. Economy & Environment	Science, Technology & Nature	Culture, Leisure & Life Style	
Democratic presidential candidate Jimmy Carter defeats incumbent Pres. Gerald Ford with a 27 electoral vote margin. The results split the U.S. virtually East-to-West as Carter wins 23 states and Wash., D.C. while Ford takes 27 states, but not those with large electoral votes.... Carter is the first man from the Deep South to be elected President since the Civil War. Ford is the first incumbent president to lose since Republican Herbert Hoover in 1932.... Eugene McCarthy, running as an independent, draws more votes in four States — Maine, Oklahoma, Iowa and Oregon — than Carter's losing margins, polling 650,000 votes.... In Senate races John Tunney (D, Calif.) loses to S.I. Hayakawa, Daniel Moynihan (D-Liberal) defeats James Buckley (Cons.-R) in N.Y., and Robert Taft Jr. (R, Ohio) loses to Howard Metzenbaum (D). Democrats maintain their 3–2 edge in the Senate and their 2–1 majority in the house.... Mass. voters reject, 3–1 the nation's first state proposal that would have required hand-gun owners to surrender their weapons to the state for reimbursement.		The Supreme Ct. rules, 5–4, in favor of the IRS on a corporate-tax question involving the carry-back of operating losses from one year to offset taxable income in prior years.... Voters in six states — Ohio, Montana, Colorado, Washington, Oregon and Arizona — decisively defeat proposals aimed at curtailing the use of nuclear power.		The Supreme Ct. divides equally, 4–4, on a case raising the issue of to what extent a company must go to accommodate the religious practices of an employe.	Nov. 2
		The Dow Jones industrial average declines 9.56 points to close at 956.53. The decline is attributed to concern over Carter's economic policies and the possibility of increased inflation.... Industry reports indicate that car sales during October rose 1.5 percent over the October 1975 level, but the increase stemmed solely from a large rise in sales of imports.			Nov. 3
Carter, in a post-election news conference, rejects the idea that his narrow margin of victory denies him a mandate for vigorous pursuit of his goals as President and pledges that he will be very aggressive in keeping his promises.	House Democratic Whip John McFall (Calif.) admits he has received $3,000 in cash from S. Korean businessman Park Tong Sun, and former Rep. Jerome Waldie (D, Calif.) is reported acknowledging that he received $2,000 in campaign contributions.	American Motors Corp. (AMC) says it has reduced the base price for the Gremlin , its lowest-priced subcompact, 7.8 percent to $2,995, making it the least expensive U.S.-made car on the market.		Baseball's draft of free agents, designed to limit the number of teams competing for any one player, is held at the Plaza Hotel, N.Y.C.	Nov. 4
Representatives of Ford and Carter meet to plan the presidential transition. Carter attributes his victory to his exposure on the three nationally televised debates.		The Nuclear Regulatory Commission will resume licensing new nuclear power plants on a conditional basis, after a court ruling to halt licensing because NRC procedures were judged to be inadequate.... The Labor Dept. says unemployment rose slightly in October, when 7.9 percent of the nation's work force, or 7.569 million, were jobless.... The Federal Reserve says consumer installment credit expanded a seasonally adjusted $1.48 billion in September, the largest monthly increase since December 1975.	Health investigators conclude that the headaches, nausea, and shortness of breath that struck 130 workers at a Pa. electronics plant were caused by chemical fumes and poor ventilation.		Nov. 5

F	G	H	I	J
Includes elections, federal-state relations, civil rights and liberties, crime, the judiciary, education, health care, poverty, urban affairs and population.	Includes formation and debate of U.S. foreign and defense policies, veterans' affairs and defense spending. (Relations with specific foreign countries are usually found under the region concerned.)	Includes business, labor, agriculture, taxation, transportation, consumer affairs, monetary and fiscal policy, natural resources, and pollution.	Includes worldwide scientific, medical and technological developments, natural phenomena, U.S. weather, natural disasters, and accidents.	Includes the arts, religion, scholarship, communications media, sports, entertainments, fashions, fads and social life.

	World Affairs	Europe	Africa & the Middle East	The Americas	Asia & the Pacific
Nov. 6		The chief prosecutor of Spain's Supreme Ct. reports that two high-ranking air force officers received commissions from Lockheed.	Meeting in Lome, Togo, representatives of 15 African nations ratify the 1975 treaty to establish the Economic Community of West African States (ECOWAS).		
Nov. 7		The British pound sterling edges up to $1.6365, near its level of Oct. 24, after hitting a record low of $1.5690 on Oct. 28.			Australian Treasurer Philip Lynch announces new steps aimed at curbing the 13.9 percent rate of inflation and easing pressure on the Australian dollar.
Nov. 8	ZAPU leader Joshua Nkomo rejects the proposed foreign-aid fund for Rhodesian development and indicates that he would favor ties with the U.S.S.R. rather than with the West.		Zaire and its creditor banks agree on a plan for Zaire to pay its overdue debts and restore its credit by immediately paying all delinquent interest — about $40 million.	Canadian destroyers seize three Cuban fishing boats that had violated Canada's 12-mile fishing limit.	Philippine Pres. Ferdinand Marcos dismisses 19 officers and 308 soldiers found guilty of various abuses, including torture, bringing to 1,604 the number removed since September 1972.
Nov. 9	The U.N. General Assembly approves 10 resolutions condemning apartheid and linking the Western powers and Israel as collaborators of the South African govt.	France's National Assembly approves a defense budget for 1977 totaling $11.3 billion, including a last-minute addition of $267.3 million announced by Defense Min. Yvon Bourges. . . . The Irish Republic's political crisis is resolved peacefully when Patrick Hillery is declared president-elect without a contest, succeeding Cearbhall O Dalaigh.	Pierre Gemayel, Phalangist Party leader, and Camille Chamoun, National Liberal Party head, give formal Lebanese Christian approval of Syria's peacekeeping role.	Two top leaders of Nicaragua's leftist Sandinista National Liberation Front, Carlos Fonsica Amador and Eduardo Contreras Escobar, are killed in shootouts with National Guard (army) troops.	
Nov. 10		British P.M. James Callaghan's Labor govt. wins narrow victories in three key procedural votes involving five bills, but loses in two votes on a crucial section of one of the bills.	About 5,000 Syrian troops, supported by tanks and artillery, enter the outskirts of Beirut to enforce the Arab League-approved truce aimed at ending the Lebanese civil war. . . . The Angolan govt. is reported to have staged an intensive drive against guerrillas of the National Union for the Total Independence of Angola (UNITA). . . . A new Egyptian Cabinet takes office following elections in which the centrist political faction that supported Pres. Anwar Sadat gained a majority in the People's Assembly.		The fiftieth anniversary of the reign of Japanese Emperor Hirohito is celebrated in Tokyo, but the ceremony is boycotted by most politicians, including Socialists and Communists.
Nov. 11	The U.N. Security Council unanimously approves a statement condemning Israel's policies in the occupied Arab lands, the first time the U.S. has joined in such council action. . . . Pres. Ford extends for another two years Alexander Haig's term as commander in chief of the European command. The posts of commander in chief and NATO supreme allied commander are usually held by the same person.	Greece and Turkey agree on procedures for future talks on continental-shelf rights in the Aegean Sea and will try to ease tension over the area while talks are in progress. . . . Plans outlining an independent republic of Northern Ireland are published under the sponsorship of the Ulster Loyalist Central Coordinating Committee, which seeks to end Britain's direct rule.	The Xhosa Republic of the Transkei orders all S. African police to leave its territory, an apparent assertion of its independence from S. Africa.		The Australian govt. says it will lift its 1972 embargo on uranium exports and will permit firms to fill their existing orders with Japan, W. Germany, and the U.S.

A	B	C	D	E
Includes developments that affect more than one world region, international organizations and important meetings of major world leaders.	Includes all domestic and regional developments in Europe, including the Soviet Union, Turkey, Cyprus and Malta.	Includes all domestic and regional developments in Africa and the Middle East, including Iraq and Iran and excluding Cyprus, Turkey and Afghanistan.	Includes all domestic and regional developments in Latin America, the Caribbean and Canada.	Includes all domestic and regional developments in Asia and Pacific nations, extending from Afghanistan through all the Pacific Islands, except Hawaii.

U.S. Politics & Social Issues	U.S. Foreign Policy & Defense	U.S. Economy & Environment	Science, Technology & Nature	Culture, Leisure & Life Style	
			Dr. Alexander Wiener, 70, co-discoverer of the Rh blood factor, dies of leukemia in N.Y.	Author Patrick Dennis, known for his novel *Auntie Mame*, dies at the age of 55 of cancer in N.Y.	Nov. 6
	Washington Post reports the Justice Dept. probe has unearthed evidence that the Korean CIA and Pak Bo Hi arranged for Rev. Sun Myung Moon's followers in the U.S. to stage demonstrations opposing former Pres. Nixon's impeachment. ... *The New York Time* reports that records of Park Tong Sun's bank account in the Bahamas show that he had brought large amounts of cash into the U.S., bolstering investigative speculation that his actual expenditures in Wash., D.C. had been large.				Nov. 7
Robert Strauss announces he is resigning as Democratic national chairman, effective Jan. 21, after four years in the party post. ... The nation's mayors, in a meeting of the U.S. Conference of Mayors, appeal to Pres.-elect Carter to set a national tone of concern for the cities. ... The Supreme Ct. refuses to stay a lower-ct. order barring the federal govt. from withholding Medicaid funds for elective abortions.		Samuel Newhouse — owner of 22 daily newspapers, five magazines, six TV stations, four radio stations, and 20 cable TV systems — acquires Booth Newspapers Inc., an 8-paper chain.			Nov. 8
Martin Gerry, director of HEW's office for civil rights, charges the N.Y.C. public school system with discrimination in hiring, promotion, and teacher assignment.		Smokey Bear, internationally recognized as the U.S. Forest Service symbol of forest-fire prevention, dies at the National Zoo in Washington, D.C., at the age of 26.		Rosina Lhevinne, 96, pianist and Juilliard teacher whose pupils included Van Cliburn and Misha Dichter, dies of a stroke in Glendale, Calif.	Nov. 9
Alameda County, Calif. is chosen as the new site of the trial of three men accused of kidnapping 25 Chowchilla, Calif. schoolchildren while they were on a school bus. The trial site is being changed because of pretrial publicity. ... Minn. Gov. Wendell Anderson (D) announces his intention to succeed Walter Mondale in the Senate when Mondale resigns to become vice president.	Commerce Dept. releases names of 111 additional companies that had filed reports of demands by their Arab customers to comply with the economic boycott of Israel.	*The New York Times* reports FRB figures indicating that loans made by U.S. banks to developing nations increased sharply in 1975–76, despite fears about repayment. ... The Dow Jones index closes at 924.04, its lowest level since Jan. 13, which is seen as reflecting concern with the changeover in economic leadership. ... The National Marine Fisheries Service's ban on commercial tuna fishing that involves the incidental killing of porpoises is upheld by a U.S. Ct. of Appeals.			Nov. 10
		FRB Chmn. Arthur Burns warns that inflation might worsen if traditional policies are used to stimulate the current sluggish economy, remarks seen as a warning directed at Pres.-elect Carter.		Alexander Calder, 78, U.S. artist known for his mobiles and stabiles, dies of a heart attack in N.Y. ... The National Conference of Catholic Bishops meets and approves the Pastoral Letter on Moral Values, a statement that reaffirms traditional Catholic teachings on sexual ethics.	Nov. 11

F	G	H	I	J
Includes elections, federal-state relations, civil rights and liberties, crime, the judiciary, education, health care, poverty, urban affairs and population.	*Includes formation and debate of U.S. foreign and defense policies, veterans' affairs and defense spending. (Relations with specific foreign countries are usually found under the region concerned.)*	*Includes business, labor, agriculture, taxation, transportation, consumer affairs, monetary and fiscal policy, natural resources, and pollution.*	*Includes worldwide scientific, medical and technological developments, natural phenomena, U.S. weather, natural disasters, and accidents.*	*Includes the arts, religion, scholarship, communications media, sports, entertainments, fashions, fads and social life.*

	World Affairs	Europe	Africa & the Middle East	The Americas	Asia & the Pacific
Nov. 12	The U.N. General Assembly approves a resolution again calling on Turkey to withdraw its troops from Cyprus. Twenty-seven nations, including the U.S. and West European countries, abstain.	London *Financial Times* says the Common Market signed a two-year agreement with Rumania to regulate its European textile exports, its first formal agreement with an Eastern European country.... France agrees to support Britain's $3.9-billion loan request from the IMF. The two countries also agree to cooperate in five industrial areas: iron and steel, textiles, automobiles, electronics, and ship-building.	In the first Moroccan elections since 1969, independents win 8,607 seats in city, town, and rural councils. The Istiqlal nationalist party wins 2,184 seats, the largest number won by an organized party.		Sri Lanka police shoot and kill a university student and wound more than 50 others, triggering a wave of student unrest.... The U.S. and Vietnam hold preliminary discussions in Paris to see if conditions are ripe for full-scale negotiations on all issues between them. It is their first formal meeting since 1975.
Nov. 13		A demonstration by 30,000 persons at the W. German Brokdorf nuclear power plant building site erupts into violence when 3,000 of the more militant try to storm the enclosed area.	Egyptian Pres. Anwar Sadat tells a U.S. Senate delegation that he and other Arab leaders are ready to negotiate a peace settlement with Israel on a sound and just basis without preconditions, and he urges U.S. Pres.-elect Carter to promote peace when he assumes office.	Members of the Guatemalan leftist Guerrilla Army of the Poor (EGP) attack the eastern town of Olopa, killing two landowners, in one of many raids throughout the country since July.	
Nov. 14		Jacques Chirac, who resigned as French prime minister in August 1975, regains his National Assembly seat in a by-election, reportedly the first step toward creating his own power base.... The Slovene ethnic minority in Carinthia, Austria's most southern province, sabotages the census held to determine how many citizens speak languages other than German, fearing goverment efforts to "Germanize" them.... Soviet CP Secy. Gen. Leonid Brezhnev, meeting with Yugoslav Pres. Tito, assures Tito that the U.S.S.R. does not pose a threat to Yugoslav autonomy.	The death in Tunisia of Moufida Bourguiba, 86, former wife of Tunisian Pres. Habib Bourguiba who worked to gain Tunisia's independence from France, is reported.... Israeli P.M. Yitzhak Rabin expresses doubt about Sadat's peaceful intentions, saying his statements were a diplomatic ploy to influence U.S. policy in the Middle East.		
Nov. 15	The U.S. vetoes the admission of Vietnam to the U.N. because of Hanoi's failure to provide an accounting of American servicemen missing in action in the Indochina war.... Geneva conference on Rhodesia chmn. Ivor Richard proposes a flexible schedule for determining the date of Rhodesian independence and majority rule, and urges delegates to focus on the organization of an interim government instead of remaining deadlocked on the actual date of independence.... China declares it has no intentions of resuming friendlier relations with the Soviet Union despite the change of leadership in Peking.		Bishop Abel Muzorewa, ANC president, and Rev. Ndabaningi Sithole, Robert Mugabe's rival for ZANU leadership, indicate willingness to accept Britain's flexible-date plan, although they favor setting the Dec. 1, 1977 date for Rhodesian independence.... Syrian peacekeeping troops move out of the eastern section of Beirut and enter the center of the capital, completing their occupation of the city and, in effect, ending the Lebanese civil war.	Rep. Robert Drinan (D, Mass.), who had visited Argentina as a member of an Amnesty International team gathering evidence of human-rights abuses, says that the team had heard incredible tales of torture being used by the Argentine govt.... Brazil's ruling ARENA party wins control of about 70 percent of the nation's mayoralties and city councils in municipal elections.... The Parti Quebecois, formed in 1968 to promote Quebec independence from Canada, scores a major upset in provincial elections, moving from a minority of six to a majority of 69.	
Nov. 16	Leaders of the two ANC factions at the Geneva conference on Rhodesia — Joshua Nkomo and Robert Mugabe — reject Ivor Richard's independence date proposal and accuse Britain of trying to widen the rift between the black delegates at Geneva. They demand setting a definite independence date of Dec. 1, 1977.... Venezuelan Pres. Carlos Andres Perez, in a talk before the U.N., says OPEC's price increases represented a decision to revalue the raw materials and products of developing nations.	French unemployment figures for the end of October pass the 1 million mark and top the November 1975 record.... A Polish-Soviet trade pact is signed that will increase trade 70 percent from 1976-80.... Newspapers and feminist groups throughout Spain openly oppose an old adultery law that effectively sanctions sexual infidelity by married men but not by married women.	A Uganda military commission that investigated Israel's Entebbe Airport raid absolves Uganda in the death of one of the hostages, Dora Bloch, who disappeared after the raid.... Iranian security police shoot and kill three terrorists and capture seven others in Teheran in an intensified drive to rid the city of guerrillas.	The National Conference of Brazilian Bishops denounces what it calls the climate of fear and violence in Brazil, a statement clearly directed against the government. ... The Nicaraguan govt. charges that Cuba is training and infiltrating Nicaraguan leftists into Nicaragua for a guerrilla war against Pres. Anatasio Somoza Debayle, and denies that Nicaragua is a base for Cuban exiles.	The national congress of the ruling Kuomintang party in Nationalist China unanimously elects Premier Chaing Ching-Kuo as the party's chairman.

A	B	C	D	E
Includes developments that affect more than one world region, international organizations and important meetings of major world leaders.	Includes all domestic and regional developments in Europe, including the Soviet Union, Turkey, Cyprus and Malta.	Includes all domestic and regional developments in Africa and the Middle East, including Iraq and Iran and excluding Cyprus, Turkey and Afghanistan.	Includes all domestic and regional developments in Latin America, the Caribbean and Canada.	Includes all domestic and regional developments in Asia and Pacific nations, extending from Afghanistan through all the Pacific Islands, except Hawaii.

U.S. Politics & Social Issues	U.S. Foreign Policy & Defense	U.S. Economy & Environment	Science, Technology & Nature	Culture, Leisure & Life Style	
		An FRB spokesman tells major U.S. newspapers that Chmn. Arthur Burns only intended to caution Congress against voting major new spending increases, not to warn Carter against cutting taxes. . . . After speaking with Burns, Rep. Henry Reuss (D, Wis.) says that he feels that Burns will cooperate with Carter's economic policies.		Walter Piston, 82, composer and teacher who won the Pulitzer Prize for Music in 1948 and 1961, dies in Belmont, Mass.	Nov. 12
	Donald Ranard, a former State Dept. official and Korean affairs director (1970–74), says that the Nixon administration was unwilling to act against the S. Korean lobby because it did not want to jeopardize its commitment of 52,000 S. Korean troops to the Vietnam War effort.				Nov. 13
Carter's hometown Baptist church ends its 11–year–old ban against attendance by blacks, reversing a 1965 resolution.	Sen. Abraham Ribicoff (D, Conn.), after visiting Cairo, says he is conviced by his talks with Egyptian Pres. Anwar Sadat that " the Arab world is ready to accept that Israel . . . has a right to exist."				Nov. 14
The U.S. Supreme Ct. stays the Calif. Supreme Ct. (Allan) Bakke ruling, which struck down as unconstitutional the admissions program of University of California Davis Medical School because it gave special consideration to minorities. . . . Carter announces the appointment of Jody Powell, 33, as presidential press secretary. Powell has been Carter's press secretary for six years.		The U.S. Postal Service reports a $15 million surplus during the quarter ending Sept. 30, the first in any quarter since 1972. A $425 deficit had been forecast. . . . Pres.-elect Carter stresses the need to reduce unemployment to 5.5 percent and thereby reduce inflation. He also stresses his commitment to a balanced budget.		Twyla Tharp premieres her new modern dance work *After All* to music by Tomaso Albioni in N.Y.C. . . . French actor of the 1930s Jean Gabin, 72, best-known for his movies *Pepe Le Moko* and *The Grand Illusion*, dies in Paris. . . . The 1976 Prix Goncourt and the Prix Renaudot, France's most prestigious literary prizes, are presented to Patrick Grainville and to Michel Henry, respectively.	Nov. 15
Convicted Utah murderer Gary Gilmore, thwarted in a bid to have his death sentence administered without delay, overdoses on barbiturates in an unsuccessful suicide attempt.		American Motors Corp. (AMC), in a second price action, offers a $253 rebate to buyers of its new 1976–77 model Pacer , a car slightly larger than the Gremlin .		Wolf Biermann, dissident poet and songwriter, is deprived of East German citizenship during a concert tour in West Germany and is barred from returning to East Germany.	Nov. 16

F	G	H	I	J
Includes elections, federal-state relations, civil rights and liberties, crime, the judiciary, education, health care, poverty, urban affairs and population.	Includes formation and debate of U.S. foreign and defense policies, veterans' affairs and defense spending. (Relations with specific foreign countries are usually found under the region concerned.)	Includes business, labor, agriculture, taxation, transportation, consumer affairs, monetary and fiscal policy, natural resources, and pollution.	Includes worldwide scientific, medical and technological developments, natural phenomena, U.S. weather, natural disasters, and accidents.	Includes the arts, religion, scholarship, communications media, sports, entertainments, fashions, fads and social life.

	World Affairs	Europe	Africa & the Middle East	The Americas	Asia & the Pacific
Nov. 17		A British left-wing coalition of unionists, public-service employes and others, in the largest political demonstration in five years, marches in London to protest the Labor Party govt.'s threatened spending cuts. . . . Austria's suicide rate, 1,813 in 1975 or 23.9 per 100,000 people, is reported to be the highest in Western Europe, but exceeded by Hungary's and Czechoslovakia's in Eastern Europe. . . . Great Britain expels as a security risk Philip Agee, former CIA officer who revealed many of the agency's secret operations after he became an investigative journalist.	Bishop Abel Muzorewa denounces the combined Nkomo-Mugabe front and rejects their charge that the Geneva conference chairman Ivor Richard is pitting the Rhodesian nationalistic factions against each other.	The Inter-American Press Assn. asks Brazilian Pres. Ernesto Geisel to use all his resources to end the terrorism wreaked by the Brazilian Anti-Communist Alliance.	Bengali leader and advocate of violence to gain East Pakistan's independence, Abdu Hamid Kha Bhashani, dies at the reported age of 97 in Bangladesh.
Nov. 18	Geneva conference chmn. Ivor Richard proposes that Dec. 20 be set as the concluding date for the conference and that the transition period to Rhodesian independence be calculated from that date, thereby shortening the original 15-month transition period set by Britain. . . . NATO Secy. Gen. Joseph Luns says NATO is considering steps to counter the probable deployment of Soviet intermediate-range ballistic missiles in central Europe.	Air France announces operating losses for 1976 of $40 million to $44 million but says it intends to lower its deficit over the next two years and break even by 1979. . . . The Spanish Parliament approves the government's political reform bill, paving the way for a new, democratically elected legislature. A national referendum is scheduled for Dec. 15. . . . Danish govt. reportedly collected a larger percentage of the nation's GNP in taxes (45.68 percent) in 1974 than other OECD members.			Australian Parliament blocks U.S. antitrust action against four Australian uranium companies, with the justification that U.S. antitrust laws operating outside the U.S. contradict accepted international law jurisdiction. . . . The Western Mining Corp., a major Australian nickel producer, reports the discovery of a large copper deposit in South Australia.
Nov. 19		The W. German opposition party, the Christian Social Union, severs its 27-year alliance with the Christian Democratic Union with major expected changes in political alignment.	A new Algerian Constitution is approved by 99.2 percent of an estimated 7.1 million voters.		
Nov. 20	The U.S.–USSR Strategic Arms Limitation Talks (SALT II), which resumed Sept. 21, are formally adjourned until after Carter's inauguration.	Tens of thousands of Spaniards pay homage to Generalissimo Francisco Franco on the first anniversary of his death. They shout opposition to the government's reform program.			The Philippines deports two U.S. missionaries, the Rev. Edward Gerlock and the Rev. Albert Booms, in a crackdown on activist church groups.
Nov. 21		U.S. Commerce Secy. Elliott Richardson, in Bucharest, signs a 10-year pact on trade and economic cooperation with Rumania, described as the broadest agreement of its kind the U.S. has ever signed with an Eastern European country.	Syrian troops, accompanied by contingents of other Arab peacekeeping forces, now have complete control of Lebanon except for a 15-mile strip along the Israeli border. . . . Lebanese Pres. Elias Sarkis praises the efforts of the Arab peacekeeping troops and says security remains our first issue.	AP reports that Argentine authorities have killed over 120 guerrillas during November, 45 of them in the previous week. . . . Enrique Rodriguez Frabregat, 81, who as Uruguayan member of the U.N. Special Committee on Palestine helped establish the state of Israel in 1948, dies of cancer in Montevideo, Uruguay.	

A	B	C	D	E
Includes developments that affect more than one world region, international organizations and important meetings of major world leaders.	Includes all domestic and regional developments in Europe, including the Soviet Union, Turkey, Cyprus and Malta.	Includes all domestic and regional developments in Africa and the Middle East, including Iraq and Iran and excluding Cyprus, Turkey and Afghanistan.	Includes all domestic and regional developments in Latin America, the Caribbean and Canada.	Includes all domestic and regional developments in Asia and Pacific nations, extending from Afghanistan through all the Pacific Islands, except Hawaii.

U.S. Politics & Social Issues	U.S. Foreign Policy & Defense	U.S. Economy & Environment	Science, Technology & Nature	Culture, Leisure & Life Style	
Jimmy Carter's presidential campaign is reported to have cost $35 million. . . . The Civil Service Commission, Justice Dept., and Labor Dept. sign new guidelines for determining bias in employers' job application tests. The EEOC calls the new guidelines, which apply to federal agencies as well as private companies with government contracts, too lenient.		NBC and the Justice Dept. settle the department's civil antitrust suit that charged NBC with monopolizing TV programming.	China conducts its fourth nuclear test of the year, estimated by U.S. experts to have a force equivalent to four million tons of TNT. . . . The 1976 Albert LaskerBasic Medical Research Award goes to Rosalyn Yalow, the first woman to win the award.	A U.S. Bicentennial exhibit in Moscow is evacuated and closed for a day after a telephoned bomb threat.	Nov. 17
		The Transportation Dept. issues policy guidelines for the reduction of aircraft noise, the first step in implementing Pres. Ford's policy directive of Oct. 21. . . . The Commerce Dept. announces the GNP increased at a slower rate during the third quarter than initially reported.	The Center for Disease Control says the death rate from septic abortions is 50 times higher among women who continue to wear IUDs after becoming pregnant than among those using other methods. . . . Philadelphia's Bellevue Stratford Hotel closes. It was headquarters of the July American Legion convention marred by the outbreak of an unidentified illness that came to be called Legionnaires disease.	U.S. painter, sculptor, and photographer Man Ray, 86, who helped found the Dadaist movement, dies in Paris from a lung infection.	Nov. 18
University of California Board of Regents votes to appeal to the U.S. Supreme Ct. a state supreme ct. ruling that struck down the university's special admissions program. . . . Patricia Hearst, the newspaper heiress convicted of bank robbery, is released from prison into her parents' custody after her family posts $1.5 million bail. . . . Carter releases a list of 11 persons representative of the interested citizens advising him on selecting personnel for his administration. Included are Rev. Theodore Hesburgh, Vernon Jordan Jr., Irving Shapiro, Lucy Benson, and Lane Kirkland.	GAO study reveals that over the span of several years the Army has spent $205 million more than budgeted by Congress. . . . The State Dept. denies that Secy. Kissinger has given Rhodesian P.M. Ian Smith assurances of U.S. military support if the Geneva talks break down.	FRB approves a reduction in the discount rate for 11 of its 12 district banks: 5.25 percent down from 5.5 percent. . . . A Harrisburg, Pa. federal grand jury indicts six Pa. coal companies and three of their present and former owners of price-fixing nationwide anthracite coal prices from 1961 through November 1974. . . . GM and UAW negotiators settle on the terms of a new three-year contract and the union promptly calls off the ministrike that began 12 hours earlier at 16 key facilities.			Nov. 19
Carter meets with Kissinger in Plains, Ga. to seek advice on the best way to prepare for the next administration. . . . State Secy. Kissinger tells Carter, in a presidential transition meeting, that he believes that foreign policy should be nonpartisan.		Asst. Atty Gen. Donald Baker says the Justice Dept. antitrust division will ask federal judges to impose 18-month prison sentences on most corporate officials convicted of price-fixing under a 1974 law.	Soviet geneticist Trofim Lysenko, whose theory that a plant's basic nature could be altered by the environment was favored by Stalin and attacked by Khrushchev, dies at the age of 78 in the Soviet Union.	Hugh D. Auchincloss Sr., 79, stockbroker, lawyer, and stepfather of Jacqueline Kennedy Onassis, dies of emphysema in Wash., D.C.	Nov. 20
				Pres. Ford dedicates a mansion on the Rockefeller family estate in Pocantico Hills, N.Y. as a national landmark. . . . Robert Wilson's and Philip Glass's surrrealist opera *Einstein on the Beach* is critically acclaimed at its Metropolitan Opera House premiere, N.Y.C.	Nov. 21

F	G	H	I	J
Includes elections, federal-state relations, civil rights and liberties, crime, the judiciary, education, health care, poverty, urban affairs and population.	Includes formation and debate of U.S. foreign and defense policies, veterans' affairs and defense spending. (Relations with specific foreign countries are usually found under the region concerned.)	Includes business, labor, agriculture, taxation, transportation, consumer affairs, monetary and fiscal policy, natural resources, and pollution.	Includes worldwide scientific, medical and technological developments, natural phenomena, U.S. weather, natural disasters, and accidents.	Includes the arts, religion, scholarship, communications media, sports, entertainments, fashions, fads and social life.

	World Affairs	Europe	Africa & the Middle East	The Americas	Asia & the Pacific
Nov. 22	UNESCO restores Israel, ousted in 1974, to full membership in its European grouping.	E. Germany says it will pay reparations to Jews in the U.S. who survived the Nazi Holocaust.... Soviet leader Leonid Brezhnev arrives on his first visit to Rumania since 1966 to a background of strained Soviet-Rumanian relations because of Rumania's independent foreign policies.	School children in the West Bank town of Nablus stage anti-Israeli demonstrations, supported by a strike of the town's shopkeepers.		Sri Lanka P.M. Sirimavo R.D. Bandaranaike assails a student boycott, called to protest the Nov. 12 police shootings of rioting students.
Nov. 23	The U.N. General Assembly approves a resolution calling on Israel to halt the transfer of Palestinian refugees in the Gaza Strip from their camps to new homes. ... OECD delegates, meeting in Paris, agree that the industrialized nations of the West face a slower and more extended period of economic growth.... Yakov Malik, Soviet Ambassador to the U.N., is removed from his post and sent back to the USSR. No reason is given for his removal and no successor is named.... Ivor Richard, British chairman of the Geneva talks on Rhodesian majority rule, tentatively sets March 1, 1978 as the date for Rhodesian independence.				The Thai govt. returns 26 Cambodian refugees to Cambodia, saying they are a threat to Thai national security.
Nov. 24	The U.N. General Assembly, 90–16, approves a resolution calling for the right of the Palestinians to establish their own state and to reclaim their former homes and properties.		The U.S. and Iran sign a contract providing for American civilian experts to train Iranian air force personnel to handle the logistics of the aircraft Iran is buying.	Venezuelan Pres. Carlos Andres Perez holds three days of talks in Moscow with Soviet Pres. Nikolai Podgorny, which he characterizes as "very positive" but "frank and sometimes tough."	
Nov. 25			Damascus reports that Syria and Iraq have withdrawn most of the troops massed on their border since June following an agreement negotiatied by Egypt.... Southern Yemen claims that its ground forces shot down one of 10 Iranian F-4 Phantom jets that violated its air space on a spy mission after taking off from Oman.	Rene Levesque is sworn in as Quebec's provincial prime minister. He favors separation of the province from Canada.... Canadian P.M. Pierre Trudeau calls for Canadian unity, saying "Quebec does not believe in separatism ... Quebeckers have chosen a new government, not a new country."	
Nov. 26	The month-long deadlock at the Geneva conference on Rhodesian majority rule is broken when two black nationalist delegates accept the British proposal for independence by March 1, 1978.... W. Ger. political leader Helmut Schmidt, in a controversial speech before the Socialist International conference in Geneva, blames bad governmental management rather than capitalism or any other ideology for the current wide disparity in world living standards.... The U.N.General Assembly votes for favorable reconsideration of Vietnam's request for admission to the U.N.	The seven member-nations of the Warsaw Pact propose the signing of a treaty renouncing first use of nuclear weapons in any conflict.		Chilean For. Min. Patricio Carvajal rejects a Peruvian plan to grant landlocked Bolivia access to the sea.	

A	B	C	D	E
Includes developments that affect more than one world region, international organizations and important meetings of major world leaders.	*Includes all domestic and regional developments in Europe, including the Soviet Union, Turkey, Cyprus and Malta.*	*Includes all domestic and regional developments in Africa and the Middle East, including Iraq and Iran and excluding Cyprus, Turkey and Afghanistan.*	*Includes all domestic and regional developments in Latin America, the Caribbean and Canada.*	*Includes all domestic and regional developments in Asia and Pacific nations, extending from Afghanistan through all the Pacific Islands, except Hawaii.*

U.S. Politics & Social Issues	U.S. Foreign Policy & Defense	U.S. Economy & Environment	Science, Technology & Nature	Culture, Leisure & Life Style	
Pres. Ford and Pres.-elect Carter meet in the White House in a demonstration of harmony in the transition of leadership.... Mary Louise Smith announces her resignation as chairman of the Republican National Committee, to become effective January 1977. ... Total college enrollment for 1976 is reported to be only .4 percent higher than in 1975, attributed to the rising percentage of student costs, enrollment ceilings, and the expiration in June of GI educational benefits for many veterans.			ErwinRingel, of the International Assn. for Suicide Prevention, notes that countries once belonging to the Austro-Hungarian empire have the highest suicide rates.		Nov. 22
A National Institute on Drug Abuse survey of 17,000 high school seniors in 130 schools finds 53 percent had tried marijuana, compared to 48 percent last year.	*The New York Times* reports that Park Tong Sun, involved in the S. Korean influence-peddling scandal, had been told by the S. Korean govt. to stay out of the U.S. until the scandal died.	The FDA proposes that warning labels be affixed to aerosol spray cans using fluorocarbon propellants, stating the flurocarbons may harm the environment by reducing the ozone layer.		French author Andre Malraux, 75, whose major novels were *Man's Fate* and *Man's Hope* and who served as minister of culture in Charles de Gaulle's govt., dies of cancer in Paris.	Nov. 23
CIA Director George Bush announces he is resigning his post, effective Jan. 20, 1977.		Top U.S. steelmakers act to raise prices on sheet and strip steel, 38.5 percent of the industry's total shipments in 1975.	An earthquake measuring 7.6 on the Richter scale kills more than 4,000 persons, injures 2,000 others, and leaves 250,000 homeless near Mount Ararat in eastern Turkey.... A House subcommittee holds hearings on the federal investigation of Legion fever. Rep. John Murphy (D, N.Y.), chairman of the subcommittee, criticizes the investigation.	Seymour Graubard, national chairman of the B'nai B'rith Anti-Defamation League, which met in Jerusalem, Nov. 16–24, endorses the Vatican guidelines issued in 1974 encouraging interfaith dialogue. He meets with Pope Paul VI in Rome.	Nov. 24
			Bacteriologist Theodor Rosebury, 72, specialist and writer on venereal disease, dies in Conway, Mass.	The Australian govt. announces it has bought the logbook kept by Captain William Bligh after he was cast adrift by the mutineers on the H.M.S. *Bounty* in 1789.	Nov. 25
					Nov. 26

F	G	H	I	J
Includes elections, federal-state relations, civil rights and liberties, crime, the judiciary, education, health care, poverty, urban affairs and population.	Includes formation and debate of U.S. foreign and defense policies, veterans' affairs and defense spending. (Relations with specific foreign countries are usually found under the region concerned.)	Includes business, labor, agriculture, taxation, transportation, consumer affairs, monetary and fiscal policy, natural resources, and pollution.	Includes worldwide scientific, medical and technological developments, natural phenomena, U.S. weather, natural disasters, and accidents.	Includes the arts, religion, scholarship, communications media, sports, entertainments, fashions, fads and social life.

	World Affairs	Europe	Africa & the Middle East	The Americas	Asia & the Pacific
Nov. 27		An Ulster peace rally in London draws an estimated 15,000 persons and is the largest gathering of the Peace Movement of Northern Ireland since its founding in August by Betty Williams and Mairead Corrigan.	Angola's ruling Council of the Revolution unanimously approves Pres. Agostinho Neto's Cabinet nominations.		
Nov. 28			Amnesty International says Iran's Savak (secret police) has imprisoned 25,000–100,000 of its citizens for political reasons and has frequently tortured them.		The Chinese govt. urges restraint in the drive against the Gang of Four — Chiang Ching, Chang Shun-chiao, Wang Hung-wen, and Yao Wen-yuan. . . . Australia devalues its currency by 17.5 percent, which lowers the Australian dollar's value from $U.S.1.2354 to $U.S.1.0174.
Nov. 29		OECD report calls Ireland's economy critical and says that the government must control incomes to fight inflation, expected to reach 18 percent.	Chief Gatsha Buthelezi of the South African KwaZulu homeland forms a political party, the Black United Front, to attract middle-class blacks and church leaders to a moderate antiapartheid movement. . . . Syrian Foreign Min. Abdel Halim Khaddam warns that Syrian troops will use military force if necessary to disarm the former combatants in the Lebanese civil war.	A number of bombs explode in Mexico City, causing police to increase security for the inauguration of Pres. Jose Lopez Portillo on Dec. 1.	Australia's devaluation of its currency is followed by devaluations in the neighboring countries of New Zealand and Papua New Guinea.
Nov. 30	Sino–Soviet border dispute talks resume in Peking, and are seen as a sign of rapprochement between the two countries under the new Chinese leaderships. . . . The U.N. Security Council approves a resolution extending for another six months the term of the U.N. Disengagement Observer Force separating Syrian and Israeli forces on the Golan Heights.	Marshal Ivan Yakubovsky, 64, Soviet deputy defense minister and commander in chief of the Warsaw Pact, dies in the U.S.S.R. . . . Greek-owned Olympic Airways pilots refuse to make night flights to all but two of Greece's airports to protest inadequate safety facilities.		A Canadian House of Commons Committee begins formal hearings in the case of unexplained payments made by Atomic Energy of Canada Ltd. in sales of nuclear reactors to S. Korea and Argentina.	Official sources report Bangladesh Gen. Ziaur Rahman, army chief of staff, assumed full power as chief martial law administrator and arrested at least 11 prominent political leaders.
Dec. 1	The U.N. General Assembly votes to admit Angola. The U.S. abstains, citing the continued presence of Cuban troops in the country.	Giovanni Agnelli, chairman of Fiat S.p.A., Italy's largest private employer and Europe's third biggest car manufacturer, announces that Libya will buy a 9.6 percent interest in the company, in a total deal involving $415 million. . . . Polish CP First Secy. Edward Gierek says investment for economic development will be cut because $1.5 million is needed for grain imports over the next year.	Syrian Foreign Min. Abdel Halim Khaddam is shot but not seriously wounded by unknown assailants with machine guns while he and his wife are riding in his car near Damascus.	Mexico's former Finance Minister Jose Lopez Portillo assumes the presidency with a call for national unity and strict austerity to overcome the country's acute economic crisis. . . . The Parti Quebecois wins a seventieth seat in the provincial parliament after a recount takes a seat from the Liberal candidate, thereby reducing the Liberal strength to 27 seats.	The Indonesian govt. releases 2,600 political prisoners and promises to free the remaining 29,000 by 1979, all held without trial after an abortive Communist coup in 1965.
Dec. 2	The U.S. Commission on Security and Cooperation in Europe reports that the 1975 Helsinki accords on security and cooperation have been more productive than the West expected.		The International Committee of the Red Cross says the Lebanese civil war has left more than 300,000, most of them Palestinians representing 25 percent of the population, destitute.		The Standing Committee of the National People's Congress of China dismisses Chiao Kuan-hua as foreign minister and replaces him with Huang Hua, China's U.N. ambassador.

A	B	C	D	E
Includes developments that affect more than one world region, international organizations and important meetings of major world leaders.	Includes all domestic and regional developments in Europe, including the Soviet Union, Turkey, Cyprus and Malta.	Includes all domestic and regional developments in Africa and the Middle East, including Iraq and Iran and excluding Cyprus, Turkey and Afghanistan.	Includes all domestic and regional developments in Latin America, the Caribbean and Canada.	Includes all domestic and regional developments in Asia and Pacific nations, extending from Afghanistan through all the Pacific Islands, except Hawaii.

U.S. Politics & Social Issues	U.S. Foreign Policy & Defense	U.S. Economy & Environment	Science, Technology & Nature	Culture, Leisure & Life Style	
			According to a Center for Disease Control report, less than one-fourth of the eligible adult U.S. population has been vaccinated against swine flu to this date.		Nov. 27
A Carter press aide, Rex Granum, confirms that Bertram Lance, president of the National Bank of Georgia, will have a Cabinet-level position, but that no decision has been made on which one.... Pres.-elect Carter's 9-year-old daughter, Amy, is to be enrolled in a public school near the White House. The school's enrollment is 60 percent black and one third are children of diplomats.		The Labor Dept. says the gap in average earnings between men and women widened over the 20 years from 1955 to 1974.		Rosalind Russell, 63, celebrated stage and screen actress of the 1930s and 1940s, dies in Beverly Hills, Calif.... A new owner, Thomas Morgan, is announced for *The Nation*, the oldest continuously published weekly magazine in the U.S. He is a former editor of the *Village Voice* .	Nov. 28
Pollster Robert Teeter cautions that the Republicans face a crippling disability through their failure to attract the black vote.... The Supreme Ct. agrees to hear a challenge by former Pres. Richard Nixon to a 1974 law giving the government control of and providing for eventual public access to Nixon's presidential papers.				The U.S. Polish National Catholic Church ends its 30-year sacramental affiliation with the Episcopal Church because it opposes the Episcopal decision to ordain women as priests.... Six women in British Columbia and Ontario are ordained as Anglican Church of Canada priests.	Nov. 29
Sen. Robert Dole (Kan.), the defeated Republican vice-presidential nominee, cautions the Republican Party against clinging to a narrow ideology and calls for a Republican version of "affirmative action" at the grass-roots level to attract more women, ethnic groups, youths, and working-class people to the party.		Federal Energy Administration (FEA) administrator Frank Zarb says that the agency opposes the proposed export of Alaskan surplus oil because the U.S. would be left vulnerable to a Middle East oil-supply cutoff.... U.S. District Judge James Parsons imposes prison terms, probation, and fines on 47 paperboard-company officials who pled no contest to price-fixing charges.	Zaire's Health Ministry says the virus that caused a recent outbreak of green monkey fever will be known as the Ebola virus. The new disease had a 91 percent fatality rate.... Martha Wolfenstein, 65, Yeshiva University psychiatry professor, child psychology specialist, and co-author with Margaret Mead of *Childhood in Contemporary Cultures*, dies in New York.	Tony Dorsett, of the University of Pittsburgh Panthers, is named winner of the 1976 Heisman Trophy as the best player in college football. ... The Vatican publishes a letter, dated Oct. 11, from Pope Paul VI to rebel Bishop Marcel Lefebvre in which the Pope sought "an act of faith and obedience" from the prelate.	Nov. 30
				George Earnshaw, 76, right-handed baseball pitcher for the Philadelphia Athletics who won 20 games in three straight years, dies in Hot Springs, Ark.	Dec. 1
	The Defense Dept. awards $704.9 million in contracts to begin production of the controversial B-1 strategic bomber. The main contract — for $526 million — goes to Rockwell International Corp..	The Council on Wage and Price Stability reports serious reservations about the steel-price increases and suggests that the industry made a "jump-the-gun" move to protect against future price controls.		Danny Murtaugh, 59, manager of the Pittsburgh Pirates who led the team to World Series titles in 1960 and 1971, dies in Chester, Pa.	Dec. 2

F	G	H	I	J
Includes elections, federal-state relations, civil rights and liberties, crime, the judiciary, education, health care, poverty, urban affairs and population.	*Includes formation and debate of U.S. foreign and defense policies, veterans' affairs and defense spending. (Relations with specific foreign countries are usually found under the region concerned.)*	*Includes business, labor, agriculture, taxation, transportation, consumer affairs, monetary and fiscal policy, natural resources, and pollution.*	*Includes worldwide scientific, medical and technological developments, natural phenomena, U.S. weather, natural disasters, and accidents.*	*Includes the arts, religion, scholarship, communications media, sports, entertainments, fashions, fads and social life.*

	World Affairs	Europe	Africa & the Middle East	The Americas	Asia & the Pacific
Dec. 3	The U.N. high commissioner for refugees, Prince Sadruddin Aga Khan, protests the forcible return of Cambodian refugees by Thailand.		South African police seal off entrances to the township and arrest more than 300 blacks in Guguletu and neighboring Nyanga as unrest continues.	The Cuban National Assembly of People's Power, its new legislature, convenes and elects Fidel Castro to be president of the new Council of State.... The Argentinean army announces it killed Norma Arrostito, a Montonero leader who participated in the 1970 assassination of ex-Pres. Pedro Eugenio Aramburu.... Eight Argentinean generals retire, including three prominent hard-liners, in an apparent move by Pres. Jorge Videla to concentrate power among moderate officers.	
Dec. 4		EEC and the five countries bordering the Rhine River sign treaties to begin a joint effort to reduce Rhine River pollution.	ANC pres. Bishop Abel Muzorewa condemns ZANU leader Robert Mugabe and ZAPU leader Joshua Nkomo for opposing elections for the interim Rhodesian government. ... The Central African Republic is officially renamed the Central African Empire by President-for-life Jean-Bedel Bokassa, reinforcing Bokassa's already complete control.		The U.S.-Philippines negotiations over American military bases in the country collapse when Pres. Ferdinand Marcos rejects the U.S. five-year offer of $1 billion in economic and military aid.... S. Korean Pres. Park Chung Hee reshuffles his Cabinet and dismisses the head of the Korean CIA, in what is seen as a reaction to the S. Korean payoff scandal involving U.S. congressmen.
Dec. 5		A firebomb attack in Londonderry, Northern Ireland destroys 16 stores and partially destroys six others, gutting half of the city's shopping district.... Jacques Chirac transforms the French Gaullist Party into a mass movement known as the Assembly for the Republic at a rally attended by 50,000 persons, and is installed as its president.... The ruling Danish Social Democratic party and four supporting non-socialist parties pass legislation freezing prices, wages, and rents for three months.	Lebanese Pres. Elias Sarkis is reported to have extended the deadline for the collection of heavy weapons from former civil war combatants to avoid using force to retrieve the arms.	*The New York Times* says hundreds of Colombians are entering Venezuela daily and staying on illegally in hope of finding work in Venezuela's expanding economy.	Japanese Premier Takeo Miki's governing Liberal Democratic Party suffers a major setback, losing its majority in nationwide elections for the expanded House of Representatives.
Dec. 6	Western European NATO defense ministers express concern over the growing military capability of the Warsaw Pact and say that substanial U.S. and Canadian forces are indispensable.	Cardinal Stefan Wyszynski, head of Poland's Roman Catholic church, repeats charges that Polish police beat workers arrested in June riots protesting food-price increases.... Libyan leader Muammar el-Qaddafi visits the U.S.S.R. for the first time since taking power in 1969 and signs agreements with Leonid Brezhnev on shipping and protocols for talks on economic and technical aid.	At least 35 are killed in clashes between rival Palestinian factions at a Lebanese refugee camp outside Tripoli.	Joao Goulart, 58, Brazil's last civilian president (1961–64), dies in exile of a heart attack in Argentina.	
Dec. 7		Maurice Bouvier, head of the French govt.'s criminal investigation dept., says the crime rate in France has increased threefold since 1963.... French Pres. Valery Giscard d'Estaing visits Yugoslavian Pres. Tito and praises Yugoslavian independence as a peace and stability factor in Europe.	The Kenyan govt. denies Tanzanian Pres. Julius Nyerere's charges that Kenya has not supported the East-African Community, a common-market arrangement between Kenya, Tanzania, and Uganda.	Grenadan P.M. Eric Gairy and his ruling Grenada United Labor Party wins a narrow victory over the opposition People's Alliance in national elections.	The Australian govt. cuts the tariffs on 900 imported items, about one-third of Australia's total imports, reportedly to offset the inflationary effect of its currency devaluation. ... Japanese Premier Takeo Miki says that he feels deep responsibility for the Liberal Democratic Party setback, the worst since it assumed power in 1955. He calls his Cabinet a caretaker and says he will resign when the Diet convenes in December.

A	B	C	D	E
Includes developments that affect more than one world region, international organizations and important meetings of major world leaders.	Includes all domestic and regional developments in Europe, including the Soviet Union, Turkey, Cyprus and Malta.	Includes all domestic and regional developments in Africa and the Middle East, including Iraq and Iran and excluding Cyprus, Turkey and Afghanistan.	Includes all domestic and regional developments in Latin America, the Caribbean and Canada.	Includes all domestic and regional developments in Asia and Pacific nations, extending from Afghanistan through all the Pacific Islands, except Hawaii.

U.S. Politics & Social Issues	U.S. Foreign Policy & Defense	U.S. Economy & Environment	Science, Technology & Nature	Culture, Leisure & Life Style	
Pres.-elect Carter says he has selected Cyrus Vance to be secretary of state and Bertram Lance to be director of the Office of Management and Budget (OMB).	Pres.-elect Carter says he has received word from Soviet leader Leonid Brezhnev that the U.S.S.R. will "bend over backward not to create any sort of test in the early days of my administration."	International City Bank & Trust Co. of New Orleans becomes the fifth-largest insured bank in U.S. history to fail and the sixteenth bank to fail in 1976. . . . The Labor Dept. announces unemployment during November was at its highest level since December 1975, 8.2 percent, and that the number of jobless has risen 200,000 since October. . . . Pres.-elect Carter renounces imposition of wage-and-price controls, barring a national emergency.	*Science* magazine reports the discovery of the first biochemical test for chronic alcoholism, and terms the test of tremendous significance in alcoholism research.		Dec. 3
				A new Protestant denomination, the Association of Evangelical Lutheran Churches, ends a two-day founding convention. It represents about 75,000 dissident moderate theologians from the Lutheran Church — Missouri Synod. . . . Benjamin Britten, 63, acclaimed as one of the twentieth century's leading composers, dies in England.	Dec. 4
		New OMB head Bertram Lance predicts that it will be very difficult to bring the unemployment rate down to Carter's stated goal of 6.5 percent by the end of 1977. . . . The last section of the 800-mile Alaskan pipelane is laid but welding is still not completed.		*The New York Times Book Review* lists *A Man Called Intrepid* by William Stevenson and *Trinity* by Leon Uris as the best-sellers for 1976 in the general and fiction categories. . . . An unprecedented Roman Catholic rite of general absolution in Memphis, Tenn. allows divorced, remarried Catholics, and other estranged church members to receive Holy Communion.	Dec. 5
Voting in caucus, House Democrats choose Rep. Thomas (Tip) O'Neill Jr. (Mass.) as speaker of the House and Rep. Jim Wright (Tex.) as majority leader. . . . A Calif. ct. dismisses a contempt-of-court action against reporter William Farr, who was cited for refusing to divulge news sources on a story about the Manson family murder trial. . . . The Supreme Ct. vacates an appellate court ruling ordering extensive busing of students in Austin, Tex..	Marine Corps pretrial hearings begin for three black marines on charges stemming from an assault on a group of white marines, who they alleged to have thought to be Marine Ku Klux Klan members.	Transportation Secy. William Coleman rules against requiring car manufacturers to equip all new cars with air bags as a protective device against accidents. Rep. John Moss (D, Calif.) and consumer activist Ralph Nader denounce the decision.	Dr. John Scudder, 76, blood-bank pioneer and advocate of "race to race" blood transfusions, dies in N.Y.		Dec. 6
A mistrial is declared in the political corruption trial of Md. Gov. Marvin Mandel after several jurors are exposed to news reports of attempted juror tampering. . . . The Supreme Ct. rules federal civil-rights law does not require company disability plans to provide pregnancy or childbirth benefits. . . . The AMA's House of Delegates endorses a national health-insurance program, but it opposes a bill sponsored by Sen. Edward Kennedy (D, Mass.) and Rep. James Corman (D, Calif.) making insurance mandatory.					Dec. 7

F	G	H	I	J
Includes elections, federal-state relations, civil rights and liberties, crime, the judiciary, education, health care, poverty, urban affairs and population.	Includes formation and debate of U.S. foreign and defense policies, veterans' affairs and defense spending. (Relations with specific foreign countries are usually found under the region concerned.)	Includes business, labor, agriculture, taxation, transportation, consumer affairs, monetary and fiscal policy, natural resources, and pollution.	Includes worldwide scientific, medical and technological developments, natural phenomena, U.S. weather, natural disasters, and accidents.	Includes the arts, religion, scholarship, communications media, sports, entertainments, fashions, fads and social life.

	World Affairs	Europe	Africa & the Middle East	The Americas	Asia & the Pacific
Dec. 8	The U.N. General Assembly reelects Kurt Waldheim by acclamation to a second five-year-term as secy. gen. after he turns back a challenge from former Mexican Pres. Luis Echeverria. . . . Rhodesian P.M. Ian Smith returns to the Geneva conference on Rhodesian majority rule after a four-week absence, and meets with British chairmam Ivor Richard. . . . The IMF sells 780,000 ounces of gold at $137 an ounce, the highest price received in the five 1976 auctions. The number of bids received was also the year's highest.	Belgian Premier Leo Tindemans wards off a potential threat to his government by redistributing Cabinet positions among the ruling parties.	Syria and Jordan announce plans to form a union of their two countries.	The Asian *Wall Street Journal* reports the Canadian Wheat Bd. announced a $C95.5 million sale of 27.9 million bushels of wheat to China.	
Dec. 9	The U.N. General Assembly adopts an Egyptian resolution calling for the reconvening of the Geneva Conference on the Middle East before March 1, 1977.	Fiat chmn. Giovanni Agnelli flies to Libya and meets with Col. Muammar el-Qaddafi, the Libyan head of state, about Libya's purchase into Fiat S.p.A., saying afterwards that he sees a potential for economic collaboration with other oil-producing countries to stimulate the Italian economy.	*The New York Times* reports an international journalists' delegation presented a formal note of protest to the S. African govt. over the government's detention of reporters.		
Dec. 10	NATO ministers veto the Warsaw Pact recommendations for a treaty to ban the first use of nuclear weapons and for a freeze on current memberships of both alliances. . . . Rhodesian P.M. Ian Smith claims he was misled by the parties who arranged the Geneva conference (a reference to Britain) into believing a change in black nationalist strategy was imminent.	Four jailed supporters of the 1968 liberal Czech govt. of Alexander Dubcek are released on probation.	Algerian Pres. Houari Boumedienne is reelected by more than 99.5 percent of the ballots cast by an estimated 96 percent of Algeria's registered voters. . . . A truce between Moslem and Christian militiamen in the south is announced by Ghassan Haidar, governor of the Bint Jbail district of Lebanon.		Violent factional fighting involving attacks on government offices is reported to have raged over the past few months in the central Chinese provinces of Yunan, Hupei, Honan, and Shansi.
Dec. 11	British For. Min. Anthony Crosland and U.S. State Secy. Henry Kissinger discuss the possibility that the governor-general, justice, and defense ministers in the proposed interim Rhodesian govt. be British.	Gunmen belonging to a Basque separatist organization kidnap Antonio de Oriol y Urquijo president of the Spanish Council of State and demand the release of 15 political prisoners.	Rhodesian guerrillas kill two blacks and a colored (mixed-race) policeman in Bulawayo.		
Dec. 12	Rhodesian P.M. Ian Smith leaves the Geneva conference on Rhodesian majority rule, saying he saw virtually no change in the deadlocked conference.	Portuguese Socialist Party candidates win 33 percent of the vote in municipal elections, thereby releasing Premier Mario Soares from having to honor his preelection offer to name members of other parties to the Cabinet. . . . Cardinal Stefan Wyszynski urges Polish workers to fight for their rights and demand more pay if they believe their salaries are inadequate. . . . EEC unemployment statistics show one out of three unemployed workers is under the age of 25, double the number reported in 1973. Women account for two-thirds of the increase.	Camille Chamoun, head of the Lebanese Nat. Liberal Party and a Christian leader, is the target of an apparent assassination attempt.		
Dec. 13		Secret U.N. reports acquired by the *London Times* reveal systematic and large-scale looting of Greek property in the Turkish-held area of Cyprus.	Upon his return from the Geneva conference on Rhodesian majority rule, ANC head Bishop Abel Muzorewa criticizes P.M. Ian Smith for his delaying tactics and calls the militant factions' opposition to elections for an interim government "an insult to our people."	Amnesty International reports that extra-judicial detentions and executions occur daily in Guatemala, and it estimates more than 20,000 have been killed or disappeared since 1966.	

A	B	C	D	E
Includes developments that affect more than one world region, international organizations and important meetings of major world leaders.	Includes all domestic and regional developments in Europe, including the Soviet Union, Turkey, Cyprus and Malta.	Includes all domestic and regional developments in Africa and the Middle East, including Iraq and Iran and excluding Cyprus, Turkey and Afghanistan.	Includes all domestic and regional developments in Latin America, the Caribbean and Canada.	Includes all domestic and regional developments in Asia and Pacific nations, extending from Afghanistan through all the Pacific Islands, except Hawaii.

U.S. Politics & Social Issues	U.S. Foreign Policy & Defense	U.S. Economy & Environment	Science, Technology & Nature	Culture, Leisure & Life Style	
Speaker of the House Thomas (Tip) O'Neill and Majority Leader Jim Wright appoint Rep. John Brademas (D, Ind.), a mainstream liberal Democrat, as majority whip, replacing Rep. John McFall (D, Calif.). . . . House Republicans elect incumbents to the top three GOP House posts: John Rhodes (Ariz.) as minority leader, Robert Michel (Ill.) as minority whip, and John Anderson (Ill.) as chairman of the House GOP Conference.		The EPA reports improvement in the nation's air quality from 1971–75, with the greatest improvements in the Northeast, Great Lakes area, and urban California. . . . The Supreme Ct. rules that a public employe cannot be barred from speaking at a public meeting on the topic of contract negotiations just because he isn't a union member.	The U.S. says the Soviet Union has agreed to sell India 200 metric tons of heavy water for its nuclear reactors. Soviet officials say international inspection and safeguards will be observed.		Dec. 8
Francois Chiappe and Miguel Russo, two members of an international narcotics ring known as the Latin American Triangle, are convicted in Brooklyn, N.Y. of conspiracy to import and distribute heroin, having allegedly smuggled $1.5 billion worth into the U.S.			The Labor Dept. Occupational Safety and Health Administration says the incidence of job-related injury, illness, and death declined significantly in 1975.	Reporter Don Bolles is posthumously named the 1976 winner of the University of Arizona's John Peter Zenger Award, given annually for distinguished service in behalf of freedom of the press.	Dec. 9
A White Plains, N.Y. jury acquits Mel Lynch and Dominic Byrne of kidnapping Samuel Bronfman II in 1975, but convicts them of extorting $2.3 million in ransom from Bronfman's father, Edgar, who heads Seagram & Son Inc..		The EPA orders Chrysler Corp. to recall 208,000 1975-model cars because improper design of carburetors led to misadjustments causing excessive carbon-monoxide emissions. . . . United Brands Co. says an internal investigation into a $1.25 million 1974 bribe to a Honduran official uncovered $1.2 million in previously undisclosed payments to foreign officials.		Washington-based journalist and broadcaster Peter Lisagor dies at the age of 61 of cancer in Va.	Dec. 10
				Philanthropist Lytle Hull, 83, who helped found the New York Opera Co. and the New York City Center, dies of post-operative complications in Poughkeepsie, N.Y.	Dec. 11
The New York Times reports a federal study that finds Detroit, Mich. has the highest proportion of heroin users of any U.S. city, and leads the nation in heroin-related deaths.				Actor and singer Jack Cassidy, 49, dies in a fire in his Los Angeles, Calif. home.	Dec. 12
The Supreme Ct. unanimously upholds a law denying divorced mothers of dependent children certain payments made to married mothers whose husbands are eligible for Social Security. . . . The Electoral College meets and casts ballots for President and Vice President as required under the Constitution. The vote is 297 for Carter–Mondale and 241 for Ford–Dole.		The strike by public school teachers in Jefferson County, Ky. ends. The settlement provides for salary increases to a range of $9,100–$16,744 from a range of $8,300–$15,000. . . . A strike by 18,000 members of the Teamsters Union against the United Parcel Service ends, and strikers return to work after almost three months.	The Journal of the American Medical Association reports a successful new rabies vaccine requiring four to six injections, compared with the current method requiring 14 to 21 injections.	The attorney representing prospective family heirs of the late Howard Hughes says he has evidence that the handwritten Mormon will under which Melvin Dummar is a beneficiary is a forgery.	Dec. 13

F	G	H	I	J
Includes elections, federal-state relations, civil rights and liberties, crime, the judiciary, education, health care, poverty, urban affairs and population.	Includes formation and debate of U.S. foreign and defense policies, veterans' affairs and defense spending. (Relations with specific foreign countries are usually found under the region concerned.)	Includes business, labor, agriculture, taxation, transportation, consumer affairs, monetary and fiscal policy, natural resources, and pollution.	Includes worldwide scientific, medical and technological developments, natural phenomena, U.S. weather, natural disasters, and accidents.	Includes the arts, religion, scholarship, communications media, sports, entertainments, fashions, fads and social life.

	World Affairs	Europe	Africa & the Middle East	The Americas	Asia & the Pacific
Dec. 14	Geneva conference on Rhodesian majority rule adjourns until January 1977. Its chairman, Ivor Richard, terms it a modest success. . . . Oleg Troyanovsky is named Soviet ambassador to the U.N., replacing Yakov Malik.	Former director of the Greek security police Evanghelos Mallios, convicted in October of torturing political prisoners during the military dictatorship, is fatally shot outside his Athens home.	The PLO Central Council formally calls for the creation of an independent Palestinian state as one of the legitimate rights of the Palestinian people. . . . A bomb blast at the international airport terminal in Baghdad, Iraq kills three, injures more than 230, and causes heavy damage to the building.		
Dec. 15		W. Ger. Chancellor Helmut Schmidt is reelected by a bare majority in the lower house of the Parliament. . . . British Exchequer Chancellor Denis Healey says he plans a $4.17-billion cut in public spending over the next two years and $470 million in new cigarette and alcohol taxes. . . . With 94.2 percent of referendum voters in favor, a Spanish reform bill, amounting to a constitutional amendment, provides for free elections in 1977.	West Bank Arabs stage a one-day general strike to protest the Israeli occupation and a new Israeli value-added tax on goods and services. . . . In Lebanon Arab League troops take over the Beirut offices of three newspapers, which continue to publish by using other facilities.	Jamaican P.M. Michael Manley and his ruling People's National Party win a decisive victory in parliamentary elections. The vote is seen as a strong endorsement of his socialist policies and ties with Fidel Castro. . . . In retaliation for the slaying of Norma Arrostito, Argentine Montoneros set off a bomb in an auditorium in the Defense Ministry building in Buenos Aires, killing nine and seriously injuring 19.	
Dec. 16		The British govt.-sponsored bill granting limited home rule to Scotland and Wales is approved by the House of Commons, but still requires referendum approval. . . . A 10-mile, 120-yard tunnel, the world's longest, is completed beneath the St. Gottard range from Goschenen, near Andermatt, on the northern side of the Alps, to Airolo. . . . The French govt. says it will ban all future sales of nuclear fuel-reprocessing plants that could be used to produce plutonium for atomic bombs, a change from its previous policy.			
Dec. 17	OPEC sets differing price increases: Saudi Arabia and the United Arab Emirates will raise oil prices by 5 percent for the first six months of 1977 while its 11 other members will increase prices by 10 percent, and by another 5 percent after July 1. . . . Financial Times says members of COMECON, the Soviet-bloc economic organization, have adopted a proposal to liberalize their currency exchange with the West.		It is reported that about half a million Lebanese who fled during the civil war have returned since the November truce. Most fled to neighboring Syria.		Japanese Premier Takeo Miki (president of the ruling Liberal Democratic Party) resigns, accepting responsibility for the party's election defeat and attributing it to the effects of the Lockheed scandal.
Dec. 18	Mediated by the U.S., the U.S.S.R. and Chile exchange two widely known political prisoners, Vladimir Bukovsky and Luis Corvalan, at a Swiss airport.	Evanghelos Mallios's assassins, members of the Greek underground group called Revolutionary Organization of 17 November, are linked by ballistic tests to the 1975 murder of Richard Welch, then head of the CIA operations in Greece. . . . The prestigious Chateau Margaux vineyard of Bordeaux, owned by the Pierre Ginestet family, is sold to the French supermarket and food chain Felix Potin for $15 million.		Chilean Ambassador to the U.S. Manuel Trucco says the only political prisoner left in Chile is Jorge Montes, the former Communist senator whom Chile proposes to exchange.	Chinese CP newspaper Jenmin Jih Pao accuses the Gang of Four of rewording a critical quote by Mao and publishing it a week after his death to make it appear that they alone were to assume his powers.
Dec. 19				Assassinations and political kidnappings are reported continuing throughout Argentina in the last quarter of 1976 as the political death toll for the year passes 1,400. . . . The body of late Argentinian Pres. Juan Peron is removed from its crypt at the Olivos presidential residence and buried in a Buenos Aires cemetery.	

A	B	C	D	E
Includes developments that affect more than one world region, international organizations and important meetings of major world leaders.	Includes all domestic and regional developments in Europe, including the Soviet Union, Turkey, Cyprus and Malta.	Includes all domestic and regional developments in Africa and the Middle East, including Iraq and Iran and excluding Cyprus, Turkey and Afghanistan.	Includes all domestic and regional developments in Latin America, the Caribbean and Canada.	Includes all domestic and regional developments in Asia and Pacific nations, extending from Afghanistan through all the Pacific Islands, except Hawaii.

U.S. Politics & Social Issues	U.S. Foreign Policy & Defense	U.S. Economy & Environment	Science, Technology & Nature	Culture, Leisure & Life Style	
	The Commission on U.S.-Latin American Relations, a private panel, urges Pres.-elect Carter to break new ground in Latin American relations and to depart sharply from the Monroe Doctrine.	Pres.-elect Carter names Michael Blumenthal, chief executive officer of Bendix Corp., as treasury Secy. and Rep. Brock Adams (D, Wash.) as transportation secy.... Carter says he plans to announce a program to stimulate the economy even before assuming office, focusing on job-producing within the existing bureaucracy.		Pres. Ford offers to donate the papers and memorabilia of his 28 years in public life to the U.S. on condition that the material be preserved and exhibited in Michigan.	Dec. 14
		The U.S. and its beef suppliers, chiefly Australia and New Zealand, agree to limit 1977 U.S. beef imports to 1.28 billion pounds, instead of mandatory U.S. quotas. ... A Liberian tanker, *Argo Merchant*, carrying 7.5 million gallons of industrial fuel oil runs aground southeast of Nantucket Island, Mass. and begins leaking oil near one of the world's richest fishing grounds.			Dec. 15
Pres.-elect Carter appoints Rep. Andrew Young (Ga.) as chief U.N. delegate, Charles Schultze as CEA chairman, and Zbigniew Brzezinski as special assistant for national security.... A U.S. District Judge rules that former Pres. Richard Nixon, former Atty. Gen. John Mitchell and Nixon aide H.R. Haldeman violated the rights of Morton Halperin, a former NSC aide, by wiretapping his home phone for 21 months.	Andrew Young, newly appointed chief U.S. delegate to the U.N., says the U.S. has a "great deal of responsibility to pursue majority rule in southern Africa." Zbigniew Brzezinski, national security adviser, says detente should be "reciprocal" and "progressively more comprehensive."	The largest corporate merger in U.S. business history to date takes place as shareholders of General Electric Co. and Utah International Inc. vote to combine the two companies.	The U.S. govt. halts its swine flu inoculation program, citing reports of Guillain-Barre syndrome (paralysis) in 51 persons who received the vaccine one to three weeks before.		Dec. 16
A federal jury in San Antonio, Tex. orders Southwestern Bell Telephone Co. to pay $1 million in damages to a former executive, James Ashley, who claimed the company wiretapped his home phone during an internal investigation.... A federal jury finds former Rep. James Hastings (R, N.Y.) guilty on counts of mail fraud and making false statements, in charges stemming from an alleged payroll kickback scheme.	Pres. Ford praises Saudi Arabia and the United Arab Emirates for their restraint on price increases and denounces the 11 other OPEC nations as irresponsible.	Transportation Secy. William Coleman says he will approve licenses for two deepwater superports to be built in the Gulf of Mexico for large oil tankers, despite environmental and antitrust objections.			Dec. 17
Congressional Quarterly reports the official popular-vote tally of the Nov. 2 presidential election gave Carter–Mondale 40,828,587 (50.1 percent) and Ford–Dole 39,147,613 (48 percent).		Pres.-elect Carter appoints Idaho Gov. Cecil Andrus (D) as interior secretary.... The Council of Economic Priorities says more than 175 U.S. companies voluntarily admitted paying bribes and making questionable payments totaling $300 million plus since 1970.			Dec. 18
Women win 13 of the 32 Rhodes Scholarships awarded to Americans, the first time the scholarships have been open to women.				Betty Ford, wife of Pres. Ford, receives an honorary Doctor of Laws degree from the University of Michigan.	Dec. 19

F	G	H	I	J
Includes elections, federal-state relations, civil rights and liberties, crime, the judiciary, education, health care, poverty, urban affairs and population.	*Includes formation and debate of U.S. foreign and defense policies, veterans' affairs and defense spending. (Relations with specific foreign countries are usually found under the region concerned.)*	*Includes business, labor, agriculture, taxation, transportation, consumer affairs, monetary and fiscal policy, natural resources, and pollution.*	*Includes worldwide scientific, medical and technological developments, natural phenomena, U.S. weather, natural disasters, and accidents.*	*Includes the arts, religion, scholarship, communications media, sports, entertainments, fashions, fads and social life.*

	World Affairs	Europe	Africa & the Middle East	The Americas	Asia & the Pacific
Dec. 20	The International Energy Agency (IEA) says the higher cost of OPEC oil will force a sharp reduction in demand and this might stem any growth of the cartel's revenues.	An EEC directive allows doctors trained in any of its nine member-countries to practice anywhere in the community.	Iraq and Iran assail Saudi Arabia for not agreeing with other OPEC members to raise its oil prices by 15 percent in 1977.		In the first elections since 1967, the Mauritius ruling Labor Party of P.M. Sir Seewoosagur Ramgoolam loses its majority to the Militant Mauritian Movement led by Paul Berenger. . . . Vietnam's governing Workers Party, at its fourth congress, renames itself the Communist Party, renames Secy. Gen. Le Duan as party leader, and ratifies a new five-year development plan.
Dec. 21	The executive directors of the World Bank approve two loans to Chile totaling $60 milion for a farm and agro-industry program and for improved electrical service. . . . The Group of 10, comprising the major Western industrialized nations and Japan, agrees to make funds available for the $3.9-billion loan to Great Britain.		Egypt and Syria announce plans to establish a unified political command as a step toward a union of the two countries.		
Dec. 22	The U.N. Gen. Assembly recesses its thirty-first session with a declaration that it might reconvene early in 1977 to assess results of the 1977 North-South conference of rich and poor nations. . . . The U.N. Security Council condemns S. Africa, without a formal vote, for its alleged attempt to force Lesotho to recognize neighboring Transkei as an independent country. . . . Freedom House reports only 19.6 percent of the world's population resides in what it says are free countries, a drop from its previous report of 19.8 percent.	Roy Jenkins, British president-designate of the European Commission, and the 12 other appointed members of the new commission meet for the first time. . . . The Swiss govt. returns Pieter Menten, a wealthy Dutchman suspected of WWII war crimes, to the Netherlands, from where he had fled hours before he was to have been arrested. . . . The E. German govt. orders the expulsion of Lothar Loewe, a W. Ger. TV correspondent who has interviewed various dissidents.		Canadian External Affairs Min. Donald Jamieson says Canada now has the most stringent conditions in the world on the sale of nuclear-reactor fuels and technology to other countries.	
Dec. 23	OPEC's Special Fund signs agreements in Vienna providing $42.7 million in interest-free 25-year loans to six developing nations: Sudan, Western Samoa, Sri Lanka, Guinea, Pakistan, and the Central African Empire.			According to documents furnished by former U.S. Ambassador to Chile Edward Korry, Anaconda Co. and other U.S. firms active in Latin America offered $500,000 to prevent the late Pres. Salvador Allende's 1970 election.	Singapore P.M. Lee Kuan Yews' ruling People's Action Party captures all 69 seats of an expanded Parliament, receiving 72 percent of the vote, up from 69 percent in 1972. . . . Chiang Ching and her three purged associates known as the Gang of Four, face possible execution, according to Chinese CP publication *Jenmin Jih Pao* editorial. . . . Indian P.M. Indira Gandhi assails the pro-Moscow Communist Party of India for criticizing her son Sanjay, but she denies she is planning to name him as her successor.

A	B	C	D	E
Includes developments that affect more than one world region, international organizations and important meetings of major world leaders.	Includes all domestic and regional developments in Europe, including the Soviet Union, Turkey, Cyprus and Malta.	Includes all domestic and regional developments in Africa and the Middle East, including Iraq and Iran and excluding Cyprus, Turkey and Afghanistan.	Includes all domestic and regional developments in Latin America, the Caribbean and Canada.	Includes all domestic and regional developments in Asia and Pacific nations, extending from Afghanistan through all the Pacific Islands, except Hawaii.

U.S. Politics & Social Issues	U.S. Foreign Policy & Defense	U.S. Economy & Environment	Science, Technology & Nature	Culture, Leisure & Life Style	
Pres.-elect Carter appoints Griffin Bell as attorney general, Juanita Kreps as commerce secy. and Rep. Bob Bergland (D, Minn.) as agriculture secretary.... The NAACP expresses great disappointment with Carter's choice of Griffin Bell as attorney general because of his record on school desegration and his membership in two clubs that do not have black or Jewish members.... Richard Daley, 74, mayor of Chicago since 1955 whose Cook County, Ill. Democratic organization was the locally dominant political force and often decisive in national party politics, dies.		The Supreme Ct. rules that a time limit for filing a civil-rights complaint with the EEOC is not extended just because a complainant chose first to file a union grievance.		*Daily Worker* editor and correspondent Joseph North, 72, dies of leukemia in San Juan, Puerto Rico. ... Outgoing State Secy. Henry Kissinger donates his official government papers to the Library of Congress, with the condition that he or persons he names control access for the longer of 25 years or five years after his death.... Oscar-winning songwriter Ned Washington, whose works include the score of Walt Disney's film *Pinocchio*, dies of a heart attack in Los Angeles.	Dec. 20
Rubin (Hurricane) Carter and John Artis are convicted, after a retrial, in N.J. of three counts of first-degree murder for the 1966 slaying of three persons.... Pres.-elect Carter appoints Harold Brown as defense secretary, Patricia Roberts Harris as HUD secretary, and Ray Marshall as labor secy.		James Storrow, publisher of *The Nation*, announces that the magazine will not be sold to Thomas Morgan, as previously announced.		Munro Leaf, 71, children's book illustrator and author, best-known for Ferdinand the Bull stories, dies of cancer in Garrett Park, Md.	Dec. 21
After criticism from the NAACP, Atty. Gen.-designate Griffin Bell announces he will resign from all his private clubs.		The Commerce Dept. announces the U.S. balance of payments swung into deficit ($1.06 billion) during the third quarter after posting a surplus during the first half of the year.... The UAW wins a union representation election at a GM plant in La., a key test for the union in face of three previous GM plant vote losses in the South.		*Your Arms Too Short To Box With God*, a musical based on the Book of Matthew, opens in N.Y.C.... Freedom House, a nongovernmental agency monitoring liberties around the world, says some 1976 international anti-press resolutions pose a threat of increased government control of the news media in some countries.... Industrial designer Russell Wright, 72, whose designs of modern dinnerware, furnishings, and other items for mass production at low prices helped popularize modern design in the U.S., dies of a heart attack in N.Y.	Dec. 22
Anthony Ulasewicz is convicted by a federal court jury of income-tax fraud involving his role in the Watergate case.... Pres.-elect Carter appoints Joseph Califano Jr. as HEW secy., Theodore Sorensen as CIA director, and James Schlesinger as special presidential assistant on energy.					Dec. 23

F	G	H	I	J
Includes elections, federal-state relations, civil rights and liberties, crime, the judiciary, education, health care, poverty, urban affairs and population.	Includes formation and debate of U.S. foreign and defense policies, veterans' affairs and defense spending. (Relations with specific foreign countries are usually found under the region concerned.)	Includes business, labor, agriculture, taxation, transportation, consumer affairs, monetary and fiscal policy, natural resources, and pollution.	Includes worldwide scientific, medical and technological developments, natural phenomena, U.S. weather, natural disasters, and accidents.	Includes the arts, religion, scholarship, communications media, sports, entertainments, fashions, fads and social life.

	World Affairs	Europe	Africa & the Middle East	The Americas	Asia & the Pacific
Dec. 24		Former French deputy foreign minister Prince Jean de Broglie, a prominent centrist politican, is shot to death on a Paris street. An extreme rightist group called the Charles Martel Club claims responsibility.	The continued rivalry between opposing Palestinian forces in Lebanon is underscored by the slaying of Abdel al -Sayed, a member of the radical Popular Front, and his wife.		Japanese Deputy Premier Takeo Fukuda is elected premier on the first ballot by the two houses of the Japanese Diet. . . . Philippine Pres. Ferdinand Marcos ends government military operations against the separatist Moslem Moro National Liberation Front in Mindanao, following a cease-fire and tentative political accord. . . . Chinese CP Chmn. Hua Kuo-feng says there will be a nationwide purge in 1977 of party and govt. officials who gained their positions through the Gang of Four. . . . The Indian govt. relinquishes control of Gujarat State, under federal rule since March 12, and a new state administration is formed by India's ruling Congress Party.
Dec. 25			Bethlehem Mayor Elias Freij receives a $20,000 check from U.S. V. P. Nelson Rockefeller for the upkeep of Manger Square. . . . Fighting erupts between rival black groups in Cape Town, South Africa over whether Christmas should be celebrated or declared a time of mourning for blacks killed by the police during rioting last summer.		Nationalist Chinese Premier Chaing Ching-kuo discloses that 254 Taiwanese are serving jail terms for antigovernment activity and insists their cases were handled legally.
Dec. 26	*The New York Times* reports that Charles Cooper, just retired as U.S. executive director of the World Bank, has voiced concern about the banks's lending policies and performance.			A book by Helio Bicudo, special prosecutor of the Brazilian death squads till his investigation closed in on powerful figures, likens the squads in Sao Paulo and Rio de Janeiro to the Mafia.	
Dec. 27			Bashir Gemayel, head of the unified command of the Christian militia forces, reports the movement of Palestinian reinforcements into southern Lebanon.		Thanat Khoman, head of the Thai National Assembly foreign relations committee, says the U.S.S.R. has built missile silos in the high mountain area of Laos.
Dec. 28		The explosion of a large bomb in a Belfast fertilizer factory signals the end of the Northern Ireland cease-fire announced by the Provisional wing of the IRA for the Christmas holidays.	The Syrian govt. is reported to have lifted its restrictions against the country's 3–4,000 Jews, who will now be allowed to travel within or outside the country and to own property. . . . Phalangist Party head Pierre Gemayel says Palestinian arms are being brought into southern Lebanon on the pretext that they would be used against Israel, but instead they are being used against Christians. . . . The S. African govt. releases 92 detainees, including Winnie Mandela and Peter Magubane, held under the Internal Security Act, keeping its promise to do so if unrest ended.	According to internal company documents cited by the *Wall Street Journal*, the Dominican Republic affiliate of Philip Morris Inc. apparently paid $1,000 a month to Pres. Joaquin Balaguer in 1973.	*Mainstream* , a newspaper often critical of the Indian govt., voluntarily ceases publication rather than submit to a pre-censorship order issued by the government.
Dec. 29		*Washington Post* reports a rise in drug addiction among upperclass Yugoslav youths.	In a *Washington Post* interview, Egyptian Pres. Anwar Sadat says he supports a formal link between any created Palestinian state and Jordan. He says Israel would have to quickly evacuate the West Bank, Gaza Strip, and other occupied Arab territories. . . . Two leading black members of Rhodesian P.M. Ian Smith's Cabinet, Jeremiah Chirau and Kayisa Ndiweni, resign to form a new political party to work for majority rule in Rhodesia.		

A	B	C	D	E
Includes developments that affect more than one world region, international organizations and important meetings of major world leaders.	Includes all domestic and regional developments in Europe, including the Soviet Union, Turkey, Cyprus and Malta.	Includes all domestic and regional developments in Africa and the Middle East, including Iraq and Iran and excluding Cyprus, Turkey and Afghanistan.	Includes all domestic and regional developments in Latin America, the Caribbean and Canada.	Includes all domestic and regional developments in Asia and Pacific nations, extending from Afghanistan through all the Pacific Islands, except Hawaii.

U.S. Politics & Social Issues	U.S. Foreign Policy & Defense	U.S. Economy & Environment	Science, Technology & Nature	Culture, Leisure & Life Style	
					Dec. 24
				Christmas observances in Bethlehem attract a record number of visitors, including American Playwright Arthur Miller and Jerusalem Mayor Teddy Kollek.... Pope Paul VI delivers a televised Christmas Mass.	**Dec. 25**
Sen. Philip Hart (D, Mich.), who sponsored civil rights, consumer, and antitrust legislation, dies at the age of 64 of cancer in Washington, D.C.				Minnesota Vikings and the Oakland Raiders win conference titles and will meet in the Super Bowl to determine the NFL championship.	**Dec. 26**
	Pres. Ford says he would reconsider the issue of a general amnesty to the Vietnam War draft resisters and deserters after the widow of Sen. Philip Hart (D, Mich.) asks him to declare the amnesty when Ford paid her a condolence call.		The EPA estimates China's Sept. 26 nuclear-test explosion could cause eventually four cases of thyroid cancer in the U.S. and notes that there has been measurable contamination of milk in some U.S. eastern states.	Leading Parisian fashion designer during the 1930s, Mainbocher (Main Rousseau Bocher), 86, dies in Munich, W. Germany.	**Dec. 27**
HEW secy.-designate Joseph Califano says welfare reform, a Carter campaign promise, might have to wait until the economy recovers.... Alderman Michael Bilandic is chosen by the Chicago City Council as acting mayor, but says he won't be a mayoral candidate in the upcoming special elections.... Alex Rose, 78, founder of New York's Liberal Party, dies after a long illness in N.Y.		The U.S. International Trade Commission rules that the domestic shoe industry was injured by competition from shoe imports valued at $1 billion a year.... The Commerce Dept. announces the U.S. posted a record deficit of $906.2 million in merchandise trade during November.... Pres. Ford rejects a CAB plan that would have given two more U.S. airlines transatlantic routes to Europe and would have opened 11 more U.S. cities for nonstop flights to Europe. ... Teamsters Union pension fund makes public a list of its loans as it continues to come under close federal scutiny.		The musical *Fiddler on the Roof* is revived on Broadway with Zero Mostel recreating his role as Tevye.... Philip Iselin, 74, New York Jets football team president, dies of an apparent heart attack in N.Y.	**Dec. 28**
Rudolph Perpich (D) becomes governor of Minnesota, succeeding Wendell Anderson, who resigned to take the Senate seat vacated by V.P.-elect Walter Mondale.	Carter says he is not committed to an absolute reduction in defense spending, but feels that $5–$7 billion can be saved annually through efficiency, economy, and better management.	The Federal Energy Administration (FEA) announces U.S. oil consumption rose to a record high in mid-December, apparently driven up by unseasonably cold weather throughout most of the country.... The Commerce Dept. announces the government's index of leading economic indicators rose 1 percent in November, following a .6 percent (revised) rise in October.			**Dec. 29**

F	G	H	I	J
Includes elections, federal-state relations, civil rights and liberties, crime, the judiciary, education, health care, poverty, urban affairs and population.	Includes formation and debate of U.S. foreign and defense policies, veterans' affairs and defense spending. (Relations with specific foreign countries are usually found under the region concerned.)	Includes business, labor, agriculture, taxation, transportation, consumer affairs, monetary and fiscal policy, natural resources, and pollution.	Includes worldwide scientific, medical and technological developments, natural phenomena, U.S. weather, natural disasters, and accidents.	Includes the arts, religion, scholarship, communications media, sports, entertainments, fashions, fads and social life.

	World Affairs	Europe	Africa & the Middle East	The Americas	Asia & the Pacific
Dec. 30		Spanish Communist Party leader Santiago Carrillo and seven comrades are freed on bail after being charged with "illegal association". Their arrests sparked protests in Madrid on Dec. 23 and 29.	*The New York Times* reports that Zambian Cultural Services Dir. Alfred Mofya has urged the government to halt Christmas celebrations in the country, calling the holiday a colonial custom.... Israel reacts favorably to Egyptian Pres. Sadat's formula for a Palestine–Jordan link, but opposes Sadat's call for a quick Israeli withdrawal from occupied Arab lands.... *Washington Post* reports the S. African govt. announced that parents of six-and seven-year-old black children will have to sign a pledge to keep them in school for at least two years.	Adepa, the Argentine press association, asks the govt. to investigate the cases of journalists, including Arturo Frers and Luis Fossatti, who have been arrested or have disappeared.	
Dec. 31		Denis Howell, British minister for water resources says the very heavy rainfall of the last two months greatly improved water supplies, but ground water sources are still seriously depleted.	Palestinian gunners shell three Christian towns in Lebanon with machine guns and artillery, according to a Christian broadcast.	The Brazilian govt. announces the inflation rate for 1976 will be 46 percent, the highest since the armed forces seized power in 1964.... The new Puerto Rican Gov. Carlos Romero Barcelo lauds Pres. Ford's advocacy of Puerto Rican statehood, but outgoing Gov. Luis Munoz Marin deplores it as contrary to the Puerto Rican people's right to self-determination.	

A	B	C	D	E
Includes developments that affect more than one world region, international organizations and important meetings of major world leaders.	*Includes all domestic and regional developments in Europe, including the Soviet Union, Turkey, Cyprus and Malta.*	*Includes all domestic and regional developments in Africa and the Middle East, including Iraq and Iran and excluding Cyprus, Turkey and Afghanistan.*	*Includes all domestic and regional developments in Latin America, the Caribbean and Canada.*	*Includes all domestic and regional developments in Asia and Pacific nations, extending from Afghanistan through all the Pacific Islands, except Hawaii.*

U.S. Politics & Social Issues	U.S. Foreign Policy & Defense	U.S. Economy & Environment	Science, Technology & Nature	Culture, Leisure & Life Style	
N.Y. Gov. Hugh Carey (D) pardons seven former Attica inmates and commutes the sentence of an eighth in a move to close the book on the Attica prison controversial 1971 uprising.			Flies, about one and two-thirds the size of house flies, are reported infesting the city of Sydney, Australia, driven from their interior breeding grounds by hot north-westerly winds.		Dec. 30
Pres. Ford advocates statehood for Puerto Rico and says that he will submit legislation to that effect to Congress. . . . The Federal Election Commission announces that the government spent $72 million to finance the 1976 presidential election, with nearly $24 million in election-fund contributions remaining.		The Dow Jones ends the year at 1,004.65, the second-highest figure to date for a year's end, exceeded only by 1,020.02 in 1972.	The first week of testimony in a hearing to determine liability for damage caused when the Liberian tanker *Argo Merchant* ran aground near Nantucket Island, Mass. ends.	Shows still running on Broadway for over a year include *A Chorus Line*, *Grease* , *Pippin* , and *Same Time, Next Year* .	Dec. 31

F	G	H	I	J
Includes elections, federal-state relations, civil rights and liberties, crime, the judiciary, education, health care, poverty, urban affairs and population.	*Includes formation and debate of U.S. foreign and defense policies, veterans' affairs and defense spending. (Relations with specific foreign countries are usually found under the region concerned.)*	*Includes business, labor, agriculture, taxation, transportation, consumer affairs, monetary and fiscal policy, natural resources, and pollution.*	*Includes worldwide scientific, medical and technological developments, natural phenomena, U.S. weather, natural disasters, and accidents.*	*Includes the arts, religion, scholarship, communications media, sports, entertainments, fashions, fads and social life.*

1977

President Anwar Sadat of Egypt is the first Arab leader to visit Israel. The purpose of his trip is to present his views on a Middle East peace settlement before the Israeli Knesset.

	World Affairs	Europe	Africa & the Middle East	The Americas	Asia & the Pacific
Jan.	P.M. Ian Smith rejects a British proposal to reconvene the Geneva conference on black majority rule in Rhodesia....The USSR withholds funds to UNEF.	A French court releases Abu Daoud, a Palestinian militant suspected of having plotted the terrorist murder of Israeli athletes at the 1972 Olympics.	Violent demonstrations against a government plan to drastically increase the price of food force the Egyptian government to cancel the program.	A Chile-Peru border dispute prompts a troop build up in area....Canadian P.M. Pierre Elliott Trudeau urges a definitive vote on Quebec independence.	China quells factional disturbances in the central provinces....Former Japanese Premier Kakuei Tanaka goes on trial on charges of accepting bribes from Lockheed Aircraft Corp.
Feb.	U.N. Secy. Gen. Kurt Waldheim tours the Middle East to sound out major parties in the Arab-Israeli dispute about prospects for peace.	Dissidents in Rumania, Czechoslovakia and the USSR step up pleas for support in their campaign for human rights.	Ethiopian head of state Teferi Bante is killed in fighting among members of the Dergue.	Riots following presidential elections in El Salvador lead to the imposition of a 30-day state of siege....Argentine President Jorge Videla narrowly escapes assassination.	Indian President Fakhruddin Ali Ahmed dies....Sri Lanka ends a state of emergency first imposed in March 1971.
March	Pres. Jimmy Carter tells U.N. General Assembly that the U.N. charter gives member nations the right and the duty to speak out about the state of human rights in other countries.	Soviet dissident Anatoly Scharansky is arrested.	Pres. Carter sets off controversy by calling for a Palestinian homeland.	The Chilean government dissolves the four political parties that had not been banned after the 1973 coup.	Indian P.M. Indira Gandhi resigns following the defeat of her party in national elections.
April	U.S. Ambassador to the U.N. Andrew Young tells British television audience that Britian was "a little chicken" in dealing with racial questions.	The Communist Party is legalized in Spain while the late Generalissimo Francisco Franco's political organization, the National Movement, is abolished.	Israeli Premier Yitzhak Rabin resigns as his ruling Labor Party's candidate for a second term after admitting that he and his wife had lied about illicit bank accounts in Washington.	Canadian P.M. Pierre Trudeau appeals for unity in face of the separatist threat posed by Quebec provincial government.	Pakistan Pres. Zulfikar Ali Bhutto assumes emergency powers and imposes martial law in Pakistan's three major cities.
May	The leaders of the world's seven major, non-Communist industrialized nations hold a summit in London and end it with commitment to continue their policies of moderate economic growth.	At a two-day meeting, NATO foreign ministers endorse Pres. Jimmy Carter's call for closer coordination of weapons production to strengthen the alliance.	Israel's ruling Labor Party, which has dominated the nation's politics since its founding, loses to the opposition right-wing Likud Party in elections held for the Knesset (parliament).	Pres. Jimmy Carter defends his emphasis on human rights in formulating U.S. foreign policy and reaffirms his commitment to negotiate a new Panama Canal Treaty.	Cambodian refugees in Thailand tell of crop failure, hunger and disease in the aftermath of purges that took hundreds of thousands of lives following the Communists' capture of Phnom Penh.
June	Carter administration releases a report criticizing the Soviet bloc for failing to fulfill its obligations under the Helsinki accords.	The stagnation of East-West detente is the main topic during a visit by Soviet President Leonid Brezhnev to French President Valery Giscard d'Estaing.	Israeli Likud Party leader Menahem Begin formally receives the designation to form a new government.	U.S. State Secy. Cyrus Vance makes a strong appeal for human rights before a meeting of the OAS in Grenada. Vance clearly ties U.S. economic aid to the observance of human rights.	U.S. and Vietnam hold another round of talks in Paris on establishing ties and trade relations.
July	OPEC delegates from Iran and Saudi Arabia say they might favor a freeze on oil prices through 1978 but spokesmen from other countries oppose the idea.	Turkish Premier Bulent Ecevit resigns after his minority government was defeated in its first National Assembly vote of confidence.	Israeli Premier Menahem Begin meets with Pres. Jimmy Carter in Washington and makes public his country's proposal for a Middle East peace settlement.	The U.K. strengthens its military presence in Belize to counter growing threats against the colony by neighboring Guatemala.	The Pakistani army overthrows the government of Prime Minister Zulfikar Ali Bhutto, imposes martial law and pledges new elections in October. Bhutto is taken into custody.
Aug.	Nigeria condemns South African apartheid as "a crime against conscience and human dignity" but falls short of calling for a complete economic and military boycott of the country.	Spyros Kyprianou is sworn in as president of Cyprus, succeeding the late Archbishop Makarios.	U.S. State Secy. Cyrus Vance ends tour of the Middle East after reporting little progress in his efforts to get Arab and Israeli leaders to agree on the reconvening of the Geneva peace conference.	Andrew Young, U.S. ambassador to the United Nations, visits 10 countries in the Caribbean region to stress the Carter Administration's interest in good relations in the area.	The Australian Parliament passes a government-backed law banning strikes by public employees.
Sept.	In its annual report, the IMF says the international economy is still unsatisfactory by past standards.	The European Community Commission bans all Soviet fishing vessels from the North Sea waters in retaliation for the Soviet Union's sudden notice that it would restrict fishing in the Barents Sea.	Controversy mounts over the death in jail of black South African student leader Steven Biko.	Pres. Carter and Panama leader Omar Torrijos sign the Panama Canal treaties in Washington.	Former Pakistani Prime Minister Zulfikar Ali Bhutto is arrested at his home in Karachi in connection with the murders of two political opponents.
Oct.	The U.S. and Soviet Union issue a joint declaration suggesting that a Middle East peace conference at Geneva guarantee "the legitimate rights of the Palestinian people."	Delegates of the 35 nations that had signed the 1975 Helsinki accords open their first formal review conference in Belgrade, Yugoslavia.	The U.S. announces that it has reached an agreement with Israel on procedures for a Middle East parley.	The Sandinista National Liberation Front begins a major offensive against the government with attacks in at least four parts of Nicaragua.	The Indian opposition Congress Party turns back a bid by former P.M. Indira Gandhi to regain her leadership of the party and instead, decides to retain K. Brahamananda Reddy as president.
Nov.	The United States withdraws from the International Labor Organization, the principal labor agency of the United Nations.	In Greece, the New Democratic Party, headed by Premier Constantine Caramanlis, wins a majority of the 300 parliamentary seats in elections.	Egyptian Pres. Anwar Sadat visits Israel, addresses the Knesset (Parliament) and meets with P.M. Menahem Begin.	U.S. State Secy. Cyrus Vance visits Argentina, Brazil and Venezuela to confer with their leaders on human rights, atomic energy, petroleum prices and various other international issues.	A military court sentences former Philippine Sen. Benigno Aquino to death on charges of subversion, murder and illegal possession of weapons.
Dec.	U.S. State Secy. Cyrus Vance reassures NATO foreign ministers that the U.S. will keep their security interests in mind when discussing an arms pact with the Soviet Union.	French Pres. Valery Giscard d'Estaing visits British P.M. James Callaghan in London to discuss industrial cooperation and world problems.	Egypt severs diplomatic relations with Syria, Iraq, Libya, Algeria and South Yemen in retaliation for their attempts to disrupt Pres. Anwar Sadat's peace overtures toward Israel.	Pres. Fidel Castro asserts that Cuba's military presence in Africa is not negotiable and has nothing to do with Cuba's relations with the U.S.	Cambodia severs diplomatic relations with Vietnam in the wake of heavy border clashes between the two countries. Fighting also erupts along the Thai-Cambodian border.

A	B	C	D	E
Includes developments that affect more than one world region, international organizations and important meetings of major world leaders.	Includes all domestic and regional developments in Europe, including the Soviet Union, Turkey, Cyprus and Malta.	Includes all domestic and regional developments in Africa and the Middle East, including Iraq and Iran and excluding Cyprus, Turkey and Afghanistan.	Includes all domestic and regional developments in Latin America, the Caribbean and Canada.	Includes all domestic and regional developments in Asia and Pacific nations, extending from Afghanistan through all the Pacific Islands, except Hawaii.

U.S. Politics & Social Issues	U.S. Foreign Policy & Defense	U.S. Economy & Environment	Science, Technology & Nature	Culture, Leisure & Life Style	
Jimmy Carter is inaugurated 39th president of the United States. . . .The U.S. Supreme Ct. rules that a suburb's refusal to change zoning laws is not inherently unconstitutional.	Pres. Carter pardons most Vietnam draft resisters. . . .Carter issues an inaugural statement to the world urging international cooperation and stressing U.S. concern for human rights.	The EPA issues rules barring the industrial discharge of PCBs directly into waterways.	Two cars of the Chicago Transit Authority elevated train plunge off overhead-tracks, killing 11 and injuring 189 others. . . .A blizzard paralyzes much of the Midwest and East.	The Oakland Raiders defeat the Minnesota Vikings 32 to 14 to win Super Bowl XI.	Jan.
A Harris Poll reports that a majority of Americans favor the death penalty. . . .The Justice Dept. issues a report maintaining that James Earl Ray acted alone in the assassination of Martin Luther King Jr.	*The Washington Post* reports that the CIA has made secret payments to a number of foreign leaders.	Pres. Carter outlines an energy plan emphasizing conservation. . . .Carter signs the Emergency Natural Gas Act, temporarily authorizing the reallocation of interstate gas.	The Midwest suffers severe fuel shortages as ice on major river systems strands fuel barges. The U.S. tests its first space shuttle.	NBC agrees to pay $35 million for the exclusive rights to televise the 1980 Moscow Olympics.	Feb.
Pres. Jimmy Carter answers questions from 42 citizens during a two-hour telephone call-in radio broadcast from the White House. It is the first such program to be conducted by a U.S. President.	The U.S. Defense Department resumes research on weapons employing nerve gas.	The Teamsters and the AFL-CIO United Farm Workers sign a five-year pact setting up jurisdictional lines to settle their organizing dispute.	The FDA says it will propose a ban on saccharin, the only artificial sweetener in the U.S.	A three-judge panel of the U.S. Circuit Court of Appeals for the District of Columbia rules that the FCC cannot ban allegedly indecent language from the airwaves.	March
Democratic Mayor Tom Bradley of Los Angeles is re-elected. . . .Pres. Jimmy Carter commutes the 20-year prison sentence of G. Gordon Liddy, one of the original Watergate-burglary defendants.	Egyptian Pres. Anwar Sadat meets with Pres. Jimmy Carter in Washington to seek U.S. military and economic aid and to press his views on a Middle East peace settlement.	Pres. Jimmy Carter presents his comprehensive new energy policy to Congress with the warning that it would require "sacrifices" from every economic sector.	The FDA modifies its proposed ban on saccharin to allow the artificial sweetener to remain on the market for limited use as a nonprescription drug.	The Fellowship of Concerned Churchmen, a coalition of 15 dissident groups opposed to liberal trends in the Episcopal Church, holds its first national congress to organize a break-away church.	April
Pres. Carter outlines his goals for reform of the U.S. welfare system.	Pres. Jimmy Carter addresses a NATO meeting in London and promises that the U.S. will join with Europe to strengthen the alliance.	Douglas Fraser is elected president of the UAW to succeed Leonard Woodcock.	The Indiana state legislature overrides Gov. Otis Bowen's veto to make Indiana the first state to authorize the manufacture, sale and use of laetrile.	The National Conference of Catholic Bishops votes to rescind the rule that automatically imposed excommunication on American Catholics who had been remarried without approval.	May
James Earl Ray, who is serving a 99-year sentence for the assassination of the Rev. Dr. Martin Luther King Jr., escapes from maximum security prison in Tennessee. Three days later he is captured.	Pres. Jimmy Carter announces he has decided against producing the B-1 bomber, a supersonic plane sought by the Air Force to replace its aging fleet of B-52 bombers.	International Telephone & Telegraph sues American Telephone & Telegraph (AT&T) on charges of antitrust violations.	Dr. Christiaan N. Barnard implants a baboon's heart into the body of a 26-year-old critically ill woman in an attempt to support her own diseased heart. The patient dies 2½ hours after the operation.	Italian film director Roberto Rossellini dies.	June
A three-judge panel prohibits the National Socialist Party of America, a neo-Nazi group, from displaying the swastika in any march or demonstration in the Illinois suburb of Skokie.	U.S. State Secy. Cyrus Vance warns that U.S.-South African relations "will inevitably suffer" unless South Africa changes its racial policies.	A massive power failure throughout New York City and suburban Westchester County leaves nine million people without electricity.	A flash flood hits Johnstown, Pa., leaving at least 68 dead and another 31 missing.	Russian-born American novelist Vladimir Nabokov dies at 78.	July
David Berkowitz, the alleged New York murderer who calls himself "Son of Sam" is arrested.	Former Pres. Gerald R. Ford and former State Secy. Henry Kissinger endorse the Panama Canal Treaties while Ronald Reagan campaigns against them.	The Dept. of Energy is created, and James Schlesinger is confirmed as its first secretary.	Volcanoes erupt in Japan, Italy and Hawaii.	Rock and Roll legend Elvis Presley dies at 42.	Aug.
The steady decline in Scholastic Aptitude Test scores of U.S. college-bound students is due to television, grade inflation and other social and educational factors, a panel of experts says.	Park Tong Sun, a central figure in the Korean lobbying scandal, is indicted on 35 counts, including conspiracy to bribe a public official and to defraud the U.S.	Bert Lance resigns as U.S. budget director in the wake of controversy over his personal financial dealings.	Voyager I, an unmanned spacecraft, is launched from Cape Canaveral, Fla., beginning a mission that will last several years as the space probe journeys to Jupiter and Saturn.	American black singer Ethel Waters dies. . . .Chris Evert wins the women's singles title in the U.S. Open tennis tournament.	Sept.
Maryland Gov. Marvin Mandel (D), convicted of federal mail fraud and racketeering charges, is sentenced to four years in prison and suspended from all powers of office.	U.S. Defense Secy. Harold Brown decides to seek funds for full-scale development of the M-X mobile missile.	In an effort to gain support in Congress for his Administration's energy program, Pres. Jimmy Carter accuses the oil industry of attempting to capitalize on the energy crisis by robbing the public.	The U.S. Enterprise, the first of a planned fleet of space shuttles, successfully passes a crucial flight test.	Authors James M. Cain and MacKinley Kantor die.	Oct.
Ernest Morial is elected mayor of New Orleans, La., the first black to be elected to that post. . . .U.S. Rep. Edward Koch is elected New York City's 105th mayor.	Paul Nitze, a former SALT negotiator releases details of negotiations, trying to illustrate a weakening of the U.S. defense posture by the Carter Administration.	Pres. Jimmy Carter signs a bill increasing the minimum wage to $3.35 an hour by 1981 from its current level of $2.30. Carter rebuts criticism that the increase would be inflationary.	The U.S. Supreme Court declines to review a lower court ruling that AT&T is subject to federal antitrust prosecution.	Archbishop John R. Quinn is elected to a three-year term as president of the National Conference of Catholic Bishops in the U.S.	Nov.
The FBI, responding to a Freedom of Information Act request, releases 40,000 pages of files it had amassed in the course of investigating the assassination of Pres. John F. Kennedy.	U.S. Navy supports assigning women to duty aboard sea-going tugs, tenders, and oceanographic research ships. Women previously had only been assigned to harbor craft and hospital ships.	James McIntyre is named director of the Office of Management and Budget, succeeding Bert Lance.	Two Soviet cosmonauts, launched into orbit aboard the Soyuz 26 spacecraft, successfully dock with and board the Salyut 6 orbiting research station.	Silent screen great Charles Chaplin dies at 88 in Switzerland.	Dec.

F	G	H	I	J
Includes elections, federal-state relations, civil rights and liberties, crime, the judiciary, education, health care, poverty, urban affairs and population.	*Includes formation and debate of U.S. foreign and defense policies, veterans' affairs and defense spending. (Relations with specific foreign countries are usually found under the region concerned.)*	*Includes business, labor, agriculture, taxation, transportation, consumer affairs, monetary and fiscal policy, natural resources, and pollution.*	*Includes worldwide scientific, medical and technological developments, natural phenomena, U.S. weather, natural disasters, and accidents.*	*Includes the arts, religion, scholarship, communications media, sports, entertainments, fashions, fads and social life.*

	World Affairs	Europe	Africa & the Middle East	The Americas	Asia & the Pacific
Jan. 1	Ivor Richard, British chairman of the adjourned Geneva conference on Rhodesian majority rule initiates a series of talks with the parties concerned, meeting with Rhodesian P.M. Ian Smith after seeing Zambian Pres. Kenneth Kaunda in Lusaka on Dec. 30, 1976.	E. German govt. imposes a $2 visa requirement for all non-German civilians crossing to E. Berlin from W. Berlin.	The Lebanese Cabinet imposes press censorship.	Peruvian Pres. Gen. Francisco Morales Bermudez denies that Peru is preparing for hostilities with Chile as tensions over their common border increase and reports circulate of Peruvian arms purchases from the Soviet Union.	The pro-Moscow Indian CP launches a nationwide series of rallies and demonstrations to protest recent cost-of-living increases, defying a recent Indian govt. ban on public political meetings.
Jan. 2		Basque demonstrators clash with police in Algorta, Spain, demanding amnesty for all political prisoners.	Israeli Cabinet weighs Egyptian Pres. Anwar Sadat's December 29, 1976 proposal for a link between any new Palestinian state and Jordan.	Carlos Romero Barcelo is inaugurated as the fifth elected governor of Puerto Rico.	
Jan. 3	IMF gives final approval for a $3.9-billion loan to Great Britain from funds made available by the Group of 10 industrialized nations.	The Icelandic govt. is reported to have kept unemployment at about .5 percent in 1976 by stimulating the economy to the extent that it had to borrow extensively from foreign sources.	Israeli Housing Min. Avraham Ofer, implicated in a police probe of corruption, commits suicide and leaves a note proclaiming his innocence.... Forty persons are killed, 50 are wounded, and 50 cars are wrecked by a bomb exploding outside the Beirut headquarters of the Lebanese Christian Phalangist Party.	Argentinian guerrilla movement losses for 1976 are reported at 4,000, with the Marxist People's Revolutionary Army (ERP) hardest hit.	
Jan. 4	After speaking with P.M. John Vorster, Ivor Richard says that his southern African trip is giving him clearer ideas about what the British role should be in the interim government leading to Rhodesian majority rule.	Foreign companies and institutions are reported having borrowed a record $6.14 billion worth of Swiss francs in 1976.	Christians in east Beirut strike to protest the bomb blast at Phalangist Party headquarters the previous day.	The Chilean govt. announces that its 1976 inflation rate dropped to 174.3 percent compared to 340.7 percent in 1975.... Eighteen suspected left-wing guerrillas and an unidentified woman are reported killed in three days of Argentinian political violence.	A Chinese govt. official confirms previous foreign press reports of provincial disturbances but asserts that they have been quelled.
Jan. 5		Royal Dutch/Shell Group and the Exxon Corp. subsidiaries sign a pact with the state-owned British National Oil Corp., (BNOC) paving the way to becoming a 51 percent owner of oil produced in their joint-venture North Sea fields.	Schools in the Johannesberg, S. African black township of Soweto reopen amid continuing but diminishing student boycotts.	Former Puerto Rican Gov. Rafael Hernandez Colon charges that Pres. Ford's statehood for Puerto Rico proposal may have been motivated by Interior Dept. designs on Puerto Rican oil deposits.	Sri Lanka govt. invokes emergency laws to deal with spreading labor unrest.
Jan. 6	The Soviet Amb. to the U.N. Oleg Troyanovsky states that the Soviet Union will withhold its $4.4 million contribution to the upkeep of the U.N. Emergency Force policing troop disengagement in the Sinai.	A manifesto protesting Czech suppression of human rights and announcing the formation of Charter 77, an association of dissidents, is published in various Western newspapers after being smuggled out of Czechoslovakia.	The Syrian govt. executes two Syrians and one Palestinian for a series of bomb attacks in Syria carried out with the complicity of Iraq. ... A fourth Rhodesian guerrilla front is reported near the Rhodesian–Zambian border. It is said to be composed of members of the Zimbabwe African People's Union (ZAPU), which is headed by Joshua Nkomo.	Eight Montoneros are killed in Argentina when 10 carloads of guerrillas attack a military convoy transferring guerrilla prisoners from one jail to another in the La Plata area.	Wall posters first appear in Peking calling for the rehabilitation of Deputy Premier Teng Hsiao-ping, who was ousted in April 1976 Inc.
Jan. 7	OECD reports a November 1976 consumer-prices increase of .5 percent for its 24-member nations.	French police in Paris arrest Abu Daoud, a Palestinian militant suspected of participating in the 1972 terrorist attack at the Olympic games in Munich that killed 17 people, including 11 Israeli athletes.		The Argentinian govt. announces that the cost of living during 1976 rose by a record 347.5 percent.... Attacks against Argentinian Jews resume, after a several-months lull, with a bomb explosion at a Jewish school in Buenos Aires and another blast that severely damages the home of Naum Kacowicz, who had been kidnapped and ransomed by terrorists in 1973.	Pakistan P.M. Zulfikar Ali Bhutto officially sets March 7 as the date for National Assembly general elections.... Philippine Pres. Ferdinand Marcos assails the U.S. State Dept. report implicating the Philippines and five other nations in human rights violations.

A	B	C	D	E
Includes developments that affect more than one world region, international organizations and important meetings of major world leaders.	Includes all domestic and regional developments in Europe, including the Soviet Union, Turkey, Cyprus and Malta.	Includes all domestic and regional developments in Africa and the Middle East, including Iraq and Iran and excluding Cyprus, Turkey and Afghanistan.	Includes all domestic and regional developments in Latin America, the Caribbean and Canada.	Includes all domestic and regional developments in Asia and Pacific nations, extending from Afghanistan through all the Pacific Islands, except Hawaii.

U.S. Politics & Social Issues	U.S. Foreign Policy & Defense	U.S. Economy & Environment	Science, Technology & Nature	Culture, Leisure & Life Style	
In his year-end report, Supreme Ct. Chief Justice Warren Burger Jr. renews his plea to have more federal judgeships created and to increase federal judges' salaries.	The house International Relations Committee releases a State Dept. report charging human-rights violations in six countries — Argentina, Haiti, Indonesia, Iran, Peru, and the Philippines — but nonetheless seeking support aid for these countries for strategic or other reasons.			Collegiate football bowl games results follow: Sugar Bowl: Pittsburgh, 27–Georgia, 3; Rose Bowl: Southern California, 14–Michigan, 6; Cotton Bowl: Houston, 30–Maryland, 21; Orange Bowl: Ohio State, 27–Colorado, 10.... The first woman Protestant Episcopal, priest Jacqueline Means, is ordained in Indianapolis, Ind.	Jan. 1
	CIA Dir. George Bush defends the agency's internal security in wake of ex-employe Edwin Moore's arrest for allegedly selling information to the Soviet Union.		Herbert Fowler, genetic psychiatrist and specialist in the inherited mental disturbances of American Indians, dies at the age of 58 of a massive hematoma in Portland, Ore.	In the Sun Bowl collegiate football championship, Texas A & M beats Florida, 37–14.... Natalia Roslavleva, 69, leading Soviet dance historian and critic, dies of cancer in Moscow.... Erroll Garner, 53, internationally acclaimed jazz pianist and composer, dies of a heart attack in Los Angeles.	Jan. 2
A federal appeals court in New Orleans, La. rules, 2–1, that members of Congress are not immune under the Constitution from charges of sex discrimination.			A group of 200 Australian scientists urges the government to ban the mining and export of uranium and to formulate, instead, a comprehensive energy conservation policy and alternative energy development program.	AP poll names the Pittsburgh Panthers and coach Johnny Mojors national collegiate football champions.	Jan. 3
		The new conflict-of-interest code announced by Pres.-elect Carter would impose regulations to close what Carter terms the revolving door between federal agencies and businesses affected by government decisions.	A Chicago rush-hour elevated train plunges off overhead tracks into one the Loop's busiest intersections, killing 11 passengers and pedestrians and injuring 189 others.		Jan. 4
Justice Dept. Issues guidelines for the FBI's use of informers.... Senate Democrats vote unanimously to create a special post, deputy president pro tempore, for Sen. Humphrey.	Army Secy. Martin Hoffman announces that the more than 150 West Point cadets implicated in the academy's cheating scandal will be readmitted, but not before the summer of 1977.				Jan. 5
		New-car sales in 1976 are reported up 17 percent to 10.1 million from the 8.6-million units sold in 1975, making 1976 the auto industry's fourth best sales year on record.		National Book Critics Circle Awards are presented for the following: fiction, October Light by John Gardner; poetry, Geography III by Elizabeth Bishop; nonfiction, The Woman Warrior by Maxime Hong Kingston; criticism, The Uses of Enchantment by Bruno Bettelheim.	Jan. 6
	Richard Gardner, a Columbia University law professor is named ambassador to Italy.	Pres.-elect Jimmy Carter reveals an economic stimulation package of $30 billion over a two-year period, including a one-time rebate tax revision and a major jobs effort. ... Australian publishing magnate Rupert Murdoch gains a controlling interest in New York magazine by reaching an out-of-court settlement with its founder, Clay Felker.			Jan. 7

F	G	H	I	J
Includes elections, federal-state relations, civil rights and liberties, crime, the judiciary, education, health care, poverty, urban affairs and population.	Includes formation and debate of U.S. foreign and defense policies, veterans' affairs and defense spending. (Relations with specific foreign countries are usually found under the region concerned.)	Includes business, labor, agriculture, taxation, transportation, consumer affairs, monetary and fiscal policy, natural resources, and pollution.	Includes worldwide scientific, medical and technological developments, natural phenomena, U.S. weather, natural disasters, and accidents.	Includes the arts, religion, scholarship, communications media, sports, entertainments, fashions, fads and social life.

	World Affairs	Europe	Africa & the Middle East	The Americas	Asia & the Pacific
Jan. 8		Czech dissidents issue a second manifesto signed by almost 300 people, which condemns the police detentions and interrogations of leading signatories of the first manifesto.... Polish dissidents appeal to the Sejm (Parliament) for an investigation into alleged police brutality against workers arrested in the June 1976 uprisings against food-price increases.	The Saudi Arabian govt. published a statement that it will require U.S. oil companies to submit reports to prove that they are passing on to consumers the benefits of the lower Saudi oil-price increases.	Four leftist Peruvian military officers are expelled from the country.	Thousands gather at Tien An Men Gate in Peking to honor Chou En-lai on the first anniversary of his death. Posters question Peking Mayor Wu Teh's trustworthiness. ... Thai former Deputy Premier Praphas Charusathien returns to Thailand after over three years of exile in Taiwan.
Jan. 9		Yugoslav Pres. Tito reportedly has rejected several bids made by Soviet CP Gen Secy. Leonid Brezhnev for closer military cooperation.	Concluding a two-day meeting in Lusaka, Zambia, representatives of the five front-line black African nations (those near or bordering Rhodesia), announce their support for the Patriotic Front of Joshua Nkomo and Robert Mugabe (ZANU and ZAPO).... The Israeli Cabinet drops the police investigation into alleged corruption by Housing Min. Avraham Ofer, who committed suicide on Jan. 3.	*Newsday*, a New York newspaper, reports that the CIA was involved in a scheme that introduced the African swine fever virus into Cuba in 1971.... The Vatican, in a rare political attack, deplores Chilean Pres. Augusto Pinochet Ugarte's recent defense of his military govt. as a totalitarian democracy necessitated by the spread of Marxism.	
Jan. 10	The Bank for International Settlements reaches an accord with Great Britain to provide $3 billion in medium-term credit as security against possible withdrawal of sterling balances from Britain by foreign creditors.		Firebombs explode in schools in the Cape Town black townships of Langa and Nyanga, despite S. African govt. efforts to ensure a peaceful school reopening after more than six months of student boycotts and violence.	Canada orders the expulsion of five Cubans, including three members of the Cuban Consulate in Montréal, on charges of recruiting and training intelligence agents to be sent to Rhodesia.... *Time* Magazine reports a Chilean–Peruvian border build-up over the two nation's inability to agree on the way to grant Bolivia an outlet to the sea.	
Jan. 11	The IMF grants Vietnam a $36-million loan for postwar reconstruction.	A Paris court releases suspected Palestinian terrorist Abu Daoud, rejecting Israeli and W. German demands that he be held for extradition hearings for the Munich Olympic games attack in 1972.	Israel recalls its Amb. to France Mordechai Gazit from Paris after a French court releases suspected terrorist Abu Daoud.		
Jan. 12		British P.M. James Callaghan announces that he will directly supervise the government's industrial policy, which calls for rapid expansion and reduced unemployment.	At an Algiers news conference following his release and expulsion from France, Palestinian militant Abu Daoud attributes his arrest to a faction of the French police that wants to sabotage French–Arab relations.... Rhodesian For. Min. Pieter van der Byl states that the front-line black states' endorsement of the Patriotic Front leaves the Rhodesian govt. with no alternative but to negotiate separately with other black groups.	A Canadian Federal Ct. judge upholds a government directive prohibiting the use of the French language in air-traffic control at Quebec's international airport.	
Jan. 13		French Premier Raymond Barre defends releasing Palestinian terrorist Abu Daoud as a judicial, not a political, decision.	A Beirut broadcast says that the Arab League peacekeeping forces in Lebanon completed its arms roundup by Jan. 12 as scheduled, but the Syrian representative, Col. Mohammed al Kholy, charges that the former combatants failed to return their heavy weapons.		Reports by a Hong Kong newspaper indicate that ousted/Chinese Deputy Premier Teng Hsiao-ping has been named premier.

A	B	C	D	E
Includes developments that affect more than one world region, international organizations and important meetings of major world leaders.	Includes all domestic and regional developments in Europe, including the Soviet Union, Turkey, Cyprus and Malta.	Includes all domestic and regional developments in Africa and the Middle East, including Iraq and Iran and excluding Cyprus, Turkey and Afghanistan.	Includes all domestic and regional developments in Latin America, the Caribbean and Canada.	Includes all domestic and regional developments in Asia and Pacific nations, extending from Afghanistan through all the Pacific Islands, except Hawaii.

U.S. Politics & Social Issues	U.S. Foreign Policy & Defense	U.S. Economy & Environment	Science, Technology & Nature	Culture, Leisure & Life Style	
				Rupert Murdoch names James Brady as the new editor of *New York* magazine and Edwin Bolwell as editor of the *New York Post*.	Jan. 8
		The Conference Board's index of consumer confidence in U.S. business conditions rises to 91.2 for the November–December 1976 period, up 11 points from September–October 1976.		The Oakland Raiders beat the Minnesota Vikings, 32–14, in the eleventh annual Super Bowl.... Second-seeded Roscoe Tanner beats top-seeded Guillermo Vilas to win $25,000 and the men's Australian Open tennis title. Kerry Reid beats Dianne Fromholtz to win the women's title.	Jan. 9
The Supreme Ct. decides, 6–3, to vacate a lower federal appeals ct. ruling upholding the dismissal of a homosexual from the U.S. Civil Service.	A Senate Foreign Relations Committee staff study recommends that a special, temporary U.S. mission be sent to Salisbury if the Rhodesian govt. accepts proposals to end racial discrimination and favors a more active U.S. role in the transition to Rhodesian majority black rule.	Both labor and management criticize Pres.-elect Jimmy Carter's economic stimulation plan.		UNESCO issues an appeal for aid to preserve and restore the Acropolis in Athens, seen endangered by a combination of age, rain, and industrial pollution.	Jan. 10
In a 5–3 ruling, the Supreme Ct. upholds suburban zoning rules that in effect bar low-income minority housing, reversing a lower court ruling on Arlington Heights, a Chicago suburb.	A former U.S. ambassador to Chile in 1967–71, Edward Korry, tells the Senate For. Rel. Committee that the CIA joined with several large U.S. corporations in a massive attempt to block Salvador Allende from winning Chile's 1964 presidential election.	Consumer group ask coffee drinkers to cut their consumption by 25 percent to force down the steadily rising price of coffee.		Ford Motor Co. chmn. Henry Ford 2nd resigns as a trustee of the Ford Foundation, expressing fundamental disagreement with its policies and direction, and accusing its staff of failing to appreciate the capitalistic system that funded it.... Melvin Dummar, a Utah service station operator who was listed as a beneficiary in the so-called Mormon will of billionaire Howard Hughes, admits that he lied about the will.	Jan. 11
		The Supreme Ct. unanimously rules that amendments added to the N.Y.S. stock transfer tax law in 1968 violate the principle of unrestricted interstate commerce, thereby reversing a N.Y.S. Appeals Ct. ruling.... In another unanimous ruling, the Supreme Ct. holds that IRS agents must have a search warrant before entering a business property to seize assets from delinquent taxpayers.... Anaconda Co., the third-ranked U.S. copper-mining company, is acquired by Atlantic Richfield Co., the nation's eighth-largest oil company.... The government's wholesale price index rises a seasonally adjusted .9 percent in December 1976, the largest monthly increase since the previous September.		French film director Henri-Georges Clouzot, 69, known for his suspense-horror film *Diabolique*, dies of a heart attack in Paris.... Henri Langlois, 62, founder and director of the French Cinematheque, dies of a heart attack in Paris.	Jan. 12
The Congressional Budget Office issues a report placing the number of U.S. families living below the official poverty line ($5,674) at 5.4 million or 6.9 percent of the total compared to Census Bureau figures of 9 million families or 11.4 percent of the total.		Pres. Ford sends to Congress a proposal for phased deregulation of the U.S. airline industry.	The U.S. National Transportation Safety Bd. reports that in 1976 a total of 42 people were killed in crashes involving U.S. airlines, the lowest fatality count since 1954.	A U.S. panel on international amateur sports competitions recommends a central amateur sports organization within the U.S. Olympic Committee.	Jan. 13
F	G	H	I	J	
Includes elections, federal-state relations, civil rights and liberties, crime, the judiciary, education, health care, poverty, urban affairs and population.	*Includes formation and debate of U.S. foreign and defense policies, veterans' affairs and defense spending. (Relations with specific foreign countries are usually found under the region concerned.)*	*Includes business, labor, agriculture, taxation, transportation, consumer affairs, monetary and fiscal policy, natural resources, and pollution.*	*Includes worldwide scientific, medical and technological developments, natural phenomena, U.S. weather, natural disasters, and accidents.*	*Includes the arts, religion, scholarship, communications media, sports, entertainments, fashions, fads and social life.*	

	World Affairs	Europe	Africa & the Middle East	The Americas	Asia & the Pacific
Jan. 14		Sir Anthony Eden, British statesman and diplomat, dies at age 79 of a liver ailment, in Wiltshire, England.	Zimbabwe African National Union (ZANU) members living in London announce they have switched their loyalty to Rev. Ndabaningi Sithole from Robert Mugabe, charging that the latter is a paid agent of the CIA.	Two bombs explode in a Cordoba, Argentina movie theater showing *Victory at Entebbe*, a film about the 1976 Israeli military operation that rescued 103 hostages held by pro-Palestinian highjackers in Uganda.	
Jan. 15		Gen. Sir John Sharp, 59, British NATO division commander, dies of a cerebral hemorrhage in Oslo, Norway.	Jordanian King Hussein and Egyptian Pres. Anwar Sadat conclude two days of talks at Aswan by agreeing to support a separate PLO delegation to Middle East peace talks in Geneva. . . . Mozambique closes its borders to all tourists and foreigners who do not have official business in the country.		
Jan. 16			Chad announces a week-long boycott of all goods and mail from South Africa to protest Pretoria's apartheid policy.		
Jan. 17		French Pres. Valery Giscard d'Estaing assails criticism of France's release of Palestinian terrorist Abu Daoud, and he implicitly criticizes West Germany for freeing the remaining three Palestinians involved in the Munich Olympics massacre in 1972.	Roman Catholic schools in S. Africa become the first white schools in the country to officially admit black and colored (mixed-race) students but emphasize their policy is a matter of conscience and not a challenge to govt. policy. . . . Bishop Abel Muzorewa, head of the Rhodesian African National Council (ANC), denounces the Rhodesian govt.'s execution of eight black nationalist ANC members, convicted of urban terrorism and sabotage.		A three-week nationwide strike by essential service employes ends in Sri Lanka.
Jan. 18	The Swiss govt. is reported having intervened in the foreign exchange market on a record scale in 1976 to slow increases in the value of the Swiss franc. . . . EEC signs agreements with Egypt, Syria, and Jordan for preferential trade status, aid, and cooperation.	Greek govt. begins a crackdown on illegal arms-smuggling traffic through Greek ports. . . . Yugoslav Federal Executive Council Pres. Dzemal Bijedic dies in a plane crash near Sarajevo with seven other persons.		Mexico formally asks Argentina to give safe-conduct passes to former Argentine Pres. Hector Campora and other Argentine refugees who received political asylum in the Mexican Embassy in Buenos Aires. . . . Seven Latin American heads of state send a letter to U.S. Pres.-elect Jimmy Carter expressing support for Panamanian demands for sovereignty over the Canal Zone.	The Indian govt. announces that parliamentary elections will be held in March and that emergency rules will be relaxed.
Jan. 19	Ivor Richard, British chairman of the adjourned Geneva conference on Rhodesia, meets with South African P.M. John Vorster to enlist his support for British proposals.	The Spanish govt. agrees to allow free display of the Basque flag and gradual use of the Basque language along with the official tongue, Castilian Spanish.	Violent riots in Alexandria and Cairo force the Egyptian govt. to cancel plans, announced on Jan. 17, to drastically increase the price of food and other staples.		
Jan. 20		British cost of living is reported to have risen 15.1 percent in 1976, thus giving Britain a higher inflation rate than any other industrialized country with the exception of Italy.		Two separate attacks by guerrillas of the September 23rd Communist League kill two policemen and two businessmen in Mexico City.	The Indian govt. announces it will lift strict press censorship and release political prisoners. Four political opposition parties announce plans to merge and pose a solid front against the ruling Congress Party in the upcoming March elections, announced two days before.

A	B	C	D	E
Includes developments that affect more than one world region, international organizations and important meetings of major world leaders.	*Includes all domestic and regional developments in Europe, including the Soviet Union, Turkey, Cyprus and Malta.*	*Includes all domestic and regional developments in Africa and the Middle East, including Iraq and Iran and excluding Cyprus, Turkey and Afghanistan.*	*Includes all domestic and regional developments in Latin America, the Caribbean and Canada.*	*Includes all domestic and regional developments in Asia and Pacific nations, extending from Afghanistan through all the Pacific Islands, except Hawaii.*

U.S. Politics & Social Issues	U.S. Foreign Policy & Defense	U.S. Economy & Environment	Science, Technology & Nature	Culture, Leisure & Life Style	
Former U.S. Sen. William (Bill) Brock (Tenn.) is elected Republican National Committee chairman.	The Justice Dept. says it will not prosecute CIA employes who had been part of the agency's clandestine mail-opening program (1953–73).	A severe cold wave throughout the U.S. with attendant unprecedented demand for heating oil, forces U.S. refineries to produce a record 1.9 million barrels of fuel per day during the previous week compared with less than 1.4 million barrels per day the year before.... The FPC unanimously approves emergency sales of naturel gas by the Houston Pipe Line Co. to pipelines serving states in the East and Gulf Coast region.		French-born novelist and diarist Anais Nin, 73, whose work explored surrealism and feminism, dies of cancer in Los Angeles.... Dissident Episcopalians form a separate denomination opposed to ordination of women.	Jan. 14
	CIA director-nominee Theodore Sorensen faces mounting opposition from CIA officials and conservative members of the Senate, focusing on an affidavit Sorensen filed in 1973 on behalf of Daniel Ellsberg and Anthony Russo during their Pentagon Papers trial.	Farmers gain a 1.5 percent increase in the prices received for their raw agricultural products in the 30-days period just ended.			Jan. 15
A Boston Schools Dept. report asserts that the quality of public education has deteriorated since the start of court-ordered desegregation.				Yuri Soloviev, a leading male dancer of the Kirov Ballet, Leningrad, is an apparent suicide at the age of 36.	Jan. 16
Convicted murderer Gary Gilmore is executed by a firing squad at the Utah State Prison, the first person in the U.S. to suffer the death penalty since 1967.	Pres. Ford's proposed budget contains substantial increases in defense spending for a total of $110.1 billion, representing 25 percent of the total federal budget and 5.4 percent of the U.S. GNP.... Theodore Sorensen withdraws his name from nomination as CIA director, fearing a confirmation fight that would handicap the new Carter administration if he were rejected and handicap his effectiveness if he were confirmed.	Pres. Ford sends a budget to Congress calling for a gradual slowdown in the growth of federal spending and for permanent income tax reductions.		A sellout crowd of 65,000 watches the American Football Conference defeat their National conference rivals, 24–27, in the NFL's annual all-star game — the Pro Bowl.	Jan. 17
The Supreme Ct. expands the use of government wiretaps by ruling, 6–3, that wiretap evidence gathered in violation of the 1968 Omnibus Crime Control and Safe Streets Act can be used to prosecute criminal defendants.... Indiana becomes the thirty-fifth state to ratify the ERA.	Outgoing Defense Secy. Donald Rumsfeld warns of a Soviet–U.S. imbalance in arms as the Soviets continue to build up their defense system and the U.S. retrenches. He calls for the U.S. to invest heavily in new strategic weapons to maintain its present balance with the U.S.S.R.	Pres. Ford sends an economic report to Congress that states a reacceleration in the pace of economic recovery but contends that an increase in business spending over government spending is the key to sustained recovery.	Center for Disease Control announces identifying a previously unknown bacterium as responsible for the outbrak of Legion fever, which killed 29 people in July 1976.	The Vatican responds cautiously to a document released in London by the Anglican-Roman Catholic International Commission that recommends recognition of papal supremacy as a means of reunifying the two churches.	Jan. 18
Following five days of hearings on Carter's nominee for attorney general, Griffin Bell, the Senate Judiciary Commitee recommends his confirmation despite criticism by the NAACP and other civil rights groups.	Pres. Ford rejects blanket amnesty to Vietnam War-era draft evaders and deserters.	EPA issues rules barring industrial discharge of PCBs directly into waterways.... The Labor Dept. reports the smallest yearly increase in the CPI in four years, a seasonally adjusted .4 percent in December 1976.	For the first time in modern history, Lake Erie, the most shallow of the Great Lakes, is frozen from bank to bank and ice spreads far enough out in Lake Michigan to require icebreakers to clear channels to oil refineries on its shores.	A nationally televised show-business tribute to incoming Pres. Jimmy Carter originates at the Kennedy Center for the Performing Arts Wash., D.C. and features a spoof of his swearing-in and satirical references to his *Playboy* magazine interview.	Jan. 19
Jimmy Carter is sworn in as the thirty-ninth President of the U.S. In his Inaugural speech he calls for a new national spirit of unity and trust and praises his predecessor, Pres. Gerald Ford, for what he had done to "heal our land."	After taking office, Pres. Carter issues a special statement, televised and broadcast around the world, assuring that U.S. foreign policy would be resposive to human needs ans would not seek to dominate nor dictate to others.	General Foods Corp. the largest U.S. coffee wholesaler, announces a 20-cents-per-pound price rise for ground coffee to $3.11 a pound, blaming the increases on a quadrupling in costs of imported green coffee beans since July 25 because of a worldwide shortage.	The U.S. Geological Survey reports that the 1976 earthquake toll — 695,000 deaths — is the highest number in modern history.		Jan. 20

F	G	H	I	J
Includes elections, federal-state relations, civil rights and liberties, crime, the judiciary, education, health care, poverty, urban affairs and population.	Includes formation and debate of U.S. foreign and defense policies, veterans' affairs and defense spending. (Relations with specific foreign countries are usually found under the region concerned.)	Includes business, labor, agriculture, taxation, transportation, consumer affairs, monetary and fiscal policy, natural resources, and pollution.	Includes worldwide scientific, medical and technological developments, natural phenomena, U.S. weather, natural disasters, and accidents.	Includes the arts, religion, scholarship, communications media, sports, entertainments, fashions, fads and social life.

	World Affairs	Europe	Africa & the Middle East	The Americas	Asia & the Pacific
Jan. 21	Ivor Richard, British chairman of the adjourned Geneva conference on Rhodesia presents a plan to Rhodesian P.M. Ian Smith that would establish a resident British commissioner with extensive executive power to ensure the smooth transition to black majority rule.	Poland is reported to have revised its economic plan to emphasize consumer goods over heavy industry in wake of June 1976 riots over food prices.	Julius Nyerere is unanimously elected head of Tanzania's new political party, the Revolutionary Party.... The Egyptian govt. blames the outlawed Egyptian communist workers' Party for Jan. 18–20 food riots in Cairo and other cities.		
Jan. 22		Soviet economy is reported having failed to meet the 1976 growth plan in key sectors, despite a record grain harvest.... Danish P.M. Anker Jorgensen dissolves the Folketing (Parliament) after negotiations with other political parties fail to reach agreements on housing policy, defense spending, and other issues, but says his minority government will stay in power until the general election scheduled for February.			
Jan. 23		U.S. V.P. Walter Mondale confers in Brussels with Belgium, NATO, and EEC officials in the first stop of a 10-day world tour.	Sudan sends Egypt over $5 million in emergency food aid.		India's opposition formally opens its election campaign, attacking Indira Gandhi's authoritarian rule and calling the government's relaxation of constitutional curbs a facade.
Jan. 24	Rhodesian P.M. Ian Smith rejects the British plan for black majority rule, charging that it would not represent the country's true black majority but a Marxist-indoctrinated minority — the Terrorist-oriented Patriotic Front.	A total of seven people are killed in Spain in two days of political violence, causing the worst crisis of the year-old monarchy.... As relations between East and West Germany deteriorate, E. Germany recalls its ambassador to Bonn for consultations.	Christian militia attack Moslem leftist and Palestinian positions around Khiam, near the Lebanese–Israeli border.		An official Chinese govt. spokesman denies a report that ousted former Deputy Premier Teng Hsiao-ping is being rehabilitated and named to the post of CP first deputy chairman.... Australia reports a record trade surplus of $600.6 million in July–September 1976.
Jan. 25	The U.S. denies Soviet charges that it has 17 defense bases in Australia, as alleged by the Soviet govt. in an attack on the Australian govt. of Malcolm Fraser.	The ruling Rumanian CP promotes Elena Ceausescu, wife of Pres. Nicolae Ceausescu, to its highest decision-making body, the Permanent Bureau.	Syrian soldiers belonging to the Arab League's Lebanese peace-keeping forces move into southern Labanon to suppress sporadic clashes between Christian and Palestinian forces and to collect weapons from the combatants.... Lebanon lifts its Jan. 1 curb on foreign press reports but continues to censor domestic press.	Quebec provincial premier Rene Levesque seeks support of U.S. investors in a speech before the Economic Club of N.Y.	
Jan. 26		French CP leader Georges Marchais attacks Czech persecution of the dissidents who signed Charter 77.... Italian trade unions and the national confederation of private employers agree to limit labor costs in a wage agreement that does not include an alteration of the quarterly cost-of-living increase system.	A reported 1,593 whites have left Rhodesia during December 1976 for a net annual loss of 7,058.	A blacklist of 21 Canadian civil servants and university professors labeled as subversives is revealed in Parliament.	
Jan. 27	Pres. Carter orders preparations for renewed arms limitation negotiations with the Soviet Union aimed at concluding SALT II which would be a replacement for an existing agreement expiring in October.				Former Japanese Premier Kakuei Tanaka and four others charged in the Lockheed bride-taking scandal go on trial in Tokyo District Ct.

A	B	C	D	E
Includes developments that affect more than one world region, international organizations and important meetings of major world leaders.	Includes all domestic and regional developments in Europe, including the Soviet Union, Turkey, Cyprus and Malta.	Includes all domestic and regional developments in Africa and the Middle East, including Iraq and Iran and excluding Cyprus, Turkey and Afghanistan.	Includes all domestic and regional developments in Latin America, the Caribbean and Canada.	Includes all domestic and regional developments in Asia and Pacific nations, extending from Afghanistan through all the Pacific Islands, except Hawaii.

U.S. Politics & Social Issues	U.S. Foreign Policy & Defense	U.S. Economy & Environment	Science, Technology & Nature	Culture, Leisure & Life Style	
ACLU co-founder Robert Dunn, 81, dies of cancer in N.Y.C.	Pres. Carter fulfills a campaign pledge and grants pardons to almost all Vietnam-era draft evaders, but not to those who entered the armed forces and then deserted.	During the previous week, stocks of petroleum distillates, including home-heating fuels, drop to 162.1 million barrels nationwide. . . . As a prolonged cold wave produces record demands for naturel gas throughout the U.S., Pres. Carter ask all Americans to set their thermostats at 65 degrees during the day and lower at night.		Exiled Soviet dissident Aleksandr Solzhenitsyn announces that he will start a nonprofit publishing business in Vermont to distribute works on Russian culture, history, and religion in the U.S. and abroad.	Jan. 21
		FPC estimates that from 200,000 to 300,000 workers have been laid off nationwide as a result of a natural gas shortage.		N.Y.C. restaurateur Bernard (Toots) Shor, dies at the age of 73 of cancer in N.Y.C.	Jan. 22
				Tom Watson wins the thirty-sixth Bing Crosby National Pro-Am golf tournament.	Jan. 23
		FEA orders oil refineries in four north-central states to produce more home heating oil for customers in Mich., Wis., Minn., and N.D. . . . Eli Lilly, 91, former president and chairman of Eli Lilly & Co. drug concern dies in Indianapolis. . . . Agriculture Dept. reports that freezing temperatures in Fla. caused an estimated $150 million in damage to its vegetable crop.			Jan. 24
Supreme Ct. 6–3, rules against an Indianapolis busing plan to achieve school desegregation. . . . Supreme Ct. restricts Miranda rights by ruling, 6–3, that a criminal suspect who voluntarily enters a police station and is not under arrest can be interrogated without being informed of his legal rights.	Defence Secy. Harold Brown indicates that he may pare former Pres. Ford's defense budget by cutting back the development or procurement of various weapons.			In the National Hockey League (NHL) all-star game, the Campbell Conference beats the Prince of Wales conference, 4–3, in Vancouver, British Columbia.	Jan. 25
In a move seen as a demonstration of its commitment to higher ethical standards by its members, House Democrats vote in caucus, 189–93, to remove Rep. Robert Sikes (D, Fla.), reprimanded by the House in 1976 on conflict-of-interest charges, from his post as chairman of an Appropriations Committee subcommittee.	The Senate Confirms, 89–3, the appointment of Andrew Young as U.S. ambassador to the U.N.	In wake of a natural gas shortage, Pres. Carter sends to Congress a proposal for emergency legislation giving the federal government temporary authority to reallocate gas from one interstate pipeline to another.			Jan. 26
The Va. State Senate blocks passage of the ERA by one vote.	State Dept. warns the Soviet Union against trying to silence dissident Andrei Sakharov, the first time the U.S. has openly defended a Soviet dissident.	Carter administration officials outline a $31.2–billion economic package of tax cuts and spending to stimulate the economy. . . . SEC files a complaint charging the General Telephone and Electronics Corp. (GTE) of making over $14 million in questionable payments in 28 countries, including the U.S., 1971–75.	N.Y. and N.J. declare full states of emergency, in wake of a crippling blizzard and cold wave.	The Vatican issues an 18-page document that definitively prohibits the ordination of women as Roman Catholic priests.	Jan. 27

F	G	H	I	J
Includes elections, federal-state relations, civil rights and liberties, crime, the judiciary, education, health care, poverty, urban affairs and population.	Includes formation and debate of U.S. foreign and defense policies, veterans' affairs and defense spending. (Relations with specific foreign countries are usually found under the region concerned.)	Includes business, labor, agriculture, taxation, transportation, consumer affairs, monetary and fiscal policy, natural resources, and pollution.	Includes worldwide scientific, medical and technological developments, natural phenomena, U.S. weather, natural disasters, and accidents.	Includes the arts, religion, scholarship, communications media, sports, entertainments, fashions, fads and social life.

	World Affairs	Europe	Africa & the Middle East	The Americas	Asia & the Pacific
Jan. 28		Spanish Premier Adolfo Suarez Gonzalez issues a decree suspending two constitutional rights for 30 days, following the worst visible political violence in the country since the 1936–39 civil war.	In a speech to the South African Parliament, P.M. John Vorster asserts that his government will not pressure Rhodesian Pres. Ian Smith to change his policy on majority rule. . . . South African P.M. Vorster rejects a bid to abolish a law requiring blacks to carry passes authorizing their presence in so-called white areas.	Canadian P.M. Pierre Trudeau says that he will stake his political career on the outcome of a proposed referendum on Quebec independence and calls on Quebec Premier Rene Levesque to resign if the referendum favors federalism.	Cambodian soldiers cross the Thai border and attack four villages, killing 30 civilians.
Jan. 29		Denmark reportedly has entered a formal protest against Great Britain's plan to use the uninhabited island of Rockall to determine its 200-mile fishing limits.			Liu Hsi-yao is appointed Chinese education minister.
Jan. 30	The Rhodesian Patriotic Front leaders refuse to meet Ivor Richard in Lusaka, Zambia because of Zambian Pres. Kenneth Kaunda's charges on the previous day that Richard called off the Geneva conference negotiations without consulting Rhodesian nationalists.		Chad releases Francoise Claustre, a French anthropologist captured in 1974, and her husband Pierre, who was captured in 1975 when he attempted to rescue her. . . . Sudanese Pres. Mohammed Gaafar el-Nimeiry reverses his position and pledges full support to the Eritreans attempting to separate from Ethiopia.		The Marxist Communist Party of India agrees to join with the Janata Party in the upcoming election drive to unseat the ruling Congress Party and its leader, P.M. Indira Gandhi
Jan. 31	Ivor Richard, British chairman of the suspended Rhodesian talks, ends his southern African shuttle, apparently conceding defeat in his efforts to solve the deadlock on the best way to achieve majority rule.	The Common Market registers a $9.5-billion trade deficit in 1976 with non-member countries.	Israeli For. Min. Yigal Allon calls for a signed agreement stating how far Syrian or Palestinian peacekeeping forces in Lebanon would come to the Israeli border.		Indian Janata Party leader Morarji Desai appeals for support at an antigovernment rally attended by 50,000 people.
Feb. 1		Edvard Hambro, 65, Norway's ambassador to France, dies of a heart attack in Paris.			Foreign travelers arriving from Canton, China report wall posters there that compare China's economy unfavorably with Japan's. . . . Australian Hight Ct. rules to clarify the formula to determine the number of seats in its Parliament, thereby reducing House membership to 123 from the current 127.

A	B	C	D	E
Includes developments that affect more than one world region, international organizations and important meetings of major world leaders.	Includes all domestic and regional developments in Europe, including the Soviet Union, Turkey, Cyprus and Malta.	Includes all domestic and regional developments in Africa and the Middle East, including Iraq and Iran and excluding Cyprus, Turkey and Afghanistan.	Includes all domestic and regional developments in Latin America, the Caribbean and Canada.	Includes all domestic and regional developments in Asia and Pacific nations, extending from Afghanistan through all the Pacific Islands, except Hawaii.

U.S. Politics & Social Issues	U.S. Foreign Policy & Defense	U.S. Economy & Environment	Science, Technology & Nature	Culture, Leisure & Life Style	
The Pa. Supreme Ct. overturns the 1974 conviction of former UMW president W.A. Tony Boyle for the 1969 murders of UMW dissident Joseph Yablonski, his wife, and his daughter.		The U.S. posts a $5.87-billion trade deficit for 1976, contrasting sharply with the record $11.01-billion surplus recorded in 1975.	A fierce blizzard with 60 mile-per-hour winds sweeps across the already frozen Midwest into the East, completely isolating Buffalo, N.Y.		Jan. 28
		In a report made public the previous day, ARA Services Inc., the largest U.S. food-service firm, tells the SEC that it had uncovered $393,000 in questionable payments made since 1970.	In Ohio, one of the U.S. states hardest hit by a widespread blizzard, Gov. James Rhodes leads a 15-minute noontime prayer service, seeking God's help to end the most severe fuel crisis in Ohio's history.	Roberto Duran successfully defends his World Boxing Association lightweight champioship with a knockout victory over Vilomar Fernandez in Miami Beach, Fla.	Jan. 29
		Federal officials report that over 1.5. million workers in 17 states have been idled temporarily because of the extreme cold wave and resultant fuel shortage.	Pres. Carter flies to Pittsburgh to see the effects of the damaging blizzard.	Tom Watson sets a golf tournament record by winning the Andy Williams–San Diego Open, after winning the Bing Crosby tournament on Jan. 23.... *Roots* , an eight-part TV dramatization of Alex Haley's best-selling semiautobiographical book about his slave ancestors, scores the highest weekly television rating average in the history of the medium.... New York Film Critics Circle Awards are given to *All the President's Men* as best film, Robert De Niro as best actor and Liv Ullmann as best actress.	Jan. 30
Federal District Ct. Judge John Lewis Smith Jr. dismisses damage suits against the FBI that stemmed from the agency's use of electronic surveillance against black leader Martin Luther King Jr.	State Secy. Cyrus Vance condemns the Rhodesian govt.'s decision to seek a separate settlement with moderate blacks and says it cannot expect U.S. support.	Pres. Carter tells Congress he plans to strengthen the Council on Wage and Price Stability.		A group of well-known poets characterize the *American Poetry Review* as racist, antifeminist, and antiyouth, and demand that a third of the publication be devoted to works by women and members of minorities.	Jan. 31
		AT&T announces record net earnings of $3.83 billion for 1976, the largest earnings ever reported by a U.S. company.... FTC Commissioner Paul Rand Dixon writes an apology to consumer advocate Ralph Nader for an ethnic slur he made about Nader's Lebanese ancestry in a Jan. 17 speech, and he also issues an apology to the National Association of Arab-Americans.... Federally chartered savings and loan associations report a record net savings gain of $34.88 billion in 1976, 17 percent higher than the previous record posted in 1975.	Marin County, Calif. enacts the nation's strictest water-rationing program, in wake of a 16-month drought.	NBC announces plans to televise the 1980 Summer Olympics from Moscow.	Feb. 1

F	G	H	I	J
Includes elections, federal-state relations, civil rights and liberties, crime, the judiciary, education, health care, poverty, urban affairs and population.	*Includes formation and debate of U.S. foreign and defense policies, veterans' affairs and defense spending. (Relations with specific foreign countries are usually found under the region concerned.)*	*Includes business, labor, agriculture, taxation, transportation, consumer affairs, monetary and fiscal policy, natural resources, and pollution.*	*Includes worldwide scientific, medical and technological developments, natural phenomena, U.S. weather, natural disasters, and accidents.*	*Includes the arts, religion, scholarship, communications media, sports, entertainments, fashions, fads and social life.*

	World Affairs	Europe	Africa & the Middle East	The Americas	Asia & the Pacific
Feb. 2	At a news conference, U.S. V.P. Walter Mondale reports on his 10-nation tour and reveals plans for an economic conference of industrialized nations.... U.N. Secy. Gen. Kurt Waldheim begins a tour of the Middle East.			Emile Gumbs is appointed chief minister of Anguilla, succeeding Ronald Webster who had lost a vote of confidence in the colonial assembly the previous day for alleged corruption and abuse of power.	Agriculture Min. Jagjivan Ram and five other leaders of India's ruling Congress Party resign and form a new political organization, Congress for Democracy, to protest P.M. Indira Gandhi's policies.
Feb. 3	Israeli Amb. to the U.N. Chaim Herzog meets privately with his Soviet counterpart Oleg Troyanovsky at U.N. headquarters in N.Y.C., where Troyanovsky is said to have reiterated Soviet insistence on PLO participation in Mideast peace talks. ... After talking with Egyptian For. Min. Ismail Fahmy in Cairo, U.N. Secy. Gen. Waldheim says that Egypt is flexible on the timing of the proposed Geneva talks on the Middle East, but adamant about having the PLO participate.		Egyptian Pres. Anwar Sadat signs a decree imposing harsh penalties to prevent a repetition of the Jan. 18–19 food riots.... Andrew Young, U.S. ambassador to the U.N., begins a week-long visit to Africa as a representative of the new Carter administration.... Ethiopian head of state Brig. Gen. Teferi Bante is killed in factional fighting among members of the Dergue, Ethiopia's ruling military council.		
Feb. 4		The Soviet Union expels AP Moscow correspondent George Krimsky, in what is seen as a move in an apparent harassment campaign against Western correspondents.... Charter 77 spokesman, Jan Patocka, reports growing support for the Czech human-rights group and notes that 448 people have come out publicly for its manifesto.	The OAU announces its support for the Patriotic Front of Robert Mugabe and Joshua Nkomo in the Rhodesian majority rule struggle. ... In a TV interview, Rhodesian P.M. Ian Smith repeats his intention to achieve a political settlement of the Rhodesian majority-rule issue by negotiating with black leaders inside Rhodesia.... Tanzania closes its border with Kenya in apparent retaliation for Kenya's closure of East Africa Airways.		Indonesian govt. reportedly opens an investigation into charges that high-ranking officials had received large payoffs from the U.S.-owned Hughes Aircraft Co. for contracts involving work on the country's new satellite communication system.
Feb. 5			At a Front for the Liberation of Mozambique (*Frelimo*) congress, which began yesterday, a program is introduced to turn Mozambique into a Marxist state.... Zambian Pres. Kenneth Kaunda says that the Carter administration should take the lead in trying to solve the problems of southern Africa.		
Feb. 6	Saudi Arabia rejects a compromise plan proposed by Qatar to end OPEC's two-tier pricing system.		Most of the estimated 400 black students who were abducted from a Rhodesian mission school on Jan. 30 are reported to have chosen to remain with nationalist guerrillas in Botswana.... Rhodesian nationalist guerrillas shoot and kill seven white Roman Catholic missionaries at a mission north of Salisbury.... Tanzanian Pres. Julius Nyerere endorses the official U.S. stance on Rhodesian majority rule but says that Britain should continue its leadership in the negotiations, and the U.S. should lend background support.	Nicaraguan Roman Catholic Church leaders accuse the government of resorting to widespread torture, rape, and summary executions in their campaign to eradicate leftist guerrillas.	A Chinese news agency reports four separate but related conferences on modernization of China's defense forces.... A Roman Catholic pastoral letter is read in Philippine churches assailing the government for intervening in evangelical work and arresting missionaries as subversives.

A	B	C	D	E
Includes developments that affect more than one world region, international organizations and important meetings of major world leaders.	*Includes all domestic and regional developments in Europe, including the Soviet Union, Turkey, Cyprus and Malta.*	*Includes all domestic and regional developments in Africa and the Middle East, including Iraq and Iran and excluding Cyprus, Turkey and Afghanistan.*	*Includes all domestic and regional developments in Latin America, the Caribbean and Canada.*	*Includes all domestic and regional developments in Asia and Pacific nations, extending from Afghanistan through all the Pacific Islands, except Hawaii.*

U.S. Politics & Social Issues	U.S. Foreign Policy & Defense	U.S. Economy & Environment	Science, Technology & Nature	Culture, Leisure & Life Style	
The House approves, 237–164, reestablishing its Select Committee on Assassinations with an $84,000 monthly budget and a March 31 deadline.... A Justice Dept. inquiry into the assassination of Martin Luther King Jr. concludes that James Earl Ray acted alone in the killing.... Clad informally in a sweater, Pres. Carter makes a televised appeal for national unity and sacrifices, citing his own elimination of unnecessary governmental luxuries such as limousine service for top officials.		In his informal televised speech, Pres. Carter reveals that his energy plan, to be ready by April 20, will emphasize conservation.... Republican senators propose a $26.2-billion economic stimulus plan as an alternative to Pres. Carter's proposed $31.2-billion plan, both for a two-year period.... Pres. Carter signs the Emergency Natural Gas Act, aimed at keeping natural gas supplies flowing to homes and essential services by temporary interstate reallocations. ... Treasury Sec. Michael Blumenthal grants a rare waiver of the Jones Act to allow Columbia Gas System Inc. to make two shipments of liquefied natural gas to Mass. from Alaska on a foreign-registered ship.	Both the Ford and Carter administrations are reported opposing a $4-billion nuclear deal between Brazil and West Germany because Brazil could use the technology to make nuclear weapons.	*Variety* lists the five top-grossing films for the previous week as follows: *Rocky*, *Silver Streak*, *King Kong*, *Pink Panther Strikes Again*, and *Search for Noah's Ark*	Feb. 2
		FRB Chmn. Arthur Burns tells the House Banking Committee that Pres. Carter's economic stimulation plan is not needed because the economy is improving on its own.			Feb. 3
Sen. Adlai Stevenson (D, Ill.) says that his Senate reorganization plan, approved 89–1, will make the Senate more democratic and spread work and responsibility among all its members.	State Secy. Cyrus Vance summons Soviet Amb. to the U.S. Anatoly Dobrynin to the State Dept. to protest AP correspondent George Krimsky's expulsion from Moscow and to express U.S. concern about the Soviet's arrest the previous day of Alexander Ginzburg, manager of a fund to aid political prisoners.	Labor Dept. announces that the January unemployment rate fell to 7.3 percent of the work force, its lowest level since May 1976.... The FPC authorizes imports of natural gas from Mexico and Algeria.		Archbishop Valerian Trifa, head of the Rumanian Orthodox Episcopate of America, is suspended from activity in the National Council of Churches until Nazi war-crime charges brought against him by the Justice Dept. and Concerned Jewish Youth are resolved.	Feb. 4
ACLU executive director Aryeh Neier condemns abuse of conservatorship laws by parents seeking to deprogram members of religious cults, seeing use against political as well as religious dissidents.			Pres. Carter declares the city of Buffalo and nine surrounding N.Y.S. counties disaster areas. He previously designated disaster areas in Fla., Va., and Md. and declared states of emergency in Mich., Pa., Ind., Ohio, and southern N.J.	Rabbi Henry Siegman of the Synagogue Council of America lauds the National Council of Churches for suspending Archbishop Valerian Trifa, charged with war crimes in Rumania in 1941.	Feb. 5
Los Angeles Times reports that the FBI used informants in an investigation of women's liberation groups for at least four years (until 1973). The investigation was promulgated by its late director J. Edgar Hoover, who insisted on determining their subversive ramifications and potential for violence.			A new wave of arctic air moves down the U.S. East Coast, and the temperature drops to a record five degrees below zero in Chicago, eight degrees in N.Y.C., and 13 degrees in Charlotte, N.C.	*The New York Times Book Review* lists *Trinity* by Leon Uris as the best-selling work of fiction for the previous week, *Roots* by Alex Haley as best-selling nonfiction, and *The Final Days* by Robert Woodward and Carl Bernstein as best-selling mass market paperback.	Feb. 6

F	G	H	I	J
Includes elections, federal-state relations, civil rights and liberties, crime, the judiciary, education, health care, poverty, urban affairs and population.	*Includes formation and debate of U.S. foreign and defense policies, veterans' affairs and defense spending. (Relations with specific foreign countries are usually found under the region concerned.)*	*Includes business, labor, agriculture, taxation, transportation, consumer affairs, monetary and fiscal policy, natural resources, and pollution.*	*Includes worldwide scientific, medical and technological developments, natural phenomena, U.S. weather, natural disasters, and accidents.*	*Includes the arts, religion, scholarship, communications media, sports, entertainments, fashions, fads and social life.*

	World Affairs	Europe	Africa & the Middle East	The Americas	Asia & the Pacific
Feb. 7		*Time* magazine says that the Soviets' arrest of Alexander Ginzburg signals a government drive against the 12 Soviet dissidents who monitor Soviet compliance with human-rights provisions in the Helsinki accords.	Mozambique Pres. Samora Machel is unanimously reelected FRELIMO leader at the first congress of the liberation movement since Mozambique became independent in June 1975.... Rev. Patrick Chakaipa, the first black Catholic archbishop of Salisbury, calls the slain Rhodesian missionaries friends of the African people and castigates their assassins as mocking the ideals they claim to serve.... Israeli For. Min. Yigal Allon says that the U.N. is not an honest broker in the Arab–Israeli dispute and that his government does not want it to participate in any peace negotiations.		The Chinese govt. urges citizens to have greater discipline in following instructions by Chmn. Hua Kuofeng to quell disorders and suppress the Gang of Four.... An Australian delegation suspends scheduled talks in the Torres Strait border dispute with Papua New Guinea.... Indian govt. frees two top Socialist Party leaders — Raj Narain and Madhu Limaye — who had been arrested at the start of emergency rule in 1975.
Feb. 8	Pres. Carter suggests that the U.S. and the Soviet Union reach a quick agreement on the ceiling for strategic arms by deferring a decision on the key unresolved issue.... The U.N. Security Council agrees to send a three-member fact-finding mission to Benin to investigate an apparent coup against the government of Lt. Col. Mathieu Kerekou.	French–Israeli relations resume with a meeting in Brussels between Israeli For. Min. Yigal Allon and French For. Min. Louis Guiringaud to settle the dispute arising from France's release of Palestinian guerrilla Abu Daoud.	Andrew Young, U.S. representative to the U.N., meets in Lagos with Angolan Pres. Agostinho Neto in the first high-level contact between the U.S. and Neto govts., which have not established diplomatic relations.	The Canadian unemployment seasonally adjusted rate of 7.5 percent in January is the highest since the government began compiling statistics in 1953.	
Feb. 9		Spain and the Soviet Union resume diplomatic ties after a 38-year hiatus.... West German sales to COMECON nations declined $100 million in 1976 from $6.57 billion in 1975, but total West German exports to all Communist countries remained near the 1975 figure of $7.2 billion.	Queen Alia of Jordan, 28, is killed in a military helicopter crash in southern Jordan.		
Feb. 10	A U.N. Secretariat report accuses the Soviet Union and four Eastern European nations of violating international trade sanctions against Rhodesia.... Andrew Young, U.S. representative to the U.N., says during an African tour that a conference among the U.S., Great Britain, black African states, and Rhodesian black nationalists should be held to solidify proposals for black majority rule in Rhodesia.... U.N. Gen. Secy. Kurt Waldheim meets with Israeli Premier Yitzhak Rabin, For. Min. Yigal Allon, and Defense Min. Shimon Peres. They reiterate their long-standing refusal to enter into peace talks with the PLO as long as it adheres to its founding principle of replacement of Israel with a secular state.	Turkey's youngest full general, Irfan Ozaydanli, protests in a letter to Premier Suleyman Demirel that the ruling conservative four-party coalition is mismanaging the government. He cites mounting violence, intraparty bickering, and the prolonged U.S. arms embargo.... In demonstrations marked by both right-and left-wing violence, an estimated 25,000 Rome high school and college students march to protest proposed reforms of the school system and the alleged revival of fascism in Italy.... Yuri Orlov, chairman of an unofficial Soviet group monitoring Soviet compliance with the Helsinki accords on human rights, is arrested one day after emerging from hiding in wake of the arrest of Alexander Ginzburg.... Alexander Dubcek, Czech CP leader in 1968, denies a report that he had refused to sign the Czech human-rights manifesto, Charter 77.	The Southern African Catholic Bishops Conference, after meeting in Pretoria, issues a statement denouncing apartheid and defending conscientious objectors.... An Egyptian plebiscite backs Pres. Anwar Sadat's political curbs.		South Korean Pres. Park Chung Hee announces plans to abandon Seoul as the seat of government and to build a new capital city.
Feb. 11	U.N. Amb. Andrew Young, back from a visit with African leaders as an envoy of the Carter administration, stops over in London where he says that a shooting war to achieve black rule would be a last and desperate resort.		South African Roman Catholics announce a widespread program to integrate church activities and to upgrade social conditions for nonwhites.... For the second day, Syrian peacekeeping forces in Lebanon clash with Palestinian guerrillas on the outskirts of Beirut, leaving three Syrians and 25 Palestinians dead.... Lt. Col. Mengistu Haile Mariam is named Ethiopian head of state.		Indian Pres. Fakhruddin Ali Ahmed dies of a heart attack, temporarily suspending India's election campaign.

A	B	C	D	E
Includes developments that affect more than one world region, international organizations and important meetings of major world leaders.	Includes all domestic and regional developments in Europe, including the Soviet Union, Turkey, Cyprus and Malta.	Includes all domestic and regional developments in Africa and the Middle East, including Iraq and Iran and excluding Cyprus, Turkey and Afghanistan.	Includes all domestic and regional developments in Latin America, the Caribbean and Canada.	Includes all domestic and regional developments in Asia and Pacific nations, extending from Afghanistan through all the Pacific Islands, except Hawaii.

U.S. Politics & Social Issues	U.S. Foreign Policy & Defense	U.S. Economy & Environment	Science, Technology & Nature	Culture, Leisure & Life Style	
A Harris Poll finds 67 percent of Americans favor capital punishment and 25 percent oppose it. The same survey in 1965 found 47 percent in favor and 38 percent in opposition.		A UPI survey finds 3 million layoffs attributed to the severe cold spell and gas shortages.	The Soviet Union launches the manned spacecraft Soyuz 24.	Former State Secy. Henry Kissinger sells his memoirs to Little, Brown & Co. of Boston for an estimated $2 million.... FTC bars directing TV advertising of "Spider-Man" vitamins specifically to children.	Feb. 7
In a case closely watched by civil libertarians as a test of the extent to which local standards can dictate the contents of national publications, a Cincinnati, Ohio court finds *Hustler* publisher and editor Larry Flynt guilty of pandering obscenity and engaging in organized crime.... Idaho rescinds its previous approval of the ERA.		Trans World Airlines (TWA) makes public a report to the SEC revealing it had made $1.3 million in questionable payments.	Pres. Carter proposes a total ban on nuclear tests.... A U.S. govt. moratorium on flu vaccinations is partially lifted following the first outbreak of A-Victoria flu.		Feb. 8
Rubin (Hurricane) Carter and John Artis, convicted a second time in December 1976 of 1966 murders, receive the same life-sentences originally imposed in 1967.		FPC statistics show that natural gas customers have drawn about 100 billion cubic feet of gas a day from interstate pipelines in December 1976 and January 1977, compared to the normal daily usage of 57 billion cubic feet.... American Airlines discloses that from 1964 to 1972 it had disbursed $275,000 in corporate funds to a secret account for illegal political campaign contributions.			Feb. 9
Pres. Carter begins a series of visits to employes of federal departments.... In its first survey of public officials' integrity, the Justice Dept. reports a mounting number of indictments between 1970–76, with a total of 1,598 for the entire seven-years period.				The revue *A Party with Betty Comden and Adolph Green* opens on Broadway.	Feb. 10
Nevada fails to ratify the ERA when its Assembly defeats the measure, 24–25.	Jerrold Schecter, a National Security Council spokesman, reveals that Pres. Carter is planning to pursue direct negotiations with Vietnam on the issue of Americans missing there.			The southern-based 950,000-member Presbyterian Church in the U.S. rejects an updated statement of doctrine that is considered to be an important step toward its unification with the 2.7 million-member northern-based United Presbyterian Church in the U.S.A.	Feb. 11

F	G	H	I	J
Includes elections, federal-state relations, civil rights and liberties, crime, the judiciary, education, health care, poverty, urban affairs and population.	*Includes formation and debate of U.S. foreign and defense policies, veterans' affairs and defense spending. (Relations with specific foreign countries are usually found under the region concerned.)*	*Includes business, labor, agriculture, taxation, transportation, consumer affairs, monetary and fiscal policy, natural resources, and pollution.*	*Includes worldwide scientific, medical and technological developments, natural phenomena, U.S. weather, natural disasters, and accidents.*	*Includes the arts, religion, scholarship, communications media, sports, entertainments, fashions, fads and social life.*

	World Affairs	Europe	Africa & the Middle East	The Americas	Asia & the Pacific
Feb. 12		Cypriot and Turkish leaders break their May 1976 negotiation deadlock and agree to meet in Vienna to discuss a compromise plan for a nonaligned two-zone federal republic of Cyprus. . . . Czechoslovakian police detain a reporter for *The New York Times*, Paul Hofmann, and confiscate his notes of interviews with dissidents and Czech officials on the activities of Charter 77, a group protesting human-rights violations in the country.	The Arab League four-power commission in Lebanon imposes new restrictions on Palestinian political and military activity in Lebanon, supplanting the 1969 Cairo agreement. . . . Cairo University students demonstrate against the new Egyptian law that sharply restricts political activities.		Yunnan province, China announces a major administrative shift, including the appointement of An Ping-sheng as CP chief, replacing Chia Chi-yun, who had been in accused in wall posters of being allied with purged former Deputy Premier Teng Hsiao-ping.
Feb. 13			Syrian troops of the Arab League peacekeeping force in southern Lebanon begin to withdraw as a result of U.S. diplomatic intervention and Israeli pressure.	French lawyers report that Brazilian police torture common criminals and minors as well as political prisoners.	
Feb. 14		An appeal for greater human-rights observances in Rumania is made by nine dissidents in a letter to participants in the Helsinki pact that is received in Belgrade, Yugoslavia. . . . Italian police form their own trade union in defiance of existing law. . . . Britain's January trade deficit of $926,8 million is called the worst ever recorded for a single month.			Vijaya Lakshmi Pandit, Indian P.M. Indira Gandhi's aunt, announces that she will campaign for the opposition Congress for Democracy Party to help end the authoritarian rule in the country.
Feb. 15	U.N. Human Rights Commission adopts a resolution, 23–3, accusing Israel of praticing torture and of pillaging archaeological and cultural property in occupied Arab territories. . . . EEC and the U.S. sign an agreement recognizing the new U.S. 200-mile coastal fishing zone.	Danish Social Democrats win enough seats in parliamentary elections to gain control of the Folketing.	U.S. State Secy. Cyrus Vance arrives in Israel on the first leg of a Mideast tour aimed at paving the way to reconvening the Geneva peace conference.		The Japenese govt. orders a probe of allegations that some politicians received kickbacks in Boeing Co.'s sale of passenger planes to Japan Air Lines. . . . Sri Lanka's state of emergency ends with the recessing of the National State Assembly.
Feb. 16	U.N. Secy. Gen. Kurt Waldheim expresses optimism for Middle East peace after his diplomatic tour of the Middle East, seeing visible evidence that Israel and the PLO want to negotiate.	Cypriot Pres. Archbishop Makarios reveals that he will resign immediately after a Cyprus settlement is signed that would safeguard Greek and Turkish peaceful coexistence there.	U.S. State Secy. Vance states that the U.S. will continue to oppose PLO participation at the Geneva peace conference unless the PLO revises its convenant refusing to accept Israel's right to exist as a state and refusing to accept U.N. Security resolutions 242 and 338. . . . Al Fatah blames rival factions within the Palestinian guerrilla movement for clashes near Beirut on Feb. 10–11	The Canadian Air Line Pilots' Association is held in contempt of court and fined for refusing to obey an injunction to end its June 1976 strike against plans for bilingual communications. . . . A Sao Paulo, Brazil military ct. rejects a request for political prisoner Aldo Silvas Arantes to be examined by a private doctor for signs of torture.	Bank of Tokyo reports that Asian economies expanded in 1976 and that their outlook for 1977 is relatively good. . . . Thai rebels kill Princess Vipaowadi Rangsit, an aide to Queen Sirkit, and seriously wound four others in an attack on a government helicopter in southern Thailand.

A	B	C	D	E
Includes developments that affect more than one world region, international organizations and important meetings of major world leaders.	Includes all domestic and regional developments in Europe, including the Soviet Union, Turkey, Cyprus and Malta.	Includes all domestic and regional developments in Africa and the Middle East, including Iraq and Iran and excluding Cyprus, Turkey and Afghanistan.	Includes all domestic and regional developments in Latin America, the Caribbean and Canada.	Includes all domestic and regional developments in Asia and Pacific nations, extending from Afghanistan through all the Pacific Islands, except Hawaii.

U.S. Politics & Social Issues	U.S. Foreign Policy & Defense	U.S. Economy & Environment	Science, Technology & Nature	Culture, Leisure & Life Style	
		Pres. Carter discloses that former State Secy. Henry Kissinger will serve as chairman of an advisory committee for a new non-governmental group formed to promote fuel consevation.		The second World Black and African Festival of Arts and Culture, held in Lagos, Nigeria, ends.... *The New York Times* reports that executives from several recording companies and a broadcaster have met with Rev. Jesse Jackson who seeks to curb sex-rock and drug-rock recordings.	Feb. 12
Atty. Gen. Griffin Bell says that the Justice Dept. report, not yet released, on the FBI investigation of Martin Luther King's assassination neither confirms nor denies that there was a conspiracy.		*The New York Times* reports that the $2-billion-a-year recorded music industry faces a major federal probe of its alleged antitrust activity.			Feb. 13
The New York Times reports that a Chicago Board of Education survey found that black children bused to predominantly white schools had done better on math and reading tests than their counterparts remaining in predominantly black schools.			Dr. Hiroo Kanamori, a California Institute of Technology geophysicist, reports a revision of the Richter scale, used since 1935 to measure earthquake intensity.... A fungus related to the potato blight is reported to have destroyed over 160,000 acres of silvertop and stringybark forests near Gippsland in Victoria, Australia.		Feb. 14
Common Cause reports that special interest political contributions to 1976 congressional candidates, a record $22.5 million, nearly doubled the $12.5 million donated for 1974 races.... The AMA, top political contributor in 1974, again heads the list, with dairy groups ranking second.... Civil Rights Commission reports that school desegregation in many cities can only be achieved by busing students between the cities and their suburbs.	Pres. Carter links improved U.S. relations with Cuba with an end to Cuba's interference in Angola and other countries and to a restoration of human rights in Cuba itself.				Feb. 15
Dr. Frank H.T. Rhodes is named Cornell University's ninth president, succeeding Dr. Dale Corson.		Housing starts reportedly declined 27 percent in January because of freezing temperatures and snow throughout most of the U.S.	*Washington Post* reports that South Africa will have the capacity to manufacture an atomic bomb within two to four years because of training and assistance by the U.S. during the early years of its nuclear program.... Pres. Carter affirms support of trial Concorde flights to the U.S. but maintains he still stands behind his campaign statements calling former Pres. Ford's approval of the trial program a mistake.	David Mamet's play *American Buffalo* opens on Broadway.	Feb. 16

F	G	H	I	J
Includes elections, federal-state relations, civil rights and liberties, crime, the judiciary, education, health care, poverty, urban affairs and population.	Includes formation and debate of U.S. foreign and defense policies, veterans' affairs and defense spending. (Relations with specific foreign countries are usually found under the region concerned.)	Includes business, labor, agriculture, taxation, transportation, consumer affairs, monetary and fiscal policy, natural resources, and pollution.	Includes worldwide scientific, medical and technological developments, natural phenomena, U.S. weather, natural disasters, and accidents.	Includes the arts, religion, scholarship, communications media, sports, entertainments, fashions, fads and social life.

	World Affairs	Europe	Africa & the Middle East	The Americas	Asia & the Pacific
Feb. 17	Andrew Young, U.S. ambassador to the U.N., calls the auto-accident deaths of Archbishop Janani Luwum and two Ugandan govt. senior ministers assassinations. The International Commission of Jurists in Geneva seeks an international investigation of the deaths.	Leading Soviet dissident Andrei Sakharov receives a letter from U.S. Pres. Jimmy Carter expressing support for Sakharov's human-rights stance.... Fighting between Communist and extreme left-wing students at Italy's Rome University erupts in wake of a speech by Communist trade unionist Luciano Lama, who had been sent to the university by Rome's Communist govt. to urge boycotting students to return to classes. ... Four signees of an open letter appealing for human rights in Rumania are placed under house arrest.	The Ugandan govt. claims that Anglican Archbishop Janani Luwum was killed the previous day in an auto accident several hours after he was accused of plotting to overthrow Ugandan Pres. Idi Amin. ... The Anglican Church, second largest religious community in South Africa, issues a statement condemning South African police brutality and its apartheid system as morally indefensible.... Egyptian Pres. Anwar Sadat makes a surprise proposal, following a two-hour talk with U.S. State Secy. Vance, that there should be an official link between the PLO and Jordan before Geneva talks on Mideast peace are held.		
Feb. 18	The World Bank approves a $60-million loan to Rumania for an irrigation project.		U.S. State Secy. Vance lauds Sadat's proposal to make the Palestinian delegation to the Geneva peace conference part of the Jordanian as showing more flexibility in the Egyptian position than he had previously thought.... Heavy fighting resumes in Lebanon as Christian milita overrun the Moslem town of Al Khiyam, two miles north of the Israeli border, killing 21 to 50 people.	Argentinian Pres. Jorge Videla narrowly escapes the third attempt on his life in 11 months when a bomb explodes in Buenos Aires' municipal airport seconds after the airplane in which he was traveling takes off.... Marxist People's Revolutionary Army (ERP), a guerrilla group presumed crippled by the slaying of its leader, Roberto Santucho in July 1976, claims responsibility for the blast.	Vietnam govt. releases over 1,000 prisoners who had been employed by the U.S. and U.S.-backed governments in South Vietnam during the Vietnam War.
Feb. 19		Anthony Crosland, 59, British foreign secy. since April 1976, dies after suffering a stroke in Oxford, England.	Jordanian King Hussein responds cautiously to the proposed link with the PLO and cautions U.S. State Secy. Vance about becoming too optimistic about a breakthrough in Mideast peace moves.... Israeli Defense Min. Shimon Peres states Israel's disappointment with the U.S. decision against selling the concussion bomb and with its Feb. 7 refusal to permit the sale of Israeli fighter jets equipped with American engines to Ecuador.		
Feb. 20		U.S. presidential envoy Clark Clifford meets a hostile reception in Ankara, where Turkish newspapers call his mission on Cyprus mistimed in light of upcoming general elections in the fall.			The *Indian Express* reports that 15,000 to 20,000 political dissidents remain in prison under the Indian govt.'s emergency rule.
Feb. 21		David Owen is appointed British foreign and commonwealth secretary to replace Anthony Crosland, who died on Feb. 19.... Rudolf Hess, 82, sole surviving imprisoned Nazi war criminal in West Berlin's Spandau Prison, attempts suicide.	Concluding his Mideast tour, U.S. State Secy. Vance says that not only are the Arabs and Israel still deeply divided on how to settle their dispute, but that the Arabs themselves cannot agree on how to solve the Palestinian problem.	Amnesty International reports that about 20,000 persons have disappeared or been executed in Guatemala since 1966.... Charging fraud, members of the National Opposition Union (UNO) demonstrate to protest the presidential election victory of the El Salvadoran govt. candidate, retired Gen. Carlos Humberto Romero.... Argentine Commission for Human Rights lawyers tell the U.N. Human Rights Commission in Geneva that 2,300 persons have been killed, 10,000 have been jailed for political reasons, and 20,000–30,000 have "disappeared" since Argentinian Pres. Jorge Videla seized power 11 months ago.	India's opposition Congress for Democracy Party promises to lift all constitutional curbs now in effect.

A	B	C	D	E
Includes developments that affect more than one world region, international organizations and important meetings of major world leaders.	Includes all domestic and regional developments in Europe, including the Soviet Union, Turkey, Cyprus and Malta.	Includes all domestic and regional developments in Africa and the Middle East, including Iraq and Iran and excluding Cyprus, Turkey and Afghanistan.	Includes all domestic and regional developments in Latin America, the Caribbean and Canada.	Includes all domestic and regional developments in Asia and Pacific nations, extending from Afghanistan through all the Pacific Islands, except Hawaii.

U.S. Politics & Social Issues	U.S. Foreign Policy & Defense	U.S. Economy & Environment	Science, Technology & Nature	Culture, Leisure & Life Style	
	In an address before the U.S. Congress, Mexican Pres. Jose Lopez Portillo urges the U.S. to establish a sensible Latin American policy and warns of a blacklash if private interests control the U.S. govt.'s economic relations.... In simultaneous announcements made in Jerusalem by State Secy. Vance and in Washington by the Carter administration, the U.S. cancels sale of the controversial concussion bomb to Israel, which had been pledged in late 1976 by then-Pres. Ford.	Interior Secy. Cecil Andrus orders an investigation into all natural gas fields leased from the federal govt. in the Gulf of Mexico to uncover whether supplies have been withheld from customers during the current gas shortage.... Racal Electronics Ltd., a British firm, emerges the winner in one of the most hotly contested acquisition battles in corporate history as it beats out Applied Digital Data Systems Inc. in acquiring enough tenders to control Milgo Electronics Corp.		Veteran Broadcaster Quincy Howe, who helped establish the field of broadcast journalism, dies of cancer at the age of 76 in N.Y.C. ... NBC announces signing a five-year contract with former State Secy. Henry Kissinger to act as its special world-affairs consultant. ... The National Football League Players Assn. (NFLPA) reaches agreement with the league's Management Council for a five-year contract that includes elimination of the Rozelle Rule by which the NFL commissioner could decide what compensation should be awarded to a team losing a free agent.... *A Symphony of Three Orchestras* by Elliott Carter receives its world premiere by the New York Philharmonic in N.Y.C., Pierre Boulez conducting.	Feb. 17
	The CIA reportedly has made secret payments totaling millions of dollars to king Hussein of Jordan each year since 1957.... SEC reverses its policy and announces that it will no longer support companies seeking to exclude stockholder resolutions on the Arab boycott of Israel.	*Wall Street Journal* reports a wave of corporate mergers after five years of diminished activity.		N.Y.C. Mayor Abraham Beame announces a settlement in the dispute between the baseball New York Mets and the NFL over playing dates at the city-owned Shea Stadium, allowing the Jets football team to play one exhibition and two regular-season games during the baseball season at Shea for the duration of their 20-year lease.	Feb. 18
	Secret CIA payments are also reported having been made to now deceased foreign leaders Chiang Kai-shek (Taiwan), Ramon Magaysay (Philippines), Syngman Rhee (South Korea), and other heads of state throughout the world. . . . Sen. Abraham Ribicoff (D, Conn.) sends a letter, signed by 35 other U.S. senators, to Soviet CP Gen. Secy. Leonid Brezhnev, protesting the jailing of a Soviet Jew for lacking an internal passport.			Grammy Awards are presented as follows: best album, *Songs in the Key of Life* by Stevie Wonder; best record, "This Masquerade" by George Benson; best male pop vocalist, Stevie Wonder; best female pop vocalist, Linda Rondstadt; and best pop group, Chicago .	Feb. 19
Substantial federal pay raises for members of Congress, federal judges, and high-level executive branch employes are made effective, after congressional blocking efforts are defeated.				*Roots* by Alex Haley is the top best-selling book in the U.S. after being on *The New York Times* best-seller list for 20 weeks.	Feb. 20
			American Association for the Advancement of Science (AAAS) opens its annual meeting in Denver, Colo., and hears evidence correlating sunspot cycles with weather extremes on Earth.		Feb. 21

F	G	H	I	J
Includes elections, federal-state relations, civil rights and liberties, crime, the judiciary, education, health care, poverty, urban affairs and population.	*Includes formation and debate of U.S. foreign and defense policies, veterans' affairs and defense spending. (Relations with specific foreign countries are usually found under the region concerned.)*	*Includes business, labor, agriculture, taxation, transportation, consumer affairs, monetary and fiscal policy, natural resources, and pollution.*	*Includes worldwide scientific, medical and technological developments, natural phenomena, U.S. weather, natural disasters, and accidents.*	*Includes the arts, religion, scholarship, communications media, sports, entertainments, fashions, fads and social life.*

	World Affairs	Europe	Africa & the Middle East	The Americas	Asia & the Pacific
Feb. 22		Following a fact-finding mission to the Aegean region, U.S. presidential envoy Clark Clifford suggests that the U.S. and Turkish positions on Cyprus are similar.		Rep. Frederick Richmond (D, N.Y.) charges Brazil with a deliberate campaign to inflate and artificially maintain coffee prices at record levels.	
Feb. 23		Exiled Soviet dissident Andrei Amalrik demonstrates outside French Pres. Valery Giscard d'Estaing's official residence to protest Giscard's refusal to meet with him on the subject of Soviet repression.	Israel's ruling Labor Party renominates Premier Yitzhak Rabin as its head, defeating challenger Defence Min. Shimon Peres, 1,445–1,404.... Rhodesian P.M. Ian Smith announces reforms intended to eliminate most of the racial barriers in Rhodesian society.... Jordanian and PLO representatives meet in Amman and tentatively agree on a strong link between Jordan and a proposed Palestinian state in the West Bank and Gaza Strip, as proposed by Egyptian Pres. Anwar Sadat.		
Feb. 24	U.N. Secy. Gen. Kurt Waldheim calls for an impartial international investigation into the reported auto-accident deaths of Anglican Archbishop Janani Luwum and two Ugandan Cabinet ministers.				ASEAN foreign ministers sign an agreement in Manila to increase mutual trade through tariff reductions, long-term contracts, and low-interest financing.
Feb. 25	Canada and the U.S. agree to seek a wheat-stabilization pact with other wheat-producing countries.	U.S. presidential envoy Clark Clifford reports real progress in talks with Cypriot Pres. Archbishop Makarios and Turkish Cypriot leader Rauf Denktash.	For the first time, Israel's ruling Labor Party agrees on an election platform that calls for ceding some of the occupied West Bank to Jordan.... Ugandan Pres. Idi Amin bans all U.S. nationals from leaving the country until he meets with them in Kampala on Feb. 28.		
Feb. 26				Brazil's highest Roman Catholic Church body charges that government repression has led to permanent insecurity among the people. ... Cuban Premier Fidel Castro meets with Benjamin Bradlee, *Washington Post* executive editor, and reportedly says that he admires Pres. Carter but questions his true concern about human rights.... Three El Salvadoran UNO demonstrators are killed in a police shootout in Santa Ana, in wake of serious protests against apparent vote fraud in the country's presidential election.	Former Bangladesh Pres. Khandakar Mushtaque Ahmed is sentenced to five years in prison on corruption and abuse-of-office charges.... Chinese news agency Hsinua announces that Chmn. Hua Kuo-feng has opened a drive to improve the army's efficiency and end the practice of putting politics ahead of military know-how.

A	B	C	D	E
Includes developments that affect more than one world region, international organizations and important meetings of major world leaders.	Includes all domestic and regional developments in Europe, including the Soviet Union, Turkey, Cyprus and Malta.	Includes all domestic and regional developments in Africa and the Middle East, including Iraq and Iran and excluding Cyprus, Turkey and Afghanistan.	Includes all domestic and regional developments in Latin America, the Caribbean and Canada.	Includes all domestic and regional developments in Asia and Pacific nations, extending from Afghanistan through all the Pacific Islands, except Hawaii.

U.S. Politics & Social Issues	U.S. Foreign Policy & Defense	U.S. Economy & Environment	Science, Technology & Nature	Culture, Leisure & Life Style	
Arlan Stangeland (R) wins an upset victory in a special election in Minnesota's Seventh Congressional District for the seat held by Rep. Bob Bergland, who resigned to become agriculture secretary in the Carter administration. . . . Four Watergate convicted burglars receive a total payment of $200,000 in an out-of-court settlement on their claim that they had been tricked into participating in the burglary by being told it was in the interests of national security.	Defense outlays in Pres. Carter's revised budget for fiscal 1978 are set at $109.7 billion, about $400 million less than in the Ford budget, but an 11.4 percent increase over $98.3 billion layed out in fiscal 1977. . . . Canadian P.M. Pierre Trudeau addresses a joint session of the U.S. Congress and promises that the Quebec separatist movement will not affect Canadian unity.	Supreme Ct. rules unanimously to overturn a lower ct. ruling that U.S. Steel Corp. had violated antitrust laws. . . . Pres. Carter submits to Congress his revisions of the Ford administration's fiscal 1978 budget, including sizeable increases in spending for social programs. . . . The FRB rules that bank-holding companies cannot own savings and loan associations.	Up to eight inches of snow falls in Aspen, Colo. hours after silver iodide crystals are seeded into the clouds over the Rocky Mountains. . . . AAAS session reveals that 35 percent of the world's food is lost to insects, weeds, and animals prior to harvest, necessitating the continued use of pesticides. . . . The 63 federally licensed nuclear-power plants in the U.S. are ordered by the Nuclear Regulatory Commission (NRC) to tighten security against terriorist attacks.	Feb. 22
E. Howard Hunt Jr., a convicted Watergate conspirator, is paroled from a Fla. federal prison.	Pres. Carter explains that his administration's human-rights concerns are worldwide and not directed solely at the Soviet Union.	Supreme Ct. unanimously upholds the EPA's authority to issue uniform restrictions to curb industrial water pollution. . . . Former CIA Dir. George Bush is elected a director of First International Bancshares Inc. of Houston.	A duststorm hits the eastern Colo. plains, destroying most of the germinating winter-wheat crop. . . . Anthropologist Margaret Mead and other delegates protest admission to the American Association for the Advancement of Science honorary board of educational psychologist Arthur Jensen, author of a 1969 article advocating that blacks' creative and abstract thinking process is genetically inferior to whites'.		Feb. 23
Rand Corp. analyst calls the 1970–75 shift by over a million Americans from urban to rural areas one of the most significant migration turnabouts in U.S. history.	Pres. Carter stresses the legitimacy of CIA activities and the need for greater secrecy, in wake of reports that the CIA had paid King Hussein of Jordan and other foreign leaders. . . . State Secy. Vance reveals Carter administration plans to reduce foreign aid to Argentina, Uruguay, and Ethiopia because of concern about human-rights violations.	Chemical Bank (N.Y.C.), the nation's sixth largest commercial bank, is indicted for failing to report over 500 cash transactions to the IRS since 1974.	British scientists report determining the sequence of 5,375 nucleatides comprising the DNA strand of a bacterial virus. . . . Commerce Dept. suspends an order issued Jan. 10 that had accelerated patent grants to companies involved in recombinant DNA research.		Feb. 24
	Andrew Young, U.S. representative to the U.N., makes the first of a series of controversial U.S. foreign policy statements when he observes in a TV interview that the presence of Cuban troops in Angola brings some stability and order. . . . In N.Y.C. poet Allen Ginsberg stages a protest outside the Soviet Mission to the U.N., and another group demonstrates outside Aeroflot offices, to protest a Soviet ban on shipping matzohs to Jews in the U.S.S.R.		Soviet cosmonauts Col. Viktor Gorbatko and Yuri Glazkov bring their Soyuz 24 spacecraft safely back to Earth.	Dr. Thomas Schelling of Harvard University tells an AAAS panel that Americans' rootless and isolated lifestyle is reflected in the wish by many to die suddenly.	Feb. 25
The New York Times reports that Sen. Daniel Inouye (D, Hawaii) had indicated at a Feb. 22 White House meeting that he had asked the FBI to oversee members and staff of the Senate Intelligence Commitee.			The New York Times reports that Soviet cosmonauts' experiments on the solidification of metals, conducted during their stay on the spacecraft Salyut 5, have demonstrated that the metal did not form perfect spheres in weightlessness as had been expected.		Feb. 26

F	G	H	I	J
Includes elections, federal-state relations, civil rights and liberties, crime, the judiciary, education, health care, poverty, urban affairs and population.	Includes formation and debate of U.S. foreign and defense policies, veterans' affairs and defense spending. (Relations with specific foreign countries are usually found under the region concerned.)	Includes business, labor, agriculture, taxation, transportation, consumer affairs, monetary and fiscal policy, natural resources, and pollution.	Includes worldwide scientific, medical and technological developments, natural phenomena, U.S. weather, natural disasters, and accidents.	Includes the arts, religion, scholarship, communications media, sports, entertainments, fashions, fads and social life.

	World Affairs	Europe	Africa & the Middle East	The Americas	Asia & the Pacific
Feb. 27			Israeli troops evict 40 members of the ultra-Orthodox Gush Emunim movement who tried to establish an unauthorized settlement in the West Bank.		
Feb. 28	Soviet-Chinese border talks end unsuccessfully. . . . Reporting on his Middle East fact-finding mission at the beginning of February, U.N. Secy. Gen. Kurt Waldheim acknowledges that he failed to break the Arab-Israeli impasse on Palestinian participation in Geneva peace conference talks.	U.S. trial lawyer Edward Bennett Williams agrees to defend imprisoned Soviet dissident Alexander Ginzburg.	Ugandan Pres. Idi Amin postpones his meeting with U.S. nationals. . . . Sudan joins the Egyptian–Syrian political command that had been formed in December 1976 to map a common strategy against Israel. . . . Rhodesian govt. announces plans to recruit an additional 12,000 men into its security forces.	A 30-day state of siege is imposed in El Salvador after members of the National Opposition Union (UNO) stage riots to protest the victory of the government's candidate in Feb. 20 presidential elections as fraudulent.	
March 1	U.N. Human Rights Commission rejects a British proposal to investigate human-rights violations in Uganda.	U.S. Embassy in Moscow delivers a protest to the Soviet govt. on its seizure the previous day of Soviet Jewish activists, Veniamin Fein and Iosif Begun, as they were attempting to enter the embassy.	Ugandan Pres. Idi Amin drops his ban on American departures from Uganda and postpones indefinitely meeting the Americans at Entebbe Airport.	Argentine and Uruguayan governments say they will refuse any U.S. aid linked to observance of human rights.	
March 2	U.S.–Brazilian talks on Brazil's nuclear-reactor deal with West Germany end abruptly the day after they began.	Soviet newspaper *Pravda* charges U.S. human-rights violations and social inequities.	Ugandan Pres. Idi Amin claims an invasion force of 2,600 U.S., British, and Israeli mercenaries is advancing on Uganda through Kenya.		
March 3	OPEC special-fund governing committee discloses that the Cambodian govt. has rejected a $3.3 million loan offer.	Lord Brian Faulkner, 56, Northern Ireland prime minister (1971–72) and head of a moderate coalition govt. (1973–74), dies in a riding accident near Belfast.		In an apparent response to foreign reports of widespread anti-Semitism in Argentina, the Argentinian government closes the publishing house Odal, which is the illegal successor to the banned pro-Nazi publisher Milicia.	
March 4	The cash price of tin hits a new all-time high of $4.92 a pound on the London Metal Exchange as members of the International Tin Council try to salvage an effective price-control mechanism.	CP officials from nine Warsaw Pact countries end a two-day meeting in Sofia, Bulgaria with a call for decisive action against human-rights activities in Eastern Europe.		Cuban For. Trade Min. Marcelo Fernandez says that Cuba is eager to open reciprocal trade relations with the U.S. . . . Over 100,000 Colombian workers march in Bogota to protest the high cost of living. . . . In a policy shift, the Canadian federal govt. backs provincial abortion clinics that would be partially funded with federal money.	China names new CP chiefs in the provinces of Heilungkiang, Chekiang, and Kiangsu. . . . Thailand and Malaysia sign a border agreement providing for joint military operations against Communist guerrillas and allowing troops of both countries to cross each other's borders in pursuit of insurgents.

	A	B	C	D	E
	Includes developments that affect more than one world region, international organizations and important meetings of major world leaders.	*Includes all domestic and regional developments in Europe, including the Soviet Union, Turkey, Cyprus and Malta.*	*Includes all domestic and regional developments in Africa and the Middle East, including Iraq and Iran and excluding Cyprus, Turkey and Afghanistan.*	*Includes all domestic and regional developments in Latin America, the Caribbean and Canada.*	*Includes all domestic and regional developments in Asia and Pacific nations, extending from Afghanistan through all the Pacific Islands, except Hawaii.*

U.S. Politics & Social Issues	U.S. Foreign Policy & Defense	U.S. Economy & Environment	Science, Technology & Nature	Culture, Leisure & Life Style	
	State Secy. Vance, appearing on CBS-TV, says he considers covert payments to foreign governments, such as those made to Jordan's King Hussein, permissible and appropriate.			Black soprano Marian Anderson is honored on her seventy-fifth birthday by a Carnegie Hall (N.Y.C.) concert, attended by Rosalynn Carter.... A national "Turn the Television Off Week," organized by Miss. clergyman Donald Wildmon, begins as part of a mounting public outcry against depictions of violence on TV.... Jack Nicklaus captures the $50,000 top prize in the Jackie Gleason–Inverray Golf Tournament, Ft. Lauderdale, Fla.... John Dickson Carr, 70, mystery writer noted for the locked-room plot, who also wrote under the pseudonyms of Carter Dickson and Carr Dickson, dies of cancer in Greenville, S.C.	Feb. 27
A longstanding land suit against the state of Maine by the Passamaquoddy and Penobscot Indians prompts the federal govt. to threaten a suit against Maine if a settlement is not reached quickly. ... Robert Mardian, former attorney general and Nixon presidential reelection campaign manager, is reinstated to the Supreme Ct. bar after his Watergate-related conviction was overturned in October 1976.	In a strong reversal of previous U.S. policy State Secy. Vance endorses the principles of strong legislation to bar participation by U.S. firms in the Arab economic boycott of Israel but opposes the two antiboycott bills now before the Senate.	The U.S. posts a record trade deficit of $1.67 billion in January.		Eddie (Rochester) Anderson, 71, comedian noted for his portrayal of Jack Benny's valet during 30 years of broadcasting, dies of a heart ailment in Los Angeles.	Feb. 28
Supreme Ct. rules that a state can use racial quotas in reapportioning its legislative districts to comply with provisions of the Voting Rights Act, 1965. Chief Justice Warren Burger dissents.... ERA is defeated in N.C., despite telephone appeals by Pres. Carter and his wife, Rosalynn.	State Secy. Vance, in discussing the U.S. stance on a proposed West German-Brazilian nuclear plant deal, says that the Carter administration would take into consideration nuclear proliferation before deciding how much economic aid to give a country.	U.S. Circuit Appeals Ct., Washington, D.C. rules that a FCC regulation prohibiting forming new joint newspaper–broadcasting ownership in the same area applies existing ownership combinations.	Dr. David Levy, child psychiatrist who coined the term sibling rivalry and developed the personality diagnosis Rorschach (ink-blot) test, dies at the age of 84 in N.Y.C.	NFL Players Assn. signs a five-year contract with the league's Management Council after a protracted period of stalled negotiations, player walkouts, and court actions since the Jan. 31, 1974 expiration of their last contract.... Supreme Ct. rules unanimously that prosecutors cannot use June 1973 obscenity standards in seeking convictions for alleged offenses prior to that date.	March 1
Supreme Ct. rules, 5–4, against a Social Security provision giving automatic benefits to widows but not to widowers with Justice John Paul Stevens casting the key vote. ... House adopts, 402–22, an ethics code that contains strong financial disclosure requirements and sets a limit on outside earnings at 15 percent of a member's current salary.					March 2
Joanne Chesimard, leader of the radical Black Liberation Army, is found guily of first-degree murder in the death of a N.J. trooper during a 1973 shootout on the New Jersey Turnpike.	Pres. Carter signs a bill permitting Japan, Spain, South Korea, and EEC nations to fish within the U.S. 200-mile fishing zone, which replaces a 12-mile zone.	U.S. International Trade Commission rules, 5–1, that sugar imports are injuring or potentially injuring the U.S. cane and sugar-beet industry.		Linda Fratianne wins the women's singles world figure skating championship in Tokyo, Japan.... Eugenie Brazier, 81, one of France's foremost chefs who emphasized freshness and simplicity in a radical departure from traditional haute cuisine, dies in Lyons, France.	March 3
Inez Garcia, convicted for murder in 1974 after fatally shooting a man involved in her alleged rape, is acquitted after a retrial in Monterey County, Calif.		Consumer credit rises sharply to a seasonally adjusted $1.92 billion in January, the third largest monthly increase on record and the biggest since March 1973.... An estimated 225,000 people lost their jobs during Febuary because of weather and energy problems. The increase from January's unemployment rate, however, is smaller than expected.	A major earthquake measuring 7.5 on the Richter scale devastates Bucharest, Rumania and several of the country's industrial centers.		March 4
F	G	H	I	J	
Includes elections, federal-state relations, civil rights and liberties, crime, the judiciary, education, health care, poverty, urban affairs and population.	*Includes formation and debate of U.S. foreign and defense policies, veterans' affairs and defense spending. (Relations with specific foreign countries are usually found under the region concerned.)*	*Includes business, labor, agriculture, taxation, transportation, consumer affairs, monetary and fiscal policy, natural resources, and pollution.*	*Includes worldwide scientific, medical and technological developments, natural phenomena, U.S. weather, natural disasters, and accidents.*	*Includes the arts, religion, scholarship, communications media, sports, entertainments, fashions, fads and social life.*	

	World Affairs	Europe	Africa & the Middle East	The Americas	Asia & the Pacific
March 5		A crime-victim compensation law goes into effect in France.		Brazil joins Argentina and Uruguay in rejecting all U.S. military assistance, in wake of the Carter administration policy of linking aid to increased observance of human rights.	
March 6			George Habash, head of the radical Popular Front for the Liberation of Palestine, threatens to withdraw from the PLO if the PLO decides at its March 12 conference to go to Geneva or to recognize Israel.		Australia signs an accord with China for two million tons of wheat to be shipped from June 1977 to January 1978 with the total sale price of $220 million to be paid in full within 12 months of the shipment.
March 7	IMF reports lending the unprecedented sum of 2.35 billion Special Drawing Rights (SDRs) from February 1976 to January 1977.		Delegates from 59 countries representing the OAU and Arab League hold their first summit conference in Cairo.... Israel reportedly has established a government agency to counter the effects of the Arab economic bycott.		Pakistani P.M. Zulfikar Ali Bhutto's ruling Pakistan People's Party (PPP) wins a heavy majority in National Assembly elections.
March 8	GATT reports that world trade increased 11 percent in volume and 12 percent in value during 1976 from the depressed 1975 levels.		Israeli Premier Itzhak Rabin does not claim that Pres. Carter supported Israel's definition of defensible borders in their Washington talks the previous day.	Jamaica's ruling People's National Party (PNP) sweeps the opposition Jamaica Labor Party (JLP) in local elections.	
March 9		Belgian P.M. Leo Tindemans dissolves Parliament and calls for a general election on April 17, following his March 4 dismissal of two Cabinet ministers who belong to the French-speaking Rassamblement Wallon Party.	The first Afro–African summit conference concludes with a speech by its initiator, Egyptian Pres. Anwar Sadat, and a pledge of formal economic and political cooperation between Arab and black African nations.	Pres. Carter announces ending travel restrictions to Cuba, the culmination of a number of qualified overtures by his administration since January.	Pres. Carter announces his intention of withdrawing American ground forces in South Korea within four to five years.
March 10			Cuban Premier Fidel Castro and Libyan leader Muammer el-Qadaffi sign an agreement to promote cultural, economic, commercial, and scientific exchanges and issue a communique denouncing imperialistic maneuvers against the Ethiopian revolution.	In a wave of labor unrest, over 100,000 Colombian state employes strike in Bogota and other cities, paralyzing more tha 40 government dependencies.	
March 11			Congolese National Liberation Front (FLNC) claims responsibility for the invasion of Zaire's Shaba province. Zaire govt. charges that Angolan troops were among the invaders.	Brazil announces cancelling its 25-year-old military assistance treaty with the U.S. because of a U.S. State Dept. report criticizing its human-rights practices.	CP newspaper *Jenmin Jih Pao* calls for a major effort to bolster China's ailing economy, reportedly plagued by serious energy, food, and industrial shortages.
March 12	Iranian, Pakistani, and Turkish foreign ministers sign the Treaty of Izmir to ratify summit-meeting decisions, made in April 1976, revitalizing the three-nation Regional Cooperation for Development, an economic and cultural body.		Egyptian Pres. Anwar Sadat says that Egypt will not cede a single inch of Arab land, in a response to U.S. Pres. Carter's March 9 distinction between Israel's future legal boundaries and forward defense lines.	Chilean govt. bans the four remaining political parties operating since the military coup.	Laotian authorities seize former King Savang Vatthana and his family in wake of fierce fighting between government and rebel forces outside the former royal capital of Luang Prabang.

A	B	C	D	E
Includes developments that affect more than one world region, international organizations and important meetings of major world leaders.	Includes all domestic and regional developments in Europe, including the Soviet Union, Turkey, Cyprus and Malta.	Includes all domestic and regional developments in Africa and the Middle East, including Iraq and Iran and excluding Cyprus, Turkey and Afghanistan.	Includes all domestic and regional developments in Latin America, the Caribbean and Canada.	Includes all domestic and regional developments in Asia and Pacific nations, extending from Afghanistan through all the Pacific Islands, except Hawaii.

U.S. Politics & Social Issues	U.S. Foreign Policy & Defense	U.S. Economy & Environment	Science, Technology & Nature	Culture, Leisure & Life Style	
Pres. Carter answers questions from 42 citizens in 26 states during a two-hour telephone call-in radio broadcast from the White House.					March 5
				The Hite Report by Shere Hite, a compilation of women's personal responses about their sexuality, is the fifth-ranking nonfiction book on the previous week's best-seller list.	March 6
HUD Dept. Secy. Patricia Roberts Harris announces a new $400-million urban development program to give the private sector more confidence in investments in depressed urban areas.	Pres. Carter meets in Washington with Israeli P.M. Yitzhak Rabin and causes a stir by appearing to support Israel's policy of refusing to return all Arab land captured in the 1967 war.	Supreme Ct. rules unanimously that states can impose taxes on interstate corporations for the privilege of doing business, overturning the so-called Spector Rule established in a 1951 ruling.	Coalition for Responsible Genetic Research announces its formation and calls for an immediate moratorium on all genetic research that would produce novel combinations between distant organisms.		March 7
	Army germ-warfare tests conducted between 1949–69 are revealed in an Army two-volume report given to a subcommittee of the Senate Committee on Human Resources.	U.S. International Trade Council warns that imports of color TV sets injure U.S. producers and workers.	*Washington Post* reports that the National Institutes of Health (NIH) is preparing the first U.S. certified P4 level laboratory where hazardous genetic experiments can be conducted.	The U.S. State Dept. authorizes sending a professional baseball team to compete in Cuba. . . . Actor Henry Hull dies at age 86 in Cornwall, England.	March 8
Hanafi Muslim gunmen take over three Washington, D.C. buildings; shoot to death Maurice Williams, a local radio reporter; and injure 19 others in apparent retaliation for the January 18, 1973 slaying of five Black Muslims of seven Hanafi sect members.	Pres. Carter announces that bans on travel to Cuba, Vietnam, Cambodia, and North Korea will be lifted on March 18.	American Petroleum Institute revised figures show that U.S. refineries' produced an average of 7.95 million barrels of oil per day in February, the first drop below the eight-million mark since 1966.	FDA proposes a ban on saccharin, the only artificial sweetener available in the U.S., because of its link to malignant bladder tumors in rats.	*Rocky*, a film about the personal triumph of a boxer played by Sylvester Stallone, is the top-grossing film for the previous week. . . . Former Pres. Gerald Ford and his wife, Betty, reportedly sign contracts for their memoirs for about $1 million each.	March 9
N.Y.C. weathers another chapter of its financial crisis when its Emergency Financial Control Bd. approves a plan to pay off a $983-million short-term debt to holders of city bonds, subject to a state-imposed moratorium on redemption of the notes' principal.		United Farm Workers head Cesar Chavez and Teamsters Union representatives sign a five-year organizational jurisdiction pact.	American Diabetic Assn. spokesman warns that lack of sugar substitutes in face of the FDA saccharin ban could have a grave impact on America's 10 million diabetic.	E. Power Biggs, 70, British-born organ virtuoso who popularized both the instument and baroque music and was an authority on Bach, dies in Boston, Mass. after surgery.	March 10
Treasury Secy. W. Michael Blumenthal releases a $255-million short-term federal loan to N.Y.C. . . . Hanafi Muslim leader Hamaas Abdul Khaalis peacefully surrenders 134 hostages seized in the takeover of three Washington buildings after ambassadors from three Islamic nations persuade him that his siege against rival Black Muslims is counter to his orthodox Moslem beliefs.		Federal bank-regulatory officials report that the list of problem banks has increased since 1976.	Center for Disease Control reports 152 cases of Reye's syndrome, representing the highest incidence of the disease since 379 cases were documented during the 1973–74 flu season.	Christopher Durang's play *A History of the American Film*, a parody of American film and image-making, opens at the Hartford Stage, Conn.	March 11
	State Dept. releases a report revealing that human-rights violations of various sorts have been noted in almost all of the 82 countries receiving U.S. security aid, with the exception of Western European nations and a few others.		Fifteen are left dead as a severe snowstorm hits Colo., Neb., Kan., and S.D.	Texas Southern University beats Campbell College of North Carolina, 71–44, to win the National Association of Intercollegiate Athletics (NAIA) basketball tournament.	March 12

F	G	H	I	J
Includes elections, federal-state relations, civil rights and liberties, crime, the judiciary, education, health care, poverty, urban affairs and population.	*Includes formation and debate of U.S. foreign and defense policies, veterans' affairs and defense spending. (Relations with specific foreign countries are usually found under the region concerned.)*	*Includes business, labor, agriculture, taxation, transportation, consumer affairs, monetary and fiscal policy, natural resources, and pollution.*	*Includes worldwide scientific, medical and technological developments, natural phenomena, U.S. weather, natural disasters, and accidents.*	*Includes the arts, religion, scholarship, communications media, sports, entertainments, fashions, fads and social life.*

	World Affairs	Europe	Africa & the Middle East	The Americas	Asia & the Pacific
March 13		Jan Patocka, 69, a former philosophy professor and spokesman for the Czech human-rights Charter 77, dies of a brain hemorrhage in Prague.	Israeli Premier Yitzhak Rabin says, in a U.S. TV interview, that he opposes Pres. Carter's calls for Israel to withdraw from all Arab land taken in 1967.	Colombian Revolutionary Armed Forces (FARC), a pro-Moscow guerrilla group, kidnaps a wealthy rancher and demands $300,000 in ransom, in a wave of politically motivated kidnappings and attacks that politicians blame on Pres. Alfonso Lopez Michelsen.	A protester demonstrating against Australia's ties with the British monarchy throws a sign at Queen Elizabeth II in Sydney during a stop in her three-week Australian tour to commemorate the twenty-fifth anniversary of her reign.
March 14			Christian militiamen attack the Lebanese Moslem village of Kafr Kila near the Israeli border, killing 12 people. . . . Cuban Premier Castro makes an unscheduled visit in Ethiopia after two-day stops in South Yemen and Somalia, where, reportedly, the main topic of discussions was Ethiopian–Somalian conflict over the future of Afars and Issas (Djibouti), scheduled for independence in June. . . . U.S. promises emergency aid to Zaire in wake of the invasion of Shaba Province.		
March 15		Soviet dissident Anatoly Shcharansky is arrested after the Soviet press charges that he is a U.S. CIA agent.	Israeli Premier Yitzhak Rabin is reported changing from his previous position of a step-by-step approach to a peace settlement to a comprehensive settlement with the Arabs as a result of Pres. Carter's basic support of the Israeli condition that the Arabs must totally accept Israel's right to exist.		Australia's population is reported to be 13.9 million as of June 30, 1976.
March 16		Over 600 people have reportedly signed the Czech human-rights Charter 77 petition. . . . The world's longest hijacking — 10,000 miles across two continents in 44 hours — ends in Zurich when an Italian auto mechanic who comandeered an Iberia Airlines flight is overpowered.	In a Clinton, Mass. speech, Pres. Carter calls for a Palestinian homeland, setting off another controversy and drawing praise from some Palestinians. . . . Lebanese leftist Moslem leader Kamal Jumblat is shot and killed by an unknown assailant near Baaklin.	Guatemala and El Salvador become the fourth and fifth Latin American countries to reject U.S. aid because of its linkage to greater observance of human rights.	
March 17	Pres. Carter emphasizes human rights in his first major foreign policy speech, telling the U.N. General Assembly that the U.N. charter gives member-nations the right and duty to speak out about human-rights abuses in other countries.	The Baader-Meinhof gang terrorism trial in Stuttgart, West Germany adjourns in wake of the disclosure that conversations between the three defendants and their lawyers had been wiretapped. . . . Spain issues a new amnesty decree for both common and political prisoners that is expected to release over 200 political prisoners.			Leaders of the Pakistan National Alliance (PNA) are arrested in wake of demonstrations against the alleged rigging of elections by P.M. Zulfikar Ali Bhutto to keep his governing Pakistan People's Party (PPP) in power.
March 18			Revenge slayings for the assassination of Lebanese Moslem leader Kamal Jumblat appear to end, with an estimated 200 Christians left dead. . . . Congo Pres. Marien Ngouabi is killed by a four-man commando squad led by former army Capt. Barthelemy Kikadidi, who escaped after the attack made in Ngouabi's Brazzaville residence. . . . Pres. Carters signs legislation to ban Rhodesian chrome imports, bringing the U.S. into compliance with a U.N. embargo imposed in 1966 as a sanction against Rhodesian white supremacist policies.	A progressive Peruvian Catholic organization endorses a previous U.S. State Dept. report finding that human rights are generally respected in Peru.	Pres. Carter says that the body of a supposed MIA, one of 12 turned over to the U.S. by the Vietnamese, was not that of a U.S. serviceman, but terms it an honest mistake.
	A *Includes developments that affect more than one world region, international organizations and important meetings of major world leaders.*	**B** *Includes all domestic and regional developments in Europe, including the Soviet Union, Turkey, Cyprus and Malta.*	**C** *Includes all domestic and regional developments in Africa and the Middle East, including Iraq and Iran and excluding Cyprus, Turkey and Afghanistan.*	**D** *Includes all domestic and regional developments in Latin America, the Caribbean and Canada.*	**E** *Includes all domestic and regional developments in Asia and Pacific nations, extending from Afghanistan through all the Pacific Islands, except Hawaii.*

U.S. Politics & Social Issues	U.S. Foreign Policy & Defense	U.S. Economy & Environment	Science, Technology & Nature	Culture, Leisure & Life Style	
		Teamsters' pension fund, under government investigation for alleged mismanagement and ties to organized crime, will be turned over to independent investment managers, necessitating the resignation of four long-time trustees, including Teamsters pres. Frank Fitzsimmons.			March 13
Fannie Lou Hamer, 59, Southern civil-rights leader during the 1960s, dies of cancer in Mount Bayou, Miss. . . . Carter administration calls for the decriminalization of marijuana.	Gerald Starek and Carl Storey, top officials of the California-based electronics firm I.I. Industries, are sentenced each to 18-month jail terms and given a $10,000 fine for selling restricted semiconductor-manufacturing equipment to the Soviet Union.	U.S. International Trade Commission recommends that Pres. Carter reduce by one-third the 7 million tons of imported sugar now allowed under existing quotas and to set the maximum import level at 4.275 million tons a year.		*Chiaroscuro*, an orchestral work by Jacob Druckman commissioned for the Bicentennial, receives its world premiere by the Cleveland Orchestra, conducted by Lorin Maazel.	March 14
	Senate by voice vote rescinds $18.6 million in fiscal 1977 appropriated for a nuclear-powered aircraft carrier.	FRB reports that industrial production rose 1 percent in February, more than offsetting a .8 percent January decline.	Official death toll for the Rumanian earthquake on March 4 is 1,541, with 11,275 injured, and 80,000 left homeless.	The Roundabout Theater, N.Y.C. presents Samuel Beckett's *Endgame* . . . . Howard Hughes, consistently tagged as a billionaire, is found to have been worth only 168.8 million, according to an estate appraisal filed in Houston and Las Vegas probate courts.	March 15
Pres. Carter appears before the Clinton, Mass. town meeting and stays overnight in the home of Edward G. Thompson, an office manager of a beer distributor, as part of his stated effort to stay close to the people.	Pres. Carter makes another controversial statement on the Israeli–Arab conflict when, in a speech in Clinton, Mass., he calls for a Palestinian homeland. He also says that the first prerequisite for a lasting peace is Arab recognition of Israel's right to exist in peace and the establishment of permanent Israeli borders. . . . State Secy. Vance tells the House International Relations Committee that the fighting in Zaire poses a threat to Zaire's copper-mining industry.			A three-judge panel rules that the FCC cannot ban allegedly indecent language from the airwaves.	March 16
	Speaking before the U.N. General Assembly, Pres. Carter says that the U.S. is ready to have normal relations throughout the world and seeks reconciliation with those countries willing to work in tandem toward global peace.	Commerce Dept. reports that U.S. personal income rose at a seasonally adjusted rate or $17.1 billion in February, or 1.2 percent from January, reflecting a substantial rise in hours worked.	House votes to spend $15 million for SST research.	Jimmy Young wins a unanimous decision over former world heavyweight boxing champion George Foreman in a 12-round bout in San Juan, Puerto Rico. . . . Baseball comr. Bowie Kuhn wins his suit against Oakland A's owner Charles Finley when U.S. Dist. Ct. Judge Frank McGarr rules in Chicago that Kuhn acted within his powers in nullifying the sale of three Oakland A's players in June 1976.	March 17
Justice Dept. files a brief endorsing Wilmington, Del. busing between city and suburbs to achieve desegregation.				The newly formed Brooklyn, Academy of Music Theater Co. opens with revivals of Langdon Mitchell's social comedy, *The New York Idea* and Anton Chekov's *Three Sisters*. ensemble members include Rosemary Harris, Ellen Burstyn, Blythe Danner, and Denholm Elliott.	March 18

F	G	H	I	J
Includes elections, federal-state relations, civil rights and liberties, crime, the judiciary, education, health care, poverty, urban affairs and population.	*Includes formation and debate of U.S. foreign and defense policies, veterans' affairs and defense spending. (Relations with specific foreign countries are usually found under the region concerned.)*	*Includes business, labor, agriculture, taxation, transportation, consumer affairs, monetary and fiscal policy, natural resources, and pollution.*	*Includes worldwide scientific, medical and technological developments, natural phenomena, U.S. weather, natural disasters, and accidents.*	*Includes the arts, religion, scholarship, communications media, sports, entertainments, fashions, fads and social life.*

	World Affairs	Europe	Africa & the Middle East	The Americas	Asia & the Pacific
March 19		Irish For. Min. Garret Fitzgerald praises the March 17 statement by four Irish–American politicians urging U.S. citizens to stop giving money to the IRA.			Pakistani post-election violence spreads, centering in Karachi where a curfew is imposed and one-third of the city placed under military control.
March 20		French government parties, led by Pres. Valery Giscard d'Estaing and Parisian Mayor Jacques Chirac — the Independent Republicans and the Gaullists — suffer their worst defeat since assuming power in 1956.	Palestinian leadership reaffirms its opposition to the existence of Israel, after a nine-day meeting of the Palestine National Council in Cairo.		Five-day elections in India result in the suprising defeat of the ruling Congress Party.
March 21		The strike against British Leyland Ltd., which began on Feb. 18, ends with its 3,000 toolmakers returning to work.			China's worst drought since 1949 is reported threatening its summer crop harvest and spring sowing. . . . The ruling Indian Congress Party lifts its state of emergency imposed since June 1975, following its defeat in nationwide elections.
March 22		British P.M. James Calaghan announces a deal between his Labor Party and the Liberal Party in which Liberal Party leader David Steel and other Liberals would comprise a shadow cabinet and be consulted before any government policies reach the House of Commons. . . . Netherlands coalition government resigns after the Cabinet fails to resolve a dispute over land expropriation.	The Ethiopian govt. is reported facing mounting opposition from widely divergent political groups within the country.	Canadian Supreme Ct. bars the use of evidence obtained by a lie-detector test in murder trials.	P.M. Indira Gandhi resigns after her Congress Party is defeated for the first time in India's 30 years of independence.
March 23		British P.M. Callaghan's Labor govt. survives a no-confidence vote in the House of Commons as the result of a deal with 13 Liberal Party members.	Tanzanian Pres. Julius Nyerere welcomes Soviet Pres. Nikolai Podgorny in Dar es Salaam and expresses thanks for Soviet military aid in nationalist movements, but asserts that Tanzania is determinedly unaligned.		Pres. Carter accepts Vietnamese Premier Pham Van Dong's invitation to reinstate U.S.–Vietnamese talks in Paris without preconditions on resuming normal relations.
March 24	Guinea-Bissau joins the IMF and World Bank.	Jailed Polish food-price protesters are released.	During a month-long African tour, Cuban Premier Fidel Castro declares that Cuba will give Angola unlimited support.		Morarji Desai, head of India's opposition Janata Party, is named prime minister, and he tells a New Delhi rally that he will drive fear of the government out of society.
March 25			Former Congolese Pres. Alphonse Massamba-Debat is executed for ploting the assassination of Pres. Marien Ngouabi on March 18.	Canadian total population reaches 23.3 million as of Jan. 1, up 308,000 during 1976.	

A	B	C	D	E
Includes developments that affect more than one world region, international organizations and important meetings of major world leaders.	Includes all domestic and regional developments in Europe, including the Soviet Union, Turkey, Cyprus and Malta.	Includes all domestic and regional developments in Africa and the Middle East, including Iraq and Iran and excluding Cyprus, Turkey and Afghanistan.	Includes all domestic and regional developments in Latin America, the Caribbean and Canada.	Includes all domestic and regional developments in Asia and Pacific nations, extending from Afghanistan through all the Pacific Islands, except Hawaii.

U.S. Politics & Social Issues	U.S. Foreign Policy & Defense	U.S. Economy & Environment	Science, Technology & Nature	Culture, Leisure & Life Style	
FBI reports that 324 fugitives from its *10 most wanted* lists have been captured since the lists' inception in 1950.			Pulitizer Prize-winning science journalist William Laurence, who covered the first atomic blast in New Mexico en 1945 and flew as an observer with the atomic bomb mission over Nagasaki, Japan, dies at the age of 89 Majorca, Spain.	Lawrence (Buck) Shaw, 77, college and pro football coach known as the Silver Fox, dies of cancer in Menlo Park, Calif.	March 19
				St. Bonaventure University defeats the University of Houston, 94–91, to win the fortieth annual National Invitational Tournament (NIT) basketball title. Greg Sanders is named MVP.	March 20
Supreme Ct. unanimously voids a Social Security provision under which retired men had to prove they were financially dependent on their wives to qualify for certain old-age benefits. . . . FALN, the radical Puerto Rican nationalist organization, claims responsibility for bombing the N.Y.C. headquarters of the FBI, injuring a passerby.	Defense Dept. reportedly is resuming research on weapons using nerve gas, spending $1.5 million to develop a bomb, code-named "Big Eye".	Transportation Secy. Brock Adams calls for mandatory air bags in all cars beginning with 1980 or 1981 models, reversing his predecessor William Coleman Jr.'s stance.	A Ford Foundation–Mitre Corp. study recommends major changes in current U.S. nuclear energy policy and discourages use of breeder reactors using plutonium reprocessing because of the potential proliferation of nuclear weapons, more easily made with the available plutonium. . . . Justice Dept. reports a total of $45 million in damage claims against the government as a result of its swine-flu inoculation program.		March 21
Supreme Ct. rules that a judge cannot sentence a defendant to death on the basis of information withheld from the defense. . . . On the deadline day for passage of the ERA, only 35 of the necessary 38 states have ratified the amendment. Three retifications have been rescinded and are the subject of a legal controversy.	Pres. Carter and Japanese Premier Takeo Fukuda issue a joint communique, after meeting in Washington, noting the importance of maintaining stability in Korea and asserting that planned U.S. troop withdrawals from South Korea would not endanger peace there.	A 9 percent increase in government price supports for milk is announced, effective April 1.	The longest-surviving heart-transplant patient to date, Betty Anick, 57, dies in Nokomis, Fla., eight years and four months after her surgery.		March 22
Supreme Ct. sidesteps the so-called Miranda rule — requiring a defendant to be informed of his rights upon arrest — and affirms an appeals court ruling, 5–4, thereby allowing the possibility that a man convicted in the rape-slaying of a 10-year-old girl could be set free.		House defeats, 217–205, a bill that would have allowed construction workers disputing only one subcontractor to picket an entire building site.	Earthquakes on Iran's southeastern coast kill 167 people.	Men's International Professional Tennis Council announces the merger of World Championship Tennis (WCT) and its former rival Grand Prix. . . . Some 200 Roman Catholic priests attending a Priests' Councils convention in Louisville, Ky. vote to ask Pope Paul VI to reconsider his declaration against the ordination of women.	March 23
		AFL–CIO Pres. George Meany denounces a Carter administration proposal to increase the federal minimum wage from $2.30 to $2.50-an-hour instead of the $3.00 proposed by the union.	A five-month drought threatens the High Plains region of the Texas Panhandle, which produces about 20 percent of U.S. cotton and sorghum and supplies more feeder cattle than any other region.	parents of five members of Rev. Sun Myung Moon's Unification Church are grated custody of their adult chidren by Calif. Superior Ct. Judge S. Lee Vavuris in a suit charging that Moon's followers had brainwashed their disciples.	March 24
U.S. District Ct. Judge Prentice Marshall rules that $28.4 million in impounded revenue-sharing funds for Chicago can be released because the Chicago police department now complies with hiring guidelines set in early 1976.			White House energy adviser James Schlesinger says that the Carter administration opposes developing plutonium fuel systems for nuclear power plants.	NFL Players' Assn. ratifies a new five-year labor agreement with the league.	March 25

F	G	H	I	J
Includes elections, federal-state relations, civil rights and liberties, crime, the judiciary, education, health care, poverty, urban affairs and population.	*Includes formation and debate of U.S. foreign and defense policies, veterans' affairs and defense spending. (Relations with specific foreign countries are usually found under the region concerned.)*	*Includes business, labor, agriculture, taxation, transportation, consumer affairs, monetary and fiscal policy, natural resources, and pollution.*	*Includes worldwide scientific, medical and technological developments, natural phenomena, U.S. weather, natural disasters, and accidents.*	*Includes the arts, religion, scholarship, communications media, sports, entertainments, fashions, fads and social life.*

	World Affairs	Europe	Africa & the Middle East	The Americas	Asia & the Pacific
March 26		Official Soviet newspapers criticize the U.S. for stalemating the 1974 SALT pact and over-emphasizing human-rights guarantees.	A joint Soviet–Tazanian communique endorses the Patriotic Front of Zimbabwe, one of three Rhodesian nationalist groups competing for African and international recognition in white-ruled Rhodesia.		Thai govt. blocks an army coup led by Gen. Chalard Hiranyasiri and aimed at toppling the ruling Administrative Reform Council headed by Sa-Ngad Chaloryu. . . . Philippine Pres. Ferdinand Marcos Formally grants autonomy to rebellious Moslems in the southwestern Philippines. . . . India's new P.M. Morarji Desai forms a 19-member Cabinet, but a Key appointee, Defense Min. Jagjivan Ram, initially rejects his appointment.
March 27		Normandy fishermen block Le Havre harbor's entrance to protest French industrial water pollution.	Arab League formally approves a six-month extension of its peace-keeping force in Lebanon.		
March 28		Portugal formally seeks entry into the EEC after having received the full endorsement of the EEC Commission on March 13.	Amnesty International charges widespread Ethiopian human-rights violations.		
March 29	Bolivia announces that it will ratify the fifth International Tin Agreement.	British Exchequer Chancellor Denis Healey presents his tenth budget in three years to the House of Commons.	*Washington Post* reports Ugandan refugees' accounts of massive killings of Christian tribesmen and purges of suspected plotters in the Ugandan army by Idi Amin's govt.		U Maung Kha is elected premier of Burma.
March 30	Soviet Union–U.S. arms limitation talks end after three days without an accord, but both sides agree to resume negotiations in Geneva in May.	Commerce Dept. reports final U.S.–Soviet agreement on a shipping pact for U.S. grain purchased by the Soviet Union.			Pakistani P.M. Zulfikar Ali Bhutto forms a new Cabinet as violent antigovernment demonstrations continue.
March 31	Soviet For. Min. Andrei Gromyko criticizes proposals for a new SALT pact that were presented by U.S. State Secy. Vance during his March 28–30 visit to Moscow.		Lebanese Christian militia units launch attacks on Palestinian guerrillas and their Lebanese Moslem leftist allies in southern Lebanon, near the Israeli border, in an attempt to capture the entire region.	Canadian Finance Min. Donald Macdonald presents a C$41.9-billion fiscal budget intended to stimulate the economy, but rules out an early end to wage and price controls.	
April 1	NATO spokesmen unofficially comment that Pres. Carter was both tough and realistic in his arms-limitation dealings with Soviet For. Min. Andrei Gromyko and say they are optimistic about an agreement later in the year.	In one of several major political reforms adopted prior to upcoming June elections, the Spanish govt. abolishes former Generalissimo Francisco Franco's political organization — the National Movement.		Quebec provincial govt. issues a white paper declaring that Quebec is a French society and rejecting bilingualism.	Indian Home Min. Charan Singh announces in Parliament that the new government will investigate corruption charges against former P.M. Indira Gandhi, her son Sanjay Gandhi, and former Defense Min. Bansi Lal.
April 2		Lucio Lombardo Radice, a senior member of the Italian CP, provokes a controversy by saying, in a Radio Free Europe interview, that a Communist Italy would side with the Soviet Union against NATO in the event of an international crisis.	Libya executes 22 officers charged with participating in an attempted coup against Col. Muammer el-Qaddafi in 1975.		The new Indian govt. announces that it is moderating the former Gandhi govt.'s birth-control policy by eliminating measures to compel or encourage sterilization.

A	B	C	D	E
Includes developments that affect more than one world region, international organizations and important meetings of major world leaders.	*Includes all domestic and regional developments in Europe, including the Soviet Union, Turkey, Cyprus and Malta.*	*Includes all domestic and regional developments in Africa and the Middle East, including Iraq and Iran and excluding Cyprus, Turkey and Afghanistan.*	*Includes all domestic and regional developments in Latin America, the Caribbean and Canada.*	*Includes all domestic and regional developments in Asia and Pacific nations, extending from Afghanistan through all the Pacific Islands, except Hawaii.*

U.S. Politics & Social Issues	U.S. Foreign Policy & Defense	U.S. Economy & Environment	Science, Technology & Nature	Culture, Leisure & Life Style	
			Nuclear researchers at the Electric Power Research Institute, Palo Alto, Calif. dispute Ford–Mitre Corp. study-findings that use of nuclear breeder reactors and of plutonium poses hazards.	China allows the music of Ludwig von Beethoven to be performed again after he had been denounced and banned during the Cultural Revolution of the late 1960s. . . . AIAW basketball championship is won for the third consecutive year by Delta State, defeating Louisiana State, 68–55.	March 26
Singer Anita Bryant, who is speargeading a campaign against a Miami, Fla. gay-rights ordinance, criticizes the White House for dignifying gay activists with serious discussion of their alleged human rights.			In the world's worst aviation disaster to date, a KLM Royal Dutch Airlines Boeing 747 crashes into a Pan American Airways 747 on the runway of a Canary Islands airport, killing over 570 people.	Chris Evert wins her fourth Virginia Slims tennis title by beating Britain's Sue Barker in the final of the $250,000 four-day championship tournament, held at N.Y.C.'s Madison Square Garden.	March 27
		Supreme Ct., 7–2, declines to review a lower ct. ruling that corporations have the same constitutional protection from double jeopardy as individuals. . . . Commerce Dept. reports a $1.87-billion seasonally adjusted U.S. trade deficit in February, the worst on record.	Eric Shipton, 69, British mountaineer and explorer who climbed Mt. Everest five times, dies in Salisbury, England.	Academy Award Oscars are presented as follows: best film, *Rocky*; best actor, the late Peter Finch; best actress, Faye Dunaway (both for *Network* roles). . . . Marquette University defeats North Carolina, 67–59, to win the NCAA basketball championship.	March 28
Richard Sprague controversial chief counsel and staff director of the House Select Committee on Assassinations, resigns.			Population Council, a private research organization, releases a report that links smoking while taking birth contol pills with an increased death rate among women over the age of 30.	Alan Ayckbourn's play *Bedroom Farce*, directed by Peter Hall, opens on Broadway after a 370-performance London run.	March 29
House votes, 230–181, to extend the life of the Select committee on Assassinations, which is investigating the deaths of former Pres. John Kennedy and civil-rights leader Martin Luther King.	State Secy. Vance says that he does not think that Pres. Carter's views on human rights had affected the nonconclusive outcome of his talks with Soviet CP leader Leonid Brezhnev on an arms-limitation agreement.	Westinghouse Electric corp. settles a contract dispute with three Pittsburgh-area utilities over its failure to deliver a promised quantity of uranium oxide.	NASA announces that Cornell University astronomers discovered rings around the planet Uranus on March 10.		March 30
Congress gives Pres. Carter the authority he requested to reorganize the executive branch of the federal government.	House Speaker Thomas (Tip) O'Neill (D, Mass.) says that Pres. Carter has bipartisan support in his arms-limitation nogotiations. Senate Minority Leader Howard Baker (D, Tenn.) also indicates Republican support, but House Minority Leader John Rhodes (R, Ariz.) attacks Carter's "spray-shot foreign policy".	U.S. District Ct. Judge James McMillan declares unconstitutional a provision of the Price–Anderson Act that limits an electric utility company's liability for a nuclear power plant accident to $560 million in damages per accident.		*The Shadow Box* by Michael Cristofer, a play about the impact of terminal illness on the patient's associates, opens on Broadway.	March 31
Following the House's example, the Senate adopts 86–9, an ethics code requiring full financial disclosure and setting a limit on a senator's earnings in addition to his salary.		March unemployment drops to 7.3 percent, compared to February's rate of 7.5 percent.	A tornado hitting two separate regions of Bangladesh kills about 900 people.	NFL team owners conclude their annual spring meeting in Phoenix, Ariz. They approve the sale of the San Francisco 49ers to Edward DeBartolo Jr., place the Tampa Bay Buccaneers permanently in the National Football Conference Central Division, expand the regular season and reduce the preseason, and adopt a new schedule formula for 1978.	April 1
		The United Shoe Workers of America and the Boot and Shoe Workers Union ask Congress to override what they term Carter's disastrous decision against shoe-import curbs and accuse him of betraying his campaign promises to organized labor.			April 2

F	G	H	I	J
Includes elections, federal-state relations, civil rights and liberties, crime, the judiciary, education, health care, poverty, urban affairs and population.	Includes formation and debate of U.S. foreign and defense policies, veterans' affairs and defense spending. (Relations with specific foreign countries are usually found under the region concerned.)	Includes business, labor, agriculture, taxation, transportation, consumer affairs, monetary and fiscal policy, natural resources, and pollution.	Includes worldwide scientific, medical and technological developments, natural phenomena, U.S. weather, natural disasters, and accidents.	Includes the arts, religion, scholarship, communications media, sports, entertainments, fashions, fads and social life.

	World Affairs	Europe	Africa & the Middle East	The Americas	Asia & the Pacific
April 3			Before his meetings in Washington with Pres. Carter, Egyptian Pres. Anwar Sadat says that all Arab states favor official relations between a proposed new Palestinian state and Jordan, and he defends the Palestine National Council's decision not to change its charter to permit recognition of Israel.... Col. Joachim Yombi Opango is named president of the Congo, succeeding the late Pres. Marien Ngouabi, who was assassinated on March 18.		
April 4			Syrian forces enter into Lebanese fighting, providing artillery support for the opening of a major Palestinian counterattack against the Christian forces.... Zaire breaks diplomatic ties with Cuba, charging Cuban support in the Shaba invasion.	Carlos Prio Soccarras, 74, Cuba's last constitutionally elected president (1948–52), dies of a self-inflicted gunshot wound in Miami, Fla.	
April 5		U.S. Amb. to the U.N. Andrew Young creates a controversy in Great Britain when he says, in a BBC interview, that Britain had institutionalized racism more than any other country in Earth's history.	Congo Pres. Joachim Yombi Opango suspends the country's four-year-old Constitution and names a new Cabinet.... Palestinians claim that their guerrillas shelled roads inside Israel to shut off supply routes into Christian-held territory in southern Lebanon with no reports of Israeli counterfire.	Canadian P.M. Pierre Trudeau denounces the Quebec white paper seeking to establish French as the official language of the province.... Ecuadoran military govt. announces that the transfer to civilian rule, scheduled for January 1978, will be delayed.	
April 6	IMF sells 524,800 ounces of gold at an average of $149.18 an ounce.	A group is created in the Soviet republic of Armenia to monitor compliance with the 1975 Helsinki accords on human rights.	Zaire govt. reports a lull in Shaba fighting as the rebel FNLC prepares to attack Kolwezi after consolidating its hold in the occupied areas near the Angolan border.... Congo's new military government dissolves the National Assembly and suspends all local government administrators.		Australian New South Wales state govt. proposes subsidizing the building of private solar energy plants and incorporating solar energy plants into any new government building in remote areas.
April 7		The West German chief federal prosecutor Siegfried Buback and his driver are shot to death in Karlsruhe en route to Buback's office.	South African P.M. John Vorster rejects a joint Western compromise plan on the future of Namibia, which is now administered by South Africa in defiance of a 1966 U.N. resolution terminating its mandate.	Democratic Sens. George McGovern and James Abourezk, both from South Dakota, and Rep. Les Aspin(D, Wis.) accompany a college basketball team to Cuba and meet with Cuban Defense Min. Raul Castro to discuss ways to improve U.S.–Cuban relations.	Indian Home Min. Charan Singh announces in Parliament that the government will establish a judicial court to investigate all abuse of power charges against the former government of Indira Gandhi during its 21-month emergency rule.
April 8	U.S. Amb. Andrew Young's remarks about British racism spark lively debates among U.N. delegates. Mauritius Amb. Radha Krishna Ramphul cites his own experiences as a 30-year resident in Britain to give Young's charges credence.	Czech govt. imposes strict censorship on foreign journalists in retaliation for their coverage of Charter 77 activities.	Israeli Premier Yitzhak Rabin resigns as his ruling Labor Party's candidate for a second term in upcoming May 17 elections after admitting that he lied about keeping an illegal personal bank account in the U.S.	Canadian P.M. Pierre Trudeau and his wife Margaret reportedly have agreed to a 90-day trial separation.	Four leading members of P.M. Zulfikar Ali Bhutto's ruling Pakistan People's Party (PPP) resign to form a new party, — the Pakistan People's Democratic Party.
April 9		West German police charge the slaying of chief federal prosecutor Siegfried Buback was planned by Siegfried Haag, a former defense lawyer for the terrorist Baader–Meinhof gang.... Spain legalizes its Communist Party, ending a 1939 ban imposed by the late Generalissimo Francisco Franco.	A Moroccan contingent of 1,500 troops flies to Kinshasa, Zaire in French transport planes to help the government resist insurgent forces, which had pushed to within 50 miles of Kolwezi after the fall of the Zaire army command center at Mutshatsha.	Sen. George McGovern (D,S.D.) and Rep. Les Aspin (D,Wis.) meet with Fidel Castro outside of Havana. Afterward Castro tells reporters that the U.S. is torn between the idealism of Pres. Carter and the realism of the country.	A U.S. delegation, including Pres. Carter's son, Chip Carter arrives in China on a goodwill visit to Peking, Hangchow, and Shanghai.

A	B	C	D	E
Includes developments that affect more than one world region, international organizations and important meetings of major world leaders.	Includes all domestic and regional developments in Europe, including the Soviet Union, Turkey, Cyprus and Malta.	Includes all domestic and regional developments in Africa and the Middle East, including Iraq and Iran and excluding Cyprus, Turkey and Afghanistan.	Includes all domestic and regional developments in Latin America, the Caribbean and Canada.	Includes all domestic and regional developments in Asia and Pacific nations, extending from Afghanistan through all the Pacific Islands, except Hawaii.

U.S. Politics & Social Issues	U.S. Foreign Policy & Defense	U.S. Economy & Environment	Science, Technology & Nature	Culture, Leisure & Life Style	
	In face of varying official opinions on the outcome of the Carter–Gromyko arms-limitation talks, State Secy. Vance acknowledges the possibility of some administration miscalculations.			Danny Edwards wins first place in the Greater Greensboro (N.C.) Open, his first victory in three years of touring with the PGA.	April 3
Supreme Ct. rules, 7–1, that federal prosecutors cannot appeal cases in which criminal defendants were acquitted by a trial judge following a jury deadlock.... A Gallup Poll finds increasing use of marijuana in the U.S., with people under 30 the most frequent users and only 5 percent of people over 50 having ever smoked it.	Pres. Carter meets Egyptian Pres. Anwar Sadat in Washington to discuss U.S. military and economic aid to Egypt and a Middle East peace settlement.	Esther Peterson is named special presidential assistant for consumer affairs, a post she held under Pres. Lyndon Johnson (1964–67).	Seventy people die in a Southern Airways DC-9 twin-engine jet crash in New Hope, Ga., in the wake of severe storm conditions.	A team of basketball players from the University of South Dakota and South Dakota State University begins a four-day competition tour of Cuba.	April 4
Handicapped people stage demonstrations and sit-ins at HEW Dept. Washington, D.C. headquarters and at regional offices throughout the U.S., demanding that HEW Secy. Joseph Califano sign regulations to implement a 1973 law that bars discrimination against the handicapped in federal-aid programs.		FRB announces that consumer installment credit posted its second largest increase on record in February, spurred by strong automotive sales.	Despite strong protests from the U.S., the West German govt. approves export licenses for blueprints of a pilot uranium-reprocessing plant and a demonstration uranium-enrichment plant to be built in Brazil.	Baseball's Texas Rangers suspend utility infielder Lenny Randle for 30 days and fine him $23,407 for a March 28 assault on manager Frank Lucchesi.	April 5
Pres. Carter signs the bill to reorganize the executive branch of the federal government.... Los Angeles Mayor Tom Bradley (D), the city's first black mayor, polls 59 percent of the vote in a nonpartisan primary election to win a second term in office.		Pres. Carter tells Congress that he seeks to establish a federal consumer protection agency to implement regulations and decisions rather than to make policy itself.	An earthquake registering 6.5 on the Richter scale hits Iran's mountainous western region, killing 352 people.... Tornadoes, heavy rains, and related flooding ravage seven states in the U.S. South and Appalachia, resulting in at least 40 deaths and property damage estimated at $275 million.	Airport 77 is the top-grossing film for the previous week.	April 6
John Kearney, a former supervisor in the FBI's N.Y.C. office, is indicted on charges that he supervised illegal surveillance activities in the FBI's efforts to find fugitive members of the Weather Underground during 1970–72.		Labor Dept. reports a wholesale price index rise of 1.1 percent in March, or 12.1 percent at an adjusted annual rate, the largest monthly increase since October 1975.	Pres. Carter signs a bill authorizing $100 million in emergency drought relief for Western and Plains states, the first installment of the administration's proposed $844-million program.	World Hockey Association (WHA) closes its 1976–77 season with the following standings: Houston Aeros have the best record, 50–24–6 and 106 points; Real Cloutier of the Quebec Nordiques has the scoring title with 66 goals and 75 assists for 141 points.	April 7
U.S. Customs officials estimate that between 27 and 30 planes loaded with marijuana currently cross the U.S.–Mexican border into the U.S. each day.			FDA warns that birth control pills can cause birth defects, tumors, blood clots, and, in women over 40, heart attacks.		April 8
Justice Dept. lawyers reportedly contend that alleged FBI illegal domestic surveillance practices are more serious than those used by the CIA and also argue that some of those activities occurred after a definite Supreme Ct. decision on their illegality.		USWA accepts a three-year contract, setting the hourly wage increase over the life of the contract at about 90 cents.	Pres. Carter declares disaster areas in three Alabama counties that were hit by tornadoes and floods, killing 20 people.		April 9

F	G	H	I	J
Includes elections, federal-state relations, civil rights and liberties, crime, the judiciary, education, health care, poverty, urban affairs and population.	Includes formation and debate of U.S. foreign and defense policies, veterans' affairs and defense spending. (Relations with specific foreign countries are usually found under the region concerned.)	Includes business, labor, agriculture, taxation, transportation, consumer affairs, monetary and fiscal policy, natural resources, and pollution.	Includes worldwide scientific, medical and technological developments, natural phenomena, U.S. weather, natural disasters, and accidents.	Includes the arts, religion, scholarship, communications media, sports, entertainments, fashions, fads and social life.

	World Affairs	Europe	Africa & the Middle East	The Americas	Asia & the Pacific
April 10	The U.S. seizes the second of two Soviet fishing vessels off the New England coast for violating the 200-mile fishing limit, which became effective on March 1.	French govt. discloses that it has sent 11 military planes to Morocco to airlift troops to Zaire, calling Zaire the victim of armed subversive activities.	Israeli Labor Party nominates Defense Min. Shimon Peres as its candidate in upcoming elections.		Three leftist parties merge into a new Socialist Front in Sri Lanka.
April 11	British For. Secy. David Owen begins a week-long tour of southern Africa to attempt to renew British–U.S. efforts for a peaceful transfer of power to the Rhodesian black majority.	Malta establishes full diplomatic ties with Cuba.		Money amounting to $17 million extorted by Argentine left-wing guerrillas, the Montoneros, in various kidnappings reportedly was invested in a wide range of commercial enterprises by the Graiver family who paid the Montoneros monthly dividends ranging from $145,000 to $175,000.	Chinese officials detail political factionalism starting in Hangchow in 1972 and becoming worse in 1975 through 1976 and charge that the Gang of Four had fomented strife by gaining political control of the city and province. . . . Laotian troops recapture the Mekong River island of Xieng Xu seized by rebels in late March. . . . The ruling Janata Party forms a government in India's Gujarat State following the collapse of the Congress Party majority there.
April 12			Zaire reportedly is receiving $13 million in U.S. non-lethal military equipment in addition to $2 million in aid sent in March.		
April 13		A goup calling itself the Ulrike Meinhof Commando claims responsibility for Siegfried Buback's murder, holding him directly accountable for the deaths in prison of three terrorists, including Ulrike Meinhof who committed suicide in prison in May 1976.	Forces of rival Palestinian groups clash briefly in the Moslem section of Beirut.		Australian federal and six state governments ask all Australians to accept a wage–price freeze for the next three months.
April 14	In a policy reversal, the U.S. says it will be willing to serve as co-sponsor with Britain of a new Rhodesian conference.	Spanish army issues a statement strongly condemning legalization of the Spanish Communist Party (PCE).	After talks with Botswanian pres. Sir Seretse Khama, British For. Secy. David Owen states his opposition to a proposed referendum among Rhodesia's blacks to choose a leader before a constitution is written.	Pres. Ernesto Geisel tightens military rule in Brazil making it virtually impossible for the opposition Brazilian Democratic Movement (MSB) to gain power through elections.	Japanese–Soviet fishing talks over rights to four disputed Soviet-held Islands in the Kurile chain collapse.
April 15			British For. Secy. David Owen arrives in Salisbury, the first top-level British official to visit Rhodesia since former For. Secy. Sir Alec Douglas-Home in 1971.		The fifth volume of the late Mao Tse-tung's *Selected Works* is published in China.
April 16			A shipment of about 30 Soviet T-34 tanks and 30 armored personnel carriers, artillery, and light arms are reported arriving in Ethiopia.		Japanese Premier Takeo Fukuda says that Japan will not prejudice its claim to the Kurile chain of islands to secure a fishry agreement with the Soviet Union.
April 17	UNCTAD reports that some $10 billion in freight revenues annually are eluding the fiscal controls of countries providing shipping flags of convenience.	Premier Leo Tindemans's Christian Social Party registers substantial gains in Belgian general elections.	Leah Rabin, wife of the Israeli premier, is fined $27,000 for holding $21,000 in a Washington, D.C. bank account.		A Philippine plebiscite rejects a government proposal to grant autonomy to 13 provinces, part of a plan reached in Tripoli, Libya to end the rebellion of the Moslem Moro National Liberation Front (MNLF). . . . P.M. Zulfikar Ali Bhutto announces legal and social reforms aimed at ending the political crisis arising from the March 7 reelection of his governing Pakistan People's Party (PPP)

A	B	C	D	E
Includes developments that affect more than one world region, international organizations and important meetings of major world leaders.	Includes all domestic and regional developments in Europe, including the Soviet Union, Turkey, Cyprus and Malta.	Includes all domestic and regional developments in Africa and the Middle East, including Iraq and Iran and excluding Cyprus, Turkey and Afghanistan.	Includes all domestic and regional developments in Latin America, the Caribbean and Canada.	Includes all domestic and regional developments in Asia and Pacific nations, extending from Afghanistan through all the Pacific Islands, except Hawaii.

U.S. Politics & Social Issues	U.S. Foreign Policy & Defense	U.S. Economy & Environment	Science, Technology & Nature	Culture, Leisure & Life Style	
	State Dept. discloses that during his historic 1972 visit to China, then Pres. Nixon pledged to the late Premier Chou En-lai that he would seek normal U.S. ties with China, but that the pledge was not implemented because of the Watergate scandal.			Tom Watson wins the forty-first Masters golf tournament in Augusta, Ga.	April 10
Ernest Boyer, commissioner of education, announces reorganization of the HEW Office of Education.	Sen. George McGovern (D,S.D.) says, after returning to Washington from Cuba, that Cuban Premier Castro had insisted on the repeal of the U.S. trade embargo as a condition for renewing the Cuba — U.S. 1973 antihijacking agreement.	The Japanese-made Honda captures third place in the U.S. auto import market during the first three months of 1977, displacing the West German-made Volkswagen . Toyota and Nissan , both Japanese-made, rank first and second.	Investigation of the March 27 collision of two Boeing 747 jumbo jets in the Canary Islands indicates that one of the pilots of the KLM Royal Dutch Airlines jet expressed doubts that the runway had been cleared less than 30 seconds before its collision into the Pan Am 747, which was taxiing down the strip.	National Book Awards are announced including the following: *World of Our Fathers* by Irving Howe; *The Spectator Bird* by Wallace Stegner; *Collected Poems 1930–1976* by Richard Eberhart, and *The Uses of Enchantment* by Bruno Bettelheim.	April 11
Pres. Carter commutes the 20-year prison sentence of G. Gordon Liddy, one of the original Watergate burglary defendants.		U.S. Customs Ct., N.Y.C., orders countervailing duties on imports of Japanese consumer electronics to offset tax rebates provided to Japanese manufacturers by the Japanese govt.	Approximately 300 Haitian children are reported to have starved to death as a result of a serious drought in the country's northwest region, the first such famine despite annual dry spells.	Philip Wrigley, 82, chewing gum magnate and owner of the Chicago Cubs baseball team, dies in Elkhorn, Wis. with an estate estimated at over $60 million.	April 12
	U.S. govt. officials are reported to be cautious about sending military aid to Zaire, fearing a repeat of the U.S. experience in Vietnam and reflecting the growing belief that the U.S. should avoid African conflicts so that the Soviet Union does not have an excuse to intervene.	AFL–CIO pres. George Meany leads a delegation of labor leaders meeting with Pres. Carter to seek clothing and textile import curbs.	A 41-nation conference on nuclear energy in Persepolis, Iran assails U.S. Pres. Jimmy Carter's nuclear energy policy which is based on the restriction of fast-breeder reactor development.	An antipornography rally at N.Y.C.'s Times Square attracts participants from the casts of over 25 Broadway shows.	April 13
About 300 FBI agents demonstrate at the federal courthouse in N.Y.C. in support of John Kearney, the FBI agent pleading not guilty to an indictment charging that he supervised illegal FBI surveillance activities, the first such indictment of an FBI agent.		Pres. Carter drops his plan to provide a $50 individual tax rebate and tax benefits for businesses, citing an economic upturn in the country.	FDA modifies its proposed saccharin ban to allow the artificial sweetener to remain on the market for limited use as a nonprescription drug, but be prohibited in commercially prepared foods and beverages.	N.Y.C. Tax commission denies Rev. Sun Myung Moon's Unification Church tax-exempt status for three pieces of church-owned property valued at $2.6 million.	April 14
HEW Dept. report finds that in May 1975 families on welfare were smaller, did not live in a major city, and stayed on welfare for a longer period of time.		Pres. Carter outlines a coordinated program to combat inflation, seeking a 4 percent level by late 1979.	Pres. Carter presents the Tyler Ecology Award to University of Georgia Prof. Eugene Odum.	NBC is reported canceling its scheduled May 15 telecast of the Emmy Awards, reacting to a bitter conflict between Los Angeles-based and N.Y.C-based members of the academy.	April 15
		East Coast longshoremen strike over a jobs issue involving containerized cargo.			April 16
			Richard Brauer, 76, pioneer in developing algebraic theory and head of the Harvard University mathematics department (1959–63), dies in Belmont, Mass.		April 17

F	G	H	I	J
Includes elections, federal-state relations, civil rights and liberties, crime, the judiciary, education, health care, poverty, urban affairs and population.	Includes formation and debate of U.S. foreign and defense policies, veterans' affairs and defense spending. (Relations with specific foreign countries are usually found under the region concerned.)	Includes business, labor, agriculture, taxation, transportation, consumer affairs, monetary and fiscal policy, natural resources, and pollution.	Includes worldwide scientific, medical and technological developments, natural phenomena, U.S. weather, natural disasters, and accidents.	Includes the arts, religion, scholarship, communications media, sports, entertainments, fashions, fads and social life.

	World Affairs	Europe	Africa & the Middle East	The Americas	Asia & the Pacific
April 18	Fifty-two journalists and government officials participate in a two-day conference in Florence, Italy on the flow of information between developed and developing countries.		The ruling Rhodesian Front gives P.M. Ian Smith full power to negotiate a constitutional settlement for black majority rule.... Finance ministers and central bankers from 20 Arab states and the PLO formally create the Arab Monetary Fund.	Canadian P.M. Pierre Trudeau begins trips to Manitoba and Saskatchewan provinces to appeal for Canadian unity in face of the separatist threat posed by Quebec's provincial government.	Indian govt. announces impounding the passports of Sanjay Gandhi and former Defense Min. Bansi Lal while their financial dealings are under investigation.
April 19		The European Court of Human Rights in Strasbourg, France begins hearings on torture charges brought by the Irish govt. against Great Britain.	Israel hands over 28 Arab terrorist prisoners to Egypt in return for the bodies of nine Israeli soldiers killed in the 1973 war and the remains of two Egyptian Jews who had been hanged as spies in Cairo in 1955.	Argentine Pres. Jorge Videla confirms that the Graivers had handled money for the Montoneros.	Over 180 people are reported killed in bloody demonstrations since the Pakistan National Alliance (PNA) began its protests of fraudulent elections that kept P.M. Bhutto's govt. in power.
April 20			Beginning a two-day French–African summit in Dakar, Pres. Leopold Sedar Senghor of Senegal calls for a joint African defense force to protect African States against foreign intervention.	Jack Horner, a key figure in the Canadian opposition Progressive Conservative Party, leaves office to join the ruling Liberals in the House of Commons after P.M. Pierre Trudeau offers him a Cabinet post.	
April 21			U.S. State Dept. reports that it turned down a request by Zaire Pres. Mobutu Sese Seko to include 16,000 cases of Coca-Cola in its military assistance package to Zaire.	Canadian Institute of Public Opinion poll finds that more Canadians believe there has been an increase in the country's racial tensions over the previous year.	Gen. Chalard Hiranyasiri is executed for his attempt to overthrow the Thai government in March.... Pres. Zulfikar Ali Bhutto assumes emergency powers and imposes martial law in Pakistan's three major cities.... Gen. Ziaur Rahman is sworn in as president of Bangladesh following the resignation of Abu Sadat Mohammed Sayem for health reasons.
April 22			Israeli Premier Yitzhak Rabin takes an extended leave of absence and turns over the duties of his office to Defense Min. Shimon Peres.	Arrests in March of Uruguay military officers critical of the government spark political debate within the armed forces, according to the *Latin American Political Report*.	Forty people are killed in politically motivated clashes throughout Pakistan, the worst day of the six-week-old crisis.
April 23	Venezuelan Pres. Carlos Andres Perez stops in Kuwait as part of his two-week tour of seven mideast oil-producing nations to attempt to negotiate an end to the OPEC oil-price dispute.		Ethiopian govt. closes five U.S. offices there as well as five other foreign consulates and orders U.S. personnel and dependents to leave the country by April 27.		
April 24	The twenty-fifth Bilderberg conference, representing nearly 100 of North America's and Europe's most influential people, concludes its three-day meeting in Torquay, England. Its three major topics were the future of mixed economies in Western democracies, U.S.–European relations, and Western relations with underdeveloped countries.	Three senior officers of the Swiss Credit Bank are arrested for complicity in the loss of up to $100 million disbursed in unauthorized loans.		In a series of left-wing guerrilla attacks since the end of March, unidentified guerrillas ambush an army patrol in Taraza, Colombia, killing two soldiers, wounding 15, and stealing arms and equipment from their victims.	

A	B	C	D	E
Includes developments that affect more than one world region, international organizations and important meetings of major world leaders.	Includes all domestic and regional developments in Europe, including the Soviet Union, Turkey, Cyprus and Malta.	Includes all domestic and regional developments in Africa and the Middle East, including Iraq and Iran and excluding Cyprus, Turkey and Afghanistan.	Includes all domestic and regional developments in Latin America, the Caribbean and Canada.	Includes all domestic and regional developments in Asia and Pacific nations, extending from Afghanistan through all the Pacific Islands, except Hawaii.

U.S. Politics & Social Issues	U.S. Foreign Policy & Defense	U.S. Economy & Environment	Science, Technology & Nature	Culture, Leisure & Life Style	
Patricia Hearst, newspaper heiress who was kidnapped by the Symbionese Liberation Army (SLA) in 1974, pleads no contest in Los Angeles Superior Ct. to charges of armed robbery and assault with a deadly weapon.		Volume on the nation's 10 commodity exchanges reportedly soared a record 67.5 percent during March, when 4.2 million futures contracts were traded, compared with 2.5 million year earlier.	Soviet Jewish scientists begin an unofficial three-day symposium.	Pulitzer Prizes are award to Michael Cristofer for *The Shadow Box* (drama); James Merrill for *Divine Comedies* (poetry), John E. Mack for *A Prince of Our Disorder: The Life of T.E. Lawrence* (biography); and posthumously to David Potter for *The Impending Crisis* (history). . . . Alex Haley is awarded a special Pulitzer Prize for his best-selling book *Roots*, called an important contribution to the literature of slavery. . . . The Boston Marathon is won by Canadian Jerome Brayton in 2 hours, 14 minutes, 46 seconds. Miki Gorman is the top woman runner, finishing en 2 hours, 48 minutes, and 44 seconds.	April 18
Supreme Ct. rules, 5–4, that school officials can spank students without violating students' constitutional rights.	Adm. James Holloway says that unionization is a real threat to the Navy.		Canada delays its saccharin ban in response to requests by food and beverage manufacturers.	Twelve U.S. Protestant and Roman Catholic leaders ask Pres. Carter to intervene on behalf of South Korean dissident Christians.	April 19
Supreme Ct. rules, 7–2, that a state cannot force an automobile owner to display an ideological message on his license plate, in a case stemming from a challenge to N.H.'s state motto, "Live Free or Die".	House approves, 364–43, a bill to ban U.S. participation in the Arab boycott of Israel, but the bill does not attempt to break the Arab League's direct boycott of Israel.	Pres. Carter presents his comprehensive energy policy to Congress with the goal of switching the U.S. from depending on oil to reviving the use of coal and, eventually, renewable energy sources, such as solar power.		William Paley, a broadcasting pioneer, announces his retirement as CBS chief executive.	April 20
		House, by voice vote, establishes a 40-member Ad Hoc Select Committee on Energy.	West German Chancellor Helmut Schmidt says that his government rejects U.S. efforts to stop the sale of sensitive atomic technology abroad.	*Annie*, a musical based on Harold Gray's comic strip *Little Orphan Annie*, opens on Broadway.	April 21
		Congress clears a $28.9-billion supplemental appropriations bill for fiscal 1977, the largest such measure since WWII.		Novelists Margaret Walker Alexander and Harold Courlander charge that Alex Haley had plagiarized passages from their novels *Jubilee* and *The African*, respectively, for use in his extremely successful best-selling novel, *Roots*	April 22
		At the closing session of the ILGWU's biennial convention, Seattle, Wash., candidates are named to vie for the post of president, vacated by the retirement of the union's founder, Harry Bridges, who served as president for 40 years.			April 23
Delegate Walter Fauntroy (D,D.C.), chairman of the House subcommittee investigating the assassination of Martin Luther King Jr., charges that some reporters covering the committee are linked to the CIA and, consequently, oppose the investigation.				David Rabe's *The Basic Training of Pavlo Hummel* is revived on Broadway with Al Pacino in the title role.	April 24

F	G	H	I	J
Includes elections, federal-state relations, civil rights and liberties, crime, the judiciary, education, health care, poverty, urban affairs and population.	Includes formation and debate of U.S. foreign and defense policies, veterans' affairs and defense spending. (Relations with specific foreign countries are usually found under the region concerned.)	Includes business, labor, agriculture, taxation, transportation, consumer affairs, monetary and fiscal policy, natural resources, and pollution.	Includes worldwide scientific, medical and technological developments, natural phenomena, U.S. weather, natural disasters, and accidents.	Includes the arts, religion, scholarship, communications media, sports, entertainments, fashions, fads and social life.

	World Affairs	Europe	Africa & the Middle East	The Americas	Asia & the Pacific
April 25		Spanish Premier Adolfo Suarez confirms his intention to run for a seat in the lower house of the new national legislature. Public opinion polls show that Suarez is the most popular political leader in Spain. . . . A Yugoslav ct. reportedly rejects a petition by 60 intellectuals challenging the government's right to deny passports to Yugoslav citizens.	Zaire army, backed by Moroccan troops, retakes its former command center of Mutshatsha from FNLC rebels.		Vietnamese Premier Pham Van Dong begins a state visit to France, his first visit to a Western nation since the Vietnamese war ended in 1975.
April 26	U.N. petroleum experts issue a report indicating the probable availability of oil and natural gas resources at substantially higher than current costs for as long as 100 years.		Syrian troops of the Arab League peacekeeping force clash with Palestinian guerrillas and Lebanese Moslems in the Moslem section of Beirut, with an estimated 40–80 people killed.		
April 27	Pres. Carter proposes that all exports of nuclear technology to countries currently without nuclear weapons be subject to IAEA safeguards and that no U.S. exports would go to countries that do not submit to international controls.		Israel echoes Pres. Carter and Jordanian King Hussein on the need for adequate preparations before reconvening the Geneva Mideast peace conference.	The National University, Bogota, Colombia closes for two weeks following repeated student disturbances.	Australian P.M. Malcolm Fraser says that his government will investigate allegations that the U.S. CIA is infiltrating Australian labor unions and supressing strikes.
April 28	Saudi Arabia says it will not raise its oil prices to conform to those of other OPEC members.	The three surviving leaders of the urban guerrilla W. Ger. Baader-Meinhof gang are sentenced to life imprisonment for the 1972 murder of four U.S. soldiers in Frankfurt and Heidelberg bomb attacks.		Ninety-one companies are reported moving their headquarters out of Quebec, Canada between November 1976, when the separatist govt. was elected, and February 1977.	France's Ekl-Aquitaine group signs a preliminary agreement with Vietnam to explore for offshore oil deposits.
April 29	An IMF panel agrees in principle to establish a temporary and supplementary loan facility to assist countries with balance-of-payments deficits.	West Berlin Mayor Klaus Schultz resigns, citing scandal within his administration.	South African P.M. John Vorster reports progress on a compromise solution for the independence of South-West Africa (Namibia).	French Gaullist Mayor of Paris Jacques Chirac endorses the Quebec independence movement.	Saudi Arabian and United Arab Emirates representatives meet with imprisoned leaders of the opposition Pakistan National Alliance (PNA) to try to settle Pakistan's seven-week-old political crisis.
April 30		An offshore Norwegian oil well in the North Sea is capped after blowing out of control for eight days, spilling an estimated 8.2 million gallons of crude oil.			Leadership of Pakistan's opposition PNA party announces plans for a peaceful march to press demands for Pres. Zulfikar Ali Bhutto's resignation.
May 1		Thirty-eight people are killed and about 200 wounded in a giant May Day rally that turns into a gun battle in Istanbul, Turkey.	Israeli authorities reportedly have banned U.S. Jewish Defense League leader Rabbi Meir Kahane from visiting the West Bank.	Eight die and 16 people are wounded in San Salvador, El Salvador during May Day clashes between security forces and demonstrating workers and peasants.	China invites the Dalai Lama to return to Tibet from his exile in India with the stipulation that he accept Chinese Communist authority.
May 2					The New York Times reports harsh conditions plaguing Cambodia, including crop failure, hunger, and disease. The Communists' program to evacuate Cambodia's cities has culminated in enforced collectivization of farms into village-wide cooperatives.

A	B	C	D	E
Includes developments that affect more than one world region, international organizations and important meetings of major world leaders.	Includes all domestic and regional developments in Europe, including the Soviet Union, Turkey, Cyprus and Malta.	Includes all domestic and regional developments in Africa and the Middle East, including Iraq and Iran and excluding Cyprus, Turkey and Afghanistan.	Includes all domestic and regional developments in Latin America, the Caribbean and Canada.	Includes all domestic and regional developments in Asia and Pacific nations, extending from Afghanistan through all the Pacific Islands, except Hawaii.

U.S. Politics & Social Issues	U.S. Foreign Policy & Defense	U.S. Economy & Environment	Science, Technology & Nature	Culture, Leisure & Life Style	
Supreme Ct. refuses to hear an appeal by murder-cultist Charles Manson and by convicted Tex. murderer Robert Excell White.	House of Representatives passes, 347–43, legislation for a $35.9-billion weapons procurement and for military research and development in fiscal 1978.	Republican national leaders suggest that Pres. Carter's proposed energy conservation taxes are a disguised general tax increase to finance welfare reform and help the President fulfill his commitment to balance the budget.		NBA referees end their 15-day strike. . . . Bantam Books Inc. announces it will reissue two novels — *Jubilee* and *The African* — whose authors charge were plagiarized by Alex Haley in his best-seller *Roots* .	April 25
In two separate decisions, the Supreme Ct. votes, 4–3, 6–3, to back the rights of illegitimate children.			FDA announces that it will require all food, drug, and cosmetic containers using fluorocarbon to be labeled with the warning that they pose a danger to public health and to the environment by reducing ozone in the upper atmosphere. . . . The first instant color motion picture system, capable of processing film in 90 seconds and projecting it on a screen, is displayed by the Polaroid Corp.	FCC announces it has increased the cash penalties for violations on citizens' band (CB) radios.	April 26
Supreme Ct. rules, 6–3, that states must provide their prison inmates with adequate legal assistance.	Christopher Boyce, on trial for espionage in the U.S., testifies in a Los Angeles court that he had seen CIA data showing that the CIA was infiltrating Australian labor unions.	U.S. registers a record trade deficit in March with imports exceeding exports by $2.39 billion.	Japan establishes its first fast-breeder experimental nuclear reactor.	Woody Allen's film *Annie Hall* is the fifth top-grossing film for the week just ended.	April 27
HEW Dept. Secy. Joseph Califano Jr, signs regulations implementing a 1973 law banning discrimination against handicapped people in federally funded programs.	Christopher Boyce is found guilty by a U.S. District Ct. in Los Angeles of transmitting U.S. defense secrets to the Soviets while he worked for TRW Systems Inc.				April 28
		The government's composite index of leading economic indicators advances 1.4 percent in March, the largest rise since July 1975.		Following a 90-minute audience with Pope Paul VI, the Archbishop of Canterbury, Dr. Frederick Donald Coggan, appeals for intercommunion — that the sacrament of communion can be given by Roman Catholic priests to Anglicans and vice versa — as a step toward unification of the two church bodies.	April 29
	State Secy. Vance says that the U.S. human-rights stance should be realistic and keep within the limits of our power and wisdom.		About 2,000 demonstrators move into the construction site of a Seabrook, N.H. nuclear power generating plant, vowing to occupy the site until building plans are abandoned.		April 30
				U.S. Davis Cup tennis team loses to Argentina, their fourth consecutive defeat in American Zone play. . . . The Archbishop of Canterbury, Dr. Frederick Donald Coggan, and the Orthodox Ecumenical Patriarch Dimitrios I meet in Istanbul, Turkey and openly dispute the ordination of women to the priesthood. . . . *Oliver's Story* by Erich Segal, a sequel to his immenseley popular *Love Story*, heads the fiction best-selling list for the previous week.	May 1
Pres. Carter outlines his welfare reform goals, calling for a totally new system.	Sen. Frank Church (D, Ida.) calls Pres. Carter's nuclear policy a formula for nuclear isolationism that would reduce U.S. influence in shaping worldwide nuclear policy.	Pres. Carter tells congressional Democratic leaders that a balanced budget by 1981 is his topmost priority.	Florida, preceded the previous day by Indiana, legalizes laetrile, an alleged anticancer agent banned by the FDA.	Basketball Hall of Fame inducts five new members: Elgin Baylor, Charles Cooper, Frank McGuire, William (Skinny) Johnson, and Lauren (Laddie) Gale.	May 2

F	G	H	I	J
Includes elections, federal-state relations, civil rights and liberties, crime, the judiciary, education, health care, poverty, urban affairs and population.	*Includes formation and debate of U.S. foreign and defense policies, veterans' affairs and defense spending. (Relations with specific foreign countries are usually found under the region concerned.)*	*Includes business, labor, agriculture, taxation, transportation, consumer affairs, monetary and fiscal policy, natural resources, and pollution.*	*Includes worldwide scientific, medical and technological developments, natural phenomena, U.S. weather, natural disasters, and accidents.*	*Includes the arts, religion, scholarship, communications media, sports, entertainments, fashions, fads and social life.*

	World Affairs	Europe	Africa & the Middle East	The Americas	Asia & the Pacific
May 3		The Labor Party loses 130 seats in Scotland's municipal elections.	Libyan leader Muammer el-Qaddafi expels 225,000 Egyptians working in Libya, effective July 1, in wake of increasing Egyptian–Libyan tensions throughout the previous month.	About 60,000 students at five separate Brazilian universities strike to protest the arrest of four students and four workers in Sao Paulo on May 1 for distributing allegedly subversive pamphlets.	U.S. and Vietnam formally open the first round of their negotiations in Paris on normalizing relations. The U.S. pledges not to veto Hanoi's admission to the U.N. and to lift its trade embargo, and Vietnam says it will provide information on MIAs.
May 4	Saudi Arabian Finance Min. Muhammad Ali Abdul-Khail balks at contributing $4-billion to the IMF's temporary lending facility, the figure expected to make the plan a success. He contends that Saudi Arabia (the richest of the OPEC nations) is really poor because its assets are only money, not wealth derived from a developed economy.		Two Arabs die and four are wounded by Israeli troops during riots in the occupied West Bank.	The Argentinian army announces that its investigation proves that David Graiver had an illicit association with the Montoneros guerrillas, investing at least $12 million for them.	Victor Marchetti, a former U.S. CIA officer, claims in an interview that the CIA had funded the Liberal and National Country parties in Australia for approximately 10 years and also had funded operations to undermine the Australian Labor Party.
May 5		Ludwig Erhard, 80, West German economics minister and chancellor who is credited with masterminding W. Germany's postwar economic recovery, dies of heart failure in Bonn.	Syrian Pres. Hafez al-Assad tells a Damascus news conference that he is prepared to accept demilitarized zones as part of a Mideast peace settlement, modifying his previous stipulation that Israel return to its pre-1967 borders.		Australian P.M. Malcolm Fraser announces the immediate reorganization of the country's intelligence and security services.... Pakistan govt. seizes most of the 27 members of the Pakistan National Alliance (PNA) general council who are still at large.
May 6			Ethiopian head of state Mengistu Haile Mariam signs a treaty of friendship and cooperation with the Soviet Union.		
May 7	Leaders of the seven major non-Communist industrialized countries meet in London for a two-day economic summit conference.	French Pres. Valery Giscard d'Estaing arrives one day late at the London economic summit conference to protest the presence of EC pres. Roy Jenkins, who is British.		Left-wing terrorists shoot and seriously wound Argentinian For. Min. Cesar Guzzetti at a Buenos Aires private medical clinic when he arrived for his weekly checkup.	
May 8	At the economic summit conference, leaders of the stronger industrialized countries set the following economic growth targets: 5.8–6 percent in the U.S.; 5 percent in West Germany; 6–7 percent for Japan.		Voters in the French Territory of Afars and Issas (Djibouti) vote overwhelmingly to become independent on June 27 after 115 years as a French colony.	Brazilian Roman Catholic Cardinal Paulo Evaristo Arns criticizes the May Day arrests of students and workers.	Over 400 people are injured and 33 arrested in demonstrations opposing the opening of Tokyo's new airport.
May 9	Venezuelan Pres. Carlos Andres Perez makes a new appeal for uniform OPEC oil prices, warning that OPEC's unity is endangered.	A private meeting between Pres. Carter and French Pres. Valery Giscard D'Estaing ends in apparent mutual respect and accord.	Pres. Carter meets with Syrian Pres. Hafez al-Assad in Geneva to discuss prospects for resolving the Arab–Israeli dispute, and praises Assad as one of the moderate leaders in the Middle East.	U.S. and Panamanian officials meet for the second round of talks on a new Panama Canal Treaty.	
May 10		In a demonstration of France's independence from its NATO allies, Pres. Giscard d'Estaing does not attend the opening session of the London NATO conference.	Saudi Arabian Crown Prince Fahd repeats a proposal, reportedly also submitted by Syrian Pres. Hafez al-Assad, that creation of a Palestinian state in the Israeli-occupied West Bank and Gaza Strip be part of an overall peace settlement.	Left-wing El Salvadoran guerrillas kill For. Min. Mauricio Borgonovo Pohl, kidnapped on April 19, after the government refuses to negotiate with them.	
May 11		A wave of strikes in Finland, begun in March, ends when the Central Federation of Technical Unions accepts the state arbitrator's compromise proposal.	U.S. State Secy. Vance assures Israeli For. Min. Yigal Allon that the U.S. will continue its special relationship with Israel and send arms and advanced technology to ensure Israeli security.		

A	B	C	D	E
Includes developments that affect more than one world region, international organizations and important meetings of major world leaders.	Includes all domestic and regional developments in Europe, including the Soviet Union, Turkey, Cyprus and Malta.	Includes all domestic and regional developments in Africa and the Middle East, including Iraq and Iran and excluding Cyprus, Turkey and Afghanistan.	Includes all domestic and regional developments in Latin America, the Caribbean and Canada.	Includes all domestic and regional developments in Asia and Pacific nations, extending from Afghanistan through all the Pacific Islands, except Hawaii.

U.S. Politics & Social Issues	U.S. Foreign Policy & Defense	U.S. Economy & Environment	Science, Technology & Nature	Culture, Leisure & Life Style	
		Congress clears legislation authorizing $4 billion for public works, the first part of Pres. Carter's economic stimulus plan to get through Congress.	An estimated 631 people are being held in National Guard armories in three N.H. towns after being arrested for occupying the construction site of the Seabrook nuclear power plant.	NFL begins its two-day draft of college players, choosing 335 in 12 rounds. Heisman Trophy-winner Tony Dorsett is the most coveted player, and he signs with the Dallas Cowboys.	May 3
	House of Representatives votes, 266–131, to bar U.S. economic aid to Vietnam.	Pres. Carter refuses to limit sugar imports into the U.S., but agrees to aid the ailing domestic sugar industry by providing subsidies.	U.S. Geological survey reports that the prolonged water shortage in Calif. is the worst drought on record.	The National Council of Catholic Bishops votes, 231–8, to rescind a 930-year-old rule that automatically excommunicated divorced Roman Catholics who remarry without church approval.	May 4
	A former CIA employe, Edwin Moore II, is found guilty of attempting to sell classified U.S. intelligence material to the Soviet Union.	Consumer installment credit rises a record $2.72 billion in March, larger than its record expansion of February 1973.			May 5
In a reversal the FCC rules 4–3, that broadcast stations do not have to give political candidates the same access to air time that they give commercial advertisers.		The U.S. unemployment rate falls to 7 percent in April from 7.3 percent in March, with a record 90,023,000 persons employed.	FDA announces it will continue its ban on the importation and sale of laetrile, an alleged cure for cancer.		May 6
				The Kentucky Derby is won by *Seattle Slew* .	May 7
				Czechoslovakia retains its world ice hockey title because of a 3–1 Swedish victory over the Soviet Union, which pushed the Soviets from top final standings.	May 8
Pres. Carter urges a substantial increase in the Social Security taxes paid by employers, coupled with a lesser increase in employe tax contributions.		U.S. Steel Corp. announces an average 6 percent price increase for its sheet, strip, bar, and plate products, effective June 19.	Dr. Hannes Alfven, a Nobel-Prize winner and Swedish AEC member, tells an IAEA conference in Salzburg, Austria that nuclear energy should be abandoned. Another Nobel-Prize winner, Dr. Hans Bethe, contends that nuclear energy is a necessity, not an option.	Novelist James Jones, 55, whose first work, *From Here to Eternity*, about pre-WWII military life in Hawaii became a bestseller and successful film, dies of heart failure in Southampton, N.Y.	May 9
		Commerce Dept. reports that U.S. per capita income rose 9.1 percent in 1976 to $6,441.00.	National Cancer Institute issues more stringent guidelines for the use of mammograms (x-rays) to detect breast cancer because of fears of radiation hazards.	Legendary Hollywood movie star Joan Crawford, who also served as a director of the Pepsi-Cola Co., dies of a heart attack in N.Y.C. at the age of about 69.	May 10
NAACP Legal Defense Fund files suit in Federal District Ct., Wash., D.C. against the HEW Dept, charging HEW with abandoning attempts to desegragate Southern vocational schools and schools for the handicapped.	Sen. Foreign Relations Committee, on the initiative of member Jacob Javits (R, N.Y.), votes to give Pres. Carter authority to halt shipments to Cuba at any time.		U.S. District Ct. Judge Milton Pollack rules illegal the ban on Concorde supersonic transport service to Kennedy International Airport, N.Y.C.	Ken Norton, rated as the prime contender for the boxing heavyweight title, demolishes Duane Bobick in the first round of a scheduled 12-round fight at Madison Square Garden, N.Y.C.	May 11

F	G	H	I	J
Includes elections, federal-state relations, civil rights and liberties, crime, the judiciary, education, health care, poverty, urban affairs and population.	*Includes formation and debate of U.S. foreign and defense policies, veterans' affairs and defense spending. (Relations with specific foreign countries are usually found under the region concerned.)*	*Includes business, labor, agriculture, taxation, transportation, consumer affairs, monetary and fiscal policy, natural resources, and pollution.*	*Includes worldwide scientific, medical and technological developments, natural phenomena, U.S. weather, natural disasters, and accidents.*	*Includes the arts, religion, scholarship, communications media, sports, entertainments, fashions, fads and social life.*

	World Affairs	Europe	Africa & the Middle East	The Americas	Asia & the Pacific
May 12		Bulgarian CP ousts high-ranking member Boris Velchev.	After conferring with Ivory Coast Pres. Felix Houphouet-Boigny, U.S. U.N. Amb. Andrew Young defends U.S. caution on the recent invasion of Zaire, saying that African problems are best dealt with by Africans.		
May 13		Canadian P.M. Pierre Trudeau tells reporters in Paris that France should stay clear of the Quebec separatism issue.		Eskimo leaders file a revised land claim to 105,000 square miles of territory along the northern shores of the Northwestern and Yukon Territories.	The opposition Pakistan National Alliance (PNA) rejects P.M. Zulfikar Ali Bhutto's announced plans for a national referendum to decide whether he should remain in office.
May 14				Representatives of Catholic, Lutheran, and Methodist churches in Bolivia announce creating a Permanent Assembly on Human Rights to be headed by former Bolivian Pres. Luis Adolfo Siles Salinas.	Seoul authorities charge that two North Korean boats fired at a South Korean ship on May 10 after it had stopped them in South Korean waters.
May 15		Centrist Jean-Jacques Servan-Schreiber is elected president of the Radical Socialist Party, one of the participants of the French coalition govt.... Kalevi Sorsa, chairman of the Social Democratic Party, takes office in Finland and forms a new coalition govt.		*The New York Times* reports Argentinian turmoil over accounts of business scandals and over the morality campaign by right-wingers in which former Pres. Alejandro Lanusse was arrested, noting allegedly anti-Semitic elements in the investigations.	Gen. Yang Sen, one of the last of mainland China's legendary warlords who joined forces in the 1920's with Chiang Kai-shek, dies in his 90s of lung cancer in Taipei.
May 16	A six-day U.N. conference in Maputo, Mozambique in support of the nationalist movements in Rhodesia and Namibia (Zimbabwe and South-West Africa) is seen as a major effort to rally world support for black majority rule in southern Africa.		Christian sources report that their militiamen killed 27 Syrian soldiers from the Arab League Lebanese peacekeeping force in May 14–15 clashes in the village of Billa.... Zambian Pres. Kenneth Kaunda declares war on Rhodesia, responding to a Rhodesian warning that its troops might attack guerrilla camps inside Zambia.		
May 17	International Commission of Jurists (ICJ) criticizes the U.N. Human Rights Commission for not investigating alleged human-rights abuses in Uganda.	The NATO Military Committee issues a report saying that Soviet increased defense spending totaled over 4 percent a year and comprised 11–12 percent of the Soviet GNP.	The Israeli Labor Party — in power since the country's founding in 1948 — is narrowly defeated in a surprising election upset by the opposition right-wing Likud Party, which is led by Menahem Begin.		A former U.S. CIA operative, Philip Agee, is reported having indentified four officials of the U.S. Embassy in Canberra, Australia as CIA agents.
May 18		After a two-day Brussels meeting, NATO defense ministers approve a 3 percent annual rise in defense expenditures for alliance members, covering a five-year period beginning in 1979.	Arab countries and the PLO denounce Israeli election results as a blow to peace.		
May 19		Rightist gunmen go on a rampage in San Sebastian, Spain, attacking citizens almost indiscriminately, in apparent response to the killing of a policeman the previous day by presumed Basque extremists.		Guatemala severs relations with Panama to protest Panama's support of independence for Belize.	Philip Agee repeats charges made by others that the CIA had infiltrated Australian labor unions.

A	B	C	D	E
Includes developments that affect more than one world region, international organizations and important meetings of major world leaders.	Includes all domestic and regional developments in Europe, including the Soviet Union, Turkey, Cyprus and Malta.	Includes all domestic and regional developments in Africa and the Middle East, including Iraq and Iran and excluding Cyprus, Turkey and Afghanistan.	Includes all domestic and regional developments in Latin America, the Caribbean and Canada.	Includes all domestic and regional developments in Asia and Pacific nations, extending from Afghanistan through all the Pacific Islands, except Hawaii.

U.S. Politics & Social Issues	U.S. Foreign Policy & Defense	U.S. Economy & Environment	Science, Technology & Nature	Culture, Leisure & Life Style	
The discovery of a stick of dynamite at Boston's South Boston High School — the scene of continuing tension since integration-related busing began in Boston — creates a disturbance resulting in the arrest of seven people and minor injuries to seven others.		Folger Coffee Co. becomes the first major U.S. coffee roaster to announce a cut in the soaring wholesale price of ground coffee, reducing its price 25-cents-a-pound to $4.18.	National Transportation Safety Bd. reports that U.S. deaths in 1976 from transportation accidents are up .15 percent from 1975, the first increase in three years.	*Wall Street Journal* reports that business support for the arts rose to about $221 million in 1976, doubling the $110 million donated in 1970.	May 12
Mohawk Indians reach an agreement with the U.S. govt. to gain control of 612 acres in N.Y.S.'s Adirondack Mountains after a three-year dispute.	U.S. Treasury Dept. says it will allow travel agents to arrange group tours to Cuba.	Major U.S. banks raise their prime lending rates to 6.5 percent on loans to top corporate customers. . . . Over 500 demonstrators, arrested and imprisoned for occupying the construction site of a Seabrook, N.H. nuclear power plant on May 1–2, are released from their National Guard armory prisons.	On a Latin American tour, U.S. Asst. State Secy. Terrence Todman says in Brasilia that Brazil's plan to purchase nuclear energy facilities from West Germany — strongly opposed by the U.S. — is an accomplished fact. . . . WHO reports that to date there is no proven evidence that saccharin causes bladder cancer.		May 13
Robert Maynard Hutchins, 78, University of Chicago president at the age of 29 and later its chancellor, dies of a kidney ailment in Santa Barbara, Calif.				Pierre Boulez retires as director of the New York Philharmonic. . . . Montreal Canadiens win their twentieth Stanley Cup in a four-game sweep over the Boston Bruins in the NHL final playoffs.	May 14
	The New York Times reports an open letter from the Coalition for a Democratic Majority to Pres. Carter, lauding his tough stand on human rights and his approach to disarmament, in wake of Sen. George McGovern's (D, S.D.) criticism of Carter for being too conservative.			Jimmy Connors wins the World Championship Tennis (WCT) singles title at the end of his first year on the circuit.	May 15
The New York Times reports that the law has become the fastest-growing profession in the U.S. over the past 10 years.	Defense Secy. Harold Brown authorizes a U.S. company to share technical information with a British company in constructing a new medium-range air-to-air missile for possible use in U.S. and European fighter planes.	U.S. industrial output continues to rise strongly in April for the third consecutive month.	A helicopter tips over one minute after landing at a heliport atop the 59-story Pan Am Building (N.Y.C.), killing four people on the landing pad and a woman walking on the street, who was hit by a falling piece of the rotor blade.	In a nationally televised fight at Capital Center Landover, Md., Muhammad Ali wins a unanimous 15-round decision over an obscure boxer, Alfredo Evangelista, in what is regarded as one of the dullest fights of Ali's career.	May 16
Chief Justice Warren Burger defends the Supreme Ct. and the federal court system against criticism that they turn away civil-rights cases.		Housing starts during April are reported dropping sharply from the record March rate, but still remaining well above the April 1976 pace.			May 17
Pres. Carter asks Congress to enact legislation requiring the government to obtain a judicial warrant if it needs to conduct electronic surveillance for national security purposes.	Defense Dept. estimates that costs for procuring the new B-1 model bomber have been revised upward to $24.8 billion for a fleet of 244 planes.	U.S. personal income in April rises $11.1 billion, or .7 percent from March.			May 18
In the third of a series of TV interviews with David Frost, former Pres. Nixon declares that a President can commit illegal acts if he deems them in he country's best interest, portraying himself as a wartime President confronted, like Abraham Lincoln, by internal dissent.	Pres. Carter outlines a six-point policy to curb U.S. arms sales abroad, with some stated exceptions.	Newly elected UAW head Douglas Fraser calls on U.S. carmakers to compete with foreign manufacturers of small cars and opposes Pres. Carter's car-oriented energy plans, especially a tax on gas guzzlers.	Kenya bans all game hunting in the country in an effort to save its dwindling wildlife population from extinction.	Sandra West, a millionaire who died on March 10 at the age of 37 in San Antonio, Tex., is buried according to her wishes — dressed in a lace nightgown and seated in her 1964 Ferrari sports car "with the seat comfortably slanted."	May 19

F	G	H	I	J
Includes elections, federal-state relations, civil rights and liberties, crime, the judiciary, education, health care, poverty, urban affairs and population.	*Includes formation and debate of U.S. foreign and defense policies, veterans' affairs and defense spending. (Relations with specific foreign countries are usually found under the region concerned.)*	*Includes business, labor, agriculture, taxation, transportation, consumer affairs, monetary and fiscal policy, natural resources, and pollution.*	*Includes worldwide scientific, medical and technological developments, natural phenomena, U.S. weather, natural disasters, and accidents.*	*Includes the arts, religion, scholarship, communications media, sports, entertainments, fashions, fads and social life.*

	World Affairs	Europe	Africa & the Middle East	The Americas	Asia & the Pacific
May 20	U.S. State Secy. Cyrus Vance and Soviet For. Min. Andrei Gromyko end three days of talks in Geneva by agreeing to end the SALT talks' stalemate prevailing since March.	Vaclav Havel, a leading spokesman for the Czech Charter 77 human-rights movement, is freed from prison, reportedly having promised to refrain from making public political statements.	Egyptian Pres. Anwar Sadat says that all Israeli premiers, no matter what party they belong to, adopt the same line when it comes to settling the Arab — Israeli conflict.		Japan agrees formally to greatly reduce the number of color television sets it exports to the U.S.
May 21	Delegates to the U.N. Maputo conference on African black nationalism adopt a declaration calling for international compliance with U.N. sanctions against South Africa and Rhodesia and for moral and material support for the nationalist groups.				Three of four national referendums on proposed changes in the Australian Constitution are approved by the required voter majority.
May 22		The Orient Express, which had provided direct train service between Paris and Istanbul since 1833 and had accrued a romantic popular image as the setting for international intrigue and high-society stories, makes its final run to Istanbul.	South African P.M. John Vorster says in Geneva that a tougher U.S. policy toward South Africa would not succeed in changing the country's apartheid policy and that it is sufficiently strong to succeed without U.S. support.		Hanoi releases U.S. documents, including a letter from Pres. Nixon to Premier Pham Van Dong, in which the U.S. allegedly had pledged postwar aid to Vietnam, and an accompanying broadcast calls for the U.S. to fulfill its pledge.
May 23		In a coordinated action in the Netherlands two groups of South Moluccan extremists seize 50 people on a hijacked train and 105 children and their six teachers in an elementary school and hold them hostage.			
May 24		Soviet Union Pres. Nikolai Podgorny is removed from the Politburo of the CP Central Committee, a move seen as ending his political career. . . . An estimated 8–10 million people strike in France against the government's wage curbs, the nation's biggest national strike since May 1968.	Israeli right-wing Likud Party appears to be easing its hard-line stance on retention of occupied Arab territories.	The Canadian Liberal Party gaines one seat in Parliament as a result of by-elections.	Allegations are reported that intelligence gathered at the top-secret U.S. base at Pine Gap, Australia is being withheld from the Australian govt. P.M. Malcolm Fraser tells Parliament that he is satisfied that the U.S. is not involved in improper activities in his country.
May 25	Returning from his 15-day tour of Africa to Britain, U.S. Amb. to the U.N. Andrew Young creates new controversy by telling reporters that the Soviets are the worst racists in the world and that the Swedes are terrible racists who treat blacks there as badly as they are treated in Queens (a N.Y.C. borough).	The deadline set by South Moluccan terrorists passes without their shooting any of their hostages as Dutch security forces surround the sites where the hostages are held and also guard the South Moluccan community from retaliation from Dutch citizens aroused by the terrorists' actions.	In two-day talks in Washington, Saudi Crown Prince Fahd assures Pres. Carter that the Saudis would not impose another oil embargo on the U.S. to force concessions from Israel to achieve a Mideast peace settlement.	Trans-Andean pipeline begins operation with crude oil flowing from Peru's Amazon jungle over the Andes to the port of Bayovar on the Pacific Ocean. . . . U.S. State Dept. says it has received reports of the arrival of 50 Cuban military advisers in Addis Ababa, Ethiopia, and warns Cuba that its intervention could impede improved U.S.–Cuban relations.	

A	B	C	D	E
Includes developments that affect more than one world region, international organizations and important meetings of major world leaders.	Includes all domestic and regional developments in Europe, including the Soviet Union, Turkey, Cyprus and Malta.	Includes all domestic and regional developments in Africa and the Middle East, including Iraq and Iran and excluding Cyprus, Turkey and Afghanistan.	Includes all domestic and regional developments in Latin America, the Caribbean and Canada.	Includes all domestic and regional developments in Asia and Pacific nations, extending from Afghanistan through all the Pacific Islands, except Hawaii.

U.S. Politics & Social Issues	U.S. Foreign Policy & Defense	U.S. Economy & Environment	Science, Technology & Nature	Culture, Leisure & Life Style	
N.C. Superior Ct. Judge George Fountain denies a new trial to the Wilmington 10, the nine black men and one white woman convicted in 1972 in connection with Wilmington racial disturbances in 1971.	Gen. Lewis Hershey, 83, director of the Selective Service system under six Presidents, dies in Angola, Ind.	Sen. Majority Leader Robert Byrd (D, W.Va.) criticizes the Japanese–U.S. color TV trade pact, charging that it does not deal with allegedly predatory Japanese pricing practices and possible antitrust violations.			**May 20**
A GAO report shows that 143 civil suits, claiming over $1 billion in damages, have been filed charging former government officials with improper spying and harassment.				*Seattle Slew* , who won the Kentucky Derby, also takes the Preakness Stakes.	**May 21**
	In a commencement speech at Notre Dame University, Pres. Carter calls for a new and broader U.S. foreign policy designed to respond to a world more politically awake.	Consumer prices rise .8 percent in April, 6.8 percent higher than in April 1976.		Vitas Gerulaitis becomes the first U.S. player in 17 years to win the men's singles title at the Italian Open matches in Rome.	**May 22**
Supreme Ct. refuses to review the Watergate cover-up convictions of John Mitchell, H.R. Haldeman, and John Ehrlichman. . . . Supreme Ct. rules, 9–0, that federal commercial fishing laws take precedence over state fishing regulations.		Supreme Ct. rules that non-union workers employed by a state or local government can be compelled to pay the equivalent of dues to the union that represented them in collective bargaining, known as the agency shop. . . . Pres. Carter proposes new penalties for air and water polluters in a message to Congress pledging firm administration support for environmental protection.	University of California (San Francisco) scientists Howard Goodman and William Rutter report successfully mass-producing the insulin gene, using the recombinant DNA technique.	Gordie Howe, 49, and his two sons, Mark 22, and Marty, 23, sign a long-term, multimillion dollar contract with the WHA New England Whalers, spurning offers from at least two National Hockey League teams. . . . Kareem Abdul-Jabbar is named the NBA's most-valuable player for the fifth time.	**May 23**
		USW ratifies a new three-year contract with major aluminum producers, providing major income-security provisions that go beyond the innovative agreements it reached with the steel industry. . . . *Wall Street Journal* reports the biggest single-family home-buying boom in history with demand far out-stripping the new-home market capacity.	A leading U.S. physicist Alfred Schild, 55, dies of an apparent heart attack in Downers Grove, Ill.		**May 24**
Madison, Wis. Judge Archie Simonson gives a light sentence to a rapist, suggesting that the victim provoked the assault with her provocative garments. . . . HEW Secy. Joseph Califano outlines a tentative version of the administration's welfare reform plan, which would divide welfare families into two classes: those who are required to work to receive federal assistance and those who do not face any work requirement.				New York Drama Critics Circle Awards are given to *Otherwise Engaged* by Simon Gray, *American Buffalo* by David Mamet and the musical *Annie* by Thomas Meehan, Charles Strouse, and Martin Charnin. . . . China lifts its ban on Shakespeare, denounced as bourgeois during the Cultural Revolution.	**May 25**

F	G	H	I	J
Includes elections, federal-state relations, civil rights and liberties, crime, the judiciary, education, health care, poverty, urban affairs and population.	*Includes formation and debate of U.S. foreign and defense policies, veterans' affairs and defense spending. (Relations with specific foreign countries are usually found under the region concerned.)*	*Includes business, labor, agriculture, taxation, transportation, consumer affairs, monetary and fiscal policy, natural resources, and pollution.*	*Includes worldwide scientific, medical and technological developments, natural phenomena, U.S. weather, natural disasters, and accidents.*	*Includes the arts, religion, scholarship, communications media, sports, entertainments, fashions, fads and social life.*

	World Affairs	Europe	Africa & the Middle East	The Americas	Asia & the Pacific
May 26	The Soviet Union announces delivering a formal note of protest to the Chinese Embassy in Moscow criticizing Peking for sabotaging efforts to improve Sino–Soviet relations.	Swedish employers and unions conclude a 1977 wage agreement for 1.3 million workers in the private sector.	South African Defense Min. Pieter Botha echoes a speech the previous day by Education Min. Pieter Koornhof endorsing the establishment of separate government councils to represent the country's non-white population (Asians and coloreds).... Zaire troops recapture the last towns held by secessionist rebels in Shaba Province, defeating the invasion that began on March 8.... Beirut sources report that the Palestinians, with the aid of Syria, have sent reinforcements into southern Lebanon in the past week in expectation of new tensions following the right-wing Likud Party's victory in Israeli elections.	Pres. Carter signs the Treaty of Tlatelolco, which bans atomic weapons in Latin America and the Caribbean, including U.S. territories Puerto Rico, the Virgin Islands, the Panama Canal Zone, and the Guantanamo naval base in Cuba. ... A group of 110 army air force colonels are reported circulating a letter calling for a return to democracy in Brazil.	
May 27	U.N. Security Council unanimously approves a resolution to close Rhodesian govt. information offices outside Rhodesia.		The Lebanese Front of right-wing Christian parties repudiates the 1969 Cairo agreement governing Palestinian activities in Lebanon and declares the Palestinian presence in the country illegal.... Israeli troops cross into southern Lebanon and clash with Palestinian forces at the border village of Yarin, their first direct clash in over two years.... Former Israeli Defense Min. Moshe Dayan resigns from the Labor Party, responding to demands that he quit because he accepted an offer to serve as foreign minister in a future Begin Likud Party govt.	Canadian federal govt. and the Quebec provincial govt. announce plans to share jurisdiction over immigration.	
May 28			In a meeting with State Secy. Cyrus Vance in Washington, Israeli Amb. to the U.S. Simcha Dinitz expresses concern that the U.S. is turning away from Israel.		
May 29				Parti Quebecois approves a series of resolutions that indicate a shift to a more moderate stance on Quebec independence.... Col. Eduardo Casanova Sandoval, El Salvador's ambassador to Guatemala, is kidnapped by members of the Guerrilla Army of the Poor, a small Guatemalan leftist group, while attending an IDB meeting in Guatemala City.	Nearly 99 percent of the voters in a Bangladesh referendum approve of Pres. Ziaur Rahman's martial law politics.
May 30		Austrian Defense Min. Karl Luetgendorf resigns to prevent being dismissed by the government for his role in a controversial arms shipment to Syria, considered to be Austria's most serious postwar scandal.		U.S. and Cuba agree to exchange diplomats by establishing "interest" offices in each other's capital, considered a significant step toward resumption of full diplomatic relations.	
May 31			Rhodesian troops capture Mapai, a village 60 miles inside Mozambique, in the stated effort to wipe out guerrilla operations there.... Angolan pres. Agostinho Neto says that hundreds of people have been arrested in the wake of a short-lived rebellion in support of two purged governement officials —Nito Alves and Jose Van Dunem. ... Iraq is reported to have called on several Arab governments to stop negotiating and to prepare for a war with Israel.	In continuing Brazilian unrest, over 20,000 University of Brasilia students strike.	

A	B	C	D	E
Includes developments that affect more than one world region, international organizations and important meetings of major world leaders.	Includes all domestic and regional developments in Europe, including the Soviet Union, Turkey, Cyprus and Malta.	Includes all domestic and regional developments in Africa and the Middle East, including Iraq and Iran and excluding Cyprus, Turkey and Afghanistan.	Includes all domestic and regional developments in Latin America, the Caribbean and Canada.	Includes all domestic and regional developments in Asia and Pacific nations, extending from Afghanistan through all the Pacific Islands, except Hawaii.

U.S. Politics & Social Issues	U.S. Foreign Policy & Defense	U.S. Economy & Environment	Science, Technology & Nature	Culture, Leisure & Life Style	
Pres. Carter's reaffirms his determination to hold federal welfare spending to its current level, reportedly alarming liberals.	SEC receives a report that Lockheed Aircraft Corp. has spent nearly $38 million in bribes, extortion payments, and other questionable outlays, 1970–75, to win foreign sales.	U.S. trade deficit reaches a record high in April when imports exceeded exports by $2.62 billion, bringing the cumulative deficit since January to $8.55 billion. . . . Congress passes, 326–49, a bill amending and weakening the 1970 Clean Air Act, particularly in delaying auto emissions curbs.		George Willig, a toy designer and amateur mountain climber, scales the 1,350-foot south tower of the World Trade Center (N.Y.C.) in three-and-a-half hours.	May 26
Noting that the U.S. has 14 times as many lawyers as Japan, Chief Justice Warren Burger tells an ABA conference that unless more legal disputes are settled outside the courtroom, the nation could be overrun by "hordes of lawyers hungry as locusts."				Quebec Nordiques win the Avco Cup, symbolic of the WHA championship, by defeating the Winnipeg Jets, 8–2. . . . Canadian P.M. Pierre Trudeau and his wife, Margaret, legally separate after six years of marriage, with P.M. Trudeau retaining custody of their three young sons.	May 27
	The New York Times reports that Pres. Carter has arranged with Sen. Henry Jackson (D, Wash.) to provide key Senate leaders with up-to-date information on SALT negotiations to prevent a major fight on the Senate floor if the treaty is ever signed.		A fire in a Ky. nightclub, four miles across the Ohio River from Cincinnati, kills 161 people and injures about 100 others. It is the worst nightclub fire since the Coconut Grove fire in Boston in 1942.		May 28
				A.J. Foyt becomes the only driver ever to win the Indianapolis 500 four times. Janet Guthrie, the only woman ever to qualify for the race, is forced to drop out because of a defective fuel pump. . . . Goddard Lieberson, 66, president of Columbia Records, dies in N.Y.C.	May 29
			Over 500 French scientists from the Grenoble area send an open letter to Pres. Giscard d'Estaing demanding that construction of a plutonium breeding plant near Lyon be stopped.		May 30
Supreme Ct. rules against recourse for minority employment bias prior to the enactment of the 1964 Civil Rights Act and does not allow retroactive seniority.				On the last day of the 1976–77 Broadway season, productions that have paid off their initial investments include California Suite, The Basic Training of Pavlo Hummel, Mark Twain Tonight!, Fiddler on the Roof, the last of which having returned 1,308 percent.	May 31

F	G	H	I	J
Includes elections, federal-state relations, civil rights and liberties, crime, the judiciary, education, health care, poverty, urban affairs and population.	Includes formation and debate of U.S. foreign and defense policies, veterans' affairs and defense spending. (Relations with specific foreign countries are usually found under the region concerned.)	Includes business, labor, agriculture, taxation, transportation, consumer affairs, monetary and fiscal policy, natural resources, and pollution.	Includes worldwide scientific, medical and technological developments, natural phenomena, U.S. weather, natural disasters, and accidents.	Includes the arts, religion, scholarship, communications media, sports, entertainments, fashions, fads and social life.

	World Affairs	Europe	Africa & the Middle East	The Americas	Asia & the Pacific
June 1		Soviet Union formally charges Anatoly Shcharansky with treason for his participation in a group monitoring compliance with the 1975 Helsinki accords on human rights.	PLO is reported to have created a new army, named Ajnadin, to fight the Israelis and the Lebanese Christian militia opposed to Palestinians in Lebanon. . . . It is reported that about 2,000 holders of Portuguese passports have been ordered to leave Mozambique by May 16.	Col. Eduardo Casanova Sandoval is released by his captors after the IDB reads their charges at the opening of IDB meetings in Guatemala City. . . . Canadian dollar drops unexpectedly to 94.8 cents (U.S.).	
June 2		Four ministers from the French-speaking wing of the Belgian Social Christians Party (PSC) refuse to appear at the palace for Cabinet swearing-in ceremonies, attributing their boycott to insufficient government post assignments to the French-speaking community.	Rhodesian troops are reported to be withdrawing from Mozambique after acknowledging that they found fewer guerrillas there than expected.		The U.S. cancels Pakistan's contract to purchase 110 A-7 attack planes because it fears upsetting the military balance on the Indian subcontinent.
June 3	The Conference on International Economic Cooperation (North-South dialogue of rich and poor nations) ends its 18-month conference in Paris inconclusively, although it agrees to establish a $1-billion aid fund for the world's poorest nations.	Belgian King Baudouin swears in a new coalition government headed by Premier Leo Tindemans, and says that he wishes to forget the previous day's incident. . . . Philip Agee, a former U.S. CIA agent, leaves Britain for the Netherlands under a government deportation order for violation of the official Secrets Act.	Independent candidates who supported King Hassan II win a substantial majority in Moroccan parliamentary elections.		Wang Hung-wen, one of the disgraced members of the Gang of Four, is accused of being the chief provocateur for some of the worst violence in provincial China in the months prior to Chmn. Mao Tsetung's death in September 1976.
June 4		The Soviet Union publishes the draft of a new Constitution that will replace the one written by Josef Stalin in 1936. The dominant role of the CP in governing the country is formally stated for the first time.			
June 5	IMF estimates that international lending by private banks will grow at a rate of over 20 percent this year, compared to 1976 when banks loaned $65 billion to foreign borrowers.	Former Premier Bulent Ecevit's Republican People's Party, regarded as mildly leftist, wins the most seats in Turkey's general election.		*The New York Times* reports that the Argentine army claims it has killed Montoneros leader Julio Roque.	Carter administration announces plans to withdraw 6,000 U.S. troops from South Korea by the end of 1978. . . . Leftists sympathetic to France Albert Rene, Seychelles prime minister, overthrow the government of Pres. James Mancham. Rene assumes the presidency and suspends the Constitution and 25-member National Assembly.
June 6	Carter administration releases a report that criticizes the Soviet bloc for failing to fulfill its obligations in all three sections of the Helsinki accords: confidence-building, economic and scientific cooperation, and human-rights observances.				Pakistani govt. lifts martial law in Karachi, Lahore, and Hyderabad, which had been imposed since April 21 in an attempt to curb violent protests against alleged rigged elections.

A	B	C	D	E
Includes developments that affect more than one world region, international organizations and important meetings of major world leaders.	Includes all domestic and regional developments in Europe, including the Soviet Union, Turkey, Cyprus and Malta.	Includes all domestic and regional developments in Africa and the Middle East, including Iraq and Iran and excluding Cyprus, Turkey and Afghanistan.	Includes all domestic and regional developments in Latin America, the Caribbean and Canada.	Includes all domestic and regional developments in Asia and Pacific nations, extending from Afghanistan through all the Pacific Islands, except Hawaii.

U.S. Politics & Social Issues	U.S. Foreign Policy & Defense	U.S. Economy & Environment	Science, Technology & Nature	Culture, Leisure & Life Style	
	In an address to the Air Force Academy graduating class, Defense Secy. Harold Brown says that the Carter administration hopes to avoid all increases in military spending except those necessitated by inflation.		The House approves a bill to impose a ceiling of 69,000 on the number of porpoises that can be killed in tuna-fishing operations in 1977.	*Star Wars*, a science-fiction film, is the top grossing movie for the week just ended.	June 1
		Under the equal-time provision for political broadcasts, Republican National Chairman Bill Brock gives a televised rebuttal to Pres. Carter's energy plan. He calls for more emphasis on mass transit, more efficient cars, and tax credits for home insulation. . . . *Black Enterprise* magazine June issue reports that total revenues for the 100 largest black-owned companies rose 24.2 percent during 1976 to $775.1 million. Motown Industries, the Detroit record co., is top-ranking with sales of $50 million.			June 2
In a *Playboy* magazine interview, U.N. Amb. Andrew Young creates more controversy by calling former Presidents Richard Nixon and Gerald Ford "racists because they had no understanding of colored people anywhere."	Republican Sen. Robert Dole (Kan) reflects the views of most Republican leaders when he says that he will introduce legislation barring any future improvement in U.S.–Cuban relations until Havana meets certain stipulations.	Record-breaking sales of foreign cars during May raise the total number of new cars sold in the U.S. to 1.054 million units, 14 percent higher than the same time last year.		Roberto Rossellini, 71, Italian neo-realistic film director widely known for his scandalous love affair with actress Ingrid Bergman, dies of a heart attack in Rome.	June 3
Chicago Puerto Rican Day festivities erupt into fighting, burning, and looting.			A group of 65 congressmen ask Pres. Carter to bar the sale of the Cyber 76 advanced computer system to the Soviet Union, arguing that the Soviets could use it for their military advantage.	John Cheever's novel *Falconer* is a top fiction best-seller for the previous week.	June 4
HEW Secy. Joseph Califano tells the graduating class of City College, N.Y.C., that the federal govt. will rely on numerical goals rather than arbitrary quotas in measuring minority access to higher education.				Portland Trail Blazers beat the Philadelphia 76ers, 109–107, to win the NBA championship in the sixth game of the final playoff round. . . . Broadway's Tony Awards recipients include the following: *Annie* (best play); Barry Bostwick; Dorothy Loudon; Lenny Baker; Dolores Hall; Tranzana Beverly; and Jonathan Price. Special awards are given to Lily Tomlin, Diana Ross, and Barry Manilow. . . . Third-seeded Guillermo Vilas of Argentina wins the French Open men's singles tennis title. Yugoslavia's Mima Jausovec wins the women's singles.	June 5
Supreme Ct. rules, 5–4, that states cannot automatically impose the death penalty for killing police officers, but leaves undecided the circumstances under which a death sentence could be constitutionally mandated. . . . FBI domestic security investigations, including those into terrorist activities, have dropped to 214 from 4,868, according to a White House report.	Supreme Ct. rules unanimously that employers must include the years an employe spent in military service when calculating pension benefits.	*Wall Street Journal* reports that sales of foreign cars in the U.S. came to about 220,000 units during May, the highest level on record and 73 percent above May 1976 sales.	*Washington Post* reports that the U.S. is about to begin production of the neutron bomb, a nuclear warhead that can kill people without destroying property.	Supreme Ct., 5–4, rules that the nature of advertising for allegedly pornographic material can be used by a jury in determining the verdict in an obscenity trial.	June 6

F	G	H	I	J
Includes elections, federal-state relations, civil rights and liberties, crime, the judiciary, education, health care, poverty, urban affairs and population.	Includes formation and debate of U.S. foreign and defense policies, veterans' affairs and defense spending. (Relations with specific foreign countries are usually found under the region concerned.)	Includes business, labor, agriculture, taxation, transportation, consumer affairs, monetary and fiscal policy, natural resources, and pollution.	Includes worldwide scientific, medical and technological developments, natural phenomena, U.S. weather, natural disasters, and accidents.	Includes the arts, religion, scholarship, communications media, sports, entertainments, fashions, fads and social life.

	World Affairs	Europe	Africa & the Middle East	The Americas	Asia & the Pacific
June 7		Italian Senate defeats a bill to legalize abortion, 156–154, surprising both the Christian Democrats, who opposed the bill, and the Communists, who supported it. . . . An estimated crowd of 1 million people line London streets for Queen Elizabeth II's ride to St. Paul's Cathedral during a week-long celebration of her twenty-fifth anniversary as the British monarch.	After being formally designated to form a new Israeli govt., the Likud Party leader, Menahem Begin, renews his appeal to the Labor Party to join a national-unity government. . . . U.S. and the Peoples's Republic of Congo formally establish diplomatic relations after a 12-year break.	A House of Commons subcommittee report charges that Canada's prison system fails to reform criminals and epitomizes injustice.	
June 8		Soviet offical news agency Tass denounces Pres. Carter as an enemy of detente who uses reactionary propaganda to defend dissidents.			
June 9	At a conference of the Commonwealth countries, Zambian Pres. Kenneth Kaunda calls for a seven-point program to topple the Rhodesian government, a statement seen as significant because of his reputation as the most moderate of the black leaders of nations surrounding Rhodesia.		*Washington Post* reports that Eritrean separatists rejected a Soviet proposal for a Eritrean–Ethiopian federation, seen as a further blow to Soviet efforts to gain influence in that region. . . . Menahem Begin offers a number of religious concessions to Agudat Israel, the ultra-Orthodox Israeli political party, to assure its inclusion in his government.	Costa Rican Pres. Daniel Oduber Quiros says he has asked fugitive U.S. financier Robert Vesco to leave Costa Rica in wake of charges and countercharges over the previous month that Vesco had given money to Oduber's political campaign.	A French dispatch from Hanoi reveals that the Vietnamese press is acknowledging that former South Vietnamese troops are attempting armed resistance in the southern part of Vietnam.
June 10		Egyptian For. Min. Ismail Fahmy confers in Moscow with Soviet For. Min. Andrei Gromyko, and Gromyko concedes that restoring normal relations between Egypt and the Soviet Union will not be simple.	South Africa formally abandons its plan to install a racially divided interim government in Namibia (South-West Africa). A new plan calls for the appointment of an administrator to govern the territory until a constituent assembly is elected.	Peru announces emergency austerity programs to deal with its financial crisis.	
June 11		Shortly before dawn, Dutch marines assault the train and schoolhouse where two contingents of South Moluccan terrorists are holding 55 Dutch citizens hostage. Six terrorists and two of the hostages on the train are killed in the raid.	A representative of SWAPO, the guerrilla group fighting South African troops in Namibia, rejects the new plan, charging that South Africa has no legal right to appoint any official to govern the territory.		
June 12	BIS warns the U.S. that its growing balance-of-payments deficits threatens the dollar, which, in turn, could cause turmoil in world monetary markets.		Libyan leader Col. Muammer el-Qaddafi urges Pres. Carter to resume full diplomatic ties.		
June 13		Israel's Democratic Movement for Change Party (DMC) votes overwhelmingly against serving in Menahem Begin's coalition govt. because it disagrees with the Likud Party's hard-line stance on occupied Arab territories.		*Wall Street Journal* reports that Robert Vesco says that he cannot leave Costa Rica until settlement of the suit pending against him by a Costa Rican who claims that Vesco had defrauded him of $224,000 invested in Investors Overseas Ltd., a mutual fund that Vesco is alleged to have looted. . . . An Argentine appeals ct. orders that former Pres. Alejandro Lanusse be released from jail.	Britain and the U.S. formally recognize the Seychelles govt. of Pres. France Albert Rene, who deposed the former Pres. James Mancham in a June 5 bloodless coup.

A	B	C	D	E
Includes developments that affect more than one world region, international organizations and important meetings of major world leaders.	Includes all domestic and regional developments in Europe, including the Soviet Union, Turkey, Cyprus and Malta.	Includes all domestic and regional developments in Africa and the Middle East, including Iraq and Iran and excluding Cyprus, Turkey and Afghanistan.	Includes all domestic and regional developments in Latin America, the Caribbean and Canada.	Includes all domestic and regional developments in Asia and Pacific nations, extending from Afghanistan through all the Pacific Islands, except Hawaii.

U.S. Politics & Social Issues	U.S. Foreign Policy & Defense	U.S. Economy & Environment	Science, Technology & Nature	Culture, Leisure & Life Style	
The House votes, 244–164, to lift most of the Hatch Act's bans against political activity by federal workers. . . . Michael Bilandic wins a special election to fill the remaining two-year term of the late mayor of Chicago, Richard Daley.	Malcolm Toon, former ambassador to Israel, is confirmed as U.S. ambassador to the Soviet Union.				June 7
HEW Dept. announces that federal Medicaid funds for 20 states will be cut by a total of $142 million because the states have failed to meet a requirement that they carry out annual reviews of nursing home care for Medicaid patients.	House Ethics Committee unanimously decides to ask every member of the House to answer a questionnaire covering his or her relationship with South Korea. It also says it has reached an agreement with the CIA giving the committee access to CIA information about Korean attemps to influence Congress.			*Variety* reports that plays on Broadways and on tour during the 1976–77 season set box office records.	June 8
Supreme Ct., 7–2, voids a N.Y.S. law that prohibited the display or advertising of contraceptives and the sale of nonprescription devices — such as condoms — to minors.		House committee and subcommittee action blocks several of Pres. Carter's key energy proposals. It approves decontrol of new natural gas, rejects Carter's proposed standby gasoline tax and tax rebates for purchasing fuel-efficient cars, and delays until 1979 the proposed tax on gas-guzzler cars.			June 9
James Earl Ray, convicted of murdering civil rights leader Martin Luther king Jr., escapes from a maximum security prison in Tenn. with six other convicts.	At a Foreign Policy Assn. meeting, Ronald Reagan reportedly criticizes Pres. Carter's "double standard" on human rights, questioning how the U.S. can ignore the issue in Panama while condemning Argentina.	The Senate passes amendments to the 1970 Clean Air Act by a 73–7 vote.			June 10
				Seattle Slew wins the Belmont Stakes, thereby sweeping the Triple Crown. He is the tenth colt to do so and the first to advance to the Crown undefeated.	June 11
		Congress completes action on a bill barring U.S. participation in the Arab League's boycott of Israel when the House passes the measure, 306–41.		Jacky Ickx of Belgium, with the aid of a relief driver, Jurgen Barth, wins the Le Mans auto endurance race in France. . . . Chako Higuchi of Japan wins the LPGA golf championship tournament.	June 12
James Earl Ray is captured after his prison break in Tenn. . . . Tom C. Clark, 77, retired Supreme Ct. justice and former attorney general who left the bench when Pres. Lyndon Johnson appointed his son Ramsey as attorney general, dies of a heart ailment in N.Y.C.		Pres. Carter decries the inordinate political influence of the auto and oil industries and warns that failure to adopt a strong energy policy would have catastrophic economic and political repercussions.	Pres. Carter approves a proposal for low-fare service between London and New York by Laker Airways.	Kareem Abdul-Jabbar, of the Los Angeles Lakers, reportedly topped all vote-getters in a sports media poll for the 1977 NBA all-star team.	June 13

F	G	H	I	J
Includes elections, federal-state relations, civil rights and liberties, crime, the judiciary, education, health care, poverty, urban affairs and population.	*Includes formation and debate of U.S. foreign and defense policies, veterans' affairs and defense spending. (Relations with specific foreign countries are usually found under the region concerned.)*	*Includes business, labor, agriculture, taxation, transportation, consumer affairs, monetary and fiscal policy, natural resources, and pollution.*	*Includes worldwide scientific, medical and technological developments, natural phenomena, U.S. weather, natural disasters, and accidents.*	*Includes the arts, religion, scholarship, communications media, sports, entertainments, fashions, fads and social life.*

	World Affairs	Europe	Africa & the Middle East	The Americas	Asia & the Pacific
June 14	Three armed Croatian nationalists invade the U.N. Yugoslav mission in N.Y.C. and surrender three hours later after throwing thousands of leaflets around calling for a free Croatian state.			U.S. State Secy. Cyrus Vance makes the Carter adminstration's strongest human-rights appeal to date in a speech before the OAS General Assembly meeting in Grenada. . . . Surinam (formerly Dutch Guinea) becomes the twenty-fifth member of the OAS.	South Korean govt. announces ending import curbs on 377 commodities effective July 1, thereby increasing imports by about $400 million annually.
June 15	Representatives from 33 Commonwealth nations, including 13 African countries, condemn the Ugandan government for its repressive acts but do not name Pres. Idi Amin.	Antoinette Spaak, daughter of the late Belgian Premier Paul-Henry Spaak, becomes the first woman to head a political party in Belgium. . . . The Union of the Democratic Center, the center-right coalition of Premier Adolfo Suarez Gonzalez, wins Spain's parliamentary elections, the first free ones since 1936. The Spanish Socialist Workers' Party runs a strong second.		Student protests in Brazil enter their seventh week as thousands demonstrate against the government in Sao Paul, Rio de Janeiro, and other cities.	
June 16		Soviet CP Gen. Secy. Leonid Brezhnev is elected president of the country, replacing Nikolai Podgorny and thus becoming the first leader in Soviet history to hold the chief post in both the party and state. . . . Former Irish P.M. John Lynch's Fianna Fail Party wins an upset victory over the existing government coalition of the Fine Gael and Labor parties, which had been in power since 1973.	Iran is hit by a nationwide energy shortage attributed to contractual problems, a sharp drop in water levels, and an underestimation of energy demand.		
June 17		Spanish Socialist Workers' Party (PSOE) bars joining a coalition govt.	In a speech described as the official position of the Carter administration, V.P. Mondale says that any Israeli withdrawal from occupied Arab territories must be coupled with Arab acceptance of a real peace with Israel. . . . V.P. Mondale reiterates the administration's view that the Palestinians should have a homeland associated with Jordan.	S.G.M. Rozendal's Democratic Party becomes the Netherlands Antilles largest political party after capturing 42 percent of the Curacao vote and six of the 22 seats in the territory's Staten (Parliament).	
June 18		British govt. is reported to be alarmed by the victory of John Lynch's Fianna Fail Party in Ireland because Liam Cosgrave's defeated government had backed British policy in Northern Ireland.	Reports circulate that Ugandan Pres. Idi Amin is wounded from an assassination attempt against him and is in hiding. . . . Twelve die in four-day riots marking the first anniversary of the June 16, 1976 Soweto uprising in South Africa.	Chile exchanges its most prominent political prisoner, Jorge Montes, for all prisoners held in East Germany and claims Montes was its last political prisoner.	
June 19				Critics of the Chilean govt. claim that political opponents are still being arrested or simply "disappearing" (murdered by the Chilean secret police).	The New York Times reports that many Vietnamese refugees, daily landing in boats along the east coast of Malaysia, are being rejected by Malaysian authorities.
June 20			The New York Times reports that the short-lived coup against Angolan Pres. Agostinho Neto on May 27 stemmed from deep political divisions in the Angolan Army, and that Cuban troops were a decisive factor in stifling the coup despite Pres. Neto's denial of Cuban participation.	Mexico's largest university, Autonomous National University, (UNAM) is closed by an indefinite strike by non-academic employes and left-wing academics.	Business Week reports that Nationalist China is encouraging foreign investments in the country in wake of a 1976 drop in investments to $141.5 million from a peak of $149 million in 1973.

A	B	C	D	E
Includes developments that affect more than one world region, international organizations and important meetings of major world leaders.	Includes all domestic and regional developments in Europe, including the Soviet Union, Turkey, Cyprus and Malta.	Includes all domestic and regional developments in Africa and the Middle East, including Iraq and Iran and excluding Cyprus, Turkey and Afghanistan.	Includes all domestic and regional developments in Latin America, the Caribbean and Canada.	Includes all domestic and regional developments in Asia and Pacific nations, extending from Afghanistan through all the Pacific Islands, except Hawaii.

U.S. Politics & Social Issues	U.S. Foreign Policy & Defense	U.S. Economy & Environment	Science, Technology & Nature	Culture, Leisure & Life Style	
Stonney Lane, warden of the Tenn. prison from which James Earl Ray escaped, rebuts charges that there had been an outside conspiracy to help Ray.		UMW reelects Arnold Miller as president after a bitterly contested election.	A three-judge panel in N.Y.C. overturns a lower court order that would have allowed the Concorde supersonic transport to land at Kennedy International Airport.		June 14
Supreme Ct. upsets, 5–4, an Ill. ban on demonstrations by a neo-Nazi group, the *Nationalist Socialist Party of America*, which had sought to hold a white supremacy rally in Skokie, Ill, a Chicago suburb with a large Jewish population.		Pres. Carter signs a bill extending the Comprehensive Employment and Training Act (CETA) for one year.		NBA votes to aid four financially troubled basketball teams — the San Antonio Spurs, the Denver Nuggets, the New York Nets, and the Indiana Pacers.	June 15
Deputy Atty. Gen Peter Flaherty says that the Justice Dept. is reexamining its authorization in May of a FBI plan to establish a computerized center that would allow police departments throughout the U.S. to exchange crime information.		U.S. Steel Corp. agrees to install $70-million worth of water pollution-control equipment at its Gary, Ind. plant and to pay a $4-million fine for not meeting the EPA's clean-water deadline.	Wernher von Braun, 65, German-born pioneer in rocketry and space travel who designed the V-2 German missile and later headed the U.S. team that in 1958 launched the first U.S. satellite, dies of cancer in Alexandria, Va.	The Supreme Ct. rules, 7–2, that employers are not required to discriminate against some employes to allow others to observe their Sabbath.	June 16
House, 201–155, bars using Medicaid funds for an abortion to save a mother's life in wake of a parliamentary maneuver by pro-abortion forces that deletes a milder version permitting such abortions.		EPA Administrator Douglas Costle says that the EPA will approve the water cooling system proposed for a nuclear power plant at Seabrook, N.H., thereby reversing a prior verdict by the Boston regional EPA administrator.			June 17
			The New York Times reports that European women continue to use Dutch abortion clinics, despite liberalized laws in their own countries, because most doctors and hospitals still refuse to perform them.	New York Yankees manager Billy Martin and outfielder Reggie Jackson shout obscenities at each other in the dugout during a nationally televised game in Boston after Martin had removed Jackson for allegedly loafing during a fielding play.	June 18
Washington Post reports that the FBI conducted ongoing surveillance and infiltration of the ACLU almost since its inception in 1920 until its late director J. Edgar Hoover's death, and maintained derogatory reports on many prominent Americans, including Felix Frankfurter, Jane Addams, and John Dewey.				Bishop John Neumann of Philadelphia, known for his development of the parochial school system, is canonized by the Roman Catholic Church, the first American male to achieve sainthood.... Hubert Green beats Lou Graham by one stroke to win the U.S. Open golf tournament.... Frank Robinson, baseball major league's first black manager, is dismissed by the Cleveland Indians.	June 19
Supreme Ct. rules, 6–3, that states are not required to fund elective abortions for indigent women. Justice Harry Blackmun dissents, saying the present rulings seriously erode the intent of the court's 1973 decision.... Supreme Ct. rules, 5–4, that states can deny welfare aid to children whose fathers had quit work, gone on strike, or been fired for misconduct.		The Trans-Alaska pipeline opens with oil from Alaska's North Slope expected to reach the port of Valdez, 789 miles away, in about 30 to 40 days.	Dr. Christiaan Barnard implants a baboon's heart into the body of a 26-year old critically ill woman, but she dies shortly after the operation.		June 20

F	G	H	I	J
Includes elections, federal-state relations, civil rights and liberties, crime, the judiciary, education, health care, poverty, urban affairs and population.	*Includes formation and debate of U.S. foreign and defense policies, veterans' affairs and defense spending. (Relations with specific foreign countries are usually found under the region concerned.)*	*Includes business, labor, agriculture, taxation, transportation, consumer affairs, monetary and fiscal policy, natural resources, and pollution.*	*Includes worldwide scientific, medical and technological developments, natural phenomena, U.S. weather, natural disasters, and accidents.*	*Includes the arts, religion, scholarship, communications media, sports, entertainments, fashions, fads and social life.*

	World Affairs	Europe	Africa & the Middle East	The Americas	Asia & the Pacific
June 21		Spain's King Juan Carlos meets with Catalan Socialists and promises them early negotiations to restore greater autonomy to Catalonia.	Menaham Begin becomes Israel's sixth premier after his new coalition govt. receives a vote of confidence from the Knesset.	Canadian federal govt. issues a white paper upholding the right of parents to chose the language in which their child is educated. . . . El Salvadoran right-wing terrorists, who call themselves the White Warrior's Union, distribute pamphlets accusing Jesuits in the country of Communist subversion and threatening to kill all priests who do not leave the country by July 21.	
June 22		Over 150,000 people demonstrate in Lisbon, Portugal to protest the government's austerity program and the rising cost of living.		OAS General Assembly, held in Grenada, ends with the issue of human rights having been the dominant and divisive topic. It issues a strongly worded document condemning torture, summary executions, or prolonged detention.	*Asian Wall Street Journal* reports a growing trend toward Australian economic grouping in Asia.
June 23	Twenty-six people hold a 12-day hunger strike at U.N. offices in Santiago, Chile to pressure the Chilean govt. to release information on 500 people who have allegedly disappeared since the 1973 Chilean military coup.	Premier Adolfo Suarez Gonzalez meets with leaders of his Union of the Democratic Center (UDC) party amidst reports that the 12-party coalition created in April to give him a potential majority in the Spanish Chamber of Deputies is internally divided.	Uganda Radio confirms that Pres. Idi Amin is alive and denounces rumors of his disappearance as a hoax. Reports from Uganda refugees, however, indicate that there had been an attempted coup against Amin by some army officers.	Brazilian Congress gives final approval to a constitutional amendment legalizing divorce.	Pres. Carter meets Australian P. M. Malcolm Fraser in Washington, D.C. and reaffirms the traditionally close ties between Australia and the U.S.
June 24	The International Whaling Commission reduces whaling quotas for the 1978 season by 36 percent.				Chinese CP newspaper *Jenmin Jih Pao* discloses a campaign against the Gang of Four and Mao Yuanhsin, a nephew of Mao Tse-tung, who is important politically in Liaoning Province.
June 25			A Cuban-trained Ethiopian peasant militia parades in Addis Ababa, marking a major offensive against antigovernment forces.		
June 26		Police in Barcelona, Spain fire rubber bullets to disperse a group of 4,000 gay-rights demonstrators, organized by the Gay Liberation Front of Catalonia.	A spokesman for the National Union for the Total Independence of Angola (UNITA) says that his movement would accept help without apology from South Africa and accuses black African nations of hypocrisy for withdrawing support from UNITA during the Angolan civil war after South Africa gave it aid.		
June 27			National Union for the Total Independence of Angola (UNITA) recaptures Cuangar, a town on Angola's border with Namibia. . . . The former French Territory of the Afars and Issas becomes the independent Republic of Djibouti. Pres. Hassan Gouled Aptidon contends that his country will maintain a nonaligned foreign policy, seek neutrality with its quarreling neighbors, and be nonsocialist in its government. . . . The U.S. reaffirms its position that Israel must withdraw from all occupied Arab territories and agree to establishment of a Palestinian homeland in return for a peace agreement with the Arabs.	Four opposition Brazilian Democratic Movement (MDB) leaders make a joint broadcast to excoriate the military Brazilian govt. and demand a return to constitutional democracy. The govt. made a late but fitile attempt to block the broadcast.	

A	B	C	D	E
Includes developments that affect more than one world region, international organizations and important meetings of major world leaders.	*Includes all domestic and regional developments in Europe, including the Soviet Union, Turkey, Cyprus and Malta.*	*Includes all domestic and regional developments in Africa and the Middle East, including Iraq and Iran and excluding Cyprus, Turkey and Afghanistan.*	*Includes all domestic and regional developments in Latin America, the Caribbean and Canada.*	*Includes all domestic and regional developments in Asia and Pacific nations, extending from Afghanistan through all the Pacific Islands, except Hawaii.*

U.S. Politics & Social Issues	U.S. Foreign Policy & Defense	U.S. Economy & Environment	Science, Technology & Nature	Culture, Leisure & Life Style	
Former Nixon aide H.R. Halderman enters a federal minimum security prison in Calif. to begin serving his sentence for his role in the Watergate cover-up.		Labor Dept. reports that the consumer price index rose a seasonally adjusted .6 percent in May.	Vladimir Timakov, 72, a microbiologist and president of the Soviet Academy of Medical Sciences, dies in Moscow.... Bruce Heezen, 53, a pioneering marine geologist who collaborated on charting the world's ocean floors, dies of an apparent heart attack aboard a submarine south of Iceland.		June 21
John Mitchell becomes the first former U.S. attorney general to serve a prison term when he enters a federal minimum-security prison in Alabama, convicted for his role in Watergate.		The U.S. registers a record $4.32-billion balance-of-payments deficit during the first quarter of the year, according to the Commerce Dept.		John Ziegler Jr. is unanimously elected NHL president.	June 22
Supreme Ct. rules, 7–2, that states can limit the activities of prison-inmate unions.			U.S. District Ct. Judge Robert Chapman overturns a Consumer Product Safety Commission ban on production and sale of children's sleepwear treated with Tris, a flame-retardant chemical believed to cause cancer.... Commerce Dept. announces that it will not grant Control Data Corp. an export license to sell its advanced Cyber 76 computer system to the Soviet Union.	*Vienna Waltzes* by George Balanchine is premiered by the New York City Ballet.... *The New York Times* reports that Philippe de Montebello has been named acting director of the Metropolitan Museum of Art, N.Y.C., an interim appointment effective July 1.	June 23
Supreme Ct. rules, 6–3, that certain forms of public aid and services can be provided parochial schools without violating church–state separation.	In a letter to Pres. Carter, Sen. Majority Leader Robert Byrd (D, W. Va.) supports Carter and argues against the B-1 bomber. He says other alternatives are less costly and vulnerable.	FHA drops its plan to convert highways signs to the metric system.			June 24
Former Black Panther Party leader Huey Newton arrives in Toronto, Canada after spending two-and-a-half years in Cuba as a fugitive from Calif. murder and assault charges.			British medical weekly *Lancet* reports studies linking cigarette smoking with early menopause.	The first Spoleto Festival U.S.A., founded by Gian-Carlo Menotti, begins in Charleston, S.C., by presenting the Tchaikovsky opera, *The Queen of Spades*.	June 25
About 40,000 protestors in San Francisco, Calif. and 60,000 spectators congregate in support of gay rights and to protest the recent Dade Country, Fla. repeal of an ordinance that had prohibited discrimination against homosexuals.		Transportation Secy. Brock Adams announces new fuel economy standards for 1981–84 cars as follows: 22 mpg. in 1982, 24 mpg in 1983, 26 mpg in 1983, and 27 mpg in 1984.	*The New York Times* reports that since the World Wildlife Fund's 1970 report that the vicuna is nearly extinct, the vicuna population has increased from 15,000 to 60,000, but its cloth is reportedly still sold illegally for $1,200 to $1,500 a yard.	Walter Kennedy, 64, NBA commissioner who helped increase basketball's popularity, dies of cancer in Stamford, Conn.	June 26
Supreme Ct. rules, 5–4, that lawyers can advertise their fees.... Supreme Ct. rules that federal courts have the power to issue school desegregation orders, including citywide busing, or to order school districts to devise remedial courses for the victims of educational bias.		Arthur Perdue, 91, founder in 1920 of Perdue Inc, a major national poultry producer based in Md., dies in Salisbury, Md.			June 27

F	G	H	I	J
Includes elections, federal-state relations, civil rights and liberties, crime, the judiciary, education, health care, poverty, urban affairs and population.	Includes formation and debate of U.S. foreign and defense policies, veterans' affairs and defense spending. (Relations with specific foreign countries are usually found under the region concerned.)	Includes business, labor, agriculture, taxation, transportation, consumer affairs, monetary and fiscal policy, natural resources, and pollution.	Includes worldwide scientific, medical and technological developments, natural phenomena, U.S. weather, natural disasters, and accidents.	Includes the arts, religion, scholarship, communications media, sports, entertainments, fashions, fads and social life.

	World Affairs	Europe	Africa & the Middle East	The Americas	Asia & the Pacific
June 28			Former Israeli Premier Yitzhak Rabin says that the U.S., statement calling for Israeli withdrawal from occupied lands reverses some assurances he had received in talks with Pres. Carter in March.	The U.S. witholds two loans to Chile, worth $7 million and $2.6 million respectively, pending developments in Chile's human-rights situation.... Chilean govt. rejects $27.5 million in U.S. aid to protest the Carter administration linkage of economic aid with human-rights observance.	
June 29		Magda Lupescu, 81, mistress of the late King Carol of Rumania for 22 years before marrying him in exile in 1947, dies in Estoril, Portugal.... EEC leaders declare that any Middle East peace settlement must provide for a Palestinian homeland and secure borders for Israel.... The Italian Christian Democratic party makes an accord with the CP to get left-wing support to pass unpopular measures dealing with the economy, education, and law enforcement.			State Secy. Cyrus Vance says that the goal of the Carter administration is full diplomatic relations with China.
June 30	Swiss govt. announces that it will not apply for U.N. membership because the majority of its citizens have doubts about the organization.	Czechoslovakia announces a general amnesty for people who fled the country after the 1968 Soviet invasion.... The Hungarian CP backs Eurocommunism.			Southeast Asia Treaty Organization (SEATO) formally disbands.
July 1		Great Britain formally nationalizes its shipbuilding industry after three years of controversy.	Israel warns it will intervene militarily in southern Lebanon if Palestinian guerrillas mass more troops along the Israeli–Lebanese border.	El Salvador inaugurates Gen. Carlos Humberto Romero to a five-year presidential term. Archbishop of San Salvador Oscar Romero boycotts the inauguration after charging torture and ill-treatment of church members by the previous government in which Romero was defense minister.... Uruguayan Pres. Aparicio Mendez signs an act to abolish the judiciary's independence. URUG Courts	
July 2			Heavy fighting rages in southern Lebanon as Christian forces seize Yarin, one mile from the Israeli border, later surrendering control of the village to Palestinian guerrillas.	Venezuelan Pres. Carlos Andres Perez concludes a six-day visit to the U.S., where he reportedly established a warm relationship with Pres. Carter.	

A	B	C	D	E
Includes developments that affect more than one world region, international organizations and important meetings of major world leaders.	Includes all domestic and regional developments in Europe, including the Soviet Union, Turkey, Cyprus and Malta.	Includes all domestic and regional developments in Africa and the Middle East, including Iraq and Iran and excluding Cyprus, Turkey and Afghanistan.	Includes all domestic and regional developments in Latin America, the Caribbean and Canada.	Includes all domestic and regional developments in Asia and Pacific nations, extending from Afghanistan through all the Pacific Islands, except Hawaii.

U.S. Politics & Social Issues	U.S. Foreign Policy & Defense	U.S. Economy & Environment	Science, Technology & Nature	Culture, Leisure & Life Style	
Supreme Ct. upholds, 7–2, a 1974 law giving the government control of former Pres. Nixon's presidential papers and tape recordings.		The ICC rejects oil transport rates proposed by Alyeska, the eight companies that own the recently opened Trans-Alaska pipeline.		Robert Lumiansky, an American scholar, reports that China has rejected a bid by U.S. academic organizations to widen scholarly and scientific exchanges with Peking.	June 28
Supreme Ct. rules, 7–2, that the death penalty cannot be imposed for the rape of an adult woman. . . . Senate approves a curb on Medicaid funding for abortions, but, unlike the House, it votes to allow relatively broad exceptions, including when the mother's life is in danger.					June 29
Irving Saypol, 71, a N.Y.S. justice for 26 years and U.S. Atty. for the Southern District of N.Y., who successfully prosecuted Julius and Ethel Rosenberg, dies of cancer in N.Y.C.	Pres. Carter announces his decision against production of the B-1 bomber and says that the U.S., instead, should begin to deploy cruise missiles to modernize its airborne nuclear deterrent force.	Transportation Secy. Brock Adams orders that new cars be equipped with air bag safety devices or passive restraint seat belts beginning with 1982 models.		Citing prohibitive costs, the Newport Jazz Festival announces it is moving from N.Y.C. to Saratoga Springs, N.Y.	June 30
	U.S. State Secy. Cyrus Vance, in the first full administration statement on U.S. policy in southern Africa, tells the annual NAACP convention that the U.S. is demanding that apartheid end in South Africa. . . . The Senate debates issues concerning the neutron bomb in a closed session Sen. Mark Hatfield (R, Ore.) introduces a motion to halt funding, which is amended by Sen. John Stennis (D, Miss.) to state that funds should be withheld until an arms-control impact statement has been filed.	Forty-five thousand copper industry workers begin a strike at the expiration of three-year contracts with 26 unions. Kennecott Copper Corp. quickly agrees to a settlement.		Britain's Virginia Wade defeats Betty Stove of the Netherlands to become the first Englishwoman to win the Wimbledon singles title since 1969.	July 1
Buddy Cochran, a truck mechanic, plunges his Jaguar XKE sports car into a crowd of 250 attending a Ku Klux Klan rally in Pres. Carter's hometown of Plains, Ga., injuring 29 people.				Eighteen-year-old Vladimir Yashcenko, sets a new world record in the high jump — 7 feet, 7 and three-quarters inches — in the Soviet–U.S. fifteenth annual track and field meet at Sochi, U.S.S.R. . . . Vladimir Nabokov, 78, Russian-born American novelist and leading literary figure who wrote the controversial novel *Lolita*, about a middle-aged man's sexual obsession with a preteen girl, dies in Montreux, Switzerland. . . . Sweden's Bjorn Borg wins his second consecutive men's singles Wimbledon tennis title, defeating top-seeded U.S. player Jimmy Connors in a 3 hour, 14 minute match, regarded as one of the best in Wimbledon's 100-year history.	July 2

F	G	H	I	J
Includes elections, federal-state relations, civil rights and liberties, crime, the judiciary, education, health care, poverty, urban affairs and population.	Includes formation and debate of U.S. foreign and defense policies, veterans' affairs and defense spending. (Relations with specific foreign countries are usually found under the region concerned.)	Includes business, labor, agriculture, taxation, transportation, consumer affairs, monetary and fiscal policy, natural resources, and pollution.	Includes worldwide scientific, medical and technological developments, natural phenomena, U.S. weather, natural disasters, and accidents.	Includes the arts, religion, scholarship, communications media, sports, entertainments, fashions, fads and social life.

	World Affairs	Europe	Africa & the Middle East	The Americas	Asia & the Pacific
July 3	Saudi Arabia and the United Arab Emirates announce a 5 percent increase in the price of their oil to $12.70 a barrel, the price charged since Jan. 1 by the 11 other members of OPEC.	Turkish Premier Bulent Ecevit resigns after his minority govt. is defeated in its first National Assembly vote of confidence, 229–217.	*London Sunday Times* carries an Israeli govt. denial of previous charges made in its June 19 edition that the Israelis had systematically tortured Arab prisoners over the past 10 years.		
July 4		A customary Fourth of July speech to be delivered over Soviet TV by U.S. Amb. Malcolm Toon is cancelled by the Soviet Govt. when Toon refuses to delete a portion dealing with Pres. Carter's position on human rights.... Valentin Turchin, head of the Moscow branch of Amnesty International, is arrested after refusing to answer a Soviet police summons the previous week.... Turkish Pres. Fahri Koruturk asks former Premier Suleyman Demirel, head of the conservative Justice Party and leader of the anti-Ecevit vote, to form a new government.	Refugees report heavy fighting in the Yarin area of southern Lebanon involving Israeli-supported Christian militiamen using tanks. Syrian troops are reported heading south toward Saida.... Egyptian Pres. Anwar Sadat accepts Israeli Premier Menahem Begin's proposal to begin Mideast peace talks in Geneva after October 10.	Canada's National Energy Bd. formally approves the Alaska Highway (Alcan) gas pipeline route to carry Alaskan natural gas down to the contiguous U.S.	Melbourne, Australia dockworkers strike for 24 hours to protest alleged police brutality during an antiuranium demonstration, July 2–3.
July 5		King Juan Carlos I swears in the new Spanish Cabinet, which, in a departure from royal tradition, is not required to kneel before the monarch as it takes the oath of office.... Soviet Pres. Leonid Brezhnev meets with U.S. Amb. Malcolm Toon to discuss their countries' relations. Afterwards Tass reports that Brezhnev had criticized aspects of U.S. policies, seen as a reference to Pres. Carter's human-rights stance.	At the end of its four-day summit conference held in Libreville, Gabon, the OAU split between radical and moderate nations remains unresolved. The organization does unite in a vaguely worded resolution opposing white minority rule in southern Africa.	Gilberto Vieyra, Colombian CP general secretary, charges that since the inauguration of Pres. Alfonso Lopez Michelsen in 1974, soldiers have killed more than 500 leftists in rural areas.	The Japanese yen's value rises to its highest point against the U.S. dollar in four years.... Pakistani army, led by Gen. Muhammad Zia ul-Haq, overthrows the government of P.M. Zulfikar Ali Bhutto, imposes martial law, and pledges new elections in October.
July 6		Soviet Union renews attacks on Spanish CP leader Santiago Carrillo, stressing that its criticism is not directed at the independent-minded Communist parties of Spain, France, and Italy, but only at Carillo, who, it charges, has long waged an open anti-soviet campaign.	A bomb believed to have been planted by Arab terrorists explodes in an open-air market in Petah Tiqva, Israel, killing one person and injuring 20.... Pres. Carter says that it is vital for the Arabs to establish full diplomatic relations with Israel as part of an overall peace settlement and cites the dangers of creating an independent Palestinian state that is not linked to Jordan.... Kenya and Sudan are reportedly seeking improved ties.	The Canadian govt. orders a probe into the activities of the Royal Canadian Mounted Police in response to charges of their widespread illegal actions.	Benigno Aquino, imprisoned as a former political rival of Philippine Pres. Ferdinand Marcos, charges he is being denied the right to express his views from his cell.
July 7	Albania's CP newspaper sharply attacks China for flagrantly departing from Marxism-Leninism, although it does not mention China by name.	U.S. Agriculture Dept. estimates a record Soviet grain crop at 225-million metric tons.	South African For. Min. Roelof Botha echoes Agricultural Min. Hendrick Schoeman in calling for the repeal of two laws forbidding interracial sexual relations, which are considered the basis of South Africa's apartheid policy.... Cairo police find the slain body of former Egyptian Religious Affairs Min. Mohammed Hussein al -Zahabi, who was kidnapped near his home on July 3 by members of a Moslem extremist group.	Britain strengthens its military strength in Belize to counter growing threats by neighboring Guatemala.	Australia lifts curbs on foreign borrowing imposed after the Australian dollar was devalued in 1976.... Australian Labor Party's National Conference unanimously approves a ban in the country on uranium mining and processing.... A Chinese pilot, Fan Yuan-yen, defects to Taiwan by flying his MiG-19 jet to a Chinese Nationalist air force base.

A	B	C	D	E
Includes developments that affect more than one world region, international organizations and important meetings of major world leaders.	Includes all domestic and regional developments in Europe, including the Soviet Union, Turkey, Cyprus and Malta.	Includes all domestic and regional developments in Africa and the Middle East, including Iraq and Iran and excluding Cyprus, Turkey and Afghanistan.	Includes all domestic and regional developments in Latin America, the Caribbean and Canada.	Includes all domestic and regional developments in Asia and Pacific nations, extending from Afghanistan through all the Pacific Islands, except Hawaii.

U.S. Politics & Social Issues	U.S. Foreign Policy & Defense	U.S. Economy & Environment	Science, Technology & Nature	Culture, Leisure & Life Style	
				Soviets and the U.S. renew their track and field rivalry in two separate meets in Sochi, U.S.S.R. and Richmond, Va. The Soviets win the Sochi meet, 207–171, and the U.S. wins the second, 213–163. . . . The book, *My Story* , Judith Campbell Exner's account of her alleged affair with the late Pres. John F. Kennedy, is reviewed by Jeff Greenfield in *The New York Times*. . . . *The Thorn Birds* by Colleen McCullough tops the fiction best-selling list for the previous week.	July 3
Protesters break up a Fourth of July Ku Klux Klan rally in Columbus, Ohio.				Large and small boats converge for the New York Harbor Festival Fourth of July celebration.	July 4
	CIA second-ranking official E. Henry Knoche submits his resignation, attributed to strong policy differences with CIA Dir. Stansfield Turner.	Time Inc. announces a $63-million merger with Book-of-the-Month Club Inc. . . . Justice Dept. files a civil antitrust suit to block United Technologies Corp.'s proposed acquisition of Babcock & Wilcox Ltd., contending that the takeover would reduce competition in the electrical generating equipment industry. . . . Xerox Corp. wins a copier patent suit it had brought against IBM's Canadian subsidiary.	Stanford Ovshinsky, chmn. of Energy Conversion Devices Inc., announces at a London press conference that advances have been made in developing amorphous semiconductors to dramatically reduce the cost of devices producing solar energy.	United Church of Christ ends its eleventh biennial general synod in Washington, D.C. by unanimously voting to review over the next two years a proposed merger with the 1.3-million-member Christian Church (Disciples of Christ.) . . . United Church of Christ reaffirms the general synod's 1975 resolution deploring violation of gay civil rights.	July 5
National Institute of Drug Abuse releases a report showing that almost 8 million Americans have tried cocaine at least once and about 1 million used it in the previous month of June. It also notes that about 9 percent of graduating high school seniors in 1975 had experimented with cocaine and that its limited availability and high price have contributed to its reputation as a status drug.	Pres. Carter meets with 40 American Jewish leaders in the White House in an attempt to reassure them, as well as Israel, that his recent statements on the Mideast peace plan do not indicate that the U.S. is reversing its support for Israel.	National charters are granted to two groups planning to open banks managed and directed chiefly by women — Women's Bank N.A. (Denver, Colo.) and Women's National Bank (Wash. D.C.). . . . Sen. Lawton Chiles (D, Fla.) charges that the SBA program for minority business is a disaster costing the taxpayers $1.5 billion. He claims that the funds are actually funneled to prosperous white-owned firms using minorities as a front.		Rock concerts in N.Y.C.'s Central Park, formerly sponsored by the Schaefer Brewing Co., open with a new sponsor, the Dr. Pepper Co.	July 6
	Rep. Bruce Caputo (R, N.Y.) says he will ask the House Ethics Committee to seek White House tapes from the former Nixon administration to try to discover if there were a cover-up of the Korean–Congress influence-buying scandal.	Commerce Dept. data reports that county, municipal, and township tax revenue came to $41.1 billion in fiscal 1976, with property tax being the major revenue source.			July 7

F	G	H	I	J
Includes elections, federal-state relations, civil rights and liberties, crime, the judiciary, education, health care, poverty, urban affairs and population.	*Includes formation and debate of U.S. foreign and defense policies, veterans' affairs and defense spending. (Relations with specific foreign countries are usually found under the region concerned.)*	*Includes business, labor, agriculture, taxation, transportation, consumer affairs, monetary and fiscal policy, natural resources, and pollution.*	*Includes worldwide scientific, medical and technological developments, natural phenomena, U.S. weather, natural disasters, and accidents.*	*Includes the arts, religion, scholarship, communications media, sports, entertainments, fashions, fads and social life.*

	World Affairs	Europe	Africa & the Middle East	The Americas	Asia & the Pacific
July 8	Former Mexican Pres. Luis Echeverria Alvarez is named as Mexico's Ambassador to UNESCO.	*Washington Post* reports Yugoslav CP publications criticizing the Soviet Union for seeking to impose its authority on individual Communist parties and comparing Soviet bloc attacks on Spanish CP leader Santiago Carrillo's Eurocommunism with Belgrade–Moscow exchanges in 1948 that ultimately expelled Yugoslavia from the Soviet bloc. . . . British Liberal Party leader David Steel says that his party's showing in the Saffron Walden by-election, where it came in second, confirms voter acceptance of the Liberals' alliance with the governing Labor Party.	Zambian Pres. Kenneth Kaunda announces he has accepted offers of Cuban and Somalian military aid to defend his country against Rhodesian attacks.	Colombian cities experience a rash of assaults and kidnappings, attributed to urban guerrillas and common criminals, with 13 kidnap victims reported still being held.	ASEAN foreign ministers conclude three days of talks in Singapore with an agreement to promote peaceful relations with the Communist states of Vietnam, Laos, and Cambodia.
July 9					
July 10			Egyptian Pres. Anwar Sadat and Jordanian King Hussein agree to assure PLO participation at any resumed Geneva peace conference by establishing an explicit link between Jordan and a Palestinian state. . . . A bombing in Damascus, Syria kills at least two people and wounds 53. It follows a July 4 bombing that killed six and injured 12. . . . Rev. Ndabaningi Sithole, one of the rivals for leadership of the Rhodesian black nationalist movement, returns to Rhodesia after two years of self-imposed exile and endorses the U.S.–Britain effort toward achieving majority rule there. . . . Eritrean rebels are reported capturing two strategic Ethiopian towns — Keren and Decamere.	The strike at Mexico City's Autonomous National University, (UNAM) is settled after the police raid the campus on July 7 and arrest hundreds of strikers.	Gen. Muhammad Zia ul-Haq imposes a series of new martial law regulations in Pakistan, banning strikes, political agitation, and trade unions, and reimposing harsh Islamic penalties for thieves and anyone who insults a woman.
July 11				Venezuelan Pres. Carlos Andres Perez announces austerity measures to control inflation, cut government spending, and reduce the amount of money in circulation.	Burmese govt.-rebel clashes reportedly have resulted in the death of more than 500 insurgents and 130 government soldiers between February and June.

A	B	C	D	E
Includes developments that affect more than one world region, international organizations and important meetings of major world leaders.	*Includes all domestic and regional developments in Europe, including the Soviet Union, Turkey, Cyprus and Malta.*	*Includes all domestic and regional developments in Africa and the Middle East, including Iraq and Iran and excluding Cyprus, Turkey and Afghanistan.*	*Includes all domestic and regional developments in Latin America, the Caribbean and Canada.*	*Includes all domestic and regional developments in Asia and Pacific nations, extending from Afghanistan through all the Pacific Islands, except Hawaii.*

U.S. Politics & Social Issues	U.S. Foreign Policy & Defense	U.S. Economy & Environment	Science, Technology & Nature	Culture, Leisure & Life Style	
		Consumer installment credit is reported expanding a seasonally adjusted $2.53 billion in May, the third largest gain on record.... Unemployment rate rises in June to a seasonaly adjusted 7.1 percent, bringing the number of unemployed to 7 million.	An explosion and subsequent fire at a pump station of the *Trans-Alaska pipeline* kills one worker and injures five others.		July 8
Alice Paul, 92, leader of the women's suffrage movement and founder of the National Woman's Party in 1913, dies in Moorestown, N.J.			Loren Eisley, 69, anthropologist, writer, and educator connected with the University of Pennsylvania for 30 years, dies of cancer in Phila., Pa.	*The New York Times* reports that the National Humanities Endowment has awarded $350,000 for pre-production of the second round of the TV series *The American Short Story* and will match dollar-for-dollar grants from private industry up to $1 million.... Tom Watson comes from behind to win the golf British Open, beating Jack Nicklaus by one shot in the final round at Turnberry, Scotland.	July 9
		White House energy adviser James Schlesinger, speaking on NBC-TV's *Meet the Press*, confirms earlier reports that the administration is studying plans to ration gasoline, but only as a standby measure in the event of a dramatic interruption of supply.		Conservative Roman Catholic Archbishop Marcel Lefebvre consecrates his first American traditionalist church in the Houston, Tex. suburb of Dickinson, celebrating the banned traditional Latin Mass.	July 10
			South African-born heart transplant pioneer Dr. Christiaan Barnard, announces that he must retire from surgery within the next few years because of crippling rheumatoid arthritis.	An editorial in *The New York Times* questions the ethics involved in Western book company representatives participating in the first Moscow International Book Fair — scheduled to open on Sept. 6 — and charges that the fair insults Soviet writers who are silenced in their own country.	July 11

F	G	H	I	J
Includes elections, federal-state relations, civil rights and liberties, crime, the judiciary, education, health care, poverty, urban affairs and population.	Includes formation and debate of U.S. foreign and defense policies, veterans' affairs and defense spending. (Relations with specific foreign countries are usually found under the region concerned.)	Includes business, labor, agriculture, taxation, transportation, consumer affairs, monetary and fiscal policy, natural resources, and pollution.	Includes worldwide scientific, medical and technological developments, natural phenomena, U.S. weather, natural disasters, and accidents.	Includes the arts, religion, scholarship, communications media, sports, entertainments, fashions, fads and social life.

	World Affairs	Europe	Africa & the Middle East	The Americas	Asia & the Pacific
July 12	Pres. Carter emphasizes that development of the neutron bomb does not affect SALT negotiations and that it is a tactical weapon — defensive not offensive.... U.N. Relief and Works Agency announces that the U.S. has pledged an additional $22 million to its aid program for Palestinian refugees.	Spain devalues the peseta in a long-awaited move to control inflation and promote exports.... Soviet Union accuses Robert Toth, Moscow correspondent for the *Los Angeles Times*, of espionage in his dealings with Soviet scientist Valery Petukhov.		Quebec's governing Parti Quebecois introduces a revised version of a bill to make French the official language of the province. It includes some modifications but retains limits on English-language education.... Former El Salvadoran Pres. Osmin Aguirre Salinas, 85, is murdered by unknown gunmen outside his El Salvador home.	Papua New Guinea holds its first national election since it began its independence process in 1972. Michael Somare's Pangu Party and its coalition partner, the People's Progress Party, win at least 60 of 109 parliamentary seats.
July 13	OPEC ministers hold their semiannual meeting in Stockholm, Sweden, focusing their discussions on existing oil price differences within member countries.... Saudi and Iranian delegates to the OPEC Stockholm meeting say they might consider an oil-price freeze through 1978, but other member countries oppose or refuse to commit themselves on the subject.... Pres. Carter reportedly agrees not to single out the Soviets for human-rights violations at the upcoming Belgrade conference on the Helsinki accords, reportedly in response to W. Ger. Chancellor Helmut Schmidt's prodding.	Leaders of Britain's Trades Union Congress (TUC) tell the government that unions will stop holding their wage increases within government guidelines, breaking the Social Contract made in 1975 to curb inflation.... Press reports indicate that meetings between W. Ger. Chancellor Helmut Schmidt and Pres. Jimmy Carter in Washington were more cordial than their previous encounters.			North Korean gunners shoot down a U.S. Army helicopter believed to have strayed into North Korean airspace near the demilitarized zone, killing three crewmen, and wounding and capturing the fourth.
July 14			Bassam Sharif, a spokesman for the Popular Front for the Liberation of Palestine (PFLP), an extremist faction of the PLO, says that the PFLP seeks the overthrow of Jordan's King Hussein and Egyptian Pres. Anwar Sadat, calling Hussein the prime enemy of the Palestinians.	Canadian P.M. Elliott Trudeau calls the education limitations in Quebec's revised language bill a serious infraction of Canadians' rights to choose the language of education for their children and charges that Quebec is acting as if it were already separated from Canada.	Sir John Kerr resigns as Australia's governor general 18 months before his five-year term expires, after political controversies surrounding his use of office.
July 15	The U.N. Conference on the Law of the Sea adjourns its sixth session in another deadlock over the seabed mining issue.			Venezuelan Pres. Carlos Andres Perez reshuffles his Cabinet.	Chinese press agency Hsinhua claims that China's economic recovery rate since the Gang of Four was overthrown has exceeded all expectations.

A	B	C	D	E
Includes developments that affect more than one world region, international organizations and important meetings of major world leaders.	*Includes all domestic and regional developments in Europe, including the Soviet Union, Turkey, Cyprus and Malta.*	*Includes all domestic and regional developments in Africa and the Middle East, including Iraq and Iran and excluding Cyprus, Turkey and Afghanistan.*	*Includes all domestic and regional developments in Latin America, the Caribbean and Canada.*	*Includes all domestic and regional developments in Asia and Pacific nations, extending from Afghanistan through all the Pacific Islands, except Hawaii.*

U.S. Politics & Social Issues	U.S. Foreign Policy & Defense	U.S. Economy & Environment	Science, Technology & Nature	Culture, Leisure & Life Style	
Pres. Carter, in his press conference, says that recent Supreme Ct. decisions against federal funding of elective abortions are fair. He notes disparity between what the wealthy and the poor can afford and says that the federal govt. cannot make opportunities exactly equal, particularly in matters of moral choice.... Local police peacefully arrest 194 demonstrators who are protesting the construction of a $6-million gym on the site where four Kent State University (Ohio) students were killed by National Guardsmen in 1970.... A three-judge Ill. panel rules that the neo-Nazi National Socialist Party of America cannot display a swastika in any march or demonstration in Skokie, Ill., a predominantly Jewish suburb of Chicago, and home of approximately 7,000 survivors of Nazi concentration camps. A previous ban on the march had been overturned by the U.S. Supreme Ct.	Pres. Carter tells a news conference that he has no explanation for current Soviet testiness toward U.S. policies.... Pres. Carter tells a news conference he is deferring a decision on deployment of the neutron bomb, but supports the bomb as an option.	Preceded by Mobil Oil Corp., Exxon Corp. and Gulf Oil Corp. withdraw from the venture to build Seadock, a proposed deep-water port for oil tankers 26 miles off the Texas coast.... Pres. Carter, in a letter disclosed by Senate Governmental Affairs Committee Chmn. Abraham Ribicoff (D, Conn.) sought, to remove a deadline for OMB Dir. Bert Lance to sell bank stock shares that Lance held because it put an undue financial burden on Lance and on the bank, The National Bank of Georgia.... The Privacy Protection Study Commission, established in 1974, submits its final report, which includes sharp criticism of an experimental electronic banking project operated with the Federal Reserve System's computer.	W. Ger. Chancellor Helmut Schmidt reports after a series of meetings in Canada with P.M. Pierre Trudeau, that Canada has agreed to a partial relaxation of its embargo on uranium exports.		July 12
Patrick Kearney is indicted in Riverside County, Calif. for three homosexual-related murders and is being investigated in connection with up to 25 unsolved slayings that authorities say might result in being the largest multiple-murder case in U.S. history.	The Senate rejects Sen. Mark Hatfield's (R, Ore) proposal to halt funds for the production of the neutron bomb.	National Bank of Georgia, whose president Bert Lance resigned in January to join the Carter administration, reports a loss of $1.25 million for the first half of 1977.	A lightning bolt knocks out power in N.Y.C.'s five boroughs and suburban Westchester County, halting transportation and affecting hospitals and other facilities.... A three-day conference of over 100 scientists is held at Oxford University to honor Benjamin Levich, a Soviet scientist denied permission to emigrate to Israel, and to send a protest letter to the Soviet Academy of Scientists.		July 13
	Congress clears legislation authorizing $36.1 billion for weapons procurement, research, and civil defense in fiscal 1978, about one-third of the proposed Defense Dept. budget.... House votes, 227–171, to create a permanent Select Committee on Intelligence that would have exclusive jurisdiction over the CIA and would share jurisdiction with other House committees over other federal intelligence services.... Rep. Edward Boland (D, Mass.) is selected to chair the new House Select Committee on Intelligence.	The two-day blackout in the N.Y.C. metropolitan area closes banks, state offices, stores, and the NYSE and Amex. It also results in rampant looting, vandalism, and other crimes resulting in the arrest of 3,700 people.... N.Y.C. Mayor Abraham Beame charges Consolidated Edison Co. with gross negligence, but a Con Ed spokesman calls the N.Y.C.-area power failure "an act of God".			July 14
Pres. Carter submits a White House reorganization plan to Congress that reportedly proposes reducing positions but not personnel.				South Africa's leading Afrikaans poet, Breyten Breytenbach, is acquitted of charges that he promoted terrorism while in prison.... The N.Y.S. Assembly passes a bill giving the Crime Victims Compensation Bd. the first claim on any money earned by criminals for selling their life stories for publication.	July 15

F	G	H	I	J
Includes elections, federal-state relations, civil rights and liberties, crime, the judiciary, education, health care, poverty, urban affairs and population.	Includes formation and debate of U.S. foreign and defense policies, veterans' affairs and defense spending. (Relations with specific foreign countries are usually found under the region concerned.)	Includes business, labor, agriculture, taxation, transportation, consumer affairs, monetary and fiscal policy, natural resources, and pollution.	Includes worldwide scientific, medical and technological developments, natural phenomena, U.S. weather, natural disasters, and accidents.	Includes the arts, religion, scholarship, communications media, sports, entertainments, fashions, fads and social life.

	World Affairs	Europe	Africa & the Middle East	The Americas	Asia & the Pacific
July 16			Egyptian Pres. Anwar Sadat discloses that the Soviet Union had cancelled its military contracts with Egypt, and that Saudi Arabia has agreed to finance development of the Egyptian armed forces.		First news that purged Chinese leader Teng Hsiao-Ping has been reinstated into the Chinese CP is seen on Peking wall posters.... North Korea returns the bodies of three U.S. crewmen shot down near the Korean DMZ as well as the captured survivor and, reportedly, are unusually cooperative in their dealings with the U.S.
July 17		Protasio Montalvo Martin, a former Socialist mayor of Cercedilla, a mountain village near Madrid, emerges from hiding in the basement of his home for 35 years (since the end of the Spanish Civil War in 1939) convinced that he would have been executed for his political beliefs.	Israeli govt. announces a major austerity plan to curb inflation, featuring an immediate 25 percent price increase in food and other basics.	Jesuits in El Salvador unanimously reject right-wing terrorist threats that if they don't leave the country they will be killed by July 21.	South Korea conditionally frees 14 political dissidents from prison in a move seen as easing Pres. Park Chung Hee's tight political rule.
July 18			Rhodesian P.M. Ian Smith dissolves Parliament and sets new elections for August 31 in wake of what he calls the failure of a British–U.S. team to come up with a workable proposal for black majority rule.... The Israeli Labor Party-dominated General Federation of Labor (Histadrut) denounces the Israeli govt's economic austerity plan and calls a one-hour protest work stoppage. ... Eritrean rebels report attacking the Ethiopian towns of Asmara and Massawa, freeing about 1,000 political prisoners.	Hector Hidalgo Sola, Argentine ambassador to Venezuela, is kidnapped in Buenos Aires by presumed security officers opposed to Pres. Jorge Videla's avowed plan to slowly return Argentina to democracy.	Vietnam and Laos sign a series of 25-year agreements to bolster military, economic, and cooperative relations. As part of their agreement, they state that their relations with the U.S. can be normalized only if Washington gives both their countries postwar reconstruction aid.
July 19			Egypt returns to Israel 19 coffins said to contain the bodies of Israeli soldiers killed in the 1973 war.... British P.M. James Callaghan condemns Rhodesian P.M. Ian Smith's decision to dissolve Parliament and call new elections as an irrelevant move since only a minority of Rhodesians can vote.	Bahaman P.M. Lynden Pindling and his Progressive Liberal Party are overwhelmingly returned to office in parliamentary elections.... A bloody strike paralyzes Lima, Peru, in the culmination of a month-long series of protests against the government's economic austerity policies.	Japan reports a record $6.64-billion trade surplus for the first half of 1977.
July 20	OECD semiannual report on its 24-member nations' economic prospects says that unemployment will increase and urges that the U.S., Japan, and West Germany expand their economies.... U.N. Security Council unanimously approves Vietnam's membership in the U.N.	British Labor govt. wins passage of its antiinflation program.	Israeli Premier Menahem Begin outlines his Middle East peace plan after discussing it with Pres. Carter at the White House. The plan deals with procedural details of the conference and contains no specific view on political or territorial terms. ... Begin refuses to consider negotiating with the PLO, but says he would accept Lebanon as a party in Mideast peace talks.... Beirut newspaper Al Anwar reports that the U.S. and the PLO have been in secret contact since May, including a meeting on June 24 between William Scranton, former chief U.S. delegate to the U.N., and Basil Akl, a member of the PLO's U.N. delegation.	The state-operated Canadian Broadcasting Corp. (CBC) is charged after a four-month investigation with failing to promote Canadian unity through biased news-topic selection.	

A	B	C	D	E
Includes developments that affect more than one world region, international organizations and important meetings of major world leaders.	Includes all domestic and regional developments in Europe, including the Soviet Union, Turkey, Cyprus and Malta.	Includes all domestic and regional developments in Africa and the Middle East, including Iraq and Iran and excluding Cyprus, Turkey and Afghanistan.	Includes all domestic and regional developments in Latin America, the Caribbean and Canada.	Includes all domestic and regional developments in Asia and Pacific nations, extending from Afghanistan through all the Pacific Islands, except Hawaii.

U.S. Politics & Social Issues	U.S. Foreign Policy & Defense	U.S. Economy & Environment	Science, Technology & Nature	Culture, Leisure & Life Style	
					July 16
		McDonald's Corp. spokesman announces suspension of the company's Glasses to Go program because of EPA tests that revealed a high lead content in the decals decorating the drinking glasses, which are given as a purchasers of McDonald's fast-food items.	Brookhaven National Laboratory, N.Y. scientists charge that increased reliance on coal as an energy source (a key element of Pres. Carter's energy plan) could substantially increase the number of premature deaths from air pollution. . . . W. Ger. Chancellor Helmut Schmidt says that West Germany will halt the export of nuclear technology that could be used to make atomic weapons.		**July 17**
The New York Times reports a Gallup Poll finding that the majority of the American public tolerates job rights for homosexuals but is evenly divided over whether homosexual behavior should be legal.		Pres. Carter asks Congress to revise the basic U.S. labor laws to strengthen collective bargaining rights. . . . AFL–CIO pres. George Meany lauds Carter's labor-law proposal while Richard Lesher, U.S. Chamber of Commerce president, denounces it. . . . Albert Zack, an AFL–CIO spokesman, says that the AFL is temporarily halting its long-standing drive to repeal a section of the Taft-Hartley Act that permits states to either bar union shops or require workers to join them.		The Mostly Mozart Festival opens in N.Y.C.'s Lincoln Center, partially sponsored by a new group, Friends of Mostly Mozart.	**July 18**
		Oil flow through the Trans-Alaska pipeline shuts down after a small accident one day after the Interior Dept. allowed the flow, stopped for environmental reasons, to resume.		Fla. Citrus Commission says that singer Anita Bryant, prominent in antihomosexual campaigns, will be retained as their advertising symbol of Fla. orange juice. . . . The NL wins its sixth straight major league All-Star Game with a 7–5 victory over the AL. The game at Yankee Stadium, N.Y.C. is dedicated to the memory of Jackie Robinson, celebrating his entry as the first black player into baseball's major leagues 30 years before.	**July 19**
ACLU calls the Carter administration's civil liberties record poor but an improvement over the Ford administration.	Former Watergate Special Prosecution Leon Jaworski agrees to serve as a special counsel to the House Ethics Committee investigation of the South Korean influence-buying scandal, popularly known as Koreagate.	Carter administration announces a federal aid program for the troubled U.S. shoe industry. . . . A N.Y.S. Supreme Ct. Justice, Nathaniel Helman, fines the UFT $50,000 for its 1975 N.Y.C. teachers' strike and fines union pres. Albert Shanker $250.		Fifty thousand people from the Roman Catholic, Protestant, and other churches attend a Conference on Charismatic Renewal in Kansas City, Mo. It is the first interdenominational gathering of charismatics, an outgrowth of the Pentecostal movement, in U.S history.	**July 20**

F	G	H	I	J
Includes elections, federal-state relations, civil rights and liberties, crime, the judiciary, education, health care, poverty, urban affairs and population.	Includes formation and debate of U.S. foreign and defense policies, veterans' affairs and defense spending. (Relations with specific foreign countries are usually found under the region concerned.)	Includes business, labor, agriculture, taxation, transportation, consumer affairs, monetary and fiscal policy, natural resources, and pollution.	Includes worldwide scientific, medical and technological developments, natural phenomena, U.S. weather, natural disasters, and accidents.	Includes the arts, religion, scholarship, communications media, sports, entertainments, fashions, fads and social life.

	World Affairs	Europe	Africa & the Middle East	The Americas	Asia & the Pacific
July 21	U.S. dollar falls to a record low of 2.2555 West German marks before Bonn intervenes to buy dollars and boost the exchange rate to 2.2640.	Suleyman Demirel, head of Turkey's conservative Justice Party, becomes premier for the fourth time after the minority govt. of Bulent Ecevit falls on a no-confidence vote after 10 days in power.	Major fighting erupts on the Egyptian–Libyan border, with both sides using planes and tanks and suffering heavy losses.	Jesuit priests are moved temporarily into heavily guarded church schools, and the El Salvadoran govt. establishes roadblocks outside San Salvador on the deadline day set by right-wing terrorists threatening to kill all Jesuits still in the country. . . . Pres. Carter tells a Miss. audience that he hopes to sign a treaty with Panama providing shared responsibility for the operation of the Panama Canal until the year 2000.	Heavy Cambodian–Thai border fighting leaves 17 Thais and 50 Cambodians dead. . . . Sri Lanka elections topple P.M. Sirimavo R.D. Bandaranaike and her ruling Freedom Party.
July 22	U.N. Economic and Social Council (ECOSOC) votes, 27–11, to admit the PLO into its Economic Commission for Western Asia, making the PLO the first non-nation to gain full membership in a U.N. agency. . . . A Soviet study of U.S. Middle East policy reportedly charges that it is determined by American Jews. It also charges Jewish domination of the U.S. media and strong influence on U.S. political parties.	Greek govt. rejects the appointement of William Schaufele as U.S. ambassador to Athens in wake of remarks Schaufele had made about the Greek–Turkish dispute over Aegean Sea islands.			China announces that purged leader Teng Hsiao-ping has been restored to power and that the Gang of Four has been ousted from the CP.
July 23		The Soviet press reportedly hails the twenty-fifth anniversary of the late Gamal Abdel Nasser's ascension to power in Egypt in what is seen as a plea for better Soviet–Egyptian relations.		*The New York Times* reports that State Dept. officials are concerned about Pres. Carter's reference to the U.S. continuing its partial sovereignty over the Panama Canal until the year 2000 as being particularly offensive to Panamanians and difficult for their leader, Omar Torrijos Herrera to accept.	Junius Richard Jayewardene is sworn in as Sri Lanka's new prime minister. He attributes his victory to the "corruption, nepotism, and family banditry" in the Freedom Party, ousted by elections.
July 24		Spanish CP leader Santiago Carrillo's book, *Eurocommunism and the New State* , reportedly is the most widely read of all clandestine publications circulating among Czech dissidents.			
July 25	U.N. Security Council committee on Rhodesian sanctions reports that the U.S. had imported 45,854 tons of minerals and other embargoed items from Rhodesia between October–December 1976.	French Pres. Valery Giscard d'Estaing, in a *Newsweek* interview, charges that Pres. Carter has violated the code of behavior by which detente is conducted.	Representatives of the five front-line nations involved in the Rhodesian nationalist fight urge Rhodesian guerrilla groups to unite. . . . An Egyptian–Libyan truce goes into effect after mediation by PLO leader Yasir Arafat, Algerian Pres. Houari Boumedienne, and Arab League and Kuwaiti officials. . . . Lebanon and the PLO agree on measures to end fighting in southern Lebanon between Christian militiamen and Palestinian guerrillas, including reducing the level of arms at Palestinian refugee camps.		
July 26		British Liberal Party extends its pact with the Labor govt.	U.S. State Dept. offers arms to Somalia to lessen its dependence on the Soviet Union. . . . Israeli govt. official approves three existing Jewish settlements on the West Bank, hitherto regarded as illegal. . . . U.S. State Secy. Vance protests the legalized Jewish West Bank settlements as an obstacle to peace efforts.	A civilian leader of Brazil's ruling ARENA Party, Jose de Magalhaes Pinto, announces his candidacy for next year's presidential election in an apparent challenge to top military leaders who want to maintain military control of the government.	A U.S. State Dept. official, Richard Holbrooke, reports that an estimated 1.2 million Cambodians may have perished since the Communist Khmer Rouge seized power in April 1975 and charges the Cambodian authorities with flagrant and systematic violations of human rights. He cites, among other offenses, their forcible relocation of urban populations and brutal treatment of political opponents. . . . U.S. accedes to a South Korean request to maintain a major portion of U.S. troops in South Korea until 1982, the last year of the planned military pullout.

A	B	C	D	E
Includes developments that affect more than one world region, international organizations and important meetings of major world leaders.	*Includes all domestic and regional developments in Europe, including the Soviet Union, Turkey, Cyprus and Malta.*	*Includes all domestic and regional developments in Africa and the Middle East, including Iraq and Iran and excluding Cyprus, Turkey and Afghanistan.*	*Includes all domestic and regional developments in Latin America, the Caribbean and Canada.*	*Includes all domestic and regional developments in Asia and Pacific nations, extending from Afghanistan through all the Pacific Islands, except Hawaii.*

U.S. Politics & Social Issues	U.S. Foreign Policy & Defense	U.S. Economy & Environment	Science, Technology & Nature	Culture, Leisure & Life Style	
Pres. Carter attends a Yazoo City, Miss. civic meeting in his effort to stay close to the people. . . . Pres. Carter tells his Yazoo City audience that the South was guilty for many years of depriving human rights to a large portion of its citizens, and that it was with great courage that the South faced change.	In a Charleston, S.C. speech, Pres. Carter appears to reassure Moscow that U.S.–Soviet detente is not endangered. . . . House International Relations subcommittee begins hearings on the human-rights situation in El Salvador and hears accounts of numerous transgressions against Jesuits and other Catholic Church representatives there who are attacked because of their support of land reforms.	Commerce Dept. reports that the real GNP rose $21 billion in the second quarter, up 6.4 percent from the previous period to a seasonally adjusted annual rate of $1.332 trillion. . . . Congress clears legislation regulating coal strip-mining to the overall approval of environmentalists and criticism from the coal industry. . . . U.S. Steel announces plans to raise prices about 6 percent on structural steel shapes and about 7 percent on tin-mill products, effective Sept. 4.		Attending a Conference on Charismatic Renewal in the Christian Churches, Pres. Carter's sister, Ruth Carter Stapleton, a leader in the movement, describes a charismatic Christian as one totally committed to Jesus Christ and adds that the President fits that description. . . . Rabbi Abraham Feldman, 84, nationally known Jewish leader and ecumenist, dies in West Hartford, Conn.	July 21
				Jacob Ben-Ami, 86, actor and founder of the Jewish Art Theater in N.Y.C., dies after a short illness in N.Y.C.	July 22
			Britain and the U.S. sign an executive agreement on commercial air service between the two countries.		July 23
In a keynote address before the National Urban League's Washington., D.C. convention, Urban League pres. Vernon Jordan Jr. accuses Pres. Carter of not living up to his political commitment to aid his black supporters.			British Airways announces that it will seek U.S. govt. approval to reduces its London–N.Y. round-trip excursion fare by 17 percent to $290.		July 24
Pres. Carter tells the National Urban League convention in Washington, D.C. that his administration need not apologize for its record in dealing with blacks and the urban poor.		Senate Govermental Affairs Committee bars a full investigation into the personal finances of OMB director Bert Lance, centering around the over 200,000 shares of stock he held in the National Bank of Georgia before, joining the Carter administration.	HEW Secy. Joseph Califano orders a ban on phenformin, a prescription drug long used by diabetics, because of overwhelming evidence that it is a prime cause of lactic acidosis, which is a metabolic disorder fatal in half the reported cases.		July 25
				Dissident Roman Catholic Archbishop Marcel Lefebvre ends a two-week tour of Colombia, Chile, and Argentina, where he celebrated the banned Tridentine Latin Mass and openly attacked Pope Paul VI.	July 26

F	G	H	I	J
Includes elections, federal-state relations, civil rights and liberties, crime, the judiciary, education, health care, poverty, urban affairs and population.	Includes formation and debate of U.S. foreign and defense policies, veterans' affairs and defense spending. (Relations with specific foreign countries are usually found under the region concerned.)	Includes business, labor, agriculture, taxation, transportation, consumer affairs, monetary and fiscal policy, natural resources, and pollution.	Includes worldwide scientific, medical and technological developments, natural phenomena, U.S. weather, natural disasters, and accidents.	Includes the arts, religion, scholarship, communications media, sports, entertainments, fashions, fads and social life.

	World Affairs	Europe	Africa & the Middle East	The Americas	Asia & the Pacific
July 27		Italian Premier Giulio Andreotti concludes two days of talks in Washington with Pres. Carter on Italy's economic and political situation.	Israeli Premier Menahem Begin rejects U.S. State Secy. Vance's protest against legalizing three Jewish West Bank settlements and insists that they do not violate international law nor harm the Arabs.	A total of 3,000 workers strike Colombian cement plants, demanding a 50 percent wage increase and paralyzing the industry.	Australian govt. begins a probe of the country,s illegal drug trade after the July 15 disappearance of a prominent antidrug campaigner, Donald MacKay, in New South Wales.
July 28	Pres. Carter announces that the U.S., Britain, and the Soviet Union will begin formal negotiations on Oct. 3 in Geneva on a comprehensive ban against nuclear testing.	Greek and U.S. governments initial a four-year defense pact in Athens that grants Greece $700 million in military assistance in exchange for American use of four military bases.	Winnie Mandela, a South African black activist, is arrested and charged with violating a government order to refrain from political activity. . . . Somalia admits that its air force is participating in the heavy fighting in the Ethiopian region of Ogaden. . . . Pres. Carter calls Israeli legalization of Jewish settlements on the West Bank an obstacle to peace but not an insurmountable problem. . . . Carter also defends Israeli Premier Menahem Begin on the settlements issue, adding that the Israeli govt. never claimed that the settlements are permanent.	Peruvian Pres. Francisco Morales Bermudez pledges in a TV speech that the military govt. will turn over its power to an elected civilian govt. in 1980.	Former Pakistani P.M. Zulfikar Ali Bhutto is released from detention. . . . Japanese exports of color TVs reportedly declined in June for the third consecutive month.
July 29			A bomb set off by Arabs explodes in a Beersheda market in Israel, wounding 29 people. . . . Israeli official, Gavriel Bach, reports incidents of five Arab terrorists, imprisoned in the West Bank Nablus prison, beating and torturing four of their fellow Arab prisoners.	Pres. Carter intervenes personally in the Panama Canal Treaty talks and urges negotiators to conclude a new treaty as soon as possible. . . . Pres. Carter sends a letter to Panamanian leader Gen. Omar Torrijos saying he is pleased that Panama Canal talks are nearly completed but warns not to expect more major U.S. concessions.	After his release from detention, deposed Pakistani P.M. Zulfikar Ali Bhutto criticizes the martial law imposed by his successor, Gen. Mohammed Zia ul-Haq.
July 30		W. Ger. Dresdner Bank chmn. Jurgen Ponto, is shot and killed in his home near Frankfurt by five terrorists, believed to be connected to the left-wing groups responsible for the April slaying of Siegfried Buback, West Germany's chief prosecutor.	Syrian troops of the Arab League peacekeeping force in Lebanon begin implementing the July 25 truce in southern Lebanon.	Bombings in Popayan, Colombia reflect the wave of violence affecting urban and rural areas throughout July.	
July 31	IMF sees an increase in protectionist trade measures in 1976 and 1977.	French antinuclear demonstrators fight police during a massive protest march at France's largest nuclear reactor complex under construction at Creys-Malville. . . . West Germans are believed to be the more militant demonstrators who began fighting with the police in the march made by an estimated 20,000 people and comprising also Swiss and Italian contingents. . . . West German press and officials stress that the passive support and sympathy for young leftists in the country is based on an erroneous belief that the terrorists are misguided social reformers. They claim that Jurgen Ponto's murder was not an action against oppression, but thrill-seeking by a bored class of youths.			The Geneva-based International Commission of Jurists (IJC) accuses the Philippine govt. of a broad range of human-rights violations that include indefinite detention, torture, and beatings.

A	B	C	D	E
Includes developments that affect more than one world region, international organizations and important meetings of major world leaders.	Includes all domestic and regional developments in Europe, including the Soviet Union, Turkey, Cyprus and Malta.	Includes all domestic and regional developments in Africa and the Middle East, including Iraq and Iran and excluding Cyprus, Turkey and Afghanistan.	Includes all domestic and regional developments in Latin America, the Caribbean and Canada.	Includes all domestic and regional developments in Asia and Pacific nations, extending from Afghanistan through all the Pacific Islands, except Hawaii.

U.S. Politics & Social Issues	U.S. Foreign Policy & Defense	U.S. Economy & Environment	Science, Technology & Nature	Culture, Leisure & Life Style	
		The U.S. posted a record $2.82-billion trade deficit during June, according to Commerce Dept. reports, raising the cumulative first-half 1977 deficit to a record $12.59 billion.... FRB Chmn. Arthur Burns tells Congress that the U.S. should protect the integrity of its currency, privately remarking that the dollar's depreciation could lead to renewed U.S. inflation.			July 27
Pres. Carter tells a news conference that the major thing he has learned in his first six months as President is how to work better with Congress.		Treas. Secy. Michael Blumenthal indicates a change in U.S. monetary policy by saying that a strong dollar is of major importance not only to the U.S. but to the rest of the world.			July 28
Congressional Black Caucus supports Vernon Jordan Jr. in his recent confrontation with Pres. Carter over programs for minorities and the urban poor.	Republican Sen. Barry Goldwater (Ariz.) charges that Pres. Carter appears overeager in his conduct of foreign policy, creating the impression that the U.S. wants settlements at any cost.			Women's Wear Daily's fall fashion round-up notes that the most startling new look of the season is called Punk, originating in London by designer Zandra Rhodes. Big shawls in luxury fabrics are another new look.	July 29
				Emory Holloway, 92, Pulitzer Prize-winning biographer of Walt Whitman, dies in Bethlehem, Pa. ... Frank Gifford, Gale Sayers, Bill Willis, Forrest Gregg, and Bart Starr are included into the Pro Football Hall of Fame.	July 30
		A July 19–20 flash flood in Johnstown, Pa. is reported leaving 68 people dead, 31 missing, at least 2,000 homeless, and damages estimated at $2 million.			July 31

F	G	H	I	J
Includes elections, federal-state relations, civil rights and liberties, crime, the judiciary, education, health care, poverty, urban affairs and population.	Includes formation and debate of U.S. foreign and defense policies, veterans' affairs and defense spending. (Relations with specific foreign countries are usually found under the region concerned.)	Includes business, labor, agriculture, taxation, transportation, consumer affairs, monetary and fiscal policy, natural resources, and pollution.	Includes worldwide scientific, medical and technological developments, natural phenomena, U.S. weather, natural disasters, and accidents.	Includes the arts, religion, scholarship, communications media, sports, entertainments, fashions, fads and social life.

	World Affairs	Europe	Africa & the Middle East	The Americas	Asia & the Pacific
Aug. 1		Britain announces a plan to give $1.6 billion to aid Northern Ireland's troubled economy and to cancel $425 million owed to the British govt. by Ulster's electricity company.	U.S. State Secy. Vance begins a 12-day tour of the Middle East to promote American efforts to reconvene the Geneva peace conference.		North Korea sets a military sea zone and a 200-mile economic zone.
Aug. 2			At a joint press conference with Secy. Vance., Pres. Sadat says he is willing to sign a peace agreement with Israel "tomorrow", but it must stipulate total Israeli withdrawal from Arab lands captured in the 1967 war.... Ethiopia appeals to the OAU to halt Somali intervention in Ogaden.		China reportedly has rehabilitated former army chief of staff Huang Ko-cheng, 80, who has been in political disgrace since 1962.
Aug. 3		Archbishop Makarios, leader of the Greek community on Cyprus and president of the Cypriot govt. since it was founded in 1960, dies at the age of 63.... Spyros Kyprianou, Cypriot Parliament president, becomes acting president of Cyprus.		The Canadian govt. rejects a proposal to divide the Northwest Territories into provinces along racial and ethnic lines.	Cambodian troops kill 28 civilians and one policeman in Thailand's Ta Phraya district, 185 miles northeast of Bangkok.
Aug. 4			Ethiopia admits that most of its southeastern Ogaden area is occupied by guerrillas of the Western Somalia Liberation Front (WSLF), who are fighting to unite Ogaden with Somalia.		Gough Whitlam, head of the Australian Labor Party, is assured by U.S. officials that the CIA will not interfere with a future Labor Party govt.... Philippines Pres. Ferdinand Marcos declares that his country will drop its claim to the Malaysian state of Sabah.
Aug. 5	The Belgrade preparatory conference to review the progress of the Helsinki accords ends with the 35 member-nation delegates agreeing on an agenda for the upcoming formal review conference, Oct. 4 – Dec. 22.		Tanzanian Pres. Julius Nyerere confers with Pres. Carter in Wash., D.C. on transition to black majority rule in Rhodesia, speaking pessimistically afterward about prospects for a peaceful solution.	Panama's chief of government Omar Torrijos Herrera meets with leaders of five neighboring countries in Bogota, Colombia to enlist their support for a new Panama Canal Treaty.... Solicitor General Francis Fox agrees to make substantial reforms in the Canadian prison system.	
Aug. 6			Somali rebels claim to have killed or captured more than 2,000 Ethiopian troops, downed more than 30 planes, and destroyed or captured masses of military equipment since July 28.... In what is declared to be the worst act of urban terrorism since the five-year-old guerrilla war in Rhodesia began, an explosion in a Salisbury department store kills 11 people and injures 76.	Leaders of Jamaica, Panama, Venezuela, Colombia, Mexico, and Costa Rica agree to create an International Coffee Fund to regulate the coffee market and control prices.... Venezuelan Pres. Carlos Andres Perez tells newsmen that Latin Americans had gained everything they wanted in Panama Canal negotiations.	Thai Premier Thanin Kraivichien confirms reports of Cambodian attacks on Vietnam and Thailand, as well as raids on Laos.

A	B	C	D	E
Includes developments that affect more than one world region, international organizations and important meetings of major world leaders.	*Includes all domestic and regional developments in Europe, including the Soviet Union, Turkey, Cyprus and Malta.*	*Includes all domestic and regional developments in Africa and the Middle East, including Iraq and Iran and excluding Cyprus, Turkey and Afghanistan.*	*Includes all domestic and regional developments in Latin America, the Caribbean and Canada.*	*Includes all domestic and regional developments in Asia and Pacific nations, extending from Afghanistan through all the Pacific Islands, except Hawaii.*

U.S. Politics & Social Issues	U.S. Foreign Policy & Defense	U.S. Economy & Environment	Science, Technology & Nature	Culture, Leisure & Life Style	
	The first in a series of reports is made about a CIA-sponsored $25-million program of secret mind-control experiments at universities, hospitals, and prisons from 1950–1973.... Francis Gary Powers, 47, who sparked a U.S.–Soviet diplomatic crisis in 1960 when the U-2 reconnaissance plane he was piloting was shot down over the Soviet Union, dies when a helicopter he was piloting as a TV reporter crashes in Encino, Calif.	USWA members strike in Minn. and northern Mich., halting 85 percent of domestic iron-ore production.	Construction begins on the atomic energy plant in Seabrook, N.H. following a July 26 NRC ruling. Opponents of the project, which has come to symbolize the controversy over nuclear power in the U.S., say they will seek new legal means to block its construction.	U.S. District Ct. Judge Earl Larson approves settlement of a class-action suit filed by the NFL Players Assn. against the NFL.	Aug. 1
	Revelations about previous CIA mind-control experiments with unwitting subjects document use of drugs, hypnosis, and behavior control devices, all aimed at developing ways to induce disorientation, amnesia, and unconsciousness in enemy agents.	U.S. Appeals Ct. for Wash., D.C. upholds the FTC's right to require advertisers to correct false claims in their ads, in wake of a challenge made by Warner-Lambert Co. on its Listerine mouthwash ads.			Aug. 2
The Puerto Rican terrorist group FALN claims responsibility for bombing two N.Y.C. office buildings.	CIA Dir. Stansfield Turner says that the CIA had been responsible for mind-control research at 80 institutions, including 44 colleges and universities, that the peak testing period had been from 1953–1963, and that the testing, now stopped, was personally abhorrent.	Pres. Carter signs the Surface Mining and Reclamation Act.		Chrysostomos of Paphos is named new archbishop to head the Cypriot Orthodox Church in wake of Archbishop Makarios's death.... Ernst Bloch, 92, German–Jewish Marxist philosopher who became the spokesman for post-WWII student radicalism, dies in Tubingen, West Germany.... Alfred Lunt, 84, American actor who, with his wife Lynn Fontanne, dominated the Broadway stage for nearly four decades, dies of cancer in Chicago.	Aug. 3
HEW Secy. Joseph Califano bans all federal subsidies for abortion except when the mother's life is in danger.	CIA Dir. Stansfield Turner is given new powers, including budgetary control, over all foreign-intelligence gathering agencies and chairmanship of two newly created intelligence policy committees.	Pres. Carter signs legislation establishing a new Energy Dept. and announces his nomination of the White House energy adviser, James Schlesinger, as its head.... Conrail reports a second-quarter net loss of $27.6 million, bringing its total loss for the first half of the year to $235.1 million.			Aug. 4
Morton Halperin, a NSC staff member during the Nixon administration, is awarded $5.00 in his $3-million wiretap suit against former Pres. Nixon and his aides, after Judge John Lewis Smith Jr. rules that although Halperin's rights were violated by the wiretaps, he could not prove that they actually damaged himself or his family.			FTC publishes a study hailing health maintenance organizations (HMOs) that offer prepaid group medical care because they create sufficient competition to keep down the cost of conventional health services.		Aug. 5
Pres. Carter reveals a plan for a comprehensive welfare revision, forsaking his previous goal of keeping costs at existing levels.		AT&T and the Communications Workers of America reach agreement on a contract to provide a 31 percent wage-benefits increase over three years. It is reached hours before a scheduled nationwide strike.	Soviet Union warns the U.S. that a South African nuclear weapons test is imminent.	Joe Namath debuts as a Los Angeles Ram in a preseason game against the Minnesota Vikings.	Aug. 6

F	G	H	I	J
Includes elections, federal-state relations, civil rights and liberties, crime, the judiciary, education, health care, poverty, urban affairs and population.	Includes formation and debate of U.S. foreign and defense policies, veterans' affairs and defense spending. (Relations with specific foreign countries are usually found under the region concerned.)	Includes business, labor, agriculture, taxation, transportation, consumer affairs, monetary and fiscal policy, natural resources, and pollution.	Includes worldwide scientific, medical and technological developments, natural phenomena, U.S. weather, natural disasters, and accidents.	Includes the arts, religion, scholarship, communications media, sports, entertainments, fashions, fads and social life.

	World Affairs	Europe	Africa & the Middle East	The Americas	Asia & the Pacific
Aug. 7			Jamshid Amouzegar replaces Amir Abbas Hoveida as Iranian premier after Hoveida resigns on Aug. 6 at the request of Shah Mohammed Riza Pahlevi, who appointed Hoveida minister of the Imperial Court.	Most of Canada's 2,200 air-traffic controllers begin a strike for wage hikes.	After four weeks of fighting a concentration of Communist rebels along their common frontier, a combined force of Thai and Malaysian troops reports progress.
Aug. 8	U.N. General Assembly's decolonization committee unanimously approves a resolution to include communications cutoffs in the boycott of Rhodesia.		Sudanese Pres. Mohammed Gaafar el-Nimeiry announces a general amnesty for all political prisoners. . . . Ugandan exiles reportedly have formed a united front in Zambia to attempt to overthrow the government of Idi Amin.	U.S. and Panamanian negotiators resume talks in Panama and predict they will have a canal treaty within the week.	Indian Industry Min. George Fernandes demands that the Coca-Cola Co. of the U.S. transfer its manufacturing formula to India and give a 60 percent share of its wholly owned American subsidiary to Indian stockholders.
Aug. 9	Soviet news agency Tass denounces Pres. Carter's decision to authorize standby funding for the neutron bomb.		State Secy. Vance encounters strong Israeli objections to returning the West Bank and Gaza Strip, to creation of a Palestinian state in the territory, or to dealing with the PLO, even if it accepts U.N. Resolution 242.	Seven policemen in Brazil are identified as members of the Rio de Janeiro, Death Squad, held responsible for 55 assassinations since July 1. . . . A Canadian govt. official reveals that lists of alleged subversives are sitll being circulated among Cabinet members, despite government denials.	
Aug. 10		Portugal passes a land reform law intended to break Communist control over the southern agricultural region and return some expropriated land to private farmers.	In wake of major fighting that began Aug. 4 in southern Lebanon, the Palestinian press agency Wafa charges that Israeli artillery had shelled Palestinian positions the previous day and cites Israeli gunboat movements near Tyre.	Panamanian and U.S. negotiators announce an agreement in principle on an new Panama Canal Treaty. The two accords give Panama complete control over the canal and zone by the year 2000, but allows the U.S. to intervene indefinitely thereafter to maintain the waterway's neutrality. . . . Canadian Parliament passes emergency legislation to return striking air controllers to work.	
Aug. 11		On the second day of her Silver Jubilee tour of Northern Ireland, Britain's Queen Elizabeth II makes as speech urging an end to violence.	Egyptian govt. indicts 54 Moslem fanatics for treason, sabotage, terrorism, and communicating with a foreign power — Libya.	At the end of a four-day visit to Cuba by U.S. Sen. Frank Church (D, Ida.), Pres. Fidel Castro announces concessions that appear to bring Cuba and the U.S. a step closer to full diplomatic relations.	
Aug. 12		Following Queen Elizabeth II's visit to Northern Ireland, a bomb explodes on the spot where she spoke the previous day, and the IRA kills a British marine and wounds three other soldiers.	Black nationalist leasder Joshua Nkomo states that one condition for ending the guerrilla war in Rhodesia is the removal from office of Rhodesian P.M. Ian Smith.	Chilean govt. announces abolishing the secret police (National Intelligence Directorate), accused of arresting, torturing, and murdering thousands of Chileans during the past four years of military rule.	The eleventh Chinese CP Congress begins in Peking.
Aug. 13		The British right-wing, antiblack National Front Party demonstrates in London, creating a riot when 3,000 left-wing militants attack the 1,000 marchers and injure 110 people. . . . Acting Pres. Spyros Kyprianou is named presidential candidate of the four main Greek Cypriot political parties to complete the five-year term of the late Archbishop Makarios.		*The New York Times* reports that several Brazilian retired military officers are joining in the movement for political freedom in the country.	
Aug. 14			Israeli govt. announces plans to grant equal rights to Arabs in the occupied West Bank and Gaza Strip, covering such social services as health care, national insurance, and free education.		Nationalist China registers a $263.5-million trade surplus in January–July 1977, compared to a $216.4-million surplus for the same period in 1976.

A	B	C	D	E
Includes developments that affect more than one world region, international organizations and important meetings of major world leaders.	Includes all domestic and regional developments in Europe, including the Soviet Union, Turkey, Cyprus and Malta.	Includes all domestic and regional developments in Africa and the Middle East, including Iraq and Iran and excluding Cyprus, Turkey and Afghanistan.	Includes all domestic and regional developments in Latin America, the Caribbean and Canada.	Includes all domestic and regional developments in Asia and Pacific nations, extending from Afghanistan through all the Pacific Islands, except Hawaii.

U.S. Politics & Social Issues	U.S. Foreign Policy & Defense	U.S. Economy & Environment	Science, Technology & Nature	Culture, Leisure & Life Style	
			The Alaska Pipeline Commission charges that $1.5 billion was wasted in construction of the Trans-Alaska pipeline through poor management, poor business practices, and maneuvers to win congressional approval.		Aug. 7
Speaking before the ABA's ninety-ninth annual convention in Chicago, V.P. Mondale says he favors legislation to prohibit domestic spying by the CIA and prevent harassment by the FBI.		Pres. Carter signs a bill delaying stiffer clean-air controls on automobile emissions.	Canada approves construction of a pipeline to bring Alaskan natural gas from Prudhoe Bay to the lower U.S.	Ernie Banks, former Chicago Cubs infielder and five others are inducted into the Baseball Hall of Fame. Former player Al Lopez is inducted as a manager.	Aug. 8
		Opinion Research Corp. poll releases a report that more U.S. workers are dissatisfied with their jobs than at any other time since 1952.	Edward Kleinschmidt, 101, who in 1914 invented the high-speed tele-type that revolutionized communications and news reporting, dies in Canaan, Conn.	NHL rejects a proposed merger with the rival WHA.	Aug. 9
David Berkowitz, is arrested outside his Yonkers, N.Y. apartment as the alleged "Son of Sam" serial murderer, after a sensational manhunt that traced him through a series of threatening anonymous notes to his neighbors and by a seemingly unrelated parking ticket. . . . ABA House of delegates votes to revise the ABA code to allow lawyers to advertise their services.	*New England*'s six states are reported having lost more than half of their defense-related jobs since 1960 because of Pentagon cutbacks, with Massachusetts being hardest hit.	Fires destroy or damage dozens of Dayton, Ohio homes during a two-day strike by 360 members of the International Assn. of Fire Fighters.	Volcanic eruptions in Japan cause an estimated $8 million in damage to agricultural crops.		Aug. 10
Calif. State Assembly overrides Gov. Edmund Brown Jr.'s veto, 54–26, and enacts the death penalty.				Mark Schorer, 69, novelist, literacy critic, and author of an extensive biography of writer Sinclair Lewis, dies following surgery in Oakland, Calif.	Aug. 11
A landmark victims' rights bill is signed by N.Y.S. Gov. Hugh Carey, which grants crime victims first rights to the proceeds earned by criminals through sale for publication of their life stories.			U.S. space shuttle Enterprise lands safely in the Mojave Desert after making its first successful solo flight test.	U.S. District Ct. Judge Walter Stapleton rules that Delaware can operate a 1977 lottery on NFL games.	Aug. 12
					Aug. 13
				Larry Wadkins wins the PGA title and $60,000 in Pebble Beach, Calif.	Aug. 14

F	G	H	I	J
Includes elections, federal-state relations, civil rights and liberties, crime, the judiciary, education, health care, poverty, urban affairs and population.	*Includes formation and debate of U.S. foreign and defense policies, veterans' affairs and defense spending. (Relations with specific foreign countries are usually found under the region concerned.)*	*Includes business, labor, agriculture, taxation, transportation, consumer affairs, monetary and fiscal policy, natural resources, and pollution.*	*Includes worldwide scientific, medical and technological developments, natural phenomena, U.S. weather, natural disasters, and accidents.*	*Includes the arts, religion, scholarship, communications media, sports, entertainments, fashions, fads and social life.*

	World Affairs	Europe	Africa & the Middle East	The Americas	Asia & the Pacific
Aug. 15		Swiss private investment firm Hervel & Co. is closed and arrest warrants are issued for its president Serge Hervel and his son, Theodore, who fled the country with $8–20 million in clients' funds. . . . Nazi war criminal Herbert Kappler excapes from a Rome military hospital and is smuggled back into West Germany by his wife, Annelise, who transports him in a large suitcase.	Joshua Nkomo, a principal Rhodesian black nationalist leader, rejects the U.S.–British approach to a formula for black majority rule in Rhodesia.	At a press conference in Port-au-Price, U.S. Amb. to the U.N. Andrew Young criticizes the repressive Haitian govt. and then meets with Pres.-for-Life Jean-Claude Duvalier, who, reportedly, tells him that Haiti "believes in human rights." . . . Amnesty International accuses the Nicaraguan National Guard of systematic and wholesale extermination of the country's peasant farmers (*campesinos*).	U.S. CIA submits a report on the Chinese economy that forecasts a mixed outlook linked to agriculture and industrial technology modernization.
Aug. 16			South African police disperce a march by white women in Pretoria demanding equal rights with men, charging that the protest is illegal under the Riotous Assemblies Act. . . . A bomb explosion in northern Israel signals the start of PLO increased military operations inside of Israel in retaliation for Israel's decision to extend social services to Arabs in the Gaza Strip and West Bank.	Nicaraguan govt. denounces Amnesty International's charges. Church and diplomatic sources concede some truth in the report, but argue that human-rights violations have significantly decreased this year because of pressure from the Carter administration.	OECD reports that the Chinese economy has expanded impressively during the past 25 years, particularly its industrial growth. . . . Pres. Suharto announces a general amnesty for FRETELIN guerrillas who fought against Indonesia's 1976 annexation of East Timor.
Aug. 17		Italian govt. formally asks West Germany to extradite Herbert Kappler, a Nazi war criminal and cancer victim who was smuggled from a Rome hospital in a suitcase by his wife, Annelise.	Israeli govt. approves plans to establish three more new Jewish settlements on the West Bank to the disapproval of the U.S. and Palestinians. . . . Three men are reported to have been executed in Uganda for producing a play alleged to be insulting to Pres. Idi Amin.	Royal Canadian Mounted Police admits that it kept surveillance files on members of Parliament and other Canadian govt. officials. . . . Canadian Labor Congress rejects P.M. Pierre Trudeau's plan to end wage and price controls — substituting voluntary wage controls — and demands, instead, an immediate end to wage controls without preconditions.	
Aug. 18		Former U.S. CIA agent Philip Agee is expelled from France as an "undersirable."	U.S. State Dept. criticizes Israel's Aug. 14 decision to extend social services to Arabs on the West Bank because the act connotes Israeli occupation.	Venezuela's opposition Social Christian Party chooses Sen. Luis Herrera Campins as its 1978 presidential candidate. . . . At the annual two-day Canadian premiers' conference in St. Andrews, New Brunswick, Quebec Premier Rene Levesque offers to modify Bill 101, Quebec's pending legislation on language rights if the other premiers make reciprocal agreements with Quebec to guarantee French-language education for their Frech-speaking minorities.	
Aug. 19		French and East German press criticize West Germany's decision against extraditing Nazi war criminal Herbert Kappler. Israel sends a protest note to the W. Ger. Embassy in Tel Aviv.	Ethiopian troops reportedly repel a major three-day attack on Diredawa by Somali-backed guerrilas.	Premiers of Canada's nine predominantly English-speaking provinces reject Quebec Premier Rene Levesque's proposal to exchange guarantees on language education.	Australian Parliament bans strikes by public employes.
Aug. 20			P.M. John Vorster proposes reorganizing the South African govt. to give more power to Asians and coloreds (mixed-race). . . . Rhodesian nationalist guerrillas massacre 16 African men, women, and children on a white-owned farm near the Mozambique border.		

A	B	C	D	E
Includes developments that affect more than one world region, international organizations and important meetings of major world leaders.	*Includes all domestic and regional developments in Europe, including the Soviet Union, Turkey, Cyprus and Malta.*	*Includes all domestic and regional developments in Africa and the Middle East, including Iraq and Iran and excluding Cyprus, Turkey and Afghanistan.*	*Includes all domestic and regional developments in Latin America, the Caribbean and Canada.*	*Includes all domestic and regional developments in Asia and Pacific nations, extending from Afghanistan through all the Pacific Islands, except Hawaii.*

U.S. Politics & Social Issues	U.S. Foreign Policy & Defense	U.S. Economy & Environment	Science, Technology & Nature	Culture, Leisure & Life Style	
	The American Conservative Union has reportedly budgeted $20,000 for newspaper advertisements against the new Panama canal treaties, termed a "giveaway" by conservatives.	U.S. govt. index of production in factories, mines, and utilities is reported rising .5 percent in July.	Pres. Carter signs a bill authorizing $884.3 million for the National Science Foundation (NSF).	U.S. Civil Rights Commission issues a study charging the TV industry with job bias and perpetuation of racial and sexual stereotypes in its programming.	Aug. 15
David Berkowitz pleads not guilty in the eight murders attributed to Son of Sam since July 29 and says he will use the defense of insanity.	Former Pres. Gerald Ford and former State Secy. Henry Kissinger, both Republicans, meet separately with Carter administration officials and announce their support of the Panama Canal treaties.	FTC releases a report charging that the funeral industry takes advantage of its customers economically and emotionally, and calls for more effective regulation and consumer education.	The Soviet atomic icebreaker *Arktika* becomes the first surface vessel in history to reach the North Pole.	Elvis Presley, 42, singer known as the "King of rock' n' roll," dies of a heart ailment in Memphis, Tenn. He had sold more records (500 million) during his career than any other performer and was seen as the embodiment of the 1950s youth–culture music.	Aug. 16
Frank M. Johnson Jr., a U.S. district ct. judge in Ala., is nominated to replace Clarence Kelley as FBI director.	Pres. Carter signs a $1.7-billion fiscal 1978 State Dept. authorization bill containing a provision that lifts the existing ban on Communist aliens entering the country.	N.Y.C. Mayor Abraham Beame scores the court ruling allowing the Concorde to land at Kennedy Airport as ignoring the best environmental interest of the people and ignoring the American tradition of home rule and local control.	U.S. District Ct. Judge Milton Pollack orders an end to the 17-month ban on Concorde supersonic transport service at Kennedy International Airport, N.Y.C.		Aug. 17
	Sens. Strom Thurmond (R, S.C.), Jesse Helms (R, N.C.), and Orrin Hatch (R, Utah) reportedly are leading a congressional effort to block ratification of the new Panama Canal treaties.	OMB Dir. Bert Lance is cleared by a government panel of criminal wrongdoing in his financial dealings while president of the National Bank of Georgia. . . . In a letter accompanying his report, Currency Comptroller John Heimann, who headed the Lance investigation, says that Lance's banking practices, which he intermingled with his personal borrowing needs, raise unresolved questions about what constitutes acceptable banking policy.		Franz Beckenbauer is voted the North American Soccer League's most valuable player. . . . Two women mourners are killed and a third critically injured when a drunken driver plunges his car into a crowd outside of the Elvis Presley mansion in Memphis during funeral services held inside.	Aug. 18
	State Dept. officials say that public opinion polls and conversations with key congressional leaders reflect strong American concern about abandoning Taiwan.	After-tax corporate profits rise 7.1 percent during the second quarter to a seasonally adjusted annual rate of $104.1 billion.	The Marble Cone fire, burning since Aug. 1, is reported destroying over 175,000 acres of the Ventana Wilderness in California's Los Padres National Forest.		Aug. 19
Gallup Poll reports that the Republican Party now has the support of only 20 percent of U.S. voters, its worst showing in 40 years.			Voyager II, an unmanned space craft is launched from Cape Canaveral, Fla. on a study-flight of the planets Jupiter and Saturn.	The book industry's largest single order — over 2 million copies — is reported being placed for *Elvis: What Happened?* , a Ballantine Books paperback by Steve Dunleavy. The book reputedly reveals Elvis Presley's drug addiction, violent outbursts, and obsession with death. . . . Groucho (Julius) Marx, 86, celebrated for his quick wit, ad-lib, and insult, and former member of the comedy quartet, the Marx Brothers, dies of pneumonia in Los Angeles.	Aug. 20

F	G	H	I	J
Includes elections, federal-state relations, civil rights and liberties, crime, the judiciary, education, health care, poverty, urban affairs and population.	*Includes formation and debate of U.S. foreign and defense policies, veterans' affairs and defense spending. (Relations with specific foreign countries are usually found under the region concerned.)*	*Includes business, labor, agriculture, taxation, transportation, consumer affairs, monetary and fiscal policy, natural resources, and pollution.*	*Includes worldwide scientific, medical and technological developments, natural phenomena, U.S. weather, natural disasters, and accidents.*	*Includes the arts, religion, scholarship, communications media, sports, entertainments, fashions, fads and social life.*

	World Affairs	Europe	Africa & the Middle East	The Americas	Asia & the Pacific
Aug. 21	Former U.S. Atty. Gen. Ramsey Clark asserts before the start of the World Peace Through Law Conference in Manila that the choice of the Philippines as the conference's site is inappropriate in face of Philippine martial law.				Chinese CP announces a new Politburo comprised of party Chmn. Hua Kuo-Feng, Defense Min. Yeh Chian-ying, and Deputy Premier Teng Hsiao-ping, who was rehabilitated in July.
Aug. 22	Addressing the opening of a U.N.-sponsored conference on apartheid, U.N. Secy. Gen. Kurt Waldheim strongly warns South Africa against creating tribal homelands for blacks.	Danish govt. asks for a $3.7-billion tax increase, spread over three years.	A U.S. State Dept. spokesman acknowledges that Israelis had been using U.S.-supplied arms in support of Christians in Lebanon. ... Helen Suzman, a leading parliamentary foe of apartheid, calls South African P.M. Vorster's government reorganization plan an illusion that gives the impression of real change but maintains white minority control.	Quebec's 4,000 Inuit (Eskimos), protest Bill 101, the Quebec govt.'s French language bill.	U.S. State Secy. Vance opens talks in Peking on establishing full diplomatic ties with China. ... Philippine Pres. Ferdinand Marcos issues a series of measures to ease maritial law.
Aug. 23	Israeli and Palestinian delegates to the World Peace Through Law Conference clash on human rights charges.		A joint Lebanese Christian–Moslem committee forms to prevent renewed clashes south of Beirut, following two days of fighting in which 17 people are killed and 19 wounded.		Former Indian Defense Min. Bansi Lal is arrested on charges of misappropriating $60,000 belonging to the youth wing of the former ruling Congress Party. ... Nine days of violence between Sri Lanka's rival racial groups leaves an estimated 54 deaths and 500 arrests.
Aug. 24		Literaturnaya Gazeta , Soviet writers' union weelkly publication, strongly condemns Benjamin Levich, the highest-ranking Soviet scientist, who has applied for emigration, and denounces the Oxford University conference held in his honor.	After U.S. Amb. to the U.N. Andrew Young meets with Nigerian head of state Lt. Gen. Olusegun Obasanjo in Lagos, details of a new Rhodesian majority-rule plan are leaked. The plans calls for the dismissal of Rhodesian P.M. Ian Smith and his replacement by an interim British administrator.	Quebec govt. issues a white paper setting forth the rules under which a referendum on Quebec separation should take place.	Indian authorities announce they have canceled an agreement with the Soviet Union for assistance in expanding the Bokaro steel plant in Bihar State and have begun negotiating with two U.S. firms because the Soviets lack the necessary sophisticated technology.
Aug. 25	At the U.N. conference on apartheid, U.S. Amb. Andrew Young warns against calling for anti-South African measures that would just be repudiated by the U.S. Congress and American public.	Joop den Uyl, caretaker head of the Netherlands govt., tells Queen Juliana he cannot form a coalition Cabinet and is released, at his request, from the assignment.			Concluding talks on establishing full U.S.–Chinese relations, U.S. State Secy. Vance says the discussions were candid, serious, and useful. ... Two thousand people march in Manila, the Philippines to protest human-rights abuses.
Aug. 26	A U.N. conference in Lagos, Nigeria condemns South African apartheid but falls short of calling for a complete economic and military boycott of the country.	During a dinner for visiting Israeli Premier Menahem Begin, Rumanian Pres. Nicolae Ceausescu calls for PLO representation at any Mideast peace conference.	Syrian Pres. Hafez al-Assad declares he would sign a peace pact to end the state of war with Israel, but that he opposes normal relations until Israel abandons its expansionism. ... PLO issues a four-point statement rejecting U.S. mediation in the Middle East and reaffirming opposition to the U.N. Security Council Resolution 242, the guideline for an overall peace settlement since 1967.	Bermuda P.M. John Sharpe resigns as the result of internal dissension in the United Bermuda Party, which he heads. ... Quebec National Assembly passes the controversial French language Bill 101. ... Two mutilated bodies are found in Cordoba as press reports contend that unexplained disappearances in Argentina are increasing.	Vietnam CP's Central Committee is reported to acknowledge major leadership policy errors, particularly in agriculture. ... Philippines Pres. Ferdinand Marcos warns that he will prolong emergency rule if antigovernment demonstrations, such as the one on the previous day, are repeated.

A	B	C	D	E
Includes developments that affect more than one world region, international organizations and important meetings of major world leaders.	Includes all domestic and regional developments in Europe, including the Soviet Union, Turkey, Cyprus and Malta.	Includes all domestic and regional developments in Africa and the Middle East, including Iraq and Iran and excluding Cyprus, Turkey and Afghanistan.	Includes all domestic and regional developments in Latin America, the Caribbean and Canada.	Includes all domestic and regional developments in Asia and Pacific nations, extending from Afghanistan through all the Pacific Islands, except Hawaii.

U.S. Politics & Social Issues	U.S. Foreign Policy & Defense	U.S. Economy & Environment	Science, Technology & Nature	Culture, Leisure & Life Style	
				Andy North wins the Westchester Golf Classic, shooting a par 71 in the last round.... The thirtieth annual Edinburgh Festival in Scotland opens with a schedule that includes productions by the Stuttgart State Theater and American actress Julie Harris repeating her U.S. success as Emily Dickinson in William Luce's *The Belle of Amherst*.	Aug. 21
	Renegotiation Bd. chairman Goodwin Chase admits his mistake in accusing the Lockheed Aircraft Corp.'s shipbuilding division of overcharging the Navy.	Touche Ross & Co., one of the largest U.S. accounting firms, and J.K. Lasser & Co., a medium-size accounting firm, merge under the Touche Ross name.		NBC dismisses Robert Howard as president of its television network and replaces him with Robert Mulholland.	Aug. 22
Md. Gov. Marvin Mandel is convicted, with five others, of mail fraud and racketeering in connection with an influence-peddling scheme. He is the first incumbent governor convicted of a federal crime since 1924.		In a press conference, Pres. Carter defends OMB Dir. Bert Lance, but concedes that government investigations into Lance's financial dealings as president of two Ga. banks reveal the need for banking regulation reforms.	P.M. John Vorster denies that South Africa is developing atomic weapons, in wake of accusations and warnings from the Soviet Union and France against nuclear testing.	Sebastian Cabot, 59, portly bearded British actor known for his roles in two American TV series, dies after a stroke in Victoria, British Columbia.	Aug. 23
			Agriculture Dept. designates 2,026 countries in 34 U.S. states, Puerto Rico, and the Virgin Islands as eligible for drought in the past century.		Aug. 24
Cook County, Ill. Democratic Party leader Jacob Arvey, 81, dies in Chicago. He is credited with launching the political careers of Ill. Gov. Adlai Stevenson Jr. and Sen. Paul H. Douglas and with playing a decisive role in Harry S. Truman's 1948 presidential victory.	Ronald Reagan says he will campaign personally to prevent ratification of the new Panama Canal treaties.	Commerce Dept. reports that the U.S. trade deficit during July was a seasonally adjusted $2.33 billion, the fourth largest ever recorded but considerably smaller than the record $2.82-billion deficit posted in June.	Australian P.M. Malcolm Fraser announces lifting a four-year govt. ban on uranium mining and export.		Aug. 25
SEC publishes a report charging that N.Y.C. Mayor Abraham Beame, Comptroller Harrison Goldin, and a group of major commercial banks deliberately failed to warn investors in N.Y.C. bonds in 1974–75 of an imminent financial crisis.... ERA supporters march in Wash., D.C. to launch a nationwide drive by the National Organization for Women (NOW) to pass the ERA before the March 1979 deadline. ... Pres. Carter calls for ERA ratification and proclaims Woman's Equality Day.		*Esquire* magazine is sold to a group headed by Clay Felker, former publisher of *New York* magazine.			Aug. 26

F	G	H	I	J
Includes elections, federal-state relations, civil rights and liberties, crime, the judiciary, education, health care, poverty, urban affairs and population.	Includes formation and debate of U.S. foreign and defense policies, veterans' affairs and defense spending. (Relations with specific foreign countries are usually found under the region concerned.)	Includes business, labor, agriculture, taxation, transportation, consumer affairs, monetary and fiscal policy, natural resources, and pollution.	Includes worldwide scientific, medical and technological developments, natural phenomena, U.S. weather, natural disasters, and accidents.	Includes the arts, religion, scholarship, communications media, sports, entertainments, fashions, fads and social life.

	World Affairs	Europe	Africa & the Middle East	The Americas	Asia & the Pacific
Aug. 27		A fire, racing through the U.S. Embassy in Moscow, causes extensive damage but no injuries.	Lebanon National Front leaders, who are Christians, blame the Palestinians for the continued fighting in Lebanon and warn that the Christians may withdraw support from Lebanese Pres. Elias Sarkis if the situation does not improve.... Front-line African states (those bordering Rhodesia) make it clear that they will not compromise on removing Rhodesian P.M. Smith from office and dismantling the Rhodesian army.		
Aug. 28		Peter Altmeier, 70, a drafter of the W. Ger. Constitution in 1949 and former president of the Rhineland–Palantine State, dies in Coblenz, West Germany.	Patriotic Front joint leaders, Robert Mugabe and Joshua Nkomo, reject a proposal for a Rhodesian interim government that would bring a U.N. peacekeeping force into Rhodesia, saying that Patriotic Front forces are the only forces entitled to supervise the transition to majority rule.	Pres. Francisco Morales Bermudez lifts the nationwide state of emergency in Peru after nearly 14 months.	U.S. State Secy. Vance expresses caution about normalizing U.S. diplomatic relations with China when he briefs Pres. Carter after his Aug. 22–25 Peking visit.
Aug. 29	Soviet–U.S. tension is seen eased by the two governments' cooperation in heading off a South African nuclear-weapons test.	Workers at British Leyland Ltd. in Birmingham, England force their shop stewards to cancel a planned strike.... Sweden devalues the krona by 10 percent and withdraws from the European Currency Cooperation Agreement, known as the snake.		Protestant School Board of Greater Montreal votes to defy Quebec's Bill 101 and admit into its English-language schools any child whose parents choose English-language education, whether or not the child meets provincial requirements.	Li Hsien-nien, a Chinese CP Politburo member, expresses displeasure with Pres. Carter's reluctance to cut ties with Taiwan.
Aug. 30	PLO leader Yasir Arafat assails U.S. intentions in the Middle East during a meeting in Moscow with Soviet For. Min. Andrei Gromyko.				Yugoslav Pres. Tito is enthusiastically received in China, where, for many years, he had been denounced. The ideological rift between the two countries is seen still existing from the fact that the Tito visit is as head of state not head of Yugoslavia's CP.
Aug. 31	Israel is reported agreeing in principle to allow UNESCO to investigate the cultural freedom of Arabs living in Israeli-occupied lands.		P.M. Ian Smith's ruling Rhodesian Front Party scores an overwhelming victory in elections, gaining all 50 white seats in the 66-seat Parliament and giving him an unequivocal mandate to negotiate a settlement with black Rhodesian leaders. Blacks boycott the elections.		Sri Lanka lifts curfews after declaring that racial violence there has ended.... Malaysia is reported easing its ban on accepting refugees from Vietnam, Cambodia, and Laos.
Sept. 1		Soviet Union officially revises its national anthem after 20 years during which the anthem could not be sung because it glorified Josef Stalin.	The first step of the Western-sponsored independence plan for Namibia goes into effect. Justice Marthinus Steyn, the Pretoria-appointed administrator general, assumes his duties with SWAPO approval.... U.S. withdraws its proposed arms aid to Somalia in face of the Ogaden conflict between Somalia and Ethiopia.	Cuban and U.S. governments establish interest sections in Havana and Wash., D.C. to function as virtual embassies in the absence of formal diplomatic relations.	Five men, including a key witness in the trial of former Philippine Sen. Benigno Aquino, are killed by unknown assailants in an ambush 60 miles north of Manila.
Sept. 2	International Institute for Strategic Studies issues a pessimistic report about the West's military strength relative to the Warsaw Pact nations.	Dutch Socialists and Christian Democrats postpone trying to settle the controversy over abortion that threatens to disrupt talks on a coalition between the two parties.	Israel discloses a settlement plan for 2 million Jews in a region stretching from the Golan Heights to the tip of the Sinai Peninsula by the end of the century as a security buffer.	Brazilian press reports that 63 ARENA congressmen met with their party's Senate leader and appealed for Democratic reforms in Brazil, which include dissolving ARENA and MDB, the country's two existing political parties, and replacing them with a mutliparty system.	

A	B	C	D	E
Includes developments that affect more than one world region, international organizations and important meetings of major world leaders.	Includes all domestic and regional developments in Europe, including the Soviet Union, Turkey, Cyprus and Malta.	Includes all domestic and regional developments in Africa and the Middle East, including Iraq and Iran and excluding Cyprus, Turkey and Afghanistan.	Includes all domestic and regional developments in Latin America, the Caribbean and Canada.	Includes all domestic and regional developments in Asia and Pacific nations, extending from Afghanistan through all the Pacific Islands, except Hawaii.

U.S. Politics & Social Issues	U.S. Foreign Policy & Defense	U.S. Economy & Environment	Science, Technology & Nature	Culture, Leisure & Life Style	
				U.S. golf team defeats the British–Irish team, 16–8, in the Walker Cup classic.	Aug. 27
N.Y.C. Comptroller Harrison Goldin challenges SEC allegations about N.Y.C.'s financial crisis, citing numerous times in 1974 and 1975 when he had publicly warned of the city's fiscal decline.			U.S.–Soviet cooperative efforts head off a planned South African nuclear-weapons test in the Kalahari Desert.	Hale Irwin wins the $50,000 top prize in the PGA Hall of Fame Classic at Pinehurst, N.C. . . . The Cosmos win their second North American Soccer League championship over the Seattle Sounders in a title game called Soccer Bowl '77 at Civic Stadium, Portland.	Aug. 28
	AFL–CIO pres. George Meany endorses the new Panama Canal treaties.	*Time* magazine gives examples of the corrosive effects inflation has had on the stock market's Dow Jones average. It also notes that seats on the NYSE are selling at under $50,000, compared with $515,000 in 1969. . . . U.S. private overseas investment rises 10.5 percent in 1976 to $137.24 billion, according to a Commerce Dept. report. . . . Pres. Carter moves to limit wheat production by asking farmers to reduce their wheat acreage by 20 percent for the 1978 crop year.	*Time* magazine reports that Italy's Mt. Etna has erupted three times within the month.	Lou Brock, of the St. Louis Cardinals, steals two bases to break the baseball Hall of Fame record held by Ty Cobb.	Aug. 29
	Sen. Ernest F. Hollings (D, S.C.) is reported stating after a visit to Argentina that the Argentine govt. is free and that the Carter administration has done too much moralizing on the human-rights issue.		South African Finance Min. Owen Horwood says that his country will develop an atomic bomb if it deems it necessary and denounces U.S. concern. Hours later, For. Min. Roelof Botha issues a statement reiterating that South Africa will not produce a nuclear weapon.		Aug. 30
A newly formed congressional workers' coalition urges an end to sex discrimination in Capitol Hill jobs and wages.		J.P. Stevens & Co. is found in contempt of prior court orders to abide by federal labor laws and refrain from interfering in unionization efforts at its Southern plants.	World Psychiatric Assn., meeting in Honolulu, Hawaii and representing 4,000 psychiatrists from 60 countries, votes to censure the Soviet Union for its systematic abuse of psychiatry for political purposes.	*The New York Times* reports adverse reaction by religious leaders and efforts to influence advertisers against the new ABC-TV comedy series *Soap*, scheduled to begin in mid-September and reported to contain much explicit sexual material.	Aug. 31
	Undersecretary of State Philip Habib says that the creation of Cuban–U.S. interest offices is significant and allows both countries to speak directly to each other.		Soviet Union bars Air France from using the wide-bodied French Airbus on its Paris–Moscow air route.	Ethel Waters, black actress and singer remembered for her roles in *Cabin in the Sky* and *Member of the Wedding*, dies at the age of 80.	Sept. 1
		Labor Dept. reports August unemployment, primarily blacks, rose to a seasonally adjusted 7.1 percent from 6.9 percent in July. . . . Dow Jones industrial average closes up at 872.31, an advance of 16.89 points in five days, after a loss of more than 40 points during the preceding six weeks.	Soviet Unin bars the French Concorde from refueling in Siberia for its Tokyo–Paris route.		Sept. 2
F	**G**	**H**	**I**	**J**	
Includes elections, federal-state relations, civil rights and liberties, crime, the judiciary, education, health care, poverty, urban affairs and population.	Includes formation and debate of U.S. foreign and defense policies, veterans' affairs and defense spending. (Relations with specific foreign countries are usually found under the region concerned.)	Includes business, labor, agriculture, taxation, transportation, consumer affairs, monetary and fiscal policy, natural resources, and pollution.	Includes worldwide scientific, medical and technological developments, natural phenomena, U.S. weather, natural disasters, and accidents.	Includes the arts, religion, scholarship, communications media, sports, entertainments, fashions, fads and social life.	

	World Affairs	Europe	Africa & the Middle East	The Americas	Asia & the Pacific
Sept. 3					Former Pakistani P.M Zulfikar Ali Bhutto is arrested at his home in Karachi and charged with the murder of two political opponents while he was in office.
Sept. 4			U.N. truce observers along the Lebanese–Israeli border are reported to be coming under increased assault from both sides.		
Sept. 5		West German industrialist Hanns-Martin Schleyer is kidnapped by armed terrorists in Cologne.	Two antiapartheid groups merge in South Africa to form the Progressive Federal Party, with 18 seats in the 171-seat Parliament.... Twelve troops are killed in a clash with Polisario Front guerrillas who are fighting for the independence of the former Spanish Sahara.	Mexican newspaper *Excelsior* reports continuing politically motivated kidnappings, torture, and murders in Guatemala.	
Sept. 6		Hanns-Martin Schleyer's kidnappers demand release of 11 of their imprisoned colleagues by the West German govt. in exchange for Schleyer.	Ethiopia claims that it has won a major military victory in Ogaden. ... The entire black faculty at 40 high schools in Soweto, South Africa resigns to protest the government policy of school segregation.	U.S. announces it has returned to Haiti 97 of 101 refugees who had sailed into the U.S. naval base at Guantanamo Bay, Cuba a month ago.... Canadian Finance Min. Donald Macdonald resigns, citing personal reasons.	Australian Atty. Gen. Robert Ellicott resigns charging that the Australian govt. had halted his investigation into possible criminal charges against former P.M. Gough Whitlam and three of his former ministers.... Pakistani martial law leader Gen. Muhammad Zia ul-Haq implicates former P.M. Zulfikar Ali Bhutto in a third political murder.
Sept. 7	A protocol attached to the second of the two-part new Panama Canal Treaty invites all nations of the world to sign the pact and acknowledge the canal's permanent neutrality.	Gangs of South Moluccan youths rampage through Assen, the Netherlands and battle police during the four-day trial of eight South Moluccan militants who seized a passenger train and a schoolhouse in May and held hostages.... British Trades Union Congress (TUC) votes to support the government's policy of limiting wage increases to once a year, which is seen as a victory for P.M. James Callaghan's govt.	Rumors circulate that Ugandan Pres. Idi Amin is in a coma the day after he signed execution orders for 15 alleged plotters against his life.	*Miami Herald* reports that the U.S. has resumed selling arms to Guatemala after a several-month hiatus caused by Guatemalan objections to Pres. Carter's human-rights policies.	Australian P.M. Malcolm Fraser rejects a trade union proposal to hold a national referendum on uranium mining and export.... New Zealand P.M. Robert Muldoon announces enacting a 200-mile fishing zone and totally banning, after Oct. 1, fishing in snapper and terakihi spawning grounds.
Sept. 8		Yugoslav Pres. Tito concludes a tour, begun Aug. 16, of the Soviet Union, North Korea, and China.... Turkish govt. imposes austerity measures to stabilize the economy. ... West German Chancellor Helmut Schmidt's Cabinet approves three bills aimed against terrorist activity.	Rhodesian Defense Min. Mark Partridge issues an outright rejection of the British–U.S. plan for Rhodesian majority rule.		South Korea says it will not force Park Tong Sun to return to the U.S. against his will to face an indictment for alleged illegal lobbying practices.... Chinese CP newspaper publishes new details of the alleged 1971 plot by the late Defense Min. Lin Piao to assassinate CP Party Chmn. Mao Tse-tung and seize power.
Sept. 9		Soviet KGB (secret police) chief Yuri Andropov calls Soviet dissidents similar to espionage agents. ... Trial of eight South Moluccans who seized a train in Assen, the Netherlands and a schoolhouse in Bovensmilde and held hostages, ends. The South Moluccan Liberation Front calls the trial a farce and demands Dutch backing for an independent homeland in Indonesia.	*Financial Times of London* reports a bloody power stuggle between the two major factions in the Ethiopian govt., which has strengthened the position of Ethiopian military leader Mengistu Haile Mariam, head of the Dergue faction.... Uganda executes 15 alleged would-be assassins of Pres. Idi Amin.	Panamanian head of government Brig. Gen. Omar Torrijos Herrera announces a plebiscite on the new Panama Canal treaties, set for Oct. 23.... Quebec Premier Rene Levesque rejects Canadian P.M. Pierre Trudeau's offer to give Quebec special status by means of a constitutional amendment guaranteeing language rights for all Canadians.	The first anniversary of Chinese Chmn. Mao Tse-tung's death is marked by a call for modification of his strict principles of government.

A	B	C	D	E
Includes developments that affect more than one world region, international organizations and important meetings of major world leaders.	Includes all domestic and regional developments in Europe, including the Soviet Union, Turkey, Cyprus and Malta.	Includes all domestic and regional developments in Africa and the Middle East, including Iraq and Iran and excluding Cyprus, Turkey and Afghanistan.	Includes all domestic and regional developments in Latin America, the Caribbean and Canada.	Includes all domestic and regional developments in Asia and Pacific nations, extending from Afghanistan through all the Pacific Islands, except Hawaii.

U.S. Politics & Social Issues	U.S. Foreign Policy & Defense	U.S. Economy & Environment	Science, Technology & Nature	Culture, Leisure & Life Style	
			Jean Rostand, 83, French essayist and biologist whose scientific work revolutionized the fields of parthenogenesis and artificial insemination and whose writings established him as a popular moralist and satirist, dies in Saint-Cloud, France.	Japanese first baseman, Sadaharu Oh, playing for Tokyo's Yomiuri Giants, becomes the highest-scoring home-run hitter in baseball history, eclipsing Hank Aaron's major league record of 755.	Sept. 3
Three masked members of a San Francisco Chinese youth gang kill five people and wound 11 others in an ambush at a San Francisco restaurant where they were apparently gunning for members of a rival Chinatown gang who were dining there.			WHO reports an upsurge of malaria cases in Guatemala, Nicaragua, El Salvador, Honduras, India, Pakistan, Sri Lanka, and Bangladesh.	The Book of Lists by David Wallechinsky, Irving Wallace, and Amy Wallace is the best-selling nonfiction book for the week just ended.	Sept. 4
			Voyager I, an unmanned spacecraft, is launched from Cape Canaveral, Fla. beginning a mission toward Jupiter and Saturn that is expected to last several years.	Unruly fans at the U.S. Open tennis matches in Forest Hills, N.Y. stage a sit-in after an announcement that a match between Guillermo Vilas and Jose Higueras would be played in the evening instead of the afternoon.	Sept. 5
Hamaas Abdul Khaalis and 11 of his Hanafi Muslim followers are sentenced to prison terms ranging from 24 to 78 years after being convicted by an all-black jury for their seizure of 149 hostages at three different buildings in Wash., D.C. on March 9.	Park Tong Sun, a central figure in the Korean congressional lobbying scandal, is indicted on 36 felony counts by a U.S. federal grand jury.	Both U.S. and foreign car sales set a record at 931,422 in August, up 17.6 percent from August 1976, with 762,422 of the units sold being domestic-made.	Canada begins converting its highway speed-limit and distance signs to the metric system, leaving only the U.S., Liberia, and South Yemen using the English system of measurement.	Soviet Union hosts its first international book fair in Moscow, which is attended by about 1,300 publishers from 63 countries, including three from Israel, and 24 from the U.S.	Sept. 6
G. Gordon Liddy is released from Danbury, Conn. federal prison after serving over four years for his role in masterminding the Watergate break-in scheme in 1972.	Pres. Carter and Brig. Gen. Omar Torrijos Herrera sign the new Panama Canal treaties in Wash., D.C. ceremonies.	Pres. Carter meets with Congressional Black Caucus members and pledges job action for blacks and equal opportunity through affirmative action.... Consumer credit posts a strong gain in July, at $2.32 billion, seen by analysts as reflecting more confidence in the economy's recovery from recession.		A survey commissioned by the AMA reportedly finds that ABC-TV programs contain the most violence and CBS-TV programs the least.... Betty Stove beats Tracy Austin, who, at 14, is the youngest tennis player ever to appear in a U.S. Open, in the quarter-finals at Forest Hills, N.Y.	Sept. 7
N.Y.C. Mayor Abraham Beame is defeated in the Democratic mayoral primary, coming in third after Rep. Edward Koch and N.Y. State Secy. Mario Cuomo. Roy Goodman wins the Republican nomination.	A $1.4-billion appropriation for production of the controversial B-1 bomber is eliminated from the defense spending bill by a House close vote of 202–199.	With new developments unfolding, OMB Dir. Bert Lance is under investigation by both houses of Congress and at least six federal units.... Senate, 74–8, passes a bill requiring newly constructed industrial plants and utilities to burn coal or other alternatives to fuel or natural gas. It is a weakened version of Pres. Carter's original energy legislation program.	Canadian P.M. Pierre Trudeau and Pres. Carter announce an agreement on the construction of a natural gas pipeline from Alaska's Prudhoe Bay through Canadian territory to the lower U.S.... EPA, OSHA, and FDA announce joint action to prevent exposure to DBCP (dibromochloropropane), a pesticide found to cause sterility among workers and cancer in laboratory animals.	Stage and screen comic actor Zero Mostel dies while on tour at the age of 62. He is best remembered as Prologus in A Funny Thing Happened On the Way to the Forum and as Tevye in Fiddler on the Roof	Sept. 8
National Governors Association endorses Pres. Carter's welfare reform proposals, 31–4, calling the proposals "audacious."	Congress clears defense appropriations of $109.75 billion in fiscal 1978.		A U.N.-sponsored conference on the problem of spreading deserts ends in Nairobi, Kenya with the adoption of a plan to establish a special U.N. account in the U.N. on which desert-threatened nations can draw.	Soviet agents are reported seizing about 16 titles brought into the Moscow book fair by U.S. publishers, including George Orwell's Animal Farm and 1984 .	Sept. 9

F	G	H	I	J
Includes elections, federal-state relations, civil rights and liberties, crime, the judiciary, education, health care, poverty, urban affairs and population.	Includes formation and debate of U.S. foreign and defense policies, veterans' affairs and defense spending. (Relations with specific foreign countries are usually found under the region concerned.)	Includes business, labor, agriculture, taxation, transportation, consumer affairs, monetary and fiscal policy, natural resources, and pollution.	Includes worldwide scientific, medical and technological developments, natural phenomena, U.S. weather, natural disasters, and accidents.	Includes the arts, religion, scholarship, communications media, sports, entertainments, fashions, fads and social life.

	World Affairs	Europe	Africa & the Middle East	The Americas	Asia & the Pacific
Sept. 10		Northern Ireland's State Secy. Roy Mason announces that British direct rule will continue indefinitely, dispelling rumors of British troop withdrawal. . . . Hamida Djandoubi, a Tunisian convicted of murdering his woman friend, is guillotined, the third murderer executed in France since Pres. Valery Giscard d'Estaing took office in 1974.			
Sept. 11	IMF economic survey calls the international economic scene unsatisfactory, citing the fall of the economic growth rate below the 1976 level and the rise in unemployment.		Idi Amin's personal adviser, Robert Astles, reports that the Ugandan president is "quite fit" although still hospitalized after suffering an alleged coma.	Brazilian newspapers are reported publishing reports that political prisoners are tortured in Rio de Janeiro and Sao Paulo jails. . . . Paraguayan Pres. Gen. Alfredo Stroessner announces that he will run for a sixth presidential term in the upcoming February 1978 election.	
Sept. 12	GATT charges that protectionism in world trade is a threat to a country's international economic growth and to international order.	Norway's ruling Labor Party makes substantial election gains, holding 78 seats in the 155-seat Parliament.	A prominent black South African student leader, Steven Biko, dies from a reported hunger strike, begun on Sept. 5 while he was held in police detention. Associates of Biko discount this police version of his death.	Costa Rica announces that U.S. fugitive financier Robert Vesco must stand trial on charges that he defrauded a Costa Rican investor of $225,000.	Exiled former Pres. Lon Nol says that more than 2.5 million people have met violent deaths in Cambodia since the Communist takeover in April 1975. . . . *Hsinhua* reports Chinese testing of guided missiles with nuclear warheads. . . . China's State Planning Commission calls for tighter economic controls and says that the government is reestablishing a system used in the late 1950s and later dropped by Chmn. Mao Tse-tung, which provides greater centralization.
Sept. 13		Maj. Gen. Alexander Knyrkov, Soviet military attache in Bonn, is the first Soviet representative ever to attend the annual NATO exercises, which begin in West Germany.	U.S. State Dept. lodges an official protest with the South African govt. over Steven Biko's death. . . . Princess Ashraf Pahlevi, twin sister of the Shah of Iran, narrowly escapes an assassination attempt while she is driving on a narrow road near the French Riviera resort, Juan les Pins.	Omar Torrijos invites the OAS to visit Panama and see first-hand the reality of human-rights policies there.	Pakistani Pres. Zulfikar Ali Bhutto is freed on bail after being held in detention since Sept. 3 on murder-conspiracy charges.
Sept. 14		The small French Left-Radical Party walks out of a conference of left-wing coalition parties to protest CP demands for changes in their common platform.	Somali-backed guerrillas capture Jijiga, a major and strategic town in Ethiopia's Ogaden region.	Left-wing guerrillas plant 40 bombs in Mexico City, Guadalajara, and Oaxaca before dawn, 23 of which explode, injuring at least five people and damaging an estimated $20-million worth of property. . . . At least 14 people are killed in a violent general strike in Colombia, called by labor unions to demand a 50 percent wage increase and other concessions from the government.	
Sept. 15		Public condemnation of Italian Premier Giulio Andreotti's govt. reportedly grows in wake of the escape from a Rome hospital of Nazi war criminal Herbert Kappler. Six political parties, including the CP, join in demanding that Defense Min. Vito Lattanzio resign.		Colombian Pres. Alfonso Lopez Michelsen goes on radio and television to denounce strikers, blames the strike deaths on political extremists, and flatly renounces their wage demands.	Pakistani govt. lifts the state of emergency imposed in 1971 just prior to the war with India.

A	B	C	D	E
Includes developments that affect more than one world region, international organizations and important meetings of major world leaders.	Includes all domestic and regional developments in Europe, including the Soviet Union, Turkey, Cyprus and Malta.	Includes all domestic and regional developments in Africa and the Middle East, including Iraq and Iran and excluding Cyprus, Turkey and Afghanistan.	Includes all domestic and regional developments in Latin America, the Caribbean and Canada.	Includes all domestic and regional developments in Asia and Pacific nations, extending from Afghanistan through all the Pacific Islands, except Hawaii.

U.S. Politics & Social Issues	U.S. Foreign Policy & Defense	U.S. Economy & Environment	Science, Technology & Nature	Culture, Leisure & Life Style	
	Sen. Majority Leader Robert Byrd (D, W.Va.) says he will not call a Senate vote to ratify the Panama Canal treaties until early 1978.	Calls for OMB Dir. Bert Lance's resignation increase as Senate Democratic Leader Robert Byrd (W.Va.) tells reporters that Lance's effectiveness has been destroyed and that his resignation is inevitable.		Susan Perkins, 23, Miss Ohio, wins the Miss America contest in Atlantic City, N.J.... Chris Evert wins the U.S. Open women's tennis singles title for the third straight year.	**Sept. 10**
Members of a rival Chinese youth gang kill one youth and injure another in a retaliatory attack for killings in a San Francisco Chinatown restaurant on Sept. 4.	Republican Sen. Barry Goldwater (Ariz.) and Democratic Sen. John Stennis (Miss.) speak out against the new Panama Canal treaties.			Guillermo Vilas of Argentina wins the U.S. Open men's tennis title. ... Emmy Awards are presented for the best TV performances as follows: best actor in a special, Ed Flanders; best actress in a special, Sally Field; best actor in a series, James Garner; best actress in a series, Lindsay Wagner. The British-made *Upstairs, Downstairs* receives the best dramatic-series award.	**Sept. 11**
	In a new policy statement, the U.S. State Dept. declares that Palestinians must be involved in the Mideast peace-making process but does not specifically refer to the PLO.... Carl Bernstein is reported charging in a *Rolling Stone* magazine article that over 400 journalists have worked with the CIA over the past 25 years, either by passing on information, performing assignments, or using employment with news organizations as covers.			Distinguished American poet Robert Lowell, 60, twice a Pulitzer Prize winner, dies of an apparent heart attack in N.Y.C.	**Sept. 12**
		OMB Dir. Bert Lance, under fire for alleged personal finances irregularities, says, "I'm not going to quit and that means I'm not going to quit." ... Chase Manhattan Bank, N.Y., raises its prime rate to 7.25 percent, the highest level since August 1976.... A ban on the sale of cars, beginning in 1980, that get less than 16 miles-per-gallon of gas is one of the provisions of the new energy bill passed by the Senate.	Space shuttle Enterprise tests well in its second landing.... Hawaii's Kilauea, the world's most active volcano, begins erupting, but does not threaten inhabited areas.... A European Space Agency communications satellite explodes one minute after its liftoff from Cape Canaveral, Fla.	Conductor Leopold Stokowski, who led the Philadelphia Orchestra for twenty-three years causing musical controversy with his orchestrations, particularly of J.S. Bach, but credited with creating rich orchestral sonorities, dies in his sleep at the age of 95 in England.	**Sept. 13**
Mark Rudd, 30, former chairman of the Students for a Democratic Society (SDS) and, later, leader of the radical Weather Underground, surrenders to N.Y.C. authorities after seven years as a fugitive.	Two former secretaries of state, Henry Kissinger and Dean Rusk, strongly endorse the Panama Canal treaties in testimony before the House International Relations Committee.			The Soviet Union's first international book fair begins in Moscow, attracting about 1,300 publishers from 63 countries, including three from Israel.... Baltimore Orioles forfeit an important baseball game in a dispute over a tarpulin at Toronto's Exhibition Stadium, giving a 9–0 victory to the Toronto Blue Jays and jeopardizing Baltimore's position in the race for the AL's Eastern Division title.	**Sept. 14**
		House votes, 309–96, to raise the minimum wage to $3.05 an hour by 1980, but rejects wage-indexing, a key legislative goal of organized labor.... OMB Dir. Bert Lance gives a point-by-point defense of his personal finances before the Senate Government Affairs Committee.	Carter administration announces a plan to set aside almost one-fourth of Alaska as national parks, wilderness areas, and wildlife refuges.	Evangelist Billy Graham, returning to the U.S. after a week-long tour of Soviet-bloc countries, says his visit showed him that the church can exist in any type of society.	**Sept. 15**

F	G	H	I	J
Includes elections, federal-state relations, civil rights and liberties, crime, the judiciary, education, health care, poverty, urban affairs and population.	Includes formation and debate of U.S. foreign and defense policies, veterans' affairs and defense spending. (Relations with specific foreign countries are usually found under the region concerned.)	Includes business, labor, agriculture, taxation, transportation, consumer affairs, monetary and fiscal policy, natural resources, and pollution.	Includes worldwide scientific, medical and technological developments, natural phenomena, U.S. weather, natural disasters, and accidents.	Includes the arts, religion, scholarship, communications media, sports, entertainments, fashions, fads and social life.

	World Affairs	Europe	Africa & the Middle East	The Americas	Asia & the Pacific
Sept. 16			Israeli troops begin a push into southern Lebanon to assist Christian militia against Palestinian guerrillas.	P.M. Pierre Trudeau shuffles his 33-member Cabinet and names Allan MacEachen to the new post of deputy prime minister. . . . Salvadoran leftist guerrillas shoot to death the rector of the National University, his driver, and a bodyguard in San Salvador.	
Sept. 17			South African Justice Min. James Kruger hints that the police might have been responsible for the death of black activist Steven Biko, first officially attributed to a self-imposed hunger strike.		Former Pakistani P.M. Zulfikar Ali Bhutto is jailed again, along with 10 other Pakistan People's Party officials, under a martial-law regulation.
Sept. 18	World Bank annual report shows that the economies of many poor countries are growing at a faster rate, in total and per capita terms, than those of richer, industrialized countries.	Polish Roman Catholic bishops strongly denounce the government-controlled media.	In a press conference, Lt. Col. Mengistu Haile Mariam, Ethiopian head of state, predicts that the Ogaden war will be long and charges that Somalia violated U.N. and OAS principles by invading the region. He also denies rumors of Cuban troops in Ethiopia. . . . James Chikerema, one of Rhodesia's first black nationalist leaders, returns to Salisbury after 13 years of self-exile.		
Sept. 19	U.N. Secy. Gen. Kurt Waldheim is pessimistic, in a press conference, about issues facing the upcoming thirty-second session of the U.N. General Assembly. He predicts stalemates on the Middle East, southern Africa, and Cyprus situations, and on North-South economic issues, but sees progress in SALT talks.		Nearly 2,000 people attend a rally outside the Johannesburg city hall to call for the dismissal of South African Justice Min. James Kruger, repeal of detention laws, and inquiries into the deaths of 21 detainees. . . . Israeli For. Min. Moshe Dayan submits his country's proposal for a Middle East peace plan at a White House meeting with Pres. Carter.	Nicaraguan govt. lifts its 33-month state of siege, apparently the price extracted by the U.S. for signing a $2.5-million military sales agreement.	
Sept. 20	The thirty-second U.N. General Assembly session convenes in N.Y.C. and approves admission of Vietnam and Djibouti.	EEC foreign ministers meeting in Brussels adopt a code calling on European businesses to abolish apartheid practices in dealing with South Africa.	South African P.M. John Vorster dissolves Parliament and sets general elections for Nov. 30, a year-and-a-half before his government's term expires. . . . A Somali official in Rome says that the Western Somalia Liberation Front is ready for cease-fire talks with the Ethiopian govt.	A power failure blacks out nearly all of Quebec for several hours, creating severe traffic jams in Montreal and stranding commuters in trains and subways.	
Sept. 21	U.S. Congress clears legislation to authorize $5.1 billion in new contributions to the World Bank and five other lending institutions. . . . H. Johannes Witteveen, announces he will resign as the IMF's managing director at the end of his five-year term in August 1978.	W. Ger. govt. rejects Italy's request to extradite convicted Nazi war criminal Herbert Kappler. . . . Turkey devalues its currency 10 percent against the U.S. dollar in face of IMF pressure.	Rhodesian P.M. Ian Smith condemns the British–U.S. formula for creating a new Rhodesian army, but says that his government is reconciled to establishing majority rule based on the plan.	Brazilian police prevent a national students' meeting in Sao Paulo, in wake of growing student protest rallies seeking a return to democracy. . . . Haitian government frees 104 political prisoners, claiming they are the last held in Haiti. . . . *Washington Post* reports that a recent Gallup Poll shows 65 percent of the Chilean population supports the military government and that 71 percent favor its economic policies.	Heavy fighting between Philippine govt. troops and Moslem rebels, which erupted yesterday, spreads to Jolo Island, just south of Basilan Island.
Sept. 22		South Moluccan hijackers are sentenced by a Dutch court to prison terms ranging from six to nine years for their role in seizing a passenger train and elementary school in May.	Following a meeting with Pres. Carter and State Secy. Vance., Egyptian For. Min. Ismail Fahmy states that the Arab nations are prepared for the first time to accept Israel as a Middle East country if Israel accepts, in return, Arab settlement terms. They include total withdrawal from occupied Arab Lands and agreement to establishment of a Palestinian state.		

A	B	C	D	E
Includes developments that affect more than one world region, international organizations and important meetings of major world leaders.	Includes all domestic and regional developments in Europe, including the Soviet Union, Turkey, Cyprus and Malta.	Includes all domestic and regional developments in Africa and the Middle East, including Iraq and Iran and excluding Cyprus, Turkey and Afghanistan.	Includes all domestic and regional developments in Latin America, the Caribbean and Canada.	Includes all domestic and regional developments in Asia and Pacific nations, extending from Afghanistan through all the Pacific Islands, except Hawaii.

U.S. Politics & Social Issues	U.S. Foreign Policy & Defense	U.S. Economy & Environment	Science, Technology & Nature	Culture, Leisure & Life Style	
Senate, 75–11, passes a bill requiring that employers must include pregnancy and childbirth benefits in any medical and disability plans they offer.	Senate votes, 72-3 to prohibit any unionization of the armed forces. . . . CBS News reports that the U.S. had wiretapped Panama Canal negotiations, beginning in 1974, and that Panamanian officials, having discovered the taps, used the issue to blackmail the U.S. into making negotiation concessions.			Operatic soprano Maria Callas dies suddenly of a heart attack at the age of 53 in Paris. She was known for her dramatic interpretations, *bel canto* roles, and stormy off-stage relations. . . . Mark Bolan, 29, British rock star and lead singer-guitarist for the group Tyrannosaurus Rex dies in a car accident in London.	Sept. 16
		The Senate inquiry into OMB Dir. Bert Lance's financial dealings focuses on the standard of ethics he followed as a banker, particularly his use of overdrafts.			Sept. 17
				Courageous defends the America's Cup for the U.S. in four straight races against the challenging yacht, *Australia* .... CBS-TV ranks last in Nielsen ratings for the week just ended, despite a $1-million cash giveaway campaign designed to increase its audience.	Sept. 18
Rep. Edward Koch wins the N.Y.C. mayoral Democratic primary, a run-off vote, against N.Y. State Secy. Mario Cuomo, who was backed by N.Y.S. Gov., Hugh Carey.	Sen. Daniel Inouye (D, Hawaii), Senate Intelligence Committee chmn., says that hearings by the committee produced no evidence to substantiate charges that alleged U.S. wiretapping affected the final outcome of Panama Canal Treaty talks.	Commerce Dept. reports that housing starts in August were 32 percent ahead of the August 1976 rate.	William Sheldon, 78, a psychologist who formulated a theory correlating personality types with physical traits, dies of a heart ailment in Cambridge, Mass.... The death toll from a flash flood that hit Kansas City, Mo. on Sept. 12-13 reaches 26.		Sept. 19
The first group of 15,000 refugees from Southeast Asia, 113 Vietnamese, authorized on August 11 by Atty. Gen. Griffin Bell to enter the U.S., arrives in San Francisco.	At Senate hearings on alleged CIA mind-control experiments on unwitting suspects, witnesses testify about attempting to spray people at a party with LSD, and developing a device to inject drugs into corked wine bottles and a chemical-coated swizzle stick.	Sen. Finance Committee votes, 11-5, against Pres. Carter's proposed auto gas-guzzler tax.	House votes, 246-162, to authorize $150 million for continued work on a plutonium-fueled liquid metal fast breeder reactor at Clinch River, near Oak Ridge, Tenn., a project opposed by Pres. Carter.... Australian Qantas Airlines annouces suspension of its weekly service to South Africa.	San Diego Padres baseball team pres. E.J. Bavasi resigns in a dispute with club owner, Ray Kroc.	Sept. 20
	AP poll reveals that the U.S. public overwhelmingly opposes the Panama Canal treaties. . . . Dr. Sidney Gottlieb, a retired CIA official who headed the CIA's 1952–65 drug experimentation program, testifies that the program was motivated by CIA fears that other countries were developing drugs that could be used covertly.	OMB Dir. Bert Lance resigns in face of allegations about past personal financial irregularities, writing in a letter to Pres. Carter that his conscience is clear.... U.S. trade deficit is measured at a record $4.6 billion during the second quarter.	Delegates at the Conference of Atomic Energy Suppliers in London approve a pact to institute uniform safeguards on sales of nuclear energy and technology among countries.	Czech-born conductor and pianist Kurt Adler, 70, dies in Berlin. He founded the Stalingrad Philharmonic Orchestra before he fled the Soviet Union, and served for many years as chorus-master and conductor at the Metropolitan Opera in N.Y.C.	Sept. 21
		Bethlehem Steel Corp. agrees, in response to a suit filed by the state of Maryland, to pay $500,000 in fines and to install $20-million worth of water pollution-control equipment in its Sparrows Point plant, near Chesapeake Bay.... Following a vote in the Senate that upholds a natural gas deregulation proposal, opponents of deregulation stage a filibuster.		Clilan Powell, 83, former editor and publisher of *The New York Amsterdam News*, which is considered the largest black community-based newspaper in the nation, dies in Briarcliff Manor, N.Y.	Sept. 22

F	G	H	I	J
Includes elections, federal-state relations, civil rights and liberties, crime, the judiciary, education, health care, poverty, urban affairs and population.	Includes formation and debate of U.S. foreign and defense policies, veterans' affairs and defense spending. (Relations with specific foreign countries are usually found under the region concerned.)	Includes business, labor, agriculture, taxation, transportation, consumer affairs, monetary and fiscal policy, natural resources, and pollution.	Includes worldwide scientific, medical and technological developments, natural phenomena, U.S. weather, natural disasters, and accidents.	Includes the arts, religion, scholarship, communications media, sports, entertainments, fashions, fads and social life.

	World Affairs	Europe	Africa & the Middle East	The Americas	Asia & the Pacific
Sept. 23	State Secy. Cyrus Vance announces that the U.S. will abide by the terms of the 1972 SALT pact, which expires on Oct. 3, after two days of talks in Washington with Soviet For. Min. Andrei Gromyko.		Heavy fighting rages around the Lebanese village of Khiam, with 15 Palestinians and three Lebanese leftists reported killed.		
Sept. 24			Five black African front-line nations give formal, but qualified, approval to the British–U.S. plan for majority rule in Rhodesia.	A Gallup Poll in Brazil shows that Sen. Jose de Magalhaes Pinto could easily defeat the leading military candidate if the president were elected by universal suffrage.	
Sept. 25	Soviet Union responds to State Secy. Vance's informal pledge on SALT observance with a tacit pledge of its own.	Swiss voters reject a proposal to legalize abortion.	At Steven Biko's funeral, 10,000 South African blacks rally to protest apartheid.... Israel accepts a U.S. plan for reconvening the Geneva conference on the Middle East. Egypt, Jordan, and Syria also accept the formula but reject a number of Israeli conditions.		Cambodian govt. announces that Premier Pol Pot has been given the additional post of CP secretary general, making him Cambodia's top leader.... Wei Kuo-ching is named head of the Chinese armed forces' political department, replacing Chang Chun-chiao, one of the Gang of Four radicals purged in October 1976.
Sept. 26		French Pres. Valery Giscard d'Estaing replaces three Cabinet ministers.	*Newsweek* magazine reports Somali accusations that the U.S. was deceptive about possible support of Somalia in its attack on the Ogaden region of Ethiopia.... The heavy fighting in southern Lebanon halts as a result of a truce aranged by the U.S. embassies in Lebanon and Israel.		
Sept. 27		French govt. announces a plan to reduce the number of immigrant workers in the country, seen as posing a serious social problem.	Israeli For. Min. Moshe Dayan says that two key Palestinian issues still block peace talks: which Palestinian group should attend and what role it should play in actual negotiations.		
Sept. 28		Two Czech dissidents who signed Charter 77 manifesto of Czech human rights are sentenced to three-and-a-half years in prison. ... British Liberal Party's annual conference overwhelmingly endorses its parliamentary agrement with the Labor govt., which was reached in March.	Pres. Carter confers separately at the White House with Syrian For. Min. Abdel Halim Khaddam and Abdul Hamid Sharaf, chief of the Jordanian royal court, both of whom oppose Israel's demand that no Mideast peace talks be held with a unified Arab delegation.... Israeli govt. bars attemps by followers of the Gush Emunim, an ultrareligious Jewish group, to establish two unauthorized settlements on the West Bank.		Five armed guerrillas of the left-wing Japanese Red Army hijack a Japan Airlines plane with more than 150 passengers and crew and divert it to Dacca, Bangladesh.

A	B	C	D	E
Includes developments that affect more than one world region, international organizations and important meetings of major world leaders.	Includes all domestic and regional developments in Europe, including the Soviet Union, Turkey, Cyprus and Malta.	Includes all domestic and regional developments in Africa and the Middle East, including Iraq and Iran and excluding Cyprus, Turkey and Afghanistan.	Includes all domestic and regional developments in Latin America, the Caribbean and Canada.	Includes all domestic and regional developments in Asia and Pacific nations, extending from Afghanistan through all the Pacific Islands, except Hawaii.

U.S. Politics & Social Issues	U.S. Foreign Policy & Defense	U.S. Economy & Environment	Science, Technology & Nature	Culture, Leisure & Life Style	
House votes, 359–4, to end mandatory retirement for federal employes at age 70.	Air Force announces that women will be assigned to launching crews of Titan 2 intercontinental ballistic missiles, which are housed in underground silos.		Center for Disease Control (CDC) reports that the mysterious legionnaires Disease, which killed 29 people in 1976, has subsequently struck 48 people in 19 states.	In a case involving Arthur Hirsch, an independent film maker producing a documentary on Karen Silkwood, a three-judge panel in Denver, Colo. rules that documentary film makers have the same First Amendment rights as print journalists, the first time a federal ct. extends protection of sources outside the recognized news media. . . . John Nash, leading British landscape painter and illustrator, and first living artist to be the subject of a major Royal Academy retrospective, dies in Colchester, England.	Sept. 23
The SAT (Scholastic Aptitude Test) scores of freshmen entering college in 1977 are reported lowest in the 51 years the test has been given. Critics charge that the tests are outdated, discriminatory, and inadequate.	Senate Majority Leader Robert Byrd (D, W.Va.) says that his mail is running 4,000 to six against the Panama Canal treaties, but sees signs in the letters suggesting that they were written as an organized effort.				Sept. 24
	Rand Corp. report calls the all-volunteer army a success and takes issue with charges that the volunteer system produces an army comprised primarily of the poor and of blacks.			Russian Orthodox Church head Patriarch Pimen rejects ordination of women as priests in talks in Moscow with the Archbishop of Canterbury Frederick Donald Coggan. . . . U.S. Olympic Committee votes, 55–39, to recommend Los Angeles as the site for the 1984 Summer Olympics, choosing it over N.Y.C.	Sept. 25
	U.S. Sen. For. Rel. Committee opens hearings on the new Panama Canal treaties, hearing as first witnesses State Secy. Vance and top canal negotiatiors, Ellsworth Bunker and Sol Linowitz.	U.S. merchandise trade deficit is reported rising in August to a seasonally adjusted $2.67 billion, the second largest deficit on record. . . . Three leading officials of federal bank regulatory agencies testify before the Senate Banking Committee that they would hire former OMB Dir. Bert Lance as a bank director despite the nature of his personal financial dealings, which forced his resignation.	More than 3,000 cases of cholera are reported throughout the Middle East, with Syria hardest hit. . . . Freddie Laker, president of the British Laker Airways, introduces London–N.Y. no-frills economy service, which requires no reservations and costs less than half of the prevailing economy air fares.	Ernie (Schnoz) Lombardi, 69, major league baseball catcher for 17 seasons, dies in Santa Cruz, Calif. . . . Uday Shankar, 76, India's foremost classical and folk dancer, who, with his brother Ravi, popularized Hindu cultural traditions worldwide, dies of heart and kidney ailments in Calcutta.	Sept. 26
	Top JCS members refute Rep. Samuel Stratton's (D, N.Y.) charges that they were coerced by Pres. Carter into supporting the Panama Canal treaties. . . . An Army study of West Point, prompted by the 1976 cheating scandal, proposes over 150 reforms to improve morale and management.	Treas. Secy. Michael Blumenthal says that the U.S. trade deficit might range from $25 billion to $30 bilion by the year's end.		Consumer advocate Ralph Nader announces plans to form a group to defend the interests of the nation's sports fans, to be called FANS (Fight to Advance the Nation's Sports).	Sept. 27
	SEC files a civil suit charging alleged Korean lobbyist Park Tong Sun, and others, with violating federal securities laws. It also charges that the Diplomat National Bank (Wash., DC.) overstated its deposits by $1 million in its 1976 quarterly statement.	Environmental Defense Fund and New York Public Interest Research Group publish a report charging that the Hudson River contains a complex spectrum of toxic and cancer-causing chemicals.			Sept. 28

F	G	H	I	J
Includes elections, federal-state relations, civil rights and liberties, crime, the judiciary, education, health care, poverty, urban affairs and population.	Includes formation and debate of U.S. foreign and defense policies, veterans' affairs and defense spending. (Relations with specific foreign countries are usually found under the region concerned.)	Includes business, labor, agriculture, taxation, transportation, consumer affairs, monetary and fiscal policy, natural resources, and pollution.	Includes worldwide scientific, medical and technological developments, natural phenomena, U.S. weather, natural disasters, and accidents.	Includes the arts, religion, scholarship, communications media, sports, entertainments, fashions, fads and social life.

	World Affairs	Europe	Africa & the Middle East	The Americas	Asia & the Pacific
Sept. 29	U.N. Security Council approves a British motion to appoint a special U.N. representative to participate in the British–U.S. initiative for Rhodesian majority rule.	France rejects a British request to modify their seabed boundary in the English Channel.	Western correspondents report that Somali-backed guerrillas, fighting to control Ethiopia's Ogaden region, have captured the strategic Gara Marda Mountain Pass, six miles west of Jijiga and have opened the way to Harar, 50 miles to the west. . . . Pres. Carter says he favors PLO participation in a Middle East peace settlement, but concedes that they are not the Palestinians' sole representatives.		Japanese Red Army guerrillas free five hostages from their hijacked Japan Airlines plane after the Japanese govt. agrees to their demands to hand over nine imprisoned guerrillas and give them $6 million in U.S. currency. . . . Pakistani govt. arrests Benazir Bhutto, daughter of the former prime minister, and warns Nusrat Bhutto, his wife, against inciting violence.
Sept. 30	IMF and World Bank end their thirty-second annual joint meetings in Washington, where discussions centered on the faltering pace of economic recovery and its consequences for world trade.	EEC bans all Soviet fishing vessels from its North Sea waters.		Canadian civil service bilingual rules revisions are announced. The provisions are aimed at ensuring that most applicants for senior government positions by 1983 will be competent in both English and French.	
Oct. 1	U.S. and the Soviet Union issue a joint statement suggesting guidelines for proposed Arab–Israeli negotiations. Israel and its U.S. backers criticize inclusion of the Soviet Union in Middle East discussions, and what they see as an erosion of traditional U.S. support for Israel.				Gen. Muhammad Zia ul-Haq announces that parliamentary elections scheduled for Oct. 18 will be postponed and that martial law will continue indefinitely in Pakistan. . . . Japanese govt. flies six of the Japanese Red Army's comrades to Dacca and hands over $6 million to the hijackers. The hijackers release, in turn, 30 more hostages, keeping the others until they escape from Dacca.
Oct. 2			Israeli govt. rejects the joint U.S.–Soviet statement, issued yesterday, stressing it will not accept PLO representation at the Geneva conference.		Premier Pol Pot defends the Cambodian govt.'s evacuation of millions of urban dwellers to rural areas after the war ended in 1975 as necessary to break up enemy spy organizations.
Oct. 3		Worker's Defense Committee, organized to help Polish workers jailed after the June 1976 riots, announces it is enlarging its scope to combat all political repression.	Michiel Botha, South African minister of Bantu (black) education, announces that he will not seek reelection to Parliament in November.	Official inquiry into the Royal Canadian Mounted Police's break-in at the office of a left-wing news agency opens in Quebec.	Japanese Red Army hijackers surrender and release the rest of their hostages after landing in Algiers, Algeria. . . . Indian govt. drops the coerced birth-control program initiated by former P.M. Indira Gandhi's govt.
Oct. 4	In a speech before the U.N. General Assembly, Pres. Carter reaffirms the U.S. commitment to Israel and stresses disarmament and control of nuclear technology. . . . Representatives of the 35 nations that signed the Helsinki accords in 1975 open their first formal review conference in Belgrade, Yugoslavia.		Pres. Carter and Israeli For. Min. Moshe Dayan meet in N.Y. to discuss Mideast peace plans.	Peru's military govt. announces that nationwide elections for a constituent assembly will be held on June 4, 1978.	Japanese govt. establishes a department within the National Policy Agency to deal specifically with terrorist activities of the revolutionary Japanese Red Army, in wake of failure to bring back Red Army gunmen from Algeria where they landed after successfully hijacking a Japan Airlines plane.

A	B	C	D	E
Includes developments that affect more than one world region, international organizations and important meetings of major world leaders.	Includes all domestic and regional developments in Europe, including the Soviet Union, Turkey, Cyprus and Malta.	Includes all domestic and regional developments in Africa and the Middle East, including Iraq and Iran and excluding Cyprus, Turkey and Afghanistan.	Includes all domestic and regional developments in Latin America, the Caribbean and Canada.	Includes all domestic and regional developments in Asia and Pacific nations, extending from Afghanistan through all the Pacific Islands, except Hawaii.

U.S. Politics & Social Issues	U.S. Foreign Policy & Defense	U.S. Economy & Environment	Science, Technology & Nature	Culture, Leisure & Life Style	
Pres. Carter signs a bill revising the food-stamp program that contains a provision, sought by antipoverty groups, to eliminate purchase requirements for food stamps.		Pres. Carter signs an agriculture bill providing target prices keyed to production costs — a controversial issue becuase Carter had called the original targets too high.... Commerce Dept. reports the index of leading economic indicators rose .8 percent in August, a sign of an economic pickup.	Three-judge panel in N.Y.C. upholds a lower court decision to allow Concorde air service at Kennedy International Airport.	Cliff Roberts, 84, a co-founder of the Augusta (Ga.) National Golf Club, home of the Masters tournament, dies of a self-inflicted gunshot wound in Augusta.... Heavyweight boxing champion Muhammad Ali wins a unanimous decision over Earnie Shavers before 15,000 spectators at Madison Square Garden, N.Y.C. The bout is seen on TV by an estimated 70 million viewers, a record TV audience for a boxing match.	Sept. 29
			A Justife Dept. memo is made public that indicates nuclear regulatory officials knew about an earthquake fault line under a nuclear power plant in Virginia, but didn't tell the federal board that licenses atomic power plants.	Mary Ford, 53, popular singer of the 1950s who, teamed with her former husband, Les Paul, developed the recording techinque of multiple harmonies, dies of pneumonia in Los Angeles, Calif.	Sept. 30
		International Longshoremen's Association (ILA) begins a selective strike in 30 ports from Maine to Texas as its contracts expire.			Oct. 1
				Alleged , a three-year-old Colt, wins the Prix de Arc de Triomphe, Europe's most prestigious horse race.... *The Silmarillion* by J.R.R. Tolkien heads the best-selling fiction list for the week just ended.	Oct. 2
Supreme Ct. lets stand a lower court decision allowing former Pres. Richard Nixon's White House tapes to be used as evidence in a civil suit against the government that names Nixon as a defendant.		In what is called one of largest civil-rights settlements ever, 300 American Airlines flight attendants, fired between 1965 and 1970 because they were pregnant, are awarded a total of $2.7 million.... Dean Witter Organization Inc. and Reynolds Securities International Inc., two of the largest firms in the securities industry, announce plans to merge by early 1978. Their consolidation, as Dean Witter Reynolds Organization Inc., is the biggest in Wall Street history.... Treasury Dept. rules that five major Japanese steel producers are dumping carbon steel-plate at below-cost prices in the U.S. and imposes a 32 percent penalty duty.	Labor Dept. proposes a new plan to protect worker exposure to cancer-causing substances.	Protestant Episcopal House of Bishops annual meeting in St. Louis, Mo., enacts a freedom-of-conscience clause to exempt dissident priests from the obligation to ordain women or to accept women priests in their parish.... Baseball comr. Bowie Kuhn waives a rule requiring players to have completed at least 10 years in the major or Negro leagues to qualify for the Hall of Fame.	Oct. 3
Federal District Judge John Sirica reduces the prison sentences of three principal Watergate figures — former Atty. Gen. John Mitchell, and former Nixon aides H.R. Haldeman and John Ehrlichman, after he hears taped personal statements of their contrition.	Sen. Robert Dole (R, Kan.) sets off a controversy over interpretation of the Panama Canal treaties by releasing a secret State Dept. cable detailing the views of one of the top canal negotiators.	Senate passes, 50–46, a natural gas deregulation bill that had been held up by a filibuster. Pres. Carter calls the bill unacceptable.... Congress clears legislation raising the temporary ceiling on the federal debt to $752 billion through March 31, 1978.		Mstislav Rostropovich conducts his first concert as the new musical director of the National Symphony Orchestra in Washington, D.C.	Oct. 4

F	G	H	I	J
Includes elections, federal-state relations, civil rights and liberties, crime, the judiciary, education, health care, poverty, urban affairs and population.	*Includes formation and debate of U.S. foreign and defense policies, veterans' affairs and defense spending. (Relations with specific foreign countries are usually found under the region concerned.)*	*Includes business, labor, agriculture, taxation, transportation, consumer affairs, monetary and fiscal policy, natural resources, and pollution.*	*Includes worldwide scientific, medical and technological developments, natural phenomena, U.S. weather, natural disasters, and accidents.*	*Includes the arts, religion, scholarship, communications media, sports, entertainments, fashions, fads and social life.*

	World Affairs	Europe	Africa & the Middle East	The Americas	Asia & the Pacific
Oct. 5	Pres. Carter signs two controversial U.N. human-right covenants – already initialed by 40 nations including the Soviet Union – which previous U.S. administrations had refused to sign because they said they intruded into U.S. affairs.	Seamus Costello, leader of the anti-British Irish Republican Socialist Party, is shot to death on a crowded Dublin street.	The U.S. and Israel reach agreement on using U.N. Security Council Resolutions 242 (post-1967 war) and 338 (post-1973 war) as the grounds for reconvening the Geneva conference.		P.M. Malcolm Fraser announces forming a royal commission to investigate Australia's growing trade in illegal drugs.
Oct. 6	ECOSOC approves a resolution entitling Vietnam to special economic assistance from U.N. agencies and outside sources.... Energy ministers from the 19-nation International Energy Agency (IEA) meet in Paris and agree to limit their oil imports to 26 million barrels a day by 1985.			Quebec Superior Ct. rules that a section of Bill 101 requiring court documents to be written in French is unconstitutional.	Chinese newspapers officially confirm that the purged radical Gang of Four was arrested on Oct. 6, 1976.
Oct. 7	The world's 72 sugar-producing nations sign an international agreement in Geneva to reestablish an export quota system and other trade restrictions aimed at regulating volatile sugar prices.	Polish CP first secy. Edward Gierek reports that current food shortages and black market activity are the result of a harvest ruined by summer floods.... Supreme Soviet approves unanimously the final draft of the Soviet Constitution, substantially the same as a draft released in June.			Police quell a demonstration of about 1,000 students at Seoul National University, South Korea.
Oct. 8		Basque leader Augusto Unceta Barrenechea is shot to death in Guernica, Spain.... Police and about 1,000 youths clash at an outdoor music festival in East Berlin, reported as the most serious outbreak of unrest in East Germany in years.			A Burmese govt. and ruling party shake-up is reported, with all purge victims known to have strong ties with Gen. San Yu, secretary general of the Socialist Program Party.
Oct. 9		A faction of ETA, the Basque separatist organization, claims responsibility for the death of Basque leader Augusto Unceta Barrenechea.			
Oct. 10	Two Irish women, Mairead Corrigan and Betty Williams, are belatedly awarded the Nobel Peace Prize for 1976 for organizing a worldwide campaign to end Roman Catholic-Protestant violence in Northern Ireland.... Amnesty International, the London-based human rights organization, is awarded the 1977 Nobel Peace Prize.	British For. Secy. David Owen and Soviet Pres. Leonid Brezhnev sign a treaty in Moscow on the prevention of accidental nuclear war.	North Yemen Pres. Ibrahim al-Hamidi and his brother, Col. Abdullah Mohammed al-Hamidi, are assassinated.		
Oct. 11			Israeli Cabinet unanimously approves a procedural paper for reconvening the Geneva Middle East peace conference.		

A	B	C	D	E
Includes developments that affect more than one world region, international organizations and important meetings of major world leaders.	Includes all domestic and regional developments in Europe, including the Soviet Union, Turkey, Cyprus and Malta.	Includes all domestic and regional developments in Africa and the Middle East, including Iraq and Iran and excluding Cyprus, Turkey and Afghanistan.	Includes all domestic and regional developments in Latin America, the Caribbean and Canada.	Includes all domestic and regional developments in Asia and Pacific nations, extending from Afghanistan through all the Pacific Islands, except Hawaii.

U.S. Politics & Social Issues	U.S. Foreign Policy & Defense	U.S. Economy & Environment	Science, Technology & Nature	Culture, Leisure & Life Style	
Pres. Carter visits the South Bronx area of N.Y.C. and calls seeing the burned-out buildings and jobless residents a "sobering experience."		UAW leaders reject attempting to reaffiliate with the AFL–CIO, which the union left in 1968.		John Allin, head of the Episcopal Church in the U.S., wins a formal vote of confidence from the House of Bishops annual meeting in St. Louis, Mo., after offering to resign in face of his personal opposition to the General Convention's 1976 vote to ordain women as priests.	Oct. 5
	Defense Secy. Harold Brown says he will seek funds to develop an experimental mobile missile, called the M-X, to replace the current Minuteman missiles.	House passes the Labor Law Reform Act, 257–163, designed to remove some barriers from union organizing efforts.		The Nobel Prize for Literature is awarded to Spanish surrealist poet Vicente Aleixandre, 79, whose work is little-known outside the Spanish-speaking world. . . . Hume Cronyn and Jessica Tandy star in *The Gin Game*, about a man and woman in a home for the aged, which opens on Broadway.	Oct. 6
Md. Gov. Marvin Mandel is sentenced to four years in prison and automatically suspended from all powers of office, after a federal mail fraud and racketeering conviction.		Council on Wage and Price Stability issues a report showing that the U.S. steel industry suffers from slack demand, high costs, slim profits, and strong foreign competition. It also notes that steel has been the problem sector of the U.S. economy for nearly 20 years.			Oct. 7
	Pres. Carter signs a bill requiring case-by-case eligibility review for veterans' benefits for those whose military discharges were upgraded under his administration's program.				Oct. 8
				New York Yankees win their second consecutive AL pennant with a 5–3 victory over the Kansas City Royals.	Oct. 9
Pres. Carter's popularity deteriorates, exemplified by a Harris Survey report showing him rating below the 50 percent public approval mark.			Swedish govt. is reported banning the use of aerosol spray cans.		Oct. 10
Supreme Ct. votes, 6–3, to nullify a lower court decision against a Mass. state law giving veterans preference in civil service jobs. . . . Chicago school authorities agree on a plan to desegregate the city's public school faculties.		Lee Way Motor Freight Inc. is ordered to pay $1.8 million in back pay to 46 black employes, the largest court-ordered amount ever obtained by the Justice Dept. on behalf of victims of employment discrimination.	The Nobel Prize for Physics is jointly presented to John Van Vleck of Harvard University, Philip Anderson of Bell Laboratories and Princeton University, and Sir Nevill Mott of Cambridge University for their contribution to modern electronic solid-state circuitry. . . . Nobel Prize for Chemistry is given to Russian-born professor at the Free University of Brussels, Ilya Prigogine, an expert in thermodynamics. . . . The Soviet spacecraft Soyuz 25 and space station Salyut 6 fail to link.	MacKinlay Kantor, 73, Pulitzer Prize-winning author of *Andersonville*, a novel depicting a Civil War prisoner-of-war camp in the South, dies in Sarasota, Fla.	Oct. 11

F	G	H	I	J
Includes elections, federal-state relations, civil rights and liberties, crime, the judiciary, education, health care, poverty, urban affairs and population.	Includes formation and debate of U.S. foreign and defense policies, veterans' affairs and defense spending. (Relations with specific foreign countries are usually found under the region concerned.)	Includes business, labor, agriculture, taxation, transportation, consumer affairs, monetary and fiscal policy, natural resources, and pollution.	Includes worldwide scientific, medical and technological developments, natural phenomena, U.S. weather, natural disasters, and accidents.	Includes the arts, religion, scholarship, communications media, sports, entertainments, fashions, fads and social life.

	World Affairs	**Europe**	**Africa & the Middle East**	**The Americas**	**Asia & the Pacific**
Oct. 12	Sweden cancels over $200 million in debts owed by eight Third World nations.	Ireland's P.M. John Lynch calls for the British govt. to acknowledge the legitimate hopes of the Irish majority for the reunification of Ireland, a departure from the previous government's stance on the issue.	The Turnhalle constitutional conference in Windhoek, the Namibian capital, formally dissolves itself.	Nicaraguan Sandinista National Liberation Front, a leftist guerrilla group thought to have been wiped out, begins a major offensive against the government. . . . Brazilian Pres. Ernesto Geisel openly intervenes in the country's presidential campaign by firing from his Cabinet a leading candidate, Army Min. Sylvio da Frota. . . . Beatriz Allende, 32, daughter of the late Chilean Pres. Salvador Allende, kills herself in Havana, Cuba.	A significant oil field is reported discovered off the Soviet-owned island of Sakhalin, which is believed to have more oil than any other site in Asia. Under terms of an agreement, both the Soviet Union and Japan will share equally in development costs.
Oct. 13		A W. Ger. group calling itself the Struggle Against World Imperialism seizes a Lufthansa jet as it takes off from the Spanish island of Majorca for Frankfurt.	Israel suspends discussions with Lebanon after protesting alleged PLO cease-fire violations.		Pakistani leader Muhammad Zia ul-Haq pledges that elections will be held in 1978, according to a report by Maulana Mufti Mahmud, the president of the Pakistan National Alliance.
Oct. 14		At its closing annual convention session, British Conservative Party leader Margaret Thatcher pledges that if returned to power, her party would take an extreme right-wing stance and engage in immediate confrontation with the unions. . . . Spain passes an amnesty bill that is expected to free most of its remaining political prisoners.		Pres. Carter and Brig. Gen. Omar Torrijos issue a joint statement to reconcile apparently conflicting U.S. and Panamanian interpretations of the Panama Canal treaties.	Pres. Ziaur Rahman bans Bangladesh's three principal political parties, charging they were behind an aborted coup on Oct. 2.
Oct. 15		Hijacked Lufthansa jet lands in Dubai, after making refueling stops in Rome, Cyprus, and Bahrain. It then takes off for Aden, where it lands despite the South Yemen government's decision to block off airport runways.			Indian opposition Congress Party denies a bid by former P.M. Indira Gandhi to regain her party leadership and retains K. Brahamananda Reddy as president.
Oct. 16		Terrorist hijackers shoot the hijacked Lufthansa jet pilot Capt. Jurgen Schumann in the head in full view of the passengers, and leave his body lying on the floor of the plane for hours.		A Sandinista leader, wounded in an attack in San Carlos, Nicaragua and hospitalized in Costa Rica, tells newsmen that the Sandinista attacks initiate a decisive struggle to overthrow the regime of Gen. Anastasio Somoza Debayle, whose family has ruled Nicaragua since the 1930s.	U.S. Justice Dept. agents arrive in Seoul, South Korea to begin talks with the South Korean govt. about interrogating Park Tong Sun, seen as the central figure in the Korean–U.S. congressional lobbying scheme.
Oct. 17		The hijacked Lufthansa jet lifts off from Aden and lands in Mogadishu, Somalia, where the terrorists push the body of the dead pilot, Jurgen Schumann, onto the runway. . . . W. Ger. Chancellor Helmut Schmidt arrives in Mogadishu and begins negotiations with the Somali govt. to permit W. Ger. armed commandos to attempt a rescue. His effort is backed by Britain, France, and the U.S.		Nicaraguan Sandinistas attack police headquarters in Masaya, 20 miles southeast of the capital, and ambush troops sent in to repel the attack. . . . Live television coverage of Canadian parliamentary debates begins.	

A	B	C	D	E
Includes developments that affect more than one world region, international organizations and important meetings of major world leaders.	Includes all domestic and regional developments in Europe, including the Soviet Union, Turkey, Cyprus and Malta.	Includes all domestic and regional developments in Africa and the Middle East, including Iraq and Iran and excluding Cyprus, Turkey and Afghanistan.	Includes all domestic and regional developments in Latin America, the Caribbean and Canada.	Includes all domestic and regional developments in Asia and Pacific nations, extending from Afghanistan through all the Pacific Islands, except Hawaii.

U.S. Politics & Social Issues	U.S. Foreign Policy & Defense	U.S. Economy & Environment	Science, Technology & Nature	Culture, Leisure & Life Style	
The Alan Guttmacher Institute, a private research organization, reports that since the Supreme Ct.'s June 20 ruling that states are not required to fund abortions for poor women, 13 states have decided to continue to use public funds for that purpose.		Federal govt. agrees to end its $250-million loan guarantees to Lockheed Aircraft Corp. at Lockheed's request because of the company's greatly improved financial condition. . . . *Washington Post* reports that since June over 18,000 U.S. steel workers have been laid off and that facilities with several million tons of operating equipment have been closed.	U.S. space shuttle Enterprise passes its crucial flight test successfully and lands safely at Edwards Air Force Base, Calif.		Oct. 12
Mark Rudd, former fugitive SDS and Weather Underground leader, is given an unconditional discharge after surrendering and pleading guilty to criminal trespassing, a pre-arranged plea bargain.		In a televised news conference, Pres. Carter calls the issue of natural gas price deregulation — which he opposes and Congress supports — the most important one he would ever face while in office, and he claims that deregulated gas prices would rise 15 times to what they had been before the 1973 oil embargo. . . . Allied Chemical Corp. and the state of Virginia announce settlement of state and local claims against the company for contamination of waterways with the toxic insecticide Kepone.	The Nobel Prize in Physiology of Medicine is shared by Rosalyn Yalow, a nuclear physicist at the VA Hospital in the Bronx, N.Y., Roger Guillemin, a French-born researcher at the Salk Institute in La Jolla, Calif., and Polish-born Andrew Schally, with the VA Hospital in New Orleans.		Oct. 13
	A Wash., D.C. federal grand jury indicts Richard Hanna, a former Democratic representative from Calif., on 40 felony charges stemming from the Korean lobbying probe. Hanna is charged with using his position as congressman to pressure the South Korean govt. to make Park Tong Sun the agent for Korean purchases of U.S. rice.	A Transportation Dept. requirement that air bags or automatic seat belts be installed in all new cars, beginning with 1982 models, goes into effect.		The Nobel Prize for Economics is awarded to two pioneers in international trade theory — Bertil Ohlin, Sweden's former commerce minister, and James Meade of Cambridge University, England. . . . Bing (Harry Lillis) Crosby, 73, world-famous American popular singer and actor, dies of a heart attack on a golf course outside of Madrid, Spain.	Oct. 14
		Farm prices rise 1 percent, Sept. 15–Oct. 15, reversing 1 percent declines in each of the previous two 30-day periods.	*Science News* reports fossil findings of single-celled organisms resembling modern blue–green algae in 3.5 million-year-old sedimentary rock from the Barberton Mountains of southeastern Swaziland.	The Metropolitan Opera performs Puccini's *La Boheme* in N.Y.C. as its first live telecast. Renata Scotto and Luciano Pavarotti sing the leading roles.	Oct. 15
			Protestors against the neutron bomb are arrested for interrupting services at the First Baptist Church in Wash., D.C., which are being attended by Pres. Carter and his family.		Oct. 16
		Supreme Ct. denies a petition to stay a lower court decision allowing the Concorde SST to land at Kennedy International Airport, N.Y.C.		Pope Paul VI offers to become a hostage on the hijacked Lufthansa plane if the passengers and crew are released. . . . Robert (Cal) Hubbard, 77, the only man in U.S. sports history to be elected to three Halls of Fame — two as a football player and one as a baseball umpire — dies of cancer in Gulfport, Fla.	Oct. 17

F	G	H	I	J
Includes elections, federal-state relations, civil rights and liberties, crime, the judiciary, education, health care, poverty, urban affairs and population.	Includes formation and debate of U.S. foreign and defense policies, veterans' affairs and defense spending. (Relations with specific foreign countries are usually found under the region concerned.)	Includes business, labor, agriculture, taxation, transportation, consumer affairs, monetary and fiscal policy, natural resources, and pollution.	Includes worldwide scientific, medical and technological developments, natural phenomena, U.S. weather, natural disasters, and accidents.	Includes the arts, religion, scholarship, communications media, sports, entertainments, fashions, fads and social life.

	World Affairs	Europe	Africa & the Middle East	The Americas	Asia & the Pacific
Oct. 18	The U.S. dollar falls to a postwar low in Tokyo, closing at 252.03 yen.	West German commandos force their way onto a hijacked Lufthansa airliner in Mogadishu, Somalia and free the 86 passengers and crew held captive by terrorists since Oct. 13. . . . West German industrialist Hanns-Martin Schleyer, who was kidnapped on Sept. 5, is slain by his abductors several hours after the capture of West German terrorist hijackers in Somalia and the suicides of Baader-Meinhof gang leaders. . . . Three members of the Czech Charter 77 human-rights group are sentenced on charges of passing subversive literature abroad.		Ecuadoran police open fire on striking sugar workers and kill at least 24 people. . . . Rio de Janeiro death squad kills 12 people in Brazil, according to a Spanish news agency.	Australian power station maintenance workers continue their nine-week strike, after briefly returning to their jobs on Oct. 14 when the arbitration board agreed to consider their requested pay hike.
Oct. 19	Gold closes at $161.60 an ounce on the London exchange, its highest price in more than two years.	Left-wing radicals in several French and Italian cities attack West German property to protest the suicides of the Baader-Meinhof gang leaders that followed the freeing of the hijacked Lufthansa aircraft. . . . The body of West German industrialist Hanns-Martin Schleyer is found with three bullets in his head and a slashed throat after what West German officials describe as the largest manhunt in the nation's history.	South African govt. bans 18 black civil-rights groups, shuts down two major black newspapers, and arrests or bans at least 50 persons, its most drastic curbs in nearly 20 years. . . . North Yemeni leader Maj. Ahmed Hussein al-Ghashmi is the target of an assassination attempt by an intruder into his home who tried to shoot him.	Nicaraguan businessmen and Catholic leaders call for political negotiations in wake of Sandinista guerrilla attacks.	Hanoi reports that over 60,000 Cambodian refugees have been granted asylum in Vietnam over the past two years.
Oct. 20			Eritrean rebel factions sign a formal merger pact in their fight for their independence from Ethiopia.		Heavy combat between Moslem rebels and Philippine govt. forces rages on the Zamboanga Peninsula. . . . Thai Premier Thanin Kraivichien's civilian govt. is overthrown in a bloodless military coup. . . . Sri Lanka National Assembly signs into law a constitutional amendment to establish a presidential-type governing system.
Oct. 21	A worldwide strike by the International Airline Pilots Assn. is cancelled after the U.N. General Assembly promises to address the issue of air safety from hijackings. . . . U.N. Security Council approves a one-year renewal of the U.N. Emergency Force separating Egyptian and Israeli troops in the Sinai.	A Dutch narcotics official is reported telling a conference on heroin traffic in Western Europe, which began on Oct. 17 in Amsterdam, that the number of identified heroin addicts in Europe has risen almost 1,000 percent in the last five years.	Rhodesian govt. takes steps to expand its black forces to fight against black nationalist guerrillas. . . . Syria and the PLO reject the U.S.–Israeli working paper on reconvening the Geneva Mideast peace conference.		Chinese govt. announces major educational reforms that require colleges to give entrance examinations and permit some high school students to go directly to college without having to put in some time working in the countryside. . . . Thailand's new ruling military junta announces that it will govern through a committee of civilians until elections are held.
Oct. 22			Soweto boycott of apartheid schools is reported extending to primary school pupils in the black township of Johannesburg, South Africa. Over 300 teachers are reported not working to support the boycott.		
Oct. 23			Pres. Carter makes public a portion of a letter from South African P.M. Vorster in which Vorster pledges that South Africa does not have nor does it intend to develop a nuclear device. Vorster denies the promise.	In a nationwide plebiscite, the Panamanian people approve the new Panama canal treaties by a two-thirds majority. It is the first free vote held in Panama since 1968.	

A	B	C	D	E
Includes developments that affect more than one world region, international organizations and important meetings of major world leaders.	Includes all domestic and regional developments in Europe, including the Soviet Union, Turkey, Cyprus and Malta.	Includes all domestic and regional developments in Africa and the Middle East, including Iraq and Iran and excluding Cyprus, Turkey and Afghanistan.	Includes all domestic and regional developments in Latin America, the Caribbean and Canada.	Includes all domestic and regional developments in Asia and Pacific nations, extending from Afghanistan through all the Pacific Islands, except Hawaii.

U.S. Politics & Social Issues	U.S. Foreign Policy & Defense	U.S. Economy & Environment	Science, Technology & Nature	Culture, Leisure & Life Style	
		Commerce Dept. reports that Americans' personal income from all sources rose $11.9 billion or .8 percent during September to a seasonally adjusted annual rate of $1.559 trillion.	Agriculture Dept. gives the meat industry until Jan. 16, 1978 to prove that bacon and other nitrate-cured meats do not cause cancer when cooked.	The New York Yankees of the AL win their first World Series in 15 years by beating the NL's Los Angeles Dodgers, 8–4, in the sixth game.	Oct. 18
Federal District Judge Frank Battisti orders Cleveland schools to remain open despite their lack of funds by using money set aside for repayment of bank loans. He bars the banks from pursuing the $15 million debt.	House clears a $6.8-billion foreign-aid appropriation for fiscal 1978. . . . House Ethics Committee begins open hearings on the South Korean lobbying effort in the U.S.		The Concorde makes its first landing at Kennedy International Airport, N.Y.C., flying from Toulouse, France in 3 hours and 45 minutes.	*Star Wars* is the top-grossing film for the week just ended.	Oct. 19
Wesley Bolin is sworn in as governor of Arizona, replacing Raul Castro, who is sworn in as ambassador to Argentina.	House narrowly defeats, by a 204—194 vote, an amendment to fiscal 1978 supplemental appropriations that would have added $1.4 billion for production of the controversial B-1 bomber.	Congress clears the minimum-wage bill and sends it to Pres. Carter. The bill would increase the minimum wage in four steps from its current $2.30 an hour to $3.35 an hour by 1981.			Oct. 20
David Berkowitz, the alleged serial murderer known as Son of Sam, is declared mentally fit to stand trial.	U.S. recalls Amb. William Bowdler from South Africa for consultation in wake of Pretoria's crackdown on antiapartheid activists. . . . Congressional Black Caucus calls for retaliatory measures against South Africa in wake of its increased repression of blacks.		Representatives of 13 nations bordering the Mediterranean Sea agree in principle to regulate dumping of industrial by-products and other wastes into the sea. . . . District Ct. Judge John Sirica orders the State Dept. to file an official objection to an International Whaling Commission ban on killing bowhead whales, which are an endangered species, thus allowing Eskimos to hunt a limited number.		Oct. 21
			CDC reports 210 cases of a penicillin-resistant strain of gonorrhea since March 1976.		Oct. 22
				Lester Markel, 83, editor of *The New York Times* Sunday edition who innovated the multisection format that became standard for Sunday newspapers, dies of cancer in N.Y.C. . . . Bill Rodgers wins the eighth annual New York City Marathon in 2 hours, 11 minutes, 28.2 seconds. Miki Gorman is the first woman to finish in 2 hours, 43 minutes, and 10 seconds.	Oct. 23

F	G	H	I	J
Includes elections, federal-state relations, civil rights and liberties, crime, the judiciary, education, health care, poverty, urban affairs and population.	Includes formation and debate of U.S. foreign and defense policies, veterans' affairs and defense spending. (Relations with specific foreign countries are usually found under the region concerned.)	Includes business, labor, agriculture, taxation, transportation, consumer affairs, monetary and fiscal policy, natural resources, and pollution.	Includes worldwide scientific, medical and technological developments, natural phenomena, U.S. weather, natural disasters, and accidents.	Includes the arts, religion, scholarship, communications media, sports, entertainments, fashions, fads and social life.

	World Affairs	Europe	Africa & the Middle East	The Americas	Asia & the Pacific
Oct. 24	*Business Week* sees the dramatic increase in the value of the Japanese yen (14 percent since January) as a part of a widespread move against the dollar that is only now being temporarily curbed by massive central-bank intervention and by rising U.S. interest rates.				
Oct. 25		Spanish Premier Adolfo Suarez and major opposition parties' leaders sign an agreement designed to reform the political system and revive the economy.... Jovanka Broz, wife of Yugoslav Pres. Tito, is reported under investigation for seeking the appointment of Serbs to high government offices and also under virtual house arrest.	Israel resumes truce discussions with Lebanese army officers.... Details of an autopsy performed on South African black activist Steven Biko, who died while in police custody, show extensive head injuries sustained over an eight-day period that had affected his circulation and caused ultimate kidney failure.		Striking Australian power workers return to their jobs without getting the pay hike they sought.
Oct. 26		Portugal formally declares public-spending cuts as part of an economic austerity program designed to satisfy, in part, the IMF in exchange for its $50-million loan.	Pres. Anwar Sadat announces that starting Jan. 1, 1978, Egypt will suspend for 10 years payments on its $4-billion in military debts to the Soviet Union because of Moscow's refusal to send Egypt more arms. ... Polisario guerrillas, the Saharan independence movement, report they attacked Moroccan and Mauritanian garrisons.	In an interview published in *The New York Times*, Sandinista leader Plutarco Hernandez insists that his guerrillas receive neither money nor arms from Cuba. He says that Sandinistas no longer favor a leftist dictatorship in Nicaragua, but believe that the country must passs through a stage of democracy.	Philippine govt. troops attack a Moslem rebel headquarters at Tabon in a move to kill or capture the Liberation Front's top leaders.
Oct. 27		Former British Liberal Party leader Jeremy Thorpe tells a press conference that he was not involved in an alleged plot to kill Norman Scott, a male model who claimed to have had homosexual relations with Thorpe.	A formal judicial inquest into the death of South African black activist Steven Biko opens in Pretoria.	Two people are killed in San Salvador when police fire into a crowd of workers and peasants protesting low wages for picking the coffee crop.... Charles Marion is released unharmed after being held for 82 days in what is described as the longest kidnapping in Canadian history. His abductors collected $50,000 in ransom.	P.M. Malcolm Fraser announces parliamentary elections will be held in Australia, 14 months before his government's term of office expires.... Fifty-five Bangladesh soldiers are reported sentenced to death for their role in an aborted army revolt on Sept. 30.
Oct. 28	U.N. General Assembly approves an Egyptian-sponsored resolution strongly deploring Israel's settlements in Arab territories.		Pres. Ali. Soilih receives a 55 percent vote of confidence in the Comoro Islands.... Israeli Finance Min. Simcha Ehrlich announces a government policy shift toward a free economy, which prompts widespread labor unrest and frantic buying sprees as consumer prices sharply rise.	Canadian Solicitor General Francis Fox reveals that the Royal Canadian Mounted Police had broken into an office of the separatist Parti Quebecois in January 1973 and copied lists of party members.	
Oct. 29		Polish CP leader Edward Gierek meets with Polish Roman Catholic leader Cardinal Stefan Wyszynski for the first time since Gierek took office in 1970.		Final vote count in the Panamanian plebiscite on the Panama Canal treaties, held on Oct. 23, is 66 percent in favor, 32 percent against, and 2 percent void.	
Oct. 30			French Pres. Valery Giscard d'Estaing sends a personal message to Algerian Pres. Houari Boumedienne threatening worsening relations between the two countries if Algeria does not pressure Polisario guerrillas to release kidnapped French nationals.		A political tour by former Indian P.M Indira Gandhi sparks clashes between police and about 5,000 demonstrators in Madras.

A	B	C	D	E
Includes developments that affect more than one world region, international organizations and important meetings of major world leaders.	Includes all domestic and regional developments in Europe, including the Soviet Union, Turkey, Cyprus and Malta.	Includes all domestic and regional developments in Africa and the Middle East, including Iraq and Iran and excluding Cyprus, Turkey and Afghanistan.	Includes all domestic and regional developments in Latin America, the Caribbean and Canada.	Includes all domestic and regional developments in Asia and Pacific nations, extending from Afghanistan through all the Pacific Islands, except Hawaii.

U.S. Politics & Social Issues	U.S. Foreign Policy & Defense	U.S. Economy & Environment	Science, Technology & Nature	Culture, Leisure & Life Style	
			Supreme Ct. Chief Justice Warren Burger refuses to alter a lower court decision banning hunting of the endangered bowhead whale, a ban opposed by Alaskan Eskimos who argue that hunting the bowhead is crucial to their diet and culture.		Oct. 24
Pres. Carter signs a bill designed to reduce Medicaid and Medicare abuses.		Robert Beasley, Firestone Tire & Rubber Co.'s former chief financial officer, is indicted on charges of embezzling $1 million. . . . SEC reports that Exxon Corp., the world's largest petroleum company, has made $56.5 million in questionable foreign payments since 1963 and then covered them up.		Orthodox Church in America selects its first American-born prelate, Bishop Theodosius of Pittsburgh, Pa. . . . Baltimore Orioles' manager Earl Weaver is named AL manager of the year. . . . Sparky Lyle of the New York Yankees becomes the first AL relief pitcher ever to win the Cy Young Award.	Oct. 25
		Bethlehem Steel Corp., second largest U.S. steel producer, posts its worst quarterly loss in U.S. business history — $477 million during the third quarter.	Space shuttle Enterprise safely returns to Edwards Air Force Base, California.	NFL concludes an agreement with the three major TV networks for the rights to broadcast NFL games in the most expensive deal in the history of televised sports — $576–656 million. . . . Marc Lalique, 78, master French glassmaker, dies in Wingen-sur-Moder, France.	Oct. 26
House passes a bill, 275–146, revising financing of the Social Security system that, among other changes, greatly increases Social Security taxes paid by upper-income workers. . . . James Earl Ray, the convicted assassin of civil rights leader Dr. Martin Luther King Jr., is sentenced to an additional one to two years in prison for attempting to escape from the state prison in Tenn. where he was serving a 99-year term.	Pres. Carter announces that the U.S. will support arms sanctions against South Africa and will extend its voluntary arms embargo to include spare parts and equipment with military value.	Treasury Dept. reports that the U.S. fiscal 1977 budget deficit has narrowed to $45.04 billion from $60.63 billion in the previous 12-month period. . . . U.S. trade deficit is the smallest since May — reported to total a seasonally adjusted $1.72 billion in September.		The Hankyu Braves beat the Yomiuri Giants, 6–3, to win the Japan Series, championship of Japanese major league baseball. . . . James M. Cain, 85, best-selling author who has been called the "poet of the potboiler" crime novel, dies in University Park, Md.	Oct. 27
Pres. Carter signs a bill to extend federal aid programs through Sept. 30, 1978 for refugees who have entered the U.S. in wake of the 1975 Communist takeover of Vietnam, Cambodia, and Laos.		The government's index of leading economic indicators is reported rising .3 percent in September to 132.4 percent of the 1967 base average.			Oct. 28
				The Act, a musical starring Liza Minnelli as a struggling young actress, opens on Broadway.	Oct. 29
				Consumer Product Safety Commission reportedly predicts that there will be 375,000 skateboard injuries in the U.S., double the amount in 1976.	Oct. 30

F	G	H	I	J
Includes elections, federal-state relations, civil rights and liberties, crime, the judiciary, education, health care, poverty, urban affairs and population.	Includes formation and debate of U.S. foreign and defense policies, veterans' affairs and defense spending. (Relations with specific foreign countries are usually found under the region concerned.)	Includes business, labor, agriculture, taxation, transportation, consumer affairs, monetary and fiscal policy, natural resources, and pollution.	Includes worldwide scientific, medical and technological developments, natural phenomena, U.S. weather, natural disasters, and accidents.	Includes the arts, religion, scholarship, communications media, sports, entertainments, fashions, fads and social life.

	World Affairs	Europe	Africa & the Middle East	The Americas	Asia & the Pacific
Oct. 31	U.S. Great Britain, and France defeat three U.N. Security Council resolutions that call for broad economic and military sanctions against South Africa and are sponsored by Benin, Libya, and Mauritius. . . . U.N. Security Council delegates unanimously approve an African-sponsored resolution condemning South Africa for "massive violence and repression" against opponents of apartheid.	British govt. floats the pound, seen as a sign of Britain's dramatic turnaround from its desperate financial situation in 1976.	An Ethiopian offensive appears to force a stalemate in the battle for the Ogaden region.	Premier Henck Arron and his National Party Alliance are voted back to office in Surinam's first national elections since it gained independence from the Netherlands in 1975.	
Nov. 1	Labor Secy. Ray Marshall annouces U.S. withdrawal from the ILO, a move supported both by the AFL–CIO and the U.S. Chamber of Commerce.				Philippine govt. troops capture a Moslem rebel camp about 50 miles north of Zamboanga City after two weeks of fierce fighting. . . . *Times of London* reports a steady increase of executions in China for political as well as common-law crimes since the October 1976 ouster of the radical Gang of Four.
Nov. 2	IMF sells 524,800 ounces of gold for $160,03 an ounce at its final gold auction of the year.	Soviet Pres. Leonid Brezhnev announces that his country's 1977 grain harvest will total 194 million metric tons, well below the planned harvest of 213 million metric tons. He blames poor weather and inefficient harvesting methods.		Quebec Premier Rene Levesque says he has known from the start that the Royal Canadian Mounted Police kept the Parti Quebecois under surveillance. . . . Argentinian troops occupy Buenos Aires subways in a futile attempt to end a strike, one of many throughout the country since Oct. 11 when 5,000 workers at the Renault auto plant in Cordoba struck for higher pay.	Sri Lanka frees people imprisoned by the previous government for crimes committed during the 1971 rebellion.
Nov. 3	U.N. General Assembly passes a resolution comdemning hijacking and asking all nations to improve airport security, the strongest antihijacking measure ever adoped by the U.N. . . . International Federation of Airline Pilots announces it will stage a 48-hour worldwide strike in wake of the U.N. resolution.	In an official visit to France, Quebec Premier Rene Levesque is made a Grand Officer of the Legion of Honor, seen marking a subtle but significant change in official French policy toward Quebec separatism.	South African P.M. John Vorster announces eased pass laws, the laws that control the movements of South African blacks in restricted white areas.	Joseph Clark, leader of the Canadian opposition Progressive Conservatives Party, announces in Parliament that an eavesdropping device had been found in a conference room next to his office in the Parliament building.	
Nov. 4	U.N. Security Council votes unanimously to impose a mandatory arms shipments embargo on South Africa. It is the first time to date that a member nation is the object of U.N. sanctions.			Canadian federal govt. diplomatically protests France's awarding its Legion of Honor to Quebec Premier Rene Levesque, who seeks Quebec separatism.	
Nov. 5			Syrian Pres. Hafez al-Assad and Lebanese Pres. Elias Sarkis meet in Damascus in a renewed effort to settle the southern Lebanese region. Assad is said to assure Sarkis that the Palestinians would withdraw and regroup in specified areas.		India and Bangladesh sign a five-year pact to share the waters of the Ganges River, ending a 25-year dispute.

A	B	C	D	E
Includes developments that affect more than one world region, international organizations and important meetings of major world leaders.	*Includes all domestic and regional developments in Europe, including the Soviet Union, Turkey, Cyprus and Malta.*	*Includes all domestic and regional developments in Africa and the Middle East, including Iraq and Iran and excluding Cyprus, Turkey and Afghanistan.*	*Includes all domestic and regional developments in Latin America, the Caribbean and Canada.*	*Includes all domestic and regional developments in Asia and Pacific nations, extending from Afghanistan through all the Pacific Islands, except Hawaii.*

U.S. Politics & Social Issues	U.S. Foreign Policy & Defense	U.S. Economy & Environment	Science, Technology & Nature	Culture, Leisure & Life Style	
Supreme Ct. bars convicted Watergate participants John Mitchell and John Ehrlichman from practicing law before the court.	House approves a resolution condemning South Africa for its repression of dissidents and expressing concern over the death of black activist Steven Biko.... Former CIA Director Richard Helms pleads no contest to two misdemeanor charges of failing to testify fully before a Senate For. Rel. Committee hearing in 1973 about CIA efforts to block the election of the late Salvador Allende as president of Chile.	Senate passes, 52–35, legislation incorporating a number of tax proposals designed to increase energy conservation and production. The bill differs sharply from tax proposals in Pres. Carter's energy plan.... United Steelworkers of America ratifies a new 40-month contract with the four major can companies.			Oct. 31
HEW Undersecretary Hale Champion announces that the Medicare program will finance second medical opinions before elective surgery for elderly patients, and urges people of all ages to get a second medical opinion before undergoing operations.		Former Atty. Gen. Richard Kleindienst tells a Senate Investigations subcommittee that he had used his friendship with Teamsters Union pres. Frank Fitzsimmons to get a $24-million insurance contract for a legal client, Joseph Hauser, and that he received part of a $250,000 finder's fee for his services.	PCP (phencyclidine), developed as an animal tranquilizer in the 1950s, is reported becoming a major health hazard among teenagers who use it alone or as a marijuana additive known as angel dust.... An HEW official cites tonsillectomies, hysterectomies, and gall bladder operations as the three most commonly abused surgical procedures.... Soviet Union inaugurates passenger supersonic transport service with a flight from Moscow to Alma-Ata, capital of the Soviet republic of Kazakhstan.	New York Yankees World series hero Reggie Jackson in acquitted in a N.Y. court of harassment charges involving the alleged beating of a 14-year-old boy, Chris Howe.	Nov. 1
A three-judge panel upholds the bank robbery conviction of Patricia Hearst, who had been kidnapped in 1974 by the radical Symbionese Liberation Army.	*The New York Times* reports that South Korean lobbyist Park Tong Sun had given $190,000 to former Rep. Otto Passman (D, La.), the largest amount given to any single congressman.	Teamsters pres. Frank Fitzsimmons challenges Richard Kleindienst's testimony and denies giving him assurances that Joseph Hauser would receive the Teamster's insurance contract.	NASA and the National Science Foundation report that University of Illinois scientists have discovered a third form of life, Mathanogens, which dates back 3.5 billion years and is distinct from the two known broad classes into which all living organisms have been divided up to now.... In Athens, Greece a torrential rainstorm and resultant flood kills at least 26 people and causes millions of dollars in damage.	Philadelphia Phillies pitcher Steve Carlton is the overwhelming choice for the NL Cy Young Award.... House communications subcommittee opens hearings on the influence of the three major TV networks on televised sports.	Nov. 2
In what is seen by feminists as a landmark ruling to establish a battered wife's right to self-defense, Francine Hughes is acquitted of first-degree murder of her former husband, James Hughes, who allegedly had beaten, choked, and threatened her.	Congress clears legislation authorizing $476 million in fiscal 1978 supplement funds for weapon and defense projects, including $220.9 million to accelerate development of the long-range cruise missile.	National Railroad Passenger Corp. (Amtrak) announces that it has canceled major service cuts on the Northeast corridor after a congressional vote approving $8 million supplemental appropriations for the 1978 fiscal year.			Nov. 3
	U.S. District Ct. Judge Barrington Parker fines former CIA Dir. Richard Helms $2,000 and gives him a suspended two-year prison sentence, charging that Helms had "dishonored his oath" and could not ignore the laws of the land in wake of his failure to testify fully to a Senate Committee investigating CIA intervention in Chile.	SBA lifts its four-month moratorium on assistance to businesses run by blacks and other disadvantaged persons.	Congress delays a proposed FDA ban on saccharin, the artificial sweetener linked with cancer.	Major League Baseball holds its second annual free-agent sale in N.Y.C.; Lyman Bostock of the Minnesota Twins is the most sought-after free agent.	Nov. 4
London-based Amnesty International human-rights organization says it is investigating the cases of 18 people imprisoned in the U.S., who are predominantly black activists.			In his first veto since assuming office, Pres. Carter vetoes a bill authorizing energy research funding because it contains an $80 million authorization for the Clinch River nuclear breeder reactor project in Oak Ridge, Tenn., which he opposes.	Guy Lombardo, 75, legendary bandleader who, since 1929, celebrated New Year's Eve by playing *Auld Lang Syne*, dies following heart surgery in Houston, Tex.	Nov. 5

F	G	H	I	J
Includes elections, federal-state relations, civil rights and liberties, crime, the judiciary, education, health care, poverty, urban affairs and population.	*Includes formation and debate of U.S. foreign and defense policies, veterans' affairs and defense spending. (Relations with specific foreign countries are usually found under the region concerned.)*	*Includes business, labor, agriculture, taxation, transportation, consumer affairs, monetary and fiscal policy, natural resources, and pollution.*	*Includes worldwide scientific, medical and technological developments, natural phenomena, U.S. weather, natural disasters, and accidents.*	*Includes the arts, religion, scholarship, communications media, sports, entertainments, fashions, fads and social life.*

	World Affairs	Europe	Africa & the Middle East	The Americas	Asia & the Pacific
Nov. 6		Denmark is reported paying the highest industrial salaries in the world, with a biginning engineer making $20,400 in 1975.	Israel rejects a proposal made by Egyptian Pres. Anwar Sadat for preliminary talks before the Geneva conference reconvenes. P.M. Menahem Begin also rejects Zbigniew Brzezinski's proposal that the West Bank be made an autonomous demilitarized zone. . . . Israel releases Archbishop Hilarion Capucci from prison following a personal appeal by Pope Paul VI.		
Nov. 7		Francisco Sa Carneiro, leader of Portugal's largest opposition party, the Social Democratic Party, resigns in a dispute over party policy toward the Socialist minority government.	Israeli Defense Min. Ezer Weizman warns that Israeli forces will act intensively and quickly to restore quiet if Palestinian guerrillas continue to shell Israeli villages.	In Argentina presumed guerrillas gun down a naval officer and a federal policeman in a Buenos Aires suburb, one of a series of attacks on executives and govenmnent officials that began in October. . . . Pres. Anastasio Somoza charges that there is an international Communist conspiracy against Nicaragua, in essence led by Cuba.	
Nov. 8		Swedish govt. announces that three of the nation's largest steel firms are merging into a single company to be owned 50 percent by the state. . . . France cancels delivery of naval equipment to South Africa in accordance with the mandatory ban on arms sales voted by the U.N. Security Council on Nov. 4.	Zambian Pres. Kenneth Kaunda, considered a moderate among the front-line African leaders, rules out the Anglo-American plan for holding elections for a Rhodesian govt. after meeting with British envoy Lord Carver and U.N. special representative Lt. Gen. Prem Chand the previous day.		
Nov. 9		Bulgaria and the U.S. agree to lift travel restrictions for diplomats. . . . British govt. tells Parliament that it will not send an ambassador to Cambodia because of human-rights violations there.	Egyptian Pres. Anwar Sadat says that he is ready to go to the Israeli Parliament to personally present his views on a Mideast peace settlement. . . . Israeli jets bomb Palestinian guerrilla strongholds in southern Lebanon, killing a reported 100 Lebanese civilians and inflicting widespread damage.	Pres. Hugo Banzer Suarez announces that elections will be held in July 1978 to restore constitutional rule in Bolivia after 14 years of military govt. . . . Canadian Solicitor-General Francis Fox confirms that the Royal Canadian Mounted Police has been illegally opening mail since 1954.	Malaysian Parliament authorizes federal govt. rule of Kelantan State, after riots erupted there in October.
Nov. 10		Dutch police in Amsterdam capture two suspected West German terrorists after a gunfight, including Christoph Wackernagel, suspected in the kidnapping–death of West German industrialist Hanns-Martin Schleyer.	South African police arrest 626 blacks, including nearly 200 schoolchildren, who were protesting in a black township complex outside of Pretoria.	AP reporter Oscar Serrat is kidnapped on his way to work at the Buenos Aires bureau in Argentina.	Thai military junta proclaims an interim Constitution that pledges elections in April 1979. . . . Pakistani Supreme Ct. upholds Pakistani leader Muhammad Zia ul-Haq's right to impose martial law. It also rejects a petition by Nusrat Bhutto, challenging the detention of her husband, former P.M. Zulfikar Ali Bhutto, and other former govt. officials.
Nov. 11		Soviet Union questions Norway's right to establish a 200-mile fisheries zone in the Arctic Ocean.	The last of the laws enforcing apartheid in Namibia are repealed.	Bolivian exiles in Mexico are reported denouncing Bolivian Pres. Hugo Banzer Suarez's election plan as a "farce."	
Nov. 12		Yefrem and Tatyana Yankelovich, Andrei Sakharov's stepdaughter and her husband, receive Soviet permission to emigrate. . . . Ingrid Schubert, 32, an imprisoned member of the West German terrorist Baader–Meinhof gang, is found hanging dead in her cell.	Ethiopian govt. announces that special identity papers will be issued to distinguish what it terms genuine revolutionaries, in wake of a wave of intensified political violence. . . . Egyptian Pres. Anwar Sadat discloses that he had suggested to Pres. Carter that an American professor of Palestinian origin represent the Palestinians at Geneva Mideast peace talks, thereby undercutting Israeli objections to dealing with an actual member of the PLO.		Australian govt. advertises in leading newspapers for applicants to fill positions in the Australian Security Intelligence Organization.
	A	**B**	**C**	**D**	**E**
	Includes developments that affect more than one world region, international organizations and important meetings of major world leaders.	*Includes all domestic and regional developments in Europe, including the Soviet Union, Turkey, Cyprus and Malta.*	*Includes all domestic and regional developments in Africa and the Middle East, including Iraq and Iran and excluding Cyprus, Turkey and Afghanistan.*	*Includes all domestic and regional developments in Latin America, the Caribbean and Canada.*	*Includes all domestic and regional developments in Asia and Pacific nations, extending from Afghanistan through all the Pacific Islands, except Hawaii.*

U.S. Politics & Social Issues	U.S. Foreign Policy & Defense	U.S. Economy & Environment	Science, Technology & Nature	Culture, Leisure & Life Style	
James Robison and Max Dunlap are convicted in Maricopa County, Ariz. of first-degree murder and conspiracy in the slaying of Don Bolles, and investigative reporter for the *Arizona Republic* .		Conference Bd. reports that the U.S. ranks sixth in engineer salaries, following Denmark, West Germany, Switzerland, Norway, and Belgium.	Thirty-nine people on the campus of Toccoa Falls Bible College in northeastern Ga. are killed in wake of a dam burst that floods the campus.	*All Things Wise and Wonderful* by James Herriot heads the best-selling nonfiction list for the week just passed.	Nov. 6
A three-judge panel, N.Y.C. rules, 2–1, that a journalist cannot be compelled to reveal his/her state of mind while preparing a story that becomes the object of a libel action, partially basing the decision on a 1964 Supreme Ct. "malice aforethought" decision.		*Business Week* reports that per capita U.S. coffee consumption has fallen 15 percent this year, largely because of its high cost.		New York Knicks basketball team files a $3.2-million suit against the New Jersey Nets stemming from a territorial infringement agreement.	Nov. 7
Supreme Ct. unanimously upholds a Social Security regulation that deprives a disabled man of his benefits if he marries a disabled woman who is not eligible for the same kind of benefits. . . . Republican John Dalton is elected governor of Va., winning against Democrat Henry Howell. . . . Democratic Gov. Brendan Byrne is reelected in N.J. in a dramatic come-from-behind victory. . . . Rep. Edward Koch (D) is elected mayor of N.Y.C.		White House acts to raise retail sugar prices.	Charles Kowal, a Hale Observatories Pasadena, Calif. astronomer, announces discovery of an object circling the sun between the orbits of Saturn and Uranus, first sighted on Oct. 18.	George Foster of the Cincinnati Reds is chosen the NL's most valuable player.	Nov. 8
William Sullivan, 65, former FBI intelligence operations head and later an outspoken critic of the late J. Edgar Hoover, who forced his retirement in 1971, dies of a hunting accident in Sugar Hill, N.H.		A U.S. Court of Appeals upholds a N.Y.S. law authorizing unemployment benefits for strikers. . . . Federal Home Loan Bank Board proposes regulations designed to curb redlining, the practice of withholding homes loans from old, deteriorating, or minority-populated areas.	Australia sends 15 nations a draft of a nuclear safeguard agreement, to be the basis for its uranium exports.		Nov. 9
N.Y.C. cancels the sale of $200 million in short-term notes after Moody's Investor Services gives the securities its lowest investment credit rating.		Amalgamated Clothing and Textile Workers Union file an antitrust suit against J.P. Stevens & Co. that accuses Stevens of violating antitrust laws in its efforts against unionization in the South. . . . SEC orders Merrill Lynch, Pierce, Fenner & Smith Inc. to pay $1.6 million to customers who had bought computer stock it recommended.	Iran signs a letter of intent with the West German firm of Kraftwerk Union AG to construct four nuclear power plants in Iran. . . . Torrential rains causing floods and landslides in northern Italy leave thousands homeless, at least 15 dead, and several million dollars in damages.	National Conference of Catholic Bishops, meeting in Wash., D.C., announces that divorced and remarried Roman Catholics will no longer face automatic excommunication.	Nov. 10
	Defense Dept. announces a total $11.3 billion in U.S. arms sales abroad for fiscal 1977.				Nov. 11
New Orleans, La. elects its first black mayor when Ernest Morial wins over Joseph DiRosa.				Metropolitan Archbishop Chrysostomos of Paphos is formally elected head of the independent Greek Orthodox Church in Cyprus.	Nov. 12

F	G	H	I	J
Includes elections, federal-state relations, civil rights and liberties, crime, the judiciary, education, health care, poverty, urban affairs and population.	*Includes formation and debate of U.S. foreign and defense policies, veterans' affairs and defense spending. (Relations with specific foreign countries are usually found under the region concerned.)*	*Includes business, labor, agriculture, taxation, transportation, consumer affairs, monetary and fiscal policy, natural resources, and pollution.*	*Includes worldwide scientific, medical and technological developments, natural phenomena, U.S. weather, natural disasters, and accidents.*	*Includes the arts, religion, scholarship, communications media, sports, entertainments, fashions, fads and social life.*

	World Affairs	Europe	Africa & the Middle East	The Americas	Asia & the Pacific
Nov. 13			Lt. Col. Atnafu Abate, vice chairman of Ethiopia's ruling military council (the Dergue), is executed for seeking to stifle the country's revolution.... In a surprise move, Somalia expels all Soviet advisers and terminates the 1974 Soviet–Somalian friendship and cooperation treaty. It also breaks diplomatic relations with Cuba.		Muhammad Zia ul-Haq extends the power of preventive detention to all four provincial martial law administrators in Pakistan.
Nov. 14		New Swiss chief of the army general staff, Hans Senn, says that the government has nuclear bomb shelters for 75 percent of its population.	U.S. State Dept. reports an estimated 400 Cuban officers and soldiers assisting Ethiopian forces in the Ogaden region.	Canadian Solicitor General Francis Fox confirms the Royal Canadian Mounted Police had obtained confidential medical files on people who allegedly threatened the national security.	
Nov. 15		Soviet Union criticizes Egyptian Pres. Anwar Sadat's projected visit to Israel.	Israeli P.M. Menahem Begin formally invites Egyptian Pres. Anwar Sadat to meet with him in Israel for discussions on the Middle East settlement.		Japanese Finance Ministry reports the Japanese trade surplus rose $1 billion in October, and $1.7 billion in September.
Nov. 16	Shah Mohammed Riza Pahlevi announces that Iran — an OPEC member — would strike to prevent an increase in OPEC oil prices in 1978, a change from his previous statement that Iran would be neutral during upcoming OPEC price deliberations.	British Labor govt. wins a test of strength in the House of Commons on its motion to limit debate time on bills to grant limited home rule to Scotland and Wales.... In a telephone interview, Soviet Nobel laureate and dissident Andrei Sakharov details official harassment of himself and his family.	Egyptian Pres. Sadat arrives in Damascus for talks with Pres. Hafez al-Assad, prior to his visit to Israel.... Libya, Iraq, and radical Palestinian groups denounce Egyptian Pres. Anwar Sadat's decision to visit Israel.		
Nov. 17			Egyptian Pres. Anwar Sadat accepts Israeli P.M. Menahem Begin's invitation to come to Israel. ... Egyptian For. Min. Ismail Fahmy resigns, apparently over Pres. Anwar Sadat's trip to Israel, followed hours later by the resignation of his replacement, Mahmoud Riad.	Mexican Pres. Jose Lopez Portillo replaces his finance and planning ministers after they cannot reconcile their differences on economic policy.	
Nov. 18		Kurt von Schuschnigg, 79, Austrian chancellor from 1934 until Hitler's invasion in March 1938, and, after emigration to the U.S., a political science professor at the University of St. Louis (Mo.), dies in Innsbruck, Austria.		Latin America Economic Report reveals that only 10 percent of Montevideo, Uruguay families earn a monthly income over $200.	

A	B	C	D	E
Includes developments that affect more than one world region, international organizations and important meetings of major world leaders.	Includes all domestic and regional developments in Europe, including the Soviet Union, Turkey, Cyprus and Malta.	Includes all domestic and regional developments in Africa and the Middle East, including Iraq and Iran and excluding Cyprus, Turkey and Afghanistan.	Includes all domestic and regional developments in Latin America, the Caribbean and Canada.	Includes all domestic and regional developments in Asia and Pacific nations, extending from Afghanistan through all the Pacific Islands, except Hawaii.

U.S. Politics & Social Issues	U.S. Foreign Policy & Defense	U.S. Economy & Environment	Science, Technology & Nature	Culture, Leisure & Life Style	
AMA and ABA endorse decriminalizing marijuana.				The final installment of the 33-year-old comic strip *L'il Abner* marks the retirement of its creator, Al Capp. . . . Minnesota quarterback Fran Tarkenton sets a NFL single-game record for passing accuracy during a 42–10 win over the Cincinnati Bengals.	**Nov. 13**
Time magazine reports that an economic boycott, initiated by NOW, of the 15 states that have failed to ratify the ERA has cost major U.S. convention cities millions of dollars in lost business. . . . Former N.Y. Knicks basketball star, Bill Bradley, announces his candidacy for the Democratic nomination for the U.S. Senate seat held by Clifford Case (R, N.J.)		Supreme Ct. votes, 4–3, to support an earlier order allowing oil companies to temporarily charge rates higher than those proposed by the government for the Trans-Alaska pipeline system. . . . *Business Week* reports a new wave of corporate takeovers that could rival the last surge of the late 1960s.	A Manila tourist landmark, the Hotel Filipinas, is destroyed by an early-morning fire that kills at least 47 people during a power outage caused by Typhoon Kim in the Philippines. . . . Peter Duncan, South Australian attorney general, says he is considering legal action to prevent uranium mining and export from the Northern Territories.	*Golda*, a play with Anne Bancroft portraying former Israeli P.M. Golda Meir, opens at the Morosco Theater in N.Y.C.	**Nov. 14**
N.Y.S. Appeals Ct. votes, 4–3, to strike down two sections of the state's death penalty law: mandating the death penalty for people convicted of intentionally killing police or corrections officers.	Professors Edward Said of Columbia University (N.Y.C.) and Ibrahim Aby Lughod of Northwestern University (Ill.) both deny that they had received offers to represent the Palestinian position at Geneva Mideast peace talks. . . . Pres. Carter signs a bill authorizing $2.6 billion in fiscal 1978 for defense and national security programs of the Energy Research and Development Administration (ERDA), including an authorization for the controversial neutron bomb.	FRB reports that industrial output rose .3 percent in October.	Canada and the U.S. agree on sales of Canadian uranium by the U.S., opening the way for the U.S. to export enriched Canadian uranium to Europe and Japan.	British composer of numerous film, theater, and TV scores, Richard Addinsell, 73, dies in London. . . . Archbishop John Quinn of San Francisco is elected to a three-year term as president of the National Conference of Catholic Bishops, meeting in Wash., D.C.	**Nov. 15**
		Commerce Dept. reports a surge in U.S. personal income, up 3.1 percent in October. . . . Housing starts in October are reported rising to their highest level since May 1973 at a seasonally adjusted annual rate of 2,179,000 units.	The Albert Lasker Medical Research Awards (clinical) are given to Swedish scientists Dr. Inge Edler and Dr. C. Hellmuth Hertz for their application of ultrasonic vibrations to heart disorder diagnosis. . . . The Albert Lasker Medical Research Awards (basic) are shared by two Swedes, Dr. K. Sune D. Bergstrom and Dr. Bengt Samuelsson, with an Englishman, Dr. John Vane, for their prostaglandins research. . . . Carter administration approves the sale of 54 tons of low-enriched uranium to Brazil for Brazil's new nuclear reactor at Angra dos Reis, south of Rio de Janeiro.	Rod Carew of the Minnesota Twins is chosen the AL's most valuable player. . . . Florida Citrus Commission votes unanimously to renew singer Anita Bryant's $100,000-a-year advertising contract through 1979, despite an orange juice boycott by several gay-rights groups, prompted by Bryant's militant stance against homosexuality.	**Nov. 16**
T. Cullen Davis, one of Texas's wealthiest men, is found not guilty in the shooting death of his 12-year-old stepdaughter, Andrea Wilborn, on Aug. 2, 1976, after the longest murder trial in Texas history.	Senators Jacob Javits (R) and Daniel Moynihan (D), both from N.Y.S., announce they have joined a committee to seek release of Soviet dissident scientist Anatoly Shcharansky, who is facing treason charges in the Soviet Union.	Commerce Dept. reports that crimes committed by employes cost U.S. businesses more than $30 billion in 1976, and that the cost is ultimately passed on to the consumers.		At their closing session, the National Conference of Catholic Bishops, meeting in Wash., D.C., approves guidelines for all Roman Catholic instruction and other proposals, which reflect Vatican II's emphasis on ecumenical relations and the augmented role of the laity.	**Nov. 17**
Robert Chambliss is convicted of first-degree murder for the 1963 bombing of the 16th Street Baptist Church in Birmingham, Ala., one of the worst racial terrorist acts during the 1960s civil rights era.	*The New York Times* publishes criticism by a former CIA analyst, Frank Snepp, that the CIA did not properly prepare to evacuate from Saigon in 1975 and thus left behind many Vietnamese allies to face Communist retaliation.	TVA files an antitrust suit against 10 foreign and three U.S. uranium producers, and says its position on its separate suit against Westinghouse Electric Corp. has not changed.	NRC closes a Mich. nuclear power plant and orders studies of 12 other plants because of possible safely hazards.	Heinemann Foundation gives the Pierpont Morgan Library, N.Y.C., a $10-million collection of books and papers.	**Nov. 18**

F	G	H	I	J
Includes elections, federal-state relations, civil rights and liberties, crime, the judiciary, education, health care, poverty, urban affairs and population.	Includes formation and debate of U.S. foreign and defense policies, veterans' affairs and defense spending. (Relations with specific foreign countries are usually found under the region concerned.)	Includes business, labor, agriculture, taxation, transportation, consumer affairs, monetary and fiscal policy, natural resources, and pollution.	Includes worldwide scientific, medical and technological developments, natural phenomena, U.S. weather, natural disasters, and accidents.	Includes the arts, religion, scholarship, communications media, sports, entertainments, fashions, fads and social life.

	World Affairs	Europe	Africa & the Middle East	The Americas	Asia & the Pacific
Nov. 19		French national Assembly passes the government's 1978 budget despite Gaullist opposition to a reduced defense appropriation.... Soviet Union continues to denounce Egyptian Pres. Sadat's Israeli trip, which it claims was masterminded by the U.S.	Egyptian Pres. Anwar Sadat receives a 21-gun salute, red carpet, and honor guard upon arriving at Ben-Gurion International Airport on the first visit by an Arab leder to the State of Israel since it was established in 1948.		
Nov. 20		Greek Premier Constantine Caramanlis's New Democracy Party wins a majority of the 300 parliamentary seats, but the size of its majority is sharply reduced by the latest election.	Egyptian Pres. Sadat tours Jerusalem's holy sites, seen as an indirect acknowledgement of Israeli sovereignty over Jerusalem.... Addressing the Israeli Knesset, Sadat promises Arab recognition of the State of Israel, but warns that there cannot be a peace settlement without the Palestinians.	U.S. State Secy. Cyrus Vance begins a three-day visit to Argentina, Brazil, and Venezuela to confer on human rights, nuclear energy, oil prices, and other international isues.	
Nov. 21		W. Ger. Chancellor Helmut Schmidt begins a visit to Poland aimed at improving relations between the two countries, which are still shadowed by residual Polish bitterness over the harsh Nazi occupation.	Israeli P.M. Menahem Begin and Egyptian Pres. Anwar Sadat hold a joint press conference in which they express hopes for peace. Sadat says that the prime reason for his visit to Israel is to eliminate the psychological barrier between the two countries.... Returning back to Egypt, Sadat receives a triumphal welcome in Cairo, with street-lined crowds chanting his praise.	After meetings with U.S. State Secy. Vance, the Argentinian govt. agrees to sign the Treaty of Tlatelolco, which bans atomic weapons in Latin America and the Caribbean.	A U.S. delegation led by Richard Rivers ends three days of talks on Japanese–U.S. trade in Tokyo in an attempt to reduce growing Japanese–U.S. friction stemming from increasing Japanese exports in the U.S.
Nov. 22	Egyptian chief delegate to the U.N. walks out on a speech by the Syrian delegate at the start of the General Assembly debate on the Middle East, the first walkout by one Arab delegate against another.	Austria and Czechoslovakia sign accords to open two new border crossings on their mutual frontier and to improve cultural and scientific cooperation.		U.S. State Secy. Vance fails to persuade Brazil to sign a nuclear nonproliferation treaty.	Peter Coleman is elected the first governor of American Samoa in a special runoff election.
Nov. 23		Malta's Premier Dom Mintoff threatens to sign a separate defense treaty with Libya if France and Italy reject Malta's request for economic and military aid, needed to replace revenues from the British and NATO bases in Malta that are scheduled to close in 1979.	Egypt expels three PLO officials from Cairo, apparently because they criticized Pres. Sadat's trip to Israel.... In the aftermath of Egyptian Pres. Sadat's visit, a number of prominent Israelis urge the government to rethink its policy on a Mideast peace settlement.	Canada's Royal Canadian Mounted Police are charged with having extensive connections with the U.S. CIA.	
Nov. 24			Rhodesian P.M. Ian Smith announces that his govt. is prepared to work out a political settlemnt with the country's black majority on the basis of universal suffrage, in light of what he calls the Anglo–American failure to reach a political settlment in the country.		
Nov. 25	U.N. condemns Israeli continued occupation of Arab lands taken in the 1967 war, by a 102–4 vote, 29 abstaining.	Bombs explode in five Portuguese towns in an apparent attempt to disrupt celebrations by conservative farmers marking the second anniversary of the suppression of a leftist revolt.	Moderate black nationalists within Rhodesia cautiously accept P.M. Smith's proposal to negotiate with them. Rhodesian Patriotic Front rejects Smith's offer.		A Manila military court sentences former Philippine Sen. Benigno Aquino to death on charges of subversion, murder, and illegal possession of weapons.
	A Includes developments that affect more than one world region, international organizations and important meetings of major world leaders.	**B** Includes all domestic and regional developments in Europe, including the Soviet Union, Turkey, Cyprus and Malta.	**C** Includes all domestic and regional developments in Africa and the Middle East, including Iraq and Iran and excluding Cyprus, Turkey and Afghanistan.	**D** Includes all domestic and regional developments in Latin America, the Caribbean and Canada.	**E** Includes all domestic and regional developments in Asia and Pacific nations, extending from Afghanistan through all the Pacific Islands, except Hawaii.

U.S. Politics & Social Issues	U.S. Foreign Policy & Defense	U.S. Economy & Environment	Science, Technology & Nature	Culture, Leisure & Life Style	
The first National Women's Conference meets in Houston, Tex., sponsored by the National Commission on the Observance of International Women's Year.... Across town from the National Women's Conference, in Houston, Tex., Phyllis Schlafly addresses 15,000 opponents of the proposed ERA and of free-choice abortions, who contend that they represent the majority of American women and support women's traditional role as wife and mother.	SEC is reported investigating an alleged $10,000 payment made by the South Korean Embassy in Wash., D.C. to Robert Smith, a retired U.S. Air Force general living in Seoul.		A TAP Portuguese Airways Boeing 727 crashes during a light rainstorm on the resort island of Madeira, killing 124 of the 156 passengers and six of the eight crew.	*Star Wars* , a space fantasy film, tops *Jaws* as the all-time leader in domestic movie theater rentals.	Nov. 19
Feminist and antifeminist factions at the National Women's Conference unite on a resolution pertaining to minority women, introduced by Coretta King, widow of slain civil-rights leader Martin Luther King Jr.	Pres. Carter calls Egyptian Pres. Anwar Sadat's arrival in Israel "a great occasion."			Paul Goma, a Rumanian dissident writer, arrives in Paris for a one-year visit as a guest of the International P.E.N. Club, a writers-editors organization.	Nov. 20
FBI releases over 50,000 pages of files detailing its counterintelligence programs against domestic dissidents. The program, known as Cointelpro, began in 1956 against the Communist Party and since then has directed its efforts against the Ku Klux Klan, black militants, and Vietnam peace groups.	*Wall Street Journal* reports that the Defense Dept. will try to award weapons manufacturing contracts simultaneously thereby maintaining competition throughout the manufacturing process to determine cost efficiency.	Energy Secy. James Schlesinger says the Carter administration might accept modifications of some of its energy proposals if other measures are left untouched by Congress.	FDA approves the first effective vaccine against bacterial pneumonia.	Steve Wolf, 34, leading rock music promoter, dies of a bullet wound received during an apparent robbery attempt at his Los Angeles home.... Didier Decoin, 32, wins France's most prestigious literary award, the Prix Goncourt.	Nov. 21
Jim McConn is elected mayor of Houston, Tex. over Frank Briscoe.	A UPI Senate poll reported in the press finds 39 senators now favoring of leaning toward the Panama Canal treaties, 29 opposed, and 32 undecided.	Polaroid Corp. announces ending sales to South Africa following disclosure that a distributor had been selling Polaroid cameras and films secretly to the South African govt. in contravention of a 1971 agreement.... Consumer prices are reported rising .3 percent in October.... Hawaiian sugar workers accept a new 15-month contract with pension and wage improvements after striking since Nov. 2.	Among those receiving the U.S. National Medal of Science are the following: Roger Guillemin, Morris Cohen, Efraim Rackler, and Hassler Whitney.... Concorde passenger service begins at Kennedy International Airport, N.Y.C.... CAB bans cigar, pipe, and cigarette smoking on commercial airlines.	The J. Paul Getty Museum in Calif. is reported paying between $3.5 and $5 million for a fourth-century B.C. bronze sculpture, said to be a record price for sculpture.... Eddie Murray, a Baltimore Orioles switch-hitting first baseman, is named AL rookie of the year.	Nov. 22
			A strong Argentinian earthquake reportedly claims 80–100 lives, injures 300 people, and leaves at least 10,000 homeless.	Andre Dawson of the Montreal Expos wins the NL rookie of the year award.	Nov. 23
	U.S. officials reportedly are emphasizing that State Secy. Vance's Latin American trip underscores the Carter administration's interest in strong relations with Latin American countries and its country-by-country approach.		A Greek archaeologist, Prof. Manolis Andronikos, announces discovering the tomb of Macedonian King Philip II, who was the father of Alexander the Great, at Vergina in northern Greece.	Mayo Smith, 62, Detroit tigers manager during their 1968 World Series victory, dies following a stroke in Boynton Beach, Fla.	Nov. 24
		EPA cites 17 federal facilities in the Midwest for violating federal clean-air and clean-water standards.... Thousands of farmers and their families drive their tractors into Plains, Ga., Pres. Carter's hometown, to dramatize their concern over low crop prices and high production costs.		Agatha Christie's play *The Mousetrap* breaks long-running theatrical records in London, celebrating in twenty-fifth birthday.	Nov. 25
F	G	H	I	J	
Includes elections, federal-state relations, civil rights and liberties, crime, the judiciary, education, health care, poverty, urban affairs and population.	Includes formation and debate of U.S. foreign and defense policies, veterans' affairs and defense spending. (Relations with specific foreign countries are usually found under the region concerned.)	Includes business, labor, agriculture, taxation, transportation, consumer affairs, monetary and fiscal policy, natural resources, and pollution.	Includes worldwide scientific, medical and technological developments, natural phenomena, U.S. weather, natural disasters, and accidents.	Includes the arts, religion, scholarship, communications media, sports, entertainments, fashions, fads and social life.	

	World Affairs	Europe	Africa & the Middle East	The Americas	Asia & the Pacific
Nov. 26		Liechtenstein issues its first death sentence in nearly 200 years.	Bishop Abel Muzorewa says he is prepared to talk with P.M. Smith, provided that Smith is genuine in his offer to negotiate on the basis of universal suffrage.... Egyptian Pres. Anwar Sadat invites all parties involved in the Middle East conflict to attend a preparatory meeting in Cairo prior to a Geneva peace conference.		
Nov. 27			Egyptian Pres. Sadat issues formal invitations to the Cairo conference to all involved parties, except the PLO. The Syrian govt. immediately rejects the bid and announces plans to convene a meeting in Tripoli, Libya of those Arab nations who also oppose Egypt's overtures to Israel. Israel accepts.... PLO says it will participate in the Tripoli rejectionist meeting and thereby shun the Cairo meeting on the Mideast peace settlement.		
Nov. 28	GATT release a report showing that protectionist trade policies tend to slow a major industrialized nation's growth rather than stimulate its domestic economy and protect jobs.... U.N. General Assembly adopts a resolution favoring independence for Belize.		Israeli P.M. Menahem Begin designates Eliahu Ben-Elissar and Meir Rosenne as Israel's envoys to the Cairo conference.... Jordan bars participating in either the Cairo or Tripoli conferences.... Rhodesian troops continue to raid Mozambique, killing about 1,200 black nationalist guerrillas since Nov. 23.		Following widespread protests, including U.S. expressions of concern, Philippine Pres. Ferdinand Marcos orders Benigno Aquino's trial reopened and permits new evidence presented.... Japanese Premier Takeo Fukuda forms a new Cabinet to include more economic experts in an effort to spur Japan's economic recovery and normalize trade relations with the U.S. and other Western nations.
Nov. 29	Japanese Amb. Masao Sawaki announces at the annual GATT assembly in Geneva that Japan is planning to lower tariffs on a wide range of products to reduce its huge trade surplus with the rest of the world.		The U.S., after several days of indecision, formally accepts Egyptian Pres. Sadat's invitation to participate in the Cairo conference.... The Soviet Union rejects a bid to participate in the Cairo Middle East peace conference.... Britain and the U.S. condemn Rhodesian raids in Mozambique.		
Nov. 30			P.M. John Vorster's National Party wins an overwhelming victory in South African parliamentary elections, an apparent mandate for continuing apartheid policies.	Quebec provincial police, with search warrants, raid the offices of the Liberal and Union National parties in Montreal and take lists of contributors.	
Dec. 1		Three of France's major labor unions stage a one-day strike to protest unemployment and the country's limit on wage increases.	Lebanon formally rejects Egypt's invitation to attend the Cairo conference to prepare for Geneva Mideast peace talks.	Brazilian Pres. Ernesto Geisel announces political reforms to abolish the institutional acts giving the military govt. dictatorial power since 1964.... Bolivan Pres. Hugo Banzer unexpectedly announces that he will not run for the presidency in the 1978 general elections.	
Dec. 2	U.N. General Assembly approves an Arab-initiated proposal to create a U.N. unit to publicize Palestinian rights.... UNCTAD talks end in failure as industrial and developing countries fail to agree on establishing a common fund to finance commodity pacts.	The Netherlands asks former U.S. CIA agent Philip Agee to leave the country after his temporary work permit expires.... Italian Interior Min. Francesco Cossiga says that 450 terrorist attacks have occurred in the country since January. He also notes the rise in common crime and prevailing street violence between left-and right-wing factions.	Five Arab hard-line states — Syria, Iraq, Libya, Algeria, and South Yemen — and the PLO meet in Tripoli, Libya to counter Egypt's peace initiatives to Israel.... South African magistrate Marthinus Prins rules that police were not responsible for the death of Steven Biko.	Bermuda Gov. Peter Ramsbotham declares a state of emergency and asks for British troops to counter riots and arson by black youth militants protesting the hangings of two black political activists who were convicted of murders in 1972, 1973, and 1974.	
	A Includes developments that affect more than one world region, international organizations and important meetings of major world leaders.	**B** Includes all domestic and regional developments in Europe, including the Soviet Union, Turkey, Cyprus and Malta.	**C** Includes all domestic and regional developments in Africa and the Middle East, including Iraq and Iran and excluding Cyprus, Turkey and Afghanistan.	**D** Includes all domestic and regional developments in Latin America, the Caribbean and Canada.	**E** Includes all domestic and regional developments in Asia and Pacific nations, extending from Afghanistan through all the Pacific Islands, except Hawaii.

U.S. Politics & Social Issues	U.S. Foreign Policy & Defense	U.S. Economy & Environment	Science, Technology & Nature	Culture, Leisure & Life Style	
Utah's Supreme Ct. rules, 4–1, that the state's death penalty is constitutional.					Nov. 26
Sen. John McClellan (D, Ark.), second most senior member of the U.S. Senate and chairman of its powerful Appropriations Committee, dies at the age of 81 in Little Rock. Ark.			National Institute on Drug Abuse (NIDA) researchers report that sleeping pills are implicated in nearly 5,000 deaths in the U.S. and in an estimated 25,000 hospital emergency ward visits a year.		Nov. 27
		Commerce Dept. reports that the U.S. trade deficit in October — a seasonally adjusted $3,1 billion — was its largest in history.... Supreme Ct. declines to review a lower court ruling that AT&T is subject to federal antitrust prosecution.	A cyclone striking India's southeastern Andhra Pradesh State is estimated killing 20,000 and leaving 2 million people homeless.	Jacques Lipchitz's final sculpture, the five-story, 23-ton *Bellerophon Taming Pegasus* , is dedicated at Columbia University, N.Y.C.... Bob Meusel, 81, former New York Yankees left fielder, dies in Downey, Calif.	Nov. 28
Frank M. Johnson Jr. withdraws as nominee for FBI director, citing personal health reasons.... Cleveland Teachers' Union votes, 3,336–2,130, not to work without pay after the financially troubled Cleveland, Ohio school system fails to meet its payroll on Nov. 23.	Navy announces that the first Trident submarine will cost $400 million more than originally estimated and take a year later to finish than originally planned.	A strike, begun Oct. 1, by Atlantic and Gulf Coast longshoremen, ends after reaching agreement on a new three-year contract that guarantees a 30.5 percent wage increase and job security.	Congress clears a bill authorizing $297.74 million for the NRC in fiscal 1978.		Nov. 29
		The Commerce Dept. reports that leading economic indicators rose .7 percent in October, the fourth increase in a row.	Congress clears a bill authorizing $16 million through fiscal 1981 to help protect endangered species.	Livingston Biddle Jr. is sworn in as National Endowment for the Arts chairman, succeeding Nancy Hanks... Sir Terence Rattigan, 66, award-winning British playwright whose scripts include the popular *Separate Tables* and *The Winslow Boy*, dies of cancer in Bermuda.	Nov. 30
		Energy Dept. announces new guidelines for coping with any fuel shortage that might arise if the winter is prolonged and cold.	California researchers announce manufacturing a human hormone, somatostatin, by using recombinant DNA research techniques.	World Boxing Council rescinds its threat to strip heavyweight champion Muhammad Ali of his title unless he negotiates a rematch with Ken Norton.	Dec. 1
Leroy (Nicky) Barnes, an elusive N.Y.C. drug dealer, is found guilty of heading a major narcotics ring that sold millions of dollars worth of heroin and cocaine annually.	CIA announces that its director, Stansfield Turner has barred agency use of journalists for intelligence operations but will allow the hiring of journalists to translate material or lecture a training course.	Interior Dept. announces conditional approval of a proposed 1,026-mile pipeline to carry Alaskan crude oil from Calif. to Tex.	A chartered Bulgarian jet carrying 159 Moslem pilgrims home from the holy city of Mecca in Saudi Arabia crashes in Libya.		Dec. 2

F	G	H	I	J
Includes elections, federal-state relations, civil rights and liberties, crime, the judiciary, education, health care, poverty, urban affairs and population.	Includes formation and debate of U.S. foreign and defense policies, veterans' affairs and defense spending. (Relations with specific foreign countries are usually found under the region concerned.)	Includes business, labor, agriculture, taxation, transportation, consumer affairs, monetary and fiscal policy, natural resources, and pollution.	Includes worldwide scientific, medical and technological developments, natural phenomena, U.S. weather, natural disasters, and accidents.	Includes the arts, religion, scholarship, communications media, sports, entertainments, fashions, fads and social life.

	World Affairs	Europe	Africa & the Middle East	The Americas	Asia & the Pacific
Dec. 3					
Dec. 4		In a referendum Swiss voters reject proposals to exempt conscientious objectors from military service and to impose uniform income-tax rates.	Central African Empire Pres.-for-Life Jean-Bedel Bokassa crowns himself His Imperial Majesty Bokassa I in an elaborate ceremony that cost an estimated $25 million.	The first divorce law in Brazilian history is cleared by both legislative houses. It limits divorce to only once in a person's lifetime.... Canadian unemployment rate for November reaches 8.4 percent, the highest rate since WWII.	Chinese CP newspaper *Jenmin Jih Pao* defends judicial use of death penalties, in face of accounts of widespread executions and the Public Security Ministry's warnings against overuse of the death penalty and of torture.
Dec. 5	U.S. Undersecretary of State Philip Habib flies to Moscow where he reportedly is seeking to persuade Soviet leaders to urge Syria to remain aloof from hard-line Arab nations opposing Egyptian Pres. Sadat's policies.	Marshal Aleksandr Vasilevsky, 82, Russian Army Chief of Staff during WWII who figured prominently in the critical battle of Stalingrad, dies in Moscow.	At the conclusion of a summit meeting in Tripoli, Libya, Arab critics of Egyptian Pres. Sadat's peace bid to Israel issue the Tripoli Declaration to establish a new Arab front for resistance to Egypt's peace initiatives.... Egypt severs diplomatic relations with Syria, Iraq, Libya, Algeria, and South Yemen in wake of their attempts to disrupt Pres. Anwar Sadat's peace overtures toward Israel.	Cuban Pres. Fidel Castro asserts that Cuba's military presence in Africa is not negotiable and has nothing to do with Cuban–U.S. relations.	Karachi police arrest 30 journalists and press workers who had been on a hunger strike since Dec. 3 to protest the Pakistani government's forced closure of *Musawat* , a newspaper owned by the family of former P.M. Zulfikar Ali Bhutto.... Former Indian P.M. Indira Gandhi persuades the executive committee of her Congress Party to issue a directive forbidding all party members from appearing as witnesses before a judicial commission investigating alleged abuses of her former government.
Dec. 6	UAE oil minister calls for replacing the U.S. dollar with an OPEC dollar as the authorized unit of payment in oil sales.	At an EEC summit conference, West German Chancellor Helmut Schmidt charges that the EEC is financing the U.S. through its support of the dollar.... NATO military committee chmn. Gen. H.F. Zeiner Gundersen, urges the alliance to increase Turkey's military aid as a move to strengthen NATO's southern defenses.	Zambian Pres. Kenneth Kaunda announces that his govt. will no longer participate in U.S.–British talks on a plan for Rhodesian majority-rule govt. and that he will throw his whole support behind the Patriotic Front, the coalition of guerrilla organizations fighting the Rhodesian minority government.	Bermuda's leaders are reported deeply concerned about the negative impact of black riots in the island's tourist industry, which is its prime income source.	
Dec. 7	An OPEC official of a special $1.6-billion fund earmarked for developing countries says that OPEC is using more of its surplus cash in direct investments in poorer countries, rather than depositing funds with U.S. banks, which then financed loans in the developing countries.	West German bankers say that the mark's steep rise against the U.S. dollar could damage West Germany's export growth and slow down the country's economic growth.... Willi Ritschard is elected president of Switzerland for 1978 by a joint session of Parliament.	Soviet support of the Arab counter Tripoli conference prompts Cairo to close Soviet cultural centers and some consulates in Egypt as well as those of four Soviet bloc countries — Czechoslovakia, Hungary, East Germany, and Poland.		Pakistan releases 30 newspeople after agreeing the day before to allow publication of *Musawat* under new management and with a new editor.... Philippines signs a most-favored-nation trade pact with East Germany.
Dec. 8	In its annual report, Amnesty International criticizes 116 U.N. members for human-rights violations.	Portuguese Socialist minority govt. loses a confidence vote in the National Assembly, thereby toppling the first democratically elected government in 50 years and leaving Portuguese politics in total confusion. Premier Mario Soares and his Socialist Cabinet remain in office in a caretaker capacity.	Egypt returns to Israel the bodies of three Israeli soldiers recently found in the Suez Canal area and believed to have been killed in the 1973 war.	Between 15 and 25 human-rights activists are kidnapped in Buenos Aires by people presumed to be Argentine plainclothed security officers.	Amnesty International cites Indonesia, which holds an estimated 50,000–100,000 political prisoners, as the worst human-rights violator within the U.N.

A	B	C	D	E
Includes developments that affect more than one world region, international organizations and important meetings of major world leaders.	Includes all domestic and regional developments in Europe, including the Soviet Union, Turkey, Cyprus and Malta.	Includes all domestic and regional developments in Africa and the Middle East, including Iraq and Iran and excluding Cyprus, Turkey and Afghanistan.	Includes all domestic and regional developments in Latin America, the Caribbean and Canada.	Includes all domestic and regional developments in Asia and Pacific nations, extending from Afghanistan through all the Pacific Islands, except Hawaii.

U.S. Politics & Social Issues	U.S. Foreign Policy & Defense	U.S. Economy & Environment	Science, Technology & Nature	Culture, Leisure & Life Style	
		Julius Shiskin, commissioner of labor statistics, says that a higher percentage of Americans held jobs in November than at any other time in U.S. history.	Indian authorities close an atomic plant at Baroda after an explosion at its heavy water facility injures about 20 people.	Karen Farmer, 26, a Detroit real estate salesperson, becomes the first black member of the Daughters of the American Revolution (DAR), a group regarded as racist since it denied black singer Marian Anderson permission to sing in the DAR Constitution Hall in Washington, D.C., back in 1939.	Dec. 3
Six congressmen, including Rep. Parren Mitchell (D, Md.) who is chairman of the Congressional Black Caucus, meet in Raleigh, N.C. with aides of Gov. James Hunt Jr. to seek release of the Wilmington 10, nine black men convicted in 1972 for firebombing a white-owned grocery store in Wilmington, N.C.	David K. Bruce, distinguished U.S. diplomat , dies at the age of 79 of a heart attack in Washington, D.C.		A hijacked Malaysian Airlines System Boeing 737, with 100 people aboard, explodes in mid-air and crashes in the Strait of Johore.	Andre Eglevsky, 60, Russian-born, French-trained classical ballet dancer who emigrated in 1937 to the U.S., dies of a heart attack in Elmira, N.Y. . . . Australia takes the 1977 Davis Cup when John Alexander beats Adriano Panatta of Italy, thus becoming the all-time leader in tennis's Davis Cup competition with 24 wins to the U.S.'s 23.	Dec. 4
Ohio Judge Paul Riley rules that Ohio's entire school financing system is unconstitutional. . . . Maine's school-financing tax law is repealed by a referendum. The law, enacted in 1973, called for equal per-pupil spending throughout the state regardless of the local tax base.		Sales of U.S.-made cars, which were strong in October, are reported to have slowed in November. November sales of imports, however, reportedly rose 21 percent above those of November 1976.	OSHA announces plans to eliminate about 1,100 obsolete job-safety regulations.		Dec. 5
Supreme Ct. unanimously rules that an employe taking maternity leave cannot be deprived of job seniority, but reaffirms its 1976 decision that employers are not legally required to provide pregnancy or childbirth benefits.		After lengthy negotiations with Japanese officials, the Carter administration unveils a plan to curb steel imports that aims to revitalize the ailing U.S. steel industry. . . . UMW strikes as its contract with the Bituminous Coal Operators Assn. expires.		A.C. Nielsen Co. reveals a significant decline in TV viewing in October and November, seen as a long-time trend.	Dec. 6
Supreme Ct. rules, 5–4, that federal judges are empowered to authorize electronic surveillance to aid criminal investigations and that they can compel telephone companies to install such devices. . . . After the House and Senate finally agree on language curbing federal funding of abortions, a bill appropriating $60.2 billion in fiscal 1978 for HEW and the Labor Dept. clears Congress.	AP reports that John Taylor, editor of *Jane's All the World's Aircraft*, questions Pres. Carter's cancellation of B-1 bomber production and disputes Carter's argument that the cruise missile is a cheaper and more effective airborne nuclear deterrent.	Congress clears legislation barring U.S. corporations from bribing foreign officials.	Peter Goldmark, 71, inventor of the long-playing phonograph record (LP) and credited with developing the first practical color-TV system, dies in a car accident in Westchester County, N.Y.	Gordie Howe of the World Hockey Assn.'s New England Whalers is the first man in the history of ice hockey to score 1,000 professional career goals.	Dec. 7
	U.S. District Ct. Judge John Lewis Smith Jr. rules that the U.S. govt. is the rightful owner of transcripts of former State Secy. Henry Kissinger's telephone conversations during his eight years as chief foreign affairs adviser and that Kissinger had "wrongfully" removed them when he left office.	Four thousand Cleveland teachers return to work.		The Heisman Trophy for the outstanding college football player of 1977 is awarded to University of Texas running back Earl Campbell. . . . Cale Yarborough wins the Olsonite driver of the year award, top honor in U.S. auto racing.	Dec. 8

F	G	H	I	J
Includes elections, federal-state relations, civil rights and liberties, crime, the judiciary, education, health care, poverty, urban affairs and population.	Includes formation and debate of U.S. foreign and defense policies, veterans' affairs and defense spending. (Relations with specific foreign countries are usually found under the region concerned.)	Includes business, labor, agriculture, taxation, transportation, consumer affairs, monetary and fiscal policy, natural resources, and pollution.	Includes worldwide scientific, medical and technological developments, natural phenomena, U.S. weather, natural disasters, and accidents.	Includes the arts, religion, scholarship, communications media, sports, entertainments, fashions, fads and social life.

	World Affairs	Europe	Africa & the Middle East	The Americas	Asia & the Pacific
Dec. 9	The Soviet Union is reported registering its first overall trade surplus with the capitalist West since 1974.		Bishop Abel Muzorewa finally joins P.M. Smith's round of talks with black leaders after boycotting the first seven days of meetings to protest the Nov. 23–27 Rhodesian raids on Mozambique guerrilla camps. . . . Eritrean rebels begin a siege of Massawa, which controls access to Asmara, the Eritrean capital, and whose fall could further erode Ethiopian control of the province.	Bolivian govt. says it has crushed a plot against Pres. Hugo Banzer Suarez. . . . Four members of the Graiver family and three of their employes are sentenced by a military court in Buenos Aires, after being found guilty of illicit association with the Montoneros, an Argentine guerrilla group for which the Graiver family allegedly invested over $17 million between 1974 and 1976.	*Washington Post* reports a massive population shift from the northern to the southern part of Vietnam as part of the government's effort to increase lagging agricultural production and to bolster central government rule.
Dec. 10	U.S. and Soviet Union conclude the third round of talks on demilitarizing the Indian Ocean. Both sides report progress.	Soviet KGB (secret police) prevent more than 20 dissidents from leaving their Moscow apartments to participate in a silent vigil protesting Soviet violation of human rights. . . . Rumania and Israel are reported planning a major expansion of their trade and economic ties.	Saudi Arabia extends its economic boycott against Israel, adding 16 foreign vessels to its blacklist.		P.M. Malcolm Fraser's coalition govt., comprised of his own Liberal Party and the more conservative National Party, wins large majorities in Australian nationwide elections. . . . Australian Labor Party head Gough Whitlam resigns.
Dec. 11	The Independent Commission on International Development Issues, headed by former West German Chancellor Willy Brandt, concludes its first meeting near Bonn. Its task over the next year-and-a-half is to devise politically acceptable ways of restructuring economic relations between the industrial and developing countries.		Angola's ruling MPLA ends its first congress. Its purpose was transforming the liberation movement into a political party committed to Marxism.	Quebec Superior Ct. rejects a third attempt by the federal govt. to halt provincial investigations into Royal Canadian Mounted Police activities in Quebec.	
Dec. 12		Baroness Clementine Spencer-Churchill of Chartwell, 92, widow of Sir Winston Churchill who had described his 57-year marriage as the most joyous and fortunate event of his life, dies of a heart attack in London.	Lebanon's main Christian political organizations stage a general strike in Beirut to protest U.S. State Secy. Cyrus Vance's upcoming visit.		
Dec. 13	U.N. Gen. Secy. Kurt Waldheim rejects an Egyptian request that a U.N. representative preside at the Cairo conference.	Soviet Union and the U.S. extend until 1982 their four-year-old agricultural cooperation agreement.	U.S. State Secy. Vance confers in Damascus with Syrian Pres. Hafez al-Assad and in Beirut with Lebanese officials, but both countries refuse to attend the Cairo meetings.	Following clashes between local students and police, the Colombian govt. closes the University of Cauca in Popayan.	
Dec. 14	U.S. and the Soviet Union begin talks on curbing the international arms trade.	A Dutch court convicts Pieter Menten, 78, of WWII war crimes and sentences him to 15 years imprisonment. . . . Cyprus Pres. Spyros Kyprianou's son, Achilleas Kyprianou, is kidnapped by a right-wing Cypriot group. . . . Soviet 1978 economic growth targets are to be significantly reduced, according to an announcement made at the opening of the Supreme Soviet's winter session.	The Cairo conference, convened to prepare procedures for a future Middle East peace parley, opens with Egypt, Israel, the U.S. and the U.N. represesented. Syria, Lebanon, Jordan, the U.S.S.R., and the PLO boycott the conference. . . . Anti-Angolan govt. National Union for the Total Independence of Angola (UNITA) has mounted 11 attacks in urban areas in past weeks, killing a number of Cuban and East European technicians.	Mexican authorities occupy Benito Juarez University of Oaxaca after campus violence reoccurs.	
Dec. 15	OECD labor ministers begin a meeting in Paris to discuss the problem of youth unemployment.	U.N. extends its peacekeeping force in Cyprus for six months. . . . Helmut Kohl, head of the West German opposition Christian Democrats Party, accuses the government of covering up a spy scandal and demands Defense Min. Georg Leber's resignation.	Grumman Corp. settles a dispute with Iran over commissions claimed by Iran in connection with the 1974 sale of 80 F-14s and agrees to provide $24-million worth of spare parts and equipment for the F-14 fighter planes free of charge.	Mexican govt. announces its 1978 budget, which somewhat relaxes the economic austerity policies adopted by Pres. Jose Lopez Portillo at the behest of the IMF. . . . U.S. govt. is reported rejecting a Peruvian govt. request for $100 million in short-term credits.	North Korea announces forming a new Cabinet, including a new premier, Li Jong-ok, in an effort to spur the nation's lagging economy.

A	B	C	D	E
Includes developments that affect more than one world region, international organizations and important meetings of major world leaders.	*Includes all domestic and regional developments in Europe, including the Soviet Union, Turkey, Cyprus and Malta.*	*Includes all domestic and regional developments in Africa and the Middle East, including Iraq and Iran and excluding Cyprus, Turkey and Afghanistan.*	*Includes all domestic and regional developments in Latin America, the Caribbean and Canada.*	*Includes all domestic and regional developments in Asia and Pacific nations, extending from Afghanistan through all the Pacific Islands, except Hawaii.*

U.S. Politics & Social Issues	U.S. Foreign Policy & Defense	U.S. Economy & Environment	Science, Technology & Nature	Culture, Leisure & Life Style	
A coalition of civil-rights groups files suit in Washington, D.C. to challenge the constitutionality of legislation designed to prevent busing of schoolchildren to achieve desegregation.		V.P. Mondale cautions the AFL–CIO biennial convention delegates against trade protectionism, saying that one out of every six American jobs depends on U.S. exports.	Scientists are reportedly successfully drilling through 1,380 feet of ice to reach an unexplored ocean shelf beneath Antarctica.	FBI is reported finding a valuable brood mare, *Fanfreluche*, after months during which it was feared that she was kidnapped.	Dec. 9
Hanna Holborn Gray, acting president of Yale University, is named president of the University of Chicago, succeeding John T. Wilson.		American Agriculture Movement launches a nationwide farmers' strike to publicize farmers' falling incomes.	Soviet Union launches the Soyuz 26 spacecraft with two cosmonauts.	Steve Cauthen, 17, becomes the first jockey in horse racing history to reach $6 million in purse earnings in a single season.	Dec. 10
Ten states representing almost a third of the U.S. population are reported having eased their marijuana penalties since 1973.			Soyuz cosmonauts successfully dock with and board the Salyut 6 orbiting space laboratory.		Dec. 11
		Supreme Ct. rules, 7–2, that employers can require workers to retire before age 65 if early retirement is a prerequisite of a company's long-standing pension plan. . . . George Meany, 83, is reelected by acclamation as AFL–CIO president.	Kenyan Pres. Jomo Kenyatta bans all sales of game skins and trophies to conserve the country's wildlife. . . . FDA bans six coloring dyes used in soaps, lipsticks, and other cosmetics because of carcinogenic hazards.	NBA comr. Lawrence O'Brien levies the largest fine in sports history — $10,000 — on a Los Angeles Laker, Kermit Washington, who injured an opponent during a Dec. 9 brawl.	Dec. 12
Atty. Gen. Griffin Bell names 10 lawyers to take over the Justice Dept. investigation into alleged break-ins and other abuses by the FBI.		AFL-CIO ends its biennial convention with a call for a protective trade policy and a $31-billion federal economic stimulus program, including $13-billion in tax cuts for low-and middle-income individuals.	The 14-member University of Evansville (Ind.) basketball team, the team's coach, and 14 other people die in a charter plane crash within a minute of takeoff in rain and dense fog.	Triple Crown winner *Seattle Slew* is named horse of the year in annual Eclipse Award voting.	Dec. 13
A young woman found murdered near downtown Los Angeles is believed to be the eleventh victim of what has come to be known as the Hillside Strangler because most of the young women victims are found choked to death.		Marshall Field & Co., Chicago's largest department store, rejects a $326-million merger offer from Carter Hawley Hale Stores Inc., which is based in Los Angeles.	Exxon Nuclear Co. reports a breakthrough in laser-use to enrich uranium.	Bishop Timotheos, 60, spiritual leader since 1967 of the Greek Orthodox Church in the Second Archdiocese, which included Ill., Wis., Iowa, Minn., Mo., and part of Ind., dies of cancer in Chicago. . . . Oakland A's owner Charles Finley sells the AL baseball team to a Denver oil magnate, Marvin Davis, for $12.5 million.	Dec. 14
Three confessed kidnappers of 26 Chowchilla schoolchildren are convicted by California State Superior Ct. Judge Leo Deegan and given life prison sentences without parole. . . . Carnegie Foundation study recommends higher education curriculum reform to strengthen the core of general education, eliminate many elective courses, and emphasize learning skills and work experiences.		U.S. and Japanese officials conclude four days of intensive trade talks in Washington to seek ways to reduce their mounting trade imbalance.	U.S. National Academy of Sciences sends a cable to Soviet Pres. Leonid Brezhnev seeking permission to send observers to the trial of Anatoly Shcharansky, a Soviet computer scientist accused of treason.		Dec. 15

F	G	H	I	J
Includes elections, federal-state relations, civil rights and liberties, crime, the judiciary, education, health care, poverty, urban affairs and population.	Includes formation and debate of U.S. foreign and defense policies, veterans' affairs and defense spending. (Relations with specific foreign countries are usually found under the region concerned.)	Includes business, labor, agriculture, taxation, transportation, consumer affairs, monetary and fiscal policy, natural resources, and pollution.	Includes worldwide scientific, medical and technological developments, natural phenomena, U.S. weather, natural disasters, and accidents.	Includes the arts, religion, scholarship, communications media, sports, entertainments, fashions, fads and social life.

	World Affairs	Europe	Africa & the Middle East	The Americas	Asia & the Pacific
Dec. 16	U.N. General Assembly passes a resolution deploring human rights abuses in Chile and expressing particular concern over the continued disappearance of Chileans. . . . U.N. General Assembly votes to seek an embargo of oil exports to and foreign investments in South Africa.	Glafkos Clerides withdraws as an opposition presidential candidate in Cyprus, saying that the nation needs to be united in face of the abduction of Pres. Spyros Kyprianou's son, Achilleas Kyprianou.	U.S. State Dept. reports that the Ethiopians have been successful in repelling Somalian assaults into Harar in late November because they received huge shipments of Soviet arms as well as increased Soviet and Cuban personnel.		
Dec. 17		French pro-government Paris daily newspaper *J'Informe* ends publication after three months of existence because of insufficient sales.	Premier Ahmed Dini Ahmed and four members of his Cabinet resign in Djibouti following months of tribal tensions between the Afars and the Issas.		
Dec. 18		Achilleas Kyprianou is released unharmed by his captors, after his father, Cyprus Pres. Spyros Kyprianou says he would sacrifice his son over his country and not meet their demands — release of 25 jailed members of their group.	An Eritrean guerrilla spokesman says that rebels had captured the garrison of Adi Caieh south of Asmara, leaving four garrisons still in Ethiopian hands.		Former P.M. Indira Gandhi resigns from the 20-member executive committee of the Congress Party.
Dec. 19		Queen Juliana swears in a new center-right coalition Cabinet headed by Premier Andreas van Agt, ending a seven-month political crisis during which the Netherlands had been without an effective government. . . . Two bomb explosions wreck Fauchon, the famous Parisian food shop, often referred to by French extreme leftists as an example of bourgeois decadence.		Canada announces a complete cutoff of official trade and economic ties with South Africa to protest apartheid.	Appearing on national television, Japanese Premier Takeo Fukuda pledges to counter Japan's growing yearly trade surplus, now nearing $17.6 billion. . . . Australian P.M. Malcolm Fraser names a new Cabinet, following his coalition govt.'s decisive victory.
Dec. 20	At the first session of the OPEC meeting, Venezuelan Pres. Carlos Andres Perez urges that OPEC hike its prices 5–8 percent and that the additional revenue be given to non-oil-exporting developing countries to help them meet their debt obligations.	EEC foreign ministers meeting in Paris agree to curb steel and textile imports. . . . Gabriele Krocher-Tiedemann and Christian Moeller, two West German terrorists, are captured after a shoot-out with Swiss custom officials.	Israeli Defense Min. Ezer Weizman holds preparatory talks in Egypt with Pres. Anwar Sadat and War Min. Mohammed Abdel Ghany el-Gamasy.	U.S. and Bolivia reach an agreement in principle that will allow Americans imprisoned in Bolivia on cocaine smuggling charges to serve out their sentences in the U.S.	Indonesian govt. announces the release of 10,000 political prisoners who had been arrested after an abortive communist coup in 1965. Amnesty International claims that an estimated 100,000 prisoners are still held.
Dec. 21	OPEC defers raising the price of crude oil after delegates meet in Caracas, Venezuela.	*The New York Times* reports that Soviet Jews are increasingly choosing to settle in Israel after emigrating from the Soviet Union, a change since May, and cites Israeli P.M. Menahem Begin's policies and recent Mideast peace initiatives as possible factors.		Three abductions are reported in Colombia, raising the number of kidnappings in 1977 to 89, with 25 victims still in the hands of their captors. . . . Bolivian govt. announces amnesty for 284 political exiles as part of its process of democratization.	Australian P.M. Malcolm Fraser fires his new minister for veteran affairs, Glenister Sheil, for advocating an apartheid system in Australia and supporting the one in South Africa.
Dec. 22			Emigration of whites from Rhodesia is reported to have slowed in November, falling below 1,000 emigres for the first time since 1975.	Washington-based Council on Hemispheric Affairs issues a report charging that Argentina is the most flagrant violator of human rights in Latin America.	William Hayden is elected leader of the opposition Australian Labor Party replacing former head Gough Whitlam, who led the party to an overwhelming defeat in the Dec. 10 general elections. . . . Cambodians are reported carrying out major attacks during November into Vietnam's Tay Ninh Province.
Dec. 23			The eight French nationals kidnapped by Saharan nationalist guerrillas in May and October are turned over to U.N. Gen. Secy. Kurt Waldheim in Algiers. . . . French govt. confirms reports that French jets supported Mauritanian troops fighting the Polisarios in Mauritania.		

A	B	C	D	E
Includes developments that affect more than one world region, international organizations and important meetings of major world leaders.	Includes all domestic and regional developments in Europe, including the Soviet Union, Turkey, Cyprus and Malta.	Includes all domestic and regional developments in Africa and the Middle East, including Iraq and Iran and excluding Cyprus, Turkey and Afghanistan.	Includes all domestic and regional developments in Latin America, the Caribbean and Canada.	Includes all domestic and regional developments in Asia and Pacific nations, extending from Afghanistan through all the Pacific Islands, except Hawaii.

U.S. Politics & Social Issues	U.S. Foreign Policy & Defense	U.S. Economy & Environment	Science, Technology & Nature	Culture, Leisure & Life Style	
Federal Election Commission files a suit against the AFL–CIO, charging it violated federal campaign spending laws.			The fully laden oil supertanker *Venoil* collides with its empty sister ship, *Venpet* , off the South African coast about 60 miles west of Port Elizabeth.	American conductor Thomas Schippers, 47, dies of lung cancer in N.Y.	Dec. 16
		GM is reported agreeing to pay $200 apiece to customers who unknowingly purchased a Buick , Oldsmobile , or Pontiac , which was powered by a Chevrolet engine. It extends the guarantees for engines and other major parts.			Dec. 17
		Marriner Eccles, 87, FRB chairman from 1936–48 who helped shape Franklin Roosevelt's New Deal policy, dies in Salt Lake City, Utah.	A chartered Swiss Caravelle jet carrying 52 passengers and a crew of five crashes into the Atlantic Ocean as it comes into a landing at one of the Madeira Islands. There are 21 survivors.	British comic actor and director Cyril Ritchard, known for his portrayal of Captain Hook in *Peter Pan*, dies at age 79. . . . Louis Untermeyer, 92, distinguished American poet, satirist, critic, and biographer who edited over 50 poetry anthologies, dies after a long illness in Newtown, Conn.	Dec. 18
Anthony (Tony Pro) Provenzano, Teamsters head in N.J. and an alleged member of organized crime, is indicted for a third time on a federal kickback charge. . . . Nellie Taylor Ross, 101, the first woman governor in U.S. history (elected 1924) dies in Washington, D.C.		Pres. Carter signs a bill that bars U.S. corporations from bribing foreign officials.			Dec. 19
Pres. Carter signs the Social Security bill that will raise taxes by about $227 billion over the next 10 years.			Canada and the EEC sign an agreement to immediately resume uranium shipments from Canada to Europe.		Dec. 20
Supreme Ct. Justice Lewis Powell Jr. refuses to set aside a temporary restraining order that prohibits the American Nazi Party from playing portions of three tape-recorded telephone messages in Houston, Tex.	*Washington Post* reports that the Navy plans to assign women to duty aboard sea-going tugs, destroyer and submarine tenders, and oceanographic research ships.	SEC charges that Goodyear Tire & Rubber Co. maintains a $1.5-million slush fund to make illegal political contributions in the U.S. and improper payments abroad.	Pres. Carter approves major expansion of air service to Europe, designating 11 U.S. cities as gateway ports.		Dec. 21
		U.S. Steel Corp., the steel industry's price-setting leader, announces it will raise prices an average 5.5 percent.	A grain elevator explosion in Westwego, La. kills 35 people. . . . Unofficial death toll from an earthquake that struck south-central Iran two days ago reaches 589.		Dec. 22
		Over 1,500 farmers, some driving tractors, demonstrate in Plains, Ga., where Pres. Carter is spending the Christmas holiday, as part of a nationwide protest for 100 percent parity support.			Dec. 23

F	G	H	I	J
Includes elections, federal-state relations, civil rights and liberties, crime, the judiciary, education, health care, poverty, urban affairs and population.	Includes formation and debate of U.S. foreign and defense policies, veterans' affairs and defense spending. (Relations with specific foreign countries are usually found under the region concerned.)	Includes business, labor, agriculture, taxation, transportation, consumer affairs, monetary and fiscal policy, natural resources, and pollution.	Includes worldwide scientific, medical and technological developments, natural phenomena, U.S. weather, natural disasters, and accidents.	Includes the arts, religion, scholarship, communications media, sports, entertainments, fashions, fads and social life.

	World Affairs	Europe	Africa & the Middle East	The Americas	Asia & the Pacific
Dec. 24			Iraq Christians are reported canceling Christmas festivities to protest Egyptian Pres. Anwar Sadat's peace bid to Israel.	Gen. Juan Velasco Alvarado, 67, president of Peru (1968–75) whose military govt. introduced various economic, social, and foreign policy reforms, dies from an inflamed pancreas in Lima.	A report from Bangkok says that Cambodian–Vietnamese fighting around Neak Luong (also called Parrot's Beak) has intensified and that the Vietnamese are using warplanes and artillery.
Dec. 25		The country home of French CP leader Georges Marchais is attacked by a group of men who fire shotguns through the front door.	Israeli Premier Menahem Begin and Egyptian Pres. Anwar Sadat begin a summit meeting at Ismailia, Egypt to draft peace guidelines. . . . About 5,000 Palestinians rally in Beirut, Lebanon to denounce Egyptian Pres. Sadat's meeting with Israeli Premier Begin.		The Vietnamese govt. is reported launching a drive to block attempts by Vietnamese to escape the country.
Dec. 26		The Corsican Liberation Front claims responsibility for a bombing attack at the Villepinte train station in Paris.	Egyptian Pres. Sadat concludes his talks with Israeli Premier Begin without agreeing on basic issues: terms for Israeli withdrawal from the Sinai, West Bank, Gaza Strip, and East Jerusalem.	Argentina announces that it will free 432 political prisoners in a holiday amnesty.	
Dec. 27	OECD issues its six-month report on the international economy, which calls for swift action by industrialized nations to avoid an economic slowdown in 1978 and urges stronger nations, such as Japan and West Germany, to stimulate their economies even at risk of causing domestic inflation.	A bomb explodes outside the apartment of a Paris judge, one of about 15 bombing incidents in the Paris area in the past two days.			The Indian Congress Party leadership splits into two factions, those supporting and those opposing Indira Gandhi.
Dec. 28		Italian Red Brigades claim responsibility for shooting and killing Angelo Pistolesi, a neo-fascist leader in Rome.	Israeli Premier Begin reveals the peace plan he had submitted to Egyptian Pres. Sadat. The plan bars the establishment of a Palestinian state in the West Bank and Gaza Strip, reaffirms Israel's claim to sovereignty over the two territories, and gives greater autonomy to Arab residents of the area. Begin proposes guaranteed access to Jerusalem's holy shrines for Jews, Christians, and Moslems. . . . Somalia charges Ethiopia with mounting air raids deep into its territory, killing and injuring civilians in the town of Hargeisa and the port of Berbera.		
Dec. 29			PLO explodes a bomb, which kills two people, in Natanya to protest Israeli Premier Menahem Begin's West Bank proposals. . . . Rhodesian black majority rule talks end after participants have problems concerning the makeup of the country's future parliament.		
Dec. 30	U.S. dollar ends the year with further losses against the world's major currencies. It stands at 2.105 W.Ger. marks, 2.11 Swiss francs, 4.7 French francs, 871.5 Italian lire, and 2.28 Dutch guilders. . . . Gold closes in London trading at $166.55 an ounce, about $20 higher than its 1976 close.	Pres. Carter holds a televised news conference in Warsaw, Poland, the first ever conducted by an American President in Eastern Europe.		Canada reduces the governmental duties of British Queen Elizabeth II to those that are purely ceremonial.	

A	B	C	D	E
Includes developments that affect more than one world region, international organizations and important meetings of major world leaders.	Includes all domestic and regional developments in Europe, including the Soviet Union, Turkey, Cyprus and Malta.	Includes all domestic and regional developments in Africa and the Middle East, including Iraq and Iran and excluding Cyprus, Turkey and Afghanistan.	Includes all domestic and regional developments in Latin America, the Caribbean and Canada.	Includes all domestic and regional developments in Asia and Pacific nations, extending from Afghanistan through all the Pacific Islands, except Hawaii.

U.S. Politics & Social Issues	U.S. Foreign Policy & Defense	U.S. Economy & Environment	Science, Technology & Nature	Culture, Leisure & Life Style	
		Pres. Carter meets with a delegation of striking farmers, expresses sympathy for their plight, but reasserts his opposition to their demand for federal support of farm prices at 100 percent parity.		Oakland Raiders advance to the AFC conference title game with a 37–31 victory over the Baltimore Colts.	Dec. 24
	Iran is reported by the Commerce Dept. as making the largest single direct foreign investment in the U.S. during 1976. Western Europe, Japan, and Canada are reported ramaining the nation's dominant foreign investors.			British-born and internationally famous stage and screen comedian Charlie Chaplin dies at the age of 88 in Switzerland.	Dec. 25
				Howard Hawks, 81, a foremost Hollywood director known for *Bringing Up Baby* and *To Have and Have Not*, dies after suffering a concussion in Palm Springs, Calif. ... In NFC playoff games the Dallas Cowboys beat the Chicago Bears, 37–7 and the Minnesota Vikings beat the heavily favored Los Angeles Rams. 14–7.	Dec. 26
	William Colby, former CIA director, defends the CIA's links with the news media before a congressional committee.		Another grain elevator explosion kills 18 in Galveston, Tex.		Dec. 27
Pres. Carter names John C. White of Texas to head the Democratic Party.		Pres. Carter appoints G. William Miller to replace Arthur F. Burns as FRB chairman.			Dec. 28
				Robert Wolff, 72, noted American abstract painter and professor emeritus at Brooklyn College, dies in New Preston, Conn.... Three University of Arkansas players, who has been suspended from playing in the 1978 Orange Bowl, drop their discrimination suit against the university after having charged that their suspension had been racially motivated.	Dec. 29
	Justice Dept. announces it has reached an agreement with the South Korean govt. and Park Tong Sun whereby Park will testify in the U.S. in criminal trials stemming from the Korean lobbying investigation and will receive immunity form prosecution for past criminal acts.	Negotiations in the 25-day-old nationwide coal strike break off indefinitely.... The Dow Jones average closes the year at 831.17, down 17.2 percent from its 1976 close of 1,004.65.			Dec. 30

F	G	H	I	J
Includes elections, federal-state relations, civil rights and liberties, crime, the judiciary, education, health care, poverty, urban affairs and population.	*Includes formation and debate of U.S. foreign and defense policies, veterans' affairs and defense spending. (Relations with specific foreign countries are usually found under the region concerned.)*	*Includes business, labor, agriculture, taxation, transportation, consumer affairs, monetary and fiscal policy, natural resources, and pollution.*	*Includes worldwide scientific, medical and technological developments, natural phenomena, U.S. weather, natural disasters, and accidents.*	*Includes the arts, religion, scholarship, communications media, sports, entertainments, fashions, fads and social life.*

	World Affairs	Europe	Africa & the Middle East	The Americas	Asia & the Pacific
Dec. 31		Turkish Premier Suleyman Demirel's conservative coalition government resigns after a no-confidence vote.... Spanish govt. gives limited autonomy to the Basque provinces.	Sheik Sabah al-Ahmed al-Sabah, ruler of Kuwait since 1965, dies of a heart attack and is succeeded by Crown Prince Sheik Jaber al-Ahmed al-Sabah.... Pres. Carter arrives in Teheran for talks with the Shah of Iran and King Hussein of Jordan.... Egyptian For. Min. Mohammed Ibrahim Kamel discloses a counterproposal to Israeli Premier Begin's Palestinian settlement plan, which states that Israel must accept the principle of total withdrawal from the West Bank and Gaza Strip and must recognize the rights to self-determination for Arabs in that area.		Cambodia severs diplomatic relations with Vietnam in wake of heavy border clashes.

A	B	C	D	E
Includes developments that affect more than one world region, international organizations and important meetings of major world leaders.	Includes all domestic and regional developments in Europe, including the Soviet Union, Turkey, Cyprus and Malta.	Includes all domestic and regional developments in Africa and the Middle East, including Iraq and Iran and excluding Cyprus, Turkey and Afghanistan.	Includes all domestic and regional developments in Latin America, the Caribbean and Canada.	Includes all domestic and regional developments in Asia and Pacific nations, extending from Afghanistan through all the Pacific Islands, except Hawaii.

U.S. Politics & Social Issues	U.S. Foreign Policy & Defense	U.S. Economy & Environment	Science, Technology & Nature	Culture, Leisure & Life Style	
				Vitas Gerulaitis takes five sets to defeat Britain's John Lloyd for the Australian Open men's singles tennis championship.	Dec. 31

F	G	H	I	J
Includes elections, federal-state relations, civil rights and liberties, crime, the judiciary, education, health care, poverty, urban affairs and population.	Includes formation and debate of U.S. foreign and defense policies, veterans' affairs and defense spending. (Relations with specific foreign countries are usually found under the region concerned.)	Includes business, labor, agriculture, taxation, transportation, consumer affairs, monetary and fiscal policy, natural resources, and pollution.	Includes worldwide scientific, medical and technological developments, natural phenomena, U.S. weather, natural disasters, and accidents.	Includes the arts, religion, scholarship, communications media, sports, entertainments, fashions, fads and social life.

1978

Over 900 followers of Rev. Jim Jones commit mass suicide at the People's Temple in Jonestown, Guyana.

	World Affairs	Europe	Africa & the Middle East	The Americas	Asia & the Pacific
Jan.	Representatives of the U.S., Britain, France, West Germany and Italy issue a statement supporting OAU efforts to promote a peaceful settlement to the war in Ethiopia.	Spyros Kyprianou, caretaker president of Cyprus, automatically wins a full five year term as president when the opposition fails to nominate a candidate to run against him.	Israeli-Egyptian Political Committee talks are abruptly halted after only one day when Egyptian Pres. Anwar Sadat recalls his nation's delegation.	Business and labor leaders in Nicaragua call a general strike following the assassination of opposition leader Pedro Joaquin Chamorro.	China and Vietnam sign a 1978 trade agreement despite strained relations between the two nations.
Feb.	The U.N. Human Rights Commission adopts a series of three resolutions condemning Israel.	The British House of Commons passes a bill to grant Scotland limited home rule.	Leaders from Syria, Libya, Algeria, South Yemen and the PLO hold a summit meeting in Algiers to plan a strategy countering Egyptian Pres. Anwar Sadat's peace initiatives in the Middle East.	Rioting plagues Nicaragua as popular opposition to the ruling Somoza regime continues to mount.	The government of China and a group of private Japanese industrialists sign an eight-year, $120 billion trade agreement.
March	After nine days of debate, the U.N. Security Council votes to reject a Rhodesian majority rule settlement reached by P.M. Ian Smith and a group of three moderate black leaders.	Former Italian Premier Aldo Moro is kidnapped by left-wing terrorists in a bloody shootout that leaves Moro's five bodyguards dead.	Israel declares a unilateral cease-fire in Lebanon while maintaining control of a large portion of southern Lebanon.	The Bolivian government breaks diplomatic ties with Chile and deploys troops to several points along Bolivia's border with Chile.	The Chinese National People's Congress ends a week-long session by announcing the reappointment of Hua Kuo-feng as premier.
April	Over 100 Western leaders attend the Bilderberg Conference which provides leaders an opportunity to discuss world affairs frankly without the threat of public disclosure.	Betty Williams, Mairead Corrigan and Ciaran McKeown, founders and leaders of the Ulster Peace Movement, resign from leadership positions in the organization.	The Lebanese Parliament approves a six-point plan banning all private Christian and Moslem militia and Palestinian guerrilla activity in the country.	Antonio Guzman defeats Pres. Joaquin Balaguer in the Dominican Republic's presidential election.	A military junta aligned to the Soviet Union seizes power in Afghanistan.
May	The U.N. General Assembly opens a special session on disarmament aimed at designing a program to end the proliferation of nuclear weapons.	The body of former Italian Premier Aldo Moro is found in a parked car in Rome.	Secessionist guerrillas invade Zaire's Shaba province.	The state of seige that existed in Paraguay since 1947 is lifted in the departments of Itapua, Central and Alto Parana, leaving only Asuncion, the capital, affected.	Relations between China and Vietnam become further strained as thousands of ethnic Chinese flee Vietnam.
June	At their annual conference ILO delegates ask the U.S. to rejoin the organization and reject an Arab-sponsored resolution condemning Israel.	Continuing violence in Northern Ireland is highlighted by youth riots in Londonderry.	Israel completes its military withdrawal from southern Lebanon.	Prior censorship of the Brazilian press formally ends as the government lifts censorship from the last four publications subject to such restrictions.	Pres. Ferdinand E. Marcos of the Philippines is sworn in as the nation's first premier.
July	The U.N. strongly endorses a Western-sponsored plan for the independence of Namibia.	The Basque region of Spain is plagued by several days of violence and protest after police open fire on a crowd in the Pamplona bull ring.	Israel rejects two peace initiatives put forward by Egyptian Pres. Anwar Sadat.	Gen. Juan Pereda Asburn topples the government of Bolivian Pres. Hugo Banzer Suarez.	France withdraws its ambassador and most of its diplomatic mission from Laos at the request of the Vientiene government.
Aug.	The U.N. conference against racism endorses a resolution calling on the Security Council to impose mandatory economic sanctions against South Africa.	Olafur Johannesson, leader of Iceland's Progressive Party, announces the formation of a new coalition government in which he will serve as premier.	Fighting breaks out between Lebanese Christian militiamen and the Syrian army in Beirut. A truce temporarily halts the fighting Aug. 9 but violence is renewed Aug. 11.	Honduran Pres. Juan Alberto Melgar Castro is overthrown in a bloodless coup by commanders of the military.	The government of Afghanistan crushes an attempted coup and arrests the leaders of the movement, Defense Minister Abdul Khadir and army chief of staff Maj. Gen. Shahpur.
Sept.	The price of gold hits a record high of $218.40 an ounce on the London bullion market.	The Italian government presents a long-range plan for economic recovery that calls for increased public investment and cuts in welfare and health programs.	After 11 days of meetings at Camp David, Egyptian Pres. Anwar Sadat and Israeli Premier Menaham Begin sign accords establishing the framework for peace between their nations.	Representatives of Colombia and the United States sign an agreement to cooperate in efforts to fight the drug traffic between the two countries.	The government of Indonesia releases 1,324 political prisoners who have been held without trial since an abortive Communist Party coup in 1965.
Oct.	The Royal Swedish Academy in Stockholm awards the 1978 Nobel Peace Prize to Egyptian Pres. Anwar Sadat and Israeli Premier Menahem Begin.	Ola Ullsten, leader of the minority Liberal Party in Sweden, becomes the nation's premier and appoints a cabinet, filling one third of the posts with women.	After a week of heavy fighting with Christian militia forces, the government of Syria declares a unilateral cease-fire in and around Beirut.	In an effort to secure better wages and working conditions, Canada's 23,000 indoor postal workers stage a 10-day strike that halts all foreign and domestic mail deliveries.	The Treaty of Peace and Understanding between Japan and the People's Republic of China is formally implemented.
Nov.	The U.N. High Commissioner for Refugees announces plans for a meeting to discuss the growing problem of S.E. Asian refugees with special focus on the "boat people."	Representatives of the seven Warsaw Pact nations meet in Moscow for their biennial summit.	Shah Mohammed Riza Pahlevi of Iran imposes martial law in an unsuccessful effort to end the violent anti-government demonstrations which have plagued the country since January.	The government of Bolivian Pres. Juan Pereda Asbun is toppled in a coup led by army commander Gen. David Padilla Arancibia.	Former P.M. Indira Gandhi of India registers a political comeback as she wins a seat in the lower house of the Indian Parliament.
Dec.	The completion of an agreement in the Strategic Arms Limitation Talks is delayed by last-minute Soviet reservations.	Leaders of the nine EEC nations approve plans for establishing a new European Monetary System.	Due to the worsening situation in Iran, the U.S. government urges the dependents of all Americans to leave the turbulent nation.	Chile and Argentina accept Pope John Paul II's offer to mediate their long-standing Beagle Channel dispute.	Afghan Premier Nur Mohammad Taraki and Soviet Pres. Leonid Brezhnev sign a 20-year treaty of friendship and cooperation.

A	B	C	D	E
Includes developments that affect more than one world region, international organizations and important meetings of major world leaders.	Includes all domestic and regional developments in Europe, including the Soviet Union, Turkey, Cyprus and Malta.	Includes all domestic and regional developments in Africa and the Middle East, including Iraq and Iran and excluding Cyprus, Turkey and Afghanistan.	Includes all domestic and regional developments in Latin America, the Caribbean and Canada.	Includes all domestic and regional developments in Asia and Pacific nations, extending from Afghanistan through all the Pacific Islands, except Hawaii.

U.S. Politics & Social Issues	U.S. Foreign Policy & Defense	U.S. Economy & Environment	Science, Technology & Nature	Culture, Leisure & Life Style	
Sen. Hubert H. Humphrey (D, Minn.) dies of cancer at his home in Waverly, Minnesota. His widow, Muriel Humphrey, is selected to fill his vacated Senate seat.	Pres. Carter concludes a nine day world tour.	Local 727 of the AFL-CIO International Association of Machinists votes to end a 12-week-old strike against Lockheed Corporation plants in Burbank and Palmdale, California.	Cosmos 954, a nuclear equipped Soviet reconnaissance satellite, falls through the atmosphere and burns. Mildly radioactive debris from the satellite is found at several sites in Canada.	The Associated Press and United Press International both choose Notre Dame as the national champion of college football.	Jan.
W.A. (Tony) Boyle, former president of the UMW is convicted of three counts of first degree murder in connection with the 1969 murder of union rival Joseph Yablonski and his family.	The U.S. Government announces plans to sell $4.8 billion worth of war planes to Egypt, Israel and Saudi Arabia.	Congress clears legislation authorizing $6.08 billion for energy research during fiscal 1978.	New England is paralyzed by the worst blizzard in the region's history.	Leon Spinks wins a split decision over Muhammad Ali in Las Vegas to gain the world heavyweight boxing title.	Feb.
The Supreme Ct. rules that Indian tribal courts do not have jurisdiction over crimes committed on reservations by non-Indians.	The U.S. Senate votes to ratify the Panama Canal treaty, guaranteeing the neutrality of the canal after its return to Panama in 1999.	The 110-day strike by 160,000 soft-coal miners comes to an end with the signing of a new three-year contract between the United Mine Workers and the Bituminous Coal Operators Association.	Soviet cosmonauts Lt. Col. Yuri Romanenko and Georgi Grechko return safely home after spending a record 96 days in space aboard their Soyuz 27 capsule.	Soviet composer-cellist Mstislav Rostropovich has his citizenship revoked by the Soviet government.	March
Gov. Hugh L. Carey of New York vetoes a bill that would restore capital punishment in the state.	Pres. Carter announces his decision to defer production of the neutron bomb.	Pres. Carter announces a new anti-inflation program that calls for limiting federal employees to 5.5% pay increases and rules out the use of mandatory wage and price controls.	The Supreme Ct. rules, 7-0, that federal courts do not have the authority to circumvent government regulations on the construction of nuclear power plants.	Officials of the Reorganized Church of Jesus Christ of Latter Day Saints install Wallace B. Smith as the church's sixth president.	April
The Senate confirms Benjamin R. Civiletti as Deputy Attorney General.	The Senate Foreign Relations Committee votes to continue the arms embargo against Turkey, stopping a Carter administration attempt to have the ban lifted.	The Supreme Court rules that the SEC does not have the authority to suspend trading of a stock for more than 10 days without a hearing.	Japanese explorer Nami Uemura successfully reaches the North Pole after a two month journey.	Pete Rose of the Cincinnati Reds gets his 3,000th career hit May 5. Rose is only the 13th player in major league history to reach the milestone.	May
The Illinois House of Representatives twice refuses to ratify the Equal Rights Amendment.	The cruise missile is tested for the first time in public at White Sands Missile Range in New Mexico.	California voters overwhelmingly approve Proposition 13, an initiative to cut property taxes by 57%.	Japan and Greece each suffer their second major earthquake of the year.	Affirmed wins horse racing's Triple Crown by capturing the Belmont Stakes.	June
Approximately 25 members of the National Socialist Party of America hold a rally in Chicago's Marquette Park.	The House Committee on Standards of Official Conduct cites four House members, all Democrats, for misconduct in connection with the Korean lobbying effort.	Washington D.C. Metro transit workers stage a seven-day wildcat strike demanding an automatic cost-of-living pay increase.	The first test-tube baby is born to John and Lesley Brown in Lancashire, England.	Bjorn Borg defeats Jimmy Connors to win his third consecutive men's singles title at the All-England lawn tennis championships at Wimbledon, England.	July
Stanford G. Ross is named commissioner of the Social Security Administration.	Pres. Carter vetoes a $37–billion weapons authorization bill, noting that the $2–billion nuclear-powered aircraft carrier in the bill was unnecessary.	The Federal Reserve tightens credit by increasing the discount rate from 7.25% to 7.75% and permitting the key interest rate on federal funds to rise to 8.125%.	Pres. Carter declares the Love Canal of Niagara Falls, New York to be a disaster area because of contamination caused by hazardous waste chemicals buried there.	Following the death of Pope Paul VI, the Sacred College of Cardinals chooses Cardinal Albino Luciani to be the 264th pope of the Roman Catholic Church. The new pontiff takes the name John Paul I.	Aug.
The House Select Committee on Assassinations concludes that John F. Kennedy was probably assassinated as a result of a conspiracy.	Pres. Carter signs a bill authorizing $2.8 billion during fiscal 1979 for foreign military and security aid.	By September 8, teachers in 13 states are on strike, causing the disruption and cancellation of classes for an estimated 625,000 students.	The Soviet Union launches 2 unmanned interplanetary probes, the Venera 11 and Venera 12, toward Venus in an effort to continue scientific exploration of the planet.	Pope John Paul I dies only 34 days after being elected pontiff of the Roman Catholic Church.	Sept.
Full rights of U.S. citizenship are posthumously restored to Jefferson Davis, president of the Confederate States of America.	Pres. Carter appoints Ralph Earle to be chief U.S. negotiator at the Strategic Arms Limitation Talks.	In its last harried hours, the 95th Congress passes a tax cut bill, energy legislation and the Humphrey-Hawkins full employment bill.	The National Science Foundation announces that the U.S. and China are ready to begin exchanging university students and scholars for the purpose of study and research.	Isaac Bashevis Singer, novelist and short story writer, is awarded the 1978 Nobel Prize for Literature.	Oct.
San Francisco Mayor George Moscone and Harvey Milk, a city supervisor, are shot to death inside San Francisco City Hall. Dan White, a former supervisor, is charged with the killings.	William P. Kampiles, a former Central Intelligence Agency employee, is convicted of selling spy-satellite secrets to the Soviet Union.	The Dow Jones industrial average achieves its largest one-day advance in history when it jumps 35.34 points to close at 827.79 on Nov. 1.	Scientists from around the world gather at the federal Center for Disease Control in Atlanta, Georgia to conduct an international symposium on Legionnaires Disease.	Nearly 1,000 members of the Peoples Temple, a California-based religious cult, die in a mass suicide/murder at the cult's agrarian commune at Jonestown, Guyana.	Nov.
The Americans for Democratic Action announces that, according to its rating system, the Senate experienced a conservative shift during 1978.	Pres. Carter announces that the U.S. and China have agreed to establish formal diplomatic relations beginning January 1, 1979.	The Carter Administration issues revised wage and price guidelines.	NASA announces that it has dropped plans to launch a mission to prevent the impending uncontrolled descent of the unmanned Skylab space station.	Soviet conductor Kirill Kondrashin defects following a concert engagement in the Netherlands.	Dec.

F	G	H	I	J
Includes elections, federal-state relations, civil rights and liberties, crime, the judiciary, education, health care, poverty, urban affairs and population.	Includes formation and debate of U.S. foreign and defense policies, veterans' affairs and defense spending. (Relations with specific foreign countries are usually found under the region concerned.)	Includes business, labor, agriculture, taxation, transportation, consumer affairs, monetary and fiscal policy, natural resources, and pollution.	Includes worldwide scientific, medical and technological developments, natural phenomena, U.S. weather, natural disasters, and accidents.	Includes the arts, religion, scholarship, communications media, sports, entertainments, fashions, fads and social life.

	World Affairs	Europe	Africa & the Middle East	The Americas	Asia & the Pacific
Jan. 1	Freedom House reports that 35.7 percent of the world population lives in free countries compared with 19.6 percent at the beginning of 1977.	Swiss govt. bans third-party trading deals involving Rhodesia, including loans or money transfers.	PLO leader Yasir Arafat tells a rally of 10,000 Palestinians in Beirut, Lebanon that U.S. Pres. Jimmy Carter cannot force the Palestinian revolution to act counter to its beliefs and calls for increased guerrilla operations against Israel.	A new Honduran electoral law becomes effective, allowing political parties to resume activities after a five-years hiatus.	Pakistani leader Gen. Muhammad Zia ul-Haq withdraws all conspiracy charges against Khan Abdul Wali Khan, president of the outlawed National Awami League, and 40 of his colleagues.
Jan. 2	World Peace Council, a Helsinki-based Soviet front organization, calls on Cambodia and Vietnam to negotiate their border dispute, which has flared into open hostilities.		After talks with U.S. Pres. Carter in Iran, Jordanian King Hussein reiterates his reasons against joining Israeli–Egyptian negotiations on the Middle East, stating that Jordan's involvement is not confined to border issues but centers on the core of the Palestinian problem.	An upcoming Chilean plebiscite called by Pres. Augusto Pinochet Ugarte is reportedly opposed by two members of his ruling military junta, the Chilean controller general, outlawed political parties, and the nation's Catholic bishops.	Indira Gandhi forms a rival political group, also called the Congress Party, after a two-day convention in New Delhi attended by several thousand of her followers.
Jan. 3		West Germany announces the second largest trade surplus in its history, officially estimated at $18.06 billion.	The family of black activist Steven Biko files a damage suit against the South African govt., seeking $204,700 for Biko's death while in police custody.	Hundreds of Chileans demonstrate in Santiago streets, handing out leaflets calling for a "no vote" in the upcoming plebiscite and shouting "peace, justice, freedom."	The Indian Congress Party ousts Indira Gandhi and her followers. . . . Cambodian govt. rejects several Vietnamese offers to negotiate their border dispute. Cambodian Premier Pol Pot is reported appealing to North Korean Pres. Kim Il Sung for his support.
Jan. 4		Turkish Premier-designate Bulent Ecevit announces that his new government's priorities include curbing domestic political violence, improving the economy, and settling the Cyprus problem. . . . Political and religious violence in Northern Ireland is reported declining in 1977 to its lowest level since 1970, with total deaths at 111 compared to 482 in 1972, at the height of unrest.	In talks with Egyptian Pres. Anwar Sadat at Aswan, Pres. Carter seeks to clarify his Dec. 28, 1977 statement in which he said he opposed an independent Palestinian state.	In the first Chilean election in nearly five years, plebiscite voters overwhelmingly back Pres. Augusto Pinochet Ugarte. Pinochet declares that no further election will be needed for at least 10 years.	China pledges to ease travel restrictions on its citizens who wish to go abroad and on overseas Chinese visits to China. . . . An Australian govt. survey warns of potential de facto racial discrimination resulting in the exclusion of the 110,000-member aboriginal population from normal Australian life.
Jan. 5	The price of gold falls on the London exchange to $165.70 an ounce.	Turkish Premier-designate Bulent Ecevit announces his new Cabinet, which includes 13 supporters from outside his own party	An organization calling itself the Voice of the Palestinian Revolution claims responsibility for the assassination in London the day before of PLO representative in Britain, Said Hammami. . . . Soviet Union is reported stopping its massive airlift of weapons and materials to Ethiopia.	Pres. Ernesto Geisel confirms his choice of Gen. Joao Baptista de Figueiredo to succeed him as Brazil's president, a choice reportedly opposed by many army leaders.	Vietnamese Premier Pham Van Dong renews his country's call for talks with Cambodia on their border dispute, but contends that the Cambodian govt. has persecuted the Vietnamese minority in Cambodia and has killed thousands. . . . Vietnam frees three Americans who were seized aboard their yacht in Vietnamese waters in October 1977.
Jan. 6	Pres. Carter visits Brussels and announces that the U.S. plans to add 8,000 more troops to its NATO contingent over next year-and-a-half.	State Secy. Cyrus Vance formally returns the crown of St. Stephen — considered symbolic of Hungary's nationhood — saying its return represents improved U.S.–Hungarian relations.	Pres. Carter discloses a U.S. plan under which the West Bank and Gaza Strip, now Israeli-occupied, would be aligned with Jordan or placed under joint Israeli–Arab administration, leaving it up to the Arabs to decide at a later date which administration they prefer.	Canada's largest insurance firm, Sun Life Assurance Co. of Canada, announces it will move its headquarters from Montreal to Toronto in wake of recent provincial legislation making French the official language of Quebec.	Cambodian–Vietnams border fighting is reported slackening, with the Vietnamese consolidating their gains in Cambodia's Parrot's Beak region.
Jan. 7		A new rash of IRA bombings in Belfast, Northern Ireland is reported.	Rhodesian govt. limits dispatches by foreign correspondents on the Rhodesian guerrilla war to government and military official versions.		Leonard Woodcock, head of the U.S. liason office in Peking, says U.S.–Chinese relations have improved in the past three months despite a continuing impasse over the issue of Taiwan.
Jan. 8	U.S. national security adviser Zbigniew Brzezinski calls the Cambodian–Vietnamese clashes the first case of a proxy war between the Soviet Union and China.	Irish P.M. Jack Lynch creates a furor by restating in a radio interview his Fianna Fail party's aim of eventually unifying Ireland.	Israeli Cabinet bars creating new Israeli settlements in the Sinai, but it approves expanding the 20 now existing and urges more Israelis to move there.		Cambodia claims that its forces have driven the Vietnamese out of the Parrot's Beak, a claim the Vietnamese counter as a fabrication.
	A	**B**	**C**	**D**	**E**
	Includes developments that affect more than one world region, international organizations and important meetings of major world leaders.	*Includes all domestic and regional developments in Europe, including the Soviet Union, Turkey, Cyprus and Malta.*	*Includes all domestic and regional developments in Africa and the Middle East, including Iraq and Iran and excluding Cyprus, Turkey and Afghanistan.*	*Includes all domestic and regional developments in Latin America, the Caribbean and Canada.*	*Includes all domestic and regional developments in Asia and Pacific nations, extending from Afghanistan through all the Pacific Islands, except Hawaii.*

U.S. Politics & Social Issues	U.S. Foreign Policy & Defense	U.S. Economy & Environment	Science, Technology & Nature	Culture, Leisure & Life Style	
In his annual State of the Judiciary message, Chief Justice Warren Burger urges states to adopt the federal court procedure that leaves jury selection to trial judges and bars attorneys from questioning prospective jurors.	Raymond Gastil, director of a Freedom House survey showing a significant gain in worldwide civil and political freedom during 1977, credits much of the gain to Pres. Jimmy Carter's emphasis on human rights.	Transportation Dept. reports that 1977 was a record year for motor vehicle safety recalls, set at 12.6 million vehicles.	An Air India 747 midair explosion and crash into the Arabian Sea claims the lives of all 213 people on board. It is the third worst disaster in aviation history to date.	Evonne Goolagong Cawley wins her fourth Autralian Open single's tennis title with a 6–3, 6–0 victory over Helen Cawley (not related). ... NFC championship is won by the Dallas Cowboys, who beat the Minnesota Vikings, 23–6. The AFC title is won by the Denver Broncos, who defeat the Oakland Raiders, 20–17.	Jan. 1
U.S. govt. is reported paying Sioux Indians $8.5 million for over 100,000 acres in South Dakota.	*U.S. News and World Report* reveals that there are 490,000 U.S. service people stationed abroad as of the end of 1977, 27,000 more than the previous year.	International Assn. of Machinists (IAM) votes to end a 12-week strike against Lockheed Corp. plants in Burbank and Palmdale, Calif., accepting a 12 percent wage hike over three years.		College football bowl games results follow: Cotton – Notre Dame 38, Texas 10; Orange – Arkansas 31, Oklahoma 6; Rose – Washington 27, Michigan 20; Sugar – Alabama 35, Ohio State 6.	Jan. 2
Calif. State Superior Ct. Judge Paul Egly holds that a controversial Los Angeles school integration plan based on mandatory busing will go into effect in September if it conforms to a 1976 Calif. Supreme Ct. mandate.		Treasury Dept. issues a partial list of trigger prices for major steel products sold in the U.S., designed to cut the import or dumping of cut-rate steel from foreign producers. ... U.S. Steel chmn. Edgar Speer Jr. reveals plans to close its Youngstown, Ohio plants because of their serious competitive disadvantages.	Signs of a sub-Saharan drought are reported as the water level of the Niger River rises to only half of its usual rate by October 1977.	Boston Celtics basketball team fires coach Tom Heinsohn and replaces him with former Boston star Tom (Satch) Sanders.	Jan. 3
A final appellate court decision in San Francisco, Calif. upholds kidnap victim Patricia Hearst's conviction for a 1976 bank robbery, while she was held by the Symbionese Liberation Army.		In a major policy shift, the U.S. Treasury Dept. and FRB announce active intervention to check a sharp year-long decline in the value of the dollar.... Eleanor Holmes Norton, EEOC chairman, reports initiating a campaign to root out systematic patterns of employment discrimination by large corporations.		*Close Encounters of the Third Kind*, a science-fiction work, heads the best-selling paperback book list and is also the top-grossing film.	Jan. 4
Wilmington 10, a group of civil-rights activists convicted for a 1971 firebombing in Wilmington, N.C., lose their final state-level court battle for a new trial.	In testimony before a House subcommittee investigating CIA relations with the press, Morton Halperin, a former NSC staff member and Defense Dept. official, details occasions in which the CIA attempted to influence press coverage within the U.S.	Foreign and domestic-made car sales for 1977 are reported to total nearly 11.2 million units, 11 percent higher than in 1976, with foreign-car sales making strong gains. ... Eleven American Stock Exchange (AMEX) floor traders are indicted for allegedly making false options reports between January and March 1976.		U.S. Tennis Assn. ranks Jimmy Connors as top men's singles player of 1977 for the second consecutive year.	Jan. 5
Mashpee, Mass. Wampanoag Indians lose the first phase of a Cape Cod land-claims suit when a Boston jury rules that they did not legally constitute a tribe at two crucial points in their history — 1870 and 1976.	*The New York Times* reports that a governmental military assessment report showing that the Soviets do not outmatch the U.S. in strategic nuclear weapons motivated the Carter administration decision to deemphasize naval expansion and develop strategic weapons, rather than increasing conventional land forces.	Dow Jones Average falls below the 800 mark, closing at 793.49 in wake of concern over the sagging U.S. dollar.... FRB unexpectedly increases the discount rate to 6.5 percent from 6 percent, seen as a symbolic move to underscore the Carter administration's determination to support the dollar.	Kitt Peak National Observatory, Ariz. astronomers report sighting a star that began burning only a few thousand years ago, which, in astronomical terms, makes it quite young.... National Transportation Safety Board reports a record 654 U.S.-based aviation deaths in 1977.	Philip C. Johnson, designer of the Glass House in New Canaan, Conn. and the Seagram and AT&T buildings in N.Y.C., wins the AIA Gold Medal for architecture.	Jan. 6
				Soviet gymnast Olga Korbut, 22, who won three gold medals in the 1977 Olympics, marries Soviet popular music singer Leonid Bortkevich, 27.	Jan. 7
		ABA panel reports that state and local government exclusionary land-use and housing policies reinforce segregation.	Two months of heavy precipitation appears to end the worst California–Pacific Northwest drought in recorded history.	Jimmy Connors wins the $100,000 Colgate Grand Prix Masters tennis tournament, defeating Bjorn Borg of Sweden.	Jan. 8

F	G	H	I	J
Includes elections, federal-state relations, civil rights and liberties, crime, the judiciary, education, health care, poverty, urban affairs and population.	*Includes formation and debate of U.S. foreign and defense policies, veterans' affairs and defense spending. (Relations with specific foreign countries are usually found under the region concerned.)*	*Includes business, labor, agriculture, taxation, transportation, consumer affairs, monetary and fiscal policy, natural resources, and pollution.*	*Includes worldwide scientific, medical and technological developments, natural phenomena, U.S. weather, natural disasters, and accidents.*	*Includes the arts, religion, scholarship, communications media, sports, entertainments, fashions, fads and social life.*

	World Affairs	Europe	Africa & the Middle East	The Americas	Asia & the Pacific
Jan. 9		Three Ulster political parties quit interparty talks on a new government following Irish P.M. Jack Lynch's comments on eventual reunification of Ireland and the prospect of power-sharing in a new Ulster govt. by Protestants and Roman Catholics.	Israeli Premier Menahem Begin criticizes Egyptian Pres. Anwar Sadat's hard-line position against keeping Israeli settlements in the Sinai after an Israeli–Egyptian peace agreement is concluded.	Canadian Solicitor General Francis Fox reveals copies of a false communique allegedly issued in 1971 by the Royal Canadian Mounted Police in the name of a Quebec terrorist group to sow disunity within the Quebec radical movement.	
Jan. 10		Sweden presents its fiscal 1978–79 budget, which contains an unusually large deficit of $6.9 billion (over 21 percent of total outlays).... Pepsico Inc. makes a new agreement with Soviet trade officials to expand sales of the soft-drink Pepsi-Cola in the U.S.S.R. and Stolichnaya vodka in the U.S.		Pedro Joaquin Chamorro, a prominent newspaper editor who opposed the Nicaraguan govt., is shot to death in Managua.... Canadian unemployment rate for December 1977 is reported increasing to a new post-1930s high — a seasonally adjusted 8.5 percent.	Vietnam and China sign a trade agreement for the year, despite strained relations over the Cambodian–Vietnamese border clashes.
Jan. 11		British P.M. James Callaghan concludes a six-day visit to India where he conferred with P.M. Morarji Desai and former P.M. Indira Gandhi.... Italian govt. bars a direct role by the Italian CP in government administration.	Israeli–Egyptian military panel convenes in Cairo to discuss Israeli withdrawal from the Sinai as part of an overall peace settlement.... South Africa's nonwhites (black, mixed-race, and Asians) meet for the first time to plan a united party to oppose the white South African govt.	After announcing that he had revealed all known Royal Canadian Mounted Police irregularities, Canadian Solicitor General Francis Fox discloses a RCMP break-in outside Quebec province.	An Indian judicial commission investigating the former rule of Indira Gandhi orders her to stand trial for contempt after she refuses to testify for the past two days.... Australia's worsening drought is reportedly expected to create financial losses of $970 million in 1978 if it continues as expected.
Jan. 12		Britain's 43,000 professional and volunteer firemen vote to end their two-month strike and return to work, accepting the government's 10 percent wage hike offer instead of holding out for the 30 percent hike they sought.	In an interview with a Cairo magazine, Egyptian Pres. Anwar Sadat says that he has absolutely no hope that upcoming Israeli–Egyptian Political Committee talks will succeed.	Nicaraguan riots and disturbances continue after the hasty burial of Pedro Joaquin Chamorro.	Vietnam signs a trade agreement with Thailand, which also covers civil aviation, economic, and technical cooperation.
Jan. 13			Israeli–Egyptian Military Committee recesses after reaching a general understanding on an Israeli proposal to divide the Sinai into three zones — a U.N. buffer strip, a demilitarized zone, and one containing a limited number of Egyptian troops.		Japan and the U.S. reach an agreement on a series of economic measures to reduce Japan's large surpluses in its balance of trade and payment accounts.
Jan. 14	*Financial Times* (London) reports that Frankfurt, West Germany is the world's most expensive city, followed by Brussels, Belgium; and Buenos Aires, Argentina.		Somalia expresses willingness to consider negotiations on the Ogaden dispute, but Ethiopia refuses as long as Somali forces occupy the region.		
Jan. 15		East Berlin refuses entry to Helmut Kohl, chairman of West Germany's opposition Christian Democratic Party.			Nusrat Bhutto, wife of the former Pakistani prime minister, is released from house arrest in Lahore.
Jan. 16		Pres. Urho Kaleva Kekkonen is reelected in Finland to his fifth consecutive term by almost 84 percent of votes cast.	South African govt. begins to raze a black squatters' camp outside of Cape Town that housed over 10,000 blacks, most of them families of black male workers within Cape Town who had been denied residence permits there.		Vietnam criticizes U.S. national security adviser Zbigniew Brzezinski's remark that Cambodian–Vietnamese fighting is a "proxy war" between the Soviet Union and China.
Jan. 17		Belgian Premier Leo Tindemans' coalition govt. agrees on a devolution plan to change the nation into a federated state by the mid-1980s. ... Bulent Ecevit's coalition government receives a vote of confidence in the Turkish National Assembly by an 11-vote margin.		U.S. V.P. Mondale announces that Canada has agreed to lift its seven-years-old freeze on natural gas sales to the U.S. in exchange for a U.S. pledge to reduce tariffs on Canadian exports.	A Taipei military court sentences six Taiwanese to prison terms ranging from three years to life on espionage charges.

A	B	C	D	E
Includes developments that affect more than one world region, international organizations and important meetings of major world leaders.	Includes all domestic and regional developments in Europe, including the Soviet Union, Turkey, Cyprus and Malta.	Includes all domestic and regional developments in Africa and the Middle East, including Iraq and Iran and excluding Cyprus, Turkey and Afghanistan.	Includes all domestic and regional developments in Latin America, the Caribbean and Canada.	Includes all domestic and regional developments in Asia and Pacific nations, extending from Afghanistan through all the Pacific Islands, except Hawaii.

U.S. Politics & Social Issues	U.S. Foreign Policy & Defense	U.S. Economy & Environment	Science, Technology & Nature	Culture, Leisure & Life Style	
Supreme Ct. refuses to review two cases involving press curbs set by trial judges. . . . Supreme Ct. declines to review two decisions allowing one-house congressional vetos.	Robert D. Murphy, 83, U.S. diplomat who was credited with helping plan the successful Allied invasion of North Africa in 1942, dies from a stroke in N.Y.C.	*The New York Times* reports that the Carter administration is halting development of an $850-million computer that the IRS would have used to monitor taxpayers' returns because it would pose a threat to citizens' privacy rights.		A Dayton, Ohio federal judge rules that high school girls cannot be barred from playing on the same sports teams as boys.	Jan. 9
Justice Dept. releases a report detailing a pattern of petty corruption practiced by former FBI Dir. J. Edgar Hoover and some of his top aides for which the statute of limitations has expired.			Supreme Ct. rules, 5–4, that the EPA has limited authority to enforce prohibitions on asbestos pollution in the air.	The North American Soccer League realigns into two conferences of three divisions each, based on the format of the National Football League.	Jan. 10
Samuel S. Leibowitz, 84, defense lawyer for the Scottsboro Boys, dies in Brooklyn, N.Y.		Supreme Ct. rules, 5–3, that foreign governments can bring antitrust suits against U.S. corporations in U.S. courts.	Two Soviet cosmonauts dock their Soyuz 27 spacecraft with the orbiting Salyut 6 space laboratory and greet the two Soyuz cosmonauts who have been living aboard the space station for a month. It is the first time a spacecraft has linked with an already manned orbiting space station.	National Book Critics Circle Awards follow: fiction, *Song of Solomon* by Toni Morrison; nonfiction, *Samuel Johnson* by Walter Jackson Bate; poetry, *Day by Day* by Robert Lowell; criticism, *On Photography* by Susan Sontag.	Jan. 11
Pres. Carter states at his press conference that he does not know of any investigation of members of Congress from the Phila., Pa. area by U.S. Atty. David Marston, who is a Republican.				*Ballo della Regina* by George Balanchine, with music from the third act of Guiseppe Verdi's opera *Don Carlo* is given its world premiere by the New York City Ballet in N.Y.C.	Jan. 12
Sen. Hubert Humphrey (D, Minn.) dies of cancer in Waverly, Minn. at the age of 66. . . . HEW issues final regulations barring discrimination against the handicapped by federal govt. agencies and by all federally funded projects.	U.S. Justice Dept investigators in Seoul begin questioning Park Tong Sun, an alleged key figure in the South Korean lobbying effort.	FTC charges Ford Motor Co. with deceptive business practices in selling faulty auto engines.		At its annual convention, the NCAA reorganizes Division I into two subdivisions for football. . . . Dick Buerkle, sets a new world record for the indoor mile — 3.54.9 — at the National Invitational Indoor Championships, College Park, Md.	Jan. 13
	La. Gov. Edwin Edwards (D) acknowledges receiving about $20,000 from Korean lobbyist Park Tong Sun while he was serving in the House.		Mathematician Kurt Godel, 71 dies in Princeton, N.J.	Joni Huntley of the Pacific Coast Club sets a new women's American indoor high-jump record of 6–4.	Jan. 14
Pres. Carter and V.P. Walter Mondale eulogize Sen. Hubert Humphrey at memorial services in the Capitol Rotunda attended by former Presidents Gerald Ford and Richard Nixon.				Dallas Cowboys defeat the Denver Broncos, 27–10, to win Super Bowl XII.	Jan. 15
	NAACP urges U.S. companies to stop doing business in South Africa, its first endorsement of a complete economic boycott of the country.	Supreme Ct. lets stand a lower court ruling allowing a rival long-distance telephone service by MCI Telecommunications Corp. to compete in limited service with AT&T.	NASA chooses 35 new astronaut candidates from 8,079 applicants for its space shuttle program. Six women, three blacks, and one Oriental are among those chosen.		Jan. 16
		Supreme Ct. rules, 6–3, that a construction union cannot legally picket a job site to enforce a so called pre-hiring agreement with a contractor if the union was not the legal bargaining agent for workers on the site.		A.C. Nielson–CBS Inc. statistics show more TV viewers for Super Bowl XII than any other event in the history of televised sports. . . . Quebec Nordiques come from behind to beat the World Hockey Association All-Stars in the WHA All-Star game in Quebec City, Canada.	Jan. 17

F	G	H	I	J
Includes elections, federal-state relations, civil rights and liberties, crime, the judiciary, education, health care, poverty, urban affairs and population.	*Includes formation and debate of U.S. foreign and defense policies, veterans' affairs and defense spending. (Relations with specific foreign countries are usually found under the region concerned.)*	*Includes business, labor, agriculture, taxation, transportation, consumer affairs, monetary and fiscal policy, natural resources, and pollution.*	*Includes worldwide scientific, medical and technological developments, natural phenomena, U.S. weather, natural disasters, and accidents.*	*Includes the arts, religion, scholarship, communications media, sports, entertainments, fashions, fads and social life.*

	World Affairs	Europe	Africa & the Middle East	The Americas	Asia & the Pacific
Jan. 18		European Court of Human Rights clears Great Britain of charges of torturing prisoners in Northern Ireland.	Egypt abruptly suspends Israeli–Egyptian Political Committee Talks, which began yesterday, charging that the Israelis were attempting to deadlock the situation.		Hanoi radio charges that Cambodian artillery has shelled all eight Vietnamese provinces along the Cambodian frontier since Jan. 9.
Jan. 19		A Swedish parliamentary commission recommends that the Swedish Lutheran Church be legally separated from the state.	Israeli Premier Menahem Begin discloses that Egypt and Israel had agreed the previous day on five of seven paragraphs in a statement of principles proposed by U.S. State Secy. Cyrus Vance.		French Premier Raymond Barre begins a five-day visit to China to seek improved economic ties.
Jan. 20			Rhodesian govt. announces that it will grant amnesty for black nationalist guerrillas who wish to return to Rhodesia.... U.S. State Secy. Vance goes to Cairo to try to persuade Pres. Sadat to reconvene talks with Israel.		Japan announces a record trade surplus of $9 billion in 1977.
Jan. 21	U.S., British, French, West German, and Italian representatives meet in Wash., D.C. to discuss the war in Ethiopia's Ogaden region, attempting to coordinate Western policy and to stem the buildup of Soviet and Cuban involvement in the area.		Egyptian Pres. Sadat convenes the People's National Assembly to defend his decision to suspend Political Committee talks. He accuses Israeli negotiators of stalling and exploiting his recognition of Israel's need for secure borders to justify its continued control over Arab territories.		
Jan. 22			Israeli Premier Menahem Begin tells newsmen that Israel is spurning U.S. efforts to return to Military Committee talks because Egypt has launched a vilification campaign against Israel.... Arab radical states opposed to Pres. Sadat's peace initiatives assail him for not completely abandoning his dialogue with Israel.		
Jan. 23		EEC imposes its first antidumping penalties on six types of steel products from seven steel-exporting nations.	In a speech before the Knesset, Israeli Premier Begin charges that the Egyptian press is anti-Semitic, noting a reference to himself as "Shylock the usurer who wants a pound of flesh..."	A general strike, called by Nicaraguan business and labor leaders, goes into effect to demand a more thorough investigation of the assassination of Pedro Joaquin Chamorro.	Pnompenh is described as a ghost city by envoys from Denmark, Sweden, and Finland after they return from a two-week visit to the Cambodian capital.
Jan. 24				Quebec Superior Ct. Chief Justice Jules Deschenes strikes down Bill 101, the core provision of a French-language law that makes French the official language of Quebec province.	Australia protests EEC limitations on Australian exports.

A	B	C	D	E
Includes developments that affect more than one world region, international organizations and important meetings of major world leaders.	Includes all domestic and regional developments in Europe, including the Soviet Union, Turkey, Cyprus and Malta.	Includes all domestic and regional developments in Africa and the Middle East, including Iraq and Iran and excluding Cyprus, Turkey and Afghanistan.	Includes all domestic and regional developments in Latin America, the Caribbean and Canada.	Includes all domestic and regional developments in Asia and Pacific nations, extending from Afghanistan through all the Pacific Islands, except Hawaii.

U.S. Politics & Social Issues	U.S. Foreign Policy & Defense	U.S. Economy & Environment	Science, Technology & Nature	Culture, Leisure & Life Style	
Supreme Ct. rules, 5–4, to expand a prosecutor's plea-bargaining power by allowing a defendant to be threatened with a second, more serious indictment, if he/she refuses to plead guilty to lesser charges.	Benjamin Civiletti, acting deputy attorney general, tells reporters that Justice Dept. investigators have not uncovered information that would lead to the indictment of current members of Congress in the Korean lobbying scandal.	Commerce Dept. reports that the U.S. personal income rose 11.1 percent in 1977 compared with 10.3 percent in 1976, the biggest increase since 1973.	The roof of the three-year-old, $70 million Hartford Civic Center (Conn.) coliseum collapses, apparently caused by the weight of accumulated snow and ice. No one is injured, but the accident is described as a financial and psychological blow to the city.	Washington Redskins fire head coach and general manager George Allen, the most successful coach in the Redskins' history, after he refused to sign his 1977 contract and disputed with team owners over policy.	Jan. 18
William Webster, a U.S. Appeals Ct. judge in St. Louis, Mo., is appointed FBI director, succeeding Clarence Kelley.	Former Calif. Gov. Ronald Reagan joins a "truth squad" led by Sen. Paul Laxalt (R, Nev.) in Denver, which is spearheading a campaign against Senate ratification of the Panama Canal treaties.	Consumer spending is reported continuing to fuel the U.S. economic recovery, rising at a rate of $36.4-billion in the fourth quarter of 1977, the largest increase since the same period of 1976.			Jan. 19
Atty. Gen. Griffin Bell dismisses Republican David Marston as U.S. attorney in Philadelphia, despite controversial political overtones in wake of Marston's successful prosecution of leading Democratic politicians accused of corruption.	Leon Jaworski, special counsel to the House committee investigating the Korean lobbying scandal, announces finding evidence of wrongdoing and possible criminal culpability by some current members of Congress.	Pres. Carter sends an economic message to Congress calling for voluntary price–wage restraint by business and labor.		NBC announces that Fred Silverman will replace Herbert Schlosser as president and chief executive officer.	Jan. 20
		A N.Y.C. federal grand jury finds that Eastman Kodak Co. has a monopoly on the photographic equipment field to the detriment of rival firm, Berkey Photo Inc.		Roberto Duran of Panama becomes the undisputed world lightweight boxing champion with a twelfth-round technical knockout of Puerto Rico's Esteban DeJesus at Caesars Palace, Las Vegas, Nev. ... NCAA Football Rules Committee revises several rules effective for the 1978 season, including adoption of a NFL regulation on the placement of the football following a missed field goal.	Jan. 21
Paul Hatfield (D) is appointed to complete the U.S. Senate term of Lee Metcalf (D, Mont.), who died on Jan. 12 of an apparent heart attack.				Leon Damas, 65, a French Guianan poet who helped found the Negritude movement in 1930s Paris — a literary–cultural movement that was a major influence on the black consciousness movement in 1960s U.S. — dies in Wash. D.C.	Jan. 22
	The fiscal 1979 defense budget request of $115.2 billion represents 23 percent of the federal budget and 5.1 percent of the GNP.... Rep. Alleln Ertel (D, Pa.) submits a resolution to the House to ask the South Korean govt. to ensure Park Tong Sun's appearance before the House committee investigating the Korean lobbying scandal.	Supreme Ct. rules that an employer who wins a job discrimination suit cannot collect legal fees unless a judges rules that the suit was frivolous or groundless.	NASA receives appropriations of nearly $4.3 billion in the fiscal 1979 federal budget, a $288-million increase over fiscal 1978.	A group of 13 former U.S. Open and PGA champions files suit against the PGA in Houston to uphold what they contend is their lifetime right to enter any PGA event of their choice without qualifying.	Jan. 23
A Justice Dept. investigation clears both Pres. Carter and Atty. Gen. Griffin Bell of obstructing justice or acting improperly in expediting Rep. Joshua Eilberg's request to replace Phila. U.S. Attorney David Marston.... Robert deLuca, assistant to the U.S. attorney in Phila., is named as temporary successor to David Marston and says that he will continue Marston's investigation of Democratic Reps. Daniel Flood and Joshua Eilberg (Pa.).	Pres. Carter's executive order gives responsibility for overseeing all counterintelligence activities to the newly created Special Coordinating Committee of the NSC, headed by National Security Adviser Zbigniew Brzezinski.		A nuclear-equipped Soviet reconnaissance satellite, Cosmos 954, falls through the atmosphere and burns up over northern Canada.	The Prince of Wales Conference wins its fourth consecutive National Hockey League All-Star game with a 3–2 overtime victory over the Campbell Conference.... Joe Namath, one of the most colorful figures in pro football, announces his retirement.	Jan. 24

F	G	H	I	J
Includes elections, federal-state relations, civil rights and liberties, crime, the judiciary, education, health care, poverty, urban affairs and population.	Includes formation and debate of U.S. foreign and defense policies, veterans' affairs and defense spending. (Relations with specific foreign countries are usually found under the region concerned.)	Includes business, labor, agriculture, taxation, transportation, consumer affairs, monetary and fiscal policy, natural resources, and pollution.	Includes worldwide scientific, medical and technological developments, natural phenomena, U.S. weather, natural disasters, and accidents.	Includes the arts, religion, scholarship, communications media, sports, entertainments, fashions, fads and social life.

	World Affairs	Europe	Africa & the Middle East	The Americas	Asia & the Pacific
Jan. 25	French Pres. Valery Giscard d'Estaing outlines a plan for a comprehensive reorganization of world disarmament negotiations and proposes disbanding the Geneva Disarmament Conference sponsored by the U.N.	West German govt. sets a target GNP growth rate of 3.5 percent for 1978.	Rhodesian P.M. Ian Smith denounces what he calls the unholy alliance of the Patriotic Front (Rhodesian black guerrilla coalition) and Great Britain, who plan to meet in Malta to discuss the transition to black majority rule in Rhodesia.	Nicaraguan Conservative Party, the coalition Union of Democratic Liberation, business, and labor leaders call for Pres. Anastasio Somoza Debayle to resign.	Hanoi radio reports that Cambodian troops have driven into the southwestern Vietnamese provincial district capital of Ha Tien.
Jan. 26		Spyros Kyprianou, caretaker president of Cyprus, automatically wins a full five-year term as president after the opposition fails to nominate a candidate.	A CIA document is released showing that as early as 1974 the CIA concluded that Israel had built atomic weapons.		Indonesian govt. security officers announce the arrest of 143 students and 15 others for allegedly panning to stage antigovernment rallies in Jakarta.
Jan. 27		Soviet statistics show that the country's economic growth, begun in the 1960s, is ending.	Black moderate Rhodesian leader Bishop Abel Muzorewa walks out of a conference with Rhodesian P.M. Ian Smith on a majority-rule settlement because he feels he was insulted by Rhodesian Finance Min. David Smith.	Nicaraguan Pres. Anastasio Somoza Debayle refuses to resign despite a wave of opposition, protests, and strikes by diverse elements in the country, including business and labor.	The main rebel hideouts of the Moslem Moro National Front in the southern Philippines are reported captured by governement forces.
Jan. 28		East and West German representatives meet in East Berlin to try to ease rising tension between the two countries.	Rhodesian white emigration totals 16,638 in 1977, with the net loss set at 10,908, the greatest since 1964.... A two-day general strike in Tunisia turns into a popular demonstration against the government of Pres. Habib Bourguiba.	In a radio speech, Pres. Anastasio Somoza Debayle calls the Nicaraguan general strike a reactionary move against the country's small businesses and working class, and he threatens to declare the Conservative Party illegal.	
Jan. 29		*The New York Times* reports recent moves by the Soviet Union to emphasize its presence in East Germany and in West Berlin.	Israeli Cabinet agrees to resume Military Committee sessions with Egypt.... Pres. Carter is reported sending a personal message to Israeli P.M. Menahem Begin expressing concern about Israel's effort to establish another settlement in the West Bank near the biblical site of Shiloh.		
Jan. 30	British For. Secy. David Owen and U.S. Amb. to the U.N. Andrew Young begin talks in Malta with the Patriotic Front — the guerrilla coalition fighting the white Rhodesian minority govt.	Portuguese Premier Mario Soares' new Cabinet is sworn in. It contains II Socialists, three Center Democrats, and two independents.... Finland posts its first trade surplus in a decade.	The Popular Movement for the Liberation of Angola (MPLA) is reported purging political dissidents.... A U.S. govt. official says that Israeli For. Min. Moshe Dayan had assured Pres. Carter, in their September 1977 meeting, that Israel would not set up any new civilian communities in the West Bank for a year.	Canadian Solicitor General Francis Fox resigns after disclosures that he had illegally obtained an abortion for a married woman with whom he had had an affair.... Nicaraguan general strike enters its second week with no sign of letting up.	Six more Japanese politicians are implicated in the Lockheed Aircraft Corp. payoff scandal, which first erupted in 1976.
Jan. 31	At the opening session of the Conference of the Committee on Disarmament in Geneva, both the U.S. and the Soviet Union express doubts about French Pres. Valery Giscard d'Estaing's plan to disband the conference.	Danish unemployment rises 7.3 percent in 1977, compared with 6.1 percent in 1976.	Israeli–Egyptian Military Committee resumes talks in Cairo on arranging a technical agreement for Israel's return of the Sinai Peninsula to Egypt.... A reported 401 people died in Rhodesian guerrilla fighting in January, one of the highest monthly death tolls since the started in 1972.	The Roman Catholic Church in Nicaragua, a traditional ally of Pres. Anastasio Somoza Debayle's regime, is reported supporting the general strike.	
Feb. 1		Michael Edwardes, the new chairman of British Leyland Ltd., announces that 12,500 people will be cut from the state-owned automobile firm's work force.	Israeli Premier Menahem Begin discusses the four controversial new Israeli settlements in the West Bank with U.S. Amb. Samuel Lewis.	U.S. State Dept. sources are reported saying that the Carter administration has decided to halt military assistance to Nicaragua in view of continuing human-rights abuses there.... *The New York Times* reports that *La Prensa*, the newspaper of assassinated editor Pedro Joaquin Chamorro, is emerging as the coordinating center of the Nicaraguan general strike.	

A	B	C	D	E
Includes developments that affect more than one world region, international organizations and important meetings of major world leaders.	*Includes all domestic and regional developments in Europe, including the Soviet Union, Turkey, Cyprus and Malta.*	*Includes all domestic and regional developments in Africa and the Middle East, including Iraq and Iran and excluding Cyprus, Turkey and Afghanistan.*	*Includes all domestic and regional developments in Latin America, the Caribbean and Canada.*	*Includes all domestic and regional developments in Asia and Pacific nations, extending from Afghanistan through all the Pacific Islands, except Hawaii.*

U.S. Politics & Social Issues	U.S. Foreign Policy & Defense	U.S. Economy & Environment	Science, Technology & Nature	Culture, Leisure & Life Style	
Muriel Humphrey is appointed to fill the U.S. Senate seat of her late husband, Hubert Humphrey (D, Minn.).			A blizzard hits the U.S. Midwest, bringing winds of 100 mph and temperatures of 50 degrees below zero.		Jan. 25
	Acting Deputy Atty. Gen. Benjamin Civiletti, reverses earlier statements and tells several congressmen that Justice Dept. questioning of Korean lobbyist Park Tong Sun has uncovered information suggesting that 15–18 current members of Congress might have violated ethical standards.	Sen. Howard Baker (R, Tenn.) criticizes Pres. Carter's emphasis on fixing energy prices.	Pres. Carter declares Ohio a federal disaster area in wake of a blizzard that dumped up to 31 inches of snow on the Midwest and caused the deaths of more than 100 people.	British actor Leo Genn, 72, best remembered for his 1952 role in the movie *Quo Vadis*, dies in London, England.	Jan. 26
Ill. Supreme Ct. upholds the right of the National Socialist Party of America (Nazi) to display swastikas at public demonstrations in Skokie, Ill., which is a predominatly Jewish suburb of Chicago.		Rep. Charles Vanik (D, Ohio) charges that in 1976 17 major U.S. firms paid no federal income taxes on $2.6 billion in earnings, noting that their returns were legal because of existing tax breaks.	Pres.Carter says he thinks that the Soviet Union handled the Cosmos 954 emergency well.	Franklin Jacobs sets a new high-jump record by leaping 7 feet, 7-and-a-quarter inches at the Wanamaker Millrose Games, N.Y.C. . . . Oscar Homolka, 79, Vienese-born character actor dies in Sussex England.	Jan. 27
					Jan. 28
	Miami Herald publishes an open letter by Egyptian Pres. Anwar Sadat appealing to American Jews to support his peace initiatives. The letter was written at the newspaper's invitation.				Jan. 29
In a nationally televised news conference, Pres. Carter defends the controversial removal by his administration of Republican David Marston from his post as U.S. attorney in Philadelphia after Marston's investigations had implicated several Democratic politicians. . . . Senate, 72–15, votes a massive revision and consolidation of federal criminal law.	Sen. For. Rel. Committee votes, 14–1, for ratification of the Panama Canal treaties on the condition that language is inserted ensuring U.S. defense and transit rights after the year 2000.		Canadian and U.S. scientists confirm that satellite debris found on Jan. 28 is from Cosmos 954 and is mildly radioactive, but does not pose a direct threat to humans. . . . In a news conference, Pres. Carter indicates favoring a ban on all orbiting vehicles carrying nuclear reactors.	Baseball comr. Bowie Kuhn cancels the sale of pitcher Vida Blue from the Oakland A's to the Cincinnati Reds because he says that the NL's competitive balance would be adversely affected.	Jan. 30
	A U.S. Information Agency official and a Vietnamese citizen living in the U.S. are reported indicted for spying for Vietnam.	United Farm Workers ends its long-standing boycotts against lettuce, table grapes, and Gallo wines, which were initiated to back up union organizing efforts.	The Aviation Consumer Action Project, fouded by Ralph Nader, scores the CAB for not defending airline passengers' rights more vigorously.		Jan. 31
	White House issues a statement that Pres. Carter has imposed an $8.6-billion ceiling on U.S. arms sales to non-allied countries.	Labor Dept. files suit against Teamsters pres. Frank Fitzsimmons and 18 others to recover losses resulting from allegedly imprudent loans from the Teamsters' Central States Pension Fund.		Movie director Roman Polanski flees California where he faces sentencing on a morals charge involving a 13-year-old girl.	Feb. 1

F	G	H	I	J
Includes elections, federal-state relations, civil rights and liberties, crime, the judiciary, education, health care, poverty, urban affairs and population.	*Includes formation and debate of U.S. foreign and defense policies, veterans' affairs and defense spending. (Relations with specific foreign countries are usually found under the region concerned.)*	*Includes business, labor, agriculture, taxation, transportation, consumer affairs, monetary and fiscal policy, natural resources, and pollution.*	*Includes worldwide scientific, medical and technological developments, natural phenomena, U.S. weather, natural disasters, and accidents.*	*Includes the arts, religion, scholarship, communications media, sports, entertainments, fashions, fads and social life.*

	World Affairs	Europe	Africa & the Middle East	The Americas	Asia & the Pacific
Feb. 2		Spain's Chamber of Deputies passes a law under which adultery and concubinage are no longer crimes.... Residents of Christiania, the so-called free city in Copenhagen, lose their court claim to the area, home for an estimed 1,000 derelicts, hippies, drug addicts, and other squatters.	Israeli Labor Party opposes and questions Premier Menahem Begin's settlements' stance, specifically the Shiloh settlement, which the Begin govt. defends as solely for archaelogical projects. ... South African govt. reportedly will take no legal action against the police for the death of Steven Biko, the black activist leader who died in police custody in September 1977.	Canadian P.M. Pierre Trudeau names Postmaster General Jean-Jacques Blais as solicitor general, replacing Francis Fox. He names J. Gilles Lamontagne as the new Postmaster General.	Following four days of talks, Cambodia and Thailand announce that they will exchange ambassadors in a renewal of diplomatic ties.
Feb. 3	U.S. govt. orders the expulsion of Vietnamese Amb. to the U.N. Dinh Ba Thi because of his alleged involvement in a Vietnamese espionage ring in the U.S.... EEC and China initial a five-year trade agreement that gives each other most-favored-nation trading status.	West German Defense Min. Georg Leber resigns, as Chancellor Helmut Schmidt carries out a major Cabinet reshuffling.... Hans Brunhart becomes Liechtenstein's premier after his Fatherland Union party wins eight of the 15 seats in the Diet.	Egyptian Pres. Anwar Sadat arrives at the White House where he meets with Pres. Carter and urges the U.S. to become the arbiter in the Arab–Israeli negotiations' dispute.		Sri Lanka govt. formally shifts to a presidential system as P.M. Junius Richard Jayewardene is sworn in as the country's first president.
Feb. 4			Arab radical states — Syria, Libya, Algeria, South Yemen, and the PLO — conclude a three-day summit meeting in Algiers where they mapped strategy against Egyptian Pres. Sadat's Mideast peace moves. Iraq boycotts the meeting. ... Pres. Carter and Egyptian Pres. Sadat begin two days of private meetings at Camp David, Md.		
Feb. 5		West German govt. is reported embarrassed by the increasingly anti-Semitic tone and visible displays of a new Nazi revival.		Rodrigo Carazo Odio, leader of a four-party coalition called the Unity Party, is elected president of Costa Rica after campaigning against the ruling party candidate, Luis Alberto Monge, on an anticorruption and antiwaste platform.	Vietnam proposes an immediate truce to end its border fighting with Cambodia.
Feb. 6	Soviet Union sharply criticizes the EEC–China trade pact.		Chad breaks diplomatic relations with Libya.... Speaking to the National Press Club in Washington, D.C., Egyptian Pres. Sadat accuses Israel of intransigence in its peace negotiations.		India and Pakistan begin two days of talks about improving relations.
Feb. 7		Austria's 1977 trade deficit is reported to have risen 35 percent over its 1976 deficit to a record $4.7 billion.	U.S. reiterates its opposition to any new Israeli settlements on the West Bank or other Israeli-occupied lands.	Nicaragua's nationwide general strike ends without achieving its intent of overthrowing Pres. Anastasio Somoza Debayle. Its failure is attributed to economic reasons.	
Feb. 8		A scandal erupts in Austria over the refusal of public health officials to report the accidental mixing of mercury-treated seed grain with grain destined for Vienna-area bakeries.	Western diplomats report that Cuba is sending new reinforcements to Ethiopia and Cubans are also flying bombing raids for the Ethiopians.... Ethiopian govt. acknowledges using terrorist tactics to rid Addis Ababa of political dissent.		Cambodia rejects Vietnam's truce offer.
Feb. 9		Herbert Kappler, the Nazi war criminal who escaped from Italian custody in August 1977, dies of cancer in Soltau, West Germany.	Over 100 casualties are reported in wake of clashes, beginning Feb. 7, between Lebanese Christian militiamen and Syrian peacekeeping troops.	Canada expels 11 Soviet diplomats and bars two others from reentering the country for running a spy ring and attempting to recruit an officer of the Royal Canadian Mounted Police's intelligence division.	A U.S. State Dept. report finds some improvement in human-rights observances by South Korea, Indonesia, and Thailand. ... Hanoi accuses Cambodia of responding to its peace proposal by launching new incursions into Vietnam.

A	B	C	D	E
Includes developments that affect more than one world region, international organizations and important meetings of major world leaders.	Includes all domestic and regional developments in Europe, including the Soviet Union, Turkey, Cyprus and Malta.	Includes all domestic and regional developments in Africa and the Middle East, including Iraq and Iran and excluding Cyprus, Turkey and Afghanistan.	Includes all domestic and regional developments in Latin America, the Caribbean and Canada.	Includes all domestic and regional developments in Asia and Pacific nations, extending from Afghanistan through all the Pacific Islands, except Hawaii.

U.S. Politics & Social Issues	U.S. Foreign Policy & Defense	U.S. Economy & Environment	Science, Technology & Nature	Culture, Leisure & Life Style	
HEW rejects college desegregation plans submitted by the states of Virginia and Georgia and rejects part of a plan submitted by North Carolina.	A Gallup Poll finds 45 percent of Americans polled favor Senate ratification of the Panama Canal treaties with 42 percent opposed. . . . Defense Secy. Harold Brown says the U.S. will have to increase its military budget by over $50 billion over the next five years to keep parity with the Soviet Union.		Labor Dept. issues new rules to limit worker exposure to benzene, a widely used chemical suspected of causing leukemia.	U.S. District Ct. in Buffalo, N.Y. rules that one-eyed player, Gregory Neeld, cannot be banned from playing by the American Hockey League, citing violation of Neeld's constitutional rights and N.Y.S.'s human-rights laws.	Feb. 2
		Time Inc. announces an agreement in principle to buy the *Washington Star* for $20 million. . . . Postal Service is reported accumulating a budget deficit of $687 million in its 1977 fiscal year, which ended in September.			Feb. 3
			Canadian and American searchers retrieve a highly radioactive piece of Cosmos 954, the Soviet satellite that fell through the atmosphere on Jan. 24 over northern Canada.	*Saturday Night Fever Soundtrack* is the best-selling album and the song "Staying Alive" is the best-selling single record — both from the movie *Saturday Night Fever*, which is the second top-grossing film.	Feb. 4
			An intense snowstorm, the worst in New England's history, paralyzes the Northeast. Boston, Mass. and Providence, R.I. have record-breaking snowfalls, 27 inches and 38 inches respectively.	James Fixx's *The Complete Book of Running* is the number two general best-selling book for the week just ended.	Feb. 5
N.Y.S. Gov. Hugh Carey and N.Y.C. Mayor Edward Koch announce an agreement under which the city will receive $200 million in new state aid.	GAO reports that it has cost $18.4 billion to switch from the draft to an all-volunteer Army.			Former OMB Dir. Bertram Lance becomes a spot TV news commentator for WXIA-TV in Atlanta, Ga. with an estimated annual salary of $50,000.	Feb. 6
			Senate passes, 88–3, legislation imposing some restrictions on the export of nuclear technology and materials.		Feb. 7
Oscar Chapman, 81, Washington lawyer and Interior Secy. (1949–53) long associated with American Indian causes, dies of pneumonia in Washington, D.C.	Senate begins debating the Panama Canal treaties. . . . Former Calif. Gov. Ronald Reagan makes a TV address to rebut Pres. Carter's recent "fireside chat" on advantages of the Panama Canal treaties.	Congress clears legislation authorizing $6.08 billion for energy research in fiscal 1978 that eliminates two features that Pres. Carter had vetoed in a very similar 1977 bill.	Mass. Gov. Michael Dukakis orders all roads and streets in the eastern part of the state closed in wake of a record blizzard. He also orders all businesses, with the exception of food stores, closed.		Feb. 8
William Webster's appointment as FBI head is confirmed by the Senate. . . . A Senate Banking Committee report states that N.Y.C. should be able to meet its financing needs and avoid bankruptcy after June 30 without further federal aid.	Senate Select Committee on Intelligence introduces legislation to restructure the U.S. intelligence community and to set curbs designed to prevent the recurrence of past abuses. . . . Frank Carlucci's nomination as deputy director of the CIA is approved by the Senate.	Senate passes the second of two separate bills to expand Redwood National Park in northern Calif.	Pentagon opens a toll-free telephone line in an effort to contact participants or spectators of atomic bomb tests who were thereby exposed to radiation.		Feb. 9

F	G	H	I	J
Includes elections, federal-state relations, civil rights and liberties, crime, the judiciary, education, health care, poverty, urban affairs and population.	Includes formation and debate of U.S. foreign and defense policies, veterans' affairs and defense spending. (Relations with specific foreign countries are usually found under the region concerned.)	Includes business, labor, agriculture, taxation, transportation, consumer affairs, monetary and fiscal policy, natural resources, and pollution.	Includes worldwide scientific, medical and technological developments, natural phenomena, U.S. weather, natural disasters, and accidents.	Includes the arts, religion, scholarship, communications media, sports, entertainments, fashions, fads and social life.

	World Affairs	Europe	Africa & the Middle East	The Americas	Asia & the Pacific
Feb. 10	Federal District Judge Albert Bryan Jr., in Wash., D.C., issues a temporary restraining order that prohibits the U.S. from ousting Vietnamese Amb. to the U.N. Dinh Ba Thi. Despite the ruling, Thi leaves the U.S.	Tass calls the expulsion of Soviet diplomats from Canada provocative and suggests it is meant to divert attention from the internal problems of the Royal Canadian Mounted Police, under investigation for alleged intelligence abuses.	U.S. State Secy. Vance says that the Soviet Union has pledged that the Ethiopians will not cross the Somalian border in their drive to retake Ogaden.... A report by two churchmen released in Lusaka charges that torture of black suspects by police and South African troops has become institutionalized in Namibia.	Argentina begins new naval maneuvers in the Beagle Channel area after a long-standing dispute with Chile over the ownership of three islands there that intensified in January.... Thousands demonstrate against the government in Managua, Nicaragua, exactly one month after the murder of opposition leader Pedro Joaquin Chamorro.	Australian Council of Trade Unions, representing 1.8 million workers, votes to honor existing uranium contracts.
Feb. 11		French Gaullist leader Jacques Chirac delivers a hard-hitting campaign speech for the upcoming March parliamentary elections in which he attacks the left, especially Socialist leader Francois Mitterrand.... A U.S. fighter-bomber accidentally drops a 500-pound bomb near a Sardinian resort town, causing a panic among residents but no injuries.	Somalia orders a general mobilization to counter what it sees as an imminent Ethiopian invasion.... Egyptian Pres. Sadat confers in Salzburg, Austria with Shimon Peres, leader of the Israeli opposition Labor Party, but claims that he is not trying to divide the Israelis.		Australian unemployment rises in January to a record total of 445,300 people or 7.2 percent of the workforce.
Feb. 12		Narcotics-related deaths in West Germany are reported at 380 during 1977.	Israeli Cabinet and Premier Begin protest U.S. State Secy. Vance's remarks about Israeli West Bank settlements, and Begin charges that the U.S. is taking sides in the peace negotiations.... Syria and Lebanon agree on measures to prevent a recurrence of fighting between their forces in Beirut.	Sandinista National Liberation Front, Nicaragua's leftist guerrillas, announces that it will soon start a civil war against Pres. Anastasio Somoza Debayle.... Paraguayan Pres. Alfredo Stroessner is reelected to a five-year term in a landslide victory.	
Feb. 13			A Lebanese spokesman reports that 150 people have been killed and 339 wounded in Feb. 7–10 clashes between Syrian peacekeeping troops on one side and combined Lebanese army regulars and Christian militiamen.		
Feb. 14	U.N. Human Rights Commission adopts three resolutions condemning Israel.	A November 1977 poll is released that shows most West Germans support limitations on personal freedoms in an effort to control terrorism.... Riccardo Palma, a Roman judge connected with the prison system, is shot and killed on a street by the Italian left-wing terrorists known as the Red Brigades.	U.S. announces plans to sell $4.8 billion worth of jet warplanes to Egypt, Saudi Arabia, and Israel, subject to congressional approval. ... Lebanese Parliament votes, 72–1, to establish a joint Syrian–Lebanese military court to try persons responsible for clashes in Beirut, a joint commission to investigate causes of the disturbances, and joint security checkpoints and roadblocks.	Argentinian govt. decrees that all religions except Roman Catholicism must register with the state or be banned.... Members of the People's Revolutionary Army, a Salvadoran leftist guerrilla group, bomb and fire on the Nicaraguan Embassy in San Salvador, leaving behind leaflets denouncing Nicaraguan Pres. Anastasio Somoza Debayle.	
Feb. 15		Rauf Denktash, leader of the Turkish-occupied portion of Cyprus, says that he would establish joint economic projects with the Cypriot Greek community.	Israeli Premier Menahem Begin deplores the Carter administration's decision to sell planes to Egypt and Saudi Arabia.... An agreement in principle to establish majority rule in Rhodesia is signed by P.M. Ian Smith and three black leaders — Bishop Abel Muzorewa, Rev. Ndabaningi Sithole, and Chief Jeremiah Chirau.	Sen. Jose de Magalhaes Pinto, the only candidate opposing Brazil's designated next president — Gen. Joao Baptista de Figueiredo — denounces the selection of Figueiredo and calls for direct elections to all political offices in Brazil.	Chinese Deputy Premier Teng Hsiao-ping is reportedly formally cleared of blame for the April 5, 1976 Peking riots that led to his temporary downfall.... Japanese Ministry of Home Affairs approves issuing an additional $229 million in municipal bonds by the Tokyo city government to help cover its $979-million deficit for the current fiscal year ending March 31.
Feb. 16		By a one-vote margin, the West German Bundestag passes a series of measures to combat terrorism.	Joshua Nkomo, co-leader of the Patriotic Front, warns that the internal settlement in Rhodesia will increase fighting there and charges that Abel Muzorewa and Ndabaningi Sithole are now part of the Smith regime.		Japan and China sign a $20-billion trade pact.... China's National People's Congress, its nominal legislature, begins a week-long meeting in Peking.

A	B	C	D	E
Includes developments that affect more than one world region, international organizations and important meetings of major world leaders.	*Includes all domestic and regional developments in Europe, including the Soviet Union, Turkey, Cyprus and Malta.*	*Includes all domestic and regional developments in Africa and the Middle East, including Iraq and Iran and excluding Cyprus, Turkey and Afghanistan.*	*Includes all domestic and regional developments in Latin America, the Caribbean and Canada.*	*Includes all domestic and regional developments in Asia and Pacific nations, extending from Afghanistan through all the Pacific Islands, except Hawaii.*

U.S. Politics & Social Issues	U.S. Foreign Policy & Defense	U.S. Economy & Environment	Science, Technology & Nature	Culture, Leisure & Life Style	
			Pres. Carter declares Mass., hit by a record blizzard, a federal disaster area. . . . California's death toll from flooding nears 20, following torrential rains, which hit the formerly drought-stricken southern region of the state.		Feb. 10
James Conant, 84, president of Harvard University (1933–53), high commissioner and subsequent ambassador to West Germany (1953–57), and during WWII, a member of U.S. govt. committees to set policy on the development of the atomic bomb, dies in Hanover, N.H.		In wake of the nationwide coal strike, Pres. Carter declares an energy emergency in Ohio, where 95 percent of electricity comes from coal.			Feb. 11
					Feb. 12
		EPA standards curbing sulfur dioxide pollution by industry in Ohio are upheld by the U.S. Sixth Circuit Appeals Ct. in Cincinnati.	Canadian External Affairs Min. Donald Jamieson says that Canada will ask the Soviet Union to pay for the cost of retrieving Cosmos 954 debris.	Spanish renowned guitarist Andres Segovia, 85, gives a golden jubilee concert in N.Y.C.	Feb. 13
In a special election in N.Y.C.'s eighteenth congressional district, S. William Green (R) wins an upset victory over Bella Abzug (D) for the seat vacated by Rep. Edward Koch (D), who became mayor of N.Y.		*Wall Street Journal* cites observers who administration's unwillingness and inability to defend the currency for the dollar's precipitous decline.	Los Angles County officials say that their Flood Control Dept. had seeded clouds hours before the rainfall that devastated the area.	Sam Shepard's play *The Curse of the Starving Class* opens at the Public Theater, N.Y.C., home of Joseph Papp's New York Shakespeare Festival.	Feb. 14
	Justice Dept. files suit in Alexandria, Va. federal ct. against Frank Snepp, a former CIA employe who had written a book, *Decent Interval*, which criticized the CIA's handling of the U.S. evacuation from Vietnam in 1975.	Pres. Carter intervenes in the nation's 73-day coal strike, the longest national strike in UMW history. . . . Retail sales are reported dropping 3.1 percent in January to their lowest point since October 1964. . . . FRB reports a .7 percent decline in industrial production, the sharpest drop since March 1975, which is attributed to severe winter weather and the continuing coal strike.	*Washington Post* reports that an estimated 300,000 military and civilian personnel have been exposed to radiation from 307 nuclear test explosions in Nevada and the Pacific between 1945–62. . . . EPA announces that it is banning 2,000 chemical pesticides because they contain potentially hazardous ingredients. . . . A bomb blows a hole in the Alaska pipeline about six miles east of Fairbanks.	Muhammad Ali, world heavyweight boxing champion for seven years, is dethroned by 24-year-old challenger Leon Spinks, who wins a split decision in the title match, nationally televised from the Las Vegas Hilton, Nev.	Feb. 15
Washington Post publishes highlights from a forthcoming book by former Nixon aide H.R. Haldeman, *The Ends of Power*, in which Haldeman charges that former Pres. Nixon initiated the Watergate break-in and participated in the cover-up from "day one."			Pres. Carter declares eight Calif. counties a major disaster area in wake of torrential rains.	Chicago Bears replace head coach Jack Pardee, who became head coach for the Washington Redskins on Jan. 25, with Neill Armstrong, formerly with the Minnesota Vikings.	Feb. 16

F	G	H	I	J
Includes elections, federal-state relations, civil rights and liberties, crime, the judiciary, education, health care, poverty, urban affairs and population.	Includes formation and debate of U.S. foreign and defense policies, veterans' affairs and defense spending. (Relations with specific foreign countries are usually found under the region concerned.)	Includes business, labor, agriculture, taxation, transportation, consumer affairs, monetary and fiscal policy, natural resources, and pollution.	Includes worldwide scientific, medical and technological developments, natural phenomena, U.S. weather, natural disasters, and accidents.	Includes the arts, religion, scholarship, communications media, sports, entertainments, fashions, fads and social life.

	World Affairs	Europe	Africa & the Middle East	The Americas	Asia & the Pacific
Feb. 17		A firebomb that explodes in a restaurant in the Protestant section of Belfast kills 12 and injures 30 people. It is the worst bombing since 1971 when 15 people died in an explosion at a Roman Catholic bar.			South Korean dissidents denounce a U.S. State Dept. report that said there is a general improvement in human rights in their country.
Feb. 18		Two Palestinian gunmen burst into the lobby of the Hilton Hotel in Nicosia, Cyprus and shoot to death Youssef el- Sebai, editor of the Egyptian newspaper Al Ahram, who is also a close confidant of Egyptian Pres. Anwar Sadat. They then seize 30 hostages.	Anti-government riots in Tabriz, Iran's second largest city, kill six people and injure 125.		Hartono Dharsono formally resigns as secretary general of ASEAN. He is replaced by another Indonesian, Umarjadi Niotowijono.
Feb. 19		An aircraft commandeered by Palestinian terrorists, carrying 11 hostages, three of whom are PLO members, returns to Larnaca airfield, Cyprus, after being refused permission to land in Kuwait, Somalia, Ethiopia, Greece, and South Yemen.... A force of 74 Egyptian commandos lands at Larnaca airport in an attempt to rescue the hijacked plane. They exchange fire with Cypriot National Guard troops, leaving 15 dead and 22 wounded. The hijackers then free their hostages and surrender.			Australia's opposition Labor Party seeks to drastically reduce immigration in face of severe unemployment in the country.
Feb. 20		The Greek Cypriot terrorist group known as EOKA-B sends letters to local newspapers announcing that it has disbanded.	Libya announces a cease-fire in the 13-year-old guerrilla war between the Chad govt. and rebels of the Chad National Liberation Front.	Former Argentinian Pres. Maria Estela (Isabel) Martinez de Peron is convicted of embezzling the equivalent of $200,000 from a public charity she headed before she was deposed in a March 1976 military coup.	
Feb. 21	British P.M. James Callaghan denounces the Soviet Union's campaign against the U.S. enhanced radiation warhead (neutron bomb).	Washington Post dispatch from Nicosia says that a 12-man unit of the PLO was seen fighting alongside the Cypriots against the Egyptians at the Larnaca airfield, Cyprus.	Ethiopian Head of State Lt. Col. Mengistu Haile Mariam reportedly makes a personal pledge to a U.S. delegation visiting Ethiopia on Feb 17–18 that Ethiopia will not invade Somalia to retaliate for the Somali invasion of Ogaden.	Demonstrations and violence in Masaya, Matagalpa, and Managua erupt as part of a nationwide campaign to oust Nicaraguan Pres. Anastasio Somoza Debayle.... Quebec Court of Appeals orders that a provincial inquiry into alleged illegal activities by the Royal Canadian Mounted Police be suspended.	Hanoi radio accuses China of arming Cambodia in its border war against Vietnam and of encouraging Pnompenh to refuse to negotiate.... Hsinhua Chinese news agency reports that the radical Gang of Four will not be executed despite their unrepentant attitude since their arrest in October 1976.
Feb. 22	Wall Street Journal reports that OPEC members dropped oil production to 29 million barrels a day in January from 32.5 million barrels a day in December 1977.	A Scottish limited home-rule bill passes the House of Commons, 297–257.	Egypt severs diplomatic relations with Cyprus for its handling of a Palestinian guerrilla hijacking at Larnaca airfield.... U.S. State Dept. announces that the U.S. will deliver equipment worth a total of $1 million to Ethiopia, which is part of a $40 million deal concluded before U.S.–Ethiopian cooperation terminated in 1977.	Amnesty International reports that Guatemalan death squads have killed or kidnapped at least 113 people for political reasons in the last four months of 1977.... Twenty-two political prisoners in Sao Paulo are reported charging that prisoners are still being tortured in Brazilian jails.	Japan rejects a bid from Soviet Pres. Leonid Brezhnev for a peace and cooperation treaty.
Feb. 23	U.S. dollar hits a new record low against the West German mark and the Swiss franc and posts sharp declines against the British pound and the French franc.... The price of gold hits $183.20 an ounce on the London exchange, its highest close in nearly four years.			Canada's 10 provincial premiers agree to guarantee freedom of choice in the language of education for school children in their provinces.	

A	B	C	D	E
Includes developments that affect more than one world region, international organizations and important meetings of major world leaders.	Includes all domestic and regional developments in Europe, including the Soviet Union, Turkey, Cyprus and Malta.	Includes all domestic and regional developments in Africa and the Middle East, including Iraq and Iran and excluding Cyprus, Turkey and Afghanistan.	Includes all domestic and regional developments in Latin America, the Caribbean and Canada.	Includes all domestic and regional developments in Asia and Pacific nations, extending from Afghanistan through all the Pacific Islands, except Hawaii.

U.S. Politics & Social Issues	U.S. Foreign Policy & Defense	U.S. Economy & Environment	Science, Technology & Nature	Culture, Leisure & Life Style	
Pres. Carter attends a Bangor, Me. town meeting on a two-day tour of New England. He endorses the ERA, but says he does not favor using federal funds for abortions except as the result of rape or incest.		Commerce Dept. reports that housing starts declined a record 29 percent during January because of crippling weather conditions.	Alice Stewart, an epidemiologist at the University of Birmingham, England, says that her study of workers at the Hanford Nuclear Plant (Wash. State) reveals a cancer death rate of 5 percent more than for the general population.		Feb. 17
Former UMW pres. W.A. (Tony) Boyle is convicted in Media, Pa. on three counts of first-degree murder in the 1969 slayings of union rival Joseph Yablonski and Yablonski's wife and daughter. His first conviction, in 1974, was set aside by the Pennsylvania Supreme Ct. in 1977 because of judicial error.		Pres. Carter warns that he will take drastic action if the coal strike is not settled.			Feb. 18
				On the Twentieth Century, a musical by Betty Comden and Adolph Green based on earlier plays, and starring Madeline Kahn, opens on Broadway.	Feb. 19
Pres. Carter attends a Democratic Party fund-raising dinner in Wilmington, Del. for Sen. Joseph Biden Jr., who is running for a second term.		AFL–CIO executive council outlines its economic stimulus proposals, recommending only about $5 billion more than the $24.5 billion proposed by Pres. Carter, but differing in its emphasis on direct-spending programs over tax cuts.			Feb. 20
Supreme Ct. declines to rule (and so leaves standing) a U.S. Circuit Ct. of Appeals decision that the University of Missouri cannot refuse to recognize Gay Lib, a student homosexual group, as an official campus organization.	At a secret Senate session, Sen. Robert Dole (R,Kan.) is believed to testify that he has documents implicating relatives of Panamanian Head of State Brig. Gen. Omar Torrijos in narcotics trafficking.			At London's Round House, the Liverpool Playhouse's British production of David Rabe's American drama *Streamers* opens.	Feb. 21
	Carter administration says it will reduce foreign military assistance by almost 10 percent in fiscal 1979. ... Opponents of the Panama Canal treaties in the Senate are defeated on a procedural motion that might have reduced the treaties' chances of ratification.	IBM rejects a proposed merger with CBS Inc.	Hal Borland, 77, writer and conservationist, who also wrote nature editorials for *The New York Times*, dies of emphysema in Sharon, Conn.	Phyllis McGinley, 72, writer of light verse and 1961 Pulitzer Prize winner, dies in N.Y.C.	Feb. 22
After saying earlier that he would give Pres. Carter a grade of "C minus" for his first years in office, AFL–CIO pres. George Meany itemizes Carter's shortcomings as follows: lacking strong leadership with Congress; reneging on campaign promises to take a liberal, bold approach to problems; and intervening in the coal strike too late.		In an EPA report on 105 urban areas, only Honolulu, Hawaii and Spokane, Wash. meet all five federal air quality standards.		Grammy Awards are presented to The Eagles (best record) and Fleetwood Mac (best album). "Evergreen " and "You Light Up My Life " tie for best song. Barbra Streisand receives two awards and Debby Boone, daughter of singer Pat Boone, is named best new artist.	Feb. 23

F	G	H	I	J
Includes elections, federal-state relations, civil rights and liberties, crime, the judiciary, education, health care, poverty, urban affairs and population.	*Includes formation and debate of U.S. foreign and defense policies, veterans' affairs and defense spending. (Relations with specific foreign countries are usually found under the region concerned.)*	*Includes business, labor, agriculture, taxation, transportation, consumer affairs, monetary and fiscal policy, natural resources, and pollution.*	*Includes worldwide scientific, medical and technological developments, natural phenomena, U.S. weather, natural disasters, and accidents.*	*Includes the arts, religion, scholarship, communications media, sports, entertainments, fashions, fads and social life.*

	World Affairs	Europe	Africa & the Middle East	The Americas	Asia & the Pacific
Feb. 24		A book, *Autobiography of Federico Sanchez* , by purged Spanish CP member Jorge Semprun reportedly sharply criticizes the party and its secretary general, Santiago Carrillo.	PLO leader Yasir Arafat accuses Egyptian Pres. Anwar Sadat of anti-Palestinian propaganda, a statement seen as reflecting PLO fears that Sadat might withdraw Egyptian recognition of the PLO as the only legitimate representative of the Palestinian people.	Chilean govt. claims that it has no record of the existence of the two suspects sought by the U.S. Justice Dept. for the killing of Orlando Letelier in Wash., D.C.	Bangkok sources report that Laotian troops shot to death a Laotian woman and her two daughters on the Laotian side of the Thai–Laotian border after the Thais had driven them back as part of a government forced repatriation of refugees policy.
Feb. 25	U.S. warns the Soviet Union that their relations will suffer if Soviet intervention in the Horn of Africa — the Ethiopian–Somalian dispute over the Ogaden region — continues. . . . In issuing its warning, the U.S. is responding to a previous-day speech by Soviet Pres. Leonid Brezhnev, in which he blames the U.S. for SALT and trade agreement stagnations.			Canada's Liberal Party's biennial convention focuses on the economy over the question of Quebec separation.	The Congress Party faction of former P.M. Indira Gandhi wins control of two of five states in Indian legislative assembly elections.
Feb. 26	The Soviet Union charges that the U.S. has premeditatively distorted the Ethiopian situation.		Israeli Cabinet decides to retain its limited policy to establish settlements in the Sinai Peninsula and the West Bank. . . . Final results of Senegal's presidential elections show incumbent Pres. Leopold Sedar Senghor to be the winner with 82 percent of the votes cast.	Speaking from a bullet-proof glass booth at a Managua rally, Nicaraguan Pres. Anastasio Somoza Debayle pledges a series of political, social, and economic reforms. Following the speech. protestors shout for his resignation.	
Feb. 27		Swiss voters approve a referendum giving the government power to take action against unemployment and inflation.	In response to the assassination of Youssef el-Sebai by two Palestinian terrorists in Cyprus and the subsequent shoot-out at the Cyprus airport, Egypt announces withdrawal of special privileges granted to the 30,000 Palestinians living in Egypt.	Colombia's ruling Liberal Party easily wins in yesterday's federal, state, and municipal elections, but three-quarters of the country's 12.3 million voters abstained from casting their ballots.	U.S. and Taiwan agree to limit Taiwan's export of textiles and apparel goods to the U.S. during the next five years in a pact similar to one recently executed by the U.S. with Hong Kong and South Korea.
Feb. 28		Six-member European Free Trade Assn. (EFTA) agrees not to increase the amount of steel it exports to the EEC in 1978.		Indians in Masaya continue to attack Nicaraguan soldiers, while students in Leon burn buses and build barricades to block traffic.	Chinese CP newspaper and news agency publicize cases of human-rights violations in the country with the indication that the abuses will be corrected. . . . Chinese govt. announces the fall reopening of graduate schools in history, law, religion, philosophy, literature, and economics — all of which were closed by the Cultural Revolution.
March 1		Turkish govt. of Premier Bulent Ecevit devalues the lire by 23 percent, its first major devaluation since 1971.	A delegation representing Christian churches in Israel visits Rome seeking Vatican support for repeal of a controversial Israeli law that the group contends implies that Christians are bribing Jews to convert.	Chile and Argentina begin negotiations in Santiago to resolve their long-standing dispute over the Beagle Channel. . . . Canadians are permitted access to personal files that the government might keep on them, including income tax, drug, civil-service employment, and prison.	
March 2	Former Australian Governor General Sir John Kerr resigns as Australian delegate to UNESCO following criticism of his appointment within Australia.	*Wall Street Journal* reports that the Soviet Union has canceled an order for 305,000 metric tons of wheat because of shipping delays by the U.S.	The National Front for the Liberation of Angola (FNLA) reports a mounting Cuban death toll in guerrilla warfare in the southern half of Angola. It also notes that the FNLA has executed over 30 Cuban officers.	U.S. officials are reported saying that the Carter administration is prepared to break relations with Chile if Chile holds back information on the Orlando Letelier murder case.	

A	B	C	D	E
Includes developments that affect more than one world region, international organizations and important meetings of major world leaders.	Includes all domestic and regional developments in Europe, including the Soviet Union, Turkey, Cyprus and Malta.	Includes all domestic and regional developments in Africa and the Middle East, including Iraq and Iran and excluding Cyprus, Turkey and Afghanistan.	Includes all domestic and regional developments in Latin America, the Caribbean and Canada.	Includes all domestic and regional developments in Asia and Pacific nations, extending from Afghanistan through all the Pacific Islands, except Hawaii.

U.S. Politics & Social Issues	U.S. Foreign Policy & Defense	U.S. Economy & Environment	Science, Technology & Nature	Culture, Leisure & Life Style	
		Pres. Carter announces a tentative settlement of the 81-day coal strike and appeals directly to the miners over prime-time TV to approve the settlement.	A derailed Louisville & Nashville Railroad Co. tanker car carrying liquid propane gas explodes in a ball of fire in Waverly, Tenn., killing 12 people and injuring 50 others. The blast destroys an entire block of downtown Waverly.	Washington Redskins football team names Bob Beatherd as general manager.	Feb. 24
			Soviet nuclear physicist Artemi Alikhanian, who pioneered during the 1930s and early 1940s in identification of atom particles and the study of cosmic rays, dies at the age of 69 in Yerevan, U.S.S.R.		Feb. 25
Portia Pittman, 94, daughter of black educator Booker T. Washington, dies in Washington, D.C. She was choir director at Tuskegee Institute, Ala. for 25 years.				Ira Levin's thriller *Deathtrap*, with John Wood and Marian Seldes, opens on Broadway.	Feb. 26
Supreme Ct. rules, 7–2, that the government can reduce federal welfare benefits for someone moving from the U.S. to Puerto Rico.		State Secy. Vance argues against protectionism in a speech before the National Governors' Assn., which is meeting in Wash., D.C.	Pentagon reports that as a result of its toll-free hot-line, 13,000 people had phoned to report having been present at atomic tests and that 241 of those said they now have cancer.		Feb. 27
		National Governors's Assn. closes its three-day Washington, D.C. meeting by adopting a resolution on water policy.	FDA approves use of an anticonvulsant drug, sodium valproate, for controlling epilepsy.	South Africa's top singles tennis player, Ray Moore, withdraws from the Davis Cup team because of the controversy surrounding his country's apartheid policy.	Feb. 28
		Postal Service selects William Bolger to succeed Benjamin Bailar as postmaster general.		*Timbuktu* !, an all-black cast version of *Kismet* transported from Arabia to Africa, opens on Broadway.	March 1
Pres. Carter submits a plan to revise the federal civil service system, allowing more flexibility for merit advancement, transfers, and firings.		OSHA imposes its heaviest fine to date — $228,700 — against Texaco Inc. for safety violations leading to the deaths of eight workers in a March 1977 fire and explosion in Port Arthur, Tex.	A patent is granted to General Electric Co. for gene-altered bacteria it has developed in its laboratories.	The coffin containing the body of comic actor Charlie Chaplin, who died in 1977, is stolen from a Swiss cemetery.	March 2

F	G	H	I	J
Includes elections, federal-state relations, civil rights and liberties, crime, the judiciary, education, health care, poverty, urban affairs and population.	*Includes formation and debate of U.S. foreign and defense policies, veterans' affairs and defense spending. (Relations with specific foreign countries are usually found under the region concerned.)*	*Includes business, labor, agriculture, taxation, transportation, consumer affairs, monetary and fiscal policy, natural resources, and pollution.*	*Includes worldwide scientific, medical and technological developments, natural phenomena, U.S. weather, natural disasters, and accidents.*	*Includes the arts, religion, scholarship, communications media, sports, entertainments, fashions, fads and social life.*

	World Affairs	Europe	Africa & the Middle East	The Americas	Asia & the Pacific
March 3		P.M. James Callaghan attacks opposition Conservative Party leader Margaret Thatcher's use of the immigration issue prior to British by-elections, saying it is a call to a prejudice-fear mixture.	Rhodesian P.M. Ian Smith and black leaders Abel Muzorewa, Ndabaningi Sithole, and Jeremiah Chirau sign an agreement to transfer power to the country's black majority by Dec. 31, 1978. Under the agreement, Smith will retain the title of prime minister, but the council of state chairmanship will rotate among the four members.... Jordan is reported freeing about 1,000 Palestinian political prisoners.		
March 4		Dutch Defense Min. Roelof Kruisinga resigns after a split with other Cabinet members over the government's position on the neutron bomb.	Israeli Premier Menahem Begin is reported informing the U.S. that he disagrees with the Carter administration's view that U.N. Security Council Resolution 242 requires Israel to withdraw from at least parts of the West Bank and Gaza Strip.		
March 5		A second bomb in two days explodes in Turin, Italy, believed to be targeted at Christian Democratic lawyer Roberto Manni and motivated by the upcoming trial of the leaders of the terrorist Red Brigades.	Ahmed Kaid, 57, Algerian freedom fighter who was exiled in 1975, dies in Rabat, Morocco.		Hua Kuo-feng is reappointed as Chinese premier at the last session of the National People's Congress, a move that surprises observers expecting that he would be replaced by First Deputy Premier Teng Hsiao-ping.
March 6	U.N. Human Rights Commission adopts a resolution stating that despite a decline in the number of political prisoners and reports of torture in Chile, the government's abuse of human rights is still systematic and institutionalized.	Yugoslav Pres. Josip Broz Tito begins an official visit to the U.S., seen as a move to emphasize the need for closer relations between the two countries.	Rhodesian groups report killing 38 guerrillas after crossing into Zambia. It is the first time that the government officially acknowledges a raid into Zambia.... Israeli Defense Min. Ezer Weizman threatens to resign over Premier Begin's policy on establishing settlements in occupied Arab areas, thereby blocking, for the time being, any further building of new settlements.	Chilean govt. announces full cooperation with the U.S. investigation of the murder of Orlando Letelier, the former Chilean foreign minister.	
March 7		Rumanian Pres. Nicolae Ceausescu dismisses Cornel Burtica and Ilie Verdet from the Political Executive Committee and the Central Committee of the Rumanian CP.	Israeli Premier Menahem Begin receives a letter from 300 Israeli army reservists that says his hardline stance on retaining West Bank and Gaza Strip occupied territories threatens peace.... Spokespeople for Dar es Salaam University announce the university's expulsion of several hundred students, including Emmy Nyerere, a son of the Tanzanian president, following their March 5 participation in an illegal demonstration against pay increases for government officials.		Indian P.M. Morarji Desai denounces India's annexation of Sikkim in 1975, but says he cannot undo the action.... Text of a new Chinese Constitution, adopted March 5, is released. It gives economic development priority over revolutionary ideology.
March 8		Cypriot Pres. Spyros Kyprianou names a new Cabinet for his full five-year term. It is larger than the one he inherited from the late Pres. Abp. Makarios.	Abu Sayed, a leading member of the radical Popular Front for the Liberation of Palestine, is killed in a machine gun and hand grenade attack by unknown assassins on the Beirut–Damascus highway in eastern Lebanon.	Bank of Canada announces it is increasing its lending rate to 8 percent from 7.5 percent.... Canada announces new immigration regulations establishing a point system for evaluating applicants.	
March 9	Patriotic Front guerrilla leaders Robert Mugabe and Joshua Nkomo denounce the internal Rhodesian majority rule pact before the U.N. Security Council.	W. Ger. Bundestag approves a law giving the legislature power to oversee operation of the intelligence services.	Israeli opposition Labor Party leaders, including former Premiers Yitzhak Rabin and Golda Meir, assail Premier Begin's position on U.N. Resolution 242.... Somalia announces that it has ordered its troops to withdraw from Ethiopia's Ogaden area.	Nicaraguan Sandinistas issue a communique saying that Reynaldo Perez Vega, the country's top military aide, was killed the day before when he resisted abduction, and charges him with having led the repression in Masaya.	

A	B	C	D	E
Includes developments that affect more than one world region, international organizations and important meetings of major world leaders.	Includes all domestic and regional developments in Europe, including the Soviet Union, Turkey, Cyprus and Malta.	Includes all domestic and regional developments in Africa and the Middle East, including Iraq and Iran and excluding Cyprus, Turkey and Afghanistan.	Includes all domestic and regional developments in Latin America, the Caribbean and Canada.	Includes all domestic and regional developments in Asia and Pacific nations, extending from Afghanistan through all the Pacific Islands, except Hawaii.

U.S. Politics & Social Issues	U.S. Foreign Policy & Defense	U.S. Economy & Environment	Science, Technology & Nature	Culture, Leisure & Life Style	
		Senate confirms G. William Miller as FRB chairman on a voice vote, after Sen. William Proxmire (D, Wis.) cast the only dissenting vote the day before in a Senate Banking Committee recommendation.	CAB approves Super-Saver fare plans for 15 airlines.	Twenty of the 26 baseball major league owners issue a statement saying they will not participate in any effort to dismiss baseball comr. Bowie Kuhn, in wake of Kuhn's refusal to allow the sale of Oakland A's pitcher Vida Blue to the Cincinnati Reds.	March 3
Ariz. Gov. Wesley Bolin (D) dies of an apparent heart attack. Atty. Gen. Bruce Babbitt (D) is sworn in to succeed him.	*The New York Times* reports that the Pentagon intends to seek repeal of legislation that bans the use of women in combat.	*Chicago Daily News*, the city's only afternoon newspaper, ceases publication. It had reportedly lost $21.7 million since 1974, and its circulation had dropped to 329,000 from a high of 614,000 in 1957.	Soviet cosmonauts Lt. Col. Yuri Romanenko and Georgi Grechko break the record of 84 days, one hour, and 17 minutes held by the U.S. for continuous time in space.		March 4
			National Weather Service declares an official end to the two-year drought that plagued parts of the U.S.	The musical *Hello, Dolly!*, with its original star, Carol Channing, is revived on Broadway as part of a trend toward reviving musicals in face of the mounting production costs and risks of new and untried shows.	March 5
A study conducted by William Bowers of Northeastern University finds that murderers of blacks are far less likely to be sentenced to death than murderers of whites. . . . Richard Speck, convicted of killing eight young nurses in 1966, admits that he was responsible for killing seven of the eight.	Defense Dept. study reported in *The New York Times* holds that the U.S. leads the Soviet Union in 15 of 32 key weapons and weapons-related systems.	Pres. Carter invokes the Taft-Hartley Act in an effort to end the 91-day coal strike by UMW members after miners vote by more than a 2–1 margin to reject ratification of a tentative contract. . . . Supreme Ct. upholds a ruling that federal law preempts state law on oil tanker regulation.		Larry Flynt, owner of the sexually explicit magazine *Hustler*, is shot on a Lawrenceville, Ga. street while returning to the state court where he is being tried for distributing obscene material.	March 6
	Pres. Carter signs a supplemental appropriations bill that rescinds $462 million appropriated in fiscal 1977 to build two B-1 bombers.	Pres. Carter signs a $7.8 billion fiscal 1978 supplemental appropriations bill, which includes funds for sewage treatment plants, SBA disaster loans, and heating-bill aid for low-income households.		An exhibition of works by 20 avant-garde Soviet artists opens in Moscow after a three-day delay.	March 7
Henry Wriston, 88, educator who was president of Brown University (1937–55), a principal in the 1954 reorganization of the U.S. Foreign Service, and chairman of the Presidential Commission on National Goals in 1960, dies in N.Y.				Hugh Leonard's Irish play, *Da*, opens in a showcase Off-off-Broadway production with Barnard Hughes in the title role.	March 8
	Carter administration begins intensely courting four Democratic senators considered to be swing votes on the Panama Canal treaties ratification — Herman Talmadge (Ga.), Sam Nunn (Ga.), Russell Long (La.), and Dennis DeConcini (Ariz.).	Procter & Gamble Co. reduces the wholesale price of its Folger-brand roasted coffee to $3.03 for a one-pound can. . . . Federal District Ct. Judge John Fullam, accepts a reorganization plan for the bankrupt Penn Central Co.		Charles Tickner wins the men's singles world figure-skating championship in Ottawa, Canada.	March 9

F	G	H	I	J
Includes elections, federal-state relations, civil rights and liberties, crime, the judiciary, education, health care, poverty, urban affairs and population.	Includes formation and debate of U.S. foreign and defense policies, veterans' affairs and defense spending. (Relations with specific foreign countries are usually found under the region concerned.)	Includes business, labor, agriculture, taxation, transportation, consumer affairs, monetary and fiscal policy, natural resources, and pollution.	Includes worldwide scientific, medical and technological developments, natural phenomena, U.S. weather, natural disasters, and accidents.	Includes the arts, religion, scholarship, communications media, sports, entertainments, fashions, fads and social life.

	World Affairs	Europe	Africa & the Middle East	The Americas	Asia & the Pacific
March 10	Amnesty International sponsors a two-day session, held in Athens, Greece, on torture and the medical profession.... Britain and the U.S. reportedly disagree over the Rhodesian internal settlement plan.	Moscow announces revoking the citizenship of former Gen. Pyotr Grigorenko, who is on a six-month visit to the U.S.	South Africa desegregates its theaters and opera houses, but keeps its movie houses segregated.	Pres. Joaquin Balaguer and leaders of the Dominican Republic's opposition Dominican Revolutionary Party agree to sign a nonaggression pact to guarantee a peaceful campaign for the May 16 presidential election.	
March 11		Italy's Christian Democrat caretaker premier, Giulio Andreotti, forms a new Cabinet with formal parliamentary support from the CP, who will now have a voice in policy-making.	In an Al Fatah guerrilla assault on the Haifa–Tel Aviv road, 35 Israeli civilians are killed.	Chile's three-and-a-half-year state of siege ends.	
March 12			Israeli accounts of the Al Fatah raid on Israel describe how the gunmen came ashore from two rubber boats and shot to death their first victim, an American woman identified as Gail Rubin, 39, a photographer and relative of U.S. Sen. Abraham Ribicoff (D, Conn.).		
March 13		Three South Moluccan terrorists enter a government building in Assen, the Netherlands and seize 71 employes as hostages, killing one during the attack.... Press reports indicate that a March 10–11 meeting between Greek and Turkish Premiers Constantine Caramanlis and Bulent Ecevit helped establish mutual confidence.	After postponing his trip to Washington, scheduled for today, Israeli Premier Menahem Begin issues a second warning against the PLO and accuses the Soviet Union of complicity in the March 11 Al Fatah attack.... Most Arab reaction to the Al Fatah attack on Israel is laudatory.	Guatemalan Congress names Gen. Romeo Lucas Garcia president-elect after determining that no candidate won more than 50 percent of the votes in the March 5 presidential election.	
March 14	U.N. Security Council votes to reject the Rhodesian majority rule settlement that was reached by P.M. Ian Smith and three moderate black leaders. The five Western members of the council abstain. ... Foreign exchange dealers are reported to be disappointed with a joint plan devised by the U.S. and West Germany to stabilize the dollar.	A special antiterrorist unit of Dutch marines storms a government building in Assen to free 70 hostages who had been held by three South Moluccan terrorists, wounding six of the hostages.... The General Confederation of Italian Labor, representing over half of Italy's labor force, votes unanimously to break with the Moscow-oriented World Federation of Trade Unions.	Blacks, Asians, and coloreds (mixed-race) establish the first interracial non-white party in South Africa, the South African Black Alliance, led by KwaZulu chief Gatsha Buthelezi.... Egyptian Pres. Anwar Sadat condemns the Al Fatah attack in Israel as irresponsible and is especially critical of the fact that Israeli civilians were its target.... Israeli ground, air, and sea forces launch a major attack against guerrilla bases and other PLO centers in Lebanon, retaliating to a Palestinian Al Fatah guerrilla assault three days before.	A riot in a prison in the outskirts of Buenos Aires, Argentina reportedly kills 55 inmates and injures 78.	Cambodian troops, assisted by naval forces, cross into Vietnam and occupy a small strip of land on the Gulf of Siam.
March 15		Portuguese govt. submits a stringent austerity budget to the National Assembly.... Soviet Union charges that the Royal Canadian Mounted Police fabricated espionage charges against a Soviet official.	Major fighting ends as the Israelis announce that they have established a security buffer in southern Lebanon after capturing major PLO strongholds there. Defense Min. Ezer Weizman says that he hopes that Syria will understand that the action is limited.... Many Palestinian and Lebanese civilians pour into Beirut to flee Israeli bombings of refugee camps in southern Lebanon where civilian casualties are reportedly heavy.		Australia announces that it will admit 2,000 Indochinese refugees by June, bringing to 9,000 the number admitted since the 1975 fall of the South Vietnamese govt.... Japan announces a series of measures to stabilize its economy and curb the rising value of the yen.

A	B	C	D	E
Includes developments that affect more than one world region, international organizations and important meetings of major world leaders.	Includes all domestic and regional developments in Europe, including the Soviet Union, Turkey, Cyprus and Malta.	Includes all domestic and regional developments in Africa and the Middle East, including Iraq and Iran and excluding Cyprus, Turkey and Afghanistan.	Includes all domestic and regional developments in Latin America, the Caribbean and Canada.	Includes all domestic and regional developments in Asia and Pacific nations, extending from Afghanistan through all the Pacific Islands, except Hawaii.

U.S. Politics & Social Issues	U.S. Foreign Policy & Defense	U.S. Economy & Environment	Science, Technology & Nature	Culture, Leisure & Life Style	
			Netherlands and the U.S. agree on a pact to liberalize bargain-fare air service between the two countries. ... Pres. Carter signs a bill to impose new and stricter controls on the export of nuclear technology and fuel to prevent the spread of nuclear weapons.	*The New York Times* reports evidence of renewed religious activity in China for the first time since the Cultural Revolution, citing small religious groups holding Sunday church services and other activities by Roman Catholics, Protestants, and Buddhists.	March 10
	Citibank, the second largest U.S. bank, says it has halted all loans to the South African govt. and government-owned corporations.			*Fast Fantasy* for cello and piano, composed by Charles Wuorinen as a birthday present for cellist Fred Sherry, is performed for the first time in Chicago by Sherry.	March 11
Labor Dept. takes issue with assertions by Westchester County, N.Y. leaders that it failed to certify applicants adequately for CETA jobs currently under investigation by Westchester District Atty. Carl Vergari, who charges "pervasive corruption" throughout the $24-million program.				Boston, Mass. postpones its annual St. Patrick's Day parade because of a large snow accumulation from its severe winter.	March 12
	In a *Wall Street Journal* interview, Sen. Abraham Ribicoff (D, Conn.) assails Israeli Premier Menahem Begin's policies and the so-called pro-Israel lobby in Washington. ... U.S. Rep. Silvio Conte (R, Mass.) calls for the release of Jacobo Timerman, a former Argentinian newspaper publisher who has been held without trial in Argentina since April 1977.	A Taft-Hartley Act return-to-work order for striking coal miners goes into effect after it was issued on March 9 (partially because of a Justice Dept. slip-up). Almost all striking miners defy the order.			March 13
	Pres. Carter is reported using political horse-trading, making a large concession, and personally approaching individual senators to win ratification of the Panama Canal treaties. His wife, Rosalynn, telephones the wife of Sen. Edward Zorinsky (D, Neb.) to seek her help in persuading her husband to vote for the treaty.	On the ninety-ninth day of the coal strike, coal industry and UMW negotiators reach agreement on terms of a new contract. ... Interior Secy. Cecil Andrus accepts a gift of 16,600 acres in Georgia to be added to the Okefenokee National Wildlife Refuge. The land is donated by Union Camp Corp. and valued at $6.6 million.	FDA revokes its 1975 regulation that prevented using claims of hypoallergenic on cosmetic labels unless scientific studies showed the product caused fewer adverse reactions than a competitive product.	Coca-Cola Co. signs an agreement with the Soviet Union to make Coca-Cola the official soft drink at the 1980 Moscow Olympics.	March 14
According to *The New York Times*, the FBI is beginning to destroy files in its field offices on criminal cases that have been closed for five or more years.	House International Relations subcommittee releases summaries of reports by U.S. intelligence agents that indicate South Korean Pres. Park Chung Hee's personal involvement in the Korean lobbying effort.	A federal ban is announced against fluorocarbon aerosol sprays, linked with depletion of the ozone layer that protects Earth from the Sun's harmful ultraviolet rays. ... Demonstrating farmers release 73 goats on the Capital steps in Washington, D.C.	N.M. District Judge J.T. Hensley awards up to $75,000 to Ramos Martinez, who claimed that his employment at the Los Alamos Scientific Laboratory had given him a neurotic and disabling fear that he would die from nuclear radiation. ... Jeremy Stone, Federation of American Scientists director, attributes strong atmospheric booms that have been heard on the East Coast in recent months to the supersonic Concorde.	Soviet Union rescinds the citizenships of composer-cellist-conductor Mstislav Rostropovich and his wife, soprano Galina Vishnevskaya, who have been living abroad on a temporary Soviet travel visa since 1974. ... Oakland A's pitcher Vida Blue is traded to the San Francisco Giants just minutes before the close of the inter-league trading deadline.	March 15

F	G	H	I	J
Includes elections, federal-state relations, civil rights and liberties, crime, the judiciary, education, health care, poverty, urban affairs and population.	Includes formation and debate of U.S. foreign and defense policies, veterans' affairs and defense spending. (Relations with specific foreign countries are usually found under the region concerned.)	Includes business, labor, agriculture, taxation, transportation, consumer affairs, monetary and fiscal policy, natural resources, and pollution.	Includes worldwide scientific, medical and technological developments, natural phenomena, U.S. weather, natural disasters, and accidents.	Includes the arts, religion, scholarship, communications media, sports, entertainments, fashions, fads and social life.

	World Affairs	Europe	Africa & the Middle East	The Americas	Asia & the Pacific
March 16		Former Italian Premier Aldo Moro is kidnapped in Rome by left-wing terrorists in a bloody shootout that kills his five-man team of bodyguards as he is driving to a special session of Parliament.... Anonymous telephone callers identify the kidnappers as members of the Red Brigades, Italy's most active left-wing terrorist group.	The U.S. suggests that Israel withdraw from the Lebanese territory it captured in yesterday's military action and its troops be replaced by an international peacekeeping force.... Diplomatic sources in Ethiopia report that Cuban troops are fighting secessionist guerrillas in the Ethiopian province of Eritrea.	Panamanian govt. indicates it will accept the Panama Canal Neutrality Treaty amendments and the reservations that Pres. Carter agreed to include to ensure its ratification by the U.S. Senate.... Renny Ottolina, a popular Venezuelan TV personality and presidential candidate, is presumed to have died when a small airplane in which he was traveling is lost off Venezuela's coast.	Cambodia calls for negotiations with Vietnam to end their conflict.
March 17	U.N. Security Council unanimously condemns a Rhodesian attack on Zambian guerrilla bases, which took place earlier this month.	Both houses of the Italian Parliament confirm the new minority Christian Democratic govt., led by Premier Giulio Andreotti, by a massive vote of confidence.... One hundred thousand people attend funeral services for the five bodyguards killed in Rome, Italy, in wake of the kidnapping of Aldo Moro.	Zaire executes eight army officers and five civilians for plotting to overthrow Pres. Mobutu Sese Seko.	Canadian federal govt. charges Peter Worthington and Douglas Creighton, editor and publisher respectively of the *Toronto Sun*, with violating the Official Secrets Act by publishing information on Soviet espionage in Canada.... Bolivia breaks diplomatic ties with Chile because of an impasse in their negotiations on an outlet for Bolivia to the Pacific Ocean.	
March 18		Italy's political and religious leaders — and some radicals who often support the Red Brigades — condemn the kidnapping of Aldo Moro.	Syria grants transit rights to Arab states wishing to funnel troops or supplies to PLO forces fighting Israelis in Lebanon.... Arabs in the Israeli-occupied West Bank stage protests against the Israeli invasion of Lebanon.		Lahore High Ct. convicts and sentences to death former Pakistani P.M. Zulfikar Ali Bhutto on charges of ordering the murder of a political opponent.
March 19	U.N. Security Council votes, 12–0, to approve a U.S. resolution calling on Israel to withdraw from southern Lebanon and establishing a 4,000-man U.N. unit to enforce a cease-fire in that region.	Contrary to political and opinion-poll predictions, the French govt. coalition of moderate and conservative parties retains its hold over Parliament.... A two-day demonstration to protest the abduction of former Italian Premier Aldo Moro draws hundreds of thousands protesters.	Richard Moose, U.S. assistant state secy. for African affairs, signs an agreement to provide Somalia with $7 million worth of food relief over a six-month period.		Cambodian Premier Pol Pot reiterates his opposition to Vietnam's alleged plan for an Indochinese federation of Vietnam, Cambodia, and Laos.
March 20	Soviet Union reports that China has rejected its offer to discuss improving relations.	British Conservative Party study group, headed by former P.M. Sir Alec Douglas-Home, proposes an extensive reorganization of the House of Lords.... The Italian CP pledges to support antiterrorist proposals.	Defense Min. Ezer Weizman claims victory in Israel's limited foray into southern Lebanon, with Israel completely controlling the area up to the Litani River with the exception of the port city of Tyre.		Australian govt. reports a sharp drop in the country's unemployment rate in February to 6.7 percent, compared with 7.2 percent in January.
March 21		Italian Cabinet announces a series of anticrime measures to fight the increasingly bold activities of terrorist groups as well as conventional criminals.... Cearbhall O Dalaigh, 67, president of the Republic of Ireland from December 1974 until his October 1976 resignation, dies of an apparent heart attack in Sneem, Ireland.	In a ceremony marking the implementation of an internal plan to transfer power to Rhodesia's black majority by the end of the year, P.M. Ian Smith, Bishop Abel Muzorewa, Rev. Ndabaningi Sithole, and Chief Jeremiah Chirau are sworn in as members of the transitional government's state council.... Israel, in apparent compliance with a U.N. resolution, declares a unilateral truce in southern Lebanon.	A commission of Argentinian Roman Catholic bishops reportedly asks Pres. Jorge Videla to free all prisoners who have not been tried. ... Maxwell Yalden, Canadian commissioner of official languages, tells Parliament that federal govt. efforts toward bilingualism have been poor.... Chile's former secret police chief, Gen. Manuel Contreras Sepulveda, resigns as head of the army's engineering command and adviser to Pres. Augusto Pinochet Ugarte.	National Assembly elects Premier Chiang Ching-kuo as president of Nationalist China.

A	B	C	D	E
Includes developments that affect more than one world region, international organizations and important meetings of major world leaders.	Includes all domestic and regional developments in Europe, including the Soviet Union, Turkey, Cyprus and Malta.	Includes all domestic and regional developments in Africa and the Middle East, including Iraq and Iran and excluding Cyprus, Turkey and Afghanistan.	Includes all domestic and regional developments in Latin America, the Caribbean and Canada.	Includes all domestic and regional developments in Asia and Pacific nations, extending from Afghanistan through all the Pacific Islands, except Hawaii.

U.S. Politics & Social Issues	U.S. Foreign Policy & Defense	U.S. Economy & Environment	Science, Technology & Nature	Culture, Leisure & Life Style	
Carter administration proposes the first major revision of drug regulation laws in 40 years, seen as an expansion of FDA powers.	U.S. Senate votes, 68–32, to ratify the Treaty Concerning the Permanent Neutrality and Operation of the Panama Canal, the first of the two treaties that guarantees neutrality of the canal after it is turned over to Panama at the end of 1999.	House passes, 257–152, the Humphrey–Hawkins bill setting the target unemployment rate at 4 percent from its current 6.1 percent level within five years of the bill's enactment. . . . House Majority Leader Jim Wright (D, Tex.) says the bill embodies what America stands for.	Soviet cosmonauts Yuri Romanenko and Georgi Grechko descend safely to Earth in their Soyuz 27 capsule after spending 96 days in space and setting a new space endurance record.		March 16
Former Rep. Richard Hanna pleads guilty to one count of fraud conspiracy, a plea bargain with the Justice Dept. on charges stemming from the Korean influence-peddling investigation. . . . *The New York Times* reports that the CIA hired American blacks to spy on the Black Panther Party in the U.S. and abroad.		Carter administration presents legislation to reduce the interim between licensing and building an atomic power plant from the current 10–12 years to about six-and-a-half years.	The supertanker *Amoco Cadiz* , carrying a full load of 1.6 million barrels of crude oil, breaks in two on rocks in heavy seas off the coast of Brittany, France. . . . The first U.S. laboratory to be approved as safe for conducting genetic recombination experiments deemed to be hazardous opens in Frederick, Md.	Thousands of demonstrators converge on Nashville, Tenn. during the tennis Davis Cup North American Zone final matches between the U.S. and South Africa to protest apartheid.	March 17
				World Boxing Council withdraws recognition of Leon Spinks as heavyweight champion and gives the title to Ken Norton, charging that Spinks had violated an agreement with the WBC to give his first title defense to Norton.	March 18
		Former OMB Dir. Bert Lance, and nine other investors in a Wash., D.C. bank-holding company, settle a civil complaint filed the previous day by the SEC.		Faith Baldwin, 84, popular author of about 85 books of light fiction, dies in Norwalk, Conn. . . . U.S. Davis Cup team defeats South Africa in North American Zone finals competition.	March 19
Leaders of the ERA movement reportedly have asked Congress to extend the time limit for ratification beyond the seven-year deadline and have asked conventions to continue to boycott states that have not ratified the amendment. . . . A House coalition of Republicans, conservative Democrats, and big-city Democrats rebuffs an attempt to get a quick vote of support for the Carter administration's proposal to expand the federal grant program to aid college students from middle-class families.	Supreme Ct. rules that the VA can restrict the type of educational courses for which veterans' benefits are available. . . . Just prior to a statute of limitations expiration, the Justice Dept. files felony charges against ITT executives Edward Gerrity Jr. and Robert Berrellez, accused of lying about ITT's clandestine attempts to prevent the election of Marxist Salvador Allende as president of Chile in 1970.	Supreme Ct. declines to review a decision upholding a United Air Lines regulation requiring a stewardess to take an unpaid maternity leave of at least seven months when she learns she is pregnant.	FDA clears the use of DMSO (dimethyl sulfoxide) for use in interstitial cystitis, which is an irritated bladder condition.		March 20
Supreme Ct. rules, 8–0, that public school students suspended without a hearing cannot collect more than one dollar in damages unless they can prove they have been harmed by their suspension. . . . Rep. John Anderson, third-ranking Republican in The House, wins renomination to a tenth term from Illinois's Sixteenth Congressional District, rebuffing a challenge by a conservative evangelical minister, Rev. Don Lyon.	House International Relations subcommittee releases documents, dated 1971 and 1972, that indicate that high officials of the Nixon administration were aware of the Korean lobbying efforts.	Senate passes, 67–26, a bill incorporating three different aid programs for farmers, despite strong criticism by Senate Budget Committee Chmn. Edmund Muskie (D, Me.)		Violinist Ani Kavafian is the first recipient of the newly established Philip M. Faucett String Prize. . . . Argentinian security police reportedly have seized 60 Jehovah's Witnesses in Mar del Plata.	March 21

F	G	H	I	J
Includes elections, federal-state relations, civil rights and liberties, crime, the judiciary, education, health care, poverty, urban affairs and population.	*Includes formation and debate of U.S. foreign and defense policies, veterans' affairs and defense spending. (Relations with specific foreign countries are usually found under the region concerned.)*	*Includes business, labor, agriculture, taxation, transportation, consumer affairs, monetary and fiscal policy, natural resources, and pollution.*	*Includes worldwide scientific, medical and technological developments, natural phenomena, U.S. weather, natural disasters, and accidents.*	*Includes the arts, religion, scholarship, communications media, sports, entertainments, fashions, fads and social life.*

	World Affairs	Europe	Africa & the Middle East	The Americas	Asia & the Pacific
March 22	French Pres. Valery Giscard d'Estaing announces that he is departing from previous policy set by the governments of Charles deGaulle and Georges Pompidou and is contributing troops to the U.N. interim peacekeeping force in Lebanon to demonstrate France's fidelity to its traditional links with Lebanon.		A 100-man vanguard of the U.N. force, comprised mainly of Iranians, arrives in Lebanon. Israel announces it will pull out shortly. ... Israeli–U.S. differences on an approach to a Middle East settlement remain unresolved as Israeli Premier Begin concludes a two-day visit to the U.S.		Pres. Suharto is unanimously reelected by the Indonesian People's Consultative Assembly to a third five-year term as president of Indonesia. ... The U.S., United Arab Emirates, Turkey, and Libya are among the nations reported seeking a repeal of former Pakistani P.M. Zulfikar Ali Bhutto's death sentence.
March 23	British P.M. James Callaghan, meeting with Pres. Carter in Washington to discuss the world trade situation, expresses concern about the industrial nations' lack of economic unity.		Richard Moose, U.S. assistant state secy., concludes talks with Somali Pres. Mohamed Siad Barre on prospects for U.S. aid, after a six-day visit to improve relations in wake of Somalia's defeat in the war for Ethiopia's Ogaden region.		
March 24		Dogan Oz, an assistant public prosecutor in Ankara, Turkey, is shot and killed by a political right-wing extremist.	Syria and the Lebanese govt. announce a ban on shipping arms and volunteers to PLO forces in southern Lebanon.		
March 25					Former Pakistani P.M. Zulfikar Ali Bhutto appeals his death sentence to the Pakistan Supreme Ct.
March 26	Chinese govt. says that talks with Moscow cannot be held while Soviet troops remain stationed on the Chinese border.	Hundreds of thousands rally in Spain's major Basque cities in the first celebration of the Basque national day since 1939, when it was abolished by Generalissimo Francisco Franco. ... Kidnappers release Baron Edouard-Jean Empain, one of the most powerful industrialists in Europe, who had been seized in France from a main Paris thoroughfare on Jan. 23.	Israeli Cabinet unanimously endorses Premier Menahem Begin's proposals for a Middle East peace settlement.	Chilean air force cmdr. Gen. Gustavo Leigh Guzman reportedly is privately criticizing Pres. Augusto Pinochet's authoritarianism and publicly calling for a rapid return to civilian rule.	Japanese demonstrators opposing the opening of Tokyo's new international airport seize and destroy the control tower during clashes with the police.
March 27			Israeli Defense Min. Ezer Weizman indicates that his troops will break their self-imposed ceasefire if the PLO continues to shell Israeli positions in southern Lebanon and Israeli towns along the Israeli-Lebanese border. ... Gunmen kill Namibian black leader Chief Clemens Kapuuo in a black township outside of Windhoek.		Pakistani leader Gen. Muhammad Zia ul-Haq says that most of the international appeals on Bhutto's behalf were based on personal relationships.
March 28	Bank of Japan purchases $1 billion in U.S. currency in an effort to halt the rise of the yen.		At its semiannual council meeting, the Arab League announces agreement on the necessity of convening an Arab summit conference, and it extends for another six months its peacekeeping force in Lebanon. ... PLO leader Yasir Arafat promises to grant all facilities to the U.N. Interim Force in Lebanon (UNIFIL) to carry out its mission. Two PLO member groups — Popular Front for the Liberation of Palestine and the Popular Democratic Front — pledge to keep fighting.	Pres. Carter, accompanied by his top foreign policy advisers, his wife, Rosalynn, and his daughter, Amy, begins a four-nation visit to Latin America in his effort to strengthen U.S. relations with developing countries.	Laotian military forces, assisted by Vietnamese troops, are reported battling a number of resistance groups, including Meo tribal guerrillas. ... Japanese govt. postpones opening the new Tokyo international airport in face of two-day violent demonstrations, which resulted in 165 arrests and scores more injured.

A	B	C	D	E
Includes developments that affect more than one world region, international organizations and important meetings of major world leaders.	Includes all domestic and regional developments in Europe, including the Soviet Union, Turkey, Cyprus and Malta.	Includes all domestic and regional developments in Africa and the Middle East, including Iraq and Iran and excluding Cyprus, Turkey and Afghanistan.	Includes all domestic and regional developments in Latin America, the Caribbean and Canada.	Includes all domestic and regional developments in Asia and Pacific nations, extending from Afghanistan through all the Pacific Islands, except Hawaii.

U.S. Politics & Social Issues	U.S. Foreign Policy & Defense	U.S. Economy & Environment	Science, Technology & Nature	Culture, Leisure & Life Style	
Supreme Ct. rules unanimously that an Indian can be tried for statutory rape in federal court despite being convicted on related charges in a tribal court.... Pres. Carter pledges to further women's rights in a meeting with a delegation from the National Women's Conference, which was held in Houston, Tex. in November 1977.		Berkey Photo Inc. wins one of the largest damage awards in history in its civil antitrust suit against Eastman Kodak Co.... President's Council on Wage and Price Stability warns that the farm-aid bill, if enacted, would be extremely inflationary.	*Amoco Cadiz*, a tanker which hit rocks off the coast of Brittany, France, leaks between 1.1 million and 1.2 million barrels of oil into the sea, almost twice the amount leaked by the previous record oil spill by a tanker in 1967.	Karl Wallenda, 73, German-born leader of a famous high-wire performing troupe that worked without nets, dies of injuries resulting from a 10-story fall from a cable strung between two hotels in San Juan, Puerto Rico.	March 22
Rep. Charles Diggs (D, Mich.) is indicted by a federal grand jury on 35 felony counts involving an alleged kickback scheme along with illegitimate payments totaling over $101,000 between 1973 and 1977.... Pres. Carter signs an executive order requiring federal regulations to be written in "plain English."		Consolidated Rail Corp. reports a net loss of $76.8 million for the fourth quarter of 1977, bringing the total loss in 1977 to $366.6 million.			March 23
	Carter administration announces that it plans to procure less than half of the 156 U.S. Navy ships proposed in a five-year plan inherited from the Ford administration.			Buffalo Bills of the NFL trade superstar running back O.J. Simpson to the San Francisco 49ers for five high draft picks.... Moslems are reported to be the second largest religious group in France, twice the number of Protestants and three times the number of Jews.	March 24
Anthony (Tony Pro) Provenzano is convicted of conspiring to arrange a $300,000 kickback on a $2.3-million loan from a Teamsters union pension fund.		UMW and Bithuminous Coal Operators Assn. representatives sign a new three-year contract and so end a 110-day strike by 160,000 soft-coal miners, the longest in the coal industry's history.		UCLA defeats the University of Maryland, 90–74, to win the AIAW basketball championship.	March 25
		NLRB administrative law judge Joel Harmatz declares that the Amalgamated Clothing and Textile Workers Union is the bargaining representative for 1,000 employes at J.P. Stevens & Co. in Wallace, N.C.			March 26
Pres. Carter unveils his urban-aid plan. Its provisions include eliminating conflicting federal regulations and procedures, creating a national development bank, providing a $3-billion public works project, giving direct financing to neighborhood self-help groups, and providing tax incentives for businesses.	U.S. State Dept. calls the internal Rhodesian settlement illegal and inadequate.	Pres. Carter signs a bill to expand Redwood National Park in northern California by 48,000 acres.	Hope is abandoned of salvaging some of the oil from the wrecked supertanker *Amoco Cadiz*, which hit reefs off the Brittany coast.	Bob Fosse's creation *Dancin '*, a revue that is a showcase for Fosse's dance vocabulary, opens on Broadway.... The NCAA basketball championship is won by the University of Kentucky, beating Duke University, 94–88.	March 27
	Defense Dept. reports that McDonnell Douglas Corp. was the top U.S. defense contractor for fiscal 1977.				March 28

F	G	H	I	J
Includes elections, federal-state relations, civil rights and liberties, crime, the judiciary, education, health care, poverty, urban affairs and population.	Includes formation and debate of U.S. foreign and defense policies, veterans' affairs and defense spending. (Relations with specific foreign countries are usually found under the region concerned.)	Includes business, labor, agriculture, taxation, transportation, consumer affairs, monetary and fiscal policy, natural resources, and pollution.	Includes worldwide scientific, medical and technological developments, natural phenomena, U.S. weather, natural disasters, and accidents.	Includes the arts, religion, scholarship, communications media, sports, entertainments, fashions, fads and social life.

	World Affairs	Europe	Africa & the Middle East	The Americas	Asia & the Pacific
March 29	Japan ceases its massive support of the U.S. dollar, allowing it to sink to yet another of its post-war lows.	Copies of a letter believed to have been written by former Italian Premier Aldo Moro, kidnapped in a bloody shootout, are delivered to newspapers in Rome and Geneva.	Israeli Knesset votes approval of Premier Begin's Mideast peace policies, 64–32, in wake of the opposition's moves to censure him because of his sharp disagreement with Pres. Carter during talks in Washington, March 21–22.	Pres. Carter receives a correct but chilly welcome in Brazil that reflects tensions between the two countries concerning human rights and nuclear nonproliferation.	
March 30		Police spokesmen suggest that Aldo Moro had been drugged or intimidated by his captors before writing letters asking that the Italian govt. submit to their demands.			
March 31		Raymond Barre is reappointed premier of France to head the new center-right coalition government.	Israeli Defense Min. Ezer Weizman leaves Cairo after two days of talks to try to revive the stalled peace negotiations. Egyptian Pres. Sadat comments that both countries remain deadlocked.	The English-language newspaper, *Buenos Aires Herald*, charges that Argentina is fomenting a policy of religious persecution unparalleled in its history in face of arrests on March 21 and 29 of members of the religious Jehovah's Witnesses sect, which had been outlawed in 1976 for refusing to salute the flag or join the armed forces.	India launches a drive toward total prohibition of alcoholic beverages by 1981.
April 1	Pravda replies negatively to a Chinese govt. condition that Soviet troops be withdrawn from the Chinese border before the two nations can hold talks on improving relations.	Press reports indicate that Pres. Carter is reversing his policy on Cyprus because of Turkish Premier Bulent Ecevit's threats to withdraw from NATO if U.S. arms aid to Turkey is not renewed.	Nine Syrian soldiers and three Syrian civilians are killed by an Israeli mine on the Golan Heights. . . . After arriving in Lagos, Nigeria the day before, Pres. Carter calls for a Cuban military withdrawal from Africa and the establishment of majority rule in South Africa and Rhodesia.		New Zealand's abortion law takes effect despite liberal groups' protests that it is the most restrictive legislation of its kind in the world.
April 2			While in Nigeria, Pres. Carter tells reporters that the U.S. and Britain are trying to arrange a meeting on the foreign-minister level of all parties in the Rhodesian dispute over majority rule transition. He proposes that participants would include representatives from the U.S., Great Britain, Patriotic Front guerrillas, P.M. Ian Smith's govt., front-line states, and if possible, the U.N.		
April 3	IMF announces changing its method of setting a value for the Special Drawing Right (SDRs), its monetary standard that serves as a kind of international money and which was created in 1969 to alleviate a shortage of gold and reserve currencies.	U.S. Amb. to the U.S.S.R. Malcolm Toon issues an unusually blunt warning that U.S.–Soviet relations could be damaged by the treatment of Anatoly Shcharansky, a Soviet dissident charged with and jailed for treason. . . . British Broadcasting Corp. (BBC) broadcasts the first of a planned series of House of Commons debates on radio. A previous 1975 attempt was stopped after listeners complained about the strong language used in the parliamentary exchanges.	Pres. Carter's Rhodesian proposal is angrily denounced by the African National Council and the United African National Council, two of the three Rhodesian black groups that have formed an interim govt. with Ian Smith.		EEC signs a five-year trade pact with China, its first with a Communist country (excepting ones with Yugoslavia and Rumania).

A	B	C	D	E
Includes developments that affect more than one world region, international organizations and important meetings of major world leaders.	*Includes all domestic and regional developments in Europe, including the Soviet Union, Turkey, Cyprus and Malta.*	*Includes all domestic and regional developments in Africa and the Middle East, including Iraq and Iran and excluding Cyprus, Turkey and Afghanistan.*	*Includes all domestic and regional developments in Latin America, the Caribbean and Canada.*	*Includes all domestic and regional developments in Asia and Pacific nations, extending from Afghanistan through all the Pacific Islands, except Hawaii.*

U.S. Politics & Social Issues	U.S. Foreign Policy & Defense	U.S. Economy & Environment	Science, Technology & Nature	Culture, Leisure & Life Style	
Supreme Ct. rules, 5–4, that cities can be sued for damages under federal antitrust law unless they are granted special protection by their state legislatures.		Pres. Carter acts to reduce the nation's wheat, corn, and cotton crops and thereby raise farm income $4 billion a year. It is a move seen as his first significant concession to militant farmers, led by the loosely organized American Agriculture Movement.		A Rolling Stones musical, *Let the Good Stones Roll*, opens in London.	March 29
Veteran civil-rights activist Bayard Rustin criticizes Pres. Carter's urban-aid plan as inadequate.... Atty. Gen. Griffin Bell says in an interview that he will consider easing secrecy contracts signed by government employes if federal courts decide that the government has the right to enforce these contracts.					March 30
	Former Rep. Otto Passman (D, La.) is indicted by a federal grand jury on charges of accepting $98,000 in bribes or illegal gratuities from South Korean businessman Park Tong Sun.	Commerce Dept. reports the worst monthly trade deficit in U.S. history during February when imports surpassed exports by a seasonally adjusted $4.52 billion.... Financially troubled American Motors Corp. (AMC) and French auto maker Renault Co. announce tentative plans for joint production and distribution.	Dr. Charles Best, 79, physician and co-discoverer of insulin treatment for diabetes, dies in Toronto, Canada.		March 31
					April 1
				Mary Simpson becomes the first woman Anglican priest to preach at Westminster Abbey as she begins a five-week tour of Great Britain to help advocates of female ordination in the Church of England.... Martina Navratilova completes her domination of the women's indoor tennis tour by winning the Virginia Slims championship over Evonne Goolagong, 7–6, 6–4, in the final match.	April 2
	In his first public testimony, Korean businessman Park Tong Sun tells an open session of the House Committee on Standards of Official Conduct (the ethics committee) that he has given a total of $850,000 in gifts and campaign contributions to U.S. politicians.	Supreme Ct. lets stand a lower court decision that upholds the FTC's power to require companies to correct false advertising claims. ... Bowing to presidential pressure, U.S. Steel Corp reduces its previously announced price increase of $10.50 a ton to $5.50 a ton.	Supreme Ct. rules, 7–0, that federal courts do not have the authority to circumvent government regulations on building nuclear power plants, specifically backing Nuclear Regulatory Commission procedures.	Woody Allen's *Annie Hall* gets the Oscar for best film and Allen wins Oscars for its original screenplay and for directing it. Diane Keaton receives the best-actress award, Richard Dreyfuss is best actor; Vanessa Redgrave best supporting actress, and Jason Robards Jr. best supporting actor. *Star Wars* wins seven awards.... A vandal with a knife slashes to pieces the seventeenth-century art masterpiece *Adoration of the Golden Calf* by Nicolas Poussin at the National Gallery in London, England.	April 3

F	G	H	I	J
Includes elections, federal-state relations, civil rights and liberties, crime, the judiciary, education, health care, poverty, urban affairs and population.	*Includes formation and debate of U.S. foreign and defense policies, veterans' affairs and defense spending. (Relations with specific foreign countries are usually found under the region concerned.)*	*Includes business, labor, agriculture, taxation, transportation, consumer affairs, monetary and fiscal policy, natural resources, and pollution.*	*Includes worldwide scientific, medical and technological developments, natural phenomena, U.S. weather, natural disasters, and accidents.*	*Includes the arts, religion, scholarship, communications media, sports, entertainments, fashions, fads and social life.*

	World Affairs	Europe	Africa & the Middle East	The Americas	Asia & the Pacific
April 4					
April 5		About 15 million workers in Spain, Italy, Greece, and Belgium participate in an Action Day walkout called by the European Trade Union Confederation to protest rising unemployment.		Chilean Pres. Augusto Pinochet announces that all civilian prisoners convicted by military courts will be pardoned or allowed to serve out their sentences in exile. The amnesty does not clarify the number of political prisoners in Chile or the whereabouts of civilians who have disappeared in the last few years.	
April 6			French govt. sources confirm that approximately 150 French military advisers have been sent to help Chad fight rebels who control much of the country's northern region.		
April 7	Soviet Union charges that Carter's decision to defer production of the neutron bomb does not indicate a significant renunciation of it. NATO Secy. Gen. Joseph Luns issues a low-keyed statement expressing understanding for the U.S. decision to postpone production.... Soviet Pres. Leonid Brezhnev blames delay in SALT negotiations on U.S. indecision and inconsistency.		U.N. peacekeeping forces come under the first major attack since the start of their mission in southern Lebanon.... In a trial considered to be one of the most important terrorist trials in South Africa since the sentencing of African National Council (ANC) leader Nelson Mandela in 1964, six black activists receive prison terms for plotting to overthrow the South African govt.		Amidst charges of fraud, Philippines Pres. Ferdinand Marcos's ruling New Society Movement wins control of the 200-seat interim National Assembly in the first nationwide elections since Marcos imposed martial law in 1972.
April 8	Gypsy delegates from 25 countries meet in Geneva to seek an end to discrimination against Gypsies and to press for official status from the U.N.	The family of former Italian Premier Aldo Moro, a kidnap victim of the terrorist Red Brigades, begins a campaign to challenge the government policy against bargaining for his release.	A decree is issued giving Marthinus Steyn, South Africa's administrator general for Namibia, the power to order the indefinite detention of anyone suspected of threatening security in wake of the assassination of Chief Clemens Kapuuo.	Chile deports Michael Townley, a suspect in the murder of former For. Min. Orlando Letelier in Wash., D.C. on the excuse that he once entered Chile using false documents.	
April 9	Chase World Information Corp. reports that the Arab petroleum-exporting countries have sharply increased their aid to developing countries since they quadrupled their oil prices in 1973 and have disbursed funds at the rate of $5 billion a year.		Fighting erupts in Beirut, Lebanon between Christian militiamen and Lebanese Moslems.		
April 10			The Xhosa Republic of the Transkei, the black homeland declared independent by South Africa in 1976, breaks its relations with South Africa, leaving it without diplomatic representation anywhere in the world.	Mariana Callejas de Townley, wife of Michael Townley who was deported two days ago from Chile, charges that the Chilean junta has betrayed her husband, who, she claims, was working for the Chilean government.... Canadian Finance Min. Jean Chretien introduces the fiscal 1979 budget, which includes tax cuts.	Thai Communist rebels, operating from neighboring Cambodia, are reported widening their control of the frontier area of Thailand.

A	B	C	D	E
Includes developments that affect more than one world region, international organizations and important meetings of major world leaders.	Includes all domestic and regional developments in Europe, including the Soviet Union, Turkey, Cyprus and Malta.	Includes all domestic and regional developments in Africa and the Middle East, including Iraq and Iran and excluding Cyprus, Turkey and Afghanistan.	Includes all domestic and regional developments in Latin America, the Caribbean and Canada.	Includes all domestic and regional developments in Asia and Pacific nations, extending from Afghanistan through all the Pacific Islands, except Hawaii.

U.S. Politics & Social Issues	U.S. Foreign Policy & Defense	U.S. Economy & Environment	Science, Technology & Nature	Culture, Leisure & Life Style	
A $22-million damage suit brought by syndicated columnist Jack Anderson against former Pres. Richard Nixon and some of his aides is dismissed by U.S. District Ct. Judge Gerhard Gesell because Anderson refused to disclose information sources.	The New York Times reports that Pres. Carter has decided not to produce the neutron bomb in the U.S. The White House and the State Dept. deny the report.			The Dutch Reformed Church of South Africa breaks away from its mother church, the Dutch Reformed Church of the Netherlands, because of the latter's vote to support the antiapartheid platform of the World Council of Churches, which includes a fund to support black liberation movements in southern Africa.	April 4
	Former CIA director George Bush testifies before the Senate Select Committee on Intelligence that some U.S. intelligence sources are drying up because foreign services don't believe that the U.S. Congress can keep secrets.... Pres. Carter names Gen. David C. Jones, Air Force chief of staff, to chair the Joint Chiefs of Staff when current chairman, Air Force Gen. George Brown retires on July 1.	Hongkong & Shanghai Banking Corp, a British bank based in Hong Kong, agrees to acquire Marine Midland Banks Inc. a Buffalo, N.Y.-based bank holding company. If approved, the takeover will be one of the largest in U.S. banking history.		Mormons install Wallace Smith as their sixth president at the church's headquarters in Independence, Mo. He succeeds his father, W. Wallace Smith, 78, who becomes president emeritus.	April 5
	Members of Congress, including Sen. Sam Nunn (D, Ga.), Senate Majority Leader Robert Byrd (D, W. Va.), and Minority Leader Howard Baker (R, Tenn.), criticize Pres. Carter's decision against neutron bomb production.				April 6
N.Y.C. implements its decisions to drop its controversial system of assigning teachers on the basis of race, which was instituted in September 1977.	After several days of public furor centering on apparent indecisiveness within the administration, Pres. Carter announces that he has decided to stop production of the neutron bomb.			A Gutenberg Bible is sold at auction in N.Y.C. for $2 million, the highest price ever paid for a printed book.... A three-judge panel in Chicago upholds the power of Baseball Comr. Bowie Kuhn to regulate player transactions.	April 7
	A Wash., D.C. federal jury convicts Hancho Kim, a Korean-born U.S. citizen, of conspiring to bribe members of Congress and of lying to a grand jury about his activities.			Ford Frick, 83, commissioner of baseball (1951–65) and president of the National League for 17 years, dies following a stroke in Bronxville, N.Y.	April 8
				NHL concludes its regular hockey season with 12 of its 18 teams qualifying for the playoffs. The Montreal Canadiens, the defending NHL champions, dominate the season and become the first team in NHL history to win the Prince of Wales, Art Ross, and Vezina trophies for three consecutive seasons.	April 9
Former FBI Dir. L. Patrick Gray III, Mark Felt, and Edward Miller, the two latter both former high-ranking FBI officials, are indicted on charges of conspiring to violate the civil rights of U.S. citizens during a three-year investigation by the Justice Dept. of suspected illegal activities by the FBI. The charges are connected to a plan to locate members of the radical anti-Vietnam War group Weathermen that included illegal break-ins and searches.	Michael Townley is arraigned in Washington and held without bail as a material witness in the murders of former Chilean For. Min. Orlando Letelier and his colleague Ronni Moffitt, who were killed in Washington in September 1976 by a bomb explosion under their car.	American Petroleum Institute survey reports that proven reserves of U.S. oil declined by the end of 1977 almost 1.5 billion barrels than the previous year. American Gas Association estimates are reported to place proven natural gas reserves down to 209 trillion cubic feet at the end of 1977 from 216 trillion cubic feet a year earlier.		National Book Awards go to Mary Lee Settle (fiction); Gloria Emerson (contemporary thought); Walter Jackson Bate (biography); David McCullough (history); Howard Nemerov (poetry); Judith and Herbert Kohl (children's literature); and Richard and Clara Winston (translation). S.L. Perelman, the author–humorist, receives a special medal.	April 10

F	G	H	I	J
Includes elections, federal-state relations, civil rights and liberties, crime, the judiciary, education, health care, poverty, urban affairs and population.	Includes formation and debate of U.S. foreign and defense policies, veterans' affairs and defense spending. (Relations with specific foreign countries are usually found under the region concerned.)	Includes business, labor, agriculture, taxation, transportation, consumer affairs, monetary and fiscal policy, natural resources, and pollution.	Includes worldwide scientific, medical and technological developments, natural phenomena, U.S. weather, natural disasters, and accidents.	Includes the arts, religion, scholarship, communications media, sports, entertainments, fashions, fads and social life.

	World Affairs	Europe	Africa & the Middle East	The Americas	Asia & the Pacific
April 11		Cyprus govt. announces arresting 22 people accused of subversion.	South African P.M. John Vorster tells Parliament that he regrets the break in relations with Transkei over land claims but says it is an independent state and can do what it pleases.... Israeli forces begin the first part of a two-phase pullback from their forward positions in southern Lebanon.	Miguel Tobias Padilla, an Agentinian Economy Ministry aide, is shot to death by left-wing terrorists in Buenos Aires. The assassination is interpreted as a warning by the Montoneros that they are still active in face of a government statement on March 27 that armed subversion had been wiped out.	Chinese broadcasts link the ousted Gang of Four to various miscarriages of justice, persecutions, and espionage.... Indonesia announces that it will free all but 200–300 of its remaining 20,000 political prisoners by the end of 1979.
April 12		West German Chancellor Helmut Schmidt says that West Germany had agreed in January to deploy the neutron bomb and warns the U.S. that misunderstandings are straining relationships between the two countries.	Sudanese Pres. Mohammed Gaafar el-Nimeiry signs a reconciliation pact with members of a right-wing exiles' coalition that had staged several unsuccessful coups against him.	Chilean Pres. Augusto Pinochet names four new civilian ministers, giving the Cabinet its first civilian majority since the 1973 military coup that overthrew Pres. Salvador Allende.... Argentine federal police admit still holding 232 of some 700 "missing persons" after the government had released the names of 158 untried prisoners three days before.	India recognizes former P.M. Indira Gandhi's breakaway Congress Party – I as the official opposition party to the Indian govt.... Cambodia reports that it has repulsed a Vietnamese attack into its territory the previous week and has killed 560 of the invaders.
April 13	In a joint communique issued at the end of talks in Washington, Pres. Carter and Rumanian Pres. Nicolae Ceausescu call for a Middle East peace settlement based on Israeli withdrawal from occupied Arab territory, respect for Israel's security and sovereignty, and respect for the Palestinians' legitimate rights.	Mileta Perovic, a pro-Moscow opponent of Yugoslav Pres. Tito, is sentenced to 20 years in prison on charges of seeking to place Yugoslavia under foreign influences.	Four days of fighting end in a truce in Lebanon, leaving 102 people killed and 294 wounded. At least five Syrian soldiers of the Arab League peacekeeping force are reported among those dead.... Polisario Front guerrillas, fighting for independence in the former Spanish Sahara, claim to have killed more than 400 Moroccan and Mauritanian troops.		Chinese CP newspaper *Jenmin Jih Pao* reports that over 10,000 Shanghai purge victims of the ousted Gang of Four have been rehabilitated, some posthumously.... Moslem rebels ambush a bus on southern Mindanao island in the Philippines, killing 30 civilian workers and 13 soldiers who were on the bus to protect the workers.
April 14		Turkish Cypriot negotiators in Vienna present U.N. Secy. Gen. Kurt Waldheim with proposals for determining Cyprus's future government.... British P.M. James Callaghan's Labor Party wins a by-election in Scotland despite a strong challenge from the Scottish Nationalist Party.... In the U.S.S.R. Georgia citizens demonstrate and force authorities to reinstate the Goergian language as the official language of the republic.	A new 18 member Council of Ministers is sworn in to replace the Cabinet of the white Rhodesian govt.	Rapidly growing opposition to the Panama Canal treaties within Panama reportedly stems from a reservation, written by U.S. Sen. Dennis DeConcini (D, Ariz.), that allows the U.S. to send troops into Panama if the canal closes for any reason after the year 2000.	
April 15		Founders of the Ulster Peace Movement in Northern Ireland, including Betty Williams and Mairead Corrigan — who won the 1976 Nobel Peace Prize — announce resigning their leadership, saying that other members should have a turn.	Patriotic Front leader Robert Mugabe rejects the concept of allowing outside representatives to assume power during a Rhodesian govt. transition. He also rejects a multiparty democracy as a luxury and asserts that the new state should have a one-party Marxist govt.		
April 16			Iranian govt. announces smashing a Soviet spy ring and arresting retired Iranian Brig. Gen. Ali Akbar Darakhshani, 85, who subsequently died in detention.... Israeli Cabinet issues a statement reaffirming its position that U.N. Security Council Resolution 242 remains the basis for negotiating a peace settlement with the Arab states and insists that the document does not apply to Israeli withdrawal from the West Bank and Gaza Strip.		

A	B	C	D	E
Includes developments that affect more than one world region, international organizations and important meetings of major world leaders.	Includes all domestic and regional developments in Europe, including the Soviet Union, Turkey, Cyprus and Malta.	Includes all domestic and regional developments in Africa and the Middle East, including Iraq and Iran and excluding Cyprus, Turkey and Afghanistan.	Includes all domestic and regional developments in Latin America, the Caribbean and Canada.	Includes all domestic and regional developments in Asia and Pacific nations, extending from Afghanistan through all the Pacific Islands, except Hawaii.

U.S. Politics & Social Issues	U.S. Foreign Policy & Defense	U.S. Economy & Environment	Science, Technology & Nature	Culture, Leisure & Life Style	
N.Y.S. Gov. Hugh Carey vetoes a bill to restore capital punishment in the state, saying that "official killing" is not a legitimate exercise of government.		Pres. Carter unveils his antiinflation program in a speech to the American Society of Newspaper Editors. He names Robert Strauss to coordinate the deceleration program in industry and labor.... Pres. Carter rules out mandatory wage and price controls for the private sector, but announces pay increase limits for federal employes and pay freezes for White House aides and high-level officials in the executive branch.		World Hockey Association finishes its season with six of its eight teams making the playoffs. The Winnipeg Jets top the league.	April 11
The Chicago, Ill. school board adopts a controversial school desegregation plan that depends on voluntary cooperation and thereby conflicts with the Illinois Board of Education requirement for compulsory desegregation.	David Graiver, an Argentine financier reported dead in 1976 after allegedly looting two banks in N.Y. and Brussels, is indicted on embezzling charges by a N.Y. federal ct., and U.S. Attorney Robert Morgenthau says there is reason to believe that he is still alive.	A CBS News–New York Times poll finds public approval of Pres. Carter's economic policy falling to a new low, with only 32 percent of those polled approving. The disapproval rate has climbed to 54 percent from 30 percent in one year.		A national study comparing black and white women's attitudes and lifestyles finds many similarities, but a divergence in attitude toward the women's liberation movement, which offends many black women who must work from necessity.	April 12
J. Wallace LaPrade, an assistant FBI director, charges that the administrations of Pres. Carter and former Pres. Gerald Ford had made political attempts to influence FBI investigations and claims that indictments against him and other officials for investigations of the radical Weathermen are part of that campaign.	During Pres. Nicolae Ceausescu's Washington visit with Pres. Carter, Rumanian exiles and human-rights activists picket the White House to protest alleged Rumanian human-rights violations.... Sources quoted by the Wall Street Journal say that Argentine financier David Graiver might be in hiding behind the Iron Curtain.	A stock rally begins with the Dow-Jones Average closing at 775.21.	New Scientist reports observations indicating a black hole at the center of the giant galaxy M87.	N.Y.S. Lt. Gov. Mary Anne Krupsak announces an elaborate financial plan to save Radio City Music Hall (N.Y.C.), known for its art deco design, the Rockettes dancing troupe, and the Music Hall Symphony.	April 13
Carter administration presents its proposal for a Cabinet-level department of education to Congress.	U.S. authorities seize two Cuban exiles in Miami, Fla. who are believed to be involved in the 1976 murder of Chilean For. Min. Orlando Letelier in Wash., D.C.	The price of the Japanese-made Toyota , top-selling auto import in the U.S., is raised for the sixth time in 12 months.... CAB proposes that air fares be deregulated by as much as 50 percent without government approval.		The Seoul Sejong Cultural Center formally opens in Seoul, South Korea.... F.R. Leavis, 82, British literary critic and author who gained wide notice in a scathing 1963 debate with novelist C.P. Snow, dies in Cambridge, England.	April 14
A report released by the Office of Population Research, Princeton University, finds that 1960s fertility rates among U.S. married white women have dropped drastically to 2.2 children, but that the decline was considerably greater among Catholics.				The New York Times notes that former U.S. Air Force officer Dr. Kenneth Cooper is known as the originator of the current jogging fad, and it also notes the growth of the jogging apparel industry in the U.S.	April 15
	Gen. Lucius Clay (ret.), 80, commander of the U.S. forces in Europe and post-WWII military governor of Germany who ordered the successful 1948–49 airlift to West Berlin, dies of emphysema in Chatham, Mass.	The stock market's rally reportedly hits a peak of frenzy with 63.5 million shares changing hands and the Dow Jones Average rising another 14.99 points. The two-day surge is unprecedented in Wall Street history.		International Tennis Federation bars South Africa from competing for either the Davis Cup or its women's counterpart, the Federation Cup, with a February 1, 1979 deadline to form a multiracial organization for administering the game.	April 16

F	G	H	I	J
Includes elections, federal-state relations, civil rights and liberties, crime, the judiciary, education, health care, poverty, urban affairs and population.	Includes formation and debate of U.S. foreign and defense policies, veterans' affairs and defense spending. (Relations with specific foreign countries are usually found under the region concerned.)	Includes business, labor, agriculture, taxation, transportation, consumer affairs, monetary and fiscal policy, natural resources, and pollution.	Includes worldwide scientific, medical and technological developments, natural phenomena, U.S. weather, natural disasters, and accidents.	Includes the arts, religion, scholarship, communications media, sports, entertainments, fashions, fads and social life.

	World Affairs	Europe	Africa & the Middle East	The Americas	Asia & the Pacific
April 17	British For. Secy. David Owen and U.S. State Secy. Vance end five days of talks with principals in the Rhodesian majority rule dispute without success in reopening talks between the Patriotic Front guerrilla coalition and the interim Rhodesian govt.	Greek Parliament passes a law requiring a mandatory death penalty for terrorist acts that result in loss of life. . . . Italian CP calls on the government to maintain its resolve not to capitulate to the demands of the terrorists who hold former Premier Aldo Moro.	Ghana's official news agency announces that 17 opponents of the country's military govt. have been arrested, including former Cabinet members of the civilian govt., which was overthrown in a bloodless 1972 coup. . . . Work resumes on a new Israeli settlement in the West Bank.	Jacobo Timerman, a former newspaper publisher who has been widely seen as a symbol of Argentinian human-rights abuse and anti-Semitism, is freed from jail one year after his arrest for unspecified economic crimes related to the Graiver guerrilla-financing scandal. He remains under house arrest.	Indian P.M. Morarji Desai confirms a previously published report in the U.S. that an American nuclear-powered spy device had been lost in the Himalayas in 1965.
April 18		An alleged message from the captors of former Italian Premier Aldo Moro says he has been executed after a people's trial, but is a hoax.		Panamanian Pres. Omar Torrijos hails U.S. ratification of the Panama Canal Treaty but adds that Panama would have resorted to violent liberation of the Canal Zone if the treaty had not been ratified.	
April 19	At the end of a two-day meeting in Denmark, defense ministers of the Nuclear Planning Group, a NATO committee, approve the U.S. decision to delay production of the neutron bomb, but stress modernizing NATO's nuclear weapons and keeping open the option of introducing neutron weapons in Europe.	Cypriot Pres. Spyros Kyprianou rejects the Turkish plan as marking the beginning of the end for Cyprus. . . . Former Soviet Gen. Pyotr Grigorenko is granted U.S. asylum one day after requesting permission to remain in the U.S. after the Soviet govt. revoked his citizenship while he was on a six-month personal visit.	Lebanese govt. resigns in wake of sectarian fighting. Premier Selim al-Hoss agrees to remain as a caretaker until he is replaced.		Chhang Song, information minister in the previous Cambodian govt., charges in a Washington news conference that a Holocaust is occuring in Cambodia, claiming that 1 million Cambodians have been slaughtered and another million appear to have perished from disease and starvation.
April 20		French National Assembly approves the new Cabinet of Premier Raymond Barre and also Barre's continued austerity measures. . . . An authentic message from the Red Brigades says that Aldo Moro is still alive and includes a photograph of him holding a newspaper dated April 19. It claims earlier messages were hoaxes and proposes to exchange him for imprisoned Communists.	U.N. Secy. Gen. Kurt Waldheim, reporting on a two-day visit to inspect U.N. peacekeeping forces in Lebanon, says that Israeli Premier Menahem Begin has assured him that Israeli troops will withdraw completely from southern Lebanon, and that he (Waldheim) will seek to increase the number of UNIFL troops there.		
April 21		The text of a previously announced Turkish plan for Cyprus is released. It calls for two separate states — a Greek and Turkish state each with its own legislature and army — and a weak central government linking them.			Pres. Carter charges that the Cambodian govt. is the worst violator of human rights in the world today.
April 22		In an apparent terrorist attack, five Alfa Romeo car showrooms in Milan, Italy are firebombed. . . . Osman Orek is named premier of the Turkish Cypriot legislative body.	Mozambique Pres. Samora Machel reorganizes his Cabinet for the first time since the country became independent in 1975.		
April 23	State Secy. Cyrus Vance reports some progress in SALT talks as a result of his Moscow visit on April 20–22. . . . The twenty-sixth Bilderberg Conference, held in Lawrence Township, N.J., concludes with more than 100 prominent North American and European leaders attending.	Pope Paul VI makes a personal plea for Aldo Moro's release by his terrorist kidnappers.	A committee of 13 Christian and Moslem Lebanese Parliament leaders draw up a national accord for the restoration of the Lebanese govt.'s authority in southern Lebanon and implementation of the U.N. Security Council resolution for the withdrawal of Israeli forces in the region.		

A	B	C	D	E
Includes developments that affect more than one world region, international organizations and important meetings of major world leaders.	Includes all domestic and regional developments in Europe, including the Soviet Union, Turkey, Cyprus and Malta.	Includes all domestic and regional developments in Africa and the Middle East, including Iraq and Iran and excluding Cyprus, Turkey and Afghanistan.	Includes all domestic and regional developments in Latin America, the Caribbean and Canada.	Includes all domestic and regional developments in Asia and Pacific nations, extending from Afghanistan through all the Pacific Islands, except Hawaii.

U.S. Politics & Social Issues	U.S. Foreign Policy & Defense	U.S. Economy & Environment	Science, Technology & Nature	Culture, Leisure & Life Style	
		Ford Motor Co. boosts prices an average $94 or 1.9 percent on small-model cars, following a similar price increase by GM on March 24. Despite the price hikes, GM's Chevette and Ford's Pinto have a competitive edge over comparable foreign imports with the Chevette prices at $3,074 and the Pinto at $3,049.		Pulitzer Prizes for Journalism are awarded, with three of the prizes going to members of *The New York Times* staff, the first time that three prizes have been won by any one newspaper. Richard L. Strout and E.B. White receive special citations.	April 17
	The Senate votes, 68–32, to ratify the second pact of the Panama Canal Treaty, thereby completing ratification of the new accords. As with the neutrality pact section, the senators added several reservations, including a compromise worked out by Sen. Dennis DeConcini (D, Ariz.).	Stock traders work on Saturday to clean up the paperwork generated by a two-day unprecedented stock-market surge. . . . Pres. Carter hails an agreement among major construction unions and contractors designed to shorten the time required to build nuclear power plants as a superb example of business–labor cooperation.		Supreme Ct. rules, 7–2, against radio, TV, and recording companies having automatic access to former Pres. Richard Nixon's White House tapes. . . . William Macomber Jr. is elected first full-time salaried president of the Metropolitan Museum of Art, N.Y.C.	April 18
Supreme Ct. strikes down, 8–0, a Tenn. law that bans members of the clergy from public office. . . . Calif. Gov. Edmund Brown Jr. formally refuses to extradite American Indian Movement (AIM) leader Dennis Banks to South Dakota where he had been convicted of assault in connection with the Wounded Knee occupation in 1973.	McGeorge Bundy, a former national security adviser, tells the Senate panel on intelligence that excessive regulations could hurt CIA morale and recruitment of qualified personnel.	The dollar is seen as a chief cause and beneficiary of the stock market surge with its value gaining added strength as the Treasury says it plans to sell some of the U.S. gold reserves to buy dollars in foreign exchange markets.	Jill Brown becomes the first black woman known to have qualified as a pilot for a major U.S. airline, Texas International Airlines Inc.		April 19
Senate passes, 95–1, a bill barring federal intelligence agencies from wiretapping in the U.S. without a court order.	Former State Secy. Henry Kissinger, who has been alleged to have ignored charges of Korean influence peddling in Congress, tells a House subcommittee that he first learned of the Korean attempts in early 1975, but the evidence was weak.	American Petroleum Institute reports that U.S. imports of foreign oil in the first quarter of 1978 were 14 percent below first quarter imports the previous year.	Nuclear Regulatory Agency refuses to approve the sale of 7.6 tons of uranium for two nuclear power plants in India.	NBC announces that its four-part TV drama *Holocaust* was seen in part or in full by 120 million people, an audience second only to the one garnered by *Roots* .	April 20
Thomas Wyatt Turner, civil rights pioneer and educator who founded the Federation of Colored Catholics and was a charter NAACP member, dies of pneumonia in Washington, D.C. at the age of 101.		House–Senate conferees report a break in the deadlock over natural gas pricing.	Kitt Peak National Observatory astronomers in Ariz. estimate that 10–20 percent of the 100 billion or more stars in the sun's galaxy probably have planets orbiting them.	The Pulitzer Prize for spot photography, in the first mix-up in the history of the prize, is given to John W. Blair, after originally being awarded to the wrong man, Jim Schweiker.	April 21
An Indian tribe's business council announces that non-Indians will not be permitted on the Ft. Hall, Idaho, Reservation, in wake of a Supreme Ct. March 6 ruling that non-Indians who break laws on reservations cannot be tried in Indian courts for criminal offenses without congressional consent.				Overseas Press Club, N.Y.C., reportedly questions the authenticity of pictures of Rhodesian soldiers and their black captives that won a Pulitzer Prize for J. Ross Baughman.	April 22
				Gary Player becomes the first man since Hubert Green in 1976 to win three consecutive events on the PGA tour and the first foreigner to win three in a row in the U.S. since fellow South African Bobby Locke accomplished that feat in 1947.	April 23

F	G	H	I	J
Includes elections, federal-state relations, civil rights and liberties, crime, the judiciary, education, health care, poverty, urban affairs and population.	Includes formation and debate of U.S. foreign and defense policies, veterans' affairs and defense spending. (Relations with specific foreign countries are usually found under the region concerned.)	Includes business, labor, agriculture, taxation, transportation, consumer affairs, monetary and fiscal policy, natural resources, and pollution.	Includes worldwide scientific, medical and technological developments, natural phenomena, U.S. weather, natural disasters, and accidents.	Includes the arts, religion, scholarship, communications media, sports, entertainments, fashions, fads and social life.

	World Affairs	Europe	Africa & the Middle East	The Americas	Asia & the Pacific
April 24		British Conservative Party opposition leader Margaret Thatcher speaks at the first meeting of European Conservative parties, the European Democratic Union in Klesheim, Austria.		Canadian Solicitor General Jean-Jacques Blais says that he will not discipline senior Royal Canadian Mounted Police officers who had authorized illegal break-ins, mail openings, and issuance of forged documents.	
April 25	U.S. govt. sources confirm that Washington and Moscow have agreed on one of the three main points that had divided them on SALT talks.	On the fourth anniversary of Portagual's successful coup against its civilian dictatorship, Pres. Antonio Ramalho Eanes says that the country's economic situation remains grave and that a period of austerity is essential.	South African P.M. John Vorster says that his govt. would accept a Western-sponsored plan for the independence of Namibia.	Sun Life Assurance Co. of Canada stockholders approve the company's decision to move its head office from Montreal to Toronto.... The Roman Catholic Church launches its Year of Human Rights in Chile.	
April 26	Arkady Shevchenko, the highest-ranking Soviet official at the U.N., announces that he has left his post and applied for asylum in the U.S., citing serious differences of political philosophy.		About 4,000 Israelis stage a rally to protest Premier Menahem Begin's West Bank settlement policies. The rally is an offshoot of a Peace Now campaign launched earlier this month by 300 Israeli military reservists and supported by intellectuals and professors.		
April 27		The British Labor Party loses two by-elections to the Conservative Party.... In an interview, Cypriot Pres. Spyros Kyprianou says that the Turkish plan for Cyprus amounts to legalizing the results of the 1974 invasion.	Lebanese Parliament approves a six-point program banning all private Christian and Moslem militia and Palestinian guerrilla activity in the country.		An OECD report scores Australia's use of trade restrictions to protect its domestic industries from competition.... A military junta seizes power in Afghanistan, killing Pres. Mohammad Daud Khan, who had, himself, seized power by a coup in 1973.
April 28			Ugandan Pres. Idi Amin assumes control of the prison system and police force.... Byron Hove, one of the two justice and law ministers in the Rhodesian transitional govt., is dismissed for criticizing Rhodesian courts and police forces.		
April 29		The British Labor Party's narrow victory in the inner London borough of Lambeth is seen as a disaster for the Labor Govt. because Lambeth is traditionally a safe Labor seat, which indicates to some observers that the government would lose heavily in a general election.... According to press reports, British Liberal Party leaders put much of the blame for their by-election losses on the party's pact with the Labor Party.... Danish Folketing (Parliament) votes to abolish the death penalty completely.			
April 30			Upper Volta holds its first legislative elections in four years, following the November 1977 referendum approving a return to civilian rule.		The Revolutionary Council proclaims a new government in Afghanistan headed by Nur Mohammad Taraki, a civilian who reportedly headed an Afghanistan CP called Khalq.

A	B	C	D	E
Includes developments that affect more than one world region, international organizations and important meetings of major world leaders.	Includes all domestic and regional developments in Europe, including the Soviet Union, Turkey, Cyprus and Malta.	Includes all domestic and regional developments in Africa and the Middle East, including Iraq and Iran and excluding Cyprus, Turkey and Afghanistan.	Includes all domestic and regional developments in Latin America, the Caribbean and Canada.	Includes all domestic and regional developments in Asia and Pacific nations, extending from Afghanistan through all the Pacific Islands, except Hawaii.

U.S. Politics & Social Issues	U.S. Foreign Policy & Defense	U.S. Economy & Environment	Science, Technology & Nature	Culture, Leisure & Life Style	
Former Rep. Richard Hanna (D, Calif.) is sentenced to serve six to 30 months in prison in connection with the Korean lobbying scandal. ... The Senate Judiciary Committee issues a report that states that there was no cover-up of any investigation when Rep. Joshua Eilberg (D, Pa.) called Pres. Carter to ask him to dismiss David Marston as U.S. attorney in Philadelphia.			French govt. denies it has exploded its own neutron bomb in the Pacific.	Soviet press agency Tass reports that American artist Andrew Wyeth has been elected an honorary member of the Soviet Academy of Arts.	April 24
Supreme Ct. rules, 6–2, that an employer who charges women more than men to participate in a pension plan is guilty of discrimination under the 1964 Civil Rights Act.	The New York Times reports that NATO's Supreme Allied Commander Gen. Alexander Haig has hinted that he would resign over the U.S. decision to halt neutron bomb production. It also cites other sources of friction between Haig and the Carter administration.	In a televised news conference Pres. Carter strongly defends his tax program.		Belgium's most famous statue, Manneken Pis, is stolen from a fountain in a square near the center of Brussels. It is the third time in this century that it has been stolen.	April 25
Supreme Ct. rules, 5–4, that under the First Amendment, corporations cannot be barred from spending money to disseminate their views on political issues. Justice Warren Burger, a member of the majority in the ruling, issues a separate opinion related to the growth of companies owning a variety of media — newspapers, magazines, TV stations, newsprint plants, and book publishing firms.	American expatriate Michael Townley is charged in Wash., D.C. with conspiring to murder Orlando Letelier, the former Chilean foreign minister. Three Cubans are also charged with the 1976 assassination.	SEC and Comptroller of the Currency file joint charges against Bert Lance, Pres. Carter's former budget director, accusing him of civil fraud and engaging in unsafe and unsound banking practices and financial irregularities.	HEW says that it is warning current and former asbestos workers about the health risk associated with working with the substance.	Among the top-grossing films for the week just ended are Annie Hall, The Goodbye Girl, and House Calls, which is in first place.... Expatriate Soviet ballet star Mikhail Baryshnikov announces that he plans to leave the American Ballet Theater to join the New York City Ballet because he wants to work with choreographers George Balanchine and Jerome Robbins.	April 26
Former White House aide John Ehrlichman is released from prison in Ariz. after serving 18 months for Watergate-realted offenses.	Washington Post reports that Michael Townley has agreed to cooperate fully with U.S. investigators in exchange for a guilty plea to a single conspiracy count in Orlando Letelier's assassination.	Pres. Carter signs an executive order to broaden the power of the White House Office of Consumer Affairs and of his consumer affairs adviser, Esther Peterson.... The stock market drops sharply after the Federal Reserve tightens credit.	Pres. Carter approves the sale of U.S. enriched uranium to India for its nuclear power plant at Tarapur, overriding an April 20 Nuclear Regulatory Agency decision to bar the sale because it would not meet Nuclear Nonproliferation Act requirements.	A plaster copy of Manneken Pis, put up in Brussels, Belgium yesterday for the benefit of tourists to replace the stolen bronze statue, is itself stolen.	April 27
Former Rep. Otto Passman (D, La.) is indicted for tax evasion after an earlier indictment on bribery and conspiracy charges stemming from the Korean lobbying scandal.	Maj. Gen. John Singlaub agress to retire from the Army after his second public criticism of Carter adminstration policies within a year.	NRC's Atomic and Safety Licensing Appeal Bd. orders a new study to find the best site for the nuclear power plant being constructed at Seabrook, N.H.			April 28
		Nuclear energy opponents begin three-day protests in South Carolina and Colorado.			April 29
Many U.S. newspapers begin publishing installments of former Pres. Richard Nixon's memoirs, RN: The Memoirs of Richard Nixon. He admits, in the excerpt, that he participated in the Watergate cover-up and had misled the public, but maintains that he committed no crime or misdemeanor that would warrant impeachment.		UMW locals in northeastern Pa. ratify a new three-year contract with the anthracite industry.... The Dow-Jones Average is at its highest level since Nov. 28, 1977.	The New York Times reports that anorexia nervosa, called the "starvation disease," affects about one in every 100 teenage girls in the U.S. Its symptom is self-starvation seen stemming from emotional causes.	Sam Snead and Gardner Dickinson share the $100,000 first prize in the Legends of Golf tournament in Austin, Tex.	April 30

F	G	H	I	J
Includes elections, federal-state relations, civil rights and liberties, crime, the judiciary, education, health care, poverty, urban affairs and population.	Includes formation and debate of U.S. foreign and defense policies, veterans' affairs and defense spending. (Relations with specific foreign countries are usually found under the region concerned.)	Includes business, labor, agriculture, taxation, transportation, consumer affairs, monetary and fiscal policy, natural resources, and pollution.	Includes worldwide scientific, medical and technological developments, natural phenomena, U.S. weather, natural disasters, and accidents.	Includes the arts, religion, scholarship, communications media, sports, entertainments, fashions, fads and social life.

	World Affairs	Europe	Africa & the Middle East	The Americas	Asia & the Pacific
May 1		French Socialist Party leader Francois Mitterrand sharply accuses the French CP of losing elections for the left-wing coalition.	PLO leader Yasir Arafat says that U.S. and Soviet guarantees for Israel and a Palestinian state are the only possible solution to a Middle East peace settlement.	More than 600 people — including workers and their relatives, two Chilean Christian Democratic labor leaders, and two reporters — are arrested in Santiago, participating in the first antigovernment May Day rallies since the 1973 military coup.	Hundreds of ethnic Chinese reportedly have fled southern Vietnam since a Vietnamese govt. announcement in March that privately owned businesses in Saigon would be nationalized.
May 2	In an interview with a West German magazine given shortly before his arrival in Bonn for talks with West German Chancellor Helmut Schmidt, Soviet Pres. Leonid Brezhnev says that the Soviet govt. would be willing to reduce its forces in Central Europe by half if the West would do the same.	European Free Trade Assn. (EFTA) announces that the combined trade deficits of its seven member-nations have risen to $12.9 billion in 1977. Finland is the only member to have a 1977 trade surplus.	Three French soldiers of the U.N. Interim Force in Lebanon (UNIFIL) are killed and 12 wounded in a clash with Lebanese left-wing guerrillas in southern Lebanon.	*Wall Street Journal* reports that Venezuelan unemployment is near an all-time low of 5 percent and its inflation rate, according to govt. statistics, is 8 percent for 1977. It adds that economists consider the latter figure unrealistic, putting the real inflation figure at 20 percent.	
May 3	U.N. General Assembly votes to ask the Security Council to impose economic sanctions on South Africa because of its refusal to relinquish control of Namibia.	The Italian press publishes a public letter from the family of Aldo Moro, which accuses leaders of the Italian Christian Democratic Party of failing to save Moro by negotiating with his kidnappers.	Idi Amin dismisses his director of police training, Ali Toweli, who is implicated in the mass killings of Ugandan citizens.		Japanese Premier Takeo Fukuda says that he has told U.S. Pres. Carter that Japan will make massive efforts to reduce its current trade account surplus, which stands at $14 billion. . . . Vietnamese govt. announces creating a single currency, merging the Northern dong and the Southern piaster into a unified dong.
May 4		Soviet Pres. Leonid Brezhnev opens his four-day visit to West Germany with a plea for deepening detente.	South African troops in Namibia cross into Angola and attack bases of the South-West Africa People's Organization (SWAPO), the guerrilla force fighting for control of Namibia.	Nicaraguan National Guardsmen in Managua open fire on several hundred students who are demonstrating in wake of ongoing unrest in Nicaragua.	In his first public speech, Afghanistan's new leader, Nur Mohammad Taraki, says that his government will be neutral and denies reports that the country would favor either the U.S. or the U.S.S.R.
May 5	Pres. Carter calls Soviet intervention in Africa a danger to U.S.–Soviet relations and charges an "innate racism toward black people in the Soviet Union."	Red Brigade terrorists send a message saying they will execute their kidnap victim, former Italian Premier Aldo Moro, because the Italian govt. refuses to negotiate with them.		Paraguay's state of siege, in effect since 1947, is lifted everywhere except in its capital, Asuncion.	Chinese Premier Hua Kuo-feng begins a visit to North Korea, his first trip abroad and the first foreign tour by a Chinese CP chairman since 1957. . . . Sanjay Gandhi, son of Indira Gandhi, begins serving a one-month jail sentence in New Delhi after his bail is canceled in a criminal case stemming from charges that he had conspired to destroy a film satirizing his mother's govt.
May 6	U.N. Security Council unanimously condemns the South African raid into Angola as a flagrant violation of Angolan sovereignty.		Angolan govt. charges that 504 Namibian refugees and 16 Angolan soldiers were killed in the South African attack on SWAPO bases.		A rally in Dacca denounces Burma's treatment and expulsions of Moslems and urges Bangladesh's leaders to raise the matter with the U.N.
May 7	Moscow denounces reports in the West that the Soviet Union had inspired the Afghanistan coup. . . . The U.S. dollar is retained as a basis for oil prices by OPEC oil ministers meeting in Taif, Saudi Arabia.	Italian kidnap victim Aldo Moro sends a farewell letter to his wife, saying that his captors, members of the Red Brigades, say they will soon kill him. . . . West Germany and the Soviet Union sign a 25-year economic pact during Soviet Pres. Leonid Brezhnev's conferences in Bonn with West German Chancellor Helmut Schmidt.	SWAPO sources claim the death toll in the South African attack in Angola to be 1,000, including women and children.		During a visit to North Korea, Chinese Premier Hua Kuo-feng assails a U.S. decision to decelerate its military withdrawal from South Korea.
May 8	World Islamic League in Mecca, Saudi Arabia expresses concern over Burma's expulsion of over 70,000 Moslems.	Leongina Shevchenko, 48, wife of Soviet defector Arkady Shevchenko, dies of an overdose of sleeping pills in Moscow.		Rodrigo Carazo Odio is inaugurated president of Costa Rica.	

A	B	C	D	E
Includes developments that affect more than one world region, international organizations and important meetings of major world leaders.	Includes all domestic and regional developments in Europe, including the Soviet Union, Turkey, Cyprus and Malta.	Includes all domestic and regional developments in Africa and the Middle East, including Iraq and Iran and excluding Cyprus, Turkey and Afghanistan.	Includes all domestic and regional developments in Latin America, the Caribbean and Canada.	Includes all domestic and regional developments in Asia and Pacific nations, extending from Afghanistan through all the Pacific Islands, except Hawaii.

U.S. Politics & Social Issues	U.S. Foreign Policy & Defense	U.S. Economy & Environment	Science, Technology & Nature	Culture, Leisure & Life Style	
Supreme Ct. declines to review a case involving the issue of competency levels of defense lawyers. . . . In the second installment of his memoirs, published in *The New York Times*, former Pres. Nixon attributes adverse public reaction to the White House tapes, once they were released, partially to the style and language of conversations.		*Newsweek* magazine reports that institutional investors accounted for 75 percent of the recent unprecedented volume on the New York Stock Exchange. . . . Federal Reserve authorizes its 5,700-member commercial banks to automatically transfer funds from savings accounts to ckecking accounts to cover overdrafts.	Japanese explorer Nami Uemura reaches the North Pole after struggling alone across over 500 miles of frozen Arctic Ocean.	Composer Richard Rodgers gives a $1-million endowment to the American Academy and Institute of Arts and Letters. . . . Aram Khachaturian, 74, Soviet composer best known for his "Sabre Dance" from the *Gayne* ballet, dies in Moscow.	May 1
N.Y.S. Senate fails by one vote to override Gov. Hugh Carey's veto of a bill to restore capital punishment.		Carter administration revises its inflation rate forecast and says it expects prices to rise in the 6.75–7 percent range — not the previously expected 6–6.25 percent range.	The U.S. Second Circuit Ct. of Appeals in N.Y.C. permanently enjoins the maker of Anacin, an aspirin-based analgesic, from claming in advertisements that Anacin gives greater pain relief than its rival product, Tylenol.		May 2
	Columbia University votes to sell its stock in selected corporations that have holdings in South Africa.	Sun Day observances are held across the U.S. in support of solar energy.	AP reports that biologists have discovered a small ocean organism that produces a chemical more powerful in killing bacteria than any other known animal-made substance.		May 3
Senate rejects a report that clears Benjamin Civiletti of any responsibility in the controversial firing of David Marston, a Republican, as U.S. attorney for Philadelphia.		GM's Chevrolet Chevette fails federal fuel-system safety tests. . . . Congress clears legislation authorizing the administration to raise target prices for grain and cotton over the next four years.	Pres. Carter tells a news conference in Portland, Ore. that a comprehensive proposal for a permanent nuclear waste disposal plan will be ready by the end of the year.		May 4
Pres. Carter attacks organized medicine as the major obstacle to health care when he speaks at a town meeting in Spokane, Wash., winding up a three-day tour of Western states.		Consumer installment credit is reported expanding a seasonally adjusted $4.07 billion during March, a record increase.		Betty Ford, wife of former Pres. Gerald Ford, ends her stay at Long Beach (Calif.) Naval Hospital after being treated at the alcohol and drug abuse center. She speaks candidly about her addiction to painkilling drugs and to alcohol. . . . Pete Rose of baseball's Cincinnati Reds makes his 3,000 base hit.	May 5
				Affirmed wins the Kentucky Derby with Steve Cauthen as jockey.	May 6
					May 7
		Fortune magazine reports that the combined sales of the 500 largest U.S. industrial companies rose 11.9 percent in 1977. GM regains the top-ranked position after an absence of three years.	Pres. Carter signs a bill providing a federal research program on ocean pollution.	Raymond Rubicam, 85, co-founder in 1923 of Young & Rubicam International Inc., one of the largest U.S. ad agencies, dies of a heart condition in Scottsdale, Ariz.	May 8

F	G	H	I	J
Includes elections, federal-state relations, civil rights and liberties, crime, the judiciary, education, health care, poverty, urban affairs and population.	*Includes formation and debate of U.S. foreign and defense policies, veterans' affairs and defense spending. (Relations with specific foreign countries are usually found under the region concerned.)*	*Includes business, labor, agriculture, taxation, transportation, consumer affairs, monetary and fiscal policy, natural resources, and pollution.*	*Includes worldwide scientific, medical and technological developments, natural phenomena, U.S. weather, natural disasters, and accidents.*	*Includes the arts, religion, scholarship, communications media, sports, entertainments, fashions, fads and social life.*

	World Affairs	Europe	Africa & the Middle East	The Americas	Asia & the Pacific
May 9		Alerted by an anonymous telephone call, Rome police find the body of former Italian Premier Aldo Moro in a parked car in the center of Rome near the political headquarters of both the Christian Democratic and Communist parties.	Antigovernment riots fomented by Moslem religious leaders sweep Iranian cities, with the worst rioting occuring in the Moslem holy city of Qom, site of previous violence.		
May 10		Italian Premier Guilio Andreotti says that Aldo Moro's assassination was an attempt by the Red Brigades to destroy the conciliation underway in Italy by the normally opposing left and right parties. . . . About 1,800 Danish fishing boats block harbor openings for the second time in a week to protest against the government's Baltic Sea fishing policy.			Government-owned newspapers deny that the Burmese army is waging an extermination campaign against Burma's Moslems. Bangladesh, however, estimates that the Moslem refugee exodus has risen to about 100,000 people.
May 11	Peking accuses Soviet border troops of striking across the Ussuri River on May 9 and attacking Chinese citizens.	British P.M. James Callaghan rejects the opposition Conservative Party's call for a vote of confidence following his government's loss of two tax votes in the House of Commons.	Israeli Chief of Staff Lt. Gen. Rafael Eitan says he questions the sincerity of Egypt's peace initiatives and believes that Israel needs to retain the West Bank and Golan Heights to defend itself. The Israeli press and political opposition charge that he has exceeded his military role and is meddling in politics. . . . Secessionist guerrillas belonging to the National Front for the Liberation of the Congo (FNLC) once again invade Zaire's southern Shaba Province and quickly occupy Kolwezi and Mutshatsha. . . . Teheran is the scene of violence for the first time, since the eruption of Moslem-inspired antigovernment rioting in Iran.	A policeman is killed in Bogota and five students sustain gunshot wounds in Neiva in wake of continuing bombings, kidnappings, strikes, and riots throughout Colombia. . . . Canadian P.M. Pierre Trudeau announces that elections will be postponed until the fall or 1979, raising the possibility that his Liberal govt. will be the first in more than 40 years to serve out a full five-year term. . . . Peruvian govt. announces new stringent austerity measures, sharp tax increases, and new investment incentives as the country's economy steadily gets worse.	
May 12			U.S. Rep. Paul McCloskey Jr. discloses that Israel has pledged not to use U.S.-supplied cluster bombs again except under special wartime conditions. Israel had used the bombs during its March invasion of southern Lebanon, contrary to previous assurances to the U.S.	In the first serious Brazilian labor unrest in a decade, 2,000 workers at the Swedish-owned Saab-Scania auto plant in Sao Bernardo strike for 20 percent above the government's declared wage increase.	China informs the Vietnamese Embassy in Peking that it will withdraw all 20 aid projects and 800 technical personnel from Vietnam starting May 19.
May 13		French press reports 18 bomb attacks in Brittany since the start of 1978, which it attributes to Breton nationalists.		Chilean govt. announces that it has approved the application of 103 political exiles to return to Chile from abroad, including Bernardo Leighton, a former Chilean vice president and leader of the outlawed Christian Democratic Party.	
May 14			Bishop Abel Muzorewa's United African National Council (UANC) votes to remain in the interim Rhodesian govt. despite the dismissal of a black minister from the Cabinet.		Robert Gordon Menzies, 83, former Australian prime minister (1939–41) and founder of the federal Liberal Party of conservatives, dies in Melbourne, Australia.
May 15		Minister for Greenland Joergen Hansen submits a bill to the Danish Folketing (parliament) to give home rule to Greenland in May 1979. Under the bill's terms, Greenland would remain part of the Danish monarchy.	Lebanese Pres. Elias Sarkis reinstates the Cabinet that resigned on April 19 after Premier Selim al-Hoss failed to create a new national unity govt.	Peru's military govt. announces a series of sharp price increases, provoking a general strike and riots in major cities.	An Indian judicial commission investigating former P.M. Indira Gandhi's govt. issues a report accusing it of illegality, widespread repression, and human-rights violation.

A	B	C	D	E
Includes developments that affect more than one world region, international organizations and important meetings of major world leaders.	Includes all domestic and regional developments in Europe, including the Soviet Union, Turkey, Cyprus and Malta.	Includes all domestic and regional developments in Africa and the Middle East, including Iraq and Iran and excluding Cyprus, Turkey and Afghanistan.	Includes all domestic and regional developments in Latin America, the Caribbean and Canada.	Includes all domestic and regional developments in Asia and Pacific nations, extending from Afghanistan through all the Pacific Islands, except Hawaii.

U.S. Politics & Social Issues	U.S. Foreign Policy & Defense	U.S. Economy & Environment	Science, Technology & Nature	Culture, Leisure & Life Style	
Newark, N.J. Mayor Kenneth Gibson wins a third four-year term. He was the first black to become a mayor of a major Northeastern city. ... Senate votes, 72–22, to confirm Benjamin Civiletti as deputy attorney general, the second-ranking post in the Justice Dept.		Justice Dept. files charges against Gulf Oil Corp. in a Pittsburgh federal court, accusing a conspiracy to fix uranium prices at an artificially high level.			May 9
		AFL–CIO pres. George Meany deals a setback to Pres. Carter's antiinflationary plan by refusing to support Carter's call for decelerated wage increases. He charges that the pressure should be applied to prices rather than wages.... EPA orders American Motors Corp. to recall almost all of its 1976 cars because of a pollutional violation. The order will cost the financially troubled company $3.1 million.	A Rockefeller Foundation-sponsored study is released that urges the U.S. to pursue research on plutonium-fueled breeder reactors in cooperation with Japan and possibly Great Britain. It takes issue with the Carter administration fear that breeder technology would encourage nuclear weapon proliferation.		May 10
	Senate For. Rel. Committee votes to continue the ban on U.S. arms aid to Turkey, a setback to the Carter administration's attempt to lift the embargo.... Margaret Brewer is named the first female general in the U.S. Marine Corps.	*The New York Times* reports the potential for garbage as an energy source, noting that 12 percent of the electricity used in Munich, West Germany, comes from burning garbage and waste.... FRB raises its discount rate to 7 percent from 6.5 percent.			May 11
		Pres. Carter agrees to scale back his $25-billion tax-reduction package to $19.4 billion and to delay its effective date by three months until Jan. 1, 1979.	A European Space Agency test satellite is successfully launched into space and placed in a stable orbit from the U.S. rocket base at Cape Canaveral, Fla.	ABC announces that former anchorman Harry Reasoner will leave in July and start work in August for the *CBS Reports* television news program.	May 12
			A federal district judge in Los Angeles reports that more than $62 million has been paid out of court in damages to more than 1,100 people as a result of the 1974 Turkish airliner crash near Paris, France in which 346 people were killed.	Joie Ray, 84, a runner who set the world's indoor mile record of 4 minutes, 12 seconds in 1924, dies in Benton Harbor, Mich.	May 13
				Alexander Kipnis, 87, Ukrainian-born opera singer best known for his Wagnerian bass roles, dies following a stroke in Westport, Conn.	May 14
Former SLA kidnap victim Patricia Hearst returns to prison in Calif., after having been free on $1.5-million bail since Nov. 19, 1976.... Supreme Ct. rules, 7–2, that federal agents need only make a reasonable effort to avoid intercepting private conversations in their use of court-ordered wiretaps in criminal investigations.	Senate votes, 54–44, to support the Carter administration's plan to sell warplanes to Saudi Arabia and Egypt, as well as Israel. The vote split follows neither party nor philosophical lines.	Supreme Ct. rules unanimously that the SEC lacks the legal authority to suspend stock trading for a period over 10 days without a hearing.	An FDA regulation requiring that blood for transfusions be clearly labeled as coming from either paid or volunteer donors takes effect. ... A final engineer's report attributes the collapse of the Hartford (Conn.) Civic Center's snow-ladden roof to design deficiencies.	Bianca Jagger files divorce papers against her husband, Mick Jagger, leader of the Rolling Stones rock group.	May 15

F	G	H	I	J
Includes elections, federal-state relations, civil rights and liberties, crime, the judiciary, education, health care, poverty, urban affairs and population.	Includes formation and debate of U.S. foreign and defense policies, veterans' affairs and defense spending. (Relations with specific foreign countries are usually found under the region concerned.)	Includes business, labor, agriculture, taxation, transportation, consumer affairs, monetary and fiscal policy, natural resources, and pollution.	Includes worldwide scientific, medical and technological developments, natural phenomena, U.S. weather, natural disasters, and accidents.	Includes the arts, religion, scholarship, communications media, sports, entertainments, fashions, fads and social life.

	World Affairs	Europe	Africa & the Middle East	The Americas	Asia & the Pacific
May 16	During a visit to Great Britain, Zambian Pres. Kenneth Kaunda says that unless the British and U.S. can implement their plan for Rhodesian majority rule, the Patriotic Front guerrillas would be free to seek outside military help, a reference to the U.S.S.R. and Cuba.	Greek For. Min. Goerge Rallis countercharges that Turkish Premier Bulent Ecevit's comment yesterday about an alleged Greek threat to Turkey proves that Turkey is seeking to remove the U.S. arms embargo to threaten Greece rather than to continue its responsibilities as a NATO ally.	Ethiopian govt. launches an offensive against Eritrean rebels.	*Washington Post* reports that in a sharp reversal of policy, the Carter administration is releasing up to $12 million in U.S. aid to Nicaragua, which had been held up because of the Nicaraguan govt.'s poor record on human rights.	
May 17	Defense ministers of 11 European NATO members agree to cooperate in outfitting three new weapons systems and training pilots for the U.S. F-16 jet fighters ordered by Europe, thereby significantly advancing integration of NATO military systems.	Italian govt., supported by the Italian CP, has strict antiterrorism laws approved by the Chamber of Deputies. . . . Lord Selwyn-Lloyd, 73, British foreign secretary (1956–60) and Speaker of the House of Commons (1971–76), dies in Oxfordshire, England.	South African Justice Min. James Kruger says that security police made errors in judgment in handling the detention of Steven Biko, a black activist who died in police custody in 1977, but the errors do not merit disciplinary action.	Dominican Republic police and army suspend the vote count of national and local elections, which took place yesterday. Opposition candidate Antonio Guzman leads Pres. Joaquin Balaguer when the voting is suspended.	Australian Immigration Min. Michael Mackellar says that Australia will admit 9,000 Indochinese refugees over a 12-month period beginning in July.
May 18	OPEC denies that it is making a concerted effort to cut back oil production. . . . The U.S. presents NATO with a plan to speed up deployment of U.S. reinforcements in Europe in the event of war.	A Moscow court sentences Yuri Orlov, founder of the group that monitored Soviet compliance with the 1975 Helsinki accord, to seven years in prison and five years of internal exile. . . . Italian Parliament completes passage of a liberalized abortion law, strongly opposed by the Roman Catholic Church, which is one of the most liberal in Europe and permits abortion on demand for women over 18. . . . Italian police find two hideouts in Rome believed to have been used by the Red Brigades terrorist group.	About 1,750 Belgian troops and 1,000 members of the French Foreign Legion are flown into Zaire to prepare to rescue more than 2,500 Europeans caught in the fighting between Zaire troops and secessionist rebels who had invaded Shaba Province.	Dominican Republic vote count resumes and the press secretary of incumbent Joaquin Balaguer's Reformist Party says he is convinced Balaguer has won.	
May 19	U.N. Conference on the Law of the Sea, held in Geneva since April 6, ends in another deadlock over the proposed formation of a Seabed Authority that would regulate deepsea mining. . . . Gen. Alexander Haig, supreme commander of NATO, says that he has accepted Pres. Carter's request that he ramain at his post.	U.S. District Ct. Judge Thomas Griesa rules that Italian financier Michele Sindona should be extradited to Italy to face fraud charges in connection with the failure of Banca Privata Italiana, a Milan bank that he had controlled.	French paratroopers are dropped into the Zairian mining town of Kolwezi. It is the first European rescue operation in Zaire since the evacuation of foreigners during the 1964 secession battle in Shaba Province, which was then called Katanga.	In a stern public warning, Pres. Carter tells incumbent Dominican Republic Pres. Joaquin Balaguer that he is seriously concerned about the military's suspension of the vote count in the presidential election two days earlier, and notes that countinuing U.S. support will be measured by the integrity of the Dominican's election process.	
May 20		French security police shoot and kill three Arab terrorists who had opened fire on French tourists in a lounge at Orly airport in Paris as they were boarding an El Al Israel Airlines flight to Israel.	A Beirut, Lebanon group, calling itself the Organization of the Sons of Southern Lebanon, claims credit for the terrorist attack at Paris's Orly airport. . . . Belgian troops follow French troops into Zaire's Shaba Province. The two forces join up and establish control over Kolwezi, beginning an airlift of Europeans.		Chiang Ching-kuo is sworn in as president of Nationalist China.
May 21			Israeli govt. announces that all its military forces will withdraw from southern Lebanon by June 13.	Diego Arria, a former Venezuelan Cabinet minister and governor of Caracas, announces that he will run as an independent in the December presidential election. . . . Dominican Republic's opposition party, the Dominican Revolutionary Party, revives charges of fraud in the vote count for the presidential election, which was interrupted by the armed forces on May 17–18.	Tokyo international airport at Narita, Japan finally opens after longstanding opposition by environmentalists and left-wing radical opponents of the government.

A	B	C	D	E
Includes developments that affect more than one world region, international organizations and important meetings of major world leaders.	Includes all domestic and regional developments in Europe, including the Soviet Union, Turkey, Cyprus and Malta.	Includes all domestic and regional developments in Africa and the Middle East, including Iraq and Iran and excluding Cyprus, Turkey and Afghanistan.	Includes all domestic and regional developments in Latin America, the Caribbean and Canada.	Includes all domestic and regional developments in Asia and Pacific nations, extending from Afghanistan through all the Pacific Islands, except Hawaii.

U.S. Politics & Social Issues	U.S. Foreign Policy & Defense	U.S. Economy & Environment	Science, Technology & Nature	Culture, Leisure & Life Style	
Ala. Gov. George Wallace (D) announces he is withdrawing from the race for the U.S. Senate seat held by retiring Sen. John Sparkman.	GAO reports that the CIA and the FBI used alleged Nazi war criminals as information sources. A CIA officials admits using these contacts only in the early 1950s.	After the House International Relations Committee unanimously passes a resolution calling for a trade embargo against Uganda because of its human-rights violations, Folger Coffee Co. announces a boycott of Ugandan coffee beans.		William Steinberg, 78, German-born former music director of the Pittsburgh (1952–76) and Boston (1969–72) Symphony orchestras, and principal guest conductor of the New York Philharmonic (1966-68), dies of an apparent heart ailment in N.Y.	May 16
		Commerce Dept. reports that personal income rose $23.3 billion in April, or 1.4 percent from March, to a seasonally adjusted annual rate of $1.68 trillion. It is the biggest increase since a $29.7-billion rise in June 1975.		The body of the late comic actor Charlie Chaplin, stolen on March 2 from a cemetery in Corsier-sur-Vevey, Switzerland, is recovered in a cornfield 10 miles east.	May 17
Charges are filed in Austin, Tex. against John Christian, a 13-year-old charged with the shooting death of his English teacher, Wilbur Grayson. The youth is the son of George Christian, a press secretary to former Pres. Lyndon Johnson.	The U.S. condemns Soviet sentencing of Yuri Orlov in its most strongly worded statement on human rights in recent months. The House approves a resolution protesting his imprisonment.	Federal Home Loan Bank Board adopts regulations to prohibit redlining, a practice which denies loans to deteriorating and minority-populated neighborhoods.		Rabbi Abraham Hecht, president of the Rabbinical Alliance of America, which represents Orthodox rabbis, announces an all-out campaign against gay rights. . . . A St. Louis, Mo. grand jury refuses to indict World Boxing Assn. heavyweight boxing champion Leon Spinks on two drug charges.	May 18
Ala. Supreme Ct. affirms the state's death penalty law by upholding the convictions of Jerry Jacobs and John Lewis Evans. . . . Senate members' personal finance reports show that at least 10 senators and possibly twice as many are millionaires.	A federal grand jury in Alexandria, Va. finds Ronald Humphrey and David Truong guilty of spying for Vietnam.	Postal Service approves increasing the cost of first-class mail from 13 cents to 15 cents for a one-ounce letter.			May 19
	FBI agents arrest two Soviet citizens as spies for allegedly attempting to get information on the U.S. Navy's antisubmarine warfare effort.		Carter administration defers approval of licenses to export nuclear fuel to 12 countries. Licenses for South Africa and Pakistan are the only ones withheld purely for political reasons.	*Affirmed* wins the Preakness Stakes with Steve Cauthen as jockey.	May 20
	A Senate Intelligence Committee report says that CIA predictions that the Soviet Union would have to import large amounts of oil by the mid-1980s were not influenced by the political objectives of the Carter administration. The panel, however, does not endorse the CIA predictions, which were widely challenged by energy experts.				May 21

F	G	H	I	J
Includes elections, federal-state relations, civil rights and liberties, crime, the judiciary, education, health care, poverty, urban affairs and population.	Includes formation and debate of U.S. foreign and defense policies, veterans' affairs and defense spending. (Relations with specific foreign countries are usually found under the region concerned.)	Includes business, labor, agriculture, taxation, transportation, consumer affairs, monetary and fiscal policy, natural resources, and pollution.	Includes worldwide scientific, medical and technological developments, natural phenomena, U.S. weather, natural disasters, and accidents.	Includes the arts, religion, scholarship, communications media, sports, entertainments, fashions, fads and social life.

	World Affairs	Europe	Africa & the Middle East	The Americas	Asia & the Pacific
May 22		Three bombs explode in Rome, damaging the outside of the Justice Ministry and two Alfa Romeo auto showrooms.	U.N. Special Secy. Roberto Guyer assures Israeli For. Min. Moshe Dayan that the U.N. Interim Force in Lebanon will use military means if necessary to prevent Palestinian guerrillas from returning to their former positions in southern Lebanon.	Limited or full strikes are reported at more than 20 Brazilian companies, including Chrysler, Volkswagenwerk, A.G., and Firestone Tire & Rubber Co.	
May 23	U.N. opens a special session of the General Assembly on disarmament, designed to formulate a program to end proliferation of nuclear weapons and reduce world military spending.		French officials estimate the European death toll in Shaba Province runs as high as 200 and the total count of blacks and whites dead in Kolwezi is about 500.... Bethlehem Mayor Elias Freij charges that Israel is planning to take over West Bank property owned by Arabs living abroad by enlarging Jewish settlements in the occupied area.	Canadian dollar continues its downward slide, closing at 89.8 U.S. cents.	
May 24	Addressing the U.N. General Assembly's special session on disarmament, V.P. Walter Mondale says that the U.S. is committed to seeking a complete ban on nuclear testing — even for peaceful purposes — as soon as the U.S.–U.S.S.R. SALT talks conclude. His speech contains several unexpectedly sharp attacks on the Soviet Union.	Italian CP newspaper publishes a front-page editorial condemning the Soviet's sentencing of dissident physicist Yuri Orlov.... An uncontested divorce ends the 18-year marriage of Britain's Princess Margaret, 47, and Lord Snowdon (Antony Armstrong-Jones), 48. The last divorce in the immediate British royal family was that of King Henry VIII, four centuries earlier.	PLO leader Yasir Arafat reaches an agreement with the Lebanese govt. to keep his guerrilla forces out of southern Lebanon.... Five factions within the PLO reject a proposal submitted by Al Fatah, the largest PLO group, that all guerrilla groups be reorganized into one Palestinian army, which the Lebanese govt. would accept as an allied force.		China accuses Vietnam of accelerating the expulsion of ethnic Chinese from Vietnam and subjecting them to harsh treatment.
May 25	Pres. Carter accuses Cuba of a key role in training and equipping the Katangan rebels who invaded Zaire from Angola, and says it is a joke to call Cuba nonaligned.... French Pres. Valery Giscard d'Estaing publicly endorses a pan-African peacekeeping force, which is also favored by Belgian Premier Leo Tindemans.		Israeli Supreme Ct. orders a temporary work halt on a new Israeli settlement at Nebi Salah in the West Bank.... French Foreign Legion paratroopers begin to withdraw from Kolwezi, the mining town in Zaire's Shaba Province, which was occupied by secessionist rebels.		Australian Deputy P.M. Douglas Anthony says that Japanese steel manufacturers will import large amounts of iron ore and pellets in the fiscal year ending March 1979.
May 26	Soviet For. Min. Andrei Gromyko responds mildly to V.P. Mondale's speech before the U.N. disarmament session. He says that the U.S.S.R. will discuss substantial cuts in nuclear weapons when the SALT treaty is concluded.		Iraq's Baathist Party-dominated govt. is reported having executed 14 members of the pro-Soviet Iraqi CP in April as the result of a growing dispute between the two factions, both of which belong to the National Progressive Front.	Dominican Republic's central elections board informs Pres. Joaquin Balaguer that he has lost the presidential election to the opposition candidate Antonio Guzman of the Dominican Revolutionary Party.	
May 27	Greek Premier Constantine Caramanlis warns before the NATO summit conference that only a fair Cyprus settlement could strengthen NATO in the eastern Mediterranean.	Two armed women free terrorist Till Meyer from West Berlin's Moabit Prison in a daring daylight raid.			Peking announces that it wants to send ships to evacuate all remaining "persecuted" Chinese from Vietnam and contends that some have been killed or wounded in violence in Ho Chi Minh City.
May 28	Zbigniew Brzezinski, U.S. national security adviser, denounces Soviet activities as violating the code of detente and accuses both the Soviets and Cuba of responsibility for the invasion of Zaire.	Polish govt. announces a 23–30 percent increase in the price of alcoholic beverages in an effort to cut down on alcoholism.... San Marino's general election fails to end a conservative-progressive deadlock over allowing the CP to join the government.		A massive security effort, called Operation Democracy, deploys about 200,000 soldiers and policemen throughout Colombia to prevent violence prior to and during the upcoming June 4 national election.	China claims that 17,700 victimized Chinese have crossed the border from Vietnam between May 21–26. Hanoi is said to attribute the country's economic decline since the end of the war in 1975 to ethnic Chinese domination of the economy.

A	B	C	D	E
Includes developments that affect more than one world region, international organizations and important meetings of major world leaders.	Includes all domestic and regional developments in Europe, including the Soviet Union, Turkey, Cyprus and Malta.	Includes all domestic and regional developments in Africa and the Middle East, including Iraq and Iran and excluding Cyprus, Turkey and Afghanistan.	Includes all domestic and regional developments in Latin America, the Caribbean and Canada.	Includes all domestic and regional developments in Asia and Pacific nations, extending from Afghanistan through all the Pacific Islands, except Hawaii.

U.S. Politics & Social Issues	U.S. Foreign Policy & Defense	U.S. Economy & Environment	Science, Technology & Nature	Culture, Leisure & Life Style	
Joseph Colombo, Sr., 54, reputed Mafia leader, dies of cardiac arrest attributed to his semicomatose condition, which resulted from gunshoot wounds inflicted in 1971.	House approves, 363–18, legislation authorizing $4.2 billion in fiscal 1979 for military construction.	Supreme Ct. rules that officers of bankrupt corporations are responsible to the government for paying withholding taxes the companies had collected for their employes. . . . *Business Week* says that the U.S. is caught in the grip of the worst, most prolonged, and most pernicious inflation in its history.		Winnipeg Jets win their second Avco Cup as World Hockey Association champions in a four-game sweep over the New England Whalers. . . . United Presbyterian Church in the U.S.A. votes against ordaining acknowledged, practicing homosexuals, but does not exclude celibate homosexuals or those seeking to become heterosexual.	May 22
Eugene, Ore. voters follow a trend set in at least four other cities and vote to repeal ordinances that prohibit discrimination against homosexuals. . . . In the Ky. primary, Rep. John Breckinridge (D) loses his bid for renomination to a fourth term in the House to state Sen. Tom Easterly. . . . Sen. Mark Hatfield (R) easily wins renomination for a third term in Oregon, gaining 65 percent of the vote.		AT&T says it will limit merit increases for its 430 top executives to less than 5 percent. . . . Supreme Ct. votes, 5–3, to uphold a lower court decision prohibiting the Occupational Safety and Health Administration (OSHA) from conducting job-safety inspections without first obtaining warrants.	Mich. Appeals Ct. rules that doctors are liable for costs and suffering of pregnancies resulting from botched vasectomies.	Supreme Ct. rules, 8–1, that juries should not consider children when applying the test of community standards to determine obscene material.	May 23
		Kennecott Copper Corp. claims victory over Curtiss-Wright Corp., which had tried to oust Kennecott's management in one of the biggest and most bitter proxy fights in Wall Street history. . . . U.S. Steel Corp. chmn. Edgar Speer refuses to commit his company to keeping prices below 8.4 percent, the average level of increases in the two previous years, as requested by Pres. Carter.		NBA names Bill Walton the most valuable player for the 1977–78 season.	May 24
		Continental Illinois National Bank & Trust Co. of Chicago raises its prime interest rate to 8.5 percent from 8.25 percent.		Montreal Canadiens win their twenty-first Stanley Cup by beating the Boston Bruins, 4–1, in the final game of the National Hockey League playoffs.	May 25
National Organization for Women (NOW) estimates that 15 states, which are being boycotted for not having ratified the ERA, already have lost over $100 million in convention revenues. . . . Sen. Edward Brooke (R, Mass.) concedes that he gave false information about a $49,000 loan in a sworn deposition taken in 1977 for his divorce proceedings.		Energy Secy. James Schlesinger says at a news conference that the oil supply forecast is bleaker than a year ago.		Ballerina Tamara Karsavina dies in London at the age of 93. Considered one of the greatest dancers in the history of ballet, she was admired both for her performance of the classics and for the many roles she created in important twentieth-century works.	May 26
		Association of American Railroads reports that the rail industry lost a total of $274 million in the first three months of 1978, the largest quarterly deficit in its history.		Czech Regina Marsikova defeats Rumanian Virginia Ruzici to win the women's tennis singles title of the Italian Open.	May 27
				Sweden's Bjorn Borg defeats Italy's Adriano Panatta to win the men's tennis singles title of the Italian Open. . . . Al Unser wins the Indianapolis 500 auto race.	May 28

F	G	H	I	J
Includes elections, federal-state relations, civil rights and liberties, crime, the judiciary, education, health care, poverty, urban affairs and population.	*Includes formation and debate of U.S. foreign and defense policies, veterans' affairs and defense spending. (Relations with specific foreign countries are usually found under the region concerned.)*	*Includes business, labor, agriculture, taxation, transportation, consumer affairs, monetary and fiscal policy, natural resources, and pollution.*	*Includes worldwide scientific, medical and technological developments, natural phenomena, U.S. weather, natural disasters, and accidents.*	*Includes the arts, religion, scholarship, communications media, sports, entertainments, fashions, fads and social life.*

	World Affairs	Europe	Africa & the Middle East	The Americas	Asia & the Pacific
May 29	Chinese For. Min. Huang Hua tells the U.N. General Assembly that China would join an international disarmament conference if the conference were truly free of superpower control. Neither China nor France participated in the international disarmament forum in Geneva.	Premiers Bulent Ecevit of Turkey and Constantine Caramanlis of Greece meet in Washington in talks encouraged by U.S. officials who fear that the Turkish–Greek disputes over Cyprus and the Aegean Sea could undermine NATO defenses in that area.... West German officials announce that Yugoslav police have arrested four of West Germany's most-wanted terrorist suspects, members of the Red Army Faction.	Yitzhak Navon is sworn in as Israel's fifth president, succeeding Ephraim Katzir.		Vietnamese CP newspaper says that Hanoi wants to preserve its friendship with China and denies that Vietnam's ethnic Chinese are being persecuted.... Ali Soilih, deposed president of the Comoro Islands, is killed when he attempts to escape house arrest.
May 30	In a speech to the opening session of the NATO summit meeting, Pres. Carter emphasizes the African situation and says the organization cannot remain indifferent to Soviet and Cuban involvement in African affairs.	A top-secret NATO study reportedly predicts that the Soviet Union will continue to place priority on military developments despite increasing economic difficulties during the 1980s.	Zairian Red Cross puts the Kolwezi death toll at 720, including 132 foreigners. Belgium says that bodies of 73 whites were recovered but almost 300 other whites are still missing.... Egyptian Pres. Anwar Sadat concedes that the Mideast peace initiative is slackening and warns that either it regains momentum in the next two months or proves a failure. The Israeli govt. rejects Sadat's deadline, saying it is impossible to set a time frame for intricate negotiations.	Police disperse rioters at the National University in Bogota, Colombia and close the campus until after the presidential elections scheduled for June 4. One person is killed.	Radio Hanoi confirms the Chinese aid cutoff to Vietnam and charges that China is attempting to sabotage Vietnam's already troubled economy.... *The New York Times* reports that Vietnam plans to move 10 million people to so-called New Economic Zones in uninhabited parts of the country during the next 20 years, with 4 million shifted by 1980.
May 31	NATO heads of government adopt a comprehensive set of guidelines for NATO defense development over the next 10–15 years at the end of a two-day summit meeting.	West Germany reportedly has requested that alleged Nazi war criminal Gustav Wagner be extradited from Brazil.	Approximately 2,500 rioting students at Iran's Teheran University cause damage estimated at $1 million in disturbances erupting after two groups of male students dispute integration of the sexes at the university, a policy instituted by the Shah five months earlier.	The Quebec provincial inquiry into the Royal Canadian Mounted Police's alleged illegal activities closes pending a ruling by the Canadian Supreme Ct. on Quebec's constitutional right to continue the hearings.	
June 1		A U.S. official reveals that eavesdropping devices have been found in the U.S. Embassy building in Moscow.... French govt. begins its promised phase-out of price controls.... British Labor Party govt. wins a significant by-election in the Scottish constituency of Hamilton, a Glasgow suburb.	The Egyptian People's Assembly overwhelming approves a 13-point measure granting Pres. Anwar Sadat authority to curb domestic criticism of his government's policies.... Several hundred women students at Teheran University, Iran conduct a peaceful demonstration against the presence of special guards in their dormitories.	A Liberal member of the Colombian House of Representatives, Heliodoro Carrillo, is kidnapped in Bogota.... A group of Chilean exiles fast in Geneva, Switzerland in a sympathy strike with the Chilean hunger strike by female relatives of Chile's disappeared persons.	IBM ends its activities in India after rejecting a government demand to reduce IBM's share of ownership to 40 percent. Its operations are immediately assumed by 180 of the employes.
June 2	Pres. Carter calls in reporters to deny a *Washington Post* report that there is a U.S. freeze on SALT talks.	Nekla Kuneralp, wife of Zehi Kuneralp, the Turkish ambassador to Spain, is slain in Madrid by three men armed with pistols. Her death is said to be an avengement of the massacre of Armenians by Turkey in the early twentieth century.	Five people are killed and 20 wounded from an Arab terrorist bomb explosion in a Jerusalem bus. Al Fatah claims responsibility. Jerusalem Mayor Teddy Kollek speculates that the attack was meant to coincide with Israel's forthcoming celebration of the eleventh anniversary of the reunification of Jerusalem.	Final reports of the Dominican Republic's May 16 general election show that Pres. Joaquin Balaguer lost to his opponent, Antonio Guzman, by a vote of 868,496-716,358. ... Canada officially bans U.S. fishing boats from its waters. The U.S. retaliates several hours later.	
June 3		About 70 people are injured in a battle in Frankfurt, West Germany between police and opponents of the neo-Nazi National Party.	Casualties in the Shaba fighting include more than 200 Zairian troops killed.		Gen. Ziaur Rahman is overwhelmingly elected to a five-year term as Bangladesh president in nationwide balloting.
June 4			U.S. airlifts Moroccan troops into Zaire's Shaba Province and removes about 350 French Legionnaires.	Colombia's former For. Min. Julio Cesar Turbay Ayala, candidate of the ruling Liberal Party, narrowly wins the presidential election over Conservative Party candidate, Belisario Betancur. Betancur refuses to concede defeat, claiming fraud.	

A	B	C	D	E
Includes developments that affect more than one world region, international organizations and important meetings of major world leaders.	Includes all domestic and regional developments in Europe, including the Soviet Union, Turkey, Cyprus and Malta.	Includes all domestic and regional developments in Africa and the Middle East, including Iraq and Iran and excluding Cyprus, Turkey and Afghanistan.	Includes all domestic and regional developments in Latin America, the Caribbean and Canada.	Includes all domestic and regional developments in Asia and Pacific nations, extending from Afghanistan through all the Pacific Islands, except Hawaii.

U.S. Politics & Social Issues	U.S. Foreign Policy & Defense	U.S. Economy & Environment	Science, Technology & Nature	Culture, Leisure & Life Style	
An FBI memorandum, dated Dec. 1, 1964, reportedly outlines talks between the FBI and an unidentified black leader to formulate a campaign to remove the late civil-rights activist Dr. Martin Luther King Jr. from the national picture.				John McEnroe of Stanford University wins the singles title of the NCAA tennis championships in Athens, Ga.	May 29
Supreme Ct. rules in two cases that states can discipline lawyers who personally seek clients for private gain but not those lawyers who represent nonprofit organizations or offer their services for free.	Joseph Califano, HEW secretary, postpones an upcoming trip in June to the U.S.S.R. as a protest against the sentence given dissident Soviet physicist Yuri Orlov.	Consumer food prices are expected to rise 8–10 percent during 1978, according to the Agriculture Dept.		Nobel Prize-winning West German Author Heinrich Boll loses a lawsuit against Mathias Walding, a journalist who had accused Boll of spiritual complicity with terrorists.	May 30
Supreme Ct. rules, 5–3, in a case involving the *Stanford Daily* , that the news media has no special immunity from court-approved searches by police officers, and that police can obtain warrants to search the property of persons not suspected of criminal wrongdoing.	House of Representatives adopts a resolution, 321–46, calling upon the South Korean govt. to cooperate with the House's inquiry into the Korean lobbying scandal.	Consumer prices rise a seasonally adjusted .9 percent in April, according to the Labor Debt. The increase is the equivalent of a double-digit 10.8 percent annual inflation rate, the biggest since February 1977.		On the last day of the 1977-78 Broadway season, the following productions have recouped their initial investments thereby qualifying as hits: *The Gin Game, Chapter Two* , *Deathtrap* , *Man of La Mancha* , and *A Touch of the Poet.*	May 31
Sen. James B. Allen (D, Ala.) dies of an apparent heart attack in Foley, Ala. at age 65. He was elected to the Senate in 1968. . . . House approves, 237–158, a bill to grant tuition tax credits to parents of college students and of pupils in private elementary and secondary schools.	Deputy Atty. Gen. Benjamin Civiletti tells reporters that he does not expect any more indictments of present or former members of Congress in connection with the Korean lobbying scandal.			Five more arrests bring to 34 the number of opera house managers and related personnel arrested in six Italian cities in wake of an investigation of alleged corruption in Italy's opera world.	June 1
	Pres. Carter briefs House and Senate leaders on CIA intelligence that is said to substantiate his claims of Cuban aid to the rebels who invaded Zaire's Shaba Province. . . . At N.J. court hearings, U.S. investigators reveal details of the 1976 assassination of former Chilean For. Min. Orlando Letelier in Wash., D.C. The details were given by Michael Townley, a former Chilean secret police agent, as the result of plea bargaining.	Gulf Oil Corp. is fined $40,000 after pleading no contest to misdemeanor charges that it had conspired to fix uranium prices at an artifically high level.		An International Tennis Federation official confirms a report that tennis champion Bjorn Borg has withdrawn from competition for the $2-million Grand Prix bonus-money pool.	June 2
Corrections Magazine reports that the state and federal prison population increased 5 percent between January 1977-78.					June 3
Arson is reported being the fastest growing and most costly of all U.S. crimes, with juveniles constituting 60 percent of those arrested.		The National Commission on Working Women reports that 80 percent of all working women are employed in low-paying, low-status jobs. The report also shows that women's 1976 median earnings for full-time jobs were 40 percent less than those of men who work full time.		Among the best-selling books for the week just ended are Richard Nixon's *R.N.: The Memoirs of Richard Nixon* , Wayne Dyer's self-help psychology book, *Pulling Your Own Strings* , and James Fixx's *The Complete Book of Running.*	June 4

F	G	H	I	J
Includes elections, federal-state relations, civil rights and liberties, crime, the judiciary, education, health care, poverty, urban affairs and population.	*Includes formation and debate of U.S. foreign and defense policies, veterans' affairs and defense spending. (Relations with specific foreign countries are usually found under the region concerned.)*	*Includes business, labor, agriculture, taxation, transportation, consumer affairs, monetary and fiscal policy, natural resources, and pollution.*	*Includes worldwide scientific, medical and technological developments, natural phenomena, U.S. weather, natural disasters, and accidents.*	*Includes the arts, religion, scholarship, communications media, sports, entertainments, fashions, fads and social life.*

	World Affairs	Europe	Africa & the Middle East	The Americas	Asia & the Pacific
June 5	Representatives from Belgium, France, Great Britain, West Germany, and the U.S. meet in Paris to discuss France's plan to create a pan-African military force to protect pre-Western African nations from threats to their security. Britain and the U.S. oppose the plan.	Job actions in many parts of France reportedly are linked to the government's austerity policies.	South African police use tear gas in a raid on the Crossroads squatters camp near Cape Town and arrest about 50 blacks.	A Venezuelan newspaper reports that Chilean Pres. Augusto Pinochet, facing a serious internal political problem over U.S. revelations about the nature of Orlando Letelier's assassination, has unsuccessfully tried earlier in the year to get his close adviser, Gen. Manuel Contreras Sepulveda, to accept full responsibility for Letelier's murder.	China reportedly has recently released about 110,000 detainees, held since the start of an antirightist campaign in 1957. The report also indicates a rehabilitation program for many lower-level CP officials, intellectuals, and others purged in the 1960s Cultural Revolution or during the 1975–76 period. . . . Port activity resumes in Australia following a two-year wage settlement.
June 6		West German Interior Min. Werner Maihofer resigns, accepting responsibility for errors that led to the escape of terrorists who had kidnapped and killed industrialist Hanns-Martin Schleyer.	Zimbabwe African People's Union (ZAPU) leader Joshua Nkomo reveals that Cubans are training his army in Zambia. He adds he has accepted Cuban and Soviet help to scare away the West from involvement in Rhodesia. . . . Shah Mohammed Riza Pahlevi dismisses Gen. Nematollah Nassiri as head of Savak, Iran's secret police, and names him ambassador to Pakistan.	Quebec's ruling Parti Quebecois presents a white paper on its aims for the cultural development of an independent Quebec.	Vietnam proposes a cease-fire in its border conflict with Cambodia.
June 7	Speaking at the U.S. Naval Academy commencement, Pres. Carter warns the U.S.S.R. that it can choose either confrontation or cooperation and criticizes almost every aspect of Soviet domestic and foreign policy.	Twenty leading Czechoslovak dissident writers issue a letter to Western authors and reporters in which they say they fear that the government has launched an intense campaign to suppress intellectual dissent. . . . Kevin Rafferty, a prominent member of the Northern Irish Sinn Fein political organization, is critically wounded in Belfast by suspected Protestant extremists.	For the second time in two days, Egyptian Pres. Anwar Sadat threatens war with Israel. . . . Gen. Nasser Moghadam replaces Gen. Nematollah Nassiri as head of Iran's secret police.	After a hunger strike, begun in Santiago on May 22, by wives and mothers of Chile's missing people, the government reverses its stance and agrees to reveal what happened to 618 Chileans listed by Roman Catholic Church sources as having disappeared since the 1973 military coup.	Australian Immigration Min. Michael Mackellar announces a new immigrant-selection system.
June 8		Soviet Union claims that bugging devices reported found in the U.S. Embassy in Moscow were used to jam U.S. espionage devices.	Tanzanian Pres. Julius Nyerere criticizes the Western-supported African peacekeeping force in Shaba.	Quebec and the Canadian federal govt. agree on a rebate plan to settle their dispute over sales-tax reduction in Quebec.	
June 9			An Israeli commando unit attacks and kills several defenders of an Al Fatah Palestinian military base on the Lebanese coast. . . . Zaire's Pres. Mobutu Sese Seko announces that an elite force will be created to defend Shaba from future attacks.	Brazil formally ends press censorship but continues radio and TV censorship. . . . In a sharp policy reversal, the Chilean govt. agrees to allow a U.N. Human Rights Commission delegation to enter Chile and investigate charges of human-rights abuses there.	
June 10		First riots in several years erupt in Londonderry, Northern Ireland after British soldiers shoot and kill IRA member Denis Heaney.	In a conciliatory gesture to Zaire, Angola says that Shaba rebels returning from Zaire will be forced to relinquish their weapons. Pres. Agostinho Neto denies that either Angola, Cuba, or the Soviet Union had aided the rebels.	About 100,000 people gather in a Panama City plaza to rally against the new Panama Canal treaties and hear former Pres. Arnulfo Arias, recently returned from exile, denounce the pacts as contrary to the country's vital interests.	
June 11		A mob of 150–200 white youths rampage through London's East End district, which is largely populated by Bengalis.			

A	B	C	D	E
Includes developments that affect more than one world region, international organizations and important meetings of major world leaders.	Includes all domestic and regional developments in Europe, including the Soviet Union, Turkey, Cyprus and Malta.	Includes all domestic and regional developments in Africa and the Middle East, including Iraq and Iran and excluding Cyprus, Turkey and Afghanistan.	Includes all domestic and regional developments in Latin America, the Caribbean and Canada.	Includes all domestic and regional developments in Asia and Pacific nations, extending from Afghanistan through all the Pacific Islands, except Hawaii.

U.S. Politics & Social Issues	U.S. Foreign Policy & Defense	U.S. Economy & Environment	Science, Technology & Nature	Culture, Leisure & Life Style	
	The New York Times reports that the U.S. has decided to reemphasize its chemical warfare program in response to a perceived sharp Soviet advantage in the field.			Stratford Festival of Canada marks its twenty-fifth anniversary, opening a season that includes productions of works by Shakespeare, Chekhov, Noel Coward, and Leonard Bernstein's Candide .	June 5
Supreme Ct. rules, 7–2, that municipalities are vulnerable to damage suits if their official policies deprive citizens of their civil rights, The decision overturns a 1961 Supreme Ct. ruling based on the 1871 Civil Rights Act.		California voters approve, by a 65–35 percent margin, Proposition 13, a primary ballot initiative to cut property taxes by 57 percent. Its passage is seen as a taxpayers' revolt that could become nationwide.... Supreme Ct. votes, 8–0, to uphold the ICC's authority to regulate the price of oil shipped through the trans-Alaska pipeline.	Tanzanian Agriculture Min. John Malecela, chairman of the seven-nation Desert Locust Control Organization of East Africa, issues an appeal for foreign aid to counter the worst locust plague to hit eastern Africa in a decade.		June 6
House leaders and Carter administration members agree on a welfare-reform bill that represents a substantial decrease in Pres. Carter's original proposals.... Calif. Gov. Edmund Brown Jr. puts an immediate freeze on the hiring of state employes after yesterday's overwhelming affirmation of Proposition 13 to cut property taxes.			In Delhi, India over 200 people reportedly have died from sunstroke or dehydration during a month-long heat wave with temperatures ranging between 105 F and 110 F.... Ethiopia declares an emergency and allocates $1 million for a control campaign against locusts, which are plaguing East Africa.	Variety lists "Shadow Dancing ", with Andy Gibbs as top-selling single record and City to City with Gerry Rafferty as top-selling album. ... NBA championship is won by the Washington Bullets, who beat the Seattle SuperSonics, 105–99, in the seventh game of the playoffs.	June 7
Pres. Carter threatens to veto not only the tuition-credits bill, but his own alternative bill to expand current grant and loan programs, which, he believes, Congress has expanded too far.			Space officials begin a series of radio commands to reorient the 84-ton Skylab space station, which has been circling Earth in a gradually deteriorating orbit since it was last manned in 1974.	The so-called Mormon will of Howard Hughes is unanimously ruled a forgery by a Las Vegas, Nev. district ct. jury. If authentic, it would have given one-fourth of Hughes' estate to the Howard Hughes Medical Institute, one-eighth to four universities, and a series of smaller shares to individuals, scholarship funds, and the Mormon church.	June 8
Democratic National Committee revises rules by which it will choose its presidential nominee in 1980. Former nominee Sen. Goerge McGovern (S.D.) charges that the changes disenfranchise dissident Democrats.	Navy and General Dynamics Corp. announce settlement of a major cost dispute over 18 attack submarines.	Pres. Carter proposes that Congress authorize 26 new water projects costing a total of $720 million to be drafted in accordance with his new national water policy.		Spencer Kimball, president of the worldwide Church of Jesus Christ of Latter-Day Saints, issues a letter rejecting the Mormon ban on black men from the church's priesthood.	June 9
				Forego , an ailing eight-year-old gelding, is retired from racing by his owner, Martha Gerry after earning $1,938 million in six years of racing. ... Affirmed wins the Belmont Stakes to become the eleventh horse to gain racing's Triple Crown. Bill Cauthen is the jockey.	June 10
	Senate Armed Service Committee report says that the components for neutron warheads should be stockpiled in the U.S., ready for quick shipment to Western Europe.			Nancy Lopez wins the LPGA golf tournament with a record 13 under par.... Bjorn Borg wins his third men's singles tennis title at the French Open with a 6–1, 6–1, 6–3 victory over Argentina's Guillermo Vilas.	June 11

F	G	H	I	J
Includes elections, federal-state relations, civil rights and liberties, crime, the judiciary, education, health care, poverty, urban affairs and population.	Includes formation and debate of U.S. foreign and defense policies, veterans' affairs and defense spending. (Relations with specific foreign countries are usually found under the region concerned.)	Includes business, labor, agriculture, taxation, transportation, consumer affairs, monetary and fiscal policy, natural resources, and pollution.	Includes worldwide scientific, medical and technological developments, natural phenomena, U.S. weather, natural disasters, and accidents.	Includes the arts, religion, scholarship, communications media, sports, entertainments, fashions, fads and social life.

	World Affairs	Europe	Africa & the Middle East	The Americas	Asia & the Pacific
June 12		In a national referendum, Italian voters overwhelmingly approve a controversial 1975 law that increases the police power in the country.	*Times of London* estimates 1,850 civilians and soldiers killed in Rhodesia's guerrilla warfare since the beginning of the year.	P.M. Elliott Trudeau presents a policy statement on a Canadian constitution to replace the British North America Act.	Pres. Ferdinand Marcos is sworn in as the Philippines first premier. While vowing to continue the martial law he imposed in 1972, Marcos says he will institute measures to make democracy real.
June 13	A study is submitted to the IEA's Trilateral Commission that charges that Western European, North American, and Japanese governments have not shown they comprehend the magnitude of the energy problems they face.... Cuban Pres. Fidel Castro tells two U.S. congressmen and three reporters that he had tried to block the invasion of Zaire when he learned it was planned several months before it happened.... Zairian govt. agrees to allow the IMF to appoint an official to a managing role in Zaire's national bank.		Israeli troops complete their withdrawal from southern Lebanon.... Two white Cape Town academics, who admit during their trial that they distributed pamphlets for banned organizations, are convicted in South Africa for participating in terrorist activities.		EEC informs the Australian govt. that it will not reduce its Australian coal imports.
June 14	U.N. Secy. Gen. Kurt Waldheim counters charges by Israeli For. Min. Moshe Dayan that UNIFIL is letting PLO guerrillas infiltrate southern Lebanese border areas evacuated by Israel and allowing them to receive arms.... Pres. Carter emphatically rejects Cuban Pres. Fidel Castro's denial of Cuban involvement in the invasion of Zaire.	In the closest vote on a confidence motion since he took office in 1976, British P.M. James Callaghan's Labor Party govt. wins, 287–282.	In wake of increasing modifications of South Africa's antiapartheid laws this year, a bill is enacted to allow blacks in urban townships to acquire 99-year leases on their homes and allows blacks to travel three miles from their homes without passbooks.... South African laws easing apartheid change the official designation "bantu" to "black" on all official documents, because bantu, the Zulu word for man, is deemed degrading by South African blacks.	In a surprise move, Quebec Finance Min. Jacques Parizeau says the tax rebate agreement worked out with the Canadian federal govt. is unacceptable.	Australian Statistics Bureau reports that the nation's sheep and cattle herds have been sharply reduced in size and that the sheep and lamb population is at its lowest level since 1954.
June 15		Italian Pres. Giovanni Leone resigns because of allegations connecting him to Lockheed bribery scandals and other improprieties.	In a TV interview, P.M. Ian Smith concedes that his government has not halted the five-year-old guerrilla war in Rhodesia.... Chief PLO representative in Kuwait, Ali Yasi, is shot to death at his home by unidentified gunmen.		
June 16	U.N. High Commissioner for Refugees and WHO reportedly condemn South Africa's extreme barbarity in its raid on Angola.		Christian forces in southern Lebanon reportely sharply disagree over their role. The dispute is marked by factional armed clashes and the house detention of Maj. Saad Haddad, Christian troop commander.	Pres. Carter and Brig. Gen. Omar Torrijos exchange the instruments of ratification of the new Panama Canal treaties at a Panama City ceremony. Later, at a rally, Carter addresses a crowd in Spanish, saying that "we stand on the threshhold of a new era of inter-American understanding and cooperation."	China is reported recalling its ambassador from Hanoi, Vietnam.
June 17	Top-level Soviet policymakers respond to Pres. Carter's June 7 speech on U.S.–Soviet relations with a commentary in the Soviet press. Their article charges that the U.S. course is fraught with danger, criticizes U.S. foreign policy on most major issues, and contends that Pres. Carter has distorted facts to a grave extent.	IRA gunmen kill a policeman belonging to the Royal Ulster Constabulary in Northern Ireland and kidnap his partner during an ambush near the Irish Republic border.			

A	B	C	D	E
Includes developments that affect more than one world region, international organizations and important meetings of major world leaders.	Includes all domestic and regional developments in Europe, including the Soviet Union, Turkey, Cyprus and Malta.	Includes all domestic and regional developments in Africa and the Middle East, including Iraq and Iran and excluding Cyprus, Turkey and Afghanistan.	Includes all domestic and regional developments in Latin America, the Caribbean and Canada.	Includes all domestic and regional developments in Asia and Pacific nations, extending from Afghanistan through all the Pacific Islands, except Hawaii.

U.S. Politics & Social Issues	U.S. Foreign Policy & Defense	U.S. Economy & Environment	Science, Technology & Nature	Culture, Leisure & Life Style	
AFL–CIO is fined $10,000 for violating federal campaign spending laws.... Supreme Ct. refuses to temporarily stay a lower court ruling that permits a neo-Nazi organization, the National Socialist Party of America, to hold a rally, set for June 25, in Skokie, Ill., a predominantly Jewish suburb of Chicago where many victims of WWII Nazi concentration camps live.	U.S. State Secy. Cyrus Vance pledges that the U.S. will not use nuclear weapons against countries that neither possess them or are allied with powers that do.	Bethlehem Steel Corp., the second largest steel producer in the U.S., announces that it will raise prices 3 percent, effective July 30.... Supreme Ct. votes, 8–0, to uphold a government regulation preventing newspapers from acquiring radio or TV stations in their communities.	Japan's main island of Honshu is rocked by an earthquake measuring 7.5 on the Richter scale. Twenty-seven people are killed and nearly 1,100 injured.... U.N. FAO official says he fears the locust plague could affect an area involving over 50 nations — from Morocco in the west to Iran and Pakistan in the east in a self-perpetuating plague.	Guy Lafleur of the Montreal Canadiens wins his second consecutive Hart Trophy as the most valuable player of the National Hockey League, the fifteenth time the honor has gone to a Montreal player.	June 12
David Berkowitz, the convicted Son of Sam killer, is sentenced in N.Y. Supreme Ct., Brooklyn to the maximum prison term for each of six murders that he committed in a year-long string of nighttime shootings before he was arrested in August 1977.				A tug-of-war between 2,200 students and teachers from the Harrisburg (Pa.) Middle School, attempting to set a world record, ends with 70 people injured when the 2,000-foot nylon rope they were using breaks.	June 13
In a series of decisions, the Supreme Ct. reinterprets the constitutional prohibition against double jeopardy (being tried twice for the same crime). In the principal case, it votes, 5–4, to reverse a doctrine it established in 1975 and 1977 rulings that held an indictment dismissed during a trial is a legal acquittal although the jury has not handed in a verdict.		Efforts to end a lengthy Senate filibuster against a revised federal labor law bill fail.		Tom Stoppard's *Every Good Boy Deserves Favour*, a musical fable about repression in Eastern Europe, is revived in London at the Mermaid Theatre.	June 14
		The $1-million Tellico Dam (Tenn.) project is indefinitely halted when the Supreme Ct. rules that the dam's construction threatens the extinction of the snail darter, a rare species of perch.	Two Soviet cosmonauts launch into orbit aboard Soyuz 29 spacecraft.		June 15
		Commerce Dept. reports that new housing starts dropped 4.9 percent below the April pace but were 4.7 percent higher than May 1977 levels.		*Grease*, the movie version of the Broadway musical about high school students in the 1950s, with John Travolta and Olivia Newton-John, is released in N.Y.C.	June 16
At an ADA convention, Sen. George McGovern says that support for California's Proposition 13, seen as a property tax-payers' revolt, has racist undertones because it reflects a desire to reduce social services to minorities.			Soviet cosmonauts board the orbiting Salyut 6 space station.	With the opening of Timon of Athens, the Oregon Shakespearean Festival accomplishes the unique feat of having produced two complete cycles of all of William Shakespeare's plays.	June 17

F	G	H	I	J
Includes elections, federal-state relations, civil rights and liberties, crime, the judiciary, education, health care, poverty, urban affairs and population.	*Includes formation and debate of U.S. foreign and defense policies, veterans' affairs and defense spending. (Relations with specific foreign countries are usually found under the region concerned.)*	*Includes business, labor, agriculture, taxation, transportation, consumer affairs, monetary and fiscal policy, natural resources, and pollution.*	*Includes worldwide scientific, medical and technological developments, natural phenomena, U.S. weather, natural disasters, and accidents.*	*Includes the arts, religion, scholarship, communications media, sports, entertainments, fashions, fads and social life.*

	World Affairs	Europe	Africa & the Middle East	The Americas	Asia & the Pacific
June 18			Israeli Cabinet issues a vaguely worded statement supporting Premier Menahem Begin's hard-line stance on the future of Israeli-occupied territory in the Gaza Strip and the West Bank. It is a response to U.S. pressure for a clear-cut statement on the future of Israeli-occupied territories to move the stalled Israeli–Egyptian peace talks.	Peruvians elect 100 members of a new Constituent Assembly, which will draft a national charter to prepare for the resumption of civilian rule in 1980. It is the first election in 10 years.	
June 19	OPEC announces that it will leave the price of oil unchanged at $12.70 a barrel through 1978.	Belgium King Baudouin formally rejects Premier Leo Tindemans' resignation, resolving a government crisis over economic policy issues.	Egypt suspends its ambassador to Portugal, Lt. Gen. Saad Eddin al-Shazli, and orders him back to Cairo to stand trial for criticizing Pres. Anwar Sadat by calling him an absolute ruler and taking issue with Sadat's Middle East peace initiative.		
June 20	U.S. State Secy. Cyrus Vance makes a major statement on U.S. African policy and says that the U.S. does not see Africa simply as an arena for East-West competition.... Yugoslav Pres. Tito warns the U.S. and U.S.S.R. that the chill in their relations threatens to precipitate another world war.		In private statements, the U.S. rejects the Israeli formula for the West Bank and the Gaza Strip as an inadequate response to U.S. peace proposals.	P.M. Pierre Trudeau introduces a bill to revise the Canadian Senate and Supreme Ct. and to enact constitutional safeguards of basic rights. The bill details his plan for a Canadian Constitution to replace the British North America Act.	Responding to China'a Hanoi Embassy closing, Vietnam orders closing its three consulates in China.
June 21		Vladimir Slepak, a dissident Soviet Jewish activist, is sentenced to five years of internal exile on charges of malicious hooliganism.	Israeli opposition Labor Party leader Shimon Peres says that he is maintaining contacts with Egyptian Pres. Sadat through intermediaries.... Donald McHenry, deputy U.S. ambassador to the U.N., visits Angola in the first official contact between the two countries since Angola won its independence in 1975.	Pres. Carter reaffirms his commitment to human rights in an opening speech to the OAS General Assembly, meeting in Wash., D.C.	
June 22		Till Meyer, who escaped from West Berlin's Moabit Prison on May 27, and three other West German terrorists are arrested in Bulgaria and immediately returned to West Germany. It is the first time a Soviet-bloc nation has returned suspected terrorists to the West.			
June 23		Twenty-nine of the 46 Red Brigades members on trial in Turin, Italy are convicted and sentenced to prison terms of up to 15 years. Sixteen are acquitted.		U.S. recalls its ambassador from Santiago, charging that the Chilean govt. is not sufficiently cooperating with its investigation of the 1976 murders of Orlando Letelier, former Chilean foreign minister, and his colleague, Ronni Moffitt, in Wash., D.C.... Quebec National Assembly passes a bill elaborating rules under which a referendum on independence will take place.	South Korean Pres. Park Chung Hee proposes forming a joint committee with North Korea to promote trade, an offer North Korea immediately rejects.
June 24			North Yemeni Pres. Ahmed Hussein al-Ghashmi is killed by a bomb that explodes in a suitcase of a visiting envoy sent by South Yemeni Pres. Salem Rubaya Ali.		

A	B	C	D	E
Includes developments that affect more than one world region, international organizations and important meetings of major world leaders.	Includes all domestic and regional developments in Europe, including the Soviet Union, Turkey, Cyprus and Malta.	Includes all domestic and regional developments in Africa and the Middle East, including Iraq and Iran and excluding Cyprus, Turkey and Afghanistan.	Includes all domestic and regional developments in Latin America, the Caribbean and Canada.	Includes all domestic and regional developments in Asia and Pacific nations, extending from Afghanistan through all the Pacific Islands, except Hawaii.

U.S. Politics & Social Issues	U.S. Foreign Policy & Defense	U.S. Economy & Environment	Science, Technology & Nature	Culture, Leisure & Life Style	
			Radioactive steam escapes into the atmosphere at a nuclear power station in Brunsbuettel, near Kiel, West Germany. Federal officials are reportedly concerned because human error played a major part in the near-disaster.... Scientists at the Goddard Space Flight Center in Greenbelt, Md. report that the San Andreas Fault in Calif. is shifting at a faster pace than expected.	Nancy Lopez, rookie of the LPGA, breaks the record for consecutive wins at the Bankers Trust Classic in Rochester, N.Y. and pushes her 1978 earnings up to $153,336 — more than any other rookie professional golfer in history.... Andy North beats J.C. Snead and Dave Stockton on the last hole in the U.S. Open golf tournament.	June 18
Supreme Ct. rules unanimously that plaintiffs in class-action lawsuits have to pay the cost of compiling the names and addresses of members of the affected class.	Senate Ethics Committee investigating the Korean lobbying scandal reports that the late Sen. John McClellan admitted before his death in 1977 that he had received an unreported campaign contribution from Tong Sun Park.	Carter administration announces final regulations to limit textile workers' exposure to cotton dust, which can produce byssinosis (brown lung disease).			June 19
Seventeen states and Wash., D.C. are reported continuing to fund all abortions for low-income women despite loss of federal matching funds.		U.S. govt.'s second gold sale does not stem the dollar's slide. Gold sells for an average $187.06 an ounce, yielding proceeds of $56.1 million.	An earthquake strikes the Salonika area in northern Greece, leaving at least 47 people dead and 150 injured. The quake registers 6.5 on the Richter scale.		June 20
Pres. Carter sends Congress a written statement protesting use of what he calls the legislative veto. ... Commerce Secy. Juanita Kreps, in a speech to the U.S. Conference of Mayors, says that tax rebellions such as Proposition 13 could contribute to urban decay.	The cruise missile is publicly tested for the first time at the White Sands Missile Range in New Mexico.	Supreme Ct. rules unanimously that under an 1897 law the Treasury Dept. is not required to impose countervailing duties on Japanese electronic products.... Commerce Dept. reports that the U.S. posted a record payments deficit in its balance-on-current-account during the first quarter.		*Evita*, a musical about the life of Argentine popular idol Eva Peron, with music by Andrew Lloyd Webber, lyrics by Tim Rice, and direction by Harold Prince, opens in London.	June 21
Illinois House of Representatives refuses for the second time in two weeks to ratify the proposed federal Equal Rights Amendment (ERA).	*Washington Post* reports that a GAO study has cleared Lockheed Shipbuilding and Construction Co. of 1977 charges of overbilling the government by about $8 million for steel used in construction of amphibious transport docks.	Energy Secy. James Schlesinger proposes a standby gasoline rationing plan in the event of an emergency.... Supreme Ct., in two separate decisions, affirms the power of labor unions to distribute their literature on company property.	Yale Medical School reports that damaged spleens surgically removed from children were replaced by regenerated new spleens in more than half the cases.... James Christy, of the U.S. Naval Observatory, discovers a hitherto unknown small moon of Pluto in orbit around it, only 12,000 miles from the planet.		June 22
N.Y.S. Supreme Ct. Justice L. Kingsley Smith rules that the state's method of funding public schools through property taxes is illegal.	On a political visit to Texas, Pres. Carter deplores efforts to make National Security Adviser Zbigniew Brzezinski a scapegoat of foreign policy criticism.	Russell Peterson, the director of a congressional research organization, tells a Senate subcommittee that the primary barrier to widespread use of on-site solar energy is not technology but economics.	Japan, France, and West Germany are reported reaching an agreement for cooperation in research on sodium-cooled breeder reactors.		June 23
Calif. Gov. Edmund Brown Jr. signs a bill allocating $5 billion of the state's $5.8-billion budget surplus to cities, counties, and schools facing drastic cutbacks because of the tax revenue loss from Proposition 13.			Clamshell Alliance begins a three-day demonstration against the controversial proposed nuclear-power plant in Seabrook, N.H. after setting ground rules for the protest with the state govt. and the Public Service Co. of New Hampshire.		June 24

F	G	H	I	J
Includes elections, federal-state relations, civil rights and liberties, crime, the judiciary, education, health care, poverty, urban affairs and population.	*Includes formation and debate of U.S. foreign and defense policies, veterans' affairs and defense spending. (Relations with specific foreign countries are usually found under the region concerned.)*	*Includes business, labor, agriculture, taxation, transportation, consumer affairs, monetary and fiscal policy, natural resources, and pollution.*	*Includes worldwide scientific, medical and technological developments, natural phenomena, U.S. weather, natural disasters, and accidents.*	*Includes the arts, religion, scholarship, communications media, sports, entertainments, fashions, fads and social life.*

	World Affairs	Europe	Africa & the Middle East	The Americas	Asia & the Pacific
June 25	Soviet Pres. Leonid Brezhnev denounces the U.S. for pitting China against the Soviet Union, in a speech that is his first public reaction to deteriorating U.S.–Soviet relations.	Moscow switches its Cyprus policy after Turkish Premier Bulent Ecevit concludes a three-day visit to the Soviet Union and now conforms to the Turkish position. The two countries issue a joint communique saying that Cyprus should resolve its dispute by direct talks between the Greek and Turkish communities there.	Israeli Cabinet rejects an Egyptian proposal on Israeli-occupied territory before it formally receives the plan, which calls for Israel to return the West Bank to Jordan and the Gaza Strip to Egypt and for Egypt and Jordan to negotiate security arrangements and Arab autonomy with Israel. . . . A three-man Military Command Council replaces assassinated North Yemeni Pres. Ahmed Hussein al-Ghashmi.		
June 26		Iceland's Cabinet, led by Premier Geir Hallgrimsson, announces that it will step down because of heavy losses in the June 25 election.	A rival faction of the pro-Soviet ruling front deposes and executes South Yemeni Pres. Salem Rubaya Ali after 12 hours of heavy fighting in Aden, the capital city.		About 100 homosexual-rights supporters throw debris at police outside a Sydney, Australia courtroom.
June 27	Soviet bloc's debt to industrialized Western nations is reported by the OECD to be rising, with a trade deficit of about $6 billion a year. . . . ILO conferees reject an Arab-sponsored resolution accusing Israel of discrimination, racism, and violation of trade union rights in Arab territories it occupies.	Paris police begin arresting Breton separatists in wake of yesterday's bombing at Versailles Palace. . . . About 1,000 workers from five Renault Co. automobile plants in France march through downtown Paris and halt afternoon traffic. The state-owned company is regarded as a weather vane in French industrial relations.			Hanoi radio reports 160 casualties in border fighting with Cambodia on June 20 and 23. Vietnam also denies a Cambodian claim that it had collaborated with the U.S. CIA to try to overthrow the Cambodian govt. in May.
June 28			Addis Ababa radio reports that there have been nine assassination attempts against Ethiopian leader Lt. Col. Mengistu Haile Mariam since September 1977.		
June 29	Vietnam becomes the tenth full member of COMECON, the Soviet bloc's economic association.		Two Israelis are killed and a least 35 injured when a bomb explodes in a market in Jerusalem.		
June 30	U.N. General Assembly's special session on disarmament closes with the adoption of a resolution to change the format of the 31-nation Conference of the Committee on Disarmament.	West German Chancellor Helmut Schmidt again defends West Germany's trade relations with South Africa in public statements in Zambia during his four-day visit to black African states.	Pres. Carter indicates that the U.S. might press for reconvening the Geneva Mideast peace conference if current U.S. efforts to break the Egyptian–Israeli deadlock fail. He calls the Egyptian peace plan inadequate, although a step in the right direction.		British Foreign Office announces that Brunei independence is set for 1983. . . . U.S. bars a jet aircraft sale to Taiwan in another gesture to strengthen its relations with China.
July 1			Syrian troops of the Arab League peacekeeping force in Lebanon engage in fierce fighting with unnumbered Christian militiamen in and around Beirut.	In his inaugural address, Guatemalan Pres. Romeo Lucas Garcia says that Guatemala will continue to claim its territorial rights in Belize. . . . Quebec provincial govt. puts into effect a law limiting the availability of construction jobs to workers from other provinces.	Australian federal govt. grants partial self-rule to the thinly populated Northern Territory, which had been directly governed from the federal capital in Canberra since 1911.

A	B	C	D	E
Includes developments that affect more than one world region, international organizations and important meetings of major world leaders.	*Includes all domestic and regional developments in Europe, including the Soviet Union, Turkey, Cyprus and Malta.*	*Includes all domestic and regional developments in Africa and the Middle East, including Iraq and Iran and excluding Cyprus, Turkey and Afghanistan.*	*Includes all domestic and regional developments in Latin America, the Caribbean and Canada.*	*Includes all domestic and regional developments in Asia and Pacific nations, extending from Afghanistan through all the Pacific Islands, except Hawaii.*

U.S. Politics & Social Issues	U.S. Foreign Policy & Defense	U.S. Economy & Environment	Science, Technology & Nature	Culture, Leisure & Life Style	
Frank Collin, leader of the American Nazi party, the National Socialist Party of America, cancels the march scheduled today in Skokie, Ill. after the U.S. Supreme Ct. refused to issue a delaying order against it. He applies for a permit to demonstrate in Marquette Park, Chicago.... Thousands of homosexuals march in San Francisco and tens of thousands march up Fifth Avenue in N.Y.C. to mark the final day of Gay and Lesbian Pride Week.				Argentina wins the eleventh World Cup soccer championship when its national team defeats the Netherlands, 3–1.	June 25
Pres. Carter's campaign committee agrees to pay a $1,200 civil penalty for illegal political use of the National Bank of Georgia's private plane. The bank was headed at the time by Bert Lance, former OMB director and Pres. Carter's friend.	In a news conference Pres. Carter stresses a unified U.S. foreign policy to counter mounting charges that the policy is beset by confusion and doubt.	Pres. Carter opens his news conference with an attack on congressional proposals to cut the capital-gains tax.	Three accidents in West German nuclear plants reportedly are arousing concern among officials and the public.	A powerful bomb explodes in France's historic Palace of Versailles, wrecking three of 14 ground-floor rooms containing precious art works. A branch of the Breton Liberation Front is suspected.... Martha Graham's dance work, *The Owl and the Pussycat*, premieres at the Metropolitan Opera House in N.Y.C.	June 26
		Sen. Robert Dole (R, Kan.) sponsors an amendment to an appropriations bill that would bar Pres. Carter from imposing import fees on oil.		Henry Rono, a Kenyan studying at Washington State University, is the first athlete in the history of track to hold four world records.	June 27
Supreme Ct. rules, 5–4, that the University of California Medical School's affirmative action minority admissions program made white applicant Allan Bakke the victim of reverse discrimination and that he must be admitted.... Another Supreme Ct. 5–4 alignment rules that although the University of California's affirmative action is illegal, universities can consider race as a factor in choosing applicants. Justice Lewis Powell Jr.. casts the deciding vote in both aspects of the case.		Economist John Kenneth Galbraith calls Proposition 13 a disguised attack on the poor, in a speech before the American Federation of State, County and Municipal Employees in Las Vegas.	Soyuz 30 docks with Slayut 6.	Martha Graham closes her run of new dance premieres at N.Y.C.'s Metropolitan Opera House with *The Flute of Pan*.	June 28
Pres. Carter issues an executive order revising federal rules that cover document classification and stripping a number of agencies of their authority to classify documents.		A *New York Times* study says that imposition of a crude oil import fee would reduce the inflow of foreign oil by only 3.5 percent by 1985.		Joseph Papp's New York Shakespeare Festival opens in the Delacorte Theater in Central Park with *All's Well That Ends Well*.	June 29
			Nuclear Regulatory Comission, 2–1, orders construction of the Seabrook, N.H. nuclear power plant suspended, effective July 21.		June 30
					July 1

F	G	H	I	J
Includes elections, federal-state relations, civil rights and liberties, crime, the judiciary, education, health care, poverty, urban affairs and population.	Includes formation and debate of U.S. foreign and defense policies, veterans' affairs and defense spending. (Relations with specific foreign countries are usually found under the region concerned.)	Includes business, labor, agriculture, taxation, transportation, consumer affairs, monetary and fiscal policy, natural resources, and pollution.	Includes worldwide scientific, medical and technological developments, natural phenomena, U.S. weather, natural disasters, and accidents.	Includes the arts, religion, scholarship, communications media, sports, entertainments, fashions, fads and social life.

	World Affairs	Europe	Africa & the Middle East	The Americas	Asia & the Pacific
July 2			Arab League freezes political and diplomatic relations with South Yemen and suspends economic and cultural ties.... V.P. Mondale reaffirms the U.S. commitment to Israel at a state dinner given in his honor.		
July 3		Corsican separatists explode 33 bombs in the largest demonstration of anti-French activity since the secessionist movement began in the early 1960s.	After meeting with Israeli Premier Menahem Begin, V.P. Mondale says they have agreed to a quick resumption of Israeli–Egyptian peace talks.... V.P. Mondale flies to Egypt where Pres. Anwar Sadat hands him a Middle East peace plan.		France withdraws its ambassador and most of its diplomatic mission from Laos at the request of the Laotian govt.... Cambodia claims that tens of thousands of Vietnamese have been killed or wounded in fighting between the two countries that started in 1975 and accelerated in December 1977.
July 4		Eight Breton nationalists are charged with numerous bombings in France, including the June blasts at Versailles Palace.... Soviet govt. allows U.S. Amb. Malcolm Toon to deliver his U.S. Independence Day speech over Soviet TV.	Christian leader Camille Chamoun denounces the Arab League peacekeeping force in Lebanon as protectors turned aggressors.... Israel claims that PLO guerrillas continue to infiltrate southern Lebanon where their forces now total over 400 men.... Libyan leader Col. Muammer el-Qaddafi promises military aid and oil supplies for Malta following talks with Maltese P.M. Dom Mintoff.		
July 5		French authorities act to prevent oil spills in coastal waters.	Egypt's formal plan for a Middle East peace is made public by the U.S. The plan provides for Israel to withdraw from the West Bank, East Jerusalem, and the Gaza Strip over a five-year period and turn transitional sovereignty over to Jordan and Egypt. Israel would also abandon immediately its settlements and military rule in the occupied territories.... The opposition United Sudanese National Front formally disbands after opposing Pres. Mohammed Gaafar el-Nimeiry for more than 20 years.	A Nicaraguan group of exiled intellectuals, priests, businessmen, and professionals, who call themselves The Twelve (although they number 10), return to Nicaragua from Costa Rica after Pres. Anastasio Somoza Debayle revokes their arrest warrants.	Pakistani military leader Gen. Muhammad Zia ul-Haq appoints a new 17-member Cabinet, replacing his advisory council.
July 6		Protesters demanding withdrawal of British troops from Ulster throw three bags of manure onto the floor of the British House of Commons. ... EEC-member heads of state end two days of meetings in Bremen, West Germany where the major topic was a French-West German proposal to form an EEC monetary zone to stabilize the European currencies' exchange rates.	A truce agreement is reached in Lebanon after Israel implies that it might intervene militarily if Syria does not stop its attacks against the Christians.	Canadian govt. calls for a halt to all land development in the northern Yukon Territory.	Chinese govt. authorizes managers of the Bank of China and 12 sister banks in Hong Kong to practice capitalistic methods as long as they are confident of making a profit.
July 7		The French-German monetary union plan would have the European countries gradually link their currencies into a joint float that would fluctuate as a unit against the U.S. dollar.	Joseph Conombo is elected premier of Upper Volta by the country's 57-member civilian Parliament.... Francisco Mendes, 38, premier of Guinea-Bissau since the country's independence from Portugal in 1974, dies in an automobile accident in Lisbon.	Domingo Laino, vice president of Paraguay's opposition Authentic Radical Liberal Party, is arrested for what the government calls his association with the extreme left. His arrest severely strains Paraguay's relations with the U.S.	Chinese CP Chmn. Hua Kuo-feng declares in a speech that China must learn from other countries' advanced experience to expand its own economy and trade.... Solomon Islands become independent after 85 years of British rule.
July 8		U.S. grants Hungary most-favored-nation trading status.... Police open fire on a crowd in the Pamplona bullring in Spain, touching off riots, demonstrations, and strikes throughout the Basque country.... The Italian Electoral Assembly elects Socialist Alessandro Pertini president of Italy by an overwhelming majority.		Following nearly two months of secret vote-counting, Antonio Guzman is declared winner of the Dominican Republic's May 16 presidential election.	Malaysia's ruling coalition led by P.M. Hussein bin Dato Onn scores a resounding victory in federal and state elections.

A	B	C	D	E
Includes developments that affect more than one world region, international organizations and important meetings of major world leaders.	Includes all domestic and regional developments in Europe, including the Soviet Union, Turkey, Cyprus and Malta.	Includes all domestic and regional developments in Africa and the Middle East, including Iraq and Iran and excluding Cyprus, Turkey and Afghanistan.	Includes all domestic and regional developments in Latin America, the Caribbean and Canada.	Includes all domestic and regional developments in Asia and Pacific nations, extending from Afghanistan through all the Pacific Islands, except Hawaii.

U.S. Politics & Social Issues	U.S. Foreign Policy & Defense	U.S. Economy & Environment	Science, Technology & Nature	Culture, Leisure & Life Style	
	Rep. Les Aspin (D, Wis.) contends that the Defense Dept. should consider lowering intelligence standards for military recruitment.			*Scruples* by Judith Krantz heads the fiction best-selling book list for the week just passed.	July 2
Supreme Ct., 7–1, strikes down Ohio's death penalty law and declines to review lower court decisions that voided capital punishment statutes in N.Y.S. and Pa. Justice William Rehnquist dissents.				James Daly, 59, a character actor best known for the TV series *Medical Center* and winner of a 1966 Emmy award, dies of a heart attack in Nyack, N.Y. . . . Supreme Ct. rules, 5–4, that the FCC can prohibit the broadcasting of language that is not legally obscene.	July 3
				Many of the activities of N.Y.C.'s Harbor Festival to celebrate Independence Day are rained out, but the rain ends in the evening to allow Macy's annual fireworks display.	July 4
			The Soviet Soyuz 30 spacecraft lands safely in the Soviet Kazakhstan, carrying a two-man crew of Col. Pyotr Klimuk and Maj. Miroslaw Hermaszewski who had gone into space on June 27.	"Shadow Dancing ", (Andy Gibbs) is the best-selling single record and *Some Girls*, (Rolling Stones) is the best-selling album. . . . *Grease* is the top-grossing film for the week just passed.	July 5
Atty. Gen. Griffin Bell is found in contempt of court for refusing to turn over the files of some FBI informants who had spied on the Socialist Workers Party.	Sen. William Proxmire (D, Wis.) charges that the Navy's proposed contract settlements with General Dynamics Corp. and Litton Industries Inc. is a move to bail-out the two ship contractors.			A Roman Catholic mass is performed in the House of Commons Chapel in Westminster Palace. It is the first performed in the chapel since the Reformation and is held in honor of the four hundredth anniversary of the birth of Thomas More, a Roman Catholic martyr condemned to death by King Henry VIII.	July 6
	U.S. District Ct. Judge Oren Lewis rules that Frank Snepp III, a former CIA employe who wrote an unauthorized book about the agency, violated his secrecy contract and must turn his earnings from the book over to the government.	Unemployment is reported declining sharply in June, when 5.7 percent of the nation's labor force was without work, bringing the jobless rate to its lowest level since August 1974, when 5.4 percent of the work force was unemployed.	U.S. Naval Observatory astronomers announce that they have discovered a moon orbiting Pluto, the planet that during most of its orbit is most distant from the sun.	Martina Navratilova downs favored Chris Evert in the final of the women's single's tennis championship at Wimbledon, England.	July 7
About 100 robed and hooded Ku Klux Klansmen parade in Davie, Fla., after repeated requests for a permit over a three-year period had been denied.		*Washington Post* reports a sharp 1976 decline in the number of rich people who paid no federal income taxes and attributes the drop to the Tax Reform Act of 1976, which tightened tax-shelter rules and increased the minimum tax.		A fire inside Rio de Janeiro's Museum of Modern Art destroys nearly a thousand paintings in 30 minutes with damage estimated between $10–$15 million. . . . Sweden's Bjorn Borg wins his third consecutive men's singles tennis title at Wimbledon, England.	July 8
F *Includes elections, federal-state relations, civil rights and liberties, crime, the judiciary, education, health care, poverty, urban affairs and population.*	**G** *Includes formation and debate of U.S. foreign and defense policies, veterans' affairs and defense spending. (Relations with specific foreign countries are usually found under the region concerned.)*	**H** *Includes business, labor, agriculture, taxation, transportation, consumer affairs, monetary and fiscal policy, natural resources, and pollution.*	**I** *Includes worldwide scientific, medical and technological developments, natural phenomena, U.S. weather, natural disasters, and accidents.*	**J** *Includes the arts, religion, scholarship, communications media, sports, entertainments, fashions, fads and social life.*	

	World Affairs	Europe	Africa & the Middle East	The Americas	Asia & the Pacific
July 9		Maltese P.M. Dominic Mintoff issues an order banning all British journals from Malta.	Israeli Cabinet formally rejects an Egyptian peace plan calling for an Israeli withdrawal from the West Bank and Gaza Strip. It accepts an American proposal for a meeting of the Israeli and Egyptian foreign ministers and U.S. State Secy. Cyrus Vance in London. . . . Former Iraqi Premier Abdul Razak al-Naif is shot in London as he walks out of his hotel toward a taxi.	Widespread confusion, irregularities, and fraud charges mark Bolivia's first election in 12 years. . . . A new wave of Nicaraguan violence begins when police in the town of Jinotepe shoot six students who, the police claim, had thrown a gasoline bomb at a police car.	An agreement is reached in which the estimated 200,000 Moslems who have fled to Bangladesh since April will be returned to Burma by the end of August.
July 10	Austrian Chancellor Bruno Kreisky and former West German Chancellor Willy Brandt, participants in talks between Egyptian Pres. Anwar Sadat and Israeli opposition party leader Shimon Peres, unveil their own plan for a Middle East peace settlement.	Israeli Premier Menahem Begin calls the trial of Soviet dissident Anatoly Shcharansky an example of traditional anti-Semitism.	Former Iraqi Premier Abdul Razak al-Naif dies after being shot twice in the head the previous day.		
July 11		One of Turkey's leading intellectuals, Bedrettin Comert, is shot and killed by gunmen in a suburb of Ankara, who are believed to be members of a right-wing terrorist group. . . . A sit-in by seven Soviet Pentecostalists at the U.S. Embassy in Moscow enters its third week.		Canada's unemployment rate for June remains at 8.6 percent for the fourth month in a row.	A Hanoi broadcast charges that Chinese fighter planes flew over Vietnamese territory on July 9.
July 12		Viscount Rothermere, 80, publisher of two London newspapers, dies in London, England.	The South-West Africa People's Organization (SWAPO) accepts the West's plan to end South African rule over Namibia after two days of talks in Luanda, Angola between SWAPO leader Sam Nujoma and the Western contact group.	A team of 10 observers from Latin American countries, Western European nations, and the U.S. issue a report asserting that the Bolivian govt. had altered the contents of ballot boxes and falsified voting records in the presidential election.	
July 13	U.S. State Secy. Vance and Soviet For. Min. Gromyko say at a joint press conference following talks on remaining obstacles to a SALT treaty that their discussions helped to introduce new proposals for reconciling the remaining conflicts.	Alexander Ginzburg, manager of a fund for Soviet political prisoners, is sentenced to eight years in a labor camp on charges of anti-Soviet agitation and propaganda.	Egyptian Pres. Anwar Sadat submits a new peace plan in an unexpected meeting with Israeli Defense Min. Ezer Weizman near Salzburg, Austria. . . . Rival Palestinian forces clash in southern Lebanon around Tyre and Saida.		In a sudden reversal of policy, Peking announces restrictions on Vietnamese ethnic Chinese wishing to enter China because Vietnam allegedly violated a joint border control accord.
July 14	U.S. dollar continues to flounder, showing no signs of correcting its fundamental weakness against major currencies.	Anatoly Shcharansky, a Soviet-Jewish dissident, is convicted of treason, espionage, and anti-Soviet agitation, and he is sentenced to three years in prison followed by 10 years in a forced labor camp.	Henri Maidou replaces Ange Patasse as premier of the Central African Empire.	Canadian govt. announces reaching tentative agreement with 2,500 Inuit (Eskimos) on land rights in the Northwest Territories.	Five leading South Koreans are arrested on corruption charges linked to a housing scandal. . . . Former Australian P.M. Gough Whitlam announces that he is leaving politics to become a university lecturer.
July 15		Pres. Carter visits Berlin where he tells West Berliners that Berlin will stay free no matter what happens, speaking the phrase in German.	Lebanese Pres. Elias Sarkis withdraws his decision to resign.		Thailand and Cambodia agree in principle to settle their long-standing border dispute and to exchange ambassadors.
July 16		A West German terrorist, Kristina Berster, is arrested near Alburg, Vt., while trying to enter the U.S. illegally from Canada. . . . Fyodor Kulakov, 60, Soviet Politburo member viewed as a possible successor to Leonid Brezhnev, dies of a heart attack in Moscow.	Israeli Cabinet defers consideration of Pres. Sadat's latest peace proposal until the Israeli–Egyptian foreign ministers' meeting concludes and debates, instead, the appropriateness of Defense Min. Ezer Weizman's meeting with Sadat, bypassing Premier Menahem Begin.	No candidate wins a majority in Ecuador's first presidential election in 10 years. A runoff between the two leading candidates, Jaime Roldos and Sixto Duran Ballen, will be held in about a month.	Spain's King Juan Carlos arrives in Peking and is greeted by Premier Hua Kuo-feng, Deputy Premier Teng Hsiao-ping, and practically the entire ambassadorial corps. He is the first European monarch to visit China and the first Spanish chief of state to visit a Communist country.

A	B	C	D	E
Includes developments that affect more than one world region, international organizations and important meetings of major world leaders.	*Includes all domestic and regional developments in Europe, including the Soviet Union, Turkey, Cyprus and Malta.*	*Includes all domestic and regional developments in Africa and the Middle East, including Iraq and Iran and excluding Cyprus, Turkey and Afghanistan.*	*Includes all domestic and regional developments in Latin America, the Caribbean and Canada.*	*Includes all domestic and regional developments in Asia and Pacific nations, extending from Afghanistan through all the Pacific Islands, except Hawaii.*

U.S. Politics & Social Issues	U.S. Foreign Policy & Defense	U.S. Economy & Environment	Science, Technology & Nature	Culture, Leisure & Life Style	
National Socialist Party of America (Nazi) rallies in Marquette Park in Chicago, Ill. before an estimated 2,000–3,000 spectators, the culmination of over a year of legal battles that reached the U.S. Supreme Ct.					July 9
		John D. Rockefeller III, 72, philanthropist and eldest of the five grandsons of the Standard Oil Co. founder, dies in an automobile accident in Pocantico Hills, N.Y.			July 10
The New York Times reports that FBI informant Gary Rowe Jr. told Ala. investigators that he had shot and killed a black man during the 1963 Birmingham riots and kept quiet about the shooting at the instruction of FBI agents.	Pres. Carter tells congressional leaders that leaks of classified information from Congress are hurting U.S. intelligence gathering. . . . Senate votes, 87–2, authorizing $36.1 billion in fiscal 1979 for weapons purchases and development.		A House health subcommittee is told that women x-rayed needlessly during pregnancy could produce 70 children a year with a predisposition to developing cancer.	NL downs the AL, 7–3, in the forty-ninth annual major league baseball All-Star game, giving the NL its seventh consecutive victory.	July 11
Justice Dept. begins an investigation to see if FBI informant, Gary Rowe Jr. had promoted and participated in violent acts with the Ku Klux Klan and whether FBI agents helped him conceal his activities.		House approves, 341–61, a $1.3-billion parks and wilderness bill, which is the largest such bill in history.	House rejects a resolution, sponsored by Rep. Richard Ottinger (D, N.Y.) that would have barred the sale of seven tons of uranium to India for a nuclear power plant.		July 12
House and Senate agree on a compromise version of a federal aid bill for N.Y.C., setting loan guarantees at $1.65 billion with Sen. William Proxmire (D, Wis.), who had opposed the legislation, instrumental in arranging the compromise.	House Ethics Committee cites four House members, all Democrats, for misconduct connected with the Korean lobbying effort. They are John McFall (Calif.), Edward Patten (N.J.), Edward Roybal (Calif.), and Charles H. Wilson (Calif.)	Henry Ford II, chairman of the Ford Motor Co., fires its president, Lee Iacocca, citing disagreement over top-level reorganization of the company.		Oliver Messel, 74, British theatrical designer for opera, ballet, movies, and the theater, whose style departed from nineteeth-century naturalism, dies of a heart attack in Barbados, West Indies.	July 13
Washington Post reports that the late rock and roll singer Elvis Presley offered to serve as an FBI informant in late 1970 and expressed his administration for J. Edgar Hoover, the then FBI director.		Los Angeles County, Calif. District Atty. John Van de Kamp announces creating a special investigative team to determine the extent of white-collar crime in the movie industry.		New York University announces it is canceling all exchange programs with the Soviet Union because of the sentences given Soviet dissidents Anatoly Shcharansky and Alexander Ginzburg.	July 14
A 2,700-mile "Longest Walk" march from Alcatraz Island, Calif. by some 1,000 American Indians and a similar number of supporters ends at the Capitol steps in Wash., D.C. Only about 20 of the original marchers, organized by the American Indian Movement (AIM), make it all the way.				Jack Nicklaus wins his third British Open golf title at St. Andrews, Scotland in a final-round duel with newcomer Simon Owen.	July 15
	Brookings Institution issues a study that questions the practicality and desirability of the Carter administration's policy of setting a dollar limit on arms sales to nonaligned countries.				July 16
F	**G**	**H**	**I**	**J**	
Includes elections, federal-state relations, civil rights and liberties, crime, the judiciary, education, health care, poverty, urban affairs and population.	*Includes formation and debate of U.S. foreign and defense policies, veterans' affairs and defense spending. (Relations with specific foreign countries are usually found under the region concerned.)*	*Includes business, labor, agriculture, taxation, transportation, consumer affairs, monetary and fiscal policy, natural resources, and pollution.*	*Includes worldwide scientific, medical and technological developments, natural phenomena, U.S. weather, natural disasters, and accidents.*	*Includes the arts, religion, scholarship, communications media, sports, entertainments, fashions, fads and social life.*	

	World Affairs	Europe	Africa & the Middle East	The Americas	Asia & the Pacific
July 17	Leaders of the world's seven major non-Communist industrial powers and an EEC representative conclude two days of talks about spurring economic growth without rekindling inflation.	A Communist-led coalition is voted into office by a one-vote majority in San Marino's Great and General Council (parliament).	The People's Council elects Col. Ali Abdullah Saleh as president of North Yemen. . . . Bishop Abel Muzorewa, a member of the multiracial Rhodesian transitional govt., arrives in Washington to begin campaigning for an end to U.S. trade sanctions against Rhodesia. . . . Two British workers who were publicly flogged in Saudi Arabia for breaking the country's strict alcohol laws are fired.		Cambodian Deputy Premier Ieng Sary embarrasses his Thai hosts by publicly assailing Vietnam while he is visiting Thailand. He also denies reports that the Cambodian govt. carried out large-scale massacres of Cambodians.
July 18	Union Bank of Switzerland release figures showing that tiny, oil-rich Kuwait was the world's wealthiest country in 1977 in terms of the ratio of its GNP to its population. The U.S. falls to fifth place from fourth in 1976 because of a deep drop in the value of the dollar.		Robert Mugabe, one of the Rhodesian guerrilla leaders, speaks before the OAU annual summit meeting on behalf of African liberation movements and praises the Western-sponsored settlement proposed for Namibia. . . . Rhodesian P.M. Ian Smith charges that black leaders have failed to keep their part of the majority rule agreement to end fighting in the country.	Bolivian opposition political candidate Hernan Siles Zuazo begins a hunger strike to protest the vote count and other alleged irregularities in the presidential elections. . . . U.S. intelligence estimates that about 1,500 Cuban soldiers have died fighting in Africa since 1975, mostly in Angola.	
July 19		A CIA report shows that the Soviet Union has a substantial civil defense program.	United African National Councils charges that failure to end fighting in Rhodesia is the responsibility of the entire transitional government, including the whites, and also charges that the whites have not made sufficient efforts to remove discrimination in Rhodesia.	Bolivian elections are annulled by the national electoral court because of widespread charges of vote fraud in favor of candidate Juan Pereda Asbun. Pereda reportedly agrees to hold new elections in six months.	
July 20	Pres. Carter says that he has not embarked on a vendetta against the Soviet Union.	Press reports claim that political killings in Turkey occur on the average of twice daily.	Israeli opposition Labor Party questions whether Premier Menahem Begin is physically and mentally fit to continue in office. . . . Israeli Knesset (parliament) approves a law exempting religious women from military service.	Sandinista guerrillas fire two rockets into a military installation in Managua, Nicaragua, killing two government officials and wounding another four.	Australian govt. announces it will introduce a bill establishing a tax on mining royalties received by Aborigines.
July 21		The British govt. announces an extension of its wage-restraint policy that would limit pay increases to 5 percent.	Angolan Pres. Agostinho Neto urges the U.S. to recognize his government.	Bolivian air force general Juan Pereda Asbun seizes control of the Bolivian govt. in a one-day military rebellion that topples Pres. Hugo Banzer Suarez. He had been the presidential candidate in July 9 elections where he claimed victory after an incomplete vote count gave him 50.13 percent of the ballots.	
July 22			Egyptian Pres. Anwar Sadat accuses Israeli Premier Menahem Begin of blocking a peace accord, saying that peace could be established within hours. . . . New fighting erupts between Lebanese Christians and Syrian troops of the Arab League peacekeeping force.	Ontario Premier William Davis requests Canadian P.M. Pierre Trudeau to question the legality of Quebec's law limiting construction jobs.	Laos gives full support to Vietnam in its dispute with China.

A	B	C	D	E
Includes developments that affect more than one world region, international organizations and important meetings of major world leaders.	Includes all domestic and regional developments in Europe, including the Soviet Union, Turkey, Cyprus and Malta.	Includes all domestic and regional developments in Africa and the Middle East, including Iraq and Iran and excluding Cyprus, Turkey and Afghanistan.	Includes all domestic and regional developments in Latin America, the Caribbean and Canada.	Includes all domestic and regional developments in Asia and Pacific nations, extending from Afghanistan through all the Pacific Islands, except Hawaii.

U.S. Politics & Social Issues	U.S. Foreign Policy & Defense	U.S. Economy & Environment	Science, Technology & Nature	Culture, Leisure & Life Style	
			Doris and John Del Zio's suit against the Columbia Presbyterian Medical Center, N.Y.C., charging that it destroyed a day-old embryo conceived by artificial insemination, goes to jury trial in Manhattan.	Britain's D'Oyle Carte Opera Co. opens a repertory of four Gilbert & Sullivan revivals at the New York State Theater in Lincoln Center with a production of *Iolanthe* .	July 17
About 25 American Indian religious leaders and elders from the "Longest Walk" protest meet privately with V.P. Walter Mondale and seek a meeting with Pres. Carter.		By a 92–6 vote, the Senate approves a bill requiring most new electric power plants and industrial facilities to use fuel other than oil or natural gas. Coal is seen as the most probable replacement fuel.	U.S. cancels the sale of an advanced computer to Tass, the Soviet news agency, in retaliation to the sentences given to dissidents Anatoly Shcharansky and Alexander Ginzburg, and Pres. Carter orders all sales of U.S. oil technology to be placed under administration review.		July 18
House, 213–196, refuses to consider legislation that would provide partial public financing for congressional elections. . . . United Paperworkers International Union president Joseph Tonelli is indicted by a N.Y. federal grand jury on charges of racketeering, embezzling $360,000 in union and pension funds, conspiracy, and accepting unlawful payments to influence pension-fund operations.		American Petroleum Institute reports that U.S. oil imports fell 12.8 percent in the first six months of 1978 compared with the same period in 1977.		*The New York Times* reports that residents of Wildwood, N.J. are trying to impose a dress code, prompted by tourists wearing skimpy bathing suits in the town. The ACLU holds that people can dress as they see fit.	July 19
Columnist Jack Anderson reports on ABC-TV that Dr. Peter Bourne had used cocaine at a Washington party in December 1977 given by the National Organization for the Reform of Marijuana Laws. Bourne's resignation as Carter's chief adviser on narcotics was more directly related to a prescription Bourne wrote for a sleeping aid.			Henri Moureu, 79, French scientist who frustrated German plans to develop an atomic bomb in WWII by keeping French stocks of heavy water out of Nazi hands, is reported dead in Pau, France. . . . Finland and Australia sign an accord setting safeguards for uranium exports from Australia to Finland.	John D. Rockefeller III's will, filed in White Plains, N.Y., bequeaths his American art collection to the Fine Arts Museum (San Francisco) and 300 art objects to the Asia Society in N.Y.C.	July 20
Benjamin Hooks, NAACP executive director, gives the Republican National Committee a prescription for winning the black vote and says that blacks resent the Democratic Party taking their vote for granted.		GNP rises 7.4 percent at a seasonally adjusted annual rate in the second quarter. The increase is the largest since the first quarter of 1976. . . . U.S. Postal Service and three unions reach a tentative agreement on a new contract calling for a 19.5 percent increase in wages and benefits over the next three years.		Following a July 3 Supreme Ct. decision upholding the FCC's right to reprimand stations broadcasting profane language, FCC Chmn. Charles Ferris assures the broadcasting industry that the FCC is not going to become a censor.	July 21
				Egyptian soccer players are assaulted by the Libyan team and its fans armed with bars and clubs at the African Games in Algiers.	July 22

F	G	H	I	J
Includes elections, federal-state relations, civil rights and liberties, crime, the judiciary, education, health care, poverty, urban affairs and population.	*Includes formation and debate of U.S. foreign and defense policies, veterans' affairs and defense spending. (Relations with specific foreign countries are usually found under the region concerned.)*	*Includes business, labor, agriculture, taxation, transportation, consumer affairs, monetary and fiscal policy, natural resources, and pollution.*	*Includes worldwide scientific, medical and technological developments, natural phenomena, U.S. weather, natural disasters, and accidents.*	*Includes the arts, religion, scholarship, communications media, sports, entertainments, fashions, fads and social life.*

	World Affairs	Europe	Africa & the Middle East	The Americas	Asia & the Pacific
July 23	Arms Control and Disarmament Agency reports the worldwide military spending in 1976 came to almost $400 billion.		Israeli Cabinet rejects a request by Pres. Sadat that Israel make a conciliatory gesture by returning Mt. Sinai and the town of El Arish, both on the Sinai Peninsula, to Egypt. . . . Pres. Omar Bongo announces the expulsion of all 10,000 Benin workers from Gabon following bloody street battles between Gabonese and the immigrant laborers.		
July 24	The U.S. dollar falls below the psychologically important barrier of 200 Japanese yen, closing at 199.05 yen in Tokyo trading.		Israeli For. Min. Moshe Dayan says that he has offered to soften Israel's stance on the West Bank and Gaza Strip in a private memo handed on July 18 to U.S. State Secy. Cyrus Vance.	Chile's Gen. Gustavo Leigh Guzman is dismissed from the military junta and from his post as air force commander. . . . Bolivian opposition presidential candidates — Hernan Siles Zuazo, Rene Bernal Escalante, and Victor Paz Estenssoro — reportedly drop out of sight after the July 21 coup.	
July 25	Foreign ministers of the 87 nonaligned nations' movement meet in Belgrade, Yugoslavia to assert the movement's importance at a time when East–West polarization seems to be increasing.		Rhodesia's multiracial transitional govt. announces that elections for a majority government will occur in December, and the actual transition of power will be made on Dec. 31. . . . At least 30 civilians are reported killed and more than 50 wounded by heavy Syrian shelling of Al Hadath, Beirut's Christian suburb.	A commission, headed by Alberta Supreme Ct. Judge James Laycraft that has been investigating Royal Canadian Mounted Police tactics, concludes that some wrongful and unethical acts were committed. . . . Chile replaces nearly all of its air force generals as the result of the dismissal of Gen. Gustavo Leigh Guzman.	Gen. Hiroomi Kurisu, chairman of the Japanese Joint Staff Council of the Self-Defense Forces, is forced to resign because of a remark he had made that appeared to question civilian control of Japan's military. . . . P.M. Albert Henry is removed from office by order of the Cook Islands High Court, which rules that he had used corrupt election practices.
July 26	At the nonaligned nations' foreign ministers conference, criticism mounts over Cuban intervention in Africa and its increasing alliance with the Soviet bloc. India warns that foreign military support could bring in the Cold War by the back door.	Increasing numbers of terrorist acts in Italy are reported being committed without clear political motives, including bombings, arson, and industrial sabotage.	Egypt expels the Israeli military mission based near Alexandria.		
July 27	U.N. Security Council gives overwhelming approval to the Western-sponsored plan for Namibia's independence. The two-part plan provides for a U.N. force to monitor a cease-fire and elections and for the unification of Walvis Bay, Namibia's only deep-water port, with an independent Namibia.	Portuguese Premier Mario Soares' Socialist six-month-old government collapses and he is dismissed by Pres. Antonio Ramalho Eanes.	U.S. announces a reduction in its embassy staff in Beirut and advises other Americans living in Lebanon to leave. . . . Iraq expels British Amb. Alexander Stirling to retaliate for Britain's ouster of the Iraqi mission in London, which was motivated by British concern about increased terrorism against Arabs in Britain.		U.S. and South Korea claim that North Korea poses a serious military threat to Seoul.
July 28	Cuban For. Min. Isidoro Malmierca answers denunciations of Cuban policy by members of the nonaligned nations group by claiming that Cuba's involvement in Africa is to support the struggle against underdevelopment inherited from colonial oppression. . . . The price of gold soars on the London bullion exchange as the dollar declines, rising above the $200 mark to close at a record $201.30 an ounce.	Iraqi Amb. to Great Britain Taha Ahmed al-Dawood escapes injury in an assassination attempt in London. The attack follows Britain's order on July 27 to oust 11 Iraqis from the country because they posed terrorist threats. . . . West German Chancellor Helmut Schmidt announces a program of budget spending and tax cuts totaling $6.12 billion in the next year to stimulate the economy.	Ethiopia announces that the government forces have broken the rebel siege around Asmara, capital of the province of Eritrea, the most significant victory in Ethiopia's 17-year campaign against separatist guerrillas there.		Cambodian Deputy Premier Ieng Sary tells foreign ministers meeting at the nonaligned nations conference that Cambodia closed its borders and emptied its cities after the Khmer Rouge victory in 1975 to prevent a civil war.
July 29			*Washington Post* cites observers who echo a June 21 claim by an Eritrean People's Liberation Front (EPLF) spokesman that Cuban troops have stopped fighting in Ethiopian troop ranks against the Eritreans, but that Cubans and Soviets are serving behind the lines as advisers.		

A	B	C	D	E
Includes developments that affect more than one world region, international organizations and important meetings of major world leaders.	*Includes all domestic and regional developments in Europe, including the Soviet Union, Turkey, Cyprus and Malta.*	*Includes all domestic and regional developments in Africa and the Middle East, including Iraq and Iran and excluding Cyprus, Turkey and Afghanistan.*	*Includes all domestic and regional developments in Latin America, the Caribbean and Canada.*	*Includes all domestic and regional developments in Asia and Pacific nations, extending from Afghanistan through all the Pacific Islands, except Hawaii.*

U.S. Politics & Social Issues	U.S. Foreign Policy & Defense	U.S. Economy & Environment	Science, Technology & Nature	Culture, Leisure & Life Style	
Medical authorities at a Health-Care Management Institute seminar in Williamsburg, Va., say that a projected surplus of doctors by 1985 will not solve the problems of rural areas or slow the growth rate of medical bills.	*Washington Post* reports that a group of U.S. senators is gathering support for lifting the trade ban on Rhodesia.			Hollis Stacy defeats JoAnne Gunderson Carner and Sally Little by one stroke to win her second consecutive U.S. Women's Open golf championship.	July 23
In a memorandum, Pres. Carter sternly advises his staff to obey the drug laws, following reports that some staff members use marijuana and that a few use cocaine.... The Third Circuit U.S. Appeals Ct. upholds a district ct. ruling to desegregate the predominantly black schools in Wilmington, Del. by busing students to 10 predominantly white suburbs.				Egypt announces that its athletes will not participate in sports events held in five Arab rejectionist states — Libya, Algeria, Syria, Iraq, and South Yemen.... New York Yankees manager Billy Martin resigns after assailing the baseball team's star player, Reggie Jackson, and its owner, George Steinbrenner.	July 24
	U.S. Senate votes, 57–42, to allow Pres. Carter to end the arms embargo on Turkey.	A strike of Wash., D.C. Metro transit workers ends after seven days during which commuters were stranded and massive traffic problems created.	The first authenticated birth of a human baby conceived in a test tube occurs in Lancashire, England. The child, Louise Brown, is delivered by Caesarian section after she was conceived by a procedure developed by Dr. Patrick Steptoe and Dr. Robert G. Edwards.	Relgious reaction by Moslem, Jewish, and Protestant leaders to the birth of Louise Brown, who was conceived in a test tube, is cautious and approval hinges on both husband and wife being parents of the child. Roman Catholics continue to oppose any form of artificial insemination.	July 25
The New York Times reports that a St. Louis, Mo. man, Russell Byers, has told the House Select Committee on Assassinations that he was offered $40,000 in late 1966 or early 1967 to arrange the murder of civil-rights leader Martin Luther King Jr.	Senate turns back an attempt to end sanctions against Rhodesia, but approves language, by a 59–36 vote, empowering the President to end the embargo if he determines that the Rhodesian govt. has made a good-faith effort to negotiate with black guerrillas and hold free elections.		A Pittsburgh, Pa. judge rules that a person cannot be compelled to be a donor for a transplant even if it might increase a patient's chance of survival.		July 26
The Sixth Circuit U.S. Appeals Ct. upholds a busing plan for desegregation of the Dayton, Ohio public schools, reversing a federal district ct. decision that busing is not necessary.... Major parties to N.Y.C.'s fiscal recovery plan tentatively agree to lend the city $2.55 billion over the next four years.	U.S. District Ct. Judge John Sirica strikes down as unconstitutional a law barring women in the Navy from serving aboard ships other than transport or hospital vessels.	Gulf Oil Corp. settles a government claim that it overcharged crude oil customers $79.1 million by agreeing to pay the government $42.2 million.			July 27
After meeting with Pres. Carter, Sen. Edward Kennedy (D, Mass.) says that Carter's national health plan, scheduled for release today, is unacceptable and accuses Carter of failure of leadership.	U.S. Senate votes, 73–1, to institute a mandatory ban on all trade with Uganda on the ground that its government is guilty of genocide.			Princess Caroline of Monaco, 21-year-old daughter of Prince Rainier III and Princess Grace, weds Philippe Junot, 38, a French financial counselor in a civil ceremony.	July 28
Pres. Carter makes public his outline for a national health plan through a news briefing by HEW Secy. Joseph Califano Jr. The plan includes 10 principles, which include that Americans should have freedom of choice in selecting their doctors, hospitals, and health delivery systems.				New York Yankees surprise the baseball world by announcing that Billy Martin will return to manage the team in 1980.	July 29
F	**G**	**H**	**I**	**J**	
Includes elections, federal-state relations, civil rights and liberties, crime, the judiciary, education, health care, poverty, urban affairs and population.	*Includes formation and debate of U.S. foreign and defense policies, veterans' affairs and defense spending. (Relations with specific foreign countries are usually found under the region concerned.)*	*Includes business, labor, agriculture, taxation, transportation, consumer affairs, monetary and fiscal policy, natural resources, and pollution.*	*Includes worldwide scientific, medical and technological developments, natural phenomena, U.S. weather, natural disasters, and accidents.*	*Includes the arts, religion, scholarship, communications media, sports, entertainments, fashions, fads and social life.*	

	World Affairs	Europe	Africa & the Middle East	The Americas	Asia & the Pacific
July 30	Depite the outcry against Cuba at the nonaligned nations conference, foreign ministers agree to hold the 1979 summit in Havanna and adopt a resolution condemning outside attempts to split the movement. They reject a resolution condemning members' foreign intervention in other countries.		Egyptian Pres. Anwar Sadat says that he opposes resuming direct peace talks with Israel because Israel's moves are negative and backward.		
July 31		An armed Arab terrorist shoots his way into the Iraqi Embassy in Paris and holds eight people hostage before surrendering to French police.	Troops of a newly reorganized Lebanese army move into the southern part of the country but are prevented by Christian militiamen from occupying their assigned positions.... Rhodesian military command says that security forces have raided 10 guerrilla training camps in Mozambique in what is described as a self-defense operation.	The Protestant School Board of Greater Montreal decides to comply with Quebec's language law that limits English-language education.... Argentine Pres. Jorge Rafael Videla retires from active duty, turning over his army command and seat on the military junta to his friend and protege, Gen. Roberto Viola.	Pnompenh radio reports that at least 1,200 Vietnamese troops have been killed and 2,500 wounded during July fighting with Cambodia.
Aug. 1		The Roman Catholic primate of Ireland, Archbishop Tomas O Fiaich, condemns conditions at Long Kesh prison in Ulster.	Beirut radio quotes Lebanese officials as saying that Israel is shelling its southern border because it does not want Lebanese authorities to reassert themselves there. Witnesses, however, reportedly say that the shelling was carried out by Christian militiamen.	The 15-year-old daughter of Argentine Vice Adm. Armando Lambruschini is killed when a powerful bomb rips through her bedroom in a Buenos Aires apartment building. The explosion is the most serious terrorist attack in Argentina this year.	U.S. intelligence reports that Vietnam is conducting heavy air strikes in support of its troops fighting inside Cambodia.
Aug. 2		Nine suspected right-wing extremists are charged under Greece's new antiterrorist laws.... British govt. announces it will increase taxes on profits made by companies extracing oil from North Sea offshore wells and will also reduce their tax deductions.	Iraqi–Arab terrorist clashes in Paris and London are believed to be linked to the growing dispute between hardline Iraq, which opposes peace negotiations with Israel, and PLO factions that favor a relatively milder stance.	Chilean Pres. Augusto Pinochet stresses that before the men indicted by the U.S. for the 1976 murder of Orlando Letelier could be extradited, the U.S. must produce proof of their involvement in Letelier's murder.	
Aug. 3			Israeli planes strike at a Palestinian guerrilla base in Lebanon after a terrorist bomb kills one person and injures 50 in a Tel Aviv market earlier in the day. The PLO claims responsibility for the explosion.... Two Arab gunmen believed linked to Iraq break into the Paris offices of the Arab League and PLO and kill two PLO officials, wounding three others.		
Aug. 4		Jeremy Thorpe, former leader of the British Liberal Party, is arrested for allegedly conspiring to murder former male model Norman Scott, who damaged Thorpe's political career in Great Britain by claiming in 1976 to have had a homosexual affair with him.			After representatives of the five-member ASEAN hold discussions with U.S. officials in Wash., D.C., a joint statement is issued that both sides have agreed to establish an integrated program for commodities.
Aug. 5			Fighting between Lebanese Christian militiamen and Syrian troops erupts in Beirut.		A PLO office is raided in Pakistan, leaving four people dead.... In one of the worst incidents in a series of clashes between Harijans (Indian caste of untouchables) and upper-caste Hindus in Maharashtra State, five people die and more than 70 are injured.

A	B	C	D	E
Includes developments that affect more than one world region, international organizations and important meetings of major world leaders.	Includes all domestic and regional developments in Europe, including the Soviet Union, Turkey, Cyprus and Malta.	Includes all domestic and regional developments in Africa and the Middle East, including Iraq and Iran and excluding Cyprus, Turkey and Afghanistan.	Includes all domestic and regional developments in Latin America, the Caribbean and Canada.	Includes all domestic and regional developments in Asia and Pacific nations, extending from Afghanistan through all the Pacific Islands, except Hawaii.

U.S. Politics & Social Issues	U.S. Foreign Policy & Defense	U.S. Economy & Environment	Science, Technology & Nature	Culture, Leisure & Life Style	
				Juan de Jesus Romero, 103, spiritual leader of the Taos Pueblo Indians, dies in Taos Pueblo, N.M.	July 30
		GAO releases a study claiming that liquefied natural gas poses serious dangers that call for more safety precautions than currently observed.... The government's composite index of leading economic indicators rises .4 percent in June.	The grasshopper invasion of Colorado and Nebraska is reported the worst since 1958. Areas in Kansas, Oklahoma, Texas, Wyoming, and South Dakota are also reporting invasions of disastrous proportions.	Pete Rose of the Cincinnati Reds hits in 44 consecutive ball games beginning June 14 and ties the NL record, but falls 12 short of the major league mark set by New York Yankee Joe DiMaggio in 1941.	July 31
Margaret Costanza's resignation as an assistant to Pres. Carter is announced, in wake of reported friction with other staff members.	U.S. House votes to allow Pres. Carter to end the embargo on arms sales to Turkey.... A grand jury in Wash., D.C. indicts three Chileans and four Cuban exiles in connection with the 1976 assassination in Wash., D.C. of Orlando Letelier, the former Chilean foreign minister.	IBM and Xerox Corp. settle an eight-year dispute over office equipment patents, which gives each company the right to use, without paying royalties, the other firm's patents currently held or applied for over the next five years.	A San Francisco sperm bank that allowed sperm to thaw, thereby spoiling it, is sued for $1.5 million in damages by a man who had made a deposit in 1972 and later became sterile.		Aug. 1
Rep. Philip Crane (R, Ill.) announces his candidacy for the presidency.	Leon Jaworski withdraws as special counsel to the House Ethics Committee's investigation of the Korean lobbying scandal, saying there is nothing else the committee can do without the testimony of Kim Dong Jo, the former South Korean ambassador to the U.S.	A congressional study reportedly says that most taxpayers will owe more taxes in 1979 than in the current year even if the $16-billion tax cut approved by the House Ways and Means Committee becomes law.	Two cases of suspected smallpox are reported in Eritrea.	Carlos Chavez 79, Mexican composer, conductor, and pianist who founded the Symphony Orchestra of Mexico in 1928, dies of a heart ailment in Mexico City.... *Star Wars* leads in worldwide film rentals, surpassing the previous record of $200 million in global rentals held by the film, *Jaws*.	Aug. 2
ABA begins its one hundredth annual convention in N.Y.C.... In Tenn. Sen. Howard Baker Jr. (R) wins nomination to a third term with 84 percent of the vote. Jane Eskind, a Nashville civic leader, wins the Democratic nomination.	A Washington judge refuses to accept Michael Townley's plea-bargaining agreement in the indictments of alleged assassins of former Chilean foreign minister Orlando Letelier.	Pres. Carter signs legislation to raise the ceiling on the national debt to $798 billion, effective March 31, 1979.	A federal study is reported that predicts 594,000 doctors in the U.S. by 1990, 25,000–50,000 more than is expected to be needed.	Rachel David, 38, and her seven children (ranging in age from six to 15 years) plunge 11 stories from the International Dunes Hotel in downtown Salt Lake City, Utah a day after her husband, Immanuel David, an excommunicated Mormon and religious cult leader, killed himself.	Aug. 3
		EPA rules that the open-ocean cooling system planned for the controversial Seabrook, N.H. nuclear power plant complies with federal water pollution laws. Environmentalists have challenged that the system would harm marine ecology.	Families are evacuated from the Love Canal, Niagara Falls, N.Y. area after N.Y.S. Health Commissioner Robert Whalen warns that there is great and imminent health peril from waste chemicals contamination, citing a significant excessive record of miscarriages and birth defects in the area.	San Diego Opera (Calif.) Verdi Festival — the only annual music festival in the world dedicated to performing the music of Giusepe Verdi — is officially launched with its first performance of *Aida*.	Aug. 4
					Aug. 5

F	G	H	I	J
Includes elections, federal-state relations, civil rights and liberties, crime, the judiciary, education, health care, poverty, urban affairs and population.	Includes formation and debate of U.S. foreign and defense policies, veterans' affairs and defense spending. (Relations with specific foreign countries are usually found under the region concerned.)	Includes business, labor, agriculture, taxation, transportation, consumer affairs, monetary and fiscal policy, natural resources, and pollution.	Includes worldwide scientific, medical and technological developments, natural phenomena, U.S. weather, natural disasters, and accidents.	Includes the arts, religion, scholarship, communications media, sports, entertainments, fashions, fads and social life.

	World Affairs	Europe	Africa & the Middle East	The Americas	Asia & the Pacific
Aug. 6			Martti Ahtisaari, U.N. representative for Namibia, arrives in Windhoek, the capital of Namibia, to discuss its transition to independence from South Africa.	Bolivia's Pres. Juan Pereda Asbun announces that general elections will be held in 1980 and that he will not be a candidate for the presidency. He adds that his government will draw up new electoral laws to prevent the anomalies that characterized the disputed July 9 elections.	
Aug. 7				Honduran Pres. Juan Alberto Melgar Castro is overthrown in a bloodless coup by commanders of the three armed forces.... Julio Cesar Turbay Ayala is sworn in as president of Colombia, promising to respect civil liberties and to promote Latin American economic integration.	Vietnam permits 29 Vietnamese women and children, separated from their American husbands and fathers after the 1975 fall of Saigon, to leave Vietnam and be reunited with their American families in the U.S.... Australian P.M. Malcolm Fraser dismisses Reginald Withers, minister for administrative services, for improperly influencing the drawing of new electoral boundaries in Queensland.
Aug. 8	World Bank approves a $60-million long-term, low interest loan to Vietnam to help finance an irrigation system to expand rice production near Ho Chi Minh City (Saigon).	Ion Pacepa, a high-ranking official in Rumania's secret police, is reported to have defected to the West while in Cologne, West Germany.	Rhodesia's ruling executive council issues a statement outlawing discrimination against blacks in public facilities, the first concrete step by the transitional government toward ending racial discrimination.... White House announces arrangements for Egyptian Pres. Anwar Sadat and Israeli Premier Menahem Begin to meet with Pres. Carter on Sept. 5 at Camp David, Md. to confer on ways to break the Middle East deadlock.	Isabel Letelier files suit in U.S. District Ct., Wash., D.C., accusing the Chilean govt. of causing the death of her husband, former For. Min. Orlando Letelier, and seeking more than $10,000 in damages.... Sen. Jose de Magalhaes Pinto announces withdrawing from the Brazilian presidential race so that the opposition will not be split.	China and Vietnam open talks in Peking on the future of ethnic Chinese in Vietnam.... A new wave of Cambodian refugees are reported moving into Thailand following another government purge in Battambang province.
Aug. 9		Portuguese Pres. Antonio Ramalho Eanes chooses Alfredo Nobre da Costa, a politically independent technocrat, as premier-designate after the major political parties fail to agree on a governing coalition. ... The Soviet grain harvest in 1978 is estimated at a record 220 million metric tons by the U.S. Agriculture Dept.	A Beirut truce is announced by both sides.... Ethiopian govt. troops capture the Eritrean town of Agordat, 75 miles nortwest of Asmara in fighting against the secessionist rebel forces.... Syria's ruling Baath Party newspaper charges that the proposed Camp David summit is a maneuver paving the way for a lightning war by Israel.		
Aug. 10			In a wave of incidents protesting the Iranian govt.'s programs supporting the liberation of women and land redistribution, Moslems stage violent demonstrations in Isfahan to protest the arrest of a local religious leader. Three people are killed and 200 wounded in Shiraz riots.	Canada's 10 provincial premiers unanimously reject P.M. Pierre Trudeau's proposals for a new Canadian Constitution to replace the British North America Act.	
Aug. 11		French air traffic controllers resume their slowdowns, which they began on July 14 and interrupted for talks with the government on Aug. 2.	Renewed clashes between Christian militiamen and Syrian troops break the Beirut truce after two days.... Lebanese army troops start to withdraw from the region near the Israeli border in the face of continued shelling by Christian militiamen.	Gen. Juan Pereda Asbun's govt. lifts the state of siege in Bolivia, imposed July 21 during his military coup.	

A	B	C	D	E
Includes developments that affect more than one world region, international organizations and important meetings of major world leaders.	Includes all domestic and regional developments in Europe, including the Soviet Union, Turkey, Cyprus and Malta.	Includes all domestic and regional developments in Africa and the Middle East, including Iraq and Iran and excluding Cyprus, Turkey and Afghanistan.	Includes all domestic and regional developments in Latin America, the Caribbean and Canada.	Includes all domestic and regional developments in Asia and Pacific nations, extending from Afghanistan through all the Pacific Islands, except Hawaii.

U.S. Politics & Social Issues	U.S. Foreign Policy & Defense	U.S. Economy & Environment	Science, Technology & Nature	Culture, Leisure & Life Style	
			Demonstrators at nuclear power plants in Ore. and Calif., and others around the U.S., commemorate the thirty-third anniversary of the atomic bombing of Hiroshima, Japan.... Victor Hasselblad, Swedish inventor and industrialist associated with the high-quality camera bearing his name, dies of cancer at age 72 in Gothenburg, Sweden.... WHO estimates that malaria cases have increased more than 25 percent in the past two years.	Pope Paul VI, spiritual leader of the world's more than 550 million Roman Catholics, dies of a heart attack at age 80. He was known as the pilgrim Pope after visiting 16 countries on six continents and was considered the most ecumenical of popes.... Edward Durell Stone, 76, architect whose successes include the Radio City Music Hall and Museum of Modern Art interiors, the GM Building, and the Kennedy Center in Wash. D.C., dies in N.Y.	Aug. 6
ABA votes, 274–136, to reject a resolution that would put it on record as favoring enactment of legislation prohibiting discrimination against homosexuals in employment, housing, and public accomodations.		AFL–CIO pres. George Meany charges that Barry Bosworth, head of the Council on Wage and Price Stability, is doing everything he possibly can to side with employers in wage negotiations.... Meany also concedes that the labor law reform bill is dead and says he does not blame Pres. Carter although it might have helped if he had been a stronger President.	Hundreds of nuclear power opponents are arrested in demonstrations against the Trojan nuclear plant near Rainier, Ore. and the Diablo Canyon plant near San Luis Obispo in California.... Pres. Carter declares the Love Canal of Niagara Falls, N.Y. a disaster area because of contamination from long-buried waste chemicals.... Australia and the Philippines sign a uranium safeguards agreement that opens the way for the sale of Australian uranium to the Philippines.		Aug. 7
Mich. Republicans renominate Sen. Robert Griffin and Gov. William Milliken, both seeking third terms.... Pres. Carter goes to N.Y.C. to sign a bill providing $1.65 billion in federal long-term loan guarantees to the city. He calls N.Y.C. the cultural, artistic, financial, and diplomatic capital of the U.S. and singles out Mayor Edward Koch (D) and N.Y.S. Gov. Hugh Carey (D) for special praise.	A congressional group calling itself the Coalition for Peace Through Strength is formed to urge a more conservative U.S. stance on defense issues. Co-chairman Sen. Robert Dole (R, Kan.) criticizes the Carter administration for vacillating.	In a study titled *The Illusion of Black Progress*, the Urban League charges that the economic gap between blacks and white is widening and that much of the increasing resistance among whites to work for racial equality is based on the misconception that black economic progress has already been sufficient to achieve equal opportunity.	U.S. and Australia sign an interim nuclear safeguards accord that will operate until the 1956 Australian-U.S. Nuclear Cooperation Agreement can be officially renegotiated. ...U.S. launches a probe, the Pioneer Venus 2, carrying equipment to gather information about Venus's atmosphere.... The worst flooding in 25 years reportedly kills 23 people in the Swiss and Italian Alps.	Calif. Superior Ct. dismisses an $11-million lawsuit charging that NBC is responsible for a sexual assault on a nine-year-old girl, Olivia Niemi, who was abused by four youths in San Francisco, four days after a TV movie, *Born Innocent*, which contained a rape scene, was broadcast by the network.	Aug. 8
Addressing the ABA convention in N.Y.C., Supreme Ct. Chief Justice Warren Burger repeats his call for added legal training for attorneys who wish to represent clients in court.... *Washington Post* reports that the majority of people surveyed in 19 opinion polls between 1972–1977 believes women should be able to get a legal abortion.	House passes a bill, 339–60, appropriating $119.2 billion for defense in fiscal 1979.... House votes, 226–163, for an amendment to a bill barring the use of any defense appropriations for abortions in the military, except when the mother's life is endangered.	Census Bureau announces that the median family income for 1977 was $16,009 compared to $14,960 in 1976. The real gain, however, is nonexistent because the 7.7 percent rise in income is erased by 1977's 6.5 percent inflation rate. ... A strike by pressmen closes down publication of N.Y.C.'s three major general newspapers— *New York Daily News*, *The New York Times*, and the *New York Post*.		James Gould Cozzens, 74, novelist who won the Pulitzer Prize in 1949 for his book *Guard of Honor*, dies of pneumonia in Stuart, Fla.	Aug. 9
		Rep. Richard Bolling (D, Mo.) characterizes the measure as a Republican bill with a Democratic label. ... Financially troubled Chrysler Corp. announces it will sell its entire European auto operations to P.S.A. Peugeot-Citroen of France for $426 million.	NRC rules, 4–0, that construction of the Seabrook N.H. nuclear power plant can immediately resume.... Six cases of poliomyelitis are confirmed in the Canadian provinces of Ontario, Alberta, and British Columbia.	National Hockey League formally approves a plan for the financial and corporate reorganization of the New York Islanders.	Aug. 10
Pres. Carter lauds Sen. Edward Kennedy (D, Mass.) and says that he expects his support when Carter runs for reelection.... Pres. Carter's Civil Service Commission reorganization plan takes effect after Congress declines to block it. ... Pres. Carter names Louis Marin as special presidential assistant on black programs and policies.	Michael Townley admits in U.S. District Ct., Wash., D.C. that he had made and planted the bomb that killed Chilean For. Min. Orlando Letelier.	Pres. Carter is characterized by the *Washington Post* as livid because of AFL–CIO pres. George Meany's continued attacks despite repeated administration attempts to accomodate him.	*Science* reports a Medical College of Virginia study that found that three monkeys chose cocaine almost exclusively over food when they had the choice.... Center of Disease Control in Atlanta announces that researchers have successfully isolated in water the bacteria causing legionnaires disease.		Aug. 11
F	**G**	**H**	**I**	**J**	
Includes elections, federal-state relations, civil rights and liberties, crime, the judiciary, education, health care, poverty, urban affairs and population.	*Includes formation and debate of U.S. foreign and defense policies, veterans' affairs and defense spending. (Relations with specific foreign countries are usually found under the region concerned.)*	*Includes business, labor, agriculture, taxation, transportation, consumer affairs, monetary and fiscal policy, natural resources, and pollution.*	*Includes worldwide scientific, medical and technological developments, natural phenomena, U.S. weather, natural disasters, and accidents.*	*Includes the arts, religion, scholarship, communications media, sports, entertainments, fashions, fads and social life.*	

	World Affairs	Europe	Africa & the Middle East	The Americas	Asia & the Pacific
Aug. 12	Soviet Union charges that the Sino-Japanese friendship pact is directed against the Soviet Union and criticizes Japan for capitulating to Peking.				China and Japan sign a 10-year treaty of peace and friendship in Peking, ending six years of talks.
Aug. 13		British submarine workers end a strike, begun on July 7, after the government offers a new pay hike.	Bishop Abel Muzorewa, a leader in the Rhodesian transitional govt., wins a confidence vote from his United African National Council (UANC).... An explosion demolishes a nine-story building in Beirut that housed the pro-Iraqi Palestine Liberation Front headquarters and offices for its rival, Al Fatah. An estimated 150–200 people are killed.		
Aug. 14		Franz-Josef Strauss, head of West Germany's conservative Christian Social Union Party, asks for a general amnesty for crimes committed during the Nazi period, excepting cases involving the murder of Jews, concentration camp atrocities, and genocide.	Israeli Cabinet decides to suspend consideration of establishing five new settlements in the West Bank, pending the outcome of the forthcoming Camp David summit.... Pres. Joachim Yhomby Opango of the Congo reveals that his government foiled a coup attempt against him.		
Aug. 15	The U.S. dollar is worth $1.9138 marks and 1.5485 Swiss francs, both record lows.				
Aug. 16	Gold Closes at $217.75 an ounce on the London exchange.	A Soviet psychiatrist, Dr. Alexander Voloshanovich, tells Western reporters that Soviet dissidents are improperly placed in mental institutions. He is motivated by the conviction of Alexander Podrabinek, a Soviet dissident who had compiled information on dissidents in mental institutions.... West German birth rate of 9.8 babies per 1,000 inhabitants is reported representing a 50 percent decline since 1968 and being the lowest in Europe and possibly in the world.		Antonio Guzman is sworn in as the new Dominican Republic president, completing the first peaceful transfer of power between constitutionally elected governments in Dominican history.... In a TV interview, P.M. Pierre Trudeau charges that Canada's provincial premiers are abetting separatism by rejecting constitutional proposals, and asserts that he is not trying to abolish the queen's status in Canada.	
Aug. 17			Gerrit Viljoen, head of the Broederbond, the Afrikaner secret society, holds an unprecedented four-hour meeting with Nthato Motlana, head of the Soweto Committee of 10, an unofficial group that represents the largest black South African township of Johannesburg.		Afghanistan govt. smashes a plot to overthrow the new leftist regime.
Aug. 18		The Moscow city court dismisses its case against two U.S. reporters — Craig Whitney of *The New York Times* amd Harold Piper of the *Baltimore Sun* — charged with slandering the Soviet Union in their dispatches and says they do not have to write retractions of their coverage of Soviet dissidents' trials.	South African press reports quote Gerrit Viljoen, head of the Afrikaner secret society Broederbond, as saying previously that the apartheid system must be modified.		
Aug. 19		Northern Ireland police say that they are convinced that IRA guerrillas were involved in eight bomb explosions the previous day in six West German towns where the British Army of the Rhine has bases.	Angolan Pres. Agostinho Neto begins a three-day visit with Zairian Pres. Mobutu Sese Seko to further improve relations.		

A	B	C	D	E
Includes developments that affect more than one world region, international organizations and important meetings of major world leaders.	Includes all domestic and regional developments in Europe, including the Soviet Union, Turkey, Cyprus and Malta.	Includes all domestic and regional developments in Africa and the Middle East, including Iraq and Iran and excluding Cyprus, Turkey and Afghanistan.	Includes all domestic and regional developments in Latin America, the Caribbean and Canada.	Includes all domestic and regional developments in Asia and Pacific nations, extending from Afghanistan through all the Pacific Islands, except Hawaii.

U.S. Politics & Social Issues	U.S. Foreign Policy & Defense	U.S. Economy & Environment	Science, Technology & Nature	Culture, Leisure & Life Style	
		Census Bureau reports that in 1977 11.6 percent of the U.S. population lived below the poverty level.	A Princeton University test reactor reportedly makes a major advance in the effort to achieve a controlled fusion reaction.	Twenty-five thousand mourners are invited to Pope Paul VI's funeral service in St. Peter's Basilica.	Aug. 12
Mayor Dennis Kucinich of Cleveland narrowly survives a recall election by a 236-vote margin.		An AP–NBC News poll finds that Americans are increasingly concerned about inflation's economic impact and about Pres. Carter's ability to stem rising prices.			Aug. 13
At the opening session of the House Assassinations Committee's public hearings on the assassination of civil-rights leader Martin Luther King Jr., the Rev. Ralph Abernathy, a chief aide to King, says he believes that King had some warning that he would be killed.		A report issued by PROD, a group of dissident Teamsters union members, charges massive mismanagement of the Teamsters' pension funds, numerous instances of bad loans, poor investment, and outright corruption.			Aug. 14
House votes a 39-month ratification extension for the ERA, pushing back the deadline to June 30, 1982.		American Friends Service Committee, a Quaker group, announces that it will sell its shares in 15 corporations that conduct business in South Africa.... Northwest Airlines pilots sign a three-year contract, ending a 109-day strike.		Diana Nyad and Stella Taylor give up their open-ocean marathon swim attempts in the Caribbean.	Aug. 15
James Earl Ray, who first confessed and then denied killing Martin Luther King Jr., tells the House Assassinations Committee that he was framed by a man named Raoul and did not kill King.		Pres. Carter expresses deep concern over the dollar's steep plunge against the Japanese yen, the West German mark, and other major currencies.... FRB, which has been criticized for its failure to intervene in the tumultuous currency trading conditions under which the dollar is sharply weakening, moves immediately to sell $20 million in Western German marks and to tighten U.S. credit.	U.S. geneticists urge the world scientific community to boycott the first international conference on genetics, which is scheduled to be held in the Soviet Union on Aug. 21-30.	NBA Philadelphia 76ers trade forward George McGinnis to the Denver Nuggets for forward Bobby Jones and guard Ralph Simpson.	Aug. 16
	Pres. Carter vetoes a $37-billion weapons authorization bill, saying that a $2-billion nuclear-powered aircraft carrier in the bill is unneeded and uses funds that should go to vital defense programs. He emphasizes that he not seeking a different weapons budget but one that has different spending allocations.	Congress clears a bill providing that foreign banks operating in the U.S. will be subject to basically the same regulations as domestic banks.... CAB lifts most restrictions on airline charter service.	Three Americans complete the first transatlantic crossing by balloon, landing their craft, the *Double Eagle II*, in a wheat field 60 miles east of Paris, France.		Aug. 17
Sen. Herman Talmadge (D, Ga.) gives a personal check to the Senate for $37,125.90 to cover improper expense claims that were made in his name from 1972–77.	Justice Dept. drops three of six felony charges against an ITT official, Edward Gerrity Jr., implicated in a U.S. plot to undermine the election of Salvador Allende in Chile, because it says that to prosecute the case would lead to disclosing national security secrets.	After-tax corporate profits rise $15.2 billion in the second quarter of 1978 to a seasonally adjusted annual rate of $117.3 billion.		Tracy Caulkins, a 15-year-old from Nashville, Tenn., enters the World Swimming Championships in West Berlin after leading a dramatic resurgence in American women's swimming records in previous meets this year.	Aug. 18
			Max Mallowan, 74, British archaeologist best known for his Middle East excavations and marriage to mystery writer Agatha Christie, dies in Oxfordshire, England.		Aug. 19
F	**G**	**H**	**I**	**J**	
Includes elections, federal-state relations, civil rights and liberties, crime, the judiciary, education, health care, poverty, urban affairs and population.	*Includes formation and debate of U.S. foreign and defense policies, veterans' affairs and defense spending. (Relations with specific foreign countries are usually found under the region concerned.)*	*Includes business, labor, agriculture, taxation, transportation, consumer affairs, monetary and fiscal policy, natural resources, and pollution.*	*Includes worldwide scientific, medical and technological developments, natural phenomena, U.S. weather, natural disasters, and accidents.*	*Includes the arts, religion, scholarship, communications media, sports, entertainments, fashions, fads and social life.*	

	World Affairs	Europe	Africa & the Middle East	The Americas	Asia & the Pacific
Aug. 20		Four Palestinian terrorists attack an El Al Israel Airlines crew bus in London, killing a stewardess and wounding nine others, including seven British bystanders.	A fire sweeping through a packed movie theater in Abadan, Iran, kills 430 people. The government charges that it is arson set by Moslem extremists opposed to the government's liberalization policies.		
Aug. 21		El Al Israel Airlines pres. Mordechai Hod holds Great Britain responsible for the terrorist attack on the El Al bus because London repeatedly rejected El Al security men's requests to be allowed to carry weapons in Britain.	Israel retaliates for the terrorist attack on an El Al Israel Airlines bus in London with an air strike against two bases of the PLO in Lebanon.... Nicolaas Diederichs, 74, president of South Africa since 1975, dies of a heart attack in Cape Town.		Brisbane and Sydney demonstrations are held to protest the austere budget presented by Australian P.M. Malcolm Fraser's govt. ... Australian P.M. Malcolm Fraser denies he is involved in the Reginald Withers scandal, which has been compared to the American Watergate scandal and sometimes dubbed Withersgate.
Aug. 22		France announces severing diplomatic relations with Laos.	Pres. Jomo Kenyatta, the leading figure in Kenya's struggle for independence, dies in his sleep while vacationing in Mombasa at the approximate age of 83.	Twenty-five Sandinistas invade the National Palace in Managua, Nicaragua and by threatening to execute several hundred hostages, obtain a cash ransom, the release of 59 political prisoners, and safe conduct to Panama.	
Aug. 23			Iranian army troops move into Abadan to control riots that broke out during mourning ceremonies for the victims of the movie house fire on Aug. 20.	Costa Rica's national election tribunal reportedly rejects Robert Vesco's appeal of a San Jose civil court decision denying him Costa Rican citizenship.	
Aug. 24					Australian opposition Labor Party leader William Hayden introduces a no-confidence motion against the Malcolm Fraser govt. in wake of the scandal involving former minister Reginald Withers.
Aug. 25			Further violence erupts in Abadan, Iran, with demonstrators shouting, "Death to the Shah."	An indefinite general strike against Nicaraguan Pres. Anastasio Somoza Debayle begins at the urging of the Broad Opposition Front, which comprises more than a dozen political business and student groups.	Peking charges that at least 400 Vietnamese troops are occupying Chinese territory in the vicinity of Friendship Pass, the frontier crossing linking Vietnam and China's Kwangsi province.
Aug. 26	U.N. conference against racism ends a two-week meeting in Geneva. It accuses Israel of military cooperation with South Africa and asks the U.N. Security Council to impose mandatory economic sanctions on South Africa.				
Aug. 27			Iran's Shah Mohammed Riza Pahlevi replaces Premier Jamshid Amouzegar with a reconciliation Cabinet headed by Jaffar Sharif Emami in an effort to defuse Moslem violence that is sweeping Iran.		The bodies of 15 U.S. servicemen killed in the Indochina war and previously listed as missing in action are returned to the U.S. by an eight-member congressional delegation that had visited Vietnam and Laos.

A	B	C	D	E
Includes developments that affect more than one world region, international organizations and important meetings of major world leaders.	Includes all domestic and regional developments in Europe, including the Soviet Union, Turkey, Cyprus and Malta.	Includes all domestic and regional developments in Africa and the Middle East, including Iraq and Iran and excluding Cyprus, Turkey and Afghanistan.	Includes all domestic and regional developments in Latin America, the Caribbean and Canada.	Includes all domestic and regional developments in Asia and Pacific nations, extending from Afghanistan through all the Pacific Islands, except Hawaii.

U.S. Politics & Social Issues	U.S. Foreign Policy & Defense	U.S. Economy & Environment	Science, Technology & Nature	Culture, Leisure & Life Style	
		Pres. Carter signs a bill creating a National Consumer Cooperative Bank, which will make loans and provide credit services to nonprofit consumer cooperatives.	Antinuclear activists from other Western European nations join in a local protest against government plans to build a nuclear plant near Carnsore Point, Ireland, 80 miles south of Dublin.	At the World Swimming Champion- ships in West Berlin, 15-year-old Tracy Caulkins, sets world records in the 200-meter individual medley.	Aug. 20
Gallup Poll finds Pres. Carter's popularity rating has stabilized and settled at a low point of 39 percent. . . . Pres. Carter and his family begin a 10-day vacation in Idaho and Wyoming.	Congress clears legislation appro- priating $3.88 billion for military construction in fiscal 1979.	Pres. Carter outlines U.S. interna- tional aviation policy, which has been in effect for several months.		Charles Eames, 71, industrial designer best known for a molded plywood chair (1940) which was later mass-produced in plastic, and for a luxurious leather and rosew- ood lounge chair and ottoman (1952), dies of a heart attack in St. Louis, Mo.	Aug. 21
Senate clears, 67–32, a proposed constitutional amendment to give Washington, D.C. full voting repre- sentation in Congress. . . . Jeffer- son County, Ky. passes an ordi- nance that cuts off county funds for abortions and requires that a woman be shown a photograph of a fetus before an abortion is permit- ted.	Carter administration rejects a proposal by Sen. George McGov- ern (D, S.D.) that an international force be sent to Cambodia to over- throw the Pnompenh govt., which, he charges, is practicing genocide against its own people.	Congress clears legislation revis- ing the federal law on oil and gas leases of the outer continental shelf.	U.S. National Academy of Sciences says that it does not endorse the boycott urged by a group of U.S. geneticists against the Soviet international conference on genetics. But its human-rights committee does say that U.S.– Soviet scientific exchanges are endangered by Soviet treatment of dissident scientists.		Aug. 22
		Sen. James McClure (R, Ida.) says that he agreed to sign a conference report compromise on the natural gas pricing bill because Pres. Carter had made a substantial commitment to support research on a liquid metal breeder reactor after having previously opposed it.	Pakistani ruler Gen. Muhammad Zia ul-Haq charges that France has backed out of its commitment to supply Pakistan with nuclear reprocessing equipment.		Aug. 23
Senate, 87–1, passes a bill incor- porating most of Pres. Carter's proposed Civil Service system reforms. . . . Stanford Ross is named Social Security Administra- tion commissioner, succeeding James Cardwell.		A coalition of 11 Democratic and seven Republican senators circu- late a letter opposing a compro- mise agreement on natural gas pricing. Conservatives oppose because natural gas price deregu- lation would be deferred until 1985. Liberals oppose because they feel consumers would pay to benefit the gas industry.	British Defense Ministry closes its Atomic Weapons Research Estab- lishment in Aldermaston after sev- eral members of the staff are found to have excessive amounts of plutonium in their lungs.	Louis Prima, 66, jazz trumpeter and bandleader dies of pneumonia after nearly three years in a coma following surgery in New Orleans.	Aug. 24
				Major league baseball umpires hold a one-day strike for improve- ments in their current contract. Amateur umpires officiate in their absence.	Aug. 25
		Sens. Mark Hatfield (R, Ore.) and Dale Bumpers (D, Ark.), both oppo- nents of the Clinch River, Tenn. fast breeder reactor project, say they are reconsidering their support of the natural gas pricing compromise.		Albino Luciani, 65, a cardinal since 1973 and patriarch of Venice since 1969, is elected 264th Pope of the Roman Catholic Church and takes the name John Paul I. His choice of a double papal name, the first in church history, is significant as a declaration to continue the work of his two predecessors.	Aug. 26
Gallup Poll survey indicates a sig- nificant decline in white prejudice toward blacks since the 1963 civil- rights march on Washington.				Cosmos win Soccer Bowl '78, the American Soccer League cham- pionship, at Giants Stadium, N.J., downing the Tampa Bay Rowdies, 3–1. . . . Pope John Paul I says that his goal is to preserve the great dis- cipline of the church intact and to follow the principles of Vatican II.	Aug. 27

F	G	H	I	J
Includes elections, federal-state rela- tions, civil rights and liberties, crime, the judiciary, education, health care, poverty, urban affairs and population.	*Includes formation and debate of U.S. foreign and defense policies, veterans' affairs and defense spending. (Relations with specific foreign countries are usually found under the region concerned.)*	*Includes business, labor, agriculture, tax- ation, transportation, consumer affairs, monetary and fiscal policy, natural resources, and pollution.*	*Includes worldwide scientific, medical and technological developments, natural phenomena, U.S. weather, natural disas- ters, and accidents.*	*Includes the arts, religion, scholarship, communications media, sports, enter- tainments, fashions, fads and social life.*

	World Affairs	Europe	Africa & the Middle East	The Americas	Asia & the Pacific
Aug. 28		Alfredo Nobre da Costa is sworn in as premier of Portugal.		Virtually all Matagalpa businesses are closed to support the general strike against Nicaraguan Pres. Anastasio Somoza Debayle. . . . Nicaraguan govt. announces that a military-civilian conspiracy against Pres. Anastasio Somoza Debayle has been uncovered and that a number of arrests have been made.	Peking reportedly calls back the Chinese delegation that is discussing the status of ethnic Chinese in Hanoi after counter accusations of who initiated clashes at the Chinese–Vietnamese border.
Aug. 29	Arms Control and Disarmament Agency reports that the U.S. currently has a greater ability than the Soviet Union to destroy targets in a nuclear war.	The Portuguese Cabinet is sworn in. Its members are technocrats and political independents, including Jose da Silva Lopes as finance minister, who is a respected economist and governor of the Bank of Portugal.	Former rebel leader Hissene Habre is named premier of Chad in a reconciliation move by Pres. Felix Malloum's government. . . . U.S. private banks are reported increasing their investments in South Africa.	Nicaraguan air force reportedly bombs and strafes Matagalpa, killing four people and wounding numerous others.	
Aug. 30		Danish Premier Anker Jorgensen announces a series of measures to stabilize the nation's economy immediately after a coalition Liberal–Social Democratic govt. is sworn in.		Archbishop Miguel Obando arrives in Managua, Nicaragua to mediate the general strike and protests against the Nicaraguan govt.	
Aug. 31		Olafur Johannesson, leader of Iceland's Progressive Party, announces that he is the premier of a new coalition govt.	John Wrathall, 65, British-born president of Rhodesia since 1976, dies of a heart attack in Salisbury. . . . Dany Chamoun, secretary general of the Christian National Liberal Party, reports that between 1,000–1,500 Syrian soldiers have been killed since the July 1 outbreak of hostilities with Christian forces in Beirut. He denounces Lebanese Pres. Elias Sarkis and praises Israel for publicizing the plight of the Christians in Lebanon.		
Sept. 1	Chinese Premier and CP Chmn. Hua Kuo-feng leaves Teheran after an unprecedented trip to Rumania, Yugoslavia, and Iran, where he signed a cultural cooperation agreement with the Shah.	Italian govt. releases a long-term economic plan (1979–81) calling for public investment to create jobs and cuts in welfare and health programs to curb inflation.		Matagalpa rebels who had occupied the Nicaraguan city for five days are dispersed by National Guardsmen. . . . Panamanian Head of State Brig. Gen Omar Torrijos announces that he will not accept the presidency after his term expires on October 11 but will remain commander of the National Guard.	New South Wales state government in Australia announces the discovery of a major new coal deposit.
Sept. 2		Former British Liberal Party leader Jeremy Thorpe faces a second charge in connection with the Norman Scott murder–conspiracy case, that of inciting David Holmes to murder Scott.	Rhodesian P.M. Ian Smith and guerrilla leader Joshua Nkomo confirm having met secretly in Zambia on Aug. 14 to discuss a possible role for the Patriotic Front guerrilla coalition in the Rhodesian transitional govt.		
Sept. 3	Albania charges that Chinese Premier Hua Kuo-feng's visit to Rumania and Yugoslavia is a ploy to stir up a new war and dominate the world.	Left-wing demonstrators throw fire bombs and set cars on fire near St. Peter's Square, Rome in a protest against visiting Argentinian Pres. Jorge Videla's policies.			Japanese govt. announces a series of measures to stimulate the economy.
Sept. 4				Jose Francisco Teran, vice president of the Nicaraguan Development Institute, which is one of the most powerful Nicaraguan business organizations, is arrested in wake of the nationwide strike.	

A	B	C	D	E
Includes developments that affect more than one world region, international organizations and important meetings of major world leaders.	Includes all domestic and regional developments in Europe, including the Soviet Union, Turkey, Cyprus and Malta.	Includes all domestic and regional developments in Africa and the Middle East, including Iraq and Iran and excluding Cyprus, Turkey and Afghanistan.	Includes all domestic and regional developments in Latin America, the Caribbean and Canada.	Includes all domestic and regional developments in Asia and Pacific nations, extending from Afghanistan through all the Pacific Islands, except Hawaii.

U.S. Politics & Social Issues	U.S. Foreign Policy & Defense	U.S. Economy & Environment	Science, Technology & Nature	Culture, Leisure & Life Style	
National Governors' Association, meeting in Boston, Mass., unanimously adopts a resolution supporting Pres. Carter's performance in office.		Nancy Teeters is nominated to the FRB to fill Arthur Burns' unexpired term.	*Los Angeles Times* reports that two eminent Chinese doctors, writing in a Chinese paper aimed at intellectuals, warn of cigarettes' health hazards and blame the Gang of Four for not issuing prior warnings against smoking.	The U.S. captures the World Swimming Championships in West Berlin, winning a total of 44 medals in the event, which gathered athletes from 49 nations. . . . Bruce Catton, 78, author and Pulitzer Prize-winning historian who wrote 13 volumes on the Civil War, dies in Frankfort, Mich. . . . Robert Shaw, 51, British-born actor and author, dies of a heart attack near Tourmakeady, Ireland.	Aug. 28
		Commerce Dept. reports the trade deficit swelled to a seasonally adjusted $2.99 billion in July, the largest since February and the fourth worst on record.	Ill. Public Health Dept. toxicologist John Spikes reveals a practical blood test to pinpoint recent marijuana use.		Aug. 29
Myron Farber, a reporter for *The New York Times*, is released from jail by a N.J. Supreme Ct. order pending appeals of Farber's conviction, which stemmed from a series of 1975 articles he had written on the mysterious deaths of 13 patients at a hospital in Oradell, N.J.	Katy Industries Inc. is the first U.S. company to be prosecuted for alleged violations of the 1977 Federal Corrupt Practices Act, which outlaws the payment of bribes overseas.	Chase Manhattan Bank in N.Y. leads commercial banks' move to raise the prime rate to 9.25 percent from 9 percent.			Aug. 30
William and Emily Harris enter guilty pleas in a complex plea bargaining agreement that would assure their 1983 release from prison for the 1974 kidnapping of Patricia Hearst.		Pres. Carter meets with a number of state governors to enlist their aid on behalf of the natural gas pricing bill. He calls the compromise fair and desperately needed, although not exactly what he wanted.			Aug. 31
		Labor Dept. reports that the nation's unemployment rate fell in August to a seasonally adjusted 5.9 percent of the work force.		An unpublished novel by Peter Benchley, *The Island*, is reported earning a record $2.15 million for its movie rights. Benchley wrote the best-selling novel *Jaws*, which was also a top-grossing film.	Sept. 1
			Aviator Charles Blair Jr., 60, who set the transatlantic speed record for his piston-engine aircraft in 1951 and won the Harmon Trophy the same year for the first single-engine solo crossing of the North Pole, dies in a plane crash near St. Thomas, Virgin Islands.	Donald Ewing, 83, retired news reporter who helped break the 1919 Chicago Black Sox scandal and wrote the story that made famous the quote, "Say it ain't so, Joe," regarding Shoeless Joe Jackson, dies in Shreveport, La.	Sept. 2
			West Germany records its strongest earthquake to date.		Sept. 3
			A helicopter dropping ping-pong balls with prize numbers at a Derry, Pa. church festival crashes into the crowd and kills seven people, injuring 19 others.	James Michener's *Chesapeake* and Erma Bombeck's *If Life Is a Bowl of Cherries—What Am I Doing in the Pits?* are best-selling fiction and general books for the previous week.	Sept. 4

F	G	H	I	J
Includes elections, federal-state relations, civil rights and liberties, crime, the judiciary, education, health care, poverty, urban affairs and population.	*Includes formation and debate of U.S. foreign and defense policies, veterans' affairs and defense spending. (Relations with specific foreign countries are usually found under the region concerned.)*	*Includes business, labor, agriculture, taxation, transportation, consumer affairs, monetary and fiscal policy, natural resources, and pollution.*	*Includes worldwide scientific, medical and technological developments, natural phenomena, U.S. weather, natural disasters, and accidents.*	*Includes the arts, religion, scholarship, communications media, sports, entertainments, fashions, fads and social life.*

	World Affairs	Europe	Africa & the Middle East	The Americas	Asia & the Pacific
Sept. 5		NATO starts its annual autumn war excerises in Europe.	ZAPU leader Joshua Nkomo declares that his guerrilla forces shot down a Rhodesian commercial jet with 56 passengers, which crashed on Sept. 3 killing 38 of those aboard.	Nicaraguan Pres. Anastasio Somoza Debayle denounces Venezuelan Pres. Carlos Andres Perez for trying to provoke a "bloodbath" in Nicaragua.... Air Canada resumes full service after reaching a labor agreement with the International Assn. of Machinists (IAM).	
Sept. 6	China assails the Soviet Union for supporting Vietnam's efforts to strengthen its international position.	Willy Stoll, on West Germany's most-wanted criminal list and a major suspect in the 1977 kidnapping and murder of industrialist Hanns-Martin Schleyer, is shot and killed in a Dusseldorf restaurant by West German police.	President Carter opens talks with Egyptian Pres. Sadat and Israeli Premier Begin at his presidential retreat at Camp David, Md.... Iranian govt. bans unauthorized demonstrations following a machine gun attack on a Teheran police station.	Colombia enacts a state of siege and curbs civil rights in wake of a wave of bombings and assassinations in the first month of Pres. Julio Cesar Turbay Ayala's administration.	*Wall Street Journal* reports that Japan is seeking stronger trade links with China in wake of domestic economic problems and export disagreements with the West.
Sept. 7	Paul Warnke, head of the Arms Control and Disarmament Agency, heads a U.S. negotiating team opening a new phase in SALT talks in Moscow.	British P.M. James Callaghan surprises observers by announcing that he will not call general elections in the fall.	An estimated 100,000 demonstrators march in Teheran to protest the Iranian govt.'s ban on unauthorized rallies and to demand the return to Iran of Ayatollah Ruholla Khomeini, an exiled Moslem religious leader, to replace the Pahlevi monarchy with an Islamic govt.... Carter, Sadat, and Begin meet for more than five hours in two separate sessions in their effort to break the deadlock on Middle East peace.		China and Vietnam resume talks in Hanoi on the status of ethnic Chinese in Vietnam.... Vietnamese Premier Pham Van Dong and Thai Premier Kriangsak Chamanand issue a joint communique that includes establishing a committee to repatriate refugees who had fled Vietnam to Thailand during the 1950s Indochina conflict.
Sept. 8			Iranian govt. imposes martial law and troops fire at several thousand antigovernment demonstrators in Teheran, leaving an estimated 95–3,000 dead, depending on the source of the estimate.	Labor Min. John Munro resigns from the Canadian Cabinet following the revelation that he had telephoned a provincial judge on the day an acquaintance was to be sentenced for assault.... Argentine Pres. Jorge Videla admits that there has been considerable political repression in Argentina in recent years but maintains that democracy will be eventually restored.	
Sept. 9		Sen. Edward Kennedy (D, Mass.) meets for two hours with Soviet Pres. Brezhnev in Moscow.		Nicaraguan Sandinista guerrillas launch what they call their final offensive to overthrow Pres. Anastasio Somoza Debayle.	
Sept. 10			Rhodesian P.M. Ian Smith announces imposition of selective martial law in unspecified areas of the country following the arrests on Sept. 9 of 20 senior members of Joshua Nkomo's ZAPU guerrilla faction.... Pres. Carter telephones the Shah of Iran to assure him of continued U.S. support but also asks for more political liberalization in Iran.		
Sept. 11			Shah of Iran says in an American TV interview that the impact of rioting in his country was unexpected.	Canadian dollar falls to a 45-year-low, closing at 85.94 U.S. cents in Toronto trading.	

A	B	C	D	E
Includes developments that affect more than one world region, international organizations and important meetings of major world leaders.	Includes all domestic and regional developments in Europe, including the Soviet Union, Turkey, Cyprus and Malta.	Includes all domestic and regional developments in Africa and the Middle East, including Iraq and Iran and excluding Cyprus, Turkey and Afghanistan.	Includes all domestic and regional developments in Latin America, the Caribbean and Canada.	Includes all domestic and regional developments in Asia and Pacific nations, extending from Afghanistan through all the Pacific Islands, except Hawaii.

U.S. Politics & Social Issues	U.S. Foreign Policy & Defense	U.S. Economy & Environment	Science, Technology & Nature	Culture, Leisure & Life Style	
Rep. Daniel Flood (D, Pa.) is indicted by a federal grand jury in Los Angeles on charges of lying about payoffs allegedly made to him and a former aide.				Metropolitan Nikodim, 48, Russian Orthodox Archbishop of Leningrad and Novgorod, dies of a heart attack during an audience with Pope John Paul I in the Vatican.	Sept. 5
Former Tex. Gov. John Connally testifies before the House Assassinations Committee as it opens its month of hearings on the 1963 assassination of Pres. John F. Kennedy. Connally was wounded by shots fired at Kennedy's car.				The single "Grease" with Frankie Valli and the album *Grease Soundtrack* rank three and two respectively on best-selling recordings lists for the previous week.	Sept. 6
House passes a bill outlawing most federal government wiretapping for national security purposes.... A stringent new La. abortion law is delayed by a federal district ct. restraining order.	House upholds Pres. Carter's veto of a $37-billion weapons authorization bill by a 206–191 vote.... White House press secy. Jody Powell dismisses reports of a proposed U.S. troop force in the Middle East as "one of the great nonexistent stories of all time."	Pan American Airways and National Airlines announce merger plans.	Pilots of a hijacked Malaysian jet airliner are reported to have been shot dead before the plane hit the ground on Dec. 4, 1977.	Keith Moon, 31, drummer for the British rock group, The Who, dies of a drug overdose in London.	Sept. 7
		A GAO report is released that blames 87 percent of the consumer food prices increase over the past five years on higher marketing costs, which are chiefly labor.... Teachers' strikes in 13 states curtail or cancel classroom instruction for an estimated 625,000 students in elementary and high schools across the country.			Sept. 8
				Jack Warner, 86, film pioneer who with his three older brothers founded Warner Brothers Studios in 1923, dies in Los Angeles, Calif.... Kylene Barker is named Miss America.	Sept. 9
			Soviet news agency Tass reports launching the first of two Venus probes, the Venera 11, from an orbiting spacecraft.	Jimmy Connors and Chris Evert win the men's and women's singles titles at the U.S. Open. Connors downs Bjorn Borg, 6–4, 6–2, 6–2, and Evert beats Pam Shriver, 7–5, 6–4.... New York Apollo beat the Los Angeles Skyhawks, 1–0, for the American Soccer League championship, playing in Woodland Hills, Calif.	Sept. 10
		Senate begins debate on the natural gas compromise bill under threat of a filibuster by the bill's opponents.... GM announces a new hiring policy to give preference at its new plants to current union employes.... National Electric Reliability Council, an industry organization, says that electricity shortages may gradually arise in the 1980s.		Swedish auto racing driver Ronnie Peterson, 34, ranked second in the world, dies of multiple injuries suffered in a 10-car crash at the start of the Italian Grand Prix in Monza, Italy.	Sept. 11

F	G	H	I	J
Includes elections, federal-state relations, civil rights and liberties, crime, the judiciary, education, health care, poverty, urban affairs and population.	*Includes formation and debate of U.S. foreign and defense policies, veterans' affairs and defense spending. (Relations with specific foreign countries are usually found under the region concerned.)*	*Includes business, labor, agriculture, taxation, transportation, consumer affairs, monetary and fiscal policy, natural resources, and pollution.*	*Includes worldwide scientific, medical and technological developments, natural phenomena, U.S. weather, natural disasters, and accidents.*	*Includes the arts, religion, scholarship, communications media, sports, entertainments, fashions, fads and social life.*

	World Affairs	Europe	Africa & the Middle East	The Americas	Asia & the Pacific
Sept. 12			South African police announce that at least 11 friends and relatives of Steven Biko, the late black activist leader, have been arrested in what is seen to be a move to forestall commemoration of the first anniversary of Biko's death while in police custody.... Iranian govt. seizes or issues arrest warrants for Moslem radicals and other anti-Shah activists.		Australian dockworkers strike, closing all major ports in the nation.
Sept. 13		Yugoslav govt. denounces West Germany for refusing to extradite Stefan Bilandzic and two other Croation nationalists to Yugoslavia, where they are wanted for terrorism.		Nicaraguan Sandinista fighting continues in Leon, and the rebels reportedly retain control of parts of Masaya, Esteli, and Cinandega.	Japan's three largest motor vehicle manufacturers and the Japan Ship Exporter's Assn. report a decline in exports, with Toyota Motor Works Ltd. revealing that its August car shipments fell by 22.4 percent against July exports.
Sept. 14		The 17-day-old govt. of Premier Alfredo Nobre da Costa falls when the Portuguese National Assembly rejects its program.... British Leyland Ltd. says its net income for January–June of 1978 was $15.6 million, a 74 percent increase from the $9-million figure for the first half of 1977.	Iranian Moslem leader Ayatollah Ruholla Khomeini calls on Iranian Moslems to practice passive resistance and urges troops to rebel if the Shah prevails in the current crisis.		A 65-page report by expelled Victoria Liberal M.P. Doug Jennings charges that Philip Lynch, Australian federal minister for industry and commerce, misappropriated campaign funds and benefited from corrupt land dealings.
Sept. 15			Israeli Premier Begin reportedly breaks an impasse in the Camp David Mideast summit meeting by agreeing to a Palestinian role during a five-year transition period in the West Bank.	Ending several months of speculation, Canadian P.M. Trudeau announces that general elections will be held in the spring of 1979.	
Sept. 16	The second session this year of the U.N. Conference on the Law of the Sea ends after general opposition to a U.S. congressional bill that would permit mining companies to tap the deep ocean floor for minerals before a treaty is signed.				Pakistani leader Muhammed Zia ul-Haq is sworn in as president.
Sept. 17		Poland's Roman Catholic clergy read a pastoral letter to their congregations denouncing censorship as a tool of totalitarian regimes.... Emphasizing that he is expressing his own not the Liberal Party's views, deputy Liberal leader John Pardoe says that the next British govt. should set a date for withdrawal of all British troops from Northern Ireland.	Israeli Premier Begin and Egyptian Pres. Sadat agree to a framework for a peace treaty between their two countries, concluding the U.S.-sponsored Middle East summit meeting at Camp David, Md.... Begin and Sadat also sign a settlement for the broader Arab–Israeli issue of the West Bank and Gaza Strip. Pres. Carter, who conducted the summit meetings, signs as a witness.		
Sept. 18		Soviet Union denounces the Camp David accords, focusing on Pres. Sadat's role.	Major points of the Camp David summit agreement between Israel and Egypt include Israeli withdrawal in stages and return to Egypt of the entire Sinai Peninsula and establishment of normal Egyptian–Israeli diplomatic relations. The final Israeli withdrawal would occur within two to three years after a peace pact is signed.		

A	B	C	D	E
Includes developments that affect more than one world region, international organizations and important meetings of major world leaders.	Includes all domestic and regional developments in Europe, including the Soviet Union, Turkey, Cyprus and Malta.	Includes all domestic and regional developments in Africa and the Middle East, including Iraq and Iran and excluding Cyprus, Turkey and Afghanistan.	Includes all domestic and regional developments in Latin America, the Caribbean and Canada.	Includes all domestic and regional developments in Asia and Pacific nations, extending from Afghanistan through all the Pacific Islands, except Hawaii.

U.S. Politics & Social Issues	U.S. Foreign Policy & Defense	U.S. Economy & Environment	Science, Technology & Nature	Culture, Leisure & Life Style	
One of the largest busing projects so far attempted — 1,200 buses transporting 64,000 fourth to eighth graders to 260 schools — peacefully launches Los Angeles, Calif.'s school integration program.		R. Manning Brown Jr. and James Finley both resign from the J.P. Stevens & Co. board of directors a day after the Amalgamated Clothing and Textile Workers Union announces plans to run independent candidates for their seats on the board of New York Life Insurance Co.			Sept. 12
House approves, 385–10, a bill incorporating most of Pres. Carter's proposed Civil Service system reforms.... House Ethics Committee charges that Rep. Joshua Eilberg (D, Pa.) had violated both House rules and federal law by accepting over $100,000 to influence a federal agency.	*Washington Post* reports that the Justice Dept. is investigating whether former U.S. Amb. to South Vietnam Graham Martin possesses CIA secret intelligence papers covering U.S. involvement in Vietnam between 1963–75.	Ford Motor Co. is indicted in the deaths of three teenage girls who were fatally burned in an August accident when the tank of their 1973 Pinto subcompact exploded after the car was hit in the rear by a van.	FDA Comr. Donald Kennedy says that the FDA has confidence in generic drugs.... A uranium find that could be the world's biggest is reported in an area of northwest Saskatchewan, Canada.	NBC announces that Jane Cahill Pfeiffer has been named board chairman as well as director of NBC's parent company, Radio Corporation of America. She will thus become the highest-ranking woman executive in the broadcasting industry.	Sept. 13
Marina Oswald Porter, widow of Lee Harvey Oswald, tells the House Select Committee on Assassinations that she believes her husband killed former Pres. John F. Kennedy.		Natural gas bill's supporters, led by Senate Majority Leader Robert Byrd (D, W. Va.), reach agreement with the bill's opponents to rule out a potential filibuster.... Ford Motor Co. claims that sales of new Pintos have fully recovered from negative publicity related to the car's fuel-system problems but says it is too early to assess the impact of yesterday's grand jury indictment.			Sept. 14
			Willy Messerschmitt, 80, German industrialist and aircraft designer who was exononerated by a de-Nazification court in 1948 for building aircraft for the German air force, dies in Munich.	Muhammad Ali defeats Leon Spinks, the World Boxing Assn. heavyweight champion, in a unanimous 15-round decision before 70,000 fans in the Louisiana Superdome, New Orleans. He thus becomes the first boxer ever to win a heavyweight title three times.	Sept. 15
College Entrance Examination Bd. reports that the average score on the Scholastic Aptitude Test (SAT) verbal section taken by the class of 1978 high school seniors was 429, the same as the previous year. The math section score dropped to 468 from 470, however.			At least 25,000 people are reported killed in an earthquake in northeast Iran that measured 7.7 on the Richter scale.	*The New York Times* reports that China has invited Pierre Cardin and Hanae Mori to Peking to act as consultants on Chinese fashion, suggesting a sharp official departure in the government's attitude toward clothes. It also notes the reappearance of skirts and dresses, which were attacked as decadent and bourgeois during the Cultural Revolution.	Sept. 16
	Pres. Carter signs a bill authorizing an undisclosed amount in fiscal 1979 for federal intelligence agencies.		The U.S. research satellite Pegasus I, launched into orbit 13 years ago, breaks up over Africa as it falls back to Earth.	Emmy Awards are presented as follows: best actor in a special, Fred Astaire; best actress in a special, Joanne Woodward; best dramatic actor in a series, Ed Asner; and best actress in a series, Sada Thompson.	Sept. 17
James Farmer, founder of the Congress of Racial Equality (CORE), charges that its convention, held Sept. 8–10, was a fraud and calls for the resignation of Roy Innis as national chairman.	Pres. Carter addresses a joint session of Congress to disclose results of the Camp David Middle East summit.... Carter lauds Sadat and Begin as two men who have made "this impossible dream a real possibility."	*Business Week* reports that U.S. corporations are holding back from investing huge cash reserves they have accumulated because they lack confidence in both the national and international economic outlook.			Sept. 18

F	G	H	I	J
Includes elections, federal-state relations, civil rights and liberties, crime, the judiciary, education, health care, poverty, urban affairs and population.	*Includes formation and debate of U.S. foreign and defense policies, veterans' affairs and defense spending. (Relations with specific foreign countries are usually found under the region concerned.)*	*Includes business, labor, agriculture, taxation, transportation, consumer affairs, monetary and fiscal policy, natural resources, and pollution.*	*Includes worldwide scientific, medical and technological developments, natural phenomena, U.S. weather, natural disasters, and accidents.*	*Includes the arts, religion, scholarship, communications media, sports, entertainments, fashions, fads and social life.*

	World Affairs	Europe	Africa & the Middle East	The Americas	Asia & the Pacific
Sept. 19	The thirty-third session of the U.N. General Assembly convenes in N.Y. Colombian For. Min. Indalecio Lievano Aguirre is elected president without opposition.... Solomon Islands are admitted as the 150th U.N. member.	A British govt.-commissioned study reveals that British oil companies —, Royal Dutch/Shell Group and British Petroleum Co. Ltd. — had defied a 1965 economic sanction against Rhodesia and had supplied Rhodesia oil through 1977.	Egyptian Pres. Sadat says he wants a comprehensive Middle East peace pact but implies that he will pursue a peace initiative alone if other Arab states refuse to join. ... Saudi Arabia and Jordan are cautiously critical of the Camp David accord while PLO leader Yasir Arafat denounces the agreement as "a dirty deal."	In a tape recording played at the House Select Committee on Assassinations hearing, Cuban Pres. Fidel Castro denies any involvement in the assassination of Pres. Kennedy.... Progressive Conservatives win an upset victory in Nova Scotian legislative elections, led by Premier-elect John Buchanan.	A dispute between the Australian govt. and the Ranger companies over who would pay Aborigines the 4.25 percent royalty for use of their land is reportedly delaying the uranium project in the Northern Territory.
Sept. 20		Corrado Alunni, a leading Red Brigades terrorist, is sentenced to a 12-year prison term for illegal possession of firearms. He is suspected for complicity in the murder of former Italian Premier Aldo Moro.... A *London Times* poll reveals that most Britons favor withdrawing British troops from Northern Ireland.	John Vorster, South Africa's prime minister since 1966, announces his resignation and says that he will seek the ceremonial position of president.... Syrian Pres. Hafez al-Assad assails Egyptian Pres. Sadat for defecting to the enemy. Lebanon expresses concern that the Camp David summit makes no provision for a Palestinian homeland.... Israeli Premier Begin concedes that Israel and the U.S. held different interpretations about Israeli settlement on the West Bank.		Afghan Deputy Premier Hafizullah Amin tells Indian reporters that his government has discovered a plot by an unnamed foreign country to overthrow the Afghan regime.
Sept. 21			State Secy. Vance arrives in Saudi Arabia after stopping in Jordan to try to gain support for the Camp David accords.... Nigerian Head of State Lt. Gen. Olusegun Obasanjo lifts the country's 12-year ban on political parties in preparation for a return to civilian rule.		Deposed Cambodian Pres. Lon Nol says that more than three million Cambodians have been killed since the Communists seized power in 1975.
Sept. 22		Soviet Pres. Brezhnev assails the Camp David accords.	Libyan leader Qaddafi and PLO Chmn. Arafat go to Jordan to confer with King Hussein, a former enemy, seeking to dissuade him from entering into negotiations with Egypt and Israel.	All members of the Ecuadoran national electoral court resign protesting what they claim was a massive vote fraud in the July 16 presidential election. They recommend that the results be annulled.... Nicaraguan National Guard finally recaptures Esteli, but the city is almost completely in ruins. The Red Cross estimates at least 400 deaths from the fighting.	
Sept. 23		West German Defense Min. Hans Apel questions the wisdom of holding large-scale NATO maneuvers in Europe.	Pres. Sadat receives a tumultuous welcome on his return to Cairo.... In his first public statement on the Camp David accords, Jordanian King Hussein expresses extreme dismay at Egyptian Pres. Sadat's peace initiative with Israel but admits that he cannot rule out a role for Jordan in a comprehensive peace settlement.		
Sept. 24			Four Arab hardline states — Syria, South Yemen, Algeria, and Libya — and the PLO end a four-day meeting in Damascus with the announcement that they are severing all economic and political relations with Egypt in face of the Camp David accords.... Fighting erupts again in Beirut.... Israeli opposition Labor Party approves the Camp David accords, 221–16.		

A	B	C	D	E
Includes developments that affect more than one world region, international organizations and important meetings of major world leaders.	Includes all domestic and regional developments in Europe, including the Soviet Union, Turkey, Cyprus and Malta.	Includes all domestic and regional developments in Africa and the Middle East, including Iraq and Iran and excluding Cyprus, Turkey and Afghanistan.	Includes all domestic and regional developments in Latin America, the Caribbean and Canada.	Includes all domestic and regional developments in Asia and Pacific nations, extending from Afghanistan through all the Pacific Islands, except Hawaii.

U.S. Politics & Social Issues	U.S. Foreign Policy & Defense	U.S. Economy & Environment	Science, Technology & Nature	Culture, Leisure & Life Style	
Mass. Gov. Michael Dukakis (D) unexpectedly loses the gubernatorial primary while Sen. Edward Brooke (R), whose political future appeared clouded by personal controversy, is renominated to a third term against a formidable conservative challenger, Avi Nelson, a radio talk-show host.		U.S. payments deficit narrows in the second quarter to a seasonally adjusted $3.26 billion, as reported by the Commerce Dept.	A poisonous cloud caused by a Genoa, Italy chemical plant accident kills three men and causes the hospitalization of many others. . . . Monsoon floods that started in late June in northern India and are now receding reportedly have claimed more than 1,200 lives and were the worst of this century.	Etienne Gilson, 94, French historian and medieval philosophy authority, dies in Cravant, France.	Sept. 19
Lowndes County, Ala. grand jury indicts Thomas Rowe Jr., an FBI informant on the Ku Klux Klan in the 1960s, for the 1965 slaying of civil-rights worker Viola Liuzzo.		Addressing a USW convention in Atlantic City, N.J. Pres. Carter vows a new antiinflation plan that will require some sacrifice from all but will not penalize labor. . . . The Republican Party begins a three-day political blitz across the country to sell the Kemp–Roth tax bill, which calls for a 33 percent cut in federal income taxes over a three-year period. The bill's sponsors are Rep. Jack Kemp (R, N.Y.) and Sen. William Roth (R, Del.).	Soviet cosmonauts Vladimir Kovalyonok and Alexander Ivanchenkov break the record for continuous time in space (96 days and 10 hours) set earlier in 1978 by Soviet cosmonauts Yuri Romanenko and Georgi Grechko.	The September 15 Superdome boxing spectacular is reported by *Variety* as having been viewed in more U.S. homes than any other sports event in TV history.	Sept. 20
Berkeley, Calif. City Council gives preliminary approval to what is believed to be the strongest homosexual-rights ordinance in the U.S. . . . Former Pres. Gerald Ford, one of three surviving members of the Warren Commission, tells the House panel investigating Pres. Kennedy's assassination that the commission would have broadened its investigation if it had been aware of the CIA plots to kill Cuban Pres. Fidel Castro.		U.S. National Council of Churches announces that it has ended ties with the Continental National Bank and Trust Co. of Chicago because the bank continues to grant loans to the South African govt. . . . Delegates to the USW convention in Atlantic City, N.J. approve new rules designed to prevent outside contributions to union election campaigns.	FDA sets regulations for the labeling of low-calorie and reduced-calorie foods.	Alex Haley is cleared of plagiarism charges when U.S. District Ct. Judge Marvin Frankel dismisses a suit that contends that Haley's best-selling book, *Roots*, was largely copied from a historical novel, *Jubilee*, by Margaret Walker.	Sept. 21
	Fifty-one House members send Pres. Carter a letter asking that he name a commission to investigate the possible hazards of a new Defense Dept. plan to make land-based missiles safe from attack.	Calif. Supreme Ct. upholds the constitutionality of Proposition 13, the ballot initiative approved by voters in June to reduce property taxes by about 57 percent. . . . Former Pres. Gerald Ford and his challenger for the 1976 Republican presidential nomination, Ronald Reagan, join in the Republican public campaign to sell the Kemp–Roth tax-cut bill.		A.J. Bakunas, 27, Hollywood stuntman who plunged 323 feet in an attempt to set a world free-fall record, dies from internal injuries sustained when the airbag on which he landed split open.	Sept. 22
				Lyman Bostock, 27, outfielder for the California Angels and one of baseball's highest-paid players, dies of a gunshot wound intended for his estranged wife in Gary, Ind. . . . Benjamin Britten's opera *Billy Budd* is premiered in N.Y.C. as the Metropolitan Opera's opening-night production.	Sept. 23
				Ruth Etting, 80, former Ziegfield show girl, radio and film star in the 1930s, and best known as a torch singer, dies in Colorado Springs.	Sept. 24

F	G	H	I	J
Includes elections, federal-state relations, civil rights and liberties, crime, the judiciary, education, health care, poverty, urban affairs and population.	*Includes formation and debate of U.S. foreign and defense policies, veterans' affairs and defense spending. (Relations with specific foreign countries are usually found under the region concerned.)*	*Includes business, labor, agriculture, taxation, transportation, consumer affairs, monetary and fiscal policy, natural resources, and pollution.*	*Includes worldwide scientific, medical and technological developments, natural phenomena, U.S. weather, natural disasters, and accidents.*	*Includes the arts, religion, scholarship, communications media, sports, entertainments, fashions, fads and social life.*

	World Affairs	Europe	Africa & the Middle East	The Americas	Asia & the Pacific
Sept. 25	Gold hits a record high when five major London dealers set a closing price of $218.40 an ounce.		State Secy. Vance returns to Washington after visiting Jordan, Saudi Arabia, and Syria to consult about the Camp David summit meeting.		Vietnam charges that China has massed its forces for an invasion of northern Vietnam on two fronts.
Sept. 26			Shah of Iran bars members of his royal family from financial dealings with the government.		China breaks off talks with Vietnam on ethnic Chinese in Vietnam. Before leaving Hanoi, Chinese Deputy For. Min. Chung Hsi-tung charges that Vietnam had used the talks to camouflage violence.
Sept. 27			Israeli Premier Begin warns that he will resign and form a new Cabinet unless a majority of his coalition's 70 members in the Knesset support the Camp David accords.		Indonesian govt. releases 1,324 political prisoners who have been detained without trial since an abortive CP coup in 1965.
Sept. 28	The U.S. dollar, remaining weak against most major currencies, moves sharply higher against the Swiss franc, trading in Zurich at 1.515 frances to the dollar.... Pres. Carter tells a Washington news conference that there should be international action under the aegis of the U.N. to end hostilities in Lebanon, which are described as the fiercest since the outbreak of civil war in 1975.		Israeli Knesset approves the Camp David accord with Egypt and the removal of Jewish settlements in the Sinai, clearing one procedural obstacle to Egyptian–Israeli peace negotiations.... Defense Min. Pieter Botha is elected by a caucus of South Africa's ruling National Party to succeed John Vorster as prime minister.	Mexican Pres. Jose Lopez Portillo's amnesty law is enacted, freeing dozens of political prisoners.	
Sept. 29	U.N. Security Council votes to give South Africa until Oct. 23 to reconsider its rejection of a U.N. plan for Namibia, and indicates that rejection of the plan would prompt a U.N. vote to impose economic sanctions.	Liechtenstein is made the twenty-second member of the Council of Europe.	South African Parliament elects John Vorster to the presidency by an overwhelming margin.	Colombia and U.S. sign an antinarcotics traffic pact.	
Sept. 30			Syrian gunners attack Christian positions in Mount Lebanon, the Christian area north of the capital where many Christian civilians have moved to escape Syrian shelling in east Beirut.... Syrian govt. rejects Pres. Carter's proposed international conference on Lebanon.	Dominican Republic Pres. Antonio Guzman surprises most observers by dismissing the army's commander in chief, Maj. Gen. Enrique Perez y Perez, and appointing him ambassador to Spain.... Nicaraguan Pres. Anastasio Somoza and leaders of the Broad Opposition Front, an umbrella group, agree to have Guatemalan, Dominican Republic, and U.S. representatives mediate the country's strife.	Tuvalu, a group of South Pacific islands formerly known as the Ellice Islands, becomes independent from the United Kingdom.
Oct. 1		A police raid on hideouts of alleged terrorists in Milan results in the arrest of a number of suspected members of Italy's ultra-left Red Brigades.	One hundred West Bank Arab leaders reject the Camp David accords and call for an independent Palestinian state governed the PLO.... The Syrian-arranged cease-fire in Lebanon is quickly shattered as shells strike three Christian districts in Beirut.		

A	B	C	D	E
Includes developments that affect more than one world region, international organizations and important meetings of major world leaders.	Includes all domestic and regional developments in Europe, including the Soviet Union, Turkey, Cyprus and Malta.	Includes all domestic and regional developments in Africa and the Middle East, including Iraq and Iran and excluding Cyprus, Turkey and Afghanistan.	Includes all domestic and regional developments in Latin America, the Caribbean and Canada.	Includes all domestic and regional developments in Asia and Pacific nations, extending from Afghanistan through all the Pacific Islands, except Hawaii.

U.S. Politics & Social Issues	U.S. Foreign Policy & Defense	U.S. Economy & Environment	Science, Technology & Nature	Culture, Leisure & Life Style	
			A mid-air collision of a Pacific Southwest Airlines jet and a single-engine training plane over San Diego, Calif. kills 150 people, the highest fatality count in U.S. aviation history.	U.S. District Ct. Judge Constance Baker Motley rules that major league baseball and the N.Y. Yankees management cannot legally bar a woman sportswriter from the locker room after a game. The suit was brought by *Sports Illustrated* reporter Melissa Ludtke.	Sept. 25
Sen. S.I. Hayakawa (R) and Rep. Leo Ryan (D), both from California, formally petition the Justice Dept. for a presidential pardon for Patricia Hearst.	Pres. Carter signs a bill authorizing $2.8 billion in fiscal 1979 for foreign military and security aid that also provides for lifting the arms embargo against Turkey.... The bill also allows U.S. economic sanctions against Rhodesia to be ended at the end of the year if specific conditions in internal Rhodesian policies are met.	Pres. Carter unveils an export promotion plan designed to shrink the enormous U.S. trade deficit.	A five-day fire that began with an explosion in a La. cavern used to store oil for the nation's strategic petroleum reserve is finally extinguished.		Sept. 26
Jose Aleman, a Cuban exile living in Miami, tells the House Select Committee on Assassinations that reputed Mafia leader Santo Trafficante had told him in the summer of 1963 that Pres. Kennedy would not be reelected because he was "going to be hit."	Pres. Carter takes direct issue with Israeli Premier Begin's version of the Camp David agreements on Israeli West Bank settlements.	Senate, 57–42, approves a compromise natural gas bill strongly promoted by Pres. Carter as central to his energy program.			Sept. 27
		A federal appeals ct. in N.Y. voids Kennecott Copper Corp.'s victory over Curtiss-Wright Corp., which was fighting to control Kennecott, the nation's biggest copper company.		Pope John Paul I, 65, dies in his Vatican apartment 34 days after he was elected spiritual leader of the Roman Catholic Church. His reign was the shortest since Pope Leo XI ruled for 18 days in 1605.... Minnesota Twins baseball team owner Calvin Griffith creates a furor in the Twin Cities area by making allegedly derogatory comments about blacks and the private lives and financial dealings of his players.	Sept. 28
A Baltimore, Md. federal grand jury indicts 18 people on charges stemming from the investigation of GSA corruption.					Sept. 29
	Pres. Carter says he is pleased to learn that Syrian Pres. Hafez al-Assad has personally brought about a Beirut cease-fire.		Pres. Carter signs a bill authorizing $4.40 billion in fiscal 1979 for NASA. The largest single authorization in the bill is $1.443 billion for the space shuttle program.	Edgar Bergen, 75, ventriloquist who starred with his monocled dummy Charlie McCarthy for almost 60 years in vaudeville, the movies, and a long-running radio show, dies in his sleep in Las Vegas, Nev.... The body of Pope John Paul I is borne from Clementine Hall to St. Peter's Basilica through the crowd of mourners in St. Peter's Square.	Sept. 30
		Commerce Dept. reports the government's composite index of leading economic indicators rose .8 percent in August after falling sharply in July.	Pres. Carter presents the new Congressional Space Medal of Honor to former astronauts Neil Armstrong, Frank Borman, Charles Conrad Jr., Alan Shepard Jr., and Sen. John Glenn Jr. (D, Ohio). He also presents a posthumous award to Virgil Grisson's widow.		Oct. 1

F	G	H	I	J
Includes elections, federal-state relations, civil rights and liberties, crime, the judiciary, education, health care, poverty, urban affairs and population.	Includes formation and debate of U.S. foreign and defense policies, veterans' affairs and defense spending. (Relations with specific foreign countries are usually found under the region concerned.)	Includes business, labor, agriculture, taxation, transportation, consumer affairs, monetary and fiscal policy, natural resources, and pollution.	Includes worldwide scientific, medical and technological developments, natural phenomena, U.S. weather, natural disasters, and accidents.	Includes the arts, religion, scholarship, communications media, sports, entertainments, fashions, fads and social life.

	World Affairs	Europe	Africa & the Middle East	The Americas	Asia & the Pacific
Oct. 2	In a meeting in Paris with U.S. national security adviser Zbigniew Brzezinski, French Pres. Valery Giscard d'Estaing proposes a peace plan for Lebanon that would have the Arab League force withdraw from regions where it has been shelling Christians. . . . South-West Africa People's Organization (SWAPO) becomes a full member of the nonaligned nations movement.		Syrian forces lay down one of the heaviest artillery barrages of the Lebanese civil war when they storm a Christian stronghold to rescue 20 of their soldiers who had been trapped there since Sept. 30. . . . Rhodesian govt. bans the *Zimbabwe Times*, the country's only daily newspaper serving a black readership. . . . Shah of Iran grants amnesty to exiled antigovernment activists including the Ayatollah Khomeini.		Supporters of imprisoned former Pakistani P.M. Zulfikar Ali Bhutto launch a self-immolation campaign to gain his release. . . . Sri Lankan Pres. Junius Richard Jayewardene announces a ban on public sector strikes and politically motivated walkouts in private industry. . . . A U.S. trade mission begins a 14-day visit to Japan to promote the sale of U.S. goods and to reduce the hugh U.S. trade deficit with Japan.
Oct. 3			Christian shelling of western Beirut cuts electricity and phone service. . . . Syrian Pres. Hafez al-Assad reportedly tells a news conference that he finds French Pres. Giscard d'Estaing's peace plan for Lebanon "rather strange." . . . South African Cabinet issues a statement that it has not rejected the U.N. plan for Namibia.		Chinese govt. marks the twenty-ninth anniversary of the founding of the People's Republic of China by calling for increased efforts to achieve economic modernization before the year 2000.
Oct. 4		A French Socialist Party motion to censure the government, also backed by the CP, falls short of a majority in the National Assembly. . . . Turkish govt. announces that it will allow the U.S. to reopen military bases closed in 1975 in retaliation for the U.S. arms embargo.	Lebanese Christian Phalangist Party radio estimates that over 500 people have been killed in the previous hours in strife in Beirut, most of them civilians caught in shelling. The presidential palace and adjacent army barracks are hit by the exchange of heavy rocket, mortar, and artillery fire.		Supporters of imprisoned former Pakistani P.M. Zulfikar Ali Bhutto riot in Multan after the arrest of his daughter, Benazir Bhutto, a member of the central executive of the Pakistan People's Party.
Oct. 5	Pres. Carter sends personal appeals to Soviet Pres. Brezhnev, Syrian Pres. Hafez al-Assad, Israeli Premier Menahem Begin, and other world leaders, requesting their cooperation with U.S. peace efforts for Lebanon at the U.N.	Norwegian Finance Min. Per Kleppe presents the socialist Labor govt.'s austerity budget to Parliament.	Israeli gunboats shell west Beirut.	During French Pres. Valery Giscard d'Estaing's four-day state visit to Brazil, he and Brazilian Pres. Ernesto Geisel sign a broad technical cooperation pact that establishes a regular exchange of technological and industrial information.	
Oct. 6	U.N. Security Council unanimously adopts a resolution for a cease-fire in Lebanon. . . . West German govt. announces it will cancel the debts of 30 of the world's poorest countries, amounting to about $2.1 billion.	The four-day annual conference of the British Labor Party ends in Blackpool. P.M. James Callaghan's proposed 5 percent limit on wage increases, a central point of his Labor govt.'s strategy to control inflation, is attacked.	Israeli authorities call the naval action of the previous day a preemptive strike against Palestinian terrorists but concede in private that it was a warning to Syria against further attacks on Christians in Beirut. . . . Shah of Iran pledges to continue his reform program despite unrest in the country.	*Los Angeles Times* reports that Chile's 16-year-old land-reform program will officially end on Dec. 31. . . . Bolivia's ex-Pres. Hugo Banzer Suarez is appointed ambassador to Argentina two months after he was ousted in a military coup.	
Oct. 7	U.N. Secretariat reportedly launches a $500,000 publicity campaign to promote the rights of the Palestinians and to improve the PLO's image.		Syria declares a unilateral cease-fire in and around Beirut after a week of fierce fighting with Christian milia. . . . As the Lebanese cease-fire goes into effect, the Syrian troops blockade Christian forces in east Beirut from other Christian areas north of the capital.		
Oct. 8			ZANU leader Robert Mugabe declares that the U.S. has lost its place in Rhodesian negotiations by permitting the transitional government, represented by P.M. Ian Smith and Rev. Ndabaningi Sithole, to visit the U.S.	About 600 peasants, armed with machetes, occupy 4,500 acres of farmland in Oaxaca State, Mexico.	

A	B	C	D	E
Includes developments that affect more than one world region, international organizations and important meetings of major world leaders.	Includes all domestic and regional developments in Europe, including the Soviet Union, Turkey, Cyprus and Malta.	Includes all domestic and regional developments in Africa and the Middle East, including Iraq and Iran and excluding Cyprus, Turkey and Afghanistan.	Includes all domestic and regional developments in Latin America, the Caribbean and Canada.	Includes all domestic and regional developments in Asia and Pacific nations, extending from Afghanistan through all the Pacific Islands, except Hawaii.

U.S. Politics & Social Issues	U.S. Foreign Policy & Defense	U.S. Economy & Environment	Science, Technology & Nature	Culture, Leisure & Life Style	
V.P. Walter Mondale announces a Carter administration program to improve rural health service.				New York Yankees beat the Boston Red Sox, 5–4, in a special one-game playoff to decide the AL Eastern Division championship after the teams ended up tied on Oct. 1. . . . Supreme Ct. declines to review a decision upholding the power of major league baseball commissioner Bowie Kuhn to regulate player sales that was challenged by Charles Finley, owner of the AL Oakland A's.	Oct. 2
William and Emily Harris are sentenced in the Alameda County, Calif. Superior Ct. to 10 years to life for the 1974 kidnapping of Patricia Hearst.			In Calcutta, India the second baby conceived outside a woman's body is born.		Oct. 3
		Council on Wage and Price Stability warns that inflation will be considerably worse this year than in the two previous years. . . . Asst. Atty. Gen. John Shenefield unveils a new Justice Dept. policy to encourage corporations to make voluntary disclosures of antitrust violations.		Ninety-two cardinals participate in a simple funeral mass for the late Pope John Paul I in St. Peter's Square.	Oct. 4
		House sustains Pres. Carter's veto of a $20.2-billion public works bill, which he called inflationary. . . . Howard Jarvis, author of California's successful Proposition 13, takes out a full-page ad in the *Washington Post* to denounce the public-works bill as an "outrage."	Consumer Product Safety Commission proposes that toys small enough, or having parts small enough, to choke children should be banned.	Isaac Bashevis Singer, 74, a Polish-born naturalized American who writes in Yiddish, is the recipient of the Nobel Prize for Literature.	Oct. 5
Senate votes, 60–36, to extend the ERA ratification deadline. . . . Phyllis Schlafly, national chairperson of Stop ERA, says that the extension will be challenged in the courts and predicts a backlash in state legislatures.		Congress approves the first major restructuring of the U.S. bankruptcy system in 40 years. . . . A bill to phase out federal regulation of the airline industry clears a congressional conference committee.			Oct. 6
Rep. Charles Diggs Jr. (D, Mich.) is convicted by a federal ct. jury in Wash., D.C. of 29 counts of mail fraud and of filing falsified congressional payroll data.				Los Angeles Dodgers and New York Yankees earn berths in the 1978 World Series by clinching the NL and AL championships respectively.	Oct. 7
Patricia Hearst's uncle, William Randolph Hearst, launches a campaign for her release from prison in a series of front-page editorials.				Los Angeles Dodger coach Jim (Junior) Gilliam, 49, dies of cardiac arrest in California after suffering a cerebral hemorrhage on Sept. 15.	Oct. 8

F	G	H	I	J
Includes elections, federal-state relations, civil rights and liberties, crime, the judiciary, education, health care, poverty, urban affairs and population.	Includes formation and debate of U.S. foreign and defense policies, veterans' affairs and defense spending. (Relations with specific foreign countries are usually found under the region concerned.)	Includes business, labor, agriculture, taxation, transportation, consumer affairs, monetary and fiscal policy, natural resources, and pollution.	Includes worldwide scientific, medical and technological developments, natural phenomena, U.S. weather, natural disasters, and accidents.	Includes the arts, religion, scholarship, communications media, sports, entertainments, fashions, fads and social life.

	World Affairs	Europe	Africa & the Middle East	The Americas	Asia & the Pacific
Oct. 9		Turkish opposition Labor Party leader Behide Boran calls the killings of six party members the previous day an extreme escalation of fascist terrorism to intimidate the party.	Lebanese Christian leader Camille Chamoun denounces Pres. Elias Sarkis as a traitor for negotiating a cease-fire with Syrian Pres. Assad.	Nicaraguan Pres. Anastasio Somoza lifts press censorship.... The president of Ecuador's Central bank says that Ecuador's oil boom has ended and its economic growth over the next two years must come exclusively from more efficient production and effective management.	
Oct. 10		British opposition Conservative Party leader Margaret Thatcher says in a BBC TV interview that the free market should determine pay levels.... Jacques Chirac, leader of the Gaullists, announces a truce in attacks on French Premier Raymond Barre's policies in the National Assembly.... Giraloma Tartaglione, a senior Rome magistrate, is shot to death by the Red Brigades terrorist group, one in a wave of politically motivated attacks that have flared throughout Italy since late September.	Lebanese Moslems stage a general strike in their section of west Beirut to protest Pres. Elias Sarkis's truce plan that would allow the Lebanese army to control Christian districts in Beirut and its suburbs and have Syrian troops withdraw to Moslem areas.... The interim Rhodesian govt. announces abolition of all racial discrimination.... Egyptian Pres. Anwar Sadat assails Syria and the Palestinians for their vehement opposition to his peace accord with Israel.		Wu Teh reportedly has been replaced by Lin Hu-chia as mayor of Peking, China after a mounting public campaign that accused him of failing to carry out CP policy and opposing Deputy Premier Teng Hsiao-ping.
Oct. 11				Aristides Royo is elected president of Panama by the National Assembly of Community Representatives, assuming executive powers previously held by Brig. Gen. Omar Torrijos. Torrijos remains National Guard commander and is still considered the most powerful man in Panama.	U.N. High Commissioner for Refugees reports a record 7,300 people have fled Vietnam by boat in September.
Oct. 12		One person is killed and six injured when three bombs explode aboard an express train from Dublin as it is about to pull into the Belfast, Northern Ireland station.	Israel and Egypt open negotiations in Wash., D.C. on drafting a bilateral peace treaty.... Negotiating teams heads — Israeli For. Min. Moshe Dayan and Egyptian Defense Min. Kamel Hassan Ali — thank Pres. Carter for his role in advancing the Middle East peace process.... Uganda accuses Tanzania of invading its western area.		
Oct. 13	At a news conference marking the end of his visit to Great Britain, Chinese For. Min. Huang Hua assails the Soviet Union, characterizing it as on the offensive while the U.S. is on the defensive.	Ola Ullsten, head of Sweden's minority Liberal Party, becomes premier when the Social Democrats and the Center Party abstain from the vote on the office.	Lebanese army units are deployed in the outskirts of Beirut for the first time since the outbreak of Syrian-Christian fighting there.... Iranian govt. lifts a press ban imposed on Oct. 11 after a protest strike by newspaper employes.	*Miami Herald* reports that evidence gathered by U.S. investigators regarding the murder of Chilean For. Min. Orlando Letelier in Wash., D.C. is being shown to one of the suspects in the case although a Chilean judge had ordered that the evidence be kept secret.... Bank of Canada raises its prime rate to a record 10.25 percent from 9.5 percent.	Cambodian For. Min. Ieng Sary invites Western observers to visit Cambodia and see for themselves whether the government has murdered thousands of its people.
Oct. 14		Soviet CP newspaper *Pravda* criticizes U.S. Amb. Malcolm Toon for "slandering" the Soviet state and acting extremely "undiplomatically."	Daniel arap Moi is officially sworn in as president of Kenya.		
Oct. 15				Gen. Joao Baptista de Figueiredo is elected president of Brazil by an electoral college dominated by his ARENA party.	

A	B	C	D	E
Includes developments that affect more than one world region, international organizations and important meetings of major world leaders.	Includes all domestic and regional developments in Europe, including the Soviet Union, Turkey, Cyprus and Malta.	Includes all domestic and regional developments in Africa and the Middle East, including Iraq and Iran and excluding Cyprus, Turkey and Afghanistan.	Includes all domestic and regional developments in Latin America, the Caribbean and Canada.	Includes all domestic and regional developments in Asia and Pacific nations, extending from Afghanistan through all the Pacific Islands, except Hawaii.

U.S. Politics & Social Issues	U.S. Foreign Policy & Defense	U.S. Economy & Environment	Science, Technology & Nature	Culture, Leisure & Life Style	
			Wall Street Journal reports that accidental contamination of cattle feed with a highly toxic chemical has spread through the food chain to most of the population of Michigan.	Jacques Brel, 49, Belgian-born singer and composer, dies of a lung embolism in Bobigny, France.	**Oct. 9**
	Army reportedly had drafted a plan aimed at young college-bound men that would reduce some enlistements to two years from three and offer a better GI bill.... Pres. Carter rules out meeting with Rhodesian P.M. Ian Smith, who is touring the U.S. to gain support for his interim government.... For the second time in a month, Pres. Carter expresses support for the embattled Shah of Iran.	Pres. Carter signs a bill to authorize minting a new one-dollar coin bearing the likeness of feminist activist Susan B. Anthony.... Pres. Carter tells a televised news conference that he will actively pursue the antiinflation program he is planning to present after Congress adjourns.		*The New York Times* reports that Orbita, a new Soviet factory, will manufacture jeans to meet the demands of Soviet teenagers.... Supreme Ct. declines to review a decision upholding La.'s "head and master" law giving a husband complete legal control over the property of a married couple.... John Bray, 99, inventor of the animated cartoon process used by almost all early animators including Walt Disney, dies in Bridgeport, Conn.	**Oct. 10**
				Living in the U.S.A., sung by Linda Ronstadt, is the best-selling record album for the week just passed.	**Oct. 11**
Rep. Daniel Flood (D, Pa.) is indicted by a federal grand jury in Wash., D.C. on 10 counts of conspiracy and bribery after being indicted by a Los Angeles grand jury in September for perjury about payoffs.	Sen. Edward Kennedy (D, Mass.) urges the Carter administration to sever all economic and military ties with Nicaragua.... Eighty U.S. senators ask State Secy. Cyrus Vance to place the issue of Cambodia's alleged human-rights violations before the U.N. Security Council.	Chase Manhattan Bank raises its prime lending rate to 10 percent, initiating an industry-wide move toward the highest prime rate since January 1975.	Nobel Prize in Medicine is shared by microbiologists Daniel Nathans, Hamilton Smith, and Werner Arber for their discovery in the late 1960s–early 1970s of restriction enzymes and their application to genetics.	Los Angeles, Calif. City Council votes, 8–4, to ratify a contract to host the 1984 Summer Olympics. ... An official Vatican statement denounces rumors that foul play might have contributed to the death of Pope John Paul I.... British punk rock guitarist Sid Vicious is charged with second-degree murder in the stabbing death of his American girlfriend, Nancy Spungen.	**Oct. 12**
Pres. Carter signs into law the Civil Service Reform Act, the first major revision of the civil service in 95 years.	Pres. Carter signs a record-breaking $117.3-billion defense appropriations bill.... House formally reprimands three Calif. Democrats — John McFall, Edward Roybal, and Charles H. Wilson — for official misconduct in the South Korean lobbying scandal (Koreagate).	House makes a crucial vote on the procedural question of dealing with the five parts of Pres. Carter's energy bill separately or as a unit, finally voting, 207–206, to deal with it as a package.			**Oct. 13**
House approves a bill that puts presidential papers in the public domain when a President leaves office and gives Americans access to the papers under the Freedom of Information Act.... House passes a bill requiring employers with medical disability plans to provide pregnancy disability payments for women on an equal basis with other medical conditions.	Pres. Carter signs the Agricultural Foreign Investment Disclosure Act, requiring foreigners buying U.S. farms to register with the federal government.	Ford Motor Co. settles an FTC complaint by agreeing to refund to consumers whose cars are repossessed any surplus money gained by dealers when the cars were sold.			**Oct. 14**
Senate follows the House in clearing a Carter administration bill to open the college student-aid program to middle-income families.	Former State Secy. Henry Kissinger reportedly has expressed support for Rhodesian P.M. Ian Smith's interim government.	Congress gives final approval after a year-and-a-half of consideration and revision to energy legislation urgently sought by Pres. Carter.... Congress completes action on a tax-revision bill that provides a cut of $18.7 billion for 1979.		Irene Miller and Vera Komarkova become the first Americans and first women to reach the summit of Annapurna I in Nepal.	**Oct. 15**
F *Includes elections, federal-state relations, civil rights and liberties, crime, the judiciary, education, health care, poverty, urban affairs and population.*	**G** *Includes formation and debate of U.S. foreign and defense policies, veterans' affairs and defense spending. (Relations with specific foreign countries are usually found under the region concerned.)*	**H** *Includes business, labor, agriculture, taxation, transportation, consumer affairs, monetary and fiscal policy, natural resources, and pollution.*	**I** *Includes worldwide scientific, medical and technological developments, natural phenomena, U.S. weather, natural disasters, and accidents.*	**J** *Includes the arts, religion, scholarship, communications media, sports, entertainments, fashions, fads and social life.*	

	World Affairs	Europe	Africa & the Middle East	The Americas	Asia & the Pacific
Oct. 16		West German mark is revalued upward against the currencies of the five other European currencies belonging to the so-called snake or joint currency float.	U.N. Western contact group on Namibia holds an emergency round of talks with South African officials to try to head off a complete breakdown of negotiations on Namibia.	Canadian governing Liberal Party suffers a severe setback in by-elections for the federal Parliament, losing 13 of 15 vacant seats.	Pakistani govt. bans all political parties whose ideology is not Islamic.... Australian Deputy P.M. Douglas Anthony says that the government will not allow Aborigines to block the country's development of uranium.
Oct. 17	Egyptian Pres. Anwar Sadat and Israeli Premier Menahem Begin share the Nobel Peace Prize. The citation specifically congratulates Sadat for his historic visit to Jerusalem in November 1977 and praises Pres. Carter's positive initiative.		Pres. Carter personally intervenes in Israeli–Egyptian peace talks in Wash., D.C. by holding separate discussions with the two delegations.... An emergency meeting of representatives of seven Arab nations works out a plan to withdraw Syrian troops from several key positions in Christian east Beirut.		Pakistani govt. imposes press censorship.
Oct. 18		New Swedish Premier Ola Ullsten names his Cabinet and gives a third of the posts to women, stating that equal status is a vital premise of his government's policy.		ILO reports that Argentina had the highest inflation rate in the world during the June 1977–78 period.	Pnompenh radio reports new fighting between invading Vietnamese forces and Cambodian soldiers in the Parrot's Beak area of Cambodia.
Oct. 19	Cambodian Deputy Premier Ieng Sary accuses the Soviet Union of playing a direct role in Vietnamese attacks on his country as part of a grand design to dominate Southeast Asia.		South African P.M. Pieter Botha unexpectedly announces that his government will accept the results of a U.N.-sponsored election on Namibia as the verdict of Namibians. But he insists that South African-sponsored elections occur before the U.N.-sponsored elections.	Argentina's military junta reportedly agrees to allow OAS delegates into the country to investigate charges of human-rights abuses.	
Oct. 20		King Baudouin swears in a new Belgian govt. in which Paul Vanden Boeynants replaces Leo Tindemans as premier.... France confirms a $700-million arms sale to China.	Concluding his U.S. tour, Rhodesian P.M. Ian Smith formally agrees to attend a conference on Rhodesia with the Patriotic Front.... Saudi Arabian troops of the Arab League force in Lebanon replace Syrian soldiers in key positions in Christian east Beirut. Christian militia leaders hail the Syrian withdrawal as a tactical victory.		
Oct. 21		First national congress of the Union of the Democratic Center meets in Madrid, Spain and reelects Premier Adolfo Suarez Gonzalez as its leader.	Joshua Nkomo, ZAPU leader, rejects the U.S. plan for a new all-party conference on Rhodesia, saying that he will hold talks only with Britain and only on the subject of an unconditional transfer of power of the Patriotic Front.	Forty-six former political prisoners and 33 relatives are flown from Havana, Cuba to Miami as part of Pres. Castro's program to send past and present political offenders to the U.S.	
Oct. 22	British For. Secy. David Owen says that it would not be in the best interest of the West for the Shah of Iran to be toppled, and concedes that although the Shah has a poor record on human rights, there is no human-rights reason to support the fanatical Moslem element that would deny all rights for women.	At least 10 Spanish police officers are reported having been shot to death in the Basque provinces since Sept. 25.... Greek opposition parties retain control of Athens and Piraeus in run-off local elections.... Anastas Mikoyan, 82, former Soviet Union president in the front rank of the Kremlin hierarchy for nearly 50 years, is reported dead from Moscow.	Syria reopens its frontier with Iraq.		

A	B	C	D	E
Includes developments that affect more than one world region, international organizations and important meetings of major world leaders.	Includes all domestic and regional developments in Europe, including the Soviet Union, Turkey, Cyprus and Malta.	Includes all domestic and regional developments in Africa and the Middle East, including Iraq and Iran and excluding Cyprus, Turkey and Afghanistan.	Includes all domestic and regional developments in Latin America, the Caribbean and Canada.	Includes all domestic and regional developments in Asia and Pacific nations, extending from Afghanistan through all the Pacific Islands, except Hawaii.

U.S. Politics & Social Issues	U.S. Foreign Policy & Defense	U.S. Economy & Environment	Science, Technology & Nature	Culture, Leisure & Life Style	
Wall Street Journal reports that the ninety-fifth Congress was not particularly liberal, despite Democratic majorities in both houses.	Senate Ethics Committee's final report on the South Korean influence-buying scandal (Koreagate) recommends that no disciplinary action be taken against any former of current senator.	Dow Jones posts its sharpest one-day decline in four years.... Herbert Simon of Carneige-Mellon University is awarded the Nobel Prize for Economics.		Karol Wojtyla, an archbishop of Krakow, Poland since 1963, is elected Pope of the Roman Catholic Church on the eighth ballot. He is the first non-Italian to be elected Pope in 456 years and the first Pole chosen. He takes the name John Paul II.	Oct. 16
Full citizenship rights are posthumously restored to Jefferson Davis, president of the Confederate States of America in the Civil War-era.		FRB reports that U.S. production increased a seasonally adjusted .5 percent in September.	Nobel Prize in Physics is shared by two American scientists, Arno Penzias and Robert W. Wilson, and Soviet scientist Pyotr Kapitsa.... Nobel Prize in Chemistry is awarded to Peter Mitchell of Britain for his contribution to the understanding of biological energy transfer through the formation of the Chemiosmotic Theory.	New York Yankees win their second straight World Series, defeating the Los Angeles Dodgers in the sixth game.	Oct. 17
Billie Sol Estes pleads guilty in U.S. District Ct., Ft. Worth, Tex. to one count of conspiracy to defraud the government through income-tax evasion schemes.		John deButts announces his retirement as chairman and chief executive officer of AT&T.... Commerce Dept. reports that U.S. personal income increased a seasonally adjusted $8.3 billion or .8 percent in September.	Spanish Ministry of Transportation reports that the pilot of the KLM Royal Dutch Airlines jet was at fault for its collision with a Pan American Airways jet on the runway at Tenerife, Canary Islands on March 27, 1977.	Ramon Mercader, 64, Spaniard who assassinated exiled Soviet revolutionary Leon Trotsky in Mexico in 1940, dies of cancer in Havana, Cuba.... Vatican officials announce that Pope John Paul II will inaugurate his reign on Oct. 22 by a celebration of mass in St. Peter's Square instead of a traditional papal coronation.	Oct. 18
		Bureau of Labor Statistics reports that the white-minority groups earnings gap is as wide as it was in 1973, the greatest minority strides being made between 1967–73.	A blood test to determine women carrying the gene causing muscular dystrophy is reported in the *New England Journal of Medicine*.	Gig Young, 60, actor who won 1969 Academy Award for his role in *They Shoot Horses, Don't They?*, dies by his own hand after apparently shooting and killing his bride of three weeks in N.Y.	Oct. 19
Pres. Carter signs a bill creating 152 new federal judgeships, the largest increase in history.... Pres. Carter signs a bill allowing deportation of all nationalized U.S. citizens who had participated in Nazi atrocities.	Pres. Carter nominates Lt. Gen. George Seignious to head the Arms Control and Disarmament Agency and Ralph Earle to be the U.S. chief negotiator at SALT sessions.	Pres. Carter refuses to place restrictions on copper imports into the U.S.... Firestone Tire & Rubber Co. announces reaching an agreement with the government to recall 10 million steel-belted radial tires. It will be the largest tire recall to date.			Oct. 20
		AFL–CIO views passage of the Humphrey–Hawkins full employment bill as more symbol than substance.			Oct. 21
		Leo Welch, 80, chairman of Standard Oil Co. of New Jersey (Exxon) (1960–63) and first chairman of Communications Satellite Corporation, dies in an automobile accident in Cuernavaca, Mexico.		Pope John Paul II celebrates mass in St. Peter's Square, Rome in a simple papal coronation ceremony in the tradition set by his predecessor, Pope John Paul I.... Bill Rodgers wins the ninth New York City Marathon in two hours, 12 minutes, 12 seconds. Grete Waitz is the first woman to finish in two hours, 32 minutes, 30 seconds.	Oct. 22

F	G	H	I	J
Includes elections, federal-state relations, civil rights and liberties, crime, the judiciary, education, health care, poverty, urban affairs and population.	Includes formation and debate of U.S. foreign and defense policies, veterans' affairs and defense spending. (Relations with specific foreign countries are usually found under the region concerned.)	Includes business, labor, agriculture, taxation, transportation, consumer affairs, monetary and fiscal policy, natural resources, and pollution.	Includes worldwide scientific, medical and technological developments, natural phenomena, U.S. weather, natural disasters, and accidents.	Includes the arts, religion, scholarship, communications media, sports, entertainments, fashions, fads and social life.

	World Affairs	Europe	Africa & the Middle East	The Americas	Asia & the Pacific
Oct. 23	U.S. State Secy. Vance and Soviet For. Min. Andrei Gromyko resume SALT talks in Moscow and report that both sides are close to an agreement although further discussions are necessary.	Workers at the Vauxhall Motors Ltd. plant in Great Britain reject calls by union negotiators to strike.	Zambian Pres. Kenneth Kaunda, main African supporter of the U.S.–British peace moves in Rhodesia, says that the U.S. erred in allowing Rhodesian P.M. Ian Smith to visit there.		The Japanese–Chinese treaty of peace and friendship, which was signed in August, is formally implemented at ceremonies attended by Japanese Premier Takeo Fukuda and Chinese Deputy Premier Teng Hsiao-ping in Tokyo. . . . Teng is quoted as saying, "Let things of the past be treated as the past," referring to the historic bitter relations between the two countries.
Oct. 24		West German economic institutes predict a real economic growth of about 4 percent in 1979 coupled with a rising inflation rate of 3.5 percent.			An upsurge in Vietnamese–Cambodian border skirmishes is reported by the Vietnam news agency. . . . Vietnam news agency charges that thousands of Chinese troops and police and some Chinese planes have crossed the frontier in 19 separate incidents between Oct. 13 and Oct. 17. . . . U.S. announces it will resume economic aid to Pakistan.
Oct. 25	Chinese Deputy Premier Teng Hsiao-ping assails the Soviet Union as interfering in other countries affairs and posing a grave threat to world peace. . . . The fifth year of mutual and balanced force reduction talks between Warsaw Pact and NATO ends without any sign of progress in reducing troop levels in central Europe.	A law professor Carlos Alberto Mota Pinto is named premier of Portugal. . . . Henri Bonnet, 90, French ambassador to the U.S. (1944–55), and a member of the League of Nations Secretariat (1920–31), dies in Paris.	Some of the 1,126 political prisoners released under an Iranian govt. amnesty to mark the Shah's fifty-ninth birthday charge that they had been tortured. . . . An Israeli announcement that it intends to expand existing settlements in the West Bank and Gaza Strip raises fears of a possible setback to the current Israeli–Egyptian peace talks in Washington. . . . Lebanese govt. issues detailed guidelines to restrict PLO guerrillas in the country.	Canada's 10-day postal strike ends when the federal government threatens to fire any workers who do not return to work as of midnight.	At a press conference, Deputy Premier Teng Hsiao-ping repeats China's three conditions for resumption of normal relations with the U.S.: abrogation of the U.S. treaty with Taiwan, withdrawal of U.S. troops from Taiwan, and severance of U.S. diplomatic ties with Taiwan.
Oct. 26	Moscow uses unusually strong terms to warn Western European countries against selling arms to China. . . . Soviets charge that Pres. Carter's approval of neutron warhead components' production could hamper SALT negotiations.				U.S. trade gap with Japan is reported narrowing to an adjusted $871 million. . . . Yasuhiro Nakasone, a leading official of Japan's ruling Liberal Democratic Party, is officially implicated in the Lockheed bribery scandal.
Oct. 27			Black students at the University of Rhodesia demonstrate to protest the transitional government's extension of compulsory military service to blacks.	Negotiations between Nicaraguan Pres. Anastasio Somoza and his civilian opponents are reported stalled over Somoza's insistence on staying in office until his term officially ends in 1981.	
Oct. 28		Washington Post reports that two-thirds of British residents polled support P.M. James Callaghan's 5 percent wage increase limitations.	London Times reports that the United African National Council (UANC) and a faction of the Zimbabwe African National Union (ZANU) have admitted they maintain private armies.		

A	B	C	D	E
Includes developments that affect more than one world region, international organizations and important meetings of major world leaders.	Includes all domestic and regional developments in Europe, including the Soviet Union, Turkey, Cyprus and Malta.	Includes all domestic and regional developments in Africa and the Middle East, including Iraq and Iran and excluding Cyprus, Turkey and Afghanistan.	Includes all domestic and regional developments in Latin America, the Caribbean and Canada.	Includes all domestic and regional developments in Asia and Pacific nations, extending from Afghanistan through all the Pacific Islands, except Hawaii.

U.S. Politics & Social Issues	U.S. Foreign Policy & Defense	U.S. Economy & Environment	Science, Technology & Nature	Culture, Leisure & Life Style	
	Paul Warnke, who announced his resignation as head of the U.S. Arms Control and Disarmament Agency on Oct. 10, is named special consultant to State Secy. Vance. He also resigns his post as chief SALT negotiator.		U.S. National Science Foundation announces an academic exchange with China.		Oct. 23
N.J. doctor Mario Jascalevich is acquitted of charges that he used injections of curare to kill three patients.... After the Jascalevich acquittal, contempt citations against *The New York Times* and reporter Myron Farber are suspended. Farber had refused to yield his source material on the alleged murders, which he had dubbed the "Dr. X" case, and the issue was tried in the N.J. Supreme Ct. as a free press-fair trial issue.		Pres. Carter reveals a new antiinflation plan designed to reduce the 1979 rate to 6–6.5 percent from its current level of more than 8 percent. He makes fiscal restraint a key feature of the plan along with voluntary wage–price guidelines. ... Republican Party chmn. Bill Brock calls Carter's plan "blatantly political" and "too little, too late."		Gaylord Perry of the San Diego Padres becomes the first pitcher to win the Cy Young Award in both the National and American Leagues. He had won the AL award in 1972.	Oct. 24
	Pres. Carter signs into law the Foreign Intelligence Surveillance Act, the first major U.S. legislation to curb national security wiretapping. ... Pres. Carter signs an authorization bill for the production of components of the controversial neutron warhead.	Many corporate and union leaders offer conditional support to Carter's antiinflation plan.... Pres. Carter names Alfred Kahn, currently CAB chairman, to head the administration's antiinflation drive, succeeding Robert Strauss.			Oct. 25
Pres. Carter signs a government-wide ethics bill into law that requires annual financial statements by 14,000 top officials.		UAW pres. Douglas Fraser expresses doubt that inflation can be controlled quickly as his 700,000-member union gives cautious endorsement to Carter's antiinflation plan.		Carlo Maria Giulini debuts as the Los Angeles Philharmonic's new music director.	Oct. 26
		Judge William Peterson in Cadillac, Mich. dismisses a suit by farmers seeking damages for PBB poisoning of their dairy herd.... Pres. Carter signs the Humphrey–Hawkins full employment bill.			Oct. 27
Congress Watch, Ralph Nader's consumer advocacy group, calls the ninety-fifth Congress the "corporate Congress," charging the influence of an increasingly powerful business lobby.... Congress Watch gives Sen. Howard Metzenbaum (D, Ohio) and Reps. Elizabeth Holtzman (D, N.Y.) and Robert Drinan (D, Mass.) highest scores for their pro-citizens'-interest votes.... Pres. Carter appears at Democratic political rallies in four Northeastern states.		Julius Shiskin, 66, Labor Dept. Bureau of Statistics commissioner since 1973, who supervised a major revision of the bureau's consumer and producer price indexes, dies of a kidney ailment in Washington.		Pavel Kohout, a Czech playwright who was a principal spokesman for the Charter 77 human-rights movement, leaves Czechoslavakia for one-year stay in Austria as a consultant to a Vienna theater.	Oct. 28

F	G	H	I	J
Includes elections, federal-state relations, civil rights and liberties, crime, the judiciary, education, health care, poverty, urban affairs and population.	Includes formation and debate of U.S. foreign and defense policies, veterans' affairs and defense spending. (Relations with specific foreign countries are usually found under the region concerned.)	Includes business, labor, agriculture, taxation, transportation, consumer affairs, monetary and fiscal policy, natural resources, and pollution.	Includes worldwide scientific, medical and technological developments, natural phenomena, U.S. weather, natural disasters, and accidents.	Includes the arts, religion, scholarship, communications media, sports, entertainments, fashions, fads and social life.

	World Affairs	Europe	Africa & the Middle East	The Americas	Asia & the Pacific
Oct. 29		Soviet For. Min. Andrei Gromyko says at the end of an official three-day visit to France that his talks with French Pres. Valery Giscard d'Estaing and For. Min. Louis de Guiringaud were designed to reinforce Moscow's special relationship with France.	Rhodesian P.M. Ian Smith virtually rules out turning the government over to the country's black majority by Dec. 31, the date set under the March internal settlement pact. . . . Thirty-four officials of Savak, Iran's secret police, are dismissed or forcibly retired in an attempt by the government to calm the country-wide unrest.		
Oct. 30	The U.S. dollar falls to new lows against the currencies of major U.S. trading partners and is worth 8.5 percent less than in February 1973, the date of its last formal devaluation.		IMF announces that Senegal has permission to purchase 21 million special drawing rights, equivalent to $25.8 million.		
Oct. 31	The dollar makes small gains against European currencies but declines to another post-war low in trading against the Japanese yen where one dollar is worth 176.08 yen.	Hungary reportedly relaxes travel restrictions on its refugees living in the West and on their relatives still in Hungary.	An estimated 40,000 Iranian oil workers strike in one of the most serious antigovernment actions yet to face the Shah. Premier Jaffar Sharif Emami calls the strike an act of treason.	Meeting with Canada's 10 provincial premiers to discuss his proposed changes in the Constitution, P.M. Pierre Trudeau agrees to consider giving certain federal powers to the provinces, a move seen as a breakthrough in the talks.	Japanese unemployment in September reportedly increased to 2.42 percent of the work force, the highest rate since February 1959.
Nov. 1	U.N. Secy. Gen. Kurt Waldheim accepts in principle an invitation from the Cambodian govt. to visit the country and make a personal assessment of the human-rights situation there. . . . The dollar sky-rockets in the international exchange market with the announcement of Pres. Carter's emergency intervention.	Queen Elizabeth II inaugurates a new session of Parliament describing the Labor Party's legislative program, which includes several proposals to gain the nationalist votes of Scotland, Wales, and the Northern Irish Ulster Unionists.	Soviet and PLO officials assail the Camp David agreement between Israel and Egypt after PLO leader Yasir Arafat visits Moscow. . . . Iranian govt. reports that 23 people have been killed and 56 injured in clashes with troops supporting the Shah.	Bolivian govt. says it has foiled a left-wing coup that had been planned for Oct. 29 and has arrested five followers of former Pres. Hernan Siles Zuazo, who claims he was cheated of victory in the July presidential election.	
Nov. 2		British Home Secy. Merlyn Rees announces an independent inquiry into the British prison system in wake of protests by both prisoners and guards.	Tanzanian Pres. Julius Nyerere vows to expel Ugandan invaders who have occupied over 700 square miles of Tanzanian territory. . . . Rhodesian planes bomb a guerrilla camp six miles from Lusaka, Zambia.	Dominica gains full independence, becoming the newest nation in the world and the smallest in the Americas. . . . Chile and Argentina end six months of negotiations without resolving the main issues in their territorial rights dispute over the Beagle Channel.	
Nov. 3				Trinidad & Tobago's natural gas reserves are reported at least 12-trillion cubic feet.	Soviet Union and Vietnam sign a 25-year treaty of friendship and cooperation, which includes reciprocal security provisions. . . . Aborigines and the Australian govt. sign an agreement opening the way to start work at the Ranger uranium mining site.
Nov. 4	Turkish Premier Bulent Ecevit warns the West that unless it responds favorably to Turkey's economic needs, Turkey will reexamine its political allegiance. . . . Soviet Union demands that the U.S. return former U.N. employes Valdik Enger and Rudolf Chernyayev, who have been convicted for spying in the U.S. and sentenced to 50-year prison terms.	Soviet Premier Alexei Kosygin announces that the 1978 grain harvest will be the largest in Soviet history, exceeding 230-million metric tons.		Cuba's Washington spokesman tells a press conference that Cuban exile leaders in the U.S. are invited to return to Havana and work out programs for the release of more political prisoners, reunification of separated families, and visits to Cuba by expatriates.	

A	B	C	D	E
Includes developments that affect more than one world region, international organizations and important meetings of major world leaders.	Includes all domestic and regional developments in Europe, including the Soviet Union, Turkey, Cyprus and Malta.	Includes all domestic and regional developments in Africa and the Middle East, including Iraq and Iran and excluding Cyprus, Turkey and Afghanistan.	Includes all domestic and regional developments in Latin America, the Caribbean and Canada.	Includes all domestic and regional developments in Asia and Pacific nations, extending from Afghanistan through all the Pacific Islands, except Hawaii.

U.S. Politics & Social Issues	U.S. Foreign Policy & Defense	U.S. Economy & Environment	Science, Technology & Nature	Culture, Leisure & Life Style	
					Oct. 29
				Eben Alexander, 79, managing editor of *Time* magazine from 1949–60, dies of pneumonia in Roslyn, N.Y.	Oct. 30
		Dow Jones industrial average falls below the 800 mark.			Oct. 31
Rep. Joshua Eilberg (D, Pa.) pleads innocent to federal conflict-of-interest charges that he accepted payment for helping a Phila., Pa. hospital obtain a $14.5-million federal grant.	Eight women ensigns report for duty aboard noncombat Navy ships, the first women in history to serve on ships other than hospital or transport ships. . . . House International Relations subcommittee chmn. Donald Fraser (D, Minn.) says that a massive, often illegal, and ultimately useless campaign by South Korea to win U.S. support of the Seoul govt. led to the Koreagate scandal.	Pres. Carter announces a series of sweeping emergency actions to halt a steep plunge in the value of the U.S. dollar. The measures include a pledge of massive intervention in currency markets, a quintupling of gold sales, and a sharp increase in the FRB's discount rate.		Bobby Hull announces that he is retiring from professional ice hockey at the age of 39 in his twenty-second pro season and his seventh with the Winnipeg Jets. . . . Ron Guidry of the New York Yankees is the overwhelming choice for the AL Cy Young Award. . . . In an interview with *The New York Times*, singer Anita Bryant describes adverse effects on her health, family, and career since she began an antihomosexual campaign in Florida in 1977.	Nov. 1
Pres. Carter signs the Middle Income Student Assistance Act that will give some 2 million students access to federal college grants and loans.		SEC files suit against ITT, charging that it made illegal, improper, corrupt, and questionable payments in at least nine countries to get business and to improperly influence their governments. It names Algeria, China, Indonesia, Iran, Italy, Mexico, Nigeria, the Philippines, and Turkey. . . . Lee Iacocca, recently fired as Ford Motor Co. president, is named president and chief operating officer of Chrysler Corp., the third largest U.S. automaker.	Soviet cosmonauts Vladimir Kovalyonok and Alexander Ivanchenkov land safely in Kazakhstan after having set a new endurance record of 139 days and 15 hours in space.	Theatrical producer Max Gordon, 86, known for his Broadway productions *My Sister Eileen* and *Born Yesterday*, dies of a heart attack in N.Y.	Nov. 2
Former Black Panther leader Huey Newton is sentenced in Oakland Calif., to two years in prison on a gun possession charge. . . . Pres. Carter appears at a political rally in Sacramento, Calif. with Calif. Gov. Edmund Brown Jr.				Major league baseball holds its third annual reentry draft of free agents in N.Y.C. where 43 players who had played out their contracts are selected by 26 teams. Interest centers on third baseman Pete Rose, who decides to leave the Cincinnati Reds after 16 seasons with the club.	Nov. 3
Pres. Carter signs the Presidential Records Act into law. . . . Former CIA agent and convicted Watergate conspirator E. Howard Hunt Jr. denies he was in Dallas the day Pres. John Kennedy was assassinated or that he was in any way involved in Kennedy's death.			A test to determine sickle cell anemia in unborn children is reported developed by Dr. Yuet Wai Kan.	National Council of Churches unanimously elects Rev. M. William Howard Jr. as its president. At age 32, he is the youngest person to head the council.	Nov. 4

F	G	H	I	J
Includes elections, federal-state relations, civil rights and liberties, crime, the judiciary, education, health care, poverty, urban affairs and population.	*Includes formation and debate of U.S. foreign and defense policies, veterans' affairs and defense spending. (Relations with specific foreign countries are usually found under the region concerned.)*	*Includes business, labor, agriculture, taxation, transportation, consumer affairs, monetary and fiscal policy, natural resources, and pollution.*	*Includes worldwide scientific, medical and technological developments, natural phenomena, U.S. weather, natural disasters, and accidents.*	*Includes the arts, religion, scholarship, communications media, sports, entertainments, fashions, fads and social life.*

	World Affairs	Europe	Africa & the Middle East	The Americas	Asia & the Pacific
Nov. 5	U.S. urges the U.N. Security Council to take preventive action against a threatened acceleration in fighting between Cambodia and Vietnam.		Iranian troops take over all Teheran's major newspapers and national radio and TV networks.... Iranian Premier Gholam Riza Azhari announces that a specially appointed commission will investigate the finances of the Shah's family, many of whom have left the country.... Arab League concludes a four-day summit meeting in Baghdad, Iraq by issuing a communique asking Egypt not to sign a peace pact with Israel.	In wake of violence in his country, Nicaraguan Pres. Anastasio Somoza tells members of his Liberal Party that if he resigns he would violate the Constitution.... Nicaraguan National Guard is reported having killed at least 14 men and boys in Nicaraguan cities in the past three days, with many of the shootings random and allegedly in cold blood.	Australian voters reject, by 50.5 percent, a plan to open the country's first nuclear power plant. ... In a political comeback, former P.M. Indira Gandhi wins a seat in the lower house of the Indian Parliament.... Chinese Deputy Premier Teng Hsiao-ping begins visits to Thailand, Malaysia, Singapore, and Burma in a major diplomatic overture to these four anti-Communist Southeast Asian countries.
Nov. 6	U.N. High Commissioner for Refugees pledges $430,000 to help thousands of Nicaraguan refugees in Honduran border camps.		Shah of Iran imposes martial rule to try to end violent antigovernment demonstrations that have been sweeping the country since January. He also launches an extensive anticorruption campaign.... Islamic opposition leader the Ayatollah Ruholla Khomeini warns that until an Islamic republic is installed in Iran, he will oppose any government, whether military or civilian-led.		Energy Secy. James Schlesinger discloses that the U.S. has offered to help China develop coal mines, design an atom smasher, and construct a huge dam on the Yangtze River.... A Chinese CP delegation visiting Pnompenh reiterates China's support for Cambodia in its border war with Vietnam.
Nov. 7		Willem Aantjes, leader of the Christian Democrats in the lower house of the Dutch Parliament, resigns following the disclosure the day before that he had belonged to the Nazi SS organization.	Ghana Supreme Military Council head Gen. Fred Akuffo declares a state of emergency and outlaws all strikes in wake of strikes by civil servants and oil refinery and electricity workers, which cripple the country.	Nicaraguan Sandinista guerrillas assassinate Sen. Ramiro Granera, a close adviser to Pres. Anastasio Somoza.	U.S. and South Korea establish a Combined Forces Command.
Nov. 8	*The New York Times* reports that U.S. banks no longer dominate the ranks of the non-Communist world's 10 largest banks because the value of their assets has fallen with the dollar.... Chinese Deputy Premier Teng Hsiao-ping assails the Soviet-Vietnamese friendship treaty and calls Vietnam the "Cuba of the Orient."		Former Iranian Premier Amir Abbas Hoveida is one of more than 15 government officials arrested by the Iranian govt.... Israel's two negotiators — Defense Min. Ezer Weizman and For. Min. Moshe Dayan — assert their government's continued opposition to linking the proposed Camp David Peace accord to an overall settlement of the Palestinian problem in the West Bank and Gaza Strip.	Venezuela reportedly is ready to halt oil shipments to Nicaragua.	
Nov. 9	OPEC Secy. Gen. Ali Mohammed Jaidah calls for help from oil-consuming nations to develop oil-refining industries.... Carter administration discloses that the U.S. has withdrawn its objections to Western European arms sales to China.	Bank of England raises its minimum lending rate to 12.5 percent from 10 percent.... P.M. James Callaghan's Labor Party wins a confidence vote on its legislative program presented in Queen Elizabeth's speech to Parliament on Nov. 1.	Meeting with U.S. State Secy. Vance, Egyptian negotiators say that Pres. Sadat wants to change some text of the Camp David accord, preferring stronger language on the linkage problem.		Australian Cabinet centralizes responsibility for the management of nuclear wastes following the embarrassing disclosure that a pound of plutonium had been buried in recoverable form at the atomic waste site at Maralinga in South Australia.
Nov. 10	U.N. High Commissioner for Refugees Paul Hartling announces a mid-December meeting on the growing problem of Southeast Asian refugees, focusing on the plight of the so-called boat people.	Tens of thousands of Spanish citizens, led by Socialist, Communist and other political party officials, march through Madrid streets to protest Basque political terrorism.	Tanzania formally recognizes the Saharan Arab Democratic Republic, the state that the Polisario guerrilla faction intends to establish in the Western Sahara.		
Nov. 11		West German Pres. Walter Scheel admits that he may have applied for membership in the Nazi Party during WWII.... Poles gather at the Tomb of the Unknown Soldier in Warsaw in an unauthorized rally to celebrate the sixtieth anniversary of Poland's independence.	PLO proposes a formal end to its dispute with Lebanese Christians on condition that they stop cooperating with Israel.... Angolan Pres. Agostinho Neto charges that South Africa is waging an undeclared war against his government.		
	A	**B**	**C**	**D**	**E**
	Includes developments that affect more than one world region, international organizations and important meetings of major world leaders.	Includes all domestic and regional developments in Europe, including the Soviet Union, Turkey, Cyprus and Malta.	Includes all domestic and regional developments in Africa and the Middle East, including Iraq and Iran and excluding Cyprus, Turkey and Afghanistan.	Includes all domestic and regional developments in Latin America, the Caribbean and Canada.	Includes all domestic and regional developments in Asia and Pacific nations, extending from Afghanistan through all the Pacific Islands, except Hawaii.

U.S. Politics & Social Issues	U.S. Foreign Policy & Defense	U.S. Economy & Environment	Science, Technology & Nature	Culture, Leisure & Life Style	
			The first increase in worldwide radioactive fallout in four years is reported occuring in 1977, triggered by a large Chinese nuclear atmospheric test in 1976.		Nov. 5
In an interview with James Reston of *The New York Times*, Pres. Carter says that at midterm of his presidency he feels more at ease and more aware of the office's powers and limitations.	U.S. expresses strong support for the Shah of Iran's imposition of martial rule.	*The New York Times* and *New York Daily News* resume publishing after an 88-day shutdown by striking unions.... Pres. Carter signs the $18.7-billion tax-cut bill.	AMA reports evidence that, syphilis and gonorrhea are increasing among homosexual males at a faster rate than among heterosexuals.	*War and Remembrance* by Herman Wouk is the best-selling fiction book for the past week and *A Distant Mirror: The Calamitous Fourteenth Century* by Barbara Tuchman is the best-selling general book.... Marilyn French's *The Women's Room* is the best-selling paperback book for the past week.	Nov. 6
The Republican Party scores solid but modest gains in midterm elections, but the Democrats retain heavy majorities in Congress and the statehouses.		The federal govt.'s campaign to deregulate the trucking industry begins with ICC Chmn. A. Daniel O'Neal presenting several proposals to his fellow commissioners, including allowing small truckers to expand their services and making it easier for railroads to acquire trucking companies.	WHO is reported continuing its final countdown on smallpox eradication from the date of the last confirmed case in Africa, which was Oct. 26, 1977.	Gene Tunney, 80, world heavyweight boxing champion (1926–28), dies in Greenwich, Conn.	Nov. 7
N.Y.C. Council rejects, 6–3, a bill aimed at outlawing discrimination against homosexuals in housing, employment, and public accomodations.	A wide range of U.S. Christian churches ask Pres. Carter to increase pressure for Nicaraguan Pres. Anastasio Somoza's resignation.	Consumer Federation of America says that U.S. consumers have been routinely betrayed by a congressional majority more concerned with wealthy campaign contributors, and charges a marked decline in the current Congress's support of consumer issues from the previous Congress.		Bobby Orr, 30, the NHL's rookie of the year in 1966–67 and the only defenseman ever to lead the NHL in scoring (1967–70 and 1974–75) announces his retirement after a career marked by an injured left knee.... Norman Rockwell, 84, illustrator and artist best known for his 317 *Saturday Evening Post* covers between 1916–1963, dies in Stockbridge, Mass.... Billy Joel's *52nd Street* is the best-selling album for the past week.	Nov. 8
House Assassinations Committee resumes its hearings on the 1968 murder of civil-rights leader Dr. Martin Luther King Jr.... AFL-CIO pres. George Meany says that the 1978 election results presage Pres. Carter losing reelection in 1980, and calls Carter "the most conservative President I have seen in my lifetime."	Pres. Carter calls on Israel and Egypt to settle their feud over linking an overall settlement of the Palestinian issue to the Camp David peace accord.	Pres. Carter signs the controversial National Energy Act of 1978, which contains a bitterly debated natural gas provision.... James Flug, head of a public affairs group called Energy Action, claims that decontrolling natural-gas prices is the functional equivalent of surrender in the moral equivalent of war.... Pres. Carter reaffirms his determination to achieve a stringent federal budget for fiscal 1980.			Nov. 9
Atlantic City, N.J. public safety comr. Edwin Roth says that street crime has risen 25 percent during the first two months of casino gambling there.		Pres. Carter signs a bill authorizing $1.2 billion for over 100 parks and preservation projects.	Ala. Health Dept. declares a rabies epidemic in a nine-county area of the southeastern section of the state.... U.S. military personnel and their dependents are reported to be the major source of measles in the U.S.	World Boxing Council heavyweight champion Larry Holmes retains his title by knocking out challenger Alfredo Evangelista in the seventh round of a fight held at Caesars Palace in Las Vegas, Nev.	Nov. 10
Former Memphis, Tenn. police and fire dir. Frank Holloman denounces theories linking the Memphis police and FBI to Martin Luther King's assassination.	Former Pres. Richard Nixon is the principal speaker at Veterans Day ceremony in Biloxi, Miss., where he tells a crowd of 8,000 that the U.S. should continue to support the current Iranian govt.				Nov. 11

F	G	H	I	J
Includes elections, federal-state relations, civil rights and liberties, crime, the judiciary, education, health care, poverty, urban affairs and population.	*Includes formation and debate of U.S. foreign and defense policies, veterans' affairs and defense spending. (Relations with specific foreign countries are usually found under the region concerned.)*	*Includes business, labor, agriculture, taxation, transportation, consumer affairs, monetary and fiscal policy, natural resources, and pollution.*	*Includes worldwide scientific, medical and technological developments, natural phenomena, U.S. weather, natural disasters, and accidents.*	*Includes the arts, religion, scholarship, communications media, sports, entertainments, fashions, fads and social life.*

	World Affairs	Europe	Africa & the Middle East	The Americas	Asia & the Pacific
Nov. 12			Employes of Iran Air return to their jobs after a strike that crippled domestic air service for two weeks. Teachers, however, stage a nation-wide strike to voice their dissatisfaction with the government.		
Nov. 13	U.N. Security Council passes a resolution warning South Africa to cancel its planned elections in Namibia or face U.N. economic sanctions.		Under pressure from the military govt., most Iranian oil workers return to their jobs, easing the crisis there.	*The New York Times* reports that a shipment of 3,249 Soviet-built Lada automobiles were quickly sold out in Canada the first time the cars were offered for sale in North America. . . . Mexican govt. announces finding a huge new oil basin with potential reserves of 100 million barrels.	
Nov. 14	GATT reports that industrial nations' oil consumption has been stable in the period from the 1973 oil crisis to the end of 1977. Developing nations' consumption expanded strongly by 7 percent annually in the same period.	A new rash of bombings coincides with the arrival in Northern Ireland of two U.S. representatives from N.Y.S. — Mario Biaggi (D) and Benjamin Gilman (R) — who are attempting to arrange a peace forum in Washington in 1979. . . . British Trades Union Congress (TUC) splits, 14–14, on endorsing a statement on pay, costs, and prices that was the product of more than a month's talks between its negotiators and the government.	South African P.M. Pieter Botha makes significant changes in his Cabinet that indicate his government favors a more liberal policy on race than the previous government. . . . Oil production in Iran rises to 3.3 million barrels for the day compared to a low of 1.1 million barrels during the workers' strike. . . . Beirut sees its worst violence since the Lebanese truce became effective on Oct. 7.		State Dept. estimates that more than 20,000 Vietnamese, about 75 percent ethnic Chinese, have fled Vietnam in the past six weeks and estimates that up to 90,000 boat people may leave Vietnam in 1978.
Nov. 15			North Yemen executes 12 people for participating in an Oct. 15 attempt to overthrow Pres. Ali Abdullah Saleh. . . . A Tanzanian battalion reportedly crossed the Kagera River and is harassing Ugandan troops.	The ruling ARENA party retains its control of both houses in the Brazilian Congress with somewhat diminished majorities. . . . Bolivian Pres. Juan Pereda Asbun initiates a program to reduce smuggling, which accounts for about $60-million worth of trade per year, much of it involving cocaine.	
Nov. 16	A delegation of U.S. senators headed by Abraham Ribicoff (D, Conn.) and Henry Bellmon (R, Okla.) engage in a bitter exchange with Premier Alexei Kosygin over the state of the SALT treaty and U.S.–Soviet relations while visiting the Soviet Union at the invitation of the Supreme Soviet.	London *Financial Times* reports that the Dutch coalition Cabinet has reached agreement on a bill to liberalize the country's abortion law.	Rhodesia's biracial transitional govt. postpones universal suffrage elections to transfer power to Rhodesia's black majority from Dec. 3 to April 1979.	Finance Min. Jean Chretien presents to the Canadian Parliament a revised 1978–79 budget, which includes spending cuts to reduce inflation.	Chinese CP newspaper *Jenmin Jih Pao* says that all CP officials who have been mistakenly purged before, during, and after the Cultural Revolution will be fully rehabilitated by the middle of 1979.
Nov. 17		Danish Parliament approves a bill granting home rule in Greenland.		On the first stop of a Latin American tour, Spanish King Juan Carlos I receives an extremely warm welcome in Mexico. . . . In what is considered its harshest report to date, the OAS Commission on Human Rights excoriates Nicaraguan Pres. Anastasio Somoza's govt. as violating human rights "in a grave, persistent, and generalized manner."	

A	B	C	D	E
Includes developments that affect more than one world region, international organizations and important meetings of major world leaders.	*Includes all domestic and regional developments in Europe, including the Soviet Union, Turkey, Cyprus and Malta.*	*Includes all domestic and regional developments in Africa and the Middle East, including Iraq and Iran and excluding Cyprus, Turkey and Afghanistan.*	*Includes all domestic and regional developments in Latin America, the Caribbean and Canada.*	*Includes all domestic and regional developments in Asia and Pacific nations, extending from Afghanistan through all the Pacific Islands, except Hawaii.*

U.S. Politics & Social Issues	U.S. Foreign Policy & Defense	U.S. Economy & Environment	Science, Technology & Nature	Culture, Leisure & Life Style	
	U.S. denies reports that Pres. Carter had offered Egyptian Pres. Sadat secret guarantees on the future of the West Bank, Gaza Strip, and East Jerusalem.			Howard Swanson, 71, composer whose works were played by major U.S. symphony orchestras and sung by major concert artists, dies in N.Y.	Nov. 12
One of convicted assassin James Earl Ray's former lawyers, Percy Foreman, tells the House panel investigating Martin Luther King's assassination, that Ray assassinated King in the hope of becoming "a hero to the white race." . . . Irwin Borowski is named to replace Vincent Alto, who voluntarily left his post as special counsel for the GSA after leading a six-month internal investigation of corruption in the agency.		Justice Dept. files a civil antitrust suit against United Technologies Corp. to prevent its planned acquisition of Carrier Corp. . . . Supreme Ct. declines to review dismissal of an antitrust suit against AT&T. . . . First National Bank of Chicago initiates a move to an 11 percent prime rate.	Labor Dept. announces its health standard to limit worker exposure to lead poisoning.		Nov. 13
FBI is reported by the *Chicago Tribune* to have placed the late Sen. Paul H. Douglas (D, Ill.) on a list of those whose arrest might be considered necessary in wartime.		Australian govt. proposes round-trip air service between Sydney and San Francisco, Calif. for $518, less than half the existing minimum fare.			Nov. 14
Congress Watch, a Ralph Nader lobbying organization, reports that candidates who outspent their opponents won 85 percent of the Nov. 7 Senate elections. Sen. Jesse Helms (R, N.C.) was the biggest spender.		Energy Secy. James Schlesinger reveals new regulations under the National Energy Act of 1978 that would require most electric utilities and industrial companies to use coal or nuclear power as a primary energy source for new installations instead of oil or natural gas. . . . Alfred Kahn, director of Pres. Carter's wage–price plan, warns that the U.S. faces a deep, deep depression if inflation continues to get worse.	About 500 scientists from 30 nations meet at the federal Center for Disease Control in Atlanta, Ga. for a symposium on legionnaires disease. They emphasize the role of air-conditioning equipment in its transmission. . . . Margaret Mead, 76, anthropologist known for her work among primitive peoples, dies of cancer in N.Y. . . . At least 183 Indonesian Moslems, returning from a pilgrimage to Mecca in Saudi Arabia, are killed when a chartered DC-8 jetliner crashes just short of the airport in Colombo, Sri Lanka.	Rep. Leo Ryan (D, Calif.) and a contingent arrive in Georgetown, Guyana to investigate reports that relatives of his constituents are being held against their will by members of the Peoples Temple — a California-based religious cult — at their commune in Jonestown, Guyana.	Nov. 15
		Chessie System Inc. and Seaboard Coast Line Industries announce a merger plan that would create the nation's largest rail system.			Nov. 16
House Assassinations Committee chief counsel G. Robert Blakey says the committee found no evidence directly linking the FBI to King's murder.				About 20 of the members of Rev. Jim Jones's Peoples Temple commune in Guyana reportedly tell Rep. Leo Ryan (D, Calif.) that they want to return to the U.S. from Jonestown and are granted permission to leave.	Nov. 17

F	G	H	I	J
Includes elections, federal-state relations, civil rights and liberties, crime, the judiciary, education, health care, poverty, urban affairs and population.	*Includes formation and debate of U.S. foreign and defense policies, veterans' affairs and defense spending. (Relations with specific foreign countries are usually found under the region concerned.)*	*Includes business, labor, agriculture, taxation, transportation, consumer affairs, monetary and fiscal policy, natural resources, and pollution.*	*Includes worldwide scientific, medical and technological developments, natural phenomena, U.S. weather, natural disasters, and accidents.*	*Includes the arts, religion, scholarship, communications media, sports, entertainments, fashions, fads and social life.*

	World Affairs	Europe	Africa & the Middle East	The Americas	Asia & the Pacific
Nov. 18			Empress Farah, wife of the Shah of Iran, visits Iraq, the first such visit by a member of the Iranian royal family.		Pakistani judge orders that Nusrat Bhutto, wife of imprisoned former P.M. Zulfikar Ali Bhutto, be released from house detention.
Nov. 19	Soviet Pres. Lenoid Brezhnev publishes a statement in *Pravda* warning the U.S. not to intervene in Iran.	Spanish protests reach a fever pitch as about 100,000 rightists rally in Madrid to mark the third anniversary of dictator Generalissimo Francisco Franco's death.	Iranian govt. frees 210 political prisoners in another move to appease the opposition.		A Peking wall poster accuses the late CP Chmn. Mao Tse-Tung of supporting the disgraced Gang of Four. It is the first time he has been publicly linked with the group, which included his widow, Chiang Ching.
Nov. 20	UNESCO unanimously approves a compromise declaration on world-wide free press.		Ethiopia signs a 20-year friendship and cooperation pact, pledging military consultation, with the U.S.S.R.	The Guyanan govt. stresses that no Guyanese were involved in the Jonestown commune murders and mass suicide and that Rev. Jim Jones, leader of the Peoples Temple cult, had presented excellent references from important U.S. officials, including First Lady Rosalynn Carter and V.P. Walter Mondale.	
Nov. 21	U.N. Economic Commission for Europe reports that a growing trade deficit with industrialized nations has forced the Soviet block to increase its borrowing from Western banks, and it estimates the Soviet bloc's total debt at $41–47 billion as of March 1978.	French Pres. Valery Giscard d'Estaing says that the powers of the European Parliament, which will be chosen in direct elections in June 1979, cannot be expanded by the Parliament itself.	Israeli Cabinet, 15–2, approves a U.S.-sponsored draft of an Israeli–Egyptian peace treaty that links the accord to self-determination for Palestinians in the West Bank and Gaza Strip, but turns down Egypt's demand for a timetable for Palestinian autonomy.	U.S. begins sending military assistance teams to Guyana in wake of the mass murder-suicide of U.S. cult members there.	
Nov. 22		Workers at Ford Motor Co.'s British subsidiary overwhelmingly approve a contract offering 16.85 percent wage increases, signaling an end to a two-month strike.		Cuban Pres. Castro says he will gradually free the nearly 3,600 remaining political prisoners in Cuba if the U.S. will admit them as immigrants.	Two hundred Vietnamese refugees die when their fishing boat tips over after it was towed away from the Malaysian shore by police at Kuala Trengganu.
Nov. 23	Great Britain announces that a new representative, Cledwyn Hughes, will go to Africa to launch another diplomatic drive to organize a peace conference on Rhodesia.	The seven Warsaw Pact nations end a two-day biennial summit meeting with a communique calling for a swift end to SALT negotiations and steps to reduce standing armies in Europe.			A large field of rubies is reported discovered in central Australia.
Nov. 24		A French court sentences four convicted U.S. Black Panthers for the 1972 hijacking of a Delta Airlines DC-8 jet from Miami to Algiers.	Zambia Pres. Kenneth Kaunda is skeptical that a new conference will achieve any results in Rhodesia. Nigerian Head of State Lt. Gen. Olusegun Obasanjo says British and U.S. efforts in Rhodesia are dead.	Canadian P.M. Trudeau forms a new Cabinet-level committee to deal with economic problems.... Gen. Juan Pereda Asbun is toppled in a bloodless coup led by Bolivian army commander Gen. David Padilla Arancibia, ending his four-month presidency.	
Nov. 25	*The New York Times* quotes State Secy. Cyrus Vance saying that he foresees improved relations with the Soviet Union.				New Zealand general elections maintain P.M. Robert Muldoon's National Party in power with a sharply reduced parliamentary majority.

A	B	C	D	E
Includes developments that affect more than one world region, international organizations and important meetings of major world leaders.	Includes all domestic and regional developments in Europe, including the Soviet Union, Turkey, Cyprus and Malta.	Includes all domestic and regional developments in Africa and the Middle East, including Iraq and Iran and excluding Cyprus, Turkey and Afghanistan.	Includes all domestic and regional developments in Latin America, the Caribbean and Canada.	Includes all domestic and regional developments in Asia and Pacific nations, extending from Afghanistan through all the Pacific Islands, except Hawaii.

U.S. Politics & Social Issues	U.S. Foreign Policy & Defense	U.S. Economy & Environment	Science, Technology & Nature	Culture, Leisure & Life Style	
	William Kampiles, a former CIA employe, is convicted in Hammond, Ind., of selling spy satellite secrets to the Soviets.... OMB Dir. James McIntyre reportedly opposes Pres. Carter's tentative decision to increase the fiscal 1980 military budget to nearly $124 billion.		A CDC spokesman says that the scientific name given legionnaires disease is Legionella pneumophilia.	U.S. Rep. Leo Ryan (D, Calif.) and four other Americans are shot to death in Guyana by members of the Peoples Temple, a California-based religious cult. Shortly afterward hundreds of American cult members either under duress or voluntarily commit suicide.	Nov. 18
Ladies Home Journal magazine article claims that the late Sen. Joseph McCarthy (R, Wis.), a major anti-Communist crusader in the early 1950s, was a morphine addict whose drugs were supplied by the federal Bureau of Narcotics and Dangerous Drugs.				Rev. Jim Jones is found with a bullet in his head along with bodies of hundreds of cult members who had been shot or had committed suicide by drinking cyanide-laced Kool-Aid.	Nov. 19
Rep. Charles Diggs (D, Mich.) is sentenced to a maximum three years in prison for his role in a payroll kickback scheme. His conviction does not preclude his membership in Congress to which he was overwhelmingly reelected on Nov. 7.		Council on Wage and Price Stability approves an increase in the price of a Hershey chocolate bar to 25 cents from 20 cents.	A U.S. State Dept.-commissioned study finds that Americans working in the U.S. Embassy in Moscow between 1953 and 1976 suffered no ill effects from Soviet microwave bombardment.	Giorgio De Chirico, 90, widely copied Italian painter who created the modern school of metaphysical art, dies of a heart attack in Rome, Italy.... Atlanta Braves Bob Horner is named NL rookie of the year.... Rookie running back Earl Campbell of the Houston Oilers pro football team runs for 199 yards and four touchdowns in a spectacular 35–30 win for his team over the Miami Dolphins.	Nov. 20
	Joint Chiefs of Staff Chmn. Gen. David C. Jones reports that the JCS recommends that draft registration be revived.	Wall Street Journal reports that labor leaders are outraged with Pres. Carter's wage–price plan to curb inflation and are threatening defiance, while businessmen are confused but pledging cooperation.		Guyanese authorities report that 409 Peoples Temple cult members were found dead either from bullets or by drinking cyanide-laced Kool-Aid. . . . Detroit Tiger Lou Whitaker is named AL rookie of the year.	Nov. 21
National Advisory Committee for Women cancels a scheduled meeting with Pres. Carter, protesting that the 15 minutes allotted for the meeting is insufficient for substantive discussion.				Same Time, Next Year, a film adaptation by Bernard Slade of his Broadway hit play about two lovers who meet once a year over a period of years, opens in N.Y.C. It stars Alan Alda and Ellen Burstyn.	Nov. 22
				NHL Colorado Rockies dismiss coach Pat Kelly and name Aldo (Bep) Guidolin to replace him.	Nov. 23
Carolyn Payton resigns as Peace Corps director in wake of a conflict with Sam Brown, head of Action, which has jurisdiction over the Peace Corps.		N.Y.'s Citibank adopts an 11.5 percent prime rate.	A hurricane hits Sri Lanka, killing an estimated 150 people with many more suspected dead.	Guyanese authorities now report that about 780 members of the Peoples Temple have been found dead.... U.S. soldiers removing corpses from the Peoples Temple mass murder-suicide site in Jonestown, Guyana become aware of the inaccuracy of the Guyanese corpse count after they remove the first 270 corpses and discover layer upon layer of bodies.	Nov. 24
	Displeased with the failure of U.S. intelligence to warn of the recent upheaval in Iran, Pres. Carter orders an improvement in the quality of U.S. political intelligence, according to Los Angeles Times reports.		Nuclear Regulatory Commission releases results of an informal safety rating of 51 nuclear power plants made in 1975, which places 10 of the plants in a "below average" category.	The New York Times says that the inadequacy of the first body count in Jonestown raises new questions about the way the Guyanese govt. handled the entire Jonestown episode.	Nov. 25

F	G	H	I	J
Includes elections, federal-state relations, civil rights and liberties, crime, the judiciary, education, health care, poverty, urban affairs and population.	Includes formation and debate of U.S. foreign and defense policies, veterans' affairs and defense spending. (Relations with specific foreign countries are usually found under the region concerned.)	Includes business, labor, agriculture, taxation, transportation, consumer affairs, monetary and fiscal policy, natural resources, and pollution.	Includes worldwide scientific, medical and technological developments, natural phenomena, U.S. weather, natural disasters, and accidents.	Includes the arts, religion, scholarship, communications media, sports, entertainments, fashions, fads and social life.

	World Affairs	Europe	Africa & the Middle East	The Americas	Asia & the Pacific
Nov. 26		Roland Faure, editor-in-chief of the French newspaper *L'Aurore* , resigns in a dispute with his publisher, Pierre Janrot. . . . Two teenage gunmen kill the deputy warden of Maze prison in Northern Ireland.		Throngs of Argentines warmly welcome Spanish King Juan Carlos I, but the country's military leaders give him a cool reception, attributed to differences between the King and the junta over human rights.	
Nov. 27	U.N. General Assembly's Political Committee approves a resolution seeking a Security Council mandatory arms embargo against Israel because of its weapons build-up and alleged military collaboration with South Africa.	Soviet Pres. Brezhnev tells the CP Central Committee that the country harvested a record 235-million tons of grain this year. . . . Soviet CP Central Committee elects Konstantin Chernenko to the Politburo.			Japanese Premier Takeo Fukuda unexpectedly loses the first round of an election for the presidency of the ruling Liberal Democratic Party to Masayoshi Ohira. . . . In an interview with U.S. correspondent Robert Novak Chinese Deputy Premier Teng Hsiaoping dismisses speculation that the current poster campaign indicates that he is at odds with Chmn. Hua Kuo-feng.
Nov. 28	Soviet CP newspaper *Pravda* says that the members of the Peoples Temple in Guyana were American dissidents whose tragic deaths cast a shadow on the prestige of the U.S. and the American way of life.	West German steelworkers begin their first strike in 50 years, seeking a 5 percent wage increase and a workweek reduction to 35 hours from 40. . . . U.S. officials confirm proposing a 12-point plan to revive talks to settle the Cyprus dispute. . . . British govt. argues that because the 16.85 percent settlement in the Ford workers' new contract is triple the 5 percent pay-restraint guideline to curb inflation, it must impose sanctions on the auto company.	Counterattacking Tanzanian troops penetrate 20 miles into Ugandan territory. . . . Ethiopian troops recapture the Eritrean city of Keren, the last city held by the secessionist rebels. . . . Iranian govt. imposes a curfew and ban on marches.	Quebec loses another court decision on Bill 101 to make French the official language of the province when the Quebec Ct. of Appeals upholds a Superior Ct. opinion that found parts of the bill unconstitutional.	A rally in Peking is attended by about 10,000 Chinese who cheer speakers demanding democracy and human rights. . . . Carter administration praises China for acknowledgment of past human-rights violations.
Nov. 29	UNESCO approves a Jordanian resolution to continue to deny Israel technical assistance funds because of its archaeological digs in Jerusalem that are said to have damaged Islamic monuments.			Four alleged members of the El Salvadoran guerrilla group, Popular Liberation Forces (FPL), including a Roman Catholic priest named Ernesto Barrera, are killed by police in San Salvador in what the police describe as a shootout stemming from a police raid on the FPL hideout.	
Nov. 30		Benjamin Levich, the highest-ranking Soviet scientist to seek emigration, leaves the U.S.S.R. with his wife to join their sons in Israel. . . . *The Times*, a 193-year-old London newspaper, suspends publication.	South African Min. Pieter Koornhof announces that the demolition of a shantytown outside of Cape Town will be indefinitely postponed for humane reasons. . . . Rhodesian interim govt.'s executive council agrees that whites will have a pivotal role in the future Cabinet. Rev. Ndabaningi Sithole, a black member of the council, defends the plan because he says it will protect the future government from a succession of coups.	A plebiscite on Nicaraguan Pres. Anastasio Somoza's staying in office, proposed by a three-member mediating team from the U.S., Guatemala, and the Dominican Republic, is accepted in principle, but each side sets conditions rejected by the other.	Australian P.M. Malcolm Fraser shuffles his Cabinet extensively. . . . Chinese authorities order a halt to wall posters indirectly critical of the late CP Chmn. Mao Tse-tung and current Chairman Hua Kuo-feng that began appearing in Peking and other major cities beginning about Nov. 20.
Dec. 1		Rumanian President and CP leader Nicolae Ceausescu concludes a week-long campaign against Soviet-bloc demands for increased military spending with a speech marking the sixtieth anniversary of the Rumanian state.	Spurred by a message from Ayatollah Khomeini from his exile in France, demonstrations begin to erupt in Teheran and other Iranian cities timed to coincide with the observance of the emotional Moslem holiday of Moharram, which begins on Dec. 2.		

A	B	C	D	E
Includes developments that affect more than one world region, international organizations and important meetings of major world leaders.	Includes all domestic and regional developments in Europe, including the Soviet Union, Turkey, Cyprus and Malta.	Includes all domestic and regional developments in Africa and the Middle East, including Iraq and Iran and excluding Cyprus, Turkey and Afghanistan.	Includes all domestic and regional developments in Latin America, the Caribbean and Canada.	Includes all domestic and regional developments in Asia and Pacific nations, extending from Afghanistan through all the Pacific Islands, except Hawaii.

U.S. Politics & Social Issues	U.S. Foreign Policy & Defense	U.S. Economy & Environment	Science, Technology & Nature	Culture, Leisure & Life Style	
Robert Groden, a photo-optical technician, tells the congressional committee investigating the late Pres. John Kennedy's assassination that blow-ups of film taken at the time dispute the Warren Commission's conclusion that Lee Harvey Oswald was a lone sniper who killed Kennedy.					Nov. 26
San Francisco Mayor George Moscone, 49, and city supervisor Harvey Milk, 48, are shot to death inside City Hall.... Supreme Ct. refuses to review the contempt of court convictions of Myron Farber, a *The New York Times* reporter who resisted a N.J. court order to turn over his personal notes relating to the Mario Jascalevich case.	Army Secy. Clifford Alexander Jr. says there is an accute shortage of doctors in the military.			Church of Jesus Christ of Latter-Day Saints (Mormon) presents a family-life award to Pres. Carter and his wife, Rosalynn Carter, in a Salt Lake City, Utah ceremony.... Miguel de Pina, 84, becomes the first surviving member of the Peoples Temple to return to the U.S. from Guyana.	Nov. 27
Statistics released by the Joint Center for Political Studies show that the number of black state legislators declined to 285 from 292 as a result of Nov. 7 elections. ... Senate Minority Leader Howard Baker Jr. (Tenn.) tells a two-day Republican Governors Assn. meeting that the party has come out of the Nov. 7 elections strong enough to start acting like the majority party.... Former Pres. Richard Nixon tells a student group at Oxford University, England that he did not lie about Watergate but said things that later "seemed to be untrue."	Atty. Gen. Griffin Bell tells Congress he is planning to admit 21,875 more Indochinese refugees — Vietnamese and Cambodians — in addition to the existing allowance of 25,000 per year.	Labor Dept. reports that consumer prices have risen a seasonally adjusted .8 percent. The October report stands at 200.9 percent of the 1967 base average, meaning that a selection of goods purchased for $100 in 1967 now costs $200.90.		Billy Sims, a junior tailback at the University of Oklahoma, wins the Heisman Trophy as the nation's finest college football player.... In a move that surprises the baseball world, the Cincinnati Reds fire manager Sparky Anderson.	Nov. 28
Dan White, 21, a former San Francisco supervisor, is charged with murdering San Francisco Mayor George Moscone and Supervisor Harvey Milk under "special circumstances" that would require the death penalty if he is convicted. Milk and Moscone reportedly had often conflicted over White's law-and-order and antihomosexual stands.	Army announces that it has given its commanders the authority to dismiss soldiers, married or unmarried, if their child-care responsibilities interfere with their military duties.	American Federation of Teachers pres. Albert Shanker announces a campaign to organize nurses and other health-care professionals under a new division of the AFT called American Federation of Nurses—AFT.... National League of Cities formally endorses Pres. Carter's anti-inflation effort.	FTC rules that the AMA has engaged in a conspiracy to illegally restrain competition among doctors by preventing them from advertising.	NBC announces it is cancelling its entire line-up of prime-time TV shows in an unprecedented move credited to NBC pres. Fred Silverman.	Nov. 29
Census Bureau study by Mark Littman finds that the former pronounced growth of black population in cities has declined for some time.	Pres. Carter tells a news conference that the basic U.S. defense policy is one of deterrence and denies reports that he is backing a $2-billion civil defense program.		Stanford Ovshinsky, a controversial scientist, says he has invented a new class of materials that could be made into an alloy to economically convert sunlight into electricity and calls for $10 million in investments in his company, Energy Conversion Devices Inc.	U.S. military officers say that a total of 911 people died in the Peoples Temple mass murder-suicides in Jonestown, Guyana, more than double the originally estimated death toll.	Nov. 30
	A U.S. federal district ct. jury convicts two Croatian terrorists on charges stemming from their August seizure of the West German consulate in Chicago.... CIA Dir. Stansfield Turner discloses that some Harvard University professors have had secret ties with the CIA.	Assn. of Western Pulp and Paper Workers files suit to have Pres. Carter's voluntary wage–price plan declared unconstitutional. They charge that the guidelines are actually mandatory controls that the President has no authority to impose.... Shell Oil Co. begins its own nationwide gas rationing by limiting dealers to 75 percent of previous monthly deliveries.	State medical boards are reported by the AMA to have increased disciplinary actions against doctors by almost six times (1971–77).		Dec. 1
F Includes elections, federal-state relations, civil rights and liberties, crime, the judiciary, education, health care, poverty, urban affairs and population.	**G** Includes formation and debate of U.S. foreign and defense policies, veterans' affairs and defense spending. (Relations with specific foreign countries are usually found under the region concerned.)	**H** Includes business, labor, agriculture, taxation, transportation, consumer affairs, monetary and fiscal policy, natural resources, and pollution.	**I** Includes worldwide scientific, medical and technological developments, natural phenomena, U.S. weather, natural disasters, and accidents.	**J** Includes the arts, religion, scholarship, communications media, sports, entertainments, fashions, fads and social life.	

	World Affairs	Europe	Africa & the Middle East	The Americas	Asia & the Pacific
Dec. 2	PLO seeks to enhance its international standing by asking to be regarded as a full-fledged recipient of United Nations development aid.	Nobel Prize-winning Soviet scientist and dissident Andrei Sakharov tells Western reporters that his Moscow apartment was ransacked on Nov. 29 and charges that it was done by the KGB.	Eritrean guerrilla sources report resisting advances by more than 45,000 Ethiopian troops using tanks, jet fighters, and helicopters.		Chinese Deputy Premier Teng Hsiao-ping says that in seeking the reunification of Taiwan with the People's Republic of China, China will accept Taiwan's higher standard of living and different political system. . . . A Vietnamese refugee boat sinks off the coast of Malaysia with as many as 143 persons reported drowned.
Dec. 3		In a national referendum, Swiss voters reject, 919,000–723,000, a proposal to create a national police force.	Iranian Premier Gholam Riza Azhari blames the turbulence of the previous two days on the outlawed Communist Tudeh Party.	Quebec's Parti Quebecois endorses Premier Rene Levesque's plan of an independent Quebec maintaining strong economic ties to the rest of Canada. . . . Opposition Social Christian Party candidate Luis Herrera Campins is elected president of Venezuela in the country's fifth consecutive free election since 1958.	Hanoi radio announces that a Kampuchean United Front for National Salvation has been formed in Cambodia to try to overthrow the Cambodian govt.
Dec. 4		U.S. Treasury Secy. Michael Blumenthal and Commerce Secy. Juanita Kreps are the first administration officials to visit the Soviet Union since Pres. Carter ordered a boycott of high-level talks to protest the trials of Soviet dissidents. They head a delegation of U.S. businessmen who are meeting with Soviet officials to discuss future U.S.–Soviet trade deals.	Thousands of antigovernment workers strike, reducing oil production by 30 percent, as anti-Shah protests intensify in Iran.		Malaysia lifts its ban on admitting Vietnamese boat people stranded off the Malaysian coast and permits approximately 600 refugees from four boats. MALAYSIA Vietnamese Refugees VIETNAM Boat People . . . Hanoi radio broadcasts a United Kampuchean Front statement assailing the Cambodian govt. as dictatorial, militarist, and fascist and echoing genocide charges brought by Cambodian refugees.
Dec. 5	NATO concludes three years of study and negotiations by agreeing to purchase the U.S. airborne warning and control system (AWACS) at a total cost of $2.44 billion.	Leaders of nine EEC nations end a two-day summit meeting in Brussels by approving plans for a new European Monetary System (EMS) to become effective JAN. 1, 1979. . . . Great Britain announces that it will not join the system, and Ireland and Italy defer decisions.	South African Judge Rudolf Erasmus releases a report confirming that South Africa's disbanded Dept. of Information officials engaged in illicit practices but leveling no charges against Pres. John Vorster and P.M. Pieter Botha.		Afghan Premier Nur Mohammad Taraki signs a 20-year treaty of cooperation and friendship with Soviet Pres. Leonid Brezhnev.
Dec. 6		Despite a surprisingly low turnout, Spanish voters overwhelmingly approve the new Constitution, which establishes a parliamentary monarchy with full individual liberties. . . . In a meeting with U.S. Treasury Secy. Michael Blumenthal and Commerce Secy. Juanita Kreps, Soviet Pres. Brezhnev affirms his country's interest in expanding trade with the U.S. . . . Gaullist leader Jacques Chirac criticizes the policies of Pres. Valery Giscard d'Estaing as a retreat from France's role as a leading world power.	Hundreds of American dependents leave Iran in wake of the turmoil there.		
Dec. 7	At the opening of their two-day annual conference, NATO foreign ministers hear a suggestion from British For. Secy. David Owen for a political dialogue with the Warsaw Pact. . . . *Wall Street Journal* reports that the U.S. endorses the European Monetary System (EMS).		South African P.M. Pieter Botha tells Parliament that the government will discontinue almost half of the secret projects funded by the former Dept. of Information. He adds that the government spent $21.9 million to subsidize the *Citizen* , a pro-government English-language newspaper.	Takakazu Suzuki, a Japanese sales manager for a Japanese-Salvadoran textile company, is the fourth foreign businessman to be kidnapped in El Salvador Since Nov. 24 by the Armed Forces of National Resistance (FARN) leftist guerrilla group. . . . Martial law and radio–TV censorship is lifted in Nicaragua by Pres. Anastasio Somoza, under pressure from U.S. mediator William Bowdler.	Over 350 people are arrested in Brisbane, Australia after a demonstration against Queensland's legislation regulating public marches. . . . Australia's economic growth Between July and September is reported to have not lived up to government expectations. . . . Masayoshi Ohira is confirmed as Japanese premier.

A	B	C	D	E
Includes developments that affect more than one world region, international organizations and important meetings of major world leaders.	Includes all domestic and regional developments in Europe, including the Soviet Union, Turkey, Cyprus and Malta.	Includes all domestic and regional developments in Africa and the Middle East, including Iraq and Iran and excluding Cyprus, Turkey and Afghanistan.	Includes all domestic and regional developments in Latin America, the Caribbean and Canada.	Includes all domestic and regional developments in Asia and Pacific nations, extending from Afghanistan through all the Pacific Islands, except Hawaii.

U.S. Politics & Social Issues	U.S. Foreign Policy & Defense	U.S. Economy & Environment	Science, Technology & Nature	Culture, Leisure & Life Style	
	Pres. Carter sends a high-level trade delegation to Moscow to discuss relaxation of export curbs.		The National Advisory Committee on Oceans and Atmosphere proposes a reorganization of U.S. government agencies and departments dealing with oceans and atmospheric programs into a new federal department.	American representational artist Edwin Dickinson dies at 87.	Dec. 2
Synanon founder, Charles Dederich, is arraigned in a hospital in Kingman, Ariz. on charges that he conspired to murder Paul Morantz by having a rattlesnake placed in his mailbox on Oct. 10. . . . A Census Bureau study finds that the historic migration of the poor from the South to the urban Northeast has reversed in the mid-1970s.			A Southern Railway System passenger train en route from Atlanta, Ga. to Washington, D.C., derails 35 miles south of Charlottesville, Va., killing six people, and injuring 60 others, five of them critically.	*Mommie Dearest* , Christina Crawford's book about her famous mother, the film star Joan Crawford, heads the best-selling general book list for the previous week. . . . Minnesota Viking Fran Tarkenton breaks the NFL pass completion record for a single season, completing 30 of 56 attempts in a 28–27 win over Philadelphia. He ends the game with 304 completions, 16 more than Sonny Jurgenson's 1967 record.	Dec. 3
House Democrats reelect Speaker Thomas O'Neill Jr. (Mass.), Majority Leader Jim Wright (Tex.), and Caucus chmn. Thomas Foley (Wash.). . . . House Republicans, in a smooth, five-hour meeting, unanimously return Minority Leader John Rhodes (Ariz.) and Minority Whip Robert Michel (Ill.) to their posts.			France concludes a trade and economic cooperation agreement with China that includes negotiating Chinese purchase of two French-built nuclear reactors valued at $2.4 billion.	Kirill Kondrashin, noted Soviet conductor, defects to the West after completing a concert in the Netherlands.	Dec. 4
FBI Dir. William Webster announces that two FBI supervisors will be fired, one demoted, and another suspended because of their involvement in illegal surveillance of the Weather Underground in the early 1970s.	Gen. George Brown (ret.), 60, JCS chairman (1974–78) and much-decorated WWII hero, dies of cancer in Wash., D.C.			Pete Rose, first choice in baseball's free agent draft, signs a four-year contract with the NL Philadelphia Phillies club for $3.2 million, making him baseball's highest-paid player.	Dec. 5
House Democrats vote for a proposal by Rep. Matthew McHugh to subject subcommittee chairmanships to approval by the full caucus if nominees have been convicted of a felony or censured by the House. The rules change means that Rep. Charles Diggs Jr. (D, Mich.) could face a caucus review if he were renominated as chairman of the House International Relations Committee's Africa subcommittee. . . . Census Bureau finds that the four largest U.S. cities have declined in population since 1970. They are N.Y.C.; Chicago, Ill.; Los Angeles, Calif.; and Philadelphia, Pa.	Pres. Carter reaffirms his human-rights policy as the soul of U.S. foreign policy. . . . Pentagon reports that the percentage of black soldiers in the Army's enlisted ranks has doubled over the past eight years and that in fiscal 1978 blacks constitute 28 percent of the Army compared to 14 percent in 1970.	U.S. auto makers are reported having sold 909,000 cars in November, about 3.2 percent more than in November 1977, but the increase is almost solely the rusult of GM sales. . . . Council on Wage and Price Stability chmn. Alfred Kahn says his office is investigating the cause of new shortages of unleaded gas.	N.H. Supreme Ct. rules that antinuclear protesters were not justified in staging illegal protests at the Seabrook N.H. nuclear plant because they had legal alternatives. . . . Gen. William Westmoreland (ret.) tells a Dade County Medical Society in Fla. that advances made in medicine as a result of the Vietnam War have saved more lives than were lost fighting in the conflict. He cites new blood transfusion techniques and malaria and trenchfoot treatment.	Barbra Streisand and Neil Diamond's single, "You Don't Bring Me Flowers ," is the best-selling record for the previous week.	Dec. 6
	Pres. Carter warns at a news conference that failure by Egypt and Israel to reach an agreement by December 17, the deadline specified in the Camp David accords, would have far-reaching adverse effects on world peace.	A study of urban mortgage lending in N.Y.S. finds that discrimination is more likely to be based on race than on so-called redlining (refusal to extend mortgage credit in certain neighborhoods.)			Dec. 7

F	G	H	I	J
Includes elections, federal-state relations, civil rights and liberties, crime, the judiciary, education, health care, poverty, urban affairs and population.	Includes formation and debate of U.S. foreign and defense policies, veterans' affairs and defense spending. (Relations with specific foreign countries are usually found under the region concerned.)	Includes business, labor, agriculture, taxation, transportation, consumer affairs, monetary and fiscal policy, natural resources, and pollution.	Includes worldwide scientific, medical and technological developments, natural phenomena, U.S. weather, natural disasters, and accidents.	Includes the arts, religion, scholarship, communications media, sports, entertainments, fashions, fads and social life.

	World Affairs	Europe	Africa & the Middle East	The Americas	Asia & the Pacific
Dec. 8		Officials of A.B. Volvo, the Swedish auto maker, and the Norwegian and Swedish governments sign an agreement allowing Norway to acquire a 40 percent interest in the company. Norway and Sweden also conclude a 30-year pact on industrial and energy cooperation.	Golda Meir, premier of Israel (1969–74), dies at age 80 in Jerusalem from malignant lymphoma, which she had fought for 12 years. She was a founder of the State of Israel and spent 40 years in its politics, but held no elective office until her appointment at age 71 as premier.	*Statistics Canada* releases a study that reveals that 263,000 unemployed Canadians had not been included in the March total of unemployed because they were not actively seeking work.	Japanese Premier Masayoshi Ohira formally announces abandonment of Japanese plans to achieve a 7 percent economic growth rate for the fiscal year ending March 31, 1979, calling the goal unrealistic.
Dec. 9		Treasury Secy. Michael Blumenthal meets with Rumanian Pres. Nicolae Ceausescu in Bucharast, a visit seen motivated by U.S. desire to support Rumania in its refusal to yield to Soviet demands for more Soviet-bloc military spending.		A Canadian public opinion poll finds that the Liberal Party would receive more of the popular vote in the country if it replaced P.M. Pierre Trudeau as party leader by former Finance Min. John Turner.	
Dec. 10	Israeli Premier Menahem Begin accepts his Nobel Peace Prize in person in Oslo, Norway ceremonies, but Egyptian Pres. Anwar Sadat stays away and is represented by an aide, who earlier denied that Sadat was boycotting the ceremonies to protest stalemated peace talks with Israel.			After a five-day fact-finding visit to El Salvador, a British panel, headed by Lord Chitnis, charges that the Salvadoran regime is one of the world's worst violators of human rights.	A Peking wall poster charging Pres. Carter to pay attention to human-rights abuses in China is immediately torn down after it is posted.
Dec. 11		Norway announces that it will not join the European Monetary System (EMS).	Amnesty International accuses the Iranian govt. of continued torture of political prisoners, despite government claims that it has stopped the practice.... Rhodesian guerrillas fire on Salisbury's central oil-storage depot, causing massive fires that destroy most of the 28 oil tankers. It is the most destructive attack in the six-year-old guerrilla war there.	A final vote count proclaims Luis Herrera Campins president-elect of Venezuela.... Nicaragua's leftist guerrilla movement, the Sandinista National Liberation Front, goes on record as opposing a plebiscite in Nicaragua because it is supposedly aimed at replacing Pres. Anastasio Somoza with a civilian conservative govt.	The Vietnamese military advance into southern Cambodia reportedly stops about 25 miles from the strategic Mekong River port of Kratie.... Former Chinese Defense Min. Peng Teh-Huai's rehabilitation is disclosed in an army newspaper.
Dec. 12	U.S. Undersecretary of State David Newsom tells a U.N. conference on the problems of refugees from Southeast Asia that the international community, not just a few nations, must respond with greatly increased offers of permanent resettlement.		Running unopposed, Zambian Pres. Kenneth Kaunda wins a second five-year term of office with an overwhelming vote majority and unexpectedly high turnout.... At least 50 people are reported killed and 500 wounded in antigovernment rioting that erupted yesterday in Isfahan, Iran's second-largest city.... Striking oil workers in Iran refuse to return to their jobs at the end of the Ashura holidays. Production drops to 1.2 million barrels.	Chilean and Argentine foreign ministers fail to agree on a mediator to help resolve their long-standing dispute over the Beagle Channel. ... Decomposed corpses of 14 people and partial remains of approximately 13 others, found in a abandoned lime kiln outside of Santiago, are speculated to be those of some of the 650 Chileans who were thought to have disappeared since the 1973 military coup.	
Dec. 13	U.S. obtains 3.04 billion marks to use in support of the dollar when the Treasury Dept. sells three- and four-year notes denominated in West German currency for the equivalent of $1.6 billion.	Alexandre Sanguinetti, a leading French Gaullist, criticizes Jacques Chirac's leadership and says that the party is in an intellectual desert. ... Italy votes to immediately enter the European Monetary System.	Speaking from his home of exile near Paris, Ayatollah Khomeini discloses that he has warned foreign heads of state that support of the Shah will deprive their countries of Iranian oil and that all treaties will be annulled if his Moslem opposition movement takes power.... Angolan Pres. Agostinho Neto cordially greets U.S. Sen. George McGovern (D, S.D.) and says that Angola wants diplomatic relations with the U.S.		China lodges a sharp protest with the Vietnamese Embassy in Peking about alleged recent Vietnamese incursions into Chinese territory and raids on Chinese fishing boats. ... Malaysian police prevent two boats carrying about 300 Vietnamese refugees from landing on the country's east coast.

A	B	C	D	E
Includes developments that affect more than one world region, international organizations and important meetings of major world leaders.	*Includes all domestic and regional developments in Europe, including the Soviet Union, Turkey, Cyprus and Malta.*	*Includes all domestic and regional developments in Africa and the Middle East, including Iraq and Iran and excluding Cyprus, Turkey and Afghanistan.*	*Includes all domestic and regional developments in Latin America, the Caribbean and Canada.*	*Includes all domestic and regional developments in Asia and Pacific nations, extending from Afghanistan through all the Pacific Islands, except Hawaii.*

U.S. Politics & Social Issues	U.S. Foreign Policy & Defense	U.S. Economy & Environment	Science, Technology & Nature	Culture, Leisure & Life Style	
Pres. Carter draws only polite applause for a half-hour speech on the opening day of the Democratic Party's midterm convention.		N.H. Gov.-elect Hugh Gallen rejects a request from William Tallman, president of the Public Service Co. of New Hamphshire, which is building the Seabrook nuclear power plant, that the state back $400 million in bonds to help build the plant.		U.S. investigators at the peoples Temple abandoned commune in Jonestown, Guyana report finding a tape-recording of the mass murder-suicide there, which reveals that cult members who objected to committing suicide were shouted down by their leader, Rev. Jim Jones.	Dec. 8
John Adamson, confessed killer of Ariz. investigative reporter Don Bolles in 1976, is sentenced to 48–49 years for planting a bomb under Bolles' car. . . . Sen. Edward Kennedy (Mass.) shouts at a workshop on national health insurance at the Democratic Party's midterm conference that he supports the fight against inflation, but that no fight can be effective or successful if it is not fair.			Pioneer Venus project manager Charles Hall calls the probe into the Venusian atmosphere for scientific data a classic mission in which everything went perfectly. . . . NRC stages a test at the Idaho National Engineering Laboratory that finds the emergency cooling system of a nuclear reactor works better than expected.		Dec. 9
The Democratic Party's midterm conference shows strong discontent with Pres. Carter's priorities. A 40 percent dissent vote is cast against his budget.		A congressional staff report charges that middleman oil companies have overcharged U.S. consumers a total of nearly $2 billion since 1974. It also claims that Energy Dept. officials in effect looked the other way.	Pioneer Venus scientists report that the probes discovered surprisingly large amounts of the gas argon, which implies that current thought about planetary evolution will have to be revised.		Dec. 10
			GAO study contends that federal agencies have failed to protect the public adequately from the potential health hazards of microwave radiation posed by household or medical equipment.	LPGA honors Nancy Lopez for her spectacular 1978 tour showing and formally names her rookie and player of the year. She is the first professional golfer, male or female, to win both titles in the same year. . . . The New York Knicks of the NBA announce replacing coach Willis Reed with Red Holzman.	Dec. 11
Pres. Carter insists at a news conference that his differences with Sen. Edward Kennedy (D, Mass.) are minor and claims there is no schism in the Democratic Party.		EEOC announces final guidelines designed to encourage employers to voluntarily hire more women and minorities by protecting the employers from reverse-discrimination charges. . . . A report prepared by officials of 36 federal govt. agencies says solar energy could provide 20 percent of U.S. energy needs by the end of the twentieth century.		*Affirmed* , the 1978 Triple Crown winner, is named Eclipse Award horse of the year. Darrel McHargue is named jockey of the year, and Laz Barrera is named top trainer.	Dec. 12
FTC issues new regulations to tighten advertising and refund policies of private vocational schools.	*The New York Times* reports that the Navy and Air Force are facing a major drain of pilots to high-paying commercial airline jobs.	Temporary Emergency Ct. of Appeals, Wash., D.C. upholds lower court decisions that the federal govt. was wrong in attempting to force 15 major oil companies in 1975–76 to refund $1.3 billion to their customers in a dispute over pricing regulations.			Dec. 13

F	G	H	I	J
Includes elections, federal-state relations, civil rights and liberties, crime, the judiciary, education, health care, poverty, urban affairs and population.	*Includes formation and debate of U.S. foreign and defense policies, veterans' affairs and defense spending. (Relations with specific foreign countries are usually found under the region concerned.)*	*Includes business, labor, agriculture, taxation, transportation, consumer affairs, monetary and fiscal policy, natural resources, and pollution.*	*Includes worldwide scientific, medical and technological developments, natural phenomena, U.S. weather, natural disasters, and accidents.*	*Includes the arts, religion, scholarship, communications media, sports, entertainments, fashions, fads and social life.*

	World Affairs	Europe	Africa & the Middle East	The Americas	Asia & the Pacific
Dec. 14		P.M. Callaghan wins a vote of confidence in the British House of Commons on his economic policies.		Canadian P.M. Trudeau denies rumors that he will resign as Liberal Party leader in wake of a poll that found his leadership detrimental to the party's voter popularity.... Buenos Aires police say that they have located 159 people reported missing since September. Local human-rights groups and relatives of missing persons claim that 3,000 Argentines have disappeared since the March 1976 military coup.	
Dec. 15	Mexico City talks between the U.S. and U.S.S.R. on limiting sales of conventional arms reach a sudden impasse in wake of a Soviet demand to discuss U.S. arms sales to Iran, China, and South Korea. ... Soviet Pres. Brezhnev reacts positively to U.S. recognition of Communist China and severance of diplomatic relations with Taiwan.	Irish P.M. Jack Lynch announces that Ireland will participate in the new European Monetary System from its inception on January 1, 1979, thus including eight of the nine Common Market countries from its inception.... British P.M. Callaghan tells Parliament that his government wants to establish a parliamentary commission to conduct a confidential investigation of British oil companies' violation of economic sanctions against Rhodesia.	The South African govt. -backed Democratic Turnhalle Alliance wins 41 of the 50 seats in the new Namibian constituent assembly and polls 82 percent of the vote. Black opposition parties boycotted the election.		In a dramatic and unexpected televised speech, Pres. Carter announces that the U.S. and China will establish diplomatic relations on Jan. 1, 1979, that Chinese Deputy Premier Teng Hsiao-ping will visit the U.S. on Jan. 29, and that both nations will exchange ambassadors and establish embassies on March 1.... Carter also says that the U.S. will sever diplomatic relations with Nationalist China on Jan. 1 and end its 1954 defense treaty on Dec. 31, 1979. ... Six Vietnamese refugees are allowed to land in Hong Kong for medical treatment.
Dec. 16				The first Nicaraguan political prisoners are freed after Pres. Anastasio Somoza signs an amnesty the previous day, one of the demands of the Broad Opposition Front (FAO)–the 14-party anti-Somoza coalition in the country.	An anti-American demonstration is staged in front of the U.S. Embassy in Taipei to protest U.S. recognition of Communist China and abrogation of its defense treaty with Taiwan.
Dec. 17	OPEC acts to raise oil prices in stages to a total increase of 14.5 percent by Oct. 1, 1979, ending a 18-month price freeze.	Irish terrorist bombs explode in five British cities, slightly injuring nine people.	PLO claims responsibility for a bomb that explodes in a crowded Jerusalem bus, injuring 17 people. ... A Polisario communique says that 10 Moroccan soldiers have been killed in separate clashes on Dec. 10 and 11 in the guerrilla group's fight for the independence of Western Sahara.... Shah of Iran names Gholam Hussein Sadiqi to form a civilian govt. in face of mounting unrest in the country, but Sadiqi fails to get National Front opposition party cooperation.	Mediators from the U.S., Guatemala, and the Dominican Republic are unable to effect a compromise between Nicaraguan Pres. Anastasio Somoza and the Broad Opposition Front Coalition, which demands that Somoza leave the country before a plebiscite is held on his continuance in office.	A State Dept. official emphasizes that the Carter administration intends to keep all existing agreements with Taiwan except for the defense treaty.
Dec. 18				British Columbia Health Min. Robert McClelland reports that a provincial law requiring compulsory treatment for heroin addicts will become effective at the beginning of 1979, in wake of an addict population estimated at 10,000 or 60 percent of the total addicts in Canada.	
Dec. 19	International Court of Justice announces it is not qualified to rule on the Greek–Turkish dispute over the continental shelf area in the Aegean Sea.	An electrical power failure blacks out most areas of France for more than two hours.		San Salvador's Archbishop Oscar Romero claims that the official explanation for the police slaying of four alleged members of the El Salvador guerrilla group FPL is not credible and that the church's investigation found strong evidence that Father Ernesto Barrera was tortured and shot and killed at close range.	The lower house of the Indian Parliament ousts former P.M. Indira Gandhi from her newly elected seat and orders her jailed for contempt and breach of privilege.

A	B	C	D	E
Includes developments that affect more than one world region, international organizations and important meetings of major world leaders.	Includes all domestic and regional developments in Europe, including the Soviet Union, Turkey, Cyprus and Malta.	Includes all domestic and regional developments in Africa and the Middle East, including Iraq and Iran and excluding Cyprus, Turkey and Afghanistan.	Includes all domestic and regional developments in Latin America, the Caribbean and Canada.	Includes all domestic and regional developments in Asia and Pacific nations, extending from Afghanistan through all the Pacific Islands, except Hawaii.

U.S. Politics & Social Issues	U.S. Foreign Policy & Defense	U.S. Economy & Environment	Science, Technology & Nature	Culture, Leisure & Life Style	
Carroll Lynn, chief of the Houston, Tex. police dept. during 1974–75, is found guilty in Federal District Ct. of extortion charges, perjury, and obstruction of justice in connection with a scheme to keep a nonexistent assassin from killing Houston oilman John Holden. The sentence comes in wake of several other cases involving criminal prosecution of Texas policemen.	Paul Reutershan, a 28-year-old Vietnam veteran who claimed his exposure to the chemical defoliant Agent Orange while serving in Southeast Asia caused him to develop cancer, dies in Norwalk, Conn. Agent Orange was sprayed over Vietnam Jungles (1961–71) to kill trees that provided cover for enemy soldiers.	Federal Home Loan Bank Board authorizes federally chartered savings and loan associations to offer three new types of home mortgages beginning Jan. 1, 1979 — variable rate, graduated payment, and reverse annuity.	University of Massachusetts scientists report finding indirect evidence for the existence of gravity waves.	Citing the high number of injuries during the past NFL season, the NFL Players Assn. calls for the league to raise the roster limit to 47 from the current 45 and establish a three-man taxi squad or reserve list in 1979. . . . *The Deer Hunter*, a film about the Vietnam War with Robert De Niro, Christopher Walken, John Savage, and Meryl Streep, is released in N.Y.	Dec. 14
	Moderate and conservative Republican politicians and some Democrats sharply criticize Carter's announcement, charging that Congress was not consulted. . . . Former Pres. Gerald Ford and former State Secy. Henry Kissinger express mild approval of Carter's decision to recognize Communist China and renounce the U.S. defense treaty with Taiwan.	FRB reports that industrial production in the U.S. rose a seasonally adjusted .7 percent in November. . . . McDonnell Douglas Corp. discloses that it made more than $18 million in foreign payments to win airplane contracts abroad in answer to a SEC suit filed the previous day. . . . Kennecott Copper Corp. and Curtiss-Wright Corp., adversaries in one of the bitterest and hardest-fought takeover battles in business history, call a truce to their nine-month dispute.			Dec. 15
Cleveland, Ohio defaults on $14 million in notes owed to six local banks.				Arizona State trounces Rutgers University, 34–18, in the first Garden State Bowl at East Rutherford, N.J. The match is the first major college bowl game played in the East in 16 years.	Dec. 16
Americans for Democratic Action (ADA), a liberal group, releases its annual rating of senators, which finds that, as a whole, the Senate became more conservative this year. Sen. Howard Metzenbaum (D, Ohio) scores a perfect liberal 100. Sen. Edward Kennedy (D, Mass.) follows with 95. James McClure (R, Idaho) and Maryon Allen (D, Ala) both score O.					Dec. 17
Supreme Ct. rules unanimously that one state cannot block another state's request for the extradition of a prisoner by investigating the basis of that request.	Sen. Barry Goldwater (R, Ariz.), who has been extremely vocal in his denunciation of the U.S. abandonment of its 23-year-old defense treaty with Taiwan, argues that Pres. Carter's act is an abuse of presidential power and urges the Senate leadership to seek a special session of Congress to deal with the issue.	Commerce Dept. reports that housing starts remain strong through most of 1978 despite high interest rates exceeding the 2-million annual rate for nine months of the year.	NASA announces that it has abandoned plans to launch a space mission to attempt to prevent the unmanned orbiting Skylab space station from falling.	An Australian movie written and directed by Peter Weir, *The Last Wave*, is released in N.Y. . . . The Soviet Embassy in Georgetown, Guyana says it wants nothing to do with an alleged bequest of millions of dollars from the Peoples Temple to the Soviet CP.	Dec. 18
Senate Ethics Committee formally charges Sen. Herman Talmadge (D, Ga.) with five possible violations of Senate rules, each involving allegations of financial wrongdoing.	White House admits that public reaction to the President's decision to recognize China is running four to one against it. A *New York Times*/CBS News poll, however, finds those surveyed neither enthusiasatic about closer ties with China nor about supporting Taiwan.	IBM announces plans for a four-for-one split of its common stock. . . . American Automobile Association (AAA) says that the average price of gasoline rose more than five cents a gallon, or 8 percent, from 1977 prices, citing a nationwide average price for regular gasoline at 67.8 cents a gallon and 71.9 cents for regular unleaded.			Dec. 19

F	G	H	I	J
Includes elections, federal-state relations, civil rights and liberties, crime, the judiciary, education, health care, poverty, urban affairs and population.	*Includes formation and debate of U.S. foreign and defense policies, veterans' affairs and defense spending. (Relations with specific foreign countries are usually found under the region concerned.)*	*Includes business, labor, agriculture, taxation, transportation, consumer affairs, monetary and fiscal policy, natural resources, and pollution.*	*Includes worldwide scientific, medical and technological developments, natural phenomena, U.S. weather, natural disasters, and accidents.*	*Includes the arts, religion, scholarship, communications media, sports, entertainments, fashions, fads and social life.*

	World Affairs	Europe	Africa & the Middle East	The Americas	Asia & the Pacific
Dec. 20		Bomb blasts damage four leading hotels in Northern Ireland.... Despite strong Soviet criticism, the Rumanian govt. announces it will cut defense spending to increase family allowances.	Israeli jets bomb Palestinian guerrilla positions in and aroud the southern Lebanese port of Tyre, which the Israelis claim are bases from which the guerrillas recently launched attacks inside Israel that killed four people and wounded 67.	Petroleos Mexicanos (Pemex), the Mexican govt. oil agency, says it will increase its basic export price of crude oil by 10.7 percent in 1979 in gradual stages.	Thousands of demonstrators riot and are arrested in major Indian cities to protest Indira Gandhi's ouster from Parliament and imprisonment.
Dec. 21	State Secy. Vance and Soviet For. Min. Gromyko begin a three-day session in Geneva amid wide expectation that a SALT pact will be concluded.	EEC officials and Greek govt. negotiators reach an agreement on Greece's entry into the Common Market but do not set a specific date.	Rhodesian warplanes bomb a Zambia military training camp north of Lusaka.	Colombian govt. raises the minimum wage by an average 35 percent, effective Jan. 1, 1979.... Fred DeGazon is elected Dominica's first president.	
Dec. 22	*Wall Street Journal* reports that a yet unresolved U.S.–Soviet dispute in current SALT talks is over a U.S. proposal to freeze the number of MIRVs the Soviets have in place on already deployed missiles.... Multilateral GATT trade talks recess without a final agreement because of major differences between the U.S. and the EEC.		South African govt. accepts a U.N. plan to establish an independent government in Namibia and agrees to admit a U.N. peacekeeping force into the territory.	Pope John Paul II announces that Argentina and Chile have accepted his offer to mediate their dispute over the territorial rights in the Beagle Channel and the South Atlantic.	Chinese CP Central Committee ends a five-day meeting in Peking by announcing that the committee is shifting the focus of party worry to the economy, seen as a reversal of one of the late CP Chmn. Mao's principles that "politics be in command."
Dec. 23	Last-minute Soviet reservations delay completion of an agreement in SALT talks... U.S. officials speculate that the delay signals Soviet displeasure with the U.S. for establishing diplomatic relations with China.	Spain abolishes the death penalty for all but military crimes committed in wartime.	Iranian terrorists shoot and kill two oil company executives, including an American, in separate attacks near Ahwaz, the oil industry's operational center in southwest Iran.		A freighter carrying more than 2,700 Vietnamese refugees is prohibited from putting its passengers ashore in Hong Kong.
Dec. 24		British Broadcasting Corp. (BBC) resumes full broadcasting four days after employes had blacked out the two BBC TV channels and reduced radio broadcasting in a dispute about wages and overtime.	State Secy. Vance confers unsuccessfully in Brussels with Egyptian and Israeli representatives in an attempt to break their deadlocked talks on a projected peace treaty.		Peking claims that dozens of Vietnamese troops invaded China the previous day and killed or wounded nine people.... CP newspaper *Jenmin Jih Pao* discloses that the Chinese CP committee meeting has decreed major economic changes, including decentralization of state-controlled factories, increased payments for grain to peasants, and other measures to halt the rapid rise in costs of urban goods.
Dec. 25			Egyptian Pres. Sadat complains that Arab countries' refusal to support his Mideast peace efforts help Israeli Premier Menahem Begin to block a settlement, claiming that it is in Begin's interest for the Arab countries to remain divided.... At a Teheran rally attended by 4,000 of his supporters, Iranian opposition party National Front leader, Karim Sanjabi, declares that the Shah must go.		Vietnamese and rebel Kampuchean United Front for National Salvation troops lauch an offensive inside eastern Cambodia.
Dec. 26	*Oil and Gas Journal* reports that because of increased oil production by communist nations, world oil production increased in 1978.	Turkey imposes martial law in 13 of its 67 provinces in wake of fighting between rival Moslem sects that erupted in southeastern Turkey four days ago.	Israeli Premier Begin says he is prepared to resume new negotiations with Egypt.		Former Indian P.M. Indira Gandhi is released from a New Delhi jail after being ousted from the lower house of Parliament for breach of privilege and contempt.

A	B	C	D	E
Includes developments that affect more than one world region, international organizations and important meetings of major world leaders.	Includes all domestic and regional developments in Europe, including the Soviet Union, Turkey, Cyprus and Malta.	Includes all domestic and regional developments in Africa and the Middle East, including Iraq and Iran and excluding Cyprus, Turkey and Afghanistan.	Includes all domestic and regional developments in Latin America, the Caribbean and Canada.	Includes all domestic and regional developments in Asia and Pacific nations, extending from Afghanistan through all the Pacific Islands, except Hawaii.

U.S. Politics & Social Issues	U.S. Foreign Policy & Defense	U.S. Economy & Environment	Science, Technology & Nature	Culture, Leisure & Life Style	
Former White House chief of staff in the Nixon administration, H.R. Haldeman, is released on parole from federal prison in Calif., after serving 18 months for his role in the Watergate cover-up. Only former Atty. Gen. John Mitchell remains in prison for Watergate-related crimes.		Chemical Bank (N.Y.C.) initiates an industry-wide move to raise the prime lending rate to 11.75 percent from 11.5 percent. . . . Leading environmentalists give Pres. Carter an outstanding rating on environmental issues in his first two years in office.	House Select Committee on Population proposes major changes in U.S. immigration policies to try to stem the flow of illegal aliens into the U.S.	Golfer Jack Nicklaus is named *Sports Illustrated* 's sportsman of the year. . . . New York Film Critics Circle Awards are voted to the following: best film *The Deer Hunter*; best actor, Jon Voight; best actress, Ingrid Bergman; best foreign-language film, *Bread and Chocolate* .	Dec. 20
Three former GSA employes are charged with taking nearly $100,000 in cash kickbacks and gifts over a three-year period from painting and repair contractors in the Wash,. D.C. area.		Environmental Defense Fund announces it has petitioned the federal govt. to have public schools inspected for asbestos dangers.	Former Interior Secy. Stewart Udall, now in private law practice, files 100 claims against the Energy Dept. seeking up to $232 million in damages for people who say they or their relatives have developed cancer or leukemia as a result of nuclear weapons testing in the Utah, Nev., and Ariz. area.	A deputy editor of a Krakow Roman Catholic weekly charges that Polish authorities extensively censored a Christmas message from Pope John Paul II to his former diocese (Krakow).	Dec. 21
	Former CIA employe William Kampiles is sentenced to 40 years in prison by Fed. district Judge Phil McNagny Jr. for selling top-secret U.S. satellite plans to the U.S.S.R. . . . Fifteen members of the House and Senate file suit in U.S. District Ct., Wash., D.C., to block the Carter administration's decision to abrogate the U.S.–Taiwan defense pact.	White House reports that Pres. Carter has restored $2 billion in planned budget cuts for social programs.		A Guyanese coroner's jury rules that all but three of the more than 900 people found dead at the Peoples Temple commune in Jonestown were murder victims, and it blames the murders on the Temple's leader, the Rev. Jim Jones.	Dec. 22
				In the Sun Bowl, Texas trounces Maryland, 42–0. In the Liberty Bowl, Missouri defeats Louisiana State, 20–15.	Dec. 23
The New York Times reports that political action committees (PACs) contributed more than twice as much money to House committee chairmen seeking reelection in 1978 than they did in the 1976 campaign.				Al Unser establishes a one-season auto racing earning record of over a half-million dollars on the 1978 U.S. Auto Club championship circuit, finishing with $591,599. . . . Advancing to the playoffs, AFC Houston Oilers defeat the Miami Dolphins, 17–9, with Oiler quarterback Dan Pastorini overcoming broken ribs and a swollen elbow to complete 20 out of 29 passes for 306 yards and a touchdown. . . . In the NFC the Atlanta Falcons edge the Philadelphia Eagles, 14–1.	Dec. 24
			Soviet probes carrying scientific instruments make their second soft landing on Venus and radio back information to Earth. . . . International Whaling Commission is reported ordering a substantial cutback in sperm whaling to 3,800 whales in 1979 from 6,444 in 1978.	Purdue crushes Georgia Tech, 41–21, in the Peach Bowl and the University of California at Los Angeles plays Arkansas to a 10–10 tie in the Fiesta Bowl.	Dec. 25
		Hershey Foods Corp. announces it will buy Friendly Ice Cream Corp. of Wilbraham, Mass. for $162 million. . . . Pres. Carter raises import duties for iron and steel nuts, bolts, and screws, reversing an earlier stand against import curbs on industrial fasteners.			Dec. 26

F	G	H	I	J
Includes elections, federal-state relations, civil rights and liberties, crime, the judiciary, education, health care, poverty, urban affairs and population.	Includes formation and debate of U.S. foreign and defense policies, veterans' affairs and defense spending. (Relations with specific foreign countries are usually found under the region concerned.)	Includes business, labor, agriculture, taxation, transportation, consumer affairs, monetary and fiscal policy, natural resources, and pollution.	Includes worldwide scientific, medical and technological developments, natural phenomena, U.S. weather, natural disasters, and accidents.	Includes the arts, religion, scholarship, communications media, sports, entertainments, fashions, fads and social life.

	World Affairs	Europe	Africa & the Middle East	The Americas	Asia & the Pacific
Dec. 27			Abdel Fattah Ismail is elected president of South Yemen.... Algerian Pres. Houari Boumedienne dies of a rare blood disease at an estimated age of 46. He had served as Algeria's president since 1965 when he ousted Ahmed Ben Bella, Algeria's first president after independence, in a bloodless coup.	An American official claims that Nicaraguan Pres. Anastasio Somoza is "stonewalling" in wake of many proposals and counter proposals by mediators, Somoza, and the Broad Opposition Front.	South Korean opposition leader Kim Dae Jung is released from jail where he had been imprisoned since March 1976 for openly criticizing the government.... Philippine authorities prohibit Vietnamese refugees from landing because officials claim that the Indochinese refugee center near Manila is already overcrowded.
Dec. 28			Oil rationing becomes effective in Iran in wake or a general strike called by the National Front opposition party to topple the Shah.		
Dec. 29	At the end of the day's trading in N.Y., the U.S. dollar had lost 19.5 percent of its value during 1978 against the Swiss franc, 19.1 percent against the Japanese yen, 13.5 percent against the West German mark, 11.1 percent against the French franc, and 6.9 percent against the British pound.	French Premier Raymond Barre announces that France is insisting on certain changes in EEC agricultural policies before it will let the new European Monetary System go into operation.	Shah of Iran appoints Shahpur Bakhtiar, a member of the country's opposition National Front, to form a new civilian govt. It will replace the military government established on Nov. 5. The appointment is motivated by growing antigovernment violence.... U.S. and Western European intelligence officials charge that Libya and the PLO have worked jointly since November to provide financial and other aid to Moslem opponents of the Shah of Iran.		Cambodia reports a new Vietnamese drive in the Mekong Valley north of Pnompenh but claims its forces repelled the assault, killing over 1,000 Vietnamese. A Vietnamese counterclaim says that Hanoi-supported Cambodian rebels killed or wounded 180 Cambodian government soldiers in Kratie province fighting, Dec. 23–26.
Dec. 30			Iran's opposition party, National Front, ousts newly appointed premier Shahpur Bakhtiar because it says his appointment does not satisfy their minimum demands for the Shah's abdication.		
Dec. 31			Iranian oil production drops to a record low of 250,000 barrels in wake of antigovernment strikes beginning Dec. 18.... Meshed, Lar, and Khurramabad in Iran are all scenes of antigovernment violence with claims that Iranian troops have killed hundreds of civilians.... U.S. urges all dependents of Americans in Iran to leave.		A Philippine–U.S. military pact is announced that will allow continued U.S. use of military bases in the Philippines in exchange for increased U.S. economic assistance to the Manila govt.... Peking calls on Taiwan to begin trade relations and permit direct postal service, shipping, and personal visits to mainland China as a first step toward reunification.

A	B	C	D	E
Includes developments that affect more than one world region, international organizations and important meetings of major world leaders.	Includes all domestic and regional developments in Europe, including the Soviet Union, Turkey, Cyprus and Malta.	Includes all domestic and regional developments in Africa and the Middle East, including Iraq and Iran and excluding Cyprus, Turkey and Afghanistan.	Includes all domestic and regional developments in Latin America, the Caribbean and Canada.	Includes all domestic and regional developments in Asia and Pacific nations, extending from Afghanistan through all the Pacific Islands, except Hawaii.

U.S. Politics & Social Issues	U.S. Foreign Policy & Defense	U.S. Economy & Environment	Science, Technology & Nature	Culture, Leisure & Life Style	
In a case that received wide press and feminist attention, John Rideout, 21, is acquitted of a first-degree rape charge brought by his wife, Greta, 23, in a Marion County, Ore. court.				Three paintings by nineteenth-century artist Paul Cezanne, valued between $2.5–3 million, are discovered missing from the Art Institute of Chicago.	Dec. 27
Gallup Poll reports Pres. Carter's popularity stabilized at the 50 percent approval mark. . . . Cleveland mayor Dennis Kucinich announces that the Cleveland Trust Co. has agreed to wait until after Feb. 27, 1979 before trying to collect on its $5 million in defaulted municipal notes.				*The Diary of Anne Frank*, a dramatization of a Jewish family hiding from the Nazis in Amsterdam during WWII, is revived on Broadway with Roberta Wallach, Eli Wallach, and Anne Jackson.	Dec. 28
	U.S. orders a naval task force to leave Subic Bay in the Philippines for the South China Sea, where it will await further orders for possible movement to the Persian Gulf.	Federal Judge Jon Newman sets aside all of the $37.3 million in damages that a jury had ordered Xerox Corp. to pay SCM Corp. for antitrust violations, charging that the damage liability cannot validly be based on any of the jury's factual findings in SCM's favor.		Clemson downs Ohio State, 17–15, in the Gator Bowl.	Dec. 29
House Select Committee on Assassinations concludes that former Pres. John F. Kennedy was probably assassinated in 1963 as the result of a conspiracy, contradicting a Warren Commission conclusion that Lee Harvey Oswald was the lone sniper who killed Kennedy. It bases its conclusion on testimony of acoustical experts whose tests showed high probability of shots from two directions.				In the AFC semifinal match, Pittsburh Steelers crush the Denver Broncos, 33–10. . . . Atlanta Falcons' championship hopes are dashed when they lose, 27–20, to the Dallas Cowboys in the NFC semifinal game. . . . Ohio State University dismisses Woody Hayes, one of the legendary coaches of college football, a day after Hayes punched a Clemson player in the Gator Bowl when Ohio State was trailing, 17–15.	Dec. 30
	Adm. Stansfield Turner retires from the Navy but remains as head of the CIA.	Dow Jones industrial average closes the year at 805.01, down 26.16 points from its 1977 finish, representing a 3.1 percent loss for the year.		Los Angeles Rams gain the NFC final against the Dallas Cowboys, trouncing the Minnesota Vikings, 34–10. . . . Houston Oilers upset the New England Patriots, 34–14, to gain the AFC final with the Pittsburgh Steelers.	Dec. 31

F	G	H	I	J
Includes elections, federal-state relations, civil rights and liberties, crime, the judiciary, education, health care, poverty, urban affairs and population.	Includes formation and debate of U.S. foreign and defense policies, veterans' affairs and defense spending. (Relations with specific foreign countries are usually found under the region concerned.)	Includes business, labor, agriculture, taxation, transportation, consumer affairs, monetary and fiscal policy, natural resources, and pollution.	Includes worldwide scientific, medical and technological developments, natural phenomena, U.S. weather, natural disasters, and accidents.	Includes the arts, religion, scholarship, communications media, sports, entertainments, fashions, fads and social life.

1979

The U.S. embassy in Teheran, Iran is captured by Iranian students who demand the return of the deposed Shah. They take 90 hostages, including 60-65 Americans.

	World Affairs	Europe	Africa & the Middle East	The Americas	Asia & the Pacific
Jan.	Pres. Carter makes Senate ratification of an expected SALT treaty with the Soviet Union his prime foreign policy goal in 1979.	A state of emergency is declared in Northern Ireland, which has been particularly hard hit by truck-and oil tanker-drivers' strikes.	Shah Mohammed Riza Pahlevi leaves Iran, ostensibly for a vacation abroad. Observers see the trip as the first move in a long and perhaps permanent exile.	Over 10,000 opponents of Pres. Anastasio Somoza march in Managua to observe the first anniversary of the assassination of opposition leader Pedro Joaquin Chammoro.	The Kampuchean United Front for National Salvation overthrows Premier Pol Pot's govt. and replaces it with a People's Revolutionary Council headed by Pres. Heng Samrin.
Feb.	OPEC members Saudi Arabia and Iraq announce that they will not increase general oil prices during the first quarter of the year.	The Soviet Union extends formal recognition to the Khomeini govt. in Iran.	Armed revolutionary followers of Ayatollah Khomeini overthrow the government of Iran as the army declares its neutrality and withdraws its troops to their barracks.	The U.S. severs military ties with Nicaragua and reduces economic aid to Somoza's regime in an effort to force it to negotiate with the Sandinistas.	China launches an invasion of Vietnam with 200,000-300,000 troops backed by planes and artillery.
March	The U.S. warns the Soviet Union against providing military aid to Afghanistan.	Wales decisively rejects a home-rule proposal and Scotland approves it by a slim margin.	Pres. Sadat and Premier Begin sign a formal peace treaty ending a 31-year state of war between Egypt and Israel.	Leaders of Canada's three major parties begin campaigning for the May general election.	China announces it is withdrawing its forces from Vietnam after having attained the goals of its February invasion.
April	Defense ministers of eight NATO countries conclude, after a two-day meeting in Florida, that the alliance should move quickly to modernize its intermediate- and short-range nuclear weapons.	Spanish Premier Adolfo Suarez Gonzalez names a Cabinet, the first constitutional government in the country since the civil war of 1936-1939.	Ayatollah Khomeini proclaims the establishment of an Islamic republic in Iran....In Uganda a group of victorious rebels form a provisional government to replace Pres. Idi Amin's eight-year regime.	Guerrillas of the Sandinista National Liberation Front resume their military-style attacks one day before Pres. Anastasio Somoza leaves on an eight-day vacation in the U.S.	The Financial Times (London) reports the Australian Export Finance and Insurance Corp. has signed an agreement to provide China with A$50-million in credit.
May	South African representatives to the U.N. take their seats in the General Assembly for the first time in five years to attend a week-long debate on Namibia.	British voters give the Conservative Party a solid parliamentary majority, thereby making its leader, Margaret Thatcher, Britain's first woman prime minister....Greece is admitted into the EEC.	A black government is formally installed in Rhodesia, completing the transition from more than 80 years of white rule. Its name is changed to Zimbabwe Rhodesia.	Canadian voters make Joseph Clark, prime minister-elect and end Liberal Party P.M. Pierre Trudeau's 11-year tenure in office.	China and the U.S. establish formal commercial relations for the first time since the Communist govt. was formed in 1949.
June	An emotionally charged ceremony in Vienna's Hofburg marks the signing of a U.S.-U.S.S.R. SALT Treaty after seven years of negotiations.	France announces that it will accept 5,000 Indochinese refugees in addition to its monthly 1,000 quota.	Pres. Carter announces that he will not lift trade sanctions against Zimbabwe Rhodesia.... An official U.S. envoy, David Halsted, arrives in Uganda after a six-year break in U.S.–Ugandan relations.	Nicaraguan National Guard troops set afire the offices of the opposition newspaper La Prensa, which symbolizes the struggle to overthrow Gen. Anastasio Somoza Debayle's regime.	The Soviet presence in Afghanistan is reported to have increased to approximately 3,000 civil and 1,000 military advisers.
July	Pres. Carter, returning from the oil summit meeting in Tokyo, reflects pessimism about U.S. economic prospects in light of recent OPEC price increases.	Austrian Chancellor Bruno Kreisky begins a Vienna conference with PLO leader Yasir Arafat, the first time a Western European head of government has formally received Arafat.	Iranian Premier Mehdi Bazargan announces nationalization of virtually all of Iran's remaining industries still privately-owned with no mention made of compensation to owners.	Pres. Anastasio Somoza Debayle resigns, ending 46-years of family rule in which his family amassed enormous wealth and power. Nicaraguan Sandinista rebels take control of Managua two days later.	The U.S. and China sign a trade agreement giving China most-favored-nation tariff treatment.
Aug.	The International Development Bank announces it is prepared to lend Nicaragua up to $500 million over the next three years to aid in rebuilding the Nicaraguan economy.	Britain's Earl Mountbatten of Burma is killed when a bomb explodes aboard his boat off Ireland.	Iran cancels $9 billion in arms agreements with the U.S. arranged by the govt. of the ousted Shah.	Paraguay strips its citizenship from Josef Mengele, the world's most-wanted Nazi fugitive....Former Canadian P.M. John Diefenbaker dies in Ottawa.	The first installment of an emergency aid program of food, medicine and other vital supplies lands in Cambodia....Indian P.M. Charan Signh resigns.
Sept.	In its annual report, the IMF says that the world faces another year of sluggish growth and high inflation in 1980, citing the effect of sharp oil increases.	Engineering and assembly-line workers strike, shutting down industry in much of Great Britain.	After 10 days of dispute, the Patriotic Front guerrillas accept the general outlines of a British-drafted constitution for an independent Zimbabwe Rhodesia.	Jacobo Timerman, held for 29 months by Argentina's military government, is released.	About 1,000 Chinese attend a rally in Peking's Tien An Men Square, denouncing special privileges among Communist Party officials and urging more human rights and free elections.
Oct.	UNICEF and the International Red Cross launch a $110 million aid program to avert starvation in Cambodia....The Nobel Peace Prize is awarded to Mother Teresa.	A Swiss jury finds Bernard Cornfeld not guilty of fraud charges in connection with the 1969 sales of shares in Investors Overseas Services Ltd.	The Israeli Cabinet approves in principle a tentative plan to station U.S., Egyptian, and Israeli observers in the Sinai to monitor the Israeli–Egyptian peace treaty.	The Bank of Canada raises its bank rate to 14 percent in a continuing effort to strengthen the Canadian dollar.	South Korean President Park Chung Hee and his chief body guard are shot to death by Kim Jae Kyu, head of the Korean Central Intelligence Agency and a life-long friend of Park's.
Nov.	A one-day U.N. conference in N.Y. pledges over $200 million for food, and medical supplies to Cambodia over the next 12 years.	The Bank of England's minimum lending rate is raised to a record level of 17 percent....The Times of London issues its first edition in more than 11 months after resolving management-labor differences.	About 500 Iranian students seize the U.S. Embassy in Teheran along with 90 hostages, including 60–65 Americans, vowing not to release their captives until the U.S. returns the Shah to stand trial in Iran.	Pierre Trudeau announces that he is resigning as head of the Liberal Party.	Masayoshi Ohira is reelected premier of Japan by a narrow margin at a special session of the lower chamber of the Japanese Diet.
Dec.	The U.N. Security Council unanimously approves a resolution demanding that Iran immediately release the 50 American hostages held in the U.S. Embassy in Teheran.	Great Britain lifts all trade sanctions against Zimbabwe Rhodesia as the country reverts to British Rule....Ireland's Fianna Fail party elects Charles Haughey to replace outgoing P.M. Jack Lynch.	Patriotic Front leaders Joshua Nkomo and Robert Mugabe and P.M. Biship Abel Muzorewa sign a cease-fire, ending seven years of guerrilla war in Zimbabwe Rhodesia.	Canadian P.M. Joseph Clark asks Gov. Gen. Edward Schreyer to dissolve the House of Commons and set elections for February 1980....The Shah of Iran leaves the U.S. for Panama.	A two-day party congress held in Cambodia replaces ousted Premier Pol Pot with Pres. Khieu Samphan.
	A *Includes developments that affect more than one world region, international organizations and important meetings of major world leaders.*	**B** *Includes all domestic and regional developments in Europe, including the Soviet Union, Turkey, Cyprus and Malta.*	**C** *Includes all domestic and regional developments in Africa and the Middle East, including Iraq and Iran and excluding Cyprus, Turkey and Afghanistan.*	**D** *Includes all domestic and regional developments in Latin America, the Caribbean and Canada.*	**E** *Includes all domestic and regional developments in Asia and Pacific nations, extending from Afghanistan through all the Pacific Islands, except Hawaii.*

U.S. Politics & Social Issues	U.S. Foreign Policy & Defense	U.S. Economy & Environment	Science, Technology & Nature	Culture, Leisure & Life Style	
Pres. Carter calls for legislation to make Jan 15, the birthday of the late civil-rights leader Martin Luther King Jr., a national holiday.	Carter administration officials say that Pres. Carter has issued new orders to keep a U.S. naval task force from proceeding to Iranian waters, a move made to downplay the Iranian crisis.	Pres. Carter sends Congress an austere budget designed primarily to restrain inflation by gently slowing the economy.	Union of Concerned Scientists, a group critical of nuclear power, recommends that 16 U.S. nuclear power plants should be shut down and repaired.	The Pittsburgh Steelers becomes the first team to win three Super Bowls with a 35-31 victory over the Dallas Cowboys.	Jan.
HEW Secy. Joseph Califano says that the U.S. could save at least 10 percent on its projected $730-billion health bill in 1990 by adopting a national health insurance plan with strict cost controls.	A U.S. Dist. Ct., Wash. D.C. jury delivers guilty verdicts against three Cuban exiles charged with the 1976 murder of Orlando Letelier, former Chilean ambassador to the U.S.	Three thousand farmers and their supporters invade Wash. D.C. causing a massive traffic snarl during the morning rush hour to demand higher price supports for their products.	A volcanic eruption in central Java, Indonesia, kills at least 175 people and injures 1,000.	Jean Renoir, 84, French-born film director best known for his classic films *The Grand Illusion* (1937) and *The Rules of the Game* (1939), dies in Beverly Hills, Calif.	Feb.
A *New York Times*-CBS News Poll finds Pres. Carter's public approval rating has risen from 37 percent to 42 percent because of his role in negotiating the Israeli-Egyptian peace treaty.	Both Egyptian Pres. Sadat and Israeli Premier Begin praise Pres. Carter's mediation and credit him with the major contribution toward achieving the peace pact between their countries.	The Energy Dept. announces easing gasoline price-control rules, increasing expected pump prices by some five cents a gallon in 1979.	A malfunction in the cooling system of a nuclear reactor at Three-Mile Island, near Harrisburg, Pa., leads to closing down of the reactor and escape of radiation into the air.	The *Washington Post* reports a survey finding a marked decline in the number of people who watch television.	March
Jane Byrne is the first woman to be elected mayor of Chicago with 82.5 percent of votes cast, beating late Mayor Richard J. Daley's record of 77.67 percent in 1975.	The U.S. announces it is withdrawing economic and military aid from Pakistan because that country is secretly constructing a uranium enrichment plant.	President Carter orders gradual decontrol of domestic oil prices to combat the worsening U.S. energy situation.	President Carter forms an independent commission to investigate the Three Mile Island accident.	Two films dealing with the Vietnam war — *Dear Hunter* and *Coming Home* — garner most of the major Academy Awards.	April
Sen. Edward Kennedy (D, Mass.) introduces a comprehensive national health insurance plan.	The Senate adopts a resolution introduced by Sen. Richard Schweiker (R, Pa.) to end economic sanctions against Rhodesia after formal installation of the newly-elected black government.	An Atlanta, Ga. federal grand jury indicts former OMB Dir. Bert Lance and three associates on charges that they conspired to obtain $20 million in bank loans for their own gain between 1970-78.	Over 65,000 protesters march peacefully against nuclear power in a Wash., D.C., demonstration that is the largest against nuclear power in the U.S. to date.	John McEnroe upsets Bjorn Borg of Sweden to win the World Championship Tennis title in Dallas, Tex....*Spectacular Bid* wins both the Kentucky Derby and the Preakness Stakes.	May
A Gallup Poll conducted over the past three days shows Pres. Carter's approval rating at a mere 29 percent of those interviewed.	The White House officially announces Pres. Carter's decision to approve full-scale development of the MX mobile intercontinental ballistic missile.	The gasoline shortage spreads throughout the U.S....Gasoline station closings are reported reaching 70 percent nationwide, with the Boston-Washington corridor hardest-hit.	Antinuclear rallies in the U.S., Spain, West Germany and France mark International Antinuclear Day.	*Spectacular Bid* loses the Belmont Stakes race to *Coastal*, thereby failing to win horse racing's Triple Crown...Actor John Wayne, 72, dies of cancer complications in Los Angeles, Calif.	June
Pres. Carter reportedly delivers a tart lecture to his Cabinet members about their unsatisfactory performance and asks for their resignations.	Testifying before the Senate For. Rel. Committee, Paul Nitze and Lt. Gen. Edward Rowny warn that the SALT II treaty would leave the U.S. in an inferior position to the U.S.S.R.	In a nationally televised speech, Pres. Carter proposes a new energy program that would cost some $140 billion over 10 years in an effort to reduce U.S. dependence on foreign oil.	Skylab, the unmanned 77-ton U.S. space station, enters the atmosphere and disintegrates over the Indian Ocean and Australia. No injuries are reported.	Arthur Fiedler, 84, conductor of the Boston Pops Orchestra for 50 years, dies of a heart ailment in Brookline, Mass.	July
The Senate confirms G. William Miller as secretary of the Treasury and Paul Volcker as chairman of the Federal Reserve.	Andrew Young resigns as U.S. ambassador to the U.N. following unauthorized direct talks with the PLO.	Pres. Carter takes the *Amtrak* Metroliner train from Washington to Baltimore to show his support for a strong mass transportation system.	An earthquake measuring 5.9 on the Richter scale hits San Francisco....Mt. Etna in Italy erupts....Two Soviet Cosmonauts return safely to Earth after spending a record 175 days in space.	Bolshoi Ballet dancer Alexander Godunov defects and is granted political asylum in the U.S....Pete Rose of the Philadelphia Phillies becomes the all-time leader in National League singles.	Aug.
In Cleveland, Ohio a school desegregation plan goes into effect climaxing a six-year court battle.	State Secy. Cyrus Vance meets with Soviet Amb. Anatoly Dobrynin in an effort to resolve the problem of the Soviet combat brigade in Cuba.	New York's Citibank raises its prime rate to a record 13.5 percent....Lee Iacocca and two of his former associates at Ford Motor Co. are named to the three top posts at Chrysler Corp.	Unmanned U.S. spacecraft Pioneer 11 flies past Saturn, gathering information on the giant planet.	The Right Rev. Robert Runcie is designated as Archbishop of Canterbury....Pope John Paul II begins a nine-day journey to Ireland and the U.S.	Sept.
Former UMW Pres. W.A. (Tony) Boyle is sentenced to life imprisonment for hiring killers to assassinate union rival Joseph Yablonski and his family.	Pope John Paul II visits Washington, D.C. and has a three-hour visit with Pres. Jimmy Carter....U.S. control of the Panama Canal Zone ends.	The Federal Reserve raises the discount rate from 11 percent to a record 12 percent....Chrysler Corp. and the UAW reach agreement on a new three-year contract.	The NRC fines Metropolitan Edison Co., operator of the Three Mile Island nuclear plant, $155,000 for serious weaknesses in the company's management and technical performance.	Humorist and author S.J. Perelman and French pianist and teacher Nadia Boulanger die.	Oct.
Sen. Howard Baker Jr. (R. Tenn.), Sen. Edward Kennedy (D. Mass.), California Gov. Edmund Brown, Jr., and former Calif. Gov. Ronald Reagan announce their candidacy for the presidency.	Thousands of protesters in Wash., D.C. rally to support the U.S. hostages in Iran, countering a demonstration by 900 Iranian students....Pres. Carter freezes all Iranian assets in the U.S.	Calif. Gov. Jerry Brown reimposes odd-even gasoline rationing....George Meany, pres. of the AFL-CIO, retires....U.S. commercial banks raise their prime rate to a record high of 15.7 percent.	An Air New Zealand DC-10 crashes in Antarctica, killing all 257 people aboard.	Cartoonist Al Capp, Broadway producer Jed Harris, composer Dimitri Tiomkin, actress Merle Oberon, Mamie Eisenhower and Zeppo Marx die.	Nov.
Pres. Carter officially declares that he is a candidate for reelection.	The U.S. lifts its ban on economic dealings with Zimbabwe Rhodesia....A powerful bomb explodes in the 11-story Soviet mission to the U.N. in N.Y.C., injuring at least six people.	David Rockefeller resigns as the chief executive officer of Chase Manhattan Bank.	Federal government files a $124.5 million suit against Occidental Petroleum Corp. over the dumping of hazardous wastes at Love Canal and three other sites in Niagara Falls, N.Y.	Film producer Darryl F. Zanuck, art collector Peggy Guggenheim, actress Joan Blondell, and archbishop Fulton J. Sheen die.	Dec.

F	G	H	I	J
Includes elections, federal-state relations, civil rights and liberties, crime, the judiciary, education, health care, poverty, urban affairs and population.	*Includes formation and debate of U.S. foreign and defense policies, veterans' affairs and defense spending. (Relations with specific foreign countries are usually found under the region concerned.)*	*Includes business, labor, agriculture, taxation, transportation, consumer affairs, monetary and fiscal policy, natural resources, and pollution.*	*Includes worldwide scientific, medical and technological developments, natural phenomena, U.S. weather, natural disasters, and accidents.*	*Includes the arts, religion, scholarship, communications media, sports, entertainments, fashions, fads and social life.*

	World Affairs	Europe	Africa & the Middle East	The Americas	Asia & the Pacific
Jan. 1	U.S., Chinese, and Egyptian representatives walk out of a public ceremony in Havana, Cuba when Pres. Fidel Castro excoriates each of their governments in an address celebrating the twentieth anniversary of the Cuban revolution.	Poland is moved from a not-free to a partly free category in a Freedom House report on world political freedom.	Ghana lifts its state of emergency, declared in November 1978, and ends a seven-year-old ban on political activities. . . . Transkei, Rhodesia, Sudan, and Iran are moved from a not-free to partly free country category in a Freedom House report on world political freedom. Upper Volta moves into the free nation category.	Freedom House survey moves Panama and Paraguay into the category of partly free country from a not-free country. It moves the Dominican Republic into the free-country category.	U.S. severs its ties with the Chinese Nationalist government on Taiwan. . . . Chinese govt. introduces a new system of transliteration called Pinyin for writing the Chinese language with the Roman alphabet. . . . In the Cambodian–Vietnamese conflict, Kampuchean United Front forces make their first victory statement of the year, claiming capture of the Mekong River town of Kratie.
Jan. 2		Italian Interior Ministry announces that kidnappings for ransom in the country declined to 42 in 1978 from the 1977 high of 76.	A draft constitution in preparation for a referendum among Rhodesia's 240,000 whites proposes that the country's name after elections for majority rule should be Zimbabwe Rhodesia instead of simply Zimbabwe, the name used by black nationalists.		Cambodian Deputy Premier Ieng Sary and Pres. Khieu Samphan appeal to the U.N. to condemn what they call Vietnamese and Soviet agression against Cambodia and to seek aid to counter the Vietnamese offensive.
Jan. 3	Gen. Alexander Haig Jr., supreme commander of NATO, announces that he will retire from both his NATO post and the U.S. Army at the end of June, giving no reason for his decision.	About 25,000 truck drivers in Scotland and the north of England strike in a wage dispute.	Iranian Premier-designate Shahpur Bakhtiar says he opposes sale of oil to Israel and South Africa. He also opposes the Shah's policy of guarding the security of the Persian Gulf, adopted from American policy.	Chilean govt. offers to restore normal labor union activities in the country, an apparent move to avert an international boycott of Chilean trade. . . . Bank of Canada raises its bankrate to 11.25 percent from 10.75 percent, the seventh increase since January 1978.	CP newspaper *Jenmin Jih Pao* strongly supports the right of the Chinese people to display wall posters to express their opinions. . . . Kampuchean United Front insurgents in Cambodia claim capturing three provincial capitals, putting them within 45 miles of Pnompenh.
Jan. 4		The funeral of Gen. Constantino Ortin Gil, the military governor of Madrid who was assassinated by the Basque ETA guerrilla group, turns into an antigovernment demonstration by right-wing military officers and civilian youths. . . . The government of Turkish Premier Bulent Ecevit survives a censure motion, brought for failing to halt political violence.	Shah of Iran signs a decree formally appointing Shahpur Bakhtiar premier. . . . Iran's opposition National Front issues a statement condemning Bakhtiar's agreement to form a government under the Shah.	Chile's inflation rate in 1978 is reported to have decreased to 30.3 percent, the lowest rate in 10 years.	Vietnamese and rebel Kampuchean United Front troops are reported pushing closer to Pnompenh and Kampong Som, Cambodia's only seaport. . . . Hu Yaopang, a close associate of Chinese Deputy Premier Teng Hsiao-ping, is reported being appointed CP secretary general and chief of the CP's propaganda department.
Jan. 5		Unemployment in West Germany is set at 993,000, the first time since 1974 when the figure has dropped below 1 million.	Iranian strikes in the oil industry and other sectors come to an end in response to appeals from opposition leaders.	Leftist guerrillas kill 55 government soldiers in two days of increased fighting in Nicaragua's northern mountain region.	U.S. officials report that China has massed troops and fighter planes on the border with Vietnam as Vietnamese forces press deeper inside Cambodia, which is China's ally. . . . Chinese Deputy Premier Teng Hsiao-ping says that China does not intend to send actual troops or military advisers to Cambodia.
Jan. 6	U.S., French, British and West German leaders conclude two days of summit talks in Guadeloupe with statements intended to relieve Soviet worries that the U.S.–Chinese rapprochement might lessen the Western nations' commitment to detente. . . . As the summit ends, British P.M. James Callaghan and West German Chancellor Helmut Schmidt specifically endorse the projected SALT accord.		As Iran's new Premier Shahpur Bakhtiar is installed, a crowd of 100,000 demonstrates against him in the holy city of Qom. . . . In his first official act as Iran's premier, Shahpur Bakhtiar ends censorship and eases martial law by reducing curfew hours.		
Jan. 7	China submits a statement to the U.N. Security Council condemning the invasion of Cambodia and accusing Vietnam of "towering crimes" and being the surrogate for the Soviet Union's expansion policy.	Soviet Union hails the capture of Pnompenh by Cambodian insurgents and Vietnamese troops.	Mobs riot in Teheran where troops open fire, reportedly killing one demonstrator and injuring a score more.		Combined force of Cambodian insurgents, the Kampuchean United Front, and Vietnamese soldiers capture Pnompenh, Cambodia's capital city.

A	B	C	D	E
Includes developments that affect more than one world region, international organizations and important meetings of major world leaders.	Includes all domestic and regional developments in Europe, including the Soviet Union, Turkey, Cyprus and Malta.	Includes all domestic and regional developments in Africa and the Middle East, including Iraq and Iran and excluding Cyprus, Turkey and Afghanistan.	Includes all domestic and regional developments in Latin America, the Caribbean and Canada.	Includes all domestic and regional developments in Asia and Pacific nations, extending from Afghanistan through all the Pacific Islands, except Hawaii.

U.S. Politics & Social Issues	U.S. Foreign Policy & Defense	U.S. Economy & Environment	Science, Technology & Nature	Culture, Leisure & Life Style	
Census Bureau reports that the U.S. population is nearly 220 million.		*Washington Star* concludes renegotiating its labor contracts and averts a threatened closing.	*Bulletin of the Atomic Scientist* says that 1978 events do not merit changing the time on the publication's doomsday clock, which has been set since 1974 at nine minutes to midnight — midnight standing for nuclear doomsday.	Alabama defeats Penn State, 14–7, in the Sugar Bowl, University of Southern California downs the University of Michigan, 17–10 in the Rose Bowl, Notre Dame nips the University of Houston, 35–34, in the Cotton Bowl, and Oklahoma beats Nebraska, 31–24, in the Orange Bowl.	Jan. 1
	Carter administration officials say that Pres. Carter has issued new orders to keep a U.S. naval task force from proceeding to Iranian waters, a move made to downplay the Iranian crisis.			UPI picks the University of Southern California as the national college football champion.	Jan. 2
	U.S. District Ct. Judge Barrington Parker, who will preside over the trial of three Cuban exiles charged in connection with the 1976 murder of former Chilean foreign minister Orlando Letelier when he was in Wash., D.C., receives a second threat against his life.	Conrad Hilton, 91, founder and chairman of Hilton Hotels Corp., dies of pneumonia in Santa Monica, Calif.... In final wage-price guidelines issued by the Carter administration, companies with net revenues of at least $250 million in the most recent fiscal year are required to submit formal plans detailing their compliance with the guidelines.	A report on a smallpox outbreak in 1978 at Birmingham University in Great Britain, which resulted in one death, charges that safety precautions were not observed in the university's laboratory where the virus was stored.	AP chooses the University of Alabama as national college football champion.... Guillermo Vilas and Chris O'Neill wins the men's and women's tennis singles titles respectively at the Australian Open in Melbourne.... AP and UPI's divergent choices for national college football champion create a storm of controversy in the sports world and renew calls for a playoff system to determine a national champion.	Jan. 3
The Ohio State Controlling Bd. approves an out-of-court settlement of the Kent State University (Ohio) civil liability case, agreeing to pay $600,000 to the parents of four students who died and to nine students who were injured in the 1970 shootings.	Acting Selective Service Dir. Robert Shuck estimates that it will cost $16–47 million annually to renew draft registration.	FCC authorizes ITT to provide domestic long-distance telephone service, mainly for business customers, to compete with AT&T and pave the way for widespread competition in the domestic telephone market.... SEC accuses Grumman Corp. and its former subsidiary, Gulfstream American Corp., of concealing more than $15 million in foreign payments to promote aircraft sales abroad.	A Johns Hopkins University study concludes that there is a definite link between use of the female hormone estrogen and uterine cancer.		Jan. 4
Dallas, Tex. police officials challenge the acoustics evidence that a second gunman fired at Pres. John Kennedy in 1963, but House Assassinations Committee investigators hold firm to that conclusion.		The Energy and Justice departments file suit against eight of the nation's largest oil companies, claiming that they had overcharged their customers for natural gas liquids by $1 billion.	Charles Masters of the U.S. Geological Survey reveals that geologists are revising their estimate of the amount of undiscovered oil in the U.S. to reflect significant new finds such as in the Green River Basin, which covers parts of Wyo., Utah, Mont., and Colorado.	Charles Mingus, 56, musician and composer of modern jazz, dies of a heart attack after suffering from Lou Gehrig's disease, in Cuernavaca, Mex.	Jan. 5
				East football all-stars edge the West, 29–24, in the Hula Bowl at Honolulu, Hawaii. The U.S. all-stars trip Team Canada, 34–14, in the second annual Can-Am Bowl at Tampa, Fla.	Jan. 6
	FBI Dir. William Webster reveals that he fears that the opening of U.S.–Chinese diplomatic relations will bring an influx of Communist Chinese spies into the U.S. under cover as students or diplomats.			Pittsburgh Steelers and Dallas Cowboys gain Super Bowl births with victories in their respective NFL conference championships.	Jan. 7

F	G	H	I	J
Includes elections, federal-state relations, civil rights and liberties, crime, the judiciary, education, health care, poverty, urban affairs and population.	*Includes formation and debate of U.S. foreign and defense policies, veterans' affairs and defense spending. (Relations with specific foreign countries are usually found under the region concerned.)*	*Includes business, labor, agriculture, taxation, transportation, consumer affairs, monetary and fiscal policy, natural resources, and pollution.*	*Includes worldwide scientific, medical and technological developments, natural phenomena, U.S. weather, natural disasters, and accidents.*	*Includes the arts, religion, scholarship, communications media, sports, entertainments, fashions, fads and social life.*

	World Affairs	Europe	Africa & the Middle East	The Americas	Asia & the Pacific
Jan. 8		Premier Giulio Andreotti nominates a slate of six men to take charge of Italy's principal state-controlled industrial companies.... Consumer prices in the nine EEC countries reportely rose 7.3 percent in 1978.		A N.Y.S. Supreme Ct. judge rules that Argentine banker David Graiver is dead and dismisses criminal charges against him of looting the American Bank & Trust Co., (N.Y.C.) of $40 million.	Insurgent Kampuchean United Front for National Salvation announces overthrowing Premier Pol Pot's govt. and replacing it by a People's Revolutionary Council of Cambodia, naming Heng Samrin president.
Jan. 9		*The New York Times* reports that Poland will keep its 1979 defense spending at the same level as in 1978, following Rumania's lead in rejecting Soviet demands for increased military spending by the Soviet bloc.	Tanzanian govt. signs an agreement with the U.S. to allow Peace Corps volunteers to return after a 10-year ban.		
Jan. 10		Disagreeing with the Soviet-bloc's line on Southeast Asia, Rumania denounces Vietnam for its intervention in Cambodia.	Bakhtiari tribe in southwest Iran, of which Premier Shahpur Bakhtiar belongs, throws its support to Ayatollah Khomeini, the exiled Islamic leader.	Over 10,000 opponents of Pres. Anastasio Somoza march in Managua to observe the first anniversary of the assassination of Pedro Joaquin Chamorro, the Nicaraguan opposition leader and newspaper editor.... Seven people are killed and dozens injured in riots opposing Jamaican P.M. Michael Manley's decision to raise gasoline prices by 13 cents to $1.99 a gallon.	Diplomatic sources in Peking disclose that Cambodian Premier Pol Pot is believed to still be in Cambodia.
Jan. 11	U.N. Security Council, convening at Cambodia's request, hears Prince Norodom Sihanouk, Cambodia's former head of state, present the Pol Pot govt.'s case against the Vietnamese invasion.	A state of emergency is declared in Northern Ireland, which has been particularly hard hit by truck and oil tanker-drivers' strikes.	Rhodesian P.M. Ian Smith tells a group of whites in the country that black rule is Rhodesia's only hope for ending the six-year-old guerrilla war.... State Secy. Cyrus Vance says that the Shah of Iran has decided to form a regency council in a few days and then "leave Iran on a vacation."	A Peru general strike is called off at the end of its second day because most workers, under intense pressure from the government, refuse to join.	Taiwan flatly rejects an offer by Deputy Premier Teng Hsiao-ping to allow Taiwan to retain its own government and armed forces in exchange for ceding sovereignty after unification with the Chinese mainland.
Jan. 12			Islamic leader Ayatollah Ruholla Khomeini says in a U.S. TV interview that he expects an Islamic state to be formed in Iran within a few days with himself as its head.		Vietnamese columns are said to have advanced as far west as Battambang, near the Cambodian–Thai border, with Cambodian govt. forces making their strongest stand in the west at Siem Reap, near the Angkor temple ruins.
Jan. 13		Jose Manuel Pagoaga, a leader of the hard-line faction of the Basque guerrilla separatist group ETA in Spain, is shot and wounded in the French town of St.-Jean-de-Luz in wake of Basque political terrorist attacks during the previous week.	The Iranian govt. announces formation of a nine-member regency council to carry out the duties of the Shah, who is leaving the country on a "vacation." ... Ayatollah Khomeini says that he has formed a Council of the Islamic Revolution, which he contends will pave the way for a transitional govt. to replace Premier Shahpur Bakhtiar. ... Palestinian guerrillas assault the Israeli town of Maalot, near the Lebanese border.		
Jan. 14					A group of 100–200 peasants from various parts of China arrive in Peking in an unsuccessful effort to present their grievances — demands for democracy, food, and work — to government officials.

A	B	C	D	E
Includes developments that affect more than one world region, international organizations and important meetings of major world leaders.	*Includes all domestic and regional developments in Europe, including the Soviet Union, Turkey, Cyprus and Malta.*	*Includes all domestic and regional developments in Africa and the Middle East, including Iraq and Iran and excluding Cyprus, Turkey and Afghanistan.*	*Includes all domestic and regional developments in Latin America, the Caribbean and Canada.*	*Includes all domestic and regional developments in Asia and Pacific nations, extending from Afghanistan through all the Pacific Islands, except Hawaii.*

U.S. Politics & Social Issues	U.S. Foreign Policy & Defense	U.S. Economy & Environment	Science, Technology & Nature	Culture, Leisure & Life Style	
		In his second inaugural speech in Sacramento, Calif., Gov. Edmund (Jerry) Brown Jr. says that the tax revolt is being heard, and that he will seek a U.S. constitutional amendment requiring that the federal budget be balanced.	*Washington Post* charges that the U.S. Public Health Service commissioned a study in 1965 and then apparently ignored and withheld its findings, which cited a definite link between excessive leukemia deaths among Utah residents and radioactive fallout from atomic bomb tests at the Nevada Proving Grounds.		Jan. 8
A three-judge panel in Wash., D.C. exempts the Socialist Workers Party from federal campaign contribution disclosure requirements after the party presents evidence that its members had been subjected to systematic harassment in the past and fears future harassment or reprisals. . . . Supreme Ct. rules, 8–1, that a Missouri law excusing women from jury duty solely on the basis of sex is illegal. . . . Supreme Ct. rules, 6–3, that a Pa. state law requiring doctors to try to preserve fetal life during abortions is illegal.	The trial of three Cuban exiles on charges stemming from the 1976 murder of Orlando Letelier opens in U.S. District Ct., Wash., D.C. The defendants are Guillermo Novo Sampol, his brother, Ignacio, and Alvin Ross Diaz.	American Express Co. offers to buy McGraw-Hill, Inc. for $830 million in cash or combined cash and stock. . . . Supreme Ct. rules, 8–1, that a judge's findings in a SEC suit against a corporation can be accepted without challenge in a private suit against the same corporation.	Federal regulatory agencies launch a drive to promote the use of cheaper generic drugs as opposed to more expensive brand name ones, saying the consumers could save as much as $4 million a year.		Jan. 9
	U.S. announces that it will send 12 advanced F-15 jets and about 300 members of the Air Force to Saudi Arabia for a short visit later in the month.	EPA proposes standards to limit soot emissions by diesel cars. GM, which is planning more diesel use to raise its products' fuel economy, calls the proposal unreasonable.		*Superman*, a movie based on the comic-strip hero, is the top-grossing film for the week. . . . Donald Graham succeeds his mother, Katharine Graham, as publisher of the *Washington Post*.	Jan. 10
A three-judge panel of the Fourth U.S. Circuit Ct. of Appeals overturns the conviction of former Md. Gov. Marvin Mandel (D) for political corruption and mail fraud, finding technical deficiencies in his trial.		Census Bureau survey finds U.S. home values have risen 118 percent, 1966–76.	U.S. Surgeon Gen. Julius Richmond issues a 1,200-page report that reaffirms and expands earlier warnings about the health dangers of cigarettes. The report concludes that women, industrial workers, and young people run special risks by smoking.	Charles Bradford is elected as the first black to head the 550,000-member Seventh-Day Adventist Church of North America.	Jan. 11
A White House aide attributes Pres. Carter's abrupt dismissal of Bella Abzug as co-chairman and member of his National Advisory Committee on Women to Abzug's attempt to lecture the President during the meeting on the duties and role of the committee.	In an open letter, over 170 retired U.S. generals and admirals warn Pres. Carter of what they see as an increasing Soviet challenge to the U.S.	CAB authorizes four airlines to offer East–West coast fares as low as $99 plus tax.	The worst blizzard to date since 1967 strikes the Midwest. . . . Two Concorde jetliners land at Dallas/Ft. Worth Airport, marking the first exclusively U.S. domestic flights of the Anglo–French supersonic transport.		Jan. 12
				Marjorie Lawrence, 71, Australian-born Wagnerian soprano who starred at the Metropolitan Opera from 1935 until stricken by infantile paralysis in 1941, dies of cardiac arrest in Little Rock, Ark.	Jan. 13
Pres. Carter calls for legislation to make Jan. 15, the birthday of the late civil-rights leader Martin Luther King Jr., a national holiday.			The world's third test-tube baby — the first boy — is born in Glasgow, Scotland.	John McEnroe downs Arthur Ashe, 6–7, 6–3, 7–5, to win the final of the Grand Prix Masters tennis tournament in Madison Square Garden, N.Y.C.	Jan. 14

F	G	H	I	J
Includes elections, federal-state relations, civil rights and liberties, crime, the judiciary, education, health care, poverty, urban affairs and population.	*Includes formation and debate of U.S. foreign and defense policies, veterans' affairs and defense spending. (Relations with specific foreign countries are usually found under the region concerned.)*	*Includes business, labor, agriculture, taxation, transportation, consumer affairs, monetary and fiscal policy, natural resources, and pollution.*	*Includes worldwide scientific, medical and technological developments, natural phenomena, U.S. weather, natural disasters, and accidents.*	*Includes the arts, religion, scholarship, communications media, sports, entertainments, fashions, fads and social life.*

	World Affairs	Europe	Africa & the Middle East	The Americas	Asia & the Pacific
Jan. 15	Soviet Union vetoes a U.N. Security Council resolution seeking the withdrawal of Vietnamese military forces from Cambodia.	Premier Giulio Andreotti's minority Christian Democratic govt. releases its economic recovery plan for 1979–81, calling for a 4.5 percent growth rate in 1979 and 4 percent in each of the next two years.	Israeli govt. announces plans to establish three new settlements on the West Bank, all military outposts. . . . An American, Martin Berkowitz, is found stabbed to death at his home in Kerman, Iran. A slogan scrawled on the wall says, "Go home to your country."		Cambodian govt. troops recapture the Gulf of Siam port of Kompong Som from Vietnamese soldiers, inflicting the first major defeat of the war on Hanoi's invading forces.
Jan. 16	U.S. Amb. to the U.N. Andrew Young suggests that the U.S. recognize the PLO's influence with the Palestinians and Arab countries.	French Premier Raymond Barre announces measures to create 11,600 new jobs. . . . British P.M. James Callaghan announces new wage proposals that would relax the government's incomes policy.	Shah Mohammed Riza Pahlevi leaves Iran ostensibly for a vacation abroad. Observers see the trip as the first move in a long and perhaps permanent exile. . . . Israeli gunboats shell a guerrilla base on the southern Lebanon coast in retaliation to a Palestinian assault two days before on Maalot.	A report by the Council for Canadian Unity concludes that, as a whole, Canadians are less interested in national unity than in economic issues. . . . Inter-American Regional Labor Organization, representing trade unions in 28 Western Hemisphere countries, decides to postpone indefinitely its planned trade boycott of Chile, Nicaragua, and Cuba.	
Jan. 17		Seventy percent of voters in a Greenland referendum approve home rule.			
Jan. 18		West German govt. announces it is abandoning its routine security checks for federal job applicants that have been in effect since 1973 to counter extremism and terrorist violence.	CIA reports closes a monitoring facility in Iran because of political turmoil there, but a second more important one is still functioning.	Mexican newspaper *Excelsior* reports that a Guatemala City death squad killed 18 people between Jan. 15–17.	Prince Norodom Sihanouk, former Cambodian head of state, says he will not return to his native land.
Jan. 19		Final figures for Soviet economic performance in 1978 show overall industrial production increased by 4.8 percent, a slower rate than the 5 percent growth rate that had been reported previously.	Israeli ground troops carry out one of their heaviest strikes inside Lebanon since their invasion in March 1978. The attack is a retaliation for a Jan. 18 bomb explosion in Jerusalem.	OAS admits Dominica as its twenty-sixth member. . . . Nicaraguan Pres. Anastasio Somoza announces that he will not accept a new compromise plan for a plebiscite to decide if he will stay in office.	South Korean Pres. Park Chung Hee proposes a meeting with North Korea to discuss prevention of another war on the Korean Peninsula and the reunification of the two countries. . . . Hong Kong authorities decide to admit temporarily 3,383 Vietnamese refugees from a boat that had been anchored in the Hong Kong harbor since Dec. 23, 1978.
Jan. 20			Iranian exiled Moslem leader Ayatollah Ruholla Khomeini announces definitive plans to return to Iran following massive countrywide demonstrations the previous day in support of his cause.	El Salvadoran soldiers attack a San Salvador parish hall and kill a Roman Catholic priest and four youths who were apparently holding a catechism class.	
Jan. 21			Two-day student riots in Bangui, the capital city of the Central African Empire, are reportedly quelled with the aid of soldiers from Zaire.	Archbishop Oscar Romero says at a requiem mass for a priest and four youths slain yesterday by El Salvadoran soldiers that the army's contention that its victims had been training as guerrillas is an outright lie.	China and Australia sign a three-year agreement for the sale of Australian wheat worth more than $1 billion.
Jan. 22		Municipal workers throughout Britain stage a one-day strike.	Sayed Jalaleddin Tehrani submits his resignation as head of Iran's regency council to Ayatollah Ruholla Khomeini at Khomeini's exile home near Paris.	*The New York Times* reports that the Inter-American Commission on Human Rights has approved a report accusing the El Salvadoran govt. of murdering political opponents, torturing citizens in secret jail cells, and systematically persecuting the Roman Catholic Church.	China pledges to support Pakistan against any foreign aggression and restates its allegiance to Pakistan in the Pakistani–Indian dispute over the state of Kashmir.

A	B	C	D	E
Includes developments that affect more than one world region, international organizations and important meetings of major world leaders.	Includes all domestic and regional developments in Europe, including the Soviet Union, Turkey, Cyprus and Malta.	Includes all domestic and regional developments in Africa and the Middle East, including Iraq and Iran and excluding Cyprus, Turkey and Afghanistan.	Includes all domestic and regional developments in Latin America, the Caribbean and Canada.	Includes all domestic and regional developments in Asia and Pacific nations, extending from Afghanistan through all the Pacific Islands, except Hawaii.

U.S. Politics & Social Issues	U.S. Foreign Policy & Defense	U.S. Economy & Environment	Science, Technology & Nature	Culture, Leisure & Life Style	
The ninety-sixth Congress convenes amid predictions that the session would see an emphasis on budget-balancing, tax cuts, and the politics of austerity.... Supreme Ct. rules, 5–4, that a lawyer does not have the constitutional right to represent a client in a state in which he is not licensed to practice.	U.S. businessmen are assured by the administration that U.S. diplomatic relations with China will not prevent the expansion of U.S. trade with Taiwan, which is estimated at $7.3 billion for 1978.			A 1978 survey of Reform Jewish rabbis shows an increase since 1973 in the number willing to perform marriages between gentiles and Jews.	Jan. 15
		Samuel Wolchok, 82, early union organizer and former CIO Retail, Wholesale and Department Store Union president (1937–48) whose organizing efforts produced the 1944 showdown with Sewell Avery of Montgomery Ward, dies in Miami Beach, Fla.	A study presented to the American Heart Assn.'s annual science writers' forum links smoking during and prior to pregnancy with a greater chance of disorders that kill the unborn and newborn.... A neurological institute report finds that pain-killers and anesthetics used during childbirth can cause subtle physical and mental impairment of newborn babies.		Jan. 16
National Urban League pres. Vernon Jordan Jr. warns that black Americans are on the brink of disaster because of the bleak federal budget picture and threatened recession.	Pres. Carter tells a news conference that he has invited former Pres. Richard Nixon to a state dinner at the White House to be held for Chinese Vice Premier Teng Hsiao-ping.	A report by the National Bank of Georgia charges that when he was chief executive of the bank, Bertram Lance had allowed Pres. Carter's family peanut business to regularly and substantially overdraw its account with the bank.	U.S. Geological Survey announces that a test well drilled in the Baltimore Canyon, 94 miles off Atlantic City, N.J., had a significant show of gas with a possibility of oil.		Jan. 17
	Michael Townley, the prosecution's key witness in the Orlando Letelier 1976 murder trial, describes how, as a secret police agent for Chile, he killed Letelier and Letelier's aide, Ronni Moffitt.	American Petroleum Institute issues figures showing that 1978 petroleum demand in the U.S. rose at the slowest rate since the recession years of 1974–75.		International Tennis Federation names Bjorn Borg of Sweden the top men's tennis player of 1978.	Jan. 18
Former Atty. Gen. John Mitchell is released on parole from a federal prison. He is the last of 25 people jailed in connection with the Watergate scandals to be freed.	Branches of the Armed Forces are reported considering removing words that could be considered sexist from their jargon, such as "she" in reference to a ship.		NRC says it has serious doubts about a 1975 study by Norman Rasmussen that concluded that a risk of a serious nuclear power plant accident is minimal.		Jan. 19
				Princeton and Rutgers universities agree to discontinue their varsity football rivalry after the 1980 game.	Jan. 20
				The Pittsburgh Steelers become the first team to win three Super Bowls with a 35–31 victory over the Dallas Cowboys.	Jan. 21
Social Security retirement, survivors, and disability outlays are budgeted to rise 13 percent to $115.2 billion in fiscal 1980.	Under cross-examination, Michael Townley, ex-American Chilean secret police agent, says he has no regrets about killing Orlando Letelier.	Pres. Carter sends Congress an austere budget designed primarily to restrain inflation by gently slowing the economy.			Jan. 22

F	G	H	I	J
Includes elections, federal-state relations, civil rights and liberties, crime, the judiciary, education, health care, poverty, urban affairs and population.	*Includes formation and debate of U.S. foreign and defense policies, veterans' affairs and defense spending. (Relations with specific foreign countries are usually found under the region concerned.)*	*Includes business, labor, agriculture, taxation, transportation, consumer affairs, monetary and fiscal policy, natural resources, and pollution.*	*Includes worldwide scientific, medical and technological developments, natural phenomena, U.S. weather, natural disasters, and accidents.*	*Includes the arts, religion, scholarship, communications media, sports, entertainments, fashions, fads and social life.*

	World Affairs	Europe	Africa & the Middle East	The Americas	Asia & the Pacific
Jan. 23		The British municipal workers' one-day strike is followed by a one-day railway engineers' strike, their third in eight days.	Shah Mohammed Riza Pahlevi of Iran postpones plans to visit the U.S., delaying his departure from Morocco in face of the uncertain political situation in Iran.		
Jan. 24			Ayatollah Ruholla Khomeini insists on returning to Iran and rejects an offer by Iranian Premier Shahpur Bakhtiar to resign and let the people decide in an election whether they want a monarchy or republic. . . . Iranian National Security Council orders all airports in the country closed until Jan. 28.		Charan Singh is sworn in as India's deputy prime minister for finance, ending a seven-month dispute within the ruling Janata Party stemming from charges that the government had failed to take action against former P.M. Indira Gandhi.
Jan. 25			Ayatollah Khomeini announces that he will arrive in Iran on Jan. 28 to fulfill his pledge to establish an Islamic republic.	After seven months of study, the Task Force on Canadian Unity issues a report calling upon Canadians to recognize Quebec's desire to preserve its cultural and linguistic distinctiveness.	Hsinhua reports that the Chinese govt. will return property seized from businessmen during the Cultural Revolution to enlist their support in the drive to modernize the country. . . . Heng Samrin, president of the People's Revolutionary Council of Cambodia, accuses leaders of Pol Pot's ousted govt. of genocide policies since they took control in April 1975.
Jan. 26		The New York Times reports that the Polish govt. has agreed to allow several Western banks to monitor its economic performance, the first time to date a Communist country has allowed capitalist institutions to have input in running its economy.	Defying an Iranian govt. ban on public rallies and angered over closure of the airports, over 100,000 supporters of Ayatollah Khomeini demonstrate, initiating one of the worst confrontations between demonstrators and the army.	Canadian P.M. Pierre Trudeau says the Canadian Unity Task Force is naive to think that provinces can be entrusted to guarantee minority language rights, maintaining that only the constitution could provide an effective guarantee of bilingual rights.	
Jan. 27	Enver Hoxha, leader of Albania's Labor (Communist) Party accuses China and the U.S. of plotting to take over the world.				
Jan. 28			PLO claims responsibility for a guerrilla bomb explosion in the Israeli coastal town of Natanya, which kills two people and wounds 34, breaking the Jan. 24 Israeli-Palestinian truce.		Bangkok sources report that Khmer Rouge troops loyal to Pol Pot's fallen government have had major successes against invading Vietnamese forces. . . . Chinese govt. confirms for the first time the death of former chief of state Liu Shao-chi.
Jan. 29	In a full dress welcoming ceremony at the White House, Chinese Deputy Premier Teng Hsiao-ping makes a speech in which he stresses the Soviet menace to world peace.	British truckers' strike that began in early January draws to a close after an arbitration panel recommends a 20.75 percent pay increase.			
Jan. 30			Rhodesian whites vote by an overwhelming margin to adopt a draft constitution bringing blacks into the government. . . . After a two-day meeting in Damascus, Syrian and Iraqi leaders postpone unification of their countries. . . . U.S. orders evacuation of all dependents and non-essential American citizens in Iran and urges all other U.S. citizens to leave in wake of new outbursts of anti-American demonstrations.		Vietnam is reported massing its troops along its border with China and deploying planes in the Hanoi area. . . . Meeting with 85 U.S. senators on Capitol Hill, Chinese Deputy Premier Teng Hsiao-ping speaks of possible Chinese military actions against Taiwan and Vietnam.
	A	B	C	D	E
	Includes developments that affect more than one world region, international organizations and important meetings of major world leaders.	Includes all domestic and regional developments in Europe, including the Soviet Union, Turkey, Cyprus and Malta.	Includes all domestic and regional developments in Africa and the Middle East, including Iraq and Iran and excluding Cyprus, Turkey and Afghanistan.	Includes all domestic and regional developments in Latin America, the Caribbean and Canada.	Includes all domestic and regional developments in Asia and Pacific nations, extending from Afghanistan through all the Pacific Islands, except Hawaii.

U.S. Politics & Social Issues	U.S. Foreign Policy & Defense	U.S. Economy & Environment	Science, Technology & Nature	Culture, Leisure & Life Style	
Pres. Carter delivers his State of the Union message, focusing his remarks on anticipated problems rather than on his administration's domestic and foreign policy accomplishments of the previous year.	In his State of the Union message, Pres. Carter makes Senate ratification of an expected SALT treaty with the Soviet Union his prime foreign policy goal in 1979.	In a departure from previous years, Pres. Carter sends his budget message to Capitol Hill before delivering his State of the Union message, which is largely devoted to defense of his budget proposals. . . . Rep. Al Ullman (D, Ore.) says that the House Ways and Means Committee will not consider Pres. Carter's new proposal to trim several Social Security benefits, including burial payments and teenage subsidies.		Actress Sophia Loren is acquitted in a Rome court of currency-smuggling charges, but her husband, producer Carlo Ponti, is found guilty.	Jan. 23
John Connally announces his candidacy for the 1980 Republican presidential nomination. . . . N.Y.C. reenters the public credit market for the first time in four years with the successful sale of $125 million in short-term notes.	House Permanent Select Committee on Intelligence blames the Carter administration and U.S. intelligence for failing to perceive the seriousness of the Iranian crisis and to predict that it could lead to the Shah's departure.	Labor Dept. reports that consumer prices rose 9 percent in 1978.	A new blizzard dumps another eight inches of snow on the same area in the Midwest stricken on January 12.	Soviet For. Min. Andrei Gromyko holds a two-hour meeting in the Vatican with Pope John Paul II on the international situation and the Roman Catholic Church's position in the U.S.S.R.	Jan. 24
	Defense Secy. Harold Brown tells the Senate Armed Services Committee that there is an uneasy balance of military power between the U.S. and the Soviet Union.	FCC votes to end Western Union's monopoly over domestic telegram service.			Jan. 25
Nelson Rockefeller, 70, former vice president of the U.S. and governor of N.Y. (1958–73) dies suddenly in N.Y.C. of cardiac arrest.	Pres. Carter defends his budget at a news conference, denying that he robbed the poor to provide for defense.		Union of Concerned Scientists, a group critical of nuclear power, recommends that 16 U.S. nuclear power plants should be shut down and repaired.	Rabbinical Council of America, an Orthodox rabbinical body, is reported differing with other Jewish groups by not endorsing the ERA.	Jan. 26
			Chicago, Ill. reports a winter accumulation to date of almost 80 inches of snow, within four inches of the city record.	Pope John Paul II opens the third meeting of the Latin American Espiscopal Conference (Roman Catholic) during a six-day visit to Mexico.	Jan. 27
	Alfred Atherton Jr. returns to Wash., D.C. after failing to revive stalled Israeli–Egyptian peace talks. Each country blames the other for the failure of his mission.				Jan. 28
				National Football Conference all-stars defeat their American Football Conference conterparts, 13–7, in the National Football League Pro Bowl.	Jan. 29
		Commerce Dept. reports that the U.S. experienced a record trade deficit in 1978 of $28.45 billion.			Jan. 30

F	G	H	I	J
Includes elections, federal-state relations, civil rights and liberties, crime, the judiciary, education, health care, poverty, urban affairs and population.	Includes formation and debate of U.S. foreign and defense policies, veterans' affairs and defense spending. (Relations with specific foreign countries are usually found under the region concerned.)	Includes business, labor, agriculture, taxation, transportation, consumer affairs, monetary and fiscal policy, natural resources, and pollution.	Includes worldwide scientific, medical and technological developments, natural phenomena, U.S. weather, natural disasters, and accidents.	Includes the arts, religion, scholarship, communications media, sports, entertainments, fashions, fads and social life.

	World Affairs	Europe	Africa & the Middle East	The Americas	Asia & the Pacific
Jan. 31		Italian Premier Giulio Andreotti submits the resignation of his Christian Democratic govt, a step expected in wake of the CP's withdrawal of support on Jan 26.		The Canadian dollar drops to 83.38 U.S. cents, the closest it has come to reaching the low of 82.47 U.S. cents it was worth in April 1933.	Pres. Carter and Chinese Deputy Premier Teng Hsiao-ping sign agreements in Wash., D.C. on cultural and scientific exchanges.
Feb. 1	Amnesty International, in a review of human-rights progress during 1978, cites violations in 110 countries, including the U.S.	Abdi Ipekci, editor of Turkey's influential newspaper *Milliyet*, is shot dead in Istanbul.	Ayatollah Ruholla Khomeini returns to Iran from France in a major bid to seize political power and establish an Islamic republic. . . . Premier Shahpur Bakhtiar pledges strong action to counter any attempt by Khomeini to proclaim a provisional Islamic govt.	El Salvador's ERP guerrillas claim credit for six bomb explosions in San Salvador and San Miguel, which kill at least 16 people and injure another 20.	Mitsuhiro Shimada, executive director of Nissho-Iwai Co. who was a key figure in an alleged payoff scandal involving the Grumman Corp., commits suicide. . . . Chinese deputy Premier Teng Hsiao-ping visits Atlanta, Ga. during his nine-day drip to the U.S. where he lays a wreath at the grave of civil-rights leader Dr. Martin Luther King Jr.
Feb. 2		A group of about 30 Soviet dissidents in Moscow announce that they will put up candidates to challenge the officially picked nominees in local elections for the Supreme Soviet. . . . British Home Secy. Merlyn Rees orders immigration officials to stop administering virginity tests to women from Pakistan, India, and Bangladesh entering Britain as financees of men living in Britain.	Eight laws prohibiting racial discrimination take effect in Rhodesia. . . . Acting Defense Min. Col. Chadli Benjedid is elected president of Algeria to succeed the late Houari Boumedienne.	Gen. Pedro Richter Prada is sworn in as Peru's prime minister, war minister, and army commander, replacing Gen. Oscar Molina Pallochia, who is retiring.	
Feb. 3	The U.S. and Britain indicate they have little hope for compromise between the Rhodesian interim govt. and the nationalist guerrillas.		Khomeini calls on the army to join his side for their own and the nation's good.		
Feb. 4	Soviet CP newspaper *Pravda* denounces the U.S. for permitting Chinese Deputy Premier Teng Hsiao-ping to attack the Soviet Union during his U.S. tour.	Yugoslav Pres. Tito, 86, is reported to have married pop singer Gertruda Munetic, 33.	U.S. Defense Dept. announces that Iran has canceled about $7 billion of the $11.56 billion of weapons it had ordered from the U.S. during the Shah's reign.		
Feb. 5			Ayatollah Ruholla Khomeini announces his appointment of Mehdi Bazargan as premier to head a proposed provisional government in Iran.		A previously secret Defense Intelligence Agency report suggests that some U.S. servicemen remained in Vietnam after the U.S. withdrawal in 1973 and collaborated with Communist forces. But it discounts claims that the Communists held back American prisoners of war after the general release in 1973.
Feb. 6		*Financial Times* reports an opinion poll that shows that 55 percent of the British electorate intends to vote Conservative, a dramatic shift in voting perferences from November 1978.	The U.S. restates its support for Iran's Bakhtiar govt. . . . Brig. Gen. Joachim Yhomby Opango voluntarily gives up his post as Congo's chief of state.	At the request of the provinces, P.M. Pierre Trudeau abandons a plan to change the status of Queen Elizabeth II as Canada's official head of state and make the governor general the official head of state instead. . . . Canada's 10 provincial premier fail to solve Canada's main constitutional problem: finding a formula for amending the constitution that would bypass the British Parliament.	Pres. Carter assures Thai Premier Kriangsak Chamanand of continued U.S. support and arms in view of fighting in neighboring Cambodia.
Feb. 7		International bankers are reported estimating that Turkey will need at least $10 billion in international aid over the next five years to maintain acceptable economic growth.	About 2,000 Lebanese doctors, both Moslem and Christian, stage a 24-hour strike to protest the general insecurity in the country and the particular dangers facing doctors.		

A	B	C	D	E
Includes developments that affect more than one world region, international organizations and important meetings of major world leaders.	*Includes all domestic and regional developments in Europe, including the Soviet Union, Turkey, Cyprus and Malta.*	*Includes all domestic and regional developments in Africa and the Middle East, including Iraq and Iran and excluding Cyprus, Turkey and Afghanistan.*	*Includes all domestic and regional developments in Latin America, the Caribbean and Canada.*	*Includes all domestic and regional developments in Asia and Pacific nations, extending from Afghanistan through all the Pacific Islands, except Hawaii.*

U.S. Politics & Social Issues	U.S. Foreign Policy & Defense	U.S. Economy & Environment	Science, Technology & Nature	Culture, Leisure & Life Style	
					Jan. 31
Patricia Hearst is released from federal prison in Pleasanton, Calif. under an executive clemency order signed by Pres. Carter.					**Feb. 1**
U.S. District Ct. Judge Frank M. Johnson Jr. places the Ala. prison system into receivership and names Gov. Forrest James Jr. as the court's agent with full powers to operate the prisons.				Aaron Douglas, 79, a leading painter during the Harlem Renaissance of the late 1920s, dies of a pulmonary embolism in Nashville, Tenn.... Sid Vicious, 21, a British punk-rock musician, dies of an apparent overdose of heroin in N.Y.	**Feb. 2**
A mistrial is declared in the bribery, conspiracy, and perjury trial of Rep. Daniel Flood (D, Pa.).	A large group of Republican Party officials declare that the total military and foreign policy relationship of the Soviet Union and the U.S. should be considered in discussions of SALT ratification.				**Feb. 3**
	Gallup Poll reports that Americans favor increased civil defense efforts in the U.S.	The Tidewater Conference of leading elected Republican Party officials rejects endorsement of a proposal to amend the Constitution to require a balanced federal budget.		The West squad beats the East team, 134–129, in the twenty-ninth annual NBA all-star game.	**Feb. 4**
Sara Jane Moore, convicted of attempting to kill Pres. Gerald Ford in 1975, is returned to prison after a failed escape attempt.		In a protest organized by the American Agriculture Movement, 3,000 farmers and their supporters snarl Wash., D.C. traffic in their demand for higher price supports for their products.			**Feb. 5**
		FRB reports that consumer credit rose a record $4.31 billion (seasonally adjusted) in December 1978, exceeding the previous May 1978 record.... White House says that Pres. Carter's appeal to the nation's 500 top companies to comply with his voluntary wage–price guidelines drew 207 pledges of support.			**Feb. 6**
Drug Enforcement Administration agents raid the Chicago Board Options Exchange just after the close of trading and arrest 10 people for allegedly selling and distributing cocaine on or near the floor of the exchange.	U.N. Amb. Andrew Young praises Ayatollah Khomeini and calls Islam "a vibrant cultural force in today's world," going further than any other Carter administration official in supporting the Iranian insurgency.	Energy Secy. James Schlesinger says that the Iranian oil crisis is prospectively more serious than the 1973 Arab oil embargo.	A coin found near Bar Harbor, Me. by an amateur archaeologist in 1961 is identified as a Norse penny minted between 1065 and 1080. ... Floods resulting from over a month of rain in east central Brazil leave 204 people dead and 200,000 homeless.		**Feb. 7**

F	G	H	I	J
Includes elections, federal-state relations, civil rights and liberties, crime, the judiciary, education, health care, poverty, urban affairs and population.	*Includes formation and debate of U.S. foreign and defense policies, veterans' affairs and defense spending. (Relations with specific foreign countries are usually found under the region concerned.)*	*Includes business, labor, agriculture, taxation, transportation, consumer affairs, monetary and fiscal policy, natural resources, and pollution.*	*Includes worldwide scientific, medical and technological developments, natural phenomena, U.S. weather, natural disasters, and accidents.*	*Includes the arts, religion, scholarship, communications media, sports, entertainments, fashions, fads and social life.*

	World Affairs	Europe	Africa & the Middle East	The Americas	Asia & the Pacific
Feb. 8	The price of gold soars and the value of the dollar tumbles as concern intensifies that the continued shutdown of Iran's oil fields will seriously affect the U.S. economy.	Italian CP demands a parliamentary investigation of the 1978 kidnap–murder of former Premier Aldo Moro, following press allegations that the kidnapping was organized by two M.P.s and a person linked to the Vatican.... Nicolai Tikhonov, 82, Soviet author and chairman of the Soviet Peace Committee, is reported dead in Moscow.	Iranian Premier Shahpur Bakhtiar announces he will accept a referendum to decide on a future government, and he dismisses plans to form an Islamic republic. ... In a generally peaceful anti-Iranian govt. demonstration, millions march in Teheran and in other major cities.... Col. Denis Sassou-Nguesso becomes Congo's new chief of state.	U.S. severs its military ties with Nicaragua and reduces economic aid to the Somoza regime to force it to negotiate with the revolutionary Sandinista movement.	
Feb. 9		Workers at British Leyland Ltd. auto plants reject a strike call by shop stewards.... British Rail says it will proceed with detailed plans for a one-track tunnel under the English Channel.	Troops of Iran's Imperial Guard loyal to the government attack civilian technicians and air force cadets who were demonstrating in support of Ayatollah Khomeini.		
Feb. 10	State Dept. reports an increasing awareness of human rights around the world in 1978, but says that torture and suppression of dissent remain widespread.		Responding to reports of fighting at Teheran's Air Force Base, thousands of pro-Khomeini civilians take to the streets and call for the overthrow of the government.		Pres. Muhammad Zia ul-Haq declares Islamic law to be the law of Pakistan.
Feb. 11			Armed revolutionary followers of Ayatollah Khomeini overthrow the government as the Iranian army declares its neutrality and withdraws its troops to their barracks. ... Iranian Premier Shahpur Bakhtiar resigns as Khomeini's appointed premier, Mehdi Bazargan, begins forming his own Cabinet.		
Feb. 12		British P.M. James Callaghan opens the Labor Party campaign for Scottish and Welsh devolution with an appearance at a Glasgow rally.... The Soviet Union extends formal recognition to the Khomeini govt. in Iran.	Loyal troops thwart an attempt to overthrow Chad's Pres. Felix Malloum.		U.S., Canada, and Australia agree to admit almost 2,000 Vietnamese refugees from the Philippines, most of whom had been aboard a ship anchored in Manila Bay since the end of December 1978.... Pakistan is believed to be the first country to officially recognize the new Iranian govt.
Feb. 13		EEC Energy Comr. Guido Brunner says that disruption of Iranian oil shipments is not a direct danger for EEC countries, but that a long-range shortage could adversely affect the economies of poor member-countries.	The Tudeh Party, Iran's CP, expresses support for Ayatollah Khomeini because he forced the Shah out of Iran.... Israeli For. Min. Moshe Dayan says that Israel cannot deny the PLO a role in a Middle East peace settlement.	During his visit to Canada, French Premier Raymond Barre refuses a suggestion by Quebec Premier Rene Levesque that he exclaim, "Long live free Quebec!"	
Feb. 14		British P.M. Callaghan unveils a 20-page concordant setting forth the economic goals that were negotiated by the government and leaders of the Trades Union Congress.	Leftist guerrillas storm the U.S. Embassy in Teheran and hold more than 100 employes, including Amb. William Sullivan, hostage for nearly two hours until they are freed by armed supporters of Khomeini.	Canadian govt. announces that it will borrow 100 billion yen (US$500 million) from Japan to support the value of the Canadian dollar.	U.S. Amb. Adolph Dubs is shot and killed in Kabul after being abducted by Afghan Moslem extremists.... The Pakistani Supreme Ct. grants former P.M. Zulfikar Ali Bhutto and four others a 10-day stay of execution to permit defense lawyers to file new appeals.... Hanoi claims that a Chinese battalion has moved deep into Vietnamese territory and appeals to all friendly countries to intervene.

A	B	C	D	E
Includes developments that affect more than one world region, international organizations and important meetings of major world leaders.	Includes all domestic and regional developments in Europe, including the Soviet Union, Turkey, Cyprus and Malta.	Includes all domestic and regional developments in Africa and the Middle East, including Iraq and Iran and excluding Cyprus, Turkey and Afghanistan.	Includes all domestic and regional developments in Latin America, the Caribbean and Canada.	Includes all domestic and regional developments in Asia and Pacific nations, extending from Afghanistan through all the Pacific Islands, except Hawaii.

U.S. Politics & Social Issues	U.S. Foreign Policy & Defense	U.S. Economy & Environment	Science, Technology & Nature	Culture, Leisure & Life Style	
Pres. Carter sends Congress his proposal for a Cabinet-level department of education, which does not contain several controversial programs that were in his 1978 request.				*Agatha*, a movie fictionalized account of the disappearance of British mystery writer Agatha Christie in 1926, starring Vanessa Redgrave and Dustin Hoffman, is released in N.Y.C.	**Feb. 8**
			Center for Disease Control says it fears that as many as 15 million people in the U.S. have undiagnosed tuberculosis.	An ancient Greek marble head valued at $150,000 is stolen from the Metropolitan Museum of Art, N.Y.C., the first major theft in the museum's 110-year history. . . . Literary critic and poet Allen Tate, 79, dies of emphysema in Nashville, Tenn. . . . Ireland's Eamonn Coghlan wins the prestigious Wanamaker Mile in 3 minutes, 55 seconds at the Millrose games.	**Feb. 9**
			A University of Southern California study reports that many blue-collar workers returning to work after being stricken by cancer face hostility from employers and coworkers.		**Feb. 10**
Immigration and Naturalization Service reports that record numbers of Mexicans and Central Americans have crossed the Rio Grande in January to seek jobs in the U.S.			Floods reportedly killed 125 Americans in 1978 and caused over $1 billion in damages.	Soviet national team defeats the National Hockey League All-Stars, 6–0, in the third and final game of the Challenge Cup series, giving the Soviets a winning edge of two games to one.	**Feb. 11**
		Speaking at a nationally televised news conference, Pres. Carter appeals for voluntary conservation of oil as the way to offset current reduction in oil supplies from Iran.			**Feb. 12**
HEW Secy. Joseph Califano says that the U.S. could save at least 10 percent on its projected $730-billion health bill in 1990 by adopting a national health insurance plan with strict cost controls.		Census Bureau data reveals that state tax collections in 50 states totaled $113.1 billion in fiscal 1978.		Israel Brodie, 83, first native-born chief rabbi of the United Hebrew Congregation of the British Commonwealth, dies in London. . . . Jean Renoir, 84, French-born film director best known for his classic films *The Grand Illusion* (1937) and *The Rules of the Game* (1939), dies in Beverly Hills, Calif.	**Feb. 13**
	A U.S. District Ct., Wash., D.C. jury delivers guilty verdicts against three Cuban exiles charged in connection with the 1976 murder of Orlando Letelier, the former Chilean ambassador to the U.S.		Utah officials claim that the AEC refused to investigate the 1953 .deaths of nearly 4,300 sheep following nuclear bomb tests in Nevada or to investigate the possibility of radiation damage to humans. . . . *New England Journal of Medicine* reports that a synthetic variation of vitamin A has been found effective in treating the most severe and scarring form of acne.	An international symposium on art security, meeting in Newark, Del., is told that the art world is suffering an unparalleled crime wave.	**Feb. 14**

F	G	H	I	J
Includes elections, federal-state relations, civil rights and liberties, crime, the judiciary, education, health care, poverty, urban affairs and population.	*Includes formation and debate of U.S. foreign and defense policies, veterans' affairs and defense spending. (Relations with specific foreign countries are usually found under the region concerned.)*	*Includes business, labor, agriculture, taxation, transportation, consumer affairs, monetary and fiscal policy, natural resources, and pollution.*	*Includes worldwide scientific, medical and technological developments, natural phenomena, U.S. weather, natural disasters, and accidents.*	*Includes the arts, religion, scholarship, communications media, sports, entertainments, fashions, fads and social life.*

	World Affairs	Europe	Africa & the Middle East	The Americas	Asia & the Pacific
Feb. 15		Nicole Alphand, 61, wife of Former French ambassador to the U.S., Herve Alphand, dies of cancer in Paris.	People's Fedayeen, a leftist guerrilla group, is seen posing serious opposition to the new Islamic regime of Ayatollah Ruhollah Khomeini by waging continuing attacks throughout Iran.... Abu Dhabi and Qatar raise the price of their light crude oils by 7–8 percent above officially determined OPEC levels in response to loss of Iranian oil exports because of workers' strikes.	Pres. Carter and Mexican Pres. Jose Lopez Portillo discuss the issue of illegal Mexican immigration into the U.S. and pledge future consultation on the problem.	Pres. Chiang Ching-kuo of Taiwan says that his government will create a new organization to continue U.S.–Taiwanese ties.
Feb. 16			Iranian radio reports that Gen. Nematollah Nassiri, former Savak head (Iranian secret police), has been executed.		
Feb. 17	Reports released by two congressional bodies indicate their doubts about NATO's effectiveness.		Iran's oil workers return to work in response to a plea by Ayatollah Khomeini's revolutionary council, but some remain on strike in sympathy with leftist groups.		China launches an invasion of Vietnam with 200,000–300,000 troops backed by planes and artillery striking along most of the 480-mile frontier.
Feb. 18	Soviet Union warns China to stop its invasion of Vietnam before it is too late.		Ayatollah Khomeini pledges to PLO leader Yasir Arafat, in a Teheran meeting, that his government will help the PLO's struggle against Israel after it consolidates its own strength.		Vietnam signs a Treaty of Peace and Friendship with the Cambodian govt. of Pres. Heng Samrin in Pnompenh.
Feb. 19	Rumania refuses to participate in the Soviet bloc's condemnation of the Chinese invasion of Vietnam. It does call on China to withdraw from Vietnam but also repeats earlier criticism of Vietnam for its troop presence in Cambodia.	Western Europe's major Communist parties denounce China for invading Vietnam.... Greek govt. publishes a law under which a person separated for more than six years from a spouse can obtain a divorce without the spouse's consent.	Israeli For. Min. Moshe Dayan expresses regret that Iran announced breaking diplomatic relations with Israel the previous day.... Chief Kaiser Dallwonga Matanzima is elected president of Transkei.... Ayatollah Khomeini warns that he considers the actions of the People's Fedayeen an uprising against the Islamic revolution in Iran.		
Feb. 20	Pres. Carter characterizes the U.S. relationship with the Soviet Union as a mixture of cooperation and competition and says he will seek both to conclude a SALT II agreement and to respond to any Soviet action that adversely affects U.S. interests.		Four more military offices are executed in Iran, apparently without the knowledge of Premier Mehdi Bazargan, leading to speculation of a possible rivalry between Bazargan and Khomeini.		Fighting intensifies between Vietnam and China, despite China's earlier statements that its drive into Vietnam is limited.
Feb. 21	U.N. Human Rights Commission adopts a resolution charging Israel with committing war crimes in occupied Arab territories.... China warns the Soviet Union not to support Vietnam militarily in wake of China's invasion of Vietnam.	Soviet Union sharply attacks Rumania for blaming both sides in the Chinese–Vietnamese conflict.	Libya follows Abu Dhabi and Qatar in raising its oil prices.... The People's Fedayeen says it will hold a rally to protest what it calls the growing gap between Khomeini and the Iranian people.	St. Lucia becomes fully independent from Great Britain.	China and Pol Pot govt. officials denounce the Cambodian–Vietnamese treaty signed in Pnompenh on Feb. 18.
Feb. 22		British Trade Min. John Smith announces that the government will write off the $320-million debt owed by the state-owned British Airways for five Concorde supersonic airlines.... Italian Pres. Sandro Pertini designates Ugo La Malfa, head of the small Republican Party, to form a new government in wake of Premier Giulio Andreotti's resignation on Jan. 31.	Rhodesian P.M. Smith says he will run in elections for the new 100-member biracial Parliament, an announcement that surprises many observers.		Reports from Bangkok say Khmer Rouge forces loyal to the fallen Cambodian govt. of Premier Pol Pot are effectively attacking troops of the central Pnompenh govt. and its Vietnamese allies.... Vietnam acknowledges that China has pushed 15 miles inside the border area up to Cao Bank, 110 miles northwest of Hanoi.

A	B	C	D	E
Includes developments that affect more than one world region, international organizations and important meetings of major world leaders.	Includes all domestic and regional developments in Europe, including the Soviet Union, Turkey, Cyprus and Malta.	Includes all domestic and regional developments in Africa and the Middle East, including Iraq and Iran and excluding Cyprus, Turkey and Afghanistan.	Includes all domestic and regional developments in Latin America, the Caribbean and Canada.	Includes all domestic and regional developments in Asia and Pacific nations, extending from Afghanistan through all the Pacific Islands, except Hawaii.

U.S. Politics & Social Issues	U.S. Foreign Policy & Defense	U.S. Economy & Environment	Science, Technology & Nature	Culture, Leisure & Life Style	
A federal study panel calls for changes in the Social Security System to eliminate discrimination against women in eligibility for benefits.		FRB reports that U.S. industrial production rose a seasonally adjusted .1 percent in January.	HEW Secy. Joseph Califano Jr. refuses to order an immediate ban on the popular painkiller Darvon manufactured by Eli Lilly & Co..		Feb. 15
		Commerce Dept. reports that Americans' personal income rose $7.8 billion or 4 percent in January to a seasonally adjusted $1.815-trillion annual rate.		Grammy Awards recipients include Billy Joel, the Bee Gees , Barry Manilow, Anne Murray, Al Jarreau, Willie Nelson, Dolly Parton, and Donna Summer.	Feb. 16
Angelo Sepe is arrested in N.Y.C. and charged by the FBI with robbery in the $5.8-million theft at the Lufthansa cargo terminal at Kennedy International Airport on Dec. 11, 1978.					Feb. 17
			A record snowstorm brings Washington, D.C. traffic, business, and Congress to a virtual standstill.		Feb. 18
	At the opening session of the AFL–CIO's Executive Council meeting, pres. George Meany criticizes Pres. Carter's foreign policy.	AFL–CIO economic policy paper, presented at its Executive Council meeting, warns that the U.S. is heading toward a recession, which can only be prevented by quick government action to control inflation.	Three little-known venereal diseases are seen posing a major health problem according to the Center for Disease Control –nongonococcal urethritis, herpes, and trichomoniasis.		Feb. 19
	In a major foreign policy speech, Pres. Carter states that the U.S. will not intervene directly in Iran or Southeast Asia.	AFL–CIO pres. George Meany tells reporters that he is thinking about retirement.	The Great Lakes are declared completely ice-clogged.		Feb. 20
U.S. District Judge Elmo Hunter upholds the right of the National Organization for Women (NOW) to undertake a convention boycott against states that have not ratified the ERA.			A volcanic eruption in central Java, Indonesia kills at least 175 people and injures 1,000.		Feb. 21
Senate votes, 78–16, to curtail tactics that had kept filibusters going after cloture was invoked. . . . Billie Sol Estes is indicted by a Dallas, Tex. federal grand jury on charges of fraud, tax evasion, and interstate transport of stolen property.	The New York Times reports a wave of CIA retirements and resignations.		A journal published by the AMA reports two new studies that find a strict vegetarian diet extremely risky for children.		Feb. 22

F	G	H	I	J
Includes elections, federal-state relations, civil rights and liberties, crime, the judiciary, education, health care, poverty, urban affairs and population.	Includes formation and debate of U.S. foreign and defense policies, veterans' affairs and defense spending. (Relations with specific foreign countries are usually found under the region concerned.)	Includes business, labor, agriculture, taxation, transportation, consumer affairs, monetary and fiscal policy, natural resources, and pollution.	Includes worldwide scientific, medical and technological developments, natural phenomena, U.S. weather, natural disasters, and accidents.	Includes the arts, religion, scholarship, communications media, sports, entertainments, fashions, fads and social life.

	World Affairs	Europe	Africa & the Middle East	The Americas	Asia & the Pacific
Feb. 23	U.N. Security Council convenes to consider ending the fighting in Vietnam as well as in Cambodia.	Greek govt. imposes a price freeze to try to stem increasing inflation.	A rally staged by the leftist-guerrilla People's Fedayeen at Teheran University draws over 50,000 Iranians, despite Ayatollah Khomeini's exhortations to ignore it.... The execution of Capt. Monir Taheri, charged with setting the August 1978 fire in an Abadan movie theater, is seen as an indication that Mehdi Bazargan has lost control to Khomeini forces.		
Feb. 24		During its annual conference, Ireland's Fianna Fail Party calls upon the government to resist pressures for large wage increases.	The Mujahedeen, an Islamic guerrilla group, supports demands by the People's Fedayeen for a role in the new Iranian govt.... Border fighting erupts between North and South Yemen, with both sides accusing the other of instigating the attacks.		
Feb. 25			Khomeini reports that former Iranian Premier Shahpur Bakhtiar has fled the country and appeals to "friends abroad" to find and help return him.	Sen Alberto Fuentes Mohr, leader of Guatemala's Authentic Revolutionary Party, is killed by a gunman in Guatemala City.	
Feb. 26	OPEC members Kuwait and Venezuela announce raising their oil prices by 9.35 percent and 15–18 percent respectively, in wake of increased oil demand tied to the political upheaval and consequent lessened oil production in Iran.	Appearing on TV, British P.M. James Callaghan rejects calling early elections, saying that the minority Labor Party govt. will remain in power until October if it possibly can.	Rhodesian warplanes penetrate Angolan territory for the first time to hit a camp housing guerrillas of Joshua Nkomo's Zimbabwe African People's Union (ZAPU).		Sanjay Gandhi, son of former P.M. Indira Gandhi, and former Indian Information Min. Vidya Charan Shukla are convicted for the theft and destruction of a film that was a political satire of the former prime minister and her rise to power.
Feb. 27	OPEC members Saudi Arabia and Iraq announce that they will not increase general oil prices during the first quarter of the year.		Iran's new revolutionary govt. says it will resume exports of crude oil on March 5.		Pres. Carter urges China to pull its troops out of Vietnam because the invasion runs risks that are unwarranted.... China reports that between Feb. 17–26 its troops have killed or wounded 17,000 Vietnamese and captured 1,600 prisoners.... Australian P.M. Malcolm Fraser says that the government's anti-inflation and economy rebuilding efforts are succeeding.
Feb. 28	On its sixth day of debate on the fighting in Vietnam and Cambodia, the U.N. Security Council finds itself blocked from acting because of the conflicting positions of China and the Soviet Union, both of which have veto power.... Gen. Bernard Rogers is accepted by European officials as the new supreme commander of NATO.	Striking French steelworkers, protesting major layoffs planned by the government as part of its effort to restructure the industry, raid the offices of the local employers' federation in Valenciennes.	Tanzanian-backed forces, determined to overthrow Ugandan Pres. Idi Amin, advance on Kampala.... Rhodesia's Parliament adjourns for the last time as a legislative body of the white minority government.		
March 1		Spain's ruling Union of the Democratic Center wins a solid victory in parliamentary elections.... Mario Tanassi, a member of the Italian Parliament and former defense minister, is convicted of corruption related to the Lockheed payments scandal.	Egyptian Pres. Sadat warns Islamic fundamentalists in Egypt that he will not tolerate religious interference in Egypt's political life.... Pres. Felix Malloum and Premier Hissene Habre, leaders of the opposing factions in Chad's civil war, accept a Nigerian offer to mediate.		Treasury Secy. W. Michael Blumenthal signs an agreement setting claims against China for U.S. property seized when the Communists took control in 1949.

A	B	C	D	E
Includes developments that affect more than one world region, international organizations and important meetings of major world leaders.	Includes all domestic and regional developments in Europe, including the Soviet Union, Turkey, Cyprus and Malta.	Includes all domestic and regional developments in Africa and the Middle East, including Iraq and Iran and excluding Cyprus, Turkey and Afghanistan.	Includes all domestic and regional developments in Latin America, the Caribbean and Canada.	Includes all domestic and regional developments in Asia and Pacific nations, extending from Afghanistan through all the Pacific Islands, except Hawaii.

U.S. Politics & Social Issues	U.S. Foreign Policy & Defense	U.S. Economy & Environment	Science, Technology & Nature	Culture, Leisure & Life Style	
					Feb. 23
Joshua Eilberg, a former congressman from Pennsylvania, pleads guilty to charges that he had illegally taken money for helping his former law firm gain a federal grant for a Philadelphia hospital. . . . HEW report shows that people ages 65 and over account for 29 percent of all public and private health spending in 1977 but represent only 11 percent of the population.					Feb. 24
Atty. Gen. Griffin Bell says he favors amending the Constitution to limit a president to a single six-year term.			Heinrich Focke, 88, German aviation pioneer, dies in Bremen, West Germany. . . . Soyuz 32 spacecraft, carrying two Soviet cosmonauts, is launched into orbit from the Baikonur space center.	Alban Berg's opera *Lulu* is presented for the first time in its original three acts at the Paris Opera.	Feb. 25
	Senate votes to confirm the nomination of Leonard Woodcock as U.S. ambassador to China.	Pres. Carter asks Congress for the power to order gasoline rationing, weekend gas station closings, and other mandatory conservation measures.	Soyuz 32 docks with the orbiting unmanned Salyut 6 space station.	N.J. Casino Control Commission votes unanimously to grant Resorts International Hotel Inc. a permanent license to run its Atlantic City gambling casino. . . . *The New York Times* reports that U.S. Christian groups are beginning to lobby on behalf of Christians who want to emigrate from the Soviet Union.	Feb. 26
Jane Byrne is the upset winner over Mayor Michael Bilandic in Chicago's Democratic mayoral primary, the first defeat for an incumbent Chicago mayor since 1955.	Pres. Carter defends his conduct of foreign policy as "an exercise of prudence."	Supreme Ct. rules, 5–4, that health insurers arrangements with pharmacies to provide drugs to subscribers for set fees are subject to federal antitrust law.		A New Orleans police strike dims Mardi Gras celebrations, with much of the pageantry taking place in the suburbs. . . . The Italian govt. is reported spending $550,000 to restore Leonardo da Vinci's masterpiece, *The Last Supper*.	Feb. 27
		Commerce Dept. reports that the U.S. balance of trade was in deficit by a seasonally adjusted $3.1 billion in January.			Feb. 28
House overwhelmingly rejects an attempt to expel Rep. Charles Diggs Jr. (D, Mich.) from Congress because he is a convicted felon.		Commerce Dept. reports that the government's composite index of leading economic indicators declined 1.2 percent in January, the steepest decline since January 1974 when the economy was entering a severe recession.	A group of 2,400 U.S. scientists pledges to break contacts with Soviet colleagues to protest the imprisonment of dissident Soviet physicist Yuri Orlov and mathematician Anatoly Shcharansky.	*Washington Post* reports a survey finding a marked decline in the number of people who watch television, a reversal of 1960 and 1970 poll findings that TV viewing was increasing.	March 1

F	G	H	I	J
Includes elections, federal-state relations, civil rights and liberties, crime, the judiciary, education, health care, poverty, urban affairs and population.	*Includes formation and debate of U.S. foreign and defense policies, veterans' affairs and defense spending. (Relations with specific foreign countries are usually found under the region concerned.)*	*Includes business, labor, agriculture, taxation, transportation, consumer affairs, monetary and fiscal policy, natural resources, and pollution.*	*Includes worldwide scientific, medical and technological developments, natural phenomena, U.S. weather, natural disasters, and accidents.*	*Includes the arts, religion, scholarship, communications media, sports, entertainments, fashions, fads and social life.*

	World Affairs	Europe	Africa & the Middle East	The Americas	Asia & the Pacific
March 2	Twenty industrial nations in the International Energy Agency (IEA) agree in Paris to reduce their collective 1979 oil demand by 5 percent.... Soviet Pres. and CP leader Leonid Brezhnev calls China the most serious threat to world peace.... Vietnam rejects a Chinese peace move, charging that it is a ruse to cover up an intensification of the war.				
March 3			Israeli Premier Begin meets with Pres. Carter in Washington to discuss a compromise U.S. proposal that modifies language linking the Israeli–Egyptian peace accord with other agreements reached at Camp David on Palestinian self-rule.	Pres. Carter assures P.M. Pierre Trudeau that the U.S. is committed to constructing the Alcan pipeline, which would bring Alaskan natural gas to the lower U.S. through Canadian territory.	
March 4		Former Pres. Nikolai Podgorny's political career ends in the U.S.S.R. with his exclusion from the newly elected Supreme Soviet (parliament).... Britain signs a $14-billion trade pact with China.	Iran severs diplomatic relations with South Africa, citing South Africa's apartheid policy.		Vietnam denies that the Chinese have taken Lang Son.
March 5	South African govt. rejects a U.N. plan for a Namibian cease-fire.	Swiss govt. rejects an Iranian request to freeze Swiss-held assets of the Shah and his family. ... Ursel Lorenzen, a secretary at NATO's Brussels headquarters, defects to East Germany with a number of secret documents.	Iran resumes oil exports, ending a 69-day interruption caused by the country's political turmoil.... In a display of support for Saudi Arabia, threatened by the fighting between North and South Yemen, the U.S. dispatches a naval task force to the Arabian Sea.		China announces it is withdrawing its forces from Vietnam after having attained the goals of its invasion.
March 6		Soviet trade with the U.S. is reported totaling a record $2.8 billion in 1978.	North and South Yemen approve an Arab League peace plan, but their actual combat intensifies past the cease-fire deadline with South Yemenese forces reported advancing 30 miles into North Yemen.	Virgin Islands voters reject a proposed constitution that would have substantially increased their self-government.	
March 7		French Pres. Valery Giscard d'Estaing says that his country is withdrawing its objections to the European Monetary System after EEC officials agreed to a compromise plan on agricultural prices.... Italian Pres. Sandro Pertini asks Giulio Andreotti to try to form a new government.	White miners strike across South Africa to protest abolishing segregation in skilled jobs.	Guyanese Supreme Ct. drops charges against Larry Layton, accused of murdering Rep. Leo Ryan (D, Calif.) and four other people who visited the Jonestown commune in Guyana in November 1978.	A Hanoi broadcast claims that Chinese troops are plundering, wantonly shelling, and looting in villages around Lang Son and Cao Bang.
March 8		French govt.-controlled steel industry halts its controversial reorganization plan following two days of demonstrations and riots against the plan by steelworkers who fear the loss of 21,000 jobs.	Pres. Carter arrives in Cairo and confers with Egyptian Pres. Anwar Sadat in a renewed U.S. effort to achieve an Israeli–Egyptian peace agreement.		Australian govt. introduces legislation to strengthen the country's security organization, giving it new authority to wiretap, intercept mail, and enter and search buildings.
March 9					

A	B	C	D	E
Includes developments that affect more than one world region, international organizations and important meetings of major world leaders.	Includes all domestic and regional developments in Europe, including the Soviet Union, Turkey, Cyprus and Malta.	Includes all domestic and regional developments in Africa and the Middle East, including Iraq and Iran and excluding Cyprus, Turkey and Afghanistan.	Includes all domestic and regional developments in Latin America, the Caribbean and Canada.	Includes all domestic and regional developments in Asia and Pacific nations, extending from Afghanistan through all the Pacific Islands, except Hawaii.

U.S. Politics & Social Issues	U.S. Foreign Policy & Defense	U.S. Economy & Environment	Science, Technology & Nature	Culture, Leisure & Life Style	
	Defense Dept. expresses concern about the fate of U.S. secret mechanical and maintenance manuals for F-14 jet fighters and for the Phoenix missile system in Iran.	Energy Dept. announces easing gasoline price-control rules.	National Academy of Sciences recommends significant congressional revision of U.S. food-safety laws, including elimination of automatic bans on any substance found to cause cancer in animals or humans.		March 2
			The New York Times reports a National Academy of Sciences recommendation to Congress that a proposed ban on saccharin be modified to keep it on the market but with greater restrictions.		March 3
Gallup Poll of Republicans' choices for their 1980 presidential nominee places Ronald Reagan of Calif. first, former Pres. Gerald Ford second, John Connally third, and Sen. Howard Baker Jr. fourth.		New Orleans police strike collapses unexpectedly as most of the force returns to work because of personal economic hardship.			March 4
Supreme Ct. rules, 6–3, that state laws requiring husbands but not divorced wives to pay alimony are unconstitutional.			Voyager I spacecraft makes its closest approach to Jupiter after a journey taking over a year, amassing sharp photographs of Jupiter and a number of its moons.		March 5
Pres. Carter opens an intense lobbying campaign for his hospital cost-control bill.					March 6
		GAO warns that higher oil prices are potentially more damaging to the U.S. economy that the actual supply reduction.... FRB reports that the U.S. govt. sold a record $6.86 billion in foreign currencies to defend the sagging U.S. dollar between Nov. 1, 1978 and Jan. 31, 1979.	Voyager I scientists announce finding a ring of dark rock particles around Jupiter, showing up as a long fuzzy streak on a photograph taken with an 11-minute exposure.	Jean Renoir bequeaths one of his father's paintings, The Hunter to the Los Angeles County Museum of Art. His father was the French Impressionist Pierre Auguste Renoir.	March 7
Atty. Gen. Griffin Bell announces a crackdown on visa policies that allow aliens to enter the U.S. under a false student status.		Labor Dept. reports that the February unemployment rate declined to a seasonally adjusted 5.7 percent of the work force.	South Burlington, Vt. firm sends recall letters to purchasers of Laetrile, the controversial anticancer substance, after a shipment was found to contain pyrogens, which are fever-causing chemicals.		March 8
	Milwuakee, Wis. District Ct. judge issues a temporary restraining order barring the Progressive, a Madison, Wis.-based monthly magazine, from publishing an article by Howard Morland that details the workings of a hydrogen bomb on grounds that the country's national security would be endangered.		WHO report ranks alcoholism and alcohol-related problems among the world's major health concerns, threatening to impede Third World economic development and overburden most countries' health services.		March 9

F	G	H	I	J
Includes elections, federal-state relations, civil rights and liberties, crime, the judiciary, education, health care, poverty, urban affairs and population.	Includes formation and debate of U.S. foreign and defense policies, veterans' affairs and defense spending. (Relations with specific foreign countries are usually found under the region concerned.)	Includes business, labor, agriculture, taxation, transportation, consumer affairs, monetary and fiscal policy, natural resources, and pollution.	Includes worldwide scientific, medical and technological developments, natural phenomena, U.S. weather, natural disasters, and accidents.	Includes the arts, religion, scholarship, communications media, sports, entertainments, fashions, fads and social life.

	World Affairs	Europe	Africa & the Middle East	The Americas	Asia & the Pacific
March 10			Pres. Carter addresses the Egyptian Parliament, the first U.S. President to do so. . . . Fifteen thousand Iranian women stage a three-hour sit-in to protest actions by the Khomeini govt. requiring that they wear Moslem-dictated clothing and abrogating the family protection law, which gives husbands certain arbitrary rights.		
March 11		A Protestant Belfast police surgeon, Robert Irwin, charges that prisoners in Northern Ireland have been beaten or subjected to other forms of brutality.			
March 12			Pres. Carter attends a Knesset session where both left- and right-wing members sharply criticize U.S. policy and denounce Israeli Premier Begin for submitting to U.S. pressure.	Luis Herrera Campins, is inaugurated president of Venezuela, promising to lead an austere administration that will emphasize education and agriculture.	
March 13		West German federal prosecutor's office reports that East German espionage agents have infiltrated the upper ranks of the opposition Christian Democratic Union. . . . EEC summit inaugurates the European Monetary System, which links all EEC-member currencies except Britain's.	PLO leader Yasir Arafat calls for an oil embargo against Egypt if it signs a peace treaty with Israel. . . . Eleven Iranian generals are executed in Teheran and two others in the provinces.	Grenada's P.M. Eric Gairy is overthrown in a virtually bloodless coup by the opposition New Jewel Movement.	
March 14		Red Brigades terrorists wound Giuliano Farina, a Fiat executive in Turin, Italy, after chaining him to his house gate.	Israeli Cabinet approves, 15-0, remaining proposals that had blocked an agreement in the Egyptian–Israeli peace treaty.		Laos charges that Chinese troops have moved two to three miles inside Laos. . . . Indian P.M. Morarji Desai and Soviet Premier Kosygin sign a pact for trade, technological, and scientific cooperation.
March 15	Soviet CP newspaper *Pravda* claims that the U.S. role in promoting an Egyptian–Israeli peace treaty is a way to extend U.S. military and political influence in the Middle East following the loss of its foothold in Iran.		The Egyptian Cabinet approves the peace treaty with Israel.	Gen. Joao Baptista de Figueiredo is inaugurated president of Brazil, pledging to democratize the country's political system.	China announces complete withdrawal of its forces from Vietnam.
March 16	Soviet Union vetoes a U.N. Security Council resolution calling for an end to Vietnam's invasion of Cambodia and China's military action in Vietnam.	Turkish Premier Bulent Ecevit announces a comprehensive economic-rescue plan.	Chad's Pres. Felix Malloum and Premier Hissene Habre sign a pact ending the country's civil war and replacing the current government with a coalition composed of Halloum, Habre, and the Moslem rebels.	Former Pres. Hugo Banzer Suarez, overthrown less than a year ago by a military coup, returns from self-imposed exile in Argentina to Bolivia where he says he will lead nationalist forces in upcoming July 1 elections.	

A	B	C	D	E
Includes developments that affect more than one world region, international organizations and important meetings of major world leaders.	Includes all domestic and regional developments in Europe, including the Soviet Union, Turkey, Cyprus and Malta.	Includes all domestic and regional developments in Africa and the Middle East, including Iraq and Iran and excluding Cyprus, Turkey and Afghanistan.	Includes all domestic and regional developments in Latin America, the Caribbean and Canada.	Includes all domestic and regional developments in Asia and Pacific nations, extending from Afghanistan through all the Pacific Islands, except Hawaii.

U.S. Politics & Social Issues	U.S. Foreign Policy & Defense	U.S. Economy & Environment	Science, Technology & Nature	Culture, Leisure & Life Style	
		GAO suggests that the federal government use commercial credit-collecting firms to collect outstanding loans, noting that in 1977 a total $118 billion was owed in unpaid student loans, benefits overpayments, royalties, and goods and services.			March 10
		Washington Post quotes Jimmy Hayes, a bonded warehouseman for Pres. Carter's family peanut business, as saying that he and the President's brother, Billy Carter, had repeatedly altered records and pledged the same collateral twice in 1976 in an effort to conceal a $500,000 payments deficit on a National Bank of Georgia loan.		Larry Nelson wins the Inverrary Classic at Lauderhill, Fla.	March 11
Sen. Lowell Weicker Jr. (Conn.) announces his candidacy for the Republican presidential nomination.		Jimmy Hayes tells reporters he disputes the *Washington Post*'s account of his alleged statements about Billy Carter's financial dealings.... Energy Secy. James Schlesinger reports that U.S. oil consumption has been at a record level in the previous weeks.	An estimated 40,000 Spaniards, many wearing gas masks, march to central Barcelona to protest a plan by the Spanish govt. to build three nuclear plants.		March 12
		Standard Oil Co. of Ohio announces abandoning plans to build a $1-billion pipeline to pump Alaskan crude oil from Long Beach, Calif. to Midland, Texas.	NRC orders the closing of five East Coast nuclear power plants because they were built with insufficient protection against damage from earthquakes.... National Cancer Institute announces delaying Laetrile experimentation on humans with untreatable tumors because the FDA has not responded to its request for permission.	A number of foreign Christian groups reportedly have been active in smuggling Bibles into the Soviet Union.	March 13
	Pres. Carter says in Washington that all of the outstanding issues between Egypt and Israel have now been successfully resolved.	Henry Ford 2nd says he plans to retire as chairman of the Ford Motor Co. by the end of the year.		A court-ordered auction of Peoples Temple property in San Francisco, Calif. attracts over 600 people and unexpectedly heavy bidding. It is sold for $300,000 to a South Korean businessman.... Christopher Nixon Cox, first child of former Pres. Richard Nixon's daughter Patricia and Edward Finch Cox, is born in N.Y.C.	March 14
		Chicago Bd. of Trade speculators are charged with trying to corner the futures market for March delivery of red soft wheat.		Pope John Paul II presents his first encyclical, which advocates priestly celibacy, ignores the issues of ordination of women and abortion, and proclaims the church's role in protecting human freedom and dignity.	March 15
				The China Syndrome, a movie about a woman investigative TV reporter who joins forces with the chief engineer of a nuclear power plant to investigate safety violations that could result in a meltdown, opens in N.Y. It stars Jane Fonda, Jack Lemmon, and Michael Douglas.	March 16

F	G	H	I	J
Includes elections, federal-state relations, civil rights and liberties, crime, the judiciary, education, health care, poverty, urban affairs and population.	Includes formation and debate of U.S. foreign and defense policies, veterans' affairs and defense spending. (Relations with specific foreign countries are usually found under the region concerned.)	Includes business, labor, agriculture, taxation, transportation, consumer affairs, monetary and fiscal policy, natural resources, and pollution.	Includes worldwide scientific, medical and technological developments, natural phenomena, U.S. weather, natural disasters, and accidents.	Includes the arts, religion, scholarship, communications media, sports, entertainments, fashions, fads and social life.

	World Affairs	Europe	Africa & the Middle East	The Americas	Asia & the Pacific
March 17			King Hussein of Jordan and PLO leader Yasir Arafat are seen moving closer to reconciliation when they declare jointly against the Egyptian–Israeli peace treaty.... A cease-fire becomes effective in the North-South Yemen border war, supervised by an Arab League border patrol.		Vietnam offers to negotiate for normalized relations with China, contingent on Chinese troop withdrawal from Vietnamese territory.
March 18			Israeli National Religious Party threatens to resign from the ruling Likud coalition if Premier Begin does not accept its demand for continued Israeli control of the West Bank and Gaza Strip.		Afghan radio charges that 7,000 Iranian troops in the guise of returning refugees crossed the border into western Afghanistan during February, attempting to undercut the Kabul govt.... Former Pres. Nixon's justification for the 1970 U.S. invasion of Cambodia is reportedly confirmed by release of a document by deposed Cambodian leader *Pol Pot*, which states that the entire Communist military operation in South Vietnam was based in Cambodia at that time.
March 19		Bulgaria's official news agency announces that doctors and nurses are forbidden to carry cigarettes in Bulgarian hospitals as part of a government antismoking campaign.	Israeli Cabinet — with Agriculture Min. Ariel Sharon and Transport Min. Chaim Landau dissenting — endorses the peace pact with Egypt.		Hanoi radio again charges that Chinese troops are remaining in Vietnamese territory, despite Peking's claim to have withdrawn all forces. The claim is substantiated by Western observers in Thailand.
March 20	U.N. Economic Commission for Europe reports the total Soviet–Soviet Bloc debt to the West will be $47 billion by the end of 1978.... An UNCTAD agreement establishes a $750-million fund for the stabilization of raw materials prices.	Irish workers hold a 24-hour strike to protest the country's tax system.	France announces it will withdraw all 2,500 of its troops from Chad as a result of the agreement between Chad's government and Moslem rebels.		
March 21		Italian Pres. Sandro Pertini swears in a new government formed by acting premier Guilio Andreotti, which includes Social Democratic and Republican members as well as Andreotti's own Christian Democrats.	Fighting continues in the northwestern Iranian city of Sanandaj between government forces and Kurdish tribesman who began their rebellion on March 18 to demand greater autonomy.		
March 22	U.N. Security Council approves, 12–0, a Jordanian-sponsored resolution to establish a three-member commission to probe Israeli settlements in occupied Arab territories.	British Amb. to the Netherlands, Richard Sykes, is killed by two gunmen as he leaves his home in The Hague.	Israeli Knesset, 95–18, approves the proposed peace treaty with Egypt.	Nine days after the abrupt overthrow of P.M. Eric Gairy, the Carter administration recognizes the New Jewel Movement in Grenada.... Manuel Colom Argueta, leader of Guatemala's Revolutionary United Front, is murdered by unknown gunmen.	Reports confirm increased fighting in Afghanistan, with the rebels' chief goal being to encourage desertions from the Afghan army.
March 23	U.S. warns the Soviet Union against providing military aid to Afghanistan in its struggle with Moslem rebels and tribal dissidents.	Riots, violence, and vandalism erupt as tens of thousands of demonstrators march through Paris to protest rising unemployment and French govt.-backed plans for steel industry layoffs.	Pres. Carter says that the U.S. wants direct relations with Palestinians living in Israeli-occupied lands but acknowledges the problems of dealing with the PLO.		
March 24					Over 1,000 Laotian troops are reported joining an estimated 100,000 Vietnamese soldiers in Cambodia battling Khmer Rouge forces of the deposed *Pol Pot* govt.

A	B	C	D	E
Includes developments that affect more than one world region, international organizations and important meetings of major world leaders.	Includes all domestic and regional developments in Europe, including the Soviet Union, Turkey, Cyprus and Malta.	Includes all domestic and regional developments in Africa and the Middle East, including Iraq and Iran and excluding Cyprus, Turkey and Afghanistan.	Includes all domestic and regional developments in Latin America, the Caribbean and Canada.	Includes all domestic and regional developments in Asia and Pacific nations, extending from Afghanistan through all the Pacific Islands, except Hawaii.

U.S. Politics & Social Issues	U.S. Foreign Policy & Defense	U.S. Economy & Environment	Science, Technology & Nature	Culture, Leisure & Life Style	
				Linda Fratianne of Calif. regains the women's figure skating crown in world championship competition held in Vienna, Austria.	March 17
					March 18
Minn. and Mass, ratify a proposed constitutional amendment giving the District of Columbia full voting representation in Congress.... House of Representatives allows for the first time live TV coverage of routine sessions.		Federal grand jury in N.Y.C. indicts Italian financier Michele Sindona on 99 counts of criminal fraud relating to the collapse of the Franklin National Bank, N.Y.	Blue Cross–Blue Shield survey shows 30 percent of surgical cases since 1976 have not been confirmed by a second opinion.		March 19
Supreme Ct. rules, 7–2, that grand jury testimony given under an immunity grant cannot be used to discredit a witness if he becomes a defendant in a criminal trial.		The White House is reported angered by the sharp rise in corporate after-tax profits in the fourth quarter of 1978 — a seasonally adjusted 9.6 percent — in face of October–December implementation of Pres. Carter's voluntary wage–price guidelines.		*The New York Times* reports that about 500 Chinese attended a Peking showing of French designer Pierre Cardin's collection of women's and men's fashions.	March 20
	House Ethics Committee decides that there is no evidence to warrant an investigation into South African former Information Dept. head, Eschel Rhoodie's, charges that U.S. congressmen were bribed to support South Africa.	Supreme Ct. rules, 6–3, that states can provide unemployment benefits to striking workers.		Indiana University beats Purdue University, 53–52, to win the National Invitation Tournament championship before 14,889 fans in Madison Square Garden, N.Y.C.	March 21
FBI Dir. William Webster says that more than 200 FBI informants have quit in the past year, fearing that their identities would be revealed.				NHL merger with its rival, the World Hockey Assn., is approved by the NHL governors board, thereby ending seven years of conflict between the leagues.	March 22
	Cuban exiles Guillermo Novo and Alvin Ross Diaz are sentenced to life imprisonment in the U.S. for the 1976 murder in Wash., D.C. of Orlando Letelier, the former Chilean foreign minister, and his colleague Ronni Moffitt.				March 23
A mistrial is declared with the jurors deadlocked, 10–2, for acquittal in the murder trial of Black Panther leader Huey Newton.				University of Minnesota downs the University of North Dakota, 4–3, to win the ice hockey championship of the NCAA.	March 24

F	G	H	I	J
Includes elections, federal-state relations, civil rights and liberties, crime, the judiciary, education, health care, poverty, urban affairs and population.	Includes formation and debate of U.S. foreign and defense policies, veterans' affairs and defense spending. (Relations with specific foreign countries are usually found under the region concerned.)	Includes business, labor, agriculture, taxation, transportation, consumer affairs, monetary and fiscal policy, natural resources, and pollution.	Includes worldwide scientific, medical and technological developments, natural phenomena, U.S. weather, natural disasters, and accidents.	Includes the arts, religion, scholarship, communications media, sports, entertainments, fashions, fads and social life.

	World Affairs	Europe	Africa & the Middle East	The Americas	Asia & the Pacific
March 25		Socialist, Communist and other left-oriented parties increase their proportion of the total vote to 54.6 percent in local French elections.	The Iranian govt. grants the Kurdish minority limited autonomy, including the freedom to run Kurdish-language schools and appoint security forces.		
March 26			Pres. Sadat and Premier Begin sign a formal peace treaty in Washington, D.C., formally ending a 31-year state of war between Egypt and Israel. Pres. Carter signs as a witness.	Canadian P.M. Pierre Trudeau dissolves Parliament and announces general elections for May 22, barely two months before his five-year term in office expires.	
March 27	OPEC's 13 member-nations agree to raise the base price of oil by 9 percent to $14.54 effective April 1.	Tass announces Soviet government signing a contract with a French company for a computer similar to one the U.S. had barred it from buying in 1978.		Leaders of Canada's three major parties begin campaigning for the May general election. P.M. Pierre Trudeau's 11 years of leadership is the focus of attacks by Progressive Conservative leader Joseph Clark and New Democratic Party leader Edward Broadbent.	India's Petroleum Min. Nannan Bahuguna scores the OPEC price increase and calls on all state organizations to cut oil consumption by 15 percent.
March 28		British Labor Party loses a House of Commons confidence vote by one vote, 311–310.	South African Finance Minster Owen Horwood presents an annual budget designed to stimulate economic growth in the country.		The real gross domestic product of Australia rose 1.3 percent in the year ended June 1978, according to Statistics Bureau reports.
March 29		British P.M. James Callaghan announces elections will be held on May 3 and Parliament dissolved on April 7 after the Labor Party's loss-of-confidence vote.... Swedish Nuclear Power Authority votes to go ahead with two new nuclear reactors.	North and South Yemen agree to unite under one government.... Egypt withdraws its diplomatic staff from Amman, Jordan, after Jordan recalls its ambassador to protest Egypt's peace treaty with Israel.	Ho Xuan Dich, a second secretary at the Vietnamese Embassy in Canada, is ordered to leave the country following charges that he intimidated the Vietnamese immigrant community in Canada.	U.S. terminates trade talks with Japan after rejecting Tokyo's proposals to give U.S. firms greater access to Japanese govt. procurement programs.
March 30		Airey Neave, a leading Conservative member of Parliament in Great Britain, is killed when a bomb explodes in his car as he is driving out of the House of Commons. Two groups associated with the IRA claim responsibility.... The parity that had existed for more than a hundred years between the Irish and British pounds is broken by Ireland to meet its obligations as a member of the European Monetary system.	Shah Mohammed Pahlevi, former ruler of Iran, leaves Morocco with his family and flies to the Bahamas for an indeterminate stay.	Fabien Roy, a member of the Quebec national assembly in Canada, is elected leader of the country's Social Credit Party.	
March 31		The coalition Cabinet in Italy, headed by Premier Giulio Andreotti, loses a confidence vote in Parliament 11 days after it was formed.	Representatives of 18 Arab League countries and the PLO adopt resolutions imposing a total economic boycott on Egypt for signing a peace treaty with Israel.		Vietnamese forces reportedly have launched a new drive in northwestern Cambodia against the Khmer Rouge guerrilla troops of the ousted Pol Pot government and forced 800 Pol Pot soldiers to flee into Thailand.
April 1		The last British sailors leave Malta, ending the 179-year military British presence there.	Ayatollah Ruhollah Khomeini proclaims the establishment of an Islamic republic in Iran, following its approval in a nationwide referendum.		Chinese authorities begin a crackdown against protesters. Workers are ordered to remove posters from walls in the center of Peking.

A	B	C	D	E
Includes developments that affect more than one world region, international organizations and important meetings of major world leaders.	Includes all domestic and regional developments in Europe, including the Soviet Union, Turkey, Cyprus and Malta.	Includes all domestic and regional developments in Africa and the Middle East, including Iraq and Iran and excluding Cyprus, Turkey and Afghanistan.	Includes all domestic and regional developments in Latin America, the Caribbean and Canada.	Includes all domestic and regional developments in Asia and Pacific nations, extending from Afghanistan through all the Pacific Islands, except Hawaii.

U.S. Politics & Social Issues	U.S. Foreign Policy & Defense	U.S. Economy & Environment	Science, Technology & Nature	Culture, Leisure & Life Style	
		Pres. Carter outlines plans to streamline the federal regulatory process, pledging to eliminate excessive costs, rules, duplication, overlap, and waste.			March 25
Supreme Ct. declines to review a Fla. death penalty appeal.	Both Egyptian Pres. Sadat and Israeli Premier Begin praise Pres. Carter's mediation as the major factor in achieving the peace pact between their countries.		Judge Robert Warren issues a preliminary injunction prohibiting the *Progressive* magazine from publishing an article on the hydrogen bomb.	Michigan State wins the national collegiate basketball championship with a 75–64 victory over Indiana State.	March 26
		State Dept. calls the OPEC price increase "untimely" and unjustified.			March 27
The Senate, by a roll-call vote, goes on record as favoring a higher limit on the amount of income its members can make from outside sources.		The U.S. balance of merchandise trade was in deficit by a seasonally adjusted $1.3 billion in February, the Commerce Dept. announces.	A malfunction in the cooling system of a nuclear reactor at Three Mile Island, a power station near Harrisburg, Pa., leads to closing down of the reactor and escape of radiation into the air.		March 28
New York Times–CBS News Poll finds Pres. Carter's public approval rating has risen to 42 percent from 37 percent in February in wake of his role in negotiating the Israeli–Egyptian peace treaty.	The Defense Dept. announces plans to close or revamp 152 military installations around the U.S., resulting in the elimination of some 15,300 jobs and transfer of thousands of defense workers.	The Carter administration tightens its price guidelines because of speculation that there is widespread noncompliance by business.	The U.S. Court for Customs and Patent Appeals reaffirms two earlier decisions that corporations are entitled to patents on microorganisms developed in their laboratories.	James Lyon, a University of California (San Diego) scholar, reveals that the FBI conducted a 13-year surveillance of German-born playwright Bertolt Brecht (1943–56) without finding any politically useful information about Brecht's alleged Communist activities.	March 29
	Justice Dept. announces it will not prosecute Graham Martin, former U.S. ambassador to South Vietnam, for alleged mishandling of classified material.	Agriculture Dept. reports that prices paid to farmers for raw agricultural products rose 2 percent in March, paced by a 9.5 percent increase in the cost of cattle.	On the third day of a continuing accident at the nuclear power plant at Three Mile Island, Pa., the Nuclear Regulatory Commission says the damaged nuclear reactor there may melt down.		March 30
			The threat of a major disaster apparently recedes on the fourth day of the nuclear accident at the Three Mile Island power plant in Pennsylvania, as federal officials note a slowdown in abnormal activity within the plant's damaged reactor.	Protestant, Roman Catholic, and Eastern Orthodox theologians from Europe, Africa, Latin America, and the U.S. end a four-day Louisville, Ky. meeting by agreeing to a document outling their understanding of the nature of baptism.	March 31
N.M. Gov Bruce King signs into law a bill reinstating the state's death penalty, which had been found unconstitutional in 1976.... Former Rep. Otto Passman is found not guilty of accepting illegal gratuities from South Korean rice dealer Tongsun Park and of related tax evasion and conspiracy counts.		The government's composite index of leading economic indicators falls for the second month in a row, dropping .9 percent in February after declining .3 percent in January, the Commerce Dept. announces.... The International Brotherhood of Teamsters calls a series of selective strikes against 73 trucking companies after union and industry bargainers fail to reach agreement on a new national master contract.	Pres. Carter visits the damaged nuclear power plant at Three Mile Island, Pa., as government officials express cautious optimism that the five-day-old crisis is easing.	Two months after her release from prison, Patricia Hearst and Bernard Shaw, a policeman and her former bodyguard, are married in San Francisco, Calif.... Soviet Union wins the World Cup of amateur wrestling in Toledo, Ohio.	April 1

F	G	H	I	J
Includes elections, federal-state relations, civil rights and liberties, crime, the judiciary, education, health care, poverty, urban affairs and population.	*Includes formation and debate of U.S. foreign and defense policies, veterans' affairs and defense spending. (Relations with specific foreign countries are usually found under the region concerned.)*	*Includes business, labor, agriculture, taxation, transportation, consumer affairs, monetary and fiscal policy, natural resources, and pollution.*	*Includes worldwide scientific, medical and technological developments, natural phenomena, U.S. weather, natural disasters, and accidents.*	*Includes the arts, religion, scholarship, communications media, sports, entertainments, fashions, fads and social life.*

	World Affairs	Europe	Africa & the Middle East	The Americas	Asia & the Pacific
April 2		A six-month government crisis in Belgium ends as King Baudouin announces that a five-party coalition has been formed.... Italian Pres. Sandro Pertini dissolves Parliament, clearing the way for national elections.	Israeli Premier Menahem Begin begins two days of talks in Cairo with Egyptian Pres. Anwar Sadat. He is the first Israeli leader to visit the Egyptian capital.		
April 3	China informs the Soviet Union that it has decided not to extend its 1950 friendship treaty when it expires in 1980.	Premier Adolfo Suarez Gonzalez's Union of the Democratic Center Party wins a country-wide popular vote majority in Spanish elections, but leftist candidates sweep municipal elections in major cities.		Canadian and Australian officials reportedly agree after talks that the two countries will not try to expand their shares of the wheat export market by underselling each other.	Australia announces resumption of cultural and scientific relations with the Soviet Union suspended in 1978 after electronic surveillance devices were found in Australia's Moscow embassy.
April 4	Soviet Union denounces China's decision to permit the Chinese–Soviet friendship treaty to lapse when it expires next year.	Greece and the EEC reach an agreement for Greece to become the community's tenth member on January 1, 1981.	Israeli Premier Menahem Begin opens a hot-line telephone link between the Israeli and Egyptian capitals.		Former Pakistan P.M. Zulfikar Bhutto is executed for conspiring to murder a political opponent in 1974.... Australia announces the immediate banning of whaling within the country's 200-mile offshore economic zone and the eventual ban on importation of whale products.
April 5		Spanish Premier Adolfo Suarez Gonzalez names a Cabinet, the first constitutional government in the country since the civil war of 1936–39.... The French govt. reveals it has approved plans to accelerate the country's shift to nuclear energy, despite the accident at Three Mile Island, Pa.			
April 6		In Great Britain the Labor Party issues a moderate campaign manifesto calling for the government to acquire greater powers over industry and promises more spending on health.			Japan and Australia sign an agreement for Japan to buy beef, other foodstuffs, and industrial goods from Australia.... *Financial Times* reports the Australian Export Finance and Insurance Corporation has signed an agreement to provide China with A$50-million in credit to finance purchases of Australian goods and services.
April 7			Egypt recalls it ambassadors from seven Arab countries in response to the Arab League decision on March 31 to sever economic and political ties with Egypt.	Guerrillas of the Sandinista National Liberation Front resume their military-style attacks one day before Pres. Anastasio Somoza is scheduled to leave on an eight-day vacation in the U.S.	Pakistani Pres. Ziaur Rahman announces lifting martial law and promises that civilian rule will be reintroduced.
April 8		In a two-day period in Italy, 16 left-wing extremists are arrested on various terrorism charges and warrants are reportedly issued for another 22 persons.		The Nicaraguan town of El Sauce is retaken one day after it had been captured by Sandanista rebels.... The Kenneth Thomson family wins control of Canada's Hudson's Bay Co. with an offer of C$37 a share for 75 percent of the company's stock.	Afghanistan claims that Pakistani troops, disguised as Afghan insurgents, raided four Afghan police stations on April 7.
April 9		In a move aimed at curbing inflation, the Bank of Italy announces new ceilings on the amount of loans that banks can make.	Saudi Arabia's deputy petroleum minister Abdul Aziz al-Turki says his country will cut back crude oil production by one million barrels a day.	Nicaraguan Pres. Anastasio Somoza tells reporters in Topeka, Kan., that he has not fled Nicaragua in favor of a provisional government formed by members of his own party.	Pakistan denies Afghanistan's charge that Pakistani troops raided Afghan police stations.

A	B	C	D	E
Includes developments that affect more than one world region, international organizations and important meetings of major world leaders.	Includes all domestic and regional developments in Europe, including the Soviet Union, Turkey, Cyprus and Malta.	Includes all domestic and regional developments in Africa and the Middle East, including Iraq and Iran and excluding Cyprus, Turkey and Afghanistan.	Includes all domestic and regional developments in Latin America, the Caribbean and Canada.	Includes all domestic and regional developments in Asia and Pacific nations, extending from Afghanistan through all the Pacific Islands, except Hawaii.

U.S. Politics & Social Issues	U.S. Foreign Policy & Defense	U.S. Economy & Environment	Science, Technology & Nature	Culture, Leisure & Life Style	
The Supreme Ct. rules, 6–3, that the FCC cannot require cable television systems to set aside channels for public, local government, and educational institutions for free or for a nominal fee.		Congress completes action on a bill raising the national debt ceiling to $830 billion through Sept. 30.	Federal and utility nuclear experts agree that a dangerous gas bubble inside the damage reactor at Three Mile Island, Pa., is shrinking, as the accident situation goes through its sixth day.	Carroll Rosenbloom, 72, Los Angeles Rams professional football team owner, drowns in waters off Golden Beach, Fla.	April 2
Jane Byrne is the first woman to be elected mayor of Chicago with 82.5 percent of votes cast, beating late Mayor Richard Daley's record of 77.67 percent in 1975.	U.S. officials say the country might resume U-2 flights to verify Soviet compliance with any SALT agreement.		NRC announces that the hydrogen bubble trapped in the damaged reactor at Three Mile Island has been eliminated.	Black filmmaker Gordon Parks Jr., 44, dies in a private plane crash in Kenya. . . . Eugene Ormandy announces that he will retire as musical director of the Philadelphia Orchestra at the end of this season after a 44-year association with the orchestra.	April 3
	In a speech to the Chicago Council on Foreign Relations, national security adviser Zbigniew Brzezinski launches a drive for Senate ratification of the expected SALT treaty with the Soviet Union.		Federal safety investigators in their first official report tell the NRC that a series of human, mechanical, and design errors contributed to the Three Mile Island accident.		April 4
	A group of 12 Republican senators say in a statement that the SALT agreement contains ambiguities that could give the Soviet Union an advantage over the U.S.	Pres. Carter orders gradual decontrol of domestic oil prices to combat the worsening U.S. energy situation. . . . The Labor Dept. announces the U.S. government's three indexes of producer prices rose 1 percent in March.	Pres. Carter forms an independent commission to investigate the Three Mile Island accident.	*Love on the Run* , fifth film in French filmmaker Francois Truffaut's series on the life of Antoine Doinel, a man who is eternally susceptible to women, opens in N.Y.	April 5
	The U.S. announces it is withdrawing economic and military aid from Pakistan because that country is secretly constructing a uranium enrichment plant capable of producing material for an atomic bomb.	U.S. consumer installment credit rose a seasonally adjusted $3.31 billion in February, according to the Federal Reserve.	A French factory that builds nuclear reactors is sabotaged by explosions that cause extensive damage.		April 6
Charles Sawyer, 92, secretary of commerce (1948–53), civic leader, and philanthropist, dies after a series of strokes in Palm Beach, Fla.				Ken Forsch of the Houston Astros pitches the earliest no-hitter ever pitched in a major league season in a 6–0 victory against the Atlanta Braves.	April 7
			NRC official Robert Bernero says that engineers have successfully stabilized the iodine, one of the principal contributors to radiation, in the Three Mile Island plant.	National Hockey League ends its 1978–79 season with the New York Islanders, Chicago Black Hawks, Boston Bruins, and Montreal Canadiens winning division titles.	April 8
		To reflect the higher cost of living, the Labor Dept. revises its figures to raise the poverty level to $6,700 annually for a family of four.	Harold Denton, NRC's top official at Three Mile Island, announces that the crisis at the crippled power plant is over.	A malpractice insurance plan for clergy and religious institutions' protection against "erroneous advice" charges is reported.	April 9

F	G	H	I	J
Includes elections, federal-state relations, civil rights and liberties, crime, the judiciary, education, health care, poverty, urban affairs and population.	*Includes formation and debate of U.S. foreign and defense policies, veterans' affairs and defense spending. (Relations with specific foreign countries are usually found under the region concerned.)*	*Includes business, labor, agriculture, taxation, transportation, consumer affairs, monetary and fiscal policy, natural resources, and pollution.*	*Includes worldwide scientific, medical and technological developments, natural phenomena, U.S. weather, natural disasters, and accidents.*	*Includes the arts, religion, scholarship, communications media, sports, entertainments, fashions, fads and social life.*

	World Affairs	Europe	Africa & the Middle East	The Americas	Asia & the Pacific
April 10				Canadian P.M. Pierre Trudeau offers the U.S. a choice of two routes for an oil pipeline to bring Alaskan petroleum into the lower U.S.	
April 11		The British Conservative Party issues its manifesto for the upcoming national elections on May 3, which calls for income tax cuts at all levels and new curbs on unions.	As a combined force of Tanzanian soldiers and Ugandan exiles triumphantly enters Kampala after six months of fighting, Ugandan exiles in Tanzania announce formation of a provisional government led by Yusufu Lule to replace Pres. Idi Amin's regime.		
April 12	A GATT-sponsored comprehensive trade agreement reducing tariffs an average 33 percent and dismantling other trade barriers is signed in Geneva.		The U.S. denounces the resumption of executions in Iran of officials who had served under the Shah.	Statistics Canada reports the consumer price index rose 1.2 percent in March, the fastest rise in eight months.	
April 13					
April 14		East Germany announces new restrictions on Western journalists in the country, including their having to get official permission to interview any East German citizen.	Rioting erupts in Monrovia, capital of Liberia, over a proposed increase in the price of rice, the country's staple food.	Nicaraguan govt. troops recapture the northern city of Esteli after a week-long siege against some 300 Sandinista guerrillas who had barricaded themselves inside the city.	
April 15			Growing opposition in Iran to the excesses of Ayatollah Khomeini's Islamic Revolutionary Council leads to the resignation of For. Min. Karim Sanjabi and the temporary departure from Teheran of Ayatollah Mahmoud Taleghani, the city's religious leader.		
April 16		Currency restrictions are introduced in East Germany to limit the circulation of West German marks there.			
April 17			Egypt is expelled from the Organization of Arab Petroleum Exporting Countries (OAPEC) in retaliation for signing a peace treaty with Israel.		

A	B	C	D	E
Includes developments that affect more than one world region, international organizations and important meetings of major world leaders.	*Includes all domestic and regional developments in Europe, including the Soviet Union, Turkey, Cyprus and Malta.*	*Includes all domestic and regional developments in Africa and the Middle East, including Iraq and Iran and excluding Cyprus, Turkey and Afghanistan.*	*Includes all domestic and regional developments in Latin America, the Caribbean and Canada.*	*Includes all domestic and regional developments in Asia and Pacific nations, extending from Afghanistan through all the Pacific Islands, except Hawaii.*

U.S. Politics & Social Issues	U.S. Foreign Policy & Defense	U.S. Economy & Environment	Science, Technology & Nature	Culture, Leisure & Life Style	
A federal grand jury indicts former Rep. Nick Galifianakis (D, N.C.), charging that he lied to Congress about taking $10,000 in cash from South Korean rice dealer Tongsun Park.	Pres. Carter signs legislation establishing unofficial relations between the U.S. and Taiwan and providing some security assistance.	A House subcommittee releases documents that show the Hooker Chemicals and Plastics Corp. was aware as early as 1958 that toxic chemicals it had dumped in the Love Canal (N.Y.) area were seeping into homes and a school playground.... A tentative accord ending a 10-day trucking strike and industry lockout is reached by negotiators for the Teamsters union and the trucking industry.	NRC says all its rules and procedures will be reevaluated in wake of the Three Mile Island accident.	National Gallery of Art in Washington, D.C. is reported acquiring a set of Gilbert Stuart portraits of the first five U.S. Presidents, known as the Gibbs–Coolidge collection.	April 10
			Pres. Carter names 11 persons to a presidential commission to investigate the nuclear accident at Three Mile Island, Pa.		April 11
			The Soviet Soyuz 33 spacecraft, launched two days ago, returns to Earth after failing to dock with the orbiting Salyut space station.		April 12
Donald David, former dean of the Harvard Graduate School of Business Administration, dies at age 83 in Hyannis, Mass.		Boston University faculty strikes for nine days before ratifying terms of a three-year contract with the board of trustees.	Personnel begin to final process to bring the damaged nuclear reactor at the Three Mile Island, Pa., power plant to cold shutdown.		April 13
		Clarence Dillon, 96, financier, retired director of many major corporations, and father of former Treasury Secy. C. Douglas Dillon, dies in Far Hills, N.J.	An estimated 4,500 residents of Crestview, Fla. complete the return to their homes after they were evacuated on April 8 because a Louisville & Nashville Railroad Co. train carrying toxic chemicals derailed, exploded, and caught fire about four miles away.	Treasury Secy. J. Michael Blumenthal and his wife, Eileen, agree to separate after a year's attempt at reconciliation.	April 14
	Billy Carter confirms that the Libyan govt. paid for his trip to Rome and Tripoli in the fall of 1978, but denies that he had any business dealings with the Qaddafi govt.		NRC files for 1978 show 2,835 reportable "occurences" at U.S. nuclear power plants.	Fuzzy Zoeller wins the Masters golf tournament in a sudden-death playoff. He is the first player to win the Masters in his initial appearance.	April 15
	CIA Dir. Stansfield Turner is reported telling the Senate that it will take the U.S. five years to replace monitoring posts that were lost in Iran, used to track Soviet missile tests.	The EPA proposes noise-control regulations for railroad yards.	St. Louis sex researchers Dr. William Masters, a gynecologist, and Virginia Johnson, a psychologist, report on therapy they claim can reverse homosexuality.	Pulitzer Prizes in Arts and Letters are awarded as follows: Fiction, John Cheever; Drama, Sam Shepard; History, Don Fehrenbacher; Biography, Leonard Baker; Poetry, Robert Penn Warren; General Nonfiction, Edward O. Wilson; Music, Joseph Schwantner.... Pulitzer Prizes in Journalism are awarded to *The Point Reyes (Calif.) Light*, the staff of *The San Diego Evening Tribune*, James Risser, Richard Ben Cramer, Herbert Block, Russell Baker, Jon Franklin, and Paul Gapp.	April 16
Supreme Ct. rules, 7-2, that a town or its residents can use the 1968 Fair Housing Act to preserve the racial balance of an integrated neighborhood.		UAW Pres. Douglas Fraser warns the Carter administration to "stay the hell away" from its contract negotiations later in the year with the automobile industry.	The strongest earthquake to hit New England in six years occurs just a few miles west of Wiscasset, Maine, home of the Maine Yankee nuclear power plant.	Tennis star Chris Evert and a less highly ranked tennis player, John Lloyd, are married in Ft. Lauderdale, Fla.	April 17

F	G	H	I	J
Includes elections, federal-state relations, civil rights and liberties, crime, the judiciary, education, health care, poverty, urban affairs and population.	Includes formation and debate of U.S. foreign and defense policies, veterans' affairs and defense spending. (Relations with specific foreign countries are usually found under the region concerned.)	Includes business, labor, agriculture, taxation, transportation, consumer affairs, monetary and fiscal policy, natural resources, and pollution.	Includes worldwide scientific, medical and technological developments, natural phenomena, U.S. weather, natural disasters, and accidents.	Includes the arts, religion, scholarship, communications media, sports, entertainments, fashions, fads and social life.

	World Affairs	Europe	Africa & the Middle East	The Americas	Asia & the Pacific
April 18		Leonid Brezhnev is reelected president of the Soviet Union. Premier Alexei Kosygin and the 38-member Presidium are also confirmed.	An estimated 100 schoolchildren are killed by soldiers in the Central African Empire after they protested a requirement to wear uniforms to school.... Christian militia commander Maj. Saad Haddad declares the independence of a six-mile-wide belt in southern Lebanon along the Israeli border.		
April 19					
April 20		A female officer at the women's prison at Armagh, Northern Ireland is killed and three other women officers injured in an IRA attack. In Belfast a sniper kills a British soldier.	Three more executions in Iran, bring to a total at least 149 people put to death by Islamic firing squads since the overthrow of the Shah.		Indian govt. rejects a demand in Parliament that the country manufacture atomic weapons in response to reports that Pakistan is doing the same.
April 21		Art officials say that rehabilitation work on the bombed Palace of the Senators in Rome will require at least a year and cost over $1 million.			
April 22		V.P. Walter Mondale finishes a 12-day visit to five Nordic countries and the Netherlands to reassure them of American interest in and commitment to their security.	Kuwait severs diplomatic relations with Egypt.... The Israeli Cabinet approves the creation of two new settlements on the West Bank.		
April 23		U.S. officials report that the Soviet Union has deployed a new tactical nuclear missile, the SS-21, in East Germany.		Argentina military junta arrests 20 of the country's most powerful labor leaders, thereby quelling a strike set for April 27 — the first threatened strike since the 1976 coup that toppled the government of Isabel Martinez de Peron.	
April 24		Pyotr Pospelov, 80, Soviet CP propagandist, principal theoretician, and longtime *Pravda* editor, is reported dead in Moscow.			
April 25	Defense ministers of eight NATO countries conclude after a two-day meeting in Florida that the alliance should move quickly to modernize its intermediate- and short-range nuclear weapons.		The Israeli–Egyptian peace treaty is formally put into effect as representatives of both countries exchange ratification documents.		
April 26	The U.N. Security Council praises Lebanon for sending troops to the south to reassert its sovereignty in the region.		A cease-fire arranged by the U.N. Interim Force in Lebanon brings to a virtual halt the sharp fighting that has raged in southern Lebanon between Israeli forces and PLO guerrillas since April 22.		After two sessions, China and Vietnam remain deadlocked in attempts to restore normal relations.

A	B	C	D	E
Includes developments that affect more than one world region, international organizations and important meetings of major world leaders.	Includes all domestic and regional developments in Europe, including the Soviet Union, Turkey, Cyprus and Malta.	Includes all domestic and regional developments in Africa and the Middle East, including Iraq and Iran and excluding Cyprus, Turkey and Afghanistan.	Includes all domestic and regional developments in Latin America, the Caribbean and Canada.	Includes all domestic and regional developments in Asia and Pacific nations, extending from Afghanistan through all the Pacific Islands, except Hawaii.

U.S. Politics & Social Issues	U.S. Foreign Policy & Defense	U.S. Economy & Environment	Science, Technology & Nature	Culture, Leisure & Life Style	
Supreme Ct. rules unanimously that private parties cannot use the Freedom of Information Act to prevent the government from disclosing information.		Commerce Dept. reports that Americans' personal income rose a seasonally adjusted $19.2 billion in March, 1 percent from February, to an adjusted annual rate of $1.85 trillion.		World Hockey Assn. concludes its season with five of its six teams qualifying for the playoffs. The Edmonton Oilers finish with the best won–lost–tied record, 48–30–2.... A North American Soccer League Players Assn. strike ends after five days.	April 18
Rogers Morton, 64, secretary of the interior (1971–75), secretary of commerce (1975–76), and Republican national chairman (1969–71), dies of cancer in Easton, Md.		The EPA issues final regulations banning the manufacture of polychlorinated biphenyls (PCBs) and phasing out most uses of the chemical.		Two films dealing with the Vietnam war — *The Deer Hunter* and *Coming Home* — win most of the major Academy Awards presented, including best picture, best director (Michael Cimino), and best supporting actor (Christopher Walken). Jane Fonda and Jon Voight win best acting awards for roles in *Coming Home*. British actress Maggie Smith wins best supporting actress award.	April 19
Pres. Carter, relaxing on a fishing trip, is attacked by a rabbit, which he beats back with a canoe paddle.	Administration officials insist that in principle the former Shah of Iran is welcome in the U.S., but they say that it is not advisable for him to come until a more stable government is established in Iran.	A federal appeals court rules that the automatic transferring of funds between savings and checking accounts at banks, savings and loan associations, and credit unions is illegal.			April 20
			Architect I.M. Pei is named to design the proposed N.Y.C. Convention and Exhibition Center, estimated to cost $375 million and be completed by the mid-1980s.	The remaining 546 bodies from the Jonestown Peoples Temple mass murder–suicide in Guyana remain unclaimed at Dover Air Force Base in Delaware.	April 21
		USW suspends its strike against the Newport News Shipbuilding and Dry Dock Co.	National Academy of Sciences' monument to Albert Einstein is unveiled in Washington, D.C. 39 days after the centennial of his birth.		April 22
Supreme Ct. declines to review, thus letting stand, a ruling that denies an Italian–American man Philip DiLeo the right to sue a law school for rejecting his application to a special admissions program.		ITT enters the domestic long-distance telephone market with a metered service known as City-Call, thus joining MCI Communications Corp. and Southern Pacific Company as AT&T competitors.		National Book Awards are announced, marked by a number of surprise winners. The fiction award is given to *Going After Cacciato* by Tim O'Brien, which depicts the horrors of the Vietnam War. Arthur Schlesinger Jr. wins for his biography, *Robert Kennedy and His Times*, and Peter Matthiessen for *The Snow Leopard*.	April 23
Supreme Court rules, 5–4, in separate cases that the father of an illegitimate child could block adoption, but could not sue for damages if the child were killed in an accident.			Calif. Gov. Jerry Brown says that the U.S. should give up on nuclear power as a future energy source, emphasizing his differences with Pres. Carter.	*Manhattan*, filmmaker Woody Allen's comedy about a successful TV writer's romances and friends, with Woody Allen, Diane Keaton, Michael Murphy, Mariel Hemingway and Meryl Streep, is released in N.Y.	April 24
Pres. Carter makes a political visit to New Hampshire for a town meeting in Portsmouth and fund-raiser in Bedford.	Pres. Carter pushes for ratification of the new SALT Treaty in a major speech in New York to a meeting of the American Newspaper Publishers Association.			Soviet Union retains its world ice hockey title with a 9–2 victory over Canada.	April 25
HEW Secy. Joseph Califano Jr. announces that Social Security benefits will be boosted 9.9 percent in July to keep up with the increased cost of living.		Cesar Chavez, president of the United Farm Workers union, announces a national boycott of iceberg lettuce in support of his union's strike against West Coast lettuce growers.			April 26

F	G	H	I	J
Includes elections, federal-state relations, civil rights and liberties, crime, the judiciary, education, health care, poverty, urban affairs and population.	*Includes formation and debate of U.S. foreign and defense policies, veterans' affairs and defense spending. (Relations with specific foreign countries are usually found under the region concerned.)*	*Includes business, labor, agriculture, taxation, transportation, consumer affairs, monetary and fiscal policy, natural resources, and pollution.*	*Includes worldwide scientific, medical and technological developments, natural phenomena, U.S. weather, natural disasters, and accidents.*	*Includes the arts, religion, scholarship, communications media, sports, entertainments, fashions, fads and social life.*

	World Affairs	Europe	Africa & the Middle East	The Americas	Asia & the Pacific
April 27	The eight session in five years of the U.N. Conference on the Law of the Sea concludes, after beginning on March 19, still with no general agreement.	Alexander Ginzburg, whose conviction in 1978 provoked worldwide protest, is among five leading Soviet dissidents flown to N.Y. in exchange for two convicted Soviet spies held in the U.S.... Soviet agreement to free the dissidents is seen motivated by the desire to rally U.S. support for the SALT treaty now under negotiations.	Morocco and Tunisia sever diplomatic relations with Egypt, bringing to 15 the number of Arab states to cut their ties in wake of Egypt's peace treaty with Israel.		
April 28					Washington Post reports that military confiscations of food in Cambodia, as well as the disruption caused by the Vietnamese–Cambodian fighting, raises the possibility of widespread famine there.
April 29		In a sudden change of policy, the Soviet Union issues an official denunciation of former Ugandan Pres. Idi Amin.	Israeli Cabinet approves, 7–5, the death penalty for Palestinian terrorists convicted of acts of "inhuman activity."	In the first Ecuadoran elections since 1968, Jaime Roldos Aguilera wins a decisive margin of votes to gain the presidency.	Thai officials report that most of an estimated 50,000–80,000 Cambodian civilians and soldiers of the ousted Pol Pot regime who fled across the border into Thailand to escape a Vietnamese-led offensive have been returned to Cambodia.
April 30	U.N. Security Council votes to condemn the Rhodesian elections and calls upon member-nations to maintain the economic boycott against Rhodesia.		The cargo ship Ashdod is the first Israeli ship to sail through the Suez Canal since Israel became a state in 1948.		
May 1	U.N. Secy. Gen. Kurt Waldheim reports after five days of mediation between China and Vietnam that both sides remain deadlocked.				Washington Post reports Chinese efforts to control population growth that include financial bonuses to one-child families.
May 2			Using new emergency powers, Liberia's Pres. William Tolbert suspends habeas corpus right for one year.... South African govt. announces that it will remove most of its restrictions on black employment, including a ban on black unions.	A nine-day strike against the Mexican national telephone company ends when striking workers agree to accept a 13.5 percent pay increase.	China reports that 20,000 of its men have been killed and wounded in the February–March war with Vietnam and that Vietnam has suffered 50,000 dead and wounded.
May 3		British voters give the Conservative Party a solid parliamentary majority, thereby making its leader, Margaret Thatcher, Britain's first woman prime minister.	U.S. Amb. to the U.N. Andrew Young calls the Rhodesian elections rigged, but says that the U.S. should support the new government of Abel Muzorewa until it agrees to negotiate with the guerrillas and prepare for new elections.		
May 4		West German police shoot and kill Elisabeth von Dyck, a suspected member of the terrorist Baader-Meinhof gang.		Popular Revolutionary Bloc guerrillas occupy the Municipal Cathedral in San Salvador and storm the French and Costa Rican embassies, taking both ambassadors as hostages.	

A	B	C	D	E
Includes developments that affect more than one world region, international organizations and important meetings of major world leaders.	Includes all domestic and regional developments in Europe, including the Soviet Union, Turkey, Cyprus and Malta.	Includes all domestic and regional developments in Africa and the Middle East, including Iraq and Iran and excluding Cyprus, Turkey and Afghanistan.	Includes all domestic and regional developments in Latin America, the Caribbean and Canada.	Includes all domestic and regional developments in Asia and Pacific nations, extending from Afghanistan through all the Pacific Islands, except Hawaii.

U.S. Politics & Social Issues	U.S. Foreign Policy & Defense	U.S. Economy & Environment	Science, Technology & Nature	Culture, Leisure & Life Style	
Pres. Carter tells a group of visiting newspaper editors that he favors limiting a President to one six-year term.		*Wall Street Journal* reports the nation's 13 largest oil companies earned 48.5 percent more in the first quarter of 1979 than they did in the first quarter of 1978.	NRC orders all operating nuclear power plants constructed by Babcock & Wilcox Co., the firm that built the Three Mile Island reactor, shut down temporarily.		April 27
	The New York Times reports that Soviet intelligence agents purchased information about several U.S. secret satellite systems expected to help the U.S. verify the proposed SALT Treaty.			Villanova takes the collegiate title at the eighty-fifth annual Penn Relays in Philadelphia.	April 28
	An estimated 100,000 people turn out for a N.Y.C. rally in support of Soviet Jewry where freed Soviet dissidents Eduard Kuznetsov and Mark Dymshits are the main attraction.		Former Pentagon analyst Daniel Ellsberg is among more than 280 protesters at the Rocky Flats, Colo. nuclear weapons plant who are arrested in waht their organizers call a deliberate act of civil disobediance.		April 29
Supreme Ct. unanimously rules that a person cannot be involuntarily committed to a mental institution without clear and convincing evidence that he or she is both mentally ill and potentially dangerous. . . . A team of doctors testifies that federal food programs have eliminated most of the gross malnutrition they had found in a 1967 study of urban slums and poor rural areas.		Pres. Carter bitterly rejects Sen. Edward Kennedy's (D, Mass.) criticism of his oil-pricing policies and proposals. . . . Sears Roebuck & Co., the largest U.S. retailer, announces reducing its spring catalogue prices 5 percent until July 31 to comply with administration price guidelines.	NRC says it believes that the uranium core of Three Mile Island No. 2, normally bathed in pressurized coolant, was left uncovered for as long as 50 minutes.	Wilt Chamberlain, a former star center in the NBA, is inducted into the Naismith Basketball Hall of Fame in Springfield, Mass.	April 30
Declaring himself a "lifelong Republican," former CIA Dir. George Bush announces his candidacy for the presidency. . . . Federal authorities announce they have broken up the largest marijuana ring in the U.S. by arresting a paramilitary group of 14 people in Miami, Fla.				Arthur Fiedler, 84, returns for his fiftieth season as conductor of the Boston Pops Orchestra.	May 1
	Lt. Gen. Edward Meyer is named Army chief of staff over 18 other three-star and four-star generals who outranked him.	Energy Dept. accuses seven major oil companies of overcharging refiners by $1.7 billion in the August 1973-March 1979 period.		*The Deer Hunter* is the top-grossing film for the previous week.	May 2
Sen. Abraham Ribicoff (D, Conn.) announces he will retire from the Senate when his third term expires in 1980.	A report commissioned by State Secy. Cyrus Vance is made public charging the State Dept. with errors and lapses in handling and evaluating information about the Peoples Temple mass murders and suicides.			Paul Mellon resigns as president and chief executive officer of the National Gallery of Art in Washington, D.C. The gallery's board also elects Ruth Carter Johnson of Ft. Worth, Tex. as its first woman trustee.	May 3
Georges May, former dean of Yale College, is named Yale University provost.		AP and NBC News poll finds that 54 percent of 1,600 adults interviewed nationwide believe that U.S. energy shortages are a hoax.			May 4

F	G	H	I	J
Includes elections, federal-state relations, civil rights and liberties, crime, the judiciary, education, health care, poverty, urban affairs and population.	Includes formation and debate of U.S. foreign and defense policies, veterans' affairs and defense spending. (Relations with specific foreign countries are usually found under the region concerned.)	Includes business, labor, agriculture, taxation, transportation, consumer affairs, monetary and fiscal policy, natural resources, and pollution.	Includes worldwide scientific, medical and technological developments, natural phenomena, U.S. weather, natural disasters, and accidents.	Includes the arts, religion, scholarship, communications media, sports, entertainments, fashions, fads and social life.

	World Affairs	Europe	Africa & the Middle East	The Americas	Asia & the Pacific
May 5			Ayatollah Ruhollah Khomeini forms a special militia responsible only to his Islamic Revolutionary Council, a move seen lessening the provisional government role of Premier Mehdi Bazargan.		Liberal Party govt. in Australia's Victoria State survives an estimated 6 percent vote swing against it to retain a narrow majority in the state legislative assembly.
May 6	U.N. Deputy High Commissioner for Refugees, Dale de Haan, announces Vietnam's agreement to a plan permitting legal emigration of Vietnamese to nations who will accept them.	Austrian Socialist Party wins 95 seats in parliamentary elections, raising its representation from 93 seats and giving Chancellor Bruno Kreisky an unprecedented fourth term.			Chinese Foreign Trade Min. Li Chiang announces cut-backs in the country's ambitious economic development program.
May 7			Israeli Premier Menahem Begin proposes an Israeli–Lebanese peace treaty, which the Lebanese govt. immediately rejects. . . . Rhodesia's black-controlled Parliament meets for the first time. The session is boycotted by 12 newly elected blacks belonging to Rev. Ndabaningi Sithole's faction of the Zimbabwe African National Union (ZANU).	Canadian postal union leader Jean-Claude Parrot is sentenced to jail for defying a government back-to-work order.	
May 8	In a speech before the WHO annual assembly's opening session in Geneva, HEW Secy. Joseph Califano urges the organization to resist Arab hard-line members' attempts to inject the Middle East dispute into its deliberations.		State Secy. Vance says that U.S.–Saudi Arabian ties have deteriorated over the Israeli–Egyptian peace treaty. . . . Israeli jets carry out two separate raids on southern Lebanon. . . . South Africa announces that the constituent assembly of Namibia will be given power to enact laws for the territory.	Serious fighting erupts around the Municipal Cathedral in San Salvador between the El Salvadoran army and supporters of the Popular Revolutionary Bloc, leaving 23 dead and 70 wounded.	
May 9		James Callaghan is unanimously reelected leader of Britain's Labor Party.	The 43-member Conference of Islamic States suspends Egypt because of its peace treaty with Israel. . . . Over 400 Israeli troops with tanks and armored vehicles cross into southern Lebanon in pursuit of three Palestinian commandos who had attempted to attack a settlement in northern Israel.		Nepal's Congress Party leader Bisheswar Prasad Koirala is freed from house arrest along with 62 other dissidents, including 24 members of the banned Congress Party and some members of the outlawed CP.
May 10		French CP reelects Georges Marchais as its secretary general at its five-day party congress.	Freedom House issues a report describing recent Rhodesian elections as relatively free. . . . Iran announces a surcharge of 60 cents a barrel on its crude oil price, raising the price to $17.17 a barrel for light crude $16.64 for heavy crude oil.	Anaconda Co., which lost its big Chuquicamata mine through expropriation in 1971, returns to copper mining in Chile. . . . Anaconda Co., which lost its big Chuquicamata mine through expropriation in 1971, returns to copper mining in Chile.	
May 11			Eleven black student activists are sentenced to prison terms of up to four years for activities during the 1976 Soweto riots in South Africa.		A Bangkok report says that more than 10,000 Cambodians have entered Thailand in the previous three days, fleeing the fighting in their country following Pol Pot's downfall.
May 12			Prompted by the May 9 execution of Habib Elghanian, a leading Jewish community leader in Iran, Aryeh Dulzin, head of the World Zionist Organization, warns the Iranian govt. that Israel will retaliate if the remaining 65,000 Jews in Iran are harmed.		South Korean govt. frees 16 student and opposition leaders, apparently motivated by Pres. Carter's upcoming visit in June.

A	B	C	D	E
Includes developments that affect more than one world region, international organizations and important meetings of major world leaders.	*Includes all domestic and regional developments in Europe, including the Soviet Union, Turkey, Cyprus and Malta.*	*Includes all domestic and regional developments in Africa and the Middle East, including Iraq and Iran and excluding Cyprus, Turkey and Afghanistan.*	*Includes all domestic and regional developments in Latin America, the Caribbean and Canada.*	*Includes all domestic and regional developments in Asia and Pacific nations, extending from Afghanistan through all the Pacific Islands, except Hawaii.*

U.S. Politics & Social Issues	U.S. Foreign Policy & Defense	U.S. Economy & Environment	Science, Technology & Nature	Culture, Leisure & Life Style	
				Spectacular Bid wins the Kentucky Derby by two and three quarters lengths over *General Assembly* .	May 5
			Over 65,000 protesters march peacefully against nuclear power in a Wash., D.C. demonstration that is the largest against nuclear power in the U.S. to date.	John McEnroe upsets Bjorn Borg of Sweden to win the final match of the World Championship Tennis title in Dallas, Tex.	May 6
		FTC Chmn. Michael Pertschuk warns that the increase in conglomerate mergers could upset the existing political balance of power in the U.S. and give more political influence to private enterprise. . . . Energy Dept. says that May gasoline supplies could run 10–15 percent below demand.			May 7
	Alfred Atherton Jr. is named as the new U.S. ambassador to Egypt to replace Hermann F. Eilts, who is retiring from the Foreign Service.	AFL–CIO Executive Council calls the Carter administration's antiinflation program a total flop.	Dade County, Fla. voters narrowly reject a proposed ordinance that would have banned cigarette smoking in many public places.	Zeizo Tanaka and Pema Sherpa reach the peak of 26,545-foot Annapurna I in Nepal.	May 8
Pres. Carter names Lynda Bird Johnson Robb to head his National Advisory Committee for Women, succeeding Bella Abzug, who was dismissed in January after an acrimonious exchange with the President.		Calif. begins an odd–even license plate plan to ration gasoline in an attempt to stem panic buying. . . . United Rubber Workers strike against Uniroyal Inc. in a contract dispute involving the Carter administration's antiinflation guidelines.	U.S. Geological Survey reports that the U.S. could tap as much energy from underground heat sources as current oil consumption would supply in 162 years.		May 9
Federal Election Commission reports that Political Action Committees (PACs) contributed $35.1 million to 1978 House and Senate candidates.		Retiring Ford Motor Co. chairman Henry Ford 2nd's bitter family feud with his nephew, Benson Ford Jr., is publicly aired at the company's annual meeting where Henry Ford speaks out against his nephew's efforts to win a seat on the board.			May 10
	Michael Townley is sentenced to between 40 months and 10 years in prison for conspiring to kill former Chilean For. Min. Orlando Letelier and an aide, Ronni Moffitt, receiving a reduced sentence for serving as a key prosecution witness in the trial.	Pres. Carter angrily assails the House for rejecting his stand-by gas rationing plan and challenges Congress to develop its own plan in the next 90 days.		Barbara Hutton, 66, Woolworth heiress whose personal misfortune earned her the nickname "poor little rich girl," dies of a heart attack in Los Angeles, Calif.	May 11
Census Bureau reports an enrollment decline in nearly all phases of education.				Bishop Addison Hosea of Lexington, Ky., leader of the largest dissident movement within the Protestant Episcopal Church, urges conservative followers opposed to the ordination of women, prayer book reform, and the church's social activism to fight for their beliefs within the church.	May 12

F	G	H	I	J
Includes elections, federal-state relations, civil rights and liberties, crime, the judiciary, education, health care, poverty, urban affairs and population.	Includes formation and debate of U.S. foreign and defense policies, veterans' affairs and defense spending. (Relations with specific foreign countries are usually found under the region concerned.)	Includes business, labor, agriculture, taxation, transportation, consumer affairs, monetary and fiscal policy, natural resources, and pollution.	Includes worldwide scientific, medical and technological developments, natural phenomena, U.S. weather, natural disasters, and accidents.	Includes the arts, religion, scholarship, communications media, sports, entertainments, fashions, fads and social life.

	World Affairs	Europe	Africa & the Middle East	The Americas	Asia & the Pacific
May 13			Ayatollah Khomeini calls for the assassination of the exiled Shah, members of his immediate family, and officials of his former government.	Leaders of Canada's three major parties hold a televised debate to climax their campaign.	U.N. Secy. Gen. Kurt Waldheim visits Cambodian refugee camps near the Thai border town of Aranyaprathet.
May 14	IMF approves a $66-million loan-package to Nicaragua, which had been the subject of controversy in wake of Nicaragua's human-rights position.		Two Israelis are killed and 32 wounded by an explosion in Tiberias, Israel, attributed to the PLO.		China and the U.S. establish formal commercial relations for the first time since the Communist govt. was formed in 1949. . . . Khmer Rouge radio gives the first official indication that deposed Cambodian Premier Pol Pot is alive and still in Cambodia.
May 15		Among Tory policies announce in Queen Elizabeth II's address from the throne is proposed repeal of the Scotland–Wales devolution acts of 1978.	U.S. Amb.-designate to Iran Walter Cutler expresses U.S. concern to Iran about ongoing executions there.		
May 16	NATO officially endorses the SALT draft treaty.		Lebanese Premier Selim al-Hoss and his eight-member Cabinet resign in a move to bring feuding Christian and Moslem factions into a national-unity coalition. . . . Two Lebanese Christian factions — the Phalangists and the National Liberal Party — announce that they are merging with their respective heads, Pierre Gemayel and Camille Chamoun, as co-leaders.		
May 17		At a Moscow dinner for visiting Pres. Tito, Soviet Pres. Brezhnev speaks to allay Yugoslav fears that the Soviet Union is trying to control Yugoslav policy.	Defense Min. Ezer Weizman, a member of the Israeli negotiating team, resigns from the delegation to protest the Israeli govt.'s plan for Palestinian self-rule.	Cuban Pres. Fidel Castro arrives in Mexico for his first visit in 23 years.	
May 18		Following Moscow talks, Yugoslav Pres. Tito and Soviet Pres. Brezhnev issue a joint statement affirming closer ties between their CPs, backing East–West detente, but ignoring their primary divisive issues related to foreign alignments	A force of 50–100 Israeli troops storms ashore from rubber boats to raid a PLO base in southern Lebanon in what is seen as a retaliatory attack. . . . Phalangists in Lebanon fight with members of the leftist National Syrian Social Party about 15 miles northeast of Beirut, leaving 14 dead.		
May 19		U.S. Secy. Gen. Kurt Waldheim announces in Nicosia that Greek and Turkish Cypriot leaders have agreed to hold new talks to try to restore the island's unity.	Over 100,000 people demonstrate in Teheran to protest Iranian govt. censorship of the press.	A group of over 100 fishermen and their sympathizers camp on the beach at Vieques, an island halfway between Puerto Rico and the U.S. Virgin Islands, to protest its use for U.S. Navy maneuvers.	About 9,000 Vietnamese refugees are reported having arrived in Malaysia, 7,000 in Indonesia, and 7,000 in Hong Kong since the beginning of May.
May 20		Voters in a referendum approve by a large margin a Swiss govt. reform package for the construction and operation of nuclear power plants.	Iran advises the U.S. to delay sending a new ambassador to Teheran, angrily responding to the U.S. Senate resolution condemning executions in Iran.		

A	B	C	D	E
Includes developments that affect more than one world region, international organizations and important meetings of major world leaders.	Includes all domestic and regional developments in Europe, including the Soviet Union, Turkey, Cyprus and Malta.	Includes all domestic and regional developments in Africa and the Middle East, including Iraq and Iran and excluding Cyprus, Turkey and Afghanistan.	Includes all domestic and regional developments in Latin America, the Caribbean and Canada.	Includes all domestic and regional developments in Asia and Pacific nations, extending from Afghanistan through all the Pacific Islands, except Hawaii.

U.S. Politics & Social Issues	U.S. Foreign Policy & Defense	U.S. Economy & Environment	Science, Technology & Nature	Culture, Leisure & Life Style	
					May 13
Sen. Edward Kennedy (D, Mass.) introduces a comprehensive national health insurance plan that would provide every American, regardless of income, complete health care for the most part privately financed by employers.		*Business Week* reports that salaries and bonuses paid to top U.S. corporate executives rose 16.7 percent in 1978, the sharpest increase of the decade.	Scientists start drilling on Maryland's Eastern Shore for water hot enough to heat homes and factories.	Jean Rhys, 84, British novelist whose theme was the plight of lonely women in a male-dominated world, dies in Exeter, England.	May 14
Pres. Carter and his wife, Rosalynn, present a bill that would revise the federal mental health programs and increase federal spending, estimated for the first year at $99.1 million.	Senate adopts a resolution, introduced by Sen. Richard Schweiker (R, Pa.), to end economic sanctions against Rhodesia after formal installation of the newly elected black government.	Pres. Carter is reported abandoning his bid to create a new Cabinet-level department of natural resources in face of opposition by Senate Democratic Leader Robert Byrd (W. Va.) and Sen. Abraham Ribicoff (D. Conn.)			May 15
Philip Randolph, 90, black labor leader and a founder of the modern U.S. civil-rights movement, dies in Washington, D.C. . . . Sen. Lowell Weicker Jr. (R, Conn.) ends his bid for the presidential nomination nine weeks after beginning it.		Pres. Carter meets Calif. Gov. Jerry Brown Jr. at the White House and promises increased gasoline for that state, which has been hit hard by tightened supplies.			May 16
	By a voice vote, the Senate unanimously adopts a resolution condemning the wave of executions in Iran and the revolutionary court's death sentence for exiled Shah Mohammed Riza Pahlevi, his family, and close officials.	Hammermill Paper Co. is cleared of noncompliance charges with Pres. Carter's price guidelines.	The presidential commission investigating the Three Mile Island nuclear accident votes to halt its probe, claiming that it cannot proceed without the right to subpoena witnesses and question them under oath.		May 17
Supreme Ct. officials announce restricted hours for reporters working at the court in an attempt to stop leaks to the press of information concerning the justices's decisions. . . . Billy Carter, the President's brother, testifies before a federal grand jury that he does not know of any money diverted from the Carter family peanut business or its bank loans to the 1976 Carter presidential campaign.			Oklahoma City federal jury awards $10.5 million in damages to the estate of Karen Silkwood, a laboratory technician contaminated by radiation in 1974 while employed at the Kerr-McGee Corp. Cimarron plutonium plant.	A three-month major league baseball umpires' strike is settled.	May 18
		Commerce Dept. reports that after-tax corporate profits rise 5.7 percent to a seasonally adjusted annual rate of $137.9 billion, for the first quarter of 1979.		*Spectacular Bid* wins the Preakness Stakes, paving the way to the Triple Crown.	May 19
Pres. Carter urges blacks to exercise their voting rights to break the hold of special interests on Congress.		Energy Dept. figures show that the use of wood as fuel has expanded at about 15 percent a year since the 1973–74 Arab oil embargo.		Winnipeg Jets win the Avco Cup, symbolic of World Hockey Assn. championship, with a 7–3 win over the Edmonton Oilers.	May 20

F	G	H	I	J
Includes elections, federal-state relations, civil rights and liberties, crime, the judiciary, education, health care, poverty, urban affairs and population.	*Includes formation and debate of U.S. foreign and defense policies, veterans' affairs and defense spending. (Relations with specific foreign countries are usually found under the region concerned.)*	*Includes business, labor, agriculture, taxation, transportation, consumer affairs, monetary and fiscal policy, natural resources, and pollution.*	*Includes worldwide scientific, medical and technological developments, natural phenomena, U.S. weather, natural disasters, and accidents.*	*Includes the arts, religion, scholarship, communications media, sports, entertainments, fashions, fads and social life.*

	World Affairs	Europe	Africa & the Middle East	The Americas	Asia & the Pacific
May 21			White House confirms that Pres. Carter has written to Saudi King Khalid urging him not to oppose Egyptian Pres. Sadat's peace treaty with Israel.	*Business Week* magazine reports that a new Chilean govt. policy encouraging private enterprise has resulted in economic growth average annual rate of 6.2 percent of and annually inflation decline to 20–25 percent annually.	Japanese govt. asks gasoline stations to close on Sundays and holidays during June. . . . Vietnam and China exchange prisoners of war, the first such trade since their February–March border war.
May 22		International Energy Agency (IEA) agrees to share oil with hard-pressed Sweden.	Britain announces it will send a permanent representative to Salisbury to have closest possible contact with the new black Rhodesian govt.	Canadian voters give the Progressive Conservative Party a 136-seat plurality in Parliament, making its leader, Joseph Clark, prime minister-elect and ending Liberal Party P.M. Pierre Trudeau's 11-year tenure in office.	
May 23	Hard-line Arab delegates to the WHO annual assembly withdraw a resolution to suspend Israel as a voting member for alleged mistreatment of Arabs in occupied territories. . . . South African representatives to the U.N. take their seats in the General Assembly for the first time in five years to attend a week-long debate on Namibia.	Karl Carstens, speaker of the Bundestag and member of the opposition Christian Democratic Party, is elected president of West Germany.	EEC foreign aid experts visit Uganda to assess its needs for economic reconstruction.	A militant guerrilla organization assassinates Carlos Antonio Herrera Rebollo, the El Salvadoran minister of education, and his chauffeur. . . . Almost half of Trudeau's 31-member Cabinet is defeated in reelection bids.	
May 24				El Salvadoran govt. orders a 30-day state of siege in response to mounting incidents of violence that culminated in yesterday's assassination of the education minister. . . . Canada's Conference Bd. reports that the government's wage and price control program (1975–78) was more effective curbing wages and salaries than keeping prices down.	Australian govt. proposes measures to raise tax revenue and cut spending to avert a deficit in the fiscal year starting July 1.
May 25		Roger Dafflon, a Communist and former construction worker, is elected mayor of Geneva, Switzerland.	Israel begins withdrawing from the Sinai Peninsula by handing back the coastal town of El Arish to Egypt, the first step under terms of the new peace treaty.	Members of the Popular Revolutionary Bloc end their 20-day occupation of San Salvador's Municipal Cathedral after the Salvadoran govt. warns that they would be forcibly removed.	
May 26	EEC talks with representatives of 57 developing nations over a new five-year assistance program to replace the 1976–80 Lome Convention collapse when the two sides can not agree on a number of issues.		Egyptian Pres. Sadat visits El Arish, receiving a tumultuous welcome from its 30,000 Egyptian inhabitants.	*Montreal Star* reports that 368 companies have moved their head offices out of Quebec since the Parti Quebecois took office in 1976.	
May 27		A four-party, left-center coalition headed by Mauno Koivisto takes office in Finland.	Israeli Premier Begin announces the opening of the Israeli–Egyptian border and other steps toward normalized relations following talks with Egyptian Pres. Sadat.		
May 28		Greek Premier Constantine Caramanlis signs a treaty with EEC representatives formally admitting Greece into the Common Market.	Josiah Zion Gumede is elected to the ceremonial post of president of the newly named Zimbabwe Rhodesia as a black majority government prepares to take over.	Five-nation Andean Group creates a Court of Justice and names Colombian Pres. Julio Cesar Turbay Ayala its negotiation representative with the EEC.	

A	B	C	D	E
Includes developments that affect more than one world region, international organizations and important meetings of major world leaders.	Includes all domestic and regional developments in Europe, including the Soviet Union, Turkey, Cyprus and Malta.	Includes all domestic and regional developments in Africa and the Middle East, including Iraq and Iran and excluding Cyprus, Turkey and Afghanistan.	Includes all domestic and regional developments in Latin America, the Caribbean and Canada.	Includes all domestic and regional developments in Asia and Pacific nations, extending from Afghanistan through all the Pacific Islands, except Hawaii.

U.S. Politics & Social Issues	U.S. Foreign Policy & Defense	U.S. Economy & Environment	Science, Technology & Nature	Culture, Leisure & Life Style	
A presidential council finds an increase in the use of marijuana in the U.S. . . . . Supreme Ct. rules unanimously that victims of alleged age discrimination must first file complaints with state agencies before seeking federal recourse.	Iranian Justice Min. Assadollah Mobasheri charges that Marion Javits, wife of Sen. Jacob Javits (R, N.Y.), was paid $507,000 to portray the exiled Shah's govt. in a good light.		Harold Denton, an NRC official, says that the NRC will not grant any new construction permits or operating licenses for nuclear power plants for at least three months in wake of the Three Mile Island accident.	Montreal Canadiens win their twenty-second Stanley Cup with a 4-1 victory over the New York Rangers in the final game of the National Hockey League playoffs. . . . Thousands of youths mob British rock singer Elton John at the opening concert in Leningrad of an eight-concert Soviet tour.	May 21
Dan White, a former San Francisco, Calif. supervisor, is convicted of voluntary manslaughter in the November 1978 killings of San Francisco Mayor George Moscone and Harvey Milk, a supervisor.		Pres. Carter asks that all federally chartered savings institutions be allowed to offer variable-rate mortgages. . . . U.S. Steel Corp. pledges to clean up nine Pittsburgh area facilities, spending $400 million to counter previous air and water pollution.		Scottish historian Micheil MacDonald advances the theory that Britain's Queen Victoria had a clandestine romance and secretly married a favorite servant after the death of Prince Albert, bearing a son named John Brown.	May 22
An indictment in N.J. for the first time names the Mafia, long used as a popular appellation for a national crime organization, and charges eight alleged members of the Vito Genovese N.Y. crime family with a long list of crimes. . . . Four House Democrats — Reps. Edward Beard (R.I.), Richard Nolan (Minn.), Richard Ottinger (N.Y.), and Fortney (Pete) Stark (Calif.) — launch a dump-Carter campaign that endorses Sen. Edward Kennedy (Mass.) as the party's 1980 presidential candidate.		An Atlanta, Ga. federal grand jury indicts former OMB Dir. Bert Lance and three associates on charges that they conspired to obtain $20 million in bank loans for their own gain between 1970–78.		Moses Malone, Houston Rockets center, is named the NBA most valuable player for the 1978–79 season.	May 23
House Administration Committee defeats a bill to provide partial public financing of House election campaigns.		After three days of debate, House Democratic Caucus formally approves a resolution opposing Pres. Carter's plan to decontrol domestic oil prices.		A futuristic science-fiction film, Alien , starring Sigourney Weaver and William Hurt, is released in N.Y.	May 24
John Spenkelink, 30, is put to death in a Florida State Prison electric chair, the first person executed in the U.S. since Gary Gilmore in 1977.		Energy Dept. adopts emergency rules aimed at easing diesel-fuel shortages for truckers hauling agricultural goods, surface mass-transit systems, and companies producing crude oil and natural gas.	All 272 people aboard an American Airlines DC-10 jet, plus three men on the ground, are killed after the plane loses one of its three engines and crashes shortly after takeoff at Chicago's O'Hare International Airport. It is the worst aviation accident to date in the U.S.		May 25
		Retail gasoline prices around the U.S. are reported rising an average of 15 cents a gallon in the first four-and-a-half months of this year.			May 26
		The New York Times reports that national average gasoline consumption per person was 531.9 gallons a year in 1978.		Rick Mears wins auto racing's Indianapolis 500.	May 27
					May 28

F	G	H	I	J
Includes elections, federal-state relations, civil rights and liberties, crime, the judiciary, education, health care, poverty, urban affairs and population.	Includes formation and debate of U.S. foreign and defense policies, veterans' affairs and defense spending. (Relations with specific foreign countries are usually found under the region concerned.)	Includes business, labor, agriculture, taxation, transportation, consumer affairs, monetary and fiscal policy, natural resources, and pollution.	Includes worldwide scientific, medical and technological developments, natural phenomena, U.S. weather, natural disasters, and accidents.	Includes the arts, religion, scholarship, communications media, sports, entertainments, fashions, fads and social life.

	World Affairs	Europe	Africa & the Middle East	The Americas	Asia & the Pacific
May 29		U.S. Embassy spokesperson in Moscow says that the Soviets have apparently stopped beaming microwave radiation at the embassy, the subject of U.S. protests since the 1960s.	Bishop Abel Muzorewa is sworn in as prime minister of the new black majority government in Zimbabwe Rhodesia. Former P.M. Ian Smith remains in the Cabinet as minister without portfolio, a sign of greatly reduced power.... Three Israeli navy landing craft sail through the Suez Canal marking the first peacetime use of the waterway by Israeli armed forces.		*Washington Post* reports that broadcasts from Hunan province criticizing Chinese Deputy Premier Teng Hsiao-ping indicate a serious split in the country's leadership.
May 30		Major Western nations agree on a $1.45 billion aid package for Turkey.	Iranian government troops battle ethnic Arabs seeking autonomy in Khuzistan province.... The body of Dora Bloch, a British–Israeli citizen who was a passenger on an airplane hijacked to Uganda in 1976, is found and identified in a shallow grave east of Uganda's capital city.	Bahamian groups reportedly are demonstrating against the exiled Shah of Iran's presence there.	Chinese officials announce that four U.S. newspapers have been allowed to open offices in Peking.
May 31	NATO foreign ministers endorse a draft treaty that concluded U.S.–U.S.S.R. SALT talks.	Twenty-two bombs explode at various locations in Paris and cause much damage but no injuries. The Corsican National Liberation Front claims responsibility.	A black government is formally installed in Rhodesia at midnight completing the transition from more than 80 years of white rule. ... Rhodesia's name is changed to Zimbabwe Rhodesia as its new Constition becomes effective.		U.S. imposes quotas on five categories of textile imports from China.
June 1			Sheik Hasham Hussendair, 72, a ranking Moslem leader who supported the Egyptian–Israeli peace treaty, is stabbed to death by a single assailant in front of his home in the Gaza Strip. The Popular Front for the Liberation of Palestine claims credit.	*Latin American Economic Report* says that although Mexico's oil-based economy is booming, industrial growth has pushed inflation about the government's target level, and the current account deficit is therefore rising.	
June 2			Iran's opposition National Democratic Front accuses Ayatollah Khomeini of being a dictator.	*The New York Times* reports that the Argentine economy has sharply rebounded from its 1978 slump but at the price of renewed inflation.	Japan and the U.S. initial an agreement in Tokyo that accepts mutual reciprocity in trade dealings.
June 3			With the capture of Koboko, the Tanzanian-led invasion of Uganda appears to be complete.... Israeli Cabinet gives final approval to establishing a new settlement of Elon Moreh near Nablus in the West Bank.		
June 4		For the first time since the end of WWII, the Italian CP loses ground in elections.	South African Pres. John Vorster resigns in wake of a revised report charging him with covering up irregularities in the former Dept. of Information.... Dissidents from Ghana's armed forces, led by Jerry Rawlings, wrest control of the country from Gen. Fred Akuffo after a first coup attempt on May 15 that failed.	In a televised ceremony, Joseph Clark is sworn in as Canada's sixteenth prime minister and its youngest head of government to date.... Nicaraguan Sandinista leaders call a general strike to bring down the government of Gen. Anastasio Somoza Debayle.	Australian P.M. Malcolm Fraser bars oil drilling on the Great Barrier Reef pending environmental impact studies.

A	B	C	D	E
Includes developments that affect more than one world region, international organizations and important meetings of major world leaders.	*Includes all domestic and regional developments in Europe, including the Soviet Union, Turkey, Cyprus, and Malta.*	*Includes all domestic and regional developments in Africa and the Middle East, including Iraq and Iran and excluding Cyprus, Turkey and Afghanistan.*	*Includes all domestic and regional developments in Latin America, the Caribbean and Canada.*	*Includes all domestic and regional developments in Asia and Pacific nations, extending from Afghanistan through all the Pacific Islands, except Hawaii.*

U.S. Politics & Social Issues	U.S. Foreign Policy & Defense	U.S. Economy & Environment	Science, Technology & Nature	Culture, Leisure & Life Style	
Supreme Ct. rules, 5–4, that prison inmates are not entitled to full protection of the Fourteenth Amendment in state parole proceedings.		Texaco Inc. says that its June 1979 allocation will be only 70 percent of the gasoline it allocated in June 1978.	FAA orders U.S. airlines to ground all DC-10 wide-bodied jets until they complete inspection of engine-mounting bolts, held responsible for the May 25 fatal crash of an American Airlines DC-10 in Chicago.	Mary Pickford, 86, Hollywood's first great film star dies following a stroke in Santa Monica, Calif.	May 29
	The New York Times publishes documents showing that Marion Javits, wife of Sen. Jacob Javits (R, N.Y.), secretly worked for an Iranian govt. lobby in the U.S. while apparently representing Iran Air.	U.S. trade deficit becomes wider with imports exceeding exports by a seasonally adjusted $2.15 billion, according to a Commerce Dept. report. . . . International Ladies Garment Workers Union announces new labor agreements covering 130,000 members in the Northeast.		Two largest denominations of the U.S. Presbyterians — the United Presbyterian Church in the U.S.A. and the Presbyterian Church in the U.S. — end a week-long joint gathering, the first time the two churches have met together since they divided in 1860 over the slavery issue.	May 30
White House releases records showing that Pres. Carter became a millionaire in 1978, with most of his assets in a trust managed by Charles Kirbo, an Atlanta lawyer.		U.S. District Ct. Judge Barrington Parker rules that the Carter administration cannot withhold federal contracts from wage–price guidelines violators. . . . AFL–CIO pres. George Meany asks the administration to abandon the guidelines and prepare a program that addresses and deals with the basic causes of inflation.			May 31
		Pres. Carter meets with consumer groups who are outspoken in criticizing Carter's program to remove oil price controls. . . . Lockheed Corp. pleads guilty in a Wash., D.C. federal district ct. to charges that it had concealed $2.6 million in payoffs to Japanese government and business officials and is fined $647,000.	Legislation passed in Iowa, Minn., Texas, and Oregon brings to 11 the number of U.S. states allowing legal access to marijuana for medical purposes.	Jan Kadar, 61, expatriate Czech film director, dies in Los Angeles, Calif. . . . Seattle SuperSonics win the NBA title by defeating the Washington Bullets, 97–93, in the fifth game of the best-of-seven final series.	June 1
Pres. Carter tells a Democratic fund-raising dinner in Indianapolis that one of the most immobilizing fears in the U.S. today is the fear of being misled and cheated. . . . Leonard Hall, 78, Republican political leader and U.S. congressman from N.Y.S. (1939–52), dies in Glen Cove, N.Y.				Pope John Paul II receives a tumultuous welcome in his native Poland when he arrives for a nine-day visit.	June 2
			Antinuclear rallies in the U.S., Spain, West Germany, and France mark International Antinuclear Day.	Two books dealing with diet — The Complete Scarsdale Medical Diet by Herman Tarnower and Samm Baker and The Pritikin Program by Nathan Pritikin — are first and fifth place respectively on the best-selling general books list for the previous week.	June 3
Gallup Poll conducted over the past three days shows Pres. Carter's approval rating at a mere 29 percent of those interviewed, barely above the approval levels former Pres. Richard Nixon had when he resigned office in 1974.		Pres. Carter names Treasury Secy. W. Michael Blumenthal as his chief economic spokesman and economic policy coordinator.			June 4

F	G	H	I	J
Includes elections, federal-state relations, civil rights and liberties, crime, the judiciary, education, health care, poverty, urban affairs and population.	*Includes formation and debate of U.S. foreign and defense policies, veterans' affairs and defense spending. (Relations with specific foreign countries are usually found under the region concerned.)*	*Includes business, labor, agriculture, taxation, transportation, consumer affairs, monetary and fiscal policy, natural resources, and pollution.*	*Includes worldwide scientific, medical and technological developments, natural phenomena, U.S. weather, natural disasters, and accidents.*	*Includes the arts, religion, scholarship, communications media, sports, entertainments, fashions, fads and social life.*

	World Affairs	Europe	Africa & the Middle East	The Americas	Asia & the Pacific
June 5	French For. Min. Jean Francois-Poncet tells a Wash., D.C. news conference that Western industrialized nations should adopt a concerted policy to end the competitive bidding that has drive up oil prices at the special market in Rotterdam.		Egyptian Pres. Sadat announces an arms agreement with China.	New Canadian P.M. Joseph Clark says he will keep a campaign promise to move the Canadian Embassy in Israel from Tel Aviv to Jerusalem.	
June 6		Soviet Union is reported proceeding with plans to build atomic power and heat-generating stations within large Soviet cities.	PLO announces that it is closing its headquarters in Tyre and withdrawing its forces from southern Lebanese villages to deprive the Israelis of a pretext for attacks.	Nicaraguan Pres. Anastasio Somoza Debayle declares a state of siege to combat a general strike and guerrilla war, thereby enabling the National Guard to make arrests without warrant and detain suspects longer than the constitutionally mandated 24 hours.	
June 7		Portuguese Premier Carlos Mota Pinto resigns in wake of Socialist and CP censure motions against the government's budget proposals.	Pres. Carter announces that he will not lift trade sanctions against Zimbabwe Rhodesia.		According to U.S. intelligence sources, the families of Afghan Pres. Nur Mohammad Taraki and Premier Hafizullah Amin have been secretly evacuated to the Soviet Union as the Islamic rebellion in Afghanistan continues.
June 8			Zimbabwe Rhodesian P.M. Abel Muzorewa strongly denounces Pres. Carter's decision against lifting sanctions and calls it an appeasement of black Africans. Zimbabwe African National Union (ZAPU) leader Robert Mugabe welcomes the decision.... Refugees from the former Ugandan regime, estimated at 100,000, are reported pouring into Sudan.	Newly elected and installed Progressive Conservative govt. in Canada orders a government employment hiring freeze.	
June 9			In Lebanon Christian militiamen clash with Dutch UNIFIL troops at Al Mansouri.		
June 10		Rolf Heissler is arrested by West German police in Frankfurt as a suspect in the 1977 murder of industrialist Hanns-Martin Schleyer.	The deposed Shah of Iran leaves his exile in the Bahamas, where his visa had expired, and flies to Mexico on a six-month tourist visa.	Army Chief of Staff Gen. Jose Cansino is shot to death in Guatemala City.	
June 11	The price of gold on the London exchange soars to a record $282.35 an ounce.... The 25-nation coordinating bureau of the nonaligned nations movement ends an eight-day meeting in Sri Lanka failing to solve two outstanding disputes: which government represents Cambodia and whether to suspend Egypt for signing a peace pact with Israel.		Robert Astles, British-born adviser to former Ugandan Pres. Idi Amin, goes on trial in Kampala on murder charges after being extradited from Kenya at the request of the new Ugandan govt.	Nicaraguan National Guard troops set afire the offices of the opposition newspaper La Prensa , which symbolizes the struggle to overthrow Gen. Anastasio Somoza Debayle's regime.	Soviet presence in Afghanistan is reported to have increased to approximately 3,000 civil advisers and 1,000 military advisers.... Thai authorities are reported turning back 30,000 Cambodian refugees in the past four days.

A	B	C	D	E
Includes developments that affect more than one world region, international organizations and important meetings of major world leaders.	Includes all domestic and regional developments in Europe, including the Soviet Union, Turkey, Cyprus and Malta.	Includes all domestic and regional developments in Africa and the Middle East, including Iraq and Iran and excluding Cyprus, Turkey and Afghanistan.	Includes all domestic and regional developments in Latin America, the Caribbean and Canada.	Includes all domestic and regional developments in Asia and Pacific nations, extending from Afghanistan through all the Pacific Islands, except Hawaii.

U.S. Politics & Social Issues	U.S. Foreign Policy & Defense	U.S. Economy & Environment	Science, Technology & Nature	Culture, Leisure & Life Style	
Supreme Ct. rules that members of Congress can be sued for sex discrimination.... Supreme Ct. rules, 7–2, that states can give veterans an advantage in public service employment without discriminating against women.		Representatives of Babcock & Wilcox Co., builders of the Three Mile Island nuclear reactors, reiterate their claim that they are blameless in the March 28 accident and charge the operating utility, Metropolitan Edison Co., with the responsibility.	Soviet Union and Turkey announce that Moscow will build a nuclear power plant in Turkey, worth $880 million, and furnish it with atomic fuel.		June 5
	U.S. District Ct. Judge Oliver Gasch dismisses a suit brought by Sen. Barry Goldwater (R, Ariz.) and 24 other congressmen that seeks to rescind the Carter administration's termination of a defense pact with Taiwan.		FAA grounds all 138 U.S.-operated McDonnell Douglas Corp. DC-10 jets indefinitely in wake of the nation's worst air disaster to date and subsequent investigations that cast doubt on the aircraft's safety. ... National Cancer Institute panel recommends that surgeons abandon radical mastectomies and use a less severe operation that has proved to be equally effective in treatment of breast cancer.		June 6
N.Y.S. Supreme Ct. Appellate Division overturns the 1978 murder convictions of Teamster officials Anthony (Tony Pro) Provenzano and Harold (Boom Boom) Konigsberg and orders new trials.		Independent truckers begin a wildcat strike against rising diesel fuel prices and scarce supplies, blockading truck stops on major highways in more than a dozen states.		Pope John Paul II visits the Auschwitz death camp.	June 7
Rep. John Anderson (Ill.) announces that he is a candidate for the Republican presidential nomination in the 1980 election.	White House officially announces Pres. Carter's decision to approve full-scale development of the MX mobile intercontinental ballistic missile.			Spencer Kimball, president of the Mormon Church, reports that thousands of blacks have been made church officers since they became eligible for the priesthood in 1978. ... Norman Hartnell, 78, dressmaker to Queen Elizabeth II, dies in Windsor, Eng. after a heart attack.	June 8
Cleveland, Ohio Mayor Dennis Kucinich and City Council leaders agree on a plan to repay the $14 million owed local banks since the city defaulted in 1978.			Voyager I is reported to have located the hottest spot in the solar system between Jupiter and Mars with a temperature between 300,000,000–400,000,000 degrees Celsius.	Chris Evert Lloyd takes her third French Open by beating Australia's Wendy Turnbull in the women's singles final.... Spectacular Bid, the odds-on favorite, loses the Belmont Stakes race to Coastal, thereby forfeiting horse racing's Triple Crown.	June 9
				Don and Bill Whittington and Klaus Ludwig win the 24 Hours of Le Mans auto race.... Sweden's Bjorn Borg wins the French Open for the fourth time with a victory over Victor Pecci of Paraguay in the men's singles tennis championship.... Donna Caponi Young wins the LPGA golf tournament.	June 10
Supreme Ct. rules unanimously that federally funded colleges do not have to admit all handicapped applicants or make extensive modifications to accomodate them.		Pres. Carter directs the Agriculture and Interior depts. to increase sales of timber from federal forests in an effort to curtail rising housing costs.		Actor John Wayne, 72, dies of cancer complications in Los Angeles, Calif.	June 11

F	G	H	I	J
Includes elections, federal-state relations, civil rights and liberties, crime, the judiciary, education, health care, poverty, urban affairs and population.	Includes formation and debate of U.S. foreign and defense policies, veterans' affairs and defense spending. (Relations with specific foreign countries are usually found under the region concerned.)	Includes business, labor, agriculture, taxation, transportation, consumer affairs, monetary and fiscal policy, natural resources, and pollution.	Includes worldwide scientific, medical and technological developments, natural phenomena, U.S. weather, natural disasters, and accidents.	Includes the arts, religion, scholarship, communications media, sports, entertainments, fashions, fads and social life.

	World Affairs	Europe	Africa & the Middle East	The Americas	Asia & the Pacific
June 12	Ayatollah Khomeini of Iran accuses the Soviet Union of assisting Afghanistan is suppressing the Islamic rebellion there and of possible interference in Iran.	The new political lineup of the European Parliament — after June 7 and 10 elections — is as follows: Socialists, 109 seats; Christian Democrats, 107 seats; Liberals and Democratics, 40 seats; European Progressive Democrats, 22 seats; European Conservatives, 63 seats, CP and allies, 46 seats; and nonaffiliates, 23 seats. . . . Ferenc Nagy, 75, the last non-Communist premier of Hungary, dies after a heart attack in Wash., D.C.			China agrees to revive a $1-billion contract with the Japanese Nippon Steel Corp. to construct a steel complex near Shanghai.
June 13	Turkey and the IMF reach agreement for a $360-million one-year standby loan and a possible $1.3 billion aid package put together by the Western powers.		U.S. officials confirm a report that deposed Ugandan Pres. Idi Amin has been given asylum in Libya.	Guerrilla fighting and consequent looting reaches Managua, Nicaragua as National Guard troops battle guerrillas who had seized the capital's outlying slums.	
June 14	U.N. Security Council approves a six-month extension of its Interim Force in Lebanon. . . . OPEC finance ministers warn that unless effective action is taken against rising oil prices, they could trigger a new inflation-generated recession similar to that in 1974–75.	Basques detonate six powerful bombs, which damage government buildings and a sports center in northern Spain.			An April speech is reported in a Hong Kong newspaper in which Chinese Vice Premier Li Hsien-nien outlines the country's serious economic problems, which include malnutrition and unemployment.
June 15	Pres. Carter and Soviet Pres. Brezhnev meet face-to-face for the first time in an informal courtesy call on Austrian Pres. Rudolf Kirchschlaeger, official host of the Vienna summit to sign the SALT Treaty.		Ariel Sharon, a member of Israel's negotiating team, accuses the U.S. of imperiling peace in the Middle East by promoting the idea of establishing a Palestinian state in the West Bank and Gaza Strip.		Malaysia announces it will expel an estimated 75,000 Vietnamese refugees from camps along its coast and shoot on sight any more who try to reach its shores. . . . Philippine Pres. Ferdinand Marcos suspends construction of a nuclear power plant on the Bataan Peninsula and names a commission to investigate its safety.
June 16	U.N. High Commissioner for Refugees Poul Hartling appeals to countries where Vietnamese refugees have arrived to receive them.			A force of 700-well-armed Sandinista guerrillas invade Nicaragua from neighboring Costa Rica.	
June 17				Amnesty International produces a list of 2,665 people who have disappeared in Argentina since the military seized control on March 24, 1976. . . . Andean Group nations issue a joint communique endorsing the Sandinistas as the legitimate force in Nicaragua attempting to overthrow Anastasio Somoza and establish a democratic govt.	
June 18	An emotionally charged ceremony in Vienna's Hofburg (palace) marks the signing of a U.S.–U.S.S.R. SALT Treaty after seven years of negotiations.	French govt. is reported reversing its May decision and will proceed to build the 2,300-kilowatt Themis solar electric power plant in the western Pyrenees.	Elections for Ghana's first civilian government since 1969 are held on schedule, but no party emerges with an absolute majority of the popular vote. . . . Ayatollah Khomeini announces a new Constitution, based on Islamic law and principles. . . . Lebanese army troops restore the government's authority in the Christian suburbs of Beirut where fighting between rival Christian groups in the past three weeks has resulted in at least 15 dead and many wounded.	Nicaraguan Sandinista guerrillas name a five-member provisional junta, held unacceptable by the U.S. because it is comprised of three leftists and two moderates. . . . Nicaraguan National Guard sends reinforcements south to try to halt the Sandinistas' advance on Rivas.	Chinese Premier and CP leader Hua Kuo-feng acknowledges that his economic goals for this year have been too ambitious.

A	B	C	D	E
Includes developments that affect more than one world region, international organizations and important meetings of major world leaders.	Includes all domestic and regional developments in Europe, including the Soviet Union, Turkey, Cyprus and Malta.	Includes all domestic and regional developments in Africa and the Middle East, including Iraq and Iran and excluding Cyprus, Turkey and Afghanistan.	Includes all domestic and regional developments in Latin America, the Caribbean and Canada.	Includes all domestic and regional developments in Asia and Pacific nations, extending from Afghanistan through all the Pacific Islands, except Hawaii.

U.S. Politics & Social Issues	U.S. Foreign Policy & Defense	U.S. Economy & Environment	Science, Technology & Nature	Culture, Leisure & Life Style	
Pres. Carter unveils a national health insurance plan that would require employers to insure workers against medical expenses above $2,500 a year and would expand Medicare coverage.... Mass. Gov. Edward King signs what is described as the strictest antiabortion law in the U.S., which permits government-funded abortions only to save a mother's life.	In a strongly worded speech, Sen. Henry Jackson (D, Wash.) charges the Carter administration with appeasing the Soviet Union in concluding the SALT Treaty.... Senate votes, 52–41, to lift economic sanctions against Zimbabwe Rhodesia in an amendment to a $40-billion weapons authorization bill sponsored by Sen. Harry Byrd (Ind. Va.).			Bryan Trottier of the New York Islanders is awarded the Hart Trophy as the most valuable player in the NHL for 1978–79.	June 12
U.S. Court of Claims awards the Sioux Nation $17.5 million for an area in the Black Hills of South Dakota, which the government obtained from the Indians in 1877. ... U.S. Conference of Mayors endorses Pres. Carter's urban and energy policies.	Senate passes, 89–7, a $40.09-billion weapons procurement bill, which is close to the funding level sought by the Carter administration.			Anatoly Kuznetsov, 49, Soviet author who defected to Great Britain in 1969 and was best known for his 1966 book, *Babi Yar*, dies after an apparent heart attack in London.	June 13
San Francisco Bay area law enforcement agents arrest 32 members of the Hell's Angels motorcycle gang on racketeering charges involving narcotics, firearms, and murder.	ACLU and Reps. Don Edwards and Ronald Dellums, both Calif. Democrats, charge that the Navy discriminates against blacks and other minorities through its entrance requirements.	Independent Truckers Assn. reports that 60 percent of the nation's long-haul interstate trucks have stopped operating in response to its call for a nationwide trucking shutdown to demand cheaper diesel fuel and a 65-mile-an-hour speed limit.		Herman Shumlin, 80, producer, and director credited with the discovery of Lillian Hellman's theatrical talent, dies of heart failure in N.Y.	June 14
		FRB reports that industrial output for May rose sharply by a seasonally adjusted 1.3 percent.			June 15
			FDA head Donald Kennedy, who has been deeply involved in efforts to ban saccharin, nitrites, and Laetrile, announces his resignation to become provost of Stanford University.		June 16
Leverett Saltonstall, 86, Republican senator and three-term governor of Massachusetts, dies of heart failure in Dover, Mass.			An express train near the Ivory Coast capital of Abidjan derails and kills 15 people, injuring 60.	Hale Irwin manages to win golf's U.S. Open although he shoots a 75 with a double bogey and a bogey on the last two holes.	June 17
Supreme Court rules, 6–2, that the legislative acts of present and former members of Congress cannot be introduced as evidence against them in criminal prosecution.		URW–B.F. Goodrich Co. reach a new contract, which is established as the pattern contract for the industry. URW. Pres. Peter Bommarito reports that the terms far exceed voluntary federal wage guidelines.	Supreme Ct. rules unanimously that the FDA has the power to ban the interstate sale and distribution of Laetrile, the controversial anticancer agent.		June 18

F	G	H	I	J
Includes elections, federal-state relations, civil rights and liberties, crime, the judiciary, education, health care, poverty, urban affairs and population.	*Includes formation and debate of U.S. foreign and defense policies, veterans' affairs and defense spending. (Relations with specific foreign countries are usually found under the region concerned.)*	*Includes business, labor, agriculture, taxation, transportation, consumer affairs, monetary and fiscal policy, natural resources, and pollution.*	*Includes worldwide scientific, medical and technological developments, natural phenomena, U.S. weather, natural disasters, and accidents.*	*Includes the arts, religion, scholarship, communications media, sports, entertainments, fashions, fads and social life.*

	World Affairs	Europe	Africa & the Middle East	The Americas	Asia & the Pacific
June 19	*Wall Street Journal* reports that Japanese banks have replaced U.S. banks as top-ranked of the world's 300 largest banks.				
June 20		French Socialist Party leader Francois Mitterrand resigns from the newly elected European Parliament to protest a recount of the French vote that cost the Socialists a seat there.	After a no-confidence vote, Ugandan Pres. Yusufu Lule gives up his post and is replaced by Godfrey Binaisa, who had served as attorney general under former Pres. Milton Obote.	ABC TV correspondent Bill Stewart, 37, is deliberately shot and killed by a Nicaraguan National Guard soldier while filming scenes of war destruction in Managua. . . . Brazil denies extradition requests from West Germany, Poland, Austria, and Israel for accused Nazi war criminal Gustav Wagner.	
June 21	Canada, Sweden, and Israel say they will accept more Indochinese refugees.		An official U.S. envoy, David Halsted, arrives in Uganda after a six-year break in U.S.–Ugandan relations.	Quebec Premier Rene Levesque announces that a Quebec sovereignty referendum will be held in spring 1980. . . . State Secy. Vance tells an emergency OAS meeting that the Somoza govt. in Nicaragua should be replaced and an OAS force sent into the country to restore order and democracy.	A 24-hour protest strike by up to 1.5 million workers strands ships in Australian ports and interferes with the country's business in a protest action against the arrest of 10 union members in West Australia for addressing public meetings without police permits.
June 22		EEC leaders meeting in Strasbourg agree to hold combined oil imports to their 1978 level through 1985. . . . Former British Liberal Party leader Jeremy Thorpe is acquitted of conspiring to murder former male model Norman Scott, who had claimed to have been Thorpe's lover.	In an incomplete count of Ghana's election returns, the People's National Party and its candidate, Hilla Limann (a virtual unknown), lead, but Limann does not have a 50 percent vote, the majority required to be president. . . . China gives Egypt 40 Shenyang F16 jets and in return receives a Soviet MiG-23.	Brazilian govt. reportedly authorizes creating a large Indian reserve on the frontier with Venezuela.	
June 23				Responding to intense pressures from Arab businessmen and Western allies, Canadian P.M. Joseph Clark announces that the proposed transfer of Canada's Embassy to Jerusalem from Tel Aviv, Israel will he postponed for at least a year.	
June 24		Turkish armed forces chief of staff Gen. Kenan Evren is quoted saying his country will not allow the U.S. to fly its U-2 spy plane over Turkish soil.	Israeli Cabinet formally accepts Defense Min. Ezer Weizman's resignation from the Israeli—Egyptian negotiating team.		
June 25	NATO Supreme Commander Alexander Haig narrowly escapes an assassination attempt when a bomb explodes just behind his car in Mons, Belgium.	British P.M. Margaret Thatcher meets for the first time with leaders of the Trades Union Congress, headed by TUC Gen. Secy. Len Murray.			Malaysia turns back more Vietnamese refugees attempting to land on its shores, forcing 13,000 in 60 boats away in the past week.
June 26		France announces that it will accept 5,000 Indochinese refugees in addition to its monthly quota of 1,000. . . . A German institute study predicts that if the country's current birth rate continues, the German population will decline to 55.9 million in the year 2000 from 61.4 million in 1976.	Two former Ghanaian heads of state, Gen. Fred Akuffo and Akwasi Afrifa, are executed by Ghana's military rulers.		Pres. Carter meets in Tokyo with Japanese Premier Masayoshi Ohira to coordinate U.S.–Japanese energy policies and discuss the plight of Indochinese refugees.

A	B	C	D	E
Includes developments that affect more than one world region, international organizations and important meetings of major world leaders.	Includes all domestic and regional developments in Europe, including the Soviet Union, Turkey, Cyprus and Malta.	Includes all domestic and regional developments in Africa and the Middle East, including Iraq and Iran and excluding Cyprus, Turkey and Afghanistan.	Includes all domestic and regional developments in Latin America, the Caribbean and Canada.	Includes all domestic and regional developments in Asia and Pacific nations, extending from Afghanistan through all the Pacific Islands, except Hawaii.

U.S. Politics & Social Issues	U.S. Foreign Policy & Defense	U.S. Economy & Environment	Science, Technology & Nature	Culture, Leisure & Life Style	
			Malfunctions in two nuclear reactors in Ontario, which had occured at least four months ago, are first reported in the Canadian press on June 16 and today.	Billy Martin returns as New York Yankees manager after almost a year-long layoff in wake of a furor over comments he had made about player Reggie Jackson and the club's principal owner, George Steinbrenner III.	June 19
Supreme Ct. rules, 5–3, that the police may use an electronic device to record the numbers dialed on a telephone without first obtaining a search warrant.		N.Y.C. begins an odd–even system of gasoline rationing, which allows service stations to sell gasoline to motorists with odd-numbered license plates on odd days of the calendar and to those with even-numbered plates on even days.			June 20
	House votes, 224–202, to implement the Panama Canal Treaties, setting up a Panama Canal Commission to run the canal through 1999.	Commerce Dept. reports that the U.S. balance of payments on current account was in surplus for the first quarter at an adjusted $157 million.		NBA governors bd. approves adoption of the three-point field goal on a one-year trial basis. . . . An article by William Safire in The New York Times notes the growing acceptance of topless swimsuits for women.	June 21
	Gen. Edward Meyer replaces Gen. Bernard Rogers as Army chief of staff while Rogers goes on to become NATO supreme commander.	U.S. Appeals Ct. in Wash., D.C. upholds Pres. Carter's authority to withhold federal contracts from companies that violated his wage–price guidelines.			June 22
		The gasoline shortage spreads throughout the U.S. with a report cited by the Automobile Association of America showing 58 percent of the nation's 6,286 service stations closed.			June 23
Americans for Democratic Action (ADA) adopts a resolution to draft Sen. Edward Kennedy (D, Mass) for the 1980 presidential race.		Nearly 70 percent of the nation's gasoline stations are reported closed, with the Boston-Washington corridor hardest-hit.			June 24
Supreme Ct. rules unanimously that a provision of the Social Security Act is unconstitutional because it provides benefits to families with unemployed fathers while denying similar benefits to families with unemployed mothers.		Odd-even license plate plan to ration gasoline takes effect in Houston, Dallas, and Ft. Worth, Texas. . . . U.S. Second Circuit Appeals Ct. reverses nearly all of an $87.1 million antitrust damage award to Berkey Photo Inc. by Eastman Kodak Co.	NRC announces that 33 of the nation's nuclear power plants will be ordered to shut down within 90 days to check for cracked cooling system pipes.	NBA holds its annual draft of college players in N.Y.C.. The first player picked is Marvin (Magic) Johnson, star guard of Michigan State University. . . . The New York Times reports the popularity of women's designer jeans, priced between $29–$70 in comparison to the $12–$15 price tag for traditional Levi Strauss or Wrangler jeans.	June 25
Supreme Ct. votes, 8–1, to narrow the definition of "public figure" as related to lawsuits for libel.		State of Md. files suit against the Energy Dept., claiming that the federal gasoline allocation formula discriminates against Northeastern states with large urban areas. . . . Labor Dept. reports that consumer prices soared in May a seasonally adjusted 1.1 percent, or 13.2. at an adjusted annual rate.			June 26

F	G	H	I	J
Includes elections, federal-state relations, civil rights and liberties, crime, the judiciary, education, health care, poverty, urban affairs and population.	Includes formation and debate of U.S. foreign and defense policies, veterans' affairs and defense spending. (Relations with specific foreign countries are usually found under the region concerned.)	Includes business, labor, agriculture, taxation, transportation, consumer affairs, monetary and fiscal policy, natural resources, and pollution.	Includes worldwide scientific, medical and technological developments, natural phenomena, U.S. weather, natural disasters, and accidents.	Includes the arts, religion, scholarship, communications media, sports, entertainments, fashions, fads and social life.

	World Affairs	Europe	Africa & the Middle East	The Americas	Asia & the Pacific
June 27	EEC and 57 developing nations agree at the end of a three day Brussels meeting to extend the 1976 Lome Convention for another five years.		Israeli and Syrian jets clash over southern Lebanon in the first aerial combat between the two countries since 1974.		Australia's arbitration commission grants the country's 6 million workers a 3.2 percent pay increase as a cost-of-living compensation.
June 28	OPEC agrees to raise the price of oil some 24 percent to a minimum price of $18 a barrel, but individual countries are allowed to charge differentials above the $18 and $20 base prices set with a maximum ceiling of $23.50 a barrel.	Greek Parliament ratifies the treaty making Greece a member of the EEC as of January 1981.	Arab League unanimously elects Tunisian Information Min. Chedli Klibi as its new secretary general. ... Syria executes 15 members of the Moslem Brotherhood on murder and subversion charges.... Saudi Arabia, Qatar, and the UAE announce they will charge the lower OPEC price of $18 a barrel.	Lawrence Pezzullo, newly appointed U.S. ambassador to Nicaragua, meets with Pres. Anastasio Somoza in an attempt to force Somoza to resign.	China informs HEW Secy. Joseph Califano that it is giving serious consideration to his proposal to establish a processing center in China for Vietnamese refugees.
June 29	At a two-day Tokyo, Japan summit conference, leaders of the seven major Western powers agree to set specific country-by-country ceilings on their oil imports through 1985.			Canadian P.M. Joseph Clark says that the price of Canadian oil must be brought into line with world oil prices.	About 2,600 Vietnamese boat people are taken into a Hong Kong detention center after their leaders deliberately let their ship run aground. It had been anchored offshore for over four months.
June 30		Italian police arrest Valerio Morucci and Adriana Faranda as suspects in the kidnap–murder of former Premier Aldo Moro.	Flight Lt. Jerry Rawlings, Ghana's military ruler, promises to end executions and pledges that Ghana will respect human rights.	William Niehous, a U.S. businessman who was kidnapped from his suburban Caracas, Venezuela home on Feb. 27, 1976, is rescued unharmed.	Pres. Carter begins an official visit in South Korea, inspecting a U.S. base near the demilitarized zone. ... At the conclusion of a three-day meeting, ASEAN foreign ministers formally announce refusal to accept any more Indochinese refugees and reserve the right to expel those already in their countries, blaming Vietnam's policies for the unending exodus.
July 1	Arriving in the U.S. from the Tokyo energy summit meeting, Pres. Carter harshly condemns OPEC's price increase as "unnecessarily high and completely unwarranted."	British P.M. Margaret Thatcher says that she expects to have British sanctions against Zimbabwe Rhodesia abolished by November.		With half of the registered votes counted, leftist-front candidate Hernan Siles Zuazo appears to be the front-runner in Bolivian presidential and congressional elections to restore constitutional civilian government after 12 years of military rule.	Carter and South Korean Pres. Park issue a joint communique that commits the U.S. to South Korea's defense, establishes a procedure toward reunification talks, and notes the importance of internationally recognized human rights. ... Pres. Carter meets separately with South Korea's most prominent dissident, Kim Young Sam, and with religious leader Kim Kwan Suk, who is a sharp critic of the South Korean govt.... China's National People's Congress ends a two-week session by appointing three economic specialists as deputy premiers: Chen Yun, Po Yi-po, and Yao Yi-lin.
July 2		Soviet Union increases prices of luxury items by 50 percent.	Saudi Arabia, the largest single source of imported oil in the U.S., announces it will increase its oil production temporarily.	The opposition Labor Party wins a decisive victory in St. Lucia's first elections as an independent nation.	U.S. State Secy. Vance confers with ASEAN ministers in Kutu, Indonesia trying to persuade them to accept Indochinese refugees temporarily until they can be given permanent homes elsewhere.

A	B	C	D	E
Includes developments that affect more than one world region, international organizations and important meetings of major world leaders.	Includes all domestic and regional developments in Europe, including the Soviet Union, Turkey, Cyprus and Malta.	Includes all domestic and regional developments in Africa and the Middle East, including Iraq and Iran and excluding Cyprus, Turkey and Afghanistan.	Includes all domestic and regional developments in Latin America, the Caribbean and Canada.	Includes all domestic and regional developments in Asia and Pacific nations, extending from Afghanistan through all the Pacific Islands, except Hawaii.

U.S. Politics & Social Issues	U.S. Foreign Policy & Defense	U.S. Economy & Environment	Science, Technology & Nature	Culture, Leisure & Life Style	
Supreme Ct. rules, 5–2, that employers and unions can establish voluntary programs, inclucing the use of quotas, to aid minorities and women even when no evidence exists of past discrimination.	Senate Minority Leader Howard Baker (R, Tenn.) comes out unequivocally in favor of amending the SALT Treaty, charging it is flatally flawed and gives the U.S.S.R. substantial strategic superiority by allowing it to keep all 308 of its heavy missiles.	U.S. foreign trade deficit widened in May with imports exceeding exports by a seasonally adjusted $2.48 billion, according to the Commerce Dept.		Theodore Bernstein, 74, assisting managing editor of *The New York Times* and an authority on the English language, dies of cancer in N.Y.	June 27
Pres. Carter announces that he will increase the quota for Indochinese refugees to be admitted into the U.S. to 14,000 from 7,000 a month.		As the truckers' energy-related strike enters its fourth week, sniper fire armed at moving rigs wounds a 14-year-old boy in Ark. and a trucker in Md. Nail sprinklings create traffic tie-ups in Ala., N.C., and Calif.			June 28
Rep. Charles Diggs (D, Mich.) admits he used his federal payroll to pay personal bills and agrees to repay the House more than $40,000 and accept censure.	Calif. Gov. Jerry Brown (D) comes out in support of the SALT II Treaty but criticizes plans to develop a U.S. mobile land-base intercontinental ballistic missile.	A six-point White House plan is credited with ending the strike of truckers protesting diesel fuel costs and other U.S. highway policies.	COMECON leaders agree to proceed with an intensive program of switching to nuclear power from fossil fuels.		June 29
					June 30
A Gallup Poll finds Pres. Carter's popularity running behind leading Republicans Ronald Reagan and Gerald Ford.	Rep. Les Aspin (D, Wis.) says that U-2 flights are not essential for the U.S. to monitor Soviet compliance with the SALT II Treaty.	Passengers holding special coupons are able to fly anywhere in the U.S. on three airlines for half fare under a plan extending until Dec. 15.			July 1
Supreme Ct. rules, 5–4, that the public and press have no constitutional right to attend pretrial criminal hearings. . . . Supreme Ct. votes, 8–1, to strike down a Mass. law that requires an unmarried minor to obtain permission of both parents or a judge before having an abortion. . . . Supreme Ct. upholds, 7–2 and 5–4, sweeping desegregation orders for two large Ohio school systems: Dayton and Columbus.		*Fortune* magazine article says that Calif.'s Proposition 13, which provides a 57 percent reduction in property taxes, has stimulated the economy.			July 2

F	G	H	I	J
Includes elections, federal-state relations, civil rights and liberties, crime, the judiciary, education, health care, poverty, urban affairs and population.	Includes formation and debate of U.S. foreign and defense policies, veterans' affairs and defense spending. (Relations with specific foreign countries are usually found under the region concerned.)	Includes business, labor, agriculture, taxation, transportation, consumer affairs, monetary and fiscal policy, natural resources, and pollution.	Includes worldwide scientific, medical and technological developments, natural phenomena, U.S. weather, natural disasters, and accidents.	Includes the arts, religion, scholarship, communications media, sports, entertainments, fashions, fads and social life.

	World Affairs	Europe	Africa & the Middle East	The Americas	Asia & the Pacific
July 3		The British pound rises sharply in value to above $2.20 for the first time in more than four years.		A group of 300 Canadian Indian chiefs protest against bringing the British North America Act, Canada's Constitution, under total Canadian control without rewriting it to give Indians a constitutional role.	
July 4		West German Chancellor Helmut Schmidt stresses an increased use of coal to cope with the country's future energy needs.	Israeli Knesset defeats, by a 54–4 vote, an opposition motion of no-confidence in the government for granting leniency to Israelis accused of murdering Arabs.... Former Algerian Pres. Ahmed Ben Bella is freed from 14 years of house arrest by Pres. Chadli Benjedid.		China is reported imposing stringent penalties to control the flood of illegal emigration to Hong Kong. ... North Korea says that it favors reunification talks but opposes the inclusion of the U.S.
July 5			Iranian Premier Mehdi Bazargan announces nationalization of virtually all of Iran's remaining industries still privately owned with no mention made of compensation to owners.	U.S. State Dept. announces it is abandoning its initial proposal to give economic aid to the Nicaraguan Sandinista junta if it adds more moderates and protects the National Guard from reprisals.	At the conclusion of its conference, ANZUS members declare that the Vietnamese refugee problem must be solved by Vietnam.
July 6		Austrian Chancellor Bruno Kreisky begins a Vienna conference with PLO leader Yasir Arafat, the first time a Western European head of government has formally received Arafat.	Egyptian and Israeli representatives at the peace talks agree to form two committees to discuss specific steps toward Palestinian autonomy on the West Bank and Gaza Strip.	Venezuela is reported suggesting names of five more conservative Nicaraguans to be added to the Sandinista guerrilla junta.	
July 7			Nigeria begins its long-awaited return to civilian rule with elections for a 95-member federal Senate. ... An Arab minority guerrilla group, identified as Black Wednesday, sabotages a pipeline carrying crude oil to the Abadan refinery in Khuzistan province, Iran.	Nicaraguan Pres. Anastasio Somoza Debayle announces that he will draft 50,000 more men for the National Guard, but he makes no mention of his apparent agreement to resign if so pressured by the U.S. govt.	U.S. and China sign a trade agreement giving China most-favored-nation tariff treatment.
July 8		Israeli govt. strongly protests Austrian Chancellor Bruno Kreisky's meeting with PLO leader Yasir Arafat, and orders its ambassador to Austria recalled for consultation.	Taghi Haj Tarkani, a strong supporter of Ayatollah Khomeini, is shot and killed by two unidentified assailants at his home in Teheran, Iran.	Nicaraguan National Guard warplanes bomb Leon, Masaya, and Rivas, but the Sandinista guerrillas continue to hold those cities as well as the military edge in most of the country.	An estimated 45,000 Vietnamese refugees reportedly have landed on Indonesian uninhabited islands in the Anambas and Riouw archipelagos.
July 9		Pres. Sandro Pertini asks Socialist Party leader Bettino Craxi to form a coalition govt. and end Italy's six-month-old political crisis.... In line with campaign promises, the British Conservative Party govt. announces proposals to curb the power of unions.	Ayatollah Khomeini declares a general amnesty for all people who committed offenses under the Shah of Iran's regime, except for those involved in murder or torture.	Chilean Pres. Augusto Pinochet's govt. issues a series of decrees aimed at curbing unions.	

A	B	C	D	E
Includes developments that affect more than one world region, international organizations and important meetings of major world leaders.	Includes all domestic and regional developments in Europe, including the Soviet Union, Turkey, Cyprus and Malta.	Includes all domestic and regional developments in Africa and the Middle East, including Iraq and Iran and excluding Cyprus, Turkey and Afghanistan.	Includes all domestic and regional developments in Latin America, the Caribbean and Canada.	Includes all domestic and regional developments in Asia and Pacific nations, extending from Afghanistan through all the Pacific Islands, except Hawaii.

U.S. Politics & Social Issues	U.S. Foreign Policy & Defense	U.S. Economy & Environment	Science, Technology & Nature	Culture, Leisure & Life Style	
Former San Francisco Supervisor Dan White is sentenced to seven years and eight months in prison for the 1978 murders of San Francisco Mayor George Moscone and Supervisor Harvey Milk.		*Look* magazine announces a reorganization that includes an end to its association with *Rolling Stone* magazine after a partial merger in May.	Rockingham County, N.H. Attorney Carleton Eldredge announces that he will not prosecute the 709 persons scheduled to go on trial on criminal trespass charges stemming from an antinuclear protest at the Seabrook, N.H. atomic plant site in 1977, citing the cost of prosecution and the fact that the cases no longer have the social significance they once did.		July 3
		Pres.Carter cancels without explanation an energy speech to the nation scheduled to be delivered July 5 from the White House.			July 4
Pres. Carter summons his domestic affairs adviser, Stuart Eizenstat, and V.P. Mondale to Camp David to confer after canceling his energy speech.... ACLU sues the FBI for $2 million on charges that it was responsible for the 1965 murder of civil-rights worker Viola Liuzzo through the actions of its onetime paid informer, Gary Rowe Jr.... NEA reports that thousands of teachers suffer from burnout caused by student violence and vandalism, inadequate salaries, and weak administrative support.			Australia and the U.S. sign a nuclear safeguards agreement, which specifically prohibits use of future Australian uranium exports to the U.S. for nuclear weapons.		July 5
	Army announces that it will again accept 17-year-old male volunteers who have not completed high school in an effort to meet the Army's strength objective of 774,000 soldiers by Oct. 1.	Presidential aide Stuart Eizenstat says that Carter canceled his July 5 speech because he became aware of how his energy decisions would have significant impact on the economy.... Labor Dept. reports that the unemployment rate fell to 5.6 percent in June, its lowest level since August 1974.	Center For Disease Control reports a 50 percent rise in U.S. rabies cases in 1979 over 1978.	Martina Navratilova beats Chris Evert Lloyd in the final of the women's tennis singles competitions at Wimbledon.	July 6
				Bjorn Borg of Sweden defeats Roscoe Tanner of the U.S. for his fourth consecutive men's singles title at the All-England tennis championships at Wimbledon.	July 7
Democratic governors approve a resolution endorsing Pres. Carter's reelection in 1980.			Shinichero Tomonaga, 73, Japanese scientist and 1965 Nobel Prize for Physics winner, dies of cancer in Tokyo, Japan.... Robert Burns Woodward, 62, Harvard University science professor who won the 1965 Nobel Prize for Chemistry, dies of a heart attack in Cambridge, Mass.	Michael Wilding, 66, British stage and screen actor most widely known as actress Elizabeth Taylor's second husband, dies from a fall in Chichester, England.	July 8
		U.S. Voyager 2 unmanned space craft makes its closest approach to Jupiter.		Cornelia Otis Skinner, 78, actress and author known for her wit and satirical humor, dies of a cerebral hemorrhage in N.Y.	July 9

F	G	H	I	J
Includes elections, federal-state relations, civil rights and liberties, crime, the judiciary, education, health care, poverty, urban affairs and population.	*Includes formation and debate of U.S. foreign and defense policies, veterans' affairs and defense spending. (Relations with specific foreign countries are usually found under the region concerned.)*	*Includes business, labor, agriculture, taxation, transportation, consumer affairs, monetary and fiscal policy, natural resources, and pollution.*	*Includes worldwide scientific, medical and technological developments, natural phenomena, U.S. weather, natural disasters, and accidents.*	*Includes the arts, religion, scholarship, communications media, sports, entertainments, fashions, fads and social life.*

	World Affairs	Europe	Africa & the Middle East	The Americas	Asia & the Pacific
July 10		Italy's CP reorganizes, electing a seven-member secretariat dominated by Enrico Berlinguer.	Hilla Limann wins a runoff election against Victor Owusu to become president of Ghana's future civilian govt.... Arab demonstrators in Iran's Khuzistan province refuse to participate in the national holiday celebrating the birthday of the twelfth Imam of the Shiite branch of Islam.	Costa Rica expels a 35-man U.S. Air Force contingent that landed there on July 8.	North Korea formally rejects a proposal for talks between the two Koreas and the U.S. to reduce tension on the Korean peninsula.
July 11	International Whaling Commission votes to make the Indian Ocean the world's largest whale sanctuary.	France and Iraq verbally agree to expand political and economic ties, including increased Iraqi oil imports.	After a two-day meeting with Israeli Premier Begin, Egyptian Pres. Sadat says he is satisfied with the pace of the negotiations on Palestinian autonomy.... Zimbabwe Rhodesian P.M. Abel Muzorewa meets with Pres. Carter in an unsuccessful attempt to convince the President to lift economic sanctions and gain U.S. recognition.	Nicaraguan Sandinista guerrilla junta issues a statement that appears to incorporate some of the U.S. demands into its national reconstruction program. These include retaining some form of the National Guard to prevent renewed violence after Pres. Anatasio Somoza Debayle's departure.	Japan is reported delaying concluding a trade agreement with Vietnam in an effort to force Vietnam to stem its refugee flow.
July 12			Libyan leader Muammer el Qaddafi promises Syria that Libya will replace every fighter plane Syria has lost in battle to Israel.		Gilbert Islands become the independent republic of Kiribati after 87 years of British rule.
July 13		Antonio Varisco, a police commandant at the Rome central courts, is killed by Italian terrorist Red Brigades as he drives to work. His is the twenty-fourth death from terrorist attacks in Italy so far this year.	Namibian National Assembly enacts a series of laws abolishing apartheid.... U.S. State Dept. announces recommending the sale of an additional $1.2 billion in arms to Saudi Arabia.		U.S. analysts cited by *The New York Times* believe that Afghanistan Pres. Nur Mohammad Taraki's pro-Communist govt. is slowly being worn down by rebel fighting.
July 14			A force of 50,000 Ethiopian govt. troops launches a new offensive against secessionist guerrillas in the coastal province of Eritrea.		
July 15					Morarji Desai resigns as India's prime minister after over 100 members of his ruling Janata Party quit to protest his policies.
July 16			Ahmed Hassan al-Bakr resigns as president of Iraq and names Gen. Saddam Hussein as his successor. ... Five members of the Arab terrorist group Black Wednesday which blew up oil pipelines in Iran's Khuzistan province, are executed yesterday and today.		A Soviet–Chinese clash on the Kazakhstan–Sinkiang border leaves one Chinese dead, one wounded, and another taken prisoner.

A	B	C	D	E
Includes developments that affect more than one world region, international organizations and important meetings of major world leaders.	Includes all domestic and regional developments in Europe, including the Soviet Union, Turkey, Cyprus and Malta.	Includes all domestic and regional developments in Africa and the Middle East, including Iraq and Iran and excluding Cyprus, Turkey and Afghanistan.	Includes all domestic and regional developments in Latin America, the Caribbean and Canada.	Includes all domestic and regional developments in Asia and Pacific nations, extending from Afghanistan through all the Pacific Islands, except Hawaii.

U.S. Politics & Social Issues	U.S. Foreign Policy & Defense	U.S. Economy & Environment	Science, Technology & Nature	Culture, Leisure & Life Style	
		Pres. Carter signs a proclamation requiring that air-conditioning in commercial, government, and many other public buildings be no lower than 78 degrees Fahrenheit (25.5 Celsius) for the summer.	FAA report is made public that attributes the nation's worst air disaster to date — the Chicago O'Hare International Airport May 25 crash — to a DC-10 maintenance procedure used by American Airlines' mechanics.	Arthur Fiedler, 84, conductor of the Boston Pops Orchestra for 50 years and one of the world's most popular musical figures, dies of a heart ailment in Brookline, Mass.	July 10
House narrowly approves a Carter administration bill to establish a separate Cabinet-level education department.	Joint Chiefs of Staff give formal support to the SALT Treaty, but call for increased U.S. military spending.		Skylab, the unmanned 77-ton U.S. space station that has been circling Earth in slowly deteriorating orbits, enters the atmosphere and disintegrates over the Indian Ocean and Australia.... Hurricane Bob, the first Atlantic hurricane given a man's name, sweeps across southeastern Louisiana and kills one person, but its damage is relatively minor.		July 11
	Testifying before the Senate For. Rel. Committee, SALT negotiator Paul Nitze and Joint Chiefs of Staff representative Lt. Gen. Edward Rowny warn that the SALT II Treaty would leave the U.S. in an inferior position to the U.S.S.R.		American Airlines disputes FAA contentions that maintenance procedures caused the May 25 crash at Chicago's O'Hare International Airport.		July 12
			FAA lifts its ban on flights by McDonnell Douglas Corp. DC-10s.	Silent screen actress Corinne Griffith, 73, dies in Santa Monica, Calif.	July 13
Bella Abzug tells the fourth biennial convention of the National Women's Political Caucus, meeting in Cincinnati, that women must form a power bloc that will have a decisive say in who is the presidential nominee in 1980.			A fire that broke out yesterday in the Hotel Corona de Aragon, a 10-story luxury hotel in Saragassa in northeastern Spain, kills 80 people and is the worst hotel fire in Spain to date.... An overcrowded bus falls into Lake Victoria in northwestern Tanzania, killing 60 passengers.		July 14
National Women's Political Caucus elects Iris Mitgang, a California lawyer, president for the next two year.		In a nationally televised speech, Pres. Carter proposes a new energy program that would cost some $140 billion over 10 years in an effort to reduce U.S. dependence on foreign oil.	Soviet cosmonauts Vladimir Lyakhov and Valery Ryumin mark their 140th day in space, breaking the previous record of 139 days and 15 hours set by another Soviet team in 1978.	An estimated 100,000 people attend a memorial concert for the late Boston Pops conductor Arthur Fiedler in Boston, Mass., where they observe a moment of silence before the Pops plays John Philip Sousa's "The Stars and Stripes Forever."	July 15
		Energy Dept. announces revised rules that would permit gas stations to increase their prices by 15.4 cents a gallon over the wholesale price.	FDA urges a ban on amphetamines as dieting aids because of the drug's widespread abuse.	A holographic manuscript of Wolfgang Amadeus Mozart's Haffner Symphony is purchased from the National Orchestral Assn. by the Pierpont Morgan Library, N.Y.C.. ... Cardinal James Francis McIntyre, 93, archbishop of Los Angeles (1948–70) and considered one of the most conservative and controversial Roman Catholic prelates, dies in Los Angeles.	July 16

F	G	H	I	J
Includes elections, federal-state relations, civil rights and liberties, crime, the judiciary, education, health care, poverty, urban affairs and population.	Includes formation and debate of U.S. foreign and defense policies, veterans' affairs and defense spending. (Relations with specific foreign countries are usually found under the region concerned.)	Includes business, labor, agriculture, taxation, transportation, consumer affairs, monetary and fiscal policy, natural resources, and pollution.	Includes worldwide scientific, medical and technological developments, natural phenomena, U.S. weather, natural disasters, and accidents.	Includes the arts, religion, scholarship, communications media, sports, entertainments, fashions, fads and social life.

	World Affairs	Europe	Africa & the Middle East	The Americas	Asia & the Pacific
July 17		After two weeks of intense negotiations, an agreement is reached on Basque autonomy in northern Spain.... Simone Veil of France is elected president of the European Parliament.... British Industry Secy. Sir Keith Joseph says that the government plans to cut its subsidies to industry in areas of high unemployment over the next three years.	Addressing the OAU summit meeting, Liberian Pres. William Tolbert, its new chairman, criticizes Africa for its silence on human-rights violations throughout the continent but specifically in Uganda.	A joint session of the Nicaraguan Congress accepts the resignation of Pres. Anastasio Somoza Debayle, who leaves several hours later for exile in Miami, Fla.	Hanoi acknowledges smashing a dissident organization in southern Vietnam that sought to overthrow the government.
July 18				For more than 12 hours, Nicaragua is virtually without a government after Somoza's successor Francisco Urcuyo Malianos flees to Guatemala, and the National Guard's acting director, Col Federico Mejia Gonzalez, breaks off negotiations with the rebel leaders.... Canadian govt. announces that it will accept 50,000 Indochinese refugees by the end of 1980 instead of the 12,000 it previously said it would accept.	Indian Pres. Neelam Sanjiva Reddy calls on opposition Congress Party leader Yeshwantrao Chavan to try to form a new government.
July 19		British House of Commons upholds the country's 14-year-old ban on capital punishment, 362–243.... Portuguese Pres. Antonio Ramalho Eanes names a 49-year-old engineer and diplomat, Maria de Lurdes Pintassilgo, to form a caretaker government until parliamentary elections are held in the fall. She is the first woman to be premier of Portugal.	Iranian Premier Mehdi Bazargan announces an agreement with Ayatollah Khomeini to share power between Bazargan's govt. and the Islamic Revolutionary Council.	Nicaraguan Sandinista rebels take control of Managua two days after Pres. Anastasio Somoza flees the country, ending a seven-week-old civil war that left over 10,000 dead and 500,000 homeless.	Australian opposition Labor Party votes, 25–20, favoring continued operation of a U.S. military base at Pine Gap, reversing its former stand and thus ensuring that the base would remain open even if the party ousts the current Fraser government.
July 20	U.N. Security Council approves a resolution calling on Israel to stop establishing settlements in its occupied Arab territories.	British Conservative govt. says it will sell a substantial minority shareholding in the state-owned British Airways to private investors.	Senegal and Gabon join Morocco in walking out of an OAU summit session after passage of a resolution calling for a U.N.-supervised referendum on the future of the Western Sahara.		Pres. Carter orders a halt to withdrawing the remaining 32,000 U.S. combat troops in South Korea until at least 1981.
July 21	After a two-day international conference, U.N. Secy. Gen Kurt Waldheim announces that Vietnam has promised to stem the flow of its refugees.				
July 22			In the heaviest of a series of attacks, Israeli planes bomb a 21-mile stretch of territory south of Beirut, killing an estimated 20 people and wounding 50.	Newly appointed head of the seven-member Nicaraguan Supreme Ct., Robert Arguello Hurtado, announces that the rebel leadership will try to avoid the excesses that characterized the Iranian revolution.	Philippine govt. reports that Vietnamese troops massacred 85 boat people after their boat ran aground on one of the Spratly Islands.... The Vietnamese-supported Cambodian govt. claims total victory over the forces of the ousted Pol Pot govt.
July 23			Ayatollah Khomeini prohibits the broadcast of all music by radio and TV in Iran, declaring that it is no different from opium and corrupts Iran's youth.	Nicaraguan Sandinistas take first steps toward reconstruction by creating a broad-based 18-member Cabinet, composed mainly of the Group of Twelve, an organization of liberal church, business, and academic leaders who were early supporters of the rebels. ... Bank of Canada raises its bank rate to a record 11.75 percent.	Dependents of U.S. Embassy employees in Kabul are ordered to begin leaving the country in face of growing violence in the Afghan capital.... An oil tanker assigned to the U.S. Seventh Fleet rescues 19 Indochinese refugees from a small boat in the South China Sea, bringing to 568 the number of boat people picked up by U.S. naval vessels so far.

A	B	C	D	E
Includes developments that affect more than one world region, international organizations and important meetings of major world leaders.	Includes all domestic and regional developments in Europe, including the Soviet Union, Turkey, Cyprus and Malta.	Includes all domestic and regional developments in Africa and the Middle East, including Iraq and Iran and excluding Cyprus, Turkey and Afghanistan.	Includes all domestic and regional developments in Latin America, the Caribbean and Canada.	Includes all domestic and regional developments in Asia and Pacific nations, extending from Afghanistan through all the Pacific Islands, except Hawaii.

U.S. Politics & Social Issues	U.S. Foreign Policy & Defense	U.S. Economy & Environment	Science, Technology & Nature	Culture, Leisure & Life Style	
Pres. Carter reportedly delivers a tart lecture to his Cabinet members about their unsatisfactory performance, asks for their resignations, and announces that he is appointing Hamilton Jordan chief of staff. ... House Assassinations Committee releases its final report, concluding that conspiracies were likely in the murders of Pres. John Kennedy and civil-rights leader Martin Luther King.				NL wins major league baseball's fiftieth annual all-star game, defeating the AL, 7–6, in the Seattle Kingdome. It was the sixteenth time in 17 years that the NL won.... Roman Catholic Church in the U.S. is reported having cost 233,144 members between 1977–78, its largest loss of the twentieth century.	July 17
Sen. Henry Jackson (D, Wash.) reflects congressional dismay over Pres. Carter's Cabinet shake-up by saying that it is unprecedented and poorly timed, destroying not rebuilding public confidence in the administration.		Commerce Dept. reports that housing starts picked up in June 5.7 percent higher than the May pace, but 7.5 percent below the June 1978 rate.			July 18
Pres. Carter dismisses Treasury Secy. Michael Blumenthal and HEW Secy. Joseph Califano Jr. and accepts the resignation of Atty. Gen. Griffin Bell. He names HUD Secy. Patricia Roberts Harris as the new HEW secretary and FRB Chmn. G. William Miller as treasury secretary. He names Deputy Atty. Gen. Benjamin Civiletti as the new attorney general.		American Petroleum Institute reports that the U.S. imported more petroleum and produced less of its own during the first six months of 1979 than it did in the same period of 1978.			July 19
Pres. Carter dismisses Energy Secy. James Schlesinger and Transportation Secy. Brock Adams, replacing them with deputy Defense Secy. Charles Duncan Jr. and Navy Secy. Graham Claytor respectively.		Commerce Dept. reports that the nation's real GNP declined 3.3 percent at a seasonally adjusted annual rate during the second quarter.			July 20
Rexford Tugwell, 88, member of Pres. Franklin Roosevelt's original brain trust and Rural Resettlement Administration head, dies of cancer in Santa Barbara, Calif.				Severiano Ballesteros wins the 108th British Open at the Royal Lytham and St. Anne's golf course.	July 21
In the keynote address for the Urban League's annual conference, Pres. Vernon Jordan Jr. refuses to commit himself to supporting any one candidate for the U.S. Presidency.					July 22
					July 23

F	G	H	I	J
Includes elections, federal-state relations, civil rights and liberties, crime, the judiciary, education, health care, poverty, urban affairs and population.	Includes formation and debate of U.S. foreign and defense policies, veterans' affairs and defense spending. (Relations with specific foreign countries are usually found under the region concerned.)	Includes business, labor, agriculture, taxation, transportation, consumer affairs, monetary and fiscal policy, natural resources, and pollution.	Includes worldwide scientific, medical and technological developments, natural phenomena, U.S. weather, natural disasters, and accidents.	Includes the arts, religion, scholarship, communications media, sports, entertainments, fashions, fads and social life.

	World Affairs	Europe	Africa & the Middle East	The Americas	Asia & the Pacific
July 24	Switzerland takes over oil-rich Kuwait's top spot as the world's richest country because of a 39 percent increase in the value of the Swiss franc.... U.N. Security Council lets expire the U.N. Emergency Force (UNEF) separating Egyptian and Israeli forces in the Sinai.		Iranian radio ignores Khomeini's directive by playing Persian folk music, classical selections, and themes of the Islamic revolution.	Pres. Carlos Humberto Romero lifts the state of siege decree that had suspended all constitutional rights in El Salvador following earlier violent demonstrations.	
July 25		A left-wing Rome newspaper publishes a document that shows that a dissident faction is criticizing the leadership of the ultraleft Red Brigades for attacking eminent people instead of building a broader base for radical social change.	In accordance with the Israeli—Egyptian peace accord, Israel returns another portion on the Sinai Peninsula to Egypt.	Sandinista govt. nationalizes five private Nicaraguan banks and curbs operations of four foreign banks.	Australia's inflation rate for the fiscal year ended June 30 is reported up 8.8 percent from the 7.9 percent rate for the previous year.
July 26		Sir Charles Clore, British financier known as one of the wealthiest men in England, dies in London.		Nearly 200 people who had taken refuge in the Salvadoran Embassy are granted safe passage out of Nicaragua, but 72 National Guard members are not allowed to leave.	
July 27		Christian Democrat Filippo Pandolfi, treasury minister in Premier Giulio Andreotti's caretaker government, agrees to try to form a new Cabinet and end Italy's month-long political crisis.... Spanish police announce they have arrested two of the country's most-wanted terrorists who have confessed to the bombing of a Madrid cafe that killed eight people on May 26.	The family of Steven Biko receives a $76,000 out-of-court settlement of its suit charging government negligence in his death.	Sandinista govt. says that water has been restored in 80 percent of Managua, electricity service in 75 percent, all telephone service, and two-thirds of the bus service.	Morarji Desai resigns as head of India's Janata Party and is replaced by Jagjivan Ram.
July 28			Iraqi press agency reports the arrest of at least five high-ranking members of Iraq's ruling Revolutionary Command Council on charges of plotting against the government with the aid of an outside power.	Nicaragua's new Interior Min. Tomas Borge meets with U.S. Amb. Lawrence Pezzullo and says afterward that he requested U.S. arms for the new Sandinista army.	Charan Singh, leader of the breakaway faction of the ruling Janata Party, is sworn in as prime minister of India.... Vietnam and Malaysia assail U.S. Navy rescues of boat people as a "show-off" operation designed to divert Americans' attention from other issues.
July 29		Basque bombs kill five and wound 113 people in Madrid's two main railway stations and the arrivals terminal of Spain's international airport.		The Nicaraguan Interior Min. Tomas Borge, a co-founder of the Sandinista Liberation Front and an avowed Marxist, is named to a three-member general command to direct the new Sandinista People's Army.	
July 30		Portuguese Premier-designate Maria de Lurdes Pintassilgo announces the formation of a 16-member all-male Cabinet to help her run the country until fall parliamentary elections.	Israeli Knesset, 58–48, defeats an opposition no-confidence motion on Premier Begin's economic policies.	U.S. Amb. to Nicaragua Lawrence Pezzullo promises that the U.S. will oppose any intervention to topple the Nicaraguan revolution.	Twenty-nine Vietnamese are picked up by a U.S. naval vessel from their 35-foot boat, 230 miles west of Luzon, the Philippines.

A	B	C	D	E
Includes developments that affect more than one world region, international organizations and important meetings of major world leaders.	Includes all domestic and regional developments in Europe, including the Soviet Union, Turkey, Cyprus and Malta.	Includes all domestic and regional developments in Africa and the Middle East, including Iraq and Iran and excluding Cyprus, Turkey and Afghanistan.	Includes all domestic and regional developments in Latin America, the Caribbean and Canada.	Includes all domestic and regional developments in Asia and Pacific nations, extending from Afghanistan through all the Pacific Islands, except Hawaii.

U.S. Politics & Social Issues	U.S. Foreign Policy & Defense	U.S. Economy & Environment	Science, Technology & Nature	Culture, Leisure & Life Style	
U.S. District Ct. Judge Aubrey Robinson Jr. approves government plans to allow the public to hear hundreds of hours of former Pres. Richard Nixon's White House tapes at 11 listening centers across the U.S.... House of Representatives defeats a proposed constitutional amendment to ban school busing by a 216–209 vote.				Boston Red Sox captain Carl Yastrzemski smashes his four hundredth major league home run in Boston, the eighteenth player in big league baseball history to reach the 400-homer level.	July 24
Pres. Carter names Hedley Donovan, former Time Inc. editor-in-chief, as senior adviser.		Sen. Edward Kennedy (D, Mass.) announces his own energy plan that relies on conservation and incentives to private industry in contrast to Pres. Carter's program, which calls for government subsidization of synthetic fuel production. ... Pres. Carter nominates Paul Volcker as FRB chairman, succeeding G. William Miller, who was named treasury secy.			July 25
The Reagan Campaign Committee, formed to explore the possibility of former Calif. Gov. Ronald Reagan making a bid for the 1980 Republican presidential nomination, has reportedly raised more than $1.4 million in campaign funds, although Reagan has not formally announced his candidacy.					July 26
N.Y.C. Mayor Edward Koch signs a bill giving himself and 50 other elected city officials substantial pay increases amid jeers from angry city residents concerned about the city's continuing fiscal problems.		Pres. Carter nominates Moon Landrieu, former mayor of New Orleans, as HUD secretary and Neil Goldschmidt, mayor of Portland, Ore. as transportation secy.			July 27
Senate Majority Leader Robert Byrd (D, W.Va.) defends Pres. Carter, saying he very well could make a strong, successful bid for reelection in 1980.	Pres. Carter's decision to use the Navy to rescue boat people is reported spurring new departures from Vietnam.		Tropical storm Claudette floods coastal and border regions of Texas and Louisiana with 25 inches of rain accompanied by 40-mile-an-hour winds. Pres. Carter declares Texas a disaster area.	George Seaton, 68, Oscar-winning motion picture director, producer, an screen writer for 40 years, dies in Los Angeles, Calif.	July 28
		Labor Dept. reports that wage increases negotiated during the first half of 1979 were larger than those won in 1978 settlements.		Herbert Marcuse, 81, German-born Marxian philospher, dies in Starnberg, West Germany.	July 29
					July 30

F	G	H	I	J
Includes elections, federal-state relations, civil rights and liberties, crime, the judiciary, education, health care, poverty, urban affairs and population.	*Includes formation and debate of U.S. foreign and defense policies, veterans' affairs and defense spending. (Relations with specific foreign countries are usually found under the region concerned.)*	*Includes business, labor, agriculture, taxation, transportation, consumer affairs, monetary and fiscal policy, natural resources, and pollution.*	*Includes worldwide scientific, medical and technological developments, natural phenomena, U.S. weather, natural disasters, and accidents.*	*Includes the arts, religion, scholarship, communications media, sports, entertainments, fashions, fads and social life.*

	World Affairs	Europe	Africa & the Middle East	The Americas	Asia & the Pacific
July 31			Nigerian govt. announces it is nationalizing all of British Petroleum Co. Ltd.'s remaining oil assets in the country.... Rev. Ndabaningi Sithole announces that he and the 11 members of his opposition Zimbabwe African National Union (ZANU) have ended their boycott of Zimbabwe Rhodesia's National Assembly.		
Aug. 1		Maria de Lurdes Pintassilgo, Portugal's first woman premier, is sworn in as head of Portugal's eleventh government since 1974.... Rumania requires all foreign travelers to pay for gasoline in hard (Western) currencies, stranding thousands of Eastern European travelers to Rumania's Black sea resorts.	Unarmed troops of the U.N. Truce Supervision Organization begin to take up positions in the Sinai Peninsula between Israeli and Egyptian forces, despite Israeli objections. ... Israel says the U.S. proposed the creation of a Palestinian state at the latest round of discussions on Palestinian autonomy held in Alexandria, Egypt.	Dominican Republic police battle hundreds of demonstrating transit drivers with tear gas and guns. The drivers were protesting a recent 60-cent rise in the price of gasoline to $1.85 a gallon.	
Aug. 2	U.S. indirectly warns the Soviet Union to halt its military intervention in Afghanistan, citing its own prudent restraint during the Iranian crisis.	An article in *Pravda*, the Soviet CP newspaper, criticizes U.S. opponents of the SALT treaty as "crudely distorting the real balance of forces between the U.S.S.R. and the U.S.A."	In a report to the United Nations, Angola says that raids on the country from South Africa in the past year have killed at least 1,383 persons and caused nearly $300 million in damage.	Former Nicaraguan Pres. Anastasio Somoza Debayle is expelled from the Bahamas, allegedly for security reasons, and is believed headed for the U.S. where his wife is a citizen.	
Aug. 3	In a speech at the Commonwealth conference, British P.M. Margaret Thatcher spells out defects in the current Zimbabwe Rhodesian Constitution: the possibility for the white minority to parliamentary check constitutional changes unwelcome to them and the overrepresentation of whites in government offices.		In nationwide balloting in Iran, Moslem clergymen and Islamic conservatives win a majority of the 73 seats in a Constituent Assembly to draft a new constitution.... Pres. Masie Nguema Biyogo is overthrown in a military coup in Equatorial Guinea and replaced by a military junta.		
Aug. 4				Inter-American Development Bank (IDB) announces it will lend Nicaragua $500 million over the next three years.	
Aug. 5		Italy swears in a three-party coalition government, headed by Francesco Cossiga, a Christian Democrat, ending a political impasse that had lasted since the end of January.	Egypt, Israel, and the U.S. meet in the fifth round of tripartite talks on procedures for Palestinian autonomy.... Mauritania formally agrees to withdraw from the war in Western Sahara under an accord signed with the Polisario Front.		
Aug. 6	Commonwealth nation heads, meeting in Lusaka, Zambia, endorse a set of proposals to draw up a new constitution for Zimbabwe Rhodesia and hold elections under British supervision.	Lawyers for Michele Sindona, an Italian financier who faces criminal charges in both the U.S. and Italy, say he has disappeared, apparently kidnapped.	Bishop Abel Muzorewa charges that the Commonwealth conference call for new elections in Zimbabwe Rhodesia is unfair and an insult to the electorate.	Walter Guevara Arze is elected provisional president of Bolivia as a compromise, the result of a congressional deadlock over two presidential candidates who did not win the 50 percent majority required.	

A	B	C	D	E
Includes developments that affect more than one world region, international organizations and important meetings of major world leaders.	Includes all domestic and regional developments in Europe, including the Soviet Union, Turkey, Cyprus and Malta.	Includes all domestic and regional developments in Africa and the Middle East, including Iraq and Iran and excluding Cyprus, Turkey and Afghanistan.	Includes all domestic and regional developments in Latin America, the Caribbean and Canada.	Includes all domestic and regional developments in Asia and Pacific nations, extending from Afghanistan through all the Pacific Islands, except Hawaii.

U.S. Politics & Social Issues	U.S. Foreign Policy & Defense	U.S. Economy & Environment	Science, Technology & Nature	Culture, Leisure & Life Style	
House votes, 414–0 to censure Rep. Charles Diggs Jr. (D, Mich.), who was convicted for taking salary kickbacks from members of his staff. . . . Donald Kennedy resigns as head of the FDA. . . . Theodore Bundy is sentenced to die in Florida's electric chair for the murders of two women at Florida State University at Tallahassee.	Pres. Carter compares the plight of the Palestinians with the U.S. civil-rights movement, charging that it is a matter of rights. At the same time, however, he rules out establishing an independent Palestinian state. . . . Former State Secy. Henry Kissinger says the U.S. Senate should approve the SALT II Treaty with the Soviet Union only if the Carter administration agrees to a substantial increase in the U.S. military budget over the next five years.	Chrysler Corp. chmn. John Riccardo states that the company lost $207.1 million in the second quarter of 1979 and seeks a $1 billion cash loan from the federal government to continue operating. . . . Commerce Dept. reports that the government's composite index of leading economic indicators declined .1 percent in June.	Kraftwerk Union AG, West Germany's largest nuclear contractor and a unit of Siemens A.G., announces that it is terminating its contract with Iran to build two nuclear power plants near the Persian Gulf port of Bushehr because Iran refuses to make $450 million in overdue payments.	The number of stations affiliated with the ABC television network is reported equal to those of the other commercial networks.	July 31
The Rev. Jesse Jackson, a black civil-rights leader from the U.S., closes out a two-week visit to South Africa after arousing the anger of conservative whites by comparing apartheid to "the ungodly acts of Hitler."	The Defense Dept. confirms that a shipment of Warsaw Pact military equipment has been bought and delivered to a U.S. Army base in New Jersey for use in training.	The U.S. Agriculture Dept. agrees to let the Soviet Union purchase up to two million metric tons of wheat over the limit set for the year ending Sept. 30.		Soviet Union's Bolshoi Ballet begins a U.S. tour.	Aug. 1
U.S. District Judge Robert Duncan orders the busing of 50,000 students in Columbus, Ohio to begin Sept. 5 after the Supreme Ct., July 2, upheld an earlier busing order by Duncan. . . . The Senate confirms G. William Miller as secretary of the Treasury and Paul Volcker as chairman of the Federal Reserve.	State Dept. announces that sale of arms to police in Northern Ireland has been suspended following pressure from some members of Congress including Rep. Mario Biaggi (D, N.Y.)	Kenny International Corp. becomes the first company prosecuted under the 1977 Foreign Corrupt Practices Act, pleading guilty to trying to rig an election in the Cook Islands so that it could continue to distribute postage stamps for the tiny South Pacific territory.	NRC releases a staff report that claims that the Three Mile Island nuclear plant accident was preventable despite some equipment failures and design inadequacies. . . . The oil tanker Atlantic Empress sinks while under tow 150 miles east of Barbados. A Lloyds of London official calls it their biggest marine loss, possibly amounting to $85 million.		Aug. 2
A fisherman is killed in the Texas coastal town of Seadrift in an outburst of tension between local crab fishermen and Vietnamese immigrants.	Assistant State Secy. Richard Holbrooke says that a U.S. decision to slow down normalization with Vietnam is not connected with U.S. recognition of China.	The Labor Dept. says the nation's unemployment rate edged up in July to seasonally adjusted 5.7 percent.			Aug. 3
The Reporters Committee for Freedom of the Press releases a survey that shows increasing attempts to close courtrooms to the public and press.				Gallup Poll releases a survey that shows increased tolerance among U.S. Catholics, Protestants, and Jews since 1952.	Aug. 4
		Outgoing Energy Secy. James Schlesinger predicts that oil prices set by OPEC will hit $40 a barrel within 10 years. Current prices range from $18 to $23.50 a barrel.		Pete Rose of the Philadelphia Phillies becomes the all-time leader in National League singles hits. . . . Baseball Hall of Fame inducts three new members: Warren Giles, Willie Mays, and Lewis (Hack) Wilson.	Aug. 5
Two high-level investigations ordered by Pres. Carter tentatively exonerate the oil industry of charges that it had deliberately hoarded gasoline supplies to create a shortage.	N.Y.S. Gov. Hugh Carey says that he has invited British and Irish officials to meet in N.Y. to discuss ways of bringing peace to Northern Ireland.	U.S. District Judge Charles Haight Jr. dismisses an antitrust suit against J.P. Stevens & Co., which was filed in November 1977 by the Amalgamated Clothing and Textile Workers Union. The union claimed that Stevens conspired with other textile concerns to deny employment to union sympathizers.	An earthquake measuring 5.9 on the Richter scale hits San Francisco, the strongest one in at least 50 years. . . . Mt. Etna in Italy erupts for the second time in three days and spews lava over a broad area. These are two of its most powerful volcanic actions of recent years.	PGA golf tournament is won by David Graham of Australia beating Ben Crenshaw on the third hole of the playoff.	Aug. 6

F	G	H	I	J
Includes elections, federal-state relations, civil rights and liberties, crime, the judiciary, education, health care, poverty, urban affairs and population.	Includes formation and debate of U.S. foreign and defense policies, veterans' affairs and defense spending. (Relations with specific foreign countries are usually found under the region concerned.)	Includes business, labor, agriculture, taxation, transportation, consumer affairs, monetary and fiscal policy, natural resources, and pollution.	Includes worldwide scientific, medical and technological developments, natural phenomena, U.S. weather, natural disasters, and accidents.	Includes the arts, religion, scholarship, communications media, sports, entertainments, fashions, fads and social life.

	World Affairs	Europe	Africa & the Middle East	The Americas	Asia & the Pacific
Aug. 7		In France leaders of both the Communist-led CGT labor confederation and the more moderate Force Ouvreiere labor group attack the government's economic policies.	Armed Islamic Revolutionary Guards occupy the Teheran offices of the independent newspaper *Ayandegan*, and the government announces that its publishers and editors will be tried for counter-revolutionary activities.	Canadians Jacques and Louise Cossette-Trudel are sentenced to two years less a day for their parts in the kidnapping of British diplomat James Richard Cross during the Quebec crisis of 1970.	
Aug. 8			Iraq executes 21 officials by firing squad for participating in an alleged plot against the government.	Paraguay strips its citizenship from Josef Mengele, the world's most-wanted Nazi fugitive.	Dockworkers return to their jobs at most of Australia's ports, ending a week-long strike. . . . About 400 Chinese stage a sit-in in front of a government building in Peking demanding jobs and assistance from the government.
Aug. 9	An OECD report states that consumer prices increased in the major Western nations at an annual rate of 11.8 percent in the first six months of 1979, compared with an average inflation rate of 7.9 percent of the OECD countries for all of 1978.			Nicaragua's new govt. announces a series of measures designed to restore normal life in the country, stimulate the economy, and define the government's role in establishing reforms.	
Aug. 10		A letter is published, apparently written by Renato Curcio and other founding members of Italy's Red Brigades, expressing support for the policy of terrorist attacks pursued by the Red Brigades' present leadership.	Iran announces that it has canceled $9 billion in arms agreements with the U.S. that had been arranged by the government of the ousted Shah Mohammed Pahlevi.	Jaime Roldos Aguilera is sworn in as president of Ecuador, the first popularly elected president in over nine years.	
Aug. 11		Protestants march in Ulster to mark the tenth anniversary of Britain's dispatch of troops to keep order in Northern Ireland. . . . Electricians and technicians for Britain's commercial television network go on strike, forcing the network off the air.	Moroccan soldiers occupy Tiris el-Gharbia, the area of the Western Sahara formerly controlled by Mauritania, completing Morocco's annexation of the entire Sahara.		*The New York Times* reports that the U.S. is intensifying its efforts to dissuade Pakistan from acquiring nuclear weapons.
Aug. 12		Italy's three-party coalition govt. headed by Premier Francesco Cossiga wins votes of confidence in both the Champer of Deputies and the Senate.	Sudanese Pres. Mohammed Gaafar el-Nimeiry dismisses Vice Pres. Abdel Kassim Mohammed Ibrahim in the wake of riots and strikes protesting sharp increases in the price of basic commodities. . . . Thousands of opponents and supporters of Ayatollah Khomeini clash in the most serious Teheran rioting since the Shah of Iran was overthrown in February.		Premier Masayoshi Ohira's govt. approves a new seven-year economic plan calling for an average annual growth rate of 5.7 percent of the Japanese economy.
Aug. 13			More than one million workers stage a two-hour strike throughout Israel is to protest rising prices.	Canadian Indian Affairs Minister Jason Epp and 11 tribes from Alberta sign an agreement that gives the Indians sole responsibility for administering all federally funded programs on their reservation.	Chinese Deputy Premier Chen Muhua is reported saying that the country is aiming to reach zero population growth between 1985 and 2000.
Aug. 14	In Geneva the Conference of the Committee on Disarmament (the Geneva Disarmament Conference) ends its 1979 session with no new resolution to present to the U.N. General Assembly.	Spanish police kill terrorist Pedro Tabanero Perez after capturing fellow terrorist Manuel Parodi Munoz on Aug. 13.	The withdrawal of the African peacekeeping force from Zaire's Shaba Province is reported to be nearly complete, as the last of the 1,500 Moroccan troops return home. . . . Israeli naval commandos land along the Beirut-Tyre coastal highway in Lebanon and ambush two trucks carrying eight PLO gunmen, killing all of them.		

A	B	C	D	E
Includes developments that affect more than one world region, international organizations and important meetings of major world leaders.	Includes all domestic and regional developments in Europe, including the Soviet Union, Turkey, Cyprus and Malta.	Includes all domestic and regional developments in Africa and the Middle East, including Iraq and Iran and excluding Cyprus, Turkey and Afghanistan.	Includes all domestic and regional developments in Latin America, the Caribbean and Canada.	Includes all domestic and regional developments in Asia and Pacific nations, extending from Afghanistan through all the Pacific Islands, except Hawaii.

U.S. Politics & Social Issues	U.S. Foreign Policy & Defense	U.S. Economy & Environment	Science, Technology & Nature	Culture, Leisure & Life Style	
Joyce Alexander is sworn in in Boston, Mass. as the first black woman U.S. magistrate.	State Secy. Vance says that Israel's use of U.S. equipment in its July 22 raids on Palestinians in southern Lebanon may have violated a 1952 U.S.–Israeli military accord.	Pres. Carter takes the Amtrak Metroliner train from Washington to Baltimore to show his support for a strong mass transportation system.			Aug. 7
Rep. John Jenrette Jr. (D, S.C.) denies published reports that a federal grand jury is investigating his alleged connection with a drug smuggling ring in South Carolina.	Pres. Carter confers at the White House with Israeli Amb. Ephraim Evron in an effort to heal the growing rift between the two countries.	IT&T settles charges brought against it by the SEC that it had made millions of dollars in illegal and questionable payments to secure foreign contracts.	The U.S. record industry reports a significant drop in profits in the first two quarters of 1979.		Aug. 8
Three FBI agents are killed in two separate incidents. This is the first time the in FBI history that three agents are killed on the same day.	A nine-member U.S. house delegation completes a five-day visit to Indochinese refuee camps in Hong Kong, Thailand, Indonesia, and Malaysia.	Pres. Carter rejects Chrysler Corp.'s plea for a $1 billion cash advance against tax credits, but offers to consider a federal loan guarantee for the financially troubled company. . . . The Labor Dept. reports the index of producer prices rose a seasonally adjusted 1.1 percent in July, the steepest rise since February.	Photographs taken by the U.S. Viking spacecraft that landed on Mars in 1976 show what scientists think in a thin layer of frost on the planet's surface.		Aug. 9
Leonel Castillo, head of the Immigration and Naturalization Service, resigns.	The Carter administration reportedly has quietly ordered American military ships and planes to challenge other nations' claims of absolute sovereignty over coastal waters beyond three miles from shore.	Texaco Inc. says it will begin test marketing of gasohol on a small-scale basis in the Boston, New York, and Indianapolis metropolitan areas.	India's first attempt to launch a satellite into orbit fails when the fourth stage of the rocket falls into the Bay of Bengal.		Aug. 10
			A flood in the western Indian town of Morvi reportedly kills 5,000–15,000 people.	Vatican's Congregation for the Doctrine of the Faith reportedly has asked five U.S. theologians to reconsider erroneous conclusions in their book *Human Sexuality: New Directions in American Catholic Thought*. The book suggests in certain situations homosexuality, premarital sex, and birth control may not be sins.	Aug. 11
The FBI reports that to date there have been over 13 percent more bank robberies in 1979 than there were in the same period in 1978.			Forest fires in Idaho, Oregon, California, Montana, and Wyoming are reported having burned at least 171,000 acres.		Aug. 12
Justice Dept. files a civil suit against the city of Philadelphia, Major Frank Rizzo, and 18 high-ranking police and city officials, charging widespread and severe police brutality.	State Dept. discloses that U.N. Amb. Andrew Young met on July 26 with Zehdi Labib Terzi, the PLO's U.N. observer at the N.Y. home of the Kuwaiti delegate to the U.N.				Aug. 13
The Immigration and Naturalization Service issues a directive ordering its agents to stop preventing foreign visitors who are suspected of being homosexual from entering the U.S. . . . Mass. Gov. Edward King signs into law a death penalty bill.	State Secy. Vance reprimands U.N. Amb. Andrew Young for violating official U.S. Middle East policy that bars direct contacts with the PLO. . . . FBI arrests Yeoman Lee Madsen, a Pentagon employe, for selling numerous top-secret U.S. intelligence and military documents.			A stamp collection compiled by New York financier Mark Haas is sold for a record $10 million in London.	Aug. 14
F	G	H	I	J	
Includes elections, federal-state relations, civil rights and liberties, crime, the judiciary, education, health care, poverty, urban affairs and population.	Includes formation and debate of U.S. foreign and defense policies, veterans' affairs and defense spending. (Relations with specific foreign countries are usually found under the region concerned.)	Includes business, labor, agriculture, taxation, transportation, consumer affairs, monetary and fiscal policy, natural resources, and pollution.	Includes worldwide scientific, medical and technological developments, natural phenomena, U.S. weather, natural disasters, and accidents.	Includes the arts, religion, scholarship, communications media, sports, entertainments, fashions, fads and social life.	

	World Affairs	Europe	Africa & the Middle East	The Americas	Asia & the Pacific
Aug. 15	Arthur McKenzie, director of the Tanker Advisory Center, predicts that tanker oil spills will increase with the world growth of super-tanker fleets.		P.M. Abel Muzorewa accepts an invitation from Great Britain to attend a new round of talks on a Zimbabwe Rhodesia political settlement.	Canadian Treasury Board President Sinclair Stevens issues a directive to government departments to cut their number of full-time jobs by 2 percent during the 1979–80 fiscal year.	Indian P.M. Charan Singh warns that his country may be forced to acquire atomic weapons if Pakistan sticks to its plans to assemble a bomb.
Aug. 16		British Shipbuilders, the state-controlled shipbuilding corporation, announces it is planning to scale down its workforce substantially and close a number of shipyards, all in Scotland, in wake of steady financial losses.	Shehu Shagari, a former minister in Nigeria's military government, is proclaimed winner of the country's presidential election, which took place Aug. 11.	Salvadoran Pres. Carlos Humberto Romero announces a general amnesty for political exiles, as civil unrest and open political protest escalate in El Salvador. . . . Former Canadian P.M. John Diefenbaker, 83, dies of an apparent heart attack in Ottawa.	
Aug. 17			The Egyptian gov. announces the arrest of more than 60 persons accused of plotting to oust Pres. Anwar Sadat and replace his administration with a communist government.	Statistics Canada reports the country's inflation rate for the year ending in July was 8.1 percent, the lowest in two years.	
Aug. 18			Masie Nguema Biyogo, deposed president of Equatorial Guinea, is captured near his native village and is brought to the city of Bata in preparation for a military trial. . . . Iranian government forces crush a Kurdish revolt that had broken out Aug. 14 in the Kurdistan province town of Paveh.		Moslem rebels announce the establishment of an Islamic regime in central Paktia province in Afghanistan, which they claim to have liberated from Afghan government forces.
Aug. 19			After three days of meetings in Cairo and Jerusalem, Israeli and Egyptian officials reject an American proposal for a U.N. resolution on Palestinian rights.	In wake of serious labor unrest in the Costa Rican port of Limon, Pres. Rodrigo Carazo Odio orders three Soviet diplomats to leave the country.	In Cambodia former Premier Pol Pot and his Deputy Premier Ieng Sary are sentenced to death in absentia on charges of killing three million people while in office.
Aug. 20		Francois Mitterand proposes that the alliance of the Socialists and Communists in France, the so-called Union of the Left that broke down in 1977, be revived. . . . Swiss police arrest Lebanese Mohsen Jaroudi on suspicion of having assassinated Zahir Mohsen, military operations chief of the PLO, in France in July.	The Iranian government closes 22 opposition newspapers in accordance with a new law prohibiting press criticism of the government. . . . The Patriotic Front guerrilla coalition in Zimbabwe accepts an invitation from Great Britain to attend Zimbabwe Rhodesian political settlement talks scheduled to begin Sept. 10.		Indian Prime Minister Charan Singh resigns because it becomes apparent that he will not be able to muster a majority in a vote of confidence in his new government.
Aug. 21		*Financial Times* (London) reports stringent economic measures in Turkey, including devaluations in the Turkish lira, have resulted in a substantial improvement in the country's account balance.	Israel, Egypt, and the U.S. remain deadlocked after another round of talks on Palestinian autonomy. . . . A third provisional government is formed for war-torn Chad by nine feuding political groups meeting in Lagos, Nigeria.	In Nicaragua the Sandanista government issues a provisional bill of rights guaranteeing basic rights under the law and promising increased social programs. . . . The Canadian government announces the implementation of bilingual air traffic control at all Quebec airports starting in 1980.	Australian P.M. Malcolm Fraser and New Zealand P.M. Robert Muldoon are reported initiating discussions to establish a common market.
Aug. 22		French railroad traffic is seriously disrupted as railroad employes launch a two-day strike to protest working conditions and staffing levels.			Figures published by the U.N. High Commissioner for Refugees show 2,458 Vietnamese boat people arrived in the countries around the China Sea in the first half of August, down from 11,919 in the first half of July.
Aug. 23	U.N. Secy. Gen. Kurt Waldheim formally takes over a $500-million office and conference complex in Vienna for his organization.			In El Salvador U.S. textile executive William Boorstein escapes after being held captive for over a week by 30 unarmed women employes of a textile factory.	Australian Defense Minister Denis Killen outlines the government's plans for improving the country's military forces, which will be financed by a 2.6 percent increase in defense spending.

A	B	C	D	E
Includes developments that affect more than one world region, international organizations and important meetings of major world leaders.	Includes all domestic and regional developments in Europe, including the Soviet Union, Turkey, Cyprus and Malta.	Includes all domestic and regional developments in Africa and the Middle East, including Iraq and Iran and excluding Cyprus, Turkey and Afghanistan.	Includes all domestic and regional developments in Latin America, the Caribbean and Canada.	Includes all domestic and regional developments in Asia and Pacific nations, extending from Afghanistan through all the Pacific Islands, except Hawaii.

U.S. Politics & Social Issues	U.S. Foreign Policy & Defense	U.S. Economy & Environment	Science, Technology & Nature	Culture, Leisure & Life Style	
The Ann Arbor, Mich. school board approves a program to teach so-called Black English to all 28 teachers at the Martin Luther King Elementary School.	Andrew Young resigns as U.S. ambassador to the U.N. following controversy over his unauthorized meeting with PLO representatives in July.	Financially troubled Chrysler Corp. launches a sales blitz with an announcement that car buyers will receive a $400 cash rebate on purchases of nearly all models of the cars and trucks it makes.		Sebastian Coe of Great Britain becomes the first runner ever to simultaneously hold world marks in the 800 meters, 1,500 meters and mile, the last of which he ran on July 17 in Oslo in 3 minutes 49 seconds.	Aug. 15
The Justice Dept. drops its 36-count indictment against South Korean businessman Tong Sun Park. The move had been promised in the agreement reached in January 1978 that had brought Park back to the U.S. to testify about South Korean government influence-buying in Congress.		The Federal Reserve raises the discount rate to a record 10.5 percent to counter strong inflationary forces in the economy and to limit the recent rapid growth of the money supply.			Aug. 16
Pres. Carter selects Washington lawyer Lloyd Cutler to be his counsel, succeeding Robert Lipshutz, who had resigned.		Pres. Carter removes federal price controls from heavy crude oil, a small portion of total domestic oil production.	The collision of two Soviet Aeroflot jetliners over the Ukraine is reported killing 173 persons.	The Vatican refuses to consider valid the naming of a new Chinese bishop, Monsignor Michael Fu Tie-shan, who was elected July 25 without papal approval.	Aug. 17
About 100 Ku Klux Klan members and over 400 black civil-rights marchers parade separately and without incident in Columbus, Ga. as heavily armed police and other law enforcement officers monitor.					Aug. 18
Black and Jewish leaders issue statements seeking to heal the growing rift between their two communities as a result of U.S. Amb. to the U.N. Andrew Young's resignation.			Soviet Cosmonauts Vladimir Lyakhov and Valery Ryumin return safely to Earth after spending a record 175 days in space.	Jack Renner comes from three shots behind in the final round to win golf's Westchester Classic at Harrison, N.Y., collecting a top prize of $72,000.	Aug. 19
Sen. Alan Cranston (D, Calif.) says he will not support Pres. Carter for the Democratic 1980 presidential nomination.	The Defense Dept. acknowledges that the armed services are having trouble finding enough volunteers to fill their ranks.		Massachusetts General Hospital, Boston, studies reveal the potentially important discovery that cancerous cells escape detection and destruction by the body's natural defense system by forming a protective cocoon around a tumor.		Aug. 20
The Veterans of Foreign Wars (VFW) votes to create a committee to endorse political candidates and contribute to their campaigns, ending an 80-year tradition of noninvolvement in the country's political process.	The Southern Christian Leadership Conference (SCLC) expresses support for the PLO after SCLC leaders meet with PLO representatives at U.N. headquarters in New York.				Aug. 21
	The American Legion gives its support to the SALT treaty at its sixty-first annual convention in Houston.			American novelist James Farrell, 75, dies in New York City of a heart attack. He is best known for the Studs Lonigan trilogy.	Aug. 22
U.S. District Judge A. Andrew Hauk rules that his court does not have jurisdiction in the 1978 antitrust suit brought by the IAM against the 13 members of OPEC, charging them with price-fixing.	The GAO reports that the Army has lowered its reserve force goals to cover up the fact that it is recruiting less than half of the reservists it needs.	Sharply criticized by members of the presidential commission on the accident at Three Mile Island, the NRC staff reverses a decision to resume processing applications for new nuclear power plants.		Alexander Godunov, a principal dancer with the Soviet Union's Bolshoi Ballet, is granted political asylum in the U.S. as he defects while his company is on a tour.	Aug. 23
F	G	H	I	J	
Includes elections, federal-state relations, civil rights and liberties, crime, the judiciary, education, health care, poverty, urban affairs and population.	Includes formation and debate of U.S. foreign and defense policies, veterans' affairs and defense spending. (Relations with specific foreign countries are usually found under the region concerned.)	Includes business, labor, agriculture, taxation, transportation, consumer affairs, monetary and fiscal policy, natural resources, and pollution.	Includes worldwide scientific, medical and technological developments, natural phenomena, U.S. weather, natural disasters, and accidents.	Includes the arts, religion, scholarship, communications media, sports, entertainments, fashions, fads and social life.	

	World Affairs	Europe	Africa & the Middle East	The Americas	Asia & the Pacific
Aug. 24	In view of a certain U.S. veto, the U.N. Security Council postpones a vote on a proposed resolution calling for self-determination, national independence and sovereignty for Palestine.		Lebanese Pres. Elias Sarkis calls on Arab states to meet to discuss the crisis resulting from the escalating violence in southern Lebanon.	Mexican Pres. Jose Lopez Portillo rejects a U.S. proposal for talks on compensation for damages caused by Mexico's Ixtoc oil well that blew out June 3.	Sen. Henry Jackson (D, Wash.) reports that China has discovered high-quality oil in a field off Hainan Island in the south of the country.
Aug. 25		One month after the Spanish Parliament approved a 10-year energy plan reaffirming the country's ambitious nuclear energy program, the Spanish government issues permits authorizing the construction of two atomic energy plants.	Polisario guerrillas fighting for Western Saharan independence report killing 800 Morocan soldiers in an ambush yesterday.		Thailand and Laos agree on a plan to halt the flow of Laotian refugees into Thailand.
Aug. 26			Fighting decreases considerably in southern Lebanon as a truce arranged by the U.N. goes into effect.	A dispute over territorial jurisdiction erupts between the U.S. and Canada when Canada seizes eight U.S. tuna-fishing boats 55 miles off Vancouver Island, Canada.	
Aug. 27		Great Britain's Earl Mountbatten of Burma is killed when a bomb explodes aboard his boat off Ireland. The Provisional IRA claims responsibility for the "execution."		The Cuban government announces pardoning 400 political prisoners, bringing to 2,800 the number of prisoners freed by the government in 1979.	
Aug. 28	Despite the Iranian revolution, which shut down oil output in that country, world oil production reportedly rose to record levels during the first six months of 1979.	The minority coalition government in Denmark of Social Democrats and Liberals cautions that its draft budget for 1980 contains assumptions that have been called into question by the latest round of oil price hikes.	In Iran an informal truce between Kurdish rebels and government forces goes into effect after six days of fierce fighting. . . . The U.S. Defense Dept. says that the U.S.S.R. has sent Syria a shipment of T-72 tanks, the most advanced in the Soviet military arsenal.	A strike, which had started July 23, ends without a settlement between the 4,500 workers at the state-owned Bauxite Industry Development Co. and the government of Guyana.	In Korea the New Democratic Party ends its sit-in at its headquarters in Seoul with a statement accusing Pres. Park Chung Hee of having lost the moral power to stay in office.
Aug. 29		Officials of the Turkish government sign an agreement in London and Zurich for the restructuring of $2.2 billion in foreign debt owed to about 250 international banks.	Israeli Foreign Minister Moshe Dayan confers in Gaza with a supporter of the PLO. The discussions are criticized by Israeli government officials, some of whom ask Dayan to resign.		A plane load of food, medicine, and other vital supplies lands in Cambodia, the first installment emergency aid program started by a group of international relief agencies earlier in the month.
Aug. 30	The price of gold surges to a record high of $319.15 an ounce on the London bullion market.	Irish police charge two suspected IRA members — Francis McGirl and Thomas McMahon — with the assassination of Great Britain's Earl Mountbatten.			The Australian oil company Ampol Petroleum announces that it plans to cooperate with Biotechnology Australia in a project to make four million tons of alcohol fuel a year from wheat.
Aug. 31		Troops and police of the Irish Republic close off the border with Northern Ireland to prevent retaliatory raids by Protestants following the assassination of Great Britain's Earl Mountbatten by IRA terrorists.		The U.S. confirms a report that the U.S.S.R. has a combat force numbering 2,000–3,000 men in Cuba. Before this, U.S. intelligence had no indication of a Soviet combat presence there.	
Sept. 1			The Syrian government sends 1,400 paratroopers to Latakia to suppress violent demonstrations by members of the minority Alawite Moslem sect after the killing of an Alawite leader.		U.S. administration sources say that the North Koreans have been discovered digging another tunnel under the demilitarized zone separating North and South Korea.
Sept. 2			Egyptian Pres. Sadat reports receiving a Moroccan request for arms and pledges 100 percent support despite Morocco's break with Egypt over the Israeli-Egyptian peace treaty.		

A	B	C	D	E
Includes developments that affect more than one world region, international organizations and important meetings of major world leaders.	Includes all domestic and regional developments in Europe, including the Soviet Union, Turkey, Cyprus and Malta.	Includes all domestic and regional developments in Africa and the Middle East, including Iraq and Iran and excluding Cyprus, Turkey and Afghanistan.	Includes all domestic and regional developments in Latin America, the Caribbean and Canada.	Includes all domestic and regional developments in Asia and Pacific nations, extending from Afghanistan through all the Pacific Islands, except Hawaii.

U.S. Politics & Social Issues	U.S. Foreign Policy & Defense	U.S. Economy & Environment	Science, Technology & Nature	Culture, Leisure & Life Style	
Pres. Carter arrives at St. Louis, completing his week's journey down the Mississippi River on the *Delta Queen* to rally support for his energy program.					Aug. 24
		The Labor Dept. reports the government's index of prices paid by urban consumers rose a seasonally adjusted 1 percent in July, the same amount as it had risen in June.	The Center for Disease Control reports that Vietnamese refugees entering the U.S. show a high rate of tuberculosis and intestinal and skin parasites.		Aug. 25
Alvin Karpis, 73, notorious criminal labeled the FBI's Public Enemy No. 1 in the 1930s for his co-leadership of the Ma Barker gang, dies in Torremolinos, Spain, a suspected suicide.				American Soccer League concludes its regular season. California Sunshine, the Western division leader, has the best won–lost–tied record, 22–3–3.	Aug. 26
	Continental Grain Co.'s Swiss subsidiary is fined $20,000 for violating U.S. regulations barring participation in the Arab boycott of Israel. This is the first prosecution under these regulations.		It is reported that scientists at SRI International have learned how to produce silicon, a key component of solar energy cells, by a new one-step method that promises to cut the cost of that material by 90 percent.		Aug. 27
Lyn Nofziger, one of Ronald Reagan's top political advisers, resigns because of differences with other advisers working on Reagan's unannounced presidential campaign.	Vice Pres. Mondale says U.S.-China ties are strengthened after two days of talks in Peking between him and China's two top leaders.	The U.S. deficit in its balance of merchandise trade narrowed in July to a seasonally adjusted $1.11 billion, the Commerce Department says.	Physicists at the Fermi National Accelerator Lab at Batavia, Ill., say that recent experiments appear to provide evidence for the existence of a subatomic particle called the gluon.	A soon-to-be released Hasting Center study strongly recommends that a course in ethics be included in college and professional school curriculums.	Aug. 28
Dr. Jeffrey MacDonald is found guilty in North Carolina of killing his pregnant wife and two daughters nearly 10 years ago and is sentenced to life.	The Navy announces that all ship and shore commanders have been ordered to use their full powers to deal effectively with racism in wake of reports of Ku Klux Klan activity aboard at least two Atlantic Fleet ships.	The Commerce Dept. reports the government's composite index of leading economic indicators declined .4 percent in July, the third decline in four months.		Vatican officials say Pope John Paul II will exclude Northern Ireland from his September visit to Ireland because of the new wave of IRA violence there.	Aug. 29
	Pres. Carter says that no Arab leader he has met privately supports an independent Palestinian state.				Aug. 30
In Chicago HEW proposes a desegregation plan that would require the Chicago school system to begin a compulsory busing program by September 1980.	Pres. Carter names Donald McHenry as U.N. ambassador succeeding Andrew Young. McHenry, a career diplomat, has been Young's chief deputy at the U.N.	New York State brings criminal charges against Hooker Chemical Co. for more than 400 violations of state law against dumping toxic chemical wastes.	A 33-year-old Baltimore woman becomes the first person known to have her spine replaced with a metal prosthesis. This is done in a 16-hour operation at the University of Maryland Hospital.	Despite a national trend toward preservation of historic buildings, the famed Baker Hotel in Dallas, Tex. is closed to make way for a new Southwestern Bell Telephone headquarters building.	Aug. 31
After studying congressional financial disclosure statements, *Congressional Quarterly* reports that one-third of the 535 members of Congress hold outside jobs.			The unmanned U.S. spacecraft Pioneer 11 flies past Saturn, gathering information on the giant planet, its spectacular ring system, and its collection of satellites.		Sept. 1
	Gen. Otto Weyland, 77, WWII and Korean War combat veteran who later headed the Tactical Air Command, dies after a stroke in San Antonio, Texas.		Rose Franzblau, 77, psychologist whose syndicated daily advice column appeared in newspapers across the country (1951–76), dies of cancer in N.Y.C.	*Sophie's Choice* by William Styron is the best-selling fiction book for the previous week. *The Complete Scarsdale Medical Diet* by Herman Tarnower and Samm Baker is the best-selling general book.	Sept. 2

F	G	H	I	J
Includes elections, federal-state relations, civil rights and liberties, crime, the judiciary, education, health care, poverty, urban affairs and population.	*Includes formation and debate of U.S. foreign and defense policies, veterans' affairs and defense spending. (Relations with specific foreign countries are usually found under the region concerned.)*	*Includes business, labor, agriculture, taxation, transportation, consumer affairs, monetary and fiscal policy, natural resources, and pollution.*	*Includes worldwide scientific, medical and technological developments, natural phenomena, U.S. weather, natural disasters, and accidents.*	*Includes the arts, religion, scholarship, communications media, sports, entertainments, fashions, fads and social life.*

	World Affairs	Europe	Africa & the Middle East	The Americas	Asia & the Pacific
Sept. 3	Following the urging of Libyan leader Col. Muammer el-Qaddafi on Sept. 2, Libyans living abroad take over seven Libyan embassies and turn them into "people's bureaus." Included are the embassies in Washington, London, and Rome.	Hungary launched a sweeping review of price and employment policy early in the year, *The New York Times* reports. As part of it, the government plans to decontrol more than 60 percent of the country's prices by the end of 1983.... In Britain a killer, terrorizing the Yorkshire region of northern England with a string of brutal slayings of young women, claims his twelfth victim.	South Africa's opposition Progressive Federal Party selects Frederick van Zyl Slabbert as its new and, at age 39, youngest leader.	Sandinista junta fixes the Nicaraguan Cordoba at 10 units to one U.S. dollar.... Juan Pablo Perez Alfonzo, 75, former Venezuelan oil minister and OPEC co-founder, dies of pancreatic cancer in Wash., D.C.	
Sept. 4	At the summit of a nonaligned nations meeting in Havana, Cuba, Iraqi Pres. Saddam Hussein charges developed nations with pretending that some developing countries are accountable for the economic scourges befalling others.		Mehabad, the center of the Kurdish rebel movement, falls to Iranian government troops as the Kurds vow to continue their fight in the hills.		
Sept. 5	At the meeting of the nonaligned nations in Havana, Cuba, Panamanian Pres. Aristides Royo praises Pres. Carter's approach to negotiating the Panama Canal treaties, but he is the only delegate to say anything good about the U.S.	In Great Britain, the funeral for Earl Mountbatten of Burma, killed Aug. 27 by IRA terrorists, is held with great ceremony in Westminster Abbey, London.... The French Cabinet approves a budget for 1980 that increases spending by 14.3 percent to $124.9 billion and has a deficit of $7.3 billion.			
Sept. 6			Egyptian Pres. Anwar Sadat and Israeli Premier Menahem Begin end three days of talks with the two remaining in disagreement over autonomy for the Palestinians.	The brother of Salvadoran Pres. Carlos Humberto Romero is machine-gunned to death by four men who burst into his home about 15 miles north of San Salvador.	The government of Taiwan announces that it is extending its territorial waters from three to 12 miles offshore.
Sept. 7			Israeli military authorities announce the arrest of 70 suspected Palestinian terrorists in the last two weeks in the occupied Gaza Strip.	The Bank of Canada raises its bank rate to 12.25 percent, continuing a trend toward record interest rates.	
Sept. 8			Morocco is reported receiving a shipment of arms from Egypt to aid in its war against Western Saharan guerrillas.		A Korean court orders Kim Young Sam removed as leader of the opposition New Democratic Party, ruling that some of the party delegates who elected Kim in May were unqualified to vote.
Sept. 9	The sixth summit of nonaligned nations ends in Havana, Cuba with clear indications of a tilt among the nations toward the U.S.S.R.				

A	B	C	D	E
Includes developments that affect more than one world region, international organizations and important meetings of major world leaders.	*Includes all domestic and regional developments in Europe, including the Soviet Union, Turkey, Cyprus and Malta.*	*Includes all domestic and regional developments in Africa and the Middle East, including Iraq and Iran and excluding Cyprus, Turkey and Afghanistan.*	*Includes all domestic and regional developments in Latin America, the Caribbean and Canada.*	*Includes all domestic and regional developments in Asia and Pacific nations, extending from Afghanistan through all the Pacific Islands, except Hawaii.*

U.S. Politics & Social Issues	U.S. Foreign Policy & Defense	U.S. Economy & Environment	Science, Technology & Nature	Culture, Leisure & Life Style	
Homer Capehart, 82, conservative Republican senator from Indiana (1945–62), dies in Indianapolis.					Sept. 3
	Sen. Frank Church (D, Ida.), chairman of the Senate Foreign Relations Committee, postpones hearings on the SALT Treaty to get reports from administration officials on the situation of Soviet combat troops in Cuba.			The Soviet Union opens it second international book fair in Moscow. The event is marred by Soviet denial of a visa to U.S. publisher Robert Bernstein and confiscation of many more books than in 1977.	Sept. 4
Rep. Morris Udall (D, Ariz.) suggests to reporters that V.P. Walter Mondale might be a possible Democratic nominee in 1980, if Pres. Carter stumbles.		Sales of U.S.-produced cars were down 6 percent in August, according to industry sources.... The U.S. Commodity Futures Trading Commission votes to kill a planned pilot project for trading commodity options on the country's exchanges.	Work crews continue cleaning up what is being called the worst spill of radioactive wastes in U.S. history. The spill at a uranium mine in New Mexico on July 16 occurred when stored radioactive waste poured through a crack in a dam.	John Cruyff, a Dutch player with the Los Angeles Aztecs, is named the most valuable player for 1979 in the North American Soccer League.	Sept. 5
As the summer tourist season ends and fuel supplies increase, the governors of N.Y.S., N.J., Pa., R.I., and Conn. announce they are ending the odd-even restrictions on gasoline sales in their states.		Revlon Inc., the beauty and health-care products company, says it has agreed in principle to buy Technicon Corp., a medical supply company, for cash and stock valued at $400 million.			Sept. 6
	Pres. Carter announces that he has approved a $33-billion plan to base the new long-range MX missile in underground shelters connected by a "racetrack" system in Western desert valleys.	Ford Motor Co.'s planned purchase of a 25 percent interest in the fourth largest Japanese auto maker, Toyo Kogyo Co., is approved by Toyo Kogyo's shareholders. Toyo Kogyo makes Mazda cars and trucks.	A report attributes at least 16 deaths in the U.S. to Hurricane David.	The Right Rev. Robert Runcie, 57, is designated as the 102nd Archbishop of Canterbury, Primate of the Church of England, and spiritual leader of 65 million Anglicans worldwide.	Sept. 7
The Ford Foundation releases a report that says programs in the U.S. to eliminate adult illiteracy are grossly inadequate.... It is reported the Scholastic Aptitude Tests (SAT) scores of America's high school seniors fell slightly in 1979, continuing a 10-year decline.		Amtrak, the National Railroad Passenger Corp., announces a record 25 percent gain in ridership in June over June 1978.		The Vancouver (Canada) Whitecaps beat the Tampa Bay (Fla.) Rowdies, 2–1, to win Soccer Bowl '79 and the championship of the North American Soccer League.	Sept. 8
Karen Stevenson, 22, a graduate of the University of North Carolina, becomes the first black American woman to win a Rhodes Scholarship.	Sen. Frank Church (D. Ida.), chairman of the Senate Foreign Relations Committee, says that in his opinion the SALT Treaty will not get the necessary two-thirds majority in the Senate unless the Soviet combat troops are removed from Cuba.			John McEnroe and Tracy Austin win the men's and women's singles titles, respectively, at the U.S. Open in N.Y.C. Austin, 16, is the youngest women's champion in the tournament's history.... The thirty-first annual Emmy Awards are presented as follows: dramatic series actor, Ron Liebman; dramatic series actress, Mariette Hartley; comedy series actor, Carroll O'Connor; comedy series actress, Ruth Gordon; outstanding series, *Lou Grant* ; outstanding drama special, *Friendly Fire* ; and outstanding children's program, *Christmas Eve On Sesame Street* .	Sept. 9

F	G	H	I	J
Includes elections, federal-state relations, civil rights and liberties, crime, the judiciary, education, health care, poverty, urban affairs and population.	*Includes formation and debate of U.S. foreign and defense policies, veterans' affairs and defense spending. (Relations with specific foreign countries are usually found under the region concerned.)*	*Includes business, labor, agriculture, taxation, transportation, consumer affairs, monetary and fiscal policy, natural resources, and pollution.*	*Includes worldwide scientific, medical and technological developments, natural phenomena, U.S. weather, natural disasters, and accidents.*	*Includes the arts, religion, scholarship, communications media, sports, entertainments, fashions, fads and social life.*

	World Affairs	Europe	Africa & the Middle East	The Americas	Asia & the Pacific
Sept. 10		*Pravda* publishes a strongly worded editorial denying that any Soviet combat troops are in Cuba. This is the first official Soviet reaction to the U.S. charge of their presence.	Agostinho Neto, first president of an independent Angola, dies in Moscow hospital.... Ayatollah Mahmoud Taleghani, the Moslem spiritual leader of Teheran and one of the few voices of moderation in Iran's religious establishment, dies of natural causes at the age of 69.		
Sept. 11		Premier Raymond Barre reaffirms nuclear weapons as the major element of French defense strategy.	Egypt and Israel reportedly have asked the U.S. for a substantial increase in economic and military aid.	In his state-of-the-nation address, Chilean Pres. Augusto Pinochet Ugarte rejects demands that he set a timetable for restoration of representative government.	The Australian Council of Trade Unions approves a statement attacking the government's wage indexation guidelines and calling for national wage hikes based on increased productivity.
Sept. 12		An OECD study concludes that Greek public officials should reduce government expenditures and channel more funds into investment in the economic infrastructure.	An Assembly of Experts in Iran, charged with revising Iran's Constitution, approve a clause that would give supreme power to an Islamic religious leader.	Amnesty International, the London-based human rights organization, says that 2,000 people have been killed in Guatemala in the past 16 months, victims of a wave of political repression.	Philippine Pres. Ferdinand Marcos orders a halt to the pre-trial military investigation of former Pres. Diosdado Macapagal on charges of sedition and rumor-mongering.
Sept. 13			The South African government formally declares the black homeland of Venda independent, although no other nation extends the country diplomatic recognition.		About 1,000 Chinese attend a rally in Peking's Tien An Men Square denouncing special privileges among Communist Party officials and urging more human rights and free elections.
Sept. 14	The price of gold rises to an unprecedented $345.80 an ounce in London trading.	The British gov. announces that the state-controlled British National Oil Corp. will not sell any of its *North Sea* oil assets after it meets with widespread opposition to such a move.			
Sept. 15	PLO leader Yasir Arafat concludes a three-day visit to Spain, part of his organization's continuing effort to gain political recognition in Europe.			In El Salvador the government of Gen. Carlos Humberto Romero cancels Independence Day celebrations because of fears that they will prompt renewed violence and political unrest in the already jittery country.	In China thousands of petitioners who have crowded into Peking in past months have been promised investigations into their complaints, a report in *Jenmin Jih Pao*, the official daily newspaper, says.
Sept. 16	The IMF in its annual report says that the world faces another year of sluggish growth and high inflation in 1980, citing the effect of sharp oil increases.	General elections in Sweden produce a one-seat parliamentary majority for three center-right groups: the Moderate, Center, and Liberal parties.	The Israeli Cabinet abrogates a 1967 law barring Israeli citizens and businesses from purchasing Arab-owned land in the occupied West Bank and Gaza Strip.... Terence Mashambanhaka, a black member of the Zimbabwe Rhodesian Parliament, is killed in an ambush by guerrillas 60 miles north of Salisbury, where he was attempting to persuade the guerrillas to accept the government's amnesty offer.		Nur Mohammad Taraki is replaced as president of Afghanistan by Premier Hafizullah Amin. Unofficial accounts say the change is the result of a government upheaval in which Taraki was shot.
Sept. 17		The Norwegian Conservative party makes substantial gains in local government elections, capturing 29 percent of the vote, seven percentage points over the 1975 municipal elections.		The last four U.S. citizens being held by Cuba on political charges are freed in response to the pardon by Pres. Carter on Sept. 6 of four Puerto Rican terrorists.	

A	B	C	D	E
Includes developments that affect more than one world region, international organizations and important meetings of major world leaders.	Includes all domestic and regional developments in Europe, including the Soviet Union, Turkey, Cyprus and Malta.	Includes all domestic and regional developments in Africa and the Middle East, including Iraq and Iran and excluding Cyprus, Turkey and Afghanistan.	Includes all domestic and regional developments in Latin America, the Caribbean and Canada.	Includes all domestic and regional developments in Asia and Pacific nations, extending from Afghanistan through all the Pacific Islands, except Hawaii.

U.S. Politics & Social Issues	U.S. Foreign Policy & Defense	U.S. Economy & Environment	Science, Technology & Nature	Culture, Leisure & Life Style	
In Cleveland, Ohio a school desegregation plan goes into effect, climaxing a six-year court battle. . . . A sweeping, two-year federal immunization program reaching nearly 90 percent of the nation's children is reported sharply decreasing cases of measles and other childhood diseases.	The Marines Corps is reported cutting its active duty strength by 10,000 men to save money.	FRB reports that expansion of consumers' installment credit slowed in July, growing at a seasonally adjusted rate of $2.44 billion, down from a growth of $2.56 billion in June.			Sept. 10
	The NAACP calls on Pres. Carter to review the U.S. policy of refusing direct negotiations with the PLO until the PLO recognizes Israel's right to exist.	Pres. Carter agrees to compromises on his energy plan including a slower and less costly construction plan for synthetic fuel plants.	Cancer specialists meeting in Copenhagen reportedly say that the drug Tamoxifen has proven effective in treating women whose breast cancer had spread beyond the breast.		Sept. 11
Former New Orleans Mayor Moon Landrieu wins unanimous confirmation by the Senate as the new secretary of housing and urban development.		Chase Manhattan raises its prime interest rate to 13 percent, an all-time high.	Hurricane Frederic strikes the central Gulf Coast of the U.S. with 130-mile-an-hour winds and torrential flooding.	Bantam Books sets a record when it purchases the paperback publishing rights to *Princess Daisy*, a novel by Judith Krantz, for $3.2 million. . . . Boston Red Sox Carl Yastrzemski becomes the first AL player to reach the 400-home-run, 3,000-hit plateau.	Sept. 12
Pres. Carter announces the appointment of Hispanic-Americans Edward Hidalgo as secretary of the Navy and Abelardo Lopez Valdez as chief of protocol, the first time Hispanic-Americans have held the positions.			Tidal waves set off by a powerful undersea earthquake destroy an Indonesian village and kill 100.		Sept. 13
The Senate Committee on Ethics recommends that Sen. Herman Talmadge (D, Ga.) be denounced by the full Senate for financial misconduct.	U.S. Defense Sec. Harold Brown says after discussions with Israeli Defense Min. Ezer Weizman that the U.S. will seriously consider an Israeli proposal to co-produce advanced U.S. fighter planes in Israeli factories.	The UAW reaches a contract settlement with GM, avoiding a strike. . . . Production in the nation's factories, mines, and utilities declined a seasonally adjusted 1.1 percent in August, the sharpest drop since April 1978, the Federal Reserve reports.			Sept. 14
	Ronald Reagan says the Senate should not ratify the SALT Treaty, charging that the treaty would not limit arms but would allow the Soviets to increase nuclear warheads.	Chrysler Corp. submits a formal request to the Carter administration for $1.2 billion in federal loan guarantees and is immediately turned down by Treasury Secy. G. William Miller, who says the request is way out of line.		Gov. Edward King of Mass. signs a bill creating the nation's first lottery in support of the arts.	Sept. 15
Republicans loyal to Ronald Reagan defeat a plan to modify California's unique winner-take-all presidential primary.		Alaska and Mississippi ranked first ($10,963) and last ($5,529) respectively, among the states in 1978 in per capita income, the Commerce Department reports.		The Sacramento (Cal.) Gold wins the championship of the American Soccer League with a 1–0 victory over the Columbus (Ohio) Magic.	Sept. 16
It is revealed that Justice William Brennan, 73, the oldest member of the Supreme Ct., suffered a mild stroke Sept. 4 but has returned to his office and is participating fully in the court schedule.	The Justice Dept. announces that it is ending its efforts to prevent the *Progressive* magazine from publishing an article on the workings of the hydrogen bomb.	CAB has sanctioned an agreement between Pan American Airways and the Civil Aviation Administration of China for air charter service to China.	The FDA notifies health officials in Minnesota, Montana, Idaho, Washington, North Dakota, and Utah that poultry and hog feed contaminated with PCBs had been distributed in their states since June from an animal feed processing concern in Billings, Mont.	Two dancers from the Soviet Union's Bolshoi Ballet — Leonid Kozlov and his wife, Valentina — are granted asylum in the U.S.	Sept. 17

F	G	H	I	J
Includes elections, federal-state relations, civil rights and liberties, crime, the judiciary, education, health care, poverty, urban affairs and population.	*Includes formation and debate of U.S. foreign and defense policies, veterans' affairs and defense spending. (Relations with specific foreign countries are usually found under the region concerned.)*	*Includes business, labor, agriculture, taxation, transportation, consumer affairs, monetary and fiscal policy, natural resources, and pollution.*	*Includes worldwide scientific, medical and technological developments, natural phenomena, U.S. weather, natural disasters, and accidents.*	*Includes the arts, religion, scholarship, communications media, sports, entertainments, fashions, fads and social life.*

	World Affairs	Europe	Africa & the Middle East	The Americas	Asia & the Pacific
Sept. 18	The thirty-fourth U.N. General Assembly convenes at U.N. headquarters in New York, with disputes over the credentials of Palestinian and Cambodian delegations the dominant issues.	A report by Great Britain's Energy Department concludes that the country's need to import energy toward the end of the century may be much greater than previously predicted.			
Sept. 19	A survey is released reporting that West Germany ranks highest and Great Britain lowest in comparative wage rates among the top ten noncommunist industrial countries.	The two leading French union confederations, the Communist-led CGT and the rival left-wing CFDT, agree on a program of opposition to the government's economic policies.	The U.S., Egypt, and Israel reach a tentative agreement for monitoring the Israeli–Egyptian peace pact in the Sinai. Its principal element is increased U.S. ground and air surveillance.		
Sept. 20		In France Pierre Goldman, a left-wing French Jewish writer is shot to death by three unidentified youths, leading to fears of a resurrection of violence on the part of anti-Semitic right-wing groups in the country. . . . Faruk Sukan, a Turkish deputy premier, resigns from the government and charges it with failing to halt the violence that is leading to the division of the country.	Central African Emperor Bokassa I is overthrown in a bloodless coup and replaced by David Dacko, former president of the land-locked nation. Dacko publicly thanks France for its help in deposing the emperor.		
Sept. 21	The U.N. General Assembly supports its Credentials Committee and votes to permit the delegation of the ousted Cambodian government of Pol Pot to retain its Assembly seat.	British and French officials meeting in London indicate that their governments will not underwrite development of a second-generation of the Concorde supersonic airliner. The action is seen as ending the controversial and costly Concorde program.		After two years of difficult negotiations, agreement is reached on the sale of Mexican natural gas to U.S. companies. . . . In El Salvador two men working for a U.S. company are kidnapped and their bodyguard killed on the road to San Salvador's airport. . . . A potentially rich deposit of oil is reported to have been discovered 195 miles southeast of Newfoundland.	
Sept. 22		Some 800 striking Dutch dockworkers cross picket lines in Rotterdam to return to work after a non-union sanctioned strike involving 7,000 dockworkers has lasted a month.			At the end of former Pres. Nixon's unofficial trip to China, a Chinese foreign ministry official praises him for opening U.S.–Chinese ties.
Sept. 23		An emergency meeting is called by Spanish Premier Adolfo Suarez to deal with the friction that has developed between the military and the government over the handling of Basque terrorism.			Afghanistan Pres. Hafizullah Amin says ousted former Pres. Nur Mohammad Taraki is being treated for an undisclosed ailment, denying earlier reports that Taraki had been killed when his government was overthrown. . . . China and the World Wildlife Fund sign an agreement to promote international exchanges to help preserve some of China's endangered animal species.
Sept. 24		The finance ministers of the countries belonging to the European Monetary System agree to a revaluation of their currencies against the West German mark. . . . Engineering and assembly-line workers begin their fourth two-day strike in four weeks, shutting down industry in much of Great Britain.	Israeli warplanes shoot down four Syrian MiG-21 fighter jets over Beirut, Israeli officials report. . . . After 10 days of dispute, the Patriotic Front guerrillas accept the general outlines of a British-drafted constitution for an independent Zimbabwe Rhodesia. . . . Hilla Limann is formally installed as president of Ghana. He heads the first completely civilian government in the country since 1966.		

A	B	C	D	E
Includes developments that affect more than one world region, international organizations and important meetings of major world leaders.	Includes all domestic and regional developments in Europe, including the Soviet Union, Turkey, Cyprus and Malta.	Includes all domestic and regional developments in Africa and the Middle East, including Iraq and Iran and excluding Cyprus, Turkey and Afghanistan.	Includes all domestic and regional developments in Latin America, the Caribbean and Canada.	Includes all domestic and regional developments in Asia and Pacific nations, extending from Afghanistan through all the Pacific Islands, except Hawaii.

U.S. Politics & Social Issues	U.S. Foreign Policy & Defense	U.S. Economy & Environment	Science, Technology & Nature	Culture, Leisure & Life Style	
		Americans' personal income rose $8.4 billion in August, or .4 percent, to a seasonally adjusted annual rate of $1.938 trillion, according to the Commerce Department.		Oleg Protopopov and Ludmila Belousova, a Soviet champion skating couple, defect to Switzerland.	Sept. 18
		The pace of residential construction slowed .4 percent in August when new houses were started at a seasonally adjusted annual rate of 1,783,000 units, the Commerce Department says.		Soviet-born Dmitri Sitkovetsky, who is a U.S. citizen, wins the International Fritz Kreisler Violin Contest in Vienna, Austria, playing the Brahms Violin Concerto.	Sept. 19
Pres. Carter orders Secret Service protection for Sen. Edward Kennedy (D, Mass.), whose consideration of a presidential campaign has raised the fear of an assassination attempt.		Lee Iacocca and two of his former associates at Ford Motor Co. are named to the three top posts at Chrysler Corp., following the sudden resignation of chairman John Riccardo.			Sept. 20
The Senate by unanimous vote confirms Neil Goldschmidt as secretary of transportation and Donald McHenry as U.S. ambassador to the U.N.			FTC releases a report stating that Americans who have stopped smoking have gained an average of two extra years of life.		Sept. 21
		Brush and forest fires fanned by hot, dry winds, which had laid waste to over 130,000 acres across California starting Sept. 10, are brought under control.... A U.S. reconnaissance satellite picks up traces of a mysterious atomic explosion in an area bounded by the Indian Ocean, the southern Atlantic, and the continent of Antarctica.		Miami Beach, Fla. tourism authority orders staff photographers to cease taking promotional pictures of bikini-clad women as not consistent with the city's support for NOW, which has imposed an economic boycott on Fla. and other states that have not ratified the proposed ERA.	Sept. 22
			More than 200,000 persons gather peacefully at a sandy landfill along the Hudson River in N.Y.C. in the nation's largest antinuclear demonstration to date.	Lou Brock of the St. Louis Cardinals steals his 935th base in a game against the Mets in N.Y.C. He sets the record to date as all-time base-stealer in baseball history.	Sept. 23
A federal judge in Chicago rules that the city's political patronage system is unconstitutional because it violates the First and Fourteenth Amendments.... AMA is ordered by the FTC to lift its ban on advertising by doctors.					Sept. 24

F	G	H	I	J
Includes elections, federal-state relations, civil rights and liberties, crime, the judiciary, education, health care, poverty, urban affairs and population.	Includes formation and debate of U.S. foreign and defense policies, veterans' affairs and defense spending. (Relations with specific foreign countries are usually found under the region concerned.)	Includes business, labor, agriculture, taxation, transportation, consumer affairs, monetary and fiscal policy, natural resources, and pollution.	Includes worldwide scientific, medical and technological developments, natural phenomena, U.S. weather, natural disasters, and accidents.	Includes the arts, religion, scholarship, communications media, sports, entertainments, fashions, fads and social life.

	World Affairs	Europe	Africa & the Middle East	The Americas	Asia & the Pacific
Sept. 25		West German Defense Min. Hans Apel rejects the French Gaullist proposal of a joint West German-French nuclear military force that would serve as a deterrent independent of the U.S.	South African P.M. Pieter Botha indicates that he is willing to consider changes in his country's laws that bar marriage and sexual relations between whites and non-white.... Labor Min. Stephanus Botha says all South African blacks, including those who officially live in the black homelands, will be allowed to join unions at their places of work, a significant concession to black demands.	Jacobo Timerman, a newspaper publisher who has been held for 29 months by Argentina's military government, is released and put on a jet for Rome.	Sources in Bangkok, Thailand report Vietnamese troops have launched a new offensive in central Cambodia against the forces of the deposed Pol Pot government.
Sept. 26		Swiss Finance Minister Georges-Andre Chevallaz proposes an austerity budget for 1980 of $10.9 billion to limit an expected deficit.		The Dominican Republic armed forces say that a plot by a group of seven military mem and three civilians to overthrow the government of Pres. Antonio Guzman has been stopped.	Japan charges that the Soviet Union has stationed troops on Shikotan, one of the islands in the Kurile group. The four southern Kurile Islands are claimed by both Japan and Russia.
Sept. 27			Egyptian, Israeli, and U.S. delegates completing their sixth round of talks on Palestinian autonomy, issue a report saying progress has been made in developing a format for holding elections in the West Bank and Gaza Strip.		Ian Sinclair, the Australian minister of primary industry and leader of the House, resigns his Cabinet post following charges of misconduct concerning his family business.
Sept. 28		Danish Premier Anker Jorgensen resigns following the collapse of the two-party coalition he headed over budgetary and economic differences.		Prospects for the repayment of the $1.6-billion external debt of Nicaragua become unclear when a leader of the new government, Daniel Ortega Saavedra, tells the U.N. that the debt must be assumed by the international community.	
Sept. 29			Masie Nguema Biyogo, the deposed ruler of Equatorial Guinea, is executed, hours after a public trial finds him guilty of mass murder, treason, and misuse of government funds.	Argentine army headquarters announces that an attempt to oust Gen. Roberto Viola, the army commander in chief, has been put down.	In a speech commemorating the thirtieth anniversary of the People's Republic of China, CP Senior Deputy Chairman Yeh Chian-ying describes the Cultural Revolution of the late 1960s as "an appalling catastrophe suffered by all our people."
Sept. 30			Toilet facilities in South African airports are integrated.		
Oct. 1			Nigeria's first civilian government in 13 years is installed as Pres. elect Shehu Shagari takes the oath of office.	A panel of five Chilean Supreme Ct. judges rejects a U.S. appeal for the extradition of three army officers indicted for the murder of former Chilean For. Min. Orlando Letelier and his aide Ronni Moffitt in Wash., D.C.	
Oct. 2	The IMF and the World Bank begin their thirty-fourth annual meetings in Belgrade, Yugoslavia, amid rising concern about the weakness of the dollar and accelerating worldwide inflation.... The price of gold reaches an unprecedented high of $437 an ounce in London.	The West German federal and state governments are reported reaching a compromise agreement aimed at facilitating the future development of nuclear power.			

A	B	C	D	E
Includes developments that affect more than one world region, international organizations and important meetings of major world leaders.	Includes all domestic and regional developments in Europe, including the Soviet Union, Turkey, Cyprus and Malta.	Includes all domestic and regional developments in Africa and the Middle East, including Iraq and Iran and excluding Cyprus, Turkey and Afghanistan.	Includes all domestic and regional developments in Latin America, the Caribbean and Canada.	Includes all domestic and regional developments in Asia and Pacific nations, extending from Afghanistan through all the Pacific Islands, except Hawaii.

U.S. Politics & Social Issues	U.S. Foreign Policy & Defense	U.S. Economy & Environment	Science, Technology & Nature	Culture, Leisure & Life Style	
Pres. Carter presides over his first town meeting in a large urban center, answering questions from an audience of 1,700 at Queens College, N.Y.C.	Yeoman Lee Madsen, a Pentagon employe, pleads guilty to selling seven top secret intelligence and military documents to an informer for the FBI.	An 11-week strike that has hampered grain shipments out of ports on Lake Superior ends when members of the American Federation of Grain Millers approve a contract settlement reached sept. 23.	A government-sponsored study is released that tentatively concludes more than 40 percent of Vietnam War veterans suffer from major emotional difficulties, such as alcoholism and narcotics abuse.	ABC wins TV rights to the 1984 summer Olympic Games in Los Angeles, Calif., offering $225 million to outbid its rivals. The amount is more than double the $87 million paid by NBC for 1980 Moscow games rights.	Sept. 25
	In a speech, former Pres. Gerald Ford opposes ratifying the SALT Treaty until the U.S. increases its defense expenditures.	The ICC orders a group of Midwestern railroads to take over freight operations of the bankrupt Chicago, Rock Island & Pacific Railroad Co., which has been shutdown by a strike since Aug. 28. . . . Pres. Carter signs the $10.8 billion fiscal 1980 energy and water development appropriations bill.		Alexandra Tolstoy, 95, the last surviving daughter of Russian author Leo Tolstoy, dies in Valley Cottage, N.Y.	Sept. 26
Murder charges against Huey Newton, co-founder of the Black Panther Party, are dropped in Alameda County, Calif,. after two trials of the charges end in hung juries.		The Department of Energy gives final approval to a $3-billion project designed to supply California with 900-million cubic feet of liquefied natural gas a day.			Sept. 27
		New York's Citibank raises its prime rate to a record 13.5 percent and is quickly followed by other major banks. . . . The AFL–CIO discloses that pres. George Meany, 85, will not seek reelection in November.			Sept. 28
				Pope John Paul II leaves on an historic nine-day journey to Ireland and the U.S., the third international trip of John Paul's papacy.	Sept. 29
	State Secy. Cyrus Vance meets for the fourth time in 16 days with Soviet Amb. Anatoly Dobrynin in an effort to resolve the problem of the Soviet combat brigade in Cuba.	Federal govt. finishes fiscal 1979 with the smallest budget deficit in five years — $27.7 billion.		Lon Hinkle wins the prestigious World Series of Golf, worth $100,000. . . . During a mass in Ireland, Pope John Paul II lashes out at the "generation of violent men" responsible for 10 years of bloodshed between Irish Catholics and Protestants.	Sept. 30
The Supreme Ct. lets stand a criminal contempt citation against Roman Catholic priest Louis Gigante, who refused to answer a grand jury's questions concerning a jail inmate on the grounds of priest-penitent confidentiality.	U.S. control of the Panama Canal Zone officially ends at midnight, the implementation of the first phase of the Panama Canal Treaties under which U.S. control of the canal itself will be surrendered to Panama by the year 2000.			Pope John Paul II arrives in Boston to begin his seven-day U.S. tour.	Oct. 1
		Marilyn McClusker, 35, hired as a coal miner in 1977 after a successful sex discrimination suit, dies in an underground mine accident in Coalport, Pa.		A PLO sports committee says that it has accepted an invitation to send a team to the 1980 summer Olympics in Moscow.	Oct. 2

F	G	H	I	J
Includes elections, federal-state relations, civil rights and liberties, crime, the judiciary, education, health care, poverty, urban affairs and population.	Includes formation and debate of U.S. foreign and defense policies, veterans' affairs and defense spending. (Relations with specific foreign countries are usually found under the region concerned.)	Includes business, labor, agriculture, taxation, transportation, consumer affairs, monetary and fiscal policy, natural resources, and pollution.	Includes worldwide scientific, medical and technological developments, natural phenomena, U.S. weather, natural disasters, and accidents.	Includes the arts, religion, scholarship, communications media, sports, entertainments, fashions, fads and social life.

	World Affairs	Europe	Africa & the Middle East	The Americas	Asia & the Pacific
Oct. 3		The U.S. Agriculture Dept. announces that the U.S.S.R. will be permitted to purchase a record amount of U.S. wheat and corn, up to 25 million metric tons, during the 12-month period that began Oct. 1. ... Western European governments have had little to say about the debate in the U.S. over Soviet combat troops in Cuba, according to an analysis by *The New York Times*.		Canadian External Affairs Min. Flora MacDonald denies that she is to blame for the loss of the sale of a nuclear reactor by Atomic Energy of Canada Ltd. to Argentina because she had criticized Argentina's human-rights record.	
Oct. 4				Over 12,000 march through the streets of San Salvador to protest the slaying of four prominent peasant leaders at a military roadblock Sept. 30. ... In Nicaragua supporters of deposed Nicaraguan Pres. Anastasio Somoza Debayle shoot and kill one of his nephews who joined the Sandinistas.	
Oct. 5		Ireland and the United Kingdom reach agreement on a package of security measures designed to reduce terrorism in Northern Ireland.			U.S. Amb. to South Korea William Gleysteen Jr. is recalled to Washington following the expulsion of a South Korean opposition leader from the National Assembly.
Oct. 6		Soviet Pres. Leonid Brezhnev announces in a speech to the East German Parliament that the U.S.S.R. will withdraw as many as 20,000 Soviet troops from the country during the next year.	Egypt displays a dozen F-4 Phantom jet fighter-bombers and 40 M-113 armored personnel carriers it received since signing the peace treaty with Israel	The Venezuelan govt. announces that the country's external debt totals $12.2 billion, a record for the country and $4.8 billion more than the government had estimated May 28.	
Oct. 7			The Israeli Cabinet approves in principle a tentative plan to station U.S., Egyptian, and Israeli observers in the Sinai to monitor the Israeli–Egyptian peace treaty.		Japanese Premier Masayoshi Ohira's ruling Liberal Democratic party retains power in national elections for the House of Representatives, but the victory is regarded as a setback for Ohira since his party captures one less seat than in the 1976 elections.
Oct. 8					Jayaprakash Narayan, 76, Indian elder statesman and advocate of non-violence who worked with Mohandas Gandhi to free India from British colonial rule, dies of a heart ailment in Patna, India.

A	B	C	D	E
Includes developments that affect more than one world region, international organizations and important meetings of major world leaders.	Includes all domestic and regional developments in Europe, including the Soviet Union, Turkey, Cyprus and Malta.	Includes all domestic and regional developments in Africa and the Middle East, including Iraq and Iran and excluding Cyprus, Turkey and Afghanistan.	Includes all domestic and regional developments in Latin America, the Caribbean and Canada.	Includes all domestic and regional developments in Asia and Pacific nations, extending from Afghanistan through all the Pacific Islands, except Hawaii.

U.S. Politics & Social Issues	U.S. Foreign Policy & Defense	U.S. Economy & Environment	Science, Technology & Nature	Culture, Leisure & Life Style	
The suit brought by militant atheist Madalyn Murray to block Pope John Paul II from celebrating mass on the Mall in Washington is dismissed by a federal court.					Oct. 3
	State Secy. Cyrus Vance reaffirms the U.S. policy of refusing to sell arms to China in response to publication in *The New York Times* of a hitherto secret Defense Dept. study suggesting that U.S. supply arms to China to assist the West in any war with the U.S.S.R.	The government's index of producer prices for finished goods rose a seasonally adjusted 1.4 percent in September, the Labor Dept. reports.		Pope John Paul II concludes his two-day visit to Philadelphia where he has taken a strongly traditionalist stance on birth control, divorce, and abortion.	Oct. 4
	Defense Dept. announces resuming shipment of spare parts for Iran's U.S.-built warplanes.	Service on the bankrupt Chicago, Rock Island & Pacific Railroad Co., halted since Aug. 28 by a strike, resumes as union members return to work.... The U.S. International Trade Commission recommends that Pres. Carter impose a three-year quota on imports from the U.S.S.R. of anhydrous ammonia, used to produce fertilizers, because the imports are disrupting the U.S. market.		The Pittsburgh Pirates win the National League 1979 title by beating the Cincinnati Reds for the third straight time in their best-three-of-five game series.	Oct. 5
	Pope John Paul II arrives in Washington and has a three-hour visit with Pres. Jimmy Carter. He is the first pope to visit the White House.	In a dramatic Saturday-night announcement, Federal Reserve Chairman Paul Volcker says the discount rate will be raised from 11 percent to a record 12 percent, as part of an intensified fight by the government against inflation and in support of the dollar.	More than 1.400 members of The Coalition for Direct Action at Seabrook are prevented from occupying the Seabrook, N.H., nuclear plant site.	The Baltimore Orioles win the 1979 American League title, taking the third game in the best three-out-of-five championship series with the California Angels.... *Affirmed* wins the Jockey Club Gold Cup over his main rival, *Spectacular Bid*, in a horse race held at Belmont Park, N.Y.	Oct. 6
			Newly declassified documents reveal that in 1950 the U.S. Army conducted tests to prove "cereal rust epidemic" could be used as a biological warfare weapon.		Oct. 7
		Trading is tumultuous in New York, the principal market for commercial paper, on the first business day following the Oct. 6 announcement of Federal Reserve steps to curb inflation.		Pavel Kohout, a Czech playwright living in Vienna since 1978, says he has been deprived of his Czech citizenship and refused permission to return to Prague.	Oct. 8

F	G	H	I	J
Includes elections, federal-state relations, civil rights and liberties, crime, the judiciary, education, health care, poverty, urban affairs and population.	*Includes formation and debate of U.S. foreign and defense policies, veterans' affairs and defense spending. (Relations with specific foreign countries are usually found under the region concerned.)*	*Includes business, labor, agriculture, taxation, transportation, consumer affairs, monetary and fiscal policy, natural resources, and pollution.*	*Includes worldwide scientific, medical and technological developments, natural phenomena, U.S. weather, natural disasters, and accidents.*	*Includes the arts, religion, scholarship, communications media, sports, entertainments, fashions, fads and social life.*

	World Affairs	Europe	Africa & the Middle East	The Americas	Asia & the Pacific
Oct. 9	*Wall Street Journal* reports foreign reaction to the Federal Reserve moves to protect the dollar are generally positive.	Thorbjorn Falldin, the leader of the Center Party and former premier, is selected to head a coalition government in Sweden made up of the three major non-socialist parties.		Canada's central bank announces that the bank rate will be increased from 12.25 percent to 13 percent, the tenth bank rate increase since the beginning of the year and another all-time high.... In the Speech from the Throne, Canada's Progressive Conservative Party outlines plans to rely on the private sector to generate economic growth and proposes to return more government-owned businesses to private hands.... The FBI says the former head of the Chilean secret police, Manuel Contreras Sepulveda paid for the defense of three Cuban-Americans later convicted of murdering Orlando Letelier.	Kabul radio announces that former Afghanistan Pres. Nur Mohammad Taraki is dead after "a severe and prolonged illness."
Oct. 10		The Italian auto maker Fiat fires 61 workers it links to labor agitation and violence at its Turin plants.	Eight persons are killed in a renewal of fighting between rival Christian groups in northern Lebanon.		The Indonesian govt. releases 2,000 prisoners detained without trial since an attempted coup by the Communist Party in 1965.... Police in the Philippines arrest 24 persons in Manila in a move against student opponents of Pres. Ferdinand Marcos.
Oct. 11	Cuban Pres. Fidel Castro comes to the U.S. for the first time in 19 years to address the U.N. General Assembly.			Bolivian Army Chief of Staff Gen. Victor Castillo and armed forces commander Gen. David Padilla persuade rebellious military officers in the Beni region to end a coup attempt.	
Oct. 12		Renault Co., France's state-owned automotive company, agrees to buy a 22.5 percent interest in American Motors Corp. for $150 million.... In Britain the Conservative Party ends its annual conference hearing a speech by P.M. Margaret Thatcher in which she calls on all union members to shun strikes.	The World Council of Churches approves a $35,000 grant to the patriotic Front, a guerrilla group in Zimbabwe Rhodesia.		
Oct. 13	UNICEF and the International Red Cross launch a $110-million aid program to avert starvation in Cambodia.	An eight-week wildcat strike in the Netherlands by more than 500 tug-boat workers at Rotterdam ends after the strikers vote to accept a lump-sum payment of about $500 each.			
Oct. 14		The U.S. press widely reports the first expression of Soviet doubts about the safety of nuclear power. Previously, Soviet scientists have stressed the reliability of Soviet reactors compared to ones in the West.	The Israeli Cabinet unanimously votes to expand seven existing Israeli civilian settlements in the occupied West Bank but decides against seizing privately owned Arab land to do it.		

A	B	C	D	E
Includes developments that affect more than one world region, international organizations and important meetings of major world leaders.	Includes all domestic and regional developments in Europe, including the Soviet Union, Turkey, Cyprus and Malta.	Includes all domestic and regional developments in Africa and the Middle East, including Iraq and Iran and excluding Cyprus, Turkey and Afghanistan.	Includes all domestic and regional developments in Latin America, the Caribbean and Canada.	Includes all domestic and regional developments in Asia and Pacific nations, extending from Afghanistan through all the Pacific Islands, except Hawaii.

U.S. Politics & Social Issues	U.S. Foreign Policy & Defense	U.S. Economy & Environment	Science, Technology & Nature	Culture, Leisure & Life Style	
The FBI reports serious crime in the U.S. increased nine percent in the first half of 1979, while violent offenses went up 13 percent in the same period.	AP reports study sponsored by the U.S. Military Academy that shows female cadets at West Point adopt so-called masculine qualities of physical prowess, competitiveness, and assertiveness to win male acceptance.				Oct. 9
The Senate votes overwhelmingly to denounce Sen. Herman Talmadge (D, Ga.) for submitting false expense accounts and diverting campaign funds to personal use.		Trading is the heaviest in the history of the New York Stock Exchange where volume soars to 81,620,000 shares as traders attempt to deal with the effects of the Federal Reserve's steps to combat inflation.		French government opens a retrospective exhibit of the works of Spanish artist Pablo Picasso. . . . Paul Paray, 93, French conductor and composer who helped give the Detroit Symphony a national reputation, dies in Monte Carlo.	Oct. 10
The Carter administration reports that the amount of home heating oil in storage has reached the government's target of 240 million barrels and, as a result, it appears the U.S. will not suffer a winter shortage. . . . In Pennsylvania former UMW President W. A. (Tony) Boyle is sentenced for the second time to life imprisonment for hiring killers to assassinate union rival Joseph Yablonski and his family. Boyle's first conviction was overturned on appeal.	Walter Fauntroy, Wash., D.C. delegate, says that the Southern Christian Leadership Conference (SCLC) has withdrawn its invitation to PLO leader Yasir Arafat to visit the U.S. because th PLO has rejected the Middle East peace plan proposed by SCLC.				Oct. 11
			Nobel prize for Medicine is awarded to Allen Cormack of the U.S. and Godfrey Hounsfield of Great Britain for their work in developing the CAT scan (computed axial tomography).		Oct. 12
Delegates pledged to Pres. Carter defeat slates committed to Sen Edward Kennedy (D, Mass.) in Florida's statewide presidential caucuses. . . . An Arab–American organization pledges $10,000 to black leader Rev. Jesse Jackson's People United to Save Humanity (Push) organization.			Two pro-nuclear groups, the Alliance for Safe Available Future Energy and Nuclear Energy for Environmental Development hold a joint rally in San Luis Obispo, Cal., to present the other side of the nuclear energy debate. . . . Two persons are killed and 43 injured when an Amtrak passenger train slams into the rear of a parked freight train about 30 miles south of Chicago.		Oct. 13
Vernon Jordan criticizes black leaders who have expressed support for the PLO. He cites the PLO's "cold-blooded murder of innocent civilians and schoolchildren." . . . Federal drug agents in Florida seize a record 384 pounds of cocaine, worth nearly $100 million.					Oct. 14

F	G	H	I	J
Includes elections, federal-state relations, civil rights and liberties, crime, the judiciary, education, health care, poverty, urban affairs and population.	Includes formation and debate of U.S. foreign and defense policies, veterans' affairs and defense spending. (Relations with specific foreign countries are usually found under the region concerned.)	Includes business, labor, agriculture, taxation, transportation, consumer affairs, monetary and fiscal policy, natural resources, and pollution.	Includes worldwide scientific, medical and technological developments, natural phenomena, U.S. weather, natural disasters, and accidents.	Includes the arts, religion, scholarship, communications media, sports, entertainments, fashions, fads and social life.

	World Affairs	Europe	Africa & the Middle East	The Americas	Asia & the Pacific
Oct. 15		A Swiss jury finds Bernard Cornfeld not guilty of fraud charges in connection with the 1969 sales of shares in Investors Overseas Ltd..	Libya raises the price of all grades of its oil bringing the price of its top crude to $26.27 and breaking the OPEC's $23.50-a-barrel price ceiling.	The military government of Gen. Carlos Humberto Romero in El Salvador is overthrown by young, lower-ranking army officers who feared that right-wing generals were planning a rebellion of their own in the country.	
Oct. 16		Turkish Premier Bulent Ecevit announces his government's resignation after parliamentary by-elections Oct. 14 gave the opposition a majority in both chambers.	Foreign ministers of six Persian Gulf states, including Saudi Arabia, Kuwait, and Bahrain, fearing Iranian attempts to annex their territories and threats to oil routes, end three days of meetings in Saudi Arabia to discuss mutual defense.	The Grenadan army announces arresting 20 persons and charged them with plotting to assassinate the country's leaders.	Loyal Afghanistan troops crush a two-day military uprising in Kabul that Radio Kabul claims was an atempt to overthrow the government of Pres. Hafizullah Amin.... Pakistan Pres. Muhammad Zia ul-Haq indefinitely postpones national elections and tightens the existing martial law by banning all political parties, outlawing strikes, and closing down publications.
Oct. 17	Soviet and Chinese representatives meet in Moscow for their first official session of talks aimed at improving relations between the two countries.... The Nobel Peace Prize is awarded to Mother Teresa of India for her work among the poor, destitute, and sick of Calcutta for more than 30 years.	Thomas J. Watson Jr., retired head of IBM, arrives in Moscow to replace Malcolm Toon as U.S. Soviet ambassador.		Eighteen hundred Marines land at the U.S. base at Guantanamo Bay in Cuba on a training exercise ordered by Pres. Carter as a response to the stationing of 2,000–3,000 Soviet combat troops in Cuba.	
Oct. 18			The Patriotic Front guerrillas in Zimbabwe Rhodesia agree to accept London's suggested constitution for the country. The government had accepted the document earlier.		
Oct. 19					
Oct. 20		Three hundred women occupy the Justice Ministry building in Madrid, Spain and over 1,357 women release a signed statement that they have had abortions to protest government prosecution of 11 working-class women, under a 1870 law, for their illegal abortions, which took place outside Spain.	Kurdish rebels in Iran are reported in control of Mehabad after heavy fighting with government troops. ... Botswana's Pres. Sir Seretse Khama is elected to a third term and his Botswana Democratic Party increases its members in the 36-seat Parliament to 29.		
Oct. 21		In Great Britain the last bar to resumption of publication by the Times of London is removed when mamagement reaches a settlement with the National Graphical Association, the only union still without a work agreement. Publication of the newspaper has been suspended since November 1978.	Moshe Dayan, Israel's foreign minister, resigns in protest over the government's hard line on the Palestinian issue.	Huber Matos, one of the most prominent political prisoners left in Cuba, is freed after serving a 20-year treason sentence for resigning his military post in protest against increasing Communist influence in the Cuban army and government.	South Korean officials report that 79 persons have been injured and 1,350 arrested during a week of student demonstrations in Pusan, Masan, and Changwon, but that calm has been restored in the three cities.

A	B	C	D	E
Includes developments that affect more than one world region, international organizations and important meetings of major world leaders.	Includes all domestic and regional developments in Europe, including the Soviet Union, Turkey, Cyprus and Malta.	Includes all domestic and regional developments in Africa and the Middle East, including Iraq and Iran and excluding Cyprus, Turkey and Afghanistan.	Includes all domestic and regional developments in Latin America, the Caribbean and Canada.	Includes all domestic and regional developments in Asia and Pacific nations, extending from Afghanistan through all the Pacific Islands, except Hawaii.

U.S. Politics & Social Issues	U.S. Foreign Policy & Defense	U.S. Economy & Environment	Science, Technology & Nature	Culture, Leisure & Life Style	
The Supreme Ct. declines to review, thus letting stand, a lower court decision finding automatic funds transfers and other banking innovations illegal.			An earthquake shakes a wide area of southern California and northern Mexico, killing at least one, injuring at least 90, and causing widespread damage. The quake, strongest in the U.S. since 1971, measures 6.4 on the Richter Scale.		Oct. 15
Justice Dept. special counsel Paul Curran says his investigation into the finances of the Carter family peanut business has cleared Pres. Carter and his brother, Billy, of any criminal wrongdoing.		Production in the nation's factories, mines, and utilities increased a seasonally adjusted .5 percent in September, the Federal Reserve reports.	Nobel Prize for Physics is awarded jointly to Steven Weinberg and Sheldon Glashow of Harvard University and to Abdus Salam, a Pakistani who worked at universities in Britain and Italy. They are cited for research toward a unifying theory that helps explain the relationship of two fundamental forces of nature. . . . Nobel Prize for Chemistry is shared by Herbert Brown of Purdue University and Georg Wittig of Heidelberg University in West Germany for their basic discoveries in the chemistry of boron and phosphorus.		Oct. 16
Supreme Ct. Justice William Brennan accuses the news media of making unjustified attacks on the Supreme Ct. for recent rulings related to freedom of the press. . . . Pres. Carter signs legislation creating a new Dept. of Education.	In a suit brought by 25 members of Congress, Federal District Judge Oliver Gasch rules that Pres. Carter cannot end the mutual defense treaty between the U.S. and Taiwan without the consent of Congress.	Nobel Prize for Economics is award to Theodore Schultz of the University of Chicago and Arthur Lewis of Princeton University for their work in the economic problems of underdeveloped nations.		Humorist and author S.J. Perelman, 75, dies of natural causes in N.Y.C. . . . The Pittsburgh Pirates of the National League win the World Series four games to three by defeating the Baltimore Orioles of the American League, 4–1.	Oct. 17
Six bombs believed planted by the FALN, the Puerto Rican independence group, explode at government facilities in Chicago and Puerto Rico.				Nobel Prize for Literature is awarded to Odysseus Elytis, a Greek poet noted for his lyric verse emphasizing the struggle for freedom and evoking the mythic past.	Oct. 18
Former Pres. Gerald Ford eliminates himself as an active candidate for the 1980 Republican presidential nomination, although he indicates availibility as a nominee in the possibility the convention deadlocks.		The nation's real gross national product rose at a 2.4 percent seasonally adjusted annual rate in the third quarter, the Commerce Dept. reports.			Oct. 19
				American John Tate succeeds retired Muhammad Ali as WBA heavyweight champion when he scores a 15-round decision over South African Gerrie Coetzee in a bout in Pretoria, South Africa. . . . Over 6,000 friends and political allies of the late Pres. John F. Kennedy, members of his family, and Pres. Carter attend ceremonies to dedicate the John F. Kennedy Library in Boston, Mass.	Oct. 20
A Georgia federal jury convicts millionaire pornographer Michael Thevis on charges of racketeering and murder conspiracy to gain control of the nation's ponography industry.					Oct. 21

F	G	H	I	J
Includes elections, federal-state relations, civil rights and liberties, crime, the judiciary, education, health care, poverty, urban affairs and population.	Includes formation and debate of U.S. foreign and defense policies, veterans' affairs and defense spending. (Relations with specific foreign countries are usually found under the region concerned.)	Includes business, labor, agriculture, taxation, transportation, consumer affairs, monetary and fiscal policy, natural resources, and pollution.	Includes worldwide scientific, medical and technological developments, natural phenomena, U.S. weather, natural disasters, and accidents.	Includes the arts, religion, scholarship, communications media, sports, entertainments, fashions, fads and social life.

	World Affairs	Europe	Africa & the Middle East	The Americas	Asia & the Pacific
Oct. 22	Chinese Premier Hua Kuo-feng, on a historic trip to Europe, meets with West German Chancellor Helmut Schmidt, who was reported concerned that the Soviet–Sino split might intrude on West Germany's detente policy with the Soviet Union.	The French National Assembly rejects the first part of the government's budget for 1980 after the ruling coalition of Gaullists and the Union pour la Democratie Francaise splits over a cost-cutting proposal.	The Israeli Supreme Ct. orders the government to remove the disputed settlement of Elon Moreh in the West Bank, upholding an appeal by Arab landowners whose property had been requisitioned for the community.	Guyana's P.M. Forbes Burnham postpones scheduled parliamentary elections amid opposition charges of corruption, mismanagement of the economy, and dictator-like ambitions.... El Salvador's new governing junta names a 12-member Cabinet representing all moderate opposition to the ousted government of Pres. Carlos Humberto Romero. Ruben Zamora is named to the key post of ministry of the presidency.	
Oct. 23		Six Czechoslovakian human-rights activists are sentenced to various prison terms after a two-day trial on charges of subversion of the state. ... In Denmark Premier Anker Jorgensen's Social Democratic Party gains four seats in parliamentary elections and, though 21 seats short of a majority, remains the largest party in the legislature.			
Oct. 24			Shah Mohammed Pahlevi undergoes surgery at the New York Hospital-Cornell Medical Center, reportedly suffering from cancer of the lymph nodes.	In Panama the government announces the arrest of five men it says are mercenaries hired by plotters seeking to overthrow the government.	Pres. Carter pledges $70 million from the U.S. for emergency food aid to fend off mass starvation in Cambodia.
Oct. 25		Voters in Spain's Basque region and Catalonia vote to accept statutes restoring autonomous regional governments.	Diplomatic sources in Damascus say that at least 200 persons have been killed in Syria since April in clashes between members of the Sunni and Alawite Islamic sects.	The Bank of Canada raises its bank rate to 14 percent in a continuing effort to check the growth of the country's money supply and to strengthen the Canadian dollar.	
Oct. 26		A three-judge court suspends the trial of 11 Spanish working-class women who admitted having illegal abortions outside the country.	Israel, Egypt, and the U.S., concluding another two days of talks on Palestinian autonomy, agree on procedures for organizing, conducting, and supervising elections in the West Bank and Gaza Strip.		South Korean Pres. Park Chung Hee and his chief bodyguard are shot to death by Kim Jae Kyu, head of the South Korean Central Intelligence Agency and a lifelong friend of Park. The Cabinet names Premier Choi Kyu Hah as acting president.
Oct. 27				The tiny Caribbean islands of St. Vincent and the Grenadines gain independence from Great Britain in a midnight flag-raising ceremony.	Cambodia rejects a proposal by three U.S. senators to truck food from Thailand to starving Cambodians, calling the bid a maneuver by the imperialists to get assistance to the guerrilla Pol Pot forces fighting the government.
Oct. 28		Environmentalists meet near Frankfurt, West Germany to form a national Green Party that would be politically nonoriented but antinuclear, nonviolent, democratic, and committed to environmental protection.			Kim Young Sam, leader of the South Korean opposition New Democratic Party and a bitter foe of murdered Pres. Park Chung Hee, calls the Oct. 26 killing a national calamity and warns North Korea not to take advantage of the situation.
Oct. 29				For the first time since the ruling junta came to power on Oct. 15 Salvadoran police open fire on a crowd of antigovernment demonstrators, killing at least 24.... Canadian P.M. Joseph Clark announces that he has canceled plans to move Canada's Embassy in Israel from Tel Aviv to Jersualem.	U.S. analysts say the Moslem rebels and the government in Afghanistan are at an impasse.

A	B	C	D	E
Includes developments that affect more than one world region, international organizations and important meetings of major world leaders.	Includes all domestic and regional developments in Europe, including the Soviet Union, Turkey, Cyprus and Malta.	Includes all domestic and regional developments in Africa and the Middle East, including Iraq and Iran and excluding Cyprus, Turkey and Afghanistan.	Includes all domestic and regional developments in Latin America, the Caribbean and Canada.	Includes all domestic and regional developments in Asia and Pacific nations, extending from Afghanistan through all the Pacific Islands, except Hawaii.

U.S. Politics & Social Issues	U.S. Foreign Policy & Defense	U.S. Economy & Environment	Science, Technology & Nature	Culture, Leisure & Life Style	
Convicted murderer Jesse Walter Bishop, 46, dies in the Nevada gas chamber, the first person to be executed in Nevada in 18 years and the third in the U.S. in the last 12.... Kenneth Bianchi pleads guilty to the murders of five Los Angeles' women, the so-called Hillside Strangler killings, and is sentenced to five concurrent life terms.		EEOC files five job discrimination suits against Sears Roebuck & Co., charging discrimination against women, blacks, and Hispanics.		French pianist and conductor Nadia Boulanger, 92, dies in Paris, France.	Oct. 22
				In what is dubbed the "John Hour," the names of nine men convicted of patronizing prostitutes are broadcast over N.Y.C.'s municipally owned broadcast stations as part of a controversial plan announced by Mayor Edward Koch to embarrass prostitutes' customers and thereby curtail street solicitation.	Oct. 23
				Eleanor Belmont, 100, N.Y. socialite and patron of the arts and charitable causes. dies in N.Y.C.	Oct. 24
	Recruiting figures released by the Defense Dept. reveal that for the first time since the draft ended in 1973, none of the military services achieved their manpower goals.	Chrysler Corp. and the UAW reach tentative agreement on a new three-year contract that is expected to save financially ailing Chrysler $203 million in the next two years.	The FAA grounds Puerto Rican International Airlines for violating the agency's safety regulations following a July 24 crash in the Virgin Islands.	Icebergs , a long-lost painting by the nineteenth-century American landscape artist Frederick Edwin Church is auctioned for a record $2.5 million.	Oct. 25
	Yeoman Lee Madsen is sentenced to eight years in prison for espionage, after pleading guilty in September to selling seven top secret documents to an FBI informer.	The government's index of consumer prices rose a seasonally adjusted 1.1 percent during September, the Labor Dept. reports.	The NRC fines Metropolitan Edison Co., operator of the Three Mile Island nuclear plant, $155,000 for serious weaknesses in the company's management and techinical performance.	Seven Eastern European women athletes are banned from international track and field competition by the International Amateur Athletic Federation because blood tests found anabolic steriods.	Oct. 26
				Rev. Charles Coughlin, 88, the Catholic radio priest famous for his weekly radio sermons preaching against what he felt were the multiple evils of communism, Wall Street, labor unions, Jews, and the New Deal, dies in Bloomfield Hills, Mich.	Oct. 27
		FRB Chmn. Paul Volcker says that the country's standard of living will drop in wake of declining production and increasing energy prices.		New York Yankees manager Billy Martin is fired by the team's principal owner, George Steinbrenner, five days after Martin was involved in an altercation in a Minn. hotel bar. Dick Howser is named as his successor.	Oct. 28
Federal investigators report flourishing commercial marijuana farms in California, which generate millions of dollars annually in illegal profits.		CAB announces that it has recommended to Pres. Carter that Pan American Airways be allowed to merge with National Airlines.	Supreme Ct. agrees to decide whether patents can be issued to living organisms.		Oct. 29

F	G	H	I	J
Includes elections, federal-state relations, civil rights and liberties, crime, the judiciary, education, health care, poverty, urban affairs and population.	Includes formation and debate of U.S. foreign and defense policies, veterans' affairs and defense spending. (Relations with specific foreign countries are usually found under the region concerned.)	Includes business, labor, agriculture, taxation, transportation, consumer affairs, monetary and fiscal policy, natural resources, and pollution.	Includes worldwide scientific, medical and technological developments, natural phenomena, U.S. weather, natural disasters, and accidents.	Includes the arts, religion, scholarship, communications media, sports, entertainments, fashions, fads and social life.

	World Affairs	Europe	Africa & the Middle East	The Americas	Asia & the Pacific
Oct. 30		The French minister of labor, 59-year-old Robert Boulin, commits suicide after being the subject of press accounts that described his allegedly unethical dealings with a real-estate operator.			
Oct. 31	Representatives of the nine-member EEC and 57 developing nations in Africa, the Caribbean, and the Pacific meet in Lome, Togo and sign a five-year extension of the 1976–80 Lome Convention that provides an aid package worth about $7.5 billion.	A contingent of British workers meet with visiting Chinese Premier Hua Kuo-feng at Highgate Cemetery, where he is laying a wreath on Karl Marx's grave, and complain about his frequent praise for British P.M. Margaret Thatcher.		A two-month strike by 24,000 teachers ends in Panama with salary increases ranging from 18 to 36 percent, about half of their demand.	
Nov. 1		Soviet police arrest three dissident activists in what is feared to be a renewed crackdown on dissent.	Iranian govt. is reported making four separate protests over the previous week about the deposed Shah of Iran's arrival in New York. The Ayatollah Khomeini denounces his entry and orders Iranian students to observe the Nov. 4 anniversary of student riots.	In Bolivia troops led by Col. Alberto Natusch Busch surround the Presidential Palace and announce that a military government will be formed with Natusch as president.... Quebec Premier Rene Levesque presents to the Canadian National assembly his government's official statement on Quebec independence, which says in part that Quebec wants a new deal with the rest of Canada based on the formula of free association between sovereign states.	Bank of Japan raises the discount rate a full point to 6.25 percent in an attempt to help check inflation and support the sagging yen.... Chinese govt. announces the first major price increases in 30 years for food items other than grain.
Nov. 2		Police kill France's most-wanted-criminal Jacques Mesrine near Paris, ending an 18-month manhunt.		Canadian P.M. Joseph Clark calls the Parti Quebecois White Paper unacceptable, and he says he will not negotiate with the province on sovereignty/association.	
Nov. 3				Bolivia's new military leader Col. Alberto Natusch Busch counters a general strike against his new regime by sending tanks and troops into the streets of La Paz.	The official Chinese CP newspaper *Jenmin Jih Pao* attacks wall posters that criticize the government.
Nov. 4		Swiss 920 megawatt nuclear power plant at Goesgen is bombed, although the plant itself is not damaged.	About 500 Iranian students seize the U.S. Embassy in Teheran along with 90 hostages, including 60–65 Americans, vowing not to release their captives until the U.S. returns the Shah to stand trial in Iran.		
Nov. 5	A one-day U.N. conference in N.Y. pledges over $200 million for food and medical supplies to Cambodia over the next 12 months, $310 million short of its target amount.	Stefan Wisniewski, a suspected terrorist arrested in France in 1978 and deported to West Germany, is charged with the murder of industrialist Hanns-Martin Schleyer.	The U.S. rejects the demands of the students who seized the U.S. Embassy in Teheran to return the Shah to Iran.		

A	B	C	D	E
Includes developments that affect more than one world region, international organizations and important meetings of major world leaders.	Includes all domestic and regional developments in Europe, including the Soviet Union, Turkey, Cyprus and Malta.	Includes all domestic and regional developments in Africa and the Middle East, including Iraq and Iran and excluding Cyprus, Turkey and Afghanistan.	Includes all domestic and regional developments in Latin America, the Caribbean and Canada.	Includes all domestic and regional developments in Asia and Pacific nations, extending from Afghanistan through all the Pacific Islands, except Hawaii.

U.S. Politics & Social Issues	U.S. Foreign Policy & Defense	U.S. Economy & Environment	Science, Technology & Nature	Culture, Leisure & Life Style	
Pres. Carter nominates Shirley Hufstedler, 54, a U.S. appeals court judge and the highest-ranking woman jurist in the country, to be head of the newly created Dept. of Education.		U.S. announces that it is setting new quotas for textile imports from China, reportedly attempting to forestall resentment in Congress against the influx of Chinese apparel and thus ease congressional approval of the recently propose trade agreement with China.	The President's Commission on the Accident at Three Mile Island urges Pres. Carter to abolish the NRC and create a new executive agency, charging that the NRC has not given sufficient consideration to safety issues in policing the nuclear power industry.	Mike Flanagan of the Baltimore Orioles is the winner of the 1979 AL Cy Young Award.	Oct. 30
		Pres. Carter unveils a plan to spur industrial innovation. It includes increased federal research grants to small businesses and grant programs for business–academic research collaboration.		The movie *10* leads as top-grossing film for the past week, followed by *Halloween* .... Switzerland grants asylum to Soviet figure skating champions Oleg Protopopov and Ludmila Belousova after they defected in late September at the end of an official tour.	Oct. 31
Sen. Howard Baker Jr. (R, Tenn.) formally declares his candidacy for the 1980 Republican presidential nomination.		The Carter administration proposes a $1.5 billion federal loan guarantee plan for financially troubled Chrysler Corp.... The government's index of producer prices for finished goods rose a seasonally adjusted 1 percent in October, the Labor Dept. reports.		Art historians announce that a mural depicting a Florentine battle for independence, painted by Leonardo da Vinci in 1505, has been detected through reflectography techniques under a fresco in Florence, Italy.... The United Methodist Church's highest court rules that an avowed homosexual can remain pastor of a N.Y.C. church.	Nov. 1
	Army announces a search for soldiers and former soldiers who were subjects of drug or chemical-biological agents tests who would consider subjecting themselves again to the risk of further testing.	Labor Dept. reports the U.S. unemployment rate rising two-tenths of a percentage point to a seasonally adjusted 6 percent in October.		In major league baseball's fourth annual reentry draft of free agents a total of 44 players who had played out their contracts are selected by 26 teams. California Angel pitcher Nolan Ryan is selected by 12 clubs.	Nov. 2
Five people are shot to death and eight wounded at a Ku Klux Klan rally in Greensboro, N.C. as Klan members open fire on anti-Klan demonstrators.... Pres. Carter leads Sen. Edward Kennedy (D, Mass.) by a 3–1 margin in a straw poll at the annual state party dinner in Iowa.					Nov. 3
A *New York Times*/CBS News Poll says Sen. Edward Kennedy (D, Mass.) is preferred by 54 percent of Democrats interviewed as the presidential candidate for 1980, against 20 percent who prefer Pres. Jimmy Carter.				A report prepared by N.Y.S. Atty. Gen. Robert Abrams shows the 1978–79 Broadway theatrical season to be one of the strongest in years with 119 productions showing a total profit of $40.6 million, an increase of $10 million over fiscal 1978.	Nov. 4
James Earl Ray, convicted assassin of Rev. Martin Luther King Jr., is recaptured inside the grounds of Brushy Mountain Prison, Tenn. as he tries to escape.				Al Capp, 79, cartoonist and creator of the satirical comic strip "Li'l Abner," dies in Cambridge, Mass.	Nov. 5

F	G	H	I	J
Includes elections, federal-state relations, civil rights and liberties, crime, the judiciary, education, health care, poverty, urban affairs and population.	Includes formation and debate of U.S. foreign and defense policies, veterans' affairs and defense spending. (Relations with specific foreign countries are usually found under the region concerned.)	Includes business, labor, agriculture, taxation, transportation, consumer affairs, monetary and fiscal policy, natural resources, and pollution.	Includes worldwide scientific, medical and technological developments, natural phenomena, U.S. weather, natural disasters, and accidents.	Includes the arts, religion, scholarship, communications media, sports, entertainments, fashions, fads and social life.

	World Affairs	Europe	Africa & the Middle East	The Americas	Asia & the Pacific
Nov. 6	In response to an appeal from the U.S., U.N. Secy. Gen Kurt Waldheim says he will use his authority to obtain the release of the hostages held by Iranian students in the U.S. Embassy in Teheran.		Iranian Premier Mehdi Bazargan resigns as a direct result of the Iranian student takeover of the U.S. Embassy, climaxing a longstanding dispute with Ayatollah Khomeini and his Islamic followers. Khomeini orders the Revolutionary Council to run the country.	Canada's Progressive Conservative govt. survives a no-confidence motion by only two votes.	Masayoshi Ohira is reelected premier of Japan by a narrow margin at a special session of the House of Representatives, the lower chamber of the Japanese Diet. . . . The South Korean Martial Law Command issues a report on the Oct. 26 assassination of Pres. Park Chung Hee that charges his assailant, South Korean CIA Director Kim Jae Kyu, had planned the killing in June as part of a coup in which he would seize power and become president.
Nov. 7		An hour-long parade of military might through Moscow marks the sixty-second anniversary of the Bolshevik Revolution.	Ugandan govt. officially rescinds the ban on Christian groups put into effect under the Idi Amin regime.	Col. Alberto Natusch Busch suspends martial law and press censorship in Bolivia but does not respond to a Nov. 6 congressional plan calling for the formation of a new military–civilian junta to rule until elections are held in May 1980.	
Nov. 8			Two PLO representatives arrive in Teheran to negotiate the release of the American hostages but are quickly rebuffed by the Iranians.	Jacques Lanctot, former member of the Front de Liberation du Quebec, is sentenced to three years in prison for the 1970 Kidnapping of British envoy James Richard Cross.	Columnist Jack Anderson in the *Washington Post* says that half of the population of the Indonesian province of East Timor has been wiped out since 1975 either by fighting between Indonesian troops and rebel forces or by disease and starvation.
Nov. 9	U.N. Security Council unanimously calls for Iran to release the U.S. hostages immediately.	Irish P.M. John Lynch, appears before the National Press Club in Wash., D.C. and charges that reunification of Ireland is the only way to end sectarian violence.	Egyptian Pres. Anwar Sadat offers to admit the Shah of Iran to Egypt for further medical treatment and political asylum.		
Nov. 10	Diplomats from Algeria, France, Sweden, Syria, and the Vatican visit the American hostages in Iran and report that their health is reasonably good.		Abolhassan Bani-Sadr assumes his duties as the new Iranian foreign minister by announcing his support for the Iranian students who have taken over the U.S. Embassy.		Acting South Korean Pres. Choi Kyu Hah announces elections under the 1972 Constitution for a successor to assassinated Pres. Park Chung Hee and is immediately criticized by the opposition New Democratic Party, which claims it had not been consulted.
Nov. 11		Heroin addiction in Western Europe is reported reaching epidemic proportions and contributing to heavy usage by American soldiers stationed there.	Israeli military authorities in the West Bank arrest Bassam Shaka, the mayor of Nablus, on charges of verbally justifying the March 1978 terrorist raid on Israel in which 35 civilians were killed. West Bank Arabs launch general strikes to protest the arrest.		
Nov. 12		British House of Commons passes an emergency bill allowing the British govt. to appoint a British governor for Zimbabwe Rhodesia when negotiations finish. . . . Basque separatist organization ETA takes responsibility for the Nov. 11 kidnapping of Javier Ruperez, head of the foreign affairs committee of the ruling Union of the Democratic Center Party in Spain.	Pres. Carter retaliates against continued detention of U.S. hostages in Teheran by suspending oil imports from Iran.	Mexico announces that it has closed its embassy in Teheran and that all of its staff has left Iran.	An American congressional group, led by Rep. Elizabeth Holtzman (D, N.Y.), visits Pnompenh to press the Vietnamese-backed Cambodian govt. to permit more emergency aid to reach the country.

A	B	C	D	E
Includes developments that affect more than one world region, international organizations and important meetings of major world leaders.	Includes all domestic and regional developments in Europe, including the Soviet Union, Turkey, Cyprus and Malta.	Includes all domestic and regional developments in Africa and the Middle East, including Iraq and Iran and excluding Cyprus, Turkey and Afghanistan.	Includes all domestic and regional developments in Latin America, the Caribbean and Canada.	Includes all domestic and regional developments in Asia and Pacific nations, extending from Afghanistan through all the Pacific Islands, except Hawaii.

U.S. Politics & Social Issues	U.S. Foreign Policy & Defense	U.S. Economy & Environment	Science, Technology & Nature	Culture, Leisure & Life Style	
Results of voting on election day across the country are mixed. Democrats retain governorships in Kentucky and Mississippi that the Republicans had eyed, but a Republican defeats the incumbent Democratic mayor of Cleveland.		Energy Dept. accuses nine major oil companies of exceeding federal price ceilings by $1.18 billion, 1973–76. . . . FRB reports that consumer installment credit rose a seasonally adjusted $4.45 billion in September, surpassing the previous record monthly high of $4.40 billion in December 1978.			Nov. 6
Sen. Edward Kennedy (D, Mass.) formally declares himself in the running for the 1980 Democratic presidential nomination.	Over half the members of the House send a letter to the Iranian Embassy in Wash., D.C. calling for quick release of the American hostages held in the U.S. Embassy in Teheran.			Bruce Sutter of the Chicago Cubs wins the NL Cy Young Award.	Nov. 7
California Gov. Edmund Brown Jr. announces his candicacy for the 1980 Democratic presidential nomination.				A $100 million donation to Emory University in Atlanta, Ga. from the Emily & Ernest Woodruff Fund Inc. is thought to be the largest single gift to date in the history of American philanthropy.	Nov. 8
	Despite pleas from Pres. Carter to remain calm, thousands of protesters in Wash., D.C. rally to support the U.S. hostages in Iran and counter a demonstration by 900 Iranian students, marching in support of Ayatollah Khomeini. . . . U.S. Military Academy Superintendent Lt. Gen. Andrew Goodpaster confirms charges that traditional hazing had turned malicious during combat training over the past summer and that some of the incidents were sexist but not racial.		NRC fines Consumers Power Co. Michigan $450,000 for leaving two radiation control valves open for 18 months at its reactor in South Haven.	The Vatican announces a projected 1979 operating deficit at $20.9 million that is expected to get worse in 1980.	Nov. 9
					Nov. 10
B'nai B'rith Anti-Defamation League publishes a survey showing that Ku Klux Klan membership in 22 states increased from 8,000 to 10,000 between 1977–79, and that the number of its sympathizers increased from 30,000 to 100,000.				A.J. Foyt becomes the first driver in the history of the U.S. Auto Club to win two national titles in the same season. . . . Dimitri Tiomkin, 85, Russian-born composer of Hollywood film scores dies after a fall in London. . . . Mamie Eisenhower, 82, widow of Dwight Eisenhower dies of heart failure in Wash., D.C.	Nov. 11
		Texaco, Inc. announces that it has found more natural gas 106 miles off the New Jersey coast in the Baltimore Canyon area of the Atlantic.		Abstract painter, sculptor, and educator Samuel Adler, 81, dies in N.Y.C.	Nov. 12

F	G	H	I	J
Includes elections, federal-state relations, civil rights and liberties, crime, the judiciary, education, health care, poverty, urban affairs and population.	Includes formation and debate of U.S. foreign and defense policies, veterans' affairs and defense spending. (Relations with specific foreign countries are usually found under the region concerned.)	Includes business, labor, agriculture, taxation, transportation, consumer affairs, monetary and fiscal policy, natural resources, and pollution.	Includes worldwide scientific, medical and technological developments, natural phenomena, U.S. weather, natural disasters, and accidents.	Includes the arts, religion, scholarship, communications media, sports, entertainments, fashions, fads and social life.

	World Affairs	Europe	Africa & the Middle East	The Americas	Asia & the Pacific
Nov. 13	Countries in Eastern and Western Europe join the U.S. and Canada in pledging to reduce air pollution moving across national borders. . . . Iranian govt. calls for a meeting of the U.N. Security Council on new proposals it has to deal with the U.S. hostage crisis. The U.S. blocks the meeting.	*Times of London* issues its first edition in more than 11 months after resolving management–labor differences. . . . West German govt. says that both it and the French govt. will join the U.S. cutoff of oil imports from Iran in wake of the hostage crisis. . . . Soviet Union informs U.S. diplomats in Moscow that it is trying to gain release of the U.S. hostages held in Iran.		Haitian President-for-Life Jean-Claude Duvalier dismisses eight of his 14 Cabinet members, a move seen motivated by Nov. 9 brawl that disrupted a meeting of about 6,000 human-rights activists in Port-au-Prince.	Pres. Carter orders an immediate airlift of food to Thailand for Cambodian and Laotian refugee camps there and authorizes $6 million to buy rice and other supplies.
Nov. 14	U.N. General Assembly approves a resolution, 91–21, calling upon Vietnam to withdraw its forces from Cambodia. . . . Eleven-member NATO Nuclear Planning Group agrees to allow new medium-range U.S. nuclear missiles to be stationed in Western Europe. . . . U.N. rejects Iran's call for a Security Council debate on its dispute with the U.S. until the American hostages are freed.	British Parliament allows part of its 1965 Southern Rhodesia Act, which imposed sanctions, to lapse at midnight, thereby allowing resumption of some trade relations between Zimbabwe Rhodesia and Britain. . . . British govt. proposes changes in immigration rules to reduce, in effect, the number of nonwhite people entering the country.	All 25 West Bank and Gaza Strip mayors resign to protest Israel's arrest of Bassam Shaka for remarks he made justifying terrorism.		
Nov. 15	Conference Bd. study shows a sharp upswing in international terrorism, primarily targeted at multinational corporations.	Bank of England's minimum lending rate is raised to the record level of 17 percent, up three percentage points from its 14 percent level. . . . P.M. Margaret Thatcher tells the House of Commons that Anthony Blunt, a distinguished art historian and artistic adviser to Queen Elizabeth II, was a Soviet agent in the 1960s — the "fourth man" in a celebrated spy ring that included Guy Burgess, Donald Maclean, and Kim Philby.	Israel returns Mt. Sinai and surrounding territory to Egypt under terms of the Israeli–Egyptian peace treaty in a goodwill gesture made more than two months before the date set for the turnover. . . . After over a week of tense negotiations, Zimbabwe Rhodesia's Patriotic Front accepts a proposal for British rule during a transition period of independence.		
Nov. 16		Great Britain announces that it will send an ambassador to Argentina in January 1980, four years after it recalled its envoy because of a dispute over ownership of the Falkland Islands.		Argentine military govt. introduces a new labor law banning the country's powerful trade unions from political activity. . . . Bolivian Congress selects Lidia Gueiler Tejada, president of the Senate, as interim president of the country to replace Col. Alberto Natusch Busch, who seized power in a Nov. 1 coup.	
Nov. 17			Ayatollah Khomeini orders the release of 12 U.S. hostages — blacks and women — citing Islam's special respect toward women and U.S. traditional "repression" of blacks.		
Nov. 18			Ayatollah Khomeini says in an interview that the remaining U.S. hostages are spies and should be tried as such.		

A	B	C	D	E
Includes developments that affect more than one world region, international organizations and important meetings of major world leaders.	Includes all domestic and regional developments in Europe, including the Soviet Union, Turkey, Cyprus and Malta.	Includes all domestic and regional developments in Africa and the Middle East, including Iraq and Iran and excluding Cyprus, Turkey and Afghanistan.	Includes all domestic and regional developments in Latin America, the Caribbean and Canada.	Includes all domestic and regional developments in Asia and Pacific nations, extending from Afghanistan through all the Pacific Islands, except Hawaii.

U.S. Politics & Social Issues	U.S. Foreign Policy & Defense	U.S. Economy & Environment	Science, Technology & Nature	Culture, Leisure & Life Style	
Former Calif. Gov. Ronald Reagan announces his candidacy for the Republican presidential nomination, calling for a spiritual revival and a renewal of confidence in government in the U.S.	Justice Dept. announces that an estimated 200,000 Iranians in the U.S. have until Dec. 14 to report to the Immigration and Naturalization Service for a formal review of their status.	Supreme Ct. rules, 5–4, that an individual investor cannot use the federal courts to recover losses caused by fraud or breach of duty by an investment adviser.... Calif. Gov. Jerry Brown reimposes odd-even gasoline rationing as a show of solidarity with Pres. Carter's decision to halt Iranian oil imports. ... GM announces it is offering $100–$400 cash rebates to spur sales of leftover 1979 models.		Willie Stargell of the Pittsburgh Pirates and Keith Hernandez of the St. Louis Cardinals are chosen the NL's most valuable players in the first tie in the 49-year history of the award.	Nov. 13
	Pres. Carter informs the State Dept. that the U.S. will not lift sanctions against Zimbabwe Rhodesia. ... Pres. Carter freezes all Iranian assets in the U.S., estimated by the U.S. to be over $6 billion although the Iranian govt. claims a $12 billion figure.	One day after hitting a 17-month high, the dollar plunges in wake of Iranian threats to pull its assets out of the U.S.		Roman Catholic bishops in the U.S. reject a proposal to replace the word "men" in prayers and liturgical rites with neutral gender references.	Nov. 14
Anthony Scotto, N.Y. longshoremen leader, is convicted on federal labor racketeering charges that he obtained more than $200,000 in cash payoffs from waterfront business.	U.S. State Dept. urges Israel not to deport Nablus Mayor Bassam Shaka because the negotiations on Palestinian autonomy could be threatened.	George Meany, 85, president of the AFL–CIO since it was formed in 1955, retires.		Broadway stage producer and director Jed Harris, 79, dies in N.Y.C.	Nov. 15
		U.S. commercial banks raise their prime rate to a record high of 15.7 percent in the aftermath of the FRB's Oct. 6 decision to severely curtail credit.... Pres. Carter and his top energy advisers ask 34 of the nation's governors to help reduce oil consumption in wake of the administration's ban on oil imports from Iran.... Philip Klutznick is named commerce secretary to succeed Juanita Kreps who resigned for personal reasons.			Nov. 16
			Immanuel Velikovsky, 84, Russian-born psychoanalyst and author known for his unorthodox theories of cosmic evolution dies of a heart ailment in Princeton, N.J.	The Rose, a movie set in 1969 about a singer whose personality resembles the late rock star Janis Joplin, is released in N.Y.C. It stars Bette Midler and Alan Bates.	Nov. 17
	The New York Times reports that while the administration was aware that admitting the Shah of Iran into the U.S. might endanger Americans in the U.S. Embassy in Teheran, it bowed to pressure from Henry Kissinger and David Rockefeller, both personal friends of the deposed Shah.		Center for Disease Control reports that incidence of gonorrhea in the U.S. has leveled off after 10 years of steady increases.	Golfer Jack Newton of Australia captures the Australian Open in Melbourne, shooting a 72-hole 288 for $27,548.	Nov. 18

F	G	H	I	J
Includes elections, federal-state relations, civil rights and liberties, crime, the judiciary, education, health care, poverty, urban affairs and population.	Includes formation and debate of U.S. foreign and defense policies, veterans' affairs and defense spending. (Relations with specific foreign countries are usually found under the region concerned.)	Includes business, labor, agriculture, taxation, transportation, consumer affairs, monetary and fiscal policy, natural resources, and pollution.	Includes worldwide scientific, medical and technological developments, natural phenomena, U.S. weather, natural disasters, and accidents.	Includes the arts, religion, scholarship, communications media, sports, entertainments, fashions, fads and social life.

	World Affairs	Europe	Africa & the Middle East	The Americas	Asia & the Pacific
Nov. 19			Zimbabwe Rhodesia's Patriotic Front criticizes Britain's cease-fire plan, which calls for a swift end to fighting, a termination of troop movements, and the presence of a small Commonwealth monitoring force. The Front wants a much larger Commonwealth force with peacekeeping capacity.	Progessive Conservative Party candidates lose two by-elections in Canada, reducing its already precarious majority in the House of Commons to one vote. . . . Bolivia's new Pres. Lidia Gueiler Tejada swears in her Cabinet, with only two ministers retaining their positions from the previous civilian administration.	
Nov. 20	U.N. Security Council refuses a U.S. appeal to publicly warn Iran against putting the remaining U.S. hostages on trial for espionage.	Anthony Blunt emerges from hiding to defend his involvement in the celebrated Soviet spy ring by saying that it was a case of political conscience vs. loyalty to country.	Pres. Carter warns Iran that the U.S. might take military action if the remaining 49 hostages held in the U.S. Embassy in Teheran are not released. . . . Pres. Kenneth Kaunda of Zambia announces that the country's 12,000-man army has been placed on full alert and that Zambia is in a full-scale war with Zimbabwe Rhodesia.		Rupert Murdoch, owner of newpapers and magazines in Australia, the U.S., and Great Britain, announces he is seeking to gain control of Australia's largest newpaper chain, the *Herald & Weekly Times Group* .
Nov. 21		In a special parliamentary debate on the Anthony Blunt espionage affair, some British M.P.s express outrage that he was not punished.		Former Canadian P.M. Pierre Trudeau announces that he is resigning as head of the Liberal Party. . . . The ruling People's United Party wins a two-thirds majority in general parliamentary elections in Belize.	A mob of Pakistanis attack and set fire to the U.S. Embassy in Islamabad, apparently spurred by baseless rumors that the U.S. and Israel were joined in a takeover of the Grand Mosque in Mecca.
Nov. 22			Zimbabwe Rhodesia's P.M. Abel Muzorewa announces an amnesty for more than 1,500 political prisoners, most supporters of the Patriotic Front guerrilla factions who were detained in late 1978 when the two black liberation organizations, ZAPU and ZANU, were banned.		
Nov. 23		East Germany condemns the seizure of the U.S. Embassy in Iran in a sudden policy switch. Statements at the beginning of the siege indicated sympathy for the Iranian occupiers. . . . Rumanian Pres. Nicolae Ceausescu is seen maintaining his domination over the country's CP at its twelfth conference, despite an unprecedented attack on his personal leadership by Constantin Pirvulescu, a former high-ranking party official.	Iranian For. Min. Abolhassan Bani-Sadr announces that Iran will not repay any of its debts incurred abroad. . . . Iran begins asking for currencies other than the U.S. dollar as payment for its oil.	Brazil raises the price of gasoline 58 percent. . . . Interim Bolivian Pres. Lidia Gueiler Tejada orders the country's army commander to resign, but he defies the order and places his troops on alert. . . . Mexico's crude oil production climbed 6.9 percent in 24 days over its daily output in October.	In wake of rumors linking the U.S. to the Mecca Grand Mosque takeover, a crowd of 1,000 people attacks the U.S. consulate in Calcutta and anti-U.S. protesters march in Dacca, Bangladesh.
Nov. 24			Egypt openly denounces the seizure of the U.S. Embassy in Iran as a "crime against Islam." Morocco and Niger, two moderate Moslem nations in Africa, also criticize the takeover. . . . Following a fierce two-day gun battle, the Saudi National Guard manages to gain control of virtually the entire Grand Mosque held by armed Islamic militants. Casualties are said to run in the hundreds.		Pakistani Secy. of Information Gen. Mujib ur-Rahman deplores the attack on the U.S. Embassy in Islamabad as un-Islamic and insists that there was no deliberate delay by the authorities in dealing with it.
Nov. 25	U.N. Gen. Secy. Kurt Waldheim formally requests the 15-member Security Council to convene for a debate on the Iranian crisis, the second time since the U.N. was established that a secretary general requested a debate.	Suleyman Demirel's new minority government in Turkey is confirmed in office by a 229–208 vote of confidence.	Rep. George Hansen (R, Idaho) is allowed to visit with 20 of the 49 U.S. hostages during an unofficial trip to Iran. He reports they looked healthy and showed no visible signs of abuse.		

A	B	C	D	E
Includes developments that affect more than one world region, international organizations and important meetings of major world leaders.	*Includes all domestic and regional developments in Europe, including the Soviet Union, Turkey, Cyprus and Malta.*	*Includes all domestic and regional developments in Africa and the Middle East, including Iraq and Iran and excluding Cyprus, Turkey and Afghanistan.*	*Includes all domestic and regional developments in Latin America, the Caribbean and Canada.*	*Includes all domestic and regional developments in Asia and Pacific nations, extending from Afghanistan through all the Pacific Islands, except Hawaii.*

U.S. Politics & Social Issues	U.S. Foreign Policy & Defense	U.S. Economy & Environment	Science, Technology & Nature	Culture, Leisure & Life Style	
The Fifth Circuit Ct. of Appeals rules that federal judges must annually disclose their personal finances under the Ethics in Government Act of 1978.	The Army announces that 427 recruiters have been fired from their jobs for enlisting an estimated 12,700 soldiers through fraud or other irregular procedures since October 1977.	Lane Kirkland is elected second president of the AFL–CIO.	Washington State Gov. Dixy Lee Ray reopens the low-level nuclear waste dump at the Hanford nuclear reservation, calling for strict controls on its use.	Pitcher Nolan Ryan, a native Texan, signs an estimated $4.5 million, four-year contract with the Houston Astros.	Nov. 19
Pres. Carter appoints Judge Charles Renfrew of San Francisco, deputy attorney general, the post vacated by Benjamin Civiletti who became attorney general.	A six-ship task force, including the aircraft carrier *Kitty Hawk*, is ordered to sail to the Indian Ocean to join another naval group of eight ships as a warning to Iran in wake of the continuing hostage crisis.			A band of 300 armed Islamic extremists, identifed as members of the ultra-conservative Oteiba tribe from southern Saudi Arabia, storm the Grand Mosque in Mecca, Islam's holiest shrine, and barricade themselves along with 50,000 worshippers inside.	Nov. 20
Campaigning for the Democratic presidential nomination in N.H., Sen. Edward Kennedy (D, Mass.) charges that Pres. Carter has left a trail of broken promises in his energy policy.				Don Baylor of the California Angels is named the AL's most valuable player.	Nov. 21
	Sale of Iranian flags in the U.S. reportedly are booming as outraged Americans use them to burn at anti-Iranian demonstrations.... Agriculture Dept. reports that under the U.S. Food for Peace plan nearly 67 billion cigarettes were sent to the world's poorer countries in 1977, twice the number sent in the early 1970s.		U.S. and other industrially advanced countries' smoking rate reportedly continues to decline in wake of high taxes and extensive warnings of health risks.	Merle Oberon, 68, film actress known for her striking beauty who starred in the film classic *Wuthering Heights*, dies after a stroke in Malibu, Calif.... Demands from the Islamic militants who seized the Grand Mosque in Saudi Arabia indicate a rising conservatism in the Islamic world. The demands include banning television, women working in public, and soccer — all fairly new elements in Saudi Arabia as a result of its contact with Western industrialized countries.	Nov. 22
Richard Rovere, 64, author and political affairs columnist for *The New Yorker* magazine, dies of emphysema in Poughkeepsie, N.Y. ... Charles Potter, 63, Republican congressman (1947–52) and senator (1952–58) from Michigan who played a leading role as a congressman in reopening hearings on alleged Communist influence in Hollywood, dies in Wash., D.C.			An earthquake measuring 6.5 on the Richter scale leaves 60 people dead, 600 injured, about 1,000 homes and buildings destroyed in Colombia. Property damage is estimated at $20 million.		Nov. 23
	GAO asserts in a study that contrary to Defense Dept. assertions, thousands of U.S. troops in Vietnam may have been exposed to the defoliant Agent Orange.	Commerce Dept. reports that the median income of American families rose 2.4 percent in 1978, after adjusting for inflation, to $17,640 — 10.2 percent higher than the 1977 median family income of $16,009.			Nov. 24
ACLU reports that Florida leads the other U.S. states in people on death row, followed by Texas, Georgia, and Alabama. Of the total 556 people awaiting execution in the U.S., 55 percent are white and 40 percent black.				Outpouring of American anger over the Iranian crisis is seen fueling a new nationwide patriotism, uniting Americans more strongly than at any time since the 1962 Cuban missile crisis.	Nov. 25

F	G	H	I	J
Includes elections, federal-state relations, civil rights and liberties, crime, the judiciary, education, health care, poverty, urban affairs and population.	*Includes formation and debate of U.S. foreign and defense policies, veterans' affairs and defense spending. (Relations with specific foreign countries are usually found under the region concerned.)*	*Includes business, labor, agriculture, taxation, transportation, consumer affairs, monetary and fiscal policy, natural resources, and pollution.*	*Includes worldwide scientific, medical and technological developments, natural phenomena, U.S. weather, natural disasters, and accidents.*	*Includes the arts, religion, scholarship, communications media, sports, entertainments, fashions, fads and social life.*

	World Affairs	Europe	Africa & the Middle East	The Americas	Asia & the Pacific
Nov. 26			*The New York Times* publishes an article that details the difficulties in assessing the deposed Shah of Iran's true financial worth because he had no investments in the U.S. in his own name.... Ayatollah Kazem Shariat Madari, the second highest religious leader in Iran, condemns the Iranian seizure of the U.S. Embassy in Teheran and says that he does not think the extradition of the Shah back to Iran is that essential.	Brazilian Finance Min. Karlos Heinz Rischbieter estimates that Brazil's inflation rate in 1979 will be over 70 percent as the result of the 58 percent increase in the price of gasoline.... The Parti Quebecois loses its sixth by-election of the year as a Liberal candidate wins by a wide margin in a suburb of Montreal.	Pakistan reports that 310,000 Afghan refugees have fled to Pakistan since the beginning of the Afghan uprising.
Nov. 27		Soviet Pres. Brezhnev castigates several govt. ministers by name for negligence, irresponsibility, or bungling that he charges contributed to the U.S.S.R.'s poor economic performance in 1979.	Iranian students occupying the U.S. Embassy in Teheran say that they have surrounded the building with explosives and planted mines in the compound to ward off any attempts to free the hostages.	Mexicana Airlines, Mexico's largest privately owned commercial airline, settles a strike of 5,750 unionized ground workers.	About 100 people are arrested in Seoul, South Korea for attending an unauthorized political gathering after 96 people were arrested the previous day in wake of antigovernment unrest.
Nov. 28				South Africa's Amb. to El Salvador, Archibald Garner Dunn, is kidnapped by a group of 15 armed men in San Salvador.	P.M. Malcolm Fraser orders an investigation of health programs for Australian Aborigines following reports that existing programs were not successful.
Nov. 29	U.S. files suit in the International Court of Justice seeking a judgment against Iran for taking hostages in the U.S. Embassy.... U.N. General Assembly adopts a resolution 75–33 declaring that the 1978 Egyptian–Israeli peace treaty is not valid for the Palestinians.	Soviet Union mounts a vigorous advertising campaign in U.S. newspapers to increase sales of the *chervonets*, its quarter-ounce gold coin. The campaign reportedly is aimed at raising foreign currency needed to pay for Western imports.	The total number of U.S. hostages held captive in Iran rises to 50 as Jerry Plotkin, an American businessman, is taken from his hotel in Teheran by the Iranians.	Mexican govt. announces that it will bar the deposed Shah of Iran from returning to Mexico.... All 11 members of Pres. Jaime Roldos Aguilera's Cabinet resign in Ecuador as a result of Roldos's power struggle with Assad Bucaram, the president of the single-chamber congress and the head of the Concentration of Popular Forces Party.	
Nov. 30		British P.M. Margaret Thatcher's call for a reduction in Britain's net contribution to the 1980–81 EEC budget is rejected by her fellow EEC leaders at their two-day summit meeting in Dublin.... The French National Assembly votes, 271–201, to make permanent a provisional five-year-law legalizing abortion.	South African P.M. Pieter Botha acknowledges that South African troops fought guerrillas in Zimbabwe Rhodesia, contradicting previous assertions that all South African troops had been withdrawn from the country in 1975.	U.S. announces measures to cut back diplomatic relations, military ties, and economic aid to Chile to retaliate for Chile's refusal to extradite three high-ranking army officers wanted by the U.S. for the murder in Wash., D.C. of Orlando Letelier.... Brazilian Pres. Joao Baptista de Figueiredo signs into law a bill reforming the country's political system.	
Dec. 1	At the opening session of the U.N. Security Council debate on the American hostages held in Iran, U.S. delegate Donald McHenry warns that freeing the hostages is not negotiable.		Most racial job restrictions are lifted in South Africa.		
Dec. 2		The Democratic Alliance, a rightist coalition led by Dr. Francisco Manuel Lumbrales de Sa Carneiro wins a majority in Portugal's National Assembly.	Shah of Iran is discharged from a N.Y. hospital where he was receiving medical treatment and flown to a hospital at Lackland Air Froce Base near San Antonio, Tex.		Vietnam News Agency reports Pnompenh govt. denials of reports that it is blocking Western relief shipments for Cambodia's starving people.

A	B	C	D	E
Includes developments that affect more than one world region, international organizations and important meetings of major world leaders.	Includes all domestic and regional developments in Europe, including the Soviet Union, Turkey, Cyprus and Malta.	Includes all domestic and regional developments in Africa and the Middle East, including Iraq and Iran and excluding Cyprus, Turkey and Afghanistan.	Includes all domestic and regional developments in Latin America, the Caribbean and Canada.	Includes all domestic and regional developments in Asia and Pacific nations, extending from Afghanistan through all the Pacific Islands, except Hawaii.

U.S. Politics & Social Issues	U.S. Foreign Policy & Defense	U.S. Economy & Environment	Science, Technology & Nature	Culture, Leisure & Life Style	
	U.S. announces that it has instructed embassies in about 10 Islamic countries to voluntarily evacuate dependents, nonessential diplomatic personnel, and private U.S. business people.	More oil is reported discovered through both offshore and onshore drilling in China.	A Pakistani jetliner carrying Moslem pilgrims returning to Pakistan from Mecca crashes about 30 miles north of Jeddah, Saudi Arabia, killing at least 156 people.	International Olympic Committee votes to recognize the two Chinas — People's Republic and Taiwan — for participation in the 1980 Olympic Games.	Nov. 26
Carnegie Council on Higher Education releases a report calling high school an alienating experience for many young people. It urges that mandatory education end at age 16, that high schools be smaller, and that rigid, five-day attendance shedules be eliminated.		Labor Dept. reports that the government's index of consumer prices rose a seasonally adjusted 1 percent in October, or 13.2 percent at an adjusted annual rate. . . . U.S. Steel Corp. announces shutting down 10 plants and closing portions of six other facilities, laying off some 13,000 of its total work force of 165,000. . . . Postmaster General William Bolger announces the Postal Service's first profit since 1946.			Nov. 27
Supreme Ct. rules, 6–3, that police authorized to search a particular place do not have the automatic right to search anyone who happens to be there.	U.S. Treasury Secy. G. William Miller says that the use of U.S. military force in Iran would irreparably harm American hopes for continued oil production by Arab states.	Productivity declined at a .7 percent seasonally adjusted annual rate during the third quarter, according to revised figures released by the Labor Dept. . . . *Wall Street Journal* reports that people are paying 18 percent of their earnings in income taxes compared to an average 12 percent in 1964, despite repeated tax-rate reductions.	An Air New Zealand DC-10 jetliner on a sightseeing flight over the South Pole crashes into a 12,400-foot mountain in Antarctica, killing all 257 people aboard. It is the third fatal DC-10 crash this year.		Nov. 28
A three-judge federal court appoints N.Y. lawyer Arthur Christy as a special prosecutor to investigate allegations that White House chief of staff Hamilton Jordan had used cocaine.					Nov. 29
	U.S. Ct. of Appeals for the District of Columbia rules that Pres. Carter has the authority to terminate unilaterally the mutual defense treaty between the U.S. and the Taiwan govt.	Farm prices are reported rising .5 percent in November, 10 percent higher than in November 1978.		Sugar Ray Leonard captures the World Boxing Council welterweight championship in Las Vegas with a fifteeth-round technical knockout of titleholder Wilfredo Benitez of Puerto Rico. . . . Zeppo Marx, 78, the last of the Marx Brothers, dies of lung cancer in Palm Springs, Calif.	Nov. 30
				Rev. William Callaghan, a Jesuit priest who has outspokenly advocated ordination of women, is reported to have been ordered by the Jesuits' worldwide director, the Very Rev. Pedro Arrupe, to break his ties with activist groups and report back to his native New England for reassignment.	Dec. 1
	Sen. Edward Kennedy (D, Mass.) stirs up a controversy by telling a TV interviewer that the Shah of Iran's regime was marked by terrorism and fundamental violations of human rights.			The U.S. Embassy in Tripoli, Libya is the target of a mob attack, which leaves the ground floor of the five-story building in ruins and the first floor heavily damaged.	Dec. 2

F	G	H	I	J
Includes elections, federal-state relations, civil rights and liberties, crime, the judiciary, education, health care, poverty, urban affairs and population.	*Includes formation and debate of U.S. foreign and defense policies, veterans' affairs and defense spending. (Relations with specific foreign countries are usually found under the region concerned.)*	*Includes business, labor, agriculture, taxation, transportation, consumer affairs, monetary and fiscal policy, natural resources, and pollution.*	*Includes worldwide scientific, medical and technological developments, natural phenomena, U.S. weather, natural disasters, and accidents.*	*Includes the arts, religion, scholarship, communications media, sports, entertainments, fashions, fads and social life.*

	World Affairs	Europe	Africa & the Middle East	The Americas	Asia & the Pacific
Dec. 3		Spanish govt. extends a tough antiterrorism law in response to the deaths of 124 people who have been killed in terrorist political violence during the year.		Bolivian Pres. Lidia Gueiler Tejada is reported having announced broad measures to deal with the country's ailing economy, including devaluation by 20 percent of the Bolivian peso, price freezes on some food items, and wage increases for most lower-paid workers.... Jose Esteban Gonzales, president of the Nicaraguan Permanent Commission on Human Rights, says in a *Los Angeles Times* interview that between 500 and 1,000 people have been illegally executed since the Sandinista junta came to power on July 19.	Soviet-block countries are reported to have supplied 124,000 tons of food to Cambodia.... Taiwan's Council for Economic Planning and Development sets an annual economic growth target of 8 percent for the 10-year period beginning in 1980.
Dec. 4	The U.N. Security Council unanimously approves a resolution demanding that Iran immediately release the 50 American hostages held in the U.S. Embassy in Teheran and allow them to leave the country.	Steingrimur Hermannsson, head of Iceland's Progressive Party, is asked to form a government after the party makes substantial election gains today.	Saudi Arabian troops take complete control of the Grand Mosque in Mecca as they rout the last of the Islamic militants who had seized the shrine on Nov. 20.	A group of 1,200 Ethiopian children is reported arriving in Cuba where an estimated 10,000 children from Angola, Congo, Mozambique, Namibia, and Guinea-Bissau are reported studying at an educational colony south of Havana.	A military court in Seoul suspends the trial of seven people charged in the Oct. 26 assassination of Pres. Park Chung Hee shortly after the proceedings started. It accepts defense lawyers' arguments that a military tribunal is not qualified to try a case for alleged offenses committed before martial law was imposed.
Dec. 5	The Soviet Union accuses the U.S. of attempting to blackmail Iran by massing forces on its frontiers instead of acceding to the Iranian govt.'s demand to return the Shah.	Irish P.M. John Lynch resigns a number of months earlier than predicted in wake of mounting criticism from some members of his Fianna Fail Party for his conciliatory approaches to Britain's policies for Northern Ireland.	Israeli authorities free West Bank Mayor Bassam Shaka of Nablus and allow him to resume his duties in an unexpected reversal of an original deportation order prompted by his espousal of Palestinian terrorism.... South Africa tentatively accepts a U.N. plan for establishing a demilitarized zone on the Angolan-Namibian border.		An international relief official at the Cambodian border says an estimated 80–90 percent of relief supplies sent to Cambodia's starving population remain in Pnompenh warehouses and at the port of Kimpong Som.
Dec. 6		Dutch Parliament's lower house rejects the production and deployment of U.S. medium-range missiles in Europe, threatening to bring down the government of Premier Andreas van Agt, who was prepared to accept the plan.		Panamanian govt. charges the U.S. with violating terms of the Panama Canal treaties by delaying naming five members to the commission responsible for the mamagement of the canal.	Chinese authorities order closing of Peking's Democracy Wall, the traditional site in the center of the city to affix wall posters and the only established public forum for free expression.... Acting Pres. Choi Kyu Hah is proclaimed president of South Korea by an overwhelming majority of the National Conference for Unification. The opposition New Democratic Party demands that he agree to hold free elections for a successor by popular vote in August 1980.
Dec. 7		The British govt. announces the appointment of Lord Soames, Conservative leader in the British House of Lords, as the governor of Zimbabwe Rhodesia.... Ireland's ruling Fianna Fail Party elects Health Min. Charles Haughey to replace outgoing P.M. John Lynch. ... Shariar Mustapha Chafik, 34, a nephew of the Shah of Iran, is shot to death in Paris by an unknown assailant.	Anglican Church in South Africa votes to refuse to apply for permits to hold integrated church gatherings.	Brazilian Pres. Joao Baptista de Figueiredo announces a series of sweeping economic measures to redirect the course of Brazil's economy, including the immediate devaluation on the cruzeiro by 30 percent.... Bahamas govt. orders a halt to the unrestricted sale of land to foreigners in an effort to end speculation causing land prices to rise beyond the means of most Bahamians.	In his first official act as president, Choi Kyu Hah lifts Emergency Decree 9, the 1975 ruling that outlawed dissident activity against the government of the late South Korean Pres. Park.
Dec. 8		The Moslem Liberation Front, a previously unknown group in Paris, joins the Iranian fundamentalist Islamic Fedayeen guerrilla group in claiming responsibility for the previous day's murder of the Shah's nephew, Shariar Mustapha Chafik.	Iranian For. Min. Sadegh Ghotbzadeh announces that Iran will form an international tribunal within 10 days to investigate American interference and wrongdoing in Iran.	Police crush a rebellion in St. Vincent's Union Island, which followed Dec. 5 general elections in which P.M. Milton Catol's ruling Labor Party won 11 of the 13 parliamentary seats.	

A	B	C	D	E
Includes developments that affect more than one world region, international organizations and important meetings of major world leaders.	Includes all domestic and regional developments in Europe, including the Soviet Union, Turkey, Cyprus and Malta.	Includes all domestic and regional developments in Africa and the Middle East, including Iraq and Iran and excluding Cyprus, Turkey and Afghanistan.	Includes all domestic and regional developments in Latin America, the Caribbean and Canada.	Includes all domestic and regional developments in Asia and Pacific nations, extending from Afghanistan through all the Pacific Islands, except Hawaii.

U.S. Politics & Social Issues	U.S. Foreign Policy & Defense	U.S. Economy & Environment	Science, Technology & Nature	Culture, Leisure & Life Style	
	State Dept. is reported unsuccessful in its attempt to find a Western country to provide a haven for the Shah of Iran.	Commerce Dept. pledges $125 million in new federal loan guarantees to create jobs for unemployed workers in Youngstown, Ohio, hard hit by the closing of U.S. Steel and Jones & Laughlin Steel Corp. plants in the city.		Charles White, a University of Southern California senior tailback, is the forty-fifth winner of the Heisman Trophy, awarded to the nation's finest collegiate football player.	Dec. 3
Pres. Carter officially declares that he is a candidate for reelection, becoming the eleventh declared presidential candidate of the two major political parties. . . . HEW issues final guidelines defining its position on Title IX of the 1972 Higher Education Act, which prohibit sex discrimination.					Dec. 4
Gallup Poll shows Pres. Carter has a 38 percent approval rating (49 percent disapproval), his highest job rating since 40 percent in April and a 6 percentage point jump in a month.	Marine Corps leaders disclose that they have been ordered to organize a 50,000-man spearhead for Pres. Carter's Rapid Deployment Force.	Sales of U.S.-made cars are reported down 21 percent in October and 22 percent in November, compared with levels a year earlier. American Motors Corp. and Volkswagen of America Inc., subsidiary of the West German company, both report sharp increases in sales during these months.		Sonia Johnson, of Sterling, Va., a fifth-generation Mormon, is formally excommunicated from the church for her outspoken advocacy of the Equal Rights Amendment.	Dec. 5
Shirley Hufstedler is sworn in as the nation's first secretary of education.	Senate Majority Leader Robert Byrd announces that a full Senate debate on the SALT Treaty will not be held until 1980.		Cecelia Payne-Gaposhkin, 79, a foremost woman in astronomy for three decades and the first to receive a tenured professorship at Harvard University, dies in Cambridge, Mass. . . . Henrietta Seiberling, 91, central figure in the founding and development of Alcoholics Anonymous, dies in N.Y.C.		Dec. 6
		Carter dismisses the chairman of the Nuclear Regulatory Commission, Joseph Henrie, and temporarily replaces him with John Ahearne, a commission member who has taken a harder line on nuclear safety.	Pres. Carter announces several changes that he says will improve the safety of nuclear energy in response to findings of the President's Commission on the Accident at Three Mile Island.	Very Rev. Pedro Arrupe, worldwide director of the Roman Catholic Jesuits, orders major leaders of the order to take firmer action to curtail liberal tendencies among priests and theologians.	Dec. 7
David Treen is elected the first Republican governor of Lousiana in 102 years.				Grease , a musical satire on the teenage scene of the 1950s, becomes Broadway's longest-running show to date, surpassing the record held by Fiddler on the Roof .	Dec. 8

F	G	H	I	J
Includes elections, federal-state relations, civil rights and liberties, crime, the judiciary, education, health care, poverty, urban affairs and population.	Includes formation and debate of U.S. foreign and defense policies, veterans' affairs and defense spending. (Relations with specific foreign countries are usually found under the region concerned.)	Includes business, labor, agriculture, taxation, transportation, consumer affairs, monetary and fiscal policy, natural resources, and pollution.	Includes worldwide scientific, medical and technological developments, natural phenomena, U.S. weather, natural disasters, and accidents.	Includes the arts, religion, scholarship, communications media, sports, entertainments, fashions, fads and social life.

	World Affairs	Europe	Africa & the Middle East	The Americas	Asia & the Pacific
Dec. 9	In its annual review of worldwide human-rights status, Amnesty International notes the increase in 1979 of kidnapping and murder of political dissenters.	Amnesty International's annual human-rights report charges British mistreatment of prisoners in Northern Ireland and Soviet use of mental institutions to imprison dissidents.... Two bombs explode in Rome, injuring nine persons.	Amnesty International's annual human-rights report criticizes both the former Shah of Iran and the current Islamic regime. It also criticizes both Israel and Egypt — Israel for mistreating Arabs in occupied territories and Egypt for arresting outspoken opponents of the peace treaty with Israel.		
Dec. 10	U.S. Atty. Gen. Benjamin Civiletti files a petition with the International Court of Justice requesting the quickest possible action to free the U.S. hostages held at the U.S. Embassy in Teheran.	State Secy. Vance seeks French and British economic moves against Iran to increase international pressure for the release of the American hostages held in Teheran.... A Warsaw court sentences four participants in an unofficial Nov. 11 independence day rally, the day in 1918 when Poland was reunited and declared an independent country, to jail terms of one to three months.	South African govt. announces that individual owners of restaurants, theaters, private hospitals, and libraries can choose to desegregate their facilities individually rather than applying annually to the government for a permit or permit renewal to integrate.	A march by 10,000 women members of the Pro-Peace Committee in El Salvador is disrupted by a group of armed leftists who hurl gasoline bombs and attack the marchers with clubs.	A spokesman for the Moslem rebels fighting Afghan govt. forces says that the Soviet Union has increased the number of its troops and advisers in the country to 25,000.
Dec. 11			Zimbabwe Rhodesia P.M. Abel Muzorewa's govt. votes to formally dissolve itself after six months in office. Parliament also repeals the unilateral declaration of independence enacted on Nov. 11, 1965, thereby ending the country's 15 years of unacknowledged independence.	White House Chief of Staff Hamilton Jordan flies to Panama to discuss arrangements with Brig. Gen. Omar Torrijos Herrera for the Shah of Iran's establishing residence there.	
Dec. 12	NATO defense and foreign ministers agree to install 572 U.S. medium-range nuclear missiles in Europe by 1983, although the Netherlands and Belgium express reservations.	A French court bars releasing $50 million in Iranian central bank funds that had been deposited in the Paris branch of Citibank.... Great Britain lifts all trade sanctions against Zimbabwe Rhodesia as the country reverts to British control.	Carter administration orders most Iranian diplomats in the U.S. to leave in view of the continued detention of 50 American hostages at the U.S. Embassy in Teheran.... Bankers and monetary officials are reported noting a steady decline in the size of Saudi Arabia's monetary assets, falling to $17 billion in September 1979 from $32 billion at the end of 1977.	Wall Street Journal reports that Mexico's staple crops of corn and beans produced a disappointing 1979 harvest in wake of a prolonged drought and early frost.	A South Korean military faction stages an apparent rebellion and arrests martial law administrator Gen. Chung Seung Hwa and 16 other senior officers.
Dec. 13		In an unprecedented action, the European Parliament rejects, 288–64, the proposed EEC budget, demanding tighter restrictions on agricultural spending, which represents over 70 percent of the $23.5 billion budget.		Canadian Supreme Ct. unanimously rules that parts of Bill 101, making French the only official language of Quebec, are unconstitutional.	U.N. relief official Henry Labouisse refutes a CIA report that charges the Soviet Union with blocking distribution of food and medicine in Cambodia, and says that supplies pile up in Cambodian centers because of a lack of transport.
Dec. 14	NATO foreign ministers end a two-day conference with a new set of proposals for the mutual and balanced force reduction talks in Vienna. NATO offers to withdraw 13,000 U.S. troops from West Germany in exchange for a Soviet withdrawal of 30,000 troops from Central Europe.	British govt. publishes figures showing an increase in retail prices of 17.4 percent over the past year. ... Turkish terrorists fatally shoot four Americans as they return from work at a NATO base.... East German amnesty, declared in September, ends with the release of 21,928 prisoners.	Iran radio reports that Iraqi troops have invaded southwestern Khuzistan province, but three hours later it denies the attack.	One of Canada's shortest-lived governments ends as P.M. Joseph Clark asks Governor General Edward Schreyer to dissolve the House of Commons and set elections for February 1980, in wake of the Commons' defeat of the budget yesterday.	An Afghan official concedes the presence of a large number of Soviet experts in Afghanistan, but denies that Soviet troops are fighting alongside government soldiers. ... Japan announces that it will reduce its purchases of Iranian oil to 620,000 barrels a day, the level before the Iranian students' seizure of the U.S. Embassy in Teheran.
Dec. 15	International Court of Justice unanimously rules that Iran must immediately free all 50 American hostages held at the U.S. Embassy in Iran.			The Shah of Iran leaves Lackland Air Force Base in Texas for Panama where he will establish residence in response to a long-standing invitation from the Panamanian govt.	U.S. is reported protesting use of U.S.–South Korean Combined Forces Command (ROK) troops in staging the South Korean army rebellion against martial law administrator Gen. Chung Seung Hwa.... Indonesia releases figures confirming that East Timor's population has been sharply reduced as the result of civil war and subsequent starvation.

A	B	C	D	E
Includes developments that affect more than one world region, international organizations and important meetings of major world leaders.	Includes all domestic and regional developments in Europe, including the Soviet Union, Turkey, Cyprus and Malta.	Includes all domestic and regional developments in Africa and the Middle East, including Iraq and Iran and excluding Cyprus, Turkey and Afghanistan.	Includes all domestic and regional developments in Latin America, the Caribbean and Canada.	Includes all domestic and regional developments in Asia and Pacific nations, extending from Afghanistan through all the Pacific Islands, except Hawaii.

U.S. Politics & Social Issues	U.S. Foreign Policy & Defense	U.S. Economy & Environment	Science, Technology & Nature	Culture, Leisure & Life Style	
In its annual assessment of world-wide human-rights abuses, Amnesty International charges the U.S. with mistreating illegal Mexican aliens and questions the existence of the death penalty whose imposition could be racially motivated.				Bjorn Borg of Sweden defeats Jimmy Connors, 6–4, 6–2, 2–6, 6–4, to win the final of the World Championship Tennis Challenge Cup.... Archbishop Fulton J. Sheen, 84, Roman Catholic clergyman, radio-TV evangelist, and author who became one of the best-known church figures in the U.S., dies of heart disease in N.Y.C.	Dec. 9
		In the costliest merger deal in U.S. corporate history to date, Shell Oil Co. acquires Belridge Oil Co. for $3.65 billion.		NBC-TV interviews a hostage held in the U.S. Embassy in Iran, Marine Cpl. William Gallegos, who says in the presence of his captors that he would give his life for any American, but doesn't see giving it for the return of the Shah.	Dec. 10
Dianne Feinstein becomes the first woman elected mayor of San Francisco, Calif. after being appointed to the post after the death in office of Mayor George Moscone in 1978.	Federal District Ct. Judge Joyce Hens Green rules that the Justice Dept.'s special investigation of Iranian students in the U.S. is unconstitutional.	Pres. Carter refuses to set trade restrictions on imports of anhydrous ammonia from the Soviet Union.		CBS and ABC, as well as the Carter administration and Congress, strongly condemn NBC-TV for yielding to Iranian conditions in its interview yesterday of one of the U.S. hostages, and charge that NBC was used by the hostages' Iranian captors.... *Affirmed* wins the Eclipse Award as horse of the year for the second straight year.	Dec. 11
	A powerful bomb explodes in the 11-story Soviet mission to the U.S. in N.Y.C., injuring at least six people, buckling steel walls inside the mission, and shattering windows along the street. An anti-Castro Cuban terrorist group claims responsibility.	Gannett Co. Inc. claims it is the largest U.S. newspaper chain in terms of circulation, which it puts at 3.52 million daily.		Nancy Lopez is named player of the year by the LPGA for the second consecutive year.	Dec. 12
House Ethics Committee formally charges Rep. Charles H. Wilson (D, Calif.) with 15 counts of violating House rules.	Supreme Ct. refuses to hear a case challenging Pres. Carter's unilateral authority to end the mutual defense treaty between the U.S. and Taiwan.			Tennis star Arthur Ashe, 36, undergoes triple-bypass heart surgery in N.Y.C. after suffering a mild heart attack on July 31.... Fired New York Yankees Manager, Billy Martin, meets with AL president, Lee MacPhail, and agrees to stop making derogatory remarks about Yankees owner, George Steinbrenner.	Dec. 13
Rep. Jack Kemp (R, N.Y.) is named Ronald Reagan's campaign chairman for policy development.				Vitas Gerulaitis and John McEnroe give the U.S. a 2–0 edge in the Davis Cup tennis series.	Dec. 14
					Dec. 15

F	G	H	I	J
Includes elections, federal-state relations, civil rights and liberties, crime, the judiciary, education, health care, poverty, urban affairs and population.	Includes formation and debate of U.S. foreign and defense policies, veterans' affairs and defense spending. (Relations with specific foreign countries are usually found under the region concerned.)	Includes business, labor, agriculture, taxation, transportation, consumer affairs, monetary and fiscal policy, natural resources, and pollution.	Includes worldwide scientific, medical and technological developments, natural phenomena, U.S. weather, natural disasters, and accidents.	Includes the arts, religion, scholarship, communications media, sports, entertainments, fashions, fads and social life.

	World Affairs	Europe	Africa & the Middle East	The Americas	Asia & the Pacific
Dec. 16		Five British soldiers are killed and another wounded in two separate bomb attacks in Northern Ireland. ... The center-right Democratic Alliance sweeps the Socialists from power in Portugal's municipal elections.	Iranian For. Min. Sadegh Ghotbzadeh says that the Shah of Iran's departure from the U.S. for Panama is another step toward the victory of the Iranian people.		
Dec. 17	By consensus the U.N. General Assembly approves a code outlawing the taking of hostages, the result of three years of West German negotiation.	New antiterrorist measures take effect in Italy that expand police powers and increase penalties for terrorist offenses. ... Warsaw masses are held to commemorate the 1970 workers' riot in Poland in which hundreds of people are believed to have died.	Patriotic Front leaders Robert Mugabe and Joshua Nkomo initial the Zimbabwe Rhodesia cease-fire after Britain grants their demand to increase the number of guerrilla assembly points for the truce.	The entire 12-member Cabinet of P.M. Michael Manley resigns in face of Jamaica's economic problems.	A two-day party congress held in Cambodia replaces ousted Premier Pol Pot with Khieu Samphan, who keeps his post as president of the country. Pol Pot is named commander-in-chief of guerrilla forces fighting the Vietnamese-supported govt. of Heng Samrin in Cambodia.
Dec. 18	U.N. General Assembly condemns, 107–16, Great Britain and the U.S. for lifting all economic sanctions against Zimbabwe Rhodesia.	Norway's Storting (parliament) approves the government's proposed extension of wage controls through March 1982.	An objection by Bishop Abel Muzorewa, delays the signing of a formal cease-fire agreement although he and the Patriotic Front leaders had initialed it over the previous four days.	Hundreds of Salvadoran troops storm two ranches and a slaughterhouse and kill 35 people who were occupying the sites to demand wage increases and economic and social changes. ... Former Canadian P.M. Pierre Trudeau accepts a call from his Liberal Party to remain their leader during the upcoming election although he announced in May that he is retiring from politics.	
Dec. 19		Renault Co., the French state-owned auto maker, agrees to purchase a 10-percent share in the passenger-car unit of Volvo, A.B., the Swedish auto company. ... Turkish Parliament extends martial law for two months in an effort to control the violence in the country.	Iran's ambassador to Sweden, Abbas Amir Entezam, is arrested at the Teheran airport on charges of collaborating with the U.S.	Argentina's military junta issues a set of guidelines to return the country to a form of democratic rule, but does not set a specific timetable.	
Dec. 20	OPEC four-day ministerial conference ends in Caracas, Venezuela without reaching agreement on a uniform pricing structure.	Dutch govt. of Premier Andreas van Agt survives a no-confidence vote on the NATO medium-range missile plan by defeating an opposition resolution that would have the government dissassociated from the missile-deployment agreement. ... British govt. announces it will provide British Leyland Ltd., the financially troubled state-owned auto maker, with up to $660 million in 1980 aid to help make it competitive again.			South Korean military court sentences seven men to death and gives another defendant a three-year sentence for the Oct. 26 assassination of Pres. Park Chung Hee.
Dec. 21	U.N. Security Council votes, 13–0, to lift economic sanctions on Zimbabwe Rhodesia as a peace agreement is signed ending the seven-year guerrilla war there. ... *Washington Post* reports that the OPEC meeting deadlock on oil prices is seen as a political defeat for Saudi Arabia, which advocated a moderate oil policy, and a victory for price hawks Iran and Libya.	In attacks in three Italian cities, terrorists shoot four men in the legs.	Patriotic Front leaders Joshua Nkomo and Robert Mugabe and P.M. Bishop Abel Muzorewa sign a cease-fire to end the seven-year guerrilla war in Zimbabwe Rhodesia.	After three days of widespread demonstrating in Panama City, riots by students opposing the presence of the deposed Shah of Iran are confined to the National University. ... Salvadoran guerrillas release Peace Corps volunteer Deborah Loff, who had been held captive along with 12 others since Dec. 13 for their protest against high rents in San Salvador's markets.	Choi Kyu Hah formally assumes office as South Korea's fourth president and expresses hope that the 1972 Constitution could be revised in about a year and subsequent steps taken to hold elections. ... U.S. reports massing of Soviet troops on the Afghanistan border, raising the Soviet military presence there to over 5,000 troops and military advisers.
Dec. 22			Palestine news service in Beirut reports that Libya has severed relations with the PLO, culminating a two-week dispute.		

A	B	C	D	E
Includes developments that affect more than one world region, international organizations and important meetings of major world leaders.	Includes all domestic and regional developments in Europe, including the Soviet Union, Turkey, Cyprus and Malta.	Includes all domestic and regional developments in Africa and the Middle East, including Iraq and Iran and excluding Cyprus, Turkey and Afghanistan.	Includes all domestic and regional developments in Latin America, the Caribbean and Canada.	Includes all domestic and regional developments in Asia and Pacific nations, extending from Afghanistan through all the Pacific Islands, except Hawaii.

U.S. Politics & Social Issues	U.S. Foreign Policy & Defense	U.S. Economy & Environment	Science, Technology & Nature	Culture, Leisure & Life Style	
	At midnight the U.S. lifts its ban on economic dealings with Zimbabwe Rhodesia.			Judge Murray Gurfein, who issued the historic ruling rejecting the Nixon administration's attempt to stop publication of the Pentagon Papers in 1971, dies of an apparent heart attack in N.Y.C. . . . U.S. wins its second consecutive tennis Davis Cup by sweeping all five matches in the final series against Italy.	Dec. 16
		Senate approves, 74–24, a windfall profits tax for the oil industry, which would increase government revenue by $178 billion from 1980–90. The House version of the bill would raise an estimated $276 billion by the year 1990.			Dec. 17
Federal Election Commission votes to approve the application for presidential campaign matching funds for Lyndon LaRouche Jr., a Labor Party candidate in 1976 who is running as a Democrat in 1980.	Carter administration again warns Iran of possible U.S. military retaliation if the hostages are placed before an international tribunal.	Mass. Gov. Edward King takes control of the financially troubled Massachusetts Bay Transporation Authority under an emergency provision of the law that created the authority.		Vatican, with the personal sanction of Pope John Paul II, censures a leading liberal theologian, the Rev. Hans Kung, declaring him guilty of heresy and barring him from teaching. His books and scholarly works question traditional tenets of the Roman Catholic Church.	Dec. 18
Republican presidential aspirant Sen. Howard Baker (Tenn.) calls for the establishment of a 50,000-member mobile force specially trained to deal with terrorists, hijacking, and kidnapping threats.		David Rockefeller announces that he is resigning as the chief executive officer of Chase Manhattan Bank effective Jan. 1, 1980 and will be succeeded by Willard Butcher, the bank's president since 1972. . . . Energy Dept. accuses seven major oil companies of overcharging customers more than $1 billion, 1973–76.		Rock'n'roll star Elvis Presley's personal physician, George Nichopoulos, is reported to have been charged with illegally and indiscriminately prescribing over 12,000 tablets of uppers, downers, and pain-killers for Presley during the 20 months before his death.	Dec. 19
	Senate Armed Services Committee releases a report that strongly criticizes the SALT treaty as not in the national security interests of the U.S.	Supreme Ct. rules unanimously that unions cannot automatically be held responsible for unauthorized (wildcat) strikes by their locals.	Federal government files a $124.5 million suit against Occidental Petroleum Corp. over the dumping of hazardous wastes at Love Canal and three other sites in Niagara Falls, N.Y.	American Ballet Theater dancers approve a new contract to end an eight-week dispute delaying the company's season.	Dec. 20
Chicago, Ill. school bd. is not able to meet its $42 million payroll after the previous two payrolls were met only with state funds advanced by Ill. Gov. James Thompson Jr.		Congress gives final approval to a bill guaranteeing the financially stricken Chrysler Corp $1.5 billion in federal backing if its officials can raise $2 billion from various sources.	National Transportation Safety Bd. votes unanimously to adopt a staff report placing the blame for the nation's worst air disaster to date — the crash of an American Airlines DC-10 jetliner near Chicago's O'Hare International Airport – on improper maintenance procedures by American Airlines.		Dec. 21
Former NATO Supreme Commander Alexander Haig announces that he will not run for the Republican presidential nomination.	State Secy. Vance revokes the passport of former CIA employe Philip Agee because his actions are seen as causing or potentially causing serious damage to national security and foreign policy.			Darryl F. Zanuck, 77, film producer and studio executive with 20th Century-Fox, dies of pneumonia in Palm Springs, Calif. . . . Philadelphia Flyers break the National Hockey League record for consecutive games without a loss, beating the Boston Bruins, 5–2, for their twenty-ninth straight game without a defeat.	Dec. 22

F	G	H	I	J
Includes elections, federal-state relations, civil rights and liberties, crime, the judiciary, education, health care, poverty, urban affairs and population.	Includes formation and debate of U.S. foreign and defense policies, veterans' affairs and defense spending. (Relations with specific foreign countries are usually found under the region concerned.)	Includes business, labor, agriculture, taxation, transportation, consumer affairs, monetary and fiscal policy, natural resources, and pollution.	Includes worldwide scientific, medical and technological developments, natural phenomena, U.S. weather, natural disasters, and accidents.	Includes the arts, religion, scholarship, communications media, sports, entertainments, fashions, fads and social life.

	World Affairs	Europe	Africa & the Middle East	The Americas	Asia & the Pacific
Dec. 23			A 1,300-man Commonwealth peacekeeping force begins to assume monitoring positions in the assembly areas of Zimbabwe Rhodesian troops and guerrillas.		
Dec. 24		Rudi Dutschke, 39, German leftist radical and Marxist scholar who was at the forefront of the student revolt in Western Europe in the late 1960s, dies of drowning after an apparent epileptic seizure in Aahrus, Denmark.			Cambodian govt. denounces a report by Red Cross operations director Jean-Pierre Hocke that very little food and medical aid sent by the Red Cross had been distributed to the people.
Dec. 25			Four clergymen chosen by Iranian militants conduct Christmas services for the U.S. hostages, but are not allowed to see all of them together as requested. . . . Israeli Knesset by a 55–50 vote nullifies a law that permitted abortion for social and economic reasons, although abortions are still legal for other restricted circumstances related to age, potential fetal damage, or endangerment of the mother's health.		
Dec. 26			Patriotic Front military leaders arrive in Salisbury to a tumultuous welcome from a crowd estimated at 20,000. They are part of the Commonwealth peacekeeping troops manning Zimbabwe Rhodesia under its cease-fire.	U.S. decides to reduce staffs at its embassy and missions in El Salvador in wake of mounting violence and leftist revolutionaries' threats.	U.S. revises its estimate of the Soviet buildup in Afghanistan to 6,000 men within the country and 50,000 deployed along the Afghan border.
Dec. 27		French Chamber of Deputies and Senate pass legislation in an emergency session authorizing the government to continue collecting taxes and other revenue in 1980.	The Zimbabwe Rhodesian truce formally goes into effect.		Afghanistan's President Hafizullah Amin is ousted in a coup backed and reportedly engineered by the Soviet Union, which airlifted thousands of Soviet troops into Afghanistan. . . . Former Deputy Premier Babrak Karmal takes over the Afghanistan govt and declares that the Afghan people have been liberated from the Hafizullah Amin regime, which he implies was controlled by the U.S.
Dec. 28	Using the Washington–Moscow hot line, Pres. Carter warns Soviet Pres. Brezhnev that the Soviet action in Afghanistan could seriously impair U.S.–Soviet relations. . . . Four exporting OPEC countries — Venezuela, Libya, Indonesia, and Iraq — announce oil price rises of 10 to 15 percent.	Soviet press agency Tass says that the new Afghan govt. had called on the U.S.S.R. to provide urgent political, moral, and economic aid, including military support.	Iranian For. Min. Sadegh Ghotbzadeh denounces Soviet intervention in Afghanistan in a note handed to Soviet Amb. Vladimir Vinogradov.	Labor groups in Canada criticize the Nova Scotia provincial government for enacting a law that makes it more difficult to unionize factories.	The new Afghan leader Babrak Karmal names a Cabinet representing elements of the Afghan left, pledges a nonalignment policy, and repeats his denunciation of Hafizullah Amin as an agent of U.S. imperialism.
Dec. 29		British P.M. Margaret Thatcher sends a message to Soviet Pres. Brezhnev saying she is profoundly disturbed by the Soviet intervention in Afghanistan.	An Israeli military committee hears an appeal of West Bank Mayor Bassam Shaka's deportation order and reportedly advises West Bank military cmdr. Benyamin Ben-Eliezer to rescind it.	U.S. gives final approval to importation of natural gas from Mexico.	The invading Soviet force in Afghanistan is estimated at over 30,000 men. Tass reports from Kabul that the government of Babrak Karmal has released a number of prominent people imprisoned by the Amin regime, including the widow of former Pres. Nur Mohammad Taraki, who was ousted by a coup in September. . . . China and Pakistan deplore Soviet intervention in Afghanistan.

A	B	C	D	E
Includes developments that affect more than one world region, international organizations and important meetings of major world leaders.	Includes all domestic and regional developments in Europe, including the Soviet Union, Turkey, Cyprus and Malta.	Includes all domestic and regional developments in Africa and the Middle East, including Iraq and Iran and excluding Cyprus, Turkey and Afghanistan.	Includes all domestic and regional developments in Latin America, the Caribbean and Canada.	Includes all domestic and regional developments in Asia and Pacific nations, extending from Afghanistan through all the Pacific Islands, except Hawaii.

U.S. Politics & Social Issues	U.S. Foreign Policy & Defense	U.S. Economy & Environment	Science, Technology & Nature	Culture, Leisure & Life Style	
				Philadelphia Eagles whip the Chicago Bears, 27–17, in the NFC wild-card game playoffs. . . . Peggy Guggenheim, 81, expatriate American millionaire and owner of one of the foremost private collections of modern art, dies after a stroke and long illness near Venice, Italy. . . . Houston Oilers beat the Denver Broncos, 13–7, in the AFC playoffs.	Dec. 23
Gov. Cliff Finch (D, Miss) announces that he is entering the presidential race.				Boston Bruin players and New York Ranger fans brawl for several minutes in Madison Square Garden (N.Y.C.) stands during a game.	Dec. 24
	U.S. State Dept. charges Iran with playing "a very cruel numbers game" by refusing to release a list of the hostages.			University of Pittsburgh defeats the University of Arizona, 16–10, in the Fiesta Bowl at Tempe, Ariz.	Dec. 25
		Alexander Haig, former NATO Supreme Commander, is named president and chief operating officer of United Technologies Corp., one of the 20 largest industrial concerns in the U.S. and a leading defense contractor.		Joan Blondell, 70, Hollywood film and TV actress known for her roles as a brash, wisecracking blonde, dies of leukemia in Santa Monica, Calif.	Dec. 26
Republican presidential aspirant John Connally wins two key endorsements in S.C. — Sen. Strom Thurmond (R, S.C.) and former Gov. James Edward.	U.S. Ct. of Appeals rules that the Carter administration has the right to check on the immigration status of Iranian students in the U.S.	IBM says it has sold $300 million worth of seven-year notes to the Saudi Arabian Monetary Agency at 10.8 percent interest, believed to be one of the single largest investments in a U.S. corportation by an oil-rich nation.			Dec. 27
Pres. Carter withdraws from participating in an Iowa debate with his competitors for the Democratic presidential nomination, citing the Iranian crisis.		Pres. Carter signs a stopgap bill to allow banks, credit unions, and savings and loan associations to continue paying interest on checking accounts until April 1, 1980. . . . Bureau of Land Management issues new rules for the protection of wild horses and burros that roam federal western lands.		Rev. John Joseph Cavanaugh, 80, president of Notre Dame University (1946–52) and close friend of the Kennedy family, dies in South Bend, Ind.	Dec. 28
F. Edward Hebert, 78, Democratic congressman from Louisiana (1941–77), dies of heart failure in New Orleans.				Underdog Tampa Bay Buccaneers beat the Philadelphia Eagles, 24–17, in a NFC semifinal game. . . . Philadelphia first baseman Pete Rose is named Player of the Decade by Sporting News . . . . Houston takes the San Diego Chargers, 17–14, in one AFC semifinal.	Dec. 29

F	G	H	I	J
Includes elections, federal-state relations, civil rights and liberties, crime, the judiciary, education, health care, poverty, urban affairs and population.	Includes formation and debate of U.S. foreign and defense policies, veterans' affairs and defense spending. (Relations with specific foreign countries are usually found under the region concerned.)	Includes business, labor, agriculture, taxation, transportation, consumer affairs, monetary and fiscal policy, natural resources, and pollution.	Includes worldwide scientific, medical and technological developments, natural phenomena, U.S. weather, natural disasters, and accidents.	Includes the arts, religion, scholarship, communications media, sports, entertainments, fashions, fads and social life.

	World Affairs	Europe	Africa & the Middle East	The Americas	Asia & the Pacific
Dec. 30		Soviet Union publicly acknowledges for the first time that it had intervened in Afghanistan. It justifies its moves on the basis of its defense treaty with the Afghan govt. and on the basis of Article 51 of the U.N. Charter, which gives any country the right to provide military aid to a member state that seeks it.	Israeli govt. extends the deadline for the evacuation of the Elon Moreh settlement, south of the West Bank town of Nablus, for five weeks to allow its residents time to prepare an alternative site at Jebel Kebir.		U.S. reaffirms its military commitment to Pakistan in face of the Soviet move into neighboring Afghanistan.
Dec. 31	U.N. Security Council approves, 11–0, a U.S.-sponsored resolution threatening Iran with economic sanctions if it does not free the American hostages in the U.S. Embassy in Teheran within a week. . . . The price of gold on the London bullion exchange reaches $524 an ounce, up an astonishing 132 percent from its 1978 closing level of $226 an ounce.			Gen. Leopoldo Fortunato Galtieri, considered a moderate who supports a return to democracy in Argentina, replaces retiring Army commander-in-chief, Gen. Roberto Viola.	Soviet forces are reported fighting a two-hour battle in the center of Kabul with dissident Afghan army troops. . . . U.S. State Dept. says it has evidence that the coup in Afghanistan had been plotted and conducted virtually without Afghan participation.

A	B	C	D	E
Includes developments that affect more than one world region, international organizations and important meetings of major world leaders.	Includes all domestic and regional developments in Europe, including the Soviet Union, Turkey, Cyprus and Malta.	Includes all domestic and regional developments in Africa and the Middle East, including Iraq and Iran and excluding Cyprus, Turkey and Afghanistan.	Includes all domestic and regional developments in Latin America, the Caribbean and Canada.	Includes all domestic and regional developments in Asia and Pacific nations, extending from Afghanistan through all the Pacific Islands, except Hawaii.

U.S. Politics & Social Issues	U.S. Foreign Policy & Defense	U.S. Economy & Environment	Science, Technology & Nature	Culture, Leisure & Life Style	
				Miami Dolphins are routed by the NFL champion Pittsburgh Steelers, 34–14, in the other AFC semifinal. . . . Richard Rodgers, 77, composer and lyricist of Broadway musical comedies, dies in N.Y.C.	Dec. 30
		Agriculture Dept. reports that raw agricultural products prices rose .5 percent in December, bringing the total increase for 1979 to 8 percent.			Dec. 31

F	G	H	I	J
Includes elections, federal-state relations, civil rights and liberties, crime, the judiciary, education, health care, poverty, urban affairs and population.	*Includes formation and debate of U.S. foreign and defense policies, veterans' affairs and defense spending. (Relations with specific foreign countries are usually found under the region concerned.)*	*Includes business, labor, agriculture, taxation, transportation, consumer affairs, monetary and fiscal policy, natural resources, and pollution.*	*Includes worldwide scientific, medical and technological developments, natural phenomena, U.S. weather, natural disasters, and accidents.*	*Includes the arts, religion, scholarship, communications media, sports, entertainments, fashions, fads and social life.*

INDEX

INDEX

The index refers to all daily entries, which are keyed to dates and column letters rather than to page numbers. Headings are arranged in letter-by-letter alphabetical order. Subject headings (e.g., AGRICULTURE, ARMAMENTS) refer to events in the U.S. unless otherwise indicated by a cross-reference or relevant subhead. For subject entries in foreign countries, see country names.

Gas, Natural
7/9/71D

North Pole
8/16/77I

Nuclear Energy
6/24/73I, 10/21/75I

Oil & Oil Products
2/24/72D

Union of Soviet Socialist Republics (USSR)
6/17/76D

Waters, Territorial
4/8/70D, 4/14/70G, 4/22/70D, 11/11/77B

Waterways
9/20/70G

ARCTIC Slope Native Assn.
10/5/71F

ARENDT, Hannah
12/4/75J

ARGAN, Giulio
8/8/76B

ARGENTINA
Accidents & Disasters
1/5/70I, 2/1/70I, 1/10/73I, 10/28/73I, 1/6/75D, 11/23/77I
Amnesties
12/26/77D
Anti-Semitism
4/17/78D
Armed Forces & Defense
12/28/72D, 12/18/73D, 5/10/74D, 1/4/75D, 1/6/75D, 8/27/75D, 12/3/76D, 9/29/79D, 12/31/79D
Arms Control & Disarmament
11/21/77D
Arms Sales
6/5/73D
Assassinations & Assassination Attempts
8/27/70D, 4/10/72D, 12/28/72D, 10/14/73D, 10/30/73D, 11/22/73D, 7/31/74D, 11/1/74D, 11/3/74D, 11/12/74D, 12/12/74D, 1/25/75D, 2/28/75D, 6/2/76D, 6/3/76D, 6/8/76D, 6/9/76D, 12/3/76D, 12/19/76D, 2/18/77D, 4/11/78D
Automobiles
8/1/74D
Aviation
1/6/75D
Awards & Grants
8/22/70J
Bank Robbery
1/30/72D
Banks & Banking
5/15/72D, 4/18/74D
Bolivia
10/6/78D
Bombs & Bombing
7/26/71D, 7/26/72D, 10/17/72D, 12/13/73D, 3/27/74D, 9/30/74D, 11/1/74D, 1/2/75D, 10/8/75D, 3/15/76D, 12/15/76D, 1/7/77D, 1/14/77D, 8/1/78D
Books & Literature
8/22/70J
Canada
10/3/79D
Casualties
9/18/74D, 4/25/75D, 5/29/75D, 9/12/75D, 10/13/75D, 12/23/75D, 1/3/76D, 4/7/76D, 5/30/76D, 7/6/76D, 7/30/76D, 9/4/76D, 11/21/76D, 1/3/77D, 1/4/77D, 2/21/77D
Censorship
2/14/70D, 3/5/70D, 6/4/74D, 5/20/75D, 3/3/77D
Chile
1/9/70D, 7/24/71D, 2/10/78D, 3/1/78D, 11/2/78D, 12/12/78D, 12/22/78D
Church-State Relations
9/25/71D, 7/22/76D, 2/14/78D, 3/21/78J, 3/31/78D
Clothing
7/10/74E
Colleges & Universities
2/24/70D, 5/30/73D, 10/20/74D
Communism
9/24/73D

Communist Party
8/23/73F
Cost of Living
1/14/78A
Coups & Attempted Coups
5/7/70D, 6/8/70D, 3/23/71D, 5/11/71D, 10/8/71D, 10/13/71D, 5/29/72D, 6/28/72D, 2/27/74D, 12/18/75D, 12/22/75D, 3/24/76D, 3/29/76D, 9/29/79D
Courts
4/1/76D
Credit
9/30/71D, 1/30/72D, 3/2/72D, 5/14/72D, 7/14/72D, 10/6/72D, 6/25/76D
Cuba
5/28/73D, 6/4/73D, 8/24/73D
Death Penalty
12/27/72D, 6/26/76D
Death Squads
9/11/76D
Deaths
7/1/74D, 9/30/74D, 10/8/74D
Democracy Moves
12/19/79D, 12/31/79D
Demonstrations & Protests
6/28/72D, 7/3/72D, 7/19/72D, 3/5/76D
Disappeared Persons
12/30/76D, 2/21/77D, 8/26/77D, 4/12/78D, 12/14/78D, 6/17/79D
Earthquakes
11/23/77I
Economy
10/9/70D, 10/22/70D, 12/24/70D, 9/2/71D, 12/3/71D, 1/19/72D, 2/23/72D, 3/1/72D, 5/14/72D, 9/20/72D, 12/2/72D, 2/14/73D, 6/9/73D, 12/21/73D, 10/21/74D, 6/4/75D, 10/10/75D, 1/5/76D, 3/5/76D, 1/7/77D, 10/18/78D, 6/2/79D
Education & Schools
1/7/71D
Elections
9/29/70D, 4/1/72D, 4/30/72D, 6/25/72D, 7/22/72D, 8/1/72D, 8/9/72D, 10/24/72D, 12/14/72D, 12/15/72D, 12/21/72D, 1/2/73D, 3/11/73D, 3/30/73D, 4/12/73D, 4/15/73D, 8/4/73D, 8/23/73F, 4/13/75D
Ethics
10/23/75D, 5/6/76D, 10/25/76D, 5/15/77D, 2/20/78D
Expatriates & Political Refugees
9/3/71D, 4/1/73D, 11/17/74D, 5/10/76D, 7/19/76D, 1/18/77D
Fish & Fishing
2/16/73D
Floods & Flooding
2/17/74I
Food Aid
11/29/74A
Foreign Aid
1/7/71D, 1/18/71D, 4/1/71A, 1/1/77G, 2/24/77G, 3/1/77D
Foreign Correspondents
11/10/77D
Foreign Investments
5/23/73D
Foreign Trade
9/13/71D, 8/24/73D, 7/10/74E
Germany, East
6/26/73D
Graiver Scandal
4/11/77D, 4/19/77D, 5/4/77D, 5/15/77D, 12/9/77D, 4/12/78G, 4/17/78D, 1/8/79D
Great Britain
7/1/71D, 1/13/76D, 2/4/76D, 11/16/79B
Guerrilla Action
1/30/72D, 4/12/73D, 5/27/73D, 2/14/74D, 5/25/74D, 8/11/74D, 9/26/74D, 10/1/74D, 11/26/74D, 12/13/74D, 2/9/75D, 10/31/75D, 11/17/75D, 11/22/75D, 12/1/75D, 12/23/75D, 11/21/76D, 1/3/77D, 2/18/77D, 11/7/77D
Hijackings
7/4/71D
Human Rights
8/26/76A, 10/31/76C, 1/1/77G, 2/21/77D, 2/24/77G, 3/1/77D,

6/10/77G, 8/30/77G, 12/8/77D, 12/22/77D, 4/17/78D, 9/8/78D, 10/19/78D, 11/26/78D, 10/3/79D
Hydroelectric Power
11/8/74D
Internal Security
6/19/71D, 5/19/73D, 5/21/74D, 6/7/74D, 10/7/74D, 11/6/74D, 11/17/75D, 11/22/75D, 3/26/76D
International Monetary Fund (IMF)
3/2/72D, 8/6/76A
Italy
9/3/78B
Jews & Judaism
1/7/77D, 1/14/77D, 3/3/77D, 5/15/77D
Kidnapping
3/28/70D, 5/29/70D, 7/16/70D, 12/16/70D, 10/29/71D, 6/5/73D, 6/7/73D, 7/29/73D, 11/11/73D, 12/6/73D, 12/15/73D, 1/4/74D, 3/13/74D, 4/12/74D, 4/29/74D, 7/15/74D, 7/20/74D, 9/19/74D, 9/30/74D, 2/28/75D, 3/8/75D, 6/20/75D, 8/22/75D, 1/8/76D, 5/18/76D, 5/20/76D, 6/2/76D, 6/3/76D, 6/8/76D, 7/10/76D, 7/19/76D, 12/19/76D, 7/18/77D, 11/10/77D, 12/8/77D
Labor
1/11/70D, 2/10/70D, 5/14/72D, 5/15/72D, 6/8/73D, 7/10/74E, 10/31/74D, 6/4/75D, 6/30/75D, 7/6/75D, 7/8/75D, 7/18/75D, 3/10/77H, 11/16/79D
Liberation Movements
7/17/75C
Libya
2/4/74D
Medicine & Health
1/24/70D
Mexico
1/18/77D
Monetary Policy & System
1/1/70D, 6/18/70D, 10/15/70D, 2/23/72D, 12/15/75D, 12/29/75D
Montoneros
9/6/74D, 9/19/74D, 9/26/74D, 6/20/75D, 7/25/75D, 8/20/76D, 12/3/76D, 12/15/76D, 1/6/77D, 4/11/77D, 4/19/77D, 5/4/77D, 6/5/77D, 12/9/77D, 4/11/78D
Nationalization of Industry
12/24/70D, 10/17/74D
Nuclear Energy
11/30/76D, 10/3/79D
Oil & Oil Products
2/4/74D
Organization of American States (OAS)
7/7/75D, 10/19/78D
Paraguay
3/28/70D
Peronistas
12/7/71D, 2/10/72D, 3/22/72D, 4/1/72D, 4/30/72D, 6/25/72D, 7/22/72D, 7/26/72D, 10/17/72D, 10/24/72D, 10/28/72D, 11/17/72D, 11/19/72D, 12/14/72D, 2/27/74D, 3/23/74D, 5/1/74D, 6/4/74D, 7/31/74D, 10/13/75D, 10/2/76D, 12/19/76D
Petrochemicals
7/12/74D
Police
3/21/73D, 5/13/74D, 6/6/74D, 7/20/74D
Political Prisoners
9/6/71D, 9/25/71D, 8/22/72D, 2/21/77D, 6/13/77D, 12/26/77D, 3/13/78G, 3/21/78D, 4/17/78D, 9/25/79D
Politics & Government
6/13/70D, 7/6/70D, 3/26/71D, 4/1/71D, 6/1/71D, 9/30/71D, 10/11/71D, 3/12/72D, 8/9/72D, 11/19/72D, 2/6/73D, 4/1/73D, 5/2/73D, 5/25/73D, 7/13/73D, 7/14/73D, 9/23/73D, 10/12/73D, 10/17/73D, 3/17/74D, 5/1/74D, 7/1/74D, 7/18/74D, 10/7/74D, 10/21/74D, 11/22/74D, 1/3/75D, 7/3/75D, 7/6/75D, 7/11/75D, 7/18/75D, 9/13/75D, 10/13/75D, 10/16/75D, 11/5/75D, 1/7/76D, 1/15/76D, 2/16/76D, 2/18/76D,

3/29/76D, 6/4/76D, 7/18/77D, 7/31/78D, 9/8/78D
Press
8/20/73D, 6/6/74D, 1/7/76D, 12/30/76D, 9/25/79D
Public Opinion
8/1/72D
Railroads
6/6/74D
Rebellion & Revolution
2/18/73D, 7/19/76D
Regional Conferences
12/7/72D
Reimbursements
4/18/74D
Riots & Violence
3/19/71D, 4/4/72D, 4/5/72D, 4/7/72D, 6/22/72D, 6/27/72D, 7/10/72D, 6/20/73D, 3/22/74D, 3/23/74D, 3/27/74D, 6/7/74D, 3/22/75D, 5/29/75D, 9/12/75D, 10/13/75D, 3/20/76D, 4/7/76D, 7/6/76D, 7/14/76D, 3/14/78D, 9/3/78B
Roman Catholic Church
3/29/70D, 8/3/71D, 7/14/76D, 9/27/76D, 10/11/76D, 7/26/77J, 2/14/78D, 3/21/78D
Spain
11/26/78D
Sports
11/11/72J, 5/1/77J, 6/25/78J
Strikes & Strike Threats
1/24/70D, 3/14/70D, 6/4/70D, 10/9/70D, 10/22/70D, 1/29/71D, 9/30/71D, 10/22/71D, 2/12/72D, 3/1/72D, 5/29/72D, 6/22/72D, 6/27/72D, 9/16/72D, 6/6/74D, 8/1/74D, 7/8/75D, 7/15/75D, 11/2/77D, 4/23/79D
Student Protests
2/24/70D
Teachers' Strike
7/5/72D
Terrorism & Terrorists
7/9/71D, 7/26/71D, 8/3/71D, 3/22/72D, 8/20/72D, 2/22/73D, 4/21/73D, 4/30/73D, 1/25/74D, 9/18/74D, 10/8/74D, 3/16/75D, 3/22/75D, 4/25/75D, 5/30/75D, 5/5/76D, 8/20/76D, 5/7/77D
Torture
5/26/72D, 10/11/76D, 11/15/76D
U.S. Relations
7/2/70F, 2/24/77G, 3/1/77D, 10/20/77F, 11/20/77D, 11/21/77D, 3/13/78G
Unemployment
7/3/72D, 10/10/75D
Uruguay
3/15/70D, 7/9/71D, 7/28/71D, 11/19/73D, 4/24/75D

ARGO Merchant (ship)
12/15/76H, 12/31/76I

ARGONAUT Insurance Co.
1/6/75F

ARGUELLO Hurtado, Robert
7/22/79D

ARIAS, Arnulfo
6/10/78D

ARIAS Navarro, Carlos
12/29/73B, 2/12/74B, 2/5/75B, 1/28/76B, 7/3/76B

ARIAS Stella, Javier
5/31/74D

ARIDA, Shafik Hussein el
1/24/74B, 5/5/74B

ARISMENDI, Rodney
1/4/75D

ARIZONA
Accidents & Disasters
12/20/70I, 5/25/73I
Crime
10/5/76F, 12/3/78F
Deaths
3/4/78F
Demonstrations & Protests
1/23/71F
Education & Schools
2/4/74F
Equal Rights Amendment

Indians, American
8/30/74F, 1/1/76F
Labor
6/11/72H
Murder
6/21/76F, 10/21/76F, 11/6/77F, 12/9/78F
Nuclear Energy
11/2/76H
Nuclear Weapons & Defense Systems
12/21/78I
Politics & Government
10/20/77F, 3/4/78F
Presidential Election of 1972
1/29/72F, 2/28/72F
Press
10/21/76F, 12/9/76J, 11/6/77F, 12/9/78F
Recall
6/11/72H
Taxation
3/27/73H
Welfare
1/27/71F
Women
2/28/72F

ARIZONA Dispatch (publication)
6/21/76F

ARIZONA Republic (publication)
6/2/76F, 11/6/77F

ARIZONA, University of
1/23/71F, 5/25/76I, 12/9/76J

ARKANSAS
Elections
9/8/70F, 5/28/74F
Government Employees
4/7/75F
Prisons & Prisoners
12/29/70F
School Desegregation
11/13/73F
Truckers' Strike
6/28/79H

ARKANSAS River
4/27/70F, 6/5/71I

ARKANSAS, University of
12/29/77J

ARKIN, Alan
12/20/72J

ARKTIKA (ship)
8/16/77I

ARLEN, Michael
4/19/76J

ARLEN, Richard
3/28/76J

ARLINGTON National Cemetery
12/27/75G

ARLINGTON, Va.
6/4/74J

ARM of the Arab Revolution
12/22/75C, 2/8/76B

ARMCO Steel Corp.
11/11/75H

ARMED Forces Day
5/16/70G

ARMED Forces & Defense — See also Airplanes, Military; Chemical & Biological Warfare; Draft; Nuclear Weapons & Defense Systems; Vietnam War; specific types of defense, e.g., Missiles & Rockets
Abortion
8/9/78G
Accidents & Disasters
11/22/75G, 2/11/78B
Air Force
11/22/72G, 5/31/74G, 12/13/78G
All-Volunteer Army
11/22/74G, 2/13/75G, 4/18/76G, 9/25/77G, 2/6/78G, 10/10/78G, 8/20/79G, 10/25/79G
All-Volunteer Army Proposals
2/21/70G, 10/12/70G
Appropriations
10/8/70G, 12/8/70G, 1/11/71G, 1/28/71G, 10/6/71G, 11/23/71G, 12/15/71G, 12/18/71G, 6/5/72G, 6/14/72G, 9/13/72G, 10/2/72G, 11/19/73G, 2/4/74G, 3/18/74G,

5/24/73I, 9/24/73I, 10/18/73I,
12/27/73I, 2/10/75I, 5/14/75I,
7/15/75I, 7/17/75I, 7/24/75I
Damages Claims
6/30/71A
Deaths
1/10/70I, 8/3/71I, 10/25/71I,
2/5/75I
Debris
1/11/75I
Docking
4/4/72I, 2/10/75I, 12/11/77I,
1/11/78I, 6/17/78I, 6/28/78I,
2/26/79I, 4/12/79I
Europe, West
5/30/75I, 5/12/78I
Explorer Missions
12/15/73I
Gas Clouds
8/21/72I
Information Exchanges
10/20/71I, 12/31/71I
International Agreements
1/21/71I, 12/9/71I, 5/24/72I
Jupiter
2/2/72I, 4/5/73I, 12/3/73I,
4/13/74I, 9/10/74I, 12/2/74I,
2/7/75I, 8/20/77I, 9/5/77I,
3/5/79I, 3/7/79I, 7/9/79I
Mars Probes
5/28/71I, 5/30/71I, 10/20/71I,
11/13/71I, 11/26/71I, 11/27/71I,
12/2/71I, 10/27/72I, 8/9/73I,
3/14/74I, 8/20/75I, 9/9/75I,
7/20/76I, 7/21/76I, 7/26/76I,
7/28/76I, 8/7/76I, 8/26/76I,
9/3/76I, 9/12/76I, 6/9/79I, 8/9/79I
Mercury
11/3/73I, 3/29/74I, 9/21/74I
Moon Landing & Orbits
4/11/70I, 4/13/70I, 4/14/70I,
4/17/70I, 9/24/70I, 11/17/70I,
1/31/71I, 2/5/71I, 2/9/71I,
7/26/71I, 7/30/71I, 8/7/71I,
9/11/71I, 10/3/71I, 10/4/71I,
4/20/72I, 4/21/72I, 4/23/72I,
4/27/72I, 12/10/72I, 12/11/72I,
12/12/72I, 12/14/72I, 1/16/73I,
6/4/73I, 6/14/73I, 5/29/74I,
11/6/74I
Moon Samples
1/21/71I, 8/23/71I, 10/15/71I,
2/14/72I, 2/21/72I, 2/25/72I,
4/23/72I, 8/3/72I, 8/11/72I,
12/12/72I
New Findings
3/5/73I, 5/25/76I, 2/26/77I,
6/9/79I
Pioneer
2/2/72I, 4/5/73I, 12/3/73I,
12/2/74I
Radiation Hazards
1/30/78I, 2/4/78I
Records & Achievements
6/19/70I, 7/26/75I, 3/4/78I,
3/16/78I, 9/20/78I, 11/2/78I,
7/15/79I, 8/19/79I
Satellites
2/11/70I, 3/31/70I, 4/8/70I,
4/22/70I, 6/19/70G, 6/26/70I,
7/31/70I, 1/25/71I, 3/13/71I,
4/15/71I, 4/24/71I, 9/28/71I,
9/29/71I, 10/21/71I, 11/5/71I,
11/15/71I, 12/9/71I, 12/19/71I,
6/16/72H, 8/21/72I, 2/13/73I,
3/6/73G, 2/17/74I, 4/13/74I,
5/17/74I, 7/26/75I, 9/17/75I,
1/24/78I, 1/27/78I, 1/30/78I,
2/4/78I, 2/13/78I, 5/12/78I
Saturn
12/2/74I, 3/30/77I, 8/20/77I,
9/5/77I, 9/1/79I
Scientific Satellites
11/22/72I, 10/25/73I, 10/31/73I,
11/3/73I, 12/27/73I, 1/22/75I,
8/8/75I, 9/27/75I, 10/16/75I,
9/17/78I
Skylab
5/14/73I, 5/26/73I, 5/28/73I,
6/22/73I, 7/28/73I, 8/10/73I,
8/24/73I, 9/7/73I, 9/25/73I,
11/11/73I, 11/16/73I, 11/22/73I,
2/8/74I, 1/11/75I, 6/8/78I,
12/18/78I, 7/11/79I
Space Centers
8/27/73I, 10/9/73I, 8/8/74I

Space Shuttles
3/15/71G, 1/5/72I, 7/26/72I,
7/14/75I, 8/12/77I, 9/13/77I,
10/12/77I, 10/26/77I, 9/30/78I
Space Vehicles
11/17/70I
Space Walks
8/6/73I, 8/24/73I, 11/22/73I,
12/25/73I, 8/22/74I
**Union of Soviet Socialist Republics
(USSR)**
4/25/71I, 6/7/71I, 6/30/71I,
2/14/72I, 2/21/72I, 2/25/72I,
4/4/72I, 9/10/72I, 5/29/74I,
7/19/74I, 11/6/74I, 12/8/74I,
2/9/75I, 2/10/75I, 5/14/75I,
5/24/75I, 7/15/75I, 7/17/75I,
7/21/75I, 7/24/75I, 7/26/75I,
9/17/75I, 9/20/75I, 10/22/75I,
9/15/76I, 2/7/77I, 2/25/77I,
2/26/77I, 10/11/77I, 12/10/77I,
12/11/77I, 1/11/78I, 1/24/78I,
1/27/78I, 1/30/78I, 2/4/78I,
2/13/78I, 3/4/78I, 3/16/78I,
6/15/78I, 6/17/78I, 6/28/78I,
7/5/78I, 9/10/78I, 9/20/78I,
11/2/78I, 12/25/78I, 2/25/79I,
2/26/79I, 4/12/79I, 7/15/79I,
8/19/79I
Venus
8/7/70I, 12/15/70I, 9/10/72I,
2/5/74I, 10/22/75I, 8/8/78I,
9/10/78I, 12/9/78I, 12/10/78I,
12/25/78I
Wages
1/5/72H, 1/13/72H
Women
1/16/78I

ASTRONOMY — See also Astronautics
Black Hole
4/13/78I
Deaths
5/24/74I, 12/6/79I
Eclipses
3/7/70I, 6/30/73I
Galaxies
6/30/75I, 4/21/78I
Meteorites
1/14/70I
Moons
6/22/78I, 7/7/78I
New Findings
1/10/71I, 1/25/73I, 6/30/75I,
3/30/77I, 11/8/77I, 1/6/78I,
6/22/78I, 7/7/78I, 12/10/78I
Sun
11/8/77I
Sunspot Cycles
2/21/77I
Women
12/6/79I

ASWAN High Dam
1/15/71I

AT&T — See American Telephone &
Telegraph Co.

ATA, Hashem al-
7/19/71C

ATALS, Charles
12/24/72J

ATHENAGORAS I
7/6/72J

ATHENS Polytechnic University
12/30/75B

ATHERTON Jr., Alfred
10/30/75G, 1/28/79G, 5/8/79G

ATIKI, Abdel Rahman al-
8/21/74C

ATKINS, Orin
7/20/73F, 11/14/73F

ATLANTA Constitution (publication)
5/22/70F, 2/20/74F, 2/23/74F,
8/4/74F, 8/30/74F, 11/28/75F,
9/17/76F

ATLANTA, Ga.
Environmental Protection
6/10/71H
Politics & Government
10/16/73F
School Desegregation
3/20/70F

Strikes & Strike Threats
4/22/70H
Teng Visit
2/1/79E
Tornado
3/24/75I
Water Supply
4/30/76I

ATLANTIC City, N.J.
11/10/78F, 2/26/79J

ATLANTIC Empress (ship)
8/2/79I

ATLANTIC Richfield Co.
Acquisition
1/12/77H
Libya
2/11/74C, 10/10/74C
Prices
11/12/70H, 3/28/73H

ATNAFU Abate
11/13/77C

ATOMIC Bomb & Weapons — See Arms
Control & Disarmament; Nuclear
Weapons & Defense Systems

ATOMIC Energy — See Nuclear Energy

ATOMIC Energy Agency, International
6/27/70A, 6/11/71A, 12/9/71A,
11/1/75I

ATOMIC Energy Commission (AEC) —
See also Nuclear Regulatory Commission
Administration
7/21/71I, 10/20/71I, 12/7/71I
Appointments
7/12/72I, 2/6/73I
Consumer Movement
10/20/71I
Environmental Protection
5/29/71I, 3/16/72H
Equal Employment Opportunity
5/6/75F
Licensing
9/3/71I, 11/24/71I, 12/13/71H,
3/16/72H, 2/4/73H
Missiles & Rockets
7/11/74G
Nuclear Energy
10/2/72H, 8/24/73H, 1/17/75I
Nuclear Reactor Accident
12/4/74I
Nuclear Tests
3/17/72I, 3/28/72I, 3/8/73I
Nuclear Waste
8/28/73H
**Nuclear Weapons & Defense Sys-
tems**
4/26/73I
Occupational Hazards & Safety
1/7/75I
Plowshare Program
3/4/71I
Radiation Hazards
3/13/70H, 8/20/70I, 2/14/79I
Replacement
10/11/74I
Safety Procedures
2/16/73H
Test Detection
7/21/70I

ATOMIC Energy of Canada Ltd.
9/27/72I, 11/30/76D

ATOMS
Research & Development
2/1/71I, 2/8/76I, 8/28/79I

ATTASSI, Nureddin al-
10/16/70C

ATTICA Prison (N.Y.)
9/9/71F, 9/13/71F, 9/17/71F,
7/19/72F, 4/5/75F, 12/22/75F,
8/23/76F, 8/28/76F, 12/30/76F

ATWOOD, William
9/1/70J

AUCHINCLOSS Sr., Hugh D.
11/20/76J

AUDEN, W.H.
9/28/73J

AUGUST 1914 (book)
11/20/72J

AUGUSTA, Ga.
Blacks
5/12/70F

AUSCHWITZ
3/10/72B

AUSTIN, Gene
1/24/72J

AUSTIN, Tex.
5/14/71F, 8/3/71F, 12/6/76F

AUSTIN, Tracy
9/7/77J, 9/9/79J

AUSTRALIA
Aborigines
1/25/72E, 2/8/72E, 7/14/72E,
7/20/72E, 11/24/72E, 10/7/76E,
1/4/78E, 7/20/78E, 9/19/78E,
10/16/78E, 11/3/78E, 11/28/79E
Abortion
5/10/73E
Accidents & Disasters
12/25/74I, 12/30/76I, 2/14/77I
Alcohol & Alcoholism
10/7/76E
Antitrust Actions & Laws
11/18/76E
Anzus Pact
11/2/71E
Apartheid
12/21/77E
Armed Forces & Defense
4/16/71E, 8/22/73E, 4/3/74E,
5/25/76E, 8/23/79E
Arms Control & Disarmament
1/23/73A, 10/1/74A
Arms Sales
3/14/73E
**Association of Southeast Asian Na-
tions (ASEAN)**
10/10/76E
Astronautics & Space
4/10/74I, 7/11/79I
Automobiles
2/12/76E
Aviation
9/20/77I, 11/14/78H
Awards & Grants
10/9/74J
Bangladesh
1/30/72E
Banks & Banking
11/5/75E
Birth Rate
10/1/76E
Budget
8/24/76E, 8/21/78E, 5/24/79E
Cambodia
7/26/73E
Canada
10/13/74E, 4/3/79D
Central Intelligence Agency (CIA)
4/27/77E, 4/27/77G, 5/4/77E,
5/17/77E, 5/19/77E, 5/24/77E,
8/4/77E
China, People's Republic of
5/13/71E, 8/1/71E, 1/9/73E,
5/19/73E, 7/24/73E, 11/4/73E,
6/12/74E, 4/6/76J, 7/29/76E,
3/6/77E, 1/21/79E, 4/6/79E
Clothing
9/20/74E
Coal
6/13/78E, 9/1/78E
Colonies & Territories
8/30/72E, 9/14/72E, 9/15/72E,
3/12/74E, 3/6/75G
Constitution
5/21/77E
Cooperative Moves & Ventures
2/25/72E, 8/13/75E
Copper
11/18/76E
Credit
8/27/74E
Deaths
5/14/78E
Demonstrations & Protests
6/26/71J, 7/14/72E, 3/13/77E,
7/4/77E, 6/26/78E, 8/21/78E,
12/7/78E
Denmark
7/31/74A
Diego Garcia
2/7/74E

Divorces
1/5/76E, 1/29/76E
Drought
9/8/76I, 10/5/76I, 1/11/78I
Economy
9/26/73E, 12/8/73E, 7/23/74E,
8/13/74E, 8/26/74E, 10/21/74E,
4/30/75E, 9/8/75E, 11/7/76E,
4/13/77E, 12/7/78E, 2/27/79E,
3/28/79E, 6/27/79E, 7/25/79E,
8/21/79E, 9/11/79E
Elections
10/10/72E, 11/2/72E, 12/2/72E,
12/7/74E, 10/16/75E, 12/13/75E,
10/27/77E, 12/10/77E, 5/5/79E
Electric Power & Light
10/18/77E, 10/25/77E
Energy & Power
12/19/73E, 10/14/75E
Environmental Protection
6/4/79E
Equal Employment Opportunity
12/5/72E
Ethics
7/2/75E, 3/7/76E, 3/17/76E,
7/14/77E, 9/6/77E, 8/7/78E,
8/21/78E, 8/24/78E, 9/14/78E,
9/27/79E
**European Economic Community
(Common Market) (EEC)**
7/31/74A, 1/24/78E, 6/13/78E
Finland
7/20/78I
Floods & Flooding
10/5/76I, 10/16/76I
Food Aid
11/29/74A
Foreign Credit
7/7/77E
Foreign Investments
10/10/74E, 8/27/75E
Foreign Payments
2/25/76E, 3/7/76E, 3/17/76E
Foreign Relations
1/21/75E
Foreign Trade
5/13/71E, 1/31/73E, 5/8/73E,
5/19/73E, 7/18/73E, 7/24/73E,
10/17/73E, 11/5/73E, 4/16/74H,
7/31/74E, 11/26/74E, 12/7/76E,
1/24/77E, 6/22/77E, 4/27/78E,
4/6/79E
Forests
2/14/77I
France
1/3/73I, 7/22/73A
Gas, Natural
2/20/73E
Gems
11/23/78E
Germany, East
11/5/73E
Government Employees
8/19/77E
Great Britain
11/12/71E, 4/25/73B, 2/27/74E,
7/31/74A, 3/13/77E
History
11/25/76J
Homosexuality
6/26/78E
Immigration & Emigration
12/26/72E, 7/23/74E, 10/2/74E,
10/30/74E, 10/1/76E, 2/19/78E,
6/7/78E
India
6/6/73E
Indian Ocean
3/25/74E
Indonesia
2/25/73E, 4/8/73E, 4/14/76E
Intelligence Organization
11/12/77E
Internal Security
7/17/76E, 5/5/77E, 3/8/79E
Iraq
3/7/76E
Ireland, Republic of (Eire)
7/31/74A
Japan
11/4/73E, 11/6/74E, 8/13/75E,
2/26/76E, 5/25/78E, 4/6/79E
Korea, North
7/31/74E, 11/8/75E
Korea, South
9/20/74E

Egypt
11/10/74C
Farm Prices
3/25/72H
Food Prices
10/31/74H
Politics & Government
1/5/73F
Racial Slur
10/1/76F, 10/2/76F, 10/3/76F,
10/4/76H
Reprimand & Resignation
11/29/74F
Rural Areas
5/7/74H
Soviet Grain Deal
7/28/74G, 10/5/74H

BUXTON, F.L.
1/4/70J

BUZAID, Alfredo
5/14/70D

BUZHARDT Jr., J. Fred
10/31/73F, 3/7/74G

BYCHOWSKI, Gustav
4/3/72I

BYERS, Russell
7/26/78F

BYKOVSKY, Valery
9/15/76I

BYNOE, Hilda
1/17/74D

BYRD, Harry
3/17/70F, 6/12/79G

BYRD, Robert
Armed Forces & Defense
6/24/77G
Arms Control & Disarmament
12/6/79G
Foreign Trade
5/20/77H
Gas, Natural
9/14/78H
Government Departments & Agencies
5/15/79H
Lance Case
9/10/77H
Natural Resources
5/15/79H
Nuclear Weapons & Defense Systems
4/6/78G
Panama Canal Treaty
9/10/77G, 9/24/77G
Presidential Election of 1976
1/9/76F, 6/10/76F
Presidential Election of 1980
7/28/79F
Vietnam War
4/8/71G

BYRNE, Brendan
11/8/77F

BYRNE, Dominic
12/10/76F

BYRNE, Jane
2/27/79F, 4/3/79F

BYRNE, Thomas
12/10/73J

BYRNE, William
2/26/73G, 4/27/73G, 5/2/73G,
5/11/73G

C

CAAMANO, Claudio
10/1/75D

CAAN, James
3/15/72J

CABANAS, Lucio
4/25/73D, 12/2/74D

CABANES, Bernard-Joseph
6/14/75B

CABARET (movie)
3/27/73J

CABINET — See specific departments;
subheads under specific president's
names: Nixon, Ford, Carter; personal
names

CABOT Prize, Maria Moors
10/29/70J, 10/22/73J

CABRAL, Amilcar
5/19/72C, 1/20/73C

CADIEUX, Leo
9/17/70D

CADILLAC Eldorado (automobile
4/21/76H

CAETANO, Marcello
12/2/70C, 7/15/73B

CAFES Suaves Centrales
3/22/75D

CAFFERY, Jefferson
4/13/74G

CAGE, John
9/29/76J

CAHILL, William
6/7/71H

CAIN, James M.
10/27/77J

CAINE, Michael
12/10/72J

CAIRNS, James
7/2/75E

CAIRO, Ill.
10/25/70F, 11/8/70F

CAIRO Conference — See under Egypt

CAIRO Opera House (Egypt)
10/28/71J

CAIRO University
1/18/72C, 2/17/72C, 12/31/72C,
1/3/73C, 2/15/73C, 2/12/77C

CALCIUM
8/29/74I

CALDER, Alexander
11/11/76J

CALDERA, Rafael
6/5/70D, 8/27/70D, 7/30/71D,
8/26/71D, 2/13/73D

CALDWELL, Earl
6/5/70F, 11/7/70F

CALDWELL, Sarah
1/13/76J, 3/31/76J

CALDWELL, William
5/3/71J

CALDWELL, Zoe
11/30/72J

CALIFANO Jr., Joseph A.
Abortion
8/4/77F
Affirmative Action
6/5/77F
Drugs & Drug Industry
2/15/79I
Handicapped
4/5/77F, 4/28/77F
Health, Education & Welfare, Dept. of
12/23/76F, 7/19/79F
Health Insurance
7/29/78F, 2/13/79F
Medicine & Health
7/25/77I
Presidential Campaign
7/27/72F
Social Security System
4/26/79F
Union of Soviet Socialist Republics (USSR)
5/30/78G
Vietnamese Refugees
6/28/79E
Welfare
12/28/76F, 5/25/77F
World Health Organization (WHO)
5/8/79A

CALIFORNIA
Accidents & Disasters
2/9/71I, 6/6/71I, 3/14/74I,
5/21/76I, 7/22/76F, 2/10/78I,
2/16/78I, 9/22/79I, 10/15/79I

Agriculture
7/29/70H, 9/17/70H, 12/23/70H,
3/26/71H, 4/15/73H, 11/15/73H,
6/5/75H
Air Pollution
1/5/76H, 12/8/76H
Archaeology & Anthropology
10/8/74I
Arts & Culture
8/4/78J
Assassinations & Assassination Attempts
9/5/75F, 9/10/75F, 9/19/75F,
9/22/75F, 10/28/75F, 11/26/75F,
12/12/75F, 12/17/75F
Bombs & Bombing
6/19/70F
Campaign Spending
6/4/74F
Colleges & Universities
5/6/70G
Death Penalty
2/18/72F, 3/20/72F, 5/30/72F,
8/11/77F
Deaths
2/23/74F, 7/9/74F, 11/18/78J
Demonstrations & Protests
8/6/78I, 8/7/78I
Draft
11/24/71G
Drought
2/1/77I, 5/4/77I, 1/8/78I, 3/5/78I
Earthquakes
1/26/75I, 8/6/79I, 10/15/79I
Economy
7/2/79H
Education & Schools
8/30/71F
Elections
6/30/70F, 5/15/73F, 5/29/73F
Endangered Species
8/19/71I
Environmental Protection
9/20/71H
Equal Employment Opportunity
6/1/71F
Ethics
10/8/70E, 12/8/75F
Euthanasia
9/30/76I
Explosions
11/1/70G
Federal Aid
1/30/71F
Fires
11/16/73I
Floods & Flooding
2/10/78I, 2/14/78I, 2/16/78I
Forest & Brush Fires
9/28/70I, 11/15/70I, 8/26/73I,
11/23/75I, 11/28/75I, 8/19/77I,
8/12/79I, 9/22/79I
Gas, Natural
9/27/79H
Gasoline Rationing
5/9/79H, 5/16/79H, 11/13/79H
Government Employees
6/7/78F
Grapes
5/1/73H, 8/21/73H, 11/15/73H
Hearst Case
2/5/74F, 2/7/74F, 2/12/74F,
2/19/74F, 2/21/74F, 4/3/74F,
5/9/74F, 5/17/74F, 5/19/74F,
5/22/74F, 6/6/74F, 3/15/75F,
10/2/75F, 11/14/75F, 11/17/75F,
9/26/78F, 10/8/78F
Hijackings
9/15/75F
Indians, American
4/8/70J, 4/19/78F
ITT Case
4/3/74F, 7/27/74F, 10/2/74F
Kidnapping
7/15/74F, 7/29/76F, 11/10/76F,
12/15/77F
Labor
6/5/75H
Legal Profession
6/29/71F
Malpractice
10/2/75F
Malpractice Insurance
5/1/75F, 2/5/76F

Murders
6/16/70F, 8/15/70F, 10/13/70F,
12/22/70F, 3/23/71F, 5/10/71F,
6/2/71F, 7/19/71F, 8/8/71F,
11/2/71F, 12/15/71F, 3/27/72F,
1/18/73F, 2/5/73F, 11/6/73F,
6/9/75F, 6/27/75F, 2/12/76J,
3/4/77F, 7/13/77F, 9/4/77F,
9/11/77F, 11/21/77J, 12/14/77F,
11/27/78F, 11/29/78F, 5/22/79F,
7/3/79F, 9/27/79F, 10/22/79F
Narcotics
10/29/79F
Nuclear Energy
1/22/73H, 2/3/76H, 6/8/76I,
8/6/78I, 8/7/78I, 4/24/79I
Oil & Oil Products
9/20/71H, 2/14/74H, 7/23/74H,
12/22/75H
Parks & Recreation Areas
4/3/70J, 7/8/70F, 2/8/72H,
2/9/78H, 3/27/78H
Peoples Temple
3/14/79J
Police
7/22/70F
Politics & Government
10/2/74F
Presidential Election of 1972
5/28/72F, 6/6/72F, 7/7/72F,
6/8/76F
Press
12/6/76F
Primaries
6/8/76F, 9/16/79F
Prisons & Prisoners
12/23/75F, 8/14/76F
Proposition 13
6/6/78H, 6/7/78F, 6/17/78F,
6/21/78F, 6/24/78F, 6/28/78H,
9/22/78H, 10/5/78H, 1/8/79H,
7/2/79H
Rape
3/4/77F
Redistricting
1/18/72F
Riots & Violence
7/8/70F
Roman Catholic Church
1/21/70J
San Andreas Fault
6/18/78I
School Desegregation
1/20/70F, 2/11/70F, 9/12/70F,
9/2/75F
Sexual Issues
5/12/75J
State Aid
6/24/78F
Strikes & Strike Threats
6/28/74H, 7/31/76H
Taxation
8/30/71F, 6/6/78H, 7/2/79H
Teachers
2/1/70F
Truckers' Strike
6/28/79H
Vietnam War
11/10/71G
Voting & Voting Rights
8/27/71F
Water Pollution
8/20/71H, 11/24/71H
Welfare
1/8/71F, 6/21/71F, 8/11/71F,
8/20/71F, 3/1/72F

CALIFORNIA Institute of Technology
1/25/73I, 3/5/73I

CALIFORNIA Suite (play)
6/10/76J, 5/31/77J

CALIFORNIA, University of
Administration
7/16/71F
Bakke Case
11/15/76F, 11/19/76F, 6/28/78F
Faculty
9/22/72F
Research & Development
4/27/70I, 1/6/71I, 2/1/71I,
5/30/73I
Sports
6/20/70J
Tuition
2/20/70F

CALL to Action
10/23/76J

CALLAGHAN, James
Arms Control & Disarmament
1/6/79A
Business & Industry
1/12/77B
Canada
9/11/76D
Cooperative Moves & Ventures
11/23/75C
Devolution
2/12/79B
Drought
8/24/76B
Economy
12/14/78B
Elections
3/23/77B, 3/3/78B, 4/14/78B,
9/7/78B, 2/26/79B, 3/29/79B
European Economic Community (Common Market) (EEC)
4/1/74B, 6/4/74B
Foreign Trade
3/23/78A
France
6/24/76B
Immigration & Emigration
3/3/78B
India
1/11/78B
Ireland, Northern (Ulster)
7/5/76B
Ireland, Republic of (Eire)
7/21/76B
Labor
2/14/79B
Oil & Oil Products
12/15/78B
Politics & Government
3/30/76B, 4/5/76B, 4/8/76B,
9/10/76B, 11/10/76B, 3/22/77B,
5/11/78B, 6/14/78B, 10/6/78B,
11/9/78B, 12/14/78B, 5/9/79B
Public Opinion
10/28/78B
Race Relations
6/15/76B
Racial Policies
3/3/78B
Rhodesia
3/22/76C, 9/24/76C, 9/26/76A,
7/19/77C, 12/15/78B
Saudi Arabia
11/23/75C
Scotland
4/14/78B
U.S. Relations
3/19/74B, 3/23/78A
Union of Soviet Socialist Republics (USSR)
2/21/78A
Wage & Price Controls
9/7/77B, 10/6/78B, 10/28/78B,
1/16/79B

CALLAGHAN, William
12/1/79J

CALLAS, Maria
9/16/77J

CALLAWAY, Howard
2/20/74G, 4/16/74G, 10/1/74G,
11/19/74G, 6/13/75G, 6/18/75F,
7/9/75F, 7/23/75F, 4/2/76F

CALLEY, William
8/14/70G, 11/12/70G, 3/29/71G,
3/31/71G, 4/3/71G, 8/20/71G,
2/16/73G, 5/14/73G, 12/21/73G,
2/27/73G, 4/16/74G, 5/4/74G,
9/25/74G, 11/19/74G, 4/5/76G,
9/8/76G

CALLOWAY, Cab
3/2/76J

CALVERT Cliffs, Md.
11/24/71I

CAMARA, Helder
11/10/73D

CAMBODIA — See also Vietnam War
Amnesty
11/4/72E
Armed Forces & Defense
8/8/72E, 7/17/73E, 2/24/75E,
3/11/75E

1/6/78D, 1/24/78D, 7/31/78D, 11/28/78D, 12/13/79D

Gas, Natural
9/29/70D, 7/9/71D, 11/19/71D, 5/23/74D, 9/20/74D, 3/18/75D, 4/10/75D, 5/5/75D, 7/16/75D, 7/4/77D, 8/8/77I, 9/8/77I, 1/17/78D, 3/3/79D

Germany, East
8/1/75D

Germany, West
7/12/77I

Gold
8/7/70D

Government Employees
12/14/72D, 2/17/75D, 3/9/75D, 3/19/75D, 1/26/77D, 9/30/77D, 6/8/79D, 8/15/79D

Great Britain
7/15/70D, 9/11/76D, 12/30/77D

Highways & Roads
9/6/77I

Hostages
10/6/70D, 10/10/70D, 10/18/70D, 11/21/70D, 11/23/70A, 12/3/70D

Housing
5/17/71D, 6/12/73D, 11/3/75D

Immigration & Emigration
3/27/72D, 8/24/72D, 2/22/74D, 10/22/74D, 7/7/75D, 11/3/76D, 5/27/77D, 3/8/78D, 3/29/79D

India
5/18/74I, 5/22/74I

Indians, American
8/11/72D, 8/25/72D, 10/25/76D, 5/13/77D, 8/22/77D, 7/14/78D, 7/3/79D, 8/13/79D

Internal Security
4/30/71D, 1/26/77D, 8/9/77D

Iran
7/9/75D

Israel
6/5/79D, 6/23/79D, 10/29/79D

Japan
9/26/74E, 10/21/76E, 2/14/79D

Kidnapping
10/5/70D, 10/16/70D, 11/7/70D, 12/28/70D, 10/27/77D, 8/7/79D, 11/8/79D

Korea, South
5/28/75I

Labor
3/23/70D, 7/16/70D, 5/15/72D, 5/19/72D, 6/6/72D, 6/11/72D, 1/16/74D, 6/3/74D, 10/13/75D, 12/28/79D

Latin America
2/2/76D

Lead
10/12/73H, 4/16/74H

Lebanon
2/23/76C

Livestock & Poultry
4/9/74D, 5/8/74D, 8/6/75D

Lumber
9/27/74H

Meat & Meat Products
4/9/74D, 6/20/74D, 8/2/74D, 11/16/74D, 8/6/75D

Medicine & Health
10/16/70D, 6/10/71I, 8/22/75D, 8/10/78I

Metric System
4/1/75D, 9/6/77I

Monetary Policy & System
5/31/70D, 3/16/73A, 2/14/74D, 6/1/77D, 5/23/78D, 9/11/78D, 1/31/79D, 2/14/79D, 10/25/79D

Murder
9/5/70D

Narcotics
8/26/71D, 5/17/72D, 7/31/72D, 6/3/75D, 7/7/75D, 12/18/78D

Nationalization of Industry
4/23/71D

Newfoundland
10/29/71D, 1/18/72D, 3/24/76D

Northwest Territories
8/3/77D

Norway
1/30/70A

Nova Scotia
9/19/78D, 12/28/79D

Nuclear Energy
9/27/72I, 7/22/73A, 5/18/74I, 5/22/74I, 9/25/74A, 11/30/76D, 12/22/76D, 6/19/79I, 10/3/79D

Oil & Oil Products
3/10/70H, 9/10/70D, 11/24/70D, 2/24/72D, 2/15/73D, 2/27/73D, 3/13/73D, 9/13/73D, 10/15/73D, 11/9/73D, 11/13/73D, 11/26/73D, 12/13/73D, 12/27/73D, 12/30/73D, 1/9/74D, 1/11/74D, 1/16/74D, 3/27/74D, 5/15/74D, 5/23/74D, 6/1/74D, 8/22/74D, 10/23/74A, 11/22/74D, 12/4/74D, 2/4/75D, 2/5/75D, 4/10/75D, 11/20/75D, 12/18/75D, 6/15/76D, 4/10/79D, 6/29/79D, 9/21/79D

Olympic Games
7/27/73J, 1/17/75J, 1/28/76J, 7/14/76J, 7/15/76J, 7/16/76J, 7/17/76J, 8/1/76J

Ontario
1/18/74D

Paper & Paper Products
7/15/75D, 7/16/75D, 10/12/75D

Parks & Recreation Areas
7/16/72D

Pipelines
8/13/70D, 6/9/72H, 1/16/74D, 6/15/76D, 8/8/77I, 9/8/77I, 3/3/79D, 4/10/79D

Police
9/26/71D, 7/21/72D

Politics & Government
9/24/70D, 3/4/71J, 4/23/71D, 4/24/71D, 4/29/71D, 6/10/71D, 6/14/71D, 1/28/72D, 11/15/72D, 11/16/72D, 11/27/72D, 1/4/73D, 1/11/73D, 9/10/73D, 12/10/73D, 1/18/74D, 5/8/74D, 8/8/74D, 9/11/75D, 9/27/75D, 11/9/75D, 2/6/76D, 2/23/76D, 6/28/76D, 9/14/76D, 11/25/76D, 12/1/76D, 4/20/77D, 9/6/77D, 9/16/77D, 10/17/77D, 1/30/78D, 2/2/78D, 9/8/78D, 12/9/78D, 12/14/78D, 3/30/79D, 6/4/79D, 8/16/79D, 11/6/79D, 11/21/79D, 12/14/79D

Population
3/25/77D

Postal System
3/27/70D, 5/7/70D, 5/27/70D, 6/21/70D, 7/6/70D, 8/17/70D, 8/19/70D, 9/4/70D, 4/19/74D, 4/26/74D, 10/21/75D, 12/3/75D, 12/12/75D, 11/9/77D, 10/25/78D, 5/7/79D

Press
9/18/71D, 2/25/76H, 3/17/78D

Prisons & Prisoners
4/18/71D, 6/11/75D, 7/2/75D, 9/27/76D, 10/1/76D, 6/7/77D, 8/5/77D

Privacy, Invasion of
12/10/72D

Provinces
9/13/74D, 8/22/75D

Public Opinion
12/9/78D, 12/14/78D

Quebec
4/29/70D, 1/18/71D, 4/7/71D, 9/26/71D, 3/28/72D, 4/22/72D, 5/19/72D, 6/6/72D, 6/11/72D, 9/27/73D, 3/14/74D, 7/30/74D, 2/20/76D, 4/13/76D, 1/25/77D, 4/1/77D, 4/5/77D, 5/27/77D, 9/20/77D, 11/30/77D, 12/11/77D, 4/25/78D, 5/31/78D, 6/8/78D, 6/14/78D, 7/1/78D, 7/22/78D, 5/26/79D, 12/13/79D

Quebec Separatists
10/5/70D, 10/6/70D, 10/10/70D, 10/16/70D, 10/18/70D, 11/7/70D, 11/21/70D, 11/23/70A, 12/1/70D, 12/3/70D, 12/28/70D, 1/13/71D, 3/13/71D, 5/20/71D, 4/7/72D, 2/22/73D, 11/15/76D, 11/25/76D, 12/1/76D, 1/28/77D, 2/22/77G, 4/18/77D, 4/28/77D, 4/29/77D, 5/13/77B, 5/29/77D, 7/14/77D, 8/24/77D, 11/3/77B, 11/4/77D, 6/6/78D, 6/23/78D, 12/3/78D, 1/16/79D, 1/25/79D, 2/13/79D, 6/21/79D, 8/7/79D, 11/1/79D, 11/2/79D, 11/8/79D, 11/26/79D

Quebec Terrorists
1/9/78D

Race Relations
4/21/77D

Radiation Hazards
1/24/78I, 1/27/78I, 1/30/78I, 2/4/78I

Radio
7/20/77D

Railroads
4/5/71D, 7/26/73D, 8/27/73D, 9/2/73D, 1/16/74D, 1/29/76D

Rhodesia
9/23/75D

Riots & Violence
4/18/71D, 10/29/71D, 6/3/76D

Royal Mounted Police Probe
7/6/77D, 8/17/77D, 10/3/77D, 10/28/77D, 11/2/77D, 11/9/77D, 11/14/77D, 11/23/77D, 12/11/77D, 1/9/78D, 1/11/78D, 2/10/78B, 2/21/78D, 4/24/78D, 5/31/78D, 7/25/78D

Scandals
1/30/78D

Science
1/17/70I, 1/30/71I

Ships & Shipping
6/9/71D, 9/1/72D, 4/5/74D, 3/27/75D, 4/28/75D

Shoes & Boots
7/16/74D

South Africa, Republic of
12/19/77D

Sports
2/13/72J, 10/28/72J, 11/25/73J, 11/24/74J

Stocks & Bonds
3/20/73D

Strikes & Strike Threats
6/21/70D, 7/6/70D, 8/17/70D, 9/15/70H, 10/16/70D, 1/25/71D, 7/12/71D, 9/26/71D, 1/17/72D, 1/27/72D, 3/28/72D, 4/22/72D, 5/15/72D, 5/19/72D, 7/21/72D, 9/1/72D, 7/26/73D, 8/27/73D, 9/2/73D, 4/5/74D, 4/19/74D, 4/26/74D, 8/26/74D, 10/11/74D, 11/3/74D, 1/17/75J, 2/17/75D, 3/9/75D, 3/19/75D, 3/27/75D, 4/19/75D, 4/28/75D, 7/15/75D, 7/16/75D, 10/10/75D, 10/12/75D, 10/21/75D, 12/3/75D, 12/12/75D, 6/20/76D, 6/28/76D, 10/14/76D, 2/16/77D, 8/7/77D, 8/10/77D, 10/25/78D, 5/7/79D

Student Protests
3/10/72D, 3/20/72D

Sweeteners, Artificial
4/19/77I

Taxation
10/14/71D, 12/17/71D, 1/16/73D, 4/18/73D, 7/4/73D, 7/16/74D, 6/8/78D, 6/14/78D

Teachers' Strike
1/16/76D, 4/13/76D, 8/31/76D, 10/1/76D

Television
5/22/70D, 9/27/73D, 7/20/77D, 10/17/77D

Tobacco
9/21/71D

Tornadoes
4/4/74I

Treaties
12/3/71D

U.S. Relations
2/2/70D, 4/24/70D, 6/23/70H, 11/20/70D, 11/24/70D, 9/7/71D, 11/4/71D, 12/3/71D, 12/6/71D, 4/15/72D, 7/26/72D, 8/28/72D, 10/17/72D, 12/10/72D, 9/10/73D, 11/13/73D, 12/17/73D, 2/1/74D, 2/28/74D, 5/8/74D, 6/1/74D, 9/25/74D, 12/4/74D, 1/23/75D, 3/18/75D, 5/9/75D, 10/15/75D, 11/27/75D, 12/15/75D, 3/22/76D, 7/26/76D, 10/4/76D, 2/22/77G, 1/17/78D, 6/2/78D, 4/10/79D, 8/26/79D

Uganda
8/24/72D, 2/6/73C

Unemployment
3/16/72D, 10/10/72D, 2/6/73D, 10/22/74D, 2/11/75D, 4/8/75D, 9/9/75D, 2/8/77D, 12/4/77D, 1/10/78D, 7/11/78D, 12/8/78D

Union of Soviet Socialist Republics (USSR)
1/24/71D, 1/30/71I, 5/19/71D, 5/28/71D, 10/17/71D, 10/26/71C, 7/19/74D, 5/9/75D, 7/23/75D, 8/13/75D, 8/28/75D, 9/26/75D, 10/10/75D, 6/17/76D, 1/24/78I, 1/27/78I, 1/30/78I, 2/4/78I, 2/9/78D, 2/10/78B, 2/13/78I, 3/15/78B, 3/17/78D, 11/13/78D

United Nations (U.N.)
11/21/70D, 11/23/70A

Uranium
3/2/70D, 3/19/70D, 5/5/70D, 7/12/77I, 11/15/77I, 12/20/77I, 9/13/78I

USSR Grain Sale
2/29/72D, 4/9/73D

Vietnam, North
2/7/73E

Vietnam, Socialist Republic of
3/29/79D

Vietnam War
3/3/73E, 4/9/73E, 4/13/73E, 5/29/73E, 7/15/73E, 7/31/73E

Vietnamese Refugees
2/12/79E, 6/21/79A, 7/18/79D

Wage Controls
6/5/70D, 12/15/75D, 3/31/77D, 8/17/77D, 5/24/79D

Water Pollution
6/23/70H, 9/8/70D, 11/20/70D, 1/14/71D, 6/10/71H, 4/15/72D

Waters, Territorial
4/8/70D, 4/14/70G, 4/22/70D

Wheat
7/31/73D, 5/31/74D, 6/26/74D, 8/26/74D, 10/11/74D, 7/17/75D, 7/24/75D, 8/13/75D, 10/10/75D, 12/8/76D, 2/25/77A, 4/3/79D

Wiretapping
1/14/74D, 11/3/77D

Women
12/7/70D, 11/27/72D, 1/18/74D

Yugoslavia
11/8/71B

Yukon Territory
7/6/78D

CANADAIR Ltd.
11/28/75D

CANADEO, Tony
2/5/74J

CANADIAN-American Committee
7/26/76D

CANADIAN National Railways
4/5/71D

CANADIAN Pacific Railroad
4/5/71D

CANADIAN Panarctic Oils Ltd.
7/9/71D

CANALAS, Maximo
11/8/71D

CANARY Islands
12/3/72I, 3/27/77I, 4/11/77I, 10/18/78I

CANCER — See also Leukemia
Asbestos
12/16/74I
Blacks
8/28/75I
Bone
5/3/76I
Breast
3/12/71I, 9/28/74J, 9/29/74I, 8/23/76I, 5/10/77I, 6/6/79I, 9/11/79I
Cervical-Vaginal
10/24/75I
Chemicals
1/29/74I, 10/1/74I, 11/8/74I, 1/19/75I, 1/31/75I, 4/26/75I, 8/28/75I, 2/8/76I, 6/23/77I, 9/28/77H, 12/12/77I, 2/2/78I
Death Rate
4/7/73I, 11/6/75I, 1/28/76I, 2/8/76I, 2/17/78I
Demographics
6/3/76I
DES Hazard
11/9/71I, 1/24/74I
Detection
1/9/74I, 8/19/75I, 10/24/75I, 8/23/76I, 5/10/77I
Diet Relationship
1/28/74I, 3/25/74I, 3/2/79I
Estrogen Hazard
11/5/75I, 6/3/76I, 4/8/77I, 1/4/79I
Federal Aid
2/13/71I, 3/9/71I, 5/11/71I, 7/7/71I, 11/15/71I, 12/7/71I, 6/23/73I, 8/17/73I, 7/23/74I
Fiber Particles
3/27/75I
Ford, Betty
9/28/74J
Information Exchanges
6/24/72I, 6/30/72I, 12/14/75I
Liver
10/1/74I
Nitrate Hazard
12/13/70I, 10/18/77I
Occupational Hazards & Safety
10/3/77I
Pesticides & Herbicides
3/23/74I, 10/1/74I, 11/19/74I, 9/8/77I
Pollution-Related
4/23/75I
Psychological Effects
2/10/79I
Radiation Hazards
12/27/76I, 2/17/78I, 2/27/78I, 7/11/78I, 12/21/78I
Red No. 2 Dye
1/19/76I
Research
7/7/71I, 4/24/73I, 8/17/73I, 2/24/74I, 3/13/79I, 8/20/79I
Respiratory
3/27/75I
Skin
5/5/75I
Smoking Link
1/10/70I, 5/29/75I, 9/14/76I, 10/15/76I
Survival Rate
7/17/75I, 8/28/75I, 11/1/75I
Sweeteners, Artificial
1/9/75I, 3/9/77I, 5/13/77I, 11/4/77I
Treatment
11/15/72I, 8/10/73I, 5/5/75I, 5/2/77I, 5/6/77I, 3/8/79I, 6/6/79I, 6/18/79I, 9/11/79I
Uterine
11/5/75I, 6/3/76I, 1/4/79I
Virus
3/12/71I, 7/2/71I, 1/14/72I, 4/3/73I, 1/8/75I

CANCER Institute, National — See National Cancer Institute

CANDELARIA, John
8/9/76J

CANDIDATE, The (movie)
6/29/72J

CANDIDE (opera)
6/5/78J

CANDY
11/20/78H

CANNES Film Festival
5/16/70J, 5/26/73J, 5/24/74J, 5/28/76J

CANNON, Howard
11/5/73F

CANNONADE (horse)
5/4/74J

CANONERO II (horse)
5/1/71J, 5/15/71J, 6/5/71J

CANSINO, Jose
6/10/79D

CAPE Hatteras, N.C.
9/24/73H

CAPE of Good Hope
10/20/74G

CAPE, Rory
10/11/70J

CAPE Verde Islands
Independence
8/26/74C, 7/5/75C

Wiretapping
5/9/76F
Yom Kippur War
10/18/73G
CONGRESS Watch
10/28/78F, 11/15/78F
CONGRESSIONAL Record (publication)
5/2/72G
CONKLIN, Chester
10/11/71J
CONNALLY, Ben
6/1/70F
CONNALLY, John
Assassinations & Assassination Attempts
9/6/78F
Balance of Payments
11/11/71E
China, People's Republic of
5/7/71G
Foreign Aid
7/10/72G
Foreign Trade
3/27/73G
Japan
11/11/71E
Monetary Policy & System
2/9/72H
Pres. Advisor
5/10/73F, 6/20/73F
Presidential Election of 1972
8/9/72F
Presidential Election of 1976
7/27/76F, 8/9/76F, 8/23/76F
Presidential Election of 1980
1/24/79F, 3/4/79F, 12/27/79F
Republican Party
5/2/73F
Taxation
9/8/71H
Treasury Dept.
2/8/71F, 2/17/71H, 5/16/72H
Watergate Affair
7/29/74F, 8/7/74F, 4/17/75F,
8/20/76F
CONNECTICUT
Abortion
4/18/72F
Accidents & Disasters
1/18/78I
Colleges & Universities
9/19/70F
Congress (U.S.)
5/3/79F
Education & Schools
3/22/71F
Gasoline Rationing
9/6/79F
Medicine & Health
7/18/76I
Oil & Oil Products
7/26/73H
Presidential Election of 1980
5/16/79F
Press
10/20/76H
Riots & Violence
8/3/70F
Welfare
1/24/72F
CONNER, Albert
8/20/71G
CONNERY, Sean
12/17/71J
CONNIFF Singers, Ray
1/28/72J
CONNOR, George
1/15/75J
CONNOR, Reginald
12/19/73E, 10/31/74I, 10/14/75E
CONNOR, Roger
8/9/76J
CONNORS, Jimmy
6/19/71J, 2/16/75J, 4/26/75J,
7/5/75J, 9/7/75J, 2/1/76J,
6/29/76J, 9/12/76J, 5/15/77J,
7/2/77J, 1/5/78J, 1/8/78J,
9/10/78J, 9/9/79J
CONOMBO, Joseph
7/7/78C

CONRAD, Anthony
12/31/75H, 9/16/76H
CONRAD, Charles
5/28/73I, 6/22/73I, 10/1/78I
CONRAIL (Consolidated Rail Corp.)
9/30/74H, 2/18/76H, 3/30/76H,
4/1/76H, 8/29/76H, 8/4/77H,
3/23/78H
CONSCIENTIOUS Objectors — See under Draft
CONSERVATION — See Environmental Protection; Natural Resources; specific subjects, e.g., Forests, National
CONSIDINE, Robert
9/25/75J
CONSOLIDATED Edison Co.
10/2/72H, 7/14/77H
CONSTANTINE, King (Greece)
5/28/73B
CONSTANTINE, Lord
7/1/71B
CONSTELLATION (ship)
11/9/72G, 11/18/72G, 11/20/72G
CONSTITUTION Hall (Wash., D.C.)
12/3/77J
CONSTITUTION (U.S.)
Copies
1/20/70J
Equal Rights Amendment
8/10/70F, 3/22/73H, 1/18/74F,
1/21/74F, 2/7/74F, 4/21/75F,
2/13/76F, 2/18/76F, 2/25/76F,
3/1/76F, 1/18/77F, 1/27/77F,
2/8/77F, 2/11/77F, 3/1/77F,
3/22/77F, 8/26/77F, 11/14/77F,
2/17/78F, 3/20/78F, 5/26/78F,
6/22/78F, 8/15/78F, 10/6/78F,
1/26/79J, 2/21/79F, 9/22/79J,
12/5/79J
Fourteenth Amendment
11/22/71F
Proposed Abortion Amendment
5/31/73F, 10/22/76F
Proposed Amendments
3/23/76F, 1/8/79H, 2/4/79H
Proposed Antibusing Amendment
4/29/72F, 11/19/75F, 7/24/79F
School Prayer Issue
11/8/71F
Vietnam War
11/9/70G
Voting & Voting Rights
3/10/71F, 3/23/71F, 6/30/71F,
3/23/76F
Wash., D.C. Representation
8/22/78F, 3/19/79F
CONSTRUCTION Industry
Accidents & Disasters
8/5/74I
Labor
2/19/70H, 12/1/70H, 1/18/71H,
2/17/71H
Minority Hiring
3/14/70H, 6/6/70H, 7/26/70H,
10/24/70H, 2/10/71H, 4/23/71H,
5/5/71H, 6/3/71H, 6/4/71H,
6/17/71H, 9/3/72F, 1/12/73H,
10/18/73H
Prices
12/1/70H, 1/18/71H, 2/17/71H
Site Picketing
7/25/75H, 11/19/75H, 1/2/76H,
1/14/76H, 3/23/77H, 1/17/78H
Vietnam War
5/8/70G, 5/12/70G
Wage & Price Controls
3/29/71H, 5/14/71H, 11/26/71H,
2/22/72H
CONSUMER Federation of America
11/8/78H
CONSUMER Movement — See also Nader, Ralph; subjects
Appropriations
10/24/73H, 8/8/74H
Automobiles
2/7/70F, 9/4/70F, 2/20/71H,
10/14/78H
Aviation
1/31/78I

Banks & Banking
8/20/78H
Carter Policies
8/7/76H, 4/4/77H, 4/6/77H
Congressional Relations
11/8/78H
Corporations
5/22/70H
Government Departments & Agencies
6/9/70F, 12/1/70F, 12/2/70F,
9/27/71H, 10/14/71F, 10/5/72H,
10/11/72H, 4/3/74H, 4/6/77H,
4/27/78H
Law & Legislation
12/15/70H, 2/22/71H
Meat Boycott
4/7/73H
Medicine & Health
11/8/70F
Milk Price Supports
10/6/72H
Oil & Oil Products
6/1/79H
Selling Practices
3/26/76H
Sports
9/27/77J
Toys
10/5/78I
CONSUMER Prices — See under Economy
CONSUMER Protection Agency (CPA)
4/3/74H
CONSUMER Protection Safety Commission
8/28/73I
CONSUMERS Power Co.
7/29/74H, 11/9/79I
CONSUMERS Union
8/30/72H
CONTAINERS & Packaging — See also Labels & Labeling
Botulism
7/7/71I
Child-Proof
6/9/71H
Health Hazards
8/28/75I, 4/26/77I
Labor
4/16/77H, 10/31/77H
Plastic
4/21/76H
Prices
4/28/72H
Strikes & Strike Threats
3/1/76H, 6/6/76H, 7/31/76H
CONTE, Silvio
3/13/78G
CONTEH, John
10/1/74J
CONTI, Haroldo
5/5/76D
CONTI, Samuel
10/28/75F
CONTINENTAL Airlines
9/15/75F
CONTINENTAL Can Co.
4/28/72H, 2/21/73B
CONTINENTAL Grain Co.
10/5/74H, 7/21/75H, 8/27/79G
CONTINENTAL National Bank and Trust Co. of Chicago
5/25/78H, 9/21/78H
CONTINENTAL Oil Co.
12/2/70H, 2/26/76B
CONTRACEPTIVES — See Birth Control and Family Planning
CONTRERAS Escobar, Eduardo
11/9/76D
CONTRERAS Sepulveda, Manuel
3/21/78D, 6/5/78D, 10/9/79D
CONTROL Data Corp.
4/4/73B, 10/24/73H, 6/23/77I
CONVERSATION, The (movie)
5/24/74J
"CONVOY" (song)
1/28/76J

CONWAY, Jill
6/25/74F
CONWAY, Rosemary Ann
8/11/75E
CONYERS Jr., John
2/5/71G
COODY, Charles
4/11/71J
COOK County, Ill.
12/20/76F
COOK, G. Bradford
5/16/73H, 3/29/74H
COOK Industries Inc.
10/5/74H, 7/16/75H
COOK Islands
2/25/72E, 7/25/78E, 8/2/79H
COOKE, Cardinal Terence
5/20/72G, 8/30/72F
COOKING
3/3/77J
COOMBS, Charles
3/11/73A
COOPER, Charles
12/26/76A, 5/2/77J
COOPER, Donald
8/5/75D
COOPER, Gladys
11/17/71J
COOPER-Hewitt Museum of Design
10/7/76J
COOPER, Irving Ben
3/4/70J, 8/12/70J
COOPER, John Sherman
Cambodian Involvement
5/11/70G, 6/22/70G, 6/30/70G,
7/9/70G
COOPER Jr., Cornelius McNeil
2/13/71G
COOPER, Kenneth
4/15/78J
COOPER, Leon
10/20/72I
COOPER, Melville
3/29/73J
COOPER, Theodore
6/2/76I
COORS, Joseph
10/30/75J
COPE, James
2/27/75E
COPPER
Australia
11/18/76E
Chile
12/21/70D, 2/10/71D, 4/2/71D,
4/9/71D, 5/12/71D, 6/1/71D,
7/11/71D, 9/1/71D, 9/28/71D,
10/11/71D, 1/4/72D, 1/5/72D,
3/31/72D, 9/19/72H, 12/1/72D,
6/5/73D, 6/20/73D, 7/2/73D,
9/28/73D, 3/12/74D, 7/17/75G,
2/3/76A, 5/10/79D
Foreign Trade
10/20/78H
Haiti
3/24/76D
International Agreements
2/20/75A
International Development
2/10/70A
Labor
8/15/74H
Mexico
8/27/71D
Nationalization of Industry
9/1/71D, 10/11/71D, 1/4/72D,
3/31/72D, 9/19/72H, 12/1/72D,
7/17/75G
Panama and Panama Canal Zone
7/14/75D
Peru
4/21/70D, 12/31/73D
Prices
3/30/70H, 3/29/71H, 5/2/74H,
6/26/74A, 12/1/74A, 2/20/75A
Strikes & Strike Threats
7/25/71H, 7/1/77H

Uganda
2/25/75C
Water Pollution
11/13/71H
Zaire
3/16/77G
COPPER Exporting Countries (CIPEC), Intergovernmental Council of
6/26/74A
COPPOLA, Francis Ford
3/15/72J, 12/12/74J
COPTIC Church — See under Orthodox Churches
COPYING Machines
12/12/72H, 11/15/74H, 7/5/77H,
8/1/78H, 12/29/78H
COPYRIGHT Laws
International Agreements
7/23/71A
Music
9/9/74J
Revision
9/30/76J
Television
4/2/76J
Union of Soviet Socialist Republics (USSR)
2/21/73B, 2/27/73A
CORCORAN, Howard
9/16/70H
CORDERO Jr., Angel
5/4/74J
CORISH, Brendan
8/30/73B
CORMACK, Allen
10/12/79I
CORMAN, James
12/7/76F
CORN
10/24/74H, 2/4/75H, 7/21/75H,
10/29/75H, 10/13/76H, 3/29/78H
CORNELL University
Administration
2/16/77F
Astronomy
3/30/77I
Bombs & Bombing
2/22/70F
CORNFELD, Bernard
3/3/71H, 12/2/71H, 5/14/73B,
10/15/79B
CORNFORTH, John
10/17/75I
CORONA, Juan
6/2/71F, 1/18/73F, 2/5/73F
CORPORATE Executives Committee for Peace
6/24/70G
CORPORATE Responsibility, Project on
3/19/70H
CORPORATION for Public Broadcasting — See Broadcasting, Corporation for Public
CORPORATIONS — See Business & Industry; Multinational Corporations; Stocks & Bonds; specific names
CORPUS Christi, Tex.
11/30/70F, 8/19/71F
CORRIGAN, Mairead
11/27/76B, 10/10/77A, 4/15/78B
CORRUPT Practices Act
8/30/78G
CORRUPTION — See Ethics subheads under organization & subject headings
CORSICA
8/18/75I, 9/2/75B, 9/7/76B,
7/3/78B, 5/31/79B
CORSICAN Liberation Front
12/26/77B
CORSON, Dale
2/16/77F
CORT, Bud
1/27/72J

Coolidge, William
2/3/75I
Cooper, Gladys
11/17/71J
Cooper, Melville
3/29/73J
Costello, John
1/5/76B
Coughlin, Charles
10/27/79J
Courant, Richard
1/27/72I
Cowan Jr., Clyde
5/24/74I
Coward, Noel
3/26/73J
Cox, Wally
2/15/73J
Cozzens, James Gould
8/9/78J
Crawford, Joan
5/10/77J
Croce, Jim
9/20/73J
Crosby, Bing (Harry Lillis)
10/14/77J
Crosland, Anthony
2/19/77B
Cross, Milton
1/3/75J
Cunningham, Imogen
6/24/76J
Cushing, Cardinal Richard
11/2/70J
Daladier, Edouard
10/10/70B
Daley, Richard
12/20/76F
Daly, James
7/3/78J
Dam, Henrik
4/17/76I
Damas, Leon
1/22/78J
Darin, Bobby
12/20/73J
David, Donald
4/13/79F
Davies, Rodger
8/19/74B
Davis, Benjamin O., Sr.
11/26/70G
Davis, Meyer
4/5/76J
Dean, Dizzy
7/17/74J
De Chirico, Giorgio
11/20/78J
de Gaulle, Charles
11/9/70B
Dell'Acqua, Cardinal Angelo
8/27/72J
Dennis, Patrick
11/6/76J
De Valera, Eamon
8/29/75B
de Vaux, Roland
9/10/71I
de Vogue, Robert-Jean
10/17/76B
Dewey, Bradley
10/14/74I
Dewey, Thomas E.
3/16/71F
DeWolfe, Billy
3/5/74J
Dickinson, Edwin
12/2/78J
Diederichs, Nicolaas
8/21/78C
Diefenbaker, John
8/16/79D
Disney, Roy O.
12/20/71J
Doi, Peter Tatsuo
2/21/70J
Dorji Wangchuk, Jigme
7/22/72E
Dos Passos, John
9/28/70J
Douglas, Aaron
2/2/79J
Douglas, Paul H
9/24/76F
Dowling, Eddie
2/18/76J

Duclos, Jacques
4/25/75B
Dulles, Foster Rhea
9/12/70J
Duncan, Donald F.
5/15/71I
Dunn, Leslie
3/19/74I
Dunn, Robert
1/21/77F
Dunning, John
8/27/75I
Dunoyer de Segonzac, Andre
9/17/74I
Dupuy, R. Ernest
4/25/75G
Durieux, Tilla
2/21/71J
Dutschke, Rudi
12/24/79B
Duvalier, François
4/21/71D
Eames, Charles
8/21/78J
Earnshaw, George
12/1/76J
Eboli, Thomas
7/16/72F
Eccles, Marriner
12/18/77H
Eden, Sir Anthony
1/14/77B
Eglevsky, Andre
12/4/77J
Egtvedt, Claire
10/19/75G
Eisenhower, Mamie
11/11/79J
Elazar, David
4/15/76C
Elifas, Chief Filemon
8/16/75C
Ellington, Duke
5/24/74J
Ely, Paul
1/16/75B
Engelhard, Charles W.
3/2/71H
Enrique, Miguel
10/5/74D
Erhard, Ludwig
5/5/77B
Ernst, Max
4/1/76J, 5/21/76F
Etting, Ruth
9/24/78J
Evans, Dame Edith
10/14/76J
Evans, Walker
4/10/75J
Ewing, Donald
9/2/78J
Ewing, W. Maurice
5/4/74I
Fabing, Howard D.
7/29/70I
Faisal, King
3/25/75C
Faith, Percy
2/9/76J
Farley, James
6/9/76F
Farrell, James
8/22/79J
Faulkner, Lord Brian
3/3/77B
Feather, Lord (Victor Feather)
7/28/76B
Feldman, Abraham
7/21/77J
Ferreira, Joaquim Camara
10/24/70D
Fiedler, Arthur
7/10/79J
Fields, Sid
9/28/75J
Fine, Larry
1/24/75J
Fishbein, Morris
9/27/76I
Focke, Heinrich
2/25/79I
Fok, Vladimir
12/28/74I
Fonseca, Carlos
10/21/73D

Ford, John
8/31/73J
Ford, Mary
9/30/77J
Foster, Marcus
11/6/73F
Fowler, Herbert
1/2/77I
Fox, Jacob Nelson (Nellie)
12/1/75J
Franco, Francisco
11/20/75B
Franklin, Sidney
4/26/76J
Franzblau, Rose
9/2/79I
Frazer, Joseph
8/7/71H
Frederick IX, King
1/14/72B
Fredes, Pablo
10/30/73D
Freed, Fred
3/31/74J
Frick, Ford
4/8/78J
Friml, Rudolf
11/12/72J
Frisch, Frankie
3/12/73J
Frizzell, William (Lefty)
7/19/75J
Fu Tso-Yi
4/25/74E
Fuentes Mohr, Alberto
2/25/79D
Gabin, Jean
11/15/76J
Galanskov, Yuri
11/4/72J
Gallico, Paul
7/15/76J
Gallo, Joseph
4/7/72F
Gambino, Carlo
10/15/76F
Garan：！, John
2/16/74G
Gardiner, Arthur
12/4/75F
Gardner, George Peabody
9/18/76J
Garner, Erroll
1/2/77J
Gaughan, Michael
6/3/74B
Genn, Leo
1/26/78J
Gentele, Goeran
7/18/72J
Geraghty, Agnes
3/1/74J
Gerard, Ralph Waldo
2/17/74I
Getty, II, George F.
6/6/73J
Getty, J. Paul
6/6/76H
Giancana, Sam
6/20/75F
Gilbert, Billy
9/23/71J
Gilliam, Jim (Junior)
10/8/78J
Gilson, Etienne
9/19/78J
Gipson, Lawrence Henry
9/26/71J
Godel, Kurt
1/14/78I
Goldberg, Rueben L.
12/7/70J
Goldfinger, Nathaniel
7/22/76H
Goldmark, Peter
12/7/77I
Goldwyn, Samuel
1/31/74J
Goodman, Paul
8/2/72J
Gorbatov, Alexander Vasilevich
12/11/73B
Gordin, Burton
3/20/70F
Gordon, Max
11/2/78J

Goslin, Leon A. (Goose)
5/15/71J
Gottlieb, Adolph
3/4/74J
Goulart, Joao
12/6/76D
Grable, Betty
7/2/73J
Grant, Jane
3/16/72J
Grechko, Andrei
4/27/76B
Griffith, Corinne
7/13/79J
Grove, Robert Moses (Lefty)
5/23/75J
Gubenkian, Nubar
1/10/72J
Guggenheim, Harry F.
1/22/71J
Guggenheim, Olga Hirsch
2/14/70J
Guggenheim, Peggy
12/23/79J
Gunther, John
5/29/70J
Gurfein, Murray
12/16/79J
Gutt, Camille
6/7/71A
Haas, George
6/30/74J
Haile Selassie
8/27/75C
Halder, Franz
4/2/72B
Haley, Harold
8/15/70F
Hall, Leonard
6/2/79F
Halliday, Richard
3/3/73J
Hambro, Edvard
2/1/77B
Hamer, Fannie Lou
3/14/77F
Hansen, Alvin
6/6/75H
Harbage, Alfred
5/2/76J
Harlan, John Marshall
12/29/71F
Harridge, Will
4/9/71J
Harris, Jed
11/15/79J
Hart, Philip
12/26/76F
Hart, Thomas C.
7/4/71G
Hartnell, Norman
6/8/79J
Harvey, Laurence
11/25/73J
Hasselblad, Victor
8/6/78I
Hatton, Raymond
10/21/71J
Hawks, Howard
12/26/77J
Hayakawa, Sessue
11/23/73J
Hayden, Carl
1/25/72F
Haynes, Henry D
8/7/71J
Hayward, Leland
3/18/71J
Hayward, Susan
3/14/75J
Hebert, F. Edward
12/29/79F
Heckel, Erich
1/27/70J
Heenan, Cardinal John Carmel
11/7/75J
Heezen, Bruce
6/21/77I
Heflin, Van
7/23/71J
Heidegger, Martin
5/26/76J
Henry, Bill
4/13/70J
Herbert, Adrian
8/17/71I

Herbert, Sir Alan P.
11/11/71J
Hernandez Castellon, Bernal
12/12/75D
Hershey, Lewis
5/20/77G
Heschel, Abraham Joshua
12/23/72J
Heyer, Georgette
7/4/74J
Hickenlooper, Bourke R.
9/4/71F
Hill, Graham
11/30/75J
Hill, Harry W.
7/19/71G
Hodges, Gil
4/2/72J
Hodgins, Eric
1/7/71J
Hoffman, Joseph
12/8/74I
Hoffman, Paul
10/8/74G
Hofstadter, Richard
10/24/70J
Hogan, Frank
4/2/74F
Holloway, Emory
7/30/77J
Homolka, Oscar
1/27/78J
Hoover, J. Edgar
5/2/72F
Hornblow Jr., Arthur
7/17/76J
Horton, Tim
2/21/74J
Howard, Moe
5/4/75J
Howe, James Wong
7/12/76J
Howe, Quincy
2/17/77J
Hubbard, Robert (Cal)
10/17/77J
Hughes-Hallet, John
4/6/72B
Hull, Henry
3/8/77J
Hull, Lytle
12/11/76J
Humphrey, Hubert
1/13/78F
Hunt, H.L.
11/29/74H
Hunter, Ivory Joe
11/8/74J
Huntley, Chet
3/20/74J
Hurok, Sol
3/5/74J
Husseini, Haj Amin el-
7/4/74C
Hutchins, Robert Maynard
5/14/77F
Hutton, Barbara
5/11/79J
Huxley, Julian
2/14/75J
Inge, William
6/10/73J
Iselin, Philip
12/28/76J
Ismail, Ahmed
12/25/74C
Jackson, George
8/21/71F
Jackson, Mahalia
1/27/72J
Jenkins, Will E.
6/8/75J
Johnson, Howard
6/20/72H
Johnson, Jerome
6/28/71F
Johnston, Perrin
5/2/75I
Jonas, Franz
4/24/74B
Jones, Bobby (Robert T.)
12/18/71J
Jones, James
5/9/77J
Joplin, Janis
10/4/70J

Jumblat, Kamal
3/16/77C
Kadar, Jan
6/1/79J
Kahn, Ben
2/5/76H
Kahn, Louis
3/17/74I
Kaid, Ahmed
3/5/78C
Kallen, Horace
2/16/74F
Kampmann, Viggo
6/3/76B
Kanafani, Ghassan
7/8/72C
Kantor, MacKinley
10/11/77J
Kappler, Herbert
2/9/78B
Karsavina, Tamara
5/26/78J
Kchessinska, Mathilde
11/7/71J
Kempe, Rudolf
5/11/76J
Kennedy, Walter
6/26/77J
Kent, Rockwell
3/13/71J
Kenyatta, Jomo
8/22/78C
Kerensky, Alexander
6/11/70B
Khachaturian, Aram
5/1/78J
Khrushchev, Nikita
9/11/71B
Kipnis, Alexander
5/14/78J
Kirchwey, Freda
1/3/76J
Kirk, Norman
8/31/74E
Kleinschmidt, Edward
8/9/77I
Klemperer, Otto
7/7/73J
Konenkov, Sergei
10/9/71J
Konev, Ivan Stepanovich
5/21/73B
Krock, Arthur
4/12/74J
Krylov, Nikolai
2/9/72B
Kulakov, Fyodor
7/16/78B
Kuznetsov, Anatoly
6/13/79J
Laddon, I.M.
1/14/76I
Lalique, Marc
10/26/77J
Lang, Fritz
8/2/76J
Lang, Walter
2/8/72J
Langlois, Henri
1/12/77J
Lapchick, Joe
8/10/70J
Laporte, Pierre
10/18/70D
Laurence, Wiliam
3/19/77I
Lavon, Pinhas
1/24/76C
Lawrence, David
2/11/73J
Lawrence, Majorie
1/13/79J
Leaf, Munro
12/21/76J
Leahy, Frank
6/21/73J
Leavis, F.R.
4/14/78J
Lee, Gypsy Rose
4/26/70J
Lee, Harold B.
12/26/73J
Lee, Manfred B.
4/2/71J
Lehman, Lotte
8/26/76J

Leibowitz, Samuel S.
1/11/78F
Leighton, Margaret
1/13/76J
Letelier, Orlando
9/21/76D
Levant, Oscar
8/14/72J
Leventritt, Rosalie Joseph
2/28/76I
Levy, David
3/1/77I
Lewis, Ted
8/25/71J
Lhevinne, Rosina
11/9/76J
Liddell Hart, Basil Henry
1/29/70J
Lieberson, Goddard
5/29/77J
Lilly, Eli
1/24/77H
Limon, Jose
12/2/72J
Lin Yutang
3/26/76J
Lincoln, George
5/24/75G
Lindbergh, Charles
8/26/74J
Lippmann, Walter
12/14/74F
Lisagor, Peter
12/10/76J
Liston, Charles (Sonny)
1/5/71J
Litton, Jerry
8/3/76F
Liu Shao-chi
10/31/74E, 1/28/79E
Lomax, Louis
7/30/70F
Lombardi, Ernie (Schnoz)
9/26/77J
Lombardi, Vince
9/3/70J
Lombardo, Guy
11/5/77J
Long, Herman
8/8/76F
Lowdermilk, Walter
5/6/74I
Lowell, Robert
9/12/77J
Lukacs, Gyorgy
6/4/71J
Lunt, Alfred
8/3/77J
Lupescu, Magda
6/29/77B
Lynd, Robert
11/1/70J
Lyons, Leonard
10/5/76J
Lysenko, Trofim
11/20/76I
MacPhail, Leland
10/1/75J
Magnani, Anna
9/26/73J
Mainbocher
12/27/76J
Makarios, Archbishop
8/3/77B
Mallowan, Max
8/19/78I
Malraux, Andre
11/23/76J
Mangrum, Lloyd
11/17/73J
Marcuse, Herbert
7/29/79J
Maritain, Jacques
4/28/73J
Markel, Lester
10/23/77J
Martinon, Jean
3/1/76J
Marx, Groucho (Julius)
8/20/77J
Marx, Zeppo
11/30/79J
Mashambanhaka, Terence
9/16/79C
Maslow, Abraham
6/8/70J

Mauze, Abby Rockefeller
5/27/76J
Mayer, Maria Goeppert
2/20/72I
McBride, Mary Margaret
4/7/76J
McClellan, John
11/27/77F
McClure, Lynn
3/13/76G
McClusker, Marilyn
10/2/79H
McCracken, Branch
6/4/70J
McDonald, Henry
6/12/76J
McGee, Frank
4/17/74J
McGinley, Phyllis
2/22/78J
McIntyre, Cardinal James Francis
7/16/79J
McKay, David O.
1/18/70J
McKeldin, Theodore Roosevelt
8/10/74F
McLaughlin, R. Samuel
1/6/72H
McMillan, Billy
4/28/75B
Mead, Margaret
11/15/78I
Medwick, Joe
3/21/75J
Melchoir, Lauritz
3/18/73J
Mendes, Francisco
7/7/78C
Menshikov, Mikhail
7/21/76B
Menzies, Robert Gordon
5/14/78E
Mercader, Ramon
10/18/78J
Mercer, Johnny
6/25/76J
Merrill Sr., John
6/10/75I
Messel, Oliver
7/13/78J
Messerschmitt, Willy
9/15/78I
Metcalf, Lee
1/22/78F
Meusel, Bob
11/28/77J
Mielziner, Jo
3/15/76J
Miessner, Benjamin Franklin
3/25/76J
Miguel, Carlos
10/8/74D
Mikoyan, Anastas
10/22/78B
Miller, William
4/12/76F
Millet, Fred
1/1/76J
Mindszenty, Cardinal Jozsef
5/6/75J
Mineo, Sal
2/12/76J
Mingus, Charles
1/5/79J
Mitchell, Martha
5/31/76J
Moe, Henry Allen
10/1/75J
Mohammed, Murtala
2/13/76C
Mohapi, Mapetla
8/5/76C
Moley, Raymond
2/18/75F
Monod, Jacques
5/31/76I
Monroe, Vaughn
5/21/73J
Montana, Bob
1/4/75J
Montgomery, Field Marshal Viscount
3/24/76B
Moon, Keith
9/7/78J

Moore, Marianne
2/5/72J
Moorehead, Agnes
4/30/74J
Moraes, Frank
5/2/74J
Morgan, Kay Sommersby
1/20/75J
Morison, Samuel Eliot
5/15/76F
Moro, Aldo
5/9/78B
Morris, Chester
9/11/70J
Morris, Glen
1/31/74J
Morse, Wayne
7/22/74F
Morton, Rogers
4/19/79F
Mostel, Zero
9/8/77J
Mountbatten of Burma, Earl
8/27/79B
Moureu, Henri
7/20/78I
Mundz Grandes, Augustin
7/11/70B
Murphy, Audie
5/28/71J
Murphy, Robert D.
1/9/78G
Murtaugh, Danny
12/2/76J
Nabokov, Vladimir
7/2/77J
Nagel, Conrad
2/24/70J
Nagy, Ferenc
6/12/79B
Naif, Abdul Razak al-
7/10/78C
Narayan, Jayaprakash
10/8/79E
Nash, John
9/23/77J
Nash, Ogden
5/19/71J
Nasser, Gamal
9/28/70C
Ndizey, Charles
4/29/72C
Neale, Earl (Greasy)
11/2/73J
Nelson, Ozzie
6/3/75J
Neruda, Pablo
9/23/73J
Neto, Agostinho
9/10/79C
Nevins, Allan
3/5/71J
Ngouabi, Marien
3/18/77C
Nicoll, Allardyce
4/17/76J
Niebuhr, Reinhold
6/1/71J
Nijinska, Bronislava
2/21/72J
Nikodim, Metropolitan
9/5/78J
Nikon, Archbishop
9/4/76J
Nilsson, Anna Q.
2/11/74J
Nin, Anais
1/14/77J
Nkrumah, Kwame
4/27/72C
North, Joseph
12/20/76J
Nurmi, Paavo
10/2/73J
Nye, Gerald P.
7/17/71F
Oberon, Merle
11/22/79J
O Dalaigh, Cearbhall
3/21/78B
O'Daniel, John
3/27/75G
Onsager, Lars
10/5/76I
Orr, Lord Boyd
6/25/71A

Ory, Edward ('Kid')
1/29/73J
Ospina Perez, Mariano
4/14/76D
Osusky, Stefan
9/27/73B
Ottolina, Renny
3/16/78D
Overney, Rene-Pierre
2/25/72B
Pagnol, Marcel
4/18/74J
Panagoulis, Alexandros
5/1/76B
Pao, Hem
2/24/75E
Paray, Paul
10/10/79J
Park Chung Hee
10/26/79E
Parks, Gordon
4/3/79J
Parsons, Louella
12/9/72J
Patchen, Kenneth
1/8/72J
Patman, Wright
3/7/76F
Patocka, Jan
3/13/77B
Paul, Alice
7/9/77F
Paul, Prince (Yugoslavia)
9/16/76B
Payne-Gaposhkin, Cecelia
12/6/79I
Payson, Joan Whitney
10/4/75J
Pearson, Lester
12/27/72D
Penfield, Wilder
4/5/76I
Penney, James Cash
2/12/71H
Perdue, Arthur
6/27/77H
Peredo, Osvaldo
10/12/70D
Perelman, S.J.
10/17/79J
Perez Alfonzo, Juan Pablo
9/3/79D
Perls, Frederick
3/14/70I
Peron, Juan
7/1/74D
Perry, Robert
6/10/70C
Peterson, Ronnie
9/11/78J
Phillips, Wendell
12/4/75H
Piatigorsky, Gregor
8/6/76J
Picasso, Pablo
4/8/73J
Piccolo, Brian
6/16/70J
Pickford, Mary
5/29/79J
Piston, Walter
11/12/76J
Pittman, Portia
2/26/78F
Polanyi, Michael
2/22/76I
Pompidou, Georges
4/2/74B
Ponce, Carlo
9/14/76D
Pons, Lily
2/13/76J
Pope-Hennessy, James
1/25/74J
Pospelov, Pyotr
4/24/79B
Post, Marjorie Merriweather
9/12/73J
Poston, Ted
1/11/74J
Potter, Charles
11/23/79F
Pound, Ezra
11/1/72J
Powell, Adam Clayton
4/4/72F

Powell, Clilan
9/22/77J

Powers, Francis Gary
8/1/77G

Prats Gonzalez, Carlos
9/30/74D

Presley, Elvis
8/16/77J

Prima, Louis
8/24/78J

Prouty, Winston L.
9/16/71F

Pyne, Joe
3/23/70J

Radford, Arthur W.
8/17/73G

Rado, Sandor
5/14/72I

Radot, Louis Pasteur-Vallery
10/9/70I

Radziwill, Prince Stanislas
6/27/76J

Raginsky, Bernard
4/26/74I

Raimundo, Jose
8/8/71D

Randolph, Philip
5/16/79F

Rattigan, Sir Terence
11/30/77J

Ray, Joie
5/13/78J

Ray, Man
11/18/76J

Razaf, Andy
2/3/73J

Reed, Sir Carol
4/25/76J

Remarque, Erich Maria
9/25/70J

Renoir, Jean
2/13/79J

Rethberg, Elisabeth
6/6/76J

Reutershan, Paul
12/14/78G

Reuther, Walter
5/9/70H

Revson, Charles
8/24/75H

Revson, Peter
3/22/74J

Reynolds, Milton
1/23/76I

Rhys, Jean
5/14/79J

Rickenbacker, Edward V.
7/23/73J

Rincon Quinones, Ramon
9/8/75D

Ritchard, Cyril
12/18/77J

Rito, Ted Fio
7/22/71J

Ritter, Tex
1/2/74J

Robeson, Paul
1/23/76J

Robinson, Edward G.
1/26/73J

Robinson, Jackie
10/24/72J

Roche, Josephine
7/29/76H

Rockefeller, John D. III
7/10/78H

Rockefeller, Winthrop
2/22/73F

Rockwell, Norman
11/8/78J

Rodgers, Richard
12/30/79J

Rodriguez Fabregat, Enrique
11/21/76D

Rollins, Walter
1/2/73J

Romero, Juan de Jesus
7/30/78J

Rose, Alex
12/28/76F

Rosebury, Theodor
11/25/76I

Rosenbloom, Carroll
4/2/79J

Rosenman, Samuel
6/24/73F

Roslavleva, Natalia
1/2/77J

Ross, Nellie Taylor
12/19/77F

Rossellini, Roberto
6/3/77J

Rostand, Jean
9/3/77I

Rothermere, Viscount
7/12/78B

Rovere, Richard
11/23/79F

Rubicam, Raymond
5/8/78J

Russell, Bertrand
2/2/70J

Russell, John (Honey)
11/15/73J

Russell Jr., Louis
11/27/74I

Russell, Richard
1/21/71F

Russell, Rossalind
11/28/76J

Rutherford, Dame Margaret
5/22/72J

Ryan, Cornelius
11/23/74J

Ryan, Leo
11/18/78J

Ryan, William Fitts
9/17/72F

Sabah al-Ahmed al-Sabah
12/31/77C

St-Laurent, Louis
7/24/73D

Salinas, Cesar Augusto
6/25/76D

Saltonstall, Leverett
6/17/79F

Sambu, Zhamsarangiin
5/20/72E

Sarnoff, David
12/12/71J

Sato, Eisaku
6/2/75E

Sawchuck, Terry
5/31/70J

Sawyer, Charles
4/7/79F

Schild, Alfred
5/24/77I

Schippers, Thomas
12/16/77J

Schoonmaker, Frank
1/11/76J

Schorer, Mark
8/11/77J

Schuschnigg, Kurt von
11/18/77B

Schuster, George
7/4/72J

Scopes, John
10/21/70J

Scudder, John
12/6/76I

Seaton, George
7/28/79J

Seiberling, Henrietta
12/6/79I

Selich, Andres
5/14/73D

Selwyn-Lloyd, Lord
5/17/78B

Shankar, Uday
9/26/77J

Sharp, Sir John
1/15/77B

Shaw, Lawrence (Buck)
3/19/77J

Shaw, Robert
8/28/78J

Shawn, Edwin Myers (Ted)
1/9/72J

Shearer, Douglas
1/5/71J

Sheean, Vincent
3/15/75J

Sheen, Fulton J.
12/9/79J

Sheldon, William
9/19/77I

Shipton, Eric
3/28/77I

Shiskin, Julius
10/28/78H

Shor, Bernard (Toots)
1/22/77J

Shriner, Eileen
4/23/70J

Shriner, Herb
4/23/70J

Shtemenko, Sergei
4/23/76B

Shumlin, Herman
6/14/79J

Shute, Denny
5/13/74J

Sim, Alastair
8/20/76J

Skinner, Cornelia Otis
7/9/79J

Smith, Gerald L.K.
4/15/76J

Smith, H. Allen
2/23/76J

Smith, Joseph Fielding
7/2/72J

Smith, Mayo
11/24/77J

Snow, Edgar
2/15/72J

Sobolev, Leonid S.
2/17/71J

Soong, T.V.
4/25/71E

Spaak, Paul-Henry
7/31/72B

Spencer-Churchill, Clementine
12/12/77B

Spingarn, Arthur B.
12/1/71F

Spivak, Robert G.
6/25/70J

Staff, Francis
2/12/76B

Stangl, Franz
6/28/71B

Stark, Paul
10/28/74I

Stehli, Edgar
7/25/73J

Steichen, Edward
3/25/73J

Steinberg, William
5/16/78J

Steiner, Max R.
12/28/71J

Stengel, Charles (Casey)
9/30/75J

Stewart, Bill
6/20/79D

Stokes, Maurice
4/6/70J

Stolz, Robert
6/27/75J

Stone, Edward Durell
8/6/78J

Strand, Paul
3/31/76J

Strauss, Lewis
1/21/74I

Stravinsky, Igor
4/6/71J

Sukarno
6/21/70E

Sullivan, Joseph M.
10/13/74J

Sullivan, Frank
2/19/76J

Sullivan, William
11/9/77F

Susann, Jacqueline
9/21/74J

Sutton, Frank
6/28/74J

Svedberg, Theodor
2/26/71I

Svenson, Andrew
8/21/75J

Swanson, Howard
11/12/78J

Taleghani, Mahmoud Ayatollah
9/10/79C

Tamm, Igor
4/12/71I

Taraki, Nur Mohammad
10/9/79E

Taruc, Pedro
10/16/70E

Tate, Allen
2/9/79J

Taylor, Sir Hugh
4/17/74I

Teferi Bante
2/3/77C

Terry, Paul H.
10/25/71J

Teyte, Maggie
5/26/76J

Thant, U
11/25/74A

Thompson Jr., Llewellyn
2/6/72G

Thorndike, Dame Sybil
6/9/76J

Tiger, Dick
12/13/71J

Tikhonov, Nicolai
2/8/79B

Tikhonravov, Mikhail
3/4/74I

Timakov, Vladimir
6/21/77I

Timoshenko, Semyon Konstantinovich
3/31/70B

Timotheos, Bishop
12/14/77J

Tiomkin, Dimitri
11/11/79J

Tobey, Mark
4/24/76J

Tolstoy, Alexandra
9/26/79J

Tomonaga, Shinichero
7/8/79I

Torres, Juan Jose
6/2/76D

Toynbee, Arnold
10/22/75J

Trardovsky, Alexander T.
12/18/71J

Traubel, Helen
7/28/72J

Traynor, Harold (Pie)
3/16/72J

Treacher, Arthur
12/14/75J

Truman, Harry S
12/26/72F

Trumbo, Dalton
9/10/76J

Tubman, William V.S.
7/23/71C

Tugwell, Rexford
7/21/79F

Tunaligil, Danis
10/22/75B

Tunnell, Emlen
7/22/75J

Tunney, Gene
11/7/78J

Turner, Thomas Wyatt
4/21/78F

Ulbricht, Walter
8/1/73B

Um Kalthoum
2/3/75J

Untermeyer, Louis
12/18/77J

Valachi, Joseph M.
4/3/71F

Van Doren, Mark
12/10/72J

Vasilevsky, Aleksandr
12/5/77B

Velasco Alvarado, Juan
12/24/77D

Velikovsky, Immanuel
11/17/79I

Vicious, Sid
2/2/79J

Vilim, Blazej
9/23/76B

Viola, Humberto
12/12/74D

Vipaowadi Rangsit, Princess
2/16/77E

Visconti, Luchino
3/30/76J

von Bismark, Otto Christian Fuerst
12/24/75B

von Braun, Wernher
6/16/77I

von Drenkmann, Gunter
11/10/74B

Wallenda, Karl
3/22/78J

Warner, Jack
9/9/78J

Warren, Earl
7/9/74F

Washington, Kenny
6/24/71J

Washington, Ned
12/20/76J

Waters, Ethel
9/1/77J

Watson, Arthur
7/26/74H

Wayne, John
6/11/79J

Webb, Del
7/4/74J

Weigle, Luther
9/2/76J

Weiss, George
8/13/72J

Welch, Leo
10/22/78H

Welch, Richard
12/23/75B

West, Sandra
5/19/77J

Westmore, George
6/23/73J

Weyland, Otto
9/2/79G

Wheat, Zach
3/11/72J

Wheeler, Burton K.
1/6/75J

Wheeler, Earle
12/18/75G

Whipper, Leigh
7/26/75J

Wiener, Alexander
11/6/76I

Wilder, Thornton
12/7/75J

Wilding, Michael
7/8/79J

Williams, David
1/8/75I

Williamson, Roger
7/29/73J

Wilson, Edmund
6/12/72J

Windsor, Duke of
5/28/72B

Winterhalter, Hugo
9/17/73J

Wodehouse, P.G.
2/14/75J

Wolchok, Samuel
1/16/79H

Wolf, Steve
11/21/77J

Wolfenstein, Martha
11/30/76I

Wolff, Robert
12/29/77J

Wolfgang, Myra
4/12/76H

Woodward, Robert Burns
7/8/79I

Wrathall, John
8/31/78C

Wright, Russell
12/22/76J

Wrigley, Philip
4/12/77J

Wriston, Henry
3/8/78F

Yablonski, Joseph
1/5/70F

Yakubovsky, Ivan
11/30/76B

Yang Sen
5/15/77E

Yangel, Mikhail K.
10/25/71I

Yarnell, Bruce
12/2/73J

York, Rudy
2/6/70J

Young, Chic
3/14/73J

Young, Whitney Jr.
3/11/71F

Zahabi, Mohammed Hussein al-
7/7/77C

Politics & Government
1/17/70F, 10/27/74F
Presidential Election of 1972
1/22/72F, 11/5/72F
Presidential Election of 1976
12/11/75F, 8/1/76E, 8/12/76F,
8/25/76F, 9/30/76F, 10/15/76F
Presidential Election of 1980
3/4/79F, 12/5/79F
Reagan, Ronald
7/1/79F
Religion
1/3/76J, 8/4/79J
Republican Party
8/20/77F
School Desegregation
9/8/73F
Terrorism
4/22/70F
Vietnam War
4/3/71G, 5/22/71G
Watergate Affair
9/2/73F

GALSTON, Arthur
5/25/71I

GALTIERI, Leopoldo Fortunato
12/31/79D

GAMASY, Mohammed Abdel Ghany el-
12/20/77C

GAMBIA
3/29/72C

GAMBINO, Carlo
3/23/70F, 10/15/76F

GAMBLING — See also Games, Lotteries & Sweepstakes
Baseball
2/19/70J, 2/24/70J
Legalized
6/19/70J, 4/7/71J, 11/10/78F,
2/26/79J
Protective Bribes
6/30/71F, 6/1/74J
Raids
1/1/70F
Sports
2/19/75J, 8/12/77J

GAMBRELL, David
2/1/71F

GAMES, Lotteries & Sweepstakes
Delaware
8/12/77J
Ethics
7/20/70J
Massachusetts
9/27/71J, 9/15/79J
Records & Achievements
1/27/76J

GANDHI, Indira
Australia
6/6/73E
Bangladesh
3/19/72E
Birth Control & Family Planning
10/3/77E
Censorship
10/21/76E, 2/26/79E
Communist Party
12/23/76E, 1/30/77E
Demonstrations & Protests
6/29/75E, 10/30/77E
Diego Garcia
2/7/74E
Dissent, Individual & Organizational
4/24/76E
Economy
10/11/72E, 11/12/73E, 7/6/74E,
7/1/75E
Elections
12/27/70E, 3/10/71E, 3/12/72E,
6/12/75E, 1/23/77E, 1/30/77E,
2/14/77E, 3/22/77E, 2/25/78E
Emergency Rule
8/4/75E, 8/15/76E
Ethics
6/12/75E, 8/6/75E, 8/10/75E,
9/19/75E, 11/7/75E, 4/1/77E,
4/7/77E, 12/5/77E, 12/18/77E,
1/11/78E, 5/15/78E, 12/19/78E,
12/20/78E, 12/26/78E, 1/24/79E
Expatriates & Political Refugees
4/24/76E

Family
2/14/77E
Great Britain
1/11/78B
Human Rights
5/15/78E
India-Pakistan War
11/16/71E, 4/4/72E, 7/3/72E,
7/14/72E
Internal Security
6/26/75E
Nationalization of Industry
2/14/70E
Nonalignment
2/12/72E
Nuclear Energy
1/19/70I
Nuclear Weapons & Defense Systems
1/14/76E
Pakistan
5/22/71E, 10/23/71E, 11/5/71E,
4/19/76E
Political Prisoners
8/4/75E
Politics & Government
3/29/70E, 11/12/73E, 7/1/75E,
10/17/76E, 12/23/76E, 2/2/77E,
10/15/77E, 12/18/77E, 12/27/77E,
1/2/78E, 1/3/78E, 4/12/78E,
11/5/78E
Public Opinion
5/7/71J
Riots & Violence
12/20/78E
Royal Family
12/15/70E
States
10/2/70E, 10/17/70E, 12/10/73E,
11/30/75E
Stocks & Bonds
7/6/74E
U.S. Relations
11/5/71E, 2/12/72E, 3/8/72E,
4/30/75E, 12/31/75E
Union of Soviet Socialist Republics (USSR)
6/11/76B
Vietnam War
4/30/75E

GANDHI, Mohandas
10/8/79E

GANDHI, Sanjay
12/23/76E, 4/1/77E, 4/18/77E,
5/5/78E, 2/26/79E

GANGES River
3/2/70E, 7/21/70E, 5/16/76E,
11/5/77E

GANNETT Co. Inc.
12/12/79H

GAPP, Paul
4/16/79J

GARAND, John
2/16/74G

GARAUDY, Roger
2/8/70B

GARBAGE — See Waste Disposal

GARCIA, Inez
3/4/77F

GARCIA Marquez, Gabriel
9/9/72J

GARDINER, Arthur
12/4/75F

GARDNER, Colleen
6/11/76F

GARDNER, George Peabody
9/18/76J

GARDNER, John
8/18/70F, 1/6/77J

GARDNER, Richard
1/7/77G

GARFUNKEL, Arthur
3/16/71J

GARLAND, Sean
3/2/75B

GARNER, Erroll
1/2/77J

GARNER, James
9/11/77J

GARNEY, Steve
11/12/74J

GARRIOTT, Owen
7/28/73I, 8/24/73I

GARRISON, Jim
6/30/71F

GARRITY, W. Arthur
12/18/74F, 12/27/74F, 1/27/75F,
5/10/75F, 12/9/75F, 2/24/76F

GARRY, Charles
6/2/75F

GARY, Ind.
6/16/77H

GAS, Natural
Accidents & Disasters
12/11/71I
Alaska
3/13/73D, 7/4/77D, 8/8/77I,
3/3/79D
Algeria
3/19/74A, 9/2/74C, 2/4/77H
Allocation
2/2/77H
Bilateral Agreements
9/29/70D, 7/9/71D, 5/19/72H,
7/31/72B, 4/8/74B, 4/26/74B
Canada
11/19/71D, 9/20/74D, 3/18/75D,
5/5/75D, 7/16/75D, 1/17/78D
Continental Shelf
8/22/78H
Denmark
4/8/75B
Distributors
8/28/75H
Exploration & Development
5/23/74D, 8/29/74B, 3/17/75H,
4/8/75B, 1/17/79I, 11/12/79H
Foreign Trade
11/19/71D, 7/16/75D, 2/4/77H,
1/17/78D
International Agreements
2/1/70B, 11/30/75E, 9/21/79D,
12/29/79D
International Incidents
6/29/73A
Law & Legislation
2/2/77H, 11/9/78H
Lay-Offs
1/22/77H
Liquefaction
9/2/74C, 7/31/78H, 1/5/79H,
9/27/79H
Mexico
2/4/77H, 9/21/79D, 12/29/79D
North Sea
8/29/74B, 7/9/76I
Offshore
12/16/71H, 4/10/73I, 3/17/75H,
1/17/79I, 11/12/79H
Pipelines
8/13/70D, 10/1/73B, 10/25/74B,
1/14/77H, 1/26/77H, 7/4/77D,
8/8/77I, 3/3/79D
Price Decontrol
10/22/75H, 2/5/76H, 6/9/77H,
9/22/77H, 10/4/77H, 10/13/77H,
4/21/78H, 8/23/78H, 8/24/78H,
8/26/78H, 8/31/78H, 9/11/78H,
9/14/78H, 9/27/78H, 11/9/78H
Prices
8/7/73H, 2/2/74H, 8/19/74C,
9/20/74D, 10/7/74H, 3/18/75D,
5/5/75D, 7/27/76H, 8/9/76H,
4/26/77A, 1/5/79H
Reserves
4/10/78H
Sales
12/30/73H, 1/14/77H
Ships & Shipping
2/2/77H
Shortage
1/13/73H, 9/6/73H, 8/28/75H,
1/21/77H, 1/22/77H, 1/26/77H,
2/2/77H, 2/7/77H, 2/9/77H,
2/17/77H
State-Federal Relations (U.S.)
3/17/75H
Trinidad & Tobago
11/3/78D
Union of Soviet Socialist Republics (USSR)
10/25/74B

GARNEY, Steve

Venezuela
8/2/71D, 8/26/71D, 5/6/74D
Weather
2/9/77H

GASCH, Oliver
6/19/74G, 6/6/79G, 10/17/79G

GASOLINE — See Automobiles; Oil & Oil Products

GATCH, Thomas
3/6/74J

GATES Jr., Thomas
3/22/76G

GATT — See General Agreement on Tariffs and Trade (GATT)

GAUGHAN, Michael
6/3/74B

GAUS, Gunter
8/12/76B

GAUVIN, Michel
3/11/73E, 5/27/73E

GAY Lib (Orgn.)
2/21/78F

GAY Rights — See Homosexuality — Civil Rights

GAZARRA, Ben
4/1/76J

GAZIT, Mordechai
1/11/77C

GEIBERGER, Al
6/20/76J

GEISEL, Ernesto
6/18/73D, 1/15/74D, 3/1/74D,
3/15/74D, 8/1/75D, 2/21/76D,
3/29/76D, 11/17/76D, 4/14/77D,
10/12/77D, 12/1/77D, 1/5/78D,
10/5/78D

GELBARD, Jose
10/21/74D

GELBER, Jack
2/22/72J

GEMAYEL, Bashir
12/27/76C

GEMAYEL, Pierre
5/10/76C, 5/11/76C, 8/7/76C,
11/9/76C, 12/28/76C, 5/16/79C

GENEEN, Harold
3/15/72F, 6/20/72H, 4/2/73G

GENERAL Accounting Office
12/25/71D, 8/26/72F, 8/27/72F,
5/19/73F

GENERAL Agreement on Tariffs and Trade (GATT)
Conferences
9/14/73A
Cotton
10/22/70A
European Economic Community (Common Market) (EEC)
5/15/73B, 6/26/73B, 12/22/78A
Organization
2/27/70A, 11/26/71A
Protectionist Policies
9/12/77A, 11/28/77A
Textiles
10/13/71A, 12/20/73A
Tokyo Round
10/24/73A, 4/12/79A
U.S. Relations
8/26/71A, 11/5/76A, 12/22/78A
United Arab Republic
4/22/70A

GENERAL Assembly (horse)
5/5/79J

GENERAL Dynamics Corp.
3/19/74H, 10/31/74G, 4/3/75B,
6/10/75B, 12/1/75H, 6/9/78G,
7/6/78G

GENERAL Electric Co. (GE)
Antitrust Actions & Laws
5/9/73H
Diamonds
5/28/70I
Job Discrimination
9/18/73H
Labor
2/3/70H

Merger
12/16/76H
Nuclear Energy
2/3/76H
Research & Development
3/2/78I
Water Pollution
9/8/76H

GENERAL Foods Corp.
1/20/77H

GENERAL Motors Corp.
Automation
3/4/72H
Consumer Movement
1/8/70F, 2/7/70F, 5/22/70H,
8/13/70F
Contracts
11/11/70H, 11/20/70H, 12/7/70H,
11/19/76H, 9/14/79H, 10/25/79H
Convertibles
4/21/76H
Corporate Policies
1/4/71H
Deaths
1/6/72H
Diesels
1/10/79H
Emissions Standards
1/14/70H, 9/24/72H, 6/17/73H,
1/10/79H
Environmental Protection
1/9/71H
Foreign Payments
8/4/75H
Foreign Trade
7/28/70G, 4/18/74D
Job Discrimination
9/18/73H
Labor
11/19/73H, 12/22/76H, 9/11/78H
Layoffs
12/28/73H, 11/8/74H, 11/29/74H,
12/18/74H, 1/9/75H, 1/29/75H,
2/14/75H
Nader Suit
9/4/70F
New Model Prices
9/29/70H
Prices
12/1/72H, 8/14/73H, 12/10/73H,
6/12/74H, 8/13/75H, 8/25/76H
Profits
5/8/78H
Rebates
11/13/79H
Recalls
1/22/71H, 12/4/71H, 4/4/72H,
5/8/72H, 7/3/72H, 2/18/75H,
12/17/77H
Safety Issue
1/13/72H, 5/4/78H
Sales
12/6/78H
Stocks & Bonds
3/19/70H
Strikes & Strike Threats
9/15/70H, 3/4/72H
Wage & Price Contols
8/29/72H

GENERAL Services Administration (GSA)
Appointments
11/13/78F
Corruption Charges
9/29/78F, 12/21/78F

GENERAL Telephone and Electronics Corp. (GTE)
1/27/77H

GENERAL Tire and Rubber Co.
5/10/76H

GENESCO Inc.
2/27/75H

GENETIC Research, Coalition for Responsible
3/7/77I

GENETICS
Aerosol Spray Hazards
8/28/73I
Artificial
6/3/70I, 1/6/73J, 2/27/75I,
12/6/75I, 8/28/76I, 3/2/78I,
10/29/79I

KREPS, Juanita
12/20/76F, 6/21/78F, 12/4/78B, 12/6/78B, 11/16/79H

KRIANGSAK Chamanand
9/7/78E, 2/6/79E

KRIMSKY, George
2/4/77B

KRISHNA River
9/3/70I

KROC, Ray
1/31/74J, 9/20/77J

KROCHER-Tiedemann, Gabriele
12/20/77B

KROCK, Arthur
4/12/74J

KROGH Jr., Egil
7/18/73F, 9/4/73G, 1/24/74F

KRUGER, James
6/25/76C, 9/2/76C, 9/17/77C, 9/19/77C, 5/17/78C

KRUISINGA, Roelof
3/4/78B

KRUMM, Philip
7/12/76J

KRUMPHOLZ, Kurt
8/4/72J

KRUPP GmbH, Fried
7/17/74C

KRUPSAK, Mary Anne
4/13/78J

KRYLOV, Nikolai
2/9/72B

KU Klux Klan
Armed Forces & Defense
8/29/79G
Demonstrations & Protests
7/8/78F, 8/18/79F
Federal Bureau of Investigation (FBI)
8/15/75F, 11/21/77F
Murder
7/12/78F, 9/20/78F
Riots & Violence
7/2/77F, 7/4/77F, 11/3/79F
School Desegregation
9/9/71F
Strength
11/11/79F

KUBISCH, Jack
8/13/74B

KUBRICK, Stanley
12/28/71J

KUCINICH, Dennis
8/13/78F, 12/28/78F, 6/9/79F

KUHN, Bowie
2/19/70J, 4/1/70J, 11/27/74J, 6/18/76J, 3/17/77J, 10/3/77J, 1/30/78J, 3/3/78J, 4/7/78J, 10/2/78J

KUKRIT Pramoj
3/19/75E, 1/12/76E, 4/4/76E

KULAKOV, Fyodor
7/16/78B

KUNERALP, Nekla
6/2/78B

KUNERALP, Zehi
6/2/78B

KUNG, Hans
2/20/75J, 12/18/79J

KUNSTLER, William
2/15/70F, 12/4/73F

KURDS — See under Iran, Iraq

KURILE Islands
4/14/77E, 4/16/77E, 9/26/79E

KURISU, Hiroomi
7/25/78E

KURUBO, G. T.
1/20/70C

KUSCSIK, Nina
4/17/72J

KUSER, Alfred
6/9/71D

KUWAIT — See also Arab League; Organization of Petroleum Exporting Countries (OPEC)
Arab Cooperative Moves
11/18/75C, 10/16/79C
Arms Sales
4/16/74B
Assassinations & Assassination Attempts
6/15/78C
Banks & Banking
11/18/75C
China, People's Republic of
3/22/71C
Deaths
12/31/77C
Economy
7/18/78A, 7/24/79A
Egypt
5/18/75C, 4/22/79C
Foreign Investments
9/12/74B
France
4/16/74B
Hijackings
12/23/73C
Hostages
9/8/73C
Hungary
12/4/74B
Iraq
3/20/73C, 3/29/73C
Jordan, Hashemite Kingdom of
3/4/71C
Lebanon
8/29/76C, 10/18/76C
Monetary Policy & System
3/14/75A
Nationalization of Industry
5/14/74C, 8/25/74C
Oil & Oil Products
1/8/73A, 5/15/73A, 10/21/73C, 1/21/74C, 1/29/74C, 2/10/74A, 2/21/74A, 5/14/74C, 7/18/74C, 8/21/74C, 8/25/74C, 9/30/74A, 10/1/74C, 2/19/75A, 12/1/75C, 2/26/79A
Palestine Liberation Organization (PLO)
6/15/78C
Politics & Government
8/29/76C, 9/6/76C, 12/31/77C
Saudi Arabia
3/29/73C
Terrorism & Terrorists
2/7/74C
U.S. Relations
7/21/74C
Yom Kippur War
10/17/73C, 1/21/74C

KUZNETSOV, Anatoly
6/13/79J

KUZNETSOV, Eduard
4/29/79G

KY, Nguyen Cao
Cambodia
6/6/70E
Elections
8/5/71E, 8/20/71E, 9/1/71E, 9/26/71E
Immigration
5/23/75G
U.S. Relations
11/15/70E, 12/8/70E, 7/18/71E

KYPRIANOU, Achilleas
12/14/77B, 12/16/77B, 12/18/77B

KYPRIANOU, Spyros
5/5/72B, 8/3/77B, 8/13/77B, 12/14/77B, 12/16/77B, 12/18/77B, 3/8/78B, 4/19/78B, 4/27/78B

L

LA IDEA (publication)
9/30/71D

LA MALFA, Ugo
2/22/79B

LA MAMA troupe
8/22/76J

LA NUEVA Provincia (publication)
10/22/73J

LABADIE, Robert
9/24/70D

LABANCA, Eduardo Rafael
5/11/71D

LABELS & Labeling
Aerosol Sprays
2/25/75H, 11/23/76H, 4/26/77I
Alcoholic Beverages
11/19/75H
Cosmetics
10/11/73F, 3/14/78I
Drugs & Drug Industry
6/4/74F
Food Products
1/12/71H, 6/4/71H, 6/13/71H, 3/13/73H, 9/4/75I, 9/21/78I
Soaps & Detergents
1/25/71H

LABOR — See also American Federation of Labor-Congress of Industrial Organizations; Economy; Government Employes; Migrant Workers; Unemployment Insurance; under country and industry headings; names of specific unions
Affirmative Action
1/18/73H, 5/3/73H, 6/12/75H, 10/22/76H, 5/31/77F, 9/7/77H, 10/11/77H, 12/12/78H, 6/27/79F
Antitrust Actions & Laws
8/6/79H
Blacks
3/10/70H, 9/2/77H
Campaign Contributions
10/2/72F
Carter, Jimmy
3/24/77H
Carter Policies
9/20/78H
Collective Bargaining
7/18/77H
Conditions
12/21/72H
Contracts
2/3/70H, 3/1/70H, 10/22/76H
Court Rulings
6/1/70H, 12/7/72H, 3/24/76H
Deaths
1/5/70F, 9/2/74H, 4/12/76H, 7/29/76H, 1/16/79H, 5/16/79F
Discrimination Charges
6/4/70F, 9/1/70H, 1/5/71H, 3/6/72F, 4/5/73H, 9/18/73H, 10/2/73H, 10/30/73H, 1/9/76H, 1/23/76F
Economy
9/7/70H, 8/19/71H, 8/13/74H, 8/29/75H, 10/2/75H, 1/10/77H, 10/26/78H, 11/21/78H, 5/8/79H
Employment Rate
12/3/77H
Energy Crisis
1/11/74H
Equal Employment Opportunity
1/12/70H, 1/25/71F, 2/6/71H, 3/8/71H, 5/12/71H, 6/1/71F, 9/16/71H, 1/26/72H, 1/30/73H, 1/8/74H, 1/31/74H, 6/3/74H, 10/17/74F, 11/12/74F, 3/24/76H, 11/17/76F, 11/28/76H, 7/18/77F, 12/6/77F, 1/23/78H, 6/4/78H, 8/8/78H, 10/14/78F, 6/5/79F
Federal Policies
6/6/70H, 6/9/70H, 10/21/78H, 10/27/78H
Government Departments & Agencies
12/30/72H
Inflation
9/20/78H
Jurisdictional Disputes
12/6/71H
Law & Legislation
10/6/77H, 3/16/78H, 6/14/78H, 8/7/78H, 10/21/78H, 10/27/78H
Layoffs
3/10/70H, 11/30/73H, 1/11/74H, 11/26/74H, 11/28/74H, 12/10/74H, 12/17/74H, 12/19/74H, 1/8/75H, 2/18/75H, 1/30/77H, 2/7/77H, 12/3/79H

Manpower Programs
12/16/70H, 12/21/70H, 3/10/71F, 6/2/71H, 6/19/71H, 7/1/71H, 7/12/71H, 8/6/71F, 5/16/75H, 5/20/75H, 5/27/75H, 5/29/75H, 6/4/75H, 6/12/75H, 9/22/76H, 6/15/77H, 3/12/78F, 12/3/79H
Medicine & Health
2/10/79I
Merit Wage Increase
11/9/72H
Minimum Wage
5/11/72H, 7/20/72H, 4/10/73H, 6/6/73H, 8/3/73H, 9/19/73H, 4/8/74H, 6/24/76H, 3/24/77H, 9/15/77H, 10/20/77H
Minority Hiring
1/27/70H, 3/14/70H, 7/4/75F
Occupational Hazards & Safety
11/17/70H, 11/24/70H, 12/29/70H, 12/7/71H, 4/7/72H, 6/6/72H, 10/1/74I, 1/19/75I, 1/31/75I, 3/27/75I, 3/31/75H, 3/2/76H, 7/1/76H, 11/5/76I, 12/9/76I, 9/8/77I, 10/3/77I, 12/5/77I, 2/2/78I, 3/2/78H, 4/26/78I, 5/23/78H, 6/19/78H, 11/13/78I
Philadelphia Plan
1/12/70H, 4/14/70G, 5/2/70H, 6/1/70H, 7/26/70H, 4/23/71H, 6/3/71H, 6/4/71H, 6/17/71H, 9/3/72F, 9/4/72F
Politics & Government
8/9/74H
Presidential Election of 1972
8/12/72F, 8/13/72F, 8/15/72F, 9/3/72F, 10/8/72G
Presidential Election of 1976
7/30/76H
Productivity
7/10/70H, 4/26/76H, 7/26/76H, 11/28/79H
Public Opinion
8/9/77H
Religion
11/2/76J, 6/16/77J
Seniority
3/24/76H
Strikes & Strike Threats
4/28/76H, 12/20/79H
Unemployment
3/6/70H, 5/8/70H, 6/5/70H, 7/2/70H, 7/22/70H, 8/3/70H, 9/4/70H, 10/2/70H, 11/6/70H, 12/4/70H, 1/8/71H, 5/7/71H, 6/4/71H, 8/30/71H, 10/8/71H, 3/3/72H, 4/7/72H, 5/5/72H, 7/7/72H, 10/26/72H, 11/3/72H, 2/2/73H, 4/6/73H, 11/2/73H, 2/1/74H, 10/6/74H, 10/13/74H, 11/1/74H, 12/7/74H, 2/7/75H, 4/4/75H, 5/3/75H, 5/29/75H, 6/8/75H, 7/3/75H, 8/7/75F, 8/30/75F, 11/8/75H, 1/9/76H, 3/5/76H, 6/4/76H, 7/2/76H, 8/6/76H, 9/3/76H, 10/8/76H, 11/5/76H, 11/15/76H, 12/3/76H, 12/5/76H, 2/4/77H, 3/4/77H, 4/1/77H, 5/6/77H, 7/8/77H, 9/2/77H, 3/16/78H, 7/7/78H, 9/1/78H, 3/8/79H, 6/9/79H, 8/3/79H, 11/2/79H
Union Shops
7/18/77H
Unionization
8/31/77H, 10/6/77H, 6/22/78H
Vietnam War
5/27/70G, 6/25/72G, 10/8/72G
Wage Indexing
9/15/77H
Wage & Price Controls
8/26/71H, 12/9/71H
Wages
11/8/70H, 2/23/71H, 2/9/73H, 2/23/73H, 7/19/73H, 1/8/74H, 10/24/75H, 7/23/76H, 11/28/76H, 6/4/78H, 10/19/78H, 7/29/79H
Watergate Affair
8/2/73F, 11/22/73F

LABOR Committee for the Election of McGovern-Shriver, National
8/14/72F

LABOR Day — See under Holidays

LABOR, Dept. of
Affirmative Action
1/27/70H
Age Discrimination
5/16/74H
Appointments
11/29/72H, 2/8/75H, 1/22/76H, 2/10/76H, 12/21/76F
Appropriations
1/26/70F, 1/28/70F, 8/16/72H, 12/19/75H, 9/30/76F, 12/7/77F
Construction Industry
10/24/70H, 5/5/71H, 6/3/71H, 6/4/71H, 6/17/71H
Economy
3/20/70H, 4/22/70H, 8/9/70H, 9/23/70H, 10/21/70H, 11/24/70H, 1/21/72H, 2/23/72H, 3/10/72H, 3/23/72H, 5/5/72H, 6/21/72H, 7/7/72H, 8/4/72H, 8/22/72H
Equal Employment Opportunity
11/17/76F
Ethics
3/12/78F
Inflation
1/19/70H
Job Discrimination
6/9/70H
Occupational Hazards & Safety
12/29/70H, 12/7/71H, 10/3/77I, 2/2/78I
Resignations
1/14/76H
Strikes & Strike Threats
4/28/76H
Teamsters, Chauffers, Warehousemen & Helpers of America, International Brotherhood of
2/1/78H
Unemployment
12/4/70H
United Mine Workers (UMW)
6/16/72H

LABOR for Peace
6/25/72G

LABOR Law Reform Act
10/6/77H

LABOR Organization, Inter-American Regional
1/16/79D

LABOR Organization, International (ILO)
Appropriations
8/24/70F
Developing Nations
6/18/76A
Finances
6/23/71A, 3/2/72A
Israel
6/27/78A
Organization
2/9/70A, 6/2/71A
Two-China Issue
11/16/71A
U.S. Relations
3/2/72A, 11/1/77A

LABOUISSE, Henry
12/13/79E

LADA (automobile)
11/13/78D

LADDON, I.M.
1/14/76I

LADIES Garment Workers — See International Ladies Garment Workers

LADY Sings the Blues (movie)
10/18/72J

LAETRILE
5/6/77I, 3/8/79I, 3/13/79I, 6/18/79I

LAFLEUR, Guy
6/12/78J

LAGOS
Ibos
2/1/70C

LAGUARDIA Airport, N.Y.C.
12/29/75F

LAGUNA, Ismael
9/26/70J

NATIONAL Catholic Education Assn.
12/12/70F

NATIONAL Collegiate Athletic Association (NCAA)
8/5/73J, 8/6/73J

NATIONAL Commission on Marijuana
1/19/72F, 2/14/73F

NATIONAL Economics Research Associates Inc.
10/11/74H

NATIONAL Education Association (NEA)
Mergers
2/1/70F
Organization
8/6/71F
School Desegregation
4/13/70F
Teacher Burnout
7/5/79F

NATIONAL Education Television
10/8/71F

NATIONAL Endowment for the Arts — See Arts, National Endowment for the

NATIONAL Gallery of Art
9/29/70J, 11/18/70J, 10/6/76J, 4/10/79J, 5/3/79J

NATIONAL Guard — See under Armed Forces & Defense

NATIONAL Gypsum Co.
7/15/75H

NATIONAL Humanities Endowment
7/9/77J

NATIONAL Institute of Arts and Letters — See Arts and Letters, National Institute of

NATIONAL Institutes of Health
7/18/72I, 4/17/73I, 12/17/74I, 6/23/76I, 3/8/77I

NATIONAL Iranian Oil Co.
1/19/74B

NATIONAL Labor Relations Board (NLRB)
Colleges & Universities
6/16/70H
Jurisdictional Disputes
12/6/71H, 3/26/78H
Medicine & Health
3/22/76H
Press
4/5/76H, 4/8/76H

NATIONAL Orchestral Assn.
7/16/79J

NATIONAL Parks — See Forests, National; Parks & Recreation Areas

NATIONAL Passenger Railroad Corp. — See AMTRAK

NATIONAL Research Act
7/12/74I

NATIONAL Review (publication)
7/28/71G

NATIONAL Science Foundation
1/26/73I, 5/6/75F, 8/15/77I, 10/23/78I

NATIONAL Security Agency
8/31/75G

NATIONAL Security Council
Counterintelligence
1/24/78G
Director
1/3/75G
Korea
8/19/76G
Power
3/7/72G
Spy Ring Issue
1/11/74G, 1/15/74G, 1/18/74G, 2/6/74G, 2/8/74G, 2/20/74G, 2/21/74G, 2/22/74G, 2/23/74G, 3/3/74G, 3/7/74G, 6/26/74G, 12/21/74G
State, Dept. of
6/28/75G
Wiretapping
12/16/76F

NATIONAL Socialist Party of America
7/12/77F, 1/27/78F, 6/12/78F, 6/25/78F, 7/9/78F

NATIONAL Symphony Orchestra
10/4/77J

NATIONAL Theatre (GB)
10/25/76J

NATIONAL University (El Salvador)
9/16/77D

NATIONAL Urban League — See Urban League, National

NATIONAL Westminster Bank
10/29/70A

NATIONAL Women's Political Caucus
2/11/73F, 5/27/76F, 7/12/76F, 7/14/79F, 7/15/79F

NATURAL Gas — See Gas, Natural

NATURAL Resources — See also specific types
Developing Nations
3/22/74A, 4/9/74A, 5/2/74A, 2/8/75A
Government Departments & Agencies
5/15/79H
Inter-American Development Bank (IDB)
4/3/74D
International Agreements
3/20/79A
Prices
5/27/75A, 3/20/79A
Shortages
8/28/74H, 10/13/76A
Stockpiles
3/15/73H

NATURAL Resources Defense Council
4/21/76H

NATURE Conservancy
8/19/71I

NATUSCH Busch, Alberto
11/1/79D, 11/3/79D, 11/7/79D, 11/16/79D

NAURU, Western Samoa
2/25/72E

NAVAJO Indians
7/26/72F, 8/30/74F, 8/13/75F

NAVAL Academy, U.S.
6/19/74G, 8/1/75G

NAVARRO, Ruben
2/12/71J

NAVON, Yitzhak
5/29/78C

NAVRATILOVA, Martina
4/5/75J, 6/14/75J, 4/2/78J, 7/7/78J, 7/6/79J

NAVY — See under Armed Forces & Defense; Ships, U.S. Navy; Submarines

NAVY, Dept. of
Appointments
4/7/72G, 9/13/79F
Resignations
4/3/72G

NAZIS
4/11/73B, 8/7/73B, 10/29/73D, 8/7/76B, 6/15/77F, 7/12/77F, 12/21/77F, 1/27/78F, 2/5/78B, 5/16/78G, 6/3/78B, 6/12/78F, 6/25/78F, 7/9/78F, 8/14/78B, 10/20/78F, 11/11/78B

NDIWENI, Kayisa
12/29/76C

NDIZEYE, Charles
4/29/72C

NDONGMO, Albert
8/27/70C

NE Win
1/2/71E, 4/20/72E

NEAHER, Edward
8/26/70A

NEALE, Earl (Greasy)
11/2/73J

NEAVE, Airey
3/30/79B

NEBRASKA
Bicentennial
7/4/76J
Courts
1/29/71F
Floods & Flooding
10/12/73I
Grasshoppers
7/31/78I
Presidential Election of 1972
5/9/72F
Presidential Election of 1976
5/11/76F
School Desegregation
8/10/73F
Tornadoes
5/6/75I
Weather
3/12/77I
Welfare
1/19/71F, 3/31/71F

NEBRASKA, University of
12/13/70I

NEEDHAM, James
4/27/76H

NEEL, Jr., Cleo
3/2/73C

NEELD, Gregory
2/2/78J

NEGROES — See Blacks

NEHRT, L.C.
4/1/75A

NEIER, Aryeh
2/5/77F

NEIL Memorial Award, Edward J.
2/18/71J

NEIMAN, David
3/5/70J

NEIZVESTNY, Ernst
3/10/76J

NELSON, Avi
9/19/78F

NELSON, Dale Merle
9/5/70D

NELSON, Harold
11/1/74F

NELSON, Larry
3/11/79J

NELSON, Ozzie
6/3/75J

NELSON, Willie
2/16/79J

NEMEROV, Howard
4/10/78J

NEMTSANOV, Sergei
7/31/76J

NEPAL
Accidents & Disasters
11/26/74I
Political Prisoners
5/9/79E
Politics & Government
8/17/72E, 2/24/75E
U.S. Relations
1/7/70E

NERUDA, Pablo
10/21/71J, 9/23/73J

NERVE Gas — See Chemical & Biological Warfare

NESSEN, Ron
2/27/73E, 11/6/74F, 11/15/74F, 4/30/75G, 4/15/76G

NETHERLANDS
Abortion
6/18/77I, 9/2/77B, 11/16/78B
Armed Forces & Defense
6/13/74A, 7/9/74B, 4/3/75B
Arms Sales
6/10/75B
Assassinations & Assassination Attempts
3/22/79B
Aviation
3/10/78I
Banks & Banking
3/7/75B
Bombs & Bombing
4/15/71B
Colonies & Territories
5/21/74B, 10/28/75D, 11/25/75D
Credit
6/4/73B, 12/6/73B
Economy
5/29/73B, 1/22/74B, 9/21/76B
Energy & Power
1/22/74B
European Economic Community (Common Market) (EEC)
1/22/72B
Foreign Payments
2/12/76B
Foreign Population
10/9/72B
Germany, West
9/2/76B, 11/10/77B
Great Britain
3/22/79B
Hijackings
11/28/73C, 6/6/74B, 9/4/76B, 9/5/76B
Indonesian Separatists
1/19/71B
Israel
10/21/73C
Land Policies
3/22/77B
Lockheed Scandal
2/8/76B, 3/4/76B, 4/13/76B, 8/26/76B, 8/30/76B, 9/1/76B, 9/2/76B
Middle East
11/4/73A, 11/28/73C
Missiles & Rockets
12/6/79B, 12/12/79A, 12/20/79B
Monetary Policy & System
5/5/71A, 5/10/71A, 3/12/73A, 9/17/73B, 2/26/75A, 7/7/75A, 12/30/77A
Narcotics
9/26/76B
North Atlantic Treaty Organization (NATO)
6/13/74A, 7/9/74B
Nuclear Energy
3/16/72I
Nuclear Weapons & Defense Systems
3/4/78B
Oil & Oil Products
10/30/73C, 11/4/73B, 11/30/73B, 12/1/73B, 12/5/73B, 1/12/74B, 6/2/74C
Political Asylum
12/4/78J
Politics & Government
7/6/71B, 7/20/72B, 8/9/72B, 5/11/73B, 3/22/77B, 8/25/77B, 9/2/77B, 12/19/77B, 3/4/78B, 11/7/78B
Riots & Violence
10/9/72B
Roman Catholic Church
1/19/70J, 8/27/70J
Royal Family
2/8/76B, 8/26/76B, 8/30/76B, 9/2/76B
Ships & Shipping
2/4/72B, 9/22/79B
South Moluccan Terrorists
12/2/75B, 12/4/75B, 12/14/75B, 12/19/75B, 5/23/77B, 5/25/77B, 6/11/77B, 9/7/77B, 9/9/77B, 9/22/77B, 3/13/78B, 3/14/78B
Sports
2/7/72J, 2/13/72J
Strikes & Strike Threats
2/4/72B, 9/22/79B, 10/13/79B
Switzerland
12/22/76B
U.S. Relations
12/7/77B, 3/10/78I, 4/22/79B
Unemployment
6/10/75B
Union of Soviet Socialist Republics (USSR)
5/6/70B
Uranium
3/4/70I
War Crimes
12/22/76B, 12/14/77B, 11/7/78B

NETHERLANDS Antilles
Politics & Government
6/5/71D, 6/17/77D

NETHERLANDS Central Bank
6/4/73B, 12/6/73B, 3/7/75B

NETO, Agostinho
6/14/72C, 11/11/75C, 5/3/76C, 7/29/76D, 10/8/76B, 11/27/76C, 2/8/77C, 5/31/77C, 6/20/77C, 6/10/78C, 7/21/78C, 8/19/78C, 11/11/78C, 12/13/78C, 9/10/79C

NETWORK (movie)
3/28/77J

NEUMANN, Bishop John
6/19/77J

NEUROBLASTOMA
3/24/72I

NEUTRON Bomb — See under Nuclear Weapons & Defense

NEVA, Franklin
12/17/74I

NEVADA
Acupuncture
4/20/73I
Crime
9/27/74F
Death Penalty
10/22/79F
Equal Rights Amendment
2/11/77F
Investments
12/19/70F
Nuclear Weapons & Defense Systems
9/21/72I, 12/21/72I, 9/26/74I, 12/21/78I, 1/8/79I, 2/14/79I

NEVINS, Allan
3/5/71J

NEVIS — See St. Kitts-Nevis-Anguilla

NEW Brunswick, N.J.
Riots & Violence
7/26/70F

NEW Deal
2/18/75F, 4/10/75J, 12/18/77H, 7/21/79F, 10/27/79J

NEW Democratic Coalition
1/29/72F

NEW England Confectionary Co.
7/15/71H

NEW Guinea — See Papua New Guinea

NEW Hampshire
Bombs & Bombing
7/14/76F
Democratic Primaries
8/8/71F, 3/7/72F, 2/24/76F
Demonstrations & Protests
6/24/78I, 12/6/78I
Elections
7/30/75F, 9/16/75F
License Plates
4/20/77F
Nuclear Energy
4/30/77I, 5/3/77I, 5/13/77H, 8/1/77I, 4/28/78H, 6/24/78I, 6/30/78I, 8/4/78H, 8/10/78I, 12/6/78I, 12/8/78H, 7/3/79I, 10/6/79I
Presidential Election of 1980
4/25/79F
Republican Primaries
3/7/72F, 2/8/76F, 2/10/76F, 2/20/76F, 2/24/76F
Taxation
5/27/71H

NEW Haven Railroad
6/29/70H

NEW Jersey
Accidents & Disasters
10/24/73I
Agriculture
6/21/75I
Blacks
12/10/73F
Church-State Relations
2/25/76F
Colleges & Universities
1/15/71F
Death Penalty
1/17/72F

Upper Volta
11/24/72B

War Crimes
2/11/72A

PONCE, Camilo
9/14/76D

PONS, Lily
2/13/76J

PONTI, Carlo
1/23/79J

PONTIAC (automobile)
12/17/77H

PONTIAC, Mich.
2/17/70F, 9/9/71F

PONTIFICAL Gregorian University
3/5/70J, 2/23/73J

PONTO, Jurgen
7/30/77B, 7/31/77B

POOR Richard's Universal Life Church
1/26/70J

POPE-Hennessey, Sir John
5/16/73J, 5/25/76J

POPE-Hennessy, James
1/25/74J

POPOVIC, Koca
11/2/72B

POPULAR Democratic Front for the Liberation of Palestine
6/23/74C

POPULAR Front for the Liberation of Palestine
3/29/70C, 9/6/70C, 9/12/70C, 9/15/70C, 9/29/70C, 5/31/72C, 7/8/72C, 7/11/72C, 8/2/72B, 1/31/74E, 2/7/74C, 6/23/74C, 2/11/75C, 3/6/77C, 7/14/77C, 3/8/78C, 3/28/78C, 6/1/79C

POPULATION — See also Birth Control
(for world population growth)
Decline Prediction
3/1/72A, 10/28/76A
Farm
10/5/76H
Foreign Statistics
8/5/72E
Growth Rate
9/1/70F, 3/1/73F, 5/18/76F
Municipal Limits
7/28/74F, 8/13/75F
Roman Catholic Church
3/13/72J
Rural Areas
2/13/71F, 2/1/72F, 2/24/77F
Shifts
7/23/74F, 2/24/77F, 12/3/78F
Statistics
11/30/70F, 4/1/75A, 5/18/76F, 1/1/79F
World Conference
9/20/72A, 8/19/74A, 8/30/74A

POPULATION Council
3/29/77I

PORGY and Bess (opera)
9/25/76J

PORNOGRAPHY
Advertising
6/6/77J
Children
5/23/78J
Convictions
2/17/72J, 4/30/76J, 10/21/79F
Court Rulings
3/1/73J, 6/21/73F, 6/24/74J, 2/8/77F, 3/1/77J, 3/16/77J, 5/23/78J, 7/3/78J, 7/21/78J
Demonstrations & Protests
4/13/77J
Interstate Prohibitions
2/15/73J
Local Standards
2/8/77F, 5/23/78J
Postal System
5/4/70F, 10/20/70F, 1/14/71F
President's Commission Report
9/30/70F, 10/24/70F
Theater
4/13/77J
Trials
3/6/78J

PORPOISES
5/11/76H, 6/11/76H, 11/10/76H, 6/1/77I

PORT Gibson, Miss.
8/9/76F

PORTER, David
5/14/74J

PORTER, Herbert
1/28/74F

PORTER, Howard
6/17/71J

PORTER, Marina Oswald
9/14/78F

PORTER, Rodney
10/12/72I

PORTER, Sylvia
10/26/75J, 1/25/76J

PORTER, William
2/1/73G, 9/25/74D, 12/15/75D

PORTUGAL
Accidents & Disasters
1/17/73I, 11/19/77I
Amnesties
10/17/75B
Angola
5/19/76C, 9/30/76B
Armed Forces & Defense
9/19/75B, 11/26/75B, 11/27/75B
Aviation
1/14/76C, 11/19/77I
Banks & Banking
3/14/75B
Bombs & Bombing
11/25/77B
Budget
3/15/78B
Censorship
6/22/74B, 9/8/75B
Church-State Relations
5/25/71C, 9/20/73C, 8/2/74J
Colonies & Territories
7/1/70C, 7/3/70B, 11/12/70C, 12/2/70C, 3/30/71B, 6/15/71B, 1/16/72B, 3/10/72A, 5/19/72C, 10/2/72A, 12/24/72B, 4/17/73C, 5/22/73A, 9/20/73C, 9/24/73C, 5/6/74C, 5/11/74C, 5/13/74C, 6/11/74C, 6/17/74C, 6/22/74B, 7/27/74C, 8/4/74A, 8/26/74C, 1/5/75C, 1/15/75C, 3/27/75C, 3/31/75C, 5/15/75C, 6/25/75C, 7/5/75C, 8/2/75C, 8/12/75E, 8/14/75C, 8/29/75C, 8/29/75E, 11/10/75C, 11/28/75E, 12/13/75E, 2/22/76C, 5/3/76C, 7/17/76E
Communist Party
5/12/70B, 9/29/71B, 5/22/75B, 7/22/75B, 8/17/75C, 10/1/76B
Constitution
4/2/76B
Council of Europe
9/22/76B
Coups & Attempted Coups
4/25/74B, 4/27/74B, 3/11/75B, 3/16/75B, 11/26/75B, 11/27/75B, 1/19/76B
Credit
12/10/71B
Czechoslovakia
6/27/74B
Demonstrations & Protests
7/19/75B, 9/25/75B, 9/30/75B, 2/1/76B, 6/22/77B
Dissent, Individual & Organizational
10/23/76B
Economy
5/25/74B, 6/22/74B, 12/20/75B, 3/13/76B, 9/9/76B, 10/8/76B, 6/22/77B, 10/26/77B, 4/25/78B
Elections
10/28/73B, 4/25/75B, 4/25/76B, 6/27/76B, 12/12/76B, 12/2/79B, 12/16/79B
European Economic Community (Common Market) (EEC)
10/7/75B, 3/28/77B
Expatriates & Political Refugees
8/10/76B, 8/12/76B
Foreign Aid
12/10/71B, 10/7/75B, 10/10/75B
Foreign Trade
1/16/73G, 12/17/75B, 10/8/76B

Germany, West
1/11/71B
Great Britain
7/15/73B, 12/17/75B
Guerrilla Action
3/10/71B, 7/10/73C
Guinea
11/22/70C, 11/28/70C, 12/1/70C, 12/8/70A, 12/11/70C
Internal Security
3/30/71B, 4/18/74B
International Monetary Fund (IMF)
10/26/77B
Labor
1/22/75B, 7/9/75B, 10/1/76B
Land Policies
2/1/76B, 9/27/76B
Land Reform
8/10/77B
Massacres
8/19/73C, 6/27/74A
Mozambique, People's Republic of
8/10/70C, 3/8/71C, 5/25/71C, 6/6/74C, 6/26/74C, 6/1/77C
Nationalization of Industry
3/14/75B
North Atlantic Treaty Organization (NATO)
6/19/74B, 10/20/74B, 3/25/75B, 5/23/75A, 5/29/75B
Political Prisoners
4/27/74B
Politics & Government
8/9/72B, 5/6/74C, 5/15/74B, 7/9/74B, 7/13/74B, 7/17/74B, 9/30/74B, 10/15/74B, 3/11/75B, 3/16/75B, 3/26/75B, 4/11/75B, 5/22/75B, 7/11/75B, 7/17/75B, 7/31/75B, 8/8/75B, 8/29/75B, 9/6/75B, 9/19/75B, 3/13/76B, 7/14/76B, 7/16/76B, 7/23/76B, 11/7/77B, 12/8/77B, 7/27/78B, 8/9/78B, 8/28/78B, 9/14/78B, 10/25/78B, 6/7/79B, 7/19/79B, 7/30/79B, 8/1/79B
Rebellion & Revolution
8/10/73C, 3/16/74B
Religion
11/2/70J
Riots & Violence
8/17/75C, 1/1/76B
Senegal
10/23/72A
Spain
5/23/70B
Strikes & Strike Threats
5/25/74B
U.S. Bases
12/10/71B, 3/3/72G
U.S. Relations
6/19/74B, 10/20/74B, 3/25/75B, 5/29/75B, 8/3/75G, 8/14/75B, 10/10/75B
Union of Soviet Socialist Republics (USSR)
6/8/70B, 6/9/74B, 8/14/75B
United Nations (U.N.)
10/2/72A, 10/23/72A, 8/4/74A
Vatican
7/3/70B
Violence
9/20/73C
Women
7/19/79B, 8/1/79B

PORTUGUESE East Africa — See Mozambique

PORTUGUESE Guinea — See also Guinea-Bissau, Republic of
7/12/70C, 5/19/72C, 1/20/73C, 5/25/74C

POSEIDON Adventure (movie)
12/12/72J

POSPELOV, Pyotr
4/24/79B

POST, Marjorie Merriweather
9/12/73J

POSTAL System
Central Intelligence Agency (CIA)
3/5/75G, 3/18/75G, 9/24/75G, 10/21/75G, 5/25/76G
China, People's Republic of
7/8/73G

Contracts
7/21/75H, 7/21/78H
Creation
8/12/70H, 7/1/71F
Finances
12/10/75H, 11/15/76H, 2/3/78H, 11/27/79H
Labor
3/3/71H, 7/20/71H
Law & Legislation
6/18/70F
Organization
12/7/71F, 3/1/78H
Pornography
5/4/70F, 10/20/70F, 1/14/71F
Rates
4/16/70H, 5/9/74H, 12/16/75H, 12/31/75H, 5/19/78H
Reorganization
4/16/70H
Resignations
10/29/71F, 1/8/75F
Strikes & Strike Threats
3/18/70H, 3/22/70H, 3/23/70H, 3/25/70H, 4/3/70H
Unsolicited Mail
4/15/70F

POSTON, Ted
1/11/74J

POSUN Yun
1/6/71E

POTIN, Felix
12/18/76B

POTOFSKY, Jacob
5/27/70G

POTTER, Charles
11/23/79F

POTTER, David
4/18/77J

POULTRY — See Livestock & Poultry

POUND, Ezra
11/1/72J

POUSSIN, Nicolas
4/3/78J

POVERTY — See also Social Services; Welfare
Abortion
6/20/77F
Civil Rights
3/2/71F
Deaths
6/12/72F
Education & Schools
4/10/72F
Federal Aid
12/17/75H
Government Programs
9/30/71F, 11/20/72F, 4/11/73F, 4/30/79F
Housing
12/16/70F
Hunger
6/21/74F, 4/30/79F
Legal Aid
6/12/72F, 1/31/74F, 7/25/74F
Level
4/9/79H
Minimum Income Guarantee
5/8/71F
Population Shifts
12/3/78F
Statistics
5/7/71F, 1/13/77F, 8/12/78H
World
8/23/75A

POWELL, Adam Clayton
4/4/72F

POWELL, Clilan
9/22/77J

POWELL, Enoch
5/24/76B

POWELL, Jody
9/22/76F, 11/15/76F, 9/7/78G

POWELL Jr., John
3/19/75F

POWELL Jr., Lewis
10/21/71F, 11/3/71F, 11/10/71F, 11/23/71F, 12/6/71F, 1/7/72F, 6/7/72F, 6/29/72F, 8/13/72J,

7/22/76F, 10/4/76F, 12/21/77F, 6/28/78F

POWER — See Energy; specific types

POWERLINE Oil Corp.
6/23/75H

POWERS, Francis Gary
8/1/77G

POWERS, Thomas
5/3/71J

PRADA, Francisco
9/25/71D

PRADO Dam (Argentina)
1/5/70I

PRAMOJ, Kukrit
6/4/75E

PRAPHAS Charusathien
8/15/76E, 8/21/76E, 8/25/76E

PRATER, William
3/26/73F, 6/3/74F

PRATS Gonzalez, Carlos
11/2/72D, 8/23/73D, 9/30/74D

PRATT, John
2/16/73F, 3/14/75F

PRATT, Mike
3/21/70J

PRAVDA (publication)
3/7/70B, 6/17/70B, 8/1/70B, 11/23/70B

PRCHLIK, Vaclav
3/26/71B

PREGNANCY — See also Abortion; Births; Menopause
Amniocentesis
10/20/75I
Armed Forces & Defense
7/7/75G
DES Hazard
11/9/71I
IUD Hazard
5/8/74I, 11/18/76I
Job-Related Issues
11/17/75H, 12/7/76F, 9/16/77F, 10/3/77H, 12/6/77F, 10/14/78F
Maternity Leave
1/21/74F, 12/6/77F, 3/20/78H
Miscarriages
8/4/78I
Radiation Hazards
7/11/78I
Smoking
1/16/79I

PRENDES Gutierrez, Orlando
10/9/70G

PRESBYTERIAN Churches
Bicentennial (U.S.)
5/21/75J
Black African Liberation
3/31/71J
Blacks
6/16/74J
Homosexuality
5/22/78J
New Branches
12/5/73J
Southern Split
8/9/73J, 6/25/74J, 2/11/77J, 5/30/79J
Vietnam War
6/19/70G, 5/22/72G

PRESCHOOL Education — See Education—Preschool; Head Start Program

PRESIDENCY (U.S.) — NOTE: Only general material is carried here. — See also names of specific presidents; Presidential Election headings
Armed Forces & Defense
6/9/71G
Economic Controls Power
7/25/73F
Executive Privilege
3/11/76F, 3/11/76G
Federal Bureau of Investigation (FBI)
12/3/75F
Fund Impoundment
10/17/72F
Libraries
4/20/75F, 10/20/79J

Floods & Flooding
7/5/70I, 7/3/75I
Foreign Trade
3/11/74G, 7/28/75G, 8/3/75B,
11/21/76B
France
6/19/70B, 1/30/73B
Germany, West
5/17/71B, 6/29/73B
Human Rights
2/14/77B, 4/13/78G
Hungary
2/24/72B
Israel
4/18/72C, 5/7/72C, 8/26/77B
Middle East
8/26/77B, 4/13/78A
Oil & Oil Products
8/1/79B
Politics & Government
3/28/74B, 6/15/76B
Textiles
11/12/76B
Travel
8/1/79B
U.S. Relations
3/11/74G, 3/22/74G, 7/28/75G,
8/3/75B, 11/21/76B, 4/13/78A,
4/13/78G, 12/9/78B
Union of Soviet Socialist Republics
(USSR)
11/22/76B, 12/20/78B, 2/21/79B
Vietnam, Socialist Republic of
1/10/79B, 2/19/79A, 2/21/79B
World Bank
2/18/77A
RUMOR, Mariano
2/7/70B, 2/28/70B, 3/27/70B,
4/17/70B, 7/6/70B, 7/8/73B,
7/22/73B, 3/2/74B, 3/6/74B,
6/10/74B, 6/20/74B, 10/3/74B
RUMSFELD, Donald
10/22/71H, 4/11/72H, 5/1/72H,
10/3/72H, 11/3/75F, 11/18/75G,
1/27/76G, 5/2/76G, 1/18/77G
RUNCIE, Robert
9/7/79J
RUNCORN, S. Keith
4/17/71I
RUNNING — See also Boston Marathon ,
4/15/78J
RUPEREZ, Javier
11/12/79B
RUPP, Adolph
3/27/72J
RURAL Areas
Cable TV
2/3/72J
Crime Rate
3/25/76F
Energy & Power
3/17/75H
Federal Aid
3/10/71F, 2/1/72F, 12/26/72H,
5/7/74H, 4/30/79F
Hunger
4/30/79F
Legal Aid
1/30/71F, 6/29/71F
Medicine & Health
7/23/78F, 10/2/78F
Population
2/13/71F, 2/24/77F
Utilities
5/11/73H
RUSH, Kenneth
3/7/74E, 6/14/74H, 7/30/74H
RUSK, Dean
7/2/71G, 9/14/77G
RUSSEL, Bill
2/8/75J
RUSSELL, Arnice
8/25/73J
RUSSELL, Bertrand
2/2/70J, 1/17/76A
RUSSELL, Dan
10/20/71F
RUSSELL, Donald
9/3/70G

RUSSELL, John (Honey)
11/15/73J
RUSSELL Jr., Louis
11/27/74I
RUSSELL, Richard
1/21/71F, 2/1/71F
RUSSELL, Rosalind
11/28/76J
RUSSIA — See Union of Soviet Socialist
Republics
RUSSO, Anthony
1/18/73G, 2/26/73G, 5/11/73G,
6/6/73G, 1/15/77G
RUSSO, Miguel
12/9/76F
RUSTIN, Bayard
3/30/78F
RUTGERS University
8/8/76I, 1/20/79J
RUTH, Babe
9/29/73J, 4/8/74J, 5/1/75J
RUTH, Henry
10/23/74F
RUTHERFORD, Dame Margaret
5/22/72J
RUTHERFORD, Johnny
5/26/74J, 5/30/76J
RUTTER, William
5/23/77I
RUZICI, Virginia
5/27/78J
RWANDA
3/8/73C, 7/22/76C
RYAN, Cornelius
11/23/74J
RYAN, Hermine Braunsteiner
8/7/73B
RYAN, Leo
9/25/76I, 9/26/78F, 11/15/78J,
11/17/78J, 11/18/78J, 3/7/79D
RYAN, Nolan
9/25/72J, 5/15/73J, 7/15/73J,
9/27/73J, 8/12/74J, 9/29/74J,
6/1/75J, 11/2/79J, 11/19/79J
RYAN, Robert
10/30/73J
RYAN, William Fitts
9/17/72F
RYLE, Sir Martin
10/15/74I
RYUKYO Islands — See Okinawa
RYUMIN, Valery
7/15/79I, 8/19/79I
RYUN, Jim
5/16/71J

S

SA CARNEIRO, Francisco
11/7/77B
SA CARNEIRO, Manuel Lumbrales de
12/2/79B
SA-Ngad Chaloryu
3/26/77E
SABAH al-Ahmad al-Jaber, Sheik
9/30/74A
SABAH al-Ahmed al-Sabah, Sheik
12/31/77C
SABBE, Osman Saleh
1/30/75C
SABENA Belgian World Airways
7/13/73B
SABIN, Albert
1/6/73I, 4/24/73I, 9/23/76I
SABRY, Aly
5/2/71C, 12/9/71C
SACCHARIN — See Sweetners, Artificial
SACOTO Montero, Julio
4/1/71D, 4/6/71D

SADAT, Anwar el-
Amnesty
1/27/74C
Arab Cooperative Moves
5/18/75C
Arab Federation Moves
10/4/71C, 7/23/72C, 8/2/72C,
8/14/74C
Arab Relations
1/13/74C, 1/22/78C, 9/19/78C,
10/10/78C, 12/25/78C
Armed Forces & Defense
11/1/71C, 12/12/73C
Arms Sales
1/29/75C, 6/5/79C
Austria
4/10/76B
Bombs & Bombing
8/15/76C
Borders & Boundaries
5/27/79C
Cairo Conference
11/27/77C, 11/29/77C,
12/20/77C, 12/25/77C, 12/26/77C
Camp David Accord
8/8/78C, 9/6/78C, 9/7/78C,
9/17/78C, 9/18/78B, 9/18/78G,
9/20/78C, 9/23/78C, 10/10/78C,
11/9/78C
Cease-Fires & Truce Developments
11/30/70C
Censorship
3/14/76C, 6/1/78C
China, People's Republic of
6/5/79C
Church-State Relations
3/1/79C
Coups & Attempted Coups
5/14/71C, 5/20/71C, 12/9/71C,
12/4/72C, 5/31/75C
Elections
10/15/70C, 9/16/76C, 11/10/76C
Food
2/3/77C
Foreign Credit
5/1/75C, 10/26/77C
France
1/29/75C
Geneva Accord
9/4/75C
Golan Heights
5/1/74C
Internal Security
8/17/79C
Iran
11/9/79C
Iraq
11/16/77C, 12/24/77C
Israel
2/6/71C, 6/26/71C, 2/17/72C,
3/30/72C, 7/26/72C, 7/27/72C,
12/28/72C, 1/17/74G, 2/19/74C,
3/13/75C, 3/12/77C, 5/20/77C,
8/2/77C, 11/9/77C, 1/12/78C,
1/20/78C, 1/21/78C, 2/6/78C,
2/11/78C, 3/14/78C, 6/7/78C,
6/21/78C, 7/30/78C
Israeli Peace Moves
11/13/76C, 11/14/76C, 11/14/76G
Israeli Peace Plan
12/28/77C, 3/31/78C
Israeli Territorial Gains
12/23/70C, 7/26/71C, 8/2/77C,
1/9/78C, 11/12/78G, 5/26/79C
Israeli Visit
11/15/77B, 11/15/77C,
11/16/77C, 11/17/77C,
11/19/77B, 11/19/77C,
11/20/77C, 11/20/77G,
11/21/77C, 11/23/77C, 12/5/77C,
10/17/78A
Jews & Judaism
1/29/78G
Jordan, Hashemite Kingdom of
12/2/70C, 2/17/77C, 2/18/77C
Libya
7/23/72C, 8/2/72C, 1/10/73C,
7/21/73C, 8/29/73C, 2/19/74C,
7/31/74C, 8/14/74C, 8/18/74C,
7/22/76C, 7/25/76C, 8/15/76C,
11/16/77C
Meir, Golda
4/28/73C
Middle East
1/4/71C, 1/8/71C, 1/12/75C

Morocco
9/2/79C
Nobel Prizes
12/10/78A
Oil & Oil Products
1/9/75C
Organization for African Unity
(OAU)
3/9/77C
Palestine Liberation Organization
(PLO)
2/27/75C, 4/7/75C, 1/15/77C,
2/17/77C, 2/18/77C, 11/16/77C,
11/23/77C
Palestinian Commandos
3/14/78C
Palestinian Dissent
7/14/77C
Palestinian Representation
7/18/74C, 11/5/75C, 11/12/77C,
2/24/78C
Palestinian Self-Determination
7/11/79C, 9/6/79C
Palestinian State Proposal
12/29/76C, 12/30/76C, 1/2/77C,
2/23/77C, 4/3/77C, 7/10/77C
Peace Pact
3/8/79C, 3/26/79C, 3/26/79G,
4/2/79C, 5/21/79C, 5/26/79C,
5/27/79C
Peace Plan
7/13/78C, 7/16/78C, 7/22/78C,
7/23/78C
Peace Proposals & Talks
2/28/71C, 6/10/71C, 2/4/72C,
1/12/75C, 2/5/75C, 7/22/75C,
1/15/77C, 2/17/77C, 2/18/77C,
7/4/77C, 11/6/77C, 11/9/77C,
11/26/77C, 1/12/78C, 1/20/78C,
1/21/78C, 2/3/78C, 2/4/78C,
2/6/78C, 7/3/78C
Political Asylum
11/9/79C
Politics & Government
10/3/70C, 5/2/71C, 9/11/71C,
9/19/71C, 2/18/72C, 3/24/73C,
3/28/73C, 4/25/74C, 9/25/74C,
4/16/75C, 10/16/76C, 2/10/77C
Riots & Violence
2/3/77C
Saudi Arabia
6/26/71C, 8/7/74C, 7/16/77C,
5/21/79C
Sinai Peninsula
2/29/76C
Soviet Equipment & Personnel
4/18/74C, 7/16/77C
Student Protests
2/17/72C
Suez Canal
4/1/71C, 4/4/71C, 10/10/71C,
1/17/74G, 3/29/75C
Syria
11/16/77C, 9/20/78C
Terrorism & Terrorists
2/18/78B
Treaty Talks
11/12/78G, 12/25/78C, 12/26/78C
U.S. Relations
10/10/71C, 5/18/72C, 4/20/74C,
5/1/74C, 10/10/74C, 11/6/74C,
3/13/75C, 5/18/75C, 6/2/75C,
7/22/75C, 10/18/75C, 10/26/75C,
11/5/75C, 2/29/76C, 11/14/76G,
4/4/77G, 11/29/77C, 1/4/78C,
1/20/78C, 2/3/78C, 2/4/78C,
7/3/78C, 11/12/78G, 3/8/79C,
3/26/79G
Union of Soviet Socialist Republics
(USSR)
1/4/71C, 1/8/71C, 5/27/71C,
10/13/71C, 2/4/72C, 4/29/72C,
7/18/72C, 7/19/72B, 8/6/72C,
8/11/72C, 10/18/73C, 1/8/75C,
2/5/75C, 5/1/75C, 9/4/75C,
4/4/76C, 10/26/77C, 11/15/77B,
9/18/78B
Yom Kippur War
10/16/73C, 10/18/73C,
10/31/73C, 1/13/74C, 10/6/74C,
1/8/75C
Yugoslavia
3/30/74C
SADEK, Mohammed
10/24/71C

SADIQI, Gholam Hussein
12/17/78C
SAEED, Muhammed Nur
8/4/76C
SAFEWAY Stores Inc.
9/15/75H
SAFIRE, William
6/21/79J
SAHARA Desert
5/12/73C
SAHARA, Western — See also Spanish
Sahara
2/27/76C, 3/7/76C, 4/14/76C,
6/21/76C, 7/3/76C, 8/26/76C,
10/26/77C, 10/30/77C,
12/23/77C, 4/13/78C, 11/10/78C,
12/17/78C, 7/20/79C, 8/5/79C,
8/11/79C, 8/25/79C, 9/2/79C,
9/8/79C
SAHARAN Arab Democratic Republic
— See Sahara, Western
SAID bin Taimur, Sultan
7/23/70C
SAID, Edward
11/15/77G
SAIJO, Shozo
2/28/71J
SAILING
9/28/70J, 9/18/77J
ST. ANTHONY Guild Press
9/29/70J
ST. CLAIR, James
5/7/74F, 7/18/74F
ST. CLAIR, Lake
3/24/70D
ST. CLAIR River
2/3/71D
ST. JEAN de Vinney, Canada
5/5/71I
ST. JOHN, Jill
12/17/71J
ST. JOHNS River
4/30/73I
ST. JOSEPH's Mining Co.
12/15/73D
ST. KITTS-Nevis-Anguilla — See also
Anguilla
5/10/71D, 11/14/71D
ST-LAURENT, Louis
7/24/73D
ST. LAWRENCE River
Port Strike
4/28/75D
Water Pollution
1/14/71D
ST. LAWRENCE Seaway
6/23/76H
ST. LOUIS, Mo.
Financial Crisis
5/26/75H
Police Shootout
2/16/72F
School Desegregation
12/27/75F
Teachers' Strike
2/18/73F
ST. LOUIS Post-Dispatch (publication)
6/25/71G
ST. LUCIA
2/21/79D, 7/2/79D
ST. MARTIN's Property Corp.
9/12/74B
ST. PATRICK's Cathedral
11/30/70J, 4/30/72F
ST. PAUL Fire & Marine Insurance Co.
10/24/75F
ST. VINCENT
11/14/71D, 10/27/79D, 12/8/79D
SAKHALIN Island
11/24/72E
SAKHAROV, Andrei
Awards & Grants
11/20/77J

U

8/14/70G, 11/12/70G, 11/20/70G,
1/14/71G, 1/22/71G, 1/29/71G,
2/5/71G, 2/26/71G, 3/8/71G,
3/18/71G, 3/29/71G, 3/31/71G,
4/3/71G, 4/12/71G, 5/19/71G,
6/11/71G, 8/16/71G, 8/20/71G,
8/23/71G, 9/22/71G, 10/15/71G,
12/17/71G, 1/18/72E, 6/3/72E,
6/4/72E, 2/16/73G, 5/14/73G,
12/21/73G, 2/27/74G, 4/16/74G,
5/4/74G, 9/25/74G, 11/19/74G,
4/5/76G, 8/3/76E

Mayday March
5/10/71G, 1/16/75G
Medicine & Health
12/6/78I
Mekong Delta
9/14/71E
Military Action
3/4/70E, 4/5/70E, 5/8/70E,
6/13/70E, 7/15/70E, 10/4/70E,
11/11/70E, 11/13/71E, 12/25/72E,
3/20/73E, 6/20/73E, 6/26/73E,
6/27/73E, 7/18/73E, 8/12/73E,
4/5/75E
Mining of Ports
5/8/72E, 5/10/72E, 5/11/72A,
5/12/72E, 5/14/72G, 5/15/72E,
5/16/72E, 5/17/72E, 5/22/72E,
7/5/72E
Missing in Action
11/11/72E, 5/21/73E, 11/10/73G,
12/24/74E, 1/21/75E, 3/2/75E,
9/11/75G, 12/5/75E, 2/22/76E,
9/14/76A, 11/15/76A, 2/11/77E,
3/18/77E, 5/3/77E, 8/27/78E
Mongolia
5/19/72E
Motion Pictures
12/14/78I, 4/19/79J
Narcotics
1/6/71G, 3/17/71G, 5/6/71G,
5/30/71G, 6/1/71G, 6/21/71G,
7/19/71G, 1/8/72G, 2/23/72G
New Zealand
8/20/70E, 8/18/71E
Nixon, Richard M.
1/4/71G, 1/25/72E, 1/27/72E,
2/9/72G, 2/10/72E, 2/10/72G,
4/26/72E, 5/5/72A, 5/11/72G,
5/12/72E, 5/31/72F, 9/30/72F,
11/2/72E, 1/15/73E, 4/9/75G,
4/30/75G, 7/9/75G, 2/1/76G,
5/22/77E
North Vietnamese Offensives
7/2/72E, 9/16/72E
North Vietnamese Troops
10/31/72E
Oil & Oil Products
12/15/73G
Pacification Program
9/4/70E, 3/1/71E
Paris Accords
1/23/73E, 1/24/73E, 1/25/73G,
1/26/73G, 1/27/73E, 1/29/73E,
2/26/73A, 4/19/73E, 5/22/73E,
5/29/73G, 6/6/73E, 6/13/73E,
10/16/73J, 10/23/73J, 1/13/75E
Paris Peace Talks
5/6/70E, 10/4/70E, 11/25/70E,
12/3/70E, 12/10/70E, 12/11/70G,
12/30/70E, 1/21/71E, 3/10/71G,
3/22/71E, 4/8/71E, 4/15/71E,
5/13/71E, 7/1/71E, 7/8/71E,
7/16/71E, 12/9/71E, 12/28/71E,
1/6/72E, 1/27/72E, 2/24/72E,
3/16/72E, 3/24/72E, 4/13/72E,
4/15/72E, 4/20/72E, 4/27/72E,
4/28/72A, 5/4/72E, 5/12/72E,
6/14/72E, 6/15/72E, 6/29/72E,
7/9/72E, 7/13/72E, 7/19/72E,
7/25/72E, 9/27/72E, 10/6/72E,
10/15/72E, 11/4/72E, 11/17/72E,
12/8/72E, 12/13/72E, 12/19/72E,
12/24/72E, 4/16/74E
Peace Proposals & Talks
2/11/70E, 4/2/70E, 4/10/70B,
5/14/70E, 6/18/70E, 7/1/70G,
8/31/70G, 9/17/70E, 10/7/70G,
10/8/70G, 10/10/70E, 10/14/70E,
7/4/71E, 1/26/72E, 1/31/72E,
2/2/72G, 2/3/72E, 2/5/72E,
2/10/72E, 6/30/72E, 9/28/72E,
11/7/72E, 1/4/73E, 1/13/73E,
1/14/73G, 3/2/73A, 5/29/73E,
5/30/73E, 10/4/73E, 3/3/75G

Pesticides & Herbicides
12/26/70E
Philippines, Republic of the
3/19/70G
Presidential Authority Issue
6/3/70G, 6/11/70G, 6/22/70G,
6/24/70G, 6/30/70G, 7/9/70G,
7/10/70G, 2/10/71G, 2/16/71G,
5/31/72F, 4/19/73G
Presidential Election of 1972
1/3/72G, 1/16/72F, 8/14/72G,
8/24/72F, 9/30/72F, 10/10/72G,
10/30/72F, 11/3/72F
Press Publication
7/1/71G
Prisoners of War
1/21/70E, 4/7/70G, 4/10/70G,
6/26/70E, 11/21/70E, 11/22/70E,
12/10/70E, 12/22/70E, 1/17/71E,
1/24/71E, 4/8/71E, 4/29/71E,
6/22/71G, 6/30/71G, 7/1/71E,
7/21/71G, 9/30/71G, 10/8/71E,
10/31/71E, 1/2/72G, 1/3/72G,
2/2/72G, 2/5/72E, 3/7/72G,
3/16/72E, 5/8/72E, 7/25/72G,
8/12/72E, 8/14/72E, 8/22/72E,
8/24/72E, 9/2/72E, 9/17/72E,
9/30/72F, 11/11/72E, 1/27/73E,
2/5/73E, 2/12/73E, 2/15/73E,
2/26/73A, 3/4/73E, 3/7/73G,
3/13/73E, 3/16/73E, 3/21/73E,
3/22/73E, 3/29/73E, 3/29/73G,
4/28/73E, 4/29/73G, 5/29/73G,
7/3/73G, 7/15/73E, 7/24/73E,
2/6/74E, 3/6/74E, 3/8/74E,
2/5/79E
Pro-Demonstrations
4/4/70G, 5/20/70G, 6/7/70G,
6/15/70G, 10/3/70G, 5/8/71G
Provisional Revolutionary Government
4/22/75E
Public Opinion
5/14/72G
Racial Issues
10/13/72G
Rain-Making Charges
6/25/72E, 7/3/72E, 5/18/74G
Refugees
5/22/70E, 5/1/72E, 5/6/72E,
6/12/72E, 12/8/73E, 3/28/75E,
4/2/75A, 4/2/75E, 4/3/75E,
4/4/75E, 4/14/75E, 4/23/75E,
4/29/75E, 5/2/75G, 5/4/75E,
5/4/75G, 5/6/75E, 5/6/75G,
5/7/75E, 5/8/75F, 5/14/75G,
5/16/75C, 5/19/75E, 5/23/75G,
5/28/75G, 6/11/75F, 6/23/75G,
7/7/75D, 9/29/75G, 10/29/75G,
10/31/75G, 12/20/75G, 2/20/76G,
3/16/76B, 3/15/78E, 5/17/78E
Relief Aid
4/18/75E
Riots & Violence
2/4/71G, 5/3/72E, 5/12/72G,
5/19/72F, 9/8/72E, 10/13/72G
Roman Catholic Church
4/9/70G, 11/19/71G
Route Interdiction
5/8/72E, 5/10/72E, 5/11/72A,
5/16/72E, 5/22/72E, 7/5/72E,
8/28/72E, 9/11/72E, 9/23/72E,
10/25/72E, 1/13/75E, 3/7/75E,
4/8/75E, 4/29/75E
Saigon, Attacks On
7/20/70E, 12/11/72E, 12/6/72E,
3/28/75E, 4/4/75E, 4/8/75E,
4/27/75E, 4/29/75E
Saigon Defenses
1/2/72E
Saigon Fall
4/30/75E
Shrines & Historic Sites
7/6/70E, 5/11/71E
South Vietnamese Advances
7/12/70E, 8/21/70E, 12/1/70E,
5/12/71E, 9/14/71E, 9/18/71E,
3/10/72E, 3/26/72E, 5/15/72E,
6/7/72E, 6/9/72E, 7/26/72E,
8/3/72E, 8/5/72E, 8/10/72E,
9/15/72E, 10/12/72E, 11/3/72E,
11/25/72E, 12/11/73E, 1/14/74E,
1/29/74E, 6/5/74E
South Vietnamese Attacks
5/13/72E, 5/21/72E, 5/28/72E,
8/15/72E, 9/11/72E

South Vietnamese Command
8/25/72E
South Vietnamese Defeat
4/15/72E, 5/5/72E, 3/20/75E,
3/20/75G, 3/22/75E, 3/24/75E,
3/25/75E, 3/30/75E, 4/2/75E,
4/2/75G, 4/3/75E, 4/4/75E,
4/7/75E, 4/16/75E, 4/19/75E,
4/22/75E, 4/29/75E, 7/9/75G,
4/24/76E
South Vietnamese Offensives
6/28/72E, 6/29/72E, 7/4/72E,
7/7/72E, 7/11/72E, 7/15/72E,
7/17/72E, 7/19/72E, 7/25/72E,
8/22/72E, 1/17/75E, 1/23/75E
South Vietnamese Retreats
9/15/70E, 4/2/72E, 4/7/72E,
4/25/72E, 5/3/72E, 5/20/72E,
7/27/72E, 4/15/75E
South Vietnamese Surrender
4/30/75E, 4/30/75G, 5/1/75B
South Vietnamese Troops
8/25/72E
Student Protests
4/25/70F, 5/1/70G, 5/3/70G,
5/4/70G, 5/5/70G, 5/8/70G,
5/9/70G, 5/12/70G, 5/14/70G,
5/20/70G, 7/11/70E, 2/7/71G,
5/30/71G, 4/20/72F, 5/5/72G,
5/9/72G, 5/11/72G
Suits & Claims
1/16/75G
Supplies
1/25/70G, 2/24/70E, 11/5/70E,
12/27/70E, 2/15/71E, 3/6/71E,
3/25/71E, 6/4/71E, 5/4/72E,
5/18/72E, 5/19/72E, 5/29/72E,
6/30/72E, 7/5/72E, 7/8/72E,
8/23/72E, 6/24/74E, 2/27/75E
Supporters
4/29/70G, 9/2/70G, 7/11/70G,
2/14/72H
Sweden
4/9/70B, 5/27/71B, 12/28/72B,
12/29/72A
Television
8/14/70G
Tet Offensive
5/24/72E
Thailand
6/7/70G, 8/28/70E, 6/30/72E
Torture
7/21/71G
Truce-Political Settlement
10/26/72E, 10/28/72E, 10/29/72E,
10/30/72E, 10/31/72E, 11/1/72E,
11/2/72E, 11/4/72E, 11/5/72E,
11/22/72E, 3/22/74E
Truce Violations
1/4/74E
U.S. Bases
11/4/70E
U.S. Command
5/16/72E, 6/12/72E, 6/20/72G,
11/15/72E
U.S. Evacuation
3/17/75E, 3/28/75E, 4/3/75E,
4/12/75E, 4/16/75G, 4/18/75E,
4/21/75G, 4/24/75G, 4/29/75E,
5/1/75G, 11/18/77G, 2/15/78G
U.S. Funds Cutoff
4/17/72G, 5/9/72G
U.S. Government Actions & Statements
1/2/70E, 2/1/70G, 2/3/70G,
5/1/70G, 6/20/70G, 7/30/70G,
11/24/70G, 2/17/71G, 2/26/71G,
8/11/72E, 1/8/73G, 3/26/75G
U.S. Inspection Tours
6/8/70E, 6/10/70G, 1/11/71E
U.S. Intelligence
12/12/70E
U.S. Relations
5/8/72A, 7/9/75G
U.S. Retreats
7/23/70E
U.S. Troops
9/7/70E, 11/2/70E, 11/9/70E,
4/26/71E, 3/2/72E, 6/5/72E
U.S. Troops Withdrawal
1/9/70E, 2/1/70E, 2/9/70G,
2/13/70E, 4/20/70G, 5/5/70B,
8/17/70G, 9/17/70E, 10/10/70E,
12/28/70G, 3/22/71G, 3/29/71G,
4/7/71G, 4/8/71E, 4/13/71G,
4/14/71G, 4/16/71G, 4/29/71E,

4/29/71G, 5/22/71G, 6/30/71G,
7/1/71E, 7/7/71G, 9/30/71G,
11/6/71E, 11/12/71G, 1/2/72G,
1/3/72G, 1/13/72E, 2/2/72G,
2/5/72E, 4/3/72E, 4/25/72J,
4/26/72E, 5/22/72G, 6/13/72E,
6/13/72G, 6/28/72E, 7/24/72G,
8/2/72G, 8/10/72G, 8/12/72E,
8/29/72E, 3/29/73E
Union of Soviet Socialist Republics (USSR)
5/4/70B, 6/11/70B, 2/8/71B,
10/25/71B, 4/16/72E, 4/28/72A,
5/9/72A, 5/11/72A, 5/16/72E,
5/18/72E, 5/19/72A, 5/20/72E,
6/15/72E, 6/18/72E, 10/25/73E,
12/21/73E, 5/1/75B
United Nations (U.N.)
5/3/70E, 5/5/70A, 11/2/70A,
5/9/72A, 5/12/72A, 9/19/72A,
4/16/74A
USO
4/14/72G
Viet Cong
7/16/71E, 10/30/72E, 3/6/73E,
3/24/73E, 3/31/73A, 4/5/73E,
6/3/73E, 8/22/73E, 10/15/73E,
11/3/73E, 11/4/73E, 11/6/73E,
12/21/73E, 5/20/74E, 6/11/74E,
4/2/75E
Vietnamization
4/2/70G, 1/8/73G
Weather
10/1/70E
Yugoslavia
5/22/71B

VIEYRA, Gilberto
7/5/77D
VIGILANT (ship)
11/23/70G
VIGNES, Alberto
1/27/75D
VILAS, Guillermo
12/15/74J, 5/9/76J, 1/9/77J,
6/5/77J, 9/5/77J, 9/11/77J,
6/11/78J, 1/3/79J
VILIM, Blazej
9/23/76B
VILJOEN, Gerrit
8/17/78C, 8/18/78C
VILLAGE Voice (publication)
2/11/76G, 2/12/76G, 2/17/76G,
2/19/76G, 2/23/76G, 11/28/76J
VILLANOVA University
3/7/70J, 5/30/70J, 5/29/71J,
6/17/71J
VILLAR, Alberto
11/1/74D, 11/3/74D
VILLAS Boas, Orlando and Claudio
2/7/73I
VINNELL Corp.
2/10/75C
VINOGRADOV, Vladimir
12/28/79C
VINS, Georgi
2/2/75B
VINYL Chloride
10/1/74I, 1/31/75I, 3/31/75H
VIOLA, Humberto
12/12/74D
VIOLA, Roberto
7/31/78D, 9/29/79D, 12/31/79D
VIPAOWADI Rangsit, Princess
2/16/77E
VIRDON, Bill
1/3/74J
VIREN, Lasse
7/30/76J
VIRGIN Airlines
Accidents & Disasters
4/27/76I
VIRGIN Islands
Accidents & Disasters
10/25/79I
Arms Control & Disarmament
5/26/77D
Drought
8/24/77I

Politics & Government
1/4/71D, 3/6/79D
VIRGINIA
Accidents & Disasters
12/1/74I, 12/3/78I
Blacks
1/13/70F, 6/5/70F
Colleges & Universities
2/2/78F
Education & Schools
5/21/73F
Elections
11/8/77F
Equal Rights Amendment
1/27/77F
Floods & Flooding
6/23/72I
Nuclear Energy
9/30/77I
Politics & Government
1/13/70F
School Desegregation
6/1/71F, 1/10/72F, 6/22/72F,
9/4/73F, 11/13/73F, 2/2/78F
Water Pollution
10/13/77H
Weather
2/5/77I
VIRGINIA Electric & Power Co.
7/29/74H
VIRUS
3/12/71I, 7/2/71I, 1/14/72I,
1/8/75I, 3/24/75I, 10/16/75I,
2/28/76I, 3/24/76I, 7/18/76I,
9/23/76I, 11/30/76I, 2/24/77I
VISCONTI, Luchino
3/30/76J
VISHNEVSKAYA, Galina
3/15/78J
VISITATION, The (painting)
1/26/76J
VITAMINS
A Vitamin
2/14/79I
Advertising
2/7/77J
C Vitamin
11/18/70I
K Vitamin
4/17/76I
VITTORI, Ottavio
8/29/75I
VOCATIONAL Schools — See under
Education & Schools
VODKA
1/10/78B
VOGAN, James
8/3/71I
VOICE of America
9/10/73B
VOICE of the Palestinian Revolution —
See Palestinian Revolution, Voice of
the
VOIGHT, Jon
7/30/72J, 10/18/74J, 12/20/78J,
4/19/79J
VOLCANIC Eruptions
Caribbean
8/30/76I, 9/2/76I
Hawaii
7/5/75I, 11/29/75I, 9/13/77I
Iceland
5/5/70I, 1/23/73I
Indonesia
2/21/79I
Italy
8/29/77I, 8/6/79I
Japan
8/10/77I
VOLCKER, Paul
2/9/72H, 9/4/72A, 2/12/73A,
3/1/73H, 7/25/79H, 8/2/79F,
10/28/79H
VOLKOV, Vladislav
6/30/71I
VOLKSWAGEN (automobile)
9/11/71H, 1/11/76H, 4/11/77H
VOLKSWAGEN of America Inc.
3/12/74H, 12/5/79H